# About the Author

James R. Lewis has worked as a professional astrologer for more than 25 years. Among astrologers, he is best known for his innovative work on Babylonian astrology and on the astrological significance of the planetary moons.

Having completed his graduate work in religious studies at the University of North Carolina, Chapel Hill, Prof. Lewis has an extensive background in history, psychology, philosophy, and comparative religion, including religious cults. He is an internationally recognized authority on nontraditional religious groups and currently teaches religious studies at the University of Wisconsin at Stevens Point.

Prof. Lewis is the author of Visible Ink's *The Death and Afterlife Book*, *Angels A to Z*, and *The Dream Encyclopedia*. Other titles include *Doomsday Prophecies: A Complete Guide to the End of the World*, *Magical Religion and Modern Witchcraft*, and *Peculiar Prophets: A Biographical Dictionary of New Religions*, and the forthcoming *Oxford Handbook of New Religious Movements*. His work has received recognition in the form of *Choice*'s Outstanding Academic Title award and Best Reference Book awards from the American Library Association and the New York Public Library Association.

# Also from Visible Ink Press

Angels A to Z

The Death and Afterlife Book: The Encyclopedia of Death, Near Death, and Life after Death

The Dream Encyclopedia

The Fortune-Telling Book: The Encyclopedia of Divination and Soothsaying

Real Ghosts, Restless Spirits, and Haunted Places

The Religion Book: Places, Prophets, Saints, and Seers

The UFO Book: Encyclopedia of the Extraterrestrial

Unexplained! Strange Sightings, Incredible Occurrences, and Puzzling Physical Phenomena

The Vampire Book: The Encyclopedia of the Undead

The Werewolf Book: The Encyclopedia of Shape-Shifting Beings

The Witch Book: The Encyclopedia of Witchcraft, Wicca, and Neo-paganism

Please visit us at visibleink.com.

# The Astrology Book

## The Encyclopedia of Heavenly Influences

For my partner and wife Eve,
who originally inspired this project,
and without whose support
this book might never have been completed.

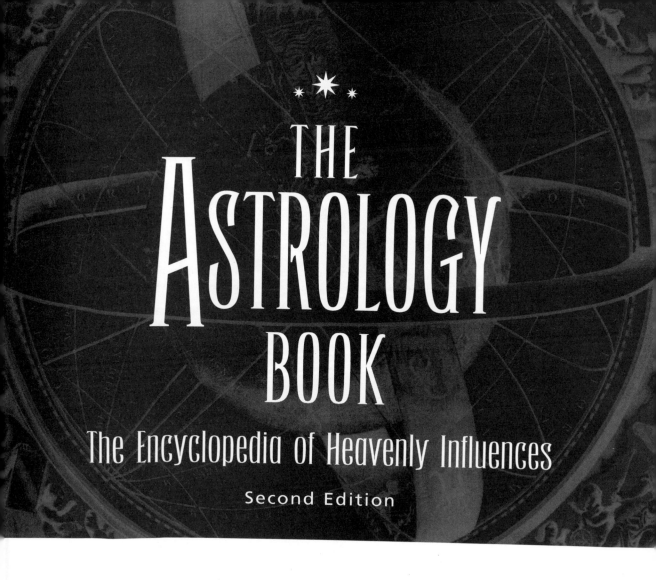

# THE ASTROLOGY BOOK

## The Encyclopedia of Heavenly Influences

Second Edition

JAMES R. LEWIS

Detroit

# THE ASTROLOGY BOOK



Visible Ink Press™
43311 Joy Road #414
Canton, MI 48187-2075

Visible Ink Press is a trademark of Visible Ink Press LLC.

Most Visible Ink Press books are available at special quantity discounts when purchased in bulk by corporations, organizations, or groups. Customized printings, special imprints, messages, and excerpts can be produced to meet your needs. For more information, contact Special Markets Director, Visible Ink Press, at www.visibleink.com.

Art Director: Mary Claire Krzewinski
Typesetting: Graphix Group

ISBN 1-57859-144-9
*The Astrology Book* is the second edition of *The Astrology Encyclopedia*.
CIP on file with the Library of Congress.

Printed in the United States of America

10 9 8 7 6 5 4 3 2 1

# Contents

# Introduction

Astrology literally means the study (or science, depending on how one translates the Greek word *logos*) of the stars (*astron*). Astrology differs from astronomy by confining its attention to the study of correlations between celestial events and humanly meaningful events. Most people are familiar with only a tiny portion of the science of the stars, namely the 12 signs of the Zodiac as they relate to the personality of individuals and the use of astrology for divinatory purposes.

The Zodiac (literally the "circle of animals" or, in its more primary meaning, the "circle of life" or "circle of living beings") is the belt constituted by the 12 signs—Aries, Taurus, Gemini, Cancer, Leo, Virgo, Libra, Scorpio, Sagittarius, Capricorn, Aquarius, and Pisces. This "belt" is said to extend 8° or 9° on either side of the ecliptic (the imaginary line drawn against the backdrop of the stars by the orbit of the Earth). The orbits of the various planets in the solar system all lie within approximately the same geometric plane, so that, from a position within the system, all of the heavenly bodies appear to move across the face of the same set of constellations. Several thousand years ago, these constellations gave their names to the Zodiac.

The notion of the Zodiac is very ancient, with roots in the early citied cultures of Mesopotamia. The first 12-sign zodiacs were named after the gods of these cultures. The Greeks adopted astrology from the Babylonians, and the Romans, in turn, adopted astrology from the Greeks. These peoples renamed the signs of the Mesopotamian Zodiac in terms of their own mythologies, which is why the familiar Zodiac of the contemporary West bears names out of Mediterranean mythology. The notion of a 12-fold division derives from the lunar cycle (the orbital cycle of the Moon around the Earth), which the Moon completes 12 times per year.

From a broad historical perspective, zodiacal symbolism can be found everywhere, and zodiacal expressions are still in use in modern English—e.g., "bull-headed" (an allusion to Taurus), "crabby" (an allusion to Cancer), etc. The popularity of Sun-sign astrology (the kind found in the daily newspaper) has kept these ancient symbols alive in modern society, so that even such prominent artifacts as automobiles have been named after some of the signs (e.g., the Taurus and the Scorpio).

The sign of the Zodiac the Sun is in at the time of a person's birth is his or her Sun sign (sometimes also called the birth sign). The Sun, as the most important celestial body for Earth-dwellers, is the most important influence in a horoscope (an astrological chart). Consequently, the sign that the Sun is in at birth will usually be the single most important influence on an individual's personality. Thus when people say that they are a certain sign, they are almost always referring to their Sun sign.

Sun-sign astrology, which is the kind of astrology one finds in newspapers and magazines, has the advantage of simplicity—all one needs to know is one's birthday to be able to figure out one's sign—but this simplicity is purchased at the price of ignoring all other astrological influences. The other important celestial bodies, for example, were all located in signs at the moment of birth. Thus, someone with a Scorpio Sun sign might also have a Sagittarius Moon sign, a Virgo Venus sign, a Libra Mercury sign, etc. Each of these other signs has an influence, which is why everyone with the same Sun sign does not have the same personality. The subsidiary influences of the sign positions of the planets is further modified by the angles between them (referred to as aspects), as well as by their house positions (another set of 12 divisions).

These other influences make Sun-sign astrology a hit-or-miss system that works sometimes but fails miserably at others. Professional astrologers tend to dislike Sun-sign astrology because it creates a misconception of the science of the stars (i.e., that astrology is entirely about Sun signs), and because its inaccuracy leads non-astrologers to reject astrology as untrue.

Similar remarks apply to predictions of the future by the 12 signs. Sun-sign prediction, in other words, is also a hit-or-miss system that sometimes works and sometimes misses the mark entirely. The columns found in popular periodicals also tend to create misperceptions about the nature of astrological prediction. In particular, readers can come away with the impression that astrological prediction is a kind of astrological fortune-telling that portrays the stars as if they foretold an irrevocable destiny for the person having her or his fortune told. Modern astrologers, however, tend to distance themselves from this tradition of predicting specific events. Instead of predicting events, most contemporary astrologers describe upcoming planetary conditions, with the understanding that clients have the free will to respond to planetary influences in different ways. Like a meteorologist, an astrologer can only predict trends and probabilities—not details.

### Understanding the Appeal of Astrology

Astrology occupies a peculiar position in the modern world. Derided by many as medieval superstition, the science of the stars nevertheless continues to exercise a fascination over the human mind. Furthermore, polls indicate that its popularity is growing rather than waning. The abysmal failure of critics to halt the expansion of astrology should be a sign that we have reached a juncture where—rather than continuing simply to dismiss astrology as a superstitious retreat from the modern world—it is appropriate to ask other kinds of questions. Simultaneously, we need to understand why this practice has evoked such passionate criticism.

Since at least the historical period known as the Enlightenment, the Western world has been home to a vocal minority of self-appointed guardians of human rationality who have railed against religion and anything else that dared to suggest that the human being was anything more than a physical-chemical organism. Astrology was lumped into the category of irrational superstition along with anything else that did not fall within a rather narrow definition of science. But just how irrational is astrology?

If you live near a seashore and is attentive to the ebb and flow of the waterline, it is easy to observe that the Sun and the Moon rule the tides. How big a step from this observation is it to assert that celestial bodies influence human beings? We cannot touch, taste, or see astrological forces, but neither can we touch, taste, or see gravity. Gravity is perceived only indirectly, in terms of its effects. It is in this way, astrologers could reply, that astrological forces are perceived—indirectly, in terms of their impact on human beings and other events in the world. Furthermore, so astrologers would assert, astrological claims can be subjected to the methods of empirical, statistical research, as has been done most notably in the work of Michel and Françoise Gauquelin. Thus, astrology is not, in the strict sense, irrational. Astrologers, in other words, do not utilize illogical principles of reasoning. Rather, astrology is labeled irrational because it has not been accepted into the mainstream of academic science.

In earlier historical periods, human beings were not so insulated from their environment as we are today. Human life was ordered according to the seasonal migration of the Sun from north to south and south to north. Also, streetlights and the other lights of a suburban/urban environment did not obstruct a view of the night sky, so that the starry heavens were a nightly experience. Aware of the relationship between Sun, Moon, and tides, as well as the correlation between such cycles as menstruation and the lunar cycle, it is not difficult to see how the human mind would seek out other kinds of correlations between celestial and terrestrial phenomena.

To shift forward in an effort to understand the attraction of astrology for the typical citizen of an industrialized society, one has to see that, even for many people with a modicum of belief in traditional religion, ordinary, everyday life—the world as it is experienced on a day-to-day basis—appears to be empty of significance. Most people feel themselves to be at the mercy of social, economic, and political forces that they can rarely understand, much less predict. Although to the outsider astrology appears to be unappealing because of its apparent determinism, it allows people to comprehend the events in their lives as part of a meaningful, predictive system over which they can gain a certain amount of control. Furthermore, even the most mundane life acquires a certain amount of cosmic significance when viewed through the lens of astrology, in the sense that the system portrays humans as beings that are basically "at home" in the universe.

## Theories of Astrological Influence

Approaches to explaining how astrology "works" move between two poles, one that stresses the study of the stars as a natural science (and that consequently attempts to distance it from occultism), and another that, while often calling astrology by the name of science, emphasizes the spiritual or occult dimension of the study of planetary influences. The former perspective, using the natural science model, tends to conceive of astrological influences in terms of forces, analogous to the forces of gravity and magnetism, that are actually "radiated" by the planets.

The latter perspective, while often speaking in terms of "occult forces," usually emphasizes that correlations between celestial and mundane spheres result from a kind of "prearranged harmony" that is built into the very structure of the cosmos. In other words, the various correspondences that astrology studies are a result of "synchronicity" (to use Carl Jung's term) rather than cause and effect. It is worth noting that a large number of astrologers attempt to adhere simultaneously to both a force and a correspondence explanation.

The cosmic interconnectedness that the second approach tends to see as fundamental to understanding astrological influence implies a kind of monistic view of the universe that is related to the worldview held in common by most strands of America's metaphysical subculture. This link is the primary reason that astrology has come in for such severe criticism from militant secularists as well as from conservative Christians.

## Christianity and Astrology

The Christian church absorbed astrology along with many other aspects of Hellenistic civilization. Some Christian thinkers worried about the tension between free will and the perceived determinism of astrology, but by and large, the science of the stars occupied an honorable position in the Western tradition. Although some of the Biblical prophets disparaged stargazing, the three wise men were clearly astrologers, and in certain other scriptural passages it is evident that God regularly utilized heavenly signs to instruct the faithful.

Despite certain tensions in the marriage, astrology and Christianity did not divorce until the fundamentalist movement emerged in the early twentieth century. For various reasons—but particularly because of astrology's association with metaphysical religion—fundamentalists, and later most other conservative Christians, rejected astrology as a delusion at best and as a tool of Satan at worst.

## The Metaphysical Subculture and Astrology

Despite the antagonism from militant secularists and conservative Christians, astrology has been growing steadily the past hundred years. This growth may well have something to do with the decreasing power of astrology's critics. While the number of conservative churches increase, their influence of traditional religion on society has been waning for more than a century. As for secular humanists, because science creates more problems than it solves, the appeal of a quasi-religious secularism tied to mainstream science has also lost its social influence. While both conservative Christianity and secular humanism have been losing ground, the West's metaphysical subculture—which has been friendly to astrology—has been growing in size and influence. Gallup polls have indicated that over one-third of Americans believe in astrology.

The metaphysical community is a loosely knit subculture. Its most distinctive institutions are the metaphysical bookstores and organizations. The largest of these organizations are the many theosophical societies and spiritualist churches, which were formed in the nineteenth century. This metaphysical community was relatively small until the late twentieth century. When the counterculture of the sixties faded away in the early seventies, many former "hippies" found themselves embarking upon spiritual quests, which radically departed from the Judeo-Christian mainstream. These new seekers swelled the ranks of the metaphysical subculture until it became a significant social force.

One important manifestation of this subculture is called the New Age movement. While segments of the metaphysical community have been referring to themselves as New Age for a long time, neither the community nor the term were familiar to the cultural mainstream until the late eighties. In North America, the single most important event prompting general awareness of this subculture was the broadcast of Shirley MacLaine's *Out on a Limb* in January 1987. The success of this television miniseries stimulated the mass media to begin investigating and, in time, to begin generating articles and programs about the New Age. The media's interest was still high at the time of the Harmonic Convergence gatherings in 1987, causing the Convergence to attract more public attention than any New Age event before or since.

The widespread interest in the New Age, which was intensified by curiosity about the Harmonic Convergence, led, in turn, to the *Time* magazine feature, "New Age Harmonies," in December 1987. This piece was the most significant general article on the movement to appear in a major news magazine. Like many previous treatments in the mainstream media, "New Age Harmonies" focused on the flashier, less substantive aspects of the movement. However, perhaps because of the greater weight of *Time*, this article, unlike earlier, similar pieces, influenced many of the more serious individuals within the movement to back away from the label "New Age."

Despite its continuities with the older metaphysical community, the New Age departed from tradition in certain ways. Of particular importance for the practice of astrology, the New Age blended metaphysics with certain other, distinct movements, such as the human potentials movement and humanistic psychology. As a consequence, the significance of such familiar occult practices as astrology and tarot were altered. Before explaining this alteration, the reader should note that in the same way that the media seized upon the expression "New Age" in the late eighties and transformed it into a term of derision, an earlier wave of media interest in the early seventies seized upon the word "occult" and succeeded in connecting it with such negative phenomena as black magic.

"Occult" comes from a root word meaning "hidden," and the original connotation of the word was that it referred to a body of esoteric beliefs and practices that were in some sense hidden from the person in the street (e.g., practices and knowledge that remain inaccessible until after an initiation). Alternately, it is sometimes said that practices were occult if they dealt with forces that operated by means that were hidden from ordinary perception (e.g., magic, tarot cards, astrology, etc.). Modern astrology is not occult in the sense of secret initiations, but it is occult in the sense that it deals with "hidden" forces.

Under the impact of the human potentials movement and humanistic psychology, astrology, tarot, and so forth were no longer regarded as mere fortune-telling devices, but became tools for self-transformation. The net result of this on the contemporary practice of astrology is that at least two kinds of astrologers can be distinguished: Astrologers who—like Joan Quigley, the astrologer to Ronald and Nancy Reagan—primarily predict events and advise clients on when to perform certain actions in the world, and astrologers who primarily see themselves as quasi-therapists, leading their clients to deeper understandings of themselves. Most contemporary astrologers would, of course, fall somewhere between these two extremes.

## Getting Started in Astrology

In addition to being a comprehensive reference work, this updated encyclopedia can be used as a foundational textbook for acquiring a basic understanding of astrology. The elements of the science of the stars are the signs and the planets. The beginning student should start by reading and studying the entries for each of the signs of the Zodiac in their natural order—Aries, Taurus, Gemini, Cancer, Leo, Virgo, Libra, Scorpio, Sagittarius, Capricorn, Aquarius, and Pisces. Read the entry on rulership, and then study the entries for the Sun, the Moon, and the planets. The planets need not be studied in any particular order. However, because the meanings of signs and planets overlap, one should refer each planet to the sign(s) that it rules. Next, you should read the entry on the houses, relating each of the signs to each of the houses. Finish up this course of reading with the entries on the ascendant, the aspects, the asteroids, and Chiron. When studying the aspects, one might also read the entries on the major aspects-conjunctions, sextiles, squares, trines, and oppositions.

To understand the basics of chart casting and chart interpretation, the student of astrology must memorize the glyphs (symbols) for the planets, the signs, and the aspects (which follow this introduction). Do not attempt to learn the symbols for the asteroids until *after* all of the other glyphs have been memorized, and, even at that point, focus on the most commonly utilized planetoids—Ceres, Pallas, Vesta, Juno, and Chiron. Read the balance of this introduction, and then the appendix on understanding your own natal chart. After completing this reading, you will have a basic grasp of natal astrology.

The next course of reading involves the various subdivisions and branches of the science of the stars. Begin this study with the entries on transits, electional astrology, solar returns, progressions, and directions. You can then read the entries on the branches of astrology, such as mundane astrology, horary astrology, medical astrology, heliocentric astrology, and so forth. The two final courses of reading focus on history—Mesopotamian astrology, the history of Western astrology, and the history of astrology in America—and the astrology of other cultures—Mesoamerican astrology, Chinese astrology, and Hindu astrology.

## Elements of Astrological Meaning

The basic building blocks of astrological meaning are the signs of the Zodiac and the planets. Beginning students of astrology are usually advised to study and acquire a good basic sense of the signs before proceeding to more complex studies. Because there is a certain similarity of meaning between particular planets and particular signs (each sign is said to be *ruled* by a particular planet), as well as a link of similar meaning between each successive sign with each successive house, a sound knowledge of the 12 signs of the Zodiac makes it easier to understand the astrological significance of the planets and the houses. A highly popular book is Linda Goodman's *Sun Signs*. While some astrologers have criticized this volume, it is a useful, entertaining book for acquiring basic information about the twelve signs of the Zodiac.

There are various ways of classifying the signs, some more useful than others. Of particular importance are the traditional elements of earth, air, fire, and water. These elements represent certain basic personality orientations: Earth represents practicality, water emotional sensitivity, air a mental orientation, and fire activity. Thus, for people who are comprised primarily of water signs (Cancer, Scorpio, and Pisces), feelings are what are most *real* in life; for a predominance of air signs (Gemini, Libra, and Aquarius), ideas are most real; for earth (Taurus, Virgo, and Capricorn), practical concerns; and for fire (Aries, Leo, and Sagittarius), activity.

The other primary system by which the signs are classified is the so-called qualities—cardinal, mutable, and fixed. Each of the 12 signs of the Zodiac is a unique combination of an element and a quality (e.g., Aries is a cardinal fire sign, Taurus is fixed earth, Gemini is mutable air, and so forth). The elemental nature of a sign is said to refer to its basic temperament, while quality is said to refer to its mode of expression. Cardinal signs are portrayed as outgoing signs that initiate new activities; fixed signs, by way of contrast, persist with their established activities; mutable signs adapt to changing circumstances. These two classification systems—elements and qualities—are helpful when one undertakes to memorize sign traits.

The interpretation of a horoscope is built around the influence of the planets as modified by three primary factors—signs, houses, and aspects (the angular relationships between the planets). An oversimplified but nonetheless useful rule of thumb is that planetary sign positions indicate personality tendencies, aspects between planets reflect how various components of one's personality interact with one another, and house positions show how the personality manifests in the world. Aspects are angular relationships between various points in an astrological chart. The term especially refers to a series of named angles, such as trines (120°) and squares (90°).

Visually in an astrological chart, houses are the 12 "pie-pieces" that together form the basic framework of the horoscope. Sign divisions (where signs begin and end) are not represented in a conventional chart. If they were, one would have to draw in another 12 lines, making a total of 24, which would result in a cluttered, aesthetically unappealing appearance. The numbers and symbols that appear around the outside of the wheel indicate where houses begin and end with respect to the signs of the 360° circle of the Zodiac. Starting at the nine o'clock position (which in most systems of house division corresponds with the eastern horizon) and moving counterclockwise, the houses are numbered from one to twelve. Thus, the first house begins at the nine o'clock position and ends at the eight o'clock position; the second house begins at eight o'clock and ends at seven o'clock; and so forth. The sign at the nine o'clock position on the chart is the rising sign or ascendant.

Let us illustrate sign-house-aspect relationships with a concrete example. The example we will use is an individual with natal Mars in the sign Virgo, that is also in a square (90°) aspect to Saturn and in the eleventh house. In the personality, Mars represents the outgoing, assertive, aggressive energies. This is what we might think of as the *basic* nature of Mars.

1. *Sign:* Individuals born when Mars was in Virgo need to organize to get anything done. They tend to be very patient with detailed work. (Organization and patience with detail are both Virgo traits.)

2. *Aspect:* In contrast to Mars, Saturn is the cautious, security-seeking side of the personality. Square aspects often indicate conflicts, so, in this case, Mars square Saturn shows, among other things, an individual who vacillates between assertiveness and caution, between excitement-seeking and security-seeking.

3. *House:* The eleventh house indicates things about friends, group associations, and ideals. Mars here shows people who have a lot of energy for friendships and ideals. They express their energy best in the context of group activities. In overly aggressive individuals, Mars placed here shows people whose assertiveness brings them into conflict with friends, as well as conflicts related to their ideals.

## Understanding and Interpreting a Natal Chart

A birth chart (usually called a natal chart by astrologers) is a symbolic map of the heavens with respect to the Earth at the moment of birth. When one examines a chart for the first time, one tends to be overwhelmed by the mass of numbers and unfamiliar symbols. The "pie-pieces" are the astrological house, and the numbers along the outer rim of the chart indicate where the houses begin and end in the signs of the Zodiac. The symbols along the rim are symbols for the zodiacal signs. Most of the symbols inside the houses are planet symbols. The meanings of some of these (e.g., the crescent moon, which is the symbol for the Moon) are intuitively obvious. The planet symbols also have numbers and sign symbols written alongside them. These indicate the location of a planet in a sign.

The 12 signs of the Zodiac, in addition to being bands of astrological influence, also provide astrologers with a system for locating planets and other points in space. A circle contains 360°, so that, when divided into 12 equal regions for the 12 signs, each sign encompasses an arc of 30°. Hence a planet located near the beginning of Aries, for instance, might be at 1° Aries; in the middle of Aries, at 15° Aries; and near the end of the sign, 29° Aries.

The ascendant, also called the rising sign, is the sign of the Zodiac that was on the eastern horizon at the moment for which a horoscope is cast (calculated and drawn). On a chart wheel, the rising sign is the sign at the nine o'clock position. In a natal chart, the ascendant indicates a significant influence on the personality; only the Sun and Moon exert stronger influences. These three signs—the rising sign, the Sun sign, and the Moon sign—are considered together when someone with a knowledge of astrology beyond Sun signs briefly describes his or her astrological make-up, e.g.: "I'm an Aquarius with Moon in Pisces and Aries rising." The astrologically informed listener then knows that the speaker, while primarily an Aquarius, is also sensitive and moody like a Pisces. She or he will also come across as an Aries in certain settings.

The planets represent various facets of one's psychological makeup. Thus Mercury represents the mind, particularly that part of the mind involved in communication and day-to-day problem solving; Venus indicates how we relate to others, especially in romance; and so forth. The sign positions of the planets—particularly the signs of the inner planets—indicate how we communicate, how we relate, etc. These positions modify the basic personality indicated by the Sun sign. Thus, for example, a person born under the sign Scorpio might have been born when Mercury was in Libra and Venus was in Sagittarius. Having natal Mercury in gentle, tactful Libra would modify this individual's communications so that they would be far less critical and sarcastic than that of a typical Scorpio, though a certain subdued tendency toward critical sarcasm would still be part of her or his makeup. Venus in idealistic Sagittarius would make this individual more romantic than a typical Scorpio, without eliminating her or his sexual intensity. As one can see from this example, the variety of influences at work in a natal chart can sometimes indicate contrary, if not actually contradictory, traits. The distinguishing mark of an experienced astrologer is her or his ability to synthesize these often competing influences into a coherent interpretation.

The "pie piece" in which a planet is found in a chart indicates its house position. Aspects are indicated in one of two ways: Traditionally, charts contained a grid that was a bit like the mileage grids one sometimes finds on maps. If two planets had an aspect between then, the aspect symbol would be drawn on the grid where one would find—to continue the map analogy—the mileage between two locations on a map. The modern tendency is to actually draw a line directly on the chart that connects the two planets in aspect. The symbol for the aspect is then drawn on or near the line.

## Going Further

If you are fascinated by astrology and want to do more than just read about the science of the stars, you do not have to commit yourself to becoming a full-time professional before exploring this field further. Astrology can be a fascinating hobby. Moreover, astrology can be a vehicle for learning more about yourself and others. Additionally, you might find yourself earning a little extra money on the side doing readings every once and a while.

Although this point should be obvious, it is important to realize that no governmental agency regulates the science of the stars. And although many of the larger astrological associations issue certifications testifying to one's astrological competence, you do not need to possess any kind of certificate to practice astrology. Consequently, if you know the basics and can tell someone else what a certain planet means in a certain house in their natal chart—even if you are doing it as a hobby and not charging money—then you can wear the title "astrologer" as legitimately as someone who has practiced astrology for 30 years and written a dozen books on the subject. It's a bit like riding a bicycle—once you know the basics, you are automatically a "cyclist" even if you've been riding a bike for less than a week.

People love to be told about themselves. If word gets around in your circle of acquaintances that you are learning astrology and can "read their horoscope," even at a very basic level, everyone and their brother will be beating down your door for a reading. This is a good thing, because the best way to develop your skills is to do free readings for friends and relatives. This gives you a chance to see how the interpretations you find in astrology books apply—or fail to apply—in the lives of flesh-and-blood human beings. And, because you're doing it for free, you can ask questions and risk being wrong (e.g., "Your Saturn conjuncts your Mercury. Do you sometimes think about things so seriously that you get depressed?") In this way, you learn some of the nuances of astrology while having meaningful, and usually enjoyable, interactions with other people.

You will definitely want to pick up at least a couple of astrological "cookbooks"—books that provide interpretations for the meanings of the planets by signs, houses, and aspects. These kinds of books are used when you take your first stabs at interpreting natal charts. If you browse through the appropriate section of a large metaphysical bookstore, you should be able to find several. If you are nowhere near such a store, you might contact the Astrology Center of America (http://www.astroamerica.com) bookstore for recommendations. Another option is your local public library, which might contain one of the older cookbooks, such as Llewellyn George's *A to Z Horoscope Maker and Delineator* or one of Grant Lewi's books. Another good source is Max Heindel's *The Message of the Stars*, an online version of which is available at http://www.rosicrucian.com/mos/moseng01.htm. A particular favorite of mine when I was learning astrology in the early 1970s was Isabel Hickey's *Astrology: A Cosmic Science*.

The astrologer's craft consists of two very different kinds of skills: (1) casting charts, meaning the mathematical construction of an astrological chart; and (2) delineation, which refers to chart interpretation. Although delineation is the very core of what astrology is all about, an accurate interpretation obviously depends on initially erecting the horoscope correctly. It used to be that the math involved with constructing an astrological chart was tedious and lengthy, which meant not only that people who hated math tended to steer away from becoming astrologers, but also that, even for people willing to do the calculations, it was easy for errors to creep in—errors that skewed the meaning of the entire chart. The personal computer revolution changed all of that.

To get started in computer chart casting, you do not need a top-end astrological calculation program (such programs currently run about $300). There are a variety of good freeware programs that can be downloaded from the Internet that accurately cast basic natal charts. At the time of this writing, Halloran Software (the maker of Astrology for Windows, which can be downloaded from http://www.halloran.com) and Cosmic Patterns (the maker of Starlite, which can be downloaded from http://www.patterns.com/freeware.htm) were both offering downloads of basic chart-casting programs for Windows. A widely available freeware program not associated with any software company is Astrolog (type "astrolog" into any search engine). Other programmers have adapted Astrolog to work with both Mac and Linux.

Astrolog offers more options, but I find it more awkward to use than the others, and the charts produced by the Astrolog program are unattractive. In addition to natal charts, Starlite will generate progressed charts; Astrology for Windows will do natal charts plus provide transits for your first chart (and for subsequent charts, but only after you send Halloran a modest registration fee). None of these programs contain an atlas, meaning you will need to look up the longitude and latitude of cities and towns where people were born. Doing an Internet search using the name of the birthplace along with the state or province plus the words "longitude" and "latitude" almost always provides this information. You also need to find out if daylight savings time was in effect on the individual's birth date (important, but not difficult to find, in most cases). Be aware of the common mistake of calculating A.M. births as P.M. births and vice versa. Also, do not charge forward with an approximate time of birth ("I think I was born sometime between midnight and 3:00 in the morning") if it is possible for your client to obtain a more precise time—a birth certificate usually includes one's time of birth. Armed with these three programs, anyone with access to a personal computer and the Internet has the basic tools necessary to handle the mathematical component of astrology.

Nevertheless, if you work with freeware programs for a while and then decide you want a more powerful program, most of the major astrological software companies offer no-frills versions of their top-end calculation programs. Top-of-the-line programs are selling for around $300; in contrast, entry-level programs are going for about $100. To encourage consumers to stay with their product line, most of these companies also offer to put all or most of the price of one's entry-level program toward the purchase of a top-end program—in the event one later decides to seek an upgrade.

As of 2002, all of the major software companies except Esoteric Technologies (the creators of Solar Fire, which is distributed outside of Australia by Astrolabe) and Time Cycles Research (the creators of Io for Macs) market no-frills programs in the $100 range. Not including Jyotish (Vedic astrology) companies, these astrological software companies are Matrix, Cosmic Patterns, Halloran, and A.I.R. Software. I have had an opportunity to examine the entry-level programs of everyone except A.I.R. All of these programs—WinStar Express (Matrix), Pegasus (Cosmic Patterns), and AstrolDeluxe for Windows (Halloran)—are absolutely excellent. Additionally and very importantly, all three companies provide excellent support. Although Time Cycles Research does not market a low-end program, their professional program for Macs is priced in the mid-range.

It is difficult to recommend one program over another, partly because the ongoing competition between astrological software companies will outdate my remarks in a very short time. With this caveat, I will nevertheless say that the WinStar Express program is easier to use (the interface is more user-friendly) than the others, but the current version of the Pegasus program contains more features. I particularly like the fact that Pegasus has a complete atlas for birthplaces in North America and Europe—although both AstrolDeluxe for Windows and WinStar Express contain good basic atlases. Alternately, if I was seriously considering Halloran's program, I would skip AstrolDeluxe for Windows and jump immediately to their high-end program, AstrolDeluxe ReportWriter, which sells for a good deal less than either Matrix's or Cosmic Pattern's corresponding high-end calculation programs, and comes bundled with a basic report program as well as with an atlas for 250,000 cities. For reviews of these and other major calculation programs, refer to Hank Friedman's software review appendix.

To return to the distinction between chart casting and delineation, one of the more problematic aspects of the application of computer methods to astrology has been the emergence of report programs that provide delineations of horoscopes. The building blocks of chart interpretation are the meanings of each particular sign position, house position, and aspect. Computer programs are perfectly capable of storing such information and generating a list of interpretations for the various components, tailored to the positions of any given person's chart. No professional astrologer, however, would simply list interpretations of each component of a horoscope. In fact, the very mark of an experienced astrologer is the ability to meaningfully synthesize such information into a coherent whole. This is especially important when two or more elements of a horoscope give contrary indications.

For example, a Capricorn moon in a natal chart usually indicates someone who is not emotionally sensitive to others. If, however, this same individual's natal moon is also in the first house, conjunct both the ascendant and Neptune, she or he will be extremely sensitive—probably overly sensitive—to other people. Experienced astrologers would immediately recognize this and avoid the mistake of telling this particular client that she or he was emotionally insensitive.

Report programs, no matter how sophisticated, cannot do much more than list the meanings of each element of a horoscope. No existing program would avoid, for instance, the error of informing Capricorn moon natives about their insensitivity. Thus, while computer readings may have a certain place as a preliminary step in astrological science, they will have to become far more sophisticated before they begin to approximate the skill of an experienced astrologer.

On the other side of the coin, report programs have developed to the point where good programs can generate better readings than those provided by inept astrologers. Based on personal experience, I would even go so far as to say that some computer reports can be more useful and more insightful than readings from even well-known, highly experienced astrologers. A lot depends a chart's complexity and on the quality of the report program. Someone with a natal chart containing a large number of strong aspects that pull the person in opposite directions is much less likely to get satisfactory results from a computer interpretation than someone with a more straightforward chart. Also, sophisticated, well-written report programs like Cosmic Patterns' short "Major Life Themes" (which is an integral part of both their high-end Kepler and their entry-level Pegasus calculation programs) or Matrix's "The Sky Within" and "Woman to Woman" (which are freestanding programs) are going to be far more insightful than certain other report programs.

I have been less impressed by predictive programs (progressions, transits, returns, etc.), though even the best astrologer can only rarely do more than predict general trends. On the other hand, I have been thoroughly impressed by the insightfulness of compatibility (synastry) reports, which I have found to offer surprisingly accurate insights into the dynamics of relationships between two people. Again, well-written programs like Cosmic Patterns' "Compatibility Report" and Matrix's "Friends & Lovers" will give you a lot more than certain other synastry reports. And there are yet other kinds of programs, such as reports on career possibilities and delineations of children's charts, that I have not worked with enough to comment on.

Report programs offer novice astrologers a number of possibilities. On the one hand, even someone with a minimum understanding of astrology can sell computer-generated reports. On the other hand, the beginning astrologer who owns an array of different report programs can generate one or more reports about a client to study beforehand as a way of preparing for a face-to-face reading. Many professional astrologers—particularly astrologers who are critical of all report programs to begin with—will be upset by this latter bit of advice, but it is nevertheless extremely useful for the novice.

Most of the major astrological software manufacturers offer a wide variety of report programs. This may change, but at present A.I.R. Software offers the fewest report programs. At the opposite end of the spectrum, Cosmic Patterns offers the most. Many high-end calculation programs (e.g., Solar Fire, Kepler, Janus, and AstrolDeluxe ReportWriter) include report modules as an integral part of their program. Additional add-on or freestanding report programs can range from $100 to $300. Matrix takes the approach of selling "hobbyist" versions (meaning that one is not licensed to sell reports) of most of their delineation software for significantly less than their professional versions. If you are not focused on making money from astrology, but just want to share astrology with friends and relatives, hobbyist report programs are a great way to go. There are also a couple of "talking" programs (e.g., one is an integral part of Kepler, and another is a free-standing program, Astro*Talk Audio, from Matrix) which, although less useful for professional astrologers, are fun for small parties and other kinds of informal gatherings.

After you have been dabbling in astrology for awhile, and particularly if the little bit of money you have been making on the side doing readings has been expanding, you may wish to consider turning your astrology hobby into a full-time job. I do not intend to go into the details of running an astrology practice here. There have been a number of good books written on this subject that you can look at, such as the Organization for Professional Astrology's *How to Start, Maintain, and Expand an Astrological Practice*, Wendy Hawks's *Nuts & Bolts of Running an Astrology Practice*, and Donna Cunningham's *The Consulting Astrologer's Guidebook* (a manual on how to give professional readings). At the time of this writing, all of these were available through Halloran.

—James R. Lewis

# Acknowledgments

Many thanks to the contributors, who trusted me with the fruits of their labor, to Alice May Kesemochen, who drew the illustrations in the glyph tables, and to Cosby Steuart, who typed sections of the final manuscript. At Visible Ink Press, I am grateful to acquisitions editor Christa Gainor and to my developmental editors—first Terri Schell and then Larry Baker. Additional thanks go to art director Mary Claire Krzewinski, copyeditor Amy Lucas, illustrations coordinator Christopher Scanlon, illustrations processor Robert J. Huffman, proofreader Susan Salter, indexer Larry Baker, and typesetter Marco Di Vita of the Graphix Group.

My understanding of astrology has been shaped by conversations with many people over the years. Each and all have my heartfelt gratitude. I would especially like to express thanks to the astrological community, which has generously supplied me with information and encouragement for this project.

# Contributors

The author wishes to thank the following contributors, who provided the entries listed.

**Tishelle Betterman:** Neptune; Pluto
**Linda R. Birch:** Uranus; Venus
**Bernadette Brady:** Fixed Stars
**Nick Campion:** Mundane Astrology
**Karen Christino:** Adams, Evangeline
**Stephanie Jean Clement, Ph.D.:** Planet-Centered Astrology; Vocational Astrology
**David Cochrane:** Harmonic Astrology
**Donna Cunningham:** Flower Remedies and Astrology
**Patrick Curry:** Lilly, William
**Michele Delemme:** Cat (Rabbit); Chinese Astrology; Dog; Dragon; Goat; Horse; Monkey; Ox (Buffalo); Pig (Boar); Rat; Roell, David R.; Snake; Tiger
**Meira B. Epstein:** Ibn Ezra, Avraham
**Michael Erlewine:** Erlewine, Michael; Matrix Astrological Software; Tibetan Astrology; Tibetan Astrology: Lunar Gaps
**Penny Farrow:** Muharta; Upaya (Remedial Measures); Yogas
**Demetra George:** Ceres; Juno; Pallas Athene; Vesta
**John Halloran:** Astrodynes
**Dennis M. Harness, Ph.D.:** The Nakshatras: The Lunar Mansions of Vedic Astrology; Vedic Astrology (Hindu Astrology)
**Dennis M. Harness, Ph.D.,** and **David Frawley:** American Council of Vedic Astrology; Vedic Astrology in the West
**Ko Hashiguchi:** Four Pillars Divination

**Madalyn Hillis-Dineen:** Uranian Astrology
**Jayj Jacobs:** The Law and Astrology
**Aidan A. Kelly:** Calendar; Humanistic Astrology; Rudhyar, Dane
**J. Lee Lehman, Ph.D.:** Horary Astrology; Hyleg; Medical Astrology; Temperaments
**Jim Lewis:** Astro*Carto*Graphy
**Lea Manders:** Kabbalah and Astrology; Manders, Lea
**Maire Masco:** Mercury; Moon
**Maria J. Mateus:** Mars; Sun
**J. Gordon Melton:** History of Astrology in America
**Ken Negus:** Kepler, Johannes
**Evelyn Dorothy Oliver:** Numerology and Astrology
**Glenn Perry, Ph.D.:** Psychological Astrology; Therapeutic Astrology
**Garry Phillipson** and **Peter Case:** Temperaments in Jungian Psychology
**Isotta Poggi:** History of Western Astrology
**David Pond:** Chakras and Astrology
**Maritha Pottenger:** Antivertex
**Irmgard Rauchhaus:** Cosmobiology
**Norma Jean Ream:** Jupiter; Saturn
**Melanie Reinhart:** Chiron
**Diana E. Roche, M.Ed., J.D.:** Sabian Symbols
**Lois M. Rodden:** Astrological Data
**Kim Rogers-Gallagher:** Rogers-Gallagher, Kim
**Barbara Schermer:** Experiential Astrology
**Bruce C. Scofield:** Mesoamerican Astrology
**Mary Fortier Shea:** Solar Return Chart
**Maria Kay Simms:** Neopagan Spirituality and Astrology
**Georgia Stathis:** Business Astrology
**Pramela Thiagesan:** Anuradha; Ardra; Ashwini; Aslesha; Bharani; Chitra; Dhanistha; Hasta; Jyeshta; Krittika; Magha; Mrigasira; Mula; Punarvasu; Purva Bhadrapada; Purva Phalguni; Purvashada; Pushya; Revati; Rohini; Satabisha; Shravana; Swati; Uttara Bhadrapada; Uttara Phalguni; Uttarashada; Visakha
**Donna Van Toen:** Gemstones and Astrology
**Angela Voss:** Ficino, Marsilio
**Sophia Wellbeloved:** Gurdjieff, George Ivanovitch
**Michael York:** Contemporary Academic Study of Astrology
**Robert Zoller:** Abū Ma‘shar; Al-Biruni; Arabic Parts; Bonatti, Guido; Charis; Masha’allah; Morin, Jean-Baptiste (Morinus)

| PLANET | COMMON ABBREVIATION | GLYPH |
|---|---|---|
| *Sun | SUN | ☉ |
| Mercury | MER | ☿ |
| Venus | VEN | ♀ |
| Earth | EAR | ⊕ |
| *Moon | MON or MOO | ☽ |
| Mars | MAR | ♂ |
| Jupiter | JUP | ♃ |
| Saturn | SAT | ♄ |
| Uranus | URA | ♅ ⛢ |
| Neptune | NEP | ♆ |
| Pluto | PLU | ♇ ♇ |

*Not planets, but traditionally listed

| SIGN | COMMON ABBREVIATION | GLYPH |
|---|---|---|
| Aries | ARI | ♈ |
| Taurus | TAR or TAU | ♉ |
| Gemini | GEM | ♊ |
| Cancer | CAN | ♋ |
| Leo | LEO | ♌ |
| Virgo | VIR | ♍ |
| Libra | LIB | ♎ |
| Scorpio | SCO | ♏ |
| Sagittarius | SAG | ♐ |
| Capricorn | CAP | ♑ |
| Aquarius | AQU | ♒ |
| Pisces | PIC or PIS | ♓ |

| OTHER POINTS | COMMON ABBREVIATION | GLYPH |
|---|---|---|
| North Node | NN | ☊ |
| South Node | SN | ☋ |
| Galactic Center | GC | [illegible] |
| Part of Fortune | P of F | ⊗ |

| ASTEROID | GLYPH |
|---|---|
| Aesculapia | |
| Amor | |
| Apollo | |
| Arachne | |
| Ariadne | |
| Astraea | % |
| Atlantis | |
| Bacchus | |
| Ceres | |
| Chiron | |
| Circe | |
| Cupido | |
| Daedalus | |
| Dembowska | |
| Demeter | |
| Diana | |
| Dike | |
| Dudu | |
| Eros | |
| Eurydike | |
| Frigga | |
| Hebe | |
| Hera | |
| Hidalgo | |
| Hopi | |
| Hybris | |

| ASTEROID | GLYPH |
|---|---|
| Hygiea | |
| Icarus | |
| Industria | |
| Isis | |
| Juno | |
| Kassandra | |
| Lilith | |
| Minerva | |
| Nemesis | |
| Niobe | |
| Orpheus | |
| Pallas | |
| Pandora | |
| Persephone | |
| Pittsburghia | |
| Proserpina | |
| Psyche | |
| Sappho | |
| Sisyphus | |
| Siva | |
| Terpsichore | |
| Themis | |
| Toro | |
| Urania | |
| Vesta | |

| IMAGINARY PLANET | GLYPH |
|---|---|
| Admetos | |
| Apollon | |
| Coda | |
| Cupido (also an asteroid name) | |
| Dido (also an asteroid name) | |
| Hades | |
| Hercules | |
| Hermes | |
| Horus (also an asteroid name) | |
| Isis (Also an asteroid name) | |
| Jason | |
| Kronos | |
| LaCroix | |
| Lilith (also an asteroid name) | |
| Lion | |
| Loki | |
| Melodia | |
| Midas (also an asteroid name) | |
| Minos | |
| Moraya | |
| Osiris (also an asteroid name) | |
| Pan (also an asteroid name) | |
| Persephone (also an asteroid name) | |
| Polyhymnia (also an asteroid name) | |
| Poseidon (also an asteroid name) | |
| Shanti | |
| Transpluto | |
| Vulcan | |
| Vulcanus (Vulkanus) | |
| Wemyss—Pluto | |
| Zeus | |

## Abū Ma'shar

The famous Persian astrologer Abū Ma'shar (787–886), whose full name was Abū Ma'shar Ja'far ibn Muhammad ibn 'Umar al-Balkhi, is perhaps the major representative of Arabic astrology from the medieval Western world. His works were widely translated in the twelfth century, were widely circulated in manuscript, and exerted a very powerful influence on the development of Western astrology. His writings were used as prototypes for astrological practice. For instance, they provided the thirteenth-century astrologer Guido Bonatti with a frequently cited source in his summa of medieval astrology, the *Liber Astronomia* (c. 1282). Episcopal clergyman Theodore Otto Wedel tells us that English poets Geoffrey Chaucer and John Gower were familiar with Abū Ma'shar's works. One can almost say that Abū Ma'shar established the standard practice for medieval astrology in general with major additional input from Messahala, Ptolemy, and Dorotheus. Abū Ma'shar's influence upon the philosophical foundations of Arabic and Latin astrology is far greater than has been recognized and to a large degree constitutes the difference between medieval astrological theory and modern astrological theory, especially with regard to fate and free will.

Abū Ma'shar's astrological writings are also an example of Hermetic influence on Arabic astrology. His works (written in Arabic) represent a fusion of Sabian Hermeticism, Persian chronology, Islam, Greek Science (especially Aristotelian), and Mesopotamian astrology. He, and his teacher Al-Kindi, were instrumental in fostering the identification of the antediluvian prophet Idris with Enoch and Hermes, thereby creating a religious syncretism that had important ramifications for the dissemination of pagan science, including astrology. Abū Ma'shar was an extremely successful practitioner of the art and traveled throughout the Middle East in service to numerous Indian, Persian, Arab, and Egyptian chiefs of state. His reputation was established in the Christian west by Peter of Abano in the thirteenth century in his *Conciliator Differentiarum Philosophorum et Precipue Medicorum* (Diff. 156), wherein Peter quotes the Al-

Mudsakaret or (Memorabilia) of Abū Sa'id Schadsan, a student of Abū Ma'shar's who recorded his teacher's answers and astrological deeds. The *Memorabilia*, which have come to be known among scholars as "Albumasar in Sadan" due to traditional corruptions of both men's names, is analyzed by Lynn Thorndike in a 1954 *ISIS* article.

The astrological works of Abū Ma'shar we have are:

*The Greater Introduction to Astrology*
*The Flores Astrologicae*
*On the Great Conjunctions and on the Revolutions of the World (Kitāb al-Qiranat)*
*On the Revolutions of Nativities*
*The Thousands (Kitāb al-Uluf)*

Abū Ma'shar was a religious Muslim. He was also an astrologer and a noted philosopher. His impact upon subsequent Arabic and Latin astrology is best understood through a consideration of his attitude toward the idea of freedom of the will as it relates to astrology. In his *Greater Introduction*, he sets forth his theory of astrological determinism in the context of a defense of astrology against its detractors.

Abū Ma'shar repeatedly mentions the divine will as the originator or director of nature. All motions, including celestial motions, are derived from one unique and unmoved source. Abū Ma'shar equated this with God. His source, Aristotle, placed it in a universal attraction at the periphery of the supreme sphere—the sphere of the fixed stars. According to Abū Ma'shar, God is the source of all motions in the universe. God's intervention in terrestrial affairs, however, never disrupts the regular operation of the system of causes and effects leading to generation in nature. This causal relationship is dependent upon the stars. This means that although Abū Ma'shar asserts frequently that Allah is omnipotent, Abū Ma'shar's universe is conceived primarily in terms of physical science and merely draped in Koranic theology.

We may be excused for questioning whether Abū Ma'shar believes that divine providence is the actual cause of natural manifestations. Where is human free will in this? Is his cosmo-conception deterministic, or can God intervene in terrestrial affairs? Is the individual human free to choose a course of action? Apart from his many assertions of orthodoxy, Abū Ma'shar leaves little room for providence because he asserts that the planets and stars intervene in the chain of causes flowing between God and nature as a kind of buffer or series of filters through which the will of God must act.

The substance of Abū Ma'shar's argument is that both the necessary and the impossible, being unchangeable, leave no room for the contingent. But accidental (i.e. possible, contingent) things happen in the world of generation. Thus a third category, "the possible," is necessary to cover these things. The greatest source of contingency in man's affairs is his ability to reason. His capacity for deliberation and the exercise of choice constitutes a principle of indetermination for future occurrences; but man's choice does not extend to things he knows to be necessary or impossible.

Abū Ma'shar asserts that contingency actually exists and gives examples taken from concrete reality. A piece of cloth may be cut up or, equally possible, it may remain whole until worn out through use. Iron or lead is at one point in time solid and at another point in time liquid. Air may receive more or less heat or cold. All such possibilities of mutations may materialize or not, but they are clear proof of the existence of contingency in some beings. On the other hand, the necessary and the impossible either are or are not absolute.

Abū Ma'shar recognizes three categories of the possible or the contingent. The first category is *contingens naturalis sive facilis;* an example is that of rain most often following the gathering of clouds. The second category is *per optacionem et difficilis;* an example is that of the non-noble man seeking to become king. The third category is *et contingens equalis;* an example is that of the pregnant woman hoping to give birth to a boy, but who has a 50-50 chance of delivering either a girl or a boy.

Possibility originates in the physical world from the capacity of matter to receive first one quality and then its opposite. Water may be cold at one time and hot in another, with varying intensity in each state. In man, possibility springs from his capacity for deliberation and choice, but also from his capacity to receive the qualities of matter in his body. Hence, though man is endowed with free choice that constitutes a first principle of contingency in him, his freedom of choice is limited, circumscribed by the matter from which his body is made.

According to Abū Ma'shar, something remarkable happens when a thing moves from potentiality to actuality. He concludes that contingency is ultimately absorbed into either the necessary or the impossible! Once a thing has come into being, its potentiality in which its contingency resided no longer subsists, and therefore it must be classified in the camp of the necessary. On the other hand, if it does not materialize, Abū Ma'shar thinks that it must be because of some sort of impossibility. Thus, Abū Ma'shar shares the fatalistic leanings of Arabic Aristotelianism.

Abū Ma'shar holds that planetary influence does not destroy contingency or freedom. He asserts that planetary influence signifies the necessary, the possible, and the impossible. With respect to contingency in matter, Abū Ma'shar holds that universal matter, formed of the four elements, is entirely dependent in all its transformations upon the stellar influences. Thus, the totality of contingency is outlined in advance in the regular motions of the stars. With respect to contingency in animated beings, Abū Ma'shar says it depends upon planetary motion, although a living thing needs more than just a natural motion to pass into action because its soul is a principle of indetermination to it as regards its future action.

Indetermination in man is no insurmountable obstacle to astrology, we are told, because there is a harmony between man's soul and the souls in the planets. The rational soul, even under the influence of the stars, has a power of deliberation and choice as a result of a similar power in the stars. Man's body, on the other hand, has the capacity to receive new qualities from the sky. Through the parallelism between the animated planets and living things in this lower world, Abū Ma'shar found it possible to ascribe an unlimited scope to the planets' influences upon the voluntary contingency in man's twofold body and soul. Within this cosmological framework, man's free will appears drastically curtailed from what it was held to be by Aristotle, the Christians, Jews, and Muslims, notwithstanding Abū Ma'shar's frequently uttered statements to the contrary inspired by his religiosity.

Having set forth his planetary theory, Abū Ma'shar reviews the various influences exerted by the planets upon man, intending to show how freedom or contingency is not destroyed. As an animated being, man possesses life, which is a necessary attribute of his nature. The animated and intelligent planets signify this for him, and in doing so they signify a modality of being that may be called of the type necessary. On the other hand, there are things incompatible with man's nature, such as the ability to fly. By excluding this eventuality from the nature of man as he comes to be, the planets signify another modality of man's being—the impossible. Finally, as man has the power of choice and reason, and the capacity to receive the impression of different physical qualities in his body by virtue of the four elements of which it is composed, human nature is open to a wide range of contingency that is nevertheless signified by the planets. Thus, the planets signify the three modes: the necessary, the impossible, and the possible.

The astrologer is only concerned with the possible. He does not inquire whether fire burns or not, but rather will fire burn tomorrow a matter that has a disposition to be burned? Will this individual talk to that one tomorrow? What the astrologer does in these cases is to make sure that the focus of the enquiry belongs to the possible. The planets can indicate that something cannot occur (impossible), that something may occur (possible), or that something must occur (necessary). If the signification holds only in the future, it will remain uncertain until the time of occurrence, when the actual event will fall into the category of the necessary. If, for instance, no impediment deprives a man from the use of his tongue, the man enjoys potentially the faculty of speaking or not. But only until he speaks. When he has spoken, his speech falls into the category of the necessary. Abū Ma'shar holds that the modes of activity of concrete beings exist potentially in them before they are translated into action. Once they have reached the stage of a completed action they fall into the category of the necessary.

Abū Ma'shar concludes that "since the planets signify the contingent in nature as well as in deliberation and choice proper to man, they indicate that man will choose only what is implied in planetary motion." If there is a providential intervention in this scheme of natural motion, it must come from outside the regular activity of nature and, presumably, against it.

Abū Ma'shar holds that the choice exercised by man's rational soul is circumscribed by its connection to the physical body, whose potentials are already limited. Man's rational soul acts in connection with his vital soul, but the latter is influenced by the animated planets. For instance, among the motions within his possibilities through the physical properties of his body, he may select walking, sitting, or standing (but not flying). Once he chooses, the possibilities of his material nature are forthwith determined to this particular motion. Moreover, man's choice is itself limited to the actual determination caused by the planetary motions.

In conclusion, what we see here is a doctrine of astrological determination that is, from one point of view, an exercise in double-talk. The planets give possibilities because they are ensouled, and, as such, they are in harmony with man's soul. So they judge and deliberate and so does man. Yet man, it turns out, judges and deliberates what the planets have already deliberated, and, thus, man's reason and choice merely reflect the celestial reason and choice. In fact there is little, if any, freedom.

Again, man's body may receive influences from the heavens or it may not. But the body exists because of heaven ordering the elements. Therefore, the body is determined already by the stars. The rational soul is free to reason. Yet the rational soul acts in concert with the vital soul, which reflects the celestial decrees. Thus, the rational soul's rational choices are adulterated by the appetitive, emotional, and instinctive inclinations of the vital soul.

Abū Ma'shar's description of the constitution of man agrees well with the esoteric teachings coming down to us from the Middle Ages, which attribute to man a rational soul, an astral soul (the soul of the middle nature, or Tree of Life), and a physical body. A fifth factor, the highest, is alluded to elliptically by the reference to the sphere of the Moon, which was associated with the intellect. There is much implied in the statement "If there is a providential intervention in this scheme of natural motion, it must come from outside the regular activity of nature and presumably against it."

Abū Ma'shar's theory of astrological influence is actually deterministic in spite of his pious posturing. As such, it is contrary not only to religious tendencies in Judaism, Christianity, and Islam, but also to the contemporary New Age idealism to which most modern (nineteenth- to twenty-first century) astrologers consciously or unconsciously ascribe. It is this difference that must be appreciated if one is to properly understand the difference between modern and medieval astrological practice.

—Robert Zoller

**Sources:**

*Alkindi's On the Stellar Rays*. Translated by Robert Zoller.

*Hermetis philosophi de revolutionibus nativitatum incerto interprete*... (bound with *Proclus In Claudii Ptolemaei quadripartium ennarator ignoti nominis Basilieae*, 1559).

Khaldūn, Ibn. *The Muqaddimah*. New York: Pantheon Books, 1958.

*L'Astrologie et la Science Occulte*. Le R. P. Festugière, O.P.

Lemay, Richard. *Abū Ma'shar and Latin Aristotelianism in the 12th Century*. Beirut, 1962.

*Studies in Islamic Exact Sciences by E. S. Kennedy, Colleagues and Former Students*. Edited by David King and Mary Hellen Kennedy. Beirut: American University of Beirut, c. 1983.

Tester, Jim. *A History of Western Astrology*. Woodbridge, Suffolk: Boydel Press, 1987.

Thorndike, Lynn. *History of Magic and Experimental Science*. Vol. 1. New York: Columbia University Press, 1923.

Wedel, Theodore Otto. *The Mediaeval Attitude Toward Astrology, Particularly in England*. New Haven: Yale University Library, 1920. Reprint, Norwood, PA: Norwood Editions, 1978.

## ABUNDANTIA

Abundantia, asteroid 151 (the 151st asteroid to be discovered, on November 1, 1875), is approximately 42 kilometers in diameter and has an orbital period of 4.1 years. Its name is Latin for "affluence" or "abundance." Abundantia's location by sign and house in a natal chart may show where one experiences the most abundance or an area that can be cultivated to achieve affluence.

**Sources:**
Kowal, Charles T. *Asteroids: Their Nature and Utilization*. Chichester, West Sussex, UK: Ellis Horwood Limited, 1988.
Room, Adrian. *Dictionary of Astronomical Names*. London: Routledge, 1988.
Schwartz, Jacob. *Asteroid Name Encyclopedia*. St. Paul, MN: Llewellyn Publications, 1995.

## Accidental Ascendant

Horary astrology is the branch of astrology in which an astrological chart is cast for the moment a question is asked. The chart is then read to determine an answer to the question. The ascendant (degree of the zodiac on the eastern horizon) for a horary chart is referred to as the accidental ascendant.

## Accidental Dignity

A planet is said to be in its dignity when it is in the sign that it rules. For example, because Pluto rules Scorpio, Pluto is in dignity when in the sign Scorpio. As the term implies, this is regarded as a fortunate placement; a planet in its dignity is traditionally regarded as being in harmony with the sign and consequently strengthened.

A planet's being in the sign of its rulership is sometimes referred to as essential dignity to distinguish it from certain other placements that tend to strengthen a planet's influence by virtue of its position in an astrological chart; these other placements are traditionally termed "accidental" dignities.

For example, the 12 signs of the zodiac correspond to the 12 astrological houses so there is a natural affinity between successive signs and successive houses (i.e., between Aries, the first sign, and the first house; Taurus, the second sign, and the second house; Gemini, the third sign, and the third house; etc.). When a planet is placed in a natal chart so that it falls in the house corresponding to the sign it rules, it is said to be "accidentally" dignified. Thus, Mars in the first house, Venus in the second house, and Mercury in the third house would be accidentally dignified because Mars rules Aries, Venus rules Taurus, and Mercury rules Gemini.

Planets are also strengthened by certain other placements, such as when a planet in the first house is conjunct the ascendant, or one in the tenth house is conjunct the midheaven. These other placements are sometimes also referred to as accidental dignities.

**Sources:**
DeVore, Nicholas. *Encyclopedia of Astrology*. New York: Philosophical Library, 1947.
Gettings, Fred. *Dictionary of Astrology*. London: Routledge & Kegan Paul, 1985.

## Achilles

Achilles, asteroid 588 (the 588th asteroid to be discovered, on February 22, 1906), is approximately 116 kilometers in diameter and has an orbital period of 11.8 years. It was named after the famous Greek hero of the Trojan War and was the first of the so-called Trojan asteroids (asteroids that travel along the same orbital path as Jupiter) to be discovered. Achilles' location by sign and house in a natal chart shows an area of exceptional strength, but at the same time the site of an Achilles' heel.

**Sources:**

Kowal, Charles T. *Asteroids: Their Nature and Utilization*. Chichester, West Sussex, UK: Ellis Horwood Limited, 1988.

Room, Adrian. *Dictionary of Astronomical Names*. London: Routledge, 1988.

Schwartz, Jacob. *Asteroid Name Encyclopedia*. St. Paul, MN: Llewellyn Publications, 1995.

## Acronycal

Acronycal (Greek for "on the edge of night") refers to a planet directly opposite the Sun that rises after sunset or sets before sunrise, which, as a consequence, is in a favorable location for astronomical observation. The *acronycal place* is the degree in the sign of the zodiac directly opposed to the Sun.

## Adad

Adad is a term from Mesopotamian astrology that refers to meteorological and astrological phenomena.

## Adams, Evangeline

Evangeline Adams, born February 8, 1868, in Jersey City, New Jersey, was the premier American astrologer of the early twentieth century. She was the daughter of George and Harriet E. (Smith) Adams and was related to U.S. presidents John Adams and John Quincy Adams. Raised in Andover, Massachusetts, she was educated there and in Chicago. She became part of the elite metaphysical community in the larger Boston area and was introduced to astrology by Dr. J. Heber Smith, a professor of medicine at Boston University. Adams also studied Hindu philosophy under Swami Vivekenanda. She eventually became so interested in the science of the stars that she chose it as her life's work.

In 1899, Adams visited New York City and stayed at the fashionable Windsor Hotel. Her first client was Warren F. Leland, owner of the Windsor. After casting his chart, she told him that he was under a planetary combination that threatened immediate disaster. The next afternoon, on March 17, 1899, the hotel burned to the ground. Adams subsequently gained much newspaper coverage, which led to her becoming an astrological superstar, and she gained many rich and powerful clients. She eventually established her studios at Carnegie Hall and was consulted by financier J. P. Morgan, tenor Enrico Caruso, playwright Eugene O'Neill, mythologist Joseph Campbell, and actress Mary Pickford, among many others.

In 1914, Adams was arrested and charged with fortune-telling. She went to court armed with reference books and proceeded to explain the principles of astrology. She concluded her defense by reading a chart of an individual unknown to her.

Impressed with the accuracy of her reading, Judge John H. Freschi remarked that "the defendant raises astrology to the dignity of an exact science" (*New York Criminal Reports*, volume XXXII, 1914 ed.). He found Adams not guilty, and the case set a precedent on how similar cases would be tried in New York City in the future.

Adams continued to practice and promote the science of the stars to the general public. She marketed monthly forecasts featuring her predictions about political and economic events (including a 1931 prediction that the United States would be at war in 1942). During the last decade of her life, she wrote some of the most popular astrology books ever published: *The Bowl of Heaven* (1926), *Astrology: Your Place in the Sun* (1928), *Astrology: Your Place Among the Stars* (1930), and *Astrology for Everyone* (1931). Much of her published work on astrology was originally done in collaboration with the English magician and occultist Aleister Crowley. On April 23, 1930, Adams began to broadcast on radio three times a week. As a result of this show, she received 150,000 requests for astrological charts over the course of the next three months. As much as a year later, requests and letters were still being received at the rate of 4,000 a day. Adams was a major contributor to the popularization of astrology in the United States. She died on November 10, 1932, in New York City.

—Karen Christino

**Sources:**

Adams, Evangeline. *Astrology for Everyone*. New York: Dodd, Mead & Co., 1931.

———. *Astrology: Your Place Among the Stars*. New York: Dodd, Mead & Co., 1930.

———. *Astrology: Your Place in the Sun*. New York: Dodd, Mead & Co., 1927.

———. *The Bowl of Heaven*. New York, Dodd, Mead & Co., 1926. Reprint, New York: Dodd, Mead & Co., 1970.

Christino, Karen, *Foreseeing the Future: Evangeline Adams and Astrology in America*. Amherst, MA: One Reed Publications, 2002.

## Adjusted Calculation Date

The adjusted calculation date is the date on which a planet in a progressed horoscope culminates (i.e., reaches the midheaven).

## Admetos

Admetos is one of the eight hypothetical planets (sometimes referred to as the trans-Neptunian points or planets, or TNPs for short) utilized in Uranian astrology. The Uranian system, sometimes referred to as the Hamburg School of Astrology, was established by Friedrich Sieggrün (1877–1951) and Alfred Witte (1878–1943). It relies heavily on hard aspects and midpoints. In decline for many decades, it has experienced a revival in recent years.

Admetos may symbolize blockage, patience, frustration, delay, hindrances, standstill, and so forth. More positively, it may represent depth, profundity, and that which is fundamental. For example, a link between the planet Mercury and Admetos may indicate limited thinking, or it may indicate deep thinking.

Based on the speculative orbits of the Uranian planets, the Kepler, Solar Fire and Win*Star software program will all locate this hypothetical planet in an astrological chart.

**Sources:**

Lang-Wescott, Martha. *Mechanics of the Future: Asteroids*. Rev. ed. Conway, MA: Treehouse Mountain, 1991.

Simms, Maria Kay. *Dial Detective: Investigation with the 90 Degree Dial*. San Diego: Astro Computing Services, 1989.

## Adorea

Adorea, asteroid 268 (the 268th asteroid to be discovered, on August 18, 1884), is approximately 122 kilometers in diameter and has an orbital period of 5.5 years. Adorea is a "concept" asteroid; the name means glory and originally referred to the gift of corn that was given to soldiers after a victory. In a natal chart, Adorea's location by sign and house position indicates where a person gives or receives recognition. When afflicted by inharmonious aspects, Adorea may indicate negative or false recognition.

**Sources:**

Kowal, Charles T. *Asteroids: Their Nature and Utilization*. Chichester, West Sussex, UK: Ellis Horwood Limited, 1988.

Room, Adrian. *Dictionary of Astronomical Names*. London: Routledge, 1988.

Schwartz, Jacob. *Asteroid Name Encyclopedia*. St. Paul, MN: Llewellyn Publications, 1995.

## Aestival Signs

The aestival signs are the summer signs, namely, Cancer, Leo, and Virgo.

## Aeternitas

Aeternitas, asteroid 446 (the 446th asteroid to be discovered, on October 27, 1899), is approximately 52 kilometers in diameter and has an orbital period of 4.7 years. Its name is Latin for "eternity," and refers to the immortality achieved by deification. When prominent in a natal chart, Aeternitas may indicate a person with interest in the "eternal verities" or one who can expect a long life.

**Sources:**

Kowal, Charles T. *Asteroids: Their Nature and Utilization*. Chichester, West Sussex, UK: Ellis Horwood Limited, 1988.

Room, Adrian. *Dictionary of Astronomical Names*. London: Routledge, 1988.

Schwartz, Jacob. *Asteroid Name Encyclopedia*. St. Paul, MN: Llewellyn Publications, 1995.

## AFFINITY

Astrologers use the term affinity to refer to compatibility between certain planets or signs. It is also used to denote attraction between people whose charts interact harmoniously and magnetically with each other.

## AFFLICTION

An affliction is (1) any difficult aspect, such as a square, or (2) a more neutral aspect, such as a conjunction, in which at least one of the planets is a "difficult" planet, such as Saturn. A planet involved in more than one such aspect, especially if there are no benefic aspects counterbalancing the hard aspects, is said to be *heavily* afflicted.

The term affliction has tended to drop out of usage among contemporary astrologers, although the revival of classical and horary astrology has also revived traditional terms. Astrologers are more likely to refer to such aspects as inharmonious, challenging, or difficult. More is involved in this change of terminology than the goal of making the language less dramatic: Some difficult aspects are necessary to bring challenges into one's life, and the modern terminology more accurately denotes challenge. People without at least a few such aspects in their natal charts usually lack character and rarely accomplish much in life.

**Sources:**

Bach, Eleanor. *Astrology from A to Z: An Illustrated Source Book*. New York: Philosophical Library, 1990.

DeVore, Nicholas. *Encyclopedia of Astrology*. New York: Philosophical Library, 1947.

## AGE OF AQUARIUS (AQUARIAN AGE)

The Age of Aquarius is one of 12 successive 2,150-year periods, each of which corresponds with one of the 12 signs of the zodiac. In the same manner in which individuals born at different times of the year are thought to be dominated by different astrological signs, astrologers also tend to view different historical periods as being dominated by the influence of particular signs. According to this view, Earth, for the past several thousand years, has been passing through a period dominated by the sign Pisces (the Age of Pisces). This succession of ages is based on a phenomenon known as the precession of equinoxes.

Due to the precession of equinoxes, the spring equinox moves slowly backward through the constellations of the zodiac, so that approximately every 2000 years, the equinox begins taking place in an earlier constellation. Thus, the spring equinox has been occurring in Pisces for the past several thousand years and will begin to occur in the constellation Aquarius in the near future. This is the background for current speculations about the so-called Age of Aquarius. The phenomenon of the precession of equinoxes also means that the spring equinox occurred in the sign Aries during the Hellenistic period (the period of Ptolemy), in Taurus several thousand years prior to the Hellenistic period, and so forth backward through the zodiac.

Because of the space between different constellations, it is difficult if not impossible to determine precisely when one age ends and another one begins, although this has not prevented many practitioners of traditional astrology, as well as esoteric astrology, from asserting that the Aquarian Age has already begun. A popular date for the beginning of the Age of Aquarius is the year 2000. If, however, the Age of Pisces began with the ministry of Jesus (as many claim), and if each age is 2,150 years in duration, then, clearly, there is a long way to go before the arrival of the Age of Aquarius.

The contemporary notion of the Age of Aquarius, developed in occult and theosophical circles in the last century, was mediated to the larger society by the counterculture of the 1960s (as in the well-known song "Age of Aquarius" that was featured in the rock musical *Hair*). The metaphysical subculture that emerged as a successor to the counterculture in the early-to-middle 1970s eventually dropped the appellation Aquarian Age in favor of New Age. Most popular accounts of the difference between the Piscean Age and the Aquarian Age emphasize the negative traits of Pisces and the positive traits of Aquarius. Thus, attention is called to the negative Piscean tendency to adopt an attitude of blind faith, and to the positive Aquarian tendency to adopt a more empirical attitude. The limits of this approach—which often ignores positive Pisces traits as well as negative Aquarius characteristics—should be clear.

A comprehensive critique of the Aquarian Age notion can be found in Nicholas Campion's important treatment, "The Age of Aquarius: A Modern Myth." Although this work is useful, contrary to Campion's argument, the ancients did put forward a theory of successive astrological ages based on the precession of equinoxes (see Mithraism and Astrology).

**Sources:**

Bach, Eleanor. *Astrology from A to Z: An Illustrated Source Book*. New York: Philosophical Library, 1990.

Campion, Nicholas. "The Age of Aquarius: A Modern Myth." In *The Astrology of the Macrocosm*. Edited by Joan McEvers. Saint Paul, MN: Llewellyn Publications, 1990.

Ulansey, David. *The Origins of the Mithraic Mysteries: Cosmology and Salvation in the Ancient World*. New York: Oxford University Press, 1989.

## Ages of Man

The Ages of Man refers to the ancient notion that the different stages of human life are ruled by different planets and the luminaries (i.e., the Sun and the Moon). The traditional schema was as follows: Moon—growth (ages 1–4); Mercury—education (5–14); Venus—emotion (15–22); Sun—virility (23–42); Mars—ambition (43–57); Jupiter—reflection (58–69); and Saturn—resignation (70–99).

## Agricultural Astrology (Planting by the Signs)

Agricultural astrology is the practice of choosing the time to plant and harvest crops according to the phase and sign of the Moon. As such, agricultural astrology is a branch of electional astrology. Planting according to the phase of the Moon—during

**The medieval Wheel of Life with the five Ages of Man: child, young man, mid-life, older, and senescent.** ***Reproduced by permission of Fortean Picture Library.***

the waxing phase for most yearly food crops that produce their yield aboveground—may be the human race's oldest astrological practice. In the more recent history of the West, agricultural astrology has been referred to as "planting by the signs"—the practice of planting seeds according to the astrological sign of the Moon, which, because of the relative shortness of the Moon's orbit, changes every two or three days. Planting by the signs has been a regular feature of almanacs, such as *The Old Farmer's Almanac*, and in some agricultural regions (e.g., rural Appalachia) it is still practiced.

Agricultural astrology is the one area of contemporary astrology in which people still rely on the traditional classification of fruitful signs and barren signs. If planted while the Moon (which rules the principle of conception) is in a fruitful sign, crops supposedly grow bigger and better; planted in a barren sign, crops are less healthy and less tasty. However, periods during which the Moon is in a barren sign are good for cultivating the soil for healthy crops and for destroying weeds.

**Sources:**

Brau, Jean-Louis, Helen Weaver, and Allan Edmands. *Larousse Encyclopedia of Astrology*. New York: New American Library, 1980.

Riotte, Louise. *Astrological Gardening: The Ancient Wisdom of Successful Planting and Harvesting by the Stars*. Pownal, VT: Storey Communications, 1989.

Starck, Marcia. *Earth Mother Astrology: Ancient Healing Wisdom*. Saint Paul, MN: Llewellyn Publications, 1989.

## Air Signs

The 12 signs of the zodiac are subdivided according to the four classical elements—earth, air, fire, and water. The three air signs (the air triplicity or air trigon) are Gemini, Libra, and Aquarius. Astrologically, air is mental. For people in whom the air element predominates, ideas and communication are the most important aspects of human life.

This mental trait shows itself somewhat differently in each of the signs of the air triplicity. Gemini's airy nature typically manifests as the ability to understand, utilize, and communicate facts; Geminis are natural teachers and communicators. As Libra's symbol, the Scales, suggests, Libra's airiness is expressed as the ability to make comparisons by weighing and balancing. This sign has a highly developed social nature that makes Libras talented hosts and insightful psychologists. Aquarius's airy quality appears as intuition and the ability to understand universal principles. Aquarius also has a natural inclination to work with others for the uplifting of humanity.

Negatively, air people can be too intellectual and too verbal. Unless counterbalanced by other factors, excess air in a natal chart indicates an individual who is stuck at the mental level, never able to manifest ideas in a practical manner. Conversely, lack of air can indicate a person who has difficulty communicating and formatting clear ideas.

**Sources:**

Hand, Robert. *Horoscope Symbols*. Rockport, MA: Para Research, 1981.

Sakoian, Frances, and Louis S. Acker. *The Astrologer's Handbook*. New York: Harper & Row, 1989.

## Albedo

Albedo (literally, "whiteness") is a measure of the power of a planet, moon, or asteroid to reflect light.

## AL-BIRUNI

Al-Biruni, whose full name is Abu'l-Rayhan Muhammad ibn Ahmad Al-Biruni, was born in 973 C.E. in what is now Khiva, Uzbekistan (formerly part of the Soviet Union). At the time of Al-Biruni's birth, the area was a suburb of Kath, the capital of Khwārizm (north and northeast of ancient Parthia on the lower Oxus River in the region south of the Aral Sea). Known to the classical Greeks and Romans as Chorasmia, Khiva was the homeland of a people related to the Sogdian Magi who lived to the south and southeast of Khwārizm on the Oxus in the eastern reaches of what had once been the Persian Empire. The proximity of Al-Biruni's general region, which was bordered on the east by the Hindu Kush, meant that Indian cultural and scientific traditions had certainly pervaded the region for centuries. Not far away, on the western shore of the Caspian Sea, lay the remnants of the Jewish empire of the Khazars, which had fallen to the duke of Kiev four years prior to Al-Biruni's birth.

Only 23 years after Al-Biruni's birth, the last of the Khwārizmshahs, Abū Abdallah Muhammad, a direct descendant of the Khusraws (the last dynasty of Persian kings before Islam), was overthrown by the Muslim emir Ma'mun ibn Muhammad. Thus, Persian-Magian traditions lingered in and around Al-Biruni's birthplace. Indeed, despite the conversion to Islam, the whole region was steeped not only in Zoroastrianism but also in Manicheanism and astrological doctrines, as is apparent from Al-Biruni's *Chronologies of Ancient Nations*, *India* and *The Book of Instruction in the Elements of the Art of Astrology*. The latter work, which was translated into English by R. Ramsay Wright in 1934, will hereafter be referred to by its Arabic short title, the *Tafhim*.

Thus, Al-Biruni came from a highly cultured society known for its mathematical, scientific, astronomical, and astrological lore. In his various works, Al-Biruni shows interest in, and familiarity with, the cultures and sciences of the peoples who surrounded him. He shows profound and advanced knowledge of scientific subjects. His mind was precise and he was a close observer of nature. He studied the Hindu numeral system and showed how to determine latitude and longitude accurately. When he visited India and viewed the Indus Valley, Al-Biruni concluded that it was an ancient sea basin filled with alluvium. In many ways, he was ahead of his time.

Al-Biruni traveled widely, leaving his birthplace for the Samanid court of Nuh ibn Mansur at Ghaznah in eastern Afghanistan, the Samanid capital, sometime after 990 C.E. In 998, he went to Gurgan with Qabus ibn Washmgir Shams al-Ma'ali. While there, Al-Biruni began his *Chronology of Ancient Nations*, which is dedicated to Qabus. In this work, completed in the year 1000, he shows advanced understanding of the comparative chronologies of the surrounding peoples. He seems to have returned to Khwa¯rizm around age 37 and to have remained there until age 46, when his patron, Abu'l-'Abbas Ma'mun ibn Ma'mun, was murdered by rebellious subjects. As a result of the murder, Mahmud of Ghaznah invaded Khwārizm and subjugated the country, exiling its ruling class (and Al-Biruni with them) to Ghaznah in the following year. Al-Biruni served Mahmud as court astrologer, but somehow found time between 1016 and 1029 to travel to India and write his classic *India*, detailing the social, religious, and scientific characteristics of the Indians. During this period he also produced the *Tafhim*, his textbook on astrology and related subjects.

The *Tafhim* is a truly remarkable book in several respects. First, it is a medieval Oriental book dedicated to a woman. This by itself is remarkable. The woman, Rayhana bint al-Hasan, was a Persian noblewoman who was apparently a student of Al-Biruni's while both were semicaptive at Mahmud's court at Ghaznah. Virtually every paragraph of the *Tafhim* is interesting. Al-Biruni seems to have written both an Arabic and a Persian version. It contains 550 paragraphs plus a colophon that Al-Biruni tells us was intended as an aide-mémoire for Rayhana in the form of questions and answers. The 1934 Wright translation deletes this feature and presents a text arranged in paragraphs with headings. Though Wright's translation shows signs of incompletion—it is typewritten, not typeset, with unpolished notes and comments, and clearly paraphrased in places—the overall composition and handling of the subject shows Al-Biruni to have possessed a mind of the highest quality and probity. As a teacher he must have been outstanding. He writes with clarity and conciseness uncharacteristic of medieval astrological writers. He tells us, at the very end of the book, that he has set forth what a beginner needs to know about astrology. He exceeds the modern standards in this regard and provides us with what amounts to an introduction to mathematics, geography, chronology, and astronomy before finally addressing judicial astrology.

As a textbook on astrology, the *Tafhim* is on a par with Ptolemy's *Tetrabiblos*. Indeed, it is superior to it, in that it contains a good deal of material contained in Ptolemy's *Almagest* as well. Much of the *Tafhim* is clearly an attempt to epitomize the *Almagest*. Its value is in the scope of its contents. In no other astrological work is there such a comprehensive survey of medieval astrological science and the subjects that supported it. The book reveals the many-faceted skills and duties of an eleventh-century Persian astrologer. Al-Biruni is also interested in the Hindu astrological traditions and how they differ or coincide with those with whom he is familiar. He also reports Magian astrological practices. The shortcoming of the book is that, written as an aide-mémoire, it lacks examples showing how to apply the methods, astrological or mathematical, so thoroughly set forth. However, the book does provide a uniquely clear window into the level of knowledge attained by a Persian astrologer in 1029. By comparison, his European counterparts were deprived.

Al-Biruni's exposition of astrology places the subject squarely in the context of the mathematical disciplines. He begins by introducing the student to geometry and arithmetic to provide the would-be astrologer with the ability to calculate. The calculations are pre-logarithmic, and geometrical trigonometry is used. Curiously absent is any mention of the forty-seventh proposition of Euclid, also known as the Pythagorean theorem, which Ptolemy used to such good effect in the first book of the *Almagest* to find the lengths of chords subtending arcs of the circle.

Al-Biruni's discussion of arithmetic is Pythagorean, based clearly on Nicomachus's *Introduction to Arithmetic*. Initially, this seems strange and possibly even esoteric, until one realizes that ancient calculation in the Middle East, insofar as it was based on Greek mathematics, was based on theoretical arithmetic such as Nicomachus's. As late as the thirteenth century, this was still true in Europe. For instance, Guido Bonatti, in *Liber Astronomiae*, asserts that the art of calculation has to do with the knowledge of numbers and tables, such as the multiplication tables and tables of roots and powers either found in Nicomachus's work or suggested by him. In practice, such tables were used in conjunction with the abacus. Throughout the geometry and arithmetic sections, he emphasizes ratio and proportion. As in Ptolemy's *Almagest*, the solution of triangles relies on the application of areas and the Pythagorean theorem.

For reasons he does not make clear, Al-Biruni discusses conic sections in the *Tafhim*, an example of the aide-mémoire character of this text. Clearly he must have explained the relevance of conic sections to astrology to Rayhana, but he does not make it clear to the reader. If it were not known that scientists in his day (and even in Ptolemy's day) knew that light expanded in cone shapes, and that the theory was fairly widely held that astrological influence was transmitted from heaven to earth via the light of the stars, there would be no hint as to why he included this discussion at all.

Al-Biruni also includes a discussion of the five regular Platonic polyhedra, equating them, in good Neoplatonic fashion, with the five elements. Paragraph 107 treats the powers of numbers from the first power to the fourth. Paragraph 108 presents the eleventh-century Persian understanding of the decimal notation of the Hindus, including the use of the cipher as a placeholder. Al-Biruni's handling of arithmetic includes an introduction to algebra, which, in his day, was truly "occult." The laws regulating it were not yet known, and his very short exposition shows this fact by its incompleteness. Al-Biruni then introduces astronomy, beginning with the sphere. Step by step he explains basic geocentric astronomy, discussing the celestial circles, their subdivisions, the movements of the luminaries (the Sun and Moon) and the planets, the constellations, and the planetary theories of his day. He, like John Dee, brings his geocentric astronomy into his geocentric astrology (paragraph 387), interpreting the meaning of planets at perigee and apogee and on different places on their epicycles. He discusses and voices skepticism about the trepidation theory, which held that the precession of the equinoxes was not constant in a retrograde direction but oscillated back and forth—an incorrect idea first put forth by Thābit ben Qurrah in the tenth century. He discusses the World Days and Year according to the Persian astrologer Abū Ma'shar and the Hindu conceptions of yugas (the four ages of Hindu world cycle), kalpas, and manvantaras as found in the Siddhantas.

Al-Biruni next discusses the size and distance of the planets and elements, the distribution of the land and water masses, and terrestrial longitude and latitude. He discusses the gnomon (a kind of sundial) and its shadow (so basic for chronology) in between discussing details of the horizon system of celestial coordinates (azimuth and altitude).

Having prepared the student with the basics, Al-Biruni then discusses geography, including the seven climates, their extent, and their characteristics. His presentation of the various cities in the climates shows that, although he has a fairly accurate mathematical sense of the terrestrial globe, his knowledge of exact latitude and longitude on Earth is approximate. One of the surprises of this book is Al-Biruni's mention in paragraph 239 of the mythological mountain Meru (the World Axis), under which angels dwell, and the island Lanka (modern Sri Lanka), where the demons dwell. This lore is Indian, not Persian, and definitely not Islamic. Could it be that the Persian Al-Biruni sought to keep ancient traditions common to both Iran and Aryan India alive? Likewise, paragraph 240 contains another surprise—red as well as white men lived in northwestern Europe. He clearly means red-skinned men, as in every one of the other cases in which he identifies the denizens of the various regions of the world by their skin color. Could it be that he was repeating reports of contact between the Viking Rus (who were in the Volga basin and Byzantium in his day) and the Amerindians?

In paragraph 242, Al-Biruni returns to astronomy to pin down with what degree a given star will culminate, rise, or set. In paragraphs 245–48 he addresses the houses of the horoscope, using equal houses from the ascendant. Next he discusses the astronomy of the anniversary on the macrocosmic level as a "Revolution of Years of the World" in medieval parlance (Aries ingress in modern) and on the microcosmic level as a solar return for an individual. Paragraph 250 deals with the Saturn-Jupiter conjunctions. Lunar motion follows, with a discussion of the phases of the Moon followed by a presentation on eclipses and the problem of parallax.

Next Al-Biruni switches to the problems of chronology, showing that the astrologer of his day was called upon to regulate the calendar and to understand how the calendar of his nation related to those of other nations who used different systems of chronology. He discusses leap years, solar and lunar years, intercalation, and the religious festivals of various peoples of the Middle and Far East, including the Indians and Sogdian Magi. There follows a description of the astrolabe and its use in astronomy, desert navigation, and trigonometrical measurements.

After the astrolabe, Al-Biruni returns to the subject of astrology, discussing the zodiacal signs and their correspondence to directions of the compass, professions, character, appearance, diseases, crops, and animals. Next he shows the relation of the signs to each other, the year, and the triplicities. He then expounds on the planets with their various correspondences. Some of his correspondences seem a bit beside the point or of little importance; for instance, he lists pimples as a Cancer "disease." Paragraph 348 presents us with a surprise, stating that the planets have a tendency to take on the gender of the sign they are in. This seems to mean that even male planets become effeminate in female signs! He discusses the Years of the Planets table found so frequently in medieval texts and consisting of Least, Mean, Great, and Greatest Years (used in predicting longevity). He confesses that he doubts that people ever lived as long as the Greatest Years (e.g., the Sun's Greatest Year is 1,461 years). He clearly does not know how to use the Greatest Years of the Planets. He then launches into the dignities and debilities of the planets, their friendships and enmities, and the halves of signs, decans, paranatellon, terms, ninths (nawamsas), and twelfths (dwadasamsas). He gives characteristics of individual degrees. Correspondences of the houses follow in natal and horary figures. The Arabic parts are discussed in paragraphs 475–80. The subject of application and separation is then addressed. He follows with more on dignities.

The vexed question of the oriental/occidental positions of the planets (i.e., whether they are in the left or right hemisphere of a horoscope) and the effect this has on their influences is the subject of paragraphs 481–86. The orientality or occidentality of the planets is found obscurely in Dorotheus's *Pentateuch* (first century C.E.) and gets a fuller and thoroughly problematical treatment in Ptolemy's *Tetrabiblos* (second century C.E.). Al-Biruni's treatment is based on Al-Kindi's. It is systematic, ultimately not at odds with Ptolemy's (in fact, he cites the *Almagest*), and has the advantage of being somewhat more rational than the available English versions of *Tetrabiblos*.

In the *Tafhim*, Al-Biruni begins his discussion of the oriental/occidental question with the position of the planets relative to the Sun. He then shows that the superior planets become occidental when 90° from the Sun (the Sun having passed them). They then go retrograde and later direct. Then comes the opposition. This divides the circle into two parts; in one, the planet is oriental, and, in the other, occidental. Al-Biruni does not say so, but he implies that the other half of the zodiac is handled in the same way. With the inferior planets a different situation holds. Neither Venus nor Mercury is ever 90° from the Sun, but both can be on either side of the Sun at an eastern or western elongation. The western elongation is oriental; presumably the eastern is occidental. Al-Biruni asserts that planets in cazimi (within 16° of the center of the Sun) are strongest. They are weakest when combust (the acceptable distance for this varies from planet to planet) and are more powerful when oriental than when occidental. There are various degrees of debility when occidental. They also change their qualities of hot, cold, wet, or dry, depending on their relation to the Sun. Al-Biruni asserts that the planets change their gender depending on their relation to the horizon, though his discussion of this dimension of the problem of orientality and occidentality is less clear than Ptolemy's in *Tetrabiblos* (in Book III, chapter 3 of Robbins's translation, and Book III, chapter 4 of the Ashmand translation).

The last section of the *Tafhim* deals with judicial astrology. It is here that the author's lack of examples is most disheartening. Case studies would have been helpful. He divides the subject of astrology into five categories: (1) meteorology, (2) mundane astrology relating to famine, plague, epidemics, etc., (3) environmental effects on the individual, (4) human activities and occupations, and (5) a division including horary and electional astrology. Al-Biruni says the foundations of this latter division are unknown: "Here astrology reaches a point which threatens to transgress its proper limits, where problems are submitted which it is impossible to solve for the most part, and where the matter leaves the solid basis of universals for particulars. Where this boundary is passed, where the astrologer is on one side and the sorcerer on the other, you enter a field of omens and divinations which has nothing to do with astrology, although the stars may be referred to in connection with them."

What today is called natal astrology is subsumed under categories 3 and 4 (environmental effects and human activities and occupations). Al-Biruni considers two initial points for natal astrology: the conception and the birth. He discusses finding the hyleg and alcocoden for longevity. He finds the length of life through the alcocoden (which he calls by its Persian name, *kadkhuda*). He defines the alcocoden as the planet with the most dignity in the place of the hyleg. The number of years attributed to the native's life is determined by whether the alcocoden is angular, succedent, or cadent. Al-Biruni is less than complete and clear here. He says "a large number" is given when the alcocoden is angular, "a mean number" when succedent, and "a small number" when cadent. The tradition is more fully expounded in other medieval works, such as Bonatti's *Liber Astronomiae* and Abū 'Ali Al-Khayyat's *The Judgements of Nativities*. From the latter two books we learn that the numbers referred to come from the Years of the Planets table. The rule varies from author to author, but is generally that Great Years are given when the alcocoden is angular, the Mean Years when it is succedent, and the Least Years when it is cadent. Yet, in addition to this, Al-Biruni, following Ptolemy, still tries to predict the exact time of death by directing the hyleg to the place of the Apheta. His complete method, therefore, is twofold and seems to be a fusion of two techniques originally used independently of each other.

He employs solar returns and progressions as well as the divisor (Ruler of the Year by profection of the ascendant) for discovering the important events in the native's life each year. He directs by profection (down to the week) and by term from year to year. He discusses rectification by the animodar of Ptolemy and the trutine of Hermes. Feeling assured that he has set forth the knowledge necessary to a beginner, he warns readers not to exceed the limits of the knowable and thereby bring scorn and derision upon themselves.

Such then is Al-Biruni's *Tafhim*. It is certainly one of the classic works in astrology and should be closely studied by all interested in the history and practice of traditional astrology. It opens a window onto the astrological and mathematical expertise of one of the world's finest astrological minds. Al-Biruni was highly regarded in his day, and his work was preserved and transmitted. As mentioned, it was a source for Guido Bonatti's thirteenth-century *Liber Astronomiae*, which was itself highly influential. Except for its failure to provide practical examples, the *Tafhim* constitutes a veritable treasure trove of astrological lore.

—Robert Zoller

**Sources:**

*Albiruni's India*. Translated by Edward C. Sachau. Delhi: S. Chand & Co., 1964.

Al-Khayyat, Abū 'Ali. *The Judgements of Nativities*. Translated by James H. Holden. Tempe, AZ: American Federation of Astrologers, 1988.

*The Book of Instruction in the Elements of the Art of Astrology*. Translated by R. Ramsay Wright. London: Luzac & Co., 1934.

Dorotheus. *Pentateuch* (published as *Carmen Astrologicum*, by Dorotheus Sidonius). Translated by Pingree. Leipzig, Germany: B. G. Teubner, 1976.

Hoyt, Edwin P. *Arab Science*. New York: Thomas Nelson, 1975.

Ptolemy, Claudius. *Ptolemy, Tetrabiblos*. Translated by F. E. Robbins. Cambridge, MA: Harvard University Press, 1964.

———. *Ptolemy's Tetrabiblos*. Translated by J. M. Ashmand. London: Foulsham & Co., 1917.

Shumaker and Heilbron. *John Dee on Astronomy: Propaedeumata Aphoristica 1558 & 1568*. Berkeley: University of California Press, 1978.

## ALCOHOLISM

Alcoholism and other forms of escapist drug addiction are associated primarily with the planet Neptune and, secondarily, with Pisces, the sign ruled by Neptune. Neptune is associated with sensitivity to the subtle dimensions of existence. When strong and positively situated in a natal chart, Neptune can manifest as musical sensitivity, mystical sensitivity, and so forth. When negatively aspected, however, Neptunian sensitivity will manifest as deceptiveness or escapism.

Charles E. O. Carter, an important astrologer of the early twentieth century, discussed alcoholism and drug addiction in *An Encyclopedia of Psychological Astrology*. Carter associated alcoholism and drug addiction with a number of different factors. In the birth chart of an alcoholic, according to Carter, the Sun and the Moon are almost always weak by sign and house position, "or else they are badly afflicted, especially in or from Fire or Water, or both." Furthermore, "the fifth house (the house of pleasure and entertainment) is nearly always afflicted by Neptune or by planets in watery signs, and Mars is very frequently afflicted by Neptune, in or from Pisces."

A more recent study, reported in Ann Parker's *Astrology and Alcoholism*, confirmed the importance of Neptune. Parker, however, also found that the planet Uranus was significantly represented in the horoscopes of alcoholics, especially Moon-Uranus aspects. She explains this unusual finding by pointing out that a Moon-Uranus contact, "even linked in good aspect, represents great emotional excitability and self-will, both charcteristic of the alchoholic." When linked by a hard aspect, "these planets produce states of fear and anxiety, extreme self will, a craving for sensation, restlessness, and a tendency to exaggerate and magnify things," all of which are associated with alcoholic personalities.

**Sources:**

Carter, Charles E. O. *An Encyclopedia of Psychological Astrology*. 1924. Reprint, London: Theosophical Publishing House, 1963.

Parker, Ann E. *Astrology and Alcoholism*. York Beach, ME: Samuel Weiser, 1982.

## Aletheia

Aletheia, asteroid 259 (the 259th asteroid to be discovered, on June 28, 1886), is approximately 103 kilometers in diameter and has an orbital period of 5.6 years. It is named after the Greek word for "truth" or "sincerity." When prominent in a natal chart, Aletheia shows a sincere person. Its location by sign and house indicates where one is most sincere or experiences sincerity. When afflicted, Aletheia may signify insincerity or confrontations with unpleasant truths.

**Sources:**

Kowal, Charles T. *Asteroids: Their Nature and Utilization*. Chichester, West Sussex, UK: Ellis Horwood Limited, 1988.

Room, Adrian. *Dictionary of Astronomical Names*. London: Routledge, 1988.

Schwartz, Jacob. *Asteroid Name Encyclopedia*. St. Paul, MN: Llewellyn Publications, 1995.

## Almagest

*Almagest* is a treatise on astronomy by the famous astronomer-mathematician Ptolemy.

## Almanac

An almanac is a book or booklet containing sets of tables, particularly calendrical tables, announcing astronomical or astrological events (such as Moon phases, eclipses, and beginnings of seasons) and carrying historical facts, information on planting by the signs, and other types of data. Older almanacs (the almanac tradition has been traced as far back as the Hellenistic period) contained prophetic announcements, a tradition carried on by modern almanacs, which usually predict the day-by-day weather on the basis of meteorological astrology. In U.S. history, the most well-known example was *Poor Richard's Almanac* (1732–1757), which was issued by Benjamin Franklin. *The Old Farmer's Almanac* remains popular in rural areas.

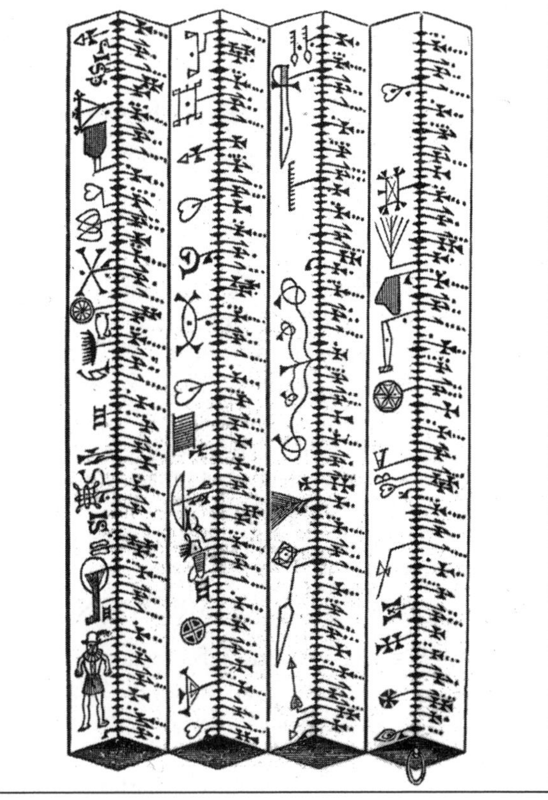

**The four sides of the clog almanac are shown extended to reveal the marks for each day. *Reproduced by permission of Fortean Picture Library.***

**Sources:**

DeVore, Nicholas. *Encyclopedia of Astrology*. New York: Philosophical Library, 1947.

Gettings, Fred. *Dictionary of Astrology*. London: Routledge & Kegan Paul, 1985.

Thomas, Robert B. *The Old Farmer's 1991 Almanac*. Dublin, NH: Yankee Publishing, 1990.

## ALMUTEN

Almuten is an Arabic term for the strongest planet in a natal chart by virtue of essential and accidental dignities.

## ALTITUDE

In astrology, altitude refers to the angular distance (i.e., measured in degrees of an arc) that a point, planet, or other heavenly body is situated above or below the horizon. Above the horizon, altitude is measured up to a maximum angular distance of 90° (directly overhead); below the horizon, down to a maximum of -90° (directly underneath).

## AMBROSIA

Ambrosia, asteroid 193 (the 193rd asteroid to be discovered, on Feburary 28, 1879), is approximately 42 kilometers in diameter and has an orbital period of 4.2 years. It was named after food of the ancient gods that was said to have bestowed immortality. Jacob Schwartz also connects Ambrosia with Saint Ambrose, the Italian bishop, musician, writer, and warrior. When prominent in a natal chart, Ambrosia may indicate long life.

**Sources:**

Kowal, Charles T. *Asteroids: Their Nature and Utilization*. Chichester, West Sussex, UK: Ellis Horwood Limited, 1988.

Room, Adrian. *Dictionary of Astronomical Names*. London: Routledge, 1988.
Schwartz, Jacob. *Asteroid Name Encyclopedia*. St. Paul, MN: Llewellyn Publications, 1995.

## American Council of Vedic Astrology

The American Council of Vedic Astrology (ACVA) was founded in November 1993. This nonprofit educational organization, located in Sedona, Arizona, is the largest Vedic astrology organization in the West and is affiliated with the Indian Council of Astrological Sciences (ICAS), founded by B. V. Raman. The ACVA has offered a forum for Vedic astrologers of all types and backgrounds, and has served as a network for them to connect and share their views. ACVA offers a 600-hour certification program for learning Vedic astrology through its approved tutors, which is the first real attempt in the West to teach Jyotish on a broad scale. The council is governed by a steering committee whose members include: Christina Collins Hill, Dennis Flaherty, David Frawley, Dennis M. Harness, Edith Hathaway, James Kelleher, William Levacy, and Chakrapani Ullal.

—Dennis M. Harness, Ph.D., and David Frawley

## American Federation of Astrologers

The American Federation of Scientific Astrologers was officially incorporated in Washington, D.C., on May 4, 1938, at 11:38 A.M., Eastern Standard Time. There were 61 charter members, of whom 29 were members of an earlier organization, the American Association of Scientific Astrologers (AASA), including Elizabeth Aldrich, Elbert and Elizabeth Benjamine, Ernest and Catharine Grant, George J. McCormack, Lewis Weston, Adrian M. Ziegler, Robert DeLuce, Llewellyn George, Keye Lloyd, and Prem H. Joshi (of India). In addition, there were 32 members of other astrological associations, including five members from other countries: Gustave Brahy of Belgium; Cyril Fagan of Ireland; and Dr. Greville Gascoigne, Charles E. O. Carter, and Rupert Gleadow of England.

Adrian M. Ziegler, president of the AASA, served as interim president of the new organization, but three days later the convention elected Ernest A. Grant as president, Ellen McCaffery as vice president, and Martha E. Knotts as secretary-treasurer. Ernest Grant served as president until 1941, when he was elected executive secretary, a post he held until 1959. He was succeeded as president by Paul R. Grell, who held that office from 1959 to 1970, after which Robert W. Cooper assumed the post. In 1979, Doris Chase Doane was elected president.

The founders intended to establish an organization to assist astrologers and astrological groups, promote the study and practice of astrology, establish a code of ethics, institute standards of astrological practice, encourage astrological research, and establish an astrological library. One of the founding cardinal ethical principles was that an astrologer should not use any method of analysis—other than astrology—without expressly stating that his or her conclusions were based in part on some other art. This principle was the signification of the word "scientific" in the original name of the organization. However, since it was later found that this was not understood by the general public, that word was dropped from the name in the early 1940s, and thereafter the organization has been known as the American Federation of Astrologers (AFA). It remained in Washington until 1975, when it moved into a new headquarters building in Tempe, Arizona.

The AFA's membership has grown from its original 61 to more than 3,000, including members in more than 30 other countries. It has held biennial conventions in most even-numbered years since 1938. These typically last five days and offer lectures and workshops on all aspects of astrology.

In 1960, the AFA began offering certification examinations for advanced and professional members and teachers.

The library has grown from a few dozen books to its present collection of thousands of books and magazines, including original copies of William Lilly's *Christian Astrology* (1647) and Ebenezer Sibly's *The Complete Illustration of the Celestial Science of Astrology* (1784). It also houses complete runs of several leading domestic and foreign astrological magazines.

The AFA has published hundreds of books and pamphlets since its founding. It issues a monthly publication, *Today's Astrologer,* and, since the organization of a research section in 1981, the *Journal of Research,* which is published annually. The AFA also offers a comprehensive correspondence course in astrology by James H. Holden, FAFA, based on Edna Carr Edmondson's *A Fifty-Year History of the American Federation of Astrologers, Inc.*

## Amicitia

Amicitia, asteroid 367 (the 367th asteroid to be discovered, on May 19, 1893), is approximately 20 kilometers in diameter and has an orbital period of 3.3 years. Its name is a personified form of the Latin word for friendship. When prominent in a natal chart, Amicitia indicates a friendly personality. The sign and house position indicate both how one interacts with friends and what one's friends are like.

**Sources:**

Kowal, Charles T. *Asteroids: Their Nature and Utilization*. Chichester, West Sussex, UK: Ellis Horwood Limited, 1988.

Room, Adrian. *Dictionary of Astronomical Names*. London: Routledge, 1988.

Schwartz, Jacob. *Asteroid Name Encyclopedia*. St. Paul, MN: Llewellyn Publications, 1995.

## Amor

Amor, asteroid 1,221 (the 1,221st asteroid to be discovered, on March 12, 1932) was named after the Roman god of love (corresponding to the Greek Eros). It has an orbital period of 2⅔ years and is only 1 kilometer in diameter. Amor is one of the more recent asteroids to be investigated by astrologers. Preliminary material on Amor can be found in Demetra George and Douglas Bloch's *Astrology for Yourself;* an ephemeris (table of celestial locations) for Amor can be found in the back of the second edition of George and Bloch's *Asteroid Goddesses*. Unlike the planets, which are associated with a wide range of phenomena, the smaller asteroids are said to represent a single principle. George and Bloch give Amor's principle as platonic "love and compassion." J. Lee Lehman associates Amor with intimacy and with nonsexual love, as well as with the loneliness and anger of being rejected. Jacob Schwartz connects the name with words like amorphous and amortization, and, similar to George and Bloch, says that this body is "astrologically interpreted as the capacity of unconditional, spiritual or platonic love and compassion."

**Sources:**

George, Demetra, with Douglas Bloch. *Asteroid Goddesses: The Mythology, Psychology and Astrology of the Reemerging Feminine*. 2d ed. San Diego: Astro Computing Services, 1990.

———. *Astrology for Yourself: A Workbook for Personal Transformation*. Berkeley, CA: Wingbow Press, 1987.

Lehman, J. Lee. *The Ultimate Asteroid Book*. West Chester, PA: Whitford Press, 1988.

Schwartz, Jacob. *Asteroid Name Encyclopedia*. St. Paul, MN: Llewellyn Publications, 1995.

## Anahita

Anahita, asteroid 270 (the 270th asteroid to be discovered, on October 8, 1887), is approximately 52 kilometers in diameter and has an orbital period of 3.3 years. It was named after a goddess of fertility and procreation in Persian mythology who was associated with Mithras. When prominent in a natal chart, Anahita can show an exceptionally productive or "fertile" individual. By sign and house location, it may show an area of great potential that need only be cultivated a little to produce results.

**Sources:**

Kowal, Charles T. *Asteroids: Their Nature and Utilization*. Chichester, West Sussex, UK: Ellis Horwood Limited, 1988.

Room, Adrian. *Dictionary of Astronomical Names*. London: Routledge, 1988.

Schwartz, Jacob. *Asteroid Name Encyclopedia*. St. Paul, MN: Llewellyn Publications, 1995.

## Androgynous Planet

Traditionally, most planets and signs were designated as either masculine or feminine. Mercury was the only planet in premodern astrology that was said to be neutral or androgynous. In contemporary astrology, Uranus has also come to be regarded as an androgynous planet.

## Angle (Angular)

The term "angle" can be used in two different ways in astrology. In its primary, traditional meaning, angle refers to one of the four "corners" (figuratively speaking) of a chart—namely, the cusps of the first, fourth, seventh, and tenth houses. Planets making a conjunction with the angles—which are sometimes called angular planets, particularly when they are in an angular house—are said to exercise an especially strong influence over the entire horoscope. In practice, astrologers pay the most attention to angular planets in the first and tenth houses. Angle is also used as an alternative term for aspect, as when one talks about the angular relationship between two planets.

## Angular Distance

The distance between points in an astrological chart is always expressed in terms of angular distance. Because the locations of the significant elements of a horoscope are expressed in terms of degrees and minutes (and, occasionally, seconds) of the zodiac, the distance between any two points is similarly expressed as so many degrees and minutes of the arc between them. For example, the angular distance between a planet located at 3°15' Aries and another planet situated at 24°27' Aries would be 21°12'.

## Angular Houses

The houses of an astrological chart are classified into three groups of four: angular houses (the first, fourth, seventh, and tenth), succedent houses (the second, fifth, eighth, and eleventh), and cadent houses (the third, sixth, ninth, and twelfth). In traditional astrology, angular houses were regarded as the most powerful houses in which planets could be positioned. Modern astrologers, however, tend to believe that planets placed in angular houses have the most influence on the outer, surface aspects of a person's life, while planets placed in the cadent houses have the most impact on one's inner life. Planets located in succedent houses mediate one's inner and outer lives.

## Angular Velocity

The core meaning of angular velocity is the angular distance, expressed in degrees and minutes of an arc, that a planet travels in the course of a day. By extension, angular velocity can also be the angular distance a heavenly body moves during any given unit of time.

## Anomalistic Period (Anomaly; Anomalistic Year)

For a planet, an anomalistic period is the time between two successive perihelions (the point in a planet's orbit where it is closest to the Sun). For the Moon, an anomalistic period is the time between two successive perigees (the point where it is closest to Earth). The expression anomalistic period is derived from anomaly, which in astronomy refers to the angular distance of a planet from its perihelion or its aphelion. By extension, an anomalistic year is the period between Earth's perihelions, which is 365.23964 days.

## Antipathy

Congruent with its use in everyday English, antipathy refers to an inharmonious relationship between certain planets, particularly when they make hard aspects to each other. The term is also used to refer to the repulsion between people whose charts interact inharmoniously with each other.

## Antiscion

Antiscion is a somewhat confusing term that has, unfortunately, come to be used for more than one notion. Picture the wheel of the zodiac and imagine a straight line from 0° Cancer to 0° Capricorn so as to divide the circle into two equal halves. If a planet is located at an angular distance of 45° away from this dividing line (e.g., at 15° Taurus), its antiscion would be 45° in the opposite direction from the line (e.g., at 15° Leo). If another planet happens to be located at or very near the antiscion of the first planet, the two planets are said to have a relationship with each other comparable to a conjunction aspect. This is the traditional meaning of the term.

Some astrologers have extended the term to apply to points at equal angular distances from the ascendant-descendant axis (i.e., at equal distances above and below the horizon) in an individual horoscope.

**Sources:**

Brau, Jean-Louis, Helen Weaver, and Allan Edmands. *Larousse Encyclopedia of Astrology*. New York: New American Library, 1980.

Gettings, Fred. *Dictionary of Astrology*. London: Routledge & Kegan Paul, 1985.

## Antivertex

The antivertex is the intersection of the ecliptic with the prime vertical in the east. (The intersection in the west forms the vertex. All horoscope angles—ascendant, midheaven, etc.—are formed by the intersections of great circles.) Some suggest interpreting the antivertex as an auxiliary ascendant—not as significant as the actual ascendant, but a secondary key to personal action and basic identity instincts. Planets closely (by three degrees) conjunct the antivertex are like conjunctions to ascendants. Planets closely conjunct the vertex are like planets conjunct the descendant—themes and issues met through interactions with other people (and may project onto other people who are likely to "overdo" those drives). Some authors have suggested a "fated" quality to the vertex, which probably is because people are not in charge with others, thus relationship issues often have a "fated" feeling. Sometimes in synastry (chart comparison) more contacts exist between committed couples involving the vertex/antivertex than the ascendant/descendant.

—Maritha Pottenger

**Sources:**

Pottenger, Maritha. *East Point and Antivertex*. San Diego: ACS Publications, 1984.

## Anubis

Anubis, asteroid 1,912 (the 1,912th asteroid to be discovered, on September 24, 1960), is approximately 11 kilometers in diameter and has an orbital period of 4.9 years. Anubis was named after the jackal-headed Egyptian god of the dead, associated with embalming, guarding tombs and, in a later period, the Greek god Hermes. According to J. Lee Lehman, individuals in whose natal chart this asteroid is prominent "may represent someone for whom death is more than a passing issue." According to Jacob Schwartz, Anubis' astrological interpretation is "death being part of a life process."

**Sources:**

Kowal, Charles T. *Asteroids: Their Nature and Utilization*. Chichester, West Sussex, UK: Ellis Horwood Limited, 1988.
Lehman, J. Lee. *The Ultimate Asteroid Book*. West Chester, PA: Whitford Press, 1988.
Schwartz, Jacob. *Asteroid Name Encyclopedia*. St. Paul, MN: Llewellyn Publications, 1995.

## Anuradha

Anuradha ("after Radha" or "success") is one of the Nakshatras (lunar mansions) of Vedic astrology. Symbolized by a row or furrow, this sign is considered another good time for marriage and other positive events. Mitra, god of friendship, presides, and the planet Saturn rules over this Nakshatra from Scorpio 3°20' to 16°40'. During this period, people may be more attractive and popular, but also grievous and secretive.

—Pramela Thiagesan

## Aphelion

Although they approximate circles, all orbits are elliptical. The point in a satellite's orbit where it is farthest from the Sun is called its aphelion (from the Greek words *apo*, meaning "away," and *helios*, meaning "sun").

## Aphrodite

Aphrodite, asteroid 1,388 (the 1,388th asteroid to be discovered, on September 24, 1935), is approximately 22 kilometers in diameter and has an orbital period of 5.2 years. Aphrodite was named after the Greek goddess of sex, love, and beauty, the equivalent of the Roman goddess Venus. J. Lee Lehman associates Aphrodite with Venus and Astarte (also divinities of sex and fertility), asserting that this asteroid is more "refined than the other two. Jacob Schwartz characterizes Aphrodite as "procreativity through refined expressions of beauty, sex and fertility."

**Sources:**

Kowal, Charles T. *Asteroids: Their Nature and Utilization*. Chichester, West Sussex, UK: Ellis Horwood Limited, 1988.
Lehman, J. Lee. *The Ultimate Asteroid Book*. West Chester, PA: Whitford Press, 1988.
Schwartz, Jacob. *Asteroid Name Encyclopedia*. St. Paul, MN: Llewellyn Publications, 1995.

## Apogee

Every orbit is elliptical. When a satellite is at its greatest distance from the Earth, it is at its apogee (from the Greek words *apo*, meaning "away," and *geios*, meaning "earth").

## Apollo

Apollo, asteroid 1,862 (the 1,862nd asteroid to be discovered, on April 24, 1932) is approximately 1.4 kilometers in diameter and has an orbital period of 1.8 years. Apol-

**The god Apollo shown in his role at Delphi, a settlement established during the Mycenaean period where the Temple of Apollo was constructed.** ***Reproduced by permission of Fortean Picture Library.***

lo was named after the Greek sun god, patron of the fine arts, medicine, music, poetry, and eloquence. According to Martha Lang-Wescott, Apollo indicates where recurrent learning experiences occur—where people are slow to learn to change our patterns.

Apollo's key phrase is "against the odds." According to J. Lee Lehman, Apollo can manifest in one of three ways—as a personification of the Sun, as a personification of the traits Greek society used to portray the ideal male, and as the giver and healer of disease. Jacob Schwartz characterizes the astrological associations of this body as "a personification of the Sun, ideal male, and the giver and healer of disease, going against the odds, naive optimism."

**Sources:**

Lang-Wescott, Martha. *Asteroids-Mechanics: Ephemerides II*. Conway, MA: Treehouse Mountain, 1990.

———. *Mechanics of the Future: Asteroids*. Rev. ed. Conway, MA: Treehouse Mountain, 1991.

Lehman, J. Lee. *The Ultimate Asteroid Book*. West Chester, PA: Whitford Press, 1988.

Schwartz, Jacob. *Asteroid Name Encyclopedia*. St. Paul, MN: Llewellyn Publications, 1995.

## Apollon

Apollon is one of the eight hypothetical planets (sometimes referred to as the trans-Neptunian points or planets, or TNPs for short) utilized in Uranian astrology. The Uranian system, sometimes referred to as the Hamburg School of Astrology, was established by Friedrich Sieggrün (1877–1951) and Alfred Witte (1878–1943). It relies heavily on hard aspects and midpoints. In decline for many decades, it has experienced a revival in recent years.

Apollon indicates expansiveness and multiplicity. It can symbolize everything from commerce and science to peace and success. In combination with other celestial bodies, Apollon means lots of (or too many) irons in the fire. It may also indicate distant career opportunities and potentials, such as in another country.

Based on the speculative orbits of the Uranian planets, the Kepler, Solar Fire and Win*Star software program will all locate this hypothetical planet in an astrological chart.

**Sources:**

Lang-Wescott, Martha. *Mechanics of the Future: Asteroids*. Rev. ed. Conway, MA: Treehouse Mountain, 1991.

Simms, Maria Kay. *Dial Detective: Investigation with the 90 Degree Dial*. San Diego: Astro Computing Services, 1989.

## Aporhoea

The Moon is said to be in aporhoea as it separates from an aspect with one planet and begins to apply an aspect with another planet.

## Apparent Motion

It has become astrological tradition to speak about the zodiac and the heavenly bodies as if they were revolving around the Earth while Earth remains stationary. So that other people do not regard astrology as locked in a pre-Copernican worldview, astrologers sometimes specify that they are talking about the *apparent* motion of the stars and planets. In this custom, astrologers are following the same tradition as everyone else who refers to the daily appearance and disappearance of the Sun—for example, as the "rising" and "setting" of the Sun—even though most people in industrialized societies know that it is the axial rotation of the Earth that causes this apparent motion.

## Applying Aspect (Approaching Aspect)

When a transiting planet begins to form an aspect vis-à-vis another planet or a house cusp, it is said to be applying. After the aspect has passed the point of being exact and the faster-moving planet is pulling away, the aspect is said to be separating. This may sound confusing, but is really quite simple. To illustrate, suppose Pluto is located at 25° in the sign Capricorn. As transiting Mars gets within about 4° of Pluto (i.e., reaches 21°, 22°, 23°, or 24° Capricorn), we say that Mars is applying to (or approaching) a conjunction with Pluto. The conjunction becomes exact when Mars reaches 25° and is separating as soon as Mars transits past 25° Capricorn.

A doubly applying (or doubly approaching) aspect occurs when both planets are moving toward an aspect. In other words, if in the preceding example Pluto had been moving retrograde (backward through the zodiac) as Mars moved direct (forward through the zodiac), the aspect would have been doubly applying. For the purpose of interpretation, applying aspects are regarded as being stronger than separating aspects. In horary astrology, separating aspects are regarded as influences that have already passed. As a consequence, the only aspects considered when judging a horary chart are applying aspects.

**Sources:**
Gettings, Fred. *Dictionary of Astrology*. London: Routledge & Kegan Paul, 1985.
Lee, Dal. *Dictionary of Astrology*. New York: Paperback Library, 1969.
Louis, Anthony. *Horary Astrology Plain & Simple*. St. Paul, MN: Llewellyn, 1998.

## Appulse

Appulse refers to either a partial occultation, a conjunction, a planet's crossing of the meridian, or the entry of the Moon into the Earth's shadow.

## Aquarius

Aquarius (from the Latin word *Aquarii*, meaning "water carrier"), the eleventh sign of the zodiac, is a fixed air sign. It is a positive, masculine sign, ruled by the planet Uranus (before the outer planets were discovered, it was said to be ruled by Saturn). Its symbol is the water bearer, and its glyph is a pair of wavy lines representing water (resulting in a frequent confusion about Aquarius's element, which is air rather than water). Aquarius is associated with the shins, ankles, and the circulatory system, and individuals with an Aquarius sun sign are susceptible to sprained ankles, hardening of the arteries, and varicose veins. The key phrase for Aquarius is "I know."

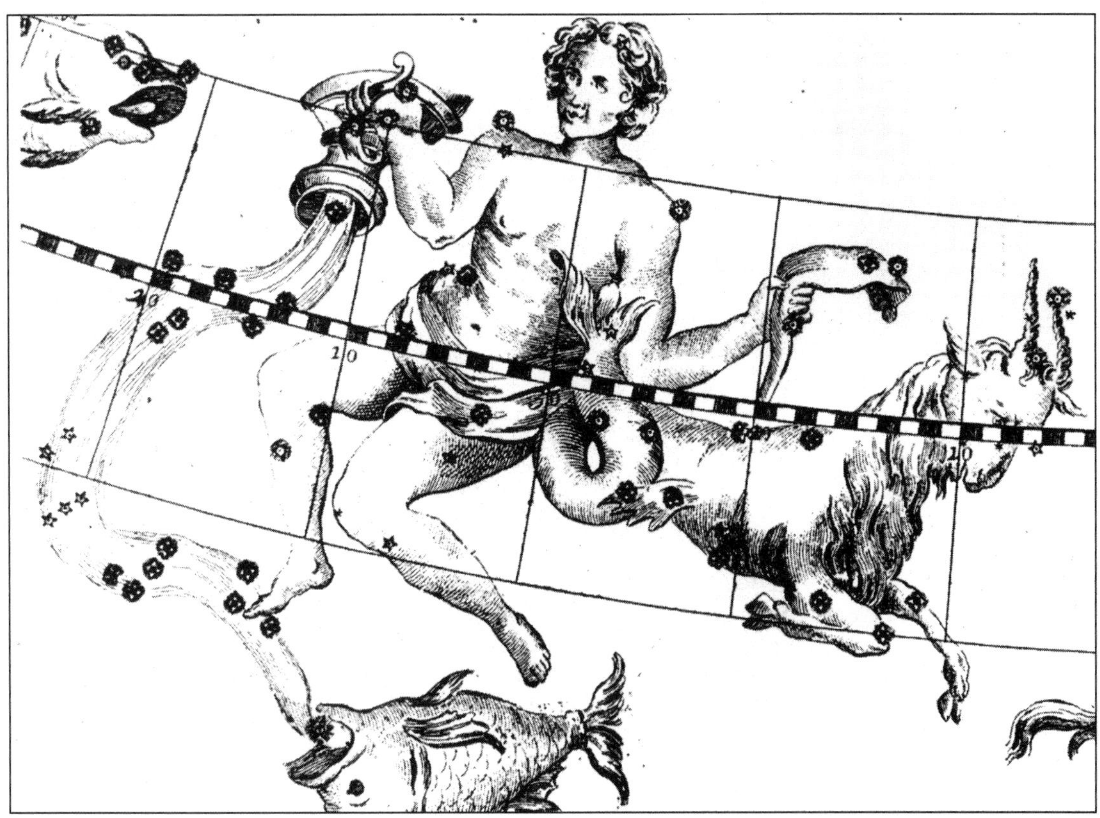

**Aquarius and Capricornus from an 18th-century engraving by Montignot. *Reproduced by permission of Fortean Picture Library.***

Like certain other zodiacal signs, Aquarius has been associated with more than one mythical figure. It is most often identified with Ganymede ("cup bearer of the gods"), a beautiful young man who, after being abducted by an eagle sent by Zeus, served as Zeus's cupbearer. Ganymede was also Zeus's lover, and was said to have been transformed into the constellation Aquarius.

Cecrops is another mythical figure sometimes associated with Aquarius. Cecrops, half human and half serpent, was a culture hero who, as king of Attica, put an end to human sacrifice (by offering cakes instead of flesh to the gods) and founded a court. He also taught his people writing, the proper manner of burying the dead, and census taking. He is particularly remembered for deciding a contest between Athena and Poseidon in favor of Athena. In anger, Poseidon responded by flooding Attica.

Despite the myth of Ganymede, there is no special connection between Aquarius and homosexuality (Neptune, ruler of Pisces, was the ancient patron of homosexuals). However, Aquarians tend to be eccentric individuals who enjoy working with other people. In line with the story of Cecrops, natives of this sign tend to be humanistic social reformers, with a special aptitude for intellectual pursuits like writing. Also in line with the Cecrops myth, census taking reflects the mathematical and scientific inclinations of Aquarius. While Aquarians are known for being open-minded, they are also unusually argumentative. They tend to avoid emotions by intellectualizing them—symbolically choosing Athena (goddess of intellect) over Poseidon (ruler of water, the symbol of emotion) until they are overwhelmed (flooded).

The sign that the Sun was in at birth is usually the single most important influence on a native's personality. Thus, when people say they are a certain sign, they are almost always referring to their sun sign. There is a wealth of information available on the characteristics of the zodiacal signs—so much that one book would not be able to contain it all. Sun-sign astrology, which is the kind of astrology found in newspaper columns and popular magazines, has the advantage of simplicity. But this simplicity is purchased at the price of ignoring other astrological influences, such as one's Moon sign, rising sign, etc. These other influences can substantially modify a person's basic sun-sign traits. As a consequence, it is the rare individual who is completely typical of her or his sign. The reader should bear this caveat in mind when perusing the following series of sun-sign interpretations.

One traditional way in which astrologers condense information is by summarizing sign and planet traits in lists of words and short phrases called key words or key phrases. The following Aquarius key words are drawn from Manly P. Hall's *Astrological Keywords:*

> *Emotional key words:* "The emotional nature is very active but in negative types not very profound; vivacious, excitable, kindly in disposition, well-liked, gentle, altruistic, domestic but changeable, unconventional, temperamental, worrying."
>
> *Mental key words:* "Inventive, intellectual, fond of literature and science, diplomatic, tolerant, reasonable, independent, discreet, optimistic, humanitarian, fixed in opinion."

At present, there are various astrology report programs that contain interpretations of each of the 12 sun signs. A selection of these for Sun in Aquarius has been excerpted below:

> You get bored with the status quo and are generally open to whatever is new. An individualist and a free spirit, you find that your friends are important to you—as long as they do not try to tie you down by making too many emotional demands. Remarkably fair-minded when dealing with large groups or broad issues, you are at the same time not always emotionally sensitive to the needs of individuals. Your thoughts are offbeat, and though you're a bit eccentric, you're not very changeable. As a matter of fact, you can be quite stubborn at times. Extremely objective, with good powers of observation, you would be qualified to study complicated technical subjects such as science, computers or maybe even astrology. (From "Professional Natal Report." Courtesy of Astrolabe [www.alabe.com].)

You are a freedom-loving, strong-willed, and independent-minded individual, and you insist upon living your own life as you see fit, even if that means ignoring convention and tradition. In personal relationships you cannot be owned or possessed, and while you are willing to share yourself with another, you do not always adjust easily to the emotional give and take of a close relationship. Though intellectually open, you can be enormously stubborn, opinionated, and inflexible on a one-to-one level. You have strong convictions and feelings about fairness and equality, and you try to live by your ideals, but your ideals about how people SHOULD treat one another don't always take into account human weaknesses, differences, and needs. You probably dislike sentimentality and traditional gender roles and "games."

You are fair, intelligent, objective, rational and often let your head rule rather than your heart. You seem rather self-sufficient and detached emotionally because you are capable of putting aside your personal feelings and viewing things dispassionately. But once you make up your mind on an issue, you are difficult to sway and can be rather dogmatic.

You think in broad terms and are concerned with the world beyond your own personal sphere—your town, nation, or even planet. You are likely to become involved in community affairs, social organizations, and groups of all kinds, or to have a keen interest in such. You enjoy being part of a group endeavor and often find yourself organizing, managing, or supervising group activities.

Forward-looking and progressive, you harbor great hopes for the future. You stay current and up to date, and respond to contemporary cultural trends, both in terms of personal style and in terms of ideas. When young you were very influenced by your peers and by group pressures and by all the "latest crazes." You have an experimental mind and are attracted by the novel.

Your strong points include your concern for human welfare and social betterment, your sense of fairness and democratic spirit, and your vision. Your faults are your stubbornness and inflexibility, and a tendency to be very obtuse and insensitive when it comes to personal feelings and human needs. (From "Merlin," by Gina Ronco and Agnes Nightingale. Courtesy of Cosmic Patterns [http://cosmic.patterns.com].)

Aquarius is the sign of geniuses—and criminals. It represents individuation, which is a five-dollar word meaning the process of being yourself. Set against your individuation are all the social forces of conformity. Buy a necktie! Shave your legs! Get hungry at noon! Outwardly, they show up as peer pressures. Inwardly, those forces are more subtle but even more formidable: all the internalized scripts that go with having once been a very little kid learning how to be human from mom, dad, and the television set.

The Aquarian part of you is odd somehow. It doesn't fit into the social environment, at least not without betraying itself. In this part of your life, the more centered you get, the weirder you'll seem—to Ann Landers and her crowd. Go for it, and pay the price of alienation or ostracism. It's high … but not as high as the price of living a life that's not your own.

With your Sun in Aquarius, the experiences that feed your solar vitality happen to be ones that most people will think are strange. There's nothing spiritually dead about "normalcy"; it just happens that you've come to a point in the soul's journey in which the path wanders through the cultural and social fringes. Don't let that stop you! Be yourself, even if doing that annoys every figure of authority for miles around.

Society will try to coerce you into living a life that's more mainstream than what's good for you. It will bribe, threaten, cajole, and intimidate you. As though that weren't enough, it will send spies inside your fortress-walls: people who love you saying, "Please compromise on this! It tears me up to think what'll happen to you if you don't!" They're sincere, but don't let them sway you. Be yourself. You're sailing in the thin, high atmosphere of true individuality. And one of the prices you pay is that, sadly, you'll have to hurt some people to do it. (From "The Sky Within," by Steven Forrest. Courtesy of Matrix Software (http://thenewage.com) and Steven Forrest (http://www.stevenforrest.com).

Among its several natal programs, Matrix Software created a unique report based on the published works of the early-twentieth-century astrologer Grant Lewi (1901–1952). Lewi's highly original delineations were recognized as creative and insightful by his contemporaries. One measure of the appeal of his work is that his books *Astrology for the Millions* and *Heaven Knows What* are still in print. The following is excerpted from the report program "Heaven Knows What":

"God must have loved the common people; he made so many of them."

"With malice toward none, with charity for all, with firmness in the right as God gives us to see the right." (*Abraham Lincoln, born in Aquarius, February 12, 1809.*)

"We face the arduous days that lie ahead in the warm courage of national unity; with the clear consciousness of seeking old and precious moral values; with the keen satisfaction that comes from the stern performance of duty by young and old alike. We aim at the assurance of a rounded and permanent national life. We do not distrust the future of essential Democracy." (*Franklin D. Roosevelt, born in Aquarius, January 30, 1882.*)

The motivating force behind Aquarius is some form of the gregarious, or herd, instinct. He likes folks. He is sociable. In a higher manifestation, he is social. In a lower manifestation, he thinks that the world—

> the folks—owe him a living. Any way you look at the Aquarian, and whatever Aquarian you look at, you will find folks at the censor of his attitude. Either he depends on them or they depend on him. The sign can go either way. Whether he is a social reformer, or a hobo, people will be around him; he will be holding them up, or they will be holding him up. He thinks himself a great individualist, and he may be, but you'll rarely find him alone. Rich or poor, great or small, deep or shallow, he is the life of the party. He may put his mind on the woes of humanity, solve their problems, give his life for theirs in a figurative or literal sense. Or he may fritter away his time in pool halls. But he will always be where there are people, in the flesh or in theory.
>
> His best expression comes when he has hitched his wagon to a star of social work or one of the social professions: invention, medicine, law, politics, architecture, literature, science, music or art with some social application. His worst expression is going places and doing things to no purpose. Some prime examples of wasted talents come in this sign—as well as some of the greatest martyrs and benefactors of the human race. Aquarius is generally misunderstood even when he has achieved greatness—and always thinks he is misunderstood when he is wasting himself. In love, Aquarius is noble but not necessarily conventional; loyal, if not faithful; affectionate, if independent, and resentful of intrusion on his private studies, which may irk the spouse because they never seem to produce anything except big electric light bills. Aquarius the social or sociable can be anything or nothing, but the one thing he will almost never be is lonesome. He may think his spirit yearns for understanding, but he will never be far from someone to listen while he attempts to explain himself. (Courtesy of Matrix Software [http://thenewage.com].)

The following excerpt comes not from a natal report program, but from David Cochrane's recent book, *Astrology for the 21st Century*. Based on lessons for astrology students, it approaches the signs of the zodiac from a somewhat different perspective than the other short delineations cited here:

> A common interpretation of Aquarius would be something like this: Aquarius is associated with inventions, discoveries, innovations, eccentricity, progressiveness, science, humanitarianism, and organizations. Aquarius is ruled by Uranus and shares many traits with Uranus. Aquarius is friendly but not intensely emotional.
>
> Of all zodiac signs, Aquarius is the one that the commonly accepted characteristics have been least easy for me to understand. I have not found eccentricity or even progressiveness to be consistent traits of Aquarius! Very often when I share this observation with other astrologers (including those whom I greatly respect and whose work I admire), they look at me in disbelief, and cannot imagine how I can fail to see these traits of Aquarius. My view of Aquarius may be com-

pletely misguided, but I will share it any way as an example of one astrologer's attempt to understand how Aquarius affects us.

> I see Aquarius as the sign of networking people and ideas. Aquarius relates ideas of different people to each other. Aquarians are social animals that typically prefer living in an urban area rather than a rural area because they prefer having access to the greater number of ideas and group activities. A person with strong Aquarian emphasis can find fulfillment in a rural setting too. Church clubs, school activities and community affairs are important in rural areas, but often Aquarius enjoys the greater number of options in an urban setting.
>
> The Aquarian inclination to network people together gives it access to many points of view and very often more ideas and information than others have. As a consequence, Aquarius does tend to have a liberal and progressive view, but Aquarius also dearly wants to preserve the organizations rather than tear them down. Aquarius joins groups, and very often participates as an employee of a large corporation. Aquarians very often like to think of themselves as great innovators, inventors, or eccentrics because they are not provincial in perspective. They are cosmopolitan and enthusiastic about modern progressive advancements. They do not cling to the past and they do not fear progress, partly because they are better acquainted with the progressive developments generated by corporations and universities, and partly because they are not sentimental or deeply emotional so the replacement of traditional methods with new ones is not offensive. However, Aquarius is a fixed sign, and like all fixed signs it is steady and consistent and not unstable and erratic like Uranus. Aquarius preserves the group activities and works to enhance and grow organizations, clubs, corporations, and groups because it needs them and values them. Aquarians may like to think of themselves as progressive, but they do not want to radically disturb the status quo; they want to preserve it. (Courtesy of Cosmic Patterns [http://cosmic.patterns.com] and David Cochrane [kepler@astrosoftware.com].)

Many specialized report programs have been developed that offer useful supplements to the generic delineations of general reports. The following sun-sign interpretation has been drawn from a program written by Gloria Star (originally part of her book, *Astrology: Woman to Woman*), that generates a specialized report for women:

> With your Sun in Aquarius you are a woman whose spirit forges into the realm of the unusual. As an individual you are unique, and you may pride yourself on the things that make you different from everyone else. But you also have a strong desire to connect to those who are like minded, and may count your friends as your most significant blessings. Since your Sun speaks of "who you think you are," you need to realize that your powerful mind, which can be strongly focused, is your link to your future, and that you are the creator of that future.

> The most friendly path toward developing and expressing your willpower and personal drive may be that of education. As an Aquarian Woman, you appreciate a well-developed mentality, and may feel most confident when you are comfortable in your knowledge about a subject or situation. However, you may have felt as a young girl that the people who knew the most were men, and you certainly may not have questioned whether or not a man had the right to be different. Although you may have felt the impulse to be different, you've never been entirely comfortable with the idea of alienating yourself from the society of which you are a part. And as you've developed your own individual identity, you may have sensed that becoming who you are might not exactly fit the model your father had in mind for you. If you're owning your personal power, you're confident about expressing your uniqueness and meeting the world on your own terms. If you've not yet embraced this part of yourself, you may by trying to accomplish it through projecting these qualities upon your husband or partner. Let him be the genius in the family! Your own genius may not fully emerge until you've consciously determined that you, too, deserve to be seen for who you really are.
>
> Even though you may have found your differences from others painful when you were a young girl, you've probably discovered that it is your uniqueness which will provide the impetus to achieving true success. Your Aquarius Sun adds a drive to attain a clear perception about yourself, and your need to make a difference in the world can give you cause to aim for something out of the ordinary. Your real goal may be to transcend the bounds of mere mortality and achieve something that will open a new pathway. Although this functions primarily at a spiritual level, it does have its implications on the physical plane. In your family, you can be the one who breaks the patterns. On the job you are the one whose vision and insight inspire new direction. (From "Woman to Woman," by Gloria Star. Courtesy of Matrix Software [http://thenew age.com] and Gloria Star [glostar@aol.com].)

Responding to the revival of interest in pre-twentieth-century astrology, J. Lee Lehman developed a report program embodying the interpretive approach of traditional astrology. The following is excerpted from her book *Classical Astrology for Modern Living* and her computer program "Classical Report":

> You are affable, courteous, unenvious, stubborn, merry and jocund, not given to quarrel, or a religious or spiritual nature, sober of speech, and strong. You can be ostentatious, but are free from maliciousness.
>
> You are an Air Sign, which means that you are "hot" and "wet." The "wet" component means, among other things, that you blur distinctions, and that you are more swayed by passion than by intellectual argument. At your worst, you see too many connections, becoming lost in conspiracies. At your best, you spot the connection that everyone

else missed. Being "hot," you react to things quickly: by expressing your anger strongly and immediately, you don't tend to harbor a grudge. This is the temperament type that is considered the most ideal, because you are the most comfortable within a social situation. You appear warm and friendly to others, and don't seem too eager to hold them to an impossible standard.

You are fixed, which means you are strong-willed and stubborn. You will want to hang onto people and things long after they have ceased to be useful to you. (Courtesy of J. Lee Lehman, Ph.D. (copyright 1998) [http://www.leelehman.com].)

Readers interested in examining interpretations for their Chinese astrological sign should refer to the relevant entry. A guide for determining one's sign in the Chinese system is provided in the entry on the Chinese zodiac.

**Sources:**


Cochrane, David. *Astrology for the 21st Century*. Gainesville, FL: Cosmic Patterns, 2002.

Forrest, Steven. *The Inner Sky: How to Make Wiser Choices for a More Fulfilling Life*. 4th ed. San Diego: ACS Publications, 1989.

Green, Landis Knight. *The Astrologer's Manual: Modern Insights into an Ancient Art*. Sebastopol, CA: CRCS Publications, 1975.

Hall, Manly P. *Astrological Keywords*. New York, Philosophical Library, 1958. Reprint, Savage, MD: Littlefield Adams Quality Paperbacks, 1975.

Lehman, J. Lee. *Classical Astrology for Modern Living: From Ptolemy to Psychology & Back Again*. Atglen, PA: Whitford Press, 1996.

Lewi, Grant. *Astrology for the Millions*. 5th rev. ed. St. Paul, MN: Llewellyn, 1978.

———. *Heaven Knows What*. Garden City, NY: Doubleday, Doran & Co., 1935. Reprint, St. Paul, MN: Llewellyn, 1995.

Star, Gloria. *Astrology: Woman to Woman*. St. Paul, MN: Llewellyn, 1999.

———. *Astrology & Your Child: A Handbook for Parents*. St. Paul, MN: Llewellyn, 2001.


## Aquinas, Thomas

Thomas Aquinas was a famous thirteenth-century Italian scholar-philosopher and the official theologian of the Catholic Church. Although not an astrologer, he made some very influential assertions about the science of the stars. While he acknowledged planetary influence, Aquinas was also concerned to reconcile the apparent determinism of astrology with free will.

For example, Aquinas asserted that one could utilize powers of rationality to overcome such forces of determinism. The basis for this assertion was the distinction Christian philosophy drew between the immortal soul (governed by reason) and the physical body (governed by sensual desire). As an artifact of this physical world, astrological forces could, according to Aquinas, affect the physical body. The soul, however, was beyond such forces. Individuals could thus exercise their reason and overcome planetary influences.

People in groups, however, were ruled more by their passions than by reason. Thus, the actions of nations, cities, and other organizations—the sphere of mundane astrology—were more "fated" than the actions of individuals. Because of the clear distinction that Aquinas drew between groups and individuals, it has been said that he was the first person to distinguish natal astrology from mundane astrology.

**Sources:**

Baigent, Michael, Nicholas Campion, and Charles Harvey. *Mundane Astrology*. 2d ed. London: Aquarian Press, 1992.

Brau, Jean-Louis, Helen Weaver, and Allan Edmands. *Larousse Encyclopedia of Astrology*. New York: North American Library, 1980.

## Ara

Ara, asteroid 849 (the 849th asteroid to be discovered, on February 9, 1912), is approximately 152 kilometers in diameter and has an orbital period of 5.6 years. Ara was named after the American Relief Administration (ARA) and represents the giving of aid. In a natal chart, its sign and house position indicates where and how one is most likely to give aid or to be aided by others. When afflicted by inharmonious aspects, Ara may indicate lack of aid or giving aid for the purpose of self-aggrandizement or as a manipulation.

**Sources:**

Kowal, Charles T. *Asteroids: Their Nature and Utilization*. Chichester, West Sussex, UK: Ellis Horwood Limited, 1988.

Room, Adrian. *Dictionary of Astronomical Names*. London: Routledge, 1988.

Schwartz, Jacob. *Asteroid Name Encyclopedia*. St. Paul, MN: Llewellyn Publications, 1995.

## Arabic Parts

The Arabic Parts are arithmetically derived points on the ecliptic (the path the Sun, from our terrestrial perspective, appears to travel during the course of a year) that represent the synthesis of two or more astrological components (e.g., planets, house cusps, or even other Arabic Parts). The longitudinal distance between them is measured and then projected from a meaningful point in the astrological chart, usually the ascendant. The degree, minute, and second of zodiacal longitude, this distance reached is called the part. Modern astrological texts (post-1800) usually do not distinguish between diurnal and nocturnal charts (astrological charts—be they natal, horary, electional, or other—are erected for times when the Sun is above the horizon or diurnal, or below the horizon or nocturnal), yet the original practice was to do so in most, if not all, cases. Thus, in diurnal charts the formula is often different from that in nocturnal charts.

For example, the most commonly used Arabic Part, the *Pars Fortunae* (Part of Fortune), is found in a diurnal figure (a traditional term for an astrological chart) by taking the distance from the Sun to the Moon, in the order of the signs, and projecting it from the ascendant, also in the order of the signs. Let it be assumed that the ascendant of a native born in the daytime with 12 Pisces 30 rising has the Sun at 4 Aquarius 46 in the eleventh house and the Moon at 0 Taurus 15. The distance between the

**An ancient Arabian zodiac.** ***Reproduced by permission of Fortean Picture Library.***

Lights (a traditional term for the Sun and the Moon) is 85°29'. When this distance is added to the ascendant, the part is found to be at 67°53' or 7 Gemini 59.

Should the figure be nocturnal, however, the Part of Fortune is found from the Moon. Thus, the distance from the Moon to the Sun, in the order of the signs, is found to be 274°31'. This distance, projected from the ascendant (12 Pisces 30) locates the part at 257°01' or 17 Sagittarius 01.

In traditional astrology (that practiced in Europe until the mid-seventeenth century), the Arabic Parts were used for several purposes. First, they were used in horary figures to assist in judgment when the planetary testimony was obscure. One circumstance in which this seems to have been done was when, in a horary figure, one planet is the significator of a matter and another planet applies to some aspect of this significator. In such a case, the astrologer may not know if the second planet will hinder or assist the business. The astrologer might take the distance from the aspect in question to the significator and—making an Arabic Part of this distance—project it from the ascendant or other relevant house cusp (say, the third, if the business is about travel, siblings, etc.). The astrologer would then judge whether the application was beneficial or not by determining if the ruler of the part was a benefic. Likewise, a judgment as to good or evil could be made in this way, again on the basis of the benefic or malefic nature of the part's ruler. The strength of the ruler of the part and its aspect (or lack of same) to the significator could also yield helpful information. This is what Guido Bonatti obscurely alludes to when he cites Albumasar in his discussion of the parts in *Liber Astronomiae*. Lynn Thorndike, in *The History of Magic and Experimental Science*, calls Bonatti "the most influential astrologer of the thirteenth century." Bonatti's work (*Liber Astronomiae*) was a major source for traditional medieval European astrological practice.

In his "146 Considerations" (Tractatus V of *Liber Astronomiae;* translated into English and published by Henry Coley in 1676, and recently republished by the American Federation of Astrologers under the title *Anima Astrologiae*), Bonatti discusses another way the concept of the parts could be used to clarify murky testimony in horary figures when the planetary indications are inscrutable. He suggests making parts of those house rulers that related to the matter considered. This is what he advocates in Considerations 144 and 146.

Jean Ganivet, in *Amicus Medicorum* (1508), provides us with an example of the use of the parts in iatromedical diagnosis. He casts a horary figure for the dean of Vienne, seeking to determine whether the dean would survive his current illness or not. He concludes, after considering the Lights, the Part of the Killing Planet, the Part of Death, the Part of Life and the Part of Fortune, all of which were adversely placed, that the dean will fall into delirium in 24 hours and die within two days. He reports that such was the case.

In natal figures, the parts were usually used to get a deeper understanding of the native's life. For instance, the Part of Fortune was called the lunar ascendant and provided the medieval astrologer with information relating to the native's inner motivation (as opposed to outer drives imposed upon one by physical and worldly demands). The Part of the Sun (*Pars Solis, Pars Futurorum, Pars Spiritus, Pars Daemonis*) signifies, Bonatti tells us, in *Libe Astonomiae*, the soul and the body and their quality, as well as faith, prophecy, religion and the culture of God, secrets, cogitations, intentions, hidden things, etc. It is found in a way different from that in which the Part of Fortune is found: In diurnal figures, the distance from the Moon to the Sun is projected from the ascendant; in nocturnal figures, the distance from the Sun to the Moon is projected from the ascendant. Bonatti's work catalogs the parts according to the themes of the houses. His parts of the seventh house contains numerous parts intended to reveal the marital fidelity of husband and wife, thus providing the astrologer with material useful in synastry, although it is here that his medieval monkish misogyny shines forth most glaringly.

The parts also had application in economic forecasting. Bonatti gives us an involved (and largely accurate) technique for commodities forecasting! In addition, the parts were used in mundane figures (ingresses; also known as Revolutions of Years of the World).

The parts were used extensively by the Arabic astrologers, who greatly increased their number. Bonatti, who relies on Arabic sources, lists 128 parts. Al-

Biruni, who is one of Bonatti's sources, lists 143. Al-Biruni advocated a rational astrology based on actual astronomical verities and expressed doubt bordering on scorn with regard to horary astrology, which he likened to sorcery. In discussing the parts (which he calls Lots), he complained, "It is impossible to enumerate the lots which have been invented for the solution of horary questions and for answering enquiries as to prosperous outcome or auspicious time for action; they increase in number daily."

This proliferation led to the superficial and promiscuous abuse of the parts by shallow practitioners who did not appreciate that the parts were never intended to replace the testimony of the primary figure. Accurate delineation of the parts depends on accurate delineation of the figure.

The history of the parts predates their Arabic usage, stretching back to the Hellenistic Period, perhaps as early as 300 B.C.E., and, conceivably, even to Greco-Babylonian times. Thus, the name "Arabic" Parts is a misnomer. The parts are found in Dorotheus's *Pentateuch* (first century C.E.) and in the *Liber Hermetis*, which Wilhelm von Gundel and Le R. P. Festugière regard as a pre-Islamic Hellenistic Hermetic text exemplifying Egyptian temple astrology of an era possibly as early as the third century B.C.E. Thus, the "Arabic" Parts might better be called Hermetic or Egyptian Parts.

The rather vague handling of the Part of the Sun and the Part Hyleg by Bonatti, Albumasar, and Al-Biruni also implies that the parts originated in pagan times. Bonatti, drawing on Albumasar and Al-Biruni, seems intentionally vague in merely mentioning that the Part of the Sun was relevant to "faith, prophesy and the culture of God." He does not elaborate on this in any way. Al-Biruni, who gives symbols for many of the parts, indicates the Part of the Sun, which he calls the Part of the Daemon, as a circle with two horns—as a crescent emerging from behind a disk. The glyph resembles the head of a medieval Roman horned demon; a figure not originally regarded as evil. In light of the well-attested fact that much of the astrological lore of Albumasar, Al-Biruni, Messahalla, and others came from the polytheistic Hermetic Sabian community at what is today Harran, Iraq, there has been a long-standing assumption on the part of some esotericists that the medieval astrological tradition was a vehicle for preserving the Hellenistic pagan Hermetic gnosis. This assumption appears correct. The reticence of both the Muslim and Christian writers (such as Albumasar, Al-Biruni, and Bonatti) was probably due to their wish to avoid censure by their respective religious authorities. The daemon referred to in the name Part of the Daemon may well be the Neoplatonic—Hermetic Agathodaemon, which was the chief deity of the pagan Sabians.

Another part that receives vague treatment by Bonatti is the Part Hyleg. Bonatti says that it is the root of the other parts and can exist without them, but they cannot exist without it and that "the ancients could have said more about it had they wanted but refrained from doing so because it was involved with other things." This statement is the very epitome of obscurity. The key to the mystery of this part is to determine how it is found and how it got its name. It is calculated as the line extending from the position of the conjunction or prevention (i.e., the new or full moon) prior to birth to the position of the Moon at the time of birth and then projected from the ascendant. It is also called the *Radix Vitae* (Root of Life) and comprehends the whole life of the native, which links it to the Gnostic and Hermetic mysteries of reincarnation discussed in the *Corpus Hermeticum* (attributed to Hermes Trismegistus). Although the *Corpus Hermeticum* we have today dates from the early centuries C.E., the cult whose doctrines it embodies began to coalesce in Egypt with Alexander's conquest (323 B.C.E.) around the notion that the Greek god Hermes and the Egyptian Thoth were one in the same, an idea that had been commonly accepted since Plato's time. The Hermetic doctrine of reincarnation, which bears resemblance to the Hindu and Buddhist concepts, is found scattered throughout the *libelli* comprising the *Corpus*, but the following are especially relevant: *Libellus I*, sections 13–18; *Libellus III*, section 4; *Libellus VIII*; and *Libellus X*, sections 16–22. In *Libellus XI*, sections 7–8a, the Moon is referred to as "the instrument by which birth and growth are wrought," and we are told that the Moon "divides the immortals from the mortals."

This new understanding of the antiquity of the parts may not be the final word. If the parts, as it now seems certain, were used as early as 300 B.C.E., we may be dealing with a tradition that is far older. The ancient usage of the parts has had an effect on modern astrological practice. Besides being resurrected in the twentieth century in the context of traditional astrology, the concepts underlying the parts have been influential in modern astrological innovations. For example, the Arabic Parts prefigure by at least 2,000 years the planetary pictures of the Hamburg School of Uranian Astrology and similar practices of the chronobiologists.

—Robert Zoller

**Sources:**

Al-Biruni, Abu'l-Rayhan Muhammad ibn Ahmad. *The Book of Instruction in the Elements of the Art of Astrology*. Translated by R. Ramsay Wright. London: Luzac & Co., 1934.

Benatti, Guidonis. *Liber Astronomiae, Traetatus V.* Translated by Henry Coley as *The Astrologer's Guide: Anima Astrologiae*. American Federation of Astrologers, Washington DC, 1970. (Originally published 1676.)

Festugière, Le R. P. *La révélation d'Hermès Trismégiste*. Paris: Librairie Lecoffre, 1950.

Ganivet, Jean. *Amicus Medicorum*. Lyons, France, 1508.

*Guidonis Bonati Forliviensis Mathematici de Astronomiae Tractatus*. Basel, Switzerland, 1550.

*Hermetica*. 4 vols. Translated and edited by Walter Scott. Dawsons of Pall Mall, London: 1968.

Thorndike, Lynn. *The History of Magic and Experimental Science*. 8 vols. New York: Columbia University Press, 1923–1964.

Von Gundel, Wilhelm. *Dekane und Dekansternbilder.* Glückstadt und Hamburg, J. J. Augustin, 1936. Reprint, Darmstadt, Germany: Wissenschaftliche Buchgesellschaft, 1969.

Zoller, Robert. *Lost Key to Prediction*. New York: Inner Traditions, 1980.

## ARACHNE

Arachne, asteroid 407 (the 407th asteroid to be discovered, on October 13, 1895), is approximately 104 kilometers in diameter and has an orbital period of 4¼ years. Arachne was named after a Greek dyer and weaver who, after a competition with Athena, hanged herself and changed into a spider. This asteroid's key words are "entangled" and "network." According to Martha Lang-Wescott, Arachne indicates "reactions to people and situations that are very involved." Jacob Schwartz gives this asteroid's astrological significance as "pride in the ability to handle intricate detail, creation of intrigue." It also represents webs (both actual and psychological), intrigue, entanglement, and perceptions of intricacy.

**Sources:**

Lang-Wescott, Martha. *Asteroids-Mechanics: Ephemerides II*. Conway, MA: Treehouse Mountain, 1990.

———. *Mechanics of the Future: Asteroids*. Rev. ed. Conway, MA: Treehouse Mountain, 1991.

Schwartz, Jacob. *Asteroid Name Encyclopedia*. St. Paul, MN: Llewellyn Publications, 1995.

## Archer

The Archer is a popular alternative name for the sign Sagittarius.

## Ardra

Ardra (moist or perspiring) is one of the Nakshatras (lunar mansions) of Vedic astrology. Rudra, the god of storms, presides over this sign, symbolized by either a teardrop or drop of sweat. Ardra lies between Gemini 6°40' and 20° and is ruled by the planet Rahu. This is considered a good time to do difficult physical work, and people may find themselves having a better memory and better skilled at manual labor, while also a bit more arrogant or reckless with their moon in this Nakshatra.

—Pramela Thiagesan

## Aries

Aries (from the Latin word for ram), the first sign of the zodiac, is a cardinal sign and a fire sign. It is a positive, masculine sign ruled by the planet Mars. Its symbol is the Ram, and its glyph is said to represent a ram's horns. It takes its name from the Greek god of war, making it one of the few signs with a well-developed mythology. Aries is associated with the head, and people with an Aries sun sign are prone to headaches and injuries to the head and face. The association of the head with Aries is the source of the word headstrong, which characterizes people with a strong Aries nature. As the first sign, the key phrase for Aries is "I am," representing the birth of awareness.

Although Zeus, king of the Greek gods, fathered many children, Aries was the only son by his wife, Hera. Aries ruled war and was said to delight in conflict. He was also impulsive, often defying the fates. According to most accounts, Aries never married but had many love affairs, best known of which was his liaison with the goddess of love, by whom he fathered Eros (source of the term "erotic"). His nature was simultaneously brave and insolent, and in ancient works of art he was portrayed as young and handsome.

Like its namesake, the sign Aries is youthful and impulsive. Arian nature can manifest positively as bravery in the act of standing up for one's rights. Negatively, the same nature can manifest as crudeness, pushiness, overaggressiveness, and even violence. Arians tend to be egotistical, though it is the unself-conscious egotism of a child (in contrast to the fully self-conscious egotism of those under a sign like Leo). They are quick to anger, but just as quick to forgive. As natives of the first sign of the zodiac, they are often pioneers, but they are infamous for the difficulties they have finishing what they begin—they enjoy the excitement of being the first into new territory but prefer to let others map it out. Like all fire sign natives, they are fond of physical and social activity.

The sign that the Sun was in at birth is usually the single most important influence on a native's personality. Thus, when people say they are a certain sign, they are almost always referring to their sun sign. There is a wealth of information available on the characteristics of the zodiacal signs—so much that one book would not be able to contain it all. Sun-sign astrology, which is the kind of astrology found in newspaper columns and popular magazines, has the advantage of simplicity. But this simplicity is purchased at the price of ignoring other astrological influences, such as one's Moon sign, rising sign, etc. These other influences can substantially modify a person's basic sun sign traits. As a consequence, it is the rare individual who is completely typical of her or his sign. The reader should bear this caveat in mind when perusing the following series of sun sign interpretations.

**A seventeenth-century manuscript page showing Aries the ram. *Reproduced by permission of Fortean Picture Library.***

One traditional way in which astrologers condense information is by summarizing sign and planet traits in lists of words and short phrases called key words or key phrases. The following Aries key words are drawn from Manly P. Hall's *Astrological Keywords:*

> *Emotional key words:* "Courageous, enthusiastic, imaginative, energetic, excitable, proud, impulsive, audacious, not domestic, hasty, brusque, sharp, passionate, quick-tempered, intemperate."
>
> *Mental key words:* "Executive, enterprising, pioneering, confident, ingenious, scientific, explorative, independent, expedient, precise, progressive or intolerant in religion [one extreme or the other], aggressive, competitive."

At present, there are various astrology report programs that contain interpretations of each of the 12 sun signs. A selection of these for Sun in Aries has been excerpted below:

By nature, you are very energetic and high-spirited. You are fiercely independent—you must be first in everything you do, and you enjoy taking risks. You are the one who will rush in where angels fear to tread. Quite brilliant at initiating new projects, you are terrible at following them through to completion. You are an enthusiastic leader but you tend to be a reluctant follower. Often you are quick to anger, but you usually recover just as fast, regretting later things you said when you were upset. One of your best traits is that you are simple and direct, blunt and honest—just be careful you do not hurt others' feelings. Your need to be competitive at all costs may provoke resistance from others, but, as long as you maintain your usual Sunny good humor, this should not prove to be a major problem for you. (From "Professional Natal Report." Courtesy of Astrolabe [http://www.alabe.com].)

You are a person who thrives on challenge, and you often feel that you must battle your way through life, depending upon no one and nothing but your own strength, intelligence, and courage. You believe in being totally honest, true to oneself and one's own vision and convictions, even if that means standing alone. Honesty, integrity, personal honor, and authenticity are your gods, and you have no sympathy for weakness of character in others.

You crave the freedom to do things in your own way, and you work very well independently. Cooperating with others or carrying out another's will is not your style. You like to be the chief—or to go it alone.

You love action and if others are settling down into a nice, comfortable little rut, then you are always ready to stir things up, do something new, make changes, bring in some fresh blood. Routine and sameness are like death to you. You are not afraid of trying something that's never been done before, and even though you may be seen as a fool sometimes, you also discover, invent, and initiate things that others will later emulate. Taking risks and following your own star are the breath of life for you, and you wilt (or get very frustrated and angry) if you cannot do this.

You are spontaneous, impulsive, direct, enthusiastic, and assertive. You believe in the power of positive thinking and positive action, and you think of yourself as a strong person—even invincible. You hate being ill or in any way in a position of dependency. Accepting your own human limitations and emotional needs is often difficult for you.

You are basically aggressive in your attitudes and have less facility in the receptive arts of relating to others, picking up subtle messages and nuances, listening, nurturing, and harmonizing. Often you are so fired up about your own projects or goals that you inadvertently run over or ignore other people's feelings and interests. Being receptive and appreciative of others' contributions, ideas, and feelings would go a long way in improving your relationships. Your impatience to get on with things causes you to be rather insensitive, and to therefore alienate others unnecessarily. You also frequently try to accomplish your ends by using anger or some version of a temper tantrum. You would gain much by learning to slow down, relax, and just let things be sometimes, but your energetic, restless nature rarely allows you to do this. (From "Merlin," by Gina Ronco & Agnes Nightingale. Courtesy of Cosmic Patterns [http://cosmic.patterns.com].)

Courage! That's what Aries is all about. Traditionally this sign is represented as the Ram—a fierce, frightening creature. That's a pretty good description of how this energy looks from the outside. Inside, it's different. Not the Ram, but the newborn robin, two days old, just hatched from its shell, living in a world full of creatures who think of it as breakfast. Does it cower? No—the little bird flaps its stubby wings and squawks its head off, demanding its right to exist. That's Aries: the raw primal urge to survive. Existential courage.

Courage is a funny virtue—it has to be scared into a person. In the evolutionary scheme of life, Aries energy has a disconcerting property: it draws stress to itself. You can choose a life of risk and adventure. Or you can choose a life of one damn thing after another. Refuse the first, you'll get the second.

With the Sun in Aries, there's a hidden spiritual agenda behind the dramatic tone of your life: you're getting braver. Every month, every year, you attract a set of challenges. As you've probably noticed, you're a magnet for stress. Sounds terrible, right? Don't worry: you have a choice. There are two kinds of stress: the kind we hate and the kind we like. The kind we like we generally call by other names, like exhilaration and adventure … which, for you, is the path of destiny. Accept it. Live the gambler's life. Risk the lows for the sake of the highs. Do it, or all that fire inside you will turn sour, emerging as tension, argumentativeness, and pointless trouble. (From "The Sky Within," by Steven Forrest. Courtesy of Matrix Software [http://thenewage.com] and Steven Forrest [http://www.stevenforrest.com.)

Among its several natal programs, Matrix Software created a unique report based on the published works of the early-twentieth-century astrologer Grant Lewi (1901–1952). Lewi's highly original delineations were recognized as creative and insightful by his contemporaries. One measure of the appeal of his work is that his books *Astrology for the Millions* and *Heaven Knows What* are still in print. The following is excerpted from the report program "Heaven Knows What":

"Here lies Thomas Jefferson, author of the Declaration of Independence, of the Statute of Virginia for religious Liberty, and founder of the University of Virginia." (*Self-written epitaph of Thomas Jefferson, born in Aries, April 13, 1743.*)

Aries' great independence is a symptom of vitality and physical energy and becomes intellectualized later in life, if at all. The highest type of

> Arian becomes capable of idealizing and universalizing his love of independence, which has its source in egocentricity. The first ambition of the Arian is to be first. He is an inveterate contestant, a professional competitor. His object is not so much the material stake as the glory of winning. He will never boast about coming in second; the also-rans he beats impress him less than the one fellow who beats him and thus steals his rightful place at the head of the procession.
>
> Literally as well as figuratively this first-ness shows. Your Arian walks one step ahead of his companions, goes through doors first, has the first word (and often the last) in any argument. He loves arguments, not as a means of arriving at truth so much as a means of demonstrating that he can come out in front. He often wins by sheer noise and vitality—that is, he makes the other fellow cry uncle. Aries is frequently original in his efforts to be first, and, when not original, is sure to be novel. Any Arian who doesn't understand the difference between originality and novelty should study the two words till he does. When an Arian is original he is a pioneer, an inventor, a great thinker. When he is only novel, he is putting first his ego ideal to be first and neglecting to make his ideas sound and his methods practical. He thus loses the benefit of his energy, his genius and his ambition. All the bugaboos of the ego beset the Arian, and he must beware of self-centeredness. This can make him arrogant, conceited, self-pitying, self-assertive, and in the face of opposition or restraint can lead to delusions of persecution in mild or acute form. To forget self, to become absorbed in mental matters, to put ideas first, and to make sure that originality (or novelties) rest on a sound basis of fact, to see the other fellow's point of view, and to regard the other fellow's needs, wishes, desires just as seriously as his own are the means by which Aries may emphasize his great good points, and insure that his desire to be first shall actually cause him to be first. (Courtesy of Matrix Software [http://thenewage.com].)

The following excerpt comes not from a natal report program, but from David Cochrane's recent book, *Astrology for the 21st Century*. Based on lessons for astrology students, it approaches the signs of the zodiac from a somewhat different perspective than the other short delineations cited here:

> The usual interpretation of Aries is that it is ruled by Mars, the warrior, and inclines a person to be strong and independent. Aries is the pioneer and prefers to blaze its own trail rather than follow the crowd.
>
> My personal observation of Aries is that it does indeed incline a person to prefer functioning independently and accordingly to their own instincts, and they often are very poor in cooperating with others. They do not solicit the opinion of others, and instead make decisions according to what seems best to them. I have not found Aries to be combative or physically forceful, although their reluctance to cooperate with others can cause problems in relationships.

> No astrologer has a monopoly on truth, and I realize that my emphasis on Aries being independent but not necessarily forceful is not a view shared by a great number of astrologers. These views of Aries are just the opinion of one astrologer, and are based on consultations with clients for many years. Progress in determining consistently accurate traits is difficult because there are many hundreds of astrological influences in the birth chart (thousands if you use some techniques) and any of these astrological influences may be responsible for the trait you are ascribing to the person, and additionally there are many ways that a person can respond to the astrological influences. I remember one particular week when I had 3 clients whose Sun sign was Aries and overall all 3 of the people were rather gentle, even passive, but all 3 of them had problems in personal relationships because of their "lone wolf" approach to life; they simply did not share openly, cooperate, or compromise, and insisted on following a career path that suited their personal taste, and all 3 were uncomfortable in an employment situation where they could not be their own boss. This kind of anecdotal evidence is generally all that we have to work from, so from a scientific perspective all astrological theory is highly speculative and there is little wonder that there are a large number of opinions. (Courtesy of Cosmic Patterns [http://cosmic.patterns.com} and David Cochrane [kepler@astrosoftware.com].)

Several specialized report programs have been developed that offer useful supplements to the generic delineations of general reports. The following sun-sign interpretation has been drawn from a program written by Gloria Star (originally part of her book, *Astrology: Woman to Woman*) that generates a specialized report for women:

> With the Sun in Aries your independent way of thinking and doing things may be quite powerful. Your ego self is driven by a need for autonomy. You need plenty of room to move, and the idea of being penned in makes you feel unsettled. You simply do not like waiting, and prefer spontaneity to planned situations. You may also be more comfortable taking the lead, which can be daunting for some of the men in your life. Since your Sun indicates "who you think you are," you may realize that if you see yourself as autonomous, then situations in your life are more likely to develop which allow you to express yourself in a more self-determined manner.
>
> Through your Aries Sun, you have the capacity to develop a strong level of autonomy and self-direction. You may be a self-starter and will prefer to address life on your own terms. However, you can have a little difficulty trying to figure out how to go after the things you want without alienating others. If your approach is too brash or abrasive, you'll meet with resistance and end up feeling that you're always defending yourself. Despite being a woman, you may be okay in situations with "the guys," especially if you're involved in sports or other activities in which there are more men than women present. Since you can be com-

> petitive, you may set up situations which provide a challenge, but you do not need to feel that you're always doing battle. You need some positive outlets through which you can develop your willpower, and may enjoy a career path which requires you to forge into new territory from time to time. You're an excellent leader, and whether you're working in the world, guiding your family through a crisis or seeking spiritual clarity, you can forge a path which others readily follow.
>
> With your Sun in Aries you'll enjoy forging a life path which challenges your sense of personal strength and courage. Your ability to blaze your way to the top in any situation is quite noticeable, although you can be a little abrasive if your eye is simply on the prize and you fail to pay attention to others around you. When a situation calls for leadership, you're the natural choice. (From "Woman to Woman," by Gloria Star. Courtesy of Matrix Software [http://thenewage.com] and Gloria Star [glostar@aol.com].)

Responding to the revival of interest in pre-twentieth-century astrology, J. Lee Lehman developed a report program embodying the interpretive approach of traditional astrology. The following is excerpted from her book *Classical Astrology for Modern Living* and her computer program "Classical Report":

> You are witty, quick to anger, yet lethargic, with a tendency toward headaches, especially migraines. You are noble-spirited, very courageous and valiant, and honorable.
>
> In astrology the sign Aries is considered to be Cardinal. This means that you are better at starting new things than you are at finishing them. Aries the Ram, being a four-footed sign, means that you have a strong sex drive. This also means that you can be vicious or violent if angered.
>
> Aries is also a Fire Sign, which, according to classical astrology is "hot" and "dry." The "dry" component means, among other things, that you see distinctions easily, and that you are more swayed by intellectual argument than by passion. Being "hot," you react to things quickly: by expressing your anger strongly and immediately, you don't tend to harbor a grudge. You may be perceived by others as angry, but that's only if they are not "hot" as well. You will be perceived as having high energy levels. You are often aware of a curious stillness amidst the seeming activity. You may need more sleep than colder types in order to recharge your batteries. (Courtesy of J. Lee Lehman, Ph.D., copyright 1998 [http://www.leelehman.com].)

Readers interested in examining interpretations for their Chinese astrological sign should refer to the relevant entry. A guide for determining one's sign in the Chinese system is provided in the entry on the Chinese zodiac.

**Sources:**

Cochrane, David. *Astrology for the 21st Century*. Gainesville, FL: Cosmic Patterns, 2002.

Forrest, Steven. *The Inner Sky: How to Make Wiser Choices for a More Fulfilling Life*. 4th ed. San Diego: ACS Publications, 1989.
Green, Landis Knight. *The Astrologer's Manual: Modern Insights into an Ancient Art*. Sebastopol, CA: CRCS Publications, 1975.
Hall, Manly P. *Astrological Keywords*. New York, Philosophical Library, 1958. Reprint, Savage, MD: Littlefield Adams Quality Paperbacks, 1975.
Lehman, J. Lee. *Classical Astrology for Modern Living: From Ptolemy to Psychology & Back Again*. Atglen, PA: Whitford Press, 1996.
Lewi, Grant. *Astrology for the Millions*. 5th ed. St. Paul, MN: Llewellyn, 1978.
———. *Heaven Knows What*. St. Paul, MN: Llewellyn, 1969.
Star, Gloria. *Astrology: Woman to Woman*. St. Paul, MN: Llewellyn, 1999.
———. *Astrology & Your Child: A Handbook for Parents*. St. Paul, MN: Llewellyn, 2001.

## Armillary Sphere

An armillary (from Latin word *armilla*, meaning "bracelet") sphere is a skeletal sphere consisting of rings that represent the more important celestial circles utilized by astrologers—the ecliptic, the meridian, the horizon, the celestial equator, etc.

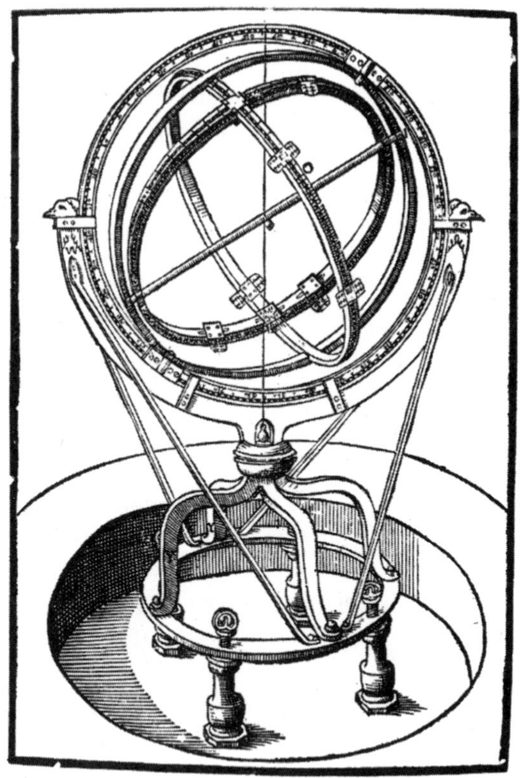

**An illustration of the type of armillary sphere used by the great scientist Tycho Brahe. *Reproduced by permission of Fortean Picture Library.***

## Armisticia

Armisticia, asteroid 1,464 (the 1,464th asteroid to be discovered, on November 11, 1939), is approximately 17 kilometers in diameter and has an orbital period of 5.2 years. Armisticia is a concept asteroid, named after armistice. J. Lee Lehman associates this asteroid with peace treaties; Jacob Schwartz associates it with peace-making as well as peace treaties.

**Sources:**

Kowal, Charles T. *Asteroids: Their Nature and Utilization*. Chichester, West Sussex, UK: Ellis Horwood Limited, 1988.
Lehman, J. Lee. *The Ultimate Asteroid Book*. West Chester, PA: Whitford Press, 1988.
Schwartz, Jacob. *Asteroid Name Encyclopedia*. St. Paul, MN: Llewellyn Publications, 1995.

## Artemis

Artemis, asteroid 105 (the 105th asteroid to be discovered, on September 16, 1868), is approximately 126 kilometers in diameter and has an orbital period of 3.6 years.

Artemis was named after the Greek goddess of the hunt. J. Lee Lehman associates this asteroid with the psychological urges evoked by "the hunt"—hunting, killing, and eating. Jacob Schwartz gives the astrological significance of Artemis as "relating to childbirth, animal husbandry, hunting and devouring as a form of emotional absorption and transmutation."

**Sources:**

Kowal, Charles T. *Asteroids: Their Nature and Utilization*. Chichester, West Sussex, UK: Ellis Horwood Limited, 1988.

Lehman, J. Lee. *The Ultimate Asteroid Book*. West Chester, PA: Whitford Press, 1988.

Room, Adrian. *Dictionary of Astronomical Names*. London: Routledge, 1988.

Schwartz, Jacob. *Asteroid Name Encyclopedia*. St. Paul, MN: Llewellyn Publications, 1995.

## Arthur

Arthur, asteroid 2,597 (the 2,597th asteroid to be discovered, on August 8, 1980), is approximately 20 kilometers in diameter and has an orbital period of 5.2 years. Arthur was named after the semi-mythic king of England. The Celtic *artos* means "bear." According to J. Lee Lehman, the person in whose natal chart this asteroid is prominent is a "hero who presides. The heroic nature of this asteroid comes from properly executing the duty of assigning someone else the job of the quest." Jacob Schwartz gives the astrological significance of Arthur as "heroism and cleverness, and delegating authority, with support from the public."

**Sources:**

Kowal, Charles T. *Asteroids: Their Nature and Utilization*. Chichester, West Sussex, UK: Ellis Horwood Limited, 1988.

Lehman, J. Lee. *The Ultimate Asteroid Book*. West Chester, PA: Whitford Press, 1988.

Schwartz, Jacob. *Asteroid Name Encyclopedia*. St. Paul, MN: Llewellyn Publications, 1995.

## Ascendant (Rising Sign)

The ascendant, also called the rising sign, is the sign of the zodiac (or, more technically, the specific degree of the zodiac) that was on the eastern horizon at the moment for which a horoscope was cast (calculated and drawn). On a zodiacal wheel, the ascendant is the sign at the nine o'clock position. In a natal chart, the ascendant indicates a significant influence on the personality; only the Sun and Moon exert stronger influences. These three signs—the ascendant, the sun sign, and the moon sign—are considered together when someone with a knowledge of astrology beyond sun signs briefly describes her or his astrological makeup (e.g., "I'm a Libra with Moon in Cancer and Leo rising"). The astrologically informed listener then knows that the speaker, while primarily a Libra, is also sensitive and moody like a Cancer and will also come across as a Leo in certain settings.

When either the Moon or the ascendant is in the same sign as the Sun, the person is said to be a double sign. If in the foregoing example, for instance, the native had been born when the Moon was in Libra instead of Cancer, the person would be referred to as a double Libra. Furthermore, continuing the same example, if the Moon was in Libra and Libra was also on the eastern horizon at the birth moment, the native would be termed a triple Libra. People who are a double or triple sign usually embody purer characteristics of their sign than other individuals. No planet is included in these specialized rubrics. In other words, if, continuing with the same example, Mercury or Venus (or any other planet for that matter) was in Libra at the moment of birth, but neither the Moon nor the ascendant was in Libra, the native would not qualify as a double or triple Libra.

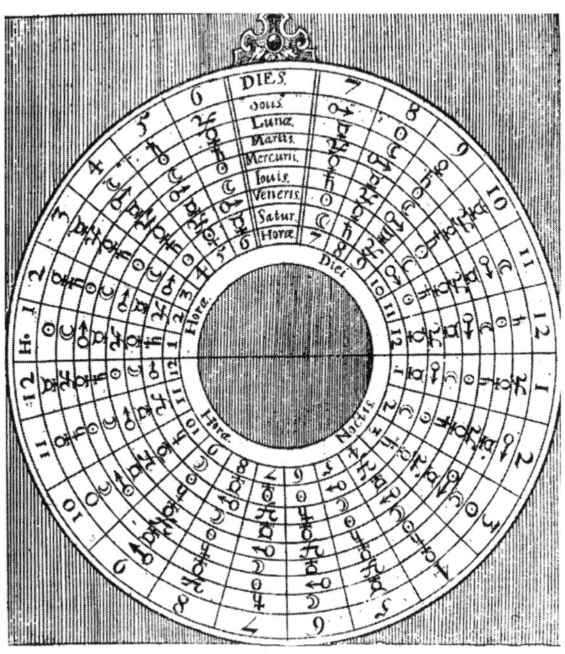


**In Grimoire literature, the planetary hours are sometimes referred to as "ascendants."** ***Reproduced by permission of Fortean Picture Library.***

Although the ascendant is important, in Western astrology it is generally regarded as exerting a more superficial influence than either the Sun or the Moon; it is usually regarded as influencing the native's appearance and certain outward traits more than the depth of her or his personality. Some astrologers, however, view the ascendant as indicating traits at least as deep as the sun sign, if not deeper. (In Vedic astrology, the ascendant or lagna is regarded as the most influential sign.) One way of resolving this disagreement is to take a clue from esoteric astrology (spiritual astrology or the astrology of the soul).

In some systems of esoteric astrology, the ascendant is said to embody positive traits that the native is supposed to be "growing toward." If one was born with Virgo on the ascendant, for example, then the native would need to learn to become more organized or more attentive to details. If this individual is indeed learning Virgo lessons, then the person's Virgo traits will have acquired "depth"; if, on the other hand, the person is not involved in the process of personal or spiritual growth, then these same traits may exert only a superficial influence on the personality. Acquaintance with one or the other of these two types of individuals (growing or nongrowing) may explain the diverging views of astrologers on the significance of the ascendant.

Whatever one's view of the greater or lesser "depth" of the ascendant, there is general agreement that the ascendant is a peculiarly sensitive point in the horoscope. In most systems of house division, the first house begins at the ascendant, and any planet in close proximity to this point—especially if it is located in the first (rather than in the twelfth) house—exerts a strong influence over the whole personality. Thus, for example, a person whose Moon is in close conjunction with the ascendant will be moody and sensitive, even if no other factor in the chart indicates this trait.

The planet that rules the ascendant is also regarded as particularly strong. Some astrologers view this planet as the "ruler" of the entire chart. In a natal chart with Taurus rising, for instance, Venus (the ruler of Taurus) would be the chart ruler. The ruler of the ascendant is more important in horary astrology than in natal astrology.

Because of the rotation of Earth, all 12 signs of the zodiac pass over the horizon during the course of any given 24-hour period. This means that the ascendant changes on the average of once every two hours. Hence, if someone's birth time is off by two hours or more, the person will be assigned an incorrect ascendant—one of the many reasons why an accurate birth time is important.

Using the ascendant as an indicator, astrologers can obtain a general idea of why a client is seeking a reading. If someone calls and makes an appointment when Libra is rising, for instance, the querent is interested in finding out about her or his marriage or some similar close personal relationship. If, on the other hand, Capricorn is rising, the querent is more interested in business and finance.

**Sources:**

Brau, Jean-Louis, Helen Weaver, and Allan Edmands. *Larousse Encyclopedia of Astrology*. New York: New American Library, 1980.

McEvers, Joan, ed. *Spiritual, Metaphysical & New Trends in Modern Astrology*. Saint Paul, MN: Llewellyn Publications, 1988.

## Ascendant Axis

The ascendant axis is the horizon axis. In an astrological chart, this corresponds to the line drawn from the ascendant to the descendant.

## Ascension, Long and Short

If one stands in front of a building, it may appear to be 20 feet wide. If one then walks 10 yards or so to the left or to the right and examines the building from a different perspective, it will appear to be narrower than before. Because the belt of the zodiac is slanted at $2\frac{3}{12}°$ to Earth's equator, we see some astrological signs from a slanted perspective. This causes, particularly at middle-latitudes, a noticeable variation in the length of time it takes for different signs to rise (ascend) over the horizon. Those requiring more time are referred to as signs of long ascension; those requiring less time, signs of short ascension. In the Northern Hemisphere, the signs of long ascension are Cancer, Leo, Virgo, Libra, Scorpio, and Sagittarius, with the "longest" signs being Virgo and Libra. The signs of short ascension are Capricorn, Aquarius, Pisces, Aries, Taurus, and Gemini, with the "shortest" signs being Pisces and Aries. This situation is reversed in the Southern Hemisphere.

**Sources:**

Brau, Jean-Louis, Helen Weaver, and Allan Edmands. *Larousse Encyclopedia of Astrology*. New York: New American Library, 1980.

Lee, Dal. *Dictionary of Astrology*. New York: Paperback Library, 1969.

## Ashwini

Ashwini (or the Horseman) is one of the Nakshatras (lunar mansions) of Vedic astrology. Most often depicted as a horse head, this moon sign resides between Aries 0° and 13°12', with Ashwinis, god of health, presiding and Ketu as the ruling planet. this is a good time to act swiftly; an individual may display behaviors of modesty and self-sufficiency during this period, but may also be stubborn and overzealous.

—Pramela Thiagesan

## Aslesha

Aslesha (the Entwiner) is one of the Nakshatras (lunar mansions) of Vedic astrology. A coiled snake represents this sign ruled by Mercury, with Sarpas presiding. This Nakshatra is found between Cancer 16°40' and 30°, and with the moon there, it is considered a good time to be fierce. An individual could find himself or herself more versatile and clever at this time, but also more impolite and depressed.

—Pramela Thiagesan

## Aspect

Aspect (from the Latin word *aspectus*, meaning "to view or to look at") refers to the angular relationship between various points in a horoscope (an astrological chart), especially to a series of named angles, such as trines (120°) and squares (90°). (For a discussion of the very different notion of aspects in Vedic Astrology, refer to the entry on drishti.)

The 12 signs of the zodiac, in addition to being bands of astrological influence, also provide astrologers with a system for locating planets and other points in space. A circle contains 360°, so when it is divided into 12 equal regions for the 12 signs, each sign encompasses an arc of 30°. Hence, a planet located near the beginning of Aries, for instance, might be at 1° Aries; in the middle of Aries, at 15° Aries; and near the end of the sign, 29° Aries. Earth, which is understood to be at the center of the horoscope (unless one is using a heliocentric or Sun-centered system), constitutes the vertex for any angle between planets or between other points in the chart. Thus, for example, if Mercury is located at 1° Aries, it would make a semisextile (30°) aspect with another planet—let us say Venus—that is located at 1° in the very next sign, which is Taurus. If we move Venus forward another 30° until it is at 1° Gemini, Mercury and Venus would form a sextile (60°) aspect. Another 30° to 1° Cancer forms a square (90°), and so forth.

The interpretation of a horoscope is built around three primary factors—signs, houses, and aspects—that make aspect interpretation one of the most fundamental components of astrology. In a natal chart, the planets represent, among other things, the various facets of one's psyche, and aspects between them indicate how these facets conflict or work together. Mars, for example, represents the forceful, outgoing, aggressive side of the self, whereas Saturn represents the security-seeking, self-disciplined side. While everyone experiences some tension between these two principles, an individual with a Mars-Saturn square (a conflict aspect) in her or his chart experiences this conflict in an exaggerated manner, often over-repressing outgoing, aggressive urges and at other times exploding with impulsive actions or words. A trine, on the other hand, represents the easy flow of energy between two points; so an individual with a Mars-Saturn trine would find that these two facets of the personality work together easily, bringing patience and discipline (Saturn) to the side of ambitious aggression (Mars), and vice versa.

The major aspects are the conjunction (0°), sextile (60°), square (90°), trine (120°), and opposition (180°). Squares and oppositions are regarded as hard aspects, meaning they usually present challenges the native must face and overcome. Sextiles and trines, on the other hand, are regarded as soft aspects, meaning the energies represented by the planets and other points in the aspect combine in an easy, harmonious manner. The conjunction indicates a powerful blending of energies that can be easy or challenging, depending on the planets involved and the aspects that other planets make to the pair in conjunction. The traditional names for hard and soft aspects (names one still finds in older astrology books) are malefic and benefic. Beyond the undesirable connotations of malefic, these terms were dropped because malefic aspects are not always "bad," nor are benefic aspects always "good." For instance, an individual with numerous soft aspects and no hard aspects can be a lazy person who is never challenged to change and grow. On the other hand, an individual who has risen to the challenge of numerous hard aspects and overcome her or his limitations can be a dynamic, powerful person.

The "traditional" minor aspects are the semisextile (30°; sometimes called a dodecile), the decile (36°), the semisquare (45°; sometimes called an octile), the quintile (72°), sesquisquare (135°; sometimes called a sesquiquadrate or sesquare), the quincunx (150°; sometimes called an injunct), and the biquintile (144°). Other minor aspects are the vigintile (18°; also called a semidecile), the semioctile (22½°; sometimes called the semi-semisquare), the quindecile (24°), the novile (40°), the septile ($51\frac{3}{7}$°), and the tredecile (108°). The ancients, who referred to the aspects as familiarities or configurations, used only the major aspects. The major hard aspects come from dividing the horoscope circle into halves and quarters, soft aspects from dividing it into thirds and sixths. Some of the minor aspects derive from further dividing the circle into eighths and sixteenths (semisquare, sesquisquare, and semioctile) and twelfths (semisextile and quincunx). Yet other minor aspects derive from 5-way and 10-way divisions (quintile, biquintile, decile, and vigintile), a 7-way division (septile), a 9-way division (novile), and a 15-way division (quindecile). For general interpretation purposes, the minor aspects are rarely used unless they are very precise.

Few aspects are ever exact (exact aspects are referred to as partile aspects). For this reason, astrologers speak of the orb—or the orb of influence—within which specific aspects are effective. For a sextile, for example, many astrologers use a 6° orb in a natal chart, which means that if any two planets are making an angle anywhere in the 54°–66° range, they are regarded as making a sextile aspect with each other. The closer an aspect is to being exact, the stronger it is. For the major aspects, astrologers often allow an orb of 8° or more; for minor aspects, 1° to 3°.

Why should some aspects produce harmony and others conflict? Although astrologers have speculated on this point (often making numerological speculations), the question has never been satisfactorily answered. In terms of the astrological tradition, it is easy to see that the trine, the primary soft aspect, usually brings a sign of one element into relationship with another sign of the same element (e.g., 15° Gemini is 120° away from 15° Libra, which is 120° away from 15° Aquarius, which, in turn, is 120° away from 15° Gemini, making a grand trine composed entirely of air signs), and signs of the same element tend to blend together harmoniously. By way of contrast, the square, which is the primary hard aspect, brings signs of very different, potentially conflicting elements into relationship (e.g., a planet in a water sign squaring a planet in a fire sign).

But such an analysis breaks down as soon as we compare oppositions and sextiles, which involve precisely the same kinds of elemental combinations (e.g., the natural opposition to a planet in a water sign is a planet in an earth sign, and the natural sextiles to water signs also involve earth signs). Thus, at this stage in our understanding, we can only observe that a certain aspect produces a certain effect, without fully knowing why. This should not be too bothersome as the situation is not much different from the natural sciences, in which one can describe the effects of, say, gravity without being able to explain why gravity works.

Because aspects are a basic part of astrological understanding, every astrology software program automatically calculates the aspects between the planets. These aspects are displayed either as lines drawn between the planets and/or in an aspect grid. All major programs also calculate and display aspects to the midheaven, the ascendant, the north lunar node, Chiron, the four major asteroid, and, depending on the program, to other points as well.

**Sources:**

Brau, Jean-Louis, Helen Weaver, and Allan Edmands. *Larousse Encyclopedia of Astrology*. New York: New American Library, 1980.

Donath, Emma Belle. *Minor Aspects Between Natal Planets*. Tempe, AZ: American Federation of Astrologers, 1981.

Hand, Robert. *Horoscope Symbols*. Rockport, MA: Para Research, 1981.

Whitman, Edward W. *Aspects and Their Meanings: Astro-kinetics*. Vol. III. London: L. N. Fowler, 1970.

## Aspectarian

An aspectarian is a chronological list of all the aspects that the planets make with one another during a particular period of time, usually a month. In addition to the planets and their aspects, the time that an aspect becomes exact is given.

## Association for Astrological Networking

The Association for Astrological Networking (AFAN) is a nonprofit organization that serves a unique function in the astrological world. While the activities of other organizations emphasize astrological education, certification, and research, AFAN focuses on advocacy and action for astrology as a whole through media watch, networking activities (including a mentoring program), and providing legal information and assistance in reversing antiquated city ordinances that forbid the practice of astrology.

The birth of AFAN was primarily due to two conditions. The first of these was the new generation of astrologers that came into the profession in the late 1960s and early 1970s. Many of these people had been caught up in the wave of interest in astrology and related subjects that had its roots in the turbulence of the late 1960s, and by the mid-1970s had begun to look on astrology as a profession. As astrologers, and as professionals, they expected to have a place at the table in making decisions that would affect astrology's future.

The second condition was inherent in the nature of astrology in the United States at the time the new generation came into its own. At that time, the dominant organization in the United States was the American Federation of Astrologers (AFA), a stable and conservative organization not inclined to rapid change. Over its several decades of existence, it had built up a large membership and a successful publishing and book distribution program, and it held a biennial conference that was at that time the largest in the astrological world.

Perhaps understandably, the AFA's old guard was content with the status quo, but the many newer members brought in on the "astrology wave" wanted change and expected participation in making that change. Because of this, the main forum for members, starting in the mid-1970s the business meetings at the biennial conventions of the AFA, became scenes of open discontent, as the new generation tried to put its issues before the membership. From the mid-1970s on, as each successive conference came along, the voices demanding change became louder, and at some conventions there were even walkouts led by discontented members. However, as the AFA restricted access to its membership list, follow-up between conventions was difficult.

Finally, the pressure for change began to take other forms, first evidenced by the forming of the short-lived Association for Professional Astrologers (APA) in 1980 after an AFA convention in New Orleans. The organization's purpose was to "create and support the profession of astrology amongst astrologers and the public." However, due to its lack of resources, and the fact that its founders were spread across North America, the APA could not get out its message or recruit members, and thus lasted only a few months.

Though the APA had failed, it pointed the way to a solution beyond the frustrating succession of vitriolic business meetings and organized walkouts. Rather than try to force change from within the AFA, the dissidents began to feel they needed to focus on the particular issues they felt were not being dealt with either by that organization, or, for that matter, by an earlier breakaway, the National Council for Geocosmic Research (NCGR). These issues centered around the need to enhance astrology's standing as a profession and to free it from its image as a fortune-telling device mainly used by either the suspicious or the superstitious, not to mention the antiquated and oppressive laws bred by that view.

## The Birth of AFAN

Despite the failure of the APA, its founders began to plan yet another assault on the conservative power structure of the AFA, to take place at its Chicago convention in 1982. The plans were put into more concrete form at an Aquarian Revelation Conference (ARC) in Michigan some months before the AFA gathering. At this time, money was raised to fund the effort, and it was decided to hold a meeting in a rented room at the AFA conference hotel on the night of August 31, 1982. Flyers announcing the meeting were circulated at the conference itself, and on the night of the meeting, nearly 300 people showed up ready to discuss the issues the meeting's organizers wanted to force the AFA to address.

At 11:52 P.M. CDT, a name for the the foundling organization was approved—The AFA Network, or AFAN. At the same time, its purpose was determined to be "to create a network among members [of the AFA], and to improve the communications between membership and the board of directors of the AFA." Various committees were formed that covered all aspects of the organization's functioning, but with the notable inclusion of activities such as networking and professionalism.

At a second meeting that night, a committee was appointed to negotiate with the AFA executive secretary on various points of interest. The meeting was held, and as a result, someone from AFAN was given a place on the official nominating committee for the next board election, thus giving the group input into AFA's political process. However, the two AFAN-linked nominees put in place by this process lost, and at this point it became clear to the reformers that they would probably have to work outside and apart from the AFA.

Unlike the APA, AFAN had a list of several hundred people who shared its goals—those who had attended that first meeting—and with contributions to fund a newsletter, and some active networking, AFAN was soon reaching nearly 500 supporters, with the original negotiating committee acting as a kind of informal leadership. At this point, a series of events helped draw the new organization together, give it more direction and focus, and finally, complete independence. The first of these was the serious illness of an astrologer named Johnny Lister, who was diagnosed with leukemia not long after the Chicago AFA convention. AFAN led an effort to collect funds to allow him to undergo costly treatments at the Gerson Therapy Center, and the resulting Johnny Lister Fund is still in existence, providing emergency support for astrologers facing illnesses and other crises.

More important for the long term, however, were two events in early 1983 involving astrolgers and the law. The first was the targeting of the Mercury Limited Bookstore in West Allis, Wisconsin, by religious fundamentalists, and an ensuing effort by the local city council to pass an antiastrology ordinance. AFAN organized a letter-writing campaign and worked with local astrologers to fight the proposed law. In the end, the proposed ordinance was defeated six to one.

Next, in April 1983, a San Jose astrologer named Shirley Sunderbruch was arrested in her home by police in the course of a chart reading for an undercover officer. Her astrological books and other materials were confiscated, and she was charged with fortune-telling and doing business without a license—despite the fact that San Jose had not issued fortune-telling licenses for ten years. Shortly thereafter, the manager of her retirement community evicted her and her husband.

The Sunderbruch affair, which required raising money for lawyers, and serious thought about how to mount a long-term challenge to laws inimical to astrology, was critical in molding AFAN's purpose and shaping its direction, and furthermore gave it a distinctive standing in the astrological community as an advocate for the rights of astrologers. Although many were timorous about getting involved in legal matters, citing the community's lack of experience and resources, others argued that the right to practice astrology was on the line—we would have to learn along the way. The activists' opinions prevailed; AFAN's Legal Information Committee was launched. Sunderbruch was eventually exonerated under the *Spiritual Psychic Church of Truth, Incorporated v. the City of Azusa* decision, two years later.

During the same period of time, it became evident to AFAN's founders that they would be unsuccessful in gaining a foothold in the AFA, so in late 1983, the ad hoc "negotiating committee" officially became the first "steering committee," AFAN's somewhat decentralized governing body. As it approached its first anniversary, AFAN's legal committee was very active and involved, either directly or in an advisory capacity, in astrologers' legal problems in New York, Alabama, Wisconsin, and several cities in California.

In 1984, AFAN held a counterconvention in a hotel down the street from the biennial AFA convention, an event firmly signaling its final move toward becoming something more than an auxiliary to the older organization. Just a little over one year later, AFAN became involved in a variety of local legal situations, city council meetings, and court cases. Near Cleveland, Ohio, a federal district court found an antiastrology law unconstitutional, influenced by material and testimony submitted by AFAN. The AFAN newsletter printed the first "What to Do in a Legal Crisis," outlining the steps to take if arrested for fortune-telling, and in Yonkers, New York, 19 people were arrested at a psychic fair. This occurred within days of the long-awaited *Azusa* decision, which resulted in Shirley Sunderbruch's exoneration.

On August 15, 1985, by a six-to-one vote, the California Supreme Court affirmed in the *Azusa* case that prohibiting astrology was an infringement on the freedom of speech guaranteed by both the California and U.S. constitutions. This decision set aside a previous decision, *Bartha,* which had held that astrology was commercial speech, and thus not entitled to such protections. Among other effects of this decision, Shirley Sunderbruch's case, AFAN's first, was dropped.

Even though the *Azusa* decision did not have force outside California, within a short time it became useful in AFAN's legal efforts, and was used to dampen the enforcement of similar laws in other states, discourage the passage of new laws, and overthrow the old ones. The lessons learned during the first two years of AFAN's legal work became the basis for its Legal Information Committee, and today a call or email to AFAN is often the first thing done by an astrologer facing a legal challenge.

Over the ensuing years, the meaning of AFAN's acronym was changed to its present form. It incorporated as a nonprofit in 1988, and it took on a variety of other tasks. Interestingly enough, one of these was the forming of the United Astrology Congress (or UAC, continuing today as the United Astrology Conference) with the International Society for Astrological Research (ISAR) and NCGR. The triennial UAC, perhaps the largest gathering of astrologers in the world, embodies many of the reforms demanded by the dissidents who created AFAN.

AFAN continues to provide legal assistance to astrologers in need and works with them to overturn antiquated local ordinances. In recent years, other projects have included monitoring the media through its Media Watch committee (now of course encompassing the Internet), and promoting International Astrology Day (IAD) on the Spring Equinox each year. AFAN actually founded this yearly event, which recognizes astrologers and educates the public about astrology. Though IAD began as a fundraising effort, it now includes informal gatherings, lectures, and other events often sponsored by local groups. AFAN also conducted a highly successful international book drive whereby books were donated and distributed throughout the world. In addition, it has instituted a mentoring program to give younger or fledgling astrologers the benefit of counsel and advice from more experienced astrologers.

Adapted with permission from *A History of AFAN* at www.afan.org.

## Astarte

Astarte, asteroid 672 (the 672nd asteroid to be discovered, on September 21, 1908), is approximately 19 kilometers in diameter and has an orbital period of 4.1 years. Astarte was named after the Middle Eastern goddess, roughly equivalent to Venus, also known as Ishtar. J. Lee Lehman associates Astarte with Venus and Aphrodite (divinities of sex and fertility), asserting that this asteroid is more "primal" than the other two. Jacob Schwartz gives the astrological significance of Astarte as "expressing primal population controls through fertility and war."

**Sources:**

Kowal, Charles T. *Asteroids: Their Nature and Utilization*. Chichester, West Sussex, UK: Ellis Horwood Limited, 1988.

Lehman, J. Lee. *The Ultimate Asteroid Book*. West Chester, PA: Whitford Press, 1988.

Room, Adrian. *Dictionary of Astronomical Terms*. London: Routledge, 1988.

Schwartz, Jacob. *Asteroid Name Encyclopedia*. St. Paul, MN: Llewellyn Publications, 1995.

## Asteroids

An asteroid (meaning starlike or small star) is one of thousands of small planets, 95 percent of whose orbits lie between the orbits of Mars and Jupiter. Some have irregular orbits that carry them inside the orbit of Mars (the Apollo and Amor groups); some, even inside the orbit of Mercury (Icarus), Earth and Venus (Bacchus and Apollo). Others travel in the same orbital path as Jupiter (the Trojan asteroids). Initially, these planetoids were given mythological names, but as telescopes increased in strength and more and more asteroids were discovered, astronomers began naming them after places (e.g., Pretoria, Toronto, and Arizona) and people (e.g., Jonathan Murray, Rockwell Kent, and Christy Carol). Some of the smaller and more recently located asteroids have been given entertaining-sounding names, such as Bilkis (the Koranic name for the Queen of Sheba), Dudu (the dancing girl in Nietzsche's *Thus Spake Zarathustra*), and Mr. Spock (named after the discoverer's cat).

While most asteroids are no more than a few miles across, many are much larger. Ceres, the largest asteroid, is 620 miles in diameter. The main group of asteroids is located where Bode's law would lead one to anticipate a planet, and one theory speculates that the asteroid belt is the debris of a former planet that has disintegrated into many pieces. Another theory speculates that at some distant time in the past when the solar system was being formed, the material circulating between Mars and Jupiter failed to coalesce into a cohesive planet, perhaps because of the disruptive influence of Jupiter's tremendous gravity.

Except for a very few whose orbital paths carry them near Earth, asteroids are invisible to the naked eye. The asteroid belt was not discovered until the nineteenth century, so asteroids were not taken into account in traditional astrology. Even after sufficient information was available to construct ephemerides (tables of positions) of the major asteroids, astrologers chose to ignore them. Alan Leo tried to interest his fellow astrologers in asteroids but was unsuccessful. Perhaps the ongoing disputes over the astrological influences of the newly discovered planets discouraged astrologers from studying the significance of these relatively tiny bodies. The sheer number of asteroids would also discourage such exploration. Whatever the explanation, the astrological study of asteroids did not begin until the last quarter of the twentieth century.

The real founder of asteroid studies was Eleanor Bach, who in the early 1970s published an ephemeris and a set of interpretations for the first four asteroids (sometimes called the Big Four) to be discovered—Ceres, Pallas, Juno, and Vesta. Zipporah Dobyns followed in 1977 with a similar work on the Big Four. Emma Belle Donath also published a set of books dealing with the four major asteroids. In 1986, Demetra George and Douglas Bloch's *Asteroid Goddesses* was published. Building on the work of its predecessors, this book quickly became the definitive study of Ceres, Pallas, Juno, and Vesta. It contained everything needed to locate and interpret the four major asteroids in a natal chart. George, the primary author, also integrated the feminist theory of the primordial goddess religion (the notion that all of our more distant ancestors were goddess worshipers) into her discussion, giving *Asteroid Goddesses* tremendous appeal in a subculture where the idea of a primordial goddess religion was widely accepted. The book enjoyed such success that a new, expanded edition was published four years later. The general availability of *Asteroid Goddesses*, the basic appeal of the goddess notion, and the integration of asteroid positions into most computer chart-casting software programs all combined to make Ceres, Pallas, Juno, and Vesta easy to use. Thus, the general acceptance and continually expanding use of the four major asteroids by the larger astrological community was ensured.

The focus on Ceres, Pallas, Juno, and Vesta by asteroid advocates has generally eased the anxiety of astrologers who resisted the introduction of hundreds of new points demanding interpretation in a horoscope. Yet, the widespread acceptance of the Big Four only made the question of the significance of the other asteroids more insistent. Those who have studied the astrological influence of asteroids have reached a consensus, which is, to quote from J. Lee Lehman's *The Ultimate Asteroid Book:* "1. The asteroids have astrological effects which may be studied. 2. The name of an asteroid has astrological significance."

The most common way of studying the influence of a new astrological factor is to study people in whose charts the factor is prominent, such as when an asteroid is in very close conjunction with a key planet or with the ascendant. The essential clue is the name of the asteroid, which gives preliminary insight into the asteroid's astrological "temperament," because the names astronomers give to newly discovered celestial bodies are not coincidental—by virtue of some nonapparent synchronistic influence, nonastrologically inclined astronomers give them astrologically significant names. For example, with regard to the asteroid Eros, an astrologer would anticipate that it was somehow related to passion, yet its name was assigned by an astronomer for whom asteroids were little more than big space rocks.

In *The Ultimate Asteroid Book* (1988), Lehman attempted to overcome some astrologers' resistance to asteroid use by asserting that asteroids have few concepts allocated to them and that their being small and numerous may allow for many very exact meanings. For example, *Eros* specifically means "passionate attachment," and so does not have a broad range of meanings. (One can only wonder about the concepts associated with asteroids such as Dudu.) Lehman contrasts this specificity with the multivalent significance of a planet like Venus, which can refer to "love, harmony, magnetic attraction, the veins, diabetes, erotica, potatoes, or a host of other things."

Beginning with a preliminary clue, such as, in the case of Eros, the idea that this small celestial body is somehow related to passion, the astrologer would place Eros in the charts of acquaintances as well as in those of famous people whose lives are open to public scrutiny. One would anticipate that natives with Eros in conjunction (or in some other close aspect) with the Sun, the ascendant, Venus, or Mars might exhibit more "erotic" inclinations than people with a less prominent Eros. One could not, however, know the specific nature of these inclinations—and how they differed from the passions of Venus, Mars, and Pluto—until after studying many people with Eros prominent in their chart. This approach to the study of new astrological factors is the same methodology utilized by astrologers to uncover the nature of the "new" planets Uranus, Neptune, and Pluto.

There were several reasons for the initial focus on the Big Four. Ceres, Pallas, Juno, and Vesta were the first asteroids to be discovered—in 1801, 1802, 1804, and 1807, respectively—and there was a 38-year gap before other asteroids were located. Thus, they belong together in a fairly natural grouping. Beyond the Big Four, however, asteroid research has not proceeded in a systematic manner. Rather than studying either the next asteroids to be discovered, or the next-largest asteroids, researchers have jumped to the study of asteroids with intriguing names such as Eros and Amor, or asteroids with eccentric orbits, such as Adonis and Icarus. These are all relatively tiny bodies: Eros is 18 miles across at its widest, Amor is approximately 2 miles in diameter, and Adonis and Icarus are both about 1 mile wide. By comparison, Hygiea (personification of health or hygiene), Psyche (personification of the soul), Kalliope (muse of epic poetry), and Laetitia (Latin for "gladness") are all larger than Juno (150 miles in diameter), but almost no information is available on any of these bodies except Psyche. (Short summary meanings of these asteroids are given in Martha Lang-Wescott's *Mechanics of the Future: Asteroids*.)

By sequence of discovery, the next four asteroids after the Big Four are Astraea, goddess of justice; Hebe, goddess of youth who took ambrosia to the gods; Iris, goddess of the rainbow who was a messenger between the gods and humanity; and Flora, goddess of flowering plants. Again, little information on any of these four asteroids is available except for short summaries in Lang-Wescott's survey. The clues that one would use to research any one of these "concept" or "goddess" asteroids—health, justice, poetry, gladness, and so forth—are all appealing, so the lack of attention they have attracted is surprising. Clearly, the next step in establishing the study of asteroids as a widely accepted branch of astrology will be the systematic exploration of the larger or the earlier asteroids, rather than the current piecemeal study of asteroids with idiosyncratic appeal.

One issue that emerged when astrological asteroid studies was beginning to attract serious interest was the question of sign rulership. It was traditionally held that the Sun and the Moon (the two luminaries) ruled one sign apiece, Leo and Cancer, respectively. The known planets each ruled two signs: Mercury ruled Virgo and Gemini; Venus ruled Taurus and Libra; Mars ruled Aries and Scorpio; Jupiter ruled Sagittarius and Pisces; and Saturn ruled Capricorn and Aquarius. When the "new" planets were discovered, astrologers determined that Uranus ruled Aquarius, Neptune ruled Pisces, and Pluto ruled Scorpio, leaving Saturn, Jupiter, and Mars as the rulers, respectively, of Capricorn, Sagittarius, and Aries. In this modified system, only Mercury and Venus still rule two signs each. The attractiveness of a balanced system in which 12 heavenly bodies rule 12 signs has often led twentieth-century astrologers to speculate that two new planets would eventually be discovered and come to be accepted as the rulers of Virgo and Libra.

Some asteroid-oriented astrologers speculated that the larger asteroids ruled these signs. Bach, the founder of astrological asteroid studies, assigned Ceres and Vesta the rulership of Virgo, and Juno and Pallas the rulership of Libra. Zipporah Dobyns, another pioneer in the field of asteroid research, accepted the Big Four as corulers (with Mercury and Venus) of these two signs. However, spreading out sign rulerships to more than one planet did not strike a favorable chord among nonasteroid astrologers. Not only did multiple rulership lack elegance, but it also made certain astrological procedures, such as identifying the significator in horary astrology, somewhat schizophrenic. Beyond the question of elegance, some of the sign associations were strained. Ceres, which embodies the quality of nurture, for example, is clearly more related to Cancer than to Virgo. Another question one might ask with respect to asteroid rulerships is: Why stop with the Big Four? The asteroid Hygiea, the personification of health and hygiene, is clearly related to Virgo; the asteroid Astraea, the goddess of justice, has definite affinities to Libra; and so forth. The point is, while various asteroids may be associated with the 12 signs of the zodiac, assigning rulerships to asteroids raised more problems than it resolved.

In more recent years, the exploration of the astrological significance of asteroids has been overshadowed, if not derailed, by two developments: the emergence of Jyotish

(Vedic astrology) and classical Western astrology as major topics of astrological interest, and the complexification of asteroid studies as the result of the discovery of numerous new objects, including hundreds of large planetoids beyond the orbit of Neptune.

As a result of translation and interpretive activities that matured in the last decades of the twentieth century, both Jyotish and classical astrology emerged as major sources of sophisticated astrological techniques that are simultaneously new (from the perspective of astrologers who matured under the influence of modern psychologically oriented astrology) and time tested. Both of these two traditions are not only rich in astrological insights, but they also completely ignore the modern planets—Uranus, Neptune, and Pluto—as well as the new planetary bodies. Thus, not only have Jyotish and classical astrology diverted interest away from new areas of astrological research, such as asteroid studies, but many of the astrologers who have become involved in this renaissance seem to have acquired an active prejudice against considering anything that was not originally a part of these traditions.

As a result of the exploration of our solar system, particularly since the advent of the Hubble space telescope, astronomers have discovered numerous new asteroids, including a host of large bodies orbiting the Sun beyond Neptune. Some of these Pluto-like bodies, referred to as plutinos, are almost as large as Charon, Pluto's moon, and in at least the case of Ixion, significantly larger than Charon. Beyond adding numerous new planetoids—which further complicates the field of astrology—these newly discovered bodies have even caused astronomers to consider dropping Pluto from the planet category. This hypothetical reclassification of Pluto would, in turn, call into question modern astrology's use of Pluto and of the other nontraditional planets and planetoids, thus dovetailing with the negative perspective of many traditional astrologers.

Despite this situation, it nevertheless seems almost certain that asteroid studies have a future as a significant field of astrological research. If nothing else, the four major asteroids have become too well established in the mainstream of contemporary astrological practice to ever be dropped. Additionally, the incorporation of asteroids beyond the Big Four into multiple astrological software programs means that the necessary tools are within easy reach of any aspiring astrological researcher. These factors and others provide a solid foundation from which asteroid studies is likely to reemerge as a major field of interest, particularly after the current fascination with traditional astrology peaks.

All major Western astrology software programs allow one to incorporate Ceres, Pallas, Vesta, and Juno into natal charts, progressed charts, etc, and in every way to treat them on par with the planets. Astrolabe and Matrix also market separate report programs for the four major asteroids. Add-on software programs for the other asteroids can be obtained for the Solar Fire calculation program from Esoteric Technologies and for the Kepler calculation program from Cosmic Patterns Software. At this writing, the current (fifth) edition of Kepler allows one to calculate the position of 1000 asteroids for any chart. An add-on program for more than 20,000 asteroids is also available. The asteroid add-on for Solar Fire allows one to calculate the positions of 10,000 asteroids. Additionally, Solar Fire can place any of these asteroids in an extra chart ring—something one cannot do in current editions of most other programs.

Mark Pottenger's freestanding asteroid DOS program can also be used to place a certain number of asteroids in the chart of his CCRS horoscope program—both available through Astrolabe. Finally, one can find the astrological positions of asteroids in a natal chart from online sites such as Astro Deinst at www.astro.com.

**Sources:**

Brau, Jean-Louis, Helen Weaver, and Allan Edmands. *Larousse Encyclopedia of Astrology*. New York: New American Library, 1980.

Dobyns, Zipporah. *Expanding Astrology's Universe*. San Diego: ACS Publications, 1983.

Donath, Emma Belle. *Asteroids in Midpoints*. 1982. Tempe, AZ: AFA, 1982.

———. *Asteroids in the Birth Chart*. 1979. Reprint, Tempe, AZ: AFA, 1991.

George, Demetra, with Douglas Bloch. *Asteroid Goddesses: The Mythology, Psychology and Astrology of the Reemerging Feminine*. 2nd ed. San Diego: ACS Publications, 1990.

Lang-Wescott, Martha. *Mechanics of the Future: Asteroids*. Rev. ed. Conway, MA: Treehouse Mountain, 1991.

Lehman, J. Lee. *The Ultimate Asteroid Book*. West Chester, PA: Whitford Press, 1988.

Press, Nona. *New Insights into Astrology*. San Diego: ACS Publications, 1993.

Schwartz, Jacob. *Asteroid Name Encyclopedia*. St. Paul, MN: Llewellyn Publications, 1995.

## Astraea

Astraea, asteroid 5 (the 5th asteroid to be discovered, on December 8, 1845, by the German amateur astronomer Karl Ludwig Hencke), is approximately 120 kilometers in diameter and has an orbital period of 4.1 years. Astraea was named after the Roman goddess of justice (the familiar blindfolded goddess who holds the scales of justice in one hand and a sword in the other), viewed as the Roman form of the Greek Dike. According to Martha Lang-Wescott, Astraea indicates where people have difficulty letting go of relationships and situations, as well as a sense of "loose ends" afterward. This asteroid's key words are "open-ended" and "witness." Jacob Schwartz gives the astrological significance of this asteroid as "problems with closure, difficulties setting limits." According to Barry McKenna, Astraea represents the most important individual needs, for which one must take exceptional personal responsibility. At the same time, it is easy for the needs indicated by this asteroid to be set aside because of other needs and external influences.

**Sources:**

Lang-Wescott, Martha. *Asteroids-Mechanics: Ephemerides II*. Conway, MA: Treehouse Mountain, 1990.

McKenna, Barry. *The Astraea Minor Planet Ephemeris*. Newtonville, MA: Astraea Publications, 1991.

Schwartz, Jacob. *Asteroid Name Encyclopedia*. St. Paul, MN: Llewellyn Publications, 1995.

## Astro*Carto*Graphy

Astro*Carto*Graphy[tm] (A*C*G) is one of many methodologies used in locational astrology, the branch of astrology that ascribes specific astrological effects to different localities. It is an elaboration of the "relocation chart," wherein the horoscope is recalculated as if the individual had been born in the new place of residence instead of the actual place of birth. In this, A*C*G differs from much older locational techniques, most of which relate geography directly to parts of the celestial sphere. The best-known classical example of these older, "geodetic" techniques is Manilius's first century C.E. ascription of areas of the ancient world to signs of the zodiac.

In contrast, A*C*G works by determining where on Earth the 10 astrological planets were angular at the moment of an individual's birth, that is, where any one of them was rising, setting, straight overhead, or anticulminating (straight underneath). For example, even though it may have been nighttime at the actual place of birth, at the moment of birth the Sun was rising someplace else on Earth. All the various localities where the Sun was rising at that moment can be displayed as a line drawn across a map of the world. Such a line is labeled SU ASC (SUn on the ASCendant) on an A*C*G map; with 10 astrological planets and four angular positions, the map will be crossed by 40 lines in all.

Interpreting an A*C*G map is easy: Since being angular enhances the expression of a planet's nature in the personality, affairs symbolized by the planet can be expected to be more prominent in the life of an individual who travels through or resides under an SU ASC line on such a map. By moving to a locality under an SU ASC line on one's A*C*G map, an individual can expect more self-confidence, theatricality, creativity, and leadership to manifest.

Although the idea of preparing such a map for applications in mundane astrology occurred to other (for the most part sidereal) astrologers in the early part of the twentieth century, it was only the development of modern computers that made maps easily enough attainable for their value to be recognized in individual astrology. Astro*Carto*Graphy pioneered the provision and interpretation of maps to tens of thousands of individuals who, by comparing their life experiences to the angular planets identified by the map, have confirmed A*C*G to be among the most reliable natal astrological techniques. It works so well because it uses only the relevant planet and angles, the two most tangible and indisputable of astrological data.

Since most people have resided at several locations during their lifetime, an A*C*G map can confirm impressions of earlier residences as well as forecast outcomes of future moves. Moreover, a location's planetary identity seems consistent even when dealt with remotely, as, for example, through people who at one time lived at a particular place or have investments or other indirect involvement there. Many people have reported that love mates were born near a place where Venus was angular, or that they met in such a zone.

In A*C*G, planet angularities are calculated by oblique ascension, that is, when the planet is bodily on the meridian or horizon, rather than when its zodiacal degree rises or culminates. Where two lines on an A*C*G map cross, they identify a place at which two planets were simultaneously angular at the moment of birth (e.g., one rising while the other occupied the midheaven). In addition to collocating a place-specific interoperation of the two planets' energies, this paran (line crossing) also establishes a latitude at which the two planets' energies are related anywhere on Earth; that is, a crossing of any two lines on an A*C*G map creates a special latitude line completely circling Earth, and on which the energies of the two planets are blended in the life of the individual. However, this "crossing" energy is far weaker than that of the planet-angle lines.

Below is the natal A*C*G for Paramahansa Yogananda, among the first of many East Indian sages to travel to the United States to transmit the highly sophisticated religious knowledge of the subcontinent. Over his native India is found the Moon ascendant (MO ASC) line, meaning that at his birth the Moon was actually rising there. Since the Moon defines the student, the child, the listener, and the "taker-in" of information, this connotes a sensitive individual, receptive, emotional, and responsive to his surroundings.

locational astrology—2 fulls. Locational Astrology: Yogananda, January 5, 1893, 8:38 P.M. Time Zone —5:33

Near the Moon line is the Uranus imum coeli (UR IC) line. The IC is perhaps the most personal and mysterious of the astrological angles, because it symbolizes what one comes into the world equipped with: one's family heritage, social class, ethnic background (and the social status it bestows), religion, etc. Uranus, the planet of individualism, at this angle suggests that Yogananda was to transform his natal social standing by developing his spiritual individuality and, coupled with the Moon line, indicates that this could be accomplished by attention to external forces and devotion. He was to transcend his social identity by discipleship to his spiritual master; he would find his true individuality by giving it up.

But the most meaningful manifestation of Yogananda's potential was to occur in Los Angeles, where he arrived in the 1930s, complete with flowing robes and long hair—unheard of in that era. In Los Angeles, he has the Sun on the ascendant (SU ASC), connoting the expression of life energy, opposite to the Moon's absorption. Moreover, the UR IC line from India to Los Angeles becomes the UR MH (midheaven) line, showing that the transcendence of Yogananda's individual cultural and family limitations is here transformed into the capacity to act out that role publicly for others—to become an exemplar of the human potential to grow beyond one's natal limitations. This, coupled with the charismatic Sun line, ensured a large following for Yogananda, who packed lecture halls in California, a state where such separation from tradition and individual self-expression have always been encouraged.

This example, while briefly delineated, makes clear how important it is to look at the whole map—not just small subsections of Earth. The reciprocal nature of the Sun and Moon lines should be obvious, as well as the interesting inversion of the Uranus line's angles, accomplished by plotting Yogananda's move half a world away. Since an individual at best is going to exemplify only one or two planetary archetypes in her or his life, knowing which parts of the world hold these lines can be vitally important in recognizing and implementing the potential of the planets they identify.

Perhaps the most powerful argument in favor of A*C*G's validity is that every modern American president whose time of birth is known has initiated armed conflict in a zone marked by Mars on his map, with the sole exception of Richard Nixon, who took over a war begun by his predecessors. In addition to using A*C*G in this fashion to forecast world events, some astrologers use national charts, which can be quite revealing, and any map can be projected forward in time through standard techniques of progression, transits, and solunar returns.

A*C*G is unique among astrological techniques in offering the individual something that she or he can do to alter the astrological indications under which she or he is laboring. Many have, upon discovering that they have been struggling under a Saturn line, relocated to a less oppressive zone and noted dramatic changes immediately. But residence in such difficult zones has its purpose also, as life cannot be all social gatherings and pleasures. In any case, knowing the astrological influence brought about by relocating—or by choosing a favorable location in advance from the A*C*G map—has proved to be an important adjunct to standard birth chart delineation. Astro*Carto*Graphy is now used universally by modern astrologers serving clients for whom travel or relocation is an option.

—Jim Lewis

**Sources:**

Harding, Michael, and Harvey, Charles. *Working with Astrology, the Psychology of Harmonics, Midpoints, and Astro*Carto*Graphy*. London: Arcana, 1990.

Hathaway, Edith. *Navigating by the Stars*. St. Paul, MN: Llewellyn Publications, 1991.

Lewis, Jim. *Astro*Carto*Graphy*. San Francisco: Astro*Carto*Graphy, 1976.

———. *Astro*Carto*Graphy Explained*. San Francisco: Astro*Carto*Graphy, 1986.

———. *The Astro*Carto*Graphy Sourcebook of Mundane Maps*. San Francisco: Astro*Carto*Graphy, 1979–1994.

———. *Cyclo*Carto*Graphy*. San Francisco: Astro*Carto*Graphy, 1982.

Lewis, Jim, and Guttman, Ariel. *The Astro*Carto*Graphy Book of Maps*. Saint Paul, MN: Llewellyn Publications, 1989.

## Astrodiagnosis

Astrodiagnosis is the subdivision of medical astrology dealing with the diagnosis of disease.

## Astrodynes

Astrodynes is a technique for obtaining a numerical overview of a person's birth chart. The technique summarizes how much power, harmony, and discord is associated with each planet, each house, and each sign in a chart. Elbert Benjamine of the Church of Light in Los Angeles adopted the terms "astrodynes," "harmodynes," and "discordynes" for the calculations of astrological energy that he and W. M. A. Drake developed in 1946. Benjamine tested, applied, and evaluated the material and conclusions sent in by Brotherhood of Light researchers around the world, according to his student Doris Chase Doane.

In 1950, Benjamine wrote in his *Astrodyne Manual*, "According to their relative power and harmony, the planets not only show the abilities and environment in which they can most successfully be used, but they also indicate the events and diseases of a particular type toward which there is a predisposition. Therefore it is very important to know as precisely as possible both the power of each planet in the birth-chart and its harmony or discord." According to the astrodynes technique, the amount of power that a planet has is determined by the house that the planet resides in and by the aspects that the planet makes or receives. The orb for the aspects varies depending on which planets are involved, from which houses the aspects originate, and what aspect is being considered.

Due to such complicated considerations, calculating astrodynes by hand for one chart takes about ten hours. In the 1970s, Astro Numeric Service and Astro Communications Services began to offer computerized printouts of the astrodynes (also known as cosmodynes) tables and summaries. Then in the mid-1980s, Church of Light member John Molfese wrote a program for the IBM personal computer to calculate and print the astrodynes tables. To quickly provide accurate planet longitudes and declinations for his calculations, Molfese linked his program to John Halloran's public domain program for calculating and saving charts. Users of Molfese's program could display the names of all the charts saved with Halloran's ASTROL96 and pick the charts for which the astrodynes program should print its tables. When Halloran released Astrology for Windows in 1994, Molfese followed suit and in 1995 released Astrodynes for Windows, which adds screen tables, bar graphs, pie charts, and other features to the astrodynes results. Halloran Software continues to distribute Astrodynes for Windows.

—John Halloran

**Sources:**

Benjamine, Elbert. *Astrodyne Manual*. Los Angeles: The Church of Light, 1950.
Doane, Doris Chase. *How to Read Cosmodynes*. Tempe, AZ: AFA, 1974.

## Astrolabe

An astrolabe is a mechanical device that, prior to the development of the sextant, was widely used by mariners. Said to have been developed by Hipparchus, greatest of the ancient Greek astronomers (although some scholars give Ptolemy the honor), the astrolabe was used by astrologers when they erected horoscopes to determine the positions of the planets. (Prior to the development of ephemerides, it was necessary to actually look at the heavens when casting a horoscope.). The term astrolabe means "taking the star" in Greek, so it could be used to refer to any instrument for observing the stellar dome. Thus, in the early medieval period, *astrolabe* was often applied to the armillary sphere, a different instrument. The device now called an astrolabe is more properly termed a planispheric astrolabe. Originally Greek, this instrument was lost to western Europe until its reintroduction by Arabic sources.

**Sources:**

DeVore, Nicholas. *Encyclopedia of Astrology*. New York: Philosophical Library, 1947.
Tester, Jim. *A History of Western Astrology*. New York: Ballantine, 1987.

## Astrologer

An astrologer is one who practices astrology. The term is usually reserved for individuals who read charts for clients, although astrological researchers can appropriately

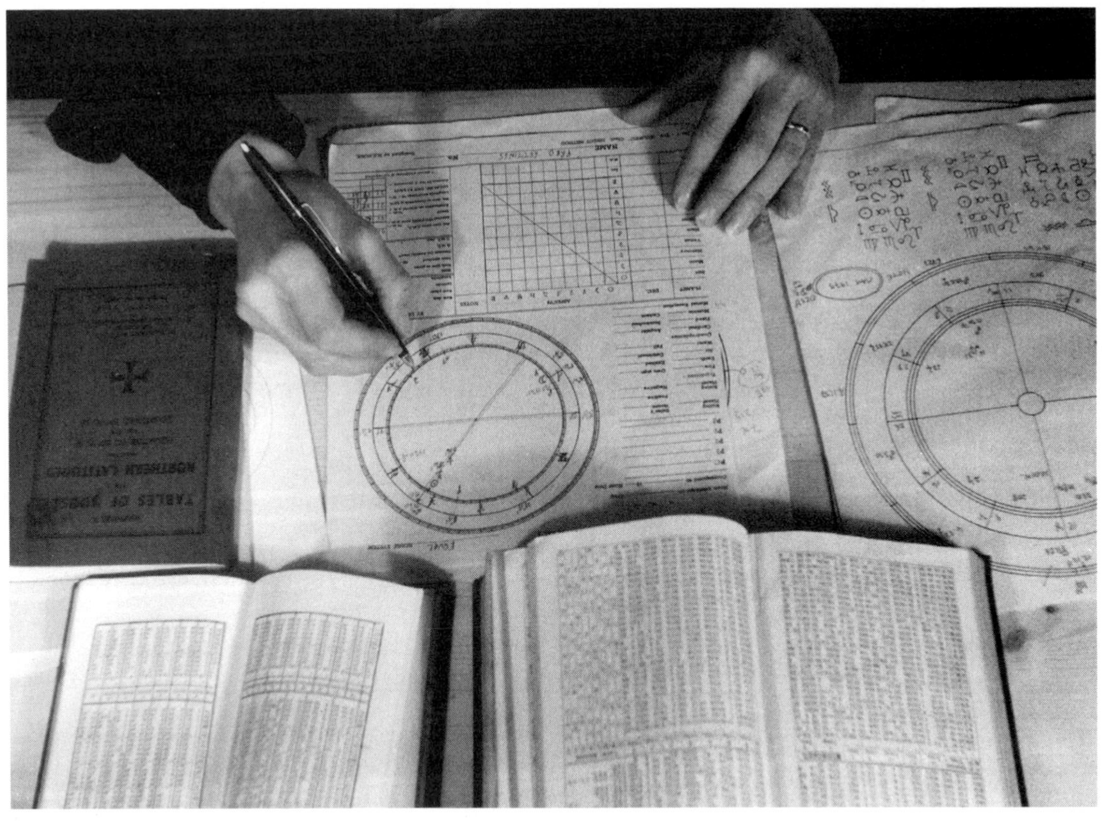

**An astrologer casting a horoscope with Tables of Houses, Ephemerides, and charts.**
***Reproduced by permission of Fortean Picture Library.***

claim the title. Because astrology is not accepted as a legitimate profession by the larger society, there presently exists no officially recognized agencies for training, testing, and certifying astrologers. While various astrological societies have established tests of astrological competence and informal certifications recognizing such skills, the nonofficial status of these examinations makes them largely ineffective for regulating the field.

## Astrological Association of Great Britain

The Astrological Association of Great Britain (AA) was founded at the deliberately elected moment of 7:22 P.M. on June 21, 1958, in London. Its founding members, notably John Addey and Roy Firebrace, were members of the Astrological Lodge of the Theosophical Society who felt their ambitions for astrology were restricted by the lodge's image and constitution, specifically its links to the Theosophical Society. Their aims were essentially twofold: to demonstrate astrology's objective validity and to enhance its public reputation, especially within the scientific community and caring professions. The founding assumption for the association was that astrological claims are both demonstrable and helpful.

The association also established itself as an umbrella organization for all astrologers, whether they adhered its objectives or not. It encouraged debate and the free exchange of information. Hence, the AA has never had a corporate view concerning the nature of astrology and has published material hostile to astrology and critical of its claims. The unfettered exchange of ideas is considered a central part of the AA's work. Its activities have centered on the organization of weekly meetings (in London from the late 1950s to the late 1980s) and an annual conference (from 1968 to the present). It has also held other events in the United Kingdom, mainly in London (though not exclusively), chiefly an annual research conference.

The AA's major publication, the *Journal*, was first published in 1959. This was followed in the 1960s by the launch of *Transit*, the newsletter. *Correlation*, its peer-reviewed journal of research into astrology, was launched in 1968 and then relaunched in 1981 after a break in publication in the 1970s. It remains the only academic journal of its kind. The *Astrology and Medicine Newsletter* is a specialist magazine containing articles on medical astrology.

**Source:**

*The Astrological Association of Great Britain*. www.astrologicalassociation.com (accessed February 21, 2003).

## Astrological Data

Astrological data are the basis for casting horoscopes and include name, date, place of birth, and time of birth. Astrologers base their studies on this data as they examine the patterns and positions of the planets and the signs as they rise, culminate, and set. Whether they are doing a research study or a personal horoscope, the accuracy of their observations depends on the accuracy of their data. Whether they are presenting a paper or delineating a chart, they cannot validate their work unless they can validate their data.

Speculative charts come from cases where the birth time is unknown and as such are pure guesswork, usually backed up with events to illustrate the supposed accuracy; rectification of a chart begins with an approximate birth time and corrects the chart to a specific minute. Historically, astrological data have not been presented with any source of origin. Magazines and journals blithely present charts and articles, and readers are apparently supposed to accept on faith that the data are accurate. Astrologers give lectures or present papers with no source given for the data. When one begins to examine the charts of historical figures and public figures, it may come as a shock to find that there are several times of birth given. There are over a dozen times of birth given for Ronald Reagan, and as many for Joseph Stalin, Clark Gable, and Evita Peron.

There is nothing wrong with speculative data—if they are presented as such. However, presenting data as factual when they are not is a falsehood; deliberate inaccuracy is ethically unforgivable; and presenting data without a source is amateurish, unprofessional, and misleading. Many astrological data are time-specific, so any chart that does not state the source is open to question, and any conclusions drawn from such a chart are not acceptable as valid conclusions. When data were scarce, astrologers took what they could get. That time is past if they ever hope to gain a reputation for conducting legitimate studies. Astrological journals, schools, and teachers have a responsibility to the next generation of astrologers to set a standard in recording information. Astrology is making great strides in the early twentieth-first century; never before has there been access to so much data or to computer-generated charts, and it is imperative that studies be built on a firm basis and employ empirical data.

The Rodden classification of astrological data is a simple, effective system. Many astrologers in the United States and Europe use it or a similar coding system. The first four letters of the English alphabet are used:

| | |
|---|---|
| AA | Accurate; recorded by the family or the state |
| A | Accurate probably; data from the person or family |
| B | Biography or autobiography |
| C | Caution; no source of origin |
| DD | Dirty data; two or more quotes with none verified |

Data are the foundation of empirical study. Astrologers should insist on quality reference works and accurate data that include the date, place, time, time zone, longitude and latitude, source, and a designation of accuracy.

—Lois M. Rodden

## Astrology

Astrology is the science or study of the stars and originally encompassed both astronomy and what today is call astrology. The word is a combination of *astron*, Greek for "star," and *logos*, a complex word originally meaning "speech" (in the sense of discourse). Astrology is discussed extensively in the introductory essay to this encyclopedia.

## Astromancy

Astromancy refers to a kind of astrological fortune-telling that views the stars as predicting an irrevocable destiny for the person having her or his fortune told. Modern astrologers tend to distance themselves from this tradition of predicting specific events. Instead of predicting events, most contemporary astrologers describe upcoming planetary conditions, with the understanding that clients have the free will to respond to planetary influences in different ways. Like meteorologists, astrologers can only predict trends and probabilities—not details.

## Astronomy

Astronomy is the branch of natural science that studies the celestial bodies. The word is a combination of *astron*, Greek for "star," and *nomos*, Greek for "law." Astrology was formerly part of astronomy, with astrological determinations being viewed as a "practical application" of astronomical knowledge. Prior to the modern period, all of the

**An illustration of the great Viennese telescope, constructed in the mid-nineteenth century.** ***Reproduced by permission of Fortean Picture Library.***

great astronomers were also astrologers, including such luminaries as Tycho Brahe and Johannes Kepler.

Several hundred years ago, however, the two fields began to diverge, and today there are two distinct communities: astrologers, who are largely ignorant of astronomy, and astronomers, who know almost nothing about astrology. For the most part, contemporary astronomers despise astrology as a medieval superstition. This is not, however, because astrology fails to pass empirical tests of validity, but because astronomers reject astrology out of hand. When skeptics have actually subjected astrology to empirical tests, they have found—sometimes to their dismay—correlations between celestial and terrestrial phenomena.

For their part, astrologers are more often than not woefully ignorant of astronomy. This ignorance is sometimes compounded by an attitude that condemns all science as narrow-minded and spiritually dead. There are, however, a handful of contemporary astrologers who have explored current astronomy for potential astrological insights, including Michael and Margaret Erlewine, whose *Astrophysical Directions* offers a starting point for astrologers interested in pursuing this line of research, and Philip Sedgwick, whose *Astrology of Deep Space* is a creative follow-up on the Erlewines' work.

**Sources:**

Brau, Jean-Louis, Helen Weaver, and Allan Edmands. *Larousse Encyclopedia of Astrology*. New York: New American Library, 1980.
Erlewine, Michael, and Margaret Erlewine. *Astrophysical Directions*. Ann Arbor, MI: Heart Center School of Astrology, 1977.
Sedgwick, Philip. *The Astrology of Deep Space*. Birmingham, MI: Seek-It Publications, 1984.

## Ate

Ate, asteroid 111 (the 111th asteroid to be discovered, on August 14, 1870), is approximately 156 kilometers in diameter and has an orbital period of 4.2 years. It was named after the goddess of blind folly, rashness, infatuation, and mischief. According to Greek tragedians, Ate was behind the avenging curse that was the ultimate cause of the Trojan War. The natal position of Ate by sign and house may indicate where one is most prone to folly. When afflicted, Ate may show where one is likely to respond to real or imagined insults in an exaggerated fashion.

**Sources:**

Kowal, Charles T. *Asteroids: Their Nature and Utilization*. Chichester, West Sussex, UK: Ellis Horwood Limited, 1988.
Room, Adrian. *Dictionary of Astronomical Names*. London: Routledge, 1988.
Schwartz, Jacob. *Asteroid Name Encyclopedia*. St. Paul, MN: Llewellyn Publications, 1995.

## Athene

Athene, asteroid 881 (the 881st asteroid to be discovered, on July 22, 1870), is approximately 12 kilometers in diameter and has an orbital period of 4.2 years.

**The temple of Athena in the Parthenon, Athens.** ***Reproduced by permission of Fortean Picture Library.***

Athene was named after the Greek warrior goddess Athena, who was born fully formed from Zeus' head and after whom the city of Athens was named. Jacob Schwartz gives the astrological significance of Athene as "protectively warlike, wise and just, associated with wisdom, handicrafts, weaving, navigation and agriculture."

J. Lee Lehman associates this asteroid, as well as the asteroids Pallas and Minerva, with "interest or ability in areas which combine the functioning of the mind and the body." Athene, in contrast with Pallas and Minerva, indicates more interest in being competent than in being right (Pallas) or accomplished (Minerva).

**Sources:**

Kowal, Charles T. *Asteroids: Their Nature and Utilization*. Chichester, West Sussex, UK: Ellis Horwood Limited, 1988.

Lehman, J. Lee. *The Ultimate Asteroid Book*. West Chester, PA: Whitford Press, 1988.

Room, Adrian. *Dictionary of Astronomical Names*. London: Routledge, 1988.

Schwartz, Jacob. *Asteroid Name Encyclopedia*. St. Paul, MN: Llewellyn Publications, 1995.

## Atlantis

Atlantis, asteroid 1,198 (the 1198th asteroid to be discovered, on September 7, 1931), is approximately 2.8 kilometers in diameter and has an orbital period of 3.4 years. Atlantis was named after a mythological continent, said by Plato to have existed in the Atlantic Ocean, that was destroyed by cataclysmic earthquakes. According to Martha Lang-Wescott, the location of Atlantis indicates where one experiences a sense of imminent doom, as well as a willingness to "pay for" real or imagined errors or unworthiness from the past. This asteroid's key words are "expiation" and "ethics." Jacob Schwartz adds "the use of karma to rationalize events" to the astrological significance of Atlantis.

**Sources:**

Lang-Wescott, Martha. *Asteroids-Mechanics: Ephemerides II*. Conway, MA: Treehouse Mountain, 1990.

———. *Mechanics of the Future: Asteroids*. Rev. ed. Conway, MA: Treehouse Mountain, 1991.

Schwartz, Jacob. *Asteroid Name Encyclopedia*. St. Paul, MN: Llewellyn Publications, 1995.

## Attila

Attila, asteroid 1489 (the 1,489th asteroid to be discovered, on April 12, 1939), is approximately 15 kilometers in diameter and has an orbital period of 5.7 years. Attila was named after the West's most famous barbarian, Attila the Hun. J. Lee Lehman associates this asteroid with power and dominance issues. Attila, she says, "signifies the fighter. The Attila type does not retire gracefully." Jacob Schwartz gives the astrological significance of this asteroid as "active dominance to get what one wants even fighting when it is unnecessary."

**Sources:**

Kowal, Charles T. *Asteroids: Their Nature and Utilization*. Chichester, West Sussex, UK: Ellis Horwood Limited, 1988.

Lehman, J. Lee. *The Ultimate Asteroid Book*. West Chester, PA: Whitford Press, 1988.

Schwartz, Jacob. *Asteroid Name Encyclopedia*. St. Paul, MN: Llewellyn Publications, 1995.

**A detail of the mythical "Lost City" from a map belonging to Nicola Sanson, c. 1600.**
***Reproduced by permission of Fortean Picture Library.***

## AUTUMNAL EQUINOX (FALL EQUINOX)

Equinox, Latin for "equal night," refers to one of the two days of the year on which daytime and nighttime are equal in duration. The autumnal equinox takes place on or around September 23, and marks the beginning of both the sign Libra and the fall season.

## Axial Rotation

Axial rotation is the turning of Earth on its axis and, by extension, the spinning of any heavenly body on its axis. It is Earth's daily rotation that is responsible for the apparent motion of the Sun, Moon, planets, and stars across the sky.

## Azimuth

One can locate a specific celestial object in several ways, most of which involve specifying two coordinates. The azimuth is one of the coordinates of such a system. Although the notion of azimuth is basically simple, it is not simple to explain. Imagine that a group of people are looking at a star. From where they are standing, they can measure the angle between the horizon and the star. This gives them one coordinate in terms of angular distance (called the altitude, for obvious reasons). Then imagine a geometric plane that, like some kind of gigantic wall, cuts through Earth, intersecting the north and south poles, the place where they are standing, and the point directly over their heads (the zenith). They then measure another angle with their surveying instrument, this time between the imaginary wall and the star. This angular distance gives them the azimuth.

**Sources:**

Filbey, John, and Peter Filbey. *The Astrologer's Companion*. Wellingborough, Northamptonshire, UK: Aquarian Press, 1986.

Gettings, Fred. *Dictionary of Astrology*. London: Routledge & Kegan Paul, 1985.

# B

## Bacchus

Bacchus is asteroid 2,063 (the 2,063rd asteroid to be discovered, on April 24, 1977). It is approximately 1.2 kilometers in diameter and has an orbital period of 1.1 years. Bacchus was named after the god of wine, the Roman equivalent of the Greek Dionysus. According to Martha Lang-Wescott, Bacchus is related to addictive syndrome, particularly to the denial, substitution, and management of uncomfortable emotions. This asteroid's key word is "denial." According to J. Lee Lehman, "Bacchus represents the way that a person seeks ecstasy through direct experience or passion." Jacob Schwartz gives the astrological significance of this asteroid as "Ecstasy to encourage sensual excess and fertility; addictive personalities and behaviors and attempts to manage feelings through substitutions."

Bacchus is also one of the names given to the hypothetical planet that some astrologers assert is orbiting beyond Pluto.

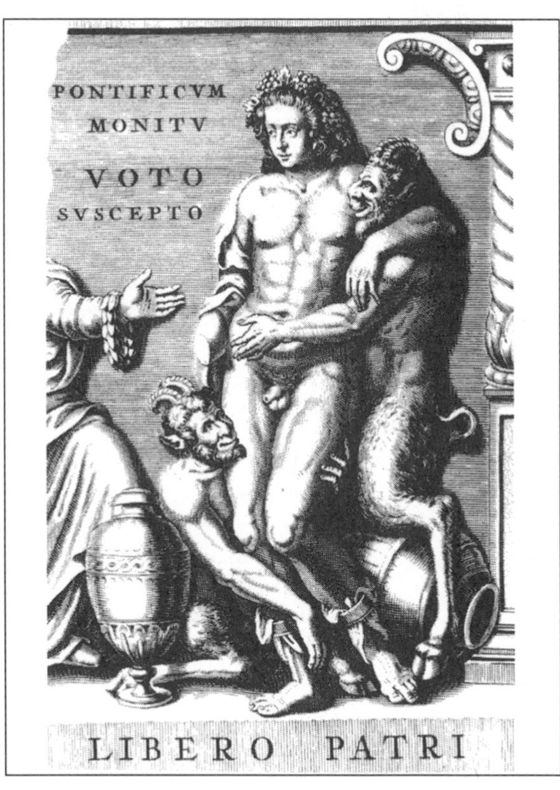


**A seventeenth-century engraving of a drunken Bacchus supported by two fauns.** ***Reproduced by permission of Fortean Picture Library.***

**Sources:**

Lehman, J. Lee. *The Ultimate Asteroid Book*. West Chester, PA: Whitford, 1988.

Lang-Wescott, Martha. *Asteroids-Mechanics: Ephemerides II*. Rev. ed. Conway, MA: Treehouse Mountain, 1990.

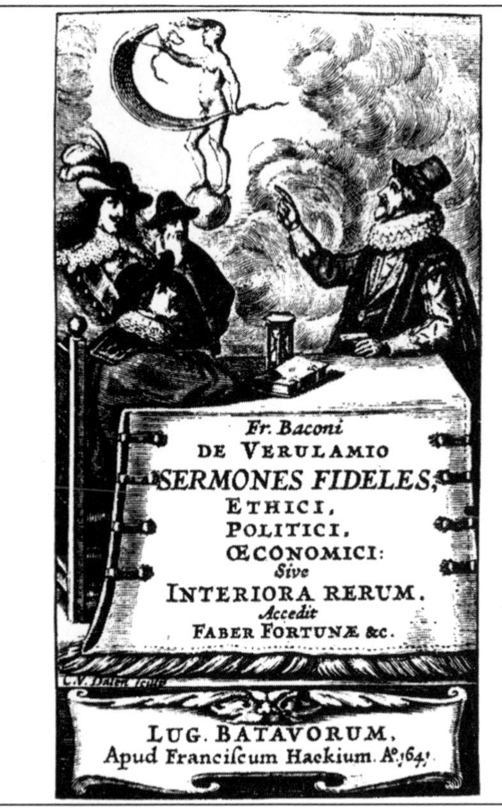


**An image of Francis Bacon from the title page of his *Sermones Fideles*, 1621. *Reproduced by permission of Fortean Picture Library.***

Schwartz, Jacob. *Asteroid Name Encyclopedia*. St. Paul, MN: Llewellyn Publications, 1995.

## Bacon, Francis

Francis Bacon (1561–1626) was an English philosopher often regarded as the father (or one of the fathers) of modern science. He was famous for his advocacy of the empirical method. Perhaps because he perceived it as resting on an empirical base, he was an ardent champion of astrology.

## Bailey, Alice A.

Alice A. Bailey, a well-known Theosophist who left the Theosophical Society to form the Arcane School in 1919, was born in Manchester, England, on June 16, 1880. Born Alice La Trobe-Bateman, she married the theosophist Foster Bailing in 1920. In the field of astrology, she is best known for a treatise on esoteric astrology that was dictated to her by Master D. K. (also known as The Tibetan). She also transcribed a volume on the astrology of countries, *The Destiny of Nations*. She asserted that she knew nothing about astrology herself. Her dense tome on esoteric astrology has been the single most influential book in this area of astrology for many decades. Bailey died in 1949.

**Sources:**

Bailey, Alice A. *The Destiny of the Nations*. New York: Lucis Publishing Co., 1949.

———. *Esoteric Astrology*. New York: Lucis Publishing Co., 1950.

———. *The Unfinished Autobiography of Alice A. Bailey*. New York: Lucis Publishing Co., 1951.

Holden, James H., and Robert A. Hughes. *Astrological Pioneers of America*. Tempe, AZ: American Federation of Astrologers, 1988.

## Bailey, E. H.

E. H. Bailey, born November 29, 1876, in Kent, England, was an astrologer and an author. It is said he became interested in astrology as a boy after reading Zadkiel's almanac, a popular astrology almanac of the time. About 1900, he worked briefly for the well-known astrologer Alan Leo. Bailey initiated the astrological periodical *Destiny* in 1904, but it was unsuccessful. He later took a job editing *The British Journal of Astrology* and became a fellow of the Astrological Society of America.

Bailey is best remembered for his work on the "prenatal epoch" (determining an individual's time of conception), a topic he became interested in after reading some pieces by W. Gorn Old (Sepharial) in *Astrologer's Magazine*. Bailey communicated with Sepharial as he developed his own theory. The basic technique for determining the conception date from the birth date goes back to antiquity and can also be utilized to rectify a birth time. Bailey and Sepharial developed the method further, but their work evoked strong opposition from certain other astrologers. Bailey studied the prenatal epoch in hundreds of cases, many of them collected from public records and others obtained with the help of obstetricians. Considering the period in which it was written, *The Prenatal Epoch* was a well-researched and well-developed book. However, astrological interest in this topic has waned considerably since Bailey's time. He died on June 4, 1959.

**Sources:**

Bailey, E. H. *The Prenatal Epoch*. N.p., 1916. Reprint, New York, S. Weiser, 1970.

Holden, James H., and Robert A. Hughes. *Astrological Pioneers of America*. Tempe, AZ: American Federation of Astrologers, 1988.

## Barren Signs

The barren signs are the signs of the zodiac traditionally said to deny children (i.e., to indicate sterility) when placed on the cusp of the fifth house, the house of children. These signs are Gemini, Leo, and Virgo. A number of other signs are regarded as being somewhat barren. The traditional barren planets are Mars and Saturn; some astrologers now add Uranus. The fertile signs and planets are referred to as fruitful. The classification of the zodiac into degrees of barrenness and fruitfulness has been largely abandoned because contemporary astrological research has failed to verify this traditional interpretation. However, some modern astrologers hold the modified view that barren signs limit the number of children, rather than actually deny them. The traditional barren signs are still regarded as unfruitful in agricultural astrology, however.

**Sources:**

Gettings, Fred. *Dictionary of Astrology*. London: Routledge & Kegan Paul, 1985.

Lee, Dal. *Dictionary of Astrology*. New York: Paperback Library, 1969.

## Beer

Beer, asteroid 1,896 (the 1,896th asteroid to be discovered, on October 26, 1971), is approximately 6.6 kilometers in diameter and has an orbital period of 3.8 years. Beer was named after the prominent astronomer, Arthur Beer, who was a spectroscopist and spectrophotometrist. J. Lee Lehman, perhaps unaware of the astronomer Beer, gives this asteroid a "literal" interpretation, associating it with addiction, particularly addiction to alcoholic substances.

**Sources:**

Kowal, Charles T. *Asteroids: Their Nature and Utilization*. Chichester, West Sussex, UK: Ellis Horwood Limited, 1988.

Lehman, J. Lee. *The Ultimate Asteroid Book*. West Chester, PA: Whitford Press, 1988.
Schwartz, Jacob. *Asteroid Name Encyclopedia*. St. Paul, MN: Llewellyn Publications, 1995.

## Beholding

Beholding signs are pairs of signs of the zodiac that have the same delineation—i.e., the signs that are equidistant from the tropical signs (Cancer and Capricorn.) These pairs of signs are Aries and Libra; Taurus and Virgo; Gemini and Leo; Aquarius and Sagittarius; and Pisces and Scorpio.

## Bellona

Bellona, asteroid 28 (the 28th asteroid to be discovered, on March 1, 1854), is approximately 124 kilometers in diameter and has an orbital period of 4.6 years. It was named after the Roman goddess of war, who some myths say was the wife of Mars; other accounts maintain that she was his sister. The goddess did not have a developed mythology of her own. The asteroid Bellona may be delineated in somewhat the same way as Mars. Its prominence in a natal chart indicates an energetic, assertive person. When inharmoniously aspected, Bellona may show a bellicose personality.

**Sources:**

Kowal, Charles T. *Asteroids: Their Nature and Utilization*. Chichester, West Sussex, UK: Ellis Horwood Limited, 1988.
Room, Adrian. *Dictionary of Astronomical Names*. London: Routledge, 1988.
Schwartz, Jacob. *Asteroid Name Encyclopedia*. St. Paul, MN: Llewellyn Publications, 1995.

## Benefic (Benefic Aspects; Benefic Planets)

Benefic is a traditional term that, after falling into disuse among modern astrologers, has experienced a revival with the renewed interest in classical astrology. It refers to aspects and planets regarded as having a fortunate, harmonious influence. Benefic aspects are angles such as trines and sextiles (often called soft aspects by current astrologers) and planets such as Venus (the Lesser Benefic) and Jupiter (the Greater Benefic). The antonym of benefic is malefic.

## Bennett, Sidney Kimball (Wynn)

Sidney Kimball Bennett, born February 10, 1892, in Chicago, was a prominent astrologer of the early twentieth century. Under the pseudonym Wynn, he published *Wynn's Astrology Magazine* in the thirties and forties. He began studying astrology as a young man (about 1915) and was practicing professionally by the twenties.

In *The Key Cycle*, Bennett relates that a number of his clients had complained that his prognostications, based on the techniques of progressions and directions, had failed. He regarded these failures as being traceable to mistaken birth times. These faulty predictions struck home, however, in May 1926 when he failed to foresee an accident in which he was almost killed by a hit-and-run driver. At the time, Bennett was traveling in California on a business trip during which he was attempting to take advantage of a "marvelous combination of progressions." However, from a business standpoint the trip was a total failure. Reflecting upon these events and calling to mind his clients' complaints, he was persuaded to give up progressions and directions.

Bennett then began to experiment with other predictive methods, such as solar return. He devised a technique for utilizing this method for intermediate dates, and this was the origin of the predictive system he called The Key Cycle.

In the early thirties, Bennett wrote an astrology column for the *New York Daily News*. In 1932, he foretold a week of financial turmoil for early March 1933. One of Franklin D. Roosevelt's first official acts as president after his inauguration on March 4, 1933, was to proclaim a "bank holiday," closing all the banks in the United States. Many banks did not reopen, and depositors suffered a complete loss. This act shook the nation and threw the financial markets into chaos. Bennett became famous for his prediction. In later life, he lived in Australia, where he is thought to have died in the late fifties.

**Sources:**

Bennett, Sidney Kimball. *Astrology, Science of Prediction*. Los Angeles: Wynn Publishing Co., 1945.

———. *Astrology: Your Path to Success*. Philadelphia: David McKay Co., 1938.

———. *The Key Cycle*. 1931. Reprint, Tempe, AZ: American Federation of Astrologers, 1970.

———. *Your Life Till 1954 ... Your Next 20 Years ... with 20-Year World Prediction, Interpreted by Wynn*. New York: Wynn Publishing Co., 1933.

Holden, James H., and Robert A. Hughes. *Astrological Pioneers of America*. Tempe, AZ: American Federation of Astrologers, 1988.

*Wynn's Astrology Magazine*. New York: Wynn Publishing Co., 1931–194[?].

## Berosus

Berosus was a famous Mesopotamian priest and astrologer born about 330 B.C.E. He left his native land, settled on the Greek island of Kos, and taught astrology. Berosus is attributed with introducing astrology to the Greeks, in whose hands it was transformed from a priestly art into an empirical science.

## Besieged

Besieged is a traditional term used to describe the situation of a planet (particularly a significator) placed between two other planets and falling within both of their orbs of influence. The conflicting connotations of the word besieged derive from the tendency of an older generation of astrologers to call attention to conjunctions in which a benefic planet (e.g., Venus) was placed between two malefics (e.g., Mars and Saturn). A planet can be favorably besieged, however, as when placed between two benefic planets.

## Bestial Signs

The bestial signs are the signs of the zodiac represented by animals. Those classified as bestial vary, but always include Aries the Ram, Taurus the Bull, Leo the Lion, and Capricorn the Goat. The three water signs are also symbolized by animals, but water sign animals are not four-footed "beasts." Hence, the water triplicity—Cancer the Crab, Scorpio the Scorpion (sometimes the Eagle), and Pisces the Fish—is sometimes included in the bestial list. Sagittarius the Archer is often represented as a centaur—half human and half horse. When represented as an archer, Sagittarius is classified as nonbestial; when represented as a centaur, bestial.

The signs that are not bestial are human signs. They are Gemini the Twins, Virgo the Virgin, Aquarius the Water Bearer, and, when considered as the Archer, Sagittarius. Only Libra is represented by a nonliving artifact, the Scales (although the old symbol for Libra was a woman holding a scale, which would make it a human sign). This grouping of signs into bestial and nonbestial contrasts with the signs found in East Asian astrological systems (e.g., Chinese astrology), all of which are bestial.

Unlike most other schemes of classification, such as the elements (earth, air, fire, and water) and the qualities (mutable, cardinal, and fixed), the bestial/nonbestial contrast does not carry practical consequences for interpretation (i.e., persons born under animal signs are not more "beastly" than others). For this reason, as well as because of the negative connotation of the term beast, the expression bestial sign has dropped out of general usage in modern astrology.

**Sources:**

Bach, Eleanor. *Astrology from A to Z: An Illustrated Source Book*. New York: Philosophical Library, 1990.

Lee, Dal. *Dictionary of Astrology*. New York: Paperback Library, 1969.

## Bettina

Bettina, asteroid 250 (the 250th asteroid to be discovered, on September 3, 1885), is approximately 128 kilometers in diameter and has an orbital period of 5.6 years. It was named after the baroness Rothschild, who, according to Jacob Schwartz, "purchased the right to name the asteroid for the fifty pounds the discoverer needed to finance a solar eclipse expedition." In a natal chart, Bettina may show where one gives or is otherwise generous with an expectation of reward.

**Sources:**

Kowal, Charles T. *Asteroids: Their Nature and Utilization*. Chichester, West Sussex, UK: Ellis Horwood Limited, 1988.

Room, Adrian. *Dictionary of Astronomical Names*. London: Routledge, 1988.

Schwartz, Jacob. *Asteroid Name Encyclopedia*. St. Paul, MN: Llewellyn Publications, 1995.

## Bharani

Bharani (or the Bearer) is one of the Nakshatras (lunar mansions) of Vedic astrology. Symbolized by a female sex organ, this Nakshatra can be found from Aries 13°20' to

26°40'. Yama, the god of death or the setting sun, presides, and the planet Venus rules Bharani. This sign implies a "cutting" energy, and is a good time to do unpleasant but necessary activities; people may be more mentally quick and spontaneous, while also exhibiting tendencies towards amorality or fickleness during this time.

—Pramela Thiagesan

## The Bible and Astrology

The Hebrew and Christian Bibles are a complex set of documents. To advocates of astrology, it is not difficult to find passages presenting the science of the stars in a positive light. If, on the other hand, one wishes to attack astrology, it is also possible to find passages condemning stargazing. Certain Scriptures appear—at least in the King James Version (KJV)—to condemn astrologers as those who keep, watch, or observe the times; e.g., "Ye shall not eat anything with the blood, neither shall ye use enchantment, nor observe times" (Lev. 19:26). This allusion to astrology, however, was an interpolation by KJV translators. In modern translations, it is clear that the original biblical condemnation was against divination in general, rather than astrology in particular: "You shall not eat meat with the blood in it. You shall not practise divination or soothsaying" (New English Bible); and "You shall not eat any flesh with the blood in it. You shall not practice augury or witchcraft" (Revised Standard Version).

Advocates of astrology, however, can point to such passages as "God created lights in the heavens, and He made them for signs and for seasons" (Gen. 1:14), which is capable of being interpreted as a reference to astrology. More generally, because the God of Western religions is a sky-god, many different scriptural passages portray God as utilizing heavenly signs to instruct the faithful. These signs are often ambiguous enough to be given an astrological interpretation. With a little reworking, it is not difficult to read many otherwise innocent passages in an astrological manner, for example, the Lord's Prayer, as noted in Don Jacobs's *Astrology's Pew in the Church)*:

Our Father who lives in the heavens,
Let your name be honored,
Let your Kingdom come,
Let your will be done down here on the earth,
As perfectly as it is in the sky.

From these examples, it is not difficult to see that both supporters and detractors must "massage" various biblical passages to get an unambiguous message on the status of astrology. One of the few biblical accounts in which we can clearly perceive the practice of astrology is the story of The Three Wise Men. The Magi were clearly astrologers, and the Star of Bethlehem, as scholars have long pointed out, was actually a major planetary conjunction. The Magi believed, as do many of our contemporaries, that our planet was on the verge of entering a "new age," and this particular conjunction was taken to indicate the birth of a new world teacher.

**Sources:**

Jacobs, Don. *Astrology's Pew in the Church*. San Francisco: The Joshua Foundation, 1979.

Simms, Maria Kay. *Twelve Wings of the Eagle: Evolution Through the Ages of the Zodiac*. San Diego: 1988.

## Bicorporeal

Bicorporeal signs are signs of the zodiac said to be "double bodied": Gemini, Sagittarius, and Pisces. As originally used by Ptolemy, bicorporeal referred to all of the mutable signs, which are the three signs mentioned above plus Virgo.

## Biquintile

A biquintile is a minor aspect of 144°, created by subdividing a circle (360°) into five parts. As the name indicates, a biquintile is equivalent to two quintiles (72° aspects). The great astronomer Johannes Kepler devised quintiles and biquintiles for his astrological work. Under-researched, a biquintile's influence is sometimes said to be similar to that of a quintile, and it is given an orb of influence of 1° to 2°.

## Birth Control, Astrological

While the expression "astrological birth control" could have several referents, it is usually taken to refer to the system discovered and elaborated by the Czech psychiatrist Eugen Jonas. His initial discoveries were summed up by his three fundamental rules—conception, determination of sex, and life capability of the fetus—which he first formulated on August 15, 1956, according to Sheila Ostrander and Lynn Schroeder's book *Astrological Birth Control:*

> 1. The time of fertility [a second period of fertility, independent of the ovulation cycle] occurs during the same phase of the moon as that in which the woman was born.
> 2. The sex of the future child will be determined by the position of the moon during the time of the woman's fertility—whether the moon is found in the positive or in the negative field [i.e., in a positive, masculine sign or in a negative, feminine sign] of the ecliptic (or zodiac).
> 3. Unfavorable distribution of gravitational forces of the nearer celestial bodies at the time of conception produces complications during pregnancy, particularly for the fetus.

These discoveries became the basis for an astrological birth control clinic that, after overcoming much resistance, Jonas was able to establish in Czechoslovakia.

The first rule became the basis for a system of birth control that is basically an elaboration and development of the old rhythm method. Rather than abstaining only during the period of a woman's ovulation, a couple also abstains on (and for several days prior to) the day that the Sun and Moon repeat the exact angle they made with each other at the moment of the woman's birth. For instance, a woman born at the exact moment of the full moon (when, with Earth as the vertex, the Sun and Moon make a 180° angle to each other) would abstain during, and for several days prior to, the full moon. When combined with abstention during ovulation, this modified rhythm method is, according to Czech researchers, 98 percent effective as a birth control method.

Jonas became interested in astrology as a student but kept this interest separate from his profession during the early part of his career. In the mid-1950s, however, neighboring Hungary legalized abortion. This motivated Jonas, a practicing Catholic, to search for alternatives, even in such unlikely subject areas as astrology. According to Ostrander and Schroeder, from the ancient system of Mesopotamian astrology, he found a fragment asserting that "woman is fertile during a certain phase of the moon." No other clues illuminating this statement survived. Using this assertion as a starting place, however, Jonas painstakingly researched birth records until he broke the code of ancient astrological science: A woman is fertile during the phase of the Moon that replicates the phase the Moon was in at the moment of her birth.

Jonas's second rule is based on the Pythagorean notion that odd numbers are male and even numbers female. Hence, since ancient times, the first, third, fifth, seventh, ninth, and eleventh signs of the zodiac (Aries, Gemini, Leo, Libra, Sagittarius, and Aquarius) were regarded as masculine, while the second, fourth, sixth, eighth, tenth, and twelfth signs (Taurus, Cancer, Virgo, Scorpio, Capricorn, and Pisces) were regarded as feminine. The Moon, as the traditional ruler of conception and motherhood, might well have been anticipated as the key to influencing the sex of a child. Using the sign of the Moon at the time of conception, Jonas found he could predict the sex of a child with 85 percent accuracy. This effect of the Moon sign was apparently known to Hellenistic astrologers.

The third rule flows out of Jonas's search for possible astrological factors in miscarriages and birth defects. Jonas found a significant correlation between such complications and the presence of opposition (180°) angles—particularly when the Sun was involved—during conception. While this particular finding has no known correlate with traditional astrology, the negative effect of an opposition aspect in a natal chart (in contrast to a conception chart) has been well known since antiquity. That the Sun, as the traditional ruler of vitality and life force, is involved in such complications is not surprising.

As Jonas's work became established and grew, his center counseled couples in all three of the areas covered by his three rules: birth control, selecting the sex of children, and avoiding birth complications. This work flourished during Czechoslovakia's "springtime of freedom," the country's short-lived experiment with an open society prior to the Soviet invasion in the late summer of 1968. Jonas's center remained in operation another year and half following the invasion before being closed by the government. The doctor was demoted and his work stopped. After the collapse of the iron curtain, Jonas revived his work, though the official website of the Centrum Jonas International indicates that Jonas is living in retirement.

Although most of the relevant research of Jonas and colleagues is contained in untranslated books, pamphlets, and articles, since 1972 the English-speaking world has had the basic information on astrological birth control available to it through Ostrander and Schroeder's *Astrological Birth Control*. The authors had discovered Jonas's work while researching their popular *Psychic Discoveries Behind the Iron Cur-*

*tain*. They collected materials on astrological birth control and, having copies of most of the relevant information at the time of the Soviet invasion, Ostrander and Schroeder decided to have the materials in their possession translated. From these and other sources they wrote *Astrological Birth Control*. (The book is also useful for its overview of scientific research on astrological effects up to 1972.) Enough technical material is included that any competent astrologer can cast an astrological birth control chart, although the authors were careful to include the caveat that they were not recommending the system. The reports from non-iron-curtain researchers who have investigated Jonas's system since the publication of Ostrander and Schroeder's book are mixed; some claim to have replicated his results, while others report disconfirmation. One can find numerous relevant websites by typing Jonas's name into any Internet search engine.

**Sources:**

*Centrum Jonas International*. http://www.centrum.jonas.com.

Naish, Francesca. *The Lunar Cycle: A Guide to Natural and Astrological Fertility Control*. Bridport, Dorset, UK: Prism Press, 1989.

Ostrander, Sheila, and Lynn Schroeder. *Astrological Birth Control*. Englewood Cliffs, NJ: Prentice-Hall, 1972. (Reissued in paperback as *Natural Birth Control*.)

———. *Psychic Discoveries Behind the Iron Curtain*. Englewood Cliffs, NJ: Prentice-Hall, 1970.

## Birth Moment

Although determining the exact birth moment—first appearance of the baby's head, delivery, severing of the umbilical cord, first breath, first cry, etc.—has sometimes been the subject of debate, the consensus among most astrologers is that the natal chart should be cast for the individual's first breath. Clients sometimes tell astrologers that their nativity should have been earlier or later than was recorded on their birth certificate (i.e., that the chart cast for their moment of birth is somehow wrong, because they were born premature). Such people misconceive the nature of astrological influence: The individual's first independent breath is like the clicking of a camera shutter, exposing the "film" of their soul to the imprint of celestial influences.

**Sources:**

Bach, Eleanor. *Astrology from A to Z: An Illustrated Source Book*. New York: Philosophical Library, 1990.

Leo, Alan. *The Complete Dictionary of Astrology*. Rochester, VT: Destiny Books, 1989.

## Birthplace System

An alternative name for the Koch house system. By extension, Koch houses are sometimes called birthplace houses.

## Bitter Signs

The expression "bitter signs" is an older term applied to the fire signs, which were said to be fiery, hot, and bitter. The antonym is sweet signs.

## Blue Moon

The Moon can sometimes appear bluish because of atmospheric conditions, but the expression "once in a blue Moon" refers to a month during which two full moons occur—one at the beginning and the other near the end of the month. This happens only once every few years.

## Bonatti, Guido

The astrologer Guido Bonatti was born in Cascia, Italy, although his birthdate is unclear. We know he was in the Italian cities of Ravenna and Bologna, in 1223, and in Forli by 1233. He was advisor to Frederick II Hohenstaufen, the Holy Roman Emperor. In 1259, Bonatti entered the service of the tyrant Ezzelino III da Romano, and the following year he became astrologer to Count Guido di Montefeltro. Bonatti was the author of the *Liber astronomicus* sometime after 1282. He died in 1297. In *History of Magic and Experimental Science* (1923), Lynn Thorndike reports that Dante put Bonatti in the eighth circle of his *Inferno*: "Vedi Guido Bonattià"—Inferno, XX, 118.

Bonatti was a well known and influential man in his day and still highly regarded in Forli and Bologna. He was an aristocrat, an adviser to the mighty, and a learned man. The chroniclers of the day—Giovanni Villani, Fossi, Salimbene di Adam—took note of him. The *Annales of Forli* report that he played a prominent part in the defense of Forli in 1282 by Guido Montefeltro against a large force sent by Pope Martin IV. Despite the high regard he was held in during his lifetime (which continues in Bologna and Forli to this day, where Guido Bonatti has the status of a kind of local hero), there are few reliable details about his life. The date of his birth is a mystery. The year of his death is debated; Thorndike thinks it closer to 1300 than 1297. Bonatti is said to have ended his life as a Franciscan monk.

Bonatti's role in the spread of astrology in western Europe in the thirteenth century was an important one. The twelfth century saw the western Christian world suddenly become obsessed with Arabic Science (called the "New Science"). Astrology played a central role in this New Science. The transmission of Arabic astrology to the Latin West and a renewal of interest in both Greek and Arabic astrology among the Byzantines led to translation projects, principally in Spain and Sicily, where translators worked avidly and prolifically to make Arabic astrological texts available to the Latins. The thirteenth century saw the widespread assimilation of this recently acquired astrological science and to ecclesiastical opposition to it. Astrology was condemned by the church in 1210, 1215, and 1277. These multiple condemnations show that no one was listening. Instead of giving up astrology, western Europeans were practicing it and comparing the many texts circulating in western Europe.

Bonatti's *Liber astronomicus* is an outstanding exemplar of the thirteenth-century dissemination and assimilation in Christian western Europe of Arabic astrology. It is a Summa of astrology based upon the author's collection, collation, comparison, and application of the existing Latin translations available to him. Bonatti was a practicing astrologer. In his day, his reputation was good.

Thorndike, in the *History of Magic and Experimental Science* calls the *Liber astronomicus* "the most important astrological work produced in Latin in the 13th century." The same work is also known as the *Liber astronomiae*. Bonatti, like Roger Bacon, uses the word "astronomy" to denote what we understand as astrology and the word "astrology" to denote astronomy. His influence is attested to by the many manuscripts and printed editions of his work. It was widely circulated in manuscript and translated into Italian and German (Basel, 1572). Segments of the text have been translated into English: his *146 Considerations*, Lilly (1676); *Tractatus* I, II, and III, by Zoller (1994), available from www.robertzoller.com; and his dicta on how to wage war using astrological elections (in *Tractatus* VI). A manuscript copy was in the library of Italian humanist Giovanni Pico della Mirandola. English mathematician and astrologer John Dee also had a manuscript copy of it; Italian philosopher Marsilio Ficino must have had one as well.

Bonatti's *Liber astronomicus* remained a standard work from the thirteenth to the eighteenth century. The English astrologer Alfred J. Pearce mentions Bonatti in his nineteenth-century *Textbook of Astrology*. Pearce's citation of Bonatti underscores the importance of the Italian's work and his lasting influence among serious astrologers. Pearce's mishandling of Bonatti's instructions regarding the keys to mundane astrological delineation and prediction are typical of the nineteenth- and twentieth-century corner-cutting simplification of real astrology, which produced a more provincial, nonthreatening astrology and opened the door to the blander version of astrology often found today.

To speak about Bonatti is to speak about his *Liber Astronomiae*. The work is 10 tractates long in 848 numbered columns (425 unpaginated pages in the 1550 Basel edition). It deals with horary, electional, natal, and mundane astrology. A text on astrometeorology is appended to the 1496 Venice and the 1550 Basel editions.

*Tractatus Primus* presents Bonatti's philosophical argument in favor of astrology. He relies heavily upon Abū Ma'shar's *Greater Introduction*. *Tractatus Secundus* gives the basics of astrology, signs, subdivisions, planets, houses, joys of the planets, dignities, melothesiae, and characteristics of degrees. *Tractatus Tertius* discusses the natures of the planets, how they interact with each other, the signs, and houses. *Tractatus Quartus* is on the consideration of certain conjunctions and of other things the astrologer ought to know. These things are the definitions of certain technical terms in astrology, the great conjunction of Saturn and Jupiter in the first term of Aries, the conjunction of the same planets in the beginning of each triplicity, the conjunction of Saturn and Mars, the conjunction of Saturn and Jupiter, the conjunction of the Sun with the other planets, the conjunction and opposition of the luminaries, the combust and incombust hours, the duodena of the Moon, and that the discovery of the ascendant when the birth time is uncertain is through the Animodar of Ptolemy.

*Tractatus Quintus* presents Bonatti's 146 Considerations pertaining to judgment. In *Tractatus Sextus*, Bonatti talks about perfection in horary astrology (interrogations). *Tractatus Septimus* discusses the special judgments of the stars (horary astrology). *Tractatus Octavus—Elections Tractatus Nonus* covers revolutions of years (solar ingresses into the cardinal signs) and the Arabic Parts. *Tractatus Decimus* deals with the topic of natal astrology, while *Tractatus de imbribus et aeris mutationibus* deals with astrometeorology.

Like most ancient and medieval texts on astrology, Bonatti's book has something to say about character analysis, but little about psychology. The emphasis is on the objective behavior of the native and others in the native's life, with an eye toward predicting the external events (the accidents of the native) rather than the subjective response to them or to their alleged significance. The *Liber astronomicus* is concrete in its interpretations. The author is direct and does not mince words. He is usually forthcoming in his appraisal of his sources. He regards Abū Ma'shar as a prince of astrology and usually accepts the Persian astrologer's opinion on most subjects. Bonatti generally arranges his discussion of astrological procedures by first presenting the reader with a detailed description of the astrological method and then bringing forward special cases and the opinions of the ancients. The fate of Bonatti's *Liber astronomicus* is the fate of western astrology.

In the Renaissance, due in part to political and military realities following the fall of Constantinople to the Muslim Turks, and to Turkish occupation of the Balkans, there was considerable fear in western Europe that Christendom would fall under the Muslim Turkish control. An intense anti-Islamic response ensued in which all things Turkish, Arabic, and Islamic were repudiated. The intelligentsia, among whom the astrologers were to be counted, turned towards scientism, in particular to Copernicus's heliocentricity, abandoning the geocentric astronomy of Ptolemy and Aristotle that had become by this time embedded in the Catholic worldview. Bonatti's astrology, which had entered Western Europe as part of the "New Science" in the twelfth century, was now regarded as typical of the old Catholic cosmology by contemporary critics who sought a new New Science 300 years after the last "renaissance."

As a result of the Turkish threat, the Reformation, the Thirty Years' War, and the beginnings of the Scientific Revolution of the seventeenth century, western European intellectuals turned increasingly toward Greek science, secularism, scientism, and rationalism. Greek science, astrology, and mathematics were regarded as superior to their Arabic counterparts. As western philology demonstrated the adulteration of pristine Greek texts of Ptolemy's *Tetrabiblos*, for instance, the Arabic astrology was increasingly regarded as corrupt.

Repudiated by the intellectually superior and educated, bona fide astrology à la Bonatti's *Liber astronomicus* was ignored on the continent, as was the entire subject of astrology until the "Occult Revival" of the nineteenth century. Perhaps because it was used for propagandistic purposes during the English Civil War (1642–1646) and during the Commonwealth (1649–1660), astrology was preserved in England. Nevertheless, it was not the "papist" medieval astrology that survived, but a "reformed" and simplified astrology intended to make the science of the stars popular and, thus, politically useful. Later, in the eighteenth century, the almanacs made astrology accessible as entertainment to the partially educated.

Bonatti's *Liber astronomicus* is an important resource for the practicing astrologer. From the point of view of the history of science, it may be viewed by some as an example of superstitious protoscience or pseudoscience. From the theological point of view, its contents, if put into practice, enable the astrologer to achieve a better than 80 percent accuracy. It thereby calls into question the doctrine of free will as it is held by religionists and by secular humanists. Philosophically, *Liber astronomicus* demands that the philosopher reexamine the conclusions of the Jewish and Arabic neoplatonists—Al-Fārābī, Ibn Sīnā, ibn Gabirol, and Ibn Rushd. From the point of view of the practice of the art, it ought to be recognized that astrology in medieval Islam was and continues to be regarded as a traditional and sacred science subordinate only to the Koran. It was as such that astrology reentered western Europe in the twelfth century.

The *Liber astronomicus* allows for the recovery of much of what was ill-advisedly tossed out as "superstition," "Arabic" (i.e., allegedly corrupt), and "papist."

—Robert Zoller

**Sources:**


Debus, Allen G. *World Who's Who in Science*. 1st ed. Chicago: Marquis' Who's Who, 1968.

Halliwell-Phillipps, J. P., ed. *The Private Library of Dr. John Dee, and the Catalogue of his Library of Manuscripts*. London: Camden Society Publications, 1842.

James, Montague R. *Lists of Manuscripts Formerly Owned by Dr. John Dee*. Oxford: Bibliographical Society, 1921.

Kibre, Pearl. *The Library of Pico Della Mirandola*. New York: Columbia University Press, 1969.

*Liber Astronomiae*. Appeared in print in Latin first in 1491 at Augsburg. Radolt was the publisher (G.W. 4643). Other Latin editions were produced in Venice (1506), and Basel (1530 and 1550).

Thorndike, Lynn. *History of Magic and Experimental Science, Vol. II*. New York: Columbia University Press, 1923.

Zoller, Robert. "The Astrologer as Military Adviser in the Middle Ages," *Astrology Quarterly*. (1992–93).


## Boomerang

A boomerang is a configuration resembling a yod but involving a fourth planet directly opposed to the "action planet" at the tip of the yod. In a yod, two planets form a sextile (60°) aspect and both in turn form a quincunx (150°) aspect with a third planet. If lines were drawn to the center of the horoscope from all three planets, the resulting pattern would look like a capital Y. The planet at the bottom tip of the Y is said to be the action planet because its house placement is where the action takes place when the configuration is activated by a transit or a progression. The interpretation often given to a yod in a natal chart is that it indicates a life that proceeds along in a certain pattern for a period of time until the established pattern is abruptly interrupted and the native is forced to proceed in a new direction, though the new direction is one for which the person had actually been preparing for some time. A completely unanticipated promotion in one's chosen profession, for example, might be brought about by an activated yod configuration.

When a fourth planet is involved in a yod so that it forms an opposition (180°) aspect to the action planet and semisextile (30°) aspects to the remaining two planets, the resulting formation is called a boomerang, a designation coined by Joan

McEvers. In a boomerang, the situation anticipated at the point of the action planet "boomerangs" when the configuration is activated. One example McEvers uses in her explanation of the boomerang is Ralph Waldo Emerson, who had such a configuration in his natal chart and who, when fortune placed the 26-year-old minister in the pulpit of Boston's Old North Church, found himself in a situation with which his nonconformist temperament had difficulty coping. He was eventually forced to leave the ministry. Thus, Emerson's opportunity "boomeranged."

**Sources:**

Escobar, Thyrza. *Side Lights of Astrology*. 3d ed. Hollywood, CA: Golden Seal Research, 1971.

McEvers, Joan. "The Boomerang: A New Configuration." In *Astrology: Old Theme, New Thoughts*. Edited by Marion D. March and Joan McEvers. San Diego: Astro Computing Services, 1984.

## Boreal Signs

Boreal signs is a traditional term referring to the northern signs, Aries through Virgo. The term is derived from *Boreas*, the Greek personification of the north wind.

## Bowl Pattern

A bowl, or hemispheric, pattern is a horoscope in which all of the planets are in half of the chart. Ideally, the planets are spread out so as to create the visual impression of a bowl.

## Bradley, Donald A. (Garth Allen)

Donald A. Bradley, born in Nebraska on May 16, 1925, was a leader of the "siderealist" movement and research director of the Llewellyn Foundation for Astrological Research. He carried out several statistical studies, including an astrological analysis of 2,492 clergymen and an extensive study of rainfall. His results, while initially greeted with enthusiasm, were later shown to be largely insignificant, either because of faulty design or neglected statistical considerations.

Bradley was an enthusiastic adherent of the sidereal zodiac as advocated by Cyril Fagan, and wrote many books and articles on siderealism. He published his early work under his own name but later used the pseudonym Garth Allen. A regular contributor to *American Astrology Magazine*, he was senior editor when he died of cancer on April 25, 1974, in Tucson, Arizona.

**Sources:**

Bradley, Donald A. *Picking Winners*. Saint Paul, MN: Llewellyn Publications, 1954.

———. *Profession and Birthdate*. Los Angeles: Llewellyn Publications, 1950.

———. *Solar and Lunar Returns*. 2d ed. Saint Paul, MN: Llewellyn Publications, 1968.

———. *Stock Market Prediction*. Los Angeles: Llewellyn Foundation for Astrological Research, 1950.

Holden, James H., and Robert A. Hughes. *Astrological Pioneers of America*. Tempe, AZ: American Federation of Astrologers, 1988.

## BRADY, BERNADETTE

Bernadette Brady is a faculty member of the Astrological Guild of Educators International; a fellow of the Federation of Australian Astrologers (FAA); coprincipal of Astro Logos, an astrological school dedicated to the education and qualification of practicing astrologers; and is currently a student at Bath Spa University in the cultural astronomy and astrology program.

Brady has published astrological software called Starlight as well as three books: *The Eagle and the Lark: A Textbook of Predictive Astrology; Brady's Book of Fixed Stars;* and *Predictive Astrology: The Eagle and the Lark.* In 1992 Brady was awarded the FAA's Inaugural Southern Cross Award for excellence in the spoken and written word. In 1996, she was awarded the FAA's Southern Cross Award for research, for her original work on Saros cycles, graphic rectification, and fixed stars. In 1998, along with Darrelyn Gunzburg, she was awarded the FAA Southern Cross award for education. In 1999, she was the recipient of the inaugural Spica Award from the United Kingdom, for her book *Predictive Astrology.* The same year, she presented the Charles Carter Memorial Lecture at the Astrological Association of Great Britain, on family hereditary patterns, a work later published in *Correlations*.

Brady has also published many articles, in Australia, and in the United Kingdom, Ireland, United States, Canada, and New Zealand. Most years she lectures at conferences in Europe and the United States.

**Sources:**

Brady, Bernadette. *Brady's Book of Fixed Stars*. York Beach, ME: S. Weiser, 1998.

———. *The Eagle and the Lark: A Textbook of Predictive Astrology*. York Beach, ME: S. Weiser, 1992.

———. *Predictive Astrology: The Eagle and the Lark*. York Beach, ME: S. Weiser, 1999.

## BRAHE, TYCHO

Tycho Brahe, an eminent Danish astronomer and astrologer, was born April 13, 1546, in Kundstorp, Denmark. He taught astronomy at the University of Copenhagen and established an observatory on the island of Hven under the patronage of King Frederick II. Brahe moved to Prague, Czechoslovakia, after the king's death, where he took Johannes Kepler as his assistant.

Dissatisfied with inexactness of most existing observations of the celestial bodies, Brahe designed instruments that enabled him to make the most precise observations of the heavens to be recorded prior to the invention of the telescope, and he discovered the phenomenon of exploding novas. (The accuracy of Brahe's observations enabled Kepler to discover some of the laws governing planetary motions.) Brahe was also a mundane astrologer. He contributed to aspect theory and did work on the connection between the natural cataclysms and conjunctions. He died October 21, 1601, in Prague.

**Sources:**

Brau, Jean-Louis, Helen Weaver, and Allan Edmands. *Larousse Encyclopedia of Astrology*. New York: New American Library, 1980.

Kitson, Annabella, ed. *History and Astrology: Clio and Urania Confer*. London: Mandala, 1989.

An engraving of the great astronomer Tycho Brahe by Gheyn near the end of the sixteenth century. *Reproduced by permission of Fortean Picture Library.*

## Broken Signs (Mutilated Signs; Imperfect Signs)

The archaic term "broken signs" (also called mutilated signs or, in more recent works, imperfect signs) refers to certain signs that, when on the ascendant and afflicted, are said to result in a twisted body or twisted limbs. The broken signs are variously listed, usually including Leo and Pisces, sometimes Scorpio or Virgo, and occasionally Capricorn and Cancer. Modern astrologers have abandoned this classification. Almost any severely afflicted planet in any sign when placed in the first house (the house of the physical body) could result in physical difficulties. The antonym term is whole sign (perfect sign).

## Broughton, Luke Dennis

Luke Dennis Broughton, a leader in the astrology revival of the late nineteenth century, was born on April 20, 1828, in Leeds, England. At a time when astrology was unpopular, his family continued to practice it. This custom originated with his grandfather, a doctor who used Nicolas Culpepper's herbal compendium (*Culpepper's English Physician and Herbal Remedies*, originally published in 1652), which correlated astrological signs with medicinal herbs. Luke Broughton's father, also a physician, followed in his father's footsteps, and Luke, in turn, followed his father. Mark Broughton, Luke's older brother, headed an astrological society in Leeds and published an almanac as well as an ephemeris (a table indicating planetary positions). After arriving in America, Mark Broughton initiated an astrological periodical, *Broughton's Monthly Horoscope*.

Luke Broughton married at age 24 and moved to the United States two years later. He intended to follow his family's medical occupation. Settling in Philadelphia, he worked as a weaver and later as a laboratory technician while as a student at Eclectic Medical College. (Eclecticism was a school of medicine based on such natural remedies as Culpepper's herbs.) After his brother's magazine ceased publication in 1860, Luke initiated *Broughton's Planet Reader and Astrological Journal*, which was published until 1869.

Antiastrology laws were passed in Philadelphia not long after Luke Broughton began his journal. It is not known whether these laws were prompted, in whole or in part, by Broughton's public astrology activity. In 1863, he moved his medical office to New York City, where he continued to practice astrology. After the Civil War, Broughton began renting a lecture hall and speaking regularly on astrology. Experiencing marked success in his lectures, he opened an office devoted completely to astrology and began dividing his time between medicine and the science of the stars. Broughton also trained astrologers, and most of the important astrologers of the early twentieth century were his students. He also distributed British astrological literature, including the technical works necessary for erecting astrological charts. He wrote *Remarks on Astrology and Astromedical Botany* (1880) as well as several texts, including *Planetary Influence* (1893) and *The Elements of Astrology* (1898).

As evidenced by the antiastrology laws adopted in Philadelphia, the astrological revival brought controversy in its wake, and Broughton situated himself in the middle of it. While he denounced astrologers he thought were incompetent or in error, he was also an outspoken defender of astrology. He served as an expert witness in cases where astrologers were arrested for telling fortunes. Broughton taught thousands of astrologers and was a pivotal individual in making astrology a widely practiced art in the United States. He died in 1898, and his daughter carried on his New York practice. Several of his sons also became astrologers.

**Sources:**

Broughton, Luke Dennis. *The Elements of Astrology*. New York: The author, 1898.
———. *Planetary Influence*. New York: The author, 1893.
———. *Remarks on Astrology and Astromedical Botany*.
*Culpepper's English Physician and Herbal Remedies*. North Hollywood, CA: Wilshire Book Co., 1971.
Holden, James H., and Robert A. Hughes. *Astrological Pioneers of America*. Tempe, AZ: American Federation of Astrologers, 1988.
Melton, J. Gordon. *New Age Encyclopedia*. Detroit: Gale Research, 1990.

## Brutish Signs

The archaic term "Brutish signs" refers to Leo and the last third (the Leo decan) of Sagittarius, which, when occupied by planets under unfavorable aspects or in some other manner afflicted, was said to produce natives with coarse, "brutish" natures. Modern astrologers have abandoned this term, as well as the connotations of afflicted planets in these two arcs.

## Bucket Pattern

A bucket pattern is a specific planetary arrangement in which all planets but one are on one side of an astrological chart. In the case of a natal chart, the isolated planet, called the handle or singleton, represents a point of focus for the native's life. Because of the focus of energies on the singleton, a bucket chart is sometimes also called a funnel chart.

## Bull

The Bull is a popular name for the sign Taurus.

## Bundle Pattern

A bundle, or cluster, pattern is a horoscope arrangement in which all of the planets are contained in one 120° arc.

## Business Astrology

Business astrology has often been included within the umbrella of financial astrology. Though both relate to business, the two are very different. Whereas financial astrology focuses on the study of movement of the financial markets, business astrology focuses on the day-to-day workings of an individual company and its leaders. Business astrology also reviews which occupations are best suited for certain individuals and assists a company in putting together a plan. However, these two types of astrology have only recently separated.

Business astrology differs from financial astrology in that it is used for such purposes as choosing the best timing to start a new venture, to market a new product, and to reorganize the structure of a company, as well for reviewing the part the employees play in the efficient workings of a company. Financial astrology deals with the much larger cycles of planetary movements and their effects on the markets, while business astrology takes a more microscopic view of an individual entity, an individual company, and its infrastructure (called organizational charts). Business astrology also provides an analysis of the first trade chart, which is calculated for the time the first trade of the company is made. The first trade chart designates volume sales and stock sales activity, while an organizational or corporate chart views the infrastructure, the situation of the employees, the public's view of the company, and so on. These are all different entities and they dance between the boundaries of both disciplines.

In an article for the International Society of Business Astrologers web site, Michael Munkasey writes:

> Business astrology is unique within the schools because it has two distinct and separate parts: consultation about business problems or questions; and also, market forecasting. Often when a person refers to their practice as "business astrology" they mean either one of these parts or the other. In truth, the parts really have little connection with each other.
>
> Consultation about business problems or questions involves having an understanding not only of various natal astrological techniques (chart reading, transits, progressions, Medieval ideas, etc.), but also of business practices. It does little good to consult with a business person who has profit in mind, when the astrologer does not understand the nature of the business. Often, questions which arise in this area involve sound business practice: should I take out a loan at this time from this bank; should I fire or hire an employee; should I move to this building; etc. Confronted with every day business questions like these the astrologer is relegated to discussions of timing. Yes, this is a good time for your business to expand (or contract); no, Tuesday is not a good day for approaching the bank about a loan; etc. Astrology can give wonderful insight into the timing of such events, but without some in-depth knowledge of contemporary business practices an astrologer can not be an effective operational consultant.
>
> Market forecasting is totally separate as a business problem from operational consulting. Market forecasting involves the use of astrological techniques to select stocks (equities), indices, futures, etc., in a satisfactory manner. Market forecasting as a discipline is much more difficult than business consulting. Also, the ideas of traditional (including

> Vedic, Greek, etc.) astrology do not apply as clearly to this practice. It is folly to think, as an accomplished professional natal astrologer, that you can immediately apply the techniques of natal astrology to selecting stocks or forecasting in the market. Astrology can be of considerable use here, but not with just using the traditional techniques. Additional insight is needed, and new ways of looking at standard techniques have to be learned. (From Munkasey, Courtesy of the International Society of Business Astrologers [www.businessastrologers.com].)

Both business and financial astrology are fairly new studies, having emerged during the twentieth century. The studies started around 1938 with the publication of Louise McWhirter's groundbreaking book, *Astrology and Stock Market Forecasting*. This book discussed the trends of the markets and is usually placed under the category of financial astrology, which is, again, a study of the markets and their cycles. Continuing with this trend, in 1959, Lt. Commander David Williams wrote *Astro-Economics* and, in 1976, Thomas Rieder wrote *Astrological Warnings and the Stock Market*.

However, in 1979 Jack Gillen wrote *The Key to Speculation on the New York Stock Exchange*, which was one of the first books to address the distinction between general financial trends and the individualism of companies. Gillen's book may well be referred to as a hybrid book that created one of the first bridges between the larger macroscopic umbrella of financial astrology and the more defined and microscopic view of companies based on their signs and placements. Granted, the Gillen book was more of a cursive study of the sun signs of the various companies, but that simple distinction offered another view of how astrology can be used in the financial world. The book that began to focus on individual companies, which is more the realm of what is called business astrology today.

### Business Astrology Publications

| Date First Published | Author | Title of Book |
|---|---|---|
| 1928 | Alfred Witte | *Rules for Planetary Pictures* |
| 1938 | Louise McWhirter | *Astrology and Stock Market Forecasting* |
| 1943 | Edward R. Dewey and Edwin Dakin | *Cycles: The Science of Prediction* |
| 1944 | George Bayer | *Turning Four Hundred Years of Astrology to Practical Use* |
| 1959 | David Williams | *Astro-Economics* |
| 1962 | Charles E. Luntz | *Vocational Guidance by Astrology* |
| 1970 | Edward R. Dewey | *Cycles—Selected Writings* |
| 1976 | Arthur M. Young | *The Geometry of Meaning* |
| 1976 | Thomas Rieder | *Astrological Warnings and the Stock Market* |
| 1977 | Raymond Merriman | *The Solar Return Book of Prediction* |
| 1977 | Raymond Merriman | *Evolutionary Astrology* |
| 1979 | Jack Gillen | *The Key to Speculation on the New York Stock Exchange* |
| 1981 | Doris Chase Doane | *Vocational Selection and Counseling* (2 vols.) |

| | | |
|---|---|---|
| 1982 | Raymond Merriman | *The Gold Book* |
| 1984 | Carol Mull | *Standard & Poor's 500* |
| 1986 | Carol Mull | *750 Over the Counter Stocks* |
| 1989 | Joan McEvers, ed. | *Financial Astrology for the 1990's* |
| 1989 | Theodore Landscheidt | *Sun-Earth-Man: A Mesh of Cosmic Oscillations* |
| 1990 | Neil F. Michelsen | *Tables of Planetary Phenomena* |
| 1991 | Michael Munkasey | *The Concept Dictionary* |
| 1991 | Michael Munkasey | *Midpoints: Unleashing the Power of the Planets* |
| 1991 | Noel Tyl | *Prediction in Astrology* |
| 1991 | Noel Tyl | *Predictions for a New Millennium* |
| 1992 | Noel Tyl | *How to Use Vocational Astrology* |
| 1993 | Barbara Koval | *Time & Money* |
| 1994 | Bill Meridian | *Planetary Stock Trading* |
| 1994 | Graham Bates and Jane Chrzanowska | *Money and the Markets* |
| 1994 | Nicholas Campion | *The Great Year* |
| 1994 | Raymond Merriman | *Merriman on Market Cycles: The Basics* |
| 1995 | Nicholas Campion | *The World Book of Horoscopes* |
| 1995 | Nicholas Campion | *The Book of World Horoscopes* |
| 1996 | Suitbert Eertel and Ken Irving | *The Tenacious Mars Effect* |
| 1998 | James A. Hyerczyk | *Pattern, Price & Time: Using Gann Theory in Trading Systems* |
| 1999 | Raymond Merriman | *Stock Market Timing* |
| 1999 | Stephanie Clement | *Charting Your Career* |
| 2000 | Garry Phillipson | *Astrology in the Year Zero* |
| 2001 | Stephanie Clement | *Power of the Midheaven* |
| 2001 | Georgia Anna Stathis | *Business Astrology 101: Weaving the Web between Business/Myth* |
| 2002 | Bill Meridian | *Planetary Stock Trading-III* |
| 2002 | Bill Meridian | *Planetary Economic Forecasting* |
| 2002 | Raymond Merriman | *The Ultimate Book on Stock Market Timing* |
| 2002 | Michael Munkasey | *Software: Corporation, First Trade, and IPO Subscription Data* |

Another individual who contributed to the development of business astrology was George Bayer, who, in 1944, wrote several books on stock market movements. He referred to such things as the position of Mercury and its speed in terms of commodities. He also looked at Venus in the same way and much more. Though his focus was on trends, he actually was one of the first to pioneer the study of commodities. His interesting work on commodities and their cycles included the study of individual planets and their operational movements.

This focus on the individual planets and their effect on the commodities they ruled was a forerunner of the inclusion of planets and their meanings within the context of individual company charts. Edward Dewey and Edwin Dakin also contributed tremendous amounts of literature to the study of cycles in their 1947 book *Cycles: The Science of Prediction* and Dewey's 1970 book *Cycles: Selected Writings*. The latter book and many others were part of the research findings found and published in their organization for the Study of Cycles for many years.

Concurrent with the publication of Dewey's and Dakin's works and the beginning of the study of financial astrology, Charles E. Luntz wrote *Vocational Guidance by Astrology*, which was another offshoot of business astrology moving into the study of vocations and the individual natal chart. This is part of the modern-day business astrology. Doris Chase Doane also wrote the two-volume *Vocational Selection and Counseling* in the early 1980s.

It was during the 1980s that a great deal of literature was published and started coming from many different sources. Carol Mull wrote *Standard and Poor's 500* in 1984 and *750 Over the Counter Stocks* in 1986. In the first book, she lists, by industry and in natal chart formats, the charts of the companies on the Standard and Poor's list at that time.

Thus began the distinction between the two disciplines. At the same time, Grace Morris began conferences on astro-economics that continue throughout the world today and include lectures from both the worlds of financial and business astrology. Many of the pioneers of this new industry are included in these conferences. Some of the first Morris conferences were in conjunction with Mull. To this day, Morris works in the field of corporate astrology and each year publishes *How to Choose Stocks That Will Outperform the Market*.

On other organizational fronts, the International Society for Business Astrologers was founded in Copenhagen, Denmark, on March 10, 1997, at 9:09 A.M. Their website is available at www.businessastrologers.com. Other organizations such as the International Society for Astrological Research (ISAR), National Council for Geocosmic Research (NCGR), Association for Astrological Networking (AFAN), and the United Astrology Congress (UAC) also present conferences with business and financial astrology as their teaching tracks.

Alice Q. Reichard of California began lecturing on real estate cycles in the late 1990s. Her groundbreaking work on the study of the transiting lunar nodes still holds today as real estate values increase and decrease along with interest rates. Her work, along with the upsurge of books on vocational astrology and the continuing study of companies and their first trades, which was pioneered by Bill Meridian in his book series *Planetary Stock Forecasting*, shuttled the study of business astrology into high gear as the early 1990s arrived. At this time, Llewellyn Publishing invited Joan McEvers to gather and edit articles from various people in the field of business and financial astrology, including such astrologers as Robert Cole, Mary Downing, Georgia Stathis, Bill Meridian, Judy Johns, Carol Mull, Pat Esclavon-Hardy, Jeanne Long, and Michael Munkasey. The resulting book, *Financial Astrology for the 1990s*, was reprinted three times, and the trend of the 1990s was set for more people becoming interested in business and financial astrology.

In the 1970s, particularly in the later part of the decade, as the personal computer became more accessible to astrologers, a number of individuals started developing their various areas of expertise. A partial list (in alphabetical order) of these individuals includes Karen Boesen (of Denmark), Tim Bost, Matt Carnicelli, Mary Downing, Pat Esclavon-Hardy , Madeline Gerwick-Brodeur, Vladimir Gorbatcevich, Robert Gover, Geraldine Hannon, Judy Johns, Barbara Koval, Maarit Laurento (of Finland), Bill Meridian, Raymond Merriman, Grace Morris, Carol Mull, Robert Mulligan, Michael Munkasey, Hannah Lund (of Denmark), Paul Yogi Niperness, Kay Shinker, Georgia Stathis, and Norman Winski (working with commodities), and Manfred Zimmel (of Austria).

As would be expected, the collection of company and first trade charts increased so heavily that software began to be written and published to help manage the data and assist in stock trends and market moves. Software pioneers include Jeanne Long, with her Galactic Trader package, and Raymond Merriman, author of the *Gold Book* and the *The Ultimate Book on Stock Market Timing* series, who designed F. A. R. software, which is sold in conjunction with Galactic Trader. Bill Meridian's data are included in Alphee Lavoie's software, Astro Analyst; David Cochrane's Cosmic Patterns software includes financial analyst tools; and Michael Munkasey is currently gathering and updating thousands of first trade charts, initial public offering dates, and incorporation dates with his subscription software.

In recent years, the news media has begun to interview both business and financial astrologers for their findings. Some of the interviews are even becoming favorable! These media entities include CNN, *Nightline*, the *Los Angeles Times*, *Fortune*, *Time*, and so forth. As a result, the use of astrology in determining business trends and cycles is becoming popular and favored because it serves as a useful tool in planning.

In 2001, Georgia Stathis, a business astrologer since the early 1980s, published *Business Astrology: Weaving the Web between Business and Myth*. This book is devoted solely to business and vocational astrology and is a hybrid publication cross-pollinating the ancient myths and stories, their relevance to the planets, and how those definitions may be incorporated into determining professions or corporation plans. Stathis incorporates the lunation cycle—an ancient study—to modern vocational and corporate development movements.

More and more individuals are requiring the service of a good business astrologer to help them understand the changing patterns of their companies, whether they are sole-proprietor organizations or large companies. As many business astrologers are beginning to collaborate with their peers to serve the greater business communities, both national and international, business astrology is slowly developing a foothold in international business. As the public becomes more exposed to business astrology and reviews its results, the usefulness of business astrology will seamlessly integrate into companies that have foresight and progressive ideas in both national and international business.

—Georgia Stathis

**Sources:**

Bayer, George. *Turning Four Hundred Years of Astrology to Practical Use, and Other Matters*. Carmel, CA: 1944.

Dewey, Edward. *Cycles: Selected Writings*. Pittsburgh: Foundation for the Study of Cycles, 1970.

Dewey, Edward, and Edwin Dakin. *Cycles: The Science of Prediction*. New York: H. Holt and Company, 1947.

Doane, Doris Chase. *Vocational Selection and Counseling*. Tempe, AZ: American Federation of Astrologers, 1981.

Gillen, Jack. *The Key to Speculation on the New York Stock Exchange*. San Antonio, TX: Bear Publishers, 1979.

Luntz, Charles E. *Vocational Guidance by Astrology*. Rev. ed. St. Paul, MN: Llewellyn Publications, 1962.

McEvers, Joan. *Financial Astrology for the 1990s*. St. Paul, MN: Llewellyn Publications, 1989.

McWhirter, Louise. *Astrology and Stock Market Forecasting*. New York: Astro Book Co., 1938.

Mull, Carol S. *750 Over-the-Counter Stocks*. Tempe, AZ: American Federation of Astrologers, 1986.

———. *Standard & Poor's 500*. Tempe, AZ: American Federation of Astrologers, 1984.

Rieder, Thomas. *Astrological Warnings and the Stock Market*. 2d ed. Toronto: Pagurian Press, 1976.

Stathis, Georgia. *Business Astrology: Weaving the Web between Business and Myth*. Pleasant Hill, CA: Starcycles Publishing, 2001.

## Cadent House

The houses of an astrological chart are classified into three groups of four: angular houses (the first, fourth, seventh, and tenth), succedent houses (the second, fifth, eighth, and eleventh), and cadent houses (the third, sixth, ninth, and twelfth). Traditionally, the cadent houses have been referred to as the mental houses, although this ascription applies best to the third house and the ninth house (the houses of the "lower" and "higher" mind). In classical astrology, cadent houses were regarded as the least powerful houses in which planets could be positioned, while angular houses were the most powerful. Modern astrologers, however, tend to think that planets placed in the angular houses have the most influence on the outer, surface aspects of a person's life, and planets placed in the cadent houses have the most impact on one's inner life. Planets located in succedent houses mediate inner and outer lives.

**Sources:**

Brau, Jean-Louis, Helen Weaver, and Allan Edmands. *Larousse Encyclopedia of Astrology*. New York: New American Library, 1980.

Hand, Robert. *Horoscope Symbols*. Rockport, MA: Para Research, 1981.

## Calendar

Astrology is built upon an accurate accounting of time. Fundamental to this accounting is a calendrical system that takes into consideration the irregular manner in which days, months, and years fit together. A calendar in the broadest sense consists of the set of rules that a society uses for deciding which days are ordinary days and which are holidays (a variant of "holy days"). Societies in the past evolved many different kinds of calendars, and a surprisingly large number of them are important for understanding the details of the Western civil calendar.

**The famous Aztec calendar can be read in terms of cycles covering thousands of years.** ***Reproduced by permission of Fortean Picture Library.***

## Origins of the Calendar

There are three natural divisions of time on Earth. The most obvious is the alternation of night and day, and all calendars are organized in terms of the 24-hour day, which is the approximate average length. However, not all calendars are organized in terms of hours with a fixed length. Our ability to measure seconds and even minutes accurately was achieved only in modern times. A medieval sundial divided the hours of sunlight into 12 hours, but, obviously, in northern latitudes an hour during a long summer day might be twice as long as an hour during a short winter day. The Western civil calendar that is now used internationally is based on hours of a precisely defined fixed length, but there are still some local or folk calendars in which the length of an hour is much more flexible.

The next most obvious way to divide time is to use the phases of the Moon. Originally, a month was a "moonth": It represented the period from one full moon or new moon to the next. We cannot know how people measured time during the tens or hundreds of millennia that all human beings existed as bands of hunters and gatherers, following the herds and the ripening fruits and grains in an annual migration north and south. During the last ice age (from roughly 20,000 to 100,000 years ago), when human beings were forced to live in caves and develop new stoneware technology in order to survive, they may have begun tallying the phases of the Moon more carefully than before in attempting to calculate the length of the lunar month. In the Western civil calendar, months are arbitrary groups of days, ranging from 28 to 31 days in length that are not correlated with the phases of the moon. All major religious calendars (Christian, Jewish, Moslem, Buddhist, and Hindu) still depend wholly or partly on having months that are exactly in phase with the Moon.

The third most obvious time division is marked by the seasons—the annual migration north and south of the Sun's rising and setting points. Probably for a long time, years were labeled only relatively, as the regnal year of a king, by the number of years since some memorable event, and so on; and this starting point would be changed with every new generation. Only rather late in the history of civilization did years begin to be numbered from some fixed point in the distant past, such as the first Olympiad, the founding of the city of Rome, or the birth of Jesus of Nazareth.

## Constructing a Calendar

As could their predecessors, agricultural villagers today can coordinate their annual activities by word of mouth, but citizens of an empire cannot. It obviously will not work to have the arrival times of people coming to a three-day festival in the capital city spread out over a week. Hence, about 5,000 years ago, the administrators in Egypt and Sumeria were faced with the problem of constructing a calendar that everyone could use to see, on each day, how many more days it would be until some scheduled event. But to construct such a calendar, these people had to deal with four basic questions:,

1. How long is a day?
2. How long is a month? (Or, equivalently, how many days are there in a month?)
3. How long is a year?
4. How many months are in a year?

Being used to our modern answers to these questions, we may think them obvious; but they are not, and adequate answers to them were found only by centuries of ongoing observations, measurements, and calculations.

## How Long Is a Day?

The technique of dividing day and night into 12 hours each was devised by the Babylonians, who calculated with a number system that used a base of 12 rather than 10. Hours were introduced into the Roman calendar only rather late in Roman history, when the seven-day week (also a Babylonian invention) was generally adopted. Originally the Romans had divided day and night into watches, each several hours in length.

In modern usage, a day is defined as being 24 hours long; an hour is defined as 60 minutes, or 3,600 seconds, long; and a second is defined as so many vibrations of a specific line in the spectrum of a specific isotope. Naturally, this definition was worked out in a way that makes 24 hours equal to the traditional average length of a day. It was finding this average length that was the problem in the ancient world, for several reasons.

First, where do you measure from? The convention of starting each calendar day at midnight was agreed upon only in modern times. In most ancient calendars, each day began at sunset and ended at the following sunset (some ancient peoples, such as the Egyptians, counted a day as running from one dawn to the next); this is why the "eve" before many traditional holidays is still important and why the Jewish Sabbath celebration begins at sunset on Friday. But exactly when is sunset? It takes about 15 minutes for the Sun to sink completely below the horizon, which appears higher on land than it does at sea. This ambiguity is why the Talmud prescribed that all activities not allowed on the Sabbath should cease two hours before sunset. Some conventional definition—such as measuring from the moment the disc of the sun first touches the horizon—had to be introduced and adhered to.

Furthermore, since the days (in the sense of hours of light) grow longer (how much longer depends on the latitude) during half the year, shorter during the other half, an accurate measurement needs to be correct to within less than a minute to be useful for constructing a calendar. But there were no accurate techniques before modern times—even measuring a quarter hour accurately was difficult—and so the ancient calendars tended to accumulate an error of a day every few years.

## How Many Days Are in a Month?

In most ancient calendars, a month was a lunar month, that is, one full cycle of the Moon's phases. We know now that the average length of a lunar month, measured from one astronomical new moon to the next, is 29.5306 days. However, an ancient month began not at the astronomical new moon, which is an invisible event, but at the first visible crescent. Many factors affect when the crescent of the new moon will be visible at a particular location. Usually the interval from each first crescent to the next will alternate between 29 and 30 days—and so the length of the months will alternate likewise—but it is easily possible for two or even three intervals of 29 days or 30 days to fall successively. Hence, it was quite late in history—long after the length of the year was well known—before the average length of the lunar cycle was known with usable accuracy.

## How Many Days Are in a Year?

We know now that the average length of the year is 365.2422 days, but this precise value was taken into account only by the Gregorian reform of the calendar in 1582. The Julian calendar (devised by Julius Caesar), which the Gregorian calendar replaced, assumed the year to be 365.25 days long (as we all do for ordinary purposes), and the earlier Roman calendar that Julius replaced apparently assumed the year to be 366.25 days. The Egyptian calendar, which Julius borrowed as the basis for his, assumed the year to be exactly 365 days.

The problem in the ancient world again was finding a fixed point from which to measure the length of (or to begin) the year. The most popular choices were the winter solstice, when the days begin growing longer again, and the spring equinox, when the hours of sunlight and darkness are equal, but many others were also used. Measuring the moment of winter solstice would seem a difficult task for ancient peoples, but it now seems clear that the people who built Stonehenge about 3000 B.C.E. could do so quite accurately. They could also predict all eclipses of the Sun and the Moon. The Egyptians seem to have solved the problem by observing the heliacal rising of Sirius each year: The fixed stars, including Sirius, appear to rotate about the Earth each sidereal day, which is always the same length. Which stars are visible in the night sky depends on where the Earth is in its annual orbit around the Sun. Sirius (and any other star) will always first become visible after sunset (weather and local conditions allowing) on the same day each year relative to the solstices and equinoxes; this is its heliacal rising. In classical times, the Mesopotamians claimed that they had also solved the problem in another way, as early as the Egyptians had, but it is not certain that they had done so before the seventh century B.C.E.

## How Many Months Are in a Year?

This is the most difficult of the four questions (and the one that causes the most differences between calendars), because the length of the solar year is not a simple multiple of the length of the lunar month. Hence, if the months are to stay in phase with the Moon, there are many problems.

Twelve months that alternate between 29 and 30 days produce a year of 29.5 x 12 = 354 days, which is 11.2422 days short of an average solar year. Every three years this difference will add up to 33.7266 days, allowing an extra lunar month—of, say, 30 days—to be added. This still leaves a difference of 3.7266 days, which will add up to 33+ days after 27 years, allowing an extra lunar month to be inserted, and so on. It seems clear, however, that people generally would not like to have a feature in their calendars that appears only once in 27 years; for example, what would this extra month be called? Would it contain any holidays?

Only two basic kinds of calendars have succeeded in dealing adequately with the various problems of timekeeping: (1) the lunisolar calendar of the Mesopotamians, which added lunar months during years three, five, and eight of eight-year cycles, and (2) the purely solar calendar, devised by the Egyptians. Despite the retention of 30- to 31-day periods that are still termed months, the Western calendar is a solar calendar.

The zodiac bears the imprint of all three means (days, months, and years),of measuring time, but does not correspond precisely with any of them. The astrological year and the solar year, for example, are of equal lengths, but the astrological year begins at the exact moment the Sun enters the sign Aries (the spring equinox) rather than on January 1. Also, the Sun resides in each sign for approximately one month, but neither the lunar months (which vary every year) nor the months of the Western calendar correspond with this residence (the Sun enters each sign between the eighteenth and the twenty-fourth of each month). For these reasons and others, astrologers must use their own calendars, termed ephemerides, to determine the precise positions of the heavenly bodies.

—Aidan A. Kelly

**Sources:**

Colson, F. H. *The Week*. Cambridge: Cambridge University Press, 1926.
Hawkins, Gerald S. *Stonehenge Decoded*. New York: Doubleday, 1965.
Hoyle, Sir Fred. *Stonehenge*. San Francisco: W. H. Freeman, 1976.
Nilsson, Martin P. *Primitive Time-Reckoning: A Study in the Origins and First Development of the Art of Counting Time Among the Primitive and Early Culture Peoples*. Lund, Norway: Gleerup, 1920.
O'Neil, W. M. *Time and the Calendars*. Sydney: Sydney University Press, 1975.
Parise, Frank, ed. *The Book of Calendars*. New York: Facts on File, 1982.
Wilson, P. W. *The Romance of the Calendar*. New York: Norton, 1937.
Wright, Lawrence. *Clockwork Man: The Story of Time, Its Origins, Its Uses, Its Tyranny*. New York: Horizon, 1968.

## Campanus System

A Campanus system of house division (advanced by Giovanni Campano, a thirteenth-century mathematician-astrologer) is generated by equally dividing the prime vertical. By the twentieth century, the system had fallen into disuse, but was partially revived as a result of the advocacy of Dane Rudhyar.

## Campion, Nicholas

Nicholas Campion was born on March 4, 1953, in Bristol England. He was educated at Queens' College, Cambridge (B.A. history, 1974; M.A. 1976) and took post-graduate courses at London University, studying Southeast Asian history at the School of Oriental and African Studies and international relations at the London School of Economics. After graduating he taught history and English and also worked in computing, housing administration, and theatre management.

Campion first became interested in astrology through newspaper sun sign columns around 1961 and had his first professional horoscope cast in 1965 at age 12. He began studying it in 1971 and his interest deepened while an undergraduate at Cambridge when he discovered that astrology was a central part of the medieval university curriculum, yet all the standard history books ignored this fact. He intended to study the history of astrology but realized that in order to do this he should study the subject in depth as well. As a result he worked as an astrological consultant (1977–84) and developed a considerable career as a teacher of astrology (1980–84 at the Camden Institute in London) and writer (he is the author of a number of popular works), alongside his scholarship in the history of astrology. His background in history and politics also enabled him to develop a second critical speciality in the astrology of history—mundane astrology. His collaboration with Michael Baigent and Charles Harvey resulted in *Mundane Astrology*, the authoritative work on the subject, published in 1984.

In 1997 Campion launched *Culture and Cosmos*, the first ever peer-reviewed journal on the history of astrology and in 2000 he began to devise and teach the first year of the new B.A. degree in astrological studies at Kepler College, near Seattle, on the history of astrology (with Demetra George, Lee Lehman and Rob Hand). Separately, in 1998, Campion began doctoral research in the Study of Religions department at Bath Spa University College in England on "the extent and nature of contemporary belief in astrology." A year later he initiated negotiations between the College and the Sophia Trust, leading to the creation of the Centre for the Study of Cultural Astronomy and Astrology, teaching (with Michael York and Patrick Curry) the first ever M.A. in the subject (from October 2002).

In 1992 Campion was awarded the Marc Edmund Jones Award for scholarly and innovative work. This was followed in 1994 by the Prix Georges Antares, in 1999 by the Spica Award for professional achievement, and in 2002 by the Marion D. March Regulus Award for Professional Image and the Charles Harvey Award for Exceptional Service to Astrology. He was president of the Astrological Lodge twice, from 1985–88 and in 1992 (and was editor of the Lodge's quarterly magazine, 1992–94), and of the Astrological Association 1994–99.

Campion's attitude to astrology remains pragmatic and he is concerned more with whether it produces results in any given situation or not, rather than whether it has a physical mechanism or a metaphysical reality, or can be demonstrated to have a universal validity. His fascination for it is based mainly on the fact that it is a contemporary cultural phenomenon, a way of looking at the world that predates modern science, Greek philosophy and Judea-Christian religion.

**Sources:**

Baigent, Michael, Nicholas Campion, and Charles Harvey. *Mundane Astrology*. Wellingborough, Northamptonshire, UK: Aquarian Press, 1984.

Campion, Nicholas. *The Book of World Horoscopes*. Wellingborough, UK: Aquarian Press, 1988.

———. *The Great Year: Astrology, Millenarianism, and History in the Western Tradition*. London: Arkana, 1994.

———. *Nick Campion's Online Astrology Resource*. www.nickcampion.com.

## CANCER

Cancer (Latin for "crab"), the fourth sign of the zodiac, is a cardinal water sign. It is a negative (in the value-neutral sense of being negatively charged), feminine sign ruled by the Moon. Its symbol is the crab, and its glyph is said to represent the two claws of a crab. A moody sign, Cancer is the source of the term "crabby." Cancer is associated with the breasts and the stomach, and people with a Cancer sun sign are prone to digestion and weight problems. The key phrase for Cancer is *I feel*.

Cancer, like many of the other signs of the zodiac, does not have a developed mythology. During the second labor of Hercules (it might be better termed the second feat or test), while he was struggling against the many-headed hydra, a giant crab bit him on the heel to create a diversion. Hercules, however, crushed it underfoot. This crab, Carcinus (Greek for "crayfish"), was an ally of Hera, queen mother of the gods, who opposed Hercules. The crab was rewarded for sacrificing loyalty when Hera promoted it to distinction as the constellation Cancer. The sign Cancer is often compared with a turtle (the symbol for Cancer in the Babylonian zodiac), and a rich source of symbolic associations for Cancer can be found in the image of the turtle, another shoreline dweller.

Cancerians are best known for their attachment to home and, like the turtle, would be happy to carry their house everywhere (if only they could!). Although homebodies, they enjoy travel if they know they have a secure home to which they can always return. Like Carcinus, they are strongly attached to their mother (or to the more nurturing parent) and tend to be nurturing parents themselves. They are highly sensitive individuals who are easily "crushed," which is why they have developed an emotional "shell" within which they can retreat. They are moodier than any of the other signs of the zodiac, and food represents emotional security to them. Like all water signs, they regard emotions as more real than any other aspect of life.

The sign that the Sun was in at birth is usually the single most important influence on a native's personality. Thus, when people say they are a certain sign, they are almost always referring to their sun sign. There is a wealth of information available on the characteristics of the zodiacal signs—so much that one book would not be able to contain it all. Sun-sign astrology, which is the kind of astrology found in newspaper columns and popular magazines, has the advantage of simplicity. But this simplicity is purchased at the price of ignoring other astrological influences, such as one's Moon sign, rising sign, etc. These other influences can substantially modify a person's basic sun sign traits. As a consequence, it is the rare individual who is completely typical of her or his sign. The reader should bear this caveat in mind when perusing the following series of sun sign interpretations.

One traditional way in which astrologers condense information is by summarizing sign and planet traits in lists of words and short phrases called keywords or key phrases. The following Cancer key words are drawn from Manly P. Hall's *Astrological Keywords:*

> *Emotional key words:* "Artistic and dreamy, maternal, kindhearted, romantic, domestic, impressionable, psychic, imaginative, serene, intuitive, restless, despondent, sometimes lazy and self-indulgent."
>
> *Mental key words:* "Versatile, self-sacrificing, receptive, expresses great veneration for ancestry and precedent, thorough, persevering, cautious, reserved, brooding."

At present, there are various astrology report programs that contain interpretations of each of the 12 sun signs. A selection of these for Sun in Cancer has been excerpted below:

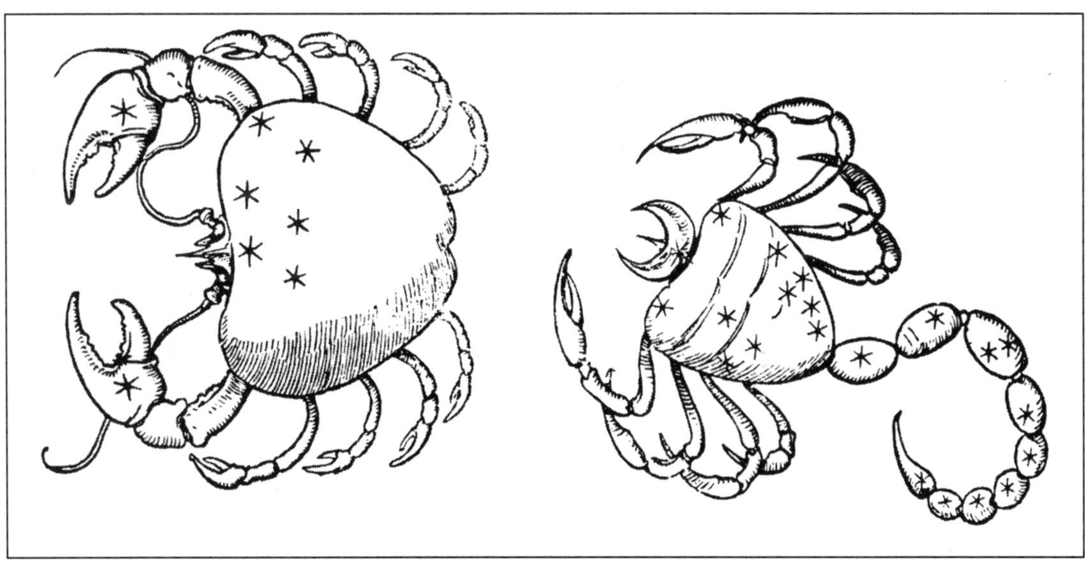

**Woodcuts of the zodiacal signs Cancer and Scorpio, from a late fifteenth-century astrological text.** ***Reproduced by permission of Fortean Picture Library.***

Very emotional and sensitive, you have an intuitive understanding of the "vibes" around you. You tend to be quite generous, giving, loving and caring, but only when your own needs for emotional support, love and security have been met. If they are not met, you tend to withdraw into yourself and become very insecure and selfish. Your home and family (especially your mother or the person who played that role for you early on) represent security for you and thus assume a larger-than-life importance. Very sentimental, you have vivid and long-enduring memories of the past. No matter how well adjusted you are, you will always need a secret quiet place of your own in order to feel at peace. Feeding others can give you great pleasure; you would enjoy being part of a large family. (From "Professional Natal Report." Courtesy of Astrolabe [http://www.alabe.com].)

You have powerful emotional attachments to the past, your family, your childhood, those places you associate with safety and security and your beginnings. Maintaining a connection with your roots and heritage and keeping family bonds strong are very important to you. Loyal, devoted, and sentimental, you tend to cling to whatever is dear to you, be it person, familiar place, or cherished possession.

You are sympathetic, nurturing, supportive, and very sensitive to the emotional needs of other people. You like to be needed, to care for others, and you often worry about the people you love. You have a very strong need for a sense of belonging and acceptance, and you center much of your life around your home. You are more concerned about people and their feelings than with power, achievement, or position in society. Kindness, consideration, and tenderness impress you more than any sort of honor the world can bestow.

You are primarily emotional and your views are often dominated by your feelings and by your own personal, subjective experiences, rather than reason, logic, or abstract principles. It is difficult for you to judge situations in a fair, objective manner for your personal sympathies and loyalties usually enter in. You take things very personally, and sometimes build a wall around yourself to protect yourself from pain and rejection. You feel rather shy and vulnerable at heart. You also tend to be moody, experiencing frequent emotional ups and downs. You need to have a place and time in your life to withdraw, introspect, dream, and replenish yourself; otherwise you become cranky and unhappy with those around you.

You function in an instinctive, nonrational manner and like to immerse yourself in creative activities where you can express your feelings, imagination, and instincts. You often love to cook, since it can be both creative and a way to nurture and nourish others. You also have a great affinity for music, because it evokes and communicates feelings that may be difficult or impossible to put into words.

Your compassion, sensitivity, and imagination are your strong points. Your faults include an inability to release the past and go forward, clannishness and prejudice, and a tendency to be self-pitying when you meet hardships in life. (From "Merlin," by Gina Ronco and Agnes Nightingale. Courtesy of Cosmic Patterns [http://cosmic.patterns.com].)

Opening the inner eye, mapping the topography of consciousness, learning to express compassion —these are Cancer's evolutionary aims. To assist in that work, Cosmic Intelligence has cranked up the volume on the Crab's ability to feel. No other sign is so sensitive—nor so vulnerable. A certain amount of self-defense is appropriate here; after all, this world isn't exactly the Garden of Eden. Trouble is, legitimate self-defense can degenerate into shyness or a fear of making changes. You really do care about the hurts that other beings suffer. That's good news. You also have an instinctive ability to soothe those hurts, homing in on the source of the pain. More good news. The bad news is that you could choose to remain forever protected within the safe (and invisible!) role of the Healer, the Counselor, or the Wise One.

With the Sun in Cancer, you feed your solar vitality by finding a role in the world in which you address the hurt in the lives of other beings. You become a nurturer or a healer of some sort. You also need to make sure that you have enough real intimacy and quiet, private time to "nurture the nurturer"—yourself, in other words.

Those methods strengthen your sense of identity. They trigger higher states of awareness in you. If you don't express your soothing wound-

> binding instincts, all the glories of the world would leave you feeling like an imposter in your own life. And without quiet time and naked intimate honesty, you'll quickly burn out on playing the role of everyone's psychotherapist.
>
> Like the crab, you're a vulnerable creature who's evolved a shell. That's fine and necessary. But again like the crab, you must eventually shed your shell and grow a larger, more inclusive one, or you'll be awfully cramped. (From "The Sky Within," by Steven Forrest. Courtesy of Matrix Software [http://thenewage.com] and Steven Forrest [http://www.stevenforrest.com].)

Among its several natal programs, Matrix Software created a unique report based on the published works of the early twentieth-century astrologer Grant Lewi (1901–1952). Lewi's highly original delineations were recognized as creative and insightful by his contemporaries. One measure of the appeal of his work is that his books *Astrology for the Millions* and *Heaven Knows What* are still in print. The following is excerpted from the report program "Heaven Knows What":

> We the people of the United States, in order to form a more perfect union, establish justice, insure domestic tranquillity, provide for the common defense, promote the general welfare, and secure the blessings of liberty for ourselves and our posterity, do ordain and establish this Constitution for the United States of America. (*Preamble to the Constitution of the United States, which as a nation was born in Cancer, July 4, 1776.*)
>
> The defensive, protective instincts dominate Cancer, whose life aims primarily at security, material and domestic. Capable of great self-sufficiency, or of being a clinging vine (male or female), the Cancer branch will take the turn as indicated by the roots, which must always be in secure soil. If independence serves security, Cancer will be independent; if security depends on another, Cancer will cling. If security requires taking a chance, Cancer will take a chance—generally, if possible, with someone else's money, and once he has put his capital or someone else's into a venture, he watches it like a hawk. His sense of responsibility toward another's money, security, etc., is as deep as if they were his own; he pays his debts and expects others to do the same. It was Coolidge, Cancer President, whose solution to the war debts was of naive simplicity: "They hired the money, didn't they?" It is this simple, direct possessiveness toward what rightfully belongs to him that makes Cancer outstandingly successful in business, where he makes his fortune buying and selling, rather than in Wall Street. Cancer will gamble when he has a nest egg, not before, and then as a game rather than as a means of livelihood.
>
> With livelihood (security), Cancer takes no chances, either in getting it or keeping it. It is therefore tops as a home-making sign; the maternal-paternal instinct is powerful; and the Cancer, male or female, will

> go to great lengths to protect, defend and improve his home, mate and children. If Cancer remains unmarried, it is because protectiveness has turned somehow into fear or selfishness; or because he feels that in some way his security is best served alone. Cancer protects himself, as well as his possessions, and may protect himself from the chances of emotional hurt by withdrawing into himself and making his security there, alone. This is a pitiable sight, because Cancer really needs a home and should have children, and few persons give the effect of incompleteness more than the introverted Cancerian who has no one to lavish his protectiveness on but himself. For in its complete development, the Cancer protectiveness becomes encompassing love that fills all its world, and warms and comforts those who are lucky enough to live in the sphere of its radiations. (Courtesy of Matrix Software [http://thenewage.com].)

The following excerpt comes not from a natal report program, but from David Cochrane's 2002 book, *Astrology for the 21st Century*. Based on lessons for astrology students, it approaches the signs of the zodiac from a somewhat different perspective than the other short delineations cited here:

> The strongest attributes of Cancer that I have noticed is very strong attachment to people and things that they are familiar with, and having their feelings hurt by loved ones. Cancer depends on close friends and family for the support and love they give, although they rarely discuss it. These views of Cancer agree closely with the findings of most astrologers. I have also observed that Cancer is easily prone to feelings of jealousy if it feels excluded from the inner circle of closeness, and sometimes is suspicious that it is being pushed away or kept out of something when this is not the case. Cancer is also inclined to be careful about spending money, and is usually aware of the exact balance in the bank account, and sometimes will go to great lengths to ensure prosperity and financial strength; money is security and protects the family, and Cancer tends not to trust the outer world to provide in the future. Cancer's concern for financial security appears to be a symptom of its tendency to be emotionally attached and bonded to close friends and family, and a fear of losing the closeness from an uncaring outer world. (Courtesy of Cosmic Patterns [http://cosmic.patterns.com] and David Cochrane [kepler@astrosoftware.com].)

A number of specialized report programs have been developed that offer useful supplements to the generic delineations of general reports. The following sun-sign interpretation has been drawn from a program written by Gloria Star (originally part of her book *Astrology: Woman to Woman*) that generates a specialized report for women:

> With your Sun in Cancer you can radiate a kind of comfort and care which comes from the core of your being. You thrive most when you're taking part in nourishing—whether you're tending your garden, teach-

> ing others, safeguarding children or fostering growth in a company. You may express strong sentimentality due to your attachment to the past, and can be especially tenacious with situations, people and your goals. Emotional sensitivity is simply a part of your essence, although your protective shell can fool people.
>
> Even when you're expressing your assertiveness and will, your emotional sensitivity acts as a filter. You innately know that expressing your masculine side has nothing do with acting like a man, but that, instead, you can assert yourself and enjoy the edge that being a woman confers. Your projection of the masculine has a feminine quality—Cancer is a feminine water sign! Before you can readily assert yourself, you must "get a feeling" for the person or situation; it's almost as though you turn inward before you turn outward. It may be difficult for you to stand up to boisterous, power-hungry individuals, and your shields are likely to go up when you're confronted with circumstances that seem to assault your vulnerability. However, once you're more at home with a situation, your sensitivity will help you navigate through it more gracefully than some of those rowdy types of individuals. You appreciate sensitive men, although you may attract men who need to be mothered. As you've discovered, there are many ways to nurture.... However, you may also think you need a man to protect you. When you step back and look at it, who is protecting whom? Your drive to accomplish recognition may be stimulated by your need to create the security you need for yourself and your family, and once you have children, they may take first priority.
>
> Regardless of your priorities, you will feel successful only when you've created a real sense of security with your Sun in Cancer. Defining this security is a very personal thing, and you must be happy with your own definition. Your work, your roles within your family, and your creativity all depend upon your sensitivity in this regard, since when you're insecure, you hang on tenaciously to everybody and everything. But when you're feeling stabilized, you don't even over-water the plants! (From "Woman to Woman," by Gloria Star. Courtesy of Matrix Software [http://thenewage.com] and Gloria Star [glostar@aol.com].)

Responding to the revival of interest in pre-twentieth-century astrology, J. Lee Lehman developed a report program embodying the interpretive approach of traditional astrology. The following is excerpted from her book *Classical Astrology for Modern Living* and her computer program "Classical Report":

> You are inconstant, easily changing your purpose, and sensitive to changes of Moon phase. You are innocent, cheerful, libidinous, and a lover of recreations like music, dancing, sports and games. If stressed, you suffer from poor digestion, and you have a tendency to edema, or water retention.
>
> You are a Water Sign, which means that you are "cold" and "wet." The "wet" component means, among other things, that you blur distinc-

tions, and that you are more swayed by passion than by intellectual argument. At your worst, you see too many connections, becoming lost in conspiracies. At your best, you spot the connection that everyone else missed. You are perceived as being "cold," which in your case simply means you may not be quickly reacting on a surface level. In the modern parlance, it fits better with "cold and dry" than with simply "cold." However, a "cold" type is basically lethargic, or slow to react. Here we have an interesting apparent contradiction: your emotions run deep, but that doesn't mean you're talking about them all the time! The quiet quality of "cold" may mislead others about what you're feeling. The "problem" with "cold" is that it makes it hard for you to forget slights. Because you don't tend to lash out immediately, it's hard for you not to allow your anger to build up.

The sign of Cancer is called a Cardinal sign in astrology, which means that you are better at starting new things than on finishing them. Laboring overlong at any task is not your strong suit. (Courtesy of J. Lee Lehman, Ph.D., copyright 1998 [http://www.leelehman.com].)

Readers interested in examining interpretations for their Chinese astrological sign should refer to the relevant entry. A guide for determining one's sign in the Chinese system is provided in the entry on the Chinese zodiac.

**Sources:**

Cochrane, David. *Astrology for the 21st Century*. Gainesville, FL: Cosmic Patterns, 2002.

Forrest, Steven. *The Inner Sky: How to Make Wiser Choices for a More Fulfilling Life*. 4th ed. San Diego: ACS Publications, 1989.

Green, Landis Knight. *The Astrologer's Manual: Modern Insights into an Ancient Art*. Sebastopol, CA: CRCS Publications, 1975.

Hall, Manly P. *Astrological Keywords*. New York, Philosophical Library, 1958. Reprint, Savage, MD: Littlefield Adams Quality Paperbacks, 1975.

Lehman, J. Lee. *Classical Astrology for Modern Living: From Ptolemy to Psychology & Back Again*. Atglen, PA: Whitford Press, 1996.

Lewi, Grant. *Astrology for the Millions*. 5th rev. ed. St. Paul, MN: Llewellyn, 1978.

———. *Heaven Knows What*. St. Paul, MN: Llewellyn, 1969.

———. *Astrology & Your Child: A Handbook for Parents*. St. Paul, MN: Llewellyn, 2001.

Star, Gloria. *Astrology: Woman to Woman*. St. Paul, MN: Llewellyn, 1999.

## Capricorn

Capricorn, the tenth sign of the zodiac, is a cardinal earth sign. It is a negative (in the value-neutral sense of being negatively charged), feminine sign ruled by the planet Saturn. Its symbol is a goat with a fish tail, and its glyph is said to reflect this symbol. It takes its name from the Latin *Capricornus*, which means "goat horn." Capricorn is associated with the bones and especially with the knees, and individuals with a Capricorn sun sign are susceptible to bone and joint problems, particularly knee problems. The key phrase for Capricorn is "I use."

**A sixteenth-century woodcut of the constellation Capricorn the goat.** ***Reproduced by permission of Fortean Picture Library.***

Capricorn has a confused association with two distinct mythological figures. Aegipan, son of Zeus and the nymph Aex, assisted Hermes with the recovery of Zeus's sinews from Typhon and then transformed himself into a goat-fish in order to escape. In gratitude, Zeus is said to have turned him into the constellation Capricorn. A more complex mythological association is the goat who suckled the newborn Zeus—usually said to be owned by the nymph Amalthea, though in other versions identified as her—and was later transformed into the star Capella. Zeus broke off the horn of the goat and gave it to Amalthea, promising her that she would be able to obtain anything she wished from the horn. This is the origin of the famous cornucopia, or horn of plenty. It was later given to the river god Achelous, who used it to replace his broken horn. Hence, Achelous became, in a sense, a blended goat and marine creature, the very image of Capricorn.

Of all the signs of the zodiac, Capricorn has the most distant relationship with its mythology. Through its association with big business, Capricorn has a certain natural connection with wealth, but it is wealth gained through work and wisdom rather than the "instant" wealth of the horn of plenty. Like the mountain goat, Capricorn's sometime symbol, Capricorns strive to climb to the top of mountains, but in a practical, cautious, self-sufficient, step-by-step manner. Capricorns are known as planners and organizers, capable of infinite patience. They tend to be reserved, conservative, sober, and highly motivated. Typically, they view pleasure-seeking as an idle waste of time. Capricorns can be intensely loyal and will go out of their way to repay a kindness. Few astrologers have pointed out that this sign's fish tail (indicating water, the symbol of emotion) indicates that there is a highly sensitive side to Capricorns, which is hidden underneath their reserved exterior.

The sign that the Sun was in at birth is usually the single most important influence on a native's personality. Thus, when people say they are a certain sign, they are almost always referring to their sun sign. There is a wealth of information available on the characteristics of the zodiacal signs—so much that one book would not be able to contain it all. Sun-sign astrology, which is the kind of astrology found in newspaper columns and popular magazines, has the advantage of simplicity. But this simplicity is purchased at the price of ignoring other astrological influences, such as one's Moon sign, rising sign, etc. These other influences can substantially modify a person's basic sun sign traits. As a consequence, it is the rare individual who is completely typical of her or his sign. The reader should bear this caveat in mind when perusing the following series of sun sign interpretations.

One traditional way in which astrologers condense information is by summarizing sign and planet traits in lists of words and short phrases called keywords or key phrases. The following Capricorn key words are drawn from Manly P. Hall's *Astrological Keywords:*

> *Emotional key words:* "Inhibited, feelings are often turned upon native himself resulting in self-pity, unforgiving, cold, irritable, timid in action, the mind rules the heart too completely."
>
> *Mental key words:* "Powerful, concentrative, laborious, forceful, cautious, economical, conservative, thrifty, scrupulous, trustworthy, detailed thinkers, fatalistic, stubborn, domineering, good friends and bad enemies, brooding, egotistic."

At present, there are various astrology report programs that contain interpretations of each of the 12 sun signs. A selection of these for Sun in Capricorn has been excerpted below:

> Extremely serious and mature, you are capable of accepting responsibilities and do so willingly. Others expect you to be dutiful as a matter of course. You may get angry when people are rewarded after not having worked nearly as hard as you have. Goal-oriented and an achiever, you are justifiably proud of the tangible results of your efforts. You are not a fast worker, but you are thorough, and you are known for being unusually persistent, tireless and tenacious in reaching your goals. When you're working, you tend to have a kind of tunnel vision that allows you to block out extraneous matters that would distract others. Your power to concentrate totally on the matter at hand enables you to be practical and efficient at managing and structuring complex, ongoing

projects. (From "Professional Natal Report." Courtesy of Astrolabe [http://www.alabe.com].)

Serious, disciplined, and quietly ambitious, you are driven to prove yourself and to achieve material accomplishments and success. Your work, your position in the world, and your contributions to society are very important to you. You will persevere through enormous hardship and frustration in order to reach a goal you have set for yourself, and you often sacrifice much in the area of personal relationships and home life in order to do so.

You have a thoughtful, quiet, and self-contained disposition and do not readily show your inner feelings and needs. You seem to be always in control, capable, efficient, and strong. You are often the person in the family or group who is given more responsibility (and more work) than the others. You are highly conscientious and even as a child you possessed great maturity, soberness, and worldly wisdom.

You are basically a pragmatic realist, and though you may have all sorts of dreams, ideals and colorful theories, you feel that the ultimate test of a concept is its practical usefulness. You have an innate shrewdness and business sense, and there is a bit of the cynic in you as well.

You are clear-headed, detached and objective, and are not swayed by emotional dramatics. Often you are authoritarian—strictly fair, but without mercy. You have a great respect for tradition and even if you do not agree with certain laws, you will abide by them or work to change them, but never flagrantly disregard them. Careful and conservative, you play by the rules.

You are subtle, understated, quiet, deep, not easy to know intimately, and never superficial. You are a modest person and sometimes overly self-critical. Giving yourself (and others) permission to feel, to play, to be spontaneous and silly, and to be weak and vulnerable sometimes, isn't easy for you.

Your strong points are your depth and thoroughness, patience, tenacity, and faithfulness. Your faults are a tendency to be rigid and inflexible, and too serious. (From "Merlin," by Gina Ronco and Agnes Nightingale. Courtesy of Cosmic Patterns [http://cosmic.patterns.com].)

Tell the truth about Capricorn and you start sounding like a voice out of the Boy Scout Handbook. Here are the key concepts: integrity, character, morality, a sense of personal honor. Those are the Sea-Goat's evolutionary themes. They all boil down to the capacity of will to dominate every other aspect of our natures, including emotion.

The Capricornian part of you needs to begin by asking itself one critical question: In the part of my life touched by the Sea-Goat, what is the highest truth I know? The rest is simple … at least simple to understand. Just live it. Keep a stiff upper lip, and do what's right. But be careful. There's nothing wrong with expressing feelings as long as they're not doing your decision-making for you. If you're tempted to do something wicked, don't be afraid to mention it. Otherwise, half the world will think you're a saint while the other half thinks you're a pompous ass. And neither half will get within a light-year of your human heart.

With your Sun in Capricorn, you feed your elemental vitality through one all-consuming activity: the accomplishment of Great Works. They may be public—like building a career that reflects the best of what you are—or they may be private, like quietly doing what's right for yourself regardless of social or practical pressures.

Capricorn is the sign of the Hermit, and accordingly, there is a theme of solitude in your life. That doesn't mean loneliness. The Sea-goat's solitude has more to do with self-sufficiency and privacy. It's certainly healthy for you to love; it's neediness on your part that leads inevitably toward frustrating emotional isolation. You're a survivor, an endurer. Those are fine qualities, and when life is hard, you'll shine. Careful you don't use them inappropriately: when you're sad or frightened, express it. Otherwise, you put yourself in pointless emotional exile. (From "The Sky Within," by Steven Forrest. Courtesy of Matrix Software [http://thenewage.com]) and Steven Forrest [http://www.stevenforrest.com].)

Among its several natal programs, Matrix Software created a unique report based on the published works of the early-twentieth-century astrologer Grant Lewi (1901–1952). Lewi's highly original delineations were recognized as creative and insightful by his contemporaries. One measure of the appeal of his work is that his books *Astrology for the Millions* and *Heaven Knows What* are still in print. The following is excerpted from the report program "Heaven Knows What":

"Let's look at the record." (*Al Smith, born in Capricorn, December 30, 1873*).

"Early to bed and early to rise makes a man healthy, wealthy, and wise." (*Benjamin Franklin, born in Capricorn, January 17, 1706.*)

"National debt, if it is not excessive, will be to us a national blessing." (*Alexander Hamilton, born in Capricorn, January 11, 1757.*)

Self-preservation aggressively carried into ambition and aspiration is the key to Capricorn activity. Not content with keeping body and soul together, Capricorn must amount to something, must have some accomplishment to point to, some property to take care of, some obligation to fulfill. His mind is subtly balanced between defense and attack; he will rarely risk either, but will pyramid his life by stepping from one to the other. Since he will never voluntarily step backward, he first shoves his security a little above his ambition, and then his ambition a little ahead of his security, till finally he is top of the heap and has taken no risks at all. He is worldly and careful; selfish, but capable of

> great devotion if he thinks it is merited; a stickler for the proprieties. He drives a hard bargain, but not an unjust one, and he asks no mercy from anyone. He has plenty of suspicion, and figures that anyone who can "put one over" on him has earned what he gets.
>
> Not the most ardent of signs in personal relations, Capricorn's love is still a much-to-be-desired thing, stable and steady, able to put up with a good deal for the sake of loyalty if not indeed for affection. He will rarely marry beneath his station, and frequently marries above it. He understands "Thee shouldst marry for love, but thou canst just as well love where there is money." He is an excellent executive and will not long remain subordinate. He rules by instinct and sometimes makes those he rules quite angry. He has little interest in seeing their point of view or answering their questions, and believes that "orders is orders": he took 'em once, and now it's someone else's turn.
>
> When the main chance requires it, Capricorn can be mild and meek as a lamb, but he'll snap off the foreman's job if he gets a chance. Once arrived, however, he can be lavishly charitable. He loves the sense of importance it gives him, the feeling that he has made the world give to him, and now he can afford to give something back to it. Underlying all his virtues and faults is the primary instinct to vindicate himself with power, to preserve himself materially in the highest structure he can build; and if some affliction in the horoscope doesn't undermine his judgment (which it often does) and cause him to overplay his hand at some critical point, he generally emerges with the world or some considerable portion of it at his feet. (Courtesy of Matrix Software [http://thenewage.com].)

The following excerpt comes not from a natal report program, but from David Cochrane's recent book, *Astrology for the 21st Century*. Based on lessons for astrology students, it approaches the signs of the zodiac from a somewhat different perspective than the other aforementioned short delineations:

> The image of the mountain goat steadily climbing to the top is a common image of Capricorn. Capricorn gives the ability to develop a plan and carefully execute it. Capricorn is serious and sometimes humorless. Capricorn is mature and responsible. Like most astrologers, I have found these descriptions of Capricorn to be accurate.
>
> In searching for a specific trait that might be central to the Capricorn's personality, I have one speculative idea: mental and emotional detachment. The most consistent feature of Capricorn seems to be its ability to look at everything objectively, as if through the lens of a camera, rather than colored by one's personal tastes and interests. The objectivity and detachment of Capricorn gives the ability to develop strategies and plans that work. Objectivity and detachment are traits that we associate with older people and accounts for the maturity of Capricorn. Detachment and objectivity require one to emotionally separate one-

> self, which is completely opposite to Scorpio's drive to fully involve itself and bond so strongly that it becomes one with the experience, or Cancer's close attachment to loved ones. Capricorn can be too dry and impersonal. In relationships Capricorn tends to be responsible and loyal, but lacking in deep feelings, and tends not to bond as strongly as most other zodiac signs. (Cosmic Patterns [http://cosmic.patterns.com] and David Cochrane [kepler@astrosoftware.com].)

Many specialized report programs have been developed that offer useful supplements to the generic delineations of general reports. The following sun-sign interpretation has been drawn from a program written by Gloria Star (originally part of her book, *Astrology: Woman to Woman*) that generates a specialized report for women:

> With your Sun in Capricorn you are a woman who needs to be in control of your own life. You've probably taken on responsibilities from a very early age, and may be strongly determined to achieve your goals and realize your aspirations. Your practical approach to life may assure that you're equally at home in the work place or making necessary repairs on your blender. It's easier for you when you can make the rules, or at the very least, enforce them!
>
> You've rarely felt satisfied unless you have a sense of accomplishment. Embracing the drive of your Capricorn Sun is a huge challenge, because once you've set your sights on something, stepping back or stopping your steady progress toward your goal is almost unthinkable. If you learned as a young girl that it was the man who could accomplish absolutely anything in the world, you may have resented that fact because you've always had a yearning to be recognized and respected. And if your relationships have seemed to support that theory, that it's a "man's world," then you may not trust your own sense of who you are. It's a question of learning about the nature of reasonable control. As a woman, you will express control differently from the way a man might. You may not care so much about submission of will. Instead, you may be most interested in asserting your will in a manner which will give you the ability to direct your own life and through which you can positively shape the lives of others.
>
> The influence of your Sun in Capricorn adds a heightened business sense to your personality, and you may love the idea of cultivating a career path. As a teacher, school administrator, business executive, administrative assistant, merchant or accountant you can outdistance the competition. Positions which allow you to be in control will be best, although you can follow orders. You'd just prefer to give them. (From "Woman to Woman," by Gloria Star. Courtesy of Matrix Software [http://thenewage.com] and Gloria Star [glostar@aol.com].)

Responding to the revival of interest in pre-twentieth-century astrology, J. Lee Lehman developed a report program embodying the interpretive approach of traditional astrology. The following is excerpted from her book *Classical Astrology for Modern Living* and her computer program "Classical Report":

> You are timid, inconstant, lecherous, and cruel. You are also just, discriminating, sometimes passionate, and you can be a good conversationalist if you put your mind to it. You are a traditionalist by temperament.
>
> You are Cardinal, which means that you are better at starting new things than on finishing them.
>
> You are an Earth Sign, which means that you are "cold" and "dry." The "dry" component means, among other things, that you see distinctions easily, and that you are more swayed by intellectual argument than by passion. You are perceived as being "cold," an outward appearance of unemotional. In the modern parlance, it fits better with "cold and dry" than with simply "cold." However, a "cold" type is basically lethargic, or slow to react. The "problem" with "cold" is that it makes it hard for you to forget slights. Because you don't tend to lash out immediately, it's hard for you not to allow your anger to build up. Combine this with a tendency, being "dry," to prefer the reasonable approach, and you can end up completely out of touch while your emotions run rampant.
>
> Being a four-footed sign, you have a strong sex drive. This also means that you can be vicious or violent if angered. (Courtesy of J. Lee Lehman, Ph.D., copyright 1998, [http://www.leelehman.com] and J. Lee Lehman [leephd@ix.netcom.com].)

Readers interested in examining interpretations for their Chinese astrological sign should refer to the relevant entry. A guide for determining one's sign in the Chinese system is provided in the entry on the Chinese zodiac.

**Sources:**

Cochrane, David. *Astrology for the 21st Century*. Gainesville, FL: Cosmic Patterns, 2002.

Forrest, Steven. *The Inner Sky: How to Make Wiser Choices for a More Fulfilling Life*. 4th ed. San Diego: ACS Publications, 1989.

Green, Landis Knight. *The Astrologer's Manual: Modern Insights into an Ancient Art*. Sebastopol, CA: CRCS Publications, 1975.

Hall, Manly P. *Astrological Keywords*. New York, Philosophical Library, 1958. Reprint, Savage, MD: Littlefield Adams Quality Paperbacks, 1975.

Lehman, J. Lee. *Classical Astrology for Modern Living: From Ptolemy to Psychology & Back Again*. Atglen, PA: Whitford Press, 1996.

Lewi, Grant. *Astrology for the Millions*. 5th rev. ed. St. Paul, MN: Llewellyn, 1978.

———. *Heaven Knows What*. St. Paul, MN: Llewellyn, 1969.

Star, Gloria. *Astrology: Woman to Woman*. St. Paul, MN: Llewellyn, 1999.

———. *Astrology & Your Child: A Handbook for Parents*. St. Paul, MN: Llewellyn, 2001.

## Caput Draconis

*Caput Draconis* (Latin for "Dragon's Head") is an older term for the north lunar node.

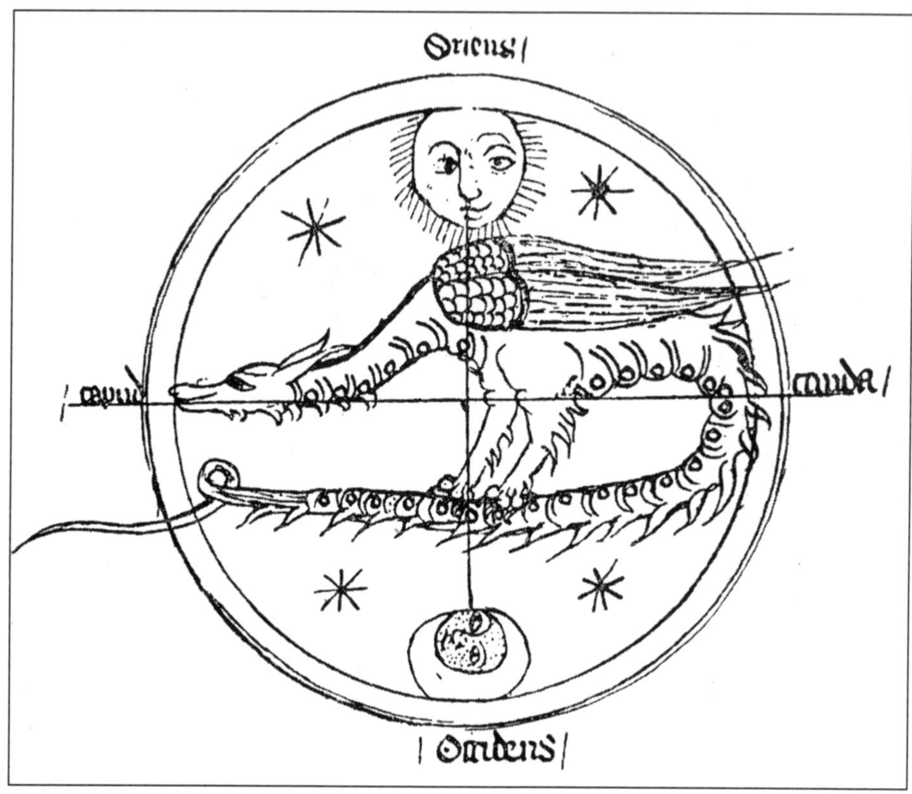


**A drawing of Caput and Cauda across the Ascendent-Descendent line from a fourteenth-century manuscript. *Reproduced by permission of Fortean Picture Library.***

## Cardinal Signs

The 12 signs of the zodiac are subdivided according to three qualities: cardinal, mutable, and fixed. The four cardinal signs (the cardinal quadruplicity or cardinal cross) are Aries, Cancer, Libra, and Capricorn. The entrance of the Sun into each of these four signs begins a new season: Aries, spring; Cancer, summer; Libra, fall; and Capricorn, winter. The identifying trait of the cardinal signs is captured by their various alternative names: initiating, moving, or movable signs. Cardinal signs thus tend to initiate new activities and to act (to "move") on the present situation. Negatively, they are said to lack staying power (a traditional characterization that applies most to Aries and not at all to Capricorn).

The same classification can be found in Vedic Astrology—Chara ("moveable" or cardinal), Dwi-Swabhava ("dual" or mutable), and Sthira ("fixed"). The three Vedic qualities, which are associated with the same signs as their Western parallels, have similar connotations.

**Sources:**

Sakoian, Frances, and Louis S. Acker. *The Astrologer's Handbook*. New York: Harper & Row, 1989.

Sutton, Komilla. *The Essentials of Vedic Astrology*. Bournemouth, UK: Wessex Astrologer, 1999.

## Carter, Charles E. O.

Charles Ernest Owen Carter, born January 31, 1887, in Parkstone, England, was a well-known and highly prolific astrologer of the early twentieth century. He graduated from the University of London and began to practice law in 1913. He also served in the army during the First World War. Carter became deeply involved with astrology in 1910 and met such eminent practitioners as Alan Leo. He started composing practitioner handbooks in the twenties, which were well received by the astrological community. He also wrote many articles that appeared in such periodicals as *The Astrologers' Quarterly*, issued by the London Astrological Lodge.

In later life, Carter came to be considered the dean of British astrologers. He served as first principal of the London Faculty of Astrological Studies, as president of the Astrological Lodge of the Theosophical Society from 1920 to 1952, and as editor of *The Astrologers' Quarterly* from 1926 to 1959. He died on October 4, 1968, in London.

**Sources:**

Carter, Charles E. O. *Astrological Aspects*. 11th ed. London: L. N. Fowler, 1971.

*Astrology of Accidents*. 2d ed. London: Theosophical Publishing House, 1961.

———. *Encyclopedia of Psychological Astrology*. 4th ed. London: Theosophical Publishing House, 1954.

———. *An Introduction to Political Astrology*. London: L. N. Fowler, 1951.

———. *Some Principles of Horoscopic Delineation*. London, 1934.

Holden, James H., and Robert A. Hughes. *Astrological Pioneers of America*. Tempe, AZ: American Federation of Astrologers, 1988.

## Casting the Horoscope

Casting the horoscope, or chart casting, refers to the process of calculating and drawing up an astrological chart. Delineating (interpreting) a chart is a distinct operation from casting a chart. Paralleling this distinction, modern astrology software programs fall into two categories—calculation programs (for casting) and report programs (for interpreting), though most major calculation programs have at least minimal delineation capabilities.

## Cat (Rabbit)

The Cat is one of the 12 animals of the Chinese zodiac. It refers to one of the 12 earthly branches, which are used in Chinese astrology, together with the 10 heavenly stems. Such a branch designates one day every 12 days: the days are named according to a sexagesimal (60) cycle, made of 10 series of 12 branches.

Lucky and hedonistic, this socialite avoids problems; looking for his comfort, he is a refined gentleman. Not very ambitious, not really cut out for fierce struggles, he is, on the other hand, very clever. Suspicious, selfish, careful, easily hedging, and tactically skilled, he proves to be very adaptable: he will always land on his feet. Studious and cultured, the Cat is also a sensitive person.

—Michele Delemme

## Cauda Draconis

*Cauda Draconis* (Latin for "Dragon's Tail") is an older term for the south lunar node.

## Cazimi

Cazimi (an Arabic term meaning "heart of the Sun") refers to a very close conjunction—within 17 minutes—between a planet and the Sun. In contrast to the wider combust conjunction, which supposedly weakened a planet, the cazimi position was traditionally said to strengthen the influence of the planet involved. Partially because modern astrologers do not regard the combust position as having a debilitating effect in a natal chart—hence, making the combust/cazimi distinction one with no practical consequence—this term has dropped out of usage.

## Celestial Coordinates

Celestial (sky) coordinates are most easily understood by comparing them to terrestrial (earthly) coordinates. Terrestrial coordinates allow a location to be specified in terms of degrees of longitude and latitude. Celestial coordinates similarly specify location in terms of two measurements of distance, expressed in terms of degrees of a circle. Rather than measuring degrees along the surface of planet Earth, however, celestial coordinates are measured against the celestial sphere, which is the sphere created by imagining that all of the objects in the sky are stuck against the inside of a gigantic, hollow sphere, with Earth located at the exact center.

There are several systems of celestial coordinates. The *altitude-azimuth system* begins from any given location on the Earth's surface, and uses the horizon, the zenith, and the north-south axis as points of reference. The *equatorial system* uses the celestial equator and the vernal point as its primary reference points. Astronomers most often use this system. The *ecliptic system* uses the ecliptic and the vernal point. Astrologers most often use the ecliptic system.

## Celestial Equator

The celestial equator, also termed the equinoctial, is the terrestrial equator imaginarily projected outward from Earth and onto the background of the stars (i.e., against the backdrop of the celestial sphere). Because of the tilt of the Earth on its axis, the celestial equator intersects the ecliptic at an angle of 23½°. Similarly, the celestial poles are the north and south poles projected outward against the backdrop of the celestial sphere.

## Celestial Sphere

The celestial sphere can be understood by imagining that all the objects in the sky are stuck against the inside of a gigantic hollow sphere, with Earth located at the exact center. The basic notion of the celestial sphere is assumed in various systems for locating celestial bodies in terms of celestial coordinates. Very much like terrestrial coordinates, which involve specifying a location in terms of longitude and latitude, celestial coordinates require two measurements of distance, expressed in terms of degrees of a circle. The *altitude-azimuth system* begins by situating itself at a specific location on the Earth's surface, and uses the horizon, the zenith, and the north-south axis as points of reference. The *equatorial system* uses the celestial equator (Earth's equator extended out into space and projected against the backdrop of the celestial sphere) and the vernal point (where the Sun is located at the point of the spring equinox) as its points of reference. Astronomers most often use the equatorial system. The *ecliptic system* uses the ecliptic (the orbit of Earth around the Sun, projected outward against the celestial sphere) and the vernal point. Astrologers use the ecliptic system.

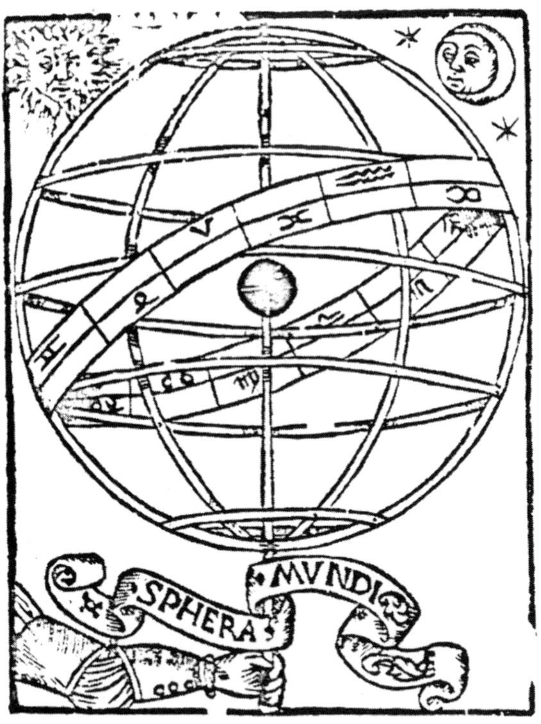


**A diagram of the celestial sphere from *Orontius Fine*, c. 1542. *Reproduced by permission of Fortean Picture Library.***

**Sources:**

Brau, Jean-Louis, Helen Weaver, and Allan Edmands. *Larousse Encyclopedia of Astrology*. New York: New American Library, 1980.

Filbey, John, and Peter Filbey. *The Astrologer's Companion*. Wellingborough, Northamptonshire, UK: Aquarian Press, 1986.

## Centaurs

Centaurs by definition originate in the Kuiper Belt, whose orbits come inside the outer planets. More specifically, a Centaur possesses a perihelion distance greater than the mean orbital distance of Jupiter from the Sun (5.2026 astronomical units [AU]) and a semi-major less than that of Neptune. (Several Centaurs exceed the semi-major axis of Neptune. Recent astrological consensus implies that if the semi-major axis is less than or about that of Pluto—39.537 AU—then the object could still be considered a Centaur). The Kuiper Belt consists of a yet undetermined number of objects made up of frozen gas and dust that orbit in the general vicinity of Pluto and Neptune. Astronomer Gerald Kuiper initially speculated about the existence of the Kuiper Belt in the 1950s.

Loosely known also as the Oort Cloud, a collection of gas and dust known to spawn comets and named for astronomer Jan Oort, the Kuiper Belt may contain thousands of objects. When the objects gain enough mass and become gravitationally perturbed by larger influences such as Neptune and Jupiter, they may be pulled inside the orbital realm of the outer planets. Technically, Pluto and Neptune's moon Triton are Kuiper Belt Objects (KBOs) or Trans-Neptunians (TNOs, not to be confused with the theoretical planets used in cosmobiology). Chiron, now known to be a comet, is a Centaur having its roots in the Kuiper Belt.

To date, the following Centaurs exist: Chiron, Pholus, Nessus, Asbolus, Chariklo, Hylonome, 31824, 32532, 1994TA, $1995SN_{55}$, $1996AR_{20}$, $1996RX_{33}$, $1998QM_{107}$, $1998SG_{35}$, $1998TF_{35}$, $1999HD_{12}$, $1999JV_{127}$ , $1999XX_{143}$, $2000CO_{104}$, $2000EC_{98}$, $2000FZ_{53}$, $2000GM_{137}$, $2000QC_{243}$, $2000SN_{331}$, $2001BL_{41}$, $2001KF_{77}$, $2001SQ_{73}$, $2001XA_{255}$, $2002CA_{249}$, $2002CB_{249}$, $2002DH_{5}$, $2002FY_{36}$, $2002GB_{10}$, and $2002GZ_{32}$. Ultimately, each of these unnumbered objects will receive a minor planet number followed by a name, but only after astronomers are relatively sure of the orbital parameters.

The KBO names refer to the year of discovery, followed by a letter to designate a two-week interval of the year, then another letter indicating order of discovery and, if necessary, a number to add final order clarification. For instance, $1995DW_2$ appeared before astronomical observers in the fourth interval (D = letter 4) of the year 1995, the 23rd object in that interval.

Astrologer Melanie Reinhart speculated that Centaur $1993HA_2$ deserved the name Nessus only to find out that a short time before it had been so named by the discovering astronomer(s). More astrological research will set the stage for appropriate name considerations. Recently $1995DW_2$ was upgraded to minor planet number 10370 and was finally named Hylonome, largely at the suggestion of astrologer Zane Stein and others in communication with Dr. Brian Mardsen of the Minor Planet Center.

Centaur loosely translates to "those who round up Bulls." These half-human, half-horse creatures bore a well-deserved reputation for wildness, lechery, lewdness, wanton ways, and an uncontrollable fondness for wine. Mavericks and sexual profligates in behavior, two notable exceptions to the debased tendencies existed.

The more evolved Centaurs were Chiron, of whom astrologers have become appreciative, and Pholus (pholis means "scale like," as in snake). Pholus maintained a reputation for being more skilled in augury than any of the other Centaurs. Versed in divination and noted for his wisdom, Pholus also kept the sacred wine left in his possession by Dionysus. One day Hercules came to visit and, after a feast of cooked meat (though Pholus ate his raw), he persuaded Pholus to uncork the good wine in honor of his visit. The aroma of the wine filled the air and attracted all the Centaurs. They came armed with trees and objects of destruction, demanding wine. Hercules drove them off with his arrows, killing many, though a good number fled. During this incident, according to some accounts, one arrow in this battle passed through the arm of Elatus and struck Chiron in the knee (thigh/hip). Pholus emerged from his cave to witness the aftermath. Fascinated by the power of the Herculean arrows he picked one up to examine. Excited, he dropped the arrow on his foot and died immediately—like

Chiron, also wounded from an arrow of Hercules. Unlike Chiron, Pholus experienced immediate death and endured no long-term suffering.

Symbolically, this Centaur refers to relinquishing the need for penance concerning an act of wrongdoing. Though the opening of the wine was not a well-thought act, no long-term punishment was required. The concept of euthanasia fits with this Centaur. The act of ending pain and suffering, no matter how it occurs, stands as a Pholus metaphor. This image could suggest the consultation of an oracle for mental and emotional relief. The process of medical intervention for physical relief or even the ending of life falls under the auspice of Pholus. Regardless, the concept of maintaining an attachment to sin and wrongdoing must fall by the wayside.

Silenius, father of Pholus, tutor of Dionysis, a part horse figure that rode an ass, often told drunken stories of far away Utopian cities. Though he generally did not tell the truth, he spoke of two streams meeting near a whirlpool. On one side trees withered and died; on the other side, everything flourished, and people reversed in age until they achieved nonexistence.

Combined with the snake derivation of his name and the metaphorical maelstrom, Pholus represents timelessness. This reversal of time suggests the ability to, within consciousness—altered or otherwise—return to a primal sense of self and restore purity of soul and reclaim innocence. Given that Centaurs at large contain bulls, they herd the beast (within), control negative urges, and bear a responsibility to the symbolic bull's-eye. This marksmanship returns to the concept of original sin, missing the mark, also denoting distance from God. Pholus implies the restoration of innocence, self-forgiveness of sin, release of infatuation with power and destruction, and pure, primal activation of the coiled serpent (Kundalini). Pholus, incidently, along with Asbolus, remain two of the reddest colored objects in the solar system.

Pholus maintains an intrinsic implication of the shedding of skin, a transformation metaphor. The exfoliation stands to signify important points of demarcation within the awareness of one's personal power. This awareness seeks a higher, well-intended use, lest it be self-damaging through unwitting self-destruction. In its worst case, ego posturing, over-embellishment of personal attributes and strength, prevails. In optimum, Pholus notes one's need to help others through similar growth intervals. Given the serpent reference of scales, the methods of homeopathy remain particularly strong as Pholus healing tools. The nature of Pholus possesses the capacity for attack of adversaries, and Pholus seeks at all cost to avoid personal conflict of a negative nature. Pholus would rather retreat, than confront. However, if cornered, Pholus will attack and attack swiftly and potently. Here it is best not to provoke the transformation of another prior to his or her willingness to accept the evolutionary process.

Pholus, in client studies, strongly indicates the effort to reduce or altogether stop consuming alcohol or caffeine. In many cases involving Neptune transits to Pholus and another personal object, especially the Moon, individuals made marked progress in recovering from alcohol misuse or abuse.

Nessus, on the other hand, did not exemplify the state of evolved consciousness of Chiron or Pholus. After the Pholus/Hercules debacle, Nessus fled to the river Evenus and became its ferryman. Nessus was approached by Hercules and his wife,

Deianira, seeking safe passage. Hercules went on his own way while assigning Nessus to carry Deianira across the river. Overcome with lust, Nessus violated Deianira. Hercules turned about to witness the deed and struck Nessus with one of his arrows, poisoned with a concoction created by Chiron. Nessus, mortally wounded, gave his blood and semen to Deianira, assuring her it would guarantee Hercules's faithfulness to her. One day, as Hercules departed for a tournament, Deianira gave him a cloak anointed with Nessus's fluids. When Hercules donned the article, he experienced excruciating pain and suffering, agonizing to his death. He raged through the land destroying everything in his path. He begged to die in dignity on a pyre of oak and olive branches. Elevated to Olympus, he was cared for by Hera, who had at his birth sought to kill him with serpents.

Melanie Reinhart, in her book *To the Edge and Beyond*, notes a Saturn-Pluto relationship with Nessus. Hercules died at the hand of Chiron and his own action of retaliation in defense of the honor of his wife—a Saturn-to-Pluto image. In the Nessus myth clearly emerges sexually transmitted disease (STD), AIDS, and those diseases transmitted by blood, like hepatitis in all its grades. Importantly, the dignity of an AIDS death must be preserved under the influence of Nessus's demise.

Asbolus became the next named Centaur. A seer, he foretold of the massacre of the Centaurs in the battle against the Lapiths during the wedding of Pirithous. Asbolus attempted in vain to dissuade his colleagues not to engage in the battle.

Like Pholus, a peaceful effort extends into the implications of Asbolus. His attempts to prevent conflict and save lives reflect a somewhat noble concern for fellow Centaurs (humans). Possibly a Centaur of negotiation, arbitration, and conflict resolution, Asbolus deserves initial recognition as a peacemaker.

The North Node and Perihelion points of Asbolus render the following possibilities: the need for self-realization because of deeds done; desire for reputation and acclaim. Negative: Reckless regard for reputation, lack of integrity, impulse driven without sense of consequence; inability to take compliments. Positive: impeccability in action; known as solid and consistent; accepting of praise with humility.

Chariklo, the next named Centaur, was not a Centaur at all but the mermaid wife of Chiron. Together they had a son, Karystos, of whom little is written. Also they had two daughters, Melanippe (black mare, also called Euippe, or good mare) and Endeis or Thetis, depending upon which mythological family tree is consulted. Melanippe had an illegal love affair with Poseidon and elected to no longer live among mortals as a consequence. Like her father, she appealed to the gods and was set into the night sky as a star.

Chariklo shows up in very few references of note. Once she attended Athene (Pallas Athena) with her bath when Teiresias, who hunted with his dogs, happened upon them. Teiresias saw the breasts and legs of Athene. The goddess placed her hands over the young man's eyes and blinded him. Chariklo, full of remorse, appealed to Athene to show mercy. Athene declared Teiresias a prophet and cleansed his ears so he could hear and understand the voices of the birds. She also gave him a staff of cornel wood so he could walk as if he had sight.

Chariklo, like Pholus and Asbolus, demonstrated compassion and a love of fairness and peacefulness. She appealed to her goddess with goodness, mercy, and fairness as tools. The justness or equality of punishment to transgression seeks balance in her delineation.

The orbital contacts (Node and Perihelion) for Chariklo offer the following: the need for definition between intimacy and personal space; seeking definition of human interaction and boundaries; desire to help without codependent interference. Negative: invasive, manipulative, and solicitous without intent to respond, aloof. Positive: a shoulder to cry upon, well-defined relating agenda, counselor of independence vs. intimacy.

Hylonome, one of the rare female centaurs, was the wife of the Centaur Cyllarus. Cyllarus was killed by a javelin thrown by an unknown warrior at the debacle of the wedding of Pirithous. Distraught with her loss, Hylonome thrust herself onto the javelin that killed her husband, thus ending her grief and pain.

Intrinsic in this Centaur is the distinction of ego and self separate from relationship. Value of self as a function of love, relating, or interaction becomes confused in the interest of regaining a clear perception of the value of self.

The processes of ending pain and grief—a consistent Centaur theme—clearly reside here. Zane Stein and his colleagues suggest that their research implies Hylonome to be significant in charts of suicide. This does not imply that transits to or from Hylonome increase the danger of self-destruction. Actually, such patterns seek resolution of what ever causes pain in life because of loss of self-esteem or loss of love. Healing of previous loves no longer present also come to the table of resolution.

The following are key point delineations for the yet-unnamed Centaurs.

31824: Expression of self and ego through word and writing. Positive: excellent communication, articulate, precise. Negative: verbose, boastful, shallow in conversation.

32532: Relational and professional attitudes based upon one another. I am what I am because of my career status or relationship ornament. Positive: balance between relationship and work, money and sexuality. Negative: object oriented, status seeking, mercenary in work ethics, stunned by glamour and beauty of partner.

1994TA: The need to assert one's accomplishments (generally professional) in the interest of recognition. Negative: solicitousness, bragging, indiscriminate flirting. Positive: sense of self-accomplishment, legacy oriented, a mentor.

1995$SN_{55}$: Urge to establish self-value regardless of relationship status. Positive: warm, supportive, nurturing in one-to-one relationship. Negative: needy, self-centered to a fault, showcase relationships.

1996$AR_{20}$: The urge to understand unresolved questions and mysteries through discussion. Positive: highly insightful ability to ask questions. Negative: incessant questioning and banal fixations.

$1996RX_{33}$: A balance of individuality for the purpose of soul fulfillment, regardless of ego. Positive: confident and self-assured in expressing uniqueness and ingenuity. Negative: cranky, weird, contentious, highly rebellious.

$1998QM_{107}$: Balancing emotions and ego as a function of professional status. Positive: giving, nurturing, and sharing to and with coworkers with extraordinary capacities. Negative: demanding, infantile in work relationships, flaunts social status as a result of accomplishments, showcases with past laurels.

$1998SG_{35}$: Need and ability to heal the ego by overcoming criticisms, both self-imposed and external. Positive: clarity, impeccability, and loyalty to personal and emotional needs, praising, complimentary. Negative: critical, judgmental, condemning both of others and self, defaming, blasphemous, solicitous.

$1998TF_{35}$: Sense of value, self-worth, economic freedom with spiritual emphasis. Positive: wealthy eccentric, affluent, humanistic, generous, spiritual involved. Negative: selfish, demanding, greedy. Manipulates with karma or projected spiritual status.

$1999HD_{12}$: Acceptance of whole and pure nurturing. Positive: acceptance of support and responsive to praise. Negative: rejecting of those attempting to help. Constant complaining about the lack of fundamental care in life.

$1999JV_{127}$: Primal sense of self. Developing a healthy self-referential attitude. Positive: confidence in raw talents. Self-assured nurturing instincts. Negative: overly subconscious in motivations. Subjective and projective. Extremely protective.

$1999XX_{143}$: Maintaining a balance of individuality and others within the domestic environment. Positive: feeling accepted by family and close friends. Negative: portraying black sheep image. Isolated and sullen at home. Doing it for family to the extreme.

$2000CO_{104}$: Emotional intensity, passionate creativity, inspirational capacity. Positive: uplifting, stimulating, infinitely artistic and creative. Negative: addicted to emotional drama, emotionally controlling and manipulative.

$2000EC_{98}$: Cosmic picture vs. detail orientation. Abstract logic vs. linear logic. Positive: balanced perspective of overviews combined with essential detail. Negative: Picky, judgmental, cantankerously weird, ungrounded.

$2000FZ_{53}$: Acute relationship awareness. Ability to negotiate relationship conflicts. Positive: clarity in relationship communication. Honest, direct, self-assured in interactions. Negative: clingy, dependent, holds back on communication based upon perceived reactions.

2000GM$_{137}$: Extreme inquisitiveness and cat-like curiosity. Relationship communication clarity. Positive: questioning and open-minded. Negative: overly scrutinizing, specializing in Pandora's box scenarios.

2000QC$_{243}$: Use of complete compassion and forgiveness toward others. Positive: understanding, compassionate, forgiving, tolerant. Negative: full of guilt and shame that is projected onto others.

2000SN$_{331}$: Highly questioning nature. Asks surface-level questions seeking the greatest depth in the answer. Positive: seeking, questioning unafraid of shadows. Negative: diverting, avoiding, asks questions to answer a question.

2001BL$_{41}$: Perceptions of an abundant universe. Positive: generous, available, and sharing. Negative: greedy, hostile regarding work position and money earned. Desperately competitive.

2001KF$_{77}$: Claiming of soul urge. Development of pure confidence and self-assuredness. Positive: strong, inspired, noncompetitive, motivated. Negative: possessive, insecure, ego proclaiming, pouting, fearful.

2001 SQ$_{73}$: Quest for ultimate individuality. Confident in all aspects of self. Positive: iron will and certainty of healthy eccentricity and imaginative ability. Negative: weird just to be contentious. Overbearing ego. Sense of intellectual superiority.

2001XA$_{255}$: Seeking fulfilling nurturing. Receptive to what feeds the spirit. Positive: receptive, integrating, responsive, proactive in the pursuit of emotional, physical needs. Negative: whiny, projects victimization by life, asks for support then rejects it.

2001 XZ$_{255}$: The quest for pure self-expression. Positive: clear, articulate, assertive, confident. Negative: accusatory, meddlesome, laborious in conversation.

2002 CA$_{249}$: Complete, uninhibited self-expression. Positive: innovative, confident, inspired, pleasantly odd. Negative: narcissistic, self-absorbed, strange for shock value.

2002 CB$_{249}$: Integrated spirituality within worldly awareness. Positive: comprehends parts/wholes theory, uses crisis/chaos to the good. Finds upside in all things. Negative: victim consciousness, resentful, critical.

2002DH$_{5}$: Perfection seeking, looking for divine order. Positive: accepting, tolerant, and compassionate. Negative: scrutinizing to a fault, viciously critical, intolerant, mean-spirited practical jokes.

2002FY$_{36}$: Seeking understanding of sacred and profane in balance. Positive: unique blend of linear and abstract minds. Negative: mentally biased and opinionated with no tractability.

2002GO$_{9}$: Need for relational support without reservation. Positive: renders and receives in relationship in healthy balance. Negative: codependent, turns intimate relationships into parent-child scenarios.

2002GB$_{10}$: Balance of emotional/nurturing give and take. Positive: encouraging, nurturing, responsive. Negative: whining, needy, clinging. Emotionally manipulates closeness, then withdraws from it.

2002GZ$_{32}$: Seeking kinship with those of great self-reliance. Positive: confident, giving, and supportive. Strong sense of bond with those of similar spirit. Negative: sullen, withdrawn, but emotionally aggressive.

Many stories about clouds prevail in Centaur mythology. The air again gains significance with these creatures. The scent of wine traveling through the air caused a major Centaur incident, as did words traversing the air. Similarly, myths involving the contamination of water exist. Overall, an environmental impact begins to form in Centaurian symbolism. Can the emphasis of the bull—money, real estate, greed—be tamed? Or will developments, population, and over-building polish off what's left of the purity of earth? Earth's air and water fall to industry and toxins. The ozone collapses, exposing earth to more dangerous radiations from space. The Centaurs declare the need to care for the earth and reverse the effects of toxic contamination.

What about the concern with sexuality, drinking, drugs, and morality? Since 1992, with the discovery of the Centaurs, and the issues of sexuality and morality being raised in that year's U.S. presidential elections, the restoration of values was called to return. A philosophical bent to Centaurs originates in the knowledge of Chiron and Pholus. The Centaurian evolution implies reestablishing clear thinking as a criteria for deciding about personal or moral situations.

Many difficult questions now face humanity. The Centaurs scratch the iceberg of these considerations. Can the animal instincts alive in human nature be controlled? Or should we go capture our own bear? Are we obsessed with the power of weaponry? Can we overcome alcoholism and drug addiction as the Centaurs demand? What about the issue of sexual harassment? Is it out of control or is balance being achieved? And these bodies contribute to our healing of relationship conflicts and physical healing and offer sanction for the difficult process of grieving.

The Centaurs hold the keys of knowledge required to transcend the human struggles. Each individual's Centaur placement works with Jupiter and Neptune (those planets bracketing Centaur orbits) to establish a clear sense of personal morality and choice independent of collective pressures. The prevailing Centaur positions relate the focus of people at large and cause reassessment of beliefs and convictions, whether original beliefs are restored or new ones chosen.

Many questions arise from the depths of space near the origins of the illusive Neptune and probing Pluto. The Centaurs point out the areas of difficulty. And as is known from augury, within the question lies the answer.

—Philip Sedgwick

## CENTILOQUIUM

The Centiloquium refers to a set of 100 astrology aphorisms, or principles, that was traditionally (but mistakenly) attributed to Ptolemy.

# Ceres

The asteroids are small planet-like bodies that orbit the Sun in a belt that lies mostly between Mars and Jupiter. They first dawned on human consciousness in the early 1800s. The first four asteroids to be sighted were given the names of four of the great goddesses of classical antiquity: Ceres (discovered in 1801), Pallas Athene (discovered in 1802), Juno (discovered in 1804), and Vesta (discovered in 1807).

Many more asteroids were soon discovered, so that by the end of the nineteenth century, over 1,000 were known. The first asteroid ephemeris (a table listing planetary positions) was made available to astrologers in 1973 by Eleanor Bach, and it covered only the original four. Today astrologers have computer software developed by Mark Pottenger that tracks the placements of over 9,000.

Among the thousands of asteroids known, Ceres, Pallas, Juno, and Vesta have a special place. While these are not necessarily the largest asteroids, they were the first to be discovered, and as such they have imprinted themselves on human consciousness in a significant way. They also complete the female pantheon of goddesses, rounding out the system of symbols begun in the usual 10 planets. Of the six great goddesses of Olympus, only Aphrodite (Venus) and Artemis (the Moon) are represented in the conventional astrological symbol system. The other four great goddesses of Graeco-Roman mythology—Demeter (Ceres), Athene (Pallas), Hera (Juno), and Hestia (Vesta)—were missing from astrology until they were reinvoked by their discovery in the early 1800s.

Appropriately, the first asteroid to be discovered was named after the Olympian goddess who most exemplifies the mother—the first human being with whom most of us have contact, the first relationship that we encounter in life. Ceres, the mother, deals with all sorts of mother-child issues. Of the four stages in a person's life, she signifies the child.

The glyph or written symbol for Ceres takes the form of a scythe. Besides signifying the goddess of agriculture, this tool for harvesting suggests both the roundness of a breast and the themes of separation and death that run through the legend of Ceres. As the mother, she brings us into life, and, like the Christian Mary who grieves over her crucified son, she also lets us go into death, thus starting another cycle. For this reason, she is associated with the imum coeli (IC) of the horoscope, the very bottom of the day cycle, where, in the system of astrological houses, life begins and ends.

Known to the Greeks as Demeter, Ceres was the goddess of agriculture who worked unceasingly to bring food and nourishment to the people of the earth. One of the great classical myths tells of her daughter Persephone's ravishment and abduction by Pluto, lord of the underworld. Grieving, Ceres wandered over the earth in search of her missing child. In her grief, depression, and anger, she caused a famine, withholding production of all food until her daughter was returned.

Meanwhile, Persephone had eaten pomegranate seeds, a symbol of sexual awareness, thus giving Pluto a claim over her so that she could not be returned permanently to her mother. A compromise was reached whereby Persephone would spend part of each year in the underworld with Pluto caring for the souls of the dead, but each spring she would be reunited with her mother in the upper world as she initiated the dead into the rites of rebirth. For over 2,000 years, this drama was celebrated regularly in ancient Greece as the initiation rites of the Eleusinian mysteries.

Ceres represents the part of our nature that longs to give birth and then to nourish and sustain the new life. She represents the essential bonding, or lack thereof, that occurs between mother and child. She is the impulse not just to nurture, but also to be nurtured by others through the giving and receiving of acceptance and unconditional love.

The story of Ceres and Persephone speaks to the complex mother-child relationship, emphasizing the interplay of closeness and separation, of nurturing, and eventual letting go as the child becomes an adult able to function on her or his own. Once the letting-go is accomplished, the child is free to reestablish the bond in a different key by becoming a friend to the parent and by producing grandchildren.

The Ceres myth also contains the themes of major physical or emotional loss, separation, abandonment, rejection, and estrangement that occur between parents and children, and later in life with other loved ones. One example of this is the anguish we face in cases of divorce or adoption when we need to share our children with their other parent. Ceres symbolizes attachment to whatever we have given birth to or created, and also the agony of losing it. If her myth is one of loss, however, it is also one of return, of death but also of rebirth. Reminding us that loss makes way for new birth, Ceres can teach us the lesson of letting go.

A central part of Ceres bonding is the giving of food as an expression of love. In our early experiences as children, this food and love may be freely given. In other instances, however, it is conditionally awarded, withheld as a form of punishment, pushed upon us, or simply neglected. Then the self-love and self-worth of the child are undermined and underdeveloped, causing a host of psychological problems.

The mythological Ceres withheld food in the midst of her grief and depression. Correspondingly, one typical kind of Ceres wound is an obsessive relationship with food, including the whole range of eating disorders and food-related illnesses. Related to this, there can also be problems with a poor body image.

In her grief, Ceres became immobilized. Thus, another Ceres problem manifests as being plunged into depths of depression or despair, making us incapable of daily functioning, work, and all other forms of productivity. To the extent that depression is associated with incomplete mourning, working through the stages of grief (shock, anger, bargaining, depression, and ultimately acceptance) can help to promote healing in times of loss.

An additional theme comes from Ceres's daughter Persephone being raped by Pluto, her mother's brother. This event points to fears that parents may have in protecting their children from similar harm. Certain Ceres placements in the chart may also point to one's having oneself experienced incest or other sexual abuse as a child.

In a desire to keep their children safe, parents with strong Ceres placements can become overly controlling and restrictive. In order to establish their own identity, their children may then struggle against the parental attachment. This, in turn, can bring up the Ceres theme of loss of the child.

On a transpersonal level, Ceres as the "mother of the world" moves us to care about the homeless and hungry, and also about the destruction of the earth's resources. She urges us to take compassionate action to provide for fundamental human needs, and to care for the body of the earth that supports and sustains us.

Ceres not only gave birth to the living, but in her aspect as Persephone she received the souls of the dead back into her womb to prepare them for rebirth. Thus Ceres can also express as a vocation for either midwifery or hospice work, facilitating the transition from death to life and back again on either the physical or the psychological level.

Ceres embodies the great truth of transformation that from death comes new life. This comes not just from the Persephone part of her story, but also from the nature of food, which always requires the taking of plant or animal life in order to sustain our own lives.

Ceres also teaches the wisdom that over-attachment and possessiveness can eventually bring loss, whereas sharing and letting go lead ultimately to reunion.

—Demetra George

**Sources:**

Dobyns, Zipporah. *Expanding Astrology's Universe*. San Diego: Astro Computing Services, 1983.

Donath, Emma Belle. *Asteroids in the Birth Chart*. Tempe, AZ: American Federation of Astrologers, 1979.

George, Demetra, with Douglas Bloch. *Asteroid Goddesses: The Mythology, Psychology and Astrology of the Reemerging Feminine*. 2d ed. rev. and enl. San Diego: Astro Computing Services, 1990.

———. *Astrology for Yourself: A Workbook for Personal Transformation*. Berkeley, CA: Wingbow Press, 1987.

Lehman, J. Lee. *The Ultimate Asteroid Book*. West Chester, PA: Whitford Press, 1988.

## Chakras and Astrology

The chakras are the seven main energy centers located from the base of the spine to the crown of the head. First described by the Hindu yogis thousands of years ago, the chakra model for understanding human consciousness has survived the test of time and cultural changes. Chakra is the Sanskrit word for "wheel," and each of these seven chakras is said to be a spinning wheel, creating a vortex of subtle life energy. The universal life energy is received by the chakras, transformed, and then distributed to the various levels of human activity associated with each chakra.

The chakras fall into two main categories: personal or lower chakras (1–3) and universal or upper chakras (4–7). There are many yogic practices and meditations for balancing the lower chakras and then raising one's consciousness to the refined energy of the upper, universal chakras.

The basic associations of each of the chakras are as follows: First Chakra, located at the base of the spine—survival and security. Second Chakra, located just above the pubic bone—pleasure and sexuality. Third Chakra, located at the solar plexus—personal power. Fourth Chakra, the heart region—love. Fifth Chakra, at the throat—creative expression. Sixth Chakra, the third-eye at the brow—intuition and inspiration. Seventh Chakra, crown of the head—divine realization.

Astrology and the chakras are two of the most profound and longstanding models for understanding the human experience. It is natural that researchers would seek the correlations between these two systems and much thought has been put forth in this direction. The difficulty of direct correlation stems from the fact that the number of chakras (7) does not readily transpose to the number of planets (ten) or signs (twelve).

C. W. Leadbeater, in his classic book *The Chakras*, cites the seventeenth-century German mystic Gichtel for planetary correspondences. Just using the seven visible planets seems natural for correspondences to the seven chakras. Gichtel's system of correspondences, which are used by Leadbeater, are as follows: First Chakra—The Moon; Second—Mercury; Third—Venus; Fourth—The Sun; Fifth—Mars; Sixth—Jupiter; and Seventh—Saturn. Although a tidy arrangement in terms of number, this system falls short. For example, Venus, the planet of pleasure, is given to Third Chakra of power; and even more unsettling, Saturn, the planet associated with limitation, is given to the seventh chakra of divine rapport beyond limitation.

Ray Grasse, author of *The Waking Dream*, presents a thorough and comprehensive model of planets and signs for each of the chakras. His correspondences are as follows: First—Saturn and its signs Capricorn and Aquarius; Second—Jupiter, with Sagittarius and Pisces; Third—Mars, with Aries and Scorpio; Fourth—Venus, with Taurus and Libra; Fifth—Mercury, with Gemini and Virgo; Sixth—Moon and Sun together with Cancer and Leo; and Seventh—beyond personal, so he does not correlate planets or signs with the crown chakra. Although Grasse's model is impressive in its scope, again there are unsettling correspondences. In the planetary model, the Sun, Moon, Mercury, Venus, and Mars are considered personal planets; Jupiter and Saturn are known as social planets. Grasse associates the social planets with the personal chakras and the personal planets with the transpersonal chakras. Also awkward is that both Grasse and Leadbeater simply ignore the outer planets of Uranus, Neptune, and Pluto.

David Pond, author of *Chakras for Beginners*, presents an alternative understanding. The planets represent concentric rings of consciousness expanding outward on a horizontal plane. The chakras represent layers of consciousness arranged on a vertical plane. Instead of the awkwardness and incompleteness of one-to-one correspondences, a vertical plane allows for an understanding of each planet at each chakra level of consciousness.

Using Mercury as an example, this planet relates to the mind—how we think, gather information, make the information useful, and communicate with others. At the first chakra level, Mercury will be consumed by thoughts concerning security. At the second chakra level, Mercury will dwell on desire for pleasure and memories of previous pleasures. At the third chakra level, Mercury will focus on its current ambitions and struggles for success. At the fourth chakra level, Mercury will pull out of its concerns for self and focus on love. At the fifth chakra level, Mercury aligns with the universal mind and will receive "flashes" of insight. At the sixth chakra level, Mercury quiets its activity and observes life from the witness point of consciousness. At the seventh chakra level, Mercury becomes totally intent upon God realization and aware of eternal, spiritual realities.

—David Pond

**Sources:**

Grasse, Ray. *The Waking Dream*. Wheaton, IL: Quest Books, 1996.

Leadbeater, C.W. *The Chakras*. Wheaton, IL: Quest Books, 1927.

Pond, David. *Chakras for Beginners*. St. Paul, MN: Llewellyn Publications, 1999.

## Chaney, W. H.

William Henry Chaney was born January 13, 1821, in Chesterville, Maine. He was called Professor Chaney (in the nineteenth century, "professor" was often applied to any prominent teacher), and taught astrology for nearly 40 years. He worked for local farmers until aged 16, worked on a fishing schooner for several years, and also spent some time in the navy. He eventually settled in Wheeling, West Virginia, where he studied and practiced law and also edited a newspaper.

In 1866, Chaney was in New York City, where he met Luke Broughton, through whom he became acquainted with astrology. He was to become Broughton's most famous pupil. Chaney thereafter devoted himself to the study, practice, and teaching of astrology.

In 1867, the *New York Herald* led a crusade against the science of the stars, resulting in Chaney's imprisonment for half a year. After his release, he resumed his practice and lecturing, and moved to California in 1869. He moved from one place to another in California, Oregon, and Washington. His fourth marriage, to Flora Wellman, took place in 1876, and this union produced the well-known novelist Jack London (who took the name of his stepfather, John London). In 1889, Chaney moved again, this time to St. Louis, where he wrote and published his major work, *Chaney's Primer of Astrology and American Urania*. Finally, in 1892, he moved to Chicago, where he married for the last time and remained until his death. His sixth wife's name was Daisy, and together they published a magazine called *The Daisy Chain*. Chaney died January 6, 1903.

**Sources:**

Chaney, W. H. *The Astrology's Vade Mecum*. Baltimore: Eureka Publishing Co., 1902.

———. *Chaney's Annual: With the magic Circle Astrology Almanac*. Saint Louis: Magic Circle Publishing Co., 1890.

———. *Chaney's Primer of Astrology and American Urania*. Saint Louis: Magic Circle Publishing Co., 1890.

Holden, James H., and Robert A. Hughes. *Astrological Pioneers of America*. Tempe, AZ: American Federation of Astrologers, 1988.

## Charis

Charis, asteroid 627 (the 627th asteroid to be discovered, on March 4, 1907), is approximately 36 kilometers in diameter, and has an orbital period of 4.9 years. It was named after a Greek goddess who was surrounded by delight, graces, and pleasures; the Charites were the three goddesses of charm and grace—Aglaia, Euphrosyne, and Thalia. In a natal chart, Charis' sign and house position indicates where and how one experiences delight. When afflicted by inharmonious aspects, Charis may show the opposite of delight or the derivation of pleasure from unhealthy activities.

**Sources:**

Kowal, Charles T. *Asteroids: Their Nature and Utilization*. Chichester, West Sussex, UK: Ellis Horwood Limited, 1988.

Room, Adrian. *Dictionary of Astronomical Names*. London: Routledge, 1988.

Schwartz, Jacob. *Asteroid Name Encyclopedia*. St. Paul, MN: Llewellyn Publications, 1995.

## Chinese Astrology

The Chinese were one of the few cultures to develop a complex system of astrology entirely independent of Mesopotamian influences. (Mesopotamian astrology is the starting point for both Western astrology and Hindu astrology.) In much the same way that popular astrology in the West is confined to knowledge of the 12 sun signs, most people's awareness of Chinese astrology is confined to the 12 animal "year signs." Many of the intricacies of the tradition dropped out of currency, even among Chinese astrologers, after the Golden Age of Chinese Astrology during the Chou and Han dynasties, but some contemporary astrologers have attempted to resuscitate classical Chinese astrology.

As might be anticipated, the Chinese system differs significantly from Mesopotamian-derived systems. In the first place, the Chinese group the stars into quite different constellations. Second, the Chinese locate heavenly bodies with respect to the celestial north pole and the celestial equator (called the Red Path by the Chinese) rather than with respect to the ecliptic (termed the Yellow Path). In the third place, while Western systems emphasize the placement of the planets along the ecliptic, the Chinese traditionally give primary importance to the Moon's placement in the daily lunar mansions (a kind of 28-sign lunar zodiac). Fourth, the Chinese assign meanings to the general appearance of a planet as modified by Earth's atmosphere, meaning that, unlike Western astrologers, who examine the stars only indirectly through tables, traditional Chinese astrologers maintain a continual watch of the heavens.

Points at which cultural traditions differ between astrological systems have naturally worked themselves out. For example, the four classical elements of the Western world—earth, air, fire, and water—are comparable to, yet contrast with, the five elements of East Asian philosophy—earth, fire, water, metal, and wood. The Chinese associated these five elements with the five visible planets—Saturn (earth), Mars (fire), Mercury (water), Venus (metal), and Jupiter (wood). The meanings the Chinese assigned to the first three planets are roughly comparable to their meanings in

**An image of the zodiacal dog from Chinese astrology.** ***Reproduced by permission of Fortean Picture Library.***

Western systems. Jupiter, the wood planet, however, is associated with birth and springtime, associations that distinguish the meaning of the Chinese Jupiter from the Western Jupiter. And Venus, as a metal planet, is associated with martial, masculine characteristics, traits alien to the Western Venus.

While all traditional civilizations evince an interest in divination, the Chinese appear to have had a peculiarly strong interest in foretelling the future. For example, some of the earliest written artifacts of Chinese civilization are found on the so-called dragon bones, inscribed pieces of tortoise shell used by the ancients for divination. In the contemporary period, one of the most widespread tools of divination is the *I Ching* (The Book of Changes), a traditional Chinese work that has become popular in the Western world. The *I Ching*, however, is much more than just a fortune-telling device. Querents seek to know not only how the future will unfold but also how and when they ought to act. Similar concerns manifest in traditional Chinese astrology, which is more concerned with divining the future and determining the proper times to act than with understanding personality characteristics.

The Chinese system contains three "Lucks": Heaven Luck is one's Fate or Destiny. Astrology deciphers Destiny, which can sometimes be improved. Earth Luck is tightly associated with the local characteristics of the specific spot in which one lives. It is the domain of *Feng Shui*. One can improve one's House, and thus improve Health and Luck. Human Luck is what one does with one's Life.

There are in fact several Chinese astrologies, which include two main techniques. The Four Pillars of the Destiny or *Ba Zi* deals with the 12 well-known animals of the Chinese zodiac (Rat, Buffalo, Tiger, etc.) but also with Yin and Yang and with the five elements (Earth, Metal, Water, Wood, and Fire). *Zi Wei Dou Shu* analyzes the location and aspects of 109 stars (or energies). These stars are located in a chart consisting of a rectangle divided into 12 boxes (these two techniques are explained in the program Izi Wai, which can be downloaded and tested at http://www.delemme.com/etelchin.htm.

Chinese astrology has nothing to do with the horoscopes found in some magazines. Many people are familiar with Yin and Yang, elements, and the 12 animals of the Chinese zodiac. To be born in the year of the Rat or some other animal year is like being born under a certain sun sign in Western astrology—it is only the beginning. *Zi Wei Dou Shu* takes 109 energies into account (the main energy, King of the Stars, as well as others such as Flying Dragon, Nullity, and Fate) located in 12 boxes (or palaces), and considers the annual transit of eleven other mobile bodies. This energy chart allows remarkable readings, revealing a person's whole life, decade after decade, year after year, moon after moon, and even hour after hour. It is thus relatively easy to distinguish between a person's periods of success, of neutrality, or of failure. Chinese astrology is a remarkable tool for obtaining precise knowledge of the nature and date of the events that take place throughout one's life.

Reading a Chinese chart is easy for the neophyte, because the person's life "program" is written practically and clearly in the houses of Destiny, Luck, Vocation. The names speak for themselves and arouse a rich association of ideas: a twinkling Fortune in the Finances box can be easily understood, while Thunder and Officer in the Vocation box suggest a military career.

*Zi Wei Dou Shu* astrology analyzes the location and aspects of 109 stars (or energies). A *Zi Wei Dou Shu* chart is therefore made up of a large rectangle (a paddy field) divided into 12 boxes or Palaces (plots of land). The distribution of these 109 energies depends on the birth data (Chinese year, Chinese moon, Chinese day and

Chinese hour) and on the sex. A Western (Gregorian) date of birth must be translated into its equivalent in the Lunar Chinese Calendar. The hour of birth is likewise converted into a Chinese hour (12 hours a day). Each energy is more or less powerful: it can be faint (&), neutral, shining (*), very shining (**) or sparkling (***), depending on the date and hour of birth. Twelve Houses are then settled, each corresponding to one of the 12 boxes. These Houses govern the particular aspects of a human life: Destiny, Parents, Luck, Vocation, etc.

| | | | |
|---|---|---|---|
| Serpent | Horse | Goat | Monkey |
| Dragon | | | Rooster |
| Cat (Rabbit) | ©http://www.delemme.com | | Dog |
| Tiger | Buffalo (Ox) | Rat | Boar (Pig) |

**Figure 1**

| | | | |
|---|---|---|---|
| Yin<br>Serpent | Yang<br>Horse | Yin<br>Goat | Yang<br>Monkey |
| Yang<br>Dragon | | | Yin<br>Rooster |
| Yin<br>Cat (Rabbit) | ©http://www.delemme.com | | Yang<br>Dog |
| Yang<br>Tiger | Yin<br>Buffalo (Ox) | Yang<br>Rat | Yin<br>Boar (Pig) |

**Figure 2**

These 12 boxes correspond to the 12 animals of the Chinese zodiac:

Rat
Buffalo
Tiger
Cat or Rabbit
Dragon
Serpent
Horse
Goat or Mutton
Monkey
Rooster
Dog
Boar or Pig

These boxes do not move. For instance, the Tiger is always on the bottom left-hand side, while the Monkey is always on the top right-hand corner. (See Figure 1.) Each box symbolizes several things. For instance, an energy acts differently, depending on whether it is located in the Rat box or in the Buffalo box. Figure 2 shows the addition of the Yin-Yang polarity.

Corresponding elements are added to Figure 3. Finally, Figure 4 includes appropriate directions for each box.

Boxes can also correspond to a given life area (parents, children, friends, etc.); a decade (life is divided into 12 periods of 10 years); a given year; a given lunar month (moon); a given day; and a given hour (a day is divided into 12 Chinese hours, which are also associated with the name of one of the 12 animals: Rat Hour, Buffalo Hour, Tiger Hour, etc.).

It is thus very important to rate these 12 boxes, because one will be able to say if a life area is harmonious or not, if the climate of a decade is tumultuous or calm, or if a year will be happy or not.

| Yin Fire Serpent | Yang Fire Horse | Yin Earth Goat | Yang Metal Monkey |
|---|---|---|---|
| Yang Earth Dragon | | | Yin Metal Rooster |
| Yin Wood Cat (Rabbit) | ©http://www.delemme.com | | Yang Earth Dog |
| Yang Wood Tiger | Yin Earth Buffalo (Ox) | Yang Water Rat | Yin Water Boar (Pig) |

**Figure 3**

| Yin Fire South-East Serpent | Yang Fire South Horse | Yin Earth South-West Goat | Yang Metal South-West Monkey |
|---|---|---|---|
| Yang Earth South-East Dragon | | | Yin Metal West Rooster |
| Yin Wood East Cat (Rabbit) | ©http://www.delemme.com | | Yang Earth North-West Dog |
| Yang Wood North-East Tiger | Yin Earth North-East Buffalo (Ox) | Yang Water North Rat | Yin Water North-West Boar (Pig) |

**Figure 4**

Depending on the birth hour and the birth moon (remember that this astrology uses the Lunar Chinese Calendar), 12 Houses, or Palaces, are associated with the 12 fixed boxes.

These 12 Houses are distributed clockwise:

House I or Destiny Palace
House II or Parents Palace
House III or Luck Palace
House IV or Real Estate Palace
House V or Vocation Palace
House VI or Friends Palace
House VII or Others Palace
House VIII or Health Palace
House IX or Finances Palace
House X or Children Palace
House XI or Union Palace
House XII or Brothers and Sisters Palace

A thirteenth House is added, which is superimposed on one of the previous 12 Houses. It is the House of the "Second World," which describes life after the age of 30. The placement depends on the Chinese birth hour.

Each box is associated with a decade, sorted out, and distributed differently depending on how the native is characterized:

Man born in a Yang Year: distributed clockwise
Woman born in a Yin Year: distributed clockwise
Man born in a Yin Year: distributed anticlockwise
Woman born in a Yang Year: distributed anticlockwise

In each box, the names of planets (Moon, Mars, Jupiter, etc.), stars (Sun, Ursa Major), or more "Chinese" energies (Yang, Virtue of the Dragon Flying Dragon, Heavenly Void, etc.) are indicated. There are 109 energies altogether, but only 36 of them are considered important. Some of them are nice companions (left column), others are more violent (right column).

Napoleon's House of Destiny is in the Tiger box (see Figure 5) which also corresponds to the Second World. The Seven-Swords energy is there, together with Officer and Seal, which both symbolize military success. Also note the presence of Void, an energy that is fatal to dictators.

The rating of the 12 boxes of a *Zi Wei Dou Shu* chart is also important at the *Feng Shui* level. *Feng Shui* is the art of harmonizing one's house with one's life, and it is important to know how to rate the boxes of one's natal chart. The most "beautiful"

| R. Estate | Vocation | Friends | Others |
|---|---|---|---|
| Sun***<br>Authorit.<br>F. Drag<br>Armour<br>Fate*<br>Nullity*<br>Tears<br>Athlete<br>Serpent Puberty 95/104 | Demolish.***<br>Flower<br>Moon.V.<br>Treasure<br>Physician<br>Recumb.<br>River<br>Horse Longevity 85/94 | V<br>B<br>Motor*<br>Lance*<br>Worries<br>Robe<br>Dream<br>Oponent<br>Detriment<br>Justice<br>Goat Nutrition 75/84 | King of Stars***<br>*Palace****<br>*Medal*<br>Joy<br>Drag.V.<br>Banner<br>Treats<br>Waylayer<br>Monkey Foetus 65/94<br>S B |
| **Luck**<br>Dance***<br>Discourse*<br>Support*<br>B. Drag*<br>Fortune<br>Benefact.<br>*Thundr.*<br>Yin<br>Lid<br>Dragon Hat 105/104 | Napoléon BONAPARTE, born on August 15th, 1769<br>Year: Buffalo of KY 11 H ) (GMT) 11 H 36 (HSL)<br>7th Hour – 14th Day – 7th Moon<br>Element: Fire of Lightning<br>Factor: Yin Male Sector: 6 Fire | | **Health**<br>Moon**<br>Phoenix**<br>DelG.<br>Luch<br>*Mars*<br>Studies<br>Tiger*<br>M.Eros<br>Messenger<br>Rooster Disappearance 55/64 |
| **Parents**<br>Servitor*<br>8Seats<br>Punish*<br>*Mourning**<br>m.Eros<br>Cat Mandarinate 115/124 | | ©http://www.delemme.com | **Finance**<br>Aphrod.**<br>*Dissert.**<br>Aid*<br>Power<br>Cloud*<br>Cel.V.<br>Widow.<br>Ancest.V.<br>Recepta<br>Beloved<br>Disease<br>Dog Interment 45/54 |
| **Destiny 2nd World**<br>7SWords***<br>Officer<br>Sceal<br>Cordon<br>Del.H.<br>Void<br>Felicity<br>*Crusher*<br>Yang<br>Solitude<br>Tiger Prosperity 5/14 | **Brothers**<br>*Honest**<br>Jupiter<br>Parasol<br>Success<br>Del.E.<br>Writings<br>Suffoc.<br>Ursa Major<br>Buffalo Decadence 15/24 | **Union**<br>*General***<br>Virgin**<br>*Laureate*<br>Arrows<br>Enigma<br>Praying<br>Rat Sickness 25/34 | **Children**<br>G.Gate*<br>G.Smile<br>Steed<br>3Steps<br>Building<br>Guest<br>Boar Death 35/44 |

**Figure 5**

boxes indicate auspicious directions, those one should respect, according to the following correspondence:

Rat = North
Buffalo + Tiger = Northeast
Cat = East
Dragon + Serpent = Southeast
Horse = South
Goat + Monkey = Southwest
Rooster = West
Dog + Boar = Northwest

An astrological chart of a house can be built, at least in the *Xuan Kong* school (flying stars), which draws up a map of the Cosmic Energy. This chart is alive (there are transits of mobile stars) and allows to forecast some events: for instance, a transit of the "bad" star N°5 on the "natal" same star N°5 is rather malevolent. *Feng Shui*, deals with the concept of Ch'i, (Qi, Ki, etc.), i.e. the Cosmic Energy.

—Michel Delemme

## Chinese Calendar

In 1912, China officially adopted the Gregorian calendar. But the old soli-lunar system (*Nong Li*) is still relevant. There are at least two Chinese calendars (solar and lunar), but they both deal with the fundamental notion of heavenly stems and earthly branches. The solar calendar is used in *Feng Shui* and in the Four Pillars of the Destiny (*Ba Zi* astrology or *Zi Ping*). The lunar calendar is mainly used in the other branch of the Chinese astrology, the *Zi Wei Dou Shu*.

The Chinese calendar is based on the sexagesimal cycle: there are 60 possible combinations (binomials) of stems and branches. This periodicity of 60 years corresponds to a new alignment of the Earth with the Moon, the Sun, Mercury, Venus, Mars and Jupiter. The first observation dates back to 2637 B.C.E., which became the first year of the first cycle of 60 years. A period of 180 years is called a grand cycle and corresponds to three cycles of 60 years (called inferior cycle, median cycle, and superior cycle) and thus to nine periods of 20 years. The current grand cycle, the 26th one, started on February 4, 1864, and will last until February 3, 2044. The period of 1984 through February 2004 is the seventh period of the current grand cycle.

The solar new year begins at the precise time when the Sun goes over the 15th degree of Aquarius, Beijing time. This corresponds to February 4 (sometimes February 5). This date is called *Li Chun* and marks the beginning of Chinese spring. Each solar month begins around the 4th or the 8th of the corresponding western month:

The first Chinese month = February (second Western month)
The second Chinese month = March (third Western month)
The eleventh Chinese month = December (twelfth Western month)
The twelfth Chinese month = January (first Western month)

The lunar new year is set on the winter solstice and can fall on any day between January 21 and February 20. A lunar year comprises 12 moons of 29 days (short moon) or 30 days (long moon), and regularly, a 13th moon must be inserted to make up the gap. (A lunar calendar consists of moons, while a solar calendar consists of solar months.)

—Michele Delemme

## Chinese Zodiac

In much the same way that popular astrology in the West is confined to a knowledge of the 12 sun signs, most people's awareness of Chinese astrology is confined to the 12 animal "year signs." The earliest Chinese zodiac was a system of lunar mansions; the 12 animal signs were incorporated into the system much later. Some speculate that these later signs originated outside of China proper, perhaps in northern central Asia. The 12 signs of East Asian astrology derive not from the 12 months of the year, but from the 12 years of the Jupiter cycle (Jupiter takes approximately a dozen years to complete one orbit of the Sun). Despite the parallelism of 12 signs in each system, attempts to correlate the Chinese zodiac with the Western zodiac have been problematic, to say the least. The 12 animal signs are:

Rat: People born in 1900, 1912, 1924, 1936, 1948, 1960, 1972, 1984, 1996, and 2008.
Ox: People born in 1901, 1913, 1925, 1937, 1949, 1961, 1973, 1985, 1997, and 2009.
Tiger: People born in 1902, 1914, 1926, 1938, 1950, 1962, 1974, 1986, 1998, and 2010.

Rabbit: People born in 1903, 1915, 1927, 1939, 1951, 1963, 1975, 1987, 1999, and 2011.

Dragon: People born in 1904, 1916, 1928, 1940, 1952, 1964, 1976, 1988, 2000, and 2012.

Snake: People born in 1905, 1917, 1929, 1941, 1953, 1965, 1977, 1989, 2001, and 2013.

Horse: People born in 1906, 1918, 1930, 1942, 1954, 1966, 1978, 1990, 2002, and 2014.

Sheep: People born in 1907, 1919, 1931, 1943, 1955, 1967, 1979, 1991, 2003, and 2015.

Monkey: People born in 1908, 1920, 1932, 1944, 1956, 1968, 1980, 1992, 2004, and 2016.

Cock: People born in 1909, 1921, 1933, 1945, 1957, 1969, 1981, 1993, 2005, and 2017.

Dog: People born in 1910, 1922, 1934, 1946, 1958, 1970, 1982, 1994, 2006, and 2018.

Pig: People born in 1911, 1923, 1935, 1947, 1959, 1971, 1983, 1995, 2007, and 2019.

In contrast to the Western year, the Chinese year begins on variable dates (on the second new moon after the winter solstice) in late January or early February. Hence, someone born on January 10, 1911, for instance, would be a Dog rather than a Pig.

In a manner that contrasts with the way in which the four classical elements of classical Western philosophy are associated with the 12 signs of the Western zodiac, the five elements of East Asian philosophy—earth, fire, water, metal, and wood—are associated with the 12 signs of the Chinese zodiac. Instead of being an integral association (e.g., Sagittarius is always a fire sign, Pisces is always a water sign, etc.), the elemental associations vary from year to year in Chinese astrology. For example, a Tiger person born in 1950 is a metal Tiger; a Tiger born in 1962 is a water Tiger; a Tiger born in 1974 is a wood tiger; etc. These elemental differences are reflected in somewhat different personality profiles. The other nuances of the Chinese system are explored in the entry on Chinese astrology.

Much is often made of the compatibility between the signs of the Chinese zodiac. Harmonious unions, particularly marriages, are regarded as best between Rats, Dragons, and Monkeys; between Oxen, Snakes, and Cocks; between Tigers, Horses, and Dogs; and between Rabbits, Sheep, and Pigs. The most inharmonious relationships are between Rats, Rabbits, Horses, and Cocks; between Oxen, Dragons, Sheep, and Dogs; and between Tigers, Snakes, Monkeys, and Pigs.

**Sources:**

Brau, Jean-Louis, Helen Weaver, and Allan Edmans. *Larousse Encyclopedia of Astrology*. New York: New American Library, 1980.

Lau, Theodora. *The Handbook of Chinese Horoscopes*. 4th ed. New York: Harper, 2000.

Logan, Daniel. *Your Eastern Star: Oriental Astrology, Reincarnation and the Future*. New York: William Morrow & Company, 1972.

Starr, Amanda. *Chinese Astrology*. Hod Hasharon, Israel: Astrolog, 2002.

Twicken, David. *Classical Five Element Chinese Astrology Made Easy*. Lincoln, NE: Writers Club, 2000.
———. *Four Pillars and Oriental Medicine*. Lincoln, NE: Writers Club, 2000.
Walters, Derek. *Chinese Astrology: Interpreting the Revelations of the Celestial Messengers*. Wellingborough, Northamptonshire, UK: Aquarian Press, 1987.
———. *The Chinese Astrology Workbook: How to Calculate and Interpret Chinese Horoscopes*. Wellingborough, Northamptonshire, UK: Aquarian Press, 1988.

## CHIRON

Before considering the meaning of Chiron in the horoscope, exploring some of its astronomy can help us reflect on its meaning. Chiron was discovered in 1977, between Saturn and Uranus, and reclassified several times until 1992, when the Kuiper Disk was discovered. This is a large disk of matter surrounding the solar system that comprises probably billions of small celestial objects and has yielded several new astronomical categories, including "Centaurs." Chiron is now considered to be the first of this group, and to date more than 20 others have been discovered, although only a few are named. The naming process itself tells us something about the astrological themes of Chiron and the Centaurs, as it is the first time in recorded history that astrologers and astronomers have cooperated in such a venture. The scientific and intuitive and the rational and inspirational have been brought together.

Chiron's discovery at this pivotal time in our history reflects the process of innovation and change by "quantum leap" and most importantly, the skills needed to deeply integrate the resulting profound changes of consciousness, belief, behavior, and lifestyle. In this sense, Chiron bridges the realms of Uranus (radical change, revolution, and the overturning of old collective structures) and Saturn (the preserver of existing forms). By weaving both impulses into a higher synthesis, more uniquely personal than either planet, Chiron's process helps us individuate beyond the various pressures of the collective to which we are all subject. Commitment to the healing of self, others, and our environment is the price was are asked to pay, and it is a lifelong journey, not a weekend workshop.

Further, Chiron and the other Centaurs all have very elliptical orbits, distinguished by the fact that they cross the orbital path of at least one other body, from Saturn outwards. Here, too, we can see that Chiron is about integrating the powerful experiences signified by the outer planets, Uranus, Neptune, and especially Pluto, which is, in fact, the largest inhabitant of the Kuiper Disk and the only orbit-crossing planet. Centaurs come into being when objects are drawn in to the solar system from the icy wastes of space in the region around Pluto, pulled by the gravitational field of Neptune. So Chiron and the Centaurs function as integrators of transpersonal experience, weaving together different levels of reality; they are the messengers of the underworld (Pluto's domain), the bringers of transformation, and the facilitators of deep healing. They preside over all rites of passage, especially those concerning our spiritual development.

### The Mythic Image

In Greek mythology, the Centaurs were a tribe of unruly creatures who were half horse, half human. Of these, very few have individual names and stories, and Chiron is perhaps the most well-known, often associated with the archetypal theme of the wounded healer. He was the son of Kronos (astrological Saturn) and a sea nymph called Philyra. Because both parents were in their horse form when he was conceived, Chiron emerged as a centaur—half horse, half human. (Note here the reference to the deep past—the conditions around our conception.) Philyra was so horrified that she prayed to be turned into anything other than what she was—the mother of a monster. Chiron was abandoned and rescued by a shepherd who took him to the Sun god Apollo. This suggests the primary level of "wounding" that Chiron can depict, in a dramatic and painful separation from his mother who rejects him. This reminds us that even with the best mothering, at the "animal" level we all suffer from a sense of abandonment at birth. Chiron's mother Philyra also demonstrates the primary state of mind that creates suffering (i.e., the inability to accept things).

Further, we can see the astronomy reflected in the mythology, in that Chiron is taken to Apollo, and fostered by the Sun god. In their elliptical orbits, Chiron and the Centaurs appear to be tending inwards to the Sun, like Chiron taken to Apollo. This detail also tells us that our suffering and our compulsions needs to be brought into the light, for Apollo was the god of healing, music, prophecy, and other skills. Chiron became the mentor of many famous Greek heroes, passing on the knowledge that would prepare them for their destinies. In the episode that earned Chiron the title of "Wounded Healer," he was accidentally wounded by Hercules, one of his students. Because Chiron was a demigod, he could not die, but neither could he heal himself as the wound was poisoned. After existing in agony for a long time, Chiron changed places with Prometheus, who was chained to a rock as a punishment for tricking Zeus, the astrological Jupiter. Note that Chiron approaches the orbit of Jupiter, cutting across the orbit of Saturn, as if trespassing the boundaries, or breaking the old model. Thus, both were released from their suffering. Chiron was able finally to die and was immortalized in the constellation of Centaurus, which flanks the Southern Cross.

## Learning through Suffering

So in the horoscope we find multilayered themes around Chiron's placement. It indicates where situations encountered in the present may trigger memories of earlier suffering in the preverbal domain. Thus, we may experience powerful reactions seemingly out of proportion and resulting in a driven quality to our behavior and interactions with others. This intensity can produce stress and anxiety, but it can also be the stimulus for enormous creativity, originality, and authenticity. Chiron in the horoscopes of famous people demonstrates this, where a cameo is revealed of precisely the person's main contribution to life, for good or ill. Chiron shows where intense and sometimes painful experiences may occur, where we might malfunction by deficiency or by overdoing it, where there is a sense of struggle for balance, and where we give more easily than receive owing to the vulnerability residing there.

Equally, Chiron may show our "destiny" as our innate gifts and wisdom seek inner recognition there, and it both locates the inner teacher and describes the nature of significant learning experiences that life will provide. The development of compassion for our own suffering and that of others is also an important Chiron theme, where we learn to tread the middle way between denial and indulgence of our pain. We discover that healing does not happen through human skill alone, but emanates from the great source, however we understand that. So around Chiron we may meet the "unfixable" as its process is intended to lead us beyond superficial "cure" to the mysteries of our participation in the cosmos and a deeper understanding of our place in it. Discerning the difference between the pain of an experience and the ongoing suffering caused by our resistance to feeling the pain is part of the healing journey of Chiron, and it asks of us that we tread the path of service as we invite healing for ourselves and others along the way.

## Ancestral Influences and Prenatal Life

With Chiron and also the other Centaurs, the "liminal" realms of ancestral influences and prenatal experiences often feature as an interesting aspect of their healing process. Examining Chiron in this light may reveal family "stories" that are incomplete, the residue of which is passed down through the generations, and, like the poisoned arrow of Hercules, lodged in our energy-body, creates pain and distress until healed through awareness. So differentiating ourselves from those who went before, but also honouring their gifts to us is part of the Chiron process. We heal the ancestral line by doing this consciously. Equally, an important but "invisible" aspect of our heritage has its roots in our intrauterine experience, where our soul is strongly impacted by the emotional experiences passing between our mother and father and other significant members of the family, and indeed their attitude to our immanent arrival. In deep psychospiritual processes occurring both in natural development, and also through shock or trauma, this area may open up and what is sometimes termed an "ego death" may result, meaning a radical transition involving the letting go of previous ways of being. Such experiences may be difficult to communicate and thus to integrate, as they belong to the precognitive realm, and may also lead into dimensions of experience that are not yet part of the traditional models used in psychotherapy, although familiar to the ancient shamanic ways of indigenous cultures. Hence, the theme of "exile" that is often felt around Chiron. We feel different, not understood, outside life, and in seeking to heal this wound, we may discover a deep thread of spiritual continuity that allows us to release our highest potential into life. Enquiring into these areas may bring significant healing as the "arrows" of ancestral issues are removed. (Note that in astrology we use the birth chart, which also embodies the major celestial patterns at work during gestation.)

## Expanding Our View

As Chiron moves between Jupiter-Saturn-Uranus, its process reflects the development of our understanding, beliefs, and perspectives as we try to live up to our highest potential, participate in creative change, and integrate new ideas. The suffering created by Saturnian resistance to the new (Uranus) is gently processed and integrated over time, so that change can truly be grounded and our participation in life is enhanced (Jupiter). It seems that a nondual perspective is trying to take root, where the opposites of mind/body, material/spiritual, and other polarities all have a place, but are not fused or confused. A "transcognitive" wisdom must develop, going beyond the split where instinct and intellect are pitted against each other. A multidimensional world view, which has compassionate space for all human experience, seems to be the Chironian view, and it is an integral part of healing. Allowing this to develop requires us to move beyond negative judgements of ourselves and others. Examining Jupiter and Uranus in the horoscope will shed light on some of the collective beliefs and stereotypes we need to release in order to be healed. Saturn's position and the conditions within the fourth, eighth, and twelfth houses may provide further clues to the ancestral heritage that needs to be transformed.

Chiron's process brings the magical, the awesome, the numinous, and the powerful. The forces of nature and the shamanic "otherworld" may open, for we will encounter the nonrational world of invisible beings, the spirits of animals, places, and people. This tricky, risky, and inviting realm is not to be entered lightly, and Chiron's process may call us to become familiar with and respect a world of dynamic energies far removed from technology, standardization, and anonymity. Personal gnosis is the soul's intention on this journey, whatever the experiences along the way. So look for the unusual, quirky, eccentric, or archaic around Chiron, and be aware that much letting go of pride and sophistication may be asked.

## Rites of Passage—The Chiron Return

Because Chiron's orbit is so elliptical, its cycle is irregular and needs to be tracked using an ephemeris. For example, Chiron's first square to its own natal position may occur anytime from about age 5 to age 23, depending on the sign. However, it returns to its natal place regularly in approximately 50 years, and this age is an important threshold crossing for both men and women. For in the few years after its return, Chiron retraces all the aspects by transit which occurred in the formative years of our life. Thus, we have the opportunity to revisit and bring healing to those areas, and very likely life will provide us with experiences that open them up.

## Studying Chiron in Your Horoscope

The easiest way to understand Chiron in your horoscope is to track its transits over time, particularly the main hard aspects: conjunction, square, and opposition. The inner and outer events occurring under these transits will often reveal a storyline that is no less than the unfolding of the soul over time, as it encounters experiences that are required for the development of wisdom, compassion, and a sense of participating in our own destiny with integrity. Start by using the same orbs as you would use for transits of Saturn and experiment as you pick up the story. As Chiron is not a planet, the traditional concept of rulership over the zodiacal signs may not apply, although being a Centaur, it does have a thematic link with the psychospiritual process of development in the sign of Sagittarius, the Archer. A new concept of emphasis is required, such as the notion of "degree zones," where Chiron is crossing the orbit of Saturn, at perihelion or aphelion, and so on. Do not expect that you can equate Chiron with healing/suffering or any other themes in the way that you can equate Mercury with communication issues. True, the ordinary astrological factors—sign, house, and aspects—often clothe an individual's Chiron "story" with astonishingly literal details. But to understand Chiron deeply, one must partake of the healing and transformation of consciousness he represents.

When the Kuiper Belt was first discovered, the scientific community declared it to be the "newest frontier of planetary science." Although Chiron and the Centaurs are not used by every astrologer, those working in depth with clients have found that Chiron and the Centaurs accurately reflect important psycho-spiritual processes not covered by the traditional planets, and address the inner world of healing and transformation in a precise manner.

—Melanie Reinhart

**Sources:**


Alexander, Marianne. *The Centaur Pholus*. Kenner, LA: Pandora Publishing, 1996.

Clow, Barbara Hand. *Chiron: Rainbow Bridge Between the Outer Planets*. St. Paul, MN: Llewellyn Publications, 1987.

Koch, Dieter, and Robert von Heeren, "The New Planet Pholus." *TMA* (July 1996).

———. *Pholus-Wandler zwischen Saturn und Neptun*. Tubingen, Germany: Chiron Verlag, 1995.

Lantero, Erminie. *The Continuing Discovery of Chiron*. York Beach, Maine: Samuel Weiser, 1983.

Nolle, Richard. *Chiron, the New Planet in Your Horoscope*. Tempe, AZ : American Federation of Astrologers, 1983.

Reinhart, Melanie. *Chiron and the Healing Journey*. Rev. ed. London: Penguin Arkana, 1999.

———. *Saturn, Chiron and the Centaurs: To the Edge and Beyond*. London: Centre for Psychological Astrology Press, 1996.

Reinhart, Melanie, and Isabella Kirton, "Spirit Child." *Apollon Magazine* (No. 3).

Steffen, Penny, "The New Centaurs Pholus and Nessus." *Journal of the Astrological Association* (Vol. 41, no. 3).

Stein, Zane. *Essence and Application: A View from Chiron*. New York: CAO Times, 1986.

Von Heeren, Robert. "The Naming of Nessus." *Journal of the Astrological Association* (Vol. 39, no. 6).


## Chitra

Chitra (Brilliant) is one of the Nakshatras (lunar mansions) of Vedic astrology. Depicted as a pearl or gem, this moon sign is located at Virgo 23°20' to Libra 6°40', with the world architect Twastri or Vishwarkarma presiding and the planet Mars ruling. Someone under this sign will tend to be more dignified and discriminating, yet quarrelsome and critical to an extent. The Hindu moon signs are also used "electionally" to decide when to do things.

—Pramela Thiagesan

## Choisnard, Paul

Paul Choisnard, born February 13, 1867, in Tours, France, was an eminent astrologer. A graduate of L'École Polytechnique in Paris, his first career was as a major in the field artillery. He became interested in astrology, especially "scientific astrology," and took it up as a significant side interest. Choisnard was particularly interested in astrological research involving statistical methods. To avoid conflict within his first profession, he used the pseudonym Paul Flambart until after he retired. He was a prolific writer, though little known in the United States.

Choisnard was important for his role in helping to revive astrology in France and for his pioneering role in applying statistical methods to astrology. He was succeeded in the latter role by the Swiss astrologer Karl Ernst Krafft, who was in turn followed by Michel Gauquelin. Choisnard died on February 9, 1930, in St. Geni-de-Saintange.

**Sources:**

Choisnard, Paul. *Étude nouvelle sur l'hérédité*. Paris: Chacornac, 1903.
———. *Influence astrale*. Paris: Chacornac, 1901.
———. *Langage astral*. Paris: Chacornac, 1903.
Holden, James H., and Robert A. Hughes. *Astrological Pioneers of America*. Tempe, AZ: American Federation of Astrologers, 1988.

## Choleric

Choleric is the traditional name for the personality temperament indicated by an excess of the element fire.

## Christianity and Astrology

Historically, astrology was integrated into the church along with other aspects of Hellenistic civilization. From time to time, various Christian thinkers worried about the tension between free will and the apparent determinism of astrology, but by and large the science of the stars occupied an honorable position in the Western tradition. Although some of the biblical prophets disparaged stargazing, the Three Wise Men were clearly astrologers, and in certain other scriptural passages it was evident that God regularly used heavenly signs to instruct the faithful.

Despite certain tensions between them, astrology and Christianity were not separated until the fundamentalist movement of the early twentieth century. For various reasons, but particularly because of astrology's association with metaphysical religion (e.g., the New Age movement), fundamentalists—and, later, most other varieties of conservative Christians—rejected astrology as a delusion at best and as a tool of Satan at worst.

**Sources:**

Jacobs, Don. *Astrology's Pew in the Church*. San Francisco: The Joshua Foundation, 1979.
Simms, Maria Kay. *Twelve Wings of the Eagle: Our Spiritual Evolution through the Ages of the Zodiac*. San Diego: Astro Computing Services, 1988.

## Christino, Karen

Karen Christino has been a consulting astrologer, lecturer, and teacher since 1977. She is the author of *Foreseeing the Future: Evangeline Adams and Astrology in America* and

*Star Success*. She has also written the popular "Choose Your Career" advice column for *American Astrology* magazine since 1992 and numerous articles for astrology journals. She has been a guest on radio programs across the country and has written astrology features for *Marie Claire*, *Modern Bride* and *Seventeen* magazines, among others.

Christino lectures regularly on astrology in the New York area, most notably for Colgate University. She teaches horary at the Online College of Astrology, and received a research grant from the New York chapter of the National Council for Geocosmic Research (NCGR) for her work on Evangeline Adams. Her other research interests include forecasting, traditional astrology, the history of astrology, and cross-cultural astrologies.

Christino is certified Level IV by the NCGR, has a B.A. in English from Colgate University, and took graduate classes at Columbia University. She studied traditional astrology with Zoltan Mason and Robert Zoller and modern techniques with Al H. Morrison. She practices yoga and meditation and has also studied zen, Reiki, and numerology.

**Sources:**

Christino, Karen. *Foreseeing the Future: Evangeline Adams and Astrology in America*. Amherst, MA: One Reed Publications, 2002.

———. *Star Success: An Astrological Guide to Your Career*. New York: Pocket Books, 1992.

## Chronocrators

The chronocrators, the "markers" or "rulers" of time, are the periodic conjunctions of Jupiter and Saturn that occur every 20 years. Because Jupiter and Saturn were the slowest-moving planets in the then-known solar system, their conjunction was perceived by the ancients as particularly significant. These celestial meetings indicated important events, as well as the beginning and ending of important periods of time. For example, some have speculated that the Star of Bethlehem was actually a Jupiter-Saturn conjunction.

Considerable traditional astrological literature exists on chronocrators. This literature develops, among other things, longer cycles out of the patterns of successive chronocrators (e.g., the two-century cycle during which chronocrators occur in the same element) and speculates about the significance of these longer time periods. Few modern astrologers have more than passing familiarity with this phase of astrology.

## Chronos

Chronos is an older name for Saturn. Mythologically, Chronos was regarded as the Greek god equivalent to the Roman god Saturn.

## Church of Light

Elbert Benjamine (C. C. Zain) incorporated the Church of Light in Los Angeles in 1932, although its roots lie in Emma Harding Britten's 1876 book *Art Magic*. The

Church of Light views itself as an outgrowth of the Brotherhood of Light, which it says separated from Egyptian theocracy in 2400 B.C.E. and subsequently became a secret order.

The Church of Light teaches that there is only one religion—the laws of nature. Astrology is emphasized as a vehicle for interpreting the laws of nature, although all occult sciences are recognized. The core teaching of the church is contained in 21 courses. After completion, members are given a Hermetic certificate. The church stresses service to others.

The Church of Light is important to the history of astrology in the United States. The church was one of the few organizations offering high-quality correspondence courses in astrology in the early twentieth century, and many older contemporary astrologers studied with the church.

**Sources:**

*Astrological Research & Reference Encyclopedia*. 2 vols. Los Angeles: Church of Light, 1972.

Burgoyne, Thomas H. *The Light of Egypt*. 2 vols. Albuquerque: Sun Publishing Company, 1980.

Wagner, H. O., comp. *A Treasure Chest of Wisdom*. Denver: H. O. Wagner, 1967.

## Circe

Circe, asteroid 34 (the 34th asteroid to be discovered, on April 6, 1855), is approximately 112 kilometers in diameter and has an orbital period of 4.4 years. Circe was named after the Greek enchantress who detained Odysseus on her island. She was a sorceress known for her knowledge of magic and poisonous herbs. According to Martha Lang-Wescott, Circe represents where one facilitates and assists others, as well as where one seeks help. This asteroid's key word is *rescue*. According to J. Lee Lehman, Circe has a magical and temptress side and indicates where one has the power to influence others, for good or for bad. Jacob Schwartz gives the astrological significance of this asteroid as "a heterosexual woman hating men but dependent on them sexually, but rescuing those in need of assistance."

**Sources:**

Lang-Wescott, Martha. *Asteroids-Mechanics: Ephemerides II*. Conway, MA: Treehouse Mountain, 1990.

———. *Mechanics of the Future: Asteroids*. Rev. ed. Conway, MA: Treehouse Mountain, 1991.

Lehman, J. Lee. *The Ultimate Asteroid Book*. West Chester, PA: Whitford, 1988.

Schwartz, Jacob. *Asteroid Name Encyclopedia*. St. Paul, MN: Llewellyn Publications, 1995.

## Clark, Vernon E.

Vernon E. Clark was born August 29, 1911, in Baltimore, Maryland. He studied art at the Maryland Institute of Art and at Columbia University Teachers College, and graduated from Columbia University. He practiced as a clinical psychologist in the U.S. Army, at Downey Veterans Hospital, and, after 1950, from his home.

In 1927, Clark became interested in astrology and joined the American Federation of Astrology in 1959. He served as a trustee of the American Federation of

Astrologers Building Fund and, in 1958, was the first American to win the Gold Medal of the Faculty of Astrological Studies in London. Clark is remembered for the blind trial experiments of natal chart interpretation that he conducted from 1959 to 1961, which generally supported the thesis that natal horoscopes are potentially indicative of the life circumstances of the natives. He died on November 6, 1967, in Evanston, Illinois.

**Sources:**

Dean, Geoffrey. *Recent Advances in Natal Astrology*. Subiaco, Australia: Analogic, 1977.

Holden, James H., and Robert A. Hughes. *Astrological Pioneers of America*. Tempe, AZ: American Federation of Astrologers, 1988.

## Clement, Stephanie Jean

Stephanie Jean Clement was born November 17, 1944, in Pueblo, Colorado. She received her B.A. degree in English literature from Colorado College in 1966; her M.A. in library science from the University of Denver in 1971; her M.A. in humanistic psychological counseling from Beacon College in 1982; and her Ph.D. in transpersonal psychology from Sierra University in 1989. She has two children and three grandchildren.

Clement began studying astrology in 1972. She has been an active member of the American Federation of Astrologers, serving on its board since 1992. She was an associate professor at Naropa University, then Naropa Institute, from 1984 to 1990, where she directed the activities of the library and taught writing and astrology classes. She is on the faculty of Kepler College and is the author of several books. From 1995 to 1998 she was the online store manager for Matrix Software. Clement has been the marketing manager for Llewellyn Worldwide, and is currently the company's acquisitions editor for astrology. She writes regularly for the National Council for Geocosmic Research's *Geocosmic Journal*, and has done extensive research on twins and on child abuse issues.

A proponent of the transpersonal perspective, Clement has focused her research and writing on dreams, planet-centered astrology and on psychological and spiritual topics related to astrology. She has lectured widely throughout the United States and Canada on astrology and psychology. Following the terrorist attacks of September 11, 2001, she compiled and edited *Civilization under Attack*, an astrology work drawing on the expertise of seven astrologers, using both traditional and contemporary astrological techniques.

**Sources:**

Clement, Stephanie Jean. *Charting Your Career*. St. Paul, MN: Llewellyn Publishing, 1999.

———. *Charting Your Spiritual Path with Astrology*. St. Paul, MN: Llewellyn Publishing, 2001.

———. *Civilization under Attack*. St. Paul, MN: Llewellyn Publishing, 2001.

———. *Counseling Techniques in Astrology*. Rev. ed. Tempe, AZ: American Federation of Astrologers, 1990.

———. *Decanates and Dwads*. Tempe, AZ: American Federation of Astrologers, 1983.

———. *Dreams: Working Interactive*. St. Paul, MN: Llewellyn Publishing, 2000.

———. *Planets and Planet-Centered Astrology*. Tempe, AZ: American Federation of Astrologers, 1992.

———. *Power of the Midheaven*. St. Paul, MN: Llewellyn Publishing, 2001.
———. *Twin Angles*. Evergreen, CO, 1978.
———. *What Astrology Can Do for You*. St. Paul, MN: Llewellyn Publishing, 2000.

## Clementina

Clementina, asteroid 252 (the 252nd asteroid to be discovered, on October 11, 1885), is approximately 45 kilometers in diameter and has an orbital period of 5.6 years. Its name, the personification of mercy (clemency), is derived from the Latin *clementia*. When prominent in a natal chart, this asteroid shows a forgiving person. Its location by sign and house indicates where one forgives or experiences forgiveness.

**Sources:**

Kowal, Charles T. *Asteroids: Their Nature and Utilization*. Chichester, West Sussex, UK: Ellis Horwood Limited, 1988.
Room, Adrian. *Dictionary of Astronomical Names*. London: Routledge, 1988.
Schwartz, Jacob. *Asteroid Name Encyclopedia*. St. Paul, MN: Llewellyn Publications, 1995.

## Climacteric Conjunction

A climacteric conjunction is a conjunction of Jupiter and Saturn. As the slowest-moving planets known to the ancients, the periodic (every 20 years) conjunction of these two celestial bodies was regarded as especially significant.

## Clio

Clio, asteroid 84 (the 84th asteroid to be discovered, in 1850), is approximately 88 kilometers in diameter and has an orbital period of 3.6 years. It was named after the muse of history. Clio's location by sign and house shows where one tends to keep alive memories—or even a written record—of the past. When prominent in a mental house (third or ninth) or in a close aspect with Mercury (planet of the mind), Clio may show a native who is always bringing the past to bear on the present. When prominent and afflicted, Clio may show someone who tends to live in the past or who is somehow stuck in the past.

**Sources:**

Kowal, Charles T. *Asteroids: Their Nature and Utilization*. Chichester, West Sussex, UK: Ellis Horwood Limited, 1988.
Room, Adrian. *Dictionary of Astronomical Names*. London: Routledge, 1988.
Schwartz, Jacob. *Asteroid Name Encyclopedia*. St. Paul, MN: Llewellyn Publications, 1995.

## Cochrane, David

David Cochrane is the founder of Cosmic Patterns Software, Inc., the company that makes the Kepler astrology software program. He also founded Avalon College and the Avalon School of Astrology, and is author of the book *Astrology for the 21st Century*. He was born on May 1, 1949, at 4:26 A.M. in East Meadow, New York.

Cochrane started a practice as an astrologer in 1973 in Gainesville, Florida. For eight years he was a full-time astrological consultant and he taught astrology classes in the evening. During this time, he also developed astrological software that ran on an IBM mainframe computer to produce computations in harmonic astrology and cosmobiology. He also developed a computerized forecast program based on transiting midpoint structures.

In 1981, Cochrane dropped his consulting business and began full-time work developing astrological software. In 1983, he found Cosmic Patterns Software and devoted himself to astrological programming. By 2000, Cosmic Patterns had grown to a staff of six full-time workers, four computer programmers, and two people who operated the company. Avalon College started out as a feature within the Kepler program, and then developed into a school that offers training in astrology.

Cochrane is internationally recognized for his contributions to astrological software, including many innovative concepts, such as treasure maps and integrated analysis and interpretations based on an integration of harmonic theory and cosmobiology. The Kepler program is widely recognized for its extraordinary comprehensiveness and flexibility.

**Sources:**

Cochrane, David. *Astrology for the 21st Century*. Gainesville, FL: Cosmic Patterns, 2002.

*Cosmic Patterns Software*. http://cosmic.patterns.com.

## Cold

The signs are numbered from 1 to 12 according to their order in the zodiac (i.e., Aries = 1, Taurus = 2, etc.). Cold and hot was one of the sets of categories used in premodern physics, and the ancients classified all even-numbered signs (all water and earth signs) as cold. Traditionally, the Moon and Saturn, and sometimes other planets, were also considered to be cold. The terms hot and cold are infrequently used in modern astrology.

## Coleman, Cathy

Cathy Coleman is the president of Kepler College of Astrological Arts and Sciences. She was born August 29, 1952, in Chillicothe, Missouri, at 8:29 P.M. She holds a doctoral degree in East-West psychology from the California Institute of Integral Studies (1991), and wrote a phenomenological dissertation on peoples' psychological experiences of the planets Saturn and Uranus. She holds a master's degree in family studies from Washington State University (1981), and has research interests in astrology, human development, and family studies. Coleman has been a student of astrology and psychology for 26 years, first studying with Jeanne Long in Houston, Texas, and has been a practitioner (consultant and teacher) for 18 years. She was in the first graduating class of the Online College of Astrology, is an ISAR certified astrological professional, and has Level II NCGR certification. She is also a Jim Lewis–certified Astro*Carto*Graphy practitioner.

Coleman worked in numerous capacities as an administrator at the California Institute of Integral Studies, an alternative institution of higher education in San Francisco, from 1982 through 2001. She served in the Peace Corps in Ecuador in 1978–79 where she learned about Astro*Carto*Graphy from a fellow volunteer. She has worked on several international conferences with the International Transpersonal Association, and pioneered the concept and development of youth conferences as part of major conferences.

## Collective Unconscious (Archetypes)

The collective unconscious, a term coined by the psychologist Carl Jung, refers to the storehouse of myths and symbols to which all human beings have access. Much of traditional Jungian analysis focuses on the interpretation of dreams. Jung found that the dreams of his clients frequently contained images with which they were completely unfamiliar but that seemed to reflect symbols that could be found somewhere in the mythological systems of world culture; the notion of the collective unconscious was used to explain this phenomenon. Jung further found that he could often interpret his patients' dreams if he studied and reflected upon the particular myth or symbol to which the dream image seemed to allude. In certain cases, deeper and more complete significance for the dream image could be uncovered by locating similar images in more than one cultural system. Researching such images in the quest for deeper meanings is referred to as amplification.

Jung's unique contribution to modern psychology begins with the observation that the basic structure of many symbols and myths is nearly universal, even between cultures with no historical influence on one another. Most traditional societies, for example, tell hero myths and use circles to represent wholeness and the sky to symbolize transcendence, etc. Jung theorized that this universality resulted from unconscious patterns (genetic or quasi-genetic predispositions to utilize certain symbolic and mythic structures) that we inherited from our distant ancestors. The reservoir of these patterns constitutes a collective unconscious, distinct from the individual, personal unconscious that is the focus of Freudian psychoanalysis.

Jung referred to the unconscious, predisposing patterns for particular myths and symbols as archetypes; hence, one can talk about the mandala (i.e., the circle) archetype, the hero archetype (which was made famous by the Jungian thinker Joseph Campbell), and so forth. Astrologers adopted this kind of language for discussions about the elements of their craft, e.g., the Mars archetype, the Venus archetype, etc.

**Sources:**

Burt, Kathleen. *Archetypes of the Zodiac*. Saint Paul, MN: Llewellyn Publications, 1990.

Valentine, Christine. *Images of the Psyche: Exploring the Planets Through Psychology and Myth*. Shaftesbury, Dorset, UK: Element Books, 1991.

## Colors and the Zodiac

Human beings have often perceived colors as constituting a kind of symbolic alphabet, so it is natural that colors would come to be associated with the signs of the zodiac as well as with the planets. There is, however, more than one system of correlations between the colors and the signs. The following color-sign associations should thus be regarded as illustrative rather than definitive:

### Colors and the Zodiac

| Sign | Colors |
|---|---|
| Aries | Red and other "flaming" colors |
| Taurus | Pink, pale blue, and other pastels |
| Gemini | Yellow and violet |
| Cancer | Green, smoky-gray, silver, and silvery-blue colors |
| Leo | Orange and gold |
| Virgo | Green and dark brown |
| Libra | Pink, pale green, and various shades of blue |
| Scorpio | Deep red, maroon, dark brown, and black |
| Sagittarius | Dark blues and purples |
| Capricorn | Brown, gray, black, dark green, and earth tones |
| Aquarius | Turquoise, aquamarine, white, and electric blue |
| Pisces | Sea green, lavender, and lilac |

Natives born under the influence of one of these signs (particularly, but not exclusively, as this influence manifests in their sun sign) usually feel a special affinity with their sign's colors. This affinity can manifest as a tendency to wear clothes of, or to decorate homes with, the associated zodiacal colors.

## Combust

A planet is said to be combust when it is within 8°30' (many would say less) of the Sun. In traditional astrology, this was regarded as having a weakening (debilitating) effect on the planet involved. Contemporary astrologers have not found that this close conjunction with the Sun weakens planets, and, to the contrary, some researchers have asserted that such a position tends to strengthen the influence of the planets involved. The notion of combust might have been based on the observation that during partile conjunctions in which the Sun actually came between a particular planet and Earth (i.e., during occultations,) the matters and processes ruled by the planet involved in the conjunction were weakened. Certain twentieth-century experiments, such as those supporting the Kolisko effect (in which the metal associated with a given planet was less reactive during the planet's occultation), would support such an interpretation.

Mercury, as the planet closest to the Sun, is most often involved in close conjunctions with the greater luminary. Observing people with combust Mercury, many modern astrologers have noted greater mental energy as well as greater powers of concentration in these natives. However, astrologers have also observed that this position, unless counteracted by other factors in the natal chart, causes people with combust Mercurys to be less able to see points of view other than their own.

M. JOHAN. BAPTISTAM Hebenſtreitt/ Auguſt.
Gymnaſij Ulmenſis Rector. Aſtrophilum.

Erſtlich Gedruckt zu Vlm / bey Johann Medern/
Anno M DC XVIII.

**A detail of the title page from a publication dealing with a comet from 1618. *Reproduced by permission of Fortean Picture Library.***

**Sources:**

Bach, Eleanor. *Astrology from A to Z: An Illustrated Source Book*. New York: Philosophical Library, 1990.

DeVore, Nicholas. *Encyclopedia of Astrology*. New York: Philosophical Library, 1947.

## Comets

A comet (from the Greek word *kometes*, meaning "longhaired") is a celestial body composed of ice, rock, and frozen gases that has been quaintly described as a dirty snowball. Almost all comets observed from Earth are part of our solar system, following long elliptical orbits that bring them from outside the orbit of Pluto, close to the Sun, and then back beyond Pluto. Many become involved with gravitational forces in the planetary system, so that they subsequently follow paths that keep them considerably inside Pluto's orbit—some even become trapped inside Jupiter's orbit. The so-called tail of a comet is produced when the comet passes close enough to the Sun for sunlight to heat it up, causing gas and dust particles to escape from the nucleus and form a glowing tail.

As extraordinary heavenly phenomena that did not appear to follow the same regular patterns as the stars or the planets, comets were traditionally regarded as signs of unusually important events. In Western countries in particular, they were regarded as omens of disaster—such as plagues, famines, and war. In China, they were also traditionally regarded as omens—either good or evil. To modern people who rarely look at the night sky—much less ever having seen a comet—this explanation appears unreasonable. To understand ancients' response to comets, one must empathize with them and understand that they saw celestial events as messages from the gods. Furthermore, our generation has not had the opportunity to view any truly spectacular comets—fiery visitors that in times past lit up the night sky with a spectacle of brilliance exceeding the glow of a full Moon. With these considerations in mind, it is easier to understand the response of the French surgeon Ambroise Paré to a comet that appeared over Europe in 1528: "It appeared to be of great length and the color of blood. At its summit was visible the figure of a bent arm, holding in its hand a great sword as if ready to strike. On either side of the tail were seen a great number of axes, knives, and bloodstained swords, among which were hideous human faces with beards and bristling hair." The comet was horrible and produced such great terror among the common people that many died of fear and many others fell sick, as noted in David Ritchie's book *Comets: The Swords of Heaven*.

Many meteors are constituted from the residue of comets. This residual matter is drawn into Earth's gravitational field, burns up as it passes through the atmosphere, and occasionally creates a visible flash that we call a falling or shooting star. Less frequently, enough mass is left after the journey through the atmosphere for a meteor to actually strike the surface of Earth. In this situation, the meteor becomes a meteorite.

Despite the importance that earlier generations of astrologers attributed to comets, modern astrologers have tended to ignore them. However, ephemeredes of such well-known comets as Halley's exist, so it is possible to place at least these in horoscopes and study their influence. It is also relevant to note that Chiron—a large planetoid orbiting between Saturn and Uranus that has been given an extraordinary amount of attention by contemporary astrologers—is a comet. It is thus entirely possible that comet studies will find a place in modern astrology in the not-too-distant future.

**Sources:**

Brandt, John C. *Comets: Readings from Scientific American*. San Francisco: W. H. Freeman and Co., 1981.

Krupp, E. C. *Beyond the Blue Horizon: Myths and Legends of the Sun, Moon, Stars, and Planets*. New York: HarperCollins, 1991.

Ritchie, David. *Comets: The Swords of Heaven*. New York: Plume, 1985.

## Commanding (Obeying)

In traditional astrology, the commanding signs were Taurus through Virgo. The complementary signs, termed obeying, were Scorpio through Pisces. The commanding/obeying schema was a way of designating equal distances from the Aries-Libra axis, rather than an assertion about the characteristics of the relevant signs.

## Common

Mercury is a neutral planet in the sense that it is neither feminine nor masculine, neither malefic nor benefic, etc. As a planet that tends to take on the traits of its sign and house placement more readily than other planets, the astrological tradition has characterized Mercury as a common (meaning, in this case, neutral) planet. "Common signs" is another designation for mutable signs (Gemini, Virgo, Sagittarius, and Pisces), which represent a kind of halfway point between the two extremes of cardinal and fixed signs and are thus common (again in the sense of neutral).

## Common Planet

The planet Mercury is sometimes refered to as a common planet, perhaps because of its androgynous character.

## Composite Chart

A composite chart is a form of synastry in which the horoscopes of two individuals (or of some other entity, such as a corporation) being compared are overlaid, the midpoints between the planets and the house cusps calculated, and a third chart generated consisting entirely of these midpoints. For example, if one individual's Sun was located at 15° Scorpio and the other person's Sun at 15° Virgo, the Sun in the composite chart would be placed at 15° Libra. The same operation is carried out for all of the planets and houses.

A composite chart, like other methods of chart comparison, is supposed to reveal how two different people or entities interact. Many astrologers, however, have criticized the composite method, finding it less than satisfactory for uncovering interpersonal dynamics. An alternative interpretation is that, rather than providing insight into the interpersonal dimension, the composite chart shows how the pair of people in the relationship operate together in the world. According to this line of interpretation, a composite chart would provide insight into the "personality" of a marriage or the "personality" of a business partnership.

All major astrological software programs will calculate a composite chart, and many software companies also market report programs that interpret composite charts.

## Concept Asteroids

Asteroids are thousands of small planetoids, 95 percent of whose orbits lie between those of Mars and Jupiter. Initially these asteroids were given mythological names, but as more asteroids were discovered, astronomers began naming them after places, people, and, eventually, concepts. Astrologers who have studied the influence of asteroids have reached the conclusion that the name of an asteroid gives one preliminary insight into the asteroid's astrological effects.

The early asteroids studied by astrologers were named after mythological figures, and an exploration of the relevant myths provided a preliminary clue to the nature of these tiny planetoids' influence. When researchers began shifting away from explicitly mythological asteroids and began examining asteroids named after concepts, they continued to follow their previous line of exploration by finding initial clues to the astrological influences of such asteroids in the concepts after which they were named. Pax, for example, is the Latin word for peace, which is a clue to the presumably "peaceful" or "pacifying" influence of the asteroid Pax.

**Sources:**

Kowal, Charles T. *Asteroids: Their Nature and Utilization*. Chichester, West Sussex, UK: Ellis Horwood Limited, 1988.

Room, Adrian. *Dictionary of Astronomical Names*. London: Routledge, 1988.

Schwartz, Jacob. *Asteroid Name Encyclopedia*. St. Paul, MN: Llewellyn Publications, 1995.

## Conception (Conception Charts)

Although genethliacal, or natal, astrology has settled on the birth time as the moment for casting the horoscope, astrologers have long felt that it would also be desirable to cast charts for the moment of conception. Ptolemy, for example, asserted that gender as well as certain other prenatal events could be deduced from the planets at the time of conception. However, the obvious difficulties involved in determining precise conception moments have effectively frustrated astrological research in this area. For the most part, the observation that Nicholas deVore made in his *Encyclopedia of Astrology* still applies: "The entire subject of prenatal cosmic stimulation is a welter of confused theorizing, which yet lacks confirmation in practice sufficient to bring about any unanimity of opinion."

Some contemporary thinkers, nevertheless, have been intrepid enough to explore this largely uncharted domain. Of greatest significance has been the work of Eugen Jonas, a Czech psychiatrist who developed a system of astrological birth control based on the discovery that women have a cycle of fertility beyond the normal ovulation cycle—one based on the phase of the Moon. Jonas found, among many other interesting things, that the sign the Moon (which rules the principal of conception and motherhood) was in during conception determined the offspring's sex—male in the case of masculine signs and female in the case of feminine signs.

In an effort to construct usable conception charts, some twentieth-century astrologers have picked up on the trutine of Hermes, an ancient principle for casting conception charts ascribed to the legendary Hermes Trismegistus that asserts that "the place of the Moon at conception was the Ascendant of the birth figure [i.e., conjunct the ascendant of the natal chart] or its opposite point [conjunct the descendant]." If Hermes was correct, then the trutine could be used to determine the precise time of conception in cases where the date and time of conception were known approximately. Prenatal charts relying on the trutine were seriously proposed in the early twentieth century by Walter Gornold (who wrote under the pen name Sepharial) in *The Solar Epoch* and by E. H. Bailey in *The Prenatal Epoch*.

**Sources:**

Bailey, E. H. *The Prenatal Epoch*. New York: S. Weiser, 1970.

Brau, Jean-Louis, Helen Weaver, and Allan Edmands. *Larousse Encyclopedia of Astrology*. New York: New American Library, 1980.

DeVore, Nicholas. *Encyclopedia of Astrology*. New York: Philosophical Library, 1947.

Gettings, Fred. *Dictionary of Astrology*. London: Routledge & Kegan Paul, 1985.

Ostrander, Sheila, and Lynn Schroeder. *Astrological Birth Control*. Englewood Cliffs, NJ: Prentice-Hall, 1972.

Sepharial. *The Solar Epoch*. New York: S. Weiser 1970.

## Conceptive Signs

The conceptive signs are the four fixed signs: Taurus, Leo, Scorpio, and Aquarius.

## Concordia

Concordia, asteroid 58 (the 58th asteroid to be discovered, on March 24, 1860), is approximately 104 kilometers in diameter and has an orbital period of 4.4 years. It was named after a Latin word for peace. Concordia shows peacefulness—or the seeking of peace—by its house and sign position (e.g., peace with relatives in the third house, peace with employees in the sixth, and so forth); also, Concordia shows agreements between people or nations.

**Sources:**

Kowal, Charles T. *Asteroids: Their Nature and Utilization*. Chichester, West Sussex, UK: Ellis Horwood Limited, 1988.

Room, Adrian. *Dictionary of Astronomical Names*. London: Routledge, 1988.

Schwartz, Jacob. *Asteroid Name Encyclopedia*. St. Paul, MN: Llewellyn Publications, 1995.

## Configuration

Traditionally, the term configuration was used to refer to any aspect. In contemporary astrology, the term is reserved for sets of interrelated aspects involving three or more planets, such as T-squares, grand trines, and so forth. By extension, the configuration is sometimes used to refer to the pattern presented by the entire horoscope.

## Conjunction

A conjunction is, as the name implies, an aspect in which two points—such as two planets—are close enough that their energies join. A conjunction is a major aspect, regarded as harmonious or inharmonious depending on the planets involved. For example, a conjunction involving planets such as Jupiter and Venus would exert a generally fortunate influence, while a conjunction involving Saturn or Pluto would be challenging, to say the least. A conjunction is sometimes called the aspect of prominence because it brings the planets involved into prominence in a chart.

## Constantia

Constantia, asteroid 315 (the 315th asteroid to be discovered, on September 4, 1891), is approximately 8 kilometers in diameter and has an orbital period of 3.4 years. Its name is a personified form of constancy, and is Latin for "steadfastness." In a natal chart, its location by sign and house indicates where one experiences or seeks constancy. When afflicted by inharmonious aspects, Constantia may show inconstancy or a false sense of stability. If prominent in a chart (e.g., conjunct the Sun or the ascendant), it may show an exceptionally fair person or someone for whom constancy and the seeking of stability and security are dominant life themes.

**Sources:**

Kowal, Charles T. *Asteroids: Their Nature and Utilization*. Chichester, West Sussex, UK Ellis Horwood Limited, 1988.

Room, Adrian. *Dictionary of Astronomical Names*. London: Routledge, 1988.

Schwartz, Jacob. *Asteroid Name Encyclopedia*. St. Paul, MN: Llewellyn Publications, 1995.

## Constellation

A constellation is a collection of stars that the ancients grouped together, identified with a figure from mythology, and named after that figure. In astrology, the names of the various signs of the zodiac are taken from 12 constellations intersected by the ecliptic. The untutored eye has a difficult time discerning the relationship between these star groups and the figures they are said to represent: Unlike the ancients, who gazed upon a sky filled with legends, heroes, and heroines, we moderns look up to see only a confused mass of tiny lights.

## Contemporary Academic Study of Astrology

Like the field of new religious movements (NRMs), mainstream academic studies of astrology are a comparatively recent development. While the scientific study of NRMs has developed for approximately 40 years, the university focus on astrology as a behavioral phenomenon developed only in the 1990s. The reflection of this novel innovation is that there are few published works that approach the subject from a detached and sophisticated perspective. The sponsorship efforts of the British-based Sophia Trust is one attempt to remedy this situation and encourage production from within a range of critical inquiries such as sociological studies of popular belief in astrology.

As a system of divination based on the positions of the sun, moon, planets, and stars, astrology finds its origins in ancient Mesopotamia and Egypt. During the days of imperial Rome, this astral method of divining flourished intermittently. Astrology died out in western Europe in the fifth century C.E. under the combined influence of the collapse of literacy and Christian hostility, but it survived in Syria, Persia, and India from where it was reintroduced into the Islamic world in the eighth to ninth centuries and from there to Europe in the twelfth century. Its popularity in the fourteenth century French court gave it a fashionable appeal that encouraged its acceptance in England. While Bede and Alcuin were both interested in the sky, in England,

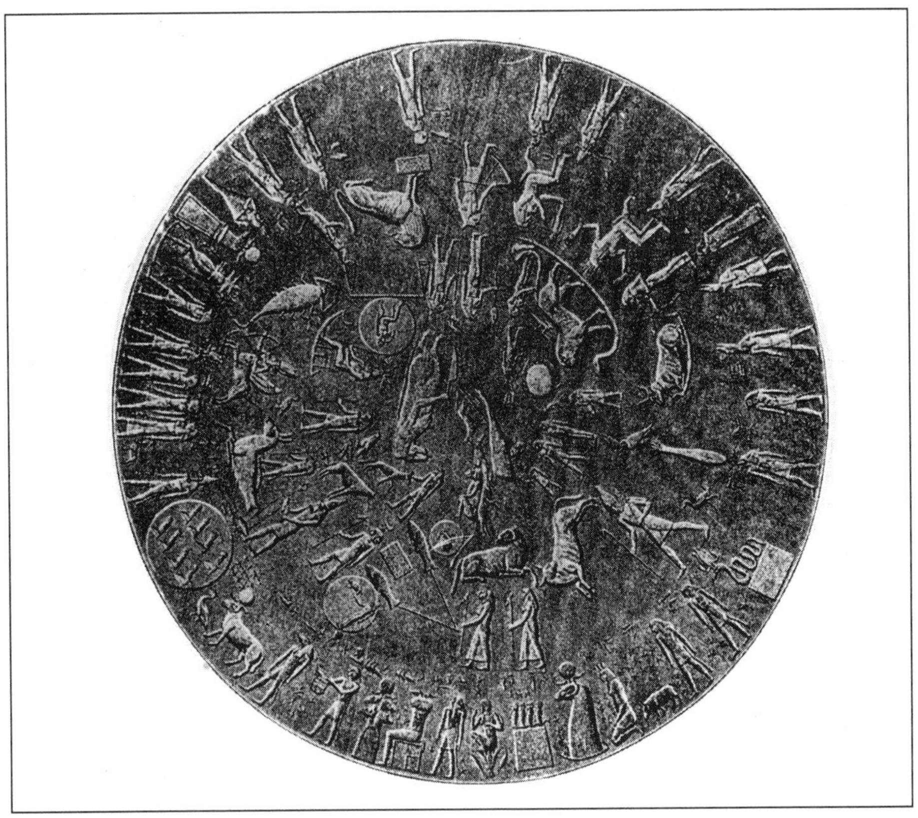

**An image of a Denderah constellation map, sometimes called the Denderah zodiac. The original is housed in the Louvre. *Reproduced by permission of Fortean Picture Library.***

astrology was practiced by such notables as Adelard of Bath, Geoffrey Chaucer, John Dee and Elias Ashmole. In the 17th century, William Lilly demarcated the ritual circle used in magical invocation for the confinement of conjured demons with astrological symbols, here being regarded in themselves as conveyors of supernatural power. In Germany, poet Johann Wolfgang von Goethe, building upon the Faustian legends, depicted his hero as an astrologer as well as a sorcerer.

The daily horoscope emerged as a journalistic feature in the 1930s. The early presentations quickly appealed to a receptive public sentiment, and the horoscope column has become a regular aspect of tabloids and syndicated newspapers ever since. Vernacular interest in astrology is a complex issue, and several scholars—with the Cultural Astronomy and Astrology (CAA) Programme funded by the Sophia Project and beyond—are currently involved with understanding the dynamics of "astrological belief" and other sociological implications from the popular Western concern with astrological prediction and character assessment. One notable factor in the standardization of stellar divination and personality types classified according to the constellations of the zodiac has been the influence of the theosophist Alan Leo (William Frederick Allen, 1860–1917). It was Leo who, as a professional astrologer, laid the foundations for the present-day understanding of what he termed the "science of the stars." Moreover, he founded the journal *Modern Astrology* and authored numerous books on the subject. In the course of the 20th century, through its links with theosophy, astrology became the *lingua franca* of the 1960s counterculture as well as many of the New Age movements that have descended from it. For New Age spirituality, use of the astronomical phenomenon of the precession of the equinoxes has become the seminal framework within which the New Age of Aquarius has been heralded. While this detection of the planet's gyroscopic motion that makes the zodiac appear from the perspective of the earth to advance incrementally is an astronomical understanding, its cultural familiarity and historical interpretation have been fostered chiefly by the legacy of astrology rather than through the findings of empirical science.

It is in fact precisely through the advent of the empirical sciences that astrology has come to receive increased criticism and skeptical attack. As Michael R. Meyer (1974) sees it, "The study of astrology was held in the highest respect by most academic institutions throughout Europe, Asia, and North Africa right up until the dawn of the 'Age of Reason'—the eighteenth century, when the 'sciences' to which astrology gave birth rationalized that it was invalid." Much of the modern-day astrophysicist antagonism to astrology culminated with the Bok "Objections to Astrology" manifesto that physicists and astronomers were asked to sign in 1975. While a standard astrological defense is to maintain that the predictive propensities of the system have themselves been acquired through empirical observation, it could be argued instead that astrological interpretation derives from religio-culturally established understandings of archetypal personalities (e.g., mercurial, jovial, and saturnine characteristics) and numerological symbolism. Already in his third-century C.E. *Enneads*, Plotinus agued that the stars are signifiers or symbols of events rather than causes.

If science tends to condemn the *a priori* as superstition—especially when it appears unsupported by empirical observation, what becomes of interest to the sociologist is the very persistence of belief that appears to fly in the face of contemporary and demonstrable aspects of rationalism. In their turn, New Age spokespeople often reject the province of science as restricted and narrow and inapplicable to the mystical "wisdom traditions." But regardless of alleged outmoded thought forms from the vantage of New Age culture, there is within the astrological community more broadly an effort to revalidate the use of nuance, metaphor and interpretation.

But if astrology must face antagonism from the preserve of canonical science, it must also deal with the antipathy engendered from traditional mainstream western religions. In particular, the socially accepted forms of established Christianity are not at all receptive to "astrological magic," which even if valid or, rather, especially if valid, is judged to be nefarious work conducted only under the sovereignty of Satan. One question contemporary researchers must invariably consider is why do people continue to resort to a form of divination that is not sanctioned by the ecclesiastical authorities. Sociologically, this opens up to the wider question of dissent and change that occurs within religion and the shifting boundaries in establishing legitimacy and permissible determination.

## Researchers of Astrology as a Social Phenomenon

In the United States, a major development has been the Seattle-based establishment of the Kepler College of Astrology and the Liberal Arts. In 2000, Kepler College was authorized by the state of Washington to offer B.A. and M.A. degrees in astrological studies. Although there are no formal methodological courses, Kepler students are nevertheless encouraged to undertake their own research. To date, several B.A. students have incorporated phenomenological investigations into their papers, and the college hopes that as its M.A. program matures, methodologically based work will become a standard part of the college's activities. In the meantime, academically sponsored sociological research into cultural astrology occurs only on an *ad hoc* basis across the nation. For example, through the sociology department of the University of California at Santa Barbara, Shoshanah Feher has conducted postgraduate research into differences between, as she noted in an article she wrote in *Perspectives on the New Age*, "those practitioners of astrology who utilize their craft as an instrument for predicting future events and those who speak of it as one tool among many in a spiritual quest." Feher collected data at the United Astrologers' Congress in New Orleans, Louisiana, in 1989, and she is particularly interested in the way gender manifests in the New Age movement.

In Spain, at the Universidad de Zaragoza, headed by Professor Jesús Navarro Artigas of the Departmento Ingeniería Electrónica y Comunicaciones, a research project has been launched in collaboration with the departments of philosophy and of history and art that concerns the interdisciplinary character of the history of astrology. This project was organized in 2001 into three main sections: astrology in antiquity: origins and gnoseology; astrology and historiography; and astrology and science. The first section is concerned with exploring such concepts as knowledge, myth, and divination. The second section is attempting to classify the various astrological schools and tendencies that have emerged in the West since the Age of Enlightenment. The third section endeavors to develop a sociology of knowledge in which scientific and astrological paradigms are compared and the study of their mutual interaction is undertaken. For the University of Zaragoza, this project represents the first step of an innovative venture.

In Great Britain, the Sophia Project, sponsored by the Sophia Trust, funds four principle initiatives in its effort "to advance the scholarly study of astrology and cultural astronomy in British institutions of higher education" (www.sophia-project.org.uk). These include short-term research fellowships (of one to three months) into any pre-1700 aspect of the history of astrology or cultural astronomy at the University of London's Warburg Institute. A second initiative is the "cosmology and divination" modules at the University of Kent at Canterbury. These are part of the mysticism and religious experience program and are divided between undergraduate coursework and the postgraduate M.A. Both modules begin with astrology as a divinatory practice in ancient, classical, Renaissance, and modern times.

The Sophia Project's other two initiatives are more sociologically oriented. These include sponsorships of the Research Group for the Critical Study of Astrology (RGCSA) at the University of Southampton and the Sophia Centre for the Study of

Cultural Astronomy and Astrology (SCSCAA) at Bath Spa University College (BSUC). The former, under the auspices of the Social Work Studies Department, concentrates on social science research and is establishing a database on research into astrology (for example, the use of astrology in counseling). The latter, an outgrowth of BSUC's Department for the Study of Religions, has its own premises at the college's Newton Park campus to promote the academic study of astrology and its practice and pursue research, scholarship, and teaching on the relationship between cosmological, astronomical and astrological beliefs, myths and theories in past and contemporary society, politics, religion, and the arts. SCSCAA offers postgraduate programs (M.A. and Ph.D) and has plans to extend its curricula to the M.B.A. level as well.

The RGCSA program comprises seven chief foci. First is the study of history and the history of science—especially in considering the central role astrology has played in the history of culture and the development of scientific thought. Secondly, there is a concern with archeology or archeoastronomy and how understanding of planetary and stellar systems and their symbolisms has been integral in the construction of ancient ritualistic centers. Works that typify the efforts in this direction are Baity (1973) and Ruggles (1999). More contemporary orientation, however, appears in the RGCSA's remaining concentrations. Its third focus is anthropological and involves the role of astrological belief in modern cultures and social systems. A fourth interest along the lines of Tyson's pursuit (1982; 1984) is described as sociological and seeks, among other things, to understand the persistence of attention to horoscopes in a scientific age. Related here is psychological research such as that undertaken by Eysenck and discerning any possible link between personality and planetary indication—e.g., connections between alleged astrological influence and the complex of health psychology. Another interest is in understanding the astrological community itself from a sociological perspective. And lastly, the RGCSA seeks to investigate both rigorously and skeptically the astrological, astronomical and biological interconnections, if any, between season-of-birth, on the one hand, and personality, career, and personal problems, on the other.

One problem for all modern researchers into cultural astronomy and astrology in particular is that they are confronted with few predecessors and accredited works on which to develop their own projects. Most effort in the field of astrological research has been toward attempting to prove or disprove astrology as a science. This usually comes down to whether predictions of future events and/or personality development that are based on the configurations of the stars and planets can be verified. There has been correspondingly little in the way of cultural and social analysis of the phenomenon itself as it affects or is used by people themselves—whether individually or collectively. An example of the use of astrology affecting an entire group would be, among others, the postponing of the date for independence by the Republic of India for a more auspicious moment in which to launch the new nation.

At best, apart from the attempts to prove or disprove stellar-based divination, astrological studies to date are chiefly historical and follow the lead of the 1899 pioneering work of Richard Allen's 1963 *Star-Names and Their Meanings*. Allen minutely investigated the folklore heritage associated with the heavenly bodies that have been recorded in the writings of the Chinese, Arabic, Mesopotamian, Biblical, Greek, and

Roman civilizations. What he has produced is a pan-cultural decipherment of historical traditions and ancient astronomical understandings. A more contemporary contribution along similar lines is Bernadette Brady's 1998 *Book of Fixed Stars*.

For a sociological rather than historical investigation of astrology, a leading contemporary effort is represented in the research being undertaken by Bath Spa University College's Nicholas Campion under the auspices of its Department for the Study of Religions. In his investigation into prophecy, cosmology, and the New Age movement, Campion is implicitly questioning whether astrology is a belief or belief system. More specifically, he wishes to determine whether astrology is a New Age belief and as such whether it is incompatible with more orthodox religious belief—namely, with mainstream Christianity. The overall import of Campion's exploration into conviction concerns the religious aspects of astrology. He is here less interested in the nature of astrology per se but rather in the external and internal perceptions of whether it is a religion.

Consequently, Campion identifies his central concern as belief. He considers faith itself to be the overarching problem that unites both the extent and nature of belief in astrology, and he argues that contemporary astrological belief is typically presented as a problematic historical issue: in historical terms, how could anyone believe in such superstition in an age of reason? Campion recognizes, accordingly, that trust in astrology threatens both scientific skeptics and religious evangelicals.

Part of Campion's study is indeed historical. In developing an understanding of the nature of astrology, he must examine its historical relationship with religion—including the origins of Christianity and astrology's conflict and accommodation with it. Campion traces contemporary astrology from the 1890s, and he is particularly concerned with the development of its esoteric and psychological schools of thought. His exploration further extends into examining the reasons given for astrological belief in religious, sociological, psychological, and scientific literature. However, his focus on New Age spirituality must address whether astrology is itself to be considered a New Age discipline. He traces the origin of the concept of the Age of Aquarius to the 19th century and argues that this construct motivated the spiritual and psychological approaches to the discipline held by such "astrological reformers" as Alan Leo, Alice Bailey, Marc Edmund Jones and Dane Rudhyar.

This historical perspective, however, extends as well into the development of newspaper and magazine astrological columns—including the development and history of popular astrology prior to 1930 in almanacs and birthday books. With the development of sun-sign astrology by Alan Leo—culminating in the horoscope column of popular post-1930 astrology—Campion is above all interested in the vernacular vocabulary that has developed as part of this process. In this light he must determine the extent of readership, the role of horoscope columns in the media, and astrologers' attitudes toward these columns. In determining the structure and nature of the horoscope column, Campion confronts the sociological question of their function, precisely, "do they offer hope?"

Methodologically, Campion is following a two-pronged approach. He wants to determine the attitudes of astrologers to astrology as well as public attitudes to and "belief" in astrology. His fieldwork requires in-depth interviews and indicative questionnaires with professional astrologers themselves—such as those he conducted during the Astrological Association gathering in Orlando, Florida, July 18–26, 2002. On the popular front, by contrast, Campion is relying on distributing questionnaires to sample groups to determine the extent of belief in astrology. Here again he is conducting in-depth interviews of people who read horoscope columns and those who are clients of professional astrologers.

In what may prove to be the most comprehensive study to date into the nature of astrological belief, Campion's research is particularly significant. He wishes to determine what is astrology and whether there is one astrology or several different astrologies. Specifically, what does astrology offer and what does this offering tell about astrology itself? Further, does astrology conform to any definitions of religion, and could it be defined as a vernacular form of religion? Campion also wishes to explore and determine the broader significances for the study of contemporary religion: expressly, sociology's secularization issue, namely, the role of belief in astrology as a possible factor in the decline of church attendance. Ultimately, the Campion study, by investigating the nature of "belief" in society as a whole, aims to elucidate what the study of astrology and its belief might tell about humans and their psychological propensities at large. Campion describes his work as "the first consistent and competent attempt to evaluate this area, and quantitative and qualitative measures are being combined to establish not just how many people believe, but what exactly it is that they believe in."

While Campion has joined the teaching staff of the SCSCAA, his colleague Patrick Curry at the Centre is involved with developing a coherent and rigorous understanding of the theory and practice of astrology from its beginnings to modern times. Curry advances to his subject from the perspective of the cultural history of ideas, but in keeping with his non-reductive approach he incorporates the subject's social, political, and material dimensions as well. He is particularly concerned with the Weberian thesis concerning disenchantment and the dynamics of reenchantment in which astrology might be playing a role.

Most other research projects into astrology explore particular aspects that may be seen as attempts to validate the discipline. For instance, British-based Sean Lovatt is seeking independently to locate correlations of TRS (tropical revolving storms, i.e., hurricanes) with the lunation cycle and the declination of both sun and moon. All the same, these investigations often retain social science dimensions nonetheless—especially those that are currently underway in consultation with the RGCSA. Among these there is the work being conducted by Bernadette Brady in Australia. Brady's current research project investigates the horoscope correlations between parents and their children. She has had informal discussions with RGCSA's Chris Bagley concerning the investigation, her statistics, and the use of Jigsaw, a software application design for research into astrology that Brady coauthored in the mid-1990s with Esoteric Technologies in Adelaide, South Australia. Her work has been inspired by the hereditary work of Michel Gauquelin and the shortcomings she perceived in that work by not fully appreciating the traditional horoscopic associations that can link one chart to another—associations such as a planet's "rulership" over a sign, its exaltation and angularity as additional ways that an astrological influence can be represented from one generation to another. Brady's research paper published in *Correlation* (July 2002) explores these types of relationships, and her results indicate that the astrological concepts of old rulership seem to be more influential than new rulerships when establishing a correlation between the charts of parents and their children. She found that these correlations hold true over a range of different experiments. However, she claims that the most interesting result in the entire project is the ancient Greek disused technique called the Noddings of the Moon. This gives surprisingly strong results when the mother's chart is considered. Nevertheless, the data can also be examined via sorting by the gender of the child, as well as order of birth. Brady has found that the emerging patterns reveal a greater frequency of correlations in the charts of the first-born child than those born later. Brady's research is a rare attempt to investigate ancient astrological claims employing modern methods.

Another RGCSA project is that of Pat Harris who is exploring the success and failure of fertility treatments in connection with planetary transits (specifically Jupiter and Saturn) to significant positions in the recipients' natal charts. In particular, using three study groups recruited through Internet fertility treatment websites, support groups, such UK publications as *Childchat* and *Child* as well as, for a phase 2 study, women's magazines, newspaper coverage on the research and the website of Jonathan Cainer (http://stars.metawire.com), Harris is endeavoring to test the null hypothesis, namely, that astrological factors have no influence on the results of fertility treatment. She is exploring the possibility entertained by such psychologists as Hans Eysenck, Carl Jung, and Alan Smithers that astrological correlates can be used as predictors of personal functioning, and in particular Harris is continuing the research into statistically significant connections suggested by Jackson (1986) and Millard (1993). In psychological terms, Greene and Sasportas (1987) argue that Saturn is traditionally associated with states of anxiety, while Valentine (1991) identifies Jupiter more or less as Saturn's positive counterpart representing optimism and confidence. The second phase is planned through the Fertility Unit of the Homerton NHS Hospital in London to test that such psychological factors as anxiety and depression (also using the Problems Relating to Infertility Questionnaire, the Spielberger Trait Anxiety Measure, the Beck Depression Inventory II, etc.) will not predict success or failure in IVF treatments. The Problems Relating to Infertility and the Pregnancy and Birth Experiences Questionnaires include sections on astrology, birth data, and the subjects' knowledge of astrology. Consequently, Harris's systematic research represents an important contribution not only to knowledge of the validity or invalidity of astrology as a diagnostic tool but also more widely to the psychological/cultural knowledge of astrology by the study participants.

## Relationship between Astrology and Science

The relationship between astrology and science conforms in general to that between religion and science. In particular, there has appeared to be a sort of religio-cultural war between scientists and astrologers with unsophisticated passions clouding objective judgment on both sides. As Victor Mansfield put it, "Unfortunately, the discussion of astrology, both by scientists who criticize it and those who uphold it, is extraordinarily strident, passionate, and often filled with outrageous statements. There is little dispassionate discussion of the issues and much poor scholarship on both sides" (Mansfield, 1997). In such efforts as the Sophia Project, the Research Group for the Critical Study of Astrology and the Sophia Centre for the Study of Cultural Astronomy and Astrology, there are concerted attempts to remedy the lacunae of proper scholarship in research into astrological and related studies.

On the one hand, attempts to "explain" astrology in scientific terms exist. For instance, Seymour's physical mechanism model for astrological influence is one such effort (Seymour 1992). In this case, however, the model is primarily speculative rather than a truly quantitative physical explanation. It is not supported by the acausal, nonlocal, and participatory character of the contemporary quantum mechanical view of nature. Instead, this last presupposes a unified view of the world as well as an acausal interconnectedness that is more supportive of astrology's fundamental assumption of personal and collective relationship to the cosmos. Current chaos or complexity theory, in fact, suggests that the universe is more nonlinear than linear. This in turn implies the possibility of acausal and nonlocal connections or correlations between the various components of the macro-system (e.g., between planets and people) (Waldrop, 1992; Mansfield, 1995).

On the other hand, the SCSCAA, in particular, seeks to employ the phenomenological approach of the sociology of religion methodology that endeavors to suspend judgments concerning the "truth" or validity of religious assertion and to look instead at how such assertions develop, are used and affect those who hold them. A particular concern is the study of astrology as a *lingua franca*. A sociology of astrology becomes a study of both a subculture and society-at-large in how it accommodates or reacts to the subculture. Astrology possesses a long history both for the West and other cultures (e.g., those of India and China), and this history and perpetually changing social dynamic that it has been and continues to be is the focus of research efforts that use social science methodologies to its study.

—Michael York

**Sources:**

Allen, Richard Hinckley. *Star Names: Their Lore and Meaning*. New York: Dover, 1963.

Baity, Elizabeth Chesley. "Archaeoastronomy and Ethnoastronomy So Far." *Current Anthropology* (October 1973): 389–449.

Barker, Eileen, ed. *New Religious Movements: A Perspective for Understanding Society*. New York: Edward Mellen, 1982.

Bok, Bart J., and Lawrence E. Jerome. *Objections to Astrology*. Buffalo: Prometheus Books, 1975.

Brady, Bernadette."The Australian Parent-Child Astrological Research Project." *Correlation* (July 2002): 4–37.

———. *Brady's Book of Fixed Stars*. York Beach, ME: 1998.

Eysenck, Hans. "Methodological Errors by Critics of Astrological Claims." *Astro-Psychological Problems* (1983): 14–17.

Eysenck, Hans, and David Nias. *Astrology: Science or Superstition?* London: Pelican, 1982.

Feher, Shoshanah. "Who Holds the Cards? Women and New Age Astrology." In *Perspectives on the New Age*. Edited by James R. Lewis and J. Gordon Melton. Albany: SUNY, 1992.

Gauquelin, Michel. *Cosmic Influences on Human Behaviour*. London: Garnstone Press, 1974.

———. *Planetary Heredity* San Diego: ACS Publications, 1988.

Gauquelin, Michel, Françoise Gauquelin, and Hans Eysenck. "Personality and Position of the Planets at Birth." *British Journal of Social and Clinical Psychology* (1979): 71–75.

Green, Liz, and Howard Sasportas. *The Development of the Personality: Seminars in Psychological Astrology* Vol. 1. London: Routledge and Kegan Paul, 1987.

Hill, Michael. *A Sociology of Religion*. London: Heinemann, 1973.

Hughes, S. "Nephrology and Astrology—Is There a Link?" *British Journal of Clinical Practice* (1990): 279.

Jackson, Eve. *Jupiter: An Astrologer's Guide*. London: Aquarian Press, 1986.

Kontos, Alkis. "The World Disenchanted, and the Return of Gods and Demons." In *The Barbarism of Reason: Max Weber and the Twilight of Enlightenment*. Edited by Asher Horowitz and Terry Maley. Toronto: University of Toronto Press, 1994.

MacKenna, Steven, trans. *Plotinus: The Enneads*. Burdett, NY: Larson Publications, 1992.

Mansfield, Victor. "An Astrophysicist's Sympathetic and Critical View of Astrology." Presentation at the Cycles and Symbols conference in San Francisco, February 14–16, 1997.

———. *Synchronicity, Science, and Soul-Making* Chicago: Open Court Publishing, 1995.

Mayo, Jeff, O. White, and Hans Eysenck. "An Empirical Study of the Relation Between Astrological Factors and Personality." *Journal of Social Psychology* (1978): 229–36.

Meyer, Michael R. *A Handbook for the Humanistic Astrologer*. Garden City, NY: Anchor Press/Doubleday, 1974.

Millard, Margaret. "In Vitro Fertilisation." *The Astrological Association Journal* (November/December 1993): 361–64.

Philipps, David P., T. E. Ruth, and L. M. Wagner. "Psychology and Survival." *Lancet* (1993): 1142–45.

Robbins, Thomas, and Dick Anthony. "New Religious Movements and the Social System: Integration, Disintegration or Transformation." *Annual Review of the Social Sciences of Religion* (1978): 1–28.

Ruggles, Clive. *Astronomy in Prehistoric Britain and Ireland*. New Haven, CT: Yale University Press, 1999.

Seymour, Percy. *The Scientific Basis of Astrology*. New York: St. Martin's Press, 1992.

Tester, Jim. *A History of Western Astrology* Woodbridge, Suffolk, UK: Boydell Press, 1987.

Tyson, G. A. "An Empirical Test of the Astrological Theory of Differences." *Personality and Individual Differences* (1984): 247–50.

———. "People Who Consult Astrologers: A Profile." *Personality and Individual Differences* (1982): 119–26).

University of London's Warburg Institute. www.sas.ac.uk/warburg.

Valentine, Christine. *Images of the Psyche: Exploring the Planets through Psychology and Myth*. Shaftsbury, England: Element Books, 1991.

Waldrop, M. Mitchell, *Complexity: The Emerging Science at the Edge of Order and Chaos*. (New York: Touchstone, 1992.

Weber, Max. "Science as Vocation." In *From Max Weber: Essays in Sociology*. Edited and translated by H. H. Gerth and C. Wright Mills. New York: Oxford University Press, 1958.

Wilson, Bryan R. "The New Religions: Some Preliminary Considerations." *Japanese Journal of Religious Studies* (1979): 193–216).

York, Michael. *The Emerging Network: A Sociology of the New Age and Neo-Pagan Movements*. Lanham, MD: Rowan and Littlefield, 1995.

## CONTRAPARALLEL

The orbits of most of the planets in the solar system lie in approximately the same geometric plane, which is why we are able to draw an astrological chart using only a two-dimensional representation rather than one with three dimensions. There is, nevertheless, a variation in the tilt or angle of these orbits, and at any given time most planets are positioned north and south of the celestial equator (the plane described by projecting the Earth's equator against the background of the stars). This variation is measured in degrees of declination. Two planets are contraparallel when they lie on opposite sides of the celestial equator and have the same degree of declination (e.g., one planet at 10° declination and the other at –10°). Planets with opposite declinations are said to have a relationship similar to an opposition. Relatively few astrologers take contraparallels into account when interpreting a horoscope.

**Sources:**

DeVore, Nicholas. *Encyclopedia of Astrology*. New York: Philosophical Library, 1947.
Hand, Robert. *Horoscope Symbols*. Rockport, MA: Para Research, 1981.

## CONTRASCION

Picture the wheel of the zodiac and draw a straight line from 0° Aries to 0° Libra so as to divide the circle into equal halves. If a planet is located at an angular distance of 45° away from this dividing line (e.g., at 15° Taurus), its contrascion would be 45° in the opposite direction from the line (i.e., at 15° Aquarius). If another planet happens to be located at or very near the contrascion of the first planet, the two planets are said to have a relationship with each other comparable to an opposition aspect.

## CONVERSE DIRECTIONS

The term "converse directions" refers to progressing planets backward rather than forward in an ephemeris during prognostication.

## CORRECTION

In astrology, correction refers to the translation of one's birth time into sidereal time.

## CORRESPONDENCES, LAW OF

The law of correspondences refers, primarily, to the notion—widely accepted in occult circles—that everything in this world is the manifestation of some spiritual principle. The expression "as above, so below" partially articulates this idea. Because the premodern world believed that celestial bodies were spiritual (or at least semispiritual), the law of correspondences was invoked to explain astrological influences. The ancient notion of correspondences is sometimes equated with the modern idea (derived from Jungian psychology) of synchronicity. However, synchronicity applies to any meaningful coincidence—not simply to parallels between events "above" and events "below." Synchronicity also does not carry the same metaphysical connotations usually associated with the law of correspondences.

## Co-significator

Co-significator, a term used particularly in horary astrology, refers to a planet or sign that in some way relates to the matter under consideration by virtue of certain traditional astrological associations.

## Cosmic Patterns Software

Cosmic Patterns Software was founded in 1983 by David Cochrane. It is best known as the developers of Kepler, a comprehensive astrological software program used by thousands of astrologers.

When the company incorporated in 2002, its four programmers were David Cochrane, Victor Ogienko, Victoria Thompson, and Thilakavathi Raja. Ogienko, from Kiev, Ukraine, joined Cosmic Patterns that year. With an extensive knowledge of many programming languages, a wealth of technical expertise, an M.S. degree in electrical engineering, and a background in developing astrological programs, Ogienko decided to join Cosmic Patterns to accelerate the development of a comprehensive software program. Thompson joined Cosmic Patterns in the early 1980s after many years as a software developer in the Boston, Massachusetts, area. Raja, who joined Cosmic Patterns in 1999, has a B.S. degree in computer science. Fei Cochrane is the business manager and directs the affairs of the entire company. There are also dozens of astrologers, translators, graphic artists, and others who provide materials and work as independent providers of services to Cosmic Patterns. In 2001, Cosmic Patterns had annual revenues in excess of $500,000, about $80,000 of which was paid out in royalties to authors of interpretive reports.

**Sources:**

*Cosmic Patterns Software*. www.astrosoftware.com.

## Cosmobiology

Cosmobiology is a contemporary form of scientific astrology that is especially popular in Europe. Cosmobiology utilizes modern methods of scientific research, such as statistics, analysis, and computer programming. The word cosmobiology was coined by the Austrian physician Dr. Friedrich Feerhow and was later used by the Swiss statistician K. E. Krafft to designate that branch of astrology working on scientific foundations and keyed to the natural sciences. Cosmobiology has, through the work of Reinhold Ebertin, become increasingly well-known within the last 50 years.

Despite the great diagnostic value of cosmobiology in the fields of characterology and psychology, one should not forget that the individual's natal constellation can only be seen and properly interpreted in connection with his or her life history (medical history, upbringing, the time and circumstances in which he or she lives, religion, manners and morals, environment, etc.).

## The Cosmogram

The cosmogram is the cosmobiological equivalent of horoscope, and designates the notation of a cosmic constellation. The foundation for casting the cosmogram is the zodiac, which the Sun moves through in one year. Each of the signs of the zodiac encompasses 30 smaller divisions called degrees. Accordingly, the whole circle contains 360 degrees.

To locate the positions of the stellar bodies in the zodiac more exactly, 1 degree is divided into 60 minutes (60') and every minute is again divided into 60 seconds (60"). The position of each stellar body is written down in degrees, minutes, and, sometimes, in seconds. To distinguish subdivisions of degrees from subdivisions of hours, one uses the symbols *h* (for hour), *m* (minute), and *s* (second) when discussing time.

## The 90° Dial

Each tradition and profession develops suitable tools with which to ease and improve its work. The most important aid for cosmobiological investigation is the 90° dial.

Traditionally, the horoscope has been divided into one of several house systems that offer further interpretations for the inquiring astrologer. Cosmobiology does not utilize a house system. Instead, the focus is on planetary influences, which are enhanced so as to dominate the interpretation of a chart.

The cosmogram, composed of two circles, is the basic form used for interpretation in cosmobiology. One circle is the standard 360° circle for the regular planetary distribution; the other is a 90° circle.

The 360° circle is a recognized measuring device for investigation. To simplify the process of investigation, we reduce the 360° circle to a fourth (i.e., the regular 360° circle is quartered and folded into four equal parts to provide a unique structure for discerning the angular distribution of the stellar bodies. The resulting 90° "circle" groups cardinal, fixed, and mutable quadruplicates together, with each quadruplicity occupying 30° of the 90° circle.

Prior to constructing a cosmogram, one must have a chart locating the stellar bodies on a 360° circle. This can be derived from standard chart erection methods, so it is suggested that the astrologer begin by constructing the type of horoscope she or he is accustomed to, then transcribe the planets to the cosmogram in their proper places; this method will prove very helpful in making the transition from traditional astrology to cosmobiology.

Cosmobiology utilizes much smaller orbs in ascertaining aspects than those used in standard methods. An orb of only 1½° on each side is allowed, except in the case of aspects' personal points (Sun, Moon, medium-coeli (MC), and Ascendant), in which an orb of 50° may be used.

As would be found in a traditional horoscope, the planets are placed in the inner circle of the cosmogram. However, because one is not using a system of any type, the ascendant (ASC) and midheaven (Medium-coeli MC) positions will not be located in the usual places. The ASC and MC are treated in the same fashion as a planet, and are placed according to sign position.

Like traditional astrology, cosmobiology utilizes the Moon's Node (Dragon's Head), but in the 90° circle there is no distinction between the North and South Nodes, as they are posited in the same place. (In the 90° circle oppositions are conjunct.) Cosmobiology pays almost no attention to sextiles and trines. The cosmogram shows only conjunctions (0°) semi-squares (45°), squares (90°), sesqui-squares (135°), and oppositions (180°). Trines and sextiles generally signify a harmonious state of affairs. However, they seldom denote concrete events. The hard aspects mentioned above indicate actual events.

The 90° (outer) circle begins with 0° (located at the top of the chart) and ends at the same spot with 90°. Each 30° sector of the 90° circle is occupied by one of the three quadruplicities, and will contain only those stellar bodies that correspond to the zodiacal signs of that particular quadruplicity. All stellar bodies are to be entered in a counterclockwise manner, beginning from point zero (0°).

A boundary line between each 30° segment of the 90° circle will aid accuracy as one inserts each stellar body on the cosmogram. If the position of the Sun, for instance, is 15° of Libra, one would locate the 15° mark in the cardinal sector of the cosmogram (0–30°) and draw on the appropriate symbol. If the Moon were posited in 27° of Scorpio, one would locate the 27° mark of the fixed sector of the cosmogram (30–60°) or, when considering the whole circle, 57° and draw in the appropriate symbol. If Venus is at 12° Virgo it will be entered at 12° of the mutable sector of the cosmogram (60–90°) or, when considering the whole circle, at 72°.

All symbols should be entered vertical to the center of the circle, so that when the sheet is turned the symbols will always be in an upright position. One should take care to be very precise, as great precision will greatly reduce errors and make the interpretative work easier.

The "individual" points in a birth chart are:

M = MC = the medium coeli
A = ASC = the ascendant

These are known as the "individual" points because they move about one degree in four minutes. With the aid of the dial, these points can be rectified and the precise time of birth confirmed. In the past, the ascendant was usually considered to be the most important individual factor. More recently, the greater importance of the MC has become evident. The ascending degree is the degree of the ecliptic rising on the eastern horizon at the time of birth, the apparent meeting point of ecliptic and horizon. We live and move on the horizontal plane and in a way the individual's ascendant can be seen as the point of contact with other people and the mutual relationship between the individual and his environment. The environment helps to shape the individual, and the individual leaves his mark upon his surroundings. However, it would seem mistaken to identify character with the ascendant. The ascendant seems to correlate much more with Jung's use of the term "persona" in its sense of a "mask" in which a person appears and through which a person plays a "part" in the world. The MC, on the other hand, seems to relate to the actual "inner life"—to one's own "ego"—including one's inner ambitions and will to make one's own decisions.

### Midpoints

In cosmobiology, not only are the so-called "hard" aspects given more attention, but a unique angular/distance relationship between two stellar bodies is utilized. The relationship is commonly known as the "midpoint."

The midpoint theory was founded centuries ago. Alfred Witte, the founder of the Hamburg School of Astrology, is credited with the introduction of the midpoint system in modern astrology. Midpoints became the object of intense research by Reinhold Ebertin, and were later incorporated by him into a system that presently dominates the astrological world.

Although midpoints are the major tools of cosmobiological interpretations, they are not the exclusive property of cosmobiology. (Uranian astrologers also use midpoints in conjunction with the 8 Trans-Neptunian planets, Cupido, Hades, Zeus, Kronos, Appolon, Admetus, Vulcanus, and Poseidon.) Midpoints have been shown to make much of traditional interpretation vague and even obsolete.

The midpoint theory, as the name implies, involves the zodiacal calculated halfway point between two stellar bodies. Midpoints (also called half sums) are calculated using the standard mathematical midpoint formula:

| | | |
|---|---|---|
| Moon | =5°51' Cancer | = 95°51' |
| Node | =1°51' Scorpio | = 211°51' |
| Sum: Moon + Node | | = 307°42' |
| Midpoint Moon/Node | | = 153°51' |
| | or | = 3°51' Virgo/Pisces |

In exact investigations, one writes the degree numbers below the names of the stellar bodies, in this way:

| | |
|---|---|
| Uranus | = Moon/Node |
| 3°46' | 3° 51' |

One can see from this equation that the midpoint is exact within 5' (minutes of arc).

In the chart below, Moon, Uranus, and the node form a grand trine, i.e., a distance approximately 120° to one another. According to the principle of traditional astrology, one would judge this stellar grouping as a "grand trine" only. But at the same time, there is a direct midpoint as well because Uranus is placed in the center of distance or in the midpoint between Moon and node, written thus:

Uranus = Moon/Node

## The Solar Arc Direction

Precise work requires not only the coordination of a number of degrees with years of life but also calculation of the individual solar arc. The solar arc for a particular year of life denotes the distance between the solar position on the day of birth and the number of days that corresponds to the year of life in question.

This is also expressible in a formula:

Birthday
\+ Days as years of life

---

= Index day
Solar position on index day
– Solar position on birthday

---

= Solar arc

Example: Male born June 20, 1971
\+ 21 days

---

= June 41

In June there are
– 30 days

---

= July 11, 1971 = index day.

The Sun is at 28°55' Gemini on June 20, 1971.
The Sun is at –19°01' Cancer on July 11, 1971.

---

18°54' = solar arc for 26 days

We now have to calculate the progressed positions to the planets by adding the solar arc of 18°54' to each planet. In order to differentiate the positions of the natal chart and the progressed positions, the natal chart is on the *inside* of the 90° wheel and planets are marked in black. The progressed positions are on the *outside* of the 90° wheel and marked in red (or any other color), thus making the relationships between the progressed cosmogram and the natal figure recognizable. Those configurations that immediately hit the eye are usually the most significant ones.

It is very important to consider the points lying opposite as well, because these constitute the semisquares and sesquiquadrates. In times past, these aspects were often ignored, because they are difficult to determine. However, statistics show that these aspects are at least equal in importance to the others. In the cosmogram they are easy to spot.

## Transits

The word transit means going over, and in cosmobiology, it refers to one planet's passage over another. Stellar bodies in the cosmogram are considered primarily to be called the radix (or natal) and each of the radical stars is marked by *r*. The planets in motion are designated "progressing," and abbreviated *pr*.

A differentiation must be made between strong and weak transits, between those that can bring about a change in life, and those that merely have a hand in shaping ordinary, everyday life. The slower the planets move, the stronger their influence. Whoever has stood under the influence of the transits of Pluto, Neptune, or Uranus will hardly be able to say he or she has felt nothing. Cosmobiologists also use midpoints for greater precision in calculation and also more exact interpretation, so that after mastering the use of transits, going on to the consideration of midpoints is highly recommendable.

Paying attention to the MC and ASC is very important. When a progressed planet is in the vicinity of the points M (MC) and A (ASC), attention should be paid to when an aspect forms. As already stated, the aspects of the planets are of greater importance than the "signs" and "houses." The orbs of the aspects are the same as in the natal chart. The closer the orbs, the more precise is the outcome (1½° on each side).

## The 45° Graphic Ephemerides

Cosmobiologists work with the 45° geocentric and heliocentric ephemerides and the 45° midpoint ephemerides. Reinhold Ebertin introduced the 45° ephemerides that excited many thousands of astrologers. This method enables one to obtain, within a few minutes of time, a survey on the year to come by writing the positions from the natal chart in the margin and then drawing straight lines through the graphic ephemerides form.

In the graphic ephemeris, the month of the year can be found at the very top, and just below, the periods of 10 years. On the both sides are the divisions into degrees; on the right-hand side this ranges from 1 to 45°, on the left-hand side the 45° with the markings for each individual sign.

By drawing horizontal lines across the page, points of intersection of the various stellar orbits will become evident. Note that the orbits of the slow-moving planets take on a fairly flat form, whereas the fast-moving planets move in an almost vertical plane. In solar motion, the small circles are marked by *N* for New Moon and *V* for Full Moon (German voll-full). An *E* in the circle indicates an eclipse.

—Irmgard Rauchhaus

**Sources:**

Ebertin, Elsbeth, and Georg Hoffman. *Fixed Stars and Their Interpretation*. Tempe, AZ: American Federation of Astrologers, 1971.

Ebertin, Reinhold. *Applied Cosmobiology*. Tempe, AZ: American Federation of Astrologers, 1972.

———. *The Combination of Stellar Influences*. Translated by Alfred G. Roosedale and Linda Kratzsch. Aalen, Germany: Ebertin, 1972. Reprint, Tempe, AZ: American Federation of Astrologers, 1994.

———. *Directions, Co-Determinants of Fate*. Tempe, AZ: American Federation of Astrologers, 1976.

———. *Transits*. Tempe, AZ: American Federation of Astrologers, 1976.

Kimmel, Eleonora A. *Patterns of Destiny: Suddenly Interrupted Lives*. Tempe, AZ: American Federation of Astrologers, 1985.

## Crab

Crab is a popular name for the sign Cancer. Its association with moody Cancer is the ultimate source of the term "crabby."

## Crescentia

Crescentia, asteroid 660 (the 660th asteroid to be discovered, on January 8, 1908), is approximately 42 kilometers in diameter and has an orbital period of 4 years. Its name is the personification of a Latin word for increasing or growing, and is related to the crescent Moon in its waxing phase. In a natal chart, its location by sign and house indicates where and how one is most likely to experience expansion. When afflicted by inharmonious aspects, Crescentia may show decrease, or less-than-desirable increase. If prominent in a chart (e.g., conjunct the Sun or the Ascendant), it may show an exceptionally expansive person.

**Sources:**

Kowal, Charles T. *Asteroids: Their Nature and Utilization*. Chichester, West Sussex, UK: Ellis Horwood Limited, 1988.

Room, Adrian. *Dictionary of Astronomical Names*. London: Routledge, 1988.

Schwartz, Jacob. *Asteroid Name Encyclopedia*. St. Paul, MN: Llewellyn Publications, 1995.

## Crowley, Aleister

Aleister Crowley, a famous English occultist and writer, was born on October 12, 8715, in Leamington, Warwick, England. He was a wealthy eccentric who inherited a fortune and was educated at Cambridge. He joined the Hermetic Order of the Golden Dawn, founded the Magical group, and wrote numerous books. He was married many times, outraged polite British society, and died of a drug overdose.

Crowley lived in the United States during World War I and had a brief association with Evangeline Adams during which he proposed a joint book on astrology—a project never manifested. Crowley did write an astrology book prior to leaving America in 1919, but this manuscript was not published until 1974. Despite the character of the author, Crowley's *Complete Astrological Writings* is suggestive and merits reading.

He also wrote a short piece, "How Horoscopes Are Faked," under the pseudonym Cor Scorpionis (Latin for "scorpion's heart") that appeared in a small-circulation New York periodical in 1917. This article was a thinly disguised attack on Adams, whom Crowley accused of practicing astrology for profit (Crowley was wealthy and did not need to work for a living) and other sins. The piece was clearly sour grapes, written after the book project was rejected. Crowley died on December 1, 1947.

**Aleister Crowley, author of *Magick* and a leader of the occultist movement of the late nineteenth century. *Reproduced by permission of Fortean Picture Library.***

**Sources:**

*Aleister Crowley/The Complete Astrological Writings*. Edited by John Symonds and Kenneth Grant. London: Gerald Duckworth & Co., 1974.

Holden, James H., and Robert A. Hughes. *Astrological Pioneers of America*. Tempe, AZ: American Federation of Astrologers, 1988.

## Culmination

Culmination usually refers to the arrival of a celestial body at the midheaven, the highest point in a chart. It may also refer to the arrival of a celestial body at a point where an aspect becomes exact.

## Culpepper, Nicolas

Nicolas Culpepper, astrologer and herbalist, was born in Ockley, England, on October 18, 1616, to a wealthy family that owned property throughout Kent and Surrey. His father died before he was born, and he was raised by his mother in Isfield, where her father was a Church of England minister with Puritan leanings. As a child, he learned Latin and Greek from his grandfather. He was sent to Cambridge, where he majored in classical studies.

Culpepper became engaged and persuaded his fiancée to run away with him and get married. However, while on her way to the rendezvous, she was struck and killed by lightning. Culpepper had a nervous breakdown; after he recovered, he refused to return to his schooling or to enter the ministry. This refusal caused him to lose his inheritance from his mother's family, and he had exhausted the inheritance from his father. He was thus apprenticed to an apothecary.

His apprenticeship was at St. Helens, Highgate, and he inherited and continued the practice of his employer. Culpepper also developed skill in astrology, a field that had intrigued him from a young age. At some point he began correlating astrology and the medicines he was studying as an apothecary. This association may have been suggested by some contemporary German books that linked the two.

Culpepper married Alice Fields in 1640 and through her wealth was able to set up practice in the east end of London, on Red Lion Street, Spitalfields. He joined the forces opposed to King Charles I in 1642 and fought in the Battle of Edgehill. He was wounded during the battle, and this wound may have triggered the tuberculosis that bothered him for the balance of his life. He evoked the hostility of the medical profession when he published an English translation of the *Pharmacopea* in 1649. Detailed information about herbs and other medical substances had been a professional secret before Culpepper's translation, and other doctors were angry. His incorporation of astrology in this publication was held up for ridicule. He continued in medical practice for the five final years of his life. His wife's money allowed him to devote his time to caring for the poor. He died at the youthful age of 38 on January 10, 1654.

Culpepper's translation of the *Pharmacopea* became known as *Culpepper's Herbal*, and gave him a certain amount of fame. It became a standard reference book and was reprinted often. When herbal medicine was making a comeback in the twentieth century, *Culpepper's Herbal* again became important for its summary of the herbal lore of earlier times. It became a resource for healers and others who wanted alternatives to the harsh chemicals of mainstream medicine.

**Sources:**

Culpepper, Nicolas. *Culpepper's English Physician and Herbal Remedies*. North Hollywood, CA: Wilshire Book Co., 1971. (Originally published in 1649.)

Inglis, Brian, and Ruth Inglis. *The Alternative Health Guide*. New York: Alfred A. Knopf, 1983.

Melton, J. Gordon. *New Age Encyclopedia*. Detroit: Gale Research, 1990.

## CULTURE AND COSMOS

Founded by Nicholas Campion in 1997, *Culture and Cosmos* is the only peer-reviewed academic journal on the history of astrology and cultural astronomy. The term "cultural astronomy" was adapted from the phrase "astronomy-in-culture," which was then increasingly used to describe the studies of nonmodern and non-Western astronomies. In Campion's definition, it "embraces the broader cultural context within which astrology exists and examines the impact of astronomical ideas on human culture, beliefs and practices. It includes the creation of calendars, astral religion and the new disciplines of discipline of 'ethnoastronomy' (which focuses on folk beliefs concerning astronomy from around the world) and archaeoastronomy (the study of astronomical alignments and symbolism in ancient buildings)." The papers published vary in scope from Mayan carvings to Indian temples, and Mesopotamian astronomy to Renaissance astrology and modern cosmology. Contributors have included Robin Heath, Nick Kollerstrom, Robert Zoller, and Patrick Curry.

## CUNNINGHAM, DONNA

Donna Cunningham is a contemporary astrologer best known for her contributions in the areas of astrology and counseling/healing. She was born in Onawa, Iowa, and holds degrees in psychology from Grinnell College (B.S., 1964, Phi Beta Kappa) and in social work from Columbia University (M.S.W., 1967). As a social worker, Cunningham was employed in such settings as hospitals and medical clinics, women's health, psychiatric clinics, and group homes for the mentally handicapped. Cunningham was licensed as a social worker in New York and California, and she served as director of social service at St. Mary's Hospital in Brooklyn, New York. She left full-time work for a private practice combining psychotherapy, astrology, and healing.

Beginning in 1968, Cunningham's main teacher was Richard Idemon, who embodied the blend of psychology and astrology. She was certified as a professional astrologer by both the American Federation of Astrologers (AFA) and Professional Astrologers Incorporated (PAI) in 1983 and as an Astro*Carto*Graphy practitioner by Jim Lewis in 1984.

Cunningham has done insight-oriented astrology consultations since 1970. She began giving classes in 1971 and taught in the National Council for Geocosmic Research (NCGR) educational program for years. She has spoken at conferences nationally since 1974. In 1986, PAI gave her its lifetime achievement award. Her materials on counseling principles for the professional astrologer filled an important need in the field. She is the author of 11 books, including *An Astrological Guide to Self-Awareness*, *Being a Lunar Type in a Solar World*, *Healing Pluto Problems*, and *The Consulting Astrologer's Guidebook*.

Since 1971, Cunningham has published hundreds of articles in astrological journals such as the *NCGR Memberletter*, *Aspects*, and *Considerations*, as well as more popular venues such as *The Mountain Astrologer*, *Dell Horoscope*, and *American Astrology*. With the January 1994 issue, she started a column, answering readers' letters using her dual skills as an astrologer and therapist. She also writes a regular column on chart interpretation for *The Mountain Astrologer*. For two years, she was editor/publisher of *Shooting Star*, an international journal combining astrology and flower remedies.

Cunningham has belonged to NCGR since the early 1970s and served on the board of NY-NCGR as newsletter editor. She joined the Association for Astrological Networking (AFAN) at its inception and served as an AFAN advisor. Most recently, she co-founded the Quimper Astrology Guild in Port Townsend, Washington, and served as program chair for three years. Currently living in Portland, Oregon, she is a member of the Oregon Astrological Association.

**Sources:**

Cunningham, Donna. *An Astrological Guide to Self-Awareness*. Sebastapol, CA: CRSC Publications, 1979.

———. *Astrology and Vibrational Healing*. San Rafael, CA: Cassandra Books, 1988.

———. *Healing Pluto Problems*. York Beach, ME: Samuel Weiser, 1982.

———. *Moon Signs: The Key to Your Inner Life*. Westminster, MD: Ballantine, 1988.

*Donna Cunningham's Web Page*. http://www.donnacunninghammsw.com/.

## CUPIDO

Cupido is one of the eight hypothetical planets (sometimes referred to as the trans-Neptunian points or planets, or TNPs) utilized in Uranian astrology. The Uranian system, sometimes referred to as the Hamburg School of Astrology, was established by Friedrich Sieggrün (1877–1951) and Alfred Witte (1878–1943). It relies heavily on hard aspects and midpoints. In decline for many decades, it has experienced a revival in recent years.

Cupido is related to small groups, such as the family. It is also, by extension, connected with attitudes toward home and property. Finally, this hypothetical planet is associated with art and the appreciation of beauty, artists, and craftspeople.

Based on the speculative orbits of the Uranian planets, the Kepler, Solar Fire and Win*Star software programs will all locate this hypothetical planet in an astrological chart.

**Sources:**

Lang-Wescott, Martha. *Mechanics of the Future: Asteroids*. Rev. ed. Conway, MA: Treehouse Mountain, 1991.

Simms, Maria Kay. *Dial Detective: Investigation with the 90 Degree Dial*. San Diego: Astro Computing Services, 1989.

## Curry, Patrick

Patrick Curry is Canadian-born but has lived in London, England for nearly 30 years. He holds a Ph.D. in the history and philosophy of science from University College London, has written two books and edited one on the history of astrology (among other subjects), and helps to edit the journal *Culture & Cosmos*. He is now an associate lecturer in the M.A. program in cultural astronomy and astrology at the Sophia Centre, Bath Spa University College, England.

## Cusp

In astrology, cusp refers to two different but related divisions. First, a cusp is the dividing line separating a sign from its preceding sign. For example, someone born just prior to the Sun's movement out of Cancer and into Leo is said to be "on the cusp of Leo" or "on the Cancer-Leo cusp." Such an individual is said to manifest traits of both signs.

Second, the cusp is the dividing line separating a house from the preceding house. For example, if an individual's seventh house begins at 10° Aries and ends at 13° Taurus, the person's seventh house cusp is at 10° Aries. Planets located at end of one house so that they are very close (usually within 5°) to the next house are said to influence the affairs of both houses. Thus, to continue using the previous example, a natal Venus located at 8° Aries in the sixth house would exert—over and above its influence in the sixth house—an influence in the seventh house because it is only 2° away from the seventh-house cusp.

**Sources:**

Brau, Jean-Louis, Helen Weaver, and Allan Edmands. *Larousse Encyclopedia of Astrology*. New York: New American Library, 1980.

Leo, Alan. *The Complete Dictionary of Astrology*. Rochester, VT: Destiny Books, 1989.

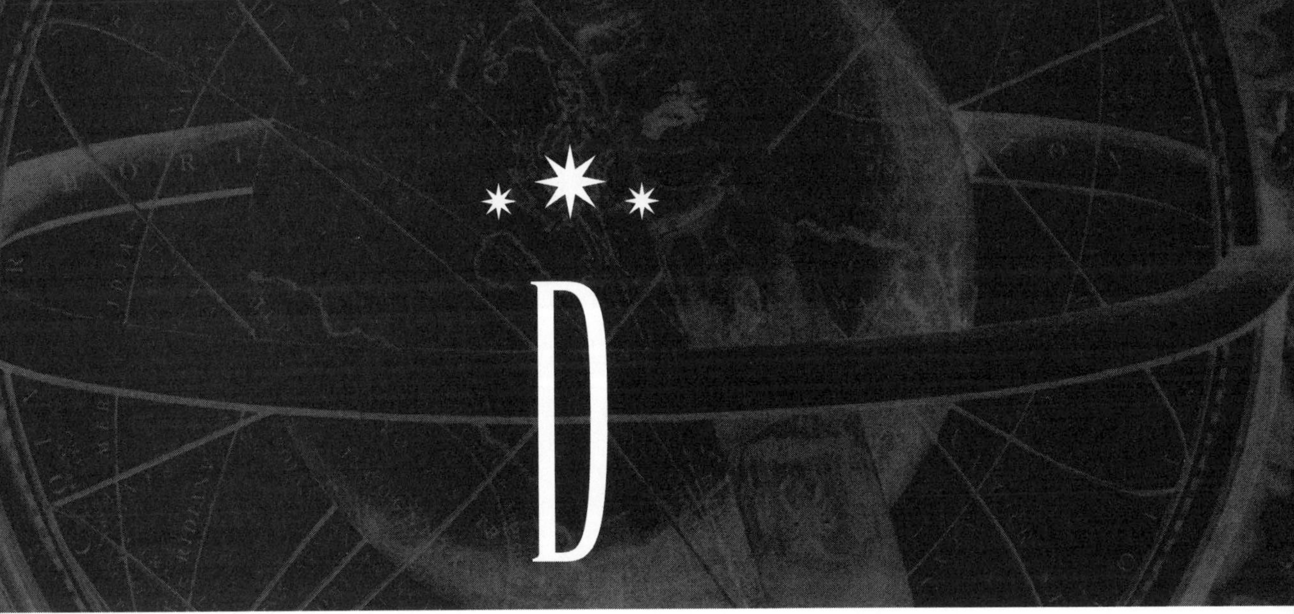


## Daily Motion

Daily motion is the angular distance, expressed in degrees and minutes of an arc, that a planet travels in the course of a day.

## Dawson, Graham

Graham Dawson holds a Federation of Australian Astrologers practitioner's certificate and diploma, and is a member of that organization. He is a student of the Ancient Wisdom teachings. He holds a master's of science degree in esotericism from the University of the Seven Rays, in Jersey City Heights, New Jersey. He also studied physics and meteorology before completing a Ph.D thesis on dynamic oceanography at Reading University, in Berkshire, England. Dawson worked as a software developer for leading oil companies in England and Australia before his professional astrology career.

## Day Horoscope

A day horoscope is a horoscope in which the Sun is above the horizon.

## Days of the Week

In ancient times, astrology was a universal language or symbolic code that was applied to the interpretation of every imaginable phenomenon. As far back as Roman times, the days of the week were correlated with the traditional planets (the Sun, the Moon, and the five planets visible to the naked eye): Monday was thought to be ruled by the Moon ("moonday"), Tuesday by Mars, Wednesday by Mercury, Thursday by Jupiter,

Friday by Venus, Saturday by Saturn ("saturnday"), and Sunday by the Sun ("sunday"). These days were regarded as lucky for people ruled by the corresponding planets (e.g., Monday was regarded as lucky for Cancer, the sign ruled by the Moon), and an activity ruled by a particular planet was said to be enhanced when carried out on a day ruled by the same planet (e.g., Mercury-ruled Wednesday was good for writing and sending letters—activities ruled by the planet Mercury). Weeks, unlike months and years, appear to be unnatural periods not correlated with any natural phenomenon; but, in fact, weeks are based on subdivisions of the lunar cycle in quarters: new moon, first quarter, full moon, and last quarter. While modern astrologers are aware of these rulerships, they are rarely utilized for practical astrological purposes.

**Sources:**

Hall, Manly P. *Astrological Keywords*. New York: Philosophical Library, 1958. Reprint, Totowa, NJ: Littlefield, Adams, 1975.

Rasmussen, Steven C. "Secrets of the Seven-Day Week." *The Mountain Astrologer* 292 (February/March 1992): 3–6.

## Death Chart

A death chart is, as the name indicates, a horoscope calculated for the time of death.

## Debility

A debility is a weakening of a planet through its placement in certain signs and houses. Planets in the sign of their detriment or fall, or in the house opposed to the natural house ruled by the planet, are said to be debilitated. The basic idea informing the notion of debility is that there are certain signs or houses whose energies are incompatible with the characteristics of certain planets, and that this inharmonious blending of energies serves to lessen the strength of a planet's influence. For various reasons, but principally because the influence of planets so placed does not actually seem to be weakened, contemporary astrologers have largely abandoned the use of this term.

## Decan (Decanate)

Each sign of the zodiac occupies an arc of 30° (the 360° of a circle divided by 12 signs equals 30° per sign). Every sign is subdivided into 3 decans or decanates of 10°, each of which is associated with three signs of the same element. Thus, for example, Scorpio, a water sign, is subdivided into a Scorpio decan (from 0° Scorpio to 10° Scorpio), a Pisces decan (from 10° Scorpio to 20° Scorpio), and a Cancer decan (from 20° Scorpio to 30° Scorpio). The uniform pattern of decans is for the first 10° of every sign to be associated with the same sign. In other words, the first decan of Aries is the Aries decan, the first decan of Taurus is the Taurus decan, and so forth.

The second decan is associated with the next sign of the same element in the natural order of the zodiac. Thus, for instance, the second decan of Aries is the Leo

**A sixteenth-century woodcut of the three decans of Pisces. *Reproduced by permission of Fortean Picture Library.***

decan (the next fire sign), the second decan of Taurus is the Virgo decan (the next earth sign), etc.

The third decan is associated with the remaining sign of the same element. To continue with the same examples, the third decan of Aries is the Sagittarius decan, and the third decan of Taurus is the Capricorn decan.

For signs placed later in the zodiac, one continues around the zodiac, past the Pisces-Aries cusp (the boundary between the last and first signs), to pick up the next signs of the same element past this cusp. For example, for the sign Aquarius, which is the last air sign in the zodiac, the first decan is the Aquarius decan, the second decan is the Gemini decan (Gemini is the next air sign after one crosses the Pisces-Aries divide), and the third decan is Libra (the next air sign in succession). These relationships are clearer in outline form:

Aries-Aries decan, 0°–10°
Leo decan, 10°–20°
Sagittarius decan, 20°–30°

Taurus-Taurus decan, 0°–10°
Virgo decan, 10°–20°
Capricorn decan, 20°–30°
Gemini-Gemini decan, 0°–10°
Libra decan, 10°–20°
Aquarius decan, 20°–30°
Cancer-Cancer decan, 0°–10°
Scorpio decan, 10°–20 °
Pisces decan, 20°–30°
Leo-Leo decan, 0°–10°
Sagittarius decan, 10°–20°
Aries decan, 20°–30°
Virgo-Virgo decan, 0°–10°
Capricorn decan, 10°–20°
Taurus decan, 20°–30°
Libra-Libra decan, 0°–10°
Aquarius decan, 10°–20°
Gemini decan, 20°–30°
Scorpio-Scorpio decan, 0°–10°
Pisces decan, 10°–20°
Cancer decan, 20°–30°
Sagittarius-Sagittarius decan, 0°–10°
Aries decan, 10°–20°
Leo decan, 20°–30°
Capricorn-Capricorn decan, 0°–10°
Taurus decan, 10°–20°
Virgo decan, 20°–30°
Aquarius-Aquarius decan, 0°–10°
Gemini decan, 10°–20°
Libra decan, 20°–30°
Pisces-Pisces decan, 0°–10°
Cancer decan, 10°–20°
Scorpio decan, 20°–30 °

The decans indicate a subsidiary influence. For example, someone born when the Sun was in the middle of Scorpio will be slightly influenced by the sign Pisces (because the Sun was in the Pisces decan of Scorpio); although the person will still be Scorpio, the normal intensity of this sign will be somewhat moderated by Pisces. This modification is relatively minor and is usually ignored, unless one is examining the subtleties of a particular chart. When decans are used at all, the focus is almost always the sun sign. For example, the decans of the planets and the other points in a natal chart, with the possible exception of the Moon and the ascendant (rising sign), are usually ignored.

**Sources:**

Bach, Eleanor. *Astrology from A to Z: An Illustrated Source Book*. New York: Philosophical Library, 1990.

Lee, Dal. *Dictionary of Astrology*. New York: Paperback Library, 1969.

## Decile

A decile is a minor aspect of 36°, created by subdividing a circle (360°) into ten parts. It is half of a quintile (72°) and is thus related to the family of aspects derived from dividing a circle into fifths. Like quintiles, deciles refer to the aptitudes or talents related to the planets involved in the aspect, though the influence of a decile is less marked. It is given an orb of influence of 1°–2°.

## Declination

The solar system lies more or less in one geometric plane, which is why astrological charts can be drawn in two dimensions. If the celestial equator (which is the terrestrial equator extended out into space, and projected against the background of the stars) is used as a point of reference, it is found that, at any given time, most celestial bodies do not lie exactly in the same plane, but, rather, are located somewhat north or south of the celestial equator. The angular distance (distance expressed in degrees and minutes) of these bodies north or south of the celestial equator is their declination. Because some astrologers regard planets at the same declination as being in aspect with one another, planets' declinations are often recorded in ephemerides.

## Decreasing or Increasing in Light

From the new to the full moon, the Moon is said to be increasing in light, for obvious reasons. Similarly, the Moon is said to be decreasing in light from full to new moon.

## Decumbiture

A decumbiture chart is a horoscope calculated for the moment one goes to bed at the start of an illness. It is sometimes used in medical astrology for prognosis.

## Degree

A degree is $\frac{1}{360}$ of the circumference of a circle. The number 360 may come from older notions about the year being 360 days in length.

## Degree Rising

The degree rising is the degree of the sign of the zodiac on the ascendant.

## Degrees, Meanings of

In astrologers' quest for subsidiary bands of influence, the 12 signs of the zodiac have been subdivided in various ways. Decans (10° arcs) and dwads (2½° arcs) are two such subdivisions. It was almost inevitable that astrologers would eventually speculate about the astrological meanings of the individual degrees of the zodiac. Unfortunately, there has been less general agreement on the meanings of the degrees than on the meaning of other subdivisions. There have been counts of not less than 17 distinct systems for assigning significance to the degrees. This lack of unanimity is less important, however, than astrologers' disagreement over other issues, because, for purposes of individual chart interpretation, degree meanings provide a level of detail that astrologers rarely have time to develop. Hence, most do not use them. Probably the most widely used system among those who do consider degree meanings is the Sabian Symbols popularized by Marc Edmund Jones and Dane Rudhyar.

**Sources:**

Jones, M.E. *The Sabian Symbols*. New York Sabian Publishing Society, 1953.
Rudhyar, Dane. *The Astrology of Personality*. New York: Lucis Trust, 1936.

## DELINEATION

Delineation is an alternative term for astrological interpretation. Traditionally, delineation meant the interpretation of specific components of an astrological chart, and the term synthesis was reserved for the interpretation of the chart as a whole. In current usage, however, delineation can mean any level of interpretation.

## DEMBOWSKA

Dembowska, asteroid 349 (the 349th asteroid to be discovered, on December 9, 1892), is approximately 164 kilometers in diameter and has an orbital period of 5 years. It was named after the Italian astronomer Baron Ercole Dembowska, who established observatories at Naples and Milan. The name of this planetoid—which seems to suggest an unusual mythological figure, but which does not appear in any mythological dictionaries—led to its inclusion in *The Asteroid Ephemeris: Dudu, Dembowska, Pittsburgh, Frigga*, Batya Stark and Mark Pottenger's tour de force of astrological humor.

**Sources:**

Kowal, Charles T. *Asteroids: Their Nature and Utilization*. Chichester, West Sussex, UK: Ellis Horwood Limited, 1988.
Room, Adrian. *Dictionary of Astronomical Names*. London: Routledge, 1988.
Schwartz, Jacob. *Asteroid Name Encyclopedia*. St. Paul, MN: Llewellyn Publications, 1995.
Stark, Batya, and Mark Pottenger. *The Asteroid Ephemeris: Dudu, Dembowska, Pittsburgh, Frigga*. San Diego: Astro Computing Services, 1982.

## DEMETER

Demeter, asteroid 1,108 (the 1,108th asteroid to be discovered, on May 31, 1929), is approximately 21 kilometers in diameter and has an orbital period of 3.8 years. Demeter, whom the Romans equated with Ceres, was one of the 12 great Olympian deities of the Greek pantheon. She was the goddess of agriculture and the guardian of the institution of marriage. Jacob Schwartz gives the astrological significance of this asteroid as "fertility, mother-child relationships and agriculture." According to

Martha Lang-Wescott, Demeter represents nurturance, which can manifest as nurturance of others or of self. This asteroid's keywords are "mother and child." J. Lee Lehman believes Demeter has an influence similar to that of the asteroid Ceres but is less practical and more spiritual than her Roman parallel. Demeter, in other words, represents more of a spiritual nurturance. Also, to take an example proffered by Lehman, Ceres represents vocational work, whereas Demeter represents more avocational work.

**Sources:**

Lang-Wescott, Martha. *Asteroids-Mechanics: Ephemerides II*. Conway, MA: Treehouse Mountain, 1990.

———. Mechanics of the Future: Asteroids. *Rev. ed. Conway, MA: Treehouse Mountain, 1991.*

Lehman, J. Lee. *The Ultimate Asteroid Book*. West Chester, PA: Whitford Press, 1988.

Schwartz, Jacob. *Asteroid Name Encyclopedia*. St. Paul, MN: Llewellyn Publications, 1995.

## Depression

In traditional astrology, depression is an alternate term for fall.

## Descendant

The descendant is the cusp (beginning) of the seventh house. In a natal chart, it corresponds to the western horizon at the moment of birth and is thus the point where, over the course of a 24-hour period, planets "descend" out of the sky. As one of the four angles—the others are the ascendant (first-house cusp), the midheaven/medium coeli (tenth-house cusp), and the nadir/imum coeli (fourth-house cusp)—the descendant is one of the more powerful locations for a planet. Thus, a planet in a close conjunction with the descendant is traditionally regarded as having a strong influence over the entire chart, although such influences are more marked in the case of planets conjunct the ascendant and the midheaven.

**Sources:**

Bach, Eleanor. *Astrology from A to Z: An Illustrated Source Book*. New York: Philosophical Library, 1990.

Fleming-Mitchell, Leslie. *Running Press Glossary of Astrology Terms*. Philadelphia: Running Press, 1977.

## Detriment

The term detriment is part of a traditional way of classifying certain sign placements of planets. A planet is said to be in its dignity when it is in the sign it rules (e.g., Mars in Aries, the Sun in Leo, etc.). There are also certain placements said to be especially favorable for a planet that are traditionally termed exaltations (to continue with the foregoing example, Mars in Capricorn, the Sun in Aries). When a planet is placed in the sign opposite its exaltation, it is said to be in its fall (Mars in Cancer, the Sun in Libra). A planet is said to be in its detriment when placed in the sign opposite the sign that it rules (Mars in Libra, the Sun in Aquarius). For example, because Venus rules

Taurus, this planet is in detriment when placed in the sign Scorpio. As the name implies, being in detriment is regarded as an unfortunate placement. A planet in its detriment is traditionally regarded as being out of harmony with the sign and consequently weakened (in a position of debility).

For the most part, contemporary Western astrological research has tended to disconfirm that a planet in its traditional detriment is weakened, particularly in a natal chart. However, it is sometimes the case that planets in detriment have unfortunate effects. In the example cited, Venus, as the planet of love, harmony, and relationships is not well placed (especially in a natal chart) in Scorpio, a sign noted for jealously, possessiveness, and sexual obsession. There are, nevertheless, certain obvious problems with this traditional understanding. The Sun, for example, rules Leo, the sign opposite Aquarius. This means that the one out of 12 people in the world born with an Aquarius sun sign have their sun in the sign of its detriment. This particular placement is not normally regarded as being unfortunate, however, making *detriment* appear inapplicable in this case. More generally, all of the traditional detriments should be regarded with caution, used when relevant to a particular individual's chart and rejected when not.

The situation is different in horary astrology, where the classical detriments have a negative bearing on the question being asked. Vedic astrology also makes extensive use of the traditional classification of planets in their signs of exaltation and fall, but not detriment in the Western sense of that term.

**Sources:**

Brau, Jean-Louis, Helen Weaver, and Allan Edmands. *Larousse Encyclopedia of Astrology*. New York: New American Library, 1980.

DeVore, Nicholas. *Encyclopedia of Astrology*. New York: Philosophical Library, 1947.

## Dexter

Dexter (from a Latin term meaning "right") refers to one of the many ways of classifying astrological aspects. The antonym is sinister (meaning "left," not "evil"). A dexter aspect occurs when a faster-moving planet makes an aspect with a slower-moving planet that is located clockwise from it (to the "right") in the zodiac. While astrologers from Ptolemy onward have regarded dexter and sinister aspects as having somewhat different influences, the differences are comparatively minor. In most general natal chart readings, this distinction is ignored.

## Dhanistha

Dhanistha (Wealthy) is one of the Nakshatras (lunar mansions) of Vedic astrology. Represented by a tabor (a type of drum) and with the deity Vasus presiding, this moon sign is ruled by the planet Mars at Capricorn 23°20' to Aquarius 6°40'. The Hindu moon signs are also used "electionally" to decide when to do things.

Considered an ideal time for many religious ceremonies, this sign usually sees people being more charitable and ambitious, while being more aggressive and overly self-seeking.

—Pramela Thiagesan

## Diana

Diana, asteroid 78 (the 78th asteroid to be discovered, on March 15, 1863), was named after the Roman goddess of the hunt and the Moon. Its orbital period is a little over 9 years, and it is 144 kilometers in diameter. Diana is one of the more recent asteroids to be investigated by astrologers. Preliminary material on Diana can be found in Demetra George and Douglas Bloch's *Astrology for Yourself*, and an ephemeris (table of celestial locations) for Diana can be found in the back of the second edition of George and Bloch's *Asteroid Goddesses*. Unlike the planets, which are associated with a wide range of phenomena, the smaller asteroids are said to represent a single principle. George and Bloch give Diana's principle as "survival and self-protection." J. Lee Lehman finds that Diana's position in a chart "shows the place and area of life in which a person expects absolute respect and obedience, as if s/he were divine." She also observes that individuals with a prominent Diana are intolerant of those they regard as "lesser types." Jacob Schwartz gives the astrological significance of this asteroid as "attunement to animal-nature, hunter-prey and conquest behaviors and attitudes; protector of whatever is contacted."

**An image of a crowned Diana of Ephesus by James Harris, c. 1765. *Reproduced by permission of Fortean Picture Library.***

**Sources:**

Dobyns, Zipporah. *Expanding Astrology's Universe*. San Diego: Astro Computing Services, 1983.
George, Demetra, with Douglas Bloch. *Astrology for Yourself: A Workbook for Personal Transformation*. Berkeley, CA: Wingbow Press, 1987.
———. *Asteroid Goddesses: The Mythology, Psychology and Astrology of the Reemerging Feminine*. 2d ed. San Diego: Astro Computing Services, 1990.
Lehman, J. Lee. *The Ultimate Asteroid Book*. West Chester, PA: Whitford Press, 1988.
Schwartz, Jacob. *Asteroid Name Encyclopedia*. St. Paul, MN: Llewellyn Publications, 1995.

## Dignity

The term dignity is part of a traditional schema for classifying certain sign placements of planets. A planet is said to be in its dignity (or in its domicile) when in the sign it rules. For example, because Mercury rules Gemini, it is in dignity when in the sign Gemini. As the name of the term implies, this is regarded as a fortunate placement; a planet in its dignity is traditionally regarded as being in harmony with the sign and consequently strengthened. For example, a person born during a period when Mercury was in Gemini has—unless other factors in the natal chart mitigate against it—a good mind and good basic communication skills.

The attitude of modern astrologers toward the traditional dignities is mixed, partly because natal planets placed in their dignities are not always the unmitigated blessings one might anticipate. The Moon in the sign of its dignity, Cancer, for example, is a highly sensitive placement that, unless counterbalanced by other factors, tends to make a person too sensitive and moody. More generally, all of the traditional dignities should be utilized with caution.

The situation is different in horary astrology, where the classical dignities have a definite bearing on the question being asked. In Vedic astrology, a planet that is placed in the sign it rules is also regarded as being fortunately placed and strong.

**Sources:**

Brau, Jean-Louis, Helen Weaver, and Allan Edmands. *Larousse Encyclopedia of Astrology*. New York: New American Library, 1980.

DeVore, Nicholas. *Encyclopedia of Astrology*. New York: Philosophical Library, 1947.

## Direct

When a planet is moving from west to east in the natural order of the zodiac, it is said to be moving direct. Direct is the antonym to retrograde, which is the apparent movement of a planet backward through the zodiac.

## Directions

Directions is an alternative designation for progressions.

## Dispositor

A planet is the dispositor of other planets when they are located in the sign the first planet rules. For instance, if both Mercury and Mars are in the sign Taurus, then Venus, the ruler of Taurus, is the dispositor of Mercury and Mars. One would say that Mercury and Mars are "disposed by" or "disposed of by" Venus. A planet in its own sign, such as Venus in Taurus, is said to dispose itself (or, sometimes, to dispose of itself). In some charts, one can trace a chain of dispositors (e.g., Venus is the dispositor of Mercury and Mars, while Jupiter is the dispositor of Venus, and so on) until stopping at a single planet that is the final or ultimate dispositor of every other planet in the chart; such a planet is regarded as having an especially strong influence over the entire horoscope.

**Sources:**

Bach, Eleanor. *Astrology from A to Z: An Illustrated Source Book*. New York: Philosophical Library, 1990.

Brau, Jean-Louis, Helen Weaver, and Allan Edmands. *Larousse Encyclopedia of Astrology*. New York: New American Library, 1980.

## Dissociate Aspects

Dissociate aspect was at one time an alternate term for quincunx. In contemporary astrology, this expression usually refers to an aspect in which the component planets are not in the anticipated signs. For example, it is normally the case that the planets making a trine aspect (120°) are in the same element. Thus, a planet in Scorpio will usually makes trines only with planets in the other water signs, Cancer and Pisces; a planet in Taurus makes trines with planets in other earth signs; etc. However, because an aspect does not have to be exact to be regarded as effective, sometimes—to continue using the trine example—two planets in a trine can be in signs of different elements. In this case, the trine would be termed dissociate.

## Dissociate Signs

Dissociate signs are signs of the zodiac that are either in adjacent signs or are five signs away from each other.

## Diurnal

Diurnal means "of or belonging to the day." In classical astrology, particular planets were classified as diurnal and others as nocturnal, no matter where they were in a horoscope. In contemporary astrology, planets are diurnal if they are located above the horizon (i.e., in houses seven through 12). Often astrologers will say that planets above the horizon line show their influence more in the public sphere, whereas planets below the horizon are more private, but this distinction clearly breaks down when considering planets in such locations as the twelfth house (a largely private house situated above the horizon). The term "diurnal arc" refers to the distance, expressed in degrees and minutes of a circle, that a planet traverses between its rising in the east and its setting in the west. Classical astrology also classified signs as diurnal (the masculine signs) and nocturnal (the feminine signs).

**Sources:**

Bach, Eleanor. *Astrology from A to Z: An Illustrated Source Book*. New York: Philosophical Library, 1990.

Brau, Jean-Louis, Helen Weaver, and Allan Edmands. *Larousse Encyclopedia of Astrology*. New York: New American Library, 1980.

## Divisional Charts

One of the powerful analytical tools of Vedic astrology, which is somewhat akin to the harmonic charts of western astrology, is the creation of a set of divisional charts by dividing the 30 degree span of each rashi or constellation by one of a defined set of discreet integers. The charts thus generated are composed of the parts of the rashi or constellation. The Sanskrit name for parts is *amsha* or *varga* and therefore these divisional charts are known in the literature as the *amsha* or *varga kundalis* (divisional wheels). As is the case with most of the classical Indian subjects, the use of the amsha charts is rich and varied. Many divisional chart techniques and traditions are less commonly known and applied; however, in the most widely used classical texts, there are 16 charts mentioned including formulas for their calculation, their names, and short descriptions of their functions and applications.

Most jyotishis and computer programmers use the system laid out in chapters 6 and 7 of the authoritative classical text, *Brihat Parashara Hora Shastra*. There are multiple names for some of the divisional charts. Those used below conform to Maharishi Parashara's work. A convention for abbreviating their names for an English-speaking audience (D-1, D-2 etc.) has been adopted as a result of the work and research of Sheshadri Iyer, a twentieth-century jyotishi from Bangalore.

The description of the 16 charts that follows represents the most popular and contemporary applications as derived from the brief verses of Parashara:

> Rashi (D-1): The Janma Kundali or conventional birth chart. Each constellation of 30° corresponds to one of the twelve houses with the ascendant fixed by the time and location of birth. This is referred to as one rashi /one bhava (one sign /one house). Parashara uses the word "physique" for this chart but it is commonly used to examine all characteristics of the individual's life.
>
> Hora (D-2): Generated by dividing the 30° span of the rashi by the integer 2 creating two horas of 15° each. This chart is used for determining wealth.
>
> Dreshkana (D-3): Generated by dividing the 30° span by 3 creating three dreshkanas of 10° each. This chart is used for a number of applications but the most classical approach is for matters relating to one's co-borns or siblings.
>
> Chaturthamsha (D-4): Generated by dividing 30° by 4 creating four parts of 7.5° each. Parashara uses the word "fortunes" for this chart. In practice, it deals with the matters of large fixed assets such as property.
>
> Sapthamsha (D-7): Generated by dividing 30° by 7 and creating seven parts of 4.285° each. This chart is classically used to assess children and grandchildren.
>
> Navamsha (D-9): Generated by dividing 30 into 9 parts of 3°20' each. This chart is given special prominence in classical literature. It is the divisional chart to assess marriage and other partnerships but is also used as a confirmatory birth chart among many other applications.
>
> Dashamsha (D-10): Generated by dividing 30 into 10 parts of 3° each. This chart details the all-important matters of career, fame, and success.
>
> Dwadashamsha (D-12): Generated by dividing 30 into 12 parts of 2°30' and used for the matter of parents and grandparents.

Shodashamsha (D-16): Generated by dividing 30 into 16 parts of 1°52'30" each. This chart is useful for information about conveyances. The modern applications are for cars, car accidents, boats, etc.

Vimshamsha (D-20): Generated by dividing 30° into 20 parts of 1°30' each. Parashara uses the word "worship" and contemporary jyotishis use it for assessment of spiritual practices (upasana).

Chaturvimshamsha (D-24): Generated by dividing 30 into 24 parts of 1°15' each. This chart is used for assessing how school and studies will go for the individual.

Saptavimshamsha (D-27): Generated by dividing 30 into 27 parts of 1°6'40" each. This chart deals with matters of strength and weakness (vitality).

Trimshamsha chart (D-30): Generated by dividing 30 into 30 parts of 1° each. Parashara uses the words "evil effects," though many jyotishis use it to assess great misfortunes and fortunes.

Khavedamsha chart (D-40): Generated by dividing 30 into 40 parts of 45' each. It is used to assess auspicious and inauspicious effects.

Akvedamsha (D-45): Generated by dividing 30 into 45 parts of 40' each and is a chart for general indications.

Shastiamsha (D-60): Generated by dividing 30 into 60 parts of 30' each. This chart is also used for general indications but has unique descriptive applications for each planetary placement.

In addition to the classical charts outlined above, the many followers of Iyer add four more amsha charts that have come through the Tajika tradition of astrology which is originally Persian or Arab and now thoroughly integrated into the Indian astrological tradition. These are the Panchamsha chart (D-5), which is used to delineate innate morality and spiritual orientation; the Shastamsha chart (D-6), which deals with health and disease; the Ashtamsha chart (D-8), which is concerned with accidents and longevity; and the Ekadashamsha chart (D-11), which details unearned wealth, conferring of honors, titles, ascension to the throne, etc.

The accuracy of the divisional charts becomes predicated on the accuracy of the birth time since the exact degree of the ascending point is the starting place for calculating the ascendant of the respective divisional charts. There is both an advantage and disadvantage in this regard. The ascendant of the more finely divided varga charts becomes less certain without a confirmed birth time. However, this can be turned around and used as a tool for arriving at a more accurate birth time as part of the process known as rectification.

There are two major categories for divisional chart analysis. One involves a quantitative evaluation of strength and the other is the more qualitative descriptive information that improves the specificity of the interpretation in the various arenas of life that fall into a given D-chart's portfolio.

Quantitatively, there are two systems for determining the overall strength factor for a planet in a given nativity through examination of the divisional chart placements. One of these systems is a complex formulation of factors to arrive at a numerical expression of "strength." This technique is known as Shad Bala. An important component of this analysis is the strength that a planet derives by its placement in certain advantageous constellations and houses in a certain defined set of divisional charts. The constellation in which a particular planet is placed in the main chart will most likely change when subjected to the mathematical formulas of divisional chart calculation. For example, Jupiter may be in the constellation of Cancer in the Rashi chart and be placed in the constellation of Capricorn in the Navamsha chart by applying the appropriate calculation and so on through the defined set of divisional charts. Some of these placements are in constellations that will add to the planet's power and some placements will detract. This is the primary idea behind the determination of a quantitative measure that becomes one of the important factors in the Shad Bala calculation.

The other quantitative system is known as Vimshopaka Bala. This system factors the placement of a planet by constellation in defined sets of divisional charts, at least one of which is the complete set. The outcome of the calculation is a specific number for each planet that correlates to that planet's strength with respect to varga chart placement. The practical application of this number is that a planet that may look weak in the birth chart can increase its strength according to its placements in the divisional charts and visa versa.

The qualitative side of divisional chart analysis is virtually endless in its possibilities with respect to interpretive richness. Each specific divisional chart can be analyzed on its own merits according to the rules of birth chart analysis and applied to that area of life it represents. This information can be correlated with what the birth chart reveals and the two can be reconciled, either resulting in greater confluence and certainty or modulating the interpretation by factoring in the appropriate divisional chart. There are techniques for more accurately predicting timing of events by combining the planetary placements in these varga charts with the dasha sequences for that native. Certain unique planetary combinations (yogas) can form exclusively in some divisional charts which greatly add to the understanding of a particular person's destiny.

For further information, the reader is invited to look at the text of the classical works as well as explore more contemporary researches into the techniques of divisional chart analysis.

## Dog

The Dog is one of the 12 animals of the Chinese zodiac. It refers to one of the 12 earthly branches that are used in Chinese astrology, together with the 10 heavenly stems. Such a branch designates one day every 12 days: the days are named according to a sexagesimal (60) cycle, made of 10 series of 12 branches.

The Dog is not a jolly fellow. Introverted and ill at ease, he seems to have self-control and to be respectable, but this is a false front. He is shy and loving, and tends to devote himself to noble causes. Modest and without ambition, but courageous and a perfectionist, he does very well with social issues, but not in business. He has a tendency to be pessimistic.

—Michele Delemme

## Dog Days

Dog days are a 40-day period, usually given as July 3 to August 11, that is regarded as being the hottest time of the year. This period was originally calculated from the heliacal rising of Sirius, the Dog Star, after which dog days received its name.

## Dolphin

The dolphin is a traditional alternate name for the sign Pisces.

## Domal Dignity

A planet is in its domal dignity when it is placed in the sign it rules. Traditional astrology referred to such a planet as domiciliated.

**An antique garnet gem showing a dog surrounded by solar ray, based on Roman superstition relating to the "dog days" between July 3 and August 11, when warm weather was thought to be caused by the rising and setting of the dog star, Sirius.** ***Reproduced by permission of Fortean Picture Library.***

## Domicile

In traditional astrology, a planet placed in the sign that it rules was said to be in domicile, a word derived from the Latin for home. Thus, a planet in domicile (e.g., Mercury in Gemini, Mars in Aries, etc.) is "at home," a location that allows the planet to express its nature freely. A planet in domicile is in the sign of its dignity, and an alternative term for domicile is domal dignity. The term domicile is infrequently used in modern astrology; when it is, it is often used in a more general sense to denote location, as when someone says that a certain planet is "domiciled" in a particular house.

## Doryphory

A doryphory, or "spearbearer," is a planet that rises shortly before the Sun rises—or shortly *after* the Moon rises—in the same or in a contiguous sign.

## Double Signs

The double signs, also called the double-bodied signs or the bicorporeal signs, are Gemini, Pisces, and Sagittarius. This expression comes from the symbols for these signs: twins for Gemini, two fish for Pisces, and a part human, part horse (centaur) for Sagittarius. Virgo is sometimes also included in this category, which would make all of the mutable signs double signs. Double signs, particularly Gemini and Pisces, are sometimes used to indicate "twos" in a chart interpretation. Thus, for example, someone with a double sign on the cusp (beginning) of her or his seventh house (the house of partnerships) might be told that she or he will have two marriages, or someone with a double sign on the cusp of the fifth house (which refers to children, among other things) might be told that she or he will have two children, with the possibility of twins.

**Sources:**

Brau, Jean-Louis, Helen Weaver, and Allan Edmands. *Larousse Encyclopedia of Astrology*. New York: New American Library, 1980.

Gettings, Fred. *Dictionary of Astrology*. London: Routledge & Kegan Paul, 1985.

## Dragon

The Dragon is one of the 12 animals of the Chinese zodiac. It refers to one of the 12 earthly branches, which are used in Chinese astrology, together with the 10 heavenly stems. Such a branch designates one day every 12 days: the days are named according to a sexagesimal (60) cycle, made of 10 series of 12 branches.

A rather distinguished-looking person with an extroverted, brilliant nature, the Dragon is attached to his independence and is shamelessly lucky. Energetic and unpredictable, he likes flattery and may easily become despotic. Wildly enthusiastic, he launches his attack, but he may lose heart if the resistance is stronger than he expected. Generous and true, he totally lacks diplomacy. Perceptive, he often gives good advice. This passionate but perhaps fragile person often proves to be very sentimental—not to say naive—when in love.

—Michele Delemme

## Dragon's Head

Dragon's head is an alternate term for the north lunar node. As a point where eclipses occur, the lunar nodes were linked to ancient mythological notions about a celestial dragon that swallowed and regurgitated the Sun—hence the name.

## Dragon's Tail

Dragon's tail is an alternate term for the south lunar node.

## Dreyer, Ronnie Gale

Ronnie Gale Dreyer is an internationally known astrological consultant, lecturer, and teacher based in New York City. She is the author of *Healing Signs: The Astrological Guide to Wholeness and Well-Being*, *Vedic Astrology: A Guide to the Fundamentals of Jyotish*, *Your Sun and Moon Guide to Love and Life*, and *Venus: The Evolution of the God-*

*dess and Her Planet*. Dreyer is also a contributor to the anthologies *Astrology for Women: Roles and Relationships*, *Hindu Astrology Lessons*, and several *Llewellyn's Sun and Moon Sign Books*. In addition to writing gift books, columns, articles, and book reviews, she has served as editorial consultant for New Age and self-help books for several major publishing companies.

Dreyer lectures extensively for astrology groups, both nationally and internationally, and has been on the faculty of conferences throughout the world sponsored by such groups as the Federation of Australian Astrologers, the Irish Astrological Association, and the Astrological Association of Great Britain. In North America, she has been on the faculty of UAC, State of the Art Conference (Canada), NORWAC, and conferences sponsored by ISAR, NCGR, and the American Council of Vedic Astrology, for which she serves as a member of its ethics committee, and tutor in its certification program. She conducts ongoing courses and workshops in Vedic astrology in several cities, and is currently working on an online correspondence course.

**Sources:**

Dreyer, Ronnie Gale. *Healing Signs: The Astrological Guide to Wholeness and Well-Being*. New York: Main Street Books, 2000.

———*Vedic Astrology: A Guide to the Fundamentals of Jyotish*. York Beach, ME: Samuel Weiser, 1997.

———. *Your Sun and Moon Guide to Love and Life* Kansas City: Andrews and McMeel, 1997.

*Venus: The Evolution of the Goddess and Her Planet*. Aquarian Press, 1994.

## Dudu

Dudu, asteroid 564 (the 564th asteroid to be discovered, on May 9, 1905), is approximately 50 kilometers in diameter and has an orbital period of 4.6 years. It was named after a character in Nietzsche's *Thus Spake Zarathustra*. The unusual name of this planetoid (the connotations of which are obvious enough) led to its inclusion in *The Asteroid Ephemeris: Dudu, Dembowska, Pittsburgh, Frigga*, Batya Stark and Mark Pottenger's tour de force of astrological humor.

**Sources:**

Kowal, Charles T. *Asteroids: Their Nature and Utilization*. Chichester, West Sussex, UK: Ellis Horwood Limited, 1988.

Room, Adrian. *Dictionary of Astronomical Names*. London: Routledge, 1988.

Stark, Batya, and Mark Pottenger. *The Asteroid Ephemeris: Dudu, Dembowska, Pittsburgh, Frigga*. San Diego: Astro Computing Services, 1982.

Schwartz, Jacob. *Asteroid Name Encyclopedia*. St. Paul, MN: Llewellyn Publications, 1995.

## Duncan, Adrian

Adrian Duncan is a full-time astrologer working from his base in Copenhagen, Denmark. He runs the website *WOW: World of Wisdom* (www.world-of-wisdom.com) both to show what's going on astrologically at any given moment and also to market his astrology software. He is Welsh but was born in York, England. During his youth he went to boarding school in Cambridge for six years.

Duncan did the opposite of what boarding school trained him to do, dropped out of university and headed out East. As a consequence of a year-long stay in India in 1970, he was gripped by the magic of astrology. His eldest son Tommy was born in Goa. At his Saturn return—aged 30—he moved to Denmark. After about five years in Denmark, he became president of the Copenhagen Astrology Society and remained so for about seven years.

During the eighties Duncan had the opportunity to speak at conferences and astrological societies in cities in the United States, Canada, ireland, England, Holland, Norway, and Sweden. Gripped by the atmosphere of New York while on tour there in 1987, he began writing his first book, *Doing Time on Planet Earth*.

In the nineties Duncan developed the World of Wisdom program. His goal with WOW is to enable ordinary people to understand their horoscopes in greater depth without needing to visit an astrologer. Sales of WOW have reached over 200,000 copies in 12 languages. In 1998 a second program, "Astrology for Lovers," designed specifically for relationships, was released.

In March 1998 Duncan moved rather suddenly from Denmark to England. The opportunity arose to be editor for the *Journal of the Astrological Association of Great Britain*. He moved back to Denmark in 2001. His latest book, *Astrology: Empowerment and Transformation*, was published by Weiser in December 2002.

## Dwad

*Dwad*, or *dwadashamsa*, derived from the Sanskrit for 12-division, refers to the 12 subdivisions of 2½° that comprise a sign. It is one of the few concepts from Vedic astrology that has been regularly utilized by Western astrologers. Each of the 12 dwads is associated with one of the 12 signs, with the first dwad being associated with the larger sign being subdivided into twelfths. The second dwad is then associated with the next sign in the order of the zodiac, and so forth through all 12 signs. Thus, for example, the first dwad of Scorpio is the Scorpio dwad; the second dwad of Scorpio is the Sagittarius dwad; the third, Capricorn; the fourth, Aquarius; etc.

The dwads indicate a subsidiary influence. Thus, for example, someone born when the Sun was at 6° Scorpio will be slightly influenced by the sign Capricorn; although she or he will still be Scorpio, the normal influence of this sign will be somewhat modified by Capricorn. This modification is relatively minor and is usually ignored by Western astrologers unless they are examining the subtleties of a particular chart. When dwads are used at all, the focus is almost always the sun sign; in Western astrology, the dwads of the other planets are usually ignored.

**Sources:**

Gettings, Fred. *Dictionary of Astrology*. London: Routledge & Kegan Paul, 1985.
Lee, Dal. *Dictionary of Astrology*. New York: Paperback Library, 1969.

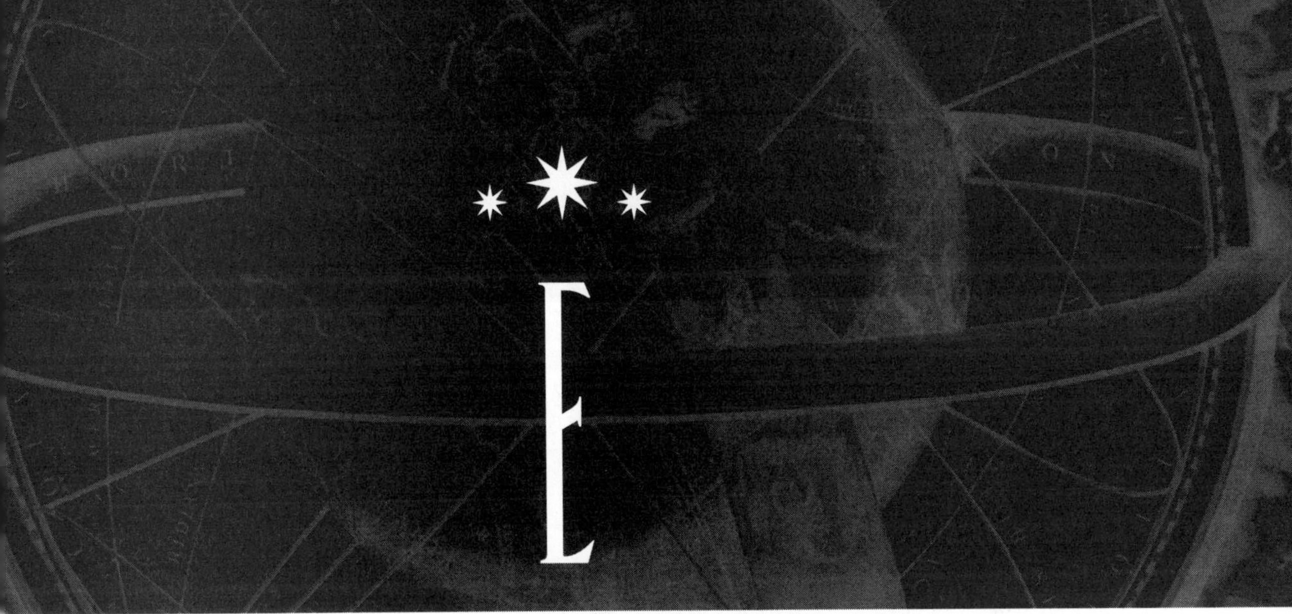

## Eagle

The constellation Aquila is an eagle, but in astrology it is sometimes taken as an alternate term for the sign Scorpio. The notion here is that Scorpio rules the principle of metamorphosis and regeneration. The lowly, stinging scorpion is an adequate symbol for the unregenerate Scorpio but does not appropriately describe transformed members of this sign. The image of the noble eagle, however, captures the highest potential of Scorpio.

## Earth Signs

The 12 signs of the zodiac are subdivided according to the four classical elements: earth, air, fire, and water. The earth signs (the earth triplicity or earth trigon) are Taurus, Virgo, and Capricorn. Astrologically, earth refers to practicality. Earth sign practicality manifests as an aptitude for the financial and material dimension of life.

The practicality of the earth element shows itself somewhat differently in each of the signs of the earth triplicity. Taurus's earthy nature emerges as interest and skill in the accumulation of material resources. Virgo's comes through as attention to details, attention to physical health, and the ability to construct material objects. Capricorn's earthy nature typically manifests as the talent to manage business.

Negative earth people can be so practical that they miss the other dimensions of life. Unless counterbalanced by other factors, excessive earth in a chart indicates an individual who is materialistic, insensitive, and unimaginative. Conversely, lack of earth can indicate a person who is impractical and unreliable.

One finds the same set of four elements and the same classification of signs by element in Vedic astrology. The connotations are basically the same as in Western astrology.

Earth is also one of the five elements of Chinese astrology—earth, water, fire, wood, and metal. In this system, the elements are not permanently associated with each of the signs of the zodiac. Rather, each one of the 12 signs of the East Asian zodiac can be a different element. For example, an individual born as an Ox in 1949 is an earth Ox; an Ox born in 1937 is a fire Ox; an Ox born in 1973 is a water Ox; etc. The connotations of earth in Chinese astrology are similar to the connotations of earth in Western astrology.

**Sources:**

Hand, Robert. *Horoscope Symbols*. Rockport, MA: Para Research, 1981.

Sakoian, Frances, and Louis S. Acker. *The Astrologer's Handbook*. New York: Harper & Row, 1989.

## Earthquakes

From the very beginning of astrology, astrologers have been concerned with the correlations between celestial events and terrestrial traumas. The Mesopotamians, as well as other ancient peoples, viewed earthquakes, plagues, droughts, and the like as being tied to such unusual heavenly occurrences as eclipses and comets. For their part, contemporary astrologers have viewed everything from the heliocentric nodes of the planets to the interaction of Uranus with specific planetary configurations as influencing earthquakes. The problem with all current methods is that, *after* an upheaval has occurred, it is easy enough to look back at a chart for the given day and point out the various factors that appear to be correlated with the event. Prediction, however, is another matter. Although many have claimed to have found the key to earthquake prediction, no factor yet discovered dependably predicts such upheavals.

The closest thing to a reliable "earthquake factor" is a syzygy (an alignment of three celestial bodies in a straight line) involving Earth, the Sun, and the Moon. Syzygies occur every new and full moon; exact syzygies occur during eclipses (a partial verification of ancient astrology). Researchers who have observed this correlation speculate that it is the larger gravitational force—generated by the combined gravity of the Sun and the Moon pulling together (or apart) along the same axis—that disturbs the crust of the Earth and sets the stage for an earthquake, which may occur immediately or within a week of the syzygy.

In addition to the exactness of the alignment, people involved in earthquake prediction, such as Jim Berkland, author and publisher of *Syzygy: An Earthquake Newsletter*, also pay attention to the distance of the Moon from Earth (and, to a lesser extent, the distance of the Sun from Earth). The Moon's orbit is elliptical rather than circular. The point farthest away from Earth is the Moon's apogee; the closest point is the Moon's perigee. The distance between Earth and the Moon varies 14 percent every 15 days. Clearly, the gravitational force exerted by the Moon on Earth is greatest during a perigee, making the potential for earthquakes greater when syzygies occur during perigees (e.g., the Santa Cruz, California, earthquake of October 1989 took place a few days after a perigean full moon). The combination of an eclipse with a lunar perigee is almost certain to lead to a terrestrial upheaval somewhere on our planet. A good reference source for determining both perigees and eclipses is Neil F. Michelsen's *Tables of Planetary Phenomena*.

Another, nonastrological factor that acts as a predictor is the odd behavior of animals prior to an earthquake. Berkland observes that the number of missing animals reported in newspapers, for instance, shoots up just before an earthquake, as if they were somehow responding to a change in Earth's magnetic field. In the March 1992 issue of his newsletter, Berkland refers to a passage in Helmut Tributsch's *When the Snakes Awake*, "based on a popular brochure printed in China in 1973," that describes the behavior of animals before an earthquake: "Cattle, sheep, mules and horses do not enter corrals. Pigs do not eat, and dogs bark madly. Ducks do not enter water and stay on shore. Chickens fly up into trees and scream loudly. Rats move their homes and flee. Hibernating snakes leave their burrows early and may freeze. Big cats pick up little ones and run. Frightened pigeons continuously fly and do not return to nests. Rabbits raise their ears, jump aimlessly and bump things. Fish are frightened and jump above water surface. Bees move their hives, making noise."

**Sources:**


Michelsen, Neil F. *Tables of Planetary Phenomena*. San Diego: Astro Computing Services Publications, 1990.

Nolle, Richard. "The Supermoon Alignment." In *The Astrology of the Macrocosm*. Edited by Joan McEvers. Saint Paul, MN: Llewellyn Publications, 1990.

Rosenberg, Diana K. "Stalking the Wild Earthquake." In *The Astrology of the Macrocosm*. Edited by Joan McEvers. Saint Paul, MN: Llewellyn Publications, 1990.

*Syzygy: An Earthquake Newsletter*. March 1992.


## East Point

The east point is sometimes used as an alternate expression to refer to the ascendant—the point where the eastern horizon intersects the ecliptic for any given astrological chart.

## Ebertin, Reinhold

Reinhold Ebertin, born February 16, 1901, in Görlitz, Saxony, was an eminent German astrologer who developed cosmobiology, which has proven popular with many astrologers, especially in Europe. He became interested in astrology in 1916 and by 1923 had taken up a career as a professional astrologer. He was initially a student of Alfred Witte's Uranian astrology but came to reject the elements of hypothetical planets and house interpretations. Ebertin also simplified Witte's midpoint combinations. The resulting system was a streamlined version of Witte's.

Ebertin initiated the periodical *Mensch in All* in 1928. It was suppressed by the Nazis but resumed after the war with the new title *Kosmobiologie*. Ebertin wrote more than 60 books. Many of his books have not been translated into other languages, although several have been translated into English. Ebertin died March 14, 1988.

**Sources:**

Ebertin. Reinhold. *Applied Cosmobiology*. Aalen, Germany: Ebertin Verlag, 1972.

———. *Combination of Stellar Influences*. Aalen, Germany: Ebertin Verlag, 1972.

Ebertin, Reinhold, and Georg Hoffman. *Fixed Stars and Their Interpretation*. Aalen, Germany: Ebertin Verlag, 1971.

Holden, James H., and Robert A. Hughes. *Astrological Pioneers of America*. Tempe, AZ: American Federation of Astrologers, 1988.

## ECCENTRIC

In astronomy, eccentricity refers to an elliptical orbit, specifically to the extent to which the ellipse described by a celestial body's orbit departs from a perfect circle, expressed by the ratio of the major to the minor axis.

## ECLIPSE

An eclipse is the full or partial obscuring of the Sun by the Moon (a solar eclipse), or the full or partial obscuring of the Moon by the Sun (a lunar eclipse). When planets and stars are obscured by another celestial body (particularly by the Moon), it is called an occultation. The orbits of the Sun and Moon intersect, but are not parallel; if they were parallel, a solar eclipse would occur during every new moon and a lunar eclipse every full moon. Eclipses can occur only when the Sun and Moon intersect the lunar nodes.

Traditionally, the influence of eclipses, whether full or partial, has been regarded as negative, portending famine, war, and the like. Also, with respect to individual natal charts, the traditional interpretation is that an eclipse exerts a malefic influence, particularly if it falls on or near (within 5° of) a natal planet or an angle. Contemporary astrologers tend to see eclipses as indicating emphasis or a crisis in the affairs related to the house in which the eclipse occurs. For instance, should an eclipse occur in a person's second house, she or he may be compelled to attend to financial matters. Should the eclipse occur near (within 5° of) a natal planet or be directly opposed to (180° away from, give or take 5°) a natal planet, the crisis will be a major one and will be colored by the nature of the planet or planets involved.

**Sources:**

Brau, Jean-Louis, Helen Weaver, and Allan Edmands. *Larousse Encyclopedia of Astrology*. New York: New American Library, 1980.

Jansky, Robert Carl. *Interpreting the Eclipses*. San Diego: Astro Computing, 1979.

Michelsen, Neil F. *Tables of Planetary Phenomena*. San Diego: Astro Computing, 1979.

## ECLIPTIC (*VIA SOLIS*, THE SUN'S PATH)

The ecliptic is the orbit of Earth as viewed from the Sun. For most astrological purposes, however, the ecliptic is taken to be the orbit that the Sun appears to describe around the Earth (the *via solis*, or the Sun's path). The *via solis* acquired the name ecliptic because it is along its path, at the points where it intersects the celestial

**Alchemical imagery from a book by German chemist Libavius Alchymia, c. 1606, depicting a black crow sitting on an eclipse while the black face above the three-headed bird represents a total lunar eclipse. *Reproduced by permission of Fortean Picture Library.***

equator (the equator of the Earth projected outward onto the background of the celestial sphere) that eclipses occur. Owing to the tilt of the Earth on its axis, the ecliptic intersects the celestial equator at an angle of 23½°. The 12 signs of the zodiac, through which the Sun appears to pass over the course of a year, lie around the outside of the ecliptic.

## Egyptian Astrology

The ancient Greeks viewed Egypt as an exotic, mysterious land, somewhat as contemporary Westerners regard India. Thus, anything Egyptian carried with it an aura of prestige that artifacts or ideas from other areas of the world did not enjoy. For this reason, Greeks such as Herodotus tended to associate astrology with Egypt, although Egyptian astrology had been adopted wholesale directly from Mesopotamian astrology, and the Egyptians had added little to the science of the stars. It was only later, after Hellenistic culture had been imposed upon the land of the Nile, that Egyptians contributed to astrology.

**A fresco of the northern constellations discovered in the lower burial chamber of Seti I.** ***Reproduced by permission of Fortean Picture Library.***

**Sources:**

Baigent, Michael, Nicholas Campion, and Charles Harvey. *Mundane Astrology*. 2d ed. London: Aquarian Press, 1992.

Brau, Jean-Louis, Helen Weaver, and Allan Edmands. *Larousse Encyclopedia of Astrology*. New York: New American Library, 1980.

## ELECTIONAL ASTROLOGY

Electional astrology is the branch of astrology dealing with selecting ("electing") the best time to initiate any given activity or project. Electional astrology is traditionally regarded as a subdivision of horary astrology because it involves a reverse application of horary principles. In other words, instead of examining an event that started at a particular time and forecasting the outcome, one determines the outcome one wishes to achieve and works backward to find an appropriate moment to start.

Electional methods have been applied to selecting the time for marriage, planting (agricultural astrology), beginning journeys, opening businesses, buying land, constructing buildings, initiating lawsuits, and so forth. Prior to the advent of modern, psychologically oriented astrology, electing the proper time to begin an activity was one of the chief reasons for consulting astrologers. There exists a vast traditional literature on the subject that stretches back to before the time of Ptolemy.

In electional astrology, the astrologer must not only construct an *inceptional figure* (electional chart) that will accomplish the intended purpose, but also select a moment that will bring concurrent influences in the client's natal chart into alignment with the desired end. In other words, contrary influences in the client's chart will counteract favorable influences in the election chart.

There is, however, a shorthand approach, using the position of the Moon, for selecting the proper moment to initiate actions. As the nearest and fastest-moving celestial body to Earth, the Moon has the most influence over the continuously changing astrological "atmosphere" of our home planet. For day-to-day choices, it is thus the most significant planet to examine. The first rule of thumb in electing actions by the position of the Moon is to pay attention to the Moon's waxing and waning cycle. Activities one hopes will quickly expand, such as a new business venture, should be initiated during a waxing moon (increasing in size from new to full). On the other hand, activities one hopes to stop or slow down, such as the growth of hair after a haircut, should be undertaken during a waning moon (decreasing in size from full to new).

A second consideration when using the position of the moon in electional astrology is the variable speed of the Moon. The Moon travels in an elliptical orbit around Earth. During its perigee (the point at which it passes closest to Earth), it is traveling faster than during its apogee (the point farthest away from Earth). As with the waxing and waning cycle, activities one wants to come quickly to fruition should be undertaken close to the Moon's perigee, and activities one wants to stop or slow down should be undertaken close to its apogee.

A third consideration is to avoid certain actions when the Moon is void of course (often abbreviated VOC). A planet is void of course after it makes its last major aspect with another planet before transiting out of a given sign. It remains void of course until it enters a new sign (referred to as ingress). The influence of void-of-course moons is on par with retrograde motion—these are poor periods during which to sign contracts, initiate new projects, or acquire new possessions. They are good times, however, to reflect and "recharge." Many of the major ephemeredes (tables of planetary positions) note when the Moon goes void of course as well as when the Moon enters a new sign. Astrologers who have studied void-of-course moons assert that the last aspect must be a major one—conjunction, sextile, square, trine, or opposition—with the Sun or one of the planets (asteroids and other celestial bodies are not considered significant for the purpose of determining VOC moons).

A fourth consideration in using the Moon's position is the nature of the Moon's last aspect before going void of course; this concluding aspect shows the outcome of any action undertaken while the Moon was in that sign. A hard aspect, such as a square or an opposition, tends to indicate an unfavorable outcome, whereas a sextile or a trine indicates a favorable one. A conjunction is usually regarded as favorable, although conjunction with a difficult planet such as Saturn might cause delays.

A fifth consideration when using the lunar position to determine timing is the next aspect the Moon makes after an action is taken (called the applying aspect). Thus, if one goes to a job interview when the Moon is applying a square to Neptune, confused communication or even a sense of deception is likely to interfere with the interview. This need not spell doom for one's job prospects, however. If the last aspect before the Moon goes void of course in the sign of the zodiac it was in during the interview gives a more positive indication, such as a trine to Jupiter, the outcome of the interview is likely to be positive.

A sixth and final consideration is the sign the Moon is in at the time a project is undertaken. For example, if one wished to undertake a project that involves attention to detail, it might be best to do so when the Moon is in Virgo (a sign associated with detailed organization); to establish a partnership, it might be best to wait until the Moon is in Libra (a sign associated with marriage and business partnerships); and so forth.

Small astrological almanacs that keep track of all the data associated with the Moon's changing signs and aspects for each year can sometimes be found at larger bookstores, though one must usually go to a specialty bookseller. In addition, the *Simplified Scientific Ephemeris* published annually by the Rosicrucian Fellowship, is widely available. These tables of ephermerides supply an aspectarian (a table that notes the day and time that aspects between planets become exact), although they do not explicitly note the last aspect the Moon makes before it goes void of course.

On a day-to-day basis, it is frequently difficult to schedule the most ideal time for any given action. Often the best one can do is to avoid the least favorable moments. Nevertheless, watching the Moon with a small pocket almanac provides anyone with a minimum of astrological expertise with a quick, rough method for electing the best times to schedule everyday tasks.

Some form of electional astrology is a part of every astrological tradition. In Vedic astrology, electional astrology is referred to as Muhurta.

**Sources:**

DeVore, Nicholas. *Encyclopedia of Astrology*. New York: Philosophical Library, 1947.

Michelsen, Neil F. *The American Ephemeris for the 20th Century*. San Diego: ACS Publications, 1988.

———. *Tables of Planetary Phenomena*. San Diego: Astro Computing Services Publications, 1990.

Morrison, Al H. "Notes on the Void-of-Course Moon." *The Mountain Astrologer* 889 (August/September 1989), pp. 11, 29.

Rosicrucian Fellowship. *Simplified Scientific Ephemeris 1993*. Oceanside, CA: Rosicrucian Fellowship, 1992.

## Elements

The primary categories by which the signs are classified are the four elements (earth, air, fire, and water) and the three qualities (cardinal, mutable, and fixed). Each of the 12 signs of the zodiac is a unique combination of an element and a quality (e.g., Aries is a cardinal fire sign, Taurus a fixed earth sign, Gemini a mutable air sign, and so forth). The elemental nature of a sign is said to refer to its basic temperament, while its quality refers to its mode of expression.

**A fifteenth-century woodcut depicting the four elements: wood (Earth) burned by flames (fire) while a bird (air) flies above the sea (water).** ***Reproduced by permission of Fortean Picture Library.***

People whose only contact with the word element was in a science class immediately think of the materials diagramed by the periodic table—oxygen, iron, hydrogen, silicon, and the like—when they hear the term. It thus strikes them as strange to consider earth, air, fire, and water by this designation. The astrological elements derive from the elements of ancient Greek philosophy. Classical philosophy and modern science share an interest in discovering the basic—the "elementary"—building blocks of the world. Prior to the advent of contemporary atomic theory, intelligent people examining the world in which they lived observed that all tangible things could be classified as solids (earth), liquids (water), or gases (air). Sources of heat and light, such as fire and the Sun, seemed to constitute a fourth factor (fire), which can be thought of as "energy." When reworded as solid, liquid, gas, and energy, this ancient scheme of classification is not really so strange.

When the ancients analyzed the human being in terms of these four factors, it appeared to them that the physical body was earthy, feeling and emotions watery, and thoughts airy. The fire element provided the spark of life that animated the human frame with activity. From this way of looking at human nature, it was but a short step to regarding sensitive, emotional people as having more of the water "element" in their constitution than their fellows, mental people as having more air, practical people as having more earth, and energetic, active people as having more fire. When astrology was being systematized in ancient Greece, this "psychological" system was applied to the 12 signs, resulting in a classification according to the four classical elements: the fire triplicity, Aries, Leo, and Sagittarius (energy signs); the earth triplicity, Taurus, Virgo, and Capricorn (practical signs); the air triplicity, Gemini, Libra, and

Aquarius (mental signs); and the water triplicity, Cancer, Scorpio, and Pisces (emotional signs).

One finds the same set of four elements and the same classification of signs by element in Vedic astrology. The connotations are basically the same as in Western astrology.

In contrast, there are five elements in Chinese astrology—earth, water, fire, wood, and metal. In this system, the elements are not permanently associated with each of the signs of the zodiac. Rather, each one of the 12 signs of the East Asian zodiac can be a different element. For example, an individual born as an Ox in 1949 is an earth Ox; an Ox born in 1937 is a fire Ox; an Ox born in 1973 is a water Ox; etc.

**Sources:**

Brau, Jean-Louis, Helen Weaver, and Allan Edmands. *Larousse Encyclopedia of Astrology*. New York: New American Library, 1980.

Hand, Robert. *Horoscope Symbols*. Rockport, MA: Para Research, 1981.

Tester, Jim. *A History of Western Astrology*. New York: Ballantine, 1987.

## Eleutheria

Eleutheria, asteroid 567 (the 567th asteroid to be discovered, on May 28, 1905), is approximately 84 kilometers in diameter and has an orbital period of 5.5 years. It was named after the Greek goddess of liberty—hence, "eleutherophobia," meaning fear of freedom, and "eleutheromania," meaning the irresistible need for freedom. There was also a festival instituted after the victory of the Greeks over the Persians that was called Eleutheria. The sign and house position of this planetoid in a natal chart indicates where and how one seeks greater freedom, as well as how one struggles for liberty. If prominent in a natal chart (e.g., conjunct the Sun or the ascendant), it may show a person for whom liberty and victory over obstacles are life themes.

**Sources:**

Kowal, Charles T. *Asteroids: Their Nature and Utilization*. Chichester, West Sussex, UK: Ellis Horwood Limited, 1988.

Room, Adrian. *Dictionary of Astronomical Names*. London: Routledge, 1988.

Schwartz, Jacob. *Asteroid Name Encyclopedia*. St. Paul, MN: Llewellyn Publications, 1995.

## Elevation

Elevation is the angular distance of a celestial body above the horizon. An elevated planet in a natal chart, especially if it is near the midheaven and in the tenth house, is said to exert a particularly strong influence on the entire chart. In traditional astrology, elevated malefic planets, especially when elevated above the Sun and Moon, were said to exert an unfavorable influence over the entire chart. Modern astrologers have largely rejected this interpretation. For instance, a well-aspected Saturn (traditionally considered the Greater Malefic) placed in the tenth house is in the house of its accidental dignity, and although this placement may indicate delay, it also indicates ultimate success (should other factors support this interpretation) in one's profession.

## Elongation

Elongation, in astrological parlance, is the maximum angular distance that Mercury and Venus travel from the Sun. Because the orbits of Mercury and Venus lie between Earth and the Sun, these two planets appear to always travel with the Sun, so that, from the position of Earth, Mercury is always within 28° of the Sun, and Venus always within 46°. Elongation also refers to the maximum apparent distance that a satellite travels from the body around which it moves (e.g., the maximum distance the Moon travels from Earth).

## Elpis

Elpis, asteroid 59 (the 59th asteroid to be discovered, on September 12, 1860), is approximately 164 kilometers in diameter and has an orbital period of 4.5 years. It was named after the Greek word for hope. The house and sign positions of Elpis in a natal chart indicate sources of hope as well as the area of life where the native invests her or his hopes. When prominent in a chart, Elpis may show a generally hopeful person. When afflicted, it may show disappointment or lack of hope.

**Sources:**

Kowal, Charles T. *Asteroids: Their Nature and Utilization*. Chichester, West Sussex, UK: Ellis Horwood Limited, 1988.

Room, Adrian. *Dictionary of Astronomical Names*. London: Routledge, 1988.

Schwartz, Jacob. *Asteroid Name Encyclopedia*. St. Paul, MN: Llewellyn Publications, 1995.

## Ephemeral Map

The ephemeral map is the astrological chart cast in horary astrology for the event in question.

## Ephemeral Motion

Ephemeral motion refers to the motion of the planets and other celestial bodies along their orbits, as distinct from progressed motion.

## Ephemeris

An ephemeris (*pl.*, ephemerides) is an astronomical/astrological almanac listing the daily positions of the Sun, the Moon, and the planets, as well as other information, including, in astrological ephemerides, certain information necessary for calculating an astrological chart. The word is derived from the Greek *ephemeros*, meaning "existing no longer than a day," from which the word "ephemeral" is also derived.

The use of such tables is very old, and ephemerides are used by navigators, astronomers, and astrologers. During the nineteenth century and the early twentieth century, most of the readily available ephemerides listed planetary positions for noon at Greenwich, England (0° longitude). By the late twentieth century, however, ephemerides had proliferated to the point that tables of planetary positions for midnight Greenwich Mean Time and noon and midnight Eastern Standard Time (North America), sidereal ephemerides, and heliocentric (Sun-centered) emphemerides were all readily available. The personal computer revolution has partially eliminated the need for such tables, as ephemerides have been incorporated into chart-casting programs.

**Sources:**

Bach, Eleanor. *Astrology from A to Z: An Illustrated Source Book*. New York: Philosophical Library, 1990.

Muise, Roxana. *A-Year-At-A-Glance: The 45 Degree Graphic Ephemeris for 101 Years, 1900–2001*. Bellevue, WA: South Western Astrology Conference, 1986.

Sepharial [W. Gorn Old]. *New Dictionary of Astrology*. New York: Arco, 1964.

## Epicycle

When Earth was viewed as the stationary center of the universe, the retrograde motion of the planets was explained in terms of epicycles—smaller orbits that circled in the reverse direction from the planets' usual motion.

## Equal House System

When the casual observer looks at an astrological chart for the first time, it is easy to make the incorrect assumption that the 12 "pie pieces" are the 12 signs of the zodiac. These lines indicate the house divisions, which can begin or end at different places in different signs. (The sign divisions are traditionally not represented; if they are, they are around the periphery of the wheel.) Astrologers disagree about how to draw the houses, although most agree that the first house should begin on the eastern horizon and the seventh house (180° away) should begin on the western horizon. All of the other divisions are disputed, although the great majority of systems begin the tenth house at the degree of the zodiac that is highest in the heavens and the fourth house at exactly 180° away from the cusp of the tenth house. The equal house system is one of the few systems of house division that utilizes a different axis for the tenth and fourth houses.

In equal house system, as the name implies, all the houses are equal in width. Thus, someone born when the eastern horizon intersected Virgo at 26° would have a first house that began at 26° Virgo, a second house that began at 26° Libra, a third house that began at 26° Scorpio, and so forth. It is an ancient system of house division that is still used in Vedic astrology, although most Vedic astrologers use the full 30° arc of the rising sign as the first house. In other words, if one's rising sign was Leo—whether 1° Leo, 29° Leo, or any point in between—the full 30° arc of Leo from 0° to 30° Leo would be the first house. Then the full 30° arc of the next sign—in this example, Virgo—would be the second house, and so forth through the natural order of the zodiac. The most ancient house system used in Western astrology was the same "whole sign" approach to houses as Vedic astrology.

For the most part, the equal house system had passed out of circulation among Western astrologers until relatively recently. Several popular astrology books, particularly Derek and Julia Parker's *The Compleat Astrologer* (first published in the United States in 1971), propagated the equal house system because it is the easiest system to use. The increasing popularity of Vedic astrology in the West, in combination with the new interest in recovering Western tradition astrology, has also helped the older whole sign house system make a comeback. Most contemporary astrologers who do not use the equal house system are severely critical of it.

**Sources:**

Frawley, David. *Astrology of the Seers*. Twin Lakes, WI: Lotus Press, 2000.

Gettings, Fred. *Dictionary of Astrology*. London: Routledge & Kegan Paul, 1985.

Hand, Robert. *Whole Sign Houses: The Oldest House System*. Reston, VA: Arhat Publications, 2000.

Parker, Derek, and Julia Parker. *The Compleat Astrologer*. New York: McGraw-Hill, 1971. Reprint, New York: Bantam, 1975.

## Equator

The equator is the imaginary line drawn around Earth (and, by extension, other celestial bodies), separating it into northern and southern hemispheres. The celestial equator refers to the circle that results when one imaginarily projects the terrestrial equator against the background of the fixed stars.

## Equinoctial Signs

The equinoctial signs are Aries, which begins on the vernal (spring) equinox, and Libra, which marks the autumnal equinox.

## Equinox

The equinoxes (from the Latin for "equal night") are the two points in the year when the length of the day is equal to that of the night. These are the vernal (spring) equinox, which occurs on the first day of spring (on or around March 21), and the autumnal equinox, which takes place on the first day of fall (on or around September 23). In astronomical terms, the equinoxes occur when Earth reaches a place in its orbit where, from our point of view, the Sun appears to be situated at the exact intersection of the celestial equator and the ecliptic. The vernal equinox is especially important for Western astrologers, who regard the Sun's position against the backdrop of the stars at the spring equinox (the vernal point) as the place where the zodiac begins.

**Sources:**

Filbey, John, and Peter Filbey. *The Astrologer's Companion*. Wellingborough, Northamptonshire, UK: Aquarian Press, 1986.

Tester, Jim. *A History of Western Astrology*. New York: Ballantine, 1987.

## ERATO

Erato, asteroid 62 (the 62nd asteroid to be discovered, on September 14, 1860), is approximately 64 kilometers in diameter and has an orbital period of 5.5 years. Erato was named after the Greek muse of love poetry. J. Lee Lehman associates this asteroid with the inspiration of love, as distinct from its consummation. Jacob Schwartz gives the astrological significance of Erato as "emotional inspiration, lyric and love poetry."

**Sources:**

Kowal, Charles T. *Asteroids: Their Nature and Utilization*. Chichester, West Sussex, UK: Ellis Horwood Limited, 1988.

Lehman, J. Lee. *The Ultimate Asteroid Book*. West Chester, PA: Whitford Press, 1988.

Room, Adrian. *Dictionary of Astronomical Names*. London: Routledge, 1988.

Schwartz, Jacob. *Asteroid Name Encyclopedia*. St. Paul, MN: Llewellyn Publications, 1995.

## ERLEWINE, MICHAEL

Astrologer Michael Erlewine founded Matrix Software, the most active center for astrological programming and research in North America, in 1977. The center includes the prestigious Heart Center Library, the largest nonprofit astrological library that is open to the public on a year-round basis.

Erlewine is active in a variety of areas, including astrology, Feng-shui, Tibetan Buddhism, music and film reviews, and producing digital videos.

Erlewine has been a practicing astrologer for over 40 years, with an international reputation in the field. Aside from nine years of counseling experience and years of teaching, he has made many original contributions to astrology including Local Space (astro-locality technique), Interface Nodes, deep-space astrology, and pioneering contributions in heliocentric astrology. Erlewine was the first astrologer to offer astrological computer programs to the general public (1977). His astrological books include *The Sun Is Shining*, *Astrophysical Directions*, *Manual of Computer Programming for Astrologers*, and *Interface Nodes*. He also served as the editor of the *Astro*Talk Bulletin*, *Matrix Journal* (a technical research journal for astrologers), and the ongoing *Astro Index Encyclopedia* project. He has won a number of awards from the astrological community including: Professional Astrologers, Inc. (PAI), the American Federation of Astrologers, and the UAC Regulus Award.

Erlewine is also very active in Tibetan Buddhism (serving on a number of boards) and directing the Heart Center Karma Thegsum Choling, a main center in North America for the translation, transcription, and publication of texts and teachings of the Karma Kagyu lineage of Tibetan Buddhism.

A former musician (he led a band in the 1960s called the Prime Movers, with Iggy Pop as its drummer), Erlewine founded and created All Media Guide (publishers of, among others, *All Music Guide* and *All Movie Guide*)—perhaps the largest database of music and film ratings and reviews on the planet. AMG has more than 14 books and many CD-ROMs published. Erlewine has worked for a wide variety of online networks and other electronic formats (such as CompuServe, E-World, AOL, and MSN).

Erlewine is currently the executive vice president for strategic planning for Alliance Entertainment Corp., of which AMG is a part. Erlewine, his wife, and his four children live in Big Rapids, Michigan.

—Michael Erlewine

## Eros

Eros, asteroid 433 (the 433rd asteroid to be discovered, on August 13, 1898), was named after the god of love in Greek mythology, the son of Ares (Mars) and Aphrodite (Venus). It was the first known asteroid to pass inside the orbit of Mars. It has an orbital period of 1¾ years and is 22 kilometers in diameter. Eros is one of the more recent asteroids to be investigated by astrologers. Preliminary material on Eros can be found in Demetra George and Douglas Bloch's *Astrology for Yourself*, and an ephemeris (table of celestial locations) for Eros can be found in the back of the second edition of George and Bloch's *Asteroid Goddesses*. Unlike the planets, which are associated with a wide range of phenomena, the smaller asteroids are said to represent a single principle. George and Bloch (1987) give Eros's principle as "vitality and passion." Zipporah Dobyns associates Eros with romantic love. J. Lee Lehman contends that Eros is the ruler of romance and passionate attachment. Lehman contrasts Sappho, which she regards as raw sexual drive, with Eros, which she sees as more mental—the conceptualization of attraction. Jacob Schwartz gives the astrological significance of this asteroid as "sexuality, eroticism, passionate romance, being 'turned on.'"

**Sources:**

Dobyns, Zipporah. *Expanding Astrology's Universe*. San Diego: Astro Computing Services, 1983.

George, Demetra, with Douglas Bloch. *Asteroid Goddesses: The Mythology, Psychology and Astrology of the Reemerging Feminine*. 2d ed. rev. San Diego: Astro Computing Services, 1990.

———. *Astrology for Yourself: A Workbook for Personal Transformation*. Berkeley, CA: Wingbow Press, 1987.

Lehman, J. Lee. *The Ultimate Asteroid Book*. West Chester, PA: Whitford Press, 1988.

Schwartz, Jacob. *Asteroid Name Encyclopedia*. St. Paul, MN: Llewellyn Publications, 1995.

## Erratics

The erratics, or erratic stars, was a term used in traditional astrology to refer to the planets, as distinct from the fixed stars.

## Esoteric Astrology

Esoteric (from the Greek *esoteros*, meaning "inner"; derived from the Greek *eso*, meaning "within") astrology is the general term for various schools of astrology whose practitioners view themselves as studying the "ancient wisdom" behind the science of the stars. The original sense of the word esoteric was that it was hidden from, or otherwise inaccessible to, the uninitiated. However, contemporary esoteric astrology is openly accessible to anyone who is able to read. The contrasting term to esoteric is exoteric (meaning external, as opposed to the "inner" significance of the esoteric approach), and, from an esoteric standpoint, all of astrology that is not esoteric is exoteric. Although modern esoteric astrology can appropriately claim an ancient lineage, the reformulation of the ancient wisdom tradition as put forward by Helena Blavatsky and the Theosophical Society in the nineteenth century has been the single most important element in the shaping of contemporary astrology.

Esoteric astrologers are more interested in utilizing the elements of astrology for philosophical speculation than in the practical application of astrology to the concerns of everyday life. Hence, the erection and interpretation of individual horoscopes plays a relatively small role. In Fred Gettings's *Dictionary of Astrology*, he describes esoteric astrology as "founded on the premise that the cosmos is a living being, that the destiny of the solar system is intimately bound up with the destiny of humanity, and that human beings reincarnate periodically onto the earth."

Sample speculations characteristic of the esoteric approach are the notion that the individual soul incarnates in each of the 12 signs of the zodiac in succession (Manly Palmer Hall) and that each of the zodiacal signs has an "esoteric ruler," different from an "exoteric ruler" (Alice A. Bailey). Other significant features are utilization of the notions of reincarnation and karma to explain hard aspects and soft aspects, the correlation of the planets with the *charkas* (the "energy centers" of the Hindu yoga tradition), and a spiritual interpretation of the elements. Beyond the aforementioned thinkers, other key shapers of modern esoteric astrology are Alan Leo, Max Heindal, and Rudolf Steiner.

**Sources:**

Gettings, Fred. *Dictionary of Astrology*. London: Routledge & Kegan Paul, 1987.

McEvers, Joan, ed. *Spiritual, Metaphysical and New Trends in Modern Astrology*. Saint Paul, MN: Llewellyn Publications, 1988.

Simms, Maria Kay. *Twelve Wings of the Eagle: Our Spiritual Evolution through the Ages of the Zodiac*. San Diego: Astro Computing Services, 1988.

## Esoteric Rulerships

In esoteric astrology, the 12 signs of the zodiac are said to have esoteric rulers—rulerships by planets other than their usual planetary rulers that are activated only in "highly evolved" (spiritually evolved) individuals.

## Esoteric Technologies

Esoteric Technologies is an Australian private limited company specializing in developing and publishing astrology software. Esoteric Technologies was formed in 1993 and launched its first product, an astrological program called Solar Fire, shortly thereafter. This was the first commercial grade astrology program to become available for the Microsoft Windows operating system.

Since that time, the Solar Fire program has become one of the world's leading western astrology programs. It now has one of the largest market shares of astrologers, from beginners through to professional consultants.

Over the following years, the company created several additional software products, which cater to a range of astrological requirements: Solar Maps, for astrolocality mapping; Solar Writer, for professional astrological report writers; Solar Spark, a real-time astrological clock; and JigSaw, for astrological research and chart group analysis.

Among the company's achievements are awards from the Federation of Australian Astrologers for research and development (1994), community service (1998), and research (1998). The company also received an editor's choice award for Solar Fire, version 4, in the February 1998 issue of the Australian *Personal Computer Magazine*.

In March 2000, Esoteric Technologies launched the fifth version of Solar Fire, and it is continuing to work on a range of astrological products and Internet-related projects. Astrologers Stephanie Johnson and Graham Dawson are its directors and authors of the Solar suite.

**Sources:**

*Esoteric Technologies Pty Ltd.* www.esotech.com.au.

## Essential Dignity

When a planet or one of the luminaries (the Sun or the Moon) is located in one of the signs of the zodiac it is said to rule, then it is in its essential dignity, as distinct from its accidental dignity. Mars, for example, would be said to be in its essential dignity if found in the sign Aries.

## Esther

Esther, asteroid 622 (the 622nd asteroid to be discovered, on November 13, 1906), is approximately 28 kilometers in diameter and has an orbital period of 3.8 years. It was named after the biblical heroine Esther, whose name was Persian for "star" or "Venus." Queen Esther, herself a Jew, intervened to prevent a genocidal campaign against the Jewish people. Like its namesake, the asteroid represents opposition to genocide and a kind of "rescuer" impulse. In a natal chart, its location by sign and house indicates where and how one is most likely to be a "rescuer." When afflicted by inharmonious aspects, Esther may show a rescuer complex—an individual who engages in rescue behavior for self-aggrandizement. If prominent in a chart (e.g., conjunct the Sun or the ascendant), it may show an individual who becomes involved in a rescue-related career or in a humanitarian group like Amnesty International.

**Sources:**

Kowal, Charles T. *Asteroids: Their Nature and Utilization*. Chichester, West Sussex, UK: Ellis Horwood Limited, 1988.

Room, Adrian. *Dictionary of Astronomical Names*. London: Routledge, 1988.

Schwartz, Jacob. *Asteroid Name Encyclopedia*. St. Paul, MN: Llewellyn Publications, 1995.

## Ethics and Astrology

Astrological organizations often promulgate explicit codes of ethics, partly because no government agencies regulate the behavior of astrologers and partly because of the tendency of astrology's critics to portray astrologers as unethical charlatans. These codes of ethics go back at least as far as Firmicus Maternus (330 B.C.E.), who in *Mathesis* set high standards for astrologers:

> Shape yourself in the image and likeness of divinity, so that you may always be a model of excellence. He who daily speaks about the gods must shape his mind to approach the likeness of divinity. Be modest, upright, sober, and content with few goods, so that the shameful love of money may not defile the glory of this divine science. Outdo the training and principles of worthy priests. For the acolyte of the Sun and Moon and the other gods, through whom all earthly things are governed, must educate his mind to be proved worthy in the sight of all mankind. See that you give your responses publicly in a clear voice, so that nothing illegal may be asked of you. Do not give a response about the condition of the Republic or the life of the Emperor—that is illegal. Have a wife, a home, friends; be constantly available to the public; keep out of quarrels; do not undertake any harmful business; do not be tempted by the offer of money; keep away from all passion of cruelty; never take pleasure in others' quarrels or capital sentences or fatal enmities.... Be generous, honest and truthful.... Be reticent about people's vices.... Do not give away the secrets of this religion to wicked men, for the astrologer must be pure.

Later astrologers, such as the seventeenth-century British astrologer William Lilly, based their ethical admonitions on those of Firmicus Maternus. In Lilly's case, this is clear from certain passages in his celebrated *Christian Astrology*, one of which, as noted in Annabella Kitson's *History and Astrology: Clio and Urania Confer*, says:

> As thou daily conversest with the heavens, so instruct and form thy mind according to the image of divinity; learn all the ornaments of vertue, be sufficiently instructed therein; be human, courteous, familiar to all ... covet not an estate, give freely to the poor ... let no worldly wealth procure an erroneous judgment from thee, or such as may dishonour the Art, or this divine Science.... Be sparing in delivering Judgment against the Commonwelth thou livest in. Give not judgment of the death of thy Prince.... Marry a wife of thy own, rejoice in the number of thy friends.

In the English-speaking world, almost all explicit ethical codes for astrologers can be traced back to Lilly. Other points usually mentioned in professional codes of ethics are confidentiality, both of personal information shared by the client and of the natal chart itself; disclaiming the ability to predict events in precise detail; de-emphasis on potentiality for future illnesses, accidents, or disasters; and avoiding approaches that would in any way encourage clients to become dependent upon the astrologer or to in any way abdicate responsibility for their own lives. Astrologers are further admonished to educate the general public on the true nature of the science of the stars; establish professional standards that exclude charlatans; propagate serious astrology through teaching, writing, and so forth; and support any serious, open-minded research on astrology.

In *The Practice of Astrology* and in other writings, Dane Rudhyar was especially concerned with the moral responsibility of the astrologer. He warned astrologers to avoid giving their clients information they were unable to assimilate, and especially to avoid inducing a state of fear. Rudhyar wrote that an astrologer failed her or his clients when, "instead of helping the client to overcome his semiconscious fears, he accentuates and gives a mysterious power to these fears by giving them a justification against which there can be no recourse." He also believed that prediction has value only as it contributes to the person's development and essential welfare. The goal of the astrologer should be to open clients to their highest potential, rather than to impress them with her or his knowledge.

**Sources:**

Brau, Jean-Louis, Helen Weaver, and Allan Edmands. *Larousse Encyclopedia of Astrology*. New York: New American Library, 1980.

Firmicus Maternus. *Mathesis*. Reprint, Paris: Les Belles Lettres, 1992–97.

Kitson, Annabella, ed. *History and Astrology: Clio and Urania Confer*. London: Mandala, 1989.

Lilly, William. *Christian Astrology Modestly Treated of in Three Books*. London: T. Brudenell, 1647.

Rudhyar, Dane. *The Practice of Astrology: As a Technique in Human Understanding*. New York: Penguin, 1968.

## EUNICE

Eunice, asteroid 185 (the 185th asteroid to be discovered, on March 1, 1878), is approximately 188 kilometers in diameter and has an orbital period of 4.5 years. It was named after one of the Greek Nereids, for good victory or happy victory. It was named in commemoration of a peace treaty that was signed between Turkey and Russia two days after this body was discovered. The asteroid indicates good luck and a fortunate outcome to activities undertaken in matters associated with its sign and house position.

**Sources:**

Kowal, Charles T. *Asteroids: Their Nature and Utilization*. Chichester, West Sussex, UK: Ellis Horwood Limited, 1988.

Room, Adrian. *Dictionary of Astronomical Names*. London: Routledge, 1988.

Schwartz, Jacob. *Asteroid Name Encyclopedia*. St. Paul, MN: Llewellyn Publications, 1995.

## EUPHROSYNE

Euphrosyne, asteroid 31 (the 31st asteroid to be discovered, on September 1, 1854), is approximately 270 kilometers in diameter and has an orbital period of 5.5 years. Euphrosyne, whose appellation means cheerfulness or joy, was named after one of the three Graces (the other two are Thalia and Aglaja). Euphrosyne was a daughter of

Zeus and Eurynome. Like its mythological namesake, the asteroid confers the "grace" of joy to natives in whose chart it is prominent.

**Sources:**

Kowal, Charles T. *Asteroids: Their Nature and Utilization*. Chichester, West Sussex, UK: Ellis Horwood Limited, 1988.

Room, Adrian. *Dictionary of Astronomical Names*. London: Routledge, 1988.

Schwartz, Jacob. *Asteroid Name Encyclopedia*. St. Paul, MN: Llewellyn Publications, 1995.

## EUTERPE

Euterpe, asteroid 27 (the 27th asteroid to be discovered, on November 8, 1853), is approximately 88 kilometers in diameter and has an orbital period of 4.3 years. It was named after the Greek muse of lyric poetry and music, who some myths say invented the flute. She also is said to have had a special affection for "wild" melodies. The prominence of Euterpe in a natal chart indicates talent in wind instruments and a preference for "wild" music.

**Sources:**

Kowal, Charles T. *Asteroids: Their Nature and Utilization*. Chichester, West Sussex, UK: Ellis Horwood Limited, 1988.

Room, Adrian. *Dictionary of Astronomical Names*. London: Routledge, 1988.

Schwartz, Jacob. *Asteroid Name Encyclopedia*. St. Paul, MN: Llewellyn Publications, 1995.

## EXALTATION

The term exaltation is part of a traditional system of classifying certain sign placements of planets. A planet is said to be in its dignity when it is in the sign it rules. These are considered to be favorable placements. Exaltations are sign positions said to be more favorable for a planet than even the signs it rules. Mars, for example, rules Aries and is said to be well placed (in its dignity) in that sign. But Mars is even better placed in Capricorn, the sign of its exaltation. This example demonstrates that while Aries would allow Mars to express its outgoing, assertive nature quite well, Capricorn would be a better placement because, without blunting one's assertiveness, Capricorn could discipline Mars so that one would not be inclined to impulsiveness (a trait characteristic of Mars in Aries).

The reception of the traditional exaltations among modern astrologers is mixed. This is partially because exalted planets are not always the unmitigated blessings that one might anticipate. Venus in the sign of its exaltation, Pisces, for example, is a highly idealistic, mystical placement that, unless counterbalanced by other factors in a natal chart, tends to make a person too impractical about human relationships, particularly romantic involvements. More generally, all of the traditional dignities should be viewed cautiously, used when relevant to a particular individual's chart, and rejected when not.

The situation is different in horary astrology, where the classical exaltations and dignities have a definite bearing on the question being asked. In Vedic astrology, a planet that is placed in the sign of its exaltation is also regarded as being extremely favorably placed and strong by virtue of this placement.

**Sources:**

Brau, Jean-Louis, Helen Weaver, and Allan Edmands. *Larousse Encyclopedia of Astrology*. New York: New American Library, 1980.

DeVore, Nicholas. *Encyclopedia of Astrology*. New York: Philosophical Library, 1947.

## Executive Type

Executive type refers to the determination of those natives born when the Sun was in one of the fixed signs—Taurus, Leo, Scorpio, or Aquarius.

## Experiential Astrology

Experiential astrology succinctly includes any technique that puts people into direct contact with their horoscopes. Its purpose is to place soul instead of prediction at the center of its inquiry. The horoscope need not remain a static, one-dimensional wheel of planetary glyphs and signs, but can become a field of planetary action that is interactive, imaginative, and vibrantly alive. Techniques include astrodrama (acting out the horoscope), group dynamics and process, in-depth therapeutic methods, artistic mandalas, contemplation of images, creating rituals and talismans, dramatic mythic storytelling, dreamwork, journaling, flower essences, and more. Many of these techniques are described in Barbara Schermer's *Astrology Alive: Experiential Astrology and the Healing Arts*.

The history of experiential astrology finds its roots 500 years ago with Marsilio Ficino, the first experiential astrologer. Ficino was the translator of the Hermetic writings, the principle translator of Plato, and the founder (under the enlightened patronage of the Medici family) of the Platonic Academy in Florence during the height of the Italian Renaissance. He was also a physician, psychotherapist, Christian theologian, musician, and astrologer. He developed a polytheistic psychology that integrated the astrological archetypes with imagination, art, music, ritual, talismans, and acts of deep contemplation.

Ficino's contemporary influence is especially felt in archetypal psychology, developed on a foundation of Jungian psychology, by James Hillman and his followers. At the core of archetypal psychology is Ficino's Neoplatonic philosophy, and Hillman acknowledges this direct influence on his thinking. An evolving archetypal psychology demonstrates room for an evolving psychological astrology. Further developments along this path have been taken by psychologist Thomas Moore, author of the bestselling *Care of the Soul*, who also wrote *The Planets Within*.

The recent history of experiential astrology includes a number of committed astrological professionals who are hard at work on its development, including Jeff Jawer, Kelley Hunter, Barbara Schermer, Wendy Ashley, Dale O'Brien, Steven MacFadden, and Susie Cox. One example is the Roots Conferences organized by Kelley Hunter of the Virgin Islands. "Roots" was a series of experiential conferences held for six consecutive summers. Always chosen for their interesting astrological transits, these events drew on the planetary energy of the moment and included four to five days of interactive and contemplative group and individual activities. The groups of 40 to 100 were facilitated by six experiential astrologers who took turns leading an evolving psychospiritual process that led toward a celebratory finale, usually a three-hour outdoor full-moon dance complete with professional conga drummers, costumes, a bonfire, a glorious night sky, and exuberant and heartfelt dancing.

Importantly, many of the major astrological conferences now have experiential tracks included in their programs. The United Astrology Congress has had such a track since its inception in 1986 (thanks in part to Marion March), as have the annual Astrological Association conference in England, the World Congress in Switzerland, and the conferences sponsored by the Chiron Center in Melbourne, Australia. In the United States, experiential workshops and tracks have been regularly included at the conferences of the International Society for Astrological Research (ISAR) and the Aquarian Revelation Conference (ARC). In addition, six astrological schools around the world now either sponsor experiential workshops, including Astrodata in Zurich, the Chiron Centre in Melbourne, and the Dublin Astrological Center in Dublin, or offer extensive experiential training programs, including the Empress Center in London, Astrologskolen in Copenhagen, and Stichting Achernar ("school for astrology") in Amsterdam. All around the world, experiential astrology is alive and well.

—Barbara Schermer

## EXTERNALIZE

Astrological influences are often thought of as affecting the inner side of life first (e.g., emotionally or mentally) and then manifesting as an event in the outer world. The term externalize is often used to describe this outward manifestation.

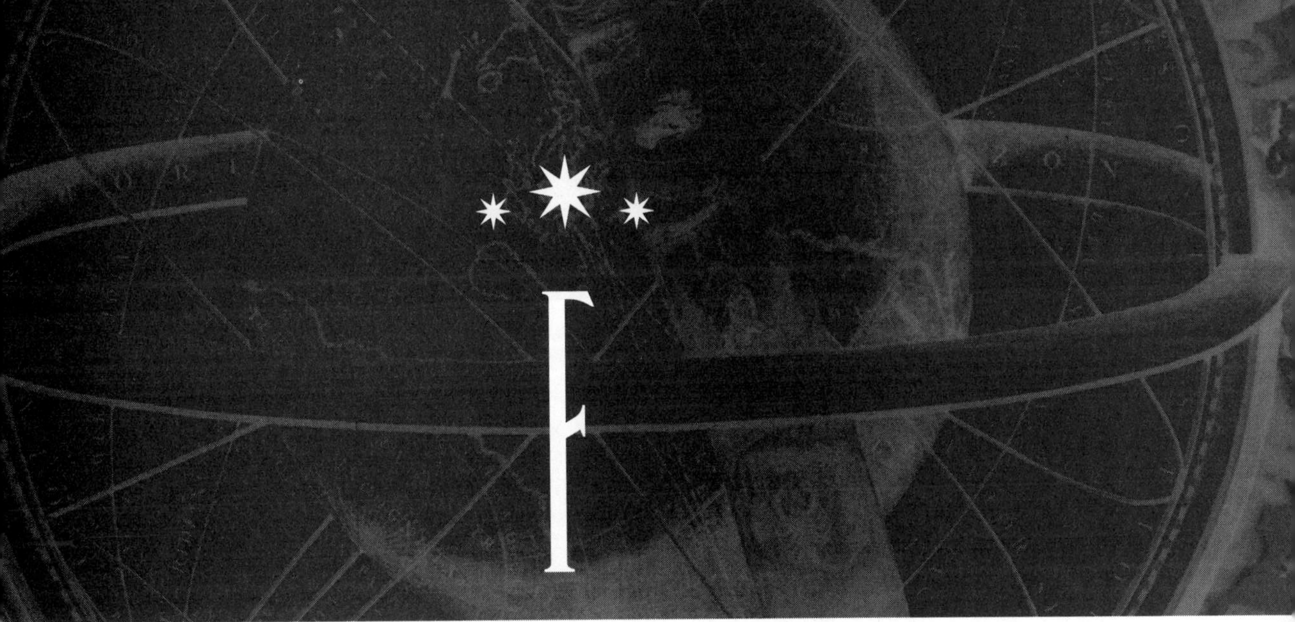

## FACE

Face is a term that refers to the division of the zodiac into 72 equal arcs of 5° each. Some astrologers have used the appellation interchangeably with decan, which divides the zodiac into 36 equal arcs of 10° each. Contemporary astrologers rarely employ the term.

## FAGAN, CYRIL

Cyril Fagan, an eminent astrologer, was born on May 22, 1896, in Dublin, Ireland, and died on January 5, 1970, in Tucson, Arizona. Deafness kept him from following the family profession—medicine—and eventually he took up astrology.

In the 1930s, Fagan founded the Irish Astrological Society, serving as president for some years. He took up the cause of the fixed or sidereal zodiac and became the leader of sidereal astrologers in America. *Zodiacs Old and New* (1950) articulates most of his ideas on siderealism. Fagan had a dogmatic style that convinced some and repelled others. Ernest Grant was the initial publisher of his *Fixed Zodiac Ephemeris for 1948*.

Despite the support of Fagan's views on siderealism, however, most astrologers continued to use the moving or tropical zodiac, and some who converted to siderealism later returned to the tropical fold. Fagan began a long-running feature, "Solunars," in *American Astrology Magazine* (1954–1970) in which he put forward his theories and also discussed horoscopes of many historical personages based on careful research into correct birth dates and birth times. Beyond siderealism, Fagan denounced the use of house rulers in natal astrology, tried to revive the ancient use of simultaneous rising stars, and advocated the Campanus house system (although he later advocated an eightfold division of the chart).

Fagan was a strong advocate of precise data and accurate calculation, and he criticized use of speculative charts and unjustified rectification of birth times. These contributions were eclipsed, however, by his advocacy of siderealism. Following Fagan's and his principal supporters' death in the 1970s, the sidereal zodiac faded from the scene. The fixed zodiac has only recently returned to prominence, in the works of Hindu astrologers.

**Sources:**

Fagan, Cyril. *Fixed Zodiac Ephemeris for 1948*. Washington, DC: National Astrology Library, 1948.
———. *Zodiacs Old and New*. 2d ed. Los Angeles: Llewellyn Publications, 1951.
Fagan, Cyril, and R. C. Firebrace. *A Primer of the Sidereal Zodiac*. London: R. C. Firebrace, 1961.
Holden, James H., and Robert A. Hughes. *Astrological Pioneers of America*. Tempe, AZ: American Federation of Astrologers, 1988.

## FALL

The term fall is part of a traditional way of classifying certain sign placements of planets. A planet is said to be in its dignity when it is in the sign it rules (e.g., Mars in Aries, the Sun in Leo). There are also certain placements said to be especially favorable for a planet that are traditionally termed exaltations (to continue with the same examples, Mars in Capricorn, the Sun in Aries). When a planet is placed in the sign opposite its dignity, it is said to be in its detriment (Mars in Libra, the Sun in Aquarius). A planet is in its fall when it is placed in the sign opposite the sign of its exaltation (Mars in Cancer, the Sun in Libra). For example, because the Moon is exalted in Taurus, it is in its fall when placed in the sign Scorpio; as the name implies, this is regarded as an unfortunate placement. A planet in its fall is traditionally regarded as being out of harmony with the sign and consequently weakened (in a position of debility).

For the most part, contemporary astrological research has tended to disconfirm that a planet in its traditional fall is weakened. However, it is sometimes the case that planets in fall have unfortunate effects. In the example cited, the Moon, as the planet of receptivity and sensitivity, is not well placed (especially in a natal chart) in Scorpio, a sign noted for possessiveness, obsessiveness, and intense emotions. There are, nevertheless, certain obvious problems with this tradition. The Sun, for example, is exalted in Aries, the sign opposite Libra. This means that the one person out of 12 in the world born with a Libra sun sign has her or his sun in its fall. This particular placement of the Sun, however, is not normally regarded as being unfortunate, making the traditional ascription appear inapplicable, at least in this case. Generally, all the traditional falls should be taken with a grain of salt when found in a natal chart.

The situation is different in horary astrology, where the classical dignities and falls have a definite bearing on the question being asked. In Vedic astrology, a planet that is placed in the sign of its fall is regarded as being unfavorably placed and weak by virtue of this placement. In fact, in contrast to Western astrology, Vedic astrology has elaborate systems for determining the strength of a planet, even assigning numerical values and ranking the strengths of the traditional planets. Sign placement is only one factor in this system, so that, in the final analysis, even a "fallen" planet may end up being a strong planet in the chart.

**Sources:**

Brau, Jean-Louis, Helen Weaver, and Allan Edmands. *Larousse Encyclopedia of Astrology*. New York: New American Library, 1980.

DeVore, Nicholas. *Encyclopedia of Astrology*. New York: Philosophical Library, 1947.

Sutton, Komilla. *The Essentials of Vedic Astrology*. Bournemouth, UK: Wessex Astrologer, 1999.

## FAMILIARITY

Familiarity is an older term for the aspects between the planets.

## FANATICA

Fanatica, asteroid 1,589 (the 1,589th asteroid to be discovered, on September 13, 1950), is approximately 14 kilometers in diameter and has an orbital period of 3.8 years. Fanatica is a concept asteroid, named after fanaticism. Fanaticism comes from the Latin *fanaticus*, meaning "one inspired" or "possessed by a deity" (specifically the priests of Cybele and other goddesses). J. Lee Lehman associates this asteroid with fanatical temperaments and activities. Jacob Schwartz associates Fanatica with "warlike behavior."

**Sources:**

Kowal, Charles T. *Asteroids: Their Nature and Utilization*. Chichester, West Sussex, UK: Ellis Horwood Limited, 1988.

Lehman, J. Lee. *The Ultimate Asteroid Book*. West Chester, PA: Whitford Press, 1988.

Schwartz, Jacob. *Asteroid Name Encyclopedia*. St. Paul, MN: Llewellyn Publications, 1995.

## FARROW, PENNY

Penny Farrow has been involved in the study of the Vedic tradition since 1971 as part of a long-standing commitment to her spiritual practice. She has studied Jyotish intensely under the personal tutelage of Hart deFouw, K. N. Rao, V. K. Choudhry, and other highly regarded masters of the subject. She has B.S. and M.S. degrees from Cornell University in biological sciences and has had extensive career experience as a teacher, researcher, and business woman. Recently, she has been a teaching assistant for deFouw in his two-week in-residence Jyotish retreats. Farrow was honored with a Jyotish Bhanu certificate from the Systems' Institute of Hindu Astrology and a certificate of honor from the Institute of Astrology (Bharatiya Vidya Bhavan) in New Delhi for promoting jyotish in the United States. She is the author of several articles that have been published in journals such as *The Mountain Astrologer* and the American Council of Vedic Astrology's *Journal*.

Farrow's ability to integrate and clearly explain the principles of Vedic astrology makes her a popular presenter at conferences and seminars. She practices Jyotish full-time and is a teacher and tutor for the American College of Vedic Astrology. Her particular interest is in integrating her predictions with guidelines on practical approaches to remedial measures as well as traditional recommendations.

## Felicia

Felicia, asteroid 294 (the 294th asteroid to be discovered, on July 15, 1890), is approximately 35 kilometers in diameter and has an orbital period of 5.5 years. Its name means lucky or happy. When prominent in a natal chart, Felicia indicates a lucky person with a generally positive attitude. Its location by sign and house indicates potential sources of luck or happiness. When involved in many inharmonious aspects, Felicia may show an unlucky or unwisely optimistic person.

**Sources:**

Kowal, Charles T. *Asteroids: Their Nature and Utilization*. Chichester, West Sussex, UK: Ellis Horwood Limited, 1988.

Room, Adrian. *Dictionary of Astronomical Names*. London: Routledge, 1988.

Schwartz, Jacob. *Asteroid Name Encyclopedia*. St. Paul, MN: Llewellyn Publications, 1995.

## Felicitas

Felicitas, asteroid 109 (the 109th asteroid to be discovered, on October 9, 1869), is approximately 76 kilometers in diameter and has an orbital period of 4.4 years. It was named after the Roman goddess of happiness. When prominent in a natal chart, Felicitas indicates a person with a generally positive attitude. Its location by sign and house position indicates potential sources of happiness. When involved in many inharmonious aspects, Felicitas may show a person who is glad about the wrong things, or an unwisely optimistic person.

**Sources:**

Kowal, Charles T. *Asteroids: Their Nature and Utilization*. Chichester, West Sussex, UK: Ellis Horwood Limited, 1988.

Room, Adrian. *Dictionary of Astronomical Names*. London: Routledge, 1988.

Schwartz, Jacob. *Asteroid Name Encyclopedia*. St. Paul, MN: Llewellyn Publications, 1995.

## Feminine Signs (Negative Signs)

The 12 signs of the zodiac are classified in a number of different ways, including a division into positive, masculine signs and negative, feminine signs (using negative and positive in the neutral sense of opposite polarities rather than as value judgments about "good" and "bad"). The feminine signs include all the earth signs (Taurus, Virgo, Capricorn) and all the water signs Cancer, Scorpio, Pisces). The gender of the signs was originally determined by the Pythagorean notion that odd numbers are male and even numbers female. This caused the signs that came second (Taurus), fourth (Cancer), sixth (Virgo), etc., in the zodiac to be classified as feminine. By comparison with the masculine signs, the feminine signs tend to be more receptive and introverted. Vedic astrology uses the same classification of signs into feminine and masculine with essentially the same characterization.

**Sources:**

Leo, Alan. *The Complete Dictionary of Astrology*. Rochester, VT: Destiny Books, 1989.

Sutton, Komilla. *The Essentials of Vedic Astrology*. Bournemouth, UK: Wessex Astrologer, 1999.
Tester, Jim. *A History of Western Astrology*. New York: Ballantine, 1987.

## FERAL

Feral is a term used to refer to a wild animal. "Feral signs" is an older designation, similar to the term bestial signs. In traditional astrology, the Moon was also sometimes said to be feral when it was void of course.

## FERONIA

Feronia, asteroid 72 (the 72nd asteroid to be discovered, on May 29, 1861), is approximately 96 kilometers in diameter and has an orbital period of 3.4 years. It was named after the Roman goddess of freed slaves (the naming came at the beginning of the American Civil War), who was also the goddess of groves, woods, and orchards. Her shrine on Mount Soracte in Etruria was the scene of an annual fire-walking ritual. In a natal chart, the asteroid's location by sign and house may indicate where one feels free from social bonds or the bondage of the past. A native with a prominent natal Feronia also feels an attraction for sylvan (related to the woods) environments.

**Sources:**

Kowal, Charles T. *Asteroids: Their Nature and Utilization*. Chichester, West Sussex, UK: Ellis Horwood Limited, 1988.
Room, Adrian. *Dictionary of Astronomical Names*. London: Routledge, 1988.
Schwartz, Jacob. *Asteroid Name Encyclopedia*. St. Paul, MN: Llewellyn Publications, 1995.

## FICINO, MARSILIO

The Florentine philosopher Marsilio Ficino (1433–1499) is chiefly remembered for his revival of Platonic philosophy into the Christian West, but has been generally less recognized for his radical revisioning of the very premises of traditional astrology. This revisioning, far from being on the periphery of his philosophical project, partook of its very essence.

In 1477 Ficino wrote, but did not publish, *Disputatio contra iudicium astrologorum*, a vehement attack on the practices of astrologers. Anyone reading this text would assume that the author found the foundations of traditional astrology fit for demolition by the power of reason and the authority of God's providence. "All this is poetic metaphor," exclaimed Ficino, surveying the absurdity of astrological terminology, "not reason or knowledge." Astrologers, he asserted, use "silly similitudes," fabricate rules—often inconsistently—attribute imaginary powers to the stars, and claim to predict concrete events. But how, asked Ficino, can they know what will happen in ten years' time, when they do not know what they themselves will be doing today?

Yet in the following year Ficino himself wrote to Pope Sixtus IV, as one "equally devoted to both prophecy and astrology," predicting various misfortunes over the coming two years from specific astrological configurations (*Letters*). Indeed, there is hardly a single letter among his vast correspondence in which he does not refer to the influence of planets on his own and his friends' natal charts, on past, present and future events. His deep familiarity with the traditional language of astrology springs from every page, yet in 1494 Ficino wrote to his friend Poliziano in firm support of Pico della Mirandola's attack on astrology, emphasising that "on no occasion" does he affirm astrological portents, and that, like Pico, he despises the "superstitious vanity" of the astrologers (*Opera omnia*).

To begin to understand this apparent anomaly, one must look briefly at the tradition of classical astrology as a rational system of apprehending the workings of the cosmos which by the fifteenth century was fully established in the West, based on the Aristotelian model of celestial causation. Greek and Arabic textbooks on astrology were passed down via Latin translations, definitively illustrated in the *Tetrabiblos* of Claudius Ptolemy, a late Hellenistic work that includes an exposition of the conceptual framework of astrology. This model implies the correlation of effects from the heavens in an "objective time" with those on earth, unfolding in a predetermined way like the cogs in a great machine of destiny. Ptolemaic astrology firmly upholds a natural process of causation, and introduces the concept of ether, an airy all-pervading substance suffused throughout creation whose quality depends on the heavenly bodies. Ptolemy promised man the ability to understand human temperament and predict events through examination of the ether, and established the primacy of the "seed moment" or moment of origin, such as birth itself, at which time the heavens stamped an impression that would indelibly mark the individual. Such a conception of direct, quantifiable astral influence presupposes an omniscient astrologer who observes objectively a fixed pattern; it appears to allow him to give an irrevocable judgment on the "fate" sealed by the birth moment. It also implies a linear unfolding of time and paves the way for modern "scientific" astrological research, based on statistical analysis, quantitative measurement, and empirical observation.

In the medieval period, orthodox Christianity found no problem with a natural astrology that understood the correspondences between the heavens and the material world, and used this knowledge in such fields as agriculture and medicine. But for denying human free will, and for attributing to the astrologer the omnipotence of God, judicial astrology was roundly condemned by theologians such as St. Augustine and Thomas Aquinas, for whom the only legitimate means of foreknowledge could be through Divine Revelation, as noted in his *Summa theologiae*.

From this position, there can never be the possibility that divine knowledge may arise through human effort or activity. The stars cannot be signs in any other way than they are effects of causes; all true insight into the workings of providence must depend on an act of grace, on the prayerful submission of the individual's will to God's. In his *Disputatio*, Ficino clearly set out to fully endorse this view, condemning the type of astrology that depends solely on human ingenuity and judgment. In his *Letters*, he urged the philosophers to gather forces against the "petty ogres" who deny the sovereignty of God, the justice of the angels, and the freewill of men, "that we may triumph over the diviners, albeit not divine but mightily profane, who have for so long been shackling us to their illusions."

This would appear to be a definitive statement of allegiance to the orthodox position. Yet a closer reading shows something new. Although Ficino rejected certain claims of astrologers, he did not deny the possibility that divinatory techniques in themselves may work. He suggested that there were three kinds of foreseeing: through the infusion of divine knowledge, which may be received through magical means and the "divining of the spheres"; through natural means, such as a melancholic temperament that more easily allows the soul contact with its own divine nature; and through what he called the "observation of heavenly patterns." In all these, he said, judgment was very difficult. But it was *not* illicit. Just as the physician may form a prognosis through the observation of an illness, so the augurs, said Ficino, "are led to penetrate all appearances of things to be apprehended here and there in single moments." Perhaps, he speculated, these things were grasped "more completely out of a certain quality of the soul than through judgement" (*Opera omnia*). This crucial observation lead some to question whether the problem is not the astrology, but the astrologers' lack of insight. Ficino was clearly talking about an understanding more akin to revelation than human reason, yet this was not a revelation directly from God to a passive recipient—it demanded the active participation of the individual through the particular way he perceives patterns and signs in nature.

The earliest astrologers of Mesopotamia were omen readers, looking to the heavens for indications of the gods' will, in the same spirit as they looked at entrails and made sacrifices. The omen appeared, either bidden or unbidden, and its significance depended on the ability of the individual to interpret the will of the god in respect to his current concerns. In other words, it was only significant if it was recognized as such, not through a theory or technique, but through the intuitive perception of a sign. As man grew more distant from his gods, so divination lost its sacred dimension and became the domain of earthly prediction of events. In astrology, it survived into the early centuries C.E., particularly in horary and inceptional techniques, but was losing hold to the influence of Stoic and Aristotelian philosophy, which demanded a reformulation of what had been a participatory experience into a theoretical structure. The great science of astrology was born. But did the "divinatory attitude" survive, and if so, how? With the condemnation of the Christian church it could hardly flourish overtly. One has to look elsewhere, to a tradition that would both hold and protect its vulnerable core in an overmantle of philosophical enquiry. Here it was not only preserved; it was reflected upon and articulated in the language of myth, poetry, revelation, and metaphysics. This was the tradition revered by Ficino as the ancient theology.

The very first of the ancient theologians, of whom Plato was the "divine" culmination, was the Egyptian sage Hermes Trismegistus, supposed author of the *Corpus Hermeticum*, Ficino's first translation from Greek. The Hermetic *corpus* is about spiritual initiation, through the individual's realization of his own immortality. In Book One, Hermes's teacher Poimandres tells a creation myth of the fall of man as he unites with the powers of nature (*Corpus Hermeticum I*). Using the metaphor of a symbolic cosmos, readers learn how man is created by the supreme mind or *nous*, and receives the qualities of the seven planets, which govern his destiny on earth. But man, who shares the essence of mind, also partakes of its absolute freedom, and he wills to "break through the circumference of the spheres" and come to know his maker. In other words, as soon as he desires to overcome fate, he can, by realizing and acting from the immortal part of his soul. All men are governed by destiny, says Poimandres, but those who are led by *nous* do not suffer as others do (*Corpus Hermeticum I*). Man is a god, he only has to recognize it, and this very recognition can change his relationship with fate. This dangerous but exhilarating message was to be the key to Ficino's transformation of astrology.

Ficino's reference to divinatory knowledge as "a gift of the soul" shows a similarity in Hermes's suggestion that divination itself is a means of *participating* in *nous*, the divine Mind who knows all. Through "dreams and signs," such as "birds, entrails, inspiration and the sacred oak," divinatory practices would seem to facilitate a mode of knowing that is at once temporal, in that man is observing an event in time, and eternal, in that his "faculty of perception" transcends time and space (*Corpus Hermeticum XII*). In the divinatory moment, these two orders would seem to be aligned as the "objective" physical event coincides with a "subjective" insight that is of another order. With specific reference to astrology, this mode of perception will not regard the stars as causal agents, but as symbols that reflect back to the human soul in its intrinsic connection with the cosmos. The signification of the astrological insight will in no way be determined by the physical configuration, but will depend on the ability, and desire, of the individual to "tune in," Ficino said. "If one pays attention to this signification, it is the thought of God who speaks that one comprehends" (*Opera omnia*).

In 1484, under a conjunction of Saturn and Jupiter, the great significators of reason and faith, Ficino published his translations of Plato. The same day, according to Ficino, Pico della Mirandola came to Florence, and persuaded him to translate Plotinus. Ficino attributed great importance to the astrological symbolism at play between himself and Pico: "It would seem to be divinely brought about that whilst Plato was, so to speak, being re-born, Pico was born under Saturn in Aquarius. In fact I too was born thirty years earlier under the same sign. And so, arriving in Florence on the day our Plato was produced, that old wish of the hero Cosimo [to translate Plotinus] which had previously been hidden from me, was divinely inspired in Pico, and through Pico in me" (*Opera omnia*). In the writings of the neoplatonists, Ficino found a philosophical justification for both symbolic astrology and practical magic.

Ficino included much of his *Disputatio* in his commentaries on Plotinus's *Enneads*, and it is easy to see why, for Plotinus's analysis of astrological effect was a clear refutation of causal thinking. Here, Ficino found confirmation of astrology as divination. In divining from the heavens, said Plotinus, people can know the nature of the all, because the stars are signs: "We may think of the stars as letters perpetually being inscribed on the heavens or inscribed once and for all," he said, and "those who know how to read this sort of writing ... can read the future from their patterns, discovering what is signified by the systematic use of analogy" (*Enneads II*). What one sees conveys the unseen, and this is the mystery at the heart of Platonism. For Plotinus, the wise man is the self-directed man, who, aligned with the higher part of his soul, has developed "another way of seeing, that all have but few use" (*Enneads I*). The Plotinian cosmos is a ballet, all parts interdependent, the hierarchies of being corresponding and mirroring each other in a cosmic energy field. It is soul, as the intermediary between intellect and body, that connects all things, sowing itself as "bait" in material forms that will naturally attract, by affinity, the soul of the human being. As it emanates from the supreme one, soul disposes the configurations of the stars, so that life experiences are announced, not caused, by their patterns. The whole process is ruled by providence, but those who are identified with their lower, material soul will not experience its law as a liberation. Rather, they will remain fate-bound.

This is reiterated by another, often neglected, spokesman for the practice of divination, the neoplatonist Iamblichus. His treatise *De mysteriis*, on the nature of Egyptian, Chaldean, and Assyrian religion, sought to penetrate to the essence of divination. "There is one correct definition and principle for all forms of divination," said Iamblichus, "and it has nothing to do with irresponsibly divining the future with things that lack foreknowledge. Rather, it is to view from the perspective of the gods—who contain in themselves the limits of the entire knowledge of reality" (*De mysteriis*).

All aspects of the material and immaterial cosmos could be used ritually and symbolically to enable the human soul to "lift" itself back to the all-knowing, divine condition it once enjoyed, but unlike Plotinus, for whom the soul was already at one with the gods, Iamblichus recognized the need for the embodied soul to use its very conditions of embodiment to begin a reascent. For this, it needed the help of the gods, which would only become available once the *magus* began to actively engage in a process of stripping off his habitual ways of conceptual thinking to come into contact with "an innate knowledge of the gods co-existent with our very essence" (*De mysteriis*). This "divine" work is *theurgy*, and Ficino dwelled at length on its implications in his *epitome* of *De mysteriis* (*Opera omnia*). He saw it as a preeminent, intuitive, experiential contact with the profoundest level of being, quite distinct from any conceptual mental activity. Conjecture, opinion, and logical reasoning will never lead to a realization of one's own divinity, rather; "the perfect efficacy of ineffable works, which are divinely performed in a way surpassing all intelligence, and the power of inexplicable symbols, which are known only to the Gods, impart theurgic union" (*De mysteriis*). Thus, images, prayers, invocations, and talismans may all contribute to the process of realigning the soul. It is important to understand that divination does not originate from the energies used in everyday life, or from human fabrications or ingenuity. Rather, the devotion, intent, and desire of the operator will allow a superior power to "perfect" the ritual and impart its authority to it. In other words, human beings may partake of divine revelation through their own efforts, and astrology, for Iamblichus, becomes an act of creative participation, an act of becoming conscious of the cosmic forces at work on the lower, "fate-bound" levels of being.

In the third part of his *Book of Life* of 1489, entited "How to fit your life to the heavens," Ficino presented the first steps in theurgy: implicit in a fully elaborated system of "natural" magic. Using Plotinus's ensouled cosmos as a philosophical framework, and drawing on Hermetic, Pythagorean, Platonic, Arabic, and Christian sources, Ficino affirmed that there was a way of achieving physical and psychological equilibrium through recognizing and contacting the hidden, but natural, powers of the universe, primarily through music and image. The magician, said Ficino, was one who used his knowledge of astrological correspondence to fashion a remedy or, image, or sing an invocation at a particular time when the cosmos is aligned with the activity; indeed, he said, "a material action, motion, or event does not obtain full or perfect efficacy *except* when the celestial harmony conduces to it from all sides" (*Liber de vita III*). Through appropriate ritual, the human spirit becomes aligned with the planetary spirit and will then automatically and naturally receive the gifts of that planet as it vibrates in sympathy, like two strings of a lute that are "similarly tuned." As in all divinatory acts, the ritual container must be perfected before the alignment occurs, and mastery of traditional astrological procedures is essential. But for psychological transformation to happen in an active sense, something else is required, and Ficino emphasized the focusing of intent, desire, and the opening of the imagination. The very word desire, from the Latin *de-sidere* ("from the star") evokes an inextricable connection between human longing and the cosmos.

It is from this ground that Ficino looked anew at his own horoscope. The malefic planet Saturn, on his ascendant, would, he said, normally indicate a "brutish" life, bowed down with the extreme of misery (*Liber de vita III*). But the god Saturn, reaching to the intelligible realm of divine knowledge, would promise something quite different. He has "taken over the things which transcend the physical" and is propitious to those who have laid aside an ordinary, worldly life in preference for a contemplative recollection of divine matters (*Liber de vita III*). In other words, the experience of Saturn—or any other planet—would depend on the ability of the individual to be freed from the literal or material levels of perception. Paradoxically, Ficino discovered that through entering into the depths of his melancholy, it began to transform into something else. It had to, because human freedom of will and initiative, for the Platonist, meant following one's destiny willingly. As Ficino wrote to Giovanni Cavalcanti, "What shall I do? I shall seek a shift; either I shall say that a nature of this kind does not issue from Saturn; or, if it should be necessary that it does issue from Saturn, I shall … say that this nature itself is a unique and divine gift" (*Letters*).

Astrology for Ficino could be justified only if it was used in this way, if its framework of techniques and the physical reality of its symbols provided the ritual "container" for the human soul to free itself from the limitations of a material consciousness, and begin to know itself as an image of God. Astrology is then in service to philosophy, and became for Ficino the primary activity of his Platonic academy. In the innermost sanctum, "philosophers will come to know their Saturn, contemplating the secrets of the heavens" (*Opera omnia*). Astrology is now indeed a poetic metaphor, but it has been transformed from the ignorant "word-mongering" of the "petty ogres" to a vehicle for the deepening of human consciousness. In one of his last works, the *Book of the Sun*, Ficino's astrological vision culminated in a triumphant conjunction of astronomy and astrology, philosophy and poetry, the divine and the human, the literal and symbolic, to produce a truly anagogic apprehension of unity.

—Angela Voss

**Sources:**

Allen, Michael J. B. *Nuptial Arithmetic: Marsilio Ficino's Commentary on the Fatal Number in Book VIII of Plato's Republic*. Berkeley: University of California Press, 1994.

Allen, Michael J. B. *The Platonism of Marsilio Ficino: A Study of His Phaedrus Commentary, Its Sources and Genesis*. Berkeley: University of California Press, 1984.

Allen, Michael J. B. *Plato's Third Eye: Studies in Marsilio Ficino's Metaphysics and Its Sources*. Brookfield, VT: Variorum, 1995.

Allen, Michael J. B. *Synoptic Art: Marsilio Ficino on the History of Platonic Interpretation*. Firenze: L. S. Olschki, 1998.

Bullard, M. "The Inward Zodiac: A Development in Ficino's Thought on Astrology." *Renaissance Quarterly*. No. 42 (1990): 687–708.

Ficino, Marsilio. *The Book of the Sun*. Translated by G. Cornelius, D. Costello, G. Tobyn, A. Voss, and V. Wells. In *Sphinx, A Journal for Archetypal Psychology and the Arts*. Vol. 6 (1994): 124–48.

———. *Commentary on Plato's Symposium on Love*. Translated by Sears Jayne. 2d rev. ed. Dallas: Spring Publications, 1985.

———. *Corpus Hermeticum*. Translated by C. Salaman, D. van Oyen, and W. Wharton as *The Way of Hermes*. Rochester, VT: Inner Traditions, 2000.

———. *Disputatio contra iudicium astrologorum*. In *Supplementum Ficinianum*. Edited by P. O. Kristeller. Florence, 1937.

———. *The Letters of Marsilio Ficino*. Translated by members of the Language Department of the School of Economic Science, London. London: Shepheard-Walwyn, 1975–1999.

———. *Opera Omnia*. 2 vols. Basle, 1576.

———. *Three Books on Life*. Edited by Carol V. Kaske and John R. Clark. Binghamton, NY: Medieval and Renaissance Texts and Studies in conjunction with the Renaissance Society of America, 1989.

Garin, Eugenio. *Astrology in the Renaissance: The Zodiac of Life*. Translated by Carolyn Jackson and June Allen. Boston: Routledge and Kegan Paul, 1983.

Iamblichus. *Iamblichus on the mysteries of the Egyptians, Chaldeans, and Assyrians*. Translated by Thomas Taylor. 3d ed. London: Stuart and Watkins, 1968.

Moore, Thomas. *The Planets Within: Marsilio Ficino's Astrological Psychology*. Lewisburg: Bucknell University Press, 1982.

Pearce, G. "Ficino and Astrology." In *Friend to Mankind*. Edited by Michael Shepherd. London: Shepheard-Walwyn, 1999.

Plato. *Timaeus*. Translated by Donald J. Zeyl. Indianapolis: Hackett, 2000.

Plotinus. *The Enneads: A New, Definitive Edition with Comparisons to Other Translations on Hundreds of Key Passages*. Translated by Stephen Mackenna. Burdett, NY: Published for the Paul Brunton Philosophic Foundation by Larson Publications, 1992.

Tomlinson, Gary. *Music in Renaissance Magic: Toward a Historiography of Others*. Chicago: University of Chicago Press, 1993.

Voss, A. "The Astrology of Marsilio Ficino: Divination or Science?" *Culture and Cosmos*. Vol.4, no. 2 (Autumn/Winter 2000): 29–46.

———. "Marsilio Ficino, the Second Orpheus." In *Music as Medicine*. Edited by Peregrine Horden. Brookfield, V.T: Ashgate, 2000.

———. "The Music of the Spheres; Marsilio Ficino and Renaissance Harmonia." *Culture and Cosmos* Vol. 2, no. 2 (Autumn/Winter 1998): 16–38.

———. "On the Knowledge of Divine Things: Ficino's Concept of Notio." *Sphinx, A Journal for Archetypal Psychology and the Arts*. Vol. 6 (1994): 149–72.

———. "Orpheus Redivivus: The Musical Magic of Marsilio Ficino." In *Marsilio Ficino, His Times, His Theology, His Philosophy, His Legacy*. Leiden, 2002.

Walker, D. P. *Spiritual and Demonic Magic from Ficino to Campanella*. London: Warburg Institute, University of London, 1958.

Yates, Frances. *Giordano Bruno and the Hermetic Tradition*. Chicago: University of Chicago Press, 1964.

## Fides

Fides, asteroid 37 (the 37th asteroid to be discovered, on October 5, 1855), is approximately 94 kilometers in diameter and has an orbital period of 4.3 years. It was named after the Roman goddess of faith, honesty, and oath. Like its mythological namesake, the asteroid confers faithfulness and honesty to natives in whose chart it is prominent (e.g., conjunct the Sun or the ascendant). Fides relates particularly to overt displays of honesty and to the outward performance of duty. Negatively, it may manifest itself as blind faith, as the tendency to use honesty as an excuse for expressing unkind remarks, or as the trait of emphasizing the duties others have toward oneself as a way of manipulating their behavior.

**Sources:**

Kowal, Charles T. *Asteroids: Their Nature and Utilization*. Chichester, West Sussex, UK: Ellis Horwood Limited, 1988.

Room, Adrian. *Dictionary of Astronomical Names*. London: Routledge, 1988.

Schwartz, Jacob. *Asteroid Name Encyclopedia*. St. Paul, MN: Llewellyn Publications, 1995.

## Fiducia

Fiducia, asteroid 380 (the 380th asteroid to be discovered, on January 8, 1894), is approximately 78 kilometers in diameter and has an orbital period of 4.4 years. Its name is a personified form of the Latin word for confidence or trust. In a natal chart, its location by sign and house position indicates where and in what manner one is most likely to be trustworthy, as well as where one experiences trust issues. When afflicted by inharmonious aspects, Fiducia can show untrustworthiness or a tendency to misplace trust. If prominent in a chart (e.g., conjunct the Sun or the ascendant), it may show an exceptionally trustworthy person or someone for whom trust is a dominant life theme.

**Sources:**

Kowal, Charles T. *Asteroids: Their Nature and Utilization*. Chichester, West Sussex, UK: Ellis Horwood Limited, 1988.

Room, Adrian. *Dictionary of Astronomical Names*. London: Routledge, 1988.

Schwartz, Jacob. *Asteroid Name Encyclopedia*. St. Paul, MN: Llewellyn Publications, 1995.

## Figure

Figure is an older term for an astrological chart.

## Fire Signs

The 12 signs of the zodiac are subdivided according to the four classical elements—earth, air, fire, and water. The three fire signs (the fire triplicity or fire trigon) are Aries, Leo, and Sagittarius. Astrologically, fire refers to activity. Fire-sign activity can manifest as inspiration and leadership. For people with a predominance of this element, action is the most important aspect of life.

The activity of the fire element shows itself somewhat differently in each of the signs of the fire triplicity. Aries's fiery nature typically manifests as bravery, curiosity, and originality. Leo's comes through in the qualities of leadership and acting ability. Sagittarius's fiery nature emerges as a striving upward toward high social or religious ideals.

Negative fire people can be egotistical, pushy, and excessively concerned about the opinions others hold of them. Unless counterbalanced by other factors, excessive fire in a chart indicates an individual who is overactive, impulsive, and even violent. Conversely, lack of fire can indicate a person who is low in energy and self-esteem.

One finds the same set of four elements and the same classification of signs by element in Vedic astrology. The connotations are basically the same as in Western astrology.

Fire is also one of the five elements of Chinese astrology—earth, water, fire, wood, and metal. In this system, the elements are not permanently associated with each of the signs of the zodiac. Rather, each one of the 12 signs of the East Asian zodiac can be a different element. For example, an individual born as a Horse in 1942 is a water Horse; a Horse born in 1954 is a wood Horse; a Horse born in 1966 is a fire horse; etc. The connotations of fire in Chinese astrology are similar to the connotations of earth in Western astrology.

**Sources:**

Hand, Robert. *Horoscope Symbols*. Rockport, MA: Para Research, 1981.

Sakoian, Frances, and Louis S. Acker. *The Astrologer's Handbook*. New York: Harper & Row, 1989.

## First Point

First point refers to zero degrees Aries, the point along the ecliptic where the zodiac begins.

## First Station

When, from the perspective of Earth, it appears that a planet pauses and then reverses direction (i.e., appears to go backward in its orbit), the point at which it pauses is called the first station.

## Fish

The fish (or fishes) is a popular name for the sign Pisces.

## Fixed Signs

The 12 signs of the zodiac are subdivided according to three qualities: cardinal, mutable, and fixed. The four fixed signs (the *fixed quadruplicity or fixed cross*) are Taurus, Leo, Scorpio, and Aquarius. The Sun moves through these signs when the seasons are at their peak: Taurus in spring, Leo in summer, Scorpio in fall, and Aquarius in winter.

The identifying trait of the fixed signs is captured by the connotation of *fixed:* In response to changing circumstances, fixed signs tend to persist in acting according to preestablished patterns. Positively, the fixed quality can manifest as strength and persistence; negatively, as inflexibility and stubbornness.

The same classification can be found in Vedic astrology—Chara ("moveable" or cardinal), Dwi-Swabhava ("dual" or mutable), and Sthira ("fixed"). The three Vedic qualities, which are associated with the same signs as their Western parallels, have similar connotations.

**Sources:**

Sakoian, Frances, and Louis S. Acker. *The Astrologer's Handbook*. New York: Harper & Row, 1989.

Sutton, Komilla. *The Essentials of Vedic Astrology*. Bournemouth, UK: Wessex Astrologer, 1999.

## Fixed Stars

There are more than 9,000 stars visible to the human eye, and, to the ancients, they belonged to the Eighth Sphere: the starry firmament. This starry sphere separated the known seven spheres of the planets, with earth at the center, from the realm of the Creator—the force that lay beyond the Eighth Sphere and caused all the inner spheres to move. Plato (360 C.E.), in his book *Timaeus*, talked of the Creator, the Demiurge, making the souls of man in the same manner as the Soul of the Universe, and that the number of these souls is the number of the fixed stars, since this was the sphere closest to the Creator. From this, the wandering stars—the planets—were singled out as the timekeepers, and it was thought that the souls moved from the fixed stars to these wanderers, and from the wanderers their power was translated onto the earth as the souls of men.

Claudius Ptolemy (100–c. 173 C.E.) took Plato's concept one step further and suggested which planet or planets were the timekeepers of each star, and consequently which planetary energy was related in similarity to each star. Ptolemy published this work in the *Tetrabiblos*, where he made such statements as: "The stars in the head of Aries possess an influence similar in its effect to that of Mars and Saturn."

What was Ptolemy trying to achieve? Inheriting the ideas of Plato, he would have considered it logical to pursue this line of thought in his attempt to conceive of some rational order in the symbolic, religious, and mythological traditions that were the foundation of the starry sky. As time passed, and Ptolemy's name grew in greatness, his suggested planet/star combinations became the central dogma for the delineation of the stars, replacing the earlier myths and religious beliefs that had been projected onto the constellations and the principal stars. Hence, works by modern authors, such as Vivian E. Robson, Reinhold Ebertin, Georg Hoffmann, and Joseph E. Rigor, show largely unsupported statements of star delineations, their origins apparently sourced in Ptolemy's star/planet associations.

In addition, the newly emerging Greek world of science was grappling with the as yet unanswered question of the rate of precession. Astronomers knew that precession occurred, but were unsure of its rate. Precession becomes apparent by observing the slow shift of the fixed stars against key calendar positions of the sun, such as the equinoxes or the solstices. Ptolemy was primarily an astronomer, and therefore this problem was one of his central preoccupations. The problem of the day was that two sets of data were required to answer the question on precession. The first was the accurate position of stars for one period in time, and the second was the same list of stars but measured for a later period. By comparing the two lists, and knowing the time period between the two, the rate of precession could be found.

The most common method of locating a star in the sky, before Ptolemy, was to use regularly repeating lunar cycles: noting the date and time, and the Moon 's degree of longitude and latitude, then marking its orientation to a star. This was a cumbersome method, as the following excerpt from Ptolemy's *Almagest* shows:

> Again, Timnicharis says he observed in Alexandria that in the year 36 of the First Callippic Period exactly at the beginning of the tenth hour, the moon appeared to overtake with its northern arc the northern star of those in the Scorpion's forehead. And this date is the year 454 of Navonassar, Egyptian wise Phaophi 16–17, 3 seasonal hours after midnight and 3⅖ equatorian hours, because the sun was 26° within the Archer, but 3⅙ hours with respect to regular solar days. At that hour the true position of the moon's centre was 31¼° from the autumn equinox and 1⅓° north of the ecliptic.

Ptolemy initially proceeded according to this method, finding the position of a particular lunation for his current date, and then calculating the star's movement. But it was tedious and not particularly accurate, so Ptolemy decided to develop a better system for recording the position of stars. His logic was that if he could clearly lay down a technique for measuring stars, and use that technique for measuring "as many stars as we could up to those of the sixth magnitude" (*Almagest*), then he would be able to produce a list of stars that could be used by future generations of astronomers to check his estimates of the rate of precession .

His method was simple. He first developed an instrument that would enable him to make the needed measurements. He then found the poles of the ecliptic, and projected every star onto the ecliptic via the lines of longitude from these poles. The point where the projected star cut the ecliptic he carefully measured, and noted the star's latitude north or south of the ecliptic. By this method, he measured 1,022 stars, and published this list in his *Almagest*.

It was an ingenious system. It meant that the position of a star could be accurately and simply recorded. It could be reproduced in years to come so that any change in the ecliptical position of the star could be easily noted. It was a huge advance for astronomers and placed Ptolemy among the giants of astronomy. However, it also altered the way that astrologers worked with fixed stars. Until that time, evidence suggests that the predominant method for working with stars in astrology was via their risings, culminations, and settings. But within several hundred years after Ptolemy, astrologers had taken his convenient list of stars with their ecliptical degrees, and were routinely using it in their horoscopes, forsaking the older, more tedious, observational methodologies. Ptolemy had developed the list as an astronomer, for astronomical needs. He was, afterall, an astronomer and the book in which he published this listing was not his book on astrology, *Tetrabiblos*, but his great astronomical work, the *Almagest*. However, later astrologers, persuaded by the eminence of his name, chose to use Ptolemy's star list of ecliptical projected degrees as the preferred methodology for working with fixed stars astrologically.

This was a slow transition, for in 379 C.E. the unknown author of *The Treatise on Bright Fixed Stars* did talk of using stars that were close to the ecliptic in this fashion. The author suggested, however, that stars further away from the ecliptic should be used when working with the older system of the "pivot points " of the chart—that is, the rising, culminating, setting, and nadir axes. This is known today as working in parans.

The voice of this unknown author (known as Anonymous of 379 C.E.), however, went unheard, and astrologers from the end of the ancient era through to modern times have used Ptolemy's convenient listing of ecliptical degrees for all their fixed star work. This list is used in the attempt to gain greater understanding of the meanings of individual stars, which have been allocated individual degrees of the ecliptic. In recent times, the New York astrologer Dianna Rosenberg has produced fine and impressive work demonstrating how individual degrees of the zodiac (and, therefore, by this logic, fixed stars) are stressed at key times.

Nevertheless, such an approach does leave unanswered another question in astrology. Michael Harding in *Hymn to the Ancient Gods* (1992) suggested that a layer of human projection, via historical events, could be linked to the individual degrees of the tropical zodiac. For example, it would be logical for astrologers to accept that the events of September 11, 2001, had projected symbolism on some particular degrees of the ecliptic that were being occupied by key planets at the time of the terrorist attacks. Such a study of the meaning of an individual degree could only be undertaken if the ecliptic of Ptolemy's projection of 1,022 stars were uncluttered. Indeed, while the ecliptic is occupied by the projection of 1,022 stars, astrologers cannot even begin to consider Harding's hypotheses.

If the individual degrees of the tropical zodiac have been influenced by the projected position of several fixed stars, then these positions would be subject to precession. For example, in the year 1 C.E., the star Algol in Perseus by projection was at 28°27' Aries. By precession this moved to 26°12' Taurus for the year 2002 C.E. Such a shift over 2,000 years gives ample opportunity for historical research into Algol, or any other star. Such an undertaking would help to resolve the question of whether the individual degrees of the tropical zodiac have meaning in their own right, or have no meaning except that derived from the projection of the fixed stars onto the ecliptic.

Yet there is the far older method of working with fixed stars, which does not require this projection. This older method allows the stars to maintain their relational positions in the celestial sphere, thereby maintaining the integrity of the dome of the night sky. The system is based in observation and, although referred to by Anonymous of 379 C.E., as previously mentioned, it is very difficult to reconstruct unless one was taking observations at the time of the event. This older system is called parans, and was absent from the astrologer's tool kit from roughly the time of Anonymous of 379 C.E. until the advent of Robert Hand's software program "Nova," published by Astrolabe in the mid-1980s. In this program, Hand produced a listing of more than 250 stars and provided astrologers with the ability to use these stars not only as projected ecliptical degrees, but, more importantly, to work with the stars in their paran relationship to each other and the planets. Thus, the addition of the computer into the astrologer's toolbox has enabled them to work with observational information, allowing them once again to be watchers of the sky, although now it is from the desktop.

Parans are the natural way of working with the daily rotation of the sky, for at any time (provided one is not at the poles) there will be stars rising on the eastern side of the circle of the horizon. They will be rising on the full half-circle of the horizon, not just due east. As a star rises, for instance, to the northeast of the point of observation, there may be, at the same time, another star in the southeast also rising. The two stars would be rising simultaneously, and are said to have a paran relationship because they are both on the line of the horizon at the same time.

Similarly, a star may be rising in the east as another star is setting on the western side of the circle of the horizon; these two stars are also in paran relationship. The important point is that the full circle of the horizon is used, not just the eastern and western points of the ecliptic.

Another very obvious point in the sky is the culmination point. Facing either north or south, an imaginary line passing directly overhead, cutting the sky in two, is the prime meridian. Where this line cuts the ecliptic is the current MC or midheaven. Stars anywhere along this line are culminating, reaching the top of their rising arc and about to start travelling downwards towards the western horizon. This culminating point adds another possible paran placement.

The Moon may be culminating just as a bright star is setting or rising. If this were the case, then the Moon would be in paran with this star. Indeed, whenever a star or planet is on any of the four major points of its diurnal movement—rising (ascendant), setting (descendant), culminating (MC), or on the nadir (IC)—and another star or planet is also on any of the four points of its diurnal motion, then the two points, star or planet, are in a paran relationship.

This is a natural approach to working with the sky. The mere act of standing and watching a night sky results in working with parans. One may note, for example, that as Venus rises a bright red star is setting; this is a paran relationship between Venus and the red star. Indeed, observations such as this make up some of the earliest recorded astronomical and astrological material.

But the night sky shows another phenomenon, which Ptolemy called star phases. Star phases have not been used in astrology for nearly 2,000 years. They were the subject of one of Ptolemy's astrological works, *The Phases of the Fixed Stars*, and were a predominant feature of any consideration concerning fixed stars in ancient life. However, as astrologers became disconnected from the sky, the astrological importance of star phases faded, first, because of the popularity of the easy technique of projecting a star onto the ecliptic, and second, because phases belonged to the older, more-difficult-to-reconstruct, visually based systems.

Nevertheless, whether astrologers observe it or not, each star does have a unique pattern of visibility for any given place on earth. Some stars will be visible in the night sky for a period of time, yet later in the year they will fail to appear and be lost to the view of the observer. Others will rise or set at night, but instead of disappearing from view altogether, they will lose touch with the horizon and spend the whole night being visible in the night sky. Yet both types of stars will eventually return to rising or setting during the night, with each individual star doing so on a particular date of the year. However, there is also another set of stars that does not partake of this pattern; these are always visible, and never sink beneath the horizon, spending every night circling around the pole.

To the Egyptians, the stars were deities, and so these annual star patterns had strong religious significance. The never-setting circumpolar stars were considered to be the Immortals, for these were the deities that never died, the stars that never set. It was therefore considered significant when a star that would normally rise or set would appear to act like a circumpolar star by being visible for the whole night. This event would always commence on the same calendar date, from one year to the next. Furthermore, and considered of even greater significance, this same star would return to the pattern of setting during the night, at another set calendar date. Such a star was considered to be a deity who spent time not only walking in the world of the Immortals, but also walking in the world of humans, and was therefore open to prayer and offerings. The return of such a star on a particular date is known as the heliacal setting star, and its phase, as named by Ptolemy, is "curtailed passage."

The stars that were never seen, the stars that never rose during the night and remained permanently out of sight, were considered by the Egyptians to be the deities that lived in the Underworld. However, at set dates some visible stars would disappear from view and fail to rise during the night. These stars were believed to be deities that died at a set time of the year and then spent time walking through the Underworld. However, such a star would reappear in the night sky (rise from the dead) by rising just before dawn at a precise calendar date. This star was considered a deity who had risen from the Underworld and now walked again upon the earth. It was believed to be the ruling deity for the period of time until the next deity returned from the land of the dead. The return of such a star is known as the heliacal rising star, and its phase, as named by Ptolemy, is arising and laying hidden.

So important were these times of the return of a star that, as Norman Lockyer (1836–1920), considered the founding father of archeoastronomy, pointed out in his work *Dawn of Astronomy* (1894), the Egyptians based their religious calendar around such events and built temples designed to capture the returning star's light onto the altar of the deity.

The principles embodied in the work of such writers as Robert Hand, Norman Lockyer, and Anonymous of 379 C.E., and also demonstrated by Ptolemy's *The Phases of the Fixed Stars*, were taken up and expanded upon by Bernadette Brady's book *Brady's Book of Fixed Stars* (1998), in which she recommends that astrologers should once again return to the older observational techniques of working with fixed stars as well as move away from the star/planet delineations of Plato and Ptolemy and, by researching the symbolism and mythology linked to the ancient constellations, use these to explore far older meanings of the stars.

—Bernadette Brady

**Sources:**

Anonymous of 379. *The Treatise on the Bright Fixed Stars*. Berkeley Springs, WV: Golden Hind Press, 1994.

Ashmand, J.M. *Ptolemy's Tetrabiblos*. New ed. North Hollywood, CA: Symbols and Signs, 1976.

Brady, Bernadette. *Brady's Book of Fixed Stars*.York Beach, ME: Weisers, 1998.

Harding, Michael. *Hymn to the Ancient Gods*. UK: Penguin, 1992.

Lockyer, J. N. *Dawn of Astronomy*. New York: Macmillan, 1894. Reprint, Cambridge, MA: MIT Press, 1964.

Ptolemy, Claudius. *The Almagest*. Multiple editions.

———. *The Phases of the Fixed Stars*. Vol. III. Translated by Robert Schmidt. Berkeley Springs, WV: The Golden Hind Press: 1993.

## Flower Remedies and Astrology

The flower remedies—also known as flower essences—are liquids that catalyze changes in problematic patterns or emotions, such as guilt or low self-esteem. They are not herbs or aromatherapy oils, but a greatly diluted essence of the flower of the plant, similar in nature to homeopathic remedies or cell salts. They are sold in many health food stores in concentrate form, four drops of which are mixed in an ounce of spring water. The resulting mixture is taken by mouth at the rate of four drops four times a day. The best known are the Bach remedies, developed in England in the 1930s, and the so-called California remedies, developed by the Flower Essence Society (FES) in the 1970s. By the 1990s, however, companies all over the world were making remedies from their local flowers.

The remedies are an easily learned tool to incorporate into the practice of astrology. The astrologer's reading clearly identifies character patterns in the birth chart and current issues brought up by transits or progressions. The astrologer can then give a mixture of remedies relevant to those patterns or issues to clients who want to continue to work with the insights gained in the reading. In taking the remedies, clients reportedly gain new perceptions and conscious awareness of where their difficulties originate. As more clarity is gained, even long-standing patterns are gradually released and are replaced with a healthier outlook and mode of behavior.

The guilt-ridden client, for instance, may be given pine by Bach, while the client with low self-esteem may benefit from FES's sunflower. The child who continually demands to be the center of attention may be given Bach's chicory. FES's lotus is useful for those who wish to pursue meditation and spiritual development. The first remedy the astrologer may wish to acquire is Bach's famous rescue remedy, which can be given to clients who are in a crisis situation or who are emotionally upset. A few drops of the concentrate to sip in a glass of water or a cup of tea are used to quickly restore calm.

As astrologers become more skilled in using the remedies, they can more easily link them with the concerns of various planets or signs. Issues related to the planet Pluto, for example, include control (treated with vine), resentment (assuaged with willow), and envy or the desire for revenge (mollified with holly)—all of these therapies for Pluto ailments are Bach remedies. FES's offerings abound with remedies for Venus concerns, such as dogwood, for gentleness and grace in relationships; bleeding heart, for the brokenhearted; and quince, for developing the positive power of love.

For the discouragement that often accompanies a Saturn transit, the astrologer may suggest Bach's elm, gentian, or gorse.

The astrologer may also be intrigued with certain formulas designed to address various chart factors. For instance, one of Desert Alchemy's founders, Cynthia Kemp, is herself an astrologer and has devised premixed formulas for transits from Jupiter and Chiron on out to Pluto. She also mixed combination formulas for the house axes, such as the axes for the first and seventh houses, the second and eighth houses, and the third and ninth houses. Pegasus Products also features remedies for issues related to the planets and several of the fixed stars in their Star-lite Elixir line. Earthfriends, founded by astrologer John Stowe, features planetary oils that incorporate both flower remedies and aromatherapy oils.

Contact information for various companies:

Alaskan Flower Essence Project
P.O. Box 1369
Homer, AK 99603
Telephone (U.S. and Canada): 800-545-9309
Outside U.S.: (907) 235-2188
Web page: http://www.alaskanessences.com
Email: info@alaskanessences.com

Australian Bush Flower Essences
45 Booralie Road
Terrey Hills, NSW, 2084, Australia
Telephone: 02 9450 1388
Fax: 02 9450 2866
International Telephone: 61 2 9450 1388
International Fax: 61 2 9450 2866
Web page: http://www.ausflowers.com.au/essence.html
Email: info@ausflowers.com.au

Desert Alchemy
P.O. Box 44189
Tucson, AZ 85733
Telephone: (800) 736-3382; (520) 325-1545
Web page: http://www.desert-alchemy.com

Earthfriends
Box 8468
Atlanta, GA 31106
Telephone: (404) 373-0111
Web page: http://www.goodweeds.com
Email: jrstowe@mindspring.com

Flower Essence Society
P.O. Box 459
Nevada City, CA 95959
Telephone: (800) 736-9222 (North America)

Web page: www.flowersociety.org
Email: info@flowersociety.org

Flower Vision Research
P.O. Box 43627
Upper Montclair, NJ 07043
Telephone: (973) 746-5798
Toll free: (800) 298-4434
Web page: http://www.flowervr.com/
Email: essences@flowervr.com

Healingherbs Ltd.
P.O. Box 65
Hereford HR2 0UW, UK
Telephone: +44(0)1873 890 218
Fax: +44(0)1873 890 314
Web page: http://www.healing-herbs.co.uk/
Email: healing-herbs@healing-herbs.co.uk

(U.S. Distributor: Flower Essence Society)
Living Essences of Australia
P.O. Box: 355
Scarborough WA 6019, Australia
Telephone: 61 8 4435600
Fax: 61 8 4435610
Web page: http://livingessences.com.au/
Email: email@livingessences.com.au

Pacific Essences
Box 8317
Victoria, BC V8W 3R9, Canada
Telephone: (250) 384-5560
Email: info@pacificessences.com

Pegasus Products, Inc.
P.O. Box 228
Boulder, CO 80306
Telephone: (970) 667-3019; (800) 527-6104
Web page: http://www.pegasusproducts.com/
Email: StarVibe@indra.com

Whole Energy Essences
P.O. Box 285
Concord, MA 01742
Telephone: (978) 369-8454
Web page: www.essences.com
Email: wessence@essences.com

Wild Earth Animal Essences
P.O. Box 407

Charlottesville, VA 22902
Telephone: (800) 871-5647
Web page: http://www.animalessence.com/
Email: info@animalessence.com

—Donna Cunningham

**Sources:**

Barnard, Julian, and Martine Barnard. *The Healing Herbs of Edward Bach*. Hereford, UK: Bach Educational Programme, 1988.

Chancellor, Philip M. *Handbook of the Bach Flower Remedies*. New Canaan, CT: Keats Health Books, 1980.

Cunningham, Donna. *Flower Remedies Handbook*. New York: Sterling Publishing, 1992.

Gurudas. *Flower Essences and Vibrational Healing*. Rev. ed. San Rafael, CA: Cassandra Press, 1989.

Kamiski, Patricia, and Richard Katz. *Flower Essence Repertory*. Rev. ed. Nevada City, CA: Flower Essence Services, 1992.

## Forming

When two planets are beginning to enter into an aspect with each other, but before the aspect has become exact, the aspect is said to be forming.

## Fortified

A planet is said to be fortified when it is elevated, favorably aspected, or in a sign that it rules.

## Fortunes

Fortunes is an older term for the so-called benefic planets—Jupiter (the Greater Fortune) and Venus (the Lesser Fortune).

## Foundation Chart

A foundation chart is a horoscope calculated for the moment construction on a building is begun. Although such charts can be cast retrospectively, in traditional astrology they were part of electional astrology—the branch that deals with the most appropriate times to begin things.

## Four Pillars Divination

The Four Pillars is the simplest of the Chinese systems for personal, heavenly divination. Properly speaking, the Four Pillars system is not a part of astrology, for it does not feature the positions of the planets or the stars as part of the natal chart. Neither are the pillars used to determine the boundaries or dimensions of the natal chart.

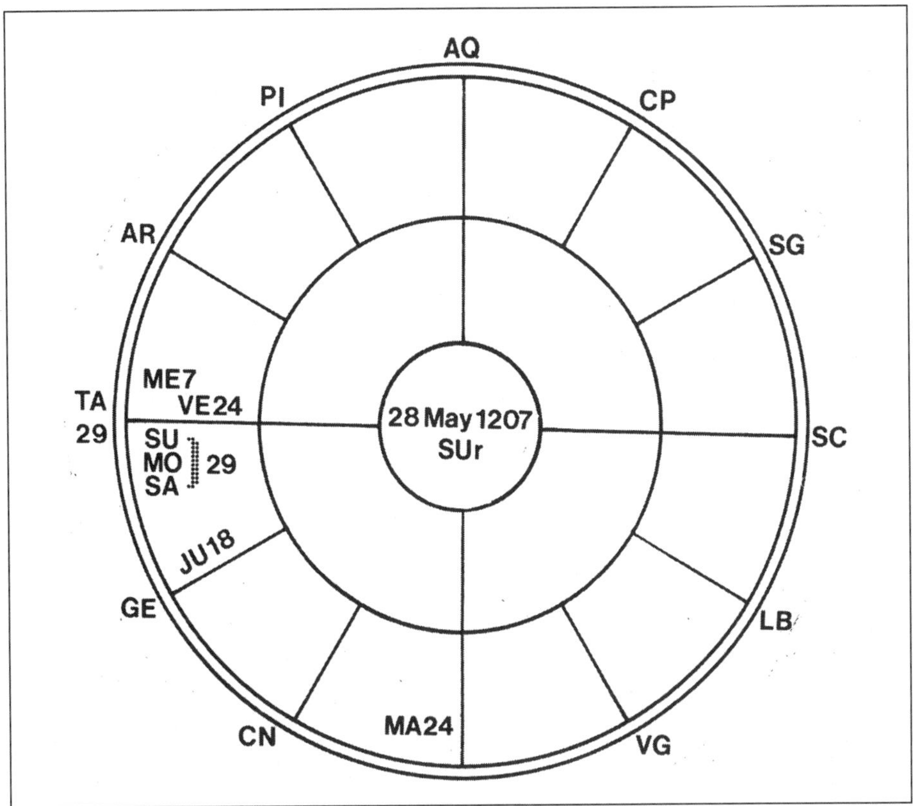


**The foundation chart of San Miniato al Monte, cast for sunrise on May 28, 1207. The chart shows the planets Mercury, Venus, and Saturn as well as the sun and moon in the constellation Taurus.** ***Reproduced by permission of Fortean Picture Library.***

The position of only one heavenly body, the Sun, is used to figure out everything contained in a Four Pillars chart. While the popular methods for working out the pillars in China involve the lunar calendar, the tables used in those popular methods are ultimately used to convert the lunar calendar into solar positions.

A Four Pillars chart consists of eight pieces of information in two rows, one row of four stacked on top of another. The pieces in the row on top are called "Heavenly Stems." The pieces in the row on the bottom are called "Earthly Branches." Each of the heavenly stems is named by a yin or a yang polarity and by one of the Taoist five elements: wood, fire, earth, metal, or water. Since there are five elements and two polarities, the heavenly stems are ten in number: yang wood, yin wood, yang fire, yin fire, yang earth, yin earth, yang metal, yin metal, yang water, and yin water. The earthly branches is the proper name for the Chinese zodiac animals: rat, ox, tiger, rabbit, dragon, snake, horse, sheep, monkey, rooster, dog, and pig.

In the Four Pillars chart a person gets one heavenly stem and one earthly branch for the year of his or her birth, one of each for the birth month, one of each for the birth day, and one of each for the double-hour period of birth. Each paired heavenly stem and earthly branch is referred to as a "pillar." The four of them together give the Four Pillars divination its name.

If one starts with heavenly stem number one (yang wood) and pairs it with earthly branch number one (rat), and runs them through in order, one will get 60 possible combinations of heavenly stem and earthly branch. This is why the sixtieth birthday is so important in the East. In effect, one has lived through all possible combinations of pillars.

The Four Pillars is unique in the astrological world for dividing up the path of the ecliptic in two different ways, one way according to the annual rotation of the Sun, another according to the daily rotation. Even though the path of the Sun is divided up in two entirely different ways, the divisions are given the same names in both rotations. Within the limits of the vastly different time periods involved, the energies associated with those like-named periods are regarded as the same as well.

The earliest Chinese astrological reference to any part of the Four Pillars system is a division of the year into 24 parts. If one takes the Western tropical signs and divides them in half, the result exactly reproduces the 24 divisions of the old Chinese year. What the Taoist Chinese do with these divisions is very different from what is done in Western astrology. In the West, the year begins at the Spring equinox, also called Zero Aries. The Chinese year begins halfway between the Winter solstice and the Spring equinox, located where the Western zodiac calls 15° of Aquarius. Fifteen degrees of Aquarius is the proper derivation of the Western ritual day of Candlemass, or Groundhog Day. The Chinese regard 15° of Aquarius—roughly February 4—as the beginning of Spring, and as the beginning of the astrological Chinese year.

A chart has a pillar for the year of a person's birth. If that person were born between 15 Aquarius 1924 and 15 Aquarius 1925, the earthly branch for that year is rat. There are five kinds of rat years: wood/rats, fire/rats, earth/rats, metal/rats, and water/rats. This refers to five different heavenly stems to go along with the rat earthly branch. Because of the order of the stems and branches, rat, tiger, dragon, horse, monkey, and dog are always associated with yang polarity heavenly stems. Ox, rabbit, snake, sheep, rooster, and pig are always associated with yin polarity heavenly stems. Between 15 Aquarius 1924 to 15 Aquarius 1925 is the yang wood/rat year. Marlon Brando, George Herbert Walker Bush, and Paul Newman were born in this period. The yang wood/rat is their year pillar.

The Chinese year is divided up very differently from the Western zodiac:

15 Aquarius to 15 Pisces is Tiger month.
15 Pisces to 15 Aries is Rabbit month.
15 Aries to 15 Taurus is Dragon month.
15 Taurus to 15 Gemini is Snake month.
15 Gemini to 15 Cancer is Horse month.
15 Cancer to 15 Leo is Sheep month.
15 Leo to 15 Virgo is Monkey month.
15 Virgo to 15 Libra is Rooster month.
15 Libra to 15 Scorpio is Dog month.

15 Scorpio to 15 Sagittarius is Pig month.
15 Sagittarius to 15 Capricorn is Rat month.
15 Capricorn to 15 Aquarius is Ox month.

Just as every 60 years covers the entire cycle of Pillars, so too, every 60 months and every 60 days cover the entire Pillars cycle as well.

The double-hours of the day are divided in a scheme that should be very familiar to students of acupuncture:

| | |
|---|---|
| 11 P.M.–1 A.M. | Rat |
| 1 A.M.–3 A.M. | Ox |
| 3 A.M.–5 A.M. | Tiger |
| 5 A.M.–7 A.M. | Rabbit |
| 7 A.M.–9 A.M. | Dragon |
| 9 A.M.–11 A.M. | Snake |
| 11 A.M.–1 P.M. | Horse |
| 1 P.M.–3 P.M. | Sheep |
| 3 P.M.–5 P.M. | Monkey |
| 5 P.M.–7 P.M. | Rooster |
| 7 P.M.–9 P.M. | Dog |
| 9 P.M.–11 P.M. | Pig |

With 12 double-hours during the day, the entire Pillars cycle runs for five days (60 double-hours) before returning to the beginning.

A person born on April 7, 1928, at 6:30 P.M. would have the following Four Pillars:

| **Hour** | **Day** | **Month** | **Year** |
|---|---|---|---|
| Yin Earth | Yin Fire | Yang Fire | Yang Earth |
| Rooster | Ox | Dragon | Dragon |

A person born on December 1, 1983, at 10:14 P.M. would have this chart:

| **Hour** | **Day** | **Month** | **Year** |
|---|---|---|---|
| Yin Water | Yin Water | Yin Water | Yin Water |
| Pig | Pig | Pig | Pig |

In effect, the year and day pillars function like the axle of a wheel, and the month and hour pillars function like the spokes. The year/month pillars divide up the annual rotation, and the day/hour pillars divide up the daily rotation. The annual rotation is divided up differently than the daily rotation, but they can—still—both have the same sign or energy.

The Four Pillars system reached maturity during the Sung Dynasty, when the subject of the chart shifted from the earthly branch of the year to the heavenly stem of the day. Even today, if you ask the Chinese "what they are," astrologically, they will give the animal of the year.

Each of the earthly branches/animals has one of the five elements attached to it, as well as a primary yin or tang polarity. The heavenly stems consist of one of the five elements and a yin or yang polarity. Using the five elements and the doctrine of yin/yang as a template, the Four Pillars astrologer judges the merit or misfortune of the nativity according to whether the chart assists/harms, strengthens/weakens, or balances/unbalances the heavenly stem of the day. The astrologer can also judge which periods of life will aid the subject or harm him.

These same techniques from Taoist philosophy can also determine the degree of compatibility between two prospective partners. In this way, the Four Pillars have been used to arrange marriages in the East for centuries.

—Ko Hashiguchi

**Sources:**

Lau, Theodora. *The Handbook of Chinese Horoscopes*. New York: Harper, 4th ed., 2000.

Starr, Amanda. *Chinese Astrology*. Hod Hasharon, Israel: Astrolog, 2002.

Twicken, David. *Four Pillars and Oriental Medicine*. Lincoln, NE: Writers Club, 2000.

Walters, Derek. *Chinese Astrology: Interpreting the Revelations of the Celestial Messengers*. Wellingborough, Northamptonshire, UK: Aquarian Press, 1987.

## Four-Footed Signs

The traditional four-footed signs were, as one might anticipate, Aries, Taurus, Leo, Sagittarius, and Capricorn.

## Fraternitas

Fraternitas, asteroid 309 (the 309th asteroid to be discovered, on April 6, 1891), is approximately 32 kilometers in diameter and has an orbital period of 4.4 years. Its name is derived from the Latin word for brotherhood. When prominent in a natal chart, Fraternitas indicates a friendly personality, interested in universal brotherhood. The sign and house position indicates how one interacts with friends.

**Sources:**

Kowal, Charles T. *Asteroids: Their Nature and Utilization*. Chichester, West Sussex, UK: Ellis Horwood Limited, 1988.

Room, Adrian. *Dictionary of Astronomical Names*. London: Routledge, 1988.

Schwartz, Jacob. *Asteroid Name Encyclopedia*. St. Paul, MN: Llewellyn Publications, 1995.

## Frieda

Frieda, asteroid 722 (the 722nd asteroid to be discovered, on October 18, 1911), is approximately 15 kilometers in diameter and has an orbital period of 3.2 years. It was named after the granddaughter of the Vienna Observatory's director, whose name means peace in German. In a natal chart, its location by sign and house indicates where and how one is most likely to seek or experience peace. When afflicted by inharmonious aspects, Frieda may show conflict or peace-seeking in situations where a peaceful response is inappropriate. If prominent in a natal chart (e.g., conjunct the Sun or the ascendant), it may show an exceptionally tranquil person.

**Sources:**

Kowal, Charles T. *Asteroids: Their Nature and Utilization*. Chichester, West Sussex, UK: Ellis Horwood Limited, 1988.

Room, Adrian. *Dictionary of Astronomical Names*. London: Routledge, 1988.

Schwartz, Jacob. *Asteroid Name Encyclopedia*. St. Paul, MN: Llewellyn Publications, 1995.

## FRIGGA

Frigga, asteroid 77 (the 77th asteroid to be discovered, on November 12, 1862), is approximately 66 kilometers in diameter and has an orbital period of 4.4 years. It was named after the Norse goddess of marriage, the wife of Odin (the Roman equivalent to Juno). The unusual name of this planetoid—which seems to suggest an obscene gesture—led to its inclusion in *The Asteroid Ephemeris: Dudu, Dembowska, Pittsburgh, Frigga*, Batya Stark and Mark Pottenger's tour de force of astrological humor.

**Sources:**

Kowal, Charles T. *Asteroids: Their Nature and Utilization*. Chichester, West Sussex, UK: Ellis Horwood Limited, 1988.

Room, Adrian. *Dictionary of Astronomical Names*. London: Routledge, 1988.

Stark, Batya, and Mark Pottenger. *The Asteroid Ephemeris: Dudu, Dembowska, Pittsburgh, Frigga*. San Diego: Astro Computing Services, 1982.

Schwartz, Jacob. *Asteroid Name Encyclopedia*. St. Paul, MN: Llewellyn Publications, 1995.

## FRUITFUL (FERTILE SIGNS AND PLANETS)

The fruitful signs are the signs of the zodiac traditionally said to indicate children (i.e., to indicate fertility) when placed on the cusp of the fifth house, the house of children. These signs are the *water triplicity*: Cancer, Scorpio, and Pisces. Several other signs are regarded as being somewhat fruitful. The fruitful planets are the Sun, the Moon, Venus, and Jupiter (with Neptune added by certain modern astrologers). Mercury is regarded as moderately fruitful. The infertile signs and planets are designated barren. The classification of the zodiac into degrees of barrenness and fruitfulness has been largely abandoned because contemporary astrological research has failed to verify this traditional interpretation. However, the traditional fruitful signs are still regarded as fertile in agricultural astrology.

**Sources:**

Lee, Dal. *Dictionary of Astrology*. New York: Paperback Library, 1969.

Leo, Alan. *The Complete Dictionary of Astrology*. Rochester, VT: Destiny Books, 1989.

## GADBURY, JOHN

John Gadbury, an English astrologer, was born in Wheatley, Oxon, England, on January 1, 1627. He was the son of a farmer, William Gadbury, and was initially apprenticed to a tailor. He left the tailor in 1644, however, when his mother's father, Sir John Curson, offered to provide the funds for an Oxford education. After graduation, Gadbury worked with a London merchant, and married in about 1648. After he returned to Oxfordshire, he studied astrology with Nicholas Fiske and in 1652 published his first book on the science of the stars. His *Doctrine of Nativities*, a general treatise on natal astrology, was published in 1658.

Gadbury became an associate of the eminent astrologer William Lilly, although they differed in their politics. Lilly even wrote an introduction to one of Gadbury's books. However, when in 1659 the Swedish king Charles X sent Lilly a gift of a gold chain and medal, Gadbury became jealous. The gift came after a favorable forecast Lilly had given Charles in his almanac of 1658. Gadbury published an opposed forecast, and, as it turned out, King Charles died unexpectedly in 1660.

This naturally led to a rift between Gadbury and Lilly, which culminated in the so-called Scorpio quarrel of 1675. Displeased with Lilly's negative characterization of Scorpio, Gadbury, who had a Scorpio ascendant, attacked Lilly in his *Obsequium Rationabile*. Gadbury was answered by some tracts and broadsides printed by Lilly's associates. The quarrel climaxed with the 1693 publication of John Partridge's *Black Life of John Gadbury*.

Gadbury is remembered primarily for his *Collectio Geniturarum*, a compilation of 150 horoscopes. This collection was often referred to by later astrologers. Gadbury also authored almanacs and tables of planetary positions, but his success was mild compared with other London astrologers, particularly Lilly. Gadbury died in London on March 28, 1704.

**Sources:**

Gadbury, John. *Collectio Geniturarum*. London: James Cottrel, 1662.

———. *Genethlialogia, or the Doctrine of Nativities*. 2d ed. London: 1661.

———. *Obsequium Rationabile*.... London, 1675.

Holden, James H., and Robert A. Hughes. *Astrological Pioneers of America*. Tempe, AZ: American Federation of Astrologers, 1988.

## Gaea

Gaea, asteroid 1,184 (the 1,184th asteroid to be discovered, on September 5, 1926), is approximately 20 kilometers in diameter and has an orbital period of 4.4 years. Gaea was named after the Greek earth goddess; *gaea* is Greek for "Earth." J. Lee Lehman associates this asteroid with what she calls the "ground of being." Jacob Schwartz gives the astrological significance of Gaea as "a personification of Mother Earth, a place rather than a player."

**Sources:**

Kowal, Charles T. *Asteroids: Their Nature and Utilization*. Chichester, West Sussex, UK: Ellis Horwood Limited, 1988.

Lehman, J. Lee. *The Ultimate Asteroid Book*. West Chester, PA: Whitford Press, 1988.

Schwartz, Jacob. *Asteroid Name Encyclopedia*. St. Paul, MN: Llewellyn Publications, 1995.

## Galactic Center

Earth is located in a spiral-shaped galaxy approximately 100,000 light-years in diameter. Our solar system lies on the outskirts of the galaxy, about 30,000 light-years away from the galactic center (GC). From Earth's perspective, the GC is located in the latter degrees of the sign Sagittarius. (Owing to the tropical or moving zodiac that most Western astrologers use, the exact position of the GC appears to be is gradually shifting.) The GC is such an intense source of infrared emissions and microwaves that astrophysicists have speculated that an explosion took place there 10 million years ago. Because our solar system is actually rotating around the GC, the GC can be thought of as a bit like the sun of our solar system. The 250 million years that it takes for our solar system to complete one rotation is called a cosmic year.

Astrologers who have studied the effects of the galactic center in horoscopes have found that it exerts a powerful influence within a narrow orb of 2°, with some effect out to 4°. Individuals with inner planets or one of the angles conjunct the GC have, as noted in Philip Sedgwick' book *The Astrology of Deep Space*, a potential link "with whatever it is behind all this." When this transpersonal link is ignored, the individual can experience stress and confusion; when it is consciously appropriated, information can be grasped that the individual may seem to have no outward way of knowing. The GC is not significant in such natural events as earthquakes, but it does appear to be prominent in important events involving technology. It also seems to play a major role in human inventiveness, especially technological inventiveness.

Given the many points occupying contemporary astrological space—heliocentric planets, multiple midpoints, thousands of asteroids, and so forth—everyone surely has some such point in the latter degrees of Sagittarius. On this basis, some astrologers find it useful to examine the position of the galactic center in every chart, and, by its house placement, determine to which area of the native's life the cosmos is "speaking." The GC was located at 26°09' Sagittarius in 1950, at 26°34' in 1980, and at 26°51' in 2000.

**Sources:**

Brau, Jean-Louis, Helen Weaver, and Allan Edmands. *Larousse Encyclopedia of Astrology*. New York: New American Library, 1980.

Sedgwick, Philip. *The Astrology of Deep Space*. Birmingham, MI: Seek-It Publications, 1984.

## Galahad

Galahad, asteroid 2,082 (the 2,082nd asteroid to be discovered, on October 17, 1960), is approximately 14 kilometers in diameter and has an orbital period of 5 years. Galahad was named after the knight of the Round Table. J. Lee Lehman associates this asteroid with the challenge of merging action and contemplation, with reminders that movement through life is a spiritual process. Jacob Schwartz gives the astrological significance of Galahad as "a mystical union between human and deity, merging action with contemplation."

**Sources:**

Kowal, Charles T. *Asteroids: Their Nature and Utilization*. Chichester, West Sussex, UK: Ellis Horwood Limited, 1988.

Lehman, J. Lee. *The Ultimate Asteroid Book*. West Chester, PA: Whitford Press, 1988.

Schwartz, Jacob. *Asteroid Name Encyclopedia*. St. Paul, MN: Llewellyn Publications, 1995.

## Galaxy

Contrary to what one might anticipate, stars are not evenly distributed throughout the universe. Instead, they cluster together in galaxies (from the Greek *gala*, meaning "milk"), which are large groupings containing billions of stars. Our galaxy is called the Milky Way.

The astrological effects of the fixed stars were the only influences from outside the solar system considered in traditional astrology. More recently, astrological researchers have begun to explore the potential astrological significance of galactic as well as extragalactic phenomena—phenomena such as the galactic center, black holes, pulsars, and quasars. This area of study is still very much in its infancy, with little information immediately applicable to the interpretation of individual natal charts.

**Sources:**

Erlewine, Michael, and Margaret Erlewine. *Astrophysical Directions*. Ann Arbor, MI: Heart Center School of Astrology, 1977.

Sedgwick, Philip. *The Astrology of Deep Space*. Birmingham, MI: Seek-It Publications, 1984.

## Galilean Moons (Moons of Jupiter)

Jupiter, the largest planet in the solar system, has, as one might anticipate, a large number of satellites —16 at last count (Saturn holds the current record of 17). Four of these, called the Galilean moons because they were discovered by Galileo, are large bodies—Ganymede (3,270 miles in diameter), Callisto (2,980 miles), Io (2,260 miles), and Europa (1,950 miles)—all larger than Pluto (estimated diameter, 1,457 miles). These moons orbit between 262,000 miles and 1.17 million miles away from Jupiter. Their orbital periods range from less than 2 terrestrial days (Io) to more than 16 (Callisto). All the non-Galilean moons are less than 120 miles in diameter, clearly distinguishing them from Jupiter's Big Four.

The moons of Mars constitute the most useful starting point for the new field in astrology of planetary moon studies. The Jovian moons are also useful for this purpose, however, particularly in the ways they contrast with the Martian system. Next to Phobos and Deimos, the Galilean moons have attracted the attention of human beings more than the moons of any other celestial body (indicating that their astrological significance should be relatively easy to retrieve from the collective unconscious). To begin with, they were the first nonterrestrial moons to be discovered, and their discovery (in 1610) was an important factor in overturning the medieval European view of extraterrestrial space: In the seventeenth century they produced a sensation, comparable to the discovery of mountains on the surface of the Moon. In more recent years, as *Pioneer* and *Voyager* probes have sailed past Jupiter and taken dramatic photographs, the Big Four Jovian moons have become the focus of considerable astronomical and popular interest.

It would be difficult to dispute the idea that four celestial bodies larger than Pluto that are, even at their greatest distance away from Earth, always more than four times nearer than Pluto's closest approach to Earth, should have some sort of astrological influence. The operative question, however, is, Does the study of Jovian satellites add anything to our understanding of Jupiter, or are these influences indistinguishably blended with Jupiter's? An initial clue from astrological studies of Phobos and Deimos is that the Jovian moons may represent a polar opposite principle (or, perhaps, another, related principle) to some key Jupiterian principle. Another clue, taken from asteroid studies, is that the mythology associated with the name of a newly explored celestial body provides an initial guide to its astrological significance.

Zeus (the Greek equivalent of the Roman Jupiter), as anyone familiar with classical mythology knows, had an unpleasant propensity to rape everyone to whom he took a fancy, and all four of the figures after whom the Galilean moons are named were victims of the god's lust. Ganymede was a young man whom Zeus kidnapped to become his lover and cupbearer, while Io, Europa, and Callisto were all young women raped by the king of the gods. Zeus, however, seems to have been plagued by guilt for his misdeeds, because he tried in various ways to make it up to his victims. In the case of Ganymede, Zeus gave the youth's royal father a pair of fine mares and a golden grapevine, and Ganymede himself was immortalized as a constellation (Aquarius). Callisto was similarly transformed into a constellation (the Big Bear), Europa was given a set of unusual gifts, and Io became a queen and the ancestress of dynasties, as well as an ancestress of the hero Hercules.

Because many of the ancient gods (including the ones after whom the outer planets are named) were portrayed as rapists, focusing on the purely sexual aspect of these tales probably does illuminate the astrological/psychological principles represented by the Jovian moons. Zeus differed from many other Olympian rapists in that he showered his victims with gifts. This, of course, ties in with Jupiter's astrological characteristic as (among other things) the principle of generosity. With some reflection, it is not difficult to see that these myths provide some less-than-pleasant insights into gift-giving: Rather than being "freely given," as the saying goes, gifts are often given to compensate victims for abuse—or, to translate this basic principle into something closer to home, to compensate for the more subtle abuse of neglect (as when parents who feel guilty about not devoting enough time to their children shower them with gifts).

In another myth, Zeus promised to give Sinope (after whom Jupiter's outermost satellite was named) anything in exchange for her favors, so she tricked him into granting her the gift of perpetual virginity. This shows another shadow side of generosity—giving gifts in order to receive something—that represents the polar opposite principle of generosity: greed. This principle is usually associated with Saturn, but Saturnian greed is a thrifty greed that flows out of a sense of deficiency. Jovian greed, by way of contrast, flows out of a sense of abundance and expansion, an expansiveness directed solely toward continuing to grow and accumulate. (In medical astrology, Jupiter is often associated with cancer.)

An analysis of these myths provides another perspective on generosity: Most people give gifts out of guilt or because they want something in return. Thus, the placement of Jupiter by sign and, especially, by house tells where one experiences at least one form of guilt (other forms of guilt are associated with Saturn) or where one is prone to be generous in order to get something (greed). This analysis of the Jovian moons provides astrologers with new meanings for Jupiter, meanings that were not part of traditional astrological thinking about the planet. And, as astrologers continue to explore the astrological meanings implicit in the Jovian system, more insights are likely to emerge.

**Sources:**

Lewis, James R. *Martian Astrology*. Goleta, CA: Jupiter's Ink, 1992.

McEvers, Joan, ed. *Planets: The Astrological Tools*. Saint Paul, MN: Llewellyn Publications, 1989.

Room, Adrian. *Dictionary of Astronomical Names*. London: Routledge, 1988.

## Ganymed

Ganymed is asteroid 1,036 (the 1,036th asteroid to be discovered, on October 23, 1924). It is approximately 40 kilometers in diameter and has an orbital period of 4.3 years. It was named after the youth who was kidnapped to become the cupbearer of Zeus. Jacob Schwartz gives the astrological significance of this asteroid as "beautiful and attractive to both genders, the mortal becoming divine by surrendering to the divine." According to J. Lee Lehman, "the asteroid Ganymed shows how we are able to submit ourselves to that which is beyond our personal power. In negative form, it is the way we evade even the awareness that there *is* anything beyond our own powers."

**Sources:**

Kowal, Charles T. *Asteroids: Their Nature and Utilization*. Chichester, West Sussex, UK: Ellis Horwood Limited, 1988.

Lehman, J. Lee. *The Ultimate Asteroid Book*. West Chester, PA: Whitford Press, 1988.

Schwartz, Jacob. *Asteroid Name Encyclopedia*. St. Paul, MN: Llewellyn Publications, 1995.

## Gauquelin, Françoise

Françoise Schneider Gauquelin, psychologist and statistician, was born in Switzerland in 1929. She first studied psychology in Geneva, then in Paris, where she met Michel Gauquelin, also a psychology student, who introduced her to the scientific investigation of astrology.

Their 30-year collaboration in this field yielded important discoveries, now often summarized as "the Gauquelin Mars effect with Sports Champions." But actually their significant findings were not confined to Mars only but involve the four most visible planets: Venus, Jupiter, Saturn, and the Moon. These bodies are not correlated with athletes only, but with all kinds of famous professionals, such as actors, politicians, scientists, writers, painters, and musicians. After investigating the data of some 15,000 professionals, the Gauquelins also explored some 16,000 parent-children pairs, which showed that similar planetary constellations preside at the birth of parents and their children in a statistically significant pattern. These outcomes appear to stem from a correlation of the planets with inborn character traits of each individual.

Although such statements are based on a sound scientific methodology, they were received with much skepticism and scorn by the scientific establishment in general. In Europe and in the United States, scientific committees joined forces to prove them fallacious. But the Gauquelins' results successfully withstood even the most severe tests. According to the famous British astrologer John Addey, "The specific importance of the Gauquelins is not in their direct contribution to the knowledge of astrological principles as such, though this has been valuable in some instances, but in the fact that, confronted by a mountain of prejudice against astrology in an age which demands secure empirical evidence, they have by dint of immense courage, tenacity, and intelligence, provided this on a massive scale and in a form which has never been refuted, despite repeated attempts by hostile critics in the scientific world."

Michel and Françoise Gauquelin's collaboration lasted until 1980. At that point each of them continued their research work separately. Françoise has written numerous technical books and articles dealing with the Gauquelin methodology. She also wrote *Psychology of the Planets* (1982), which shows how strikingly similar are the traditional psychological traits associated with the planets and the modern outcomes of the Gauquelins' statistical studies. Her research journal *Astro-Psychological Problems*

(1982–88) convincingly shows that not only are famous professionals born under typical planetary constellations, but unknown individuals as well. *The Horoscope Revisited* explains how to use the Gauquelin findings in current practice.

**Sources:**

Gauquelin, Françoise. *Series A: Professional Notabilities*. 6 vols. Paris: Laboratoire d'Etude des Relations entre Rythmes Cosmiques et Psychophysiologiques, 1970–71.

———. *Series B: Heredity Experiments*. 6 vols. Paris: Laboratoire d'Etude des Relations entre Rythmes Cosmiques et Psychophysiologiques, 1970–71.

———. *Series C: Psychological Monographs*. 5 vols. Paris: Laboratoire d'Etude des Relations entre Rythmes Cosmiques et Psychophysiologiques, 1972–77.

———. *Series D: Scientific Documents*. 10 vols. Paris: Laboratoire d'Etude des Relations entre Rythmes Cosmiques et Psychophysiologiques, 1976–82.

## Gauquelin, Michel

Michel Gauquelin, a French researcher prominent for his statistical investigation of astrology, was born on November 13, 1928, in Paris. He received his doctorate in psychology and statistics from the Sorbonne. He and his wife, Françoise Gauquelin, provided the most rigorous scientific evidence for the validity of astrology, although their work departs from traditional astrology on certain points.

Investigating earlier statistical studies of astrology, the Gauquelins found them lacking proper controls and other elements of sound research. Beginning in 1949, they collected birth data on thousands of people from records across Europe and analyzed natal planetary positions with respect to such factors as profession and personality. Their most celebrated discovery was that for specific professions—particularly for writers, sports champions, and scientists—the positions of certain planets were found in statistically significant patterns. The planet Mars, for instance, was often found to be near the horizon or near the meridian of the birth charts of sports champions (the so-called Mars effect). The horoscopes of eminent scientists exhibited a similar pattern with respect to the planet Saturn; the writers' with respect to the Moon.

The Gauquelins' studies have withstood repeated attacks, and replications of their research by others have verified the original findings. Through their laboratory they published a complete record of their research, which filled 23 volumes. They also published numerous short works, including *The Cosmic Clocks* (1967), *The Scientific Basis of Astrology* (1969), *Cosmic Influences on Human Behavior* (1973), and *Birthtimes: A Scientific Investigation of the Secrets of Society* (1983). To avoid professional prejudice against them, the Gauquelins tended to discuss their findings in terms of "cosmic genetics," "planetary heredity," or "cosmobiology."

Because the Gauquelins' work differs in many respects from traditional astrology, astrologers tend to refer to it as neoastrology. The significance of their work is such that no research validating astrology is more frequently cited. Michel Gauquelin died in Paris on May 20, 1991.

**Sources:**

Brau, Jean-Louis, Helen Weaver, and Allan Edmands. *Larousse Encyclopedia of Astrology*. New York: Plume, 1980.

"In Memoriam: Michel Gauquelin—November 13, 1928–May 20, 1991." *Astroflash* (Summer 1991): 9–10.

## Gemini

Gemini, the third sign of the zodiac, is a mutable air sign. It is a positive, masculine sign ruled by the planet Mercury. Its symbol is the twins, its glyph is said to represent twins, and it takes its name from the Latin word for twins. Gemini is associated with the shoulders, arms, hands, and lungs. Individuals with a Gemini sun sign are prone to lung problems and to accidents involving the arms. The key phrase for Gemini is "I think."

While Gemini has been associated with different pairs of people, the primary association is with Castor and Pollux (the Roman version of the Greek Castor and Polydeuces). Castor and Pollux were the sons of Leda, who coupled with the god Zeus and then, in some accounts, lay with her husband, King Tyndareus. The resulting offspring were Pollux, the son of Zeus, and Castor, the son of Tyndareus. They were warriors and members of the Argonauts' crew (the band of mythological adventurers who sailed with Jason in quest of the Golden Fleece) and came to be regarded as patron deities of sailors and navigators. During a cattle-stealing adventure, Castor was slain. Pollux, the immortal brother, asked Zeus that either he might die also or his dead brother might share his immortality. In deference to his son's wish, Zeus allowed the brothers to alternate so that one spent a day in the underworld while the other was among the gods; on successive days they traded places.

The primary Gemini trait reflected in this tale is the sign's well-known dual nature. People who do not understand Geminis frequently regard them as "two-faced," but people born under this sign are, more often than not, sincerely schizophrenic—they sincerely identify with both their personalities. Positively, this dual nature manifests as an ability to see both sides of every disagreement; a typical Gemini remark is, "There are two sides to everything." Like Castor and Pollux, Geminis are highly social beings with greatly developed communication skills. Also like the twins of mythology, they are associated with travel and trade (and sometimes "cattle rustling") and enjoy travel. Like all air signs, they are at home in the mental realm; many academics and teachers are Geminis.

The sign that the Sun was in at birth is usually the single most important influence on a native's personality. Thus, when people say they are a certain sign, they are almost always referring to their sun sign. There is a wealth of information available on the characteristics of the zodiacal signs—so much that one book would not be able to contain it all. Sun-sign astrology, which is the kind of astrology found in newspaper columns and popular magazines, has the advantage of simplicity. But this simplicity is purchased at the price of ignoring other astrological influences, such as one's Moon sign, rising sign, etc. These other influences can substantially modify a person's basic sun sign traits. As a consequence, it is the rare individual who is completely typical of her or his sign. The reader should bear this caveat in mind when perusing the following series of sun-sign interpretations.

**An image of the constellation Gemini from the late fifteenth century. *Reproduced by permission of Fortean Picture Library.***

One traditional way in which astrologers condense information is by summarizing sign and planet traits in lists of words and short phrases called keywords or key phrases. The following Gemini keywords are drawn from Manly P. Hall's *Astrological Keywords:*

> *Emotional keywords:* "Lack concentration, sensitive, eloquent, humane, travel, not domestic, changeable, unsympathetic but genial, quick-tempered."
>
> *Mental keywords:* "Dextrous in manual expression, inventive, literary, versatile, adaptable, self-expressive, democratic, curious, analytical if highly evolved, sometimes scatterbrained, tricky."

At present, there are various astrology report programs that contain interpretations of each of the 12 sun signs. A selection of these for Sun in Gemini has been excerpted below:

> You have a quick, bright and agile mind, but an extremely short attention span. You love the external, kaleidoscopic aspects of life, but you

tend to avoid (and even fear) deep, close emotional involvements. As such, you seem to enjoy travel and sightseeing and generally being "on-the-go." You get quite listless when things around you become static and dull, but your excitement returns whenever you are stimulated by a new idea. Chatty, inquisitive and quite playful, you enjoy practical jokes and games in general. Your moods change quickly and often—you are very restless and constantly in motion. You are known for your versatility and adaptability. Your vivaciousness enlivens any social gathering. (From "Professional Natal Report." Courtesy of Astrolabe [http://www.alabe.com].)

You are, in many ways, an eternal child. Your mind is bright, alert, curious, flexible, playful, and always eager for new experiences—and your attention span is often quite brief. You grasp ideas quickly and once your initial curiosity has been satisfied, you want to go on to something else. You crave frequent change, variety, meeting new situations and people.

It may be hard for you to decide just where your talents and true vocation lie, for you have a multitude of interests and are loathe to limit yourself by concentrating on just one. You are easily distracted by all of the other fascinating possibilities. Your curiosity and restlessness propel you into many different experiences in life, and you are willing to taste or try anything once. Doing the same thing over and over again, even if it is something you do well, is real drudgery for you.

You live in your head a great deal—reading, observing, thinking, spinning ideas around—and you need mental stimulation every bit as much as you need food and drink. In fact, if you had to choose between a good book or movie and a good lunch, you would very likely choose the former. You have a creative mind and often live by your wits.

You are also a very social creature, with a strong need to communicate and to interact with people. You enjoy using and playing with words and have a real flair for getting your ideas across in a clever, interesting, articulate manner. Writing or speaking are areas you have talent for.

You also have a rather light and mischievous sense of humor, and often do not take anything too seriously. Though you crave emotional involvement, it is hard for you to achieve it, for you are frequently unwilling to commit yourself to anything, to take responsibility, or to limit your personal freedom and mobility.

Your happiness lies in using your creativity and your language skills to communicate something meaningful, to teach, inspire, or bring people together. You have an unbiased mind and can usually offer a fresh, clear, uncluttered perspective. Your faults are your lack of constancy and persistence, and your tendency to overlook or ignore deep emotional issues and other people's feelings. (From "Merlin," by Gina Ronco and Agnes Nightingale. Courtesy of Cosmic Patterns [http://cosmic.patterns.com].)

> Wonder, amazement, astonishment, a sense of the miraculous—those states of consciousness are the best of what Gemini symbolizes. Although this is an Air sign and therefore rather mental in its orientation, the Twins represent something more primal than thinking. They represent perception itself: all the raw, undigested stuff that pours in through our senses. Thinking too much about that material removes us from its immediate, moment-to-moment reality. We start to inhabit theories instead of the actual world of perception. "Authority" creeps in. So does "rightness." And "mental clarity." And the Twins wither. Nourish your Geminian energies with an endless diet of newness and change. They're hungry for anything they've not seen or felt before. Feed them! Give them conversation, books, travel, education ... anything but boredom.
>
> With your Sun in Gemini, you're blessed with high levels of physical and mental energy. Use them! There's a quickness about you, an aliveness to the moment. People probably imagine you to be younger than you really are. Your deepest nature is driven by one force above all others: curiosity. You're happiest when faced with surprises. You thrive on the unexpected. And you wither in the face of rigid predictability.
>
> Spiritually, you're learning to keep your mind wide open, to view life as a crash course in amazement. Feed your vitality with new relationships—or old relationships with people who themselves are always new. Stimulate yourself with books and travel. When in doubt, look through a telescope! Take a course in Etruscan history! Do anything you've never done before. (From "The Sky Within," by Steven Forrest. Courtesy of Matrix Software [http://thenewage.com] and Steven Forrest [http://www.stevenforrest.com].)

Among its several natal programs, Matrix Astrological Software created a unique report based on the published works of the early-twentieth-century astrologer Grant Lewi (1901–1952). Lewi's highly original delineations were recognized as creative and insightful by his contemporaries. One measure of the appeal of his work is that his books *Astrology for the Millions* and *Heaven Knows What* are still in print. The following is excerpted from the report program "Heaven Knows What":

> "I celebrate myself and sing myself." (*Walt Whitman, born in Gemini, May 31, 1819.*)
>
> "Whoso would be a man must be a non-conformist." (*Ralph Waldo Emerson, born in Gemini, May 25, 1803.*)
>
> "Democracy wishes to elevate mankind, to teach it to think, to set it free." (*Thomas Mann, born in Gemini, June 6, 1875.*)
>
> Into strange paths leads the Gemini's desire to be himself, to think for himself, to do for himself, and, ultimately and in its highest form, to become his best self. It takes him a long time to learn that he can't possibly be anything except himself. The self he wants to be is at first not

well defined, except that it has to be different from what his father, or his mother, or his brother, is. If the urge remains ... Gemini stays a bad child all his life, breaking rules, rebelling against authority, dashing hither and yon over the geographical, social and emotional world in order to make sure that he doesn't yield his individuality to one place or one wife (or husband). Education or other discipline must come to Gemini through his own volition, and when it does is his salvation; for then the passion to be different turns into creative originality in business or the arts, and Gemini forges ahead. He will generally be found in the camp of liberalism, because it is against the status quo if for no other reason.

Sometimes Gemini rebels against the status quo of his own life.... But if his life gives him sufficient scope to be himself, Gemini stays settled. The more his concept of what it means to be himself diverges from the early, rebellious, sensational, adventurous urges toward intellectual excellence and a sense of social responsibility, the higher Gemini gets in the world, for his sense of what constitutes his best self is not limited. It often starts with free love, breaking school rules and talking back to cops. But here, with any luck at all, the Gemini versatility breaks in; also the Gemini practical good sense. He discovers that his self might just as well be something more stable, sets his self development along another line, and gratifies his desire to be himself in progress rather than in destruction. Everything depends on his subjective reaction to himself; and it therefore becomes his moral obligation to develop to the point where he is inwardly satisfied by what is constructive. He will never do anything because someone, or a convention, tells him to; but he may, and often does, grow up to the point where his behavior satisfies himself best when it is going somewhere in a straight line, instead of nowhere in a circle. (Courtesy of Matrix Software [http://thenew age.com].)

Curious, versatile, clever, and able to jump quickly from one area to another are well known traits of Gemini. I have not found anything to add or subtract to the widely held ideas of Gemini. (Courtesy of Cosmic Patterns [http://cosmic.patterns.com] and David Cochrane [kepler@astrosoftware.com].)

A number of specialized report programs has been developed that offer useful supplements to the generic delineations of general reports. The following sun-sign interpretation has been drawn from a program written by Gloria Star (originally part of her book, *Astrology: Woman to Woman*) that generates a specialized report for women:

With your Sun in Gemini your inquisitive manner and quick wit may be your trademarks. You need variety, and whether in relationships, career opportunities or creative endeavors will prefer to create a life which gives you plenty of options. You may radiate an air of intelligence, and most enjoy people and situations which stimulate your

> mind. The old truth, "you are what you think," is especially clear to you, and you have the ability to shift your consciousness and create a whole new realm of life experience by first altering your mental focus.
>
> Your expression of your masculine sensibilities through your Gemini Sun is filtered through your intellect. Your admiration for others who are knowledgeable and communicative is a direct result of your own desire to know as much as possible. If your early impulse was to think that a man had more knowledgeable authority than a woman, that has probably changed radically as you have matured. In fact, you may even challenge that assumption through your choices in career. However, you may not think in terms of man versus woman: you're more into dealing with people for who they are, and may assume that others will also take that stance. You may even have a knack for communicating quite effectively with both men and women, and may make strides in bridging the gender gap. You can waffle a bit in situations which require you to take control, and may sit on the fence a bit too long some of the time, it just takes a little objectivity to get this under control, especially in new circumstances. But once you know how things work, you can be the maven of juggling your priorities.
>
> To experience a real feeling of success, you may feel that you have to learn something from the experience. You are multitalented with your Sun in Gemini, and may even change your career direction in order to experience a new range of possibilities. Sometimes, it may seem that you're living at least two lifetimes at once. Or you may find that you're living a dual life, juggling a mixed list of priorities in your many roles. Although this may keep things interesting, you've probably found that you are happier when the juggling act involves keeping fewer things in the air at once. (From "Woman to Woman," by Gloria Star. Courtesy of Matrix Software [http://thenewage.com] and Gloria Star [glostar@aol.com].)

Responding to the revival of interest in pre-twentieth-century astrology, J. Lee Lehman developed a report program embodying the interpretive approach of traditional astrology. The following is excerpted from her book *Classical Astrology for Modern Living* and her computer program "Classical Report":

> You are a lover of arts and sciences, curiosities, and learning. You are judicious in worldly affairs, witty, affable, courteous, with excellent understanding, but telling the truth is not your strongest suit, because embellishing can be such fun. Because you have a strong imagination, you can be quite creative. You are skilled at the sciences, or areas of knowledge.
>
> You are an Air Sign, which means that you are "hot" and "wet." The "wet" component means, among other things, that you blur distinctions, and that you are more swayed by passion than by intellectual argument. At your worst, you see too many connections, becoming lost in conspiracies. At your best, you spot the connection that everyone

else missed. Being "hot," you react to things quickly: by expressing your anger strongly and immediately, you don't tend to harbor a grudge. This is the temperament type that is considered the most ideal, because you are the most comfortable within a social situation. You appear warm and friendly to others, and don't seem too eager to hold them to an impossible standard.

You are mutable, which means that you adapt easily to change. However, you adapt so easily compared to others that they may wonder if you are capable of maintaining a permanent stance about anything. (Courtesy of J. Lee Lehman, Ph.D. (copyright 1998) [http://www.leelehman.com].)

Readers interested in examining interpretations for their Chinese astrological sign should refer to the relevant entry. A guide for determining one's sign in the Chinese system is provided in the entry on the Chinese zodiac.

**Sources:**

Cochrane, David. *Astrology for the 21st Century*. Gainesville, FL: Cosmic Patterns, 2002.

Forrest, Steven. *The Inner Sky: How to Make Wiser Choices for a More Fulfilling Life*. 4th ed. San Diego, CA: ACS Publications, 1989.

Green, Landis Knight. *The Astrologer's Manual: Modern Insights into an Ancient Art*. Sebastopol, CA: CRCS Publications, 1975.

Lehman, J. Lee. *Classical Astrology for Modern Living: From Ptolemy to Psychology & Back Again*. Atglen, PA: Whitford Press, 1996.

Lewi, Grant. *Astrology for the Millions*. 5th rev. ed. St. Paul, MN: Llewellyn, 1978.

———. *Heaven Knows What*. St. Paul, MN: Llewellyn, 1969.

Star, Gloria. *Astrology: Woman to Woman*. St. Paul, MN: Llewellyn, 1999.

———. *Astrology & Your Child: A Handbook for Parents*. St. Paul, MN: Llewellyn, 2001.

Hall, Manly P. *Astrological Keywords*. New York: Philosophical Library, 1958. Reprint, Savage, MD: Littlefield Adams Quality Paperbacks, 1975.

## Gemstones and Astrology

Quite a bit has been written on the correlation between gemstones and astrology. Unfortunately, much of that has not been in agreement. Some of the disagreement stems from the fact that Vedic astrologers have a very different philosophy from Western astrologers. Additionally, confusion in the Western system seems to stem from the gem industry's attempt to "translate" these correlations into "birthstones" for each month, even though the signs "straddle" two months rather than starting and ending neatly with the beginning and end of each month. This confusion is compounded because European birthstone selections, especially those from German-speaking countries, do not always coincide with the North American birthstones. Some of this may very well be attributed to the difference in availability of stones in Europe and in North America.

The rationale for correlating gemstones with astrological placements is that since everything is energy and everything is interrelated, correspondence between gems, signs, and planets can be made by looking at properties (e.g., hardness, color, mineral families, crystal systems, chemical elements, and inclusions) and other things, including mythology. In the Vedic system, each planet has only one primary gem, although some authors consider secondary gems. In all cases in the Vedic system, gems should be as close to flawless as possible and color is an extremely important factor. The primary stone correlations in Vedic astrology come from antiquity, and authorities are in general agreement about both the primary and secondary stones. In the Western system, confusion again arises, in part from subjectivity (e.g., what is "red" to one person may be "blackish red" or "purple-red" to another); in part because while sign and gem correlations are similar, they do not necessarily tally 100%; and because Western astrologers feel that even inclusions and flaws have meaning, and, therefore no two gemstones are precisely alike. Western astrologers therefore subscribe to the philosophy that just as one does not find a person who is, for instance, purely Cancer energy, one likewise does not find too many gemstones that partake "purely" of one planet. For example, while one may be content to call a certain stone an agate, agates can be a variety of colors and may be banded, layered, or a single color. Moreover, agates are a form of chalcedony, which is part of the quartz family. Furthermore, agate nodules, such as geodes, may contain opal, quartz crystal, or calcite, among other things.

Vedic astrologers do not work with signs per se. Their approach is more purist than that of Western astrology. The Western astrologer will make use of sign correlations in order to "blend" planet-sign combinations and will differentiate between, for instance, Venus in Sagittarius and Venus in Pisces, in addition to taking house positions and aspects into account. Both Vedic and Western astrologers who are trained in working with gems can, through the premise that everything is energy, suggest certain stones to enhance, balance, or redirect certain energies symbolized by natal planets or transits. However, contrary to some systems of magic, astrologers do not believe that one can use a gem to create a potential that is not inherently present in the natal chart. Nor can a gemstone be used for protection from the consequences of one's actions. They can, however, be used to increase awareness of potential consequences, thus possibly acting as a discouragement from taking inappropriate action.

Where Western astrologers will work with any planet of the client's choosing according to the client's natal chart, progressions, and transits, the Vendic astrologer works according to certain strict criteria to come up with one specific stone, which may change from time to time according to changes in *dasas* (planetary periods) and transits. For example, the Vedic astrologer will first look at the ascendant. If the ruler is in an auspicious sign, then the gem of choice would most likely be that of the ruler of the ascendant. Next, the Moon's sign and the ruler of that sign are considered, along with the ruler of the *naksatra* (lunar mansion). Planets in rulership and exaltation are also considered, as their gemstones may also be used to theiradvantage according to the Vedic system.

Where Vedic astrologers caution that wearing an inauspicious stone can cause misfortune, Western astrologers are more inclined to say, "If you like it, wear it, as it's saying something about you at the moment." This is not to say they disregard the inherent symbolism, but rather that they place great stock on free will and on the awareness level of the client. So where Western astrologers will select the class of gem appropriate to the clients' concerns, they will encourage clients to select the gem themselves, the theory being that the clients will choose a stone that has color correlations or inclusions or even flaws that have personal meaning. This runs counter to Vedic astrology in which the astrologer "prescribes" the gem, the color, and even the specific weight and will either select and set the gem for the client themselves or send the client to a specialist who will "fill the prescription" for the client. Client preference is generally of only minimal importance in the Vedic system. There are also specific contraindications in terms of combining certain stone combinations in the Vedic system, though there is such a thing as a nine-gem setting called a Nava-Ratna, which is an exception to the contraindication rule. Western astrologers are less stringent about cautioning against various gem combinations, though some will advise against certain of these.

Following is a list of commonly accepted correspondences between gems and planets. Note that even when Vedic and Western correlations are in agreement, there is a high likelihood that the gem of choice will be different for the same chart when viewed in both the Vedic and Western systems. This is because Vedic astrologers use the sidereal zodiac while Western astrologers use the tropical zodiac. Note that for each planet, "secondary" correlations are in parentheses:

*Sun:* Western: Ruby (golden yellow chrysoberyl, champagne [yellow] diamond, amber, gold); Vedic: Ruby (red spinel, garnet, rubellite). All of these should be set in gold.

*Moon:* Western: Pearl (moonstone, emerald, calcite, chalcedony); Vedic: Pearl (moonstone).

*Mercury:* Western: Agate (yellow sapphire, yellow topaz, lodestone, cinnabar); Vedic: Emerald (green jade, peridot, green tourmaline, diopside)

*Venus:* Western: Blue or pink sapphire (padparadschah sapphire, hyacinth zircon, chrysoprase, copper); Vedic: Diamond (zircon, quartz, topaz, white sapphire). Venus stones should be free of opaque patches.

*Mars:* Western: Diamond (red garnet, star ruby, hematite, red coral); *Vedic:* Red coral (carnelian, bloodstone).

*Jupiter:* Western: Blue topaz (lapis lazuli, star sapphire, blue spinel, iris agate); Vedic: Yellow sapphire (yellow topaz, citrine, heliodor).

*Saturn:* Western: Turquoise (aquamarine, black spinel, obsidian, black coral); Vedic: Blue sapphire (blue spinel, amethyst, indicolite).

*Uranus:* Western: Amethyst (aventurine quartz, quartz crystal, barite, green garnet); Vedic: Not used.

*Neptune:* Western: Bloodstone (rainbow moonstone, shells in general, fluorite, amethyst quartz [striped with milky quartz]); Vedic: Not used.

*Pluto:* Western: Opal (alexandrite, flint, kunzite, rhodochrosite); Vedic: Not used.

*Rahu (Moon's North Node):* Western: Depends on sign and sign's ruler. Vedic: Hessonite garnet (orange zircon, spessartine garnet).

Ketu (Moon's South Node): Western: Depends on sign and sign's ruler; Vedic: Cat's eye chrysoberyl (cat's eye apatite, tourmaline, beryl).

—Donna Van Toen

**Sources:**

Bauer, Jarsolav, and Vladimir Bouska. *A Guide in Color to Precious and Semi-Precious Stones*. Secausus, NJ: Chartwell Books, 1989.

Matteson, Barbara J. *Mystic Minerals*. Seattle: Cosmic Resources, 1985.

Raphaell, Katrina. *Crystal Enlightenment*. Vol. 1. New York: Aurora Press, 1986.

Schumann, Walter. *Gemstones of the World*. New York: Sterling, 1984.

Uyldert, Mellie. *The Magic of Precious Stones*. Northamptonshire, UK: Turnstone Press, 1984.

## Genethliacal Astrology

Genethliacal (from the Greek *genos*, meaning "birth") astrology is the traditional term for natal astrology, the branch of the science of the stars that interprets the significance of individual birth charts. Genethliacal astrology is distinguished from such other branches of astrology as mundane astrology, which interprets the significance of celestial events for nations, cultural trends, and world affairs.

## Genetics and Astrology

Adherents as well as critics of astrology sometimes ask the question, How do astrological influences interact with the "forces" of genetic heritage to determine human nature? In the hands of critics, this issue becomes the assertion that genetics can explain any inborn traits. A subsequent assertion is then that contrary astrological influences cannot possibly overcome genetic factors, and hence astrology is false. However, this way of stating the problem does not do justice to the manner in which astrologers would actually approach the issue.

Instead of conceiving celestial influences as external forces that affect Earth like some kind of extraterrestrial radiation, most astrologers view the universe as an interconnected whole, and astrological "forces" as working in synchronicity. Synchronism refers to the occurrences of events at one place simultaneously with those in another part of the universe, even though there is no causal link between them. Consider an analogy: Imagine the relationship between two clocks, both registering the same time. Their indicating the same time does not mean that one clock forces the other clock to read the same. Rather, they are both set to run parallel courses.

In a similar manner, astrological influences do not work by competing with and overcoming terrestrial forces, such as genetic inheritance. Instead, the universe runs in such a manner that events on the terrestrial sphere mirror events in the celestial sphere (the patterns of the planets). Thus, occasions do not arise in which genetics and astrology conflict with each other.

## Geniture

Geniture is an older term for a personal horoscope.

## Geocentric Astrology

Geocentric means Earth-centered, and geocentric astrology refers to any astrological system that uses Earth as the point of reference from which to record the positions of celestial bodies. All traditional systems were geocentric, but some astrologers have experimented with heliocentric (Sun-centered) systems, creating heliocentric astrology.

## Geographical Astrology

Geographical astrology is a subdivision of mundane astrology, which deals with the astrological associations between the zodiac and geographical locations.

## George, Demetra

Demetra George has been a practitioner of astrology for over 30 years. She is the coauthor of *Astrology for Yourself* and the author of *Asteroid Goddesses*, *Mysteries of the Dark Moon*, and *Finding Our Way through the Dark*. Her earlier pioneering work synthesized ancient history and archetypal mythology with contemporary astrology, and currently she translates ancient Greek astrological manuscripts. Listed in *World Who's Who of Women*, Demetra lectures internationally and leads pilgrimages to the sacred sites in the Mediterranean. She is on the faculty of Kepler College and the Astrological Institute, where she teaches the history of ancient and medieval astrology and the methods and philosophy of Hellenistic astrology. George received her B.A. in philosophy and her M.A. in the classics.

## George, Llewellyn

Llewellyn George, born August 17, 1876, in Swansea, Wales, was a prominent astrologer, author, and founder of Llewellyn Publications. His father died when he was young, and his mother remarried and moved to the United States. George's younger half-brother, Griff Abrams, was his partner in the astrological publishing field for many years.

George began studying astrology in Portland, Oregon, under L. H. Weston. Later George moved to Los Angeles, where his publishing business was highly successful. He began publishing the *Astrological Bulletin* in 1905 and *The Moon Sign Book* in 1906.

Throughout a busy lifetime, George supported astrologers, astrology, and astrological organizations. He seldom accepted office in these organizations, but did serve on committees. The American Federation of Astrologers (AFA) honored him by awarding him honorary life membership in 1939, and the *Astrological Bulletin* of August 22, 1941, called him the "dean of American astrologers." In 1948, he contributed to the AFA building fund, and when the AFA library was being expanded, he contributed money for a bookcase dedicated to his brother, Griff Abrams, and filled it with copies of all available Llewellyn Publications.

During a period of legal problems in California in the mid-1940s, he cofounded and served as president of Educational Astrology, Inc., in Los Angeles. This organization was established to fight antiastrology legislation and ordinances. Toward the end of the decade, he established the Llewellyn Foundation for Astrological Research, with Donald A. Bradley as research director. George died on July 11, 1954, in Los Angeles.

**Sources:**

George, Llewellyn. *The New A to Z Horoscope Maker and Delineator.* 13th ed. Edited by Marylee Bytheriver. St. Paul, MN: Llewellyn Publications, 1986.

———. *Astrologer's Searchlight*. 2d ed. rev. Los Angeles: Llewellyn Publications, 1933.

———. *(The New Improved) Planetary Hour Book*. Portland, OR: Portland School of Astrology, 1907.

———. *Practical Astrology for Everybody*. Portland, OR: Bulletina Publishing, 1911.

Holden, James H., and Robert A. Hughes. *Astrological Pioneers of America*. Tempe, AZ: American Federation of Astrologers, 1988.

## Georgium Sidus

*Georgium Sidus* (Latin for "George's Star") was the name given to the newly discovered Uranus by Sir William Herschel in honor of his patron, George III. Needless to say, astronomers in other countries of the world were not pleased with Herschel's choice of name, so *Georgium Sidus* never became widely used.

## Gilgamesh

Gilgamesh, asteroid 1,812 (the 1,812th asteroid to be discovered, on September 24, 1960), is approximately 14 kilometers in diameter and has an orbital period of 5.2 years. It was named after the Sumerian hero of the *Gilgamesh* epic. Gilgamesh was a king of Uruk who, after his best friend died, embarked on an unsuccessful quest for immortality. The asteroid represents an interest in death and physical immortality. The sign and house position of Gilgamesh in a natal chart indicates how this interest manifested. If prominent in a chart (e.g., conjunct the Sun or the ascendant), it may show a person for whom this interest is a major life theme.

**Sources:**

Kowal, Charles T. *Asteroids: Their Nature and Utilization*. Chichester, West Sussex, UK: Ellis Horwood Limited, 1988.

Room, Adrian. *Dictionary of Astronomical Names*. London: Routledge, 1988.

Schwartz, Jacob. *Asteroid Name Encyclopedia*. St. Paul, MN: Llewellyn Publications, 1995.

## Glyphs

Astrological glyphs are symbols that represent celestial bodies, signs, or other components of a horoscope. Glyphs constitute a kind of shorthand that allows astrologers to concentrate a large amount of information in a small space. To many new students of astrology, these symbols seem to constitute an unnecessary and difficult hurdle: Why not just write the names of the planets into the chart? But, once memorized, they are easy to use and are far preferable to drawing in other kinds of abbreviations. The increasing use of asteroids by astrologers has led to the proliferation of new, not particularly memorable, glyphs, as well as questions about who should have the final say on adopting new symbols. One proposal is that an interorganizational glyph committee, parallel to the International Astronomical Union nomenclature committee, be created to standardize new glyphs.

**A Babylonian relief of God pursuing the demon Gilgamesh.** ***Reproduced by permission of Fortean Picture Library.***

**Sources:**

Brau, Jean-Louis, Helen Weaver, and Allan Edmands. *Larousse Encyclopedia of Astrology*. New York: New American Library, 1980.

Foreman, Patricia. *Computers and Astrology: A Universal User's Guide and Reference*. Burlington, VT: Good Earth Publications, 1992.

## Goat

The Goat is one of the 12 animals of the Chinese zodiac. It refers to one of the 12 earthly branches that are used in Chinese astrology, together with the 10 heavenly stems. Such a branch designates one day every 12 days: the days are named according to a sexagesimal (60) cycle, made of 10 series of 12 branches.

Kind and gentle, the Goat is emotional and even shy. He tries to be liked by everyone. Touchy, passive and lazy, not really ambitious, very imaginative, and artistic, he hates to be disturbed in his dreams. Eccentric, he likes neither routine nor discipline, and never arrives on time. He loves to stay at home. Generous and attracted by mysticism, he hates violence.

The Goat is also a popular name for the sign Capricorn. The original Mesopotamian creature associated with this sign was half goat and half fish.

—Michele Delemme

## Grand Cross (Cosmic Cross)

The configuration of a cross formed in a horoscope by four or more planets is referred to as a grand cross. Each planet successively makes a square (an aspect of 90°) to the preceding planet, and the planets directly across the chart from each other are involved in oppositions (180° aspects). Because astrological signs at 90° angles to each other belong to the same quality (cardinal, mutable, or fixed), grand crosses tend to involve planets in all four signs of one quality. Thus, grand crosses can be classified as cardinal crosses, mutable crosses, or fixed crosses (grand crosses that involve planets in signs of different qualities are referred to as mixed crosses).

Because all the aspects contained in a grand cross are hard aspects, an individual with such a configuration in her or his natal chart is presented with more challenges than the average person, and these natives sometimes feel "crucified" by life. On the other hand, once the challenges proffered by a grand cross have been adequately met, the individual becomes an unusually well integrated person, with the power to accomplish great tasks.

## Grand Trine

A trine aspect is a 120° angle between two planets in an astrological chart. When a third planet on the other side of the chart makes trine aspects to the two planets forming the first trine, the resulting configuration is called a grand trine. Because astrological signs at 120° angles to each other belong to the same element (earth, air, fire, or water), grand trines tend to involve planets in all three signs of one element. Thus, grand trines can be classified as grand earth trines, grand air trines, grand fire trines, or grand water trines (grand trines that involve planets in signs of different elements are referred to as mixed grand trines).

Because trines are soft aspects, a person with a grand trine in her or his natal chart tends to be unusually lucky, particularly in matters related to the houses and signs affected by this configuration. However, unless there are also some hard aspects in the chart, such individuals are often not presented with enough challenges to develop strong wills. Thus, this seemingly beneficial configuration can actually handicap the native. A more ideal configuration is a kite, which is a grand trine plus a fourth planet that makes an opposition to one of the other three planets.

## Grant, Ernest A.

Ernest A. Grant, one of the founders of the American Federation of Astrologers, was born on June 4, 1893, in Detroit, Michigan. Around 1906, he moved to the nation's capital. He initially worked as a stenographer and court reporter for the Norfolk Navy

Yard and was later employed by different members of the U.S. Congress and by lobby groups. He worked, for example, for Senator Wallace Humphrey White of Maine, for the Methodist Board of Temperance Promotion and Public Morals, for Senator Theodore Burton of Ohio, for the Securities and Exchange Committee, and so forth.

Grant's future wife, Catherine, taught him astrology, and soon after their marriage he became an astrologer, lecturer, and teacher. In 1938, he was one of the three incorporators of the American Federation of Astrologers (AFA), one of the oldest astrology organizations in America. He was the AFA's first president (1938–1941) as well as its first executive secretary (1941–1959). Federation work was centered in his home from 1938 to 1951, when the federation moved to a small building in Library Court, adjacent to the Library of Congress. This building served as its headquarters until the early 1970s, when the AFA moved to Arizona.

Grant and his wife also founded the National Astrological Library, a book publishing organization that was later acquired by the AFA. Despite his heavy organizational involvement, he found time to teach and write about astrology. Grant was an ardent student of political astrology. He researched the astrological history of the United States and, with Ralph Kraum, wrote *Astrological Americana*. Grant died on March 6, 1968, in Washington, D.C.

**Sources:**

Grant, Ernest A. *Tables of Diurnal Planetary Motion*. Washington, DC: National Astrology Library, 1948.

Grant, Ernest A., and Ralph Kraum. *Astrological Americana*. 1949. Reprint, Tempe, AZ: American Federation of Astrologers, n.d.

Holden, James H., and Robert A. Hughes. *Astrological Pioneers of America*. Tempe, AZ: American Federation of Astrologers, 1988.

## Gratia

Gratia, asteroid 424 (the 424th asteroid to be discovered, on December 31, 1896), is approximately 44 kilometers in diameter and has an orbital period of 4.6 years. It was named after the three Graces of Greek mythology. Like its mythological namesake, the asteroid confers "grace" upon natives in whose natal chart it is prominent. The house and sign position of Gratia indicate where and how one expresses gracefulness.

**Sources:**

Kowal, Charles T. *Asteroids: Their Nature and Utilization*. Chichester, West Sussex, UK: Ellis Horwood Limited, 1988.

Room, Adrian. *Dictionary of Astronomical Names*. London: Routledge, 1988.

Schwartz, Jacob. *Asteroid Name Encyclopedia*. St. Paul, MN: Llewellyn Publications, 1995.

## Great Circle

A great circle is any circle drawn on a sphere, the plane of which also passes through the inside of the sphere. Great circles are the basis of various systems for locating terrestrial and celestial bodies in terms of sets of coordinates expressed in degrees of a circle.

Longitude and latitude are the most familiar of these coordinates. Astrology utilizes several systems of celestial coordinates. Parallel to the manner in which terrestrial coordinates are great circles drawn on the surface of Earth, celestial coordinates are great circles drawn on the inside of the celestial sphere. The ecliptic, the celestial equator, and the prime vertical are examples of some of the great circles used in astrology.

## Greenwich Time

Because of the variation in time caused by various time changes as one moves east or west across Earth, astrologers have found it convenient to construct tables such as ephemerides (tables of planetary positions) with the time at Greenwich, England, as a benchmark. Greenwich lies exactly on the 0° longitude line, which makes it relatively easy to determine the number of hours to add or subtract to local time in order to obtain Greenwich time (15° = 1 hour).

**Sources:**

Brau, Jean-Louis, Helen Weaver, and Allan Edmands. *Larousse Encyclopedia of Astrology*. New York: New American Library, 1980.

Filbey, John, and Peter Filbey. *The Astrologer's Companion*. Wellingborough, Northamptonshire, UK: Aquarian Press, 1986.

## Gurdjieff, George Ivanovitch

George Ivanovitch Gurdjieff (1866?–1949) was not an astrologer. However, his cosmology was largely derived from Western European occult sources and has much in common with the popular Theosophical cosmology/astrology of his day. Gurdjieff's two primary cosmological laws, the Law of Seven and the Law of Three, have their origins in Mesopotamian astronomy/astrology, echoes of which are also found in Judaism, Christianity, Hinduism, Islam, and in Western European occult and esoteric thinking derived from Pythagoras.

The forms that Gurdjieff's oral and written teaching took—occult cosmology and psychology, dance, psychological exercises, and storytelling—can be related to prevailing contemporary interests in the places where he taught. In Russia, these were Western European occultism, especially Theosophy, and ballet; in Paris, occultism, literary modernism, the archaic epic, and dance.

Gurdjieff was born in Alexandropol, Armenia, of Greek and Armenian parents. He travelled widely in the Middle and Far East, and arrived back in Moscow in 1912. There he began to teach an occult cosmological and psychological "system" of ideas, which, according to his unverifiable, mythologized writings, he had gathered from hidden places of sacred learning during his travels.

Leaving Russia because of the Bolshevik Revolution, Gurdjieff travelled via Tiblisi and Constantinople to Europe, arriving in France in 1922. In France he established his Institute for the Harmonious Development of Man, which attracted English and American pupils. Gurdjieff also gave his teaching in a form of sacred dancing, and demonstrations of these were open to the public. During the 1920s, Gurdjieff had a high profile in Paris and the reputation of a "mage." He took his dancers to America in 1924, but a near-fatal car accident on his return caused him to reassess his mode of teaching. Reducing the activity of the institute, he began to put his teaching into a written form. He made eight further visits to America to establishing his teaching there. Gurdjieff spent the World War II years teaching in Paris and died there in 1949.

The following is a discussion of some of the aspects of Gurdjieff's teaching that are related to zodiacal structure, number symbolism, and the multivalent and interpretive mode of enquiry that is part of astrological thinking.

## The Law of Seven and the Seven Known Planets of the Ancient World

Gurdjieff applies a synthesis of ideas derived from Pythagoras's relation of the musical octave to the ratio of distances between the seven known planets of the ancient world to his own Law of Seven, which is also known as the Law of Octaves. For example, the law is expressed in his oral and written teaching in relation to the colors of the light ray, the days of the week, the proportions of the human body, the digestion of food, and as the Ray of Creation, which describes the creation of the universe in the form of a descending octave, from the Absolute All to Absolute Nothing. Many of Gurdjieff's cosmological ideas are related to this fundamental law. For example, Gurdjieff relates levels of the Ray of Creation with the physical, astral, mental, or causal bodies of man, and each level has a specific density of matter and a specified number of laws. Thus, man on earth, subject to 48 laws, is gnostically distant from the Absolute towards which however, he can ascend through his own efforts and by so doing he develops new bodies.

| Ray of Creation | Notes | Number of Laws Subject to | Bodies |
|---|---|---|---|
| The Absolute/All | DO | 1 | - |
| All Worlds | SI | 3 | - |
| All Suns | LA | 6; 3 from all worlds and 3 of its own | Causal body |
| Our Sun | SOL | 12; 6 from all suns and 6 of its own | Mental body |
| The Planets | FA | 24; 12 from our sun and 12 of their own | Astral body |
| The Earth | MI | 48; 24 from the planets and 24 of the Earth | Physical body |
| The Moon | RE | 96; 48 from the Earth and 48 of its own | - |
| Absolute/Nothing | DO | - | - |

Gurdjieff connects the Law of Seven with number symbolism and stresses that the Ray of Creation should not be taken literally.

## The Law of Three and Astrological Modes

All events or actions throughout the universe are the result of the interaction of three forces: the positive/active, the negative/passive, and the reconciling that may be either active or passive. These forces can be equated in astrological terms with the cardinal, fixed, and mutable modes. The Law of Three can also be seen operating in the Ray of Creation (see previous chart) in the number of laws functioning at each level of the universe. Movement through the Ray of Creation is downward, or involutionary, as a result of a passively reconciling third force, and upward, or evolutionary, as a result of an actively reconciling third force.

### Elements

Gurdjieff followed occultist Helena Blavatsky in renaming the occult elements of fire, earth, air, and water, respectively, "carbon," "oxygen," "nitrogen," and "hydrogen." Each substance can be the conductor of an active, passive, or reconciling force. When the force is active the substance is termed "carbon," when passive "oxygen," and when reconciling "nitrogen." A substance that does not conduct a force is termed "hydrogen." Taken together, Gurdjieff's three forces in relation to the four elements may be expressed in astrological terms as the zodiac of 12 signs, in which each of the four elements is expressed in the cardinal, fixed, and mutable modes.

### Types and Signs of the Zodiac

Gurdjieff referred to a "science of types" that could be recognized only through study. Elsewhere Gurdjieff wrote of the necessity of finding the 28 types he needed for his own observations, which might be equated with lunar rather than solar types.

Astrology deals only with a man's essence, and Gurdjieff equates essence with type. Astrological signs were "invented" to synthesize the specific characteristics a person would have to struggle against during his or her life.

### Planetary Influence

Gurdjieff taught that "planets have a tremendous influence" on mankind as a whole. For example, they are a cause of war, and they influence individuals whose lives are "colored" by the planetary influence received at birth and who remain slaves to these influences throughout life.

### Fate

Astrology effects only a person's "essence" (i.e., his essential nature) and determines a person's fate. The Law of Accident controls his or her personality. Fate may be worse than accident, but has the advantage that it can be foreseen, while accident cannot.

### Gurdjieff's Enneagram as a Symbol of the Zodiac

Gurdjieff's cosmic laws are integrated in this diagram. The 3-6-9 triangle represents the Law of Three. The sequence of numbers 1 through 7 represents the Law of Seven. This recurring sequence is derived from the division of 1 by 7. Gurdjieff expands the Law of Seven numerologically to nine by including "intervals" or semitones, places where "shocks are required for the octave to flow on." Here points 3, 6, and 9 represent "intervals."

In Cabalistic terms, the Laws of Three and Seven may be represented by the Tree of Life in the three realms of Kether, Binah, and Chokmah, and the seven realms of

Geburah, Hesed, Tipareth, Hod, Netzach, Hod, and Yesod. Like the Tree, the Enneagram is a symbol that may be recoded in diverse ways, including that of a zodiac, the planets, and the correspondences belonging to them. As such, it represents the relationship between macrocosm and microcosm. Gurdjieff urged his pupils to experience the functioning of these cosmic laws in everyday life and also in their inner world: "Inside us we also have a moon, a sun and so on. We are a whole system. If you know what your moon is and does, you can understand the whole system." Gurdjieff referred to the Enneagram as a moving symbol and expressed this motion through his sacred dances.

## The Enneagram of Personality Types

The Enneagram of Personality Types is an aspect of Gurdjieff's teaching that has achieved a popular form and is continuing to develop its own set of teachings. Enneagram of Personality publications usually give secret Sufi origins for the Enneagram. This appropriation of the Enneagram stems from the Sufi Idries Shah, who convinced the Gurdjieff teacher J. G. Bennett of its truth. Although there is no record of any direct evidence offered for this view, the mythology of Sufi origins is now well established.

In *The Theory of Celestial Influence: Man the Universe and Cosmic Mystery* (1954), Rodney Collin, who learned about the Enneagram from Gurdjieff's pupil P. D. Ouspensky, reintroduced Gurdjieff's cosmic laws in his own synthesis that makes evident their zodiacal and astrological foundations. His Enneagram of planets, related to planetary types of people, provides the link between Gurdjieff's Enneagram and the Enneagram of Personality, which developed from the teaching of Oscar Ichazo at his Arica Institute in Chile. In 1970, Claudio Naranjo, psychiatrist researching personality typology, together with others from the Esalen Institute in California, took Ichazo's course. Kathleen Riordan Speeth and Robert (Bob) Ochs were pupils in the group that Naranjo taught on his return to the United States. Ochs, a Jesuit with a Ph.D. in theology from the Institut Catholique of Paris, adapted the Enneagram types into "the nine faces of God." He taught this version of the Enneagram at Loyola University in Chicago and also at the Graduate Theological Union of the University of California at Berkeley. These classes are the direct origin of the introduction of the Enneagram into Jesuit retreats, which, in turn, lead to the publication of Don Riso's *Personality Types: Using the Enneagram for Self Discovery* (1987) and also influenced Helen Palmer's *The Enneagram: Understanding Yourself and the Others in Your Life* (1988).

## Gurdjieff's Texts and Zodiacal Structure

Gurdjieff used the structure of the zodiac in his writings. For example, *Beelzebub's Tales to His Grandson* has 48 chapters, four in each sign of the zodiac, while *Meetings with Remarkable Men* is structured as a zodiac, in which the 11 remarkable men and one woman are personifications of the 12 zodiacal signs. In *Tales*, the journey through the zodiac is in accordance with the flow of time, from Aries to Pisces, and thus involutionary, like the involutionary flow of the Ray of Creation. The zodiac in *Meetings* is evolutionary in that it moves backwards against the flow of time from Aquarius to Pisces.

The zodiacal structure of his texts enables Gurdjieff to incorporate the myths and symbols connected to the signs and their ruling planets and to the sets of correspondences in astrology and other occult traditions. Here Gurdjieff was in accord with modernist literary interests in Theosophical astrology and in the archaic epic expressed as a solar journey; as well as becoming part of a long tradition of the numerological and astrological structuring of texts.

## Interpretation of Gurdjieff's Texts and Astrological Interpretation

Gurdjieff warns that his ideas should not to be taken literally and speaks of the necessity for the multivalence of symbols. Symbols taken in one meaning only become fixed and dead. Gurdjieff favored indirect methods of teaching so that his pupils would make their own efforts to understand. In addition to his use of symbolism, he arouses questioning in his reader by the use of anomaly, metaphor, paradox, and contradictions in the narrative.

The use of astrological correspondences and number symbolism enables Gurdjieff to suggest virtually inexhaustible variant readings of his texts in relation to other occult astrological systems, from the Sumerian, Greek, Roman, Renaissance, and nineteenth-century occult revival in which the zodiac is encoded. Thus, although Gurdjieff's writings demand interpretation, they defy any attempt at a fixed or closed reading and are also in tune with the contemporary interest in the integration of astrology and psychology.

## Gurdjieff's Influence

Gurdjieff's teaching continues and its occult cosmological/astrological influence can be seen in popular astrology, popular occult-archaeology in the occult, and in twentieth-century literature.

—Sophia Wellbeloved

**Sources:**


Blake, Anthony G. E. *The Intelligent Enneagram*. London: Shambala, 1996.

Collin, Rodney *The Theory of Celestial Influence: Man, the Universe, and Cosmic Mystery*. London: Vincent Stuart, 1954. Reprint, Boulder, CO: Shambhala, 1984.

Gurdjieff, Georges Ivanovitch. *All and Everything*, Ten Books in Three Series: First Series: *Beelzebub's Tales to His Grandson: An Objectively Impartial Criticism of the Life of Man*. London: Routledge & Kegan Paul, 1950; Second Series: *Meetings with Remarkable Men*. Translated by A. R. Orage. London: Picador, 1978; Third Series: *Life Is Real Only Then, When "I Am."* London: Viking Arkana, 1991.

———. *The Herald of Coming Good*. Paris, 1933. Reprint, New York: S. Weiser, 1971.

———.*Views from the Real World*. London: Routledge & Kegan Paul, 1976.

Ouspensky P. D. *In Search of the Miraculous: Fragments of an Unknown Teaching*. New York: Harcourt, Brace, 1949. Reprint, San Diego: Harcourt, 2001.

Palmer, Helen, *The Enneagram: Understanding Yourself and the Others in Your Life*. New York: Harper Collins, 1995.

Riso, Don Richard, *Personality Types: Using the Enneagram for Self Discovery*. Boston: Houghton Mifflin, 1987.

Taylor, Paul Beekman. *Gurdjieff and Orage: Brothers in Elysium*. York Beach, ME: Weiser Books, 2001.

———. *Shadows of Heaven: Gurdjieff and Toomer*. York Beach, ME: Weiser Books, 1998.

Wellbeloved, Sophia. *Gurdjieff: The Key Concepts*. New York: Routledge, 2003.

## Guttman, Arielle

Arielle Guttman has been involved with many aspects of astrology—research, writing, lecturing, teaching and counseling—since 1974. She has taught astrological seminars in many countries around the world. She has carried on much of the work of the late astrologer Jim Lewis with whom she had conducted many projects within the field of locational astrology and locality mapping. She has also worked personally with Robert Hand in the field of astrolocality mapping. Now, Guttman serves on the faculty and the board of directors of the Wisdom School in Santa Fe, New Mexico. She is the author of three books on astrology: *Astro-Compatibility*, *Mythic Astrology* (with Kenneth Johnson), and *The Astro*Carto*Graphy Book of Maps* (with Jim Lewis). Her astrological work also involves leading groups on pilgrimages to the sacred sites in Greece to study mythology and astrology at the sites themselves.

## Hades

Hades is one of the eight hypothetical planets (sometimes referred to as the trans-Neptunian points or planets, or TNPs for short) utilized in Uranian astrology. The Uranian system, sometimes referred to as the Hamburg School of Astrology, was established by Friedrich Sieggrün (1877–1951) and Alfred Witte (1878–1943). It relies heavily on hard aspects and midpoints. In decline for many decades, it has experienced a revival in recent years.

Hades is associated with such negative conditions and substances as poverty, ugliness, garbage, dirt, sickness, bacteria, loneliness, debasement, vulgarity, and crime. It is also connected with "past lifetimes," the ancient past, and secrets, and in certain combinations can even represent ancient wisdom and the older sciences. This hypothetical planet can have positive meanings, particularly when found in the horoscopes of individuals who deal with such Hades matters as the healing of disease.

Based on the speculative orbits of the Uranian planets, the Kepler, Solar Fire and Win*Star software program will all locate this hypothetical planet in an astrological chart.

**Sources:**


Lang-Wescott, Martha. *Mechanics of the Future: Asteroids*. Rev. ed. Conway, MA: Treehouse Mountain, 1991.

Simms, Maria Kay. *Dial Detective: Investigation with the 90 Degree Dial*. San Diego: Astro Computing Services, 1989.


## Hagar

Hagar, asteroid 682 (the 682nd asteroid to be discovered, on June 17, 1909), is approximately 12 kilometers in diameter and has an orbital period of 4.3 years. It is

**A woodcut of an Assyrian seal depicting the descent of Ishtar into Hades.** ***Reproduced by permission of Fortean Picture Library.***

named after the biblical Hagar, Sarah's maid, who fathered Ishmael through Abraham and was later driven away and left to die in the desert. Muslims trace their lineage to Ishmael. In Hebrew, *hagar* means "forsaken." When prominent in a natal chart, the asteroid Hagar can show an individual who creates for another person but is later rejected out of jealousy of her or his work and creativity. Like the biblical Hagar, this person can later become an independent creator.

**Sources:**

Kowal, Charles T. *Asteroids: Their Nature and Utilization*. Chichester, West Sussex, UK: Ellis Horwood Limited, 1988.

Room, Adrian. *Dictionary of Astronomical Names*. London: Routledge, 1988.

Schwartz, Jacob. *Asteroid Name Encyclopedia*. St. Paul, MN: Llewellyn Publications, 1995.

## HALLORAN SOFTWARE

Halloran Software began in October 1985 when John Halloran was dialed into a bulletin board system (BBS) based in Glendale, California, and noticed a message from a woman inquiring if there were any free or inexpensive computer programs for astrology. Having already searched for these, he knew nothing was available, but Halloran, who started studying astrology in the late 1960s, had purchased a copy of Michael Erlewine's 1980 *Manual of Computer Programming for Astrologers*. Within two weeks, Halloran had figured out how to bypass the typographical errors in this book and released into the public domain an astrology calculation program that ran in the Basic interpreter on CP/M computers.

Mac programmer David C. Oshel discovered Halloran's program and rewrote it in modular form, which allowed Halloran to add chart comparison to its capabilities. Version 7, also called ASTROLPC.BAS, was the last version released with source code. When versions 8 and 9 added support for saved charts, a dating service search engine, a transits list, and an on-screen graphic wheel that even the commercial programs did not have at that time, Halloran began charging a modest registration fee to access the program's more advanced features. By this time, in 1986, IBM PC and XT clones were becoming popular, and Halloran ported the program and compiled it for the IBM PC. In 1987, in response to a complaint from Matrix, Michael Erlewine's company, Halloran deleted the calculation routines taken from Erlewine's book and replaced them with faster, more accurate astronomical routines. In addition to collecting shareware registration fees, Halloran sold many program copies from a classified ad in the back of *Computer Shopper* magazine, from which astrology magazine editors such as Richard Nolle and Kenneth Irving discovered and reviewed the program.

Besides improving his shareware calculation program, Halloran wrote an astrological research program called TimeSearch that reverse-engineers an astrology chart. In collaboration with other programmers, such as John Molfese, author of the Astrodynes program, James Davis, author of the Self Search and Handwriting Analyzer programs, and at the urging of the late Joseph Hettiger, owner of a Texas company selling astrology programs for the Commodore 64 computer, Halloran wrote his first report writer program, LifeTrends, with transits interpretations by San Antonio radio astrologer Deanna Christensen. By 1989, Halloran was able to quit his technical writer/quality assurance job with an HMO data processing department to create and sell astrology software full time.

In June 1990, Halloran Software announced the first version of AstrolDeluxe, which proceeded to sell one thousand copies in the first six months. This program added color printing and advanced calculations, such as progressed and return charts, as well as Chiron and the major asteroids. In the same year, Halloran began a productive collaboration with astrologer/journalism student Janice Barsky, who had written original natal, compatibility, and transits interpretations on her word processor and was cutting and pasting inexpensive reports for clients who could not pay for a professional reading. Out of this collaboration came the StarMatch and Natal Professional report writer programs. The last MS-DOS-based report writer was the hobbyist-priced Natal Profiles program with interpretations by Hollywood-based metaphysical astrologer Carolyne Lacy.

Microsoft's Windows operating system began to loom on the horizon, so while Halloran worked to finish Natal Professional, he began collaborating with Robert Brown, a Gemini friend who already owned 20 Windows programs, on AstrolDeluxe for Windows, the first copies of which sold in December 1992. The Windows environment allowed this AstrolDeluxe to create graphic chartwheels on any Windows-supported printer without the program having to supply and work with particular printer drivers, which was a big advance. Natal Professional and AstrolDeluxe for Windows also started providing access to the PC Atlas, produced by the company Astro Communications Services founded in San Diego by the late Neil F. Michelsen, based on research by Thomas G. Shanks. Then, for use with the AstrolDeluxe for Windows program, Halloran Software designed TrueType fonts with 130 astrological glyphs and assembled a collection of 4,100 famous charts especially for the program's data research module, which executes 20 different types of searches.

In December 1994, Halloran Software first released Astrology for Windows, a combination freeware and shareware program. Ed Perrone, moderator of the Astrology RoundTable on the GEnie online network, wrote at the time, "In terms of non-commercial Windows astrology programs (i.e., shareware and freeware), it is really the only contender. I've only seen a couple of Windows chart-calculation programs at all, and none of them compare to this one for ease of use, clarity of display, and other features." A unique feature of this program was to externalize all of its messages and captions, with the result that volunteer translators soon made it available in 14 different languages. For a year, this program could only be downloaded from GEnie and other online networks such as Compuserve and America Online, but in 1996, the Internet took off and Halloran Software launched its own web site from which anyone could download the latest version of Astrology for Windows and order the company's commercial astrology software.

Beginning in 1996 with version 3, Halloran and Brown integrated a report writing engine into the AstrolDeluxe for Windows calculation program, with the result that after using the program to perform a natal, comparison, transits, progressions, or return chart calculation, a user with the appropriate interpretation files could easily create a customizable 30-page report. AstrolDeluxe ReportWriter gives the user about 70 commands that are like a programming language for custom-designing interpretation reports, and it comes with an easy-to-use interpretations editor. Halloran collaborated with astrologer Tony Louis in developing program features for progressions, career analysis, and return reports.

In 2002, Halloran Software released version 6 of its AstrolDeluxe ReportWriter program. Version 6 runs on 32-bit versions of Windows from Windows 95 to Windows XP, and comes bundled with the full ACS PC Atlas and Carolyne Lacy's Spirit Success natal interpretations.

## Hamburg School

The Hamburg school is another name for Uranian astrology.

## Hansa

Hansa, asteroid 480 (the 480th asteroid to be discovered, on May 21, 1901), is approximately 64 kilometers in diameter and has an orbital period of 4.3 years. This asteroid was named after the merchant guild that gave its name to the Hanseatic League. Hansa shows mercantile ability, particularly in associations with others.

**Sources:**

Kowal, Charles T. *Asteroids: Their Nature and Utilization*. Chichester, West Sussex, UK: Ellis Horwood Limited, 1988.

Room, Adrian. *Dictionary of Astronomical Names*. London: Routledge, 1988.

Schwartz, Jacob. *Asteroid Name Encyclopedia*. St. Paul, MN: Llewellyn Publications, 1995.

## HARD ASPECTS

Hard aspects are aspects that present a native with challenges—squares, oppositions, semisquares, and the like. Hard aspects is the preferred contemporary term for the aspects that were traditionally termed malefic aspects (malefic dropping out of usage because of its negative connotations).

## HARMONIA

Harmonia, asteroid 40 (the 40th asteroid to be discovered, on March 31, 1856), is approximately 116 kilometers in diameter and has an orbital period of 3.4 years. Harmonia was named after the Greek daughter of Aries (Mars) and Aphrodite (Venus). J. Lee Lehman associates this asteroid with musical as well as social harmony. Jacob Schwartz gives the astrological significance of Harmonia as "balance between forces, singing."

**Sources:**

Kowal, Charles T. *Asteroids: Their Nature and Utilization*. Chichester, West Sussex, UK: Ellis Horwood Limited, 1988.

Lehman, J. Lee. *The Ultimate Asteroid Book*. West Chester, PA: Whitford Press, 1988.

Room, Adrian. *Dictionary of Astronomical Names*. London: Routledge, 1988.

Schwartz, Jacob. *Asteroid Name Encyclopedia*. St. Paul, MN: Llewellyn Publications, 1995.

## HARMONIC ASTROLOGY

Harmonic astrology is the term used for a system of astrological analysis developed by British astrologer John Addey in the 1960s and 1970s. Many of the concepts used in harmonic astrology have roots going back hundreds of years. Johannes Kepler developed a theory of aspects and planetary relationships that closely mirrors many of Addey's ideas, and some of the varga charts used in Vedic astrology are equivalent to the harmonic charts used by Addey and other harmonic astrologers. However, Addey formulated many ideas that go beyond the scope of what had been developed before, and he supported his ideas with a great amount of research.

In harmonic astrology an aspect is viewed as a fraction of a circle. For example, a trine aspect of 120° is $\frac{1}{3}$ of a circle, a square is $\frac{1}{4}$ of a circle, a sextile is $\frac{1}{6}$ of a circle, a quincunx is $\frac{5}{12}$, and so on.

According to the theory of harmonic astrologer, aspects with the same denominator have a great deal in common. For example, a $\frac{1}{7}$ aspect, a $\frac{2}{7}$ aspect, and a $\frac{3}{7}$

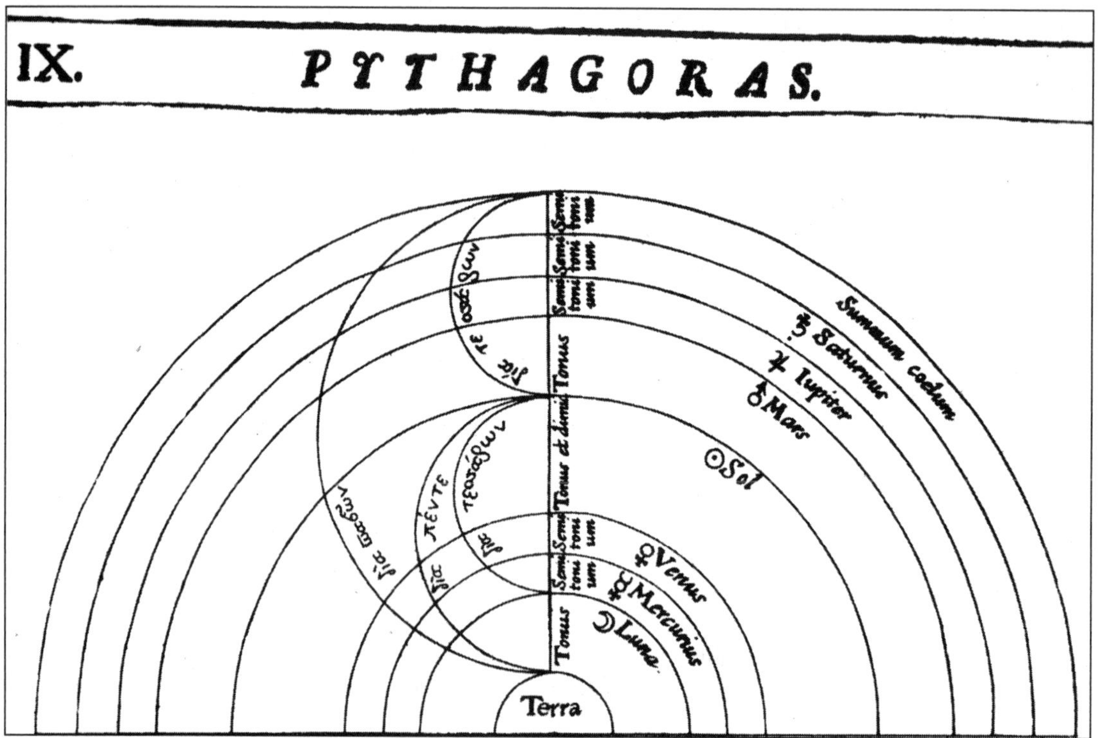


**An eighteenth-century engraving of the planetary spheres and the harmonies of the spheres, which relate to musical intervals.** ***Reproduced by permission of Fortean Picture Library.***

aspect have a similar meaning. The denominator is often referred to as the harmonic, so two planets that are in $\frac{1}{7}$ aspect or $\frac{2}{7}$ aspect, for example, can also be referred to as being in the seventh harmonic.

Another belief of harmonic astrologers is that doubling the denominator results in an aspect with a similar meaning. This theory is consonant with some beliefs in traditional astrology, such as, for example, that a trine aspect ($\frac{1}{3}$ aspect) has a similar meaning to a sextile aspect ($\frac{1}{6}$ aspect). Also, a $\frac{1}{2}$ (opposition) and $\frac{1}{4}$ (square) aspect are hard aspects, and some astrologers also use the $\frac{1}{8}$ (semisquare) and $\frac{3}{8}$ aspect (sesquiquadrate) and also believe that these are hard aspects. Hard aspects are challenging and motivating. The $\frac{1}{3}$ and $\frac{1}{6}$ aspect, on the other hand, are harmonious and pleasant.

Harmonic astrologers believe that astrological aspects have much in common with sound waves. Interestingly, if a plucked guitar string is shortened to half its length, the resulting note is an octave higher. Musical notes that are an octave apart have a very similar musical quality even though the pitch of the two notes is very different. Similarly the sextile aspect is $\frac{1}{2}$ the distance of a trine aspect and both aspects have a similar meeting. Similarly the $\frac{1}{4}$ and $\frac{1}{2}$ aspects have similar meanings. These similarities between sound and astrological aspects incline harmonic astrologers to believe that waves similar to sound waves are the basis of astrological aspects. Harmonic astrology is not yet widely used, and there is not yet agreement on the meanings of different harmonics.

John Addey wrote several books that explain the theory and application of harmonic astrology in detail. Others have wirtten books in more recent times that have further developed and applied the concepts of harmonic astrology described by Addey.

—David Cochrane

**Sources:**

Brau, Jean-Louis, Helen Weaver, and Allan Edmands. *Larousse Encyclopedia of Astrology*. New York: New American Library, 1980.

Harvey, Charles, and Michael Harding. *Working with Astrology: The Psychology of Harmonics, Midpoints and Astro*Carto*Graphy*. New York: Arkana, 1990.

## Harmonic Chart

A harmonic chart is a secondary chart constructed by multiplying all of the various factors in the radix (initial) chart by the harmonic number under consideration. Although there exists much interesting research on harmonic theory, harmonic charts are rarely used in day-to-day astrological practice, except in Hindu astrology.

## Hasta

Hasta (Hand) is one of the Nakshatras (lunar mansions) of Vedic astrology. This Nakshatra, symbolized by the five fingers of the hand, or a clenched fist, is found from Virgo 10° to 23°20', and is a wise time for "getting a grip" on new situations; during this period, a person can be quite intelligent and persuasive, though controlling and even cruel at times.

—Pramela Thiagesan

## Heavy Planets

The heavy planets are more commonly known as the outer planets, which take longer to travel through the zodiac and which thus seem to be "heavier" than the others. The heavy planets are Jupiter, Saturn, Uranus, Neptune, and Pluto.

## Hebe

Hebe, asteroid 6 (the 6th asteroid to be discovered, on July 1, 1847, by the German amateur astronomer Karl Ludwig Hencke), is approximately 204 kilometers in diameter and has an orbital period of 3.8 years. Hebe was named after the Greek goddess of youth who took ambrosia to the Olympian deities. According to Martha Lang-Wescott, Hebe "deals with codependency—the ways that one 'enables' the egocentricity and emotional immaturity of others." Jacob Schwartz adds the further trait of "granting leeway." This asteroid's key word is "serving."

**Sources:**

Lang-Wescott, Martha. *Asteroids-Mechanics: Ephemerides II*. Conway, MA: Treehouse Mountain, 1990.

———. *Mechanics of the Future: Asteroids*. Rev. ed. Conway, MA: Treehouse Mountain, 1991.

Schwartz, Jacob. *Asteroid Name Encyclopedia*. St. Paul, MN: Llewellyn Publications, 1995.

## Heindel, Max

Max Heindel, founder of the Rosicrucian Fellowship, was born July 23, 1865, as Carl Louis von Grasshof, the oldest son in an aristocratic German family. He went to Glasgow, Scotland, to study maritime engineering at age 16 and eventually became chief engineer on an ocean liner. He moved to New York City in 1895, worked as a consulting engineer, and married. He moved to Los Angeles eight years later. There he began occult studies, soon joining the Theosophical Society in America, led by Katherine Tingley. Heindel served as vice president of the Los Angeles branch in 1904–5. He became interested in astrology and began lecturing on it in various cities on the West Coast.

In Germany in 1907, according to Heindel, a spiritual being later identified as an elder brother of the Rosicrucian order appeared in his room, informing him that he had passed a test. He subsequently traveled to the Temple of the Rosy Cross near the border of Germany and Bohemia and remained for a month. There he received information that became *The Rosicrucian Cosmo-Conception*. He then returned to the United States, and in Columbus, Ohio, established the first center of the Rosicrucian Fellowship in 1908.

Heindel's teachings differ from the Theosophical Society's in their greater emphasis on astrology, Christianity, Christian symbols, and a Rosicrucian heritage. His ideas reflect those of Rudolf Steiner.

Following the Ohio center, Heindel soon established centers in Seattle, Washington; North Yakima, Washington; Portland, Oregon; and Los Angeles, California. He had a heart problem and was hospitalized in March 1910. While there, he had an out-of-body experience that showed him plans for future work. In August 1910, he married Augusta Foss, a woman he had known before his first wife died in 1905. Part of his hospital vision was fulfilled when Rosicrucian headquarters were established at Mt. Ecclesia near Oceanside, California, in 1911. The grounds included a sanctuary, offices, a woman's dormitory, cottages, and a vegetarian cafeteria.

Heindel's final years were productive ones in which he wrote several volumes and a regular column in the Rosicrucian Fellowship's monthly, *Rays from the Rosy Cross*. The fellowship was a major force in the spread and popularization of astrology. Astrologers not connected with the fellowship nevertheless use the annual ephemeris and table of houses, both published in Oceanside. Heindel's wife assumed leadership of the fellowship after he passed away in 1919.

**Sources:**

Heindel, Max. *The Message of the Stars*. Oceanside, CA: Rosicrucian Fellowship, 1963.

———. *The Rosicrucian Cosmo-Conception*. Seattle: Rosicrucian Fellowship, 1909.

———. *Simplified Scientific Astrology*. Oceanside, CA: Rosicrucian Fellowship, 1928.

Melton, J. Gordon. *Religious Leaders of America*. Detroit: Gale, 1991.

## HEKATE

Hekate, asteroid 100 (the 100th asteroid to be discovered, on July 11, 1868), is approximately 84 kilometers in diameter and has an orbital period of 5.4 years. Hekate was named after a Greek goddess of the underworld. J. Lee Lehman asserts that people with this asteroid strongly positioned in their natal charts "tend to break down other people's images of themselves, as well as their own." Jacob Schwartz gives the astrological significance of Hekate as "the end of the old before the beginning of the new; assertion of the older woman."

**Sources:**

Kowal, Charles T. *Asteroids: Their Nature and Utilization*. Chichester, West Sussex, UK: Ellis Horwood Limited, 1988.

Lehman, J. Lee. *The Ultimate Asteroid Book*. West Chester, PA: Whitford Press, 1988.

Room, Adrian. *Dictionary of Astronomical Names*. London: Routledge, 1988.

Schwartz, Jacob. *Asteroid Name Encyclopedia*. St. Paul, MN: Llewellyn Publications, 1995.

## HELIACAL

Heliacal means associated with the Sun (from the Greek *helios*, meaning "sun"). The heliacal rising of a star is its first appearance following a period of invisibility due to its conjunction with the Sun. Similarly, the heliacal setting of a star refers to its last appearance before entering into a conjunction with the Sun.

## HELIO

Helio, asteroid 895 (the 895th asteroid to be discovered, on July 11, 1918), is approximately 68 kilometers in diameter and has an orbital period of 5.7 years. Helio was named after the Greek god of the Sun. J. Lee Lehman asserts that the person with this asteroid prominent in her or his natal chart "does her/his job, and expects to shine as a result of it." Jacob Schwartz gives the astrological significance of Helio as "consistent confidence and delivery of creative energy."

**Sources:**

Kowal, Charles T. *Asteroids: Their Nature and Utilization*. Chichester, West Sussex, UK: Ellis Horwood Limited, 1988.

Lehman, J. Lee. *The Ultimate Asteroid Book*. West Chester, PA: Whitford Press, 1988.

Room, Adrian. *Dictionary of Astronomical Names*. London: Routledge, 1988.

Schwartz, Jacob. *Asteroid Name Encyclopedia*. St. Paul, MN: Llewellyn Publications, 1995.

## HELIOCENTRIC ASTROLOGY

Although traditional astrology is geocentric (Earth-centered), some astrologers have undoubtedly considered using a heliocentric (Sun-centered) system ever since the Copernican revolution. The argument against heliocentric astrology is that, since we are situated on Earth, we need to focus on Earth's relationship to the other celestial bodies—a Sun-centered astrology would make sense only if we were born on the Sun.

This argument was persuasive enough to prevent the emergence of a true heliocentric astrology until relatively recently. The two factors behind this emergence were (1) the discovery that scientists had found a correlation between sunspot activity and angles between the planets (the same basic aspects that are used in geocentric astrology) and (2) the personal computer revolution, which made casting heliocentric horoscopes quite easy. Use by NASA scientists of a form of heliocentric astrology—under the rubric "gravitational vectoring"—to predict high sunspot activity was not just an important verification of astrological principles; it also, because of the well-known effects of such activity on weather conditions, on radio wave propagation, and on other terrestrial events, alerted astrologers to the possibility that astrological forces impacting the solar sphere had an influence on Earth's astrological "atmosphere."

The early solar charts presented a barren appearance: There were no house divisions, no ascendant, no Sun, and, sometimes, no zodiac (because for the tropical zodiac, the first sign always begins at the spring equinox, a notion that has no meaning from a heliocentric viewpoint). Earth, which is always 180° away from where the Sun would be in a geocentric chart, is drawn in as a cross surrounded by a circle (like the symbol for the Part of Fortune, only shifted 45°). Because the Sun in traditional astrology represents one's deepest "soul" self, some heliocentric astrologers have proposed that solar horoscopes chart the astrology of the soul.

Heliocentric astrologers began with the principle that the heliocentric perspective would supplement rather than supplant the geocentric perspective. This principle paved the way for a newer approach to heliocentric astrology that represents the heliocentric and the geocentric positions in the same horoscope. These are technically "geo-helio" charts. Astrologers who use this system claim that including the heliocentric positions is like "finding the missing half of the horoscope." The heliocentric planets have the same meaning as when used geocentrically, although they are said to manifest their influence in a different manner. This newer approach did not entirely overturn the older heliocentric system, so there are now at least two distinct heliocentric approaches, one purely heliocentric (but which does not reject the validity of a geocentric chart, using it only in an entirely separate phase of the operation), and the other a mixed geo-helio approach in which the two charts are merged.

Most contemporary astrologers, although not actually opposed to heliocentric astrology, have not integrated it into their practice, primarily because there are so many new techniques that no one astrologer can possibly master them all. The heliocentric perspective is just one tool among a multitude available to the astrological practitioner. Many astrologers have adopted the attitude that very good astrologers are rare enough, so why not just stick to mastering the basics? This argument has more than a little merit. And, after all, if we adopt a Sun-centered astrology, why not also make use of the many insights that are probably waiting to be discoved in a Moon-centered or a Mars-centered or even a Ceres-centered astrology? If a heliocentric chart cast for one's birth time gives valid insights for a native of Earth, then it should be possible to apply the same principles to any planet or planetoid in the solar system!

Such considerations have caused many astrologers to greet heliocentric methods with indifference. At the same time, the widespread availability of chart-casting programs that include heliocentric positions as a standard option makes it almost inevitable that the astrologers who buy them will experiment with these positions, resulting in more astrologers who use heliocentric or geo-helio charts. Thus, the future of heliocentric astrology as a continuing presence within the astrological community seems ensured.

**Sources:**

Brau, Jean-Louis, Helen Weaver, and Allan Edmands. *Larousse Encyclopedia of Astrology*. New York: New American Library, 1980.

Davis, T. Patrick. *Revolutionizing Astrology with Heliocentric*. Windermere, FL: Davis Research Reports, 1980.

Sedgwick, Philip. *The Sun at the Center: A Primer of Heliocentric Astrology*. St. Paul, MN: Llewellyn Publications, 1990.

## Hemisphere

Hemisphere literally means a half sphere. In geography, hemisphere refers to the division of Earth into northern, southern, eastern, and western hemispheres. In astrology, hemisphere usually refers to the division of a horoscope into upper and lower halves (using the ascendant-descendant axis as the dividing line) or into left and right halves (using the midheaven–imum coeli axis as the dividing line). The upper and lower hemispheres of a chart are technically termed the diurnal (day, because it is above the horizon) arc and the nocturnal (night, because it is below the horizon) arc, respectively. The left and right hemispheres are termed the oriental (eastern) arc and the occidental (western) arc. These technical terms are rarely used by contemporary astrologers.

In the interpretation of a natal chart, the occurence of many planets above the horizon is said to indicate extroversion; many planets below the horizon indicates introversion. Also, a chart with a preponderance of planets in the left hemisphere is said to indicate an individual who shapes her or his environment, and a preponderance in the right hemisphere indicates an individual who adapts to the environment. These interpretations are tentative, "first impression" delineations and can be quickly abandoned if other factors in a birth chart give contrary indications.

**Sources:**

Brau, Jean-Louis, Helen Weaver, and Allan Edmands. *Larousse Encyclopedia of Astrology*. New York: New American Library, 1980.

Gettings, Fred. *Dictionary of Astrology*. London: Routledge & Kegan Paul, 1985.

## Hera

Hera, asteroid 103 (the 103rd asteroid to be discovered, on September 7, 1868), is approximately 96 kilometers in diameter and has an orbital period of 4.4 years. Hera was named after the Greek goddess of women and childbirth. She was the sister and wife of Zeus, king of the Olympian deities. Hera was the most jealous wife in ancient mythology, and she persecuted both her husband's lovers and the children of Zeus's many love affairs. Jacob Schwartz gives the astrological significance of this asteroid as "maintaining the balance between power and justice; issues of rights and partnership dynamics." According to Martha Lang-Wescott, Hera "illustrates the relationship model of the parents as perceived by the individual—and the way that model is acted out in present roles through assumptions about equality, fidelity and commitment in relationship." This asteroid's key phrase is "keeping accounts."

**Sources:**

Lang-Wescott, Martha. *Asteroids-Mechanics: Ephemerides II*. Conway, MA: Treehouse Mountain, 1990.

———. *Mechanics of the Future: Asteroids*. Rev. ed. Conway, MA: Treehouse Mountain, 1991.

Schwartz, Jacob. *Asteroid Name Encyclopedia*. St. Paul, MN: Llewellyn Publications, 1995.

## Herschel

Herschel was the original designation of Uranus. It was named after Sir William Herschel, the astronomer who discovered Uranus. British astrologers persisted in using the name long after the rest of the world had switched to Uranus.

William Herschel was born Friedrich Wilhelm Herschel in Hanover, Germany, on November 15, 1738, and anglicized his name after he moved to England. His original profession was music, and music students were said to have flocked to him because of his talent, amiability, and teaching ability. He became interested in astronomy and took it up as a hobby; in time, it consumed him. He taught himself calculus and optics and, dissatisfied with the quality of existing telescopes, designed and built his own (later declared to be far better than any other in existence). He was creative and resourceful. Concerned about the welfare of his sister Caroline, whose brilliance was being wasted by parents who held very traditional ideas about the proper place of women, Herschel arranged for her to move to England and become his partner in the music (and later astronomy) business.

A modest individual, he brought Uranus to the attention of other astronomers with the announcement that he had discovered a new "comet." When, after he had become famous, the king wished to honor him with an official appointment, he made certain that his sister also received a royal subsidy—making her the first woman in history to become a professional astronomer. Herschel also went into the telescope-manufacturing business: It was through a Herschel telescope that the first asteroid, Ceres, was discovered.

**Sources:**

Littmann, Mark. *Planets Beyond: Discovering the Outer Solar System*. 2d ed. New York: John Wiley & Sons, 1990.

Paul, Haydn. *Revolutionary Spirit: Exploring the Astrological Uranus*. Shaftesbury, Dorset, UK: Element Books, 1989.

Room, Adrian. *Dictionary of Astronomical Names*. London: Routledge & Kegan Paul, 1988.

## Hesperus

Hesperus is the name given to the planet Venus when it appears as the Evening Star.

## Hestia

Hestia, asteroid 46 (the 46th asteroid to be discovered, on August 16, 1857), is approximately 164 kilometers in diameter and has an orbital period of 4 years. It was named after the Greek virgin goddess of the hearth and symbol of the home (parallel to the Roman Vesta). Hestia was the oldest and most sacred of the 12 Olympian dieties. As with the asteroid Vesta, the natal location of Hestia by sign and house indicates something about the native's domestic inclinations. When prominent in a natal chart (e.g., conjunct the Sun or the ascendant), it can indicate a homebody.

**Sources:**

Kowal, Charles T. *Asteroids: Their Nature and Utilization*. Chichester, West Sussex, UK: Ellis Horwood Limited, 1988.

Room, Adrian. *Dictionary of Astronomical Names*. London: Routledge, 1988.

Schwartz, Jacob. *Asteroid Name Encyclopedia*. St. Paul, MN: Llewellyn Publications, 1995.

## Hidalgo

Hidalgo, asteroid 944 (the 944th asteroid to be discovered, on October 31, 1920) was named after the revolutionary priest who attempted to overthrow Spanish rule in Mexico. It is about 28½ kilometers in diameter and has an eccentric orbit that is the longest (14 years) of any asteroid. Hidalgo is one of the more recent asteroids to be investigated by astrologers. Preliminary material on Hidalgo can be found in Demetra George and Douglas Bloch's *Astrology for Yourself*, and an ephemeris (table of celestial locations) for Hidalgo can be found in the second edition of George and Bloch's *Asteroid Goddesses*. Unlike the planets, which are associated with a wide range of phenomena, the smaller asteroids are said to represent a single principle. Bloch and George (1987) give Hidalgo's principle as "protecting and fighting for one's beliefs"; their tentative key phrase for Hidalgo is "My capacity for self-assertion in defense of my principles." Zipporah Dobyns associates Hidalgo with Saturn, finding that it often aspects that planet in the charts of women who reach positions of success and power. J. Lee Lehman finds that Hidalgo represents "an assertion of will *over* others." This influence can be used in fighting for other people's rights, but "Hidalgo *expects* to be in control, to be the general in all situations." Lehman describes Hidalgo as a "macho" asteroid. Jacob Schwartz gives the astrological significance of this asteroid as "fighting for others' rights; exchanges based on integrity or principles."

**Sources:**

Dobyns, Zipporah. *Expanding Astrology's Universe*. San Diego: Astro Computing Services, 1983.

George, Demetra, with Douglas Bloch. *Astrology for Yourself: A Workbook for Personal Transformation*. Berkeley, CA: Wingbow Press, 1987.

———. *Goddesses: The Mythology, Psychology and Astrology of the Reemerging Feminine*. 2d ed. rev. San Diego: Astro Computing Services, 1990.

Lehman, J. Lee. *The Ultimate Asteroid Book*. West Chester, PA: Whitford Press, 1988.
Schwartz, Jacob. *Asteroid Name Encyclopedia*. St. Paul, MN: Llewellyn Publications, 1995.

## Hillis-Dineen, Madalyn

Madalyn Hillis-Dineen is the director of marketing of Astrolabe, Inc., the largest privately owned astrological software company in the world. She is also a well-known Uranian astrologer, teacher, author, and lecturer and is a certified Astro*Carto*Graphy interpreter. She began her study of astrology in 1979 and started working as an astrologer full time in 1990. From 1990 to 1994, she served as executive secretary of the National Council for Geocosmic Research (NCGR) where she concentrated her efforts on conference planning and public relations. She also edited the NCGR membership letter from 1986 to 1994. Hillis-Dineen is active in a number of astrological organizations and she was the winner of the 1995 United Astrology Congress (UAC) Regulus Award for Community Service. Currently, she serves as the Clerk and Parliamentarian of the NCGR National Board of Directors.

During the course of her astrological career, she has been a frequent lecturer at astrology conferences throughout the United States and Canada. She was UAC's track coordinator for Uranian/Cosmobiology in 1992, 1995, and 2002. Her astrological consultations center around relationships, women's issues, relocation (Astro*Carto*Graphy) and choosing good times to begin ventures (electional astrology). From 1991 to 1993, Hillis-Dineen had a monthly column on astrological money management in *Horoscope Guide* magazine. She is the author of a chapter called "On Singleness: Choosing to Be Me" in the Llewellyn anthology entitled *Astrology for Women: Roles and Relationships*. She was also a frequent contributor for www.stariq.com. She holds a certification as a consulting astrologer from the NCGR and is a certified Astro*Carto*Graphy interpreter. She is also an active member of the Business and Professional Women/USA and was president of the Lower Cape Cod (MA) Chapter.

Hillis-Dineen was born and raised in Brooklyn, New York, and was educated in a small, private Catholic girl's academy during the 1950s and 1960s. Interestingly enough, two other professional astrologers also attended that same academy during those years. She earned a B.S. degree in marketing from St. John's University in 1972.

## Hipparchus

Hipparchus, the preeminent ancient Greek astronomer, lived from approximately 190 B.C.E. to 120 B.C.E. He developed trigonometry, recorded the location of more than a thousand stars, and originated the idea of latitude and longitude. He is said to have discovered the phenomenon known as the precession of the equinoxes. Hipparchus was also a practicing astrologer.

## History of Astrology in America

Astrology came to America during the colonial era along with the entire body of occult teachings available in Europe in the seventeenth century. The first American astrologers, the Rosicrucians, under the leadership of Johannes Kelpius (1673–1708), established an astrological library and conservatory on Wissahickon Creek in what is now the Germantown section of Philadelphia, Pennsylvania. Among other activities, they helped upgrade the almanac already being published by Daniel Leeds, and, in 1698, one of their better astrologers, Johann Seelig, was commissioned to cast the horoscope for the Swedish Lutheran church in Wisaco, Pennsylvania, in order to determine the best date to commence the new building. After the demise of the Chapter of Perfection, as Kelpius's group was known, surviving members became the first hexmeisters, the well-known folk magicians of eastern Pennsylvania.

## European Background

Through the eighteenth and nineteenth centuries, Americans attracted to astrology derived their interest from a flow of material from Europe, even though several almanacs, which passed along astrological data for farming and doctoring, were published in America. After reaching a low point in the eighteenth century, a distinct new era for astrology began in England in the early nineteenth century. This new era can be marked by the 1816 publication of James Wilson's *A Complete Dictionary of Astrology*, which for the first time gave its readers the basic kind of astrological information they needed to construct astrological charts and interpret them. A decade later, Robert C. Smith (1795–1832), writing under the pen name Raphael, launched the first successful astrological publishing house. His first book, *Manual of Astrology*, was an immediate success, but more importantly, he produced an ephemeris, a book of charts showing the position of the planets in the sky day by day. The annual *Raphael's Ephemeris* remains a standard astrological textbook. After Smith's death, a succession of individuals carried on his work, providing the material necessary for those who wished to follow its practice. Wilson, the various Raphaels, and the two men who wrote under the pseudonym of Zadkiel (Richard James Morrison and Alfred J. Pearce) produced the initial library of books that circulated in the United States and through which Americans rediscovered astrology.

At the end of the century, astrology received additional support from the Theosophical Society. The first important Theosophical astrologer, Walter Gorn Old, also assumed a pen name, Sepharial. As popular as Sepharial became—and his books are still in print—his work was eclipsed by that of a man he introduced into the society and to astrology, William Frederick Allen (1860–1917), better known by his pen name, Alan Leo. Allen launched the very successful *The Astrologer's Magazine* (later renamed *Modern Astrology*), and, in 1896, he and Old organized the first modern astrological society. This Astrological Society, soon reconstituted as the Society for Astrological Research, survives today as the Astrological Lodge of the Theosophical Society. Among its outstanding members were Allen's wife, known under her pen name, Bessie Leo, and one of the first British astrologers not to use a pen name, Charles E. O. Carter.

## New Beginnings in America

Throughout the colonial era, America had never been without astrology. As with Europe, astrology had been pushed to the hinterland and for many years survived only in the annual farmers' almanacs. It experienced an initial revival in 1840 when Thomas Hayes began the *Hayes United States Horoscope and Scientific and Literary Messenger,* which lasted for eight years, followed by Mark Broughton's *Monthly Horoscope.* However, it was not until the 1880s with the emergence of Luke Dennis Broughton (1828–1898), Mark's younger brother, that astrology experienced the foretaste of its present success.

Broughton came from a family of astrologers. His grandfather, a physician, had become an enthusiastic student of astrology after reading Culpepper's *Herbal,* which gave information of an astrological nature about each medicinal plant then in a physician's bag. The grandfather passed the interest to Luke's father, who in turn passed it to Luke and his brothers. Mark had begun publishing an almanac and an ephemeris while still living in England, and after migrating to the United States, began his magazine when Hayes's initial effort ceased. In 1860, Luke began issuing *Broughton's Monthly Planet Reader and Astrological Journal* from his Philadelphia home. Three years later, he and his magazine moved to New York City where he launched that city's astrological establishment. He became the major American distributor of British astrological books and the teacher of the next generation of American astrologers.

Broughton authored several astrology books himself. His *Elements of Astrology,* issued the year of his death, summarized astrological knowledge to that point. It its pages the reader could find a history of astrology, a survey of astrological theory, information on horoscope interpretation, and a lengthy apology for astrology in response to its major critics.

The four decades of Broughton's career saw the movement of astrology from an almost nonexistent state to the point where practitioners could be found in all the major cities. Broughton claimed that in 1860 he knew "nearly every man in the United States who had any knowledge of the subject, and probably at that time there were not twenty persons that knew enough of Astrology to be able to erect a horoscope, and they were all either French, English, or German." But 40 years later, Broughton could say, "At the present day [1898] there are many thousand American people who are studying Astrology, and some have become quite proficient in the science."

The growth of astrology in the 1880s and 1890s did not go unnoticed, and attacks upon it were frequent. Broughton assigned himself the role of defender of the faith and at every opportunity made the case for the fledgling science. He went on the offensive against laws that prevented astrologers from freely doing their work. In 1886, he came to the defense of a Mr. Romaine who had been sentenced to 18 months imprisonment for practicing astrology. He accused Romaine's attackers of ignorance. Why, he asked, is "astrology the only science or art in existence concerning which expert testimony is entirely discarded, and in regard to which only the opinions of men who are the most ignorant of the subject are entertained." Broughton would go on to do battle with other debunkers of the heavenly art such as *New York Sun* editor Charles A. Dana, astronomer Richard A. Proctor, and popular encyclopedists Thomas Dick and William and Robert Chambers.

Broughton was, of course, neither the only astrologer nor the only astrology teacher in the late nineteenth century. Boston had developed its own astrological establishment that included astronomer Joseph G. Dalton, who, in 1898, published an American ephemeris. Also, at least three astrological religions had emerged. The first dates to 1876 when Emma Harding Britten published her book *Art Magic*, within which she included the teachings of an occult order, the Brotherhood of Light, which she claimed dated from ancient Egypt. During the early years of the Brotherhood of Light, a young lumberjack, forced out of the business by an accident that cost him several fingers, retired to a hermit's life in rural California. He began to have visions that he shared with others. A group of 12 formed around him and, pooling their resources, moved to Applegate, California, where they formed the Esoteric Fraternity. Hiram Butler, the ex-lumberjack, taught them what he called Esoteric Christianity, a form of Christian occultism. Butler called his astrological teachings *Solar Biology*. It differed from Broughton's more orthodox astrology due to the adjustment Butler made in light of the Copernican insights on the position of the sun. The practical effect of Butler's alternations was to reverse the signs so that a Libyan in solar biology would have all the characteristics of a person born under Aries in the more traditional system.

A third astrological religion, The Order of the Magi (in this case, magi refers to astrologer) was founded in 1889 in Chicago. Its founder, Olney H. Richmond, had begun his occult career while a soldier in the Civil War. Eventually, Richmond became a teacher to a group of 30 men and women and opened an initial temple in Chicago on South Division Street. The following year, a second temple opened in Lansing, Michigan. The emergence of the Order of the Magi and other astrological religions merely underscore the genuine revival of astrology and the occult in general that was occurring in America during the last half of the nineteenth century.

## The Astrological Universe

In trying to present itself anew to the culture that had previously banished it and, therefore, to a public largely ignorant of it, astrology aligned itself to the increasingly influential world of science. The single affirmation common to all of the nineteenth century astrologers was that "astrology is a science." As F. M. Lupton asserted in his book *Astrology Made Easy*, "Astrology is an exact science, and … as a science, is pure mathematics, and there is no guesswork about it." This affirmation was made in the opening paragraph of almost every book published in the nineteenth century on astrology and was repeated frequently throughout the texts.

Like other new "sciences" of the era, such as psychology, astrology had a specific realm of knowledge assigned to it. Astrology described the nature of planetary influences upon human life, and thus the astrologer's task was to know and describe the zodiacal forces and the laws that govern them. Most astrology books would take the reader systematically through each of the signs of the zodiac and the planets and minutely describe the influences exerted by each.

As a science, the astrologers claimed, astrology was not really new, but, rather, thousands of years old. It dated to ancient Chaldea and Egypt. Its influence in biblical times was obvious from the many Old Testament references, and more than one astrologer reminded readers that the New Testament opened with the account of Chaldean astrologers following the star to the Christ child. Astrology as it was practiced in the nineteenth century—and as it is known in the twenty-first century—is ancient. It derived from Ptolemy, the second-century Greek author of the *Tetrabiblos*. In fact, rather than developing a new body of "scientific" knowledge, nineteenth century astrologers merely copied Ptolemy's system and took their information on the significance of the signs and planets from his book.

While affirming astrology as a science, astrologers had to admit it was a science with a slight difference. It was an "occult" science, by which they meant that it described the hidden (and some would say "spiritual") forces of the universe. Astrologers claimed that centuries of observations had demonstrated the truth of their assertions that the planetary movements through the zodiac effected human life. They were, however, at a loss to pinpoint the exact nature of the force or connection between the stars and the earth. They had to fall back upon an esoteric or occult connection.

Most astrologers postulated a universe of heavenly correspondences to earthly conditions. Thomas Burgoyne of the Brotherhood of Light described it succinctly in his book *The Light of Egypt:*

> Astrology, per se, is a combination of two sciences, viz.: astronomy and correspondences. These two are related to each other as hand and glove; the former deals with suns, moons, planets and stars, and the motion, while the latter deals with the spiritual and physical influences of the same bodies; first upon each other, then upon earth, and lastly upon the organism of man.

This law of correspondences had been a major building block of Emanuel Swedenborg's thought in the previous century and ultimately derived from the hermetic principle, "As above, so below." Hermetics assume that the individual was a microcosm of the universe, which was the macrocosm. For astrology, the movement of the planets through the zodiac activated the correspondences. Only in the twentieth century would some astrologers move away from the hermetic approach, though, even today, many rely upon it.

As an occult science, astrology tried to have the best of both worlds. As a science, it was as new and modern as the latest scientific journal and aligned to the wave of the future. As an occult body of thought, it was allowed to make "religious" affirmations about the place of individuals in a universe of meaning, purpose, and morals. Minimally, these affirmations might be little more than reflections about the nature of life, but astrology, taken to its natural conclusion, led directly to the religion of the stars.

Astrologers, even the most secular, were quite aware that they were offering a "religious" alternative to Christianity. In his book *Evolutionism*, Olney Richmond decried as unscientific the traditional Creator Deity who he saw as a mere convenience for those who pretended to give people the directives of the Almighty. "A far off God and a remote heaven," said Eleanor Kirk, in her book *The Influence of the Zodiac upon the Human Life*, "are no longer attractive. The quickening spirit has breathed a thought to those who have ears to hear and hearts to feel, of the Eternal Now, and a God and a heaven in every human soul." The astrologer's God was an impersonal but immanent force or a principle of order and causation. In his book *Solar Biology*, Hiram Butler described God as the Cause World.

The astrological universe, which replaced the traditional Christian one, once pictured God and nature and humanity as intimately connected in a matrix of correlates. God was not someone or something apart from human beings. Each individual, affirmed F. M. Lupton, in his book *Astrology Made Easy*, was a soul that comes from God "and is a part of It—a part of the Great One."

## Astrology and Religion

The twofold nature of the occult science provides the major clue as to astrology's place in the developing culture of the West. Beginning with Deism in the eighteenth century and continuing through Free Thought in the next, religious skeptics conducted an intense attack upon the essential "supernatural" elements in Christianity. In the name of science, critics questioned the existence of a personal Creator God, the viability of prayer, revelation, moral law, and the legitimacy of the church. In the face of a new understanding of the world, the spiritual world of traditional religion was seen the same way as was astrology—simply worthless superstition.

Astrology, as occultism in general, however, aligned itself with this critique of the supernatural in general and Christianity in particular, and throughout the nineteenth century, Free Thought and the occult made common cause. Yet Free Thought had a problem. Few could live with the cold hard universe within which it seemed content to leave humanity. The new occultism offered free thinkers a way both to accept the very compelling critique of supernaturalism and yet to retain a "spiritual" vision that offered many of the benefits of traditional religion without its ecclesiastical trappings. Astrology replaced the controversy between science and religion with a complete capitulation to science, an approach that has allowed it to accept and feed off of each new scientific insight. Most especially, astrology rejoiced in scientific descriptions of the subtle and invisible forces of the universe—from radio waves to gamma rays—as welcome confirmation of its previous insights. More recently, new trends in psychology have been integrated into the astrological universe. Astrology tied itself to the rising wave of science and has ridden that wave to new heights of success and acceptance.

## Astrology in Twentieth-Century America, 1900–1920

The twentieth century for astrology began a year early in a fiery explosion as a new astrological light appeared in the person of Evangeline Adams. A member of the Massachusetts family that had given the country two presidents, Adams was reared in the conservative atmosphere of Andover, a Boston suburb. Though not in Boston itself, she was not so far away to be isolated from the large occult community developing there and in nearby Cambridge. This community included the former president of the Society for Psychical Research, William James, and a number of his academic colleagues. One of these, Dr. J. Heber Smith, a professor of medicine at Boston University, introduced Adams to the practice of astrology and to Eastern religion. Smith introduced the young woman to astrology while she was recovering from a broken leg. She went on to become a serious student of Eastern religion after seeing an Andover professor manhandled in a heresy trial.

In 1899, having chosen astrology already as her life's profession, Adams moved to New York City and took up residence in the Windsor Hotel. A Mr. Leland, the proprietor, became her first client. Since he believed the following day, Friday, March 17, 1899, would bring bad luck, he felt in need of advice. Adams cast his chart only to find him under the "worst possible combination of planets." Danger was imminent and would possibly overtake him the following day. A second check on Friday merely reinforced Adams' opinion that disaster was imminent. Leland walked out of her hotel room to find his fashionable hotel on fire.

Saturday morning, New Yorkers awoke to read of the fire and to a new celebrity in their midst. In bold type on the front page, the newspapers printed Leland's statement that Adams had predicted the fire. Adams became an instant astrological superstar, America's first, and after finding a new office, she began a career as astrologer to the rich, famous, and powerful. She also gave astrology a new level of respectability. By 1914, she had gained enough leverage to challenge and have stricken down New York's statute against "fortune telling," at least as it applied to astrologers.

While astrology continued a powerful force in the East, Chicago, the new occult center of the era, developed its astrological community. At its center was Professor Alfred F. Seward, who for many years published astrological books, taught astrology by mail, and claimed to be America's largest dealer in astrological and occult books. Such proliferation in the East and Midwest set the stage for the emergence of three new astrological giants on the West Coast—Elbert Benjamine, Max Heindel, and Llewellyn George.

Elbert Benjamine (1882–1951) had been a member of the Brotherhood of Light for nine years when, in 1909, he was summoned to the home of one of its governing three and informed that they wanted Benjamine as the order's astrologer. They also wanted him to undertake the task of writing a complete set of lessons on the 21 branches of occult science. The next year he agreed to take the position and assume the task. After five years of preparing himself, in 1915 he began conducting classes to brotherhood members and in 1918 to the public at large. Work on the 21 volumes began in 1914 and took the next two decades. In this task Benjamine wrote under the pen name C. C. Zain, a name he assumed to separate his official Brotherhood of Light lessons from his other numerous writings. He wrote a series of 12 reference books on astrology, a number of booklets and pamphlets, and many articles in astrological and occult periodicals. Under Benjamine's leadership, the Brotherhood of Light developed into a large occult body with centers across the United States and international centers in England, Mexico, Canada, and Chile. It was one of the major teachers of astrologers for the century.

Max Heindel migrated to the United States from his native Germany in 1903. He had been a Theosophist and headed the Los Angeles Lodge in 1904–1905. He was also a student of German theosophist Rudolf Steiner. On a trip to Germany in 1907, Heindel claimed that a being described as an elder brother of the Rosicrucian Order appeared to him. The Rosicrucian led Heindel to a secret temple near the border between Germany and Bohemia and taught him the material later published in *The Rosicrucian Cosmo-Conception*, Heindel's main book. In 1908, Heindel formed the Rosicrucian Fellowship with its first chapter in Columbus, Ohio. Within two years, chapters appeared in Los Angeles; Seattle; Portland; and North Yakima, Washington. In 1911, headquarters were moved to Oceanside, California, where they remain to this day.

While teaching the whole range of occultism, astrology was one of several main interests. Heindel wrote several popular astrological texts, all still in print and used far beyond the fellowship's borders. The fellowship began the publication of an annual *Ephemeris* and a *Table of Houses*, the two necessary reference books used by astrologers. Like the Brotherhood of Light, the fellowship became a national and international organization during the first decades of its existence.

But as outstanding as Benjamine and Heindel were, neither approached in accomplishments Llewellyn George. Born in Wales in 1876, George moved to Chicago as a child and grew up there. At the turn of the century he moved to Portland, Oregon, and in 1901 established the Llewellyn Publishing Company and the Portland School of Astrology. In 1906, he began the annual *Moon Sign Book*, and two years later he began the *Astrological Bulletina*. George's career gained significance by his lifelong attempt to separate astrology from occultism. Such an attempt, which could only be partially successful, was a natural outcome of the articulation of astrology as a science and the growing status that science was gaining in society in general.

George could be successful to the extent he could make his publishing house, school, and magazine concentrate solely upon astrology to the exclusion of such occult topics as card reading, tarot, palmistry, and numerology. He could and did drop much of the traditional occult language of astrology, but failed in separating astrology from the occult in that astrology still had to fall back upon occult explanations of its operation. But George did try to move away from the magical (i.e. hermetic) explanation of astrology. Instead of talking about correspondences between individual and universal phenomena, he spoke of planetary vibrations. Some of these cosmic vibrations were plainly physical (e.g., gravity, radiation, etc.). "A radio broadcasting station," asserted George, in his book *Astrological Charts*, "vibrates all those receiving sets within range which are attuned to it.... Each station sends out its own particular program.... In astrology every planet is a broadcasting station: the nervous system of every person is a 'receiving set'."

George also effectively associated astrology with the findings in the natural sciences rather than the ongoing development of occult thought. He lauded experiments in astrology that demonstrated the truth of particular astrological propositions, while denouncing the misuse of astrology for fortune-telling. But ultimately George's success could only be relative.

Astrology was, and still is, intimately linked to the occult, and no physical "vibrations" or influences were ever located to account for all the astrological effects. Also, most people attracted to astrology were also attracted to the occult in general. Both served the effect of offering a "religious" world view to those who were attracted to science, but who found the various secular philosophies, such as rational humanism, personally cold and unsatisfying. In the end, George's publishing arm, Llewellyn Publications, began circulating its catalog offering hundreds of books on progressive subjects, including psychism, hypnotism, prophecy, spiritualism, character reading, magic, personality, prayer, yogi, personal-development, careers, diet and health, employment, business success, etc.

## Expansion Between the Wars, 1920–1940

Astrology moved into the roaring twenties formally established across the United States and with a growing clientele. However, it still needed to break into the mass market. The two decades between World War I and World War II were the years of that accomplishment.

Prior to 1920, most astrology books were privately published. Only two received the imprint of a major American publisher, Katherine Taylor Craig's *Stars of Destiny* (E. P. Dutton, 1916) and Yarmo Vedra's (a pseudonym) *Heliocentric Astrology* (David McKay, 1910). The attention by major publishers to astrology changed in 1924 when Dodd, Mead and Company published the first of four major volumes by Evangeline Adams, *The Bowl of Heaven*. Within the decade, both J. B. Lippincott and Doubleday had published a line of astrological titles and opened a whole new audience to the wonders of astrological speculations.

Astrology was ready for a growth period in the 1920s and responded to its popularity by fostering a number of successful periodicals. Prior to World War I, several periodicals had been started and attained some degree of success within the astrological community, but as a whole they had been unable to break into the large mass markets or the newsstands. That situation changed in 1923 when Paul G. Clancy began *American Astrology*, the single longest-running astrological periodical. His effort was followed the next year by that of Sidney K. Bennett, better known by his pen name Wynn. *Wynn's Magazine* quickly joined *American Astrology* on the newsstands, and Wynn's books flooded the popular astrology market.

Though several astrological societies had been formed before 1920, the first organizations to claim widespread membership were formed after World War I. In 1923, Llewellyn George and A. Z. Stevenson founded the American Astrological Society, and George helped found the National Astrological Society four years later. That same year, a group of New York astrologers founded the Astrologers' Guild of America. The various national and regional organizations spurred the formation of many local groups, such as the Oakland (California) Astrological Society founded in 1925 and the Friends of Astrology founded in Chicago in 1938. They also led to the formation of the American Federation of Astrologers (AFA) in 1938. The AFA, the most prestigious of the several astrological organizations, has been the most effective force in bringing professionalism to the field and creating a favorable public image for its members.

The massive growth of astrology in the 1920s and 1930s set the stage for another spurt after World War II. Only one step—the spread of the sun-sign columns now carried in most daily newspapers and many monthly magazines—remained to create the popularity level so evident today. Since the turn of the century, astrologers had tried to break into the popular press. Sepharial had a column briefly, but in the end his forecasting ended in disaster for both him and the cause of astrology. Not until 1930 did a successful column appear in England. P. I. H. Naylor wrote it, but it was suppressed in 1942 as England began to use astrology in its intelligence efforts against Hitler. After the war, newspapers on both sides of the Atlantic began to publish astrology columns and quickly recognized their popularity with the public.

## Since World War II

The spectacular spread of astrology through the culture in the second part of the twentieth century was made possible by several developments, the most important being its gradual movement from a base in the hard sciences to one in psychology. The most significant thinker in that transition was Dane Rudhyar (1895–1985). Rudhyar developed what he initially termed harmonic astrology, now called humanistic astrology. Deeply moved by Eastern metaphysics, theosophy and the teachings of Alice Bailey, and the occult speculations of psychiatrist Carl Jung, he was at the same time disturbed by the problems of the older astrology with it psychologically questionable analysis of good and bad points in individual horoscopes, not to mention the irresponsible predictions traditional astrology seemed periodically to suggest to its practitioners. Thus in the 1960s, Rudhyar founded the International Committee for a Humanistic Astrology, which would attempt to orient astrology to the fulfillment of the individual person and to undergird astrological practice with a sound philosophical and psychological perspective.

The transformation of astrological thinking by Rudhyar and his students has been the most significant intellectual development of the discipline, and the least understood by astrology's traditional critics. Using Jung's category of synchonicity, Rudhyar suggested that stellar and planetary bodies did not directly effect humans, merely that the astrological chart has a coincidental relationship to the individual human peculiar psychological makeup (students of astrology will recognize his argument as a very sophisticated recasting of the correspondences theory). By this means, Rudhyar removed the need to find specific physical forces that operated on humans causing the behavioral consequences predicted by astrology. Rudhyar went beyond his predecessors, however, in his suggestion that astrology dealt in possibilities and potentialities inherent within the individual, rather than forces operating on him or her from outside, either from physical or occult forces. Thus, Rudhyar completely discarded any need for empirical verification for astrological insight while at the same time distancing it of its main albatross—determinism. Astrological forces did not determine the future; they merely suggested a future with which the individual could fruitfully cooperate.

Rudhyar's insights finally stripped astrology of the remnant of its "fortune-telling" image and recast it as a psychological helping profession. Contemporary astrologers have little problem with stepping into the role of professional counselors assisting their clients, much as do clinical psychologists and psychotherapists. Psychological counselors have had little base from which to critique their new astrological competitors as their own field has fragmented into numerous competing camps, none of which has a strong empirical base.

Meanwhile, those astrologers who still wish to operate out of a base in hard science have continued to look for specific scientific findings that would support their faith in the direct influence of the planetary bodies on human life. Some spectacular underpinnings came from the study of biological rhythms. The work of biologist Frank A. Brown at Northwestern University demonstrated celestial influences on plant and animal life, and brought the results of the studies of natural rhythms by other scientists to the attention of the astrological community. Even more spectacular, Michel

Gauquelin continued to demonstrate the coincidence of astrological delineations in large samples of various occupational groups. He found that particular planets would be prominent in the ascendant and midheaven of outstanding representatives of the differing occupations tested—scientists, military leaders, sports stars, doctors, and musicians. While Gauquelin presented much data against traditional astrology, only the positive results attracted attention.

In the end, however, the scientific work has had little influence on the developing practice of astrology. Like empirical behavioral studies, empirical studies in astrology have continued but have had little to do with the developing trends in psychological counseling practice.

## Astrology Today

The new wave of astrological thought set in motion by Rudhyar, recent attempts to create a neo-astrology based on science, the continuing allegiance to more traditional astrological schools, and some new forms of astrological practice have mixed and matched to create numerous schools of astrology. They are all inheritors of the efforts of the astrological pioneers who operated in the nineteenth and early-twentieth century without the broad popular acceptance and legal protections that today's astrologers accept as a matter of fact. Given the growth of astrology through the twentieth century, there is no reason to believe that it will not continue to grow and prosper.

In the meantime, all of the astrological schools of thought have been equally affected by the advent of the computer. Given the mathematical nature of the horoscope, the computer arrived on the astrological scene in the 1970s as if it had been created just for the field. Computer programs will not only draw the basic horoscope and note the major aspects, they will run progressions and midpoints, place asteroids, and execute any number of other manipulations. Today, astrologers find their workload immensely reduced by the computer, and all astrologers use them.

—J. Gordon Melton

**Sources:**

Broughton, Luke D. *The Elements of Astrology*. New York: The Author, 1893.

Burgoyne, Thomas H. *The Light of Egypt*. 2 vols. San Francisco: Religio-Philosophical Publishing House, 1884.

Butler, Hiram E. *Solar Biology*. 25th ed. Applegate, CA: Esoteric Publishing Co., 1887.

George, Llewellyn. *Astrological Charts*. Los Angeles: Llewellyn Publications, 1941.

———. *Astrology/What Is It/What It Is Not*. Los Angeles: Llewellyn Publishing Co., 1931.

Heindel, Augusta Foss. *The Birth of the Rosicrucian Fellowship*. Oceanside, CA: The Rosicrucian Fellowship, n.d.

Kirk, Eleanor. *The Influence of the Zodiac upon the Human Life*. New Life: The Author, 1894.

Lupton, F. M. *Astrology Made Easy*. Baltimore: I. & M. Ottenheimer, 1897.

Melton, J. Gordon. *A Bibliography of Astrology in America, 1840–1940*. Santa Barbara, CA: Institute for the Study of American Religion, 1987.

———. *Biographical Dictionary of Cult and Sect Leaders*. New York: Garland Publishing, 1986.

Richmond, Olney H. *Evolutionism*. Chicago: Temple Publishing Co., 1896.

———. *Temple Lectures*. Chicago: The Author, 1891.

## History of Western Astrology

The investigation of the heavenly bodies, in the forms that are now distinguished as astrology and astronomy, began in the European world at the beginning of Greek civilization. The word "astrology" comes from the Greek *astron*, meaning "star," and *logos*, meaning "study"). The study of the stars had both scientific and religious purposes. The rhythms of the stars provided the basis for calculating calendars. The stars also represented a kind of natural watch in a clockless age and provided spatial reference points, important for such practical matters as navigation.

Berosus, a Chaldean priest from Belus who settled in Cos to teach, probably in the early fourth century B.C.E., is traditionally regarded as having introduced astrology to Greece. The Greeks were interested in the study of the stars much earlier, however. The pre-Socratic philosopher Thales (c. 625–c. 547 B.C.E.), who founded the Ionian school, and Pythagoras of Samos (c. 580–500 B.C.E.), founder of Pythagoreanism, had already devoted attention to the stars and speculated about the nature and constitution of the heavenly bodies. The fourth century B.C.E. was particularly fertile for the proliferation of astrology. Plato and Aristotle had a unified view of the universe (Aristotle even spoke of connections between the heavenly bodies and the sublunar world), reflecting Greek culture's Eastern heritage.

Astrology also influenced the study of medicine, as is evident in the work of Hippocrates (c. 460–c. 377 B.C.E.), who lived on the island of Cos. Hippocrates defined the four humors, which are based on the status of blood (warm and moist), yellow bile (warm and dry), black bile (cold and dry), and phlegm (cold and wet), and set forth a correspondence of the humors with the planets. In 140 B.C.E., Hipparchus of Bythnia catalogued 1,081 stars, while a few decades later the Syrian Posidonius of Apamea spread his knowledge of magic and astrology in the school he founded in Rhodes, where both Romans and Greeks studied. Marcus Manilius was probably influenced by Posidonius of Apamea when he wrote his verses entitled "Astronomica."

The Romans, who had an indigenous form of divination traditionally practiced by augurs, received astrology in the second century B.C.E. from Greeks living in the colonies of southern Italy. The Romans adopted the Greek system of the zodiac, naming the planets after Roman-Latin deities (names that are still in use) and naming the seven days of the week after the corresponding planets and deities. This tradition also influenced the English names of the days of the week, which still reflect the ancient connection (e.g., "Saturn-day," "Sun-day," and "Moon-day"). In about 270 B.C.E., judicial astrology and medical astrology were mentioned in the poem "Diosemeia" by the Greek Aratus of Soli. Aratus's poem was translated into Latin and influenced the Romans.

In ancient Rome judicial astrology survived the years of the Republic despite antiastrology efforts by such famous intellectuals as Cato and Cicero (*De divinatione*). In 139 B.C.E., after the unrest of the slaves and the lower class in Rome, astrologers were expelled from the city and from the Roman borders of Italy. Despite this opposition, astrology gradually came to be accepted among intellectuals toward the end of the first century B.C.E., largely as a result of the spread of Stoicism (which had adopted astrology as part of its system). Although during the imperial age astrology was several times forbidden as a private practice, astrologers continued to be consulted by the court. As the empire became Christianized, the Christian church began to officially oppose certain kinds of astrology in the fourth century C.E. (for example, in the writings of the Council of Laodicea).

During Hellenistic times, astrology began to bloom in Egypt through the Alexandrian school, where Babylonian and Egyptian astrological lore mingled with Greek philosophy. The earliest Greek Hermetic literature, in the second century B.C.E., focused on astrology. Fragments of these texts, among which are the Salmeschiniaka and the textbook of Nechepso and Petosiris, have survived in the *Catalogus codicum astrologum Graecorum*, as quotations in some Arabic works of the ninth century, and in later Latin writings. Within the Hermetic tradition, iatromathematics, or medical astrology (through which the various anatomical parts are associated with planets, herbs, and minerals), also developed, deriving its name from the Greek *iatromathematikos*. A poem on astrology, "Astronomica," of which five books still exist, was composed in the early first century C.E. by Manilius. He compiled contemporary knowledge of this science, often in contradictory forms and under the influence of the Stoicist vision of cosmic sympathy and correlation between macrocosm and microcosm. In the second century C.E., Vettius Valens, an Antiochian intellectual operating in Alexandria, Egypt, compiled the *Anthology*, a work on astrology that shows the new concept of this field as a secret art learned through initiation.

Ptolemy, one of the most influential intellectuals in the history of Western astrology, also lived in Alexandria in the second century. His main works were the *Almagest* (Greek, meaning "greatest") and the *Tetrabiblos* (*Quadripartitum* in Latin). The *Almagest* was an astronomy work that taught how to predict celestial phenomena, mostly through the use of mathematics. The *Tetrabiblos* became a major text for astrologers and occultists in the western world for several centuries. Ptolemy gathered the knowledge of Egyptian and Chaldean astrology and interpreted it in the light of Greek philosophy, Stoicism in particular. The Stoic idea that all matter is bound together in a cosmic sympathy became a rational explanation for the relationship between the changes in the universe (macrocosm) and in man (microcosm). Magic and such traditions as number symbolism, chiromancy, and geomancy became attached to astrological divination, although these did not change the basic principles of astrology.

Ptolemy's work was authoritative for centuries, particularly in Constantinople (Byzantium), the capital of the eastern part of the empire, where Greek remained the spoken language. In 500 C.E., Rhetorius introduced, among other new elements, the division of the signs of the zodiac into triplicities, corresponding to the four classical elements (still used in modern astrology). Although some theological schools in Byzantium accepted astrology, several Christian emperors (such as Constantius, Teodosius, and Valerianus) began to proscribe astrology and threatened astrologers with exile. Earlier, in the fifth century, in the Platonic Academy of Athens, the last bulwark of the Greek pre-Christian culture, Proclo (410–485) had commented on the *Tetrabiblos* with regard to the stars as a "secondary cause of earthly events." But in 529, the emperor Justinian (527–565) closed the academy, claiming it was a center of pagan thinking, and many of the scholars from Athens fled to Persia and Syria.

The *Catalogus Codicum Astrologorum Graecorum* shows the large amount of astrology literature that had been produced in Byzantium, although most of the extant manuscripts belong to the twelfth century. In this same century, despite the opposition of the church, there was interest in astrology—sometimes even within the church itself—although the stars were now considered to be signs rather than causes of events.

In the western world the study of the stars, called astronomy, was one of the seven *artes liberales* comprising the education curriculum of the time (along with grammar, rhetoric, dialectic, arithmetic, geometry, and music). The fathers of the Latin church condemned astrology as magic and as pagan. Augustine, referring to astrology in *De civitate Dei* (The City of God), asserted that it was mere superstition. The fundamental astrology text, the *Tetrabiblos*, was not yet known to the Latins, who had only a few sources on astronomy (such as a chapter on astronomy in *The Marriage of Mercury and Phylologiae* by Martianus Capella, the *Commentary* by Macrobius in the fourth century, and the works of Isidore and Bede during the seventh century).

In the sixth century, astronomy was defined by Cassiodoro (490–583), secretary at the court of Teodoricus, the Ostrogoth king of Italy, as the science that examines the heavenly bodies and their relation to one another and to Earth. It was not until the early seventh century that an effort was made to distinguish between astronomy and astrology—in the *Etymologiae* of Isidore, bishop of Seville. The definitions in the *Etymologiae* show how in antiquity it was impossible to consider as independent two arts considered as complementary as these. The study of the stars and the *computus* (the art of computing the calendar) were also part of monastic education, as a tool for calendrical reference to the course of time through the year.

A reawakened interest in astrology in the Western world began under the influence of the Arabs, who had been settled in Spain and Sicily since the eighth century. The Arabs were the heirs of the philosophy and culture of Hellenistic Greece—a heritage they blended with Syrian, Indian, and Persian cultures—and this knowledge began to spread to the schools of northwestern Europe. Although in Islamic culture astrology was generally opposed for many of the same reasons as in Christianity, scientific and intellectual interest in the movements of the stars persisted in the work of such Muslim astrologers as Masha'allah, al-Kindi, Abū Ma'shar, and al-Battani. The works of these scholars were eventually translated into Latin. Al-Kindi and Abū Ma'shar (ninth century) especially provided philosophical underpinnings for astrology, under the influence of Aristotelianism, Neoplatonism, Neopythagoreanism, and Stoicism.

In the early 1100s Ptolemy's *Tetrabiblos* was translated, possibly by Plato of Tivoli, from an Arabic edition that also contained information on Persian and Indian astrology. It became attractive for Western Latin intellectuals to study the astrological system of the Arabs, with its new terminology and complexity, alongside Ptolemy's *Tetrabiblos* and *Almagest*. Also, the discovery of Aristotle's *Physics*, among other works, was instrumental in the following centuries in supporting the validity of astrology in understanding natural science (medicine, alchemy, and meteorology). The intellectual milieu in which this new literature was accepted—the only intellectual milieu of the time before the first universities were founded in the thirteenth century—was that created by the Church. In Europe, paganism had disappeared and the superstitious aspect of astrology, which had been such a cause of concern for Saint Augustine, was now no longer an issue. The scientific aspect of astrology (its relation to alchemy, medicine, and meteorology) was still of interest in this environment.

With the founding of Oxford University (in 1249), astronomy was included in the liberal arts curriculum for its contribution in understanding medicine, meteorology, and alchemy. Judicial astrology, however, was explicitly opposed in the writings of Robert Grosseteste, bishop of Lincoln and chancellor of Oxford University, on the basis of Augustine's position (that astrology denies the will of God). The opposition of the Church to astrology also surfaced in 1277 in the list of statements of condemnation by the bishop of Paris, Stephen of Tempier, who condemned astrology and authors who connected astrology with the sublunar world. Some scholastic theologians (who were influenced by Saint Augustine and later by Aristotelianism), including Albertus Magnus of Cologne (Albert the Great, 1206–1280), accepted the influence of the planets on the lower world. Nevertheless, they denied planetary influence over the human will, because they believed the soul is the image of God. Albertus Magnus recommended the *Almagest* for the study of astronomy and the *Tetrabiblos* for astrology (in their Latin translations). Thomas Aquinas (1255–1274), Magnus's pupil and one of the greatest scholastic theologians, declared, in *Summa theologica* that heavenly bodies indirectly influence the human intellect and thus astrologers can make true predictions. In *De sortibus* and *De judiciis astrorum*, however, he expressed his opposition to horoscopes and election of propitious days.

Although Church intellectuals of the thirteenth century were opposed to the superstitious aspects of astrology, Roger Bacon (1214–1294), the greatest scientist of his time, fully accepted medical astrology. In the following century also, intellectual churchmen were using astrology as an instrument for further understanding science (and for interpreting the Scriptures). Judicial astrology, however, is not even mentioned by such authors as Thomas Bradwardine (archbishop of Canterbury) and Henry of Langestein. The "scientific" application of astrology is reflected in the efforts of the University of Paris to explain the Black Death epidemic that ravaged Europe from 1347 to 1350; contemporary intellectuals were more inclined to attribute the plague to conjunctions of the stars rather than to conduct physical and medical investigations. At the University of Bologna, founded in 1119 for the education of a lay public and less influenced by the Church (though still under its control), students of medicine were required to undertake a four-year program in astrology, which culminated with the *Tetrabiblos* and the *Almagest*. Guido Bonatti, one of the most famous astrologers of the 13th century, was professor at this university and author of *De Astronomia*.

There were a number of other famous astrologers in this period. Michael Scot was court astrologer for Frederick II in Sicily and wrote the *Liber introductorius* as a student manual. Campanus of Novara, one of the few good mathematicians of the time, according to Bacon, wrote the *Sphaera* and the *Theorica planetarum*. In 1327, during the Inquisition, Cecco d'Ascoli was burned at the stake as a heretic. He was an astrologer and magician who had lectured at the University of Bologna and applied astrology to the birth and death of Christ. Although there were undoubtedly political factors behind Cecco's execution, the charge of heresy nevertheless reflected the concern of the Church over astrological matters.

Following the discovery of Arabic texts, the Church absorbed astrology and disapproved of it only when it seemed to imply fatalistic determinism (as in the case of Cecco d'Ascoli), which contradicted man's free will and God's omnipotence. Also, the writings of intellectuals in the fourteenth and fifteenth centuries, such as Nicole d'Oresme, Peter d'Ailly, and Jean Gerson, show that astrology was still part of contemporary science, and few doubts about its validity appear.

In the early Renaissance, various cultural and historical factors contributed to the development of interest in astrology. First, the technological improvement of printing techniques favored the production of ephemerides, almanacs, charts and calendars, and so on. In 1474, the first ephemeris, *Ephemeris ad XXXII annos futuros*, by Regiomantanus (Johann Müller, 1436–1476), eminent mathematician and astronomer, was printed in Nuremberg, and a second edition in Venice in 1484. In 1489, the *Introductorium in astronomia* by Abū Ma'shar was translated into Latin from Arabic.

Another important factor in the new interest in astrology was increased appreciation of the rediscovered classical authors of antiquity, beginning with the first humanists at the end of the fourteenth century. One reason for the new interest in the ancients was the siege of the city of Constantinople by the Turks in 1453, which forced Greek scholars to flee from the city (taking with them their literature) to Italy, a country that had already shown a renewed interest in the classics of the ancient world. Some Greek scholars were already settled in Italy before the siege of Constantinople. Manuel Chrysoloras, whose nephew, Marsilio Ficino (1433–1499), was one of the most important figures in the history of occultism during the Renaissance, went to teach Greek in Florence in 1396. The Florentine court of Cosimo de' Medici was also one of the first cultural centers to offer refuge to the Greeks and, as a consequence, to develop an interest in astrology.

At the Medici court, Ficino and Giordano Bruno (1548–1600) worked as the translators of Plato's writings (thus rediscovering Neoplatonism). Ficino also wrote the *Pimander*, a hermetic work full of astrological elements. A physician as well as an intellectual, Ficino also wrote *De vita libri tres*, a medical treatise on the health of the intellectual; in the third part of the book, "De vita coelitus comparanda," he describes his vision of astrology and planetary influences on one's health.

The intellectuals of the early fifteenth century could read the *Picatrix*, an Arab compilation translated into Spanish (in 1256), which dealt largely with astrological magic and influenced Ficino and his student Pico della Mirandola (1463–1494). The application of astrology to medicine (iatromathematics) received attention from Paracelsus (Bombast von Hohenheim, 1493–1541), who considered astrology a means of understanding one's innate physical disposition and allowing better control of one's life. Medical astrology was also the focus of the *Amicus medicorum*, written in 1431 by Jean Ganivet and in use for the following two centuries throughout the Western world.

Although court astrologers continued to enjoy their position as consultants to kings and princes, their way of doing astrology was the object of an ongoing intellectual debate. The astrology of natal charts and forecasting the future, called judicial astrology, was considered superstitious by the intellectuals of the period. This kind of astrology was contrasted with iatromathematics, the study of the influence of the planets on the physical body. Ficino always disapproved of the use of judicial astrology for divinatory purposes, but devoted the entire third chapter of *De vita* to medical astrology. According to Ficino, however, the planets have an influence only at the moment of birth, while the balance of one's life is determined by one's own will.

The debate over judicial and medical astrology was especially animated after the publication in 1496 of Pico della Mirandola's *Disputationes contra astrologiam*. In this work the author attacked judicial astrology, demonstrated it to be fallible and arbitrary, lacking consensus on its basic principles, and ruled by a materialistic determinism. He argued that astrology cannot be true because it requires an accuracy that is impossible to obtain in interpreting the movements of the stars. But the accusation he leveled against astrologers concerned their use of unclear and contradictory Latin sources in place of Ptolemy, whose work on astrology Pico did consider to be accurate. He was thus not attacking astrology itself. His *Disputationes* became an important work for its influence on the debate over astrology.

A response soon came from Pico's contemporary, Pietro Pomponazzi (1462–1524), a teacher in various Italian universities, who found Pico's observations unscientific and took apart his arguments against astrology. In 1508, Luca Gaurico, author of *Tractatus astrologicus*, published the *Oratio de inventoribus et astrologiae laudibus* to defend astrology. About the same time, the German occultist Cornelius Agrippa (1486–1535), in his *De occulta philosophia*, connected astrology with other magic arts, such as palmistry and alchemy, and laid the groundwork for the future development of astrology in the occultist milieu that arose during the Enlightenment.

One of the most prominent astrologers from Italy in the sixteenth century, the Dominican Tommaso Campanella (1568–1639), wrote six books on astrology free of the superstitious aspects caused by Arabic and Jewish influence and concordant with the teachings of Church theologians (i.e., disapproving of astrological determinism). He also wrote a defense of Galileo, *Apologia pro Galilaeo* (1616). He was twice imprisoned on charges of heresy.

The debate over astrology became intense during the sixteenth century, fueled by Copernicus's (1473–1543) postulation of heliocentrism (and continued into the next century as a result of Galileo's advocacy of that theory). The sixteenth century was also the time of the Reformation and the counter-Reformation, when the Church was particularly sensitive to heresies. In 1533, at the Council of Trent, the Church condemned judicial astrology. In 1586 and again in 1631, a bull was issued condemning astrology, and at the end of the century the Church officially disassociated itself from it. Galileo was denounced for his *Letters on the Solar Spots* (1613) and was condemned by the Church in 1632 for his heliocentrism.

In the same period the English scientist Francis Bacon (1561–1626) demonstrated the invalidity of astrology as commonly practiced, and suggested a system purified of all superstitious elements and in agreement with basic scientific principles. According to Bacon, astrology cannot be applied to the individual but can help to predict mass changes and movements of heavenly bodies or people. Although Bacon attacked all superstition, as a scientist of the seventeenth century he still accepted astrology as a divinatory system.

Astrology still survived in the academic milieu as iatromathematics in the seventeenth century. But with the progress of medicine as an empirical science, medicine ultimately became a distinct field of investigation. At the same time, the slow process of the evolution of astronomy as a descriptive science, which had begun with the new Copernican tables (1551), gradually widened the gap between divinatory astrology and scientific astronomy.

Astrology continued to be practiced throughout the sixteenth century in various parts of western Europe. In France, another member of the Medici family, Catherine, previously in contact with the astrologer Luca Gaurico, contributed to the spread of astrology in that country. She married Henry II and, after many years without children, consulted astrologers. The birth of her first child strengthened her faith in astrology. Among the astrologers invited to work at her court was Nostradamus (Michel de Nostredame, 1503–1566), an astrologer who became notorious for his prophecies written in quatrain in the poem called *Centuries* (1555). Working at Henry II's court, Nostradamus became known throughout the whole country, publishing almanacs and medical works that advocated the use of astrology for medical purposes.

While Copernicus's heliocentrism was gradually introduced into England through the works of Thomas Digges and Thomas Bretnor, lay societies of professionals, not necessarily tied to the universities or to the Church, began to organize to discuss the new science. In England the Royal Society of London was chartered in 1662 by Charles II. At the time, England and Holland were the only two countries in Europe to offer freedom of thought during a period of strict censorship by both the Catholic and Protestant churches in all the other European countries. Astrology was not included among the principal subjects discussed by the Royal Society, but some of its members were practicing it.

In the seventeenth century, astrology was no longer debated in European universities. Also, there is little in the historical record regarding astrologers in the 1700s and 1800s. Astrology did not die during this period; it was merely neglected in academic and scientific debate. Modern thought, which began with the Enlightenment, excluded astrology as an empirical science. It was not included, or even mentioned, in the entry on astronomy in Diderot and d'Alembert's extensive *Encyclopedia* in 1781.

Astrology and its symbolism survived the Enlightenment, however, in esoteric circles. Various occultists revived the magic writings of the *Picatrix* and the *Corpus hermeticum* of the Renaissance and kabbala to give a new, more esoteric interpretation, of the movements of the stars. Precursors of this "modern" vision of astrology were Emanuel Swedenborg (1688–1772) and Franz Anton Mesmer (1733–1815). The European astrological revival in the nineteenth century began in England. Francis Barrett, who wrote *The Magus* (1815), an important synthesis of magical lore, and Nicolas Culpepper, an astrologer, had already devoted their time to the study of occultism. But interest in astrology reawakened with the publication of certain books on the subject. In 1816, James Wilson wrote *A Complete Dictionary of Astrology*, and a few years later Robert C. Smith (1795–1832), whose pen name was Raphael, wrote the *Manual of Astrology* and compiled his *Ephemeris*. New works on astrology followed, such as Ely Star's *Les mystères de l'horoscope* in 1887. Also important was Eliphas Lévi

(1810–1875), the modern magician, who synthesized ancient esotericism and developed a new form of magic. A relevant work on astrology was written in 1915 by Aleister Crowley (1875–1947), a famous English occultist. He was a member of the Hermetic Order of the Golden Dawn, a magical society founded by S. L. MacGregor Mathers, who was learned in kabbala and magic. Crowley wrote *Astrology* in 1915, in which he taught a scientific astrology that reinterpreted the science of the stars in light of the discovery of the last two planets, Neptune (1846) and Uranus (1781).

A revival of astrology also took place within the Theosophical movement, started by Madame Helena Blavatsky in 1875 in the United States. Astrology became the focus of the Astrological Lodge of the Theosophical Society (which publishes *Astrology Quarterly*), founded in 1915 by Alan Leo (1860–1917), an important author in the British revival of astrology. Leo was initiated into theosophy by his friend W. Gorn Old (1864–1929), whose pen name was Sepharial, a man learned in astrology and kabbala. From the theosophical movement and the Astrological Lodge—where another famous astrologer, Charles Carter, was trained in astrology—the Faculty of Astrology and the Astrological Association were founded in England a few decades later. Leo's work also influenced the German Uranian system (Hamburg Astrology School, founded by Alfred Witte and Friedrich Sieggrün in the 1930s), cosmobiology (a scientific school of astrology founded by Reinhold Ebertin in the 1930s that averred the existence of a physical connection between the movements of the stars and human behavior), and the Dutch Ram School. Within the theosophical milieu, Alice Bailey (1880–1949), founder of the Arcane School, devoted the third volume of the trilogy *A Treatise on the Seven Rays* to astrology. According to D. K., the Tibetan master channeled by Alice Bailey, astrology was the most occult science. Bailey's work contributed to the revival of astrology in the twentieth century.

Astrology also developed in France through the symbolist school. It drew upon the depth psychology of famous psychologist and psychiatrist Carl Jung (1875–1961), who explained astrology via his notion of synchronicity. For Jung, astrology embodied some of the archetypes that play an important role in the development of the human mind. The French symbolist school, in the same way, aimed at freeing astrology from its rigid mechanistic structure to enable a more descriptive approach to personality through the understanding of astrological symbols.

Under Jung's influence, astrology was also revived for application to psychology in humanistic astrology as the North American counterpart of the French symbolist school. As such, astrology's focus is not centered on events but on the person. Humanistic astrology was initially formulated by Dane Rudhyar, whose benchmark work in the field was *The Astrology of Personality: A Reformulation of Astrological Concepts and Ideals in Terms of Contemporary Psychology and Philosophy* (1936). Rudhyar was particularly influenced by the humanistic psychology of Abraham Maslow.

An effort to use a scientific approach, based on the application of statistical methodology, to astrology was carried out in the early twentieth century by Paul Choisnard and Karl Krafft. Their studies convinced them that "astrology exists." In 1950, Michel and Françoise Gauquelin again applied statistics to the study of astrology, testing a large number of individuals (approximately 25,000) according to profession. They found a correlation different from the traditional astrological one. The resulting controversy polarized modern astrology into humanistic astrology (which opposes the mechanical determinism of the scientific school) and scientific astrology (which claims to be empirical).

The French astrologer André Barbault wrote *De la psychanalyse a l'astrologie* (1961), in which he demonstrated the similarity between the psychological determinism of certain contemporary trends of psychoanalysis and the cosmic determinism of ancient astrology. Barbault was also the first to design a computer program that enabled astrologers to cast horoscopes. While Barbault's work continued the tradition of scientific astrology, a British astrologer, Sybil Leek (1923–1983), strengthened the occultist aspect of this ancient art. Leek moved to the United States later in her life, and through her several books, many of them on astrology, she contributed to the spread of witchcraft (she was a "white" witch) and astrology.

More recently, a revival of astrology has occurred within the subculture referred to as the New Age movement. The New Age began in the late 1960s in the United States and arrived in Europe soon afterward. The New Age, which was originally called the Age of Aquarius, is conceived of in terms of astrological symbolism. The New Age movement also draws upon a holistic vision of reality that is reminiscent of the unified vision of the cosmos of the ancients. The unity and correspondence of micro- and macro-cosmo legitimizes the use of an ancient art that, for the scientific milieu and for mainstream religion, is mere superstition. Today, astrological horoscopes are included in a great majority of popular magazines and other "checkout counter" literature. Periodical publications specializing in astrology are published all over Europe and in the United States for all kinds of audiences, from the most popular to the most sophisticated Although astrological charts are no longer cast for princes and kings, and astrology is no longer used to interpret major historical and natural phenomena, it still plays a large role in modern society. Today, astrology is the tool of individuals for the interpretation of their everyday life, from business to love affairs. In this form, astrology seems certain to survive into the future.

—Isotta Poggi

**Sources:**

Brau, Jean-Louis, Helen Weaver, and Allan Edmands. *Larousse Encyclopedia of Astrology*. New York: New American Library, 1980.

Filbey, John, and Peter Filbey. *The Astrologer's Companion*. Wellingborough, Northamptonshire, UK: Aquarian Press, 1986.

Gettings, Fred. *Dictionary of Astrology*. London: Routledge & Kegan Paul, 1985.

Kitson, Annabella, ed. *History and Astrology: Clio and Urania Confer*. London: Mandala, 1989.

Tester, Jim. *A History of Western Astrology*. New York: Ballantine, 1987.

## Hoen, Joyce

Joyce Hoen was born on January 24, 1953, in the Netherlands. She taught medical astrology at a school for natural health in the Netherlands from 1988 to 1995. During that time, in 1991, she created and taught at the Centre of Humanistic and Transpersonal Astrology in her hometown of Zutphen. In 1996, she organized an international astrology conference in Amsterdam (at the now extinct Oibibio Centre) after having organized with Tees Reitsma of Astrokring many spiritual astrology workshops between 1988 and 1993.

From 1997 to 1999, Hoen had her own national spiritual and astrology radio program on Q Radio until the station had to stop because of a lack of funds. In 1998 she started email courses in astrology. She is the vice president for the Netherlands branch of the International Society for Astrological Research (ISAR) and she edits its weekly email newsletter. She is a freelance astrologer for the Dutch health magazine *Sante* and provides chart interpretations for a weekly television program.

Hoen also has a busy consulting practice and has done thousands of charts. She conducts spiritual master classes in astrology in a nature resort with students and astrologers from all over the Netherlands and Belgium. She lectures in Europe and the United States and taught at the Faculty of Astrological Studies in the summer of 2002. Her take on astrology is spiritual and is influenced by Dane Rudhyar's and Alexander Ruperti's approach.

## Homosexuality and Astrology

The treatment of homosexuality in astrology has tended to reflect the social conditions and the attitude toward homosexuals at the time. Ptolemy, the father of Western astrology, very matter-of-factly mentions patterns that distinguish homosexuals from heterosexuals in his classic work *Tetrabiblos*. If Venus (the ruler of romantic relationships) and Jupiter precede the Sun in a man's chart, and if the former two planets also aspect Mars (the ruler of passion), then he will be sexually interested only in other males. If, on the other hand, Mars and Venus are in masculine signs in a woman's chart, she will be inclined to lesbianism. In another place, Ptolemy notes that links between Mercury (corresponding to the Greek Hermes) and Venus (Greek Aphrodite) indicates an attraction to young men. This interpretation may have been suggested by the joining of the Greek names of these two planets, which results in *Hermaphroditos*.

By way of contrast, astrologers who matured during a period of time when society viewed homosexuality as a behavior disorder tend to attribute interest in the same sex to certain afflictions in a horoscope. Charles E. O. Carter, an important astrologer of the early twentieth century, discussed homosexuality under the heading "Immorality (Sexual)" in his *Encyclopedia of Psychological Astrology*. Carter saw the key to homosexuality in Uranus (ruler of, among other traits, eccentricity) and Neptune (ruler of, among other characteristics, secrets, deception, and hidden things). A native with a poorly aspected Uranus, particularly when Venus was involved, was thought to be a prime candidate.

As homosexuality has acquired a more acceptable position on the sexual landscape, astrological speculations that attributed same-sex preference to difficult aspects and unfavorable placements have been quietly put aside. The contemporary astrological community is highly tolerant of unconventional sexual orientations, and there now exist sun-sign guides to love and romance expressly for homosexuals (e.g.,

Michael Jay's *Gay Love Signs*). There is no general agreement, however, on the process of determining sexual orientation from a birth chart.

**Sources:**

Carter, Charles E. O. *An Encyclopedia of Psychological Astrology*. 1924. Reprint, London: Theosophical Publishing House, 1963.

Dynes, Wayne R. *Encyclopedia of Homosexuality*. 2 vols. New York: Garland, 1990.

van Dam, Wim. *Astrology and Homosexuality*. York Beach, ME: Samuel Weiser, 1985.

## Hopi

Hopi, asteroid 2,938 (the 2,938th asteroid to be discovered, on June 14, 1980), is approximately 25.4 kilometers in diameter and has an orbital period of 5.6 years. Hopi was named after the Hopi tribe of North American Indians. Jacob Schwartz gives the astrological significance of this asteroid as "territorial disputes, minority experiences, Native Americans." According to Martha Lang-Wescott, Hopi represents the awareness of oppression and prejudice. This asteroid also represents the principle of "ambush," including psychological ambush. This asteroid's key words are "prejudice" and "ambush."

**Sources:**

Lang-Wescott, Martha. *Asteroids-Mechanics: Ephemerides II*. Conway, MA: Treehouse Mountain, 1990.

———. *Mechanics of the Future: Asteroids*. Rev. ed. Conway, MA: Treehouse Mountain, 1991.

Schwartz, Jacob. *Asteroid Name Encyclopedia*. St. Paul, MN: Llewellyn Publications, 1995.

## Horary Astrology

Horary astrology is one of three branches of the general category of interrogatory astrology, literally, the astrology of questions. The other two branches are electional and event interpretation.

Horary astrology requires a question to be posed by a querent; and the simpler and clearer the question, the better. The purpose of horary method is then to provide a means to answer the question.

As a technology for answering a specific question using astrological methods, horary can also be considered a type of divination. As such, it is akin to I-Ching, tarot, geomancy, and many other divinatory practices.

The horary process can, for simplicity's sake, be divided into three components:

Defining and asking the question
Describing the circumstances surrounding the question, i.e., proving the question
Providing an answer to the question

## Defining and Asking the Question

A good horary question is clear, answerable, and can only be asked once. In order to avoid the consequences of asking the same question twice, it is possible to limit a question to a particular time interval. Thus, one may encourage the querent to prefer the wording, "Will I get married within two years (or another time interval)?" to "Will I *ever* get married?"

Taking the time and noting the place of a horary question are important. The clock time taken for a horary question is when the querent finds it almost impossible to not know the answer any longer. This is called the moment. Deciding which location to use if the querent and the astrologer are separated by distance varies depending on the educational lineage of the astrologer. Schools deriving primarily from classical methods favor using the astrologer's location, while schools deriving from Ivy Goldstein-Jacobson prefer the querent's location.

## Describing the Circumstances Surrounding the Question

By the medieval period, astrologers had begun to notice certain general chart configurations that portended specific answers. These came to be called the "considerations against judgment." While it seems that every astrologer had a somewhat different list, the concept is simple: if one of the considerations is present, there is a problem related to the asking of the question. This is where the astrologer decides whether the question can and should be answered.

In the twentieth century, it became common to use the considerations as a reason *not* to answer the question, but no evidence exists showing this being done consistently before the modern era. In most cases, the considerations themselves become part of the delineation of the answer.

The main considerations are:

The placement of Saturn: If in the first house, the querent may be lying or misleading. In the seventh, the astrologer may not be properly placed to answer this question unless it is of a seventh house nature, in which case Saturn simply becomes part of that delineation. (For example, if the question concerns marriage, and Saturn is in the seventh house, then it may become a significator of the quesited or tell something about the potential marriage partner. Since seventh-house questions include marriage, buying and selling, and theft, it is very common for this consideration to not apply. It is then not considered to be a warning concerning the astrologer. Also, if Saturn is dignified, these house placements may not qualify as true considerations, because then Saturn is not considered so malefic.) In the tenth house, the querent may damage the reputation of the horary astrologer.

Ascendant or Moon in the *Via Combusta* (the zone from 15° Libra to 15° Scorpio: This is considered to be a malefic section of the zodiac. As there have been other degree spans mentioned by the ancient astrologers, it is unclear exactly what the *Via* is. It is also not known whether the reference is tropical or sidereal.

Ascendant too early or too late: An early ascendant of 3° or less may mean either that it is too early to ask the question, or that there is much free will in place to presume to give an answer. A late ascendant, generally 27° or later, means that there is nothing that the querent can do to change the outcome: other plans and events have happened rendering the question moot.

Moon void-of-course: As the Moon traverses a sign it (usually) makes aspects to the Sun and other planets. It is as if the Moon still has work to do. After the Moon has completed the last aspect to a planet, its condition is said to be void-of-course, or *vacua cursus*. The aspects in use were the five ptolemaic aspects and the bodies, the Sun through Saturn. In classical times, the Moon was not void-of-course if occupying four signs: Cancer, Taurus, Sagittarius, and Pisces (i.e., the Moon's own sign and exaltation sign, and Jupiter's two signs). There are multiple interpretations to what this means in practice. The simplest starting point is to be aware that most timing in a horary comes from the Moon: when void-of-course, there are no events being recorded by the Moon.

The planetary hour matches the ascendant ruler by triplicity (i.e., their signs are in the same element). The use of planetary hours in modern times has dwindled, but traditionally, these were supposed to match, sharing an affinity between the question and the moment.

The traditional purpose of the considerations was to look for issues that would make judgment difficult.

### Providing an Answer to the Question

Generally, the astrologer needs to be able to do the following things to delineate the question:

1. Describe the querent.
2. Describe the quesited (that which is asked about).
3. See if there is any relationship between the two.
4. Provide some detail on how the querent does or does not attain the desired end.

The querent is always given by the first house. The possible significators for the querent are:

The Ascendant itself
The Ascendant Ruler
Planets in the first house
The Moon, occasionally, but this is problematic, because what the Moon really shows in the chart is the sequence of events

A similar list can be drawn up for the quesited, but which house rules (if any) the quesited must be decided first. The quesited is shown by:

The House represented by the nature of the Question
The Ruler of that house
Planets in that house

The following list shows house rulerships for various types of questions, done in the classical style.

First House: Longevity, health (disease is sixth), happiness, moving vehicles (planes, trains, and automobiles), best period in life, the visiting team in most sporting events.

Second House: Money, financial instruments directly convertible into cash (bank accounts, CDs, guaranteed bonds), salary, moveable objects (things you can pick up and carry by yourself), lawyer acting in your behalf in a lawsuit (i.e., barrister).

Third House: Neighbors, siblings, cousins of the same generation in age, primary education, short trips, religious matters, whether the rumor is true, writing.

Fourth House: Your father (usually), property (whether land or buildings), hidden or buried treasure, your home, inheritance of land, the home team in many sporting events, gardeners or other workers who do landscaping or other outside work.

Fifth House: Entertainment, sex, pleasure, gambling, ambassadors, bribery, gifts, the stock market and other riskier investments, alcohol and recreational drugs, children, procreation.

Sixth House: Pets, disease, accidents (e.g., car accidents), employees or day laborers, small animals (i.e., smaller than a sheep, but also includes large but domesticated dogs such as St. Bernards), birds, labor unions (the unions themselves, not labor actions).

Seventh House: Marriage and marriage partners, partnerships of all sorts (business as well as intimate), open enemies, thieves, the other party in a buying and selling transaction, a contract labor or subcontractor situation, the default other person, the other side in a lawsuit or negotiation, the other possibility for the home team in a sporting event, removals (or moving house).

Eighth House: Death, taxes, wills, insurance, your partner's money, inheritances other than of property, lawyer representing the other side in a lawsuit.

Ninth House: Travel, long trips, philosophy, religion, prophetic dreams, lawyers, higher education.

Tenth House: Your mother (usually), honors and awards, promotions, high managerial jobs, judge in a lawsuit, arbiter in a negotiation, bosses higher up in the corporate ladder, perks given out at the whim of someone higher up.

Eleventh House: Friends, associations, organizations, funding bodies of government agencies, hopes and wishes.

Twelfth House: Witchcraft, hidden enemies, imprisonment, all institutions of confinement, hospitals, self-undoing, large animals (horses, elephants, whales).

Having defined querent and quesited, the astrologer has three steps left. First, there may be specific rules that apply to the particular type of question. For example, there are specific rules for determining whether an object is lost or stolen that are considerably more complex than simply determining the house rulership of the object.

Second, the astrologer needs to decide whether the question is resolved through perfection or emplacement. A perfection horary requires that some sort of action(s) or event(s) happen in order for the result to be brought about. An emplacement horary relies purely on where the planets are positioned at the time of the horary, not where they will be sometime later. Lost items, and missing people or animal horaries are the emplacement type horaries. Most other horary questions require the significators' perfection.

The most common perfection is an approaching aspect of the querent's planet to the planet symbolizing the quesited. Usually, only the ptolemaic aspects (conjunction, sextile, square, trine, and opposition) are allowed, but differing horary systems may include the parallel or quincunx. In a perfection, the faster-moving body must catch up to the slower, generally, without the planets changing sign.

Many authors also allow for perfection by mutual reception between the significators of the querent and quesited.

The next most common means of perfection is translation. In translation, a fast-moving body (generally the Moon, but occasionally Venus or Mercury) separates from one of the significators, and applies to the other one.

There is one very rare means of translation, which is very powerful: collection, which occurs when the faster moving body is separating from the slower moving one, but both are applying to yet a slower body. The slowest one then "collects" the other two.

In addition to these means of achieving perfection, there are also other ways to thwart a perfection. These include:

Refranation: In this case, the two bodies are moving toward perfection, but before the aspect becomes exact, the faster-moving body turns retrograde, and the aspect never happens until after that body goes direct again, if at all in the same sign. This is one of the most frustrating scenarios, because everything appears to be moving in the right direction until things suddenly veer off.

Frustration: In this case, again the significators appear to be moving to perfection, but this time the slower-moving planet achieves a partile aspect with a different body before the faster moving body catches up. Again, this scenario shows hope until the person represented by the slower-moving significator goes off in a different direction.

Prohibition: The significators are moving to perfection, but a swifter body intervenes and completes aspects with both bodies first.

Besiegement: If a significator is between two malefics, it is besieged. It is not at all clear how large an orb should be allowed for this. The concept for besieged is: between a rock and a hard place. A besieged planet is not free to act as it is hemmed in on all sides.

If the outcome of the question is negative, the horary astrologer is finished at this point. If the outcome is positive, then there is one more job: attempting to determine the timing of the events leading to the result, or determining the spatial relationship to the object in question in the case of a lost object.

Timing comes from looking for a degree separation between any of the following:

The significators of the two parties in a simple perfection
The Moon and one of the significators
A significator and a nearby house cusp
The number of degrees until the Moon changes sign, especially if the Moon is in the late degrees of a sign.

There are actually two scales of time: symbolic and ephemeris. Symbolic time (a difference of degrees between the two significators applied to produce time units through the following table) is used most of the time, unless some significant ephemeris event itself may impact the outcome. If, for example, a significant planet is about to go retrograde or direct, it is common to refer to the actual station date as the critical timing date. The units of time to go with these numbers are given in the following table.

### Units of Time Based on the Qualities of the Significators

| **Angular** | **Succedent** | **Cadent** |
|---|---|---|
| Cardinal = days | Cardinal = weeks | Cardinal = months |
| Mutable = weeks | Mutable = months | Mutable = years |
| Fixed = months | Fixed = years | Fixed = unknown |

Of course, much of the time one gets mixed indicators: for example, one significator will be cardinal cadent, while the other is fixed succedent. In these cases, an adjustment of the units of time may be in order. The units of time also vary according to the nature of the question itself.

Direction is not always so obvious, in part because of the frequency of having mixed indicators. The general idea is to take the major significators in the chart and examine their location by sign and by house. If the bulk of the planets are either in one house or one sign, then one can translate this into compass location using the cardinal points of the chart: the ascendant as east, etc.

Horary was already well developed by the first century C.E., as demonstrated by the work of Dorotheus of Sidon. In this remarkable work, Dorotheus presented interrogatory methods for such questions as building or demolishing a building, buying and selling, requesting a gift, marriage, whether a pregnancy will come to term, debt, travel, buying or building a ship, imprisonment, lawsuits, theft, fugitives, illness, and bewitchment. While a modern horary astrologer would not likely follow all of his methods, his presentation is quite readable and logical to modern eyes.

The viewpoint that infused Dorotheus was that all forms of interrogations are interpreted with the same methods, except where the type of interrogation forces a change in usage. Furthermore, there is a hierarchy among the three branches, which applies to deciding upon the appropriate time to use for a question. For example, when it comes to theft, if the time of the theft is known, then a chart for the event is drawn. A horary is used only if that time is not known. While the differences between reading an event chart and a horary are often not explicitly mentioned, the most important is that in a horary, the ascendant gives the querent, while in either event interpretation or electional, the ascendant gives the event itself. Event interpretation is generally for a past event, horary for the present, and electional for the future.

Most likely, horary is much older than the first or second century in which Dorotheus lived. This is because Dorotheus's work looks too sophisticated to be a first-generation codification, and because Vedic astrology has an absolutely equivalent branch called *prashna*, which is probably equally ancient. At this time, it is impossible, based on manuscripts and artifacts alone, to decisively nail down the exact nature of the cross-fertilization of Western and Hindu methods. It is clear that there was extensive sharing of knowledge between the two cultures. For example, the words used by Vedic astrologers for the planets are transliterations of the Greek planet words. It was easy to postulate that the major source of "sharing" occurred when Alexander the Great invaded Western India in 327 C.E. However, it now appears that sharing between cultures was far more extensive and over a far greater time period than had been previously thought possible.

There are several extant *katarche* (the Greek word for interrogation) from the fifth-century astrologer Palchus. Mixed in with questions about taming lions and ships at sea, Palchus included charts of political events: a disastrous crowning of a king and the time when a prefect entered Alexandria.

Horary was passed on as one of many techniques when large numbers of Greek manuscripts were translated into Arabic in the period around the eighth century C.E. Because the Islamic expansion extended into India, this was another period of technique-sharing between East and West. Dorotheus was one of the authors translated into Arabic, so his methodology became generally known and influential on subsequent generations of astrologers. Later authors expanded on the Hellenistic authors. William Lilly, the great seventeenth-century horary astrologer, cited Zael, one of the ninth-century Jewish horary astrologers. The tenth-century astrologer Al-Biruni (973–1048?) also included horary as part of his work.

Just as the eighth century represented a bonanza for Arabic-speaking intellectuals, the twelfth century was the same for Latin-speaking ones, as that marked the watershed for the translation of Arabic materials into Latin. To fully understand the significance of this transmission, it is important to recall what actually happened to astrology in the Arabic period:

> Hellenistic (and Persian, i.e., Babylonian) methods were translated into Arabic and studied.
> Vedic methods were also translated in Arabic.
> Hellenistic (Western) and Vedic methods could be combined and synthesized.
> The Arabic-speaking practitioners themselves added and modified the inheritance they received.

The influx of material into the Latin West was even more extensive than that experienced by the Arabic scholars four centuries before. Thus, when Guido Bonatti wrote on horary in the thirteenth century, the tradition he built upon was already rich.

The medieval horary astrologer practicing in the West navigated turbulent waters since the very essence of horary astrology—divination—was at best an uncomfortable topic for the Christian church, and at worst, a mortal sin. Church philosophers postulated that if one can really predict human behavior, then the individual is not "free" to choose Christ and salvation. While other branches of astrology can adopt the position that the stars incline, but do not compel, doing so for horary would destroy its very substance, which is the prediction of human behavior. The church had effectively restricted prophesy as its own perquisite, banning and anathematicizing it in other quarters. So despite brilliant individual horary astrologers like Bonatti, most portions of horary apart from medical usage were outside the pale of acceptable astrological behavior for much of the Middle Ages. Yet somehow, its rules continued to be transmitted to future generations, and no doubt individual astrologers continued to answer their own questions.

The survival of horary astrology is due in no small part to the fact that people continued to ask the kind of questions that are the grist for horary astrology: Will I marry X? Is she a virgin? Where is my brother's ship? Will my son die in the war? The people wanted the answers, while the church said it either was not possible to have them, or the answers were from a demonic source. This hardly represented a stable situation.

Ultimately, every town had its own cunning man or woman. He or she would either "fix" the problem, or at least explain what was going to happen. These people were often the targets of the Inquisition in Catholic countries, but they flourished in Protestant ones, as long as they kept a low profile. *How* they did their job might vary, with prayer a frequent accompaniment, but there were herbalists, palmists, readers of bird lore, physiognomists, scryers, talisman makers, psychics, and some astrologers. The astrology practiced might have been primitive by the usual standards, but as literacy increased and books became more available, astrological technique became increasingly available.

The Renaissance had opened the door on classical learning, and it was never completely closed again after that. Part of what this opening represented was an alternate source of knowledge, one not controlled by the church. Distracted by the rise of Protestantism, the Catholic Church was never able to regain the keys to knowledge. It was in this heady mix of the sixteenth and seventeenth centuries that horary once again flourished. The foremost practitioner of this period, who still influences horary, was William Lilly (1602–1681). His 854-page masterwork, *Christian Astrology* (1647), is one of the most significant works on the subject. What made Lilly's work both great and enduring was that he not only covered the theory, but he also provided sufficient examples so that the reader could really work through his method.

By the time of Lilly's death, unfortunately, horary astrology had gone increasingly out of fashion. Lilly had been involved in producing political propaganda in the form of almanacs and broadsides for the Parliamentary faction in the English Civil War. While that side "won" the war in the sense that they ousted (and beheaded) the king, after a relatively short period, the monarchy was restored. In this new social climate, prophesy that could have religious and political implications was frowned upon. In addition, the "new" scientific (i.e., secular) paradigm had asserted itself, and all forms of the occult became suspect. Astrology went into decline.

Fortunately, astrology was revived in the eighteenth century. Ebenezer Sibly's large work in 1817 on astrology, which went to many editions both before and after his death, included a substantial section on horary technique with his own chart examples. Sibly's technique was on a par with late-seventeenth-century astrologers, an observation that unfortunately does not hold true for the next generations. The nineteenth-century environment in which astrology again flourished was one in which matters of the occult generally had become increasingly popular, in part as a reaction to excessive reason in the century prior.

Zadkiel (Richard James Morrison, 1795–1874) is today the best known of the nineteenth-century horary cohort. Zadkiel thought highly enough of Lilly to produce an abridged version with his own material tacked on, a work that still confuses modern horary astrologers, who often mistake it for the original *Christian Astrology*. Zadkiel and his contemporary Raphael (Robert Cross Smith, 1795–1832) both substantially simplified the astrology of their ancestors, with Zadkiel going in a "scientific" direction that would have been frankly unrecognizable to Lilly.

Many, if not most, astrologers dabbled with horary, even if it was not the bulk of their practice. For example, *The Astrologer's Magazine* featured a regular horary column by "E. Casael." This magazine was published by Alan Leo and his wife Bessie.

In the early part of the twentieth century, Leo substantially changed his astrological method to emphasize character analysis over predictive technique. It was from these changes that both psychological astrology and esoteric astrology were ultimately based.

In the wake of these new forms of astrology, it is not surprising that one of the major trends of twentieth-century horary was to add natal methods to horary delineation, and to combine horary with natal method.

Among the significant twentieth-century horary astrologers were:

Marc Edmund Jones (1888–1980): While Jones's method is often opaque, in great part because of a lack of examples, his philosophical discussion of "Phrasing the Question" and "Locating the Question" are useful reading even to classicists.

Ivy Goldstein-Jacobson (1893–1990) practiced in California, writing a number of books. She adapted some classical methods, adding the use of the word "cautions" for the considerations against judgment, and was adamant that the horary had to be calculated for the location of the querent, not the horary astrologer. She was inadvertently the originator of the idea that planets in mutual reception "swap" or "exchange" places. She also popularized the use of the parallel and added decanates to horary delineation.

Barbara Watters (1907–1984) allowed the quincunx as an aspect, brought back the use of eclipses in horary delineation, and used the word "strictures" for the considerations against judgment (thereby allowing later horary astrologers to refer to the "cautions and strictures" and to attempt to distinguish between them).

Olivia Barclay (1919–2001) was largely responsible for the current popularity of William Lilly and the revival of classical methods in horary astrology. Originally trained in Goldstein-Jacobson's methods, Barclay switched when she accidentally found a partial original copy of Lilly in a used-book shop.

—J. Lee Lehman, Ph.D.

**Sources:**

Al-Biruni, Abu'l-Rayhan Muhammed ibn Ahmad. *The Book of Instruction in the Elements of Astrology*. 1029. Translated by R. Ramsay Wright. London: Luzac & Co., 1934.

Barclay, Olivia. *Horary Astrology Rediscovered*. West Chester, PA: Whitford Press, 1990.

Chevalier, Jacques M. *A Postmodern Revelation: Signs of Astrology and the Apocalypse*. Toronto: University of Toronto Press, 1997.

Cornelius, Geoffrey. *The Moment of Astrology*. New York: Penguin, 1994.

Curry, Patrick. *A Confusion of Prophets: Victorian and Edwardian Astrology*. London: Collins & Brown, 1992.

———. *Prophesy and Power*. Princeton, NJ: Princeton University Press, 1989.

Dorotheus of Sidonius. *Carmen Astrologicum*. Translated by David Pingree. B. G. Teubner Verlagsgesellschaft: Leipzig, Germany: 1976.

Goldstein-Jacobson, Ivy M. *Simplified Horary Astrology*. Alhambra, CA: Frank Severy Publishing, 1960.

Jones, Marc Edmund. *Horary Astrology*. Santa Fe, NM: Aurora Press, 1993.

Lehman, J. Lee. *The Martial Art of Horary Astrology*. West Chester, PA: Whitford Press, 2002.

Lilly, William. *Christian Astrology*. London: T. Brudenell, 1647. Reprint, London: Regulus, 1985.

McEvilley, Thomas. *The Shape of Ancient Thought: Comparative Studies in Greek and Indian Philosophies*. New York: Allworth Press, 2002.

Neugebuaer, Otto, and Van Hoesen. *Greek Horoscopes*. Philadelphia: American Philosophical Society, 1959.

Rupertus, Stella. *An Astrologian's Guide in Horary Astrology*. London: Simpkin and Marshall, 1832.

Sibly, Ebenezer. *A New and Complete Illustration of the Celestial Science of Astrology*. London: W. Nicol, 1784–1797.

Thomas, Keith. *Religion and the Decline of Magic*. Oxford: Oxford University Press, 1971.

Watters, Barbara. *Horary Astrology and the Judgment of Events*. Washington, DC: Valhalla, 1973.

Zadkiel. *An Introduction to Astrology: By William Lilly with Numerous Emendations, Adapted to the Improved State of the Science; Also a Grammar of Astrology and Tables for Calculating Nativities*. 1852. Many editions.

## HORARY TIME

Horary time is measured by dividing by 12 either the length of the day between sunrise and sunset, or the length of the night between sunset and sunrise.

## HORIZON

The term horizon has the same meaning in astrology as in other contexts, although in astrological practice it usually refers only to the eastern and western horizons. Extended out into space and projected against the background of the stars, the eastern horizon is referred to as the ascendant, which is the same as the cusp of the first house. Similarly, the western horizon projected against the background of the stars is the descendant, which is also the cusp of the seventh house. A distinction can be made between the tropocentric horizon, which is the horizon from a particular spot on the surface of Earth, and the geocentric horizon, which is a "horizon" created by drawing through the middle of Earth an imaginary line (or great circle) that is parallel to the tropocentric horizon. When extended out into space, the geocentric horizon is called the rational horizon. For most astrological work, the difference between the tropocentric horizon and the geocentric horizon is insignificant.

**Sources:**

Brau, Jean-Louis, Helen Weaver, and Allan Edmands. *Larousse Encyclopedia of Astrology*. New York: New American Library, 1980.

Filbey, John, and Peter Filbey. *The Astrologer's Companion*. Wellingborough, Northamptonshire, UK: Aquarian Press, 1986.

## HORIZON SYSTEM

The horizon system is a system of house division in which the horizon is split into 12 arcs of 30 degrees.

## HOROSCOPE (ASTROLOGICAL CHART)

Among contemporary astrologers, the term horoscope (from the Greek *hora*, meaning "hour," and *skopos*, meaning "watcher") is used to refer to any astrological chart. Because of the popularity of newspaper astrology, which often presents itself as a "horoscope," the word has become synonymous with "daily prediction" in the minds of the general public. Prior to the eighteenth century, however, a horoscope was applied only to the ascendant, which is the sign on the eastern horizon at the moment for which the chart is constructed.

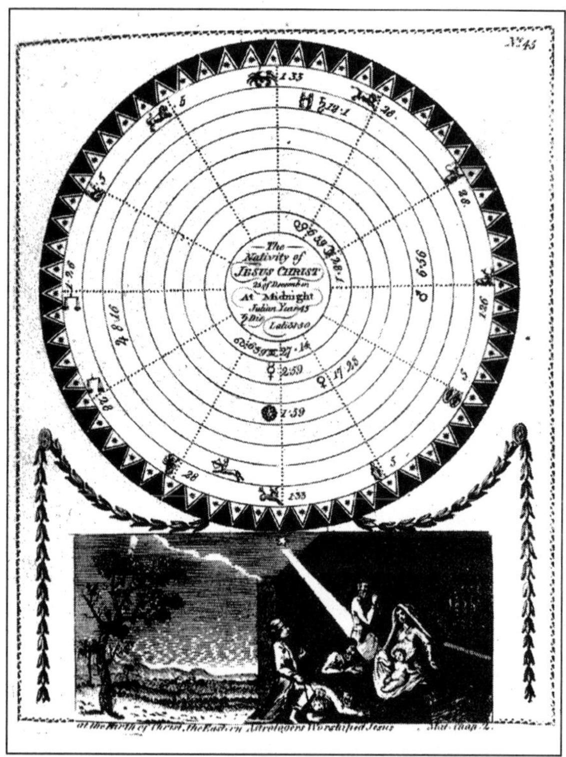

**An engraving of the famous horoscope of Jesus Christ's birthdate from Ebenezer Sibly's *A New and Complete Illustration of the Occult Sciences*, 1790. *Reproduced by permission of Fortean Picture Library.***

## Horse

The Horse is one of the 12 animals of the Chinese zodiac. It refers to one of the 12 earthly branches, which are used in Chinese astrology, together with the 10 heavenly stems. Such a branch designates one day every 12 days: the days are named according to a sexagesimal (60) cycle, made of 10 series of 12 branches.

With his fiery nature, the Horse quickly gets worked up. Happy and not complicated, a little naive and sometimes weak, this socialite likes to entertain and to be entertained; he is appreciated everywhere. This enthusiastic worker is ambitious, persuasive, and a great improviser. He often does well in his plans, but he is not noted for his inordinate intelligence. He likes travelling, mostly abroad, and has a rather fickle nature.

—Michele Delemme

## Horus

Horus, asteroid 1,924 (the 1,924th asteroid to be discovered, on September 24, 1960), is approximately 8.2 kilometers in diameter and has an orbital period of 3.6 years. Horus was named after an Egyptian sky-god who in later mythology became the son of Osiris. J. Lee Lehman associates Horus with "far-sightedness and avenging nature." Jacob Schwartz gives the astrological significance of this asteroid as "synthesis resolving thesis and antithesis (Osiris and Isis); farsightedness."

**Sources:**

Kowal, Charles T. *Asteroids: Their Nature and Utilization*. Chichester, West Sussex, UK: Ellis Horwood Limited, 1988.

Lehman, J. Lee. *The Ultimate Asteroid Book*. West Chester, PA: Whitford Press, 1988.

Schwartz, Jacob. *Asteroid Name Encyclopedia*. St. Paul, MN: Llewellyn Publications, 1995.

## Hot

The signs are numbered from 1 to 12 according to their order in the zodiac (e.g., from Aries, 1, to Pisces, 12). Hot and cold made up one of the sets of categories utilized in premodern physics, and the ancients classified all odd-numbered signs (all fire and air signs) as hot. Traditionally, the Sun and Mars were also considered to be hot, while Jupiter and Venus were regarded as warm (an intermediate category). The terms hot and cold are rarely used in modern astrology.

**An image of Horus and Anubis from *The Dawn of Civilization: Egypt and Chaldea* by G. Maspero, 1894. *Reproduced by permission of Fortean Picture Library.***

## Hours

In traditional astrology, the period between sunrise and sunset was subdivided into 12 hours, each ruled by a different planet. The tradition, to which there have been no serious modifications since the discovery of planets beyond Saturn, stipulates that the day should be divided into 12 equal segments between sunrise and sunset, which will thus vary in length according to the season. On a particular day, the first of these hours is ruled by the planet ruling that day of the week. In other words, on Saturday, the first hour would be ruled by Saturn; on Sunday, the first hour would be ruled by the Sun; and so forth. The succeeding hours are ruled by the next planet in the following order: Saturn, Jupiter, Mars, the Sun, Venus, and the Moon. After reaching the Moon, one begins again with Saturn and repeats the same order.

Ancient astrologers were careful to carry out certain activities during appropriate hours. It was said, for example, that Paracelsus (a sixteenth-century German alchemist and physician) always chose to prepare chemical compounds on days and during hours when the ruling planet matched the therapeutic intent behind his compounds. Despite the importance given this subject by the ancients, modern astrologers have largely ignored the planetary hours.

**Sources:**
DeVore, Nicholas. *Encyclopedia of Astrology*. New York: Philosophical Library, 1947.
Hall, Manly P. *Astrological Keywords*. Savage, MD: Littlefield, Adams, 1975.

## Houses

Houses, sometimes termed mundane houses, are one of the basic building blocks of astrological meaning. Astrological influences manifest themselves primarily through the planets (for astrological purposes, the Sun and Moon are both regarded as planets). These basic influences are modified according to (1) the signs of the zodiac (i.e., the familiar 12 astrological signs—Aries, Taurus, Gemini, etc.) in which the planets are placed, (2) the aspects (geometric angles) between them, and (3) the houses in which they are placed. An oversimplified but nonetheless useful rule of thumb is that planetary sign positions indicate personality tendencies, aspects between planets reflect how various components of one's personality interact with one another, and house positions show how the personality manifests in the world.

As an illustration of these relationships, consider an individual with natal Mars in Virgo, who is also square to Saturn and in the eleventh house. As to personality, Mars represents outgoing, assertive, aggressive energies; this is what might be considered the basic nature of Mars.

> *Sign:* Individuals born when Mars was in Virgo need to organize to get anything done. They tend to be very patient with detailed work. (Organization and patience with detail are both Virgo traits.)
>
> *Aspect:* In contrast to Mars, Saturn is the cautious, security-seeking side of the personality. Square aspects often indicate conflicts, so, in this case, Mars square Saturn shows, among other things, an individual who vacillates between assertiveness and caution, between excitement-seeking and security-seeking.
>
> *House:* The eleventh house indicates things about friends, group associations, and ideals. Mars here shows someone who has a lot of energy for friendships and ideals; such a person expresses that energy best in the context of group activities. In overaggressive individuals, Mars placed here shows a person whose assertiveness causes conflict with friends, as well as conflicts related to that person's ideals.

Visually in an astrological chart, houses are the 12 "pie pieces" that together form the basic framework of the horoscope. Sign divisions (where signs begin and end) are not traditionally represented in a conventional chart, though sometimes—particularly in computer-generated charts—the sign divisions are indicated around the periphery of the chart wheel. If they were represented in the chart itself, one would have to draw in another 12 lines, making a total of 24 (which would result in a cluttered, aesthetically unappealing appearance). The numbers and symbols that appear around the outside of the wheel indicate where houses begin and end with respect to the signs of the zodiac. Starting at the 9:00 position (which in most systems of house division corresponds with the eastern horizon) and moving counterclockwise, the houses are numbered from 1 to 12. Thus, the first house begins at the 9:00 position and ends at the 8:00 position; the second house begins at 8:00 and ends at 7:00, and so forth.

The zodiac is traditionally thought of as beginning with Aries. The subsequent order of the signs is then counterclockwise around the ecliptic. Because the signs and houses both contain 12 members, astrologers have often noted a special relationship between sequentially corresponding signs and houses; in other words, they have often noted certain parallels of meaning between Aries and the first house, Taurus and the second house, Gemini and the third house, etc. The following list, which is by no means exhaustive, outlines some of the principal meanings of corresponding signs and houses. It is taken from Ralph William Holden's *The Elements of House Division*. Note how sign traits indicate internal, psychological characteristics, while house traits tend to indicate external factors, as well as how personality traits manifest themselves in the world (houses tend to represent "signs in action," in Holden's words).

> *First sector*—Aries: Energy, drive, force, heat, initiative, courage, pugnacious, selfish; First house: The appearance, disposition, and manner of the native, outlook on life, carriage, capacity for self development, vitality, health, inherent strength and physical condition, mental and emotional qualities.
>
> *Second sector*—Taurus: Reliable, careful, trustworthy, hospitable, possessive, conservative, affectionate, greedy, grasping, obstinate; Second house: Hereditary and social background, financial standing, money, movable possessions and property, gain and loss of income, earning and spending capacity, personal debts, manner in which money is acquired and in which obligations are met.
>
> *Third sector*—Gemini: Intelligent, lively, quick, versatile, inquisitive, communicative, restless, unstable, not dependable, erratic, oversmart; Third house: Power of mind, dexterity, cleverness, education, short journey, near relatives, neighbors, writing, communications, recording, lecturing.
>
> *Fourth sector*—Cancer: Emotional, instinctive, protective, sensitive, maternal, domestic, moody, sullen; Fourth house: The home and domestic affairs, recollections, residence, base, end of life, private affairs, old age, early home life, lands, houses, estates, mines, things stored up, the hidden or unconscious, social care and concern, the sea.
>
> *Fifth sector*—Leo: Proud, dignified, commanding, generous, reliable, strong-willed, confident, leadership, creative, sincere, wholehearted, reckless, power conscious, conceited, domineering; Fifth house: Offspring, creative and procreative urges, recreation, games, pleasures, artistic efforts, romantic affairs, gaming, speculation, risks, acting, theater.

*Sixth sector*—Virgo: Worker, servant, neatness, carefulness, precision, detail, sensible, critical, retiring, fault-finding, fussy, pinpricking, hygienic, clean; Sixth house: Food, clothing, pets, capacity to serve, employees, health, diseases, employment, daily work, servants, diet, hygiene.

*Seventh sector*—Libra: Companionable, harmonious, evenly balanced, diplomatic, indecisive, vacillating; Seventh house: Partnership, cooperation, marriage, war, legal contracts, lawsuits, divorce, treaties, enemies.

*Eighth sector*—Scorpio: Passionate, secretive, sexual, sensual, penetrating, resentful, mystical, unfathomable; Eighth house: Birth, death, regeneration, sexual instincts, occultism, legacies, others' property, investigation, afterlife.

*Ninth sector*—Sagittarius: Intellectual, exploration, research, wide-ranging, far-reaching, freedom loving, sporty, traveler, religious, moral; Ninth house: Philosophy, religion, law, travel, exploration, research, foreign lands or people, higher education, publishing.

*Tenth sector*—Capricorn: Cautious, practical, prudent, ambitious, grave, stern, restrained, disciplined, authoritarian; Tenth house: The personal image, authority, honor, prestige, career, ambition, father, organizations, rulers, employers.

*Eleventh sector*—Aquarius: Original, independent, detached, scientific, cool, humane, freedom loving, congenial, social, reformer, eccentric; Eleventh house: Friends, contacts, clubs, social groups, humanitarian enterprises, altruism, hopes and wishes.

*Twelfth sector*—Pisces: Intuitive, expansive, sensitive, sympathetic, intangible mystical, artistic, occult, sacrificial, confused, deceived, escapist, sentimental; Twelfth house: Sacrificial service, repressions, neurosis, hidden enemies, prisons, asylums, institutions, occultism, mysticism, secrets.

According to Holden, the notion of a belt of zodiacal signs that modify planetary influences according to the sign in which planets are placed originated over 2,500 years ago in the ancient Near East. At least 300 more years passed before the notion of houses was developed, probably by the Egyptian astrologer Petosiris in the mid-second century B.C.E. The earliest house system, which was the system put forward by Ptolemy, was an equal house system.

An equal house system, as the name implies, draws all houses equal in width with respect to the ecliptic (the great circle at the center of the belt of the zodiac). Most systems of equal houses, including the earliest, begin the first house on the eastern horizon. Thus, someone born when the eastern horizon intersected Virgo at 26° would have a first house that began at 26° Virgo, a second house that began at 26° Libra, a third house that began at 26° Scorpio, and so forth. It is an ancient system of house division that is still used in Vedic astrology, although most Vedic astrologers use the full 30° arc of the rising sign as the first house. In other words, if someone's rising sign was Leo—whether 1° Leo, 29° Leo, or any point in between—the full 30° arc of Leo from 0° to 30° Leo would be the first house. Then the full 30° arc of the next sign—in this example, Virgo—would be the second house, and so forth through the natural order of the zodiac. The most ancient house system used in Western astrology was the same—whole sign—approach to houses as Vedic astrology.

For the most part the equal house system had passed out of circulation among Western astrologers until relatively recently. Several popular astrology books, particularly Derek and Julia Parker's *The Compleat Astrologer* (first published in the United States in 1971), propagated the equal house system because it is the easiest system to use. The increasing popularity of Vedic astrology in the West in combination with the new interest in recovering Western tradition astrology has also helped the older whole sign house system make a comeback. Most contemporary astrologers who do not use the equal house system are severely critical of it.

The other house systems that enjoy widespread acceptance begin the tenth house at the degree of the zodiac that is highest in the heavens (termed the midheaven or medium coeli [MC]), and the fourth house exactly 180° away from the cusp (beginning) of the tenth house (termed the nadir). Because of the tilt of Earth's axis and the resulting inclination of the belt of the zodiac at a 23° angle (the angle of obliquity) away from the plane of the Earth's rotation, the highest degree of the zodiac for any given point on Earth is often not 90° along the ecliptic from the zodiacal degree on the eastern horizon, even though the zenith and the horizon do, of course, lie at a 90° angle to each other. Why this is so is difficult to understand unless one is familiar with spherical geometry. Suffice it to say that the substantial angle between the zodiacal belt and the plane of Earth's rotation results in either lengthening or shortening zodiacal degrees when the zodiac is superimposed on the plane of the horizon and the zenith.

Other than the equal house system, the systems of house division in popular use now all take the axis of the eastern and western horizon as demarcating the cusps of the first house (east) and the seventh house (west), and the axis of the medium coeli and the nadir as demarcating the beginnings of the tenth house (MC) and the fourth house (nadir). These systems differ in the various approaches they take to determining the other eight house cusps. Precisely how they differ is hard to explain unless one has thoroughly grasped all the notions related to the celestial sphere and celestial coordinates. The following brief summaries are provided in lieu of elaborately detailed explanations:

> *Porphyry Houses:* The second-oldest house system was devised by the third-century astrologer Porphyry. The positions of the house cusps for the second, third, fifth, sixth, eighth, ninth, eleventh, and twelfth house are determined by dividing the arcs of the ecliptic contained in the four quadrants of a chart into even divisions of three. Few contemporary astrologers use this system.
>
> *Campanus Houses:* Devised by Johannes Campanus, a thirteenth-century mathematician who was also chaplain to Pope Urban IV. Roughly similar to the Porphyry system, except that Campanus trisected the prime vertical in each quadrant, rather than the ecliptic. This system has enjoyed a modest revival because it was the system favored by the influential modern astrologer Dane Rudhyar.

*Regiomontanus Houses:* In the century after Campanus, Johannes Müller (who wrote under the name Regiomontanus), a professor of astronomy at Vienna, developed a similar system that trisected the celestial equator. Few contemporary astrologers use this system.

*Placidian Houses:* A seventeenth-century Italian monk and professor of mathematics named Placidus de Tito developed this system by trisecting the time it takes a degree of the zodiac to rise from the eastern horizon to the midheaven. Due to the widespread availability of Placidian tables of houses, this was the most popular house system in the early twentieth century, and it still enjoys widespread use.

*Koch Houses*. This is a very recent system, put forward in 1971 by Walter Koch, that also works by trisecting time. Although Holden characterizes it as possibly the least acceptable of all the time systems, it has enjoyed a surge of popularity over the past decade or so.

Although this overabundance of competing house systems may seem overwhelming, there are numerous other systems, of both ancient and modern origin, that have not been mentioned. These include, among others, Albategnian houses, Alcabitian houses, horizontal houses, meridian houses, morinus houses, and topocentric houses.

Because the differences between the various systems that share the midheaven-nadir axis as the cusps of the tenth and fourth houses are comparatively small, the most significant disagreement between competing popular house systems lies in the divergence between these midheaven-nadir systems and the equal house system. Thus, any attempt to find the "best" system should begin with an examination of this disagreement.

The chief argument in favor of midheaven-nadir approaches is that much informal astrological research has found that the midheaven is a sensitive point in a natal chart for career matters, whereas the nadir is sensitive to matters having to do with house and home. Because these correspond with the traditional meanings of the tenth and fourth houses, it seems inescapable that the midheaven and the nadir should be utilized as the cusps of these houses.

One encounters problems with midheaven-nadir houses, however, when attempting to construct charts for high latitudes. Using of any of these systems at high latitudes can result in exaggeratedly large houses (encompassing arcs of over 60°) as well as extremely tiny ones (less than 10°). Thus, in a location like Fairbanks, Alaska, for example, it is unlikely that one would find professional astrologers using anything other than the equal house system as their primary system. Any serious consideration of the problem of high-latitude chart casting seems to present an incontrovertible argument in favor of some kind of equal house approach.

These competing considerations suggest that any house system capable of becoming universally accepted among astrologers must somehow integrate the long-standing astrological experience that stands behind the use of the midheaven-nadir axis for the tenth- and fourth-house cusps with the need to produce houses of reasonable width for individuals born in high latitudes. The basic incompatibility of these two requirements makes the likelihood of resolving the problem of competing house systems highly unlikely in the foreseeable future.

**Sources:**

Frawley, David. *Astrology of the Seers*. Twin Lakes, WI: Lotus Press, 2000.

Gettings, Fred. *Dictionary of Astrology*. London: Routledge & Kegan Paul, 1985.

Hand, Robert. *Whole Sign Houses: The Oldest House System*. Reston, VA: Arhat Publications, 2000.

Holden, Ralph William. *The Elements of House Division*. Essex, UK: L. N. Fowler, 1977.

McEvers, Joan. *The Houses: Power Places of the Horoscope*. St. Paul, MN: Llewellyn Publications, 1991.

Parker, Derek, and Julia Parker. *The Compleat Astrologer*. New York: McGraw-Hill, 1971. Reprint, New York: Bantam, 1975.

Rudhyar, Dane. *The Astrological Houses: The Spectrum of Individual Experience*. Garden City, NY: Doubleday, 1972.

## Huberta

Huberta, asteroid 260 (the 260th asteroid to be discovered, on October 3, 1886), is approximately 98 kilometers in diameter and has an orbital period of 6.3 years. This asteroid was named after Hubert, the patron saint of hunters. When Huberta is prominent in a natal chart, it indicates someone for whom hunting, searching, researching, or investigating is a life theme. The sign and house position of Huberta indicates how and where this searching drive manifests itself.

**Sources:**

Kowal, Charles T. *Asteroids: Their Nature and Utilization*. Chichester, West Sussex, UK: Ellis Horwood Limited, 1988.

Room, Adrian. *Dictionary of Astronomical Names*. London: Routledge, 1988.

Schwartz, Jacob. *Asteroid Name Encyclopedia*. St. Paul, MN: Llewellyn Publications, 1995.

## Human Signs

The human signs are the signs of the zodiac represented by human figures. The signs classified as human vary, but always include Gemini the Twins, Virgo the Virgin, and Aquarius the Water Bearer. Although the symbol for Libra the Scales is a nonliving artifact, Libra is usually considered a human sign because the older symbol of Libra was a woman holding scales. Sagittarius the Archer is often represented as a centaur—half human, half horse. When represented as an archer, Sagittarius is classified as human; when represented as a centaur, nonhuman. The signs not represented by human figures are referred to as bestial. The human/bestial contrast does not carry practical consequences for interpretation (e.g., persons born under human signs are not more humane or less "beastly" than others). For this reason, as well as the negative connotations of the term beast, this distinction has dropped out of general usage in modern astrology.

**Sources:**

Bach, Eleanor. *Astrology from A to Z: An Illustrated Source Book*. New York: Philosophical Library, 1990.

Lee, Dal. *Dictionary of Astrology*. New York: Paperback Library, 1969.

## Humanistic Astrology

Humanistic astrology was created in the 1930s by Dane Rudhyar, who followed the lead of Marc Edmund Jones in reinterpreting traditional astrology in terms of modern psychology. Rudhyar combined the Theosophical approach to astrology that he had learned at the Krotona Institute with the insights of Carl Jung's depth psychology, whose works he read during the summer of 1933.

By the 1940s, Rudhyar was trying to create an astrology based on a philosophy "freed not only from the materialistic biases of our Western tradition, but also from the glamour surrounding so much of what today passes for esoteric revelations and unprovable occult claims," as noted in his book *My Stand on Astrology*. By this time, the letters he was receiving about his regular columns in *American Astrology* had alerted him to "the psychological danger involved in careless astrological statements about birth-charts. I therefore tried to stress the psychological responsibility of the practitioner, and to develop theoretically a consistent approach to those astrological factors which were more particularly related to the individuality and the potentiality of growth of the person whose chart was being studied. I increasingly emphasized the need to take a holistic approach to the birth-chart." In this approach, Rudhyar reinterpreted factors in the birth chart that had traditionally been called malefic or evil as being instead weaknesses in personality structure; and these he saw, not as tragic flaws, but as opportunities for learning and growth.

Rudhyar went on to emphasize that "astrology is a *symbolic language* … attempting to formulate, by means of symbols based on the common experience of men facing the all-surrounding sky, an immensely complex structure of relationships between the universe and man." He proposed, for example, that the signs of the zodiac refer not to the vastly distant constellations they were named for, but to 12 zones in Earth's magnetic aura through which Earth turns every day.

Rudhyar stresses the concept that astrology should be "person-centered," that the individual birth chart is intended as a guide for telling a person how best to actualize as fully as possible her or his birth potential. If the chart is to do this, then those elements in it that apply to mankind as a whole should not be emphasized; instead, those that reveal a person's unique individuality should be stressed. Behind this lies the concept common to all modern astrology, psychology, and therapy: The individual personality is not fixed and unchangeable. It can be revised, rewritten, reprogrammed, restructured, and any means that gives the individual some insights into her or his internal patterns can be used for such work on oneself. Rudhyar's belief—which goes back to his reading, as a youth, of Nietzsche—is that the goal of the fully actualized individual is to become totally free "from the Collective and from an unconscious, compulsive bondage to the values of one's particular culture—values which a person takes for granted because they have been stamped during childhood upon his sensitive mind by the teachings and even more the example of his elders, and also by the ambience of his society" and to develop one's own unique qualities as fully as possible.

Rudhyar says that the birth chart is "a set of instructions … showing you how in your particular case the ten basic energies of human nature should be used to the best advantage.… In modern astrology, these basic energies are represented by the ten planets (the Sun and the Moon included). Where these planets are located indicates where (by zodiacal signs and especially by houses) they can be used by you to produce the most valuable results."

Rudhyar also believed that humanistic astrology needed to be founded on certain basic principles that would guide the astrologer in deciding how to interpret a chart and would function as a code of ethics in helping the astrologer decide what to tell a client, just as a therapist would choose not to state "facts" that would merely damage a patient's perhaps already eroded self-esteem. The central principle is that every individual has a right "to stand, erect and open, at the center of the universe around him."

Finally, Rudhyar says, "It is evident that many astrologers … mainly think of astrology in terms of conformism—if not to the goal of financial profit, at least to popular expectations and the wishes of their clients' egos. I believe instead in an astrology of transformation.… I hope to awaken the sleeping god in every person. By sounding the 'true name' of an individual one may arouse to life the divine within him. Every person is a 'celestial,' if only he gains the strength and has the courage to stand by the truth of his being and to fulfill his place and function on this earth by following the 'celestial set of instruction' revealed by the sky."

In *From Humanistic to Transpersonal Psychology*, Rudhyar expands on *My Stand on Astrology* to discuss astrology as a spiritual discipline whose highest goal is to assist the individual to manifest his or her own special relationship to divinity. From this viewpoint, he argues against the use of statistics and other research to provide a "scientific" basis for astrology, on the grounds that, were astrology to be socially sanctioned, licensed, and regulated, it would become a force for conformity, not for actualization of individual potentials. He thought that the situation would be as ridiculous as looking to the American Medical Association for spiritual guidance. Rudhyar specifically allied himself with the Eleusinian Mysteries against Aristotle, with the Gnostics against the fathers of the church, with the Albigensians against the pope and the king, with the alchemists against the chemists, and with the Romantics against the scientific materialism and bourgeois boredom and mediocrity of the Victorian Age. Consequently, his popularity with the young during the 1970s and 1980s is not at all difficult to understand.

—Aidan A. Kelly

**Sources:**

Rudhyar, Dane. *From Humanistic to Transpersonal Astrology*. Palo Alto, CA: The Seed Center, 1975.

———. *My Stand on Astrology*. Palo Alto, CA: The Seed Center, 1972.

## HUNTER, KELLEY

Kelley Hunter has studied the sky as a professional astrologer, mythologist, and amateur astronomer for over 30 years. An internationally known astrologer, she is a speaker at national and international conferences and was the cofounder of the Roots of Astrology experiential conferences. She is the astrologer-in-residence for the Omega Institute programs in the Caribbean and on the faculty of the Self Centre at Caneel Bay resort. Holding degrees in drama and in depth psychology / creative communication, Hunter has taught at various colleges as well as in special programs for high schools. She is presently pursuing doctoral studies in world cosmologies and myth.

A dramatic artist and workshop leader, Hunter worked for years with Dragon Dance Theater and has performed at Bread and Puppet Circus and the United Nations. A feature writer for the *International Astrologer* and other journals, she is the author of *Black Moon Lilith* and a contributing author to *Astrology for Women*. Hunter resides in St. John, Virgin Islands (U.S.) and leads stargazing nights at local resorts.

## Hurtful Signs

The term "hurtful signs" is an older designation for the signs Aries, Taurus, Cancer, Scorpio, and Capricorn. They are so called because the animal symbols of these zodiacal signs appear capable of "hurting" human beings.

## Hygeia

Hygeia, asteroid 10 (the 10th asteroid to be discovered, on April 12, 1849, by the Italian astronomer Annibale de Gasparis), is approximately 430 kilometers in diameter and has an orbital period of 5.5 years. Hygeia was the daughter of Aesculapius and the goddess of health and hygiene. According to Martha Lang-Wescott, the position of Hygeia and the aspects to it provide some indications of the native's health. This asteroid's key words are "health" and "hygiene."

**Sources:**

Lang-Wescott, Martha. *Asteroids-Mechanics: Ephemerides II*. Conway, MA: Treehouse Mountain, 1990.

———. *Mechanics of the Future: Asteroids*. Rev. ed. Conway, MA: Treehouse Mountain, 1991.

Schwartz, Jacob. *Asteroid Name Encyclopedia*. St. Paul, MN: Llewellyn Publications, 1995.

## Hyleg

The Hyleg (Arabic), Apheta (Greek), Prorogator (Latin), or Giver of Life, was a planet or point that was calculated as part of the process to evaluate both the life expectancy and periods when the native was at mortal risk. When this point was directed (using what are now called primary directions) to an Anareta (or killing point; there may be more than one), or vice versa, death occurs. In their book *Greek Horoscopes*, Otto Neugerbauer and Henry Bartlett Van Hoesen noted that early versions, such as that of the Roman astrologer Babillus, allowed any planet to be hyleg; later versions restricted the hyleg, except under relatively rare circumstances, to being one of the hylegical points: Sun, Moon, ascendant, or Part of Fortune.

House placement is critical to the definition of the hyleg. The earliest Greek houses were what is now referred to as whole sign: if the ascendant was in Cancer, then the first house was Cancer, regardless of the degree of the ascendant. This is similar to traditional Vedic usage as well. In this system, the words "sign" and "house" become literally interchangeable, as in, "The Sun is in his own house" being equivalent to saying "The Sun is in Leo." Ptolemy, who represents the later Greek period, used equal houses from the ascendant, where the first house was comprised of the region from 5° before the ascendant, through 25° after. Each of the following houses was constructed the same way. Using this definition, Ptolemy then defined the prorogational or hylegical places, or houses: the first, seventh, ninth, tenth, and eleventh houses, as noted in his *Tetrabiblos*. In Ptolemy's definition, the Part of Fortune was always taken using the daytime formula; unlike many classical sources, he did not reverse the calculation by day and by night.

In calculations of the hyleg, the general procedure is to examine particular hylegical points in a given sequence. Determine if the first planet or point in question is in a hylegical house. If it is, and it meets all other specified criteria, then that body or point is declared the hyleg, and the procedure ends. If it is not, then the next body or point in the sequence is examined, then the next, as necessary.

Ptolemy's method begins with no provision other than whether the body or point is in a prorogational or hylegical place. The sequence of placements examined depends on whether the chart is diurnal or nocturnal.

If diurnal, examine first the Sun, then the Moon, then the planet that has the most types of rulership (all five essential dignities) over the Sun, the prenatal new Moon, and the ascendant. If none of these bodies or points is in a prorogational house, then the ascendant is prorogator or hyleg.

If nocturnal, the Moon, then the Sun, then the planet that has the most types of rulership (all five essential dignities) over the Moon, the prenatal Full Moon, and the Part of Fortune. If none of these bodies is in a prorogational house, then the ascendant is prorogator or hyleg *if* the prenatal syzygy (i.e., lunation) was a new Moon; otherwise if the prenatal syzygy was a full Moon, use the Part of Fortune as hyleg.

Ptolemy then uses the prorogator and principally its aspects to benefic and malefic planets to calculate the length of life.

By contrast, here is the system of calculation according to Guido Bonatti, as noted in Robert Zoller's book *Tools and Techniques of the Medieval Astrologers*. At Bonatti's time, 30° houses were not used in the "placement in a house." In Bonatti's system, if a body was on the cadent side of an angle, it was still angular if it was within 7° of the cusp. If it was on the angular side of a succedent house, it was still succedent if it was within 5° of the cusp. And, if a planet was on the succedent side of a cadent house, it was still cadent if it was within 3° of the cusp. In this table, the hyleg is found once a statement is true.

1. The Sun in first, tenth, or eleventh house in a masculine or feminine sign.
2. The Sun in seventh, eighth, or ninth house in a masculine sign only.
3. Moon is in an angular house or in a succedent house, and in a feminine sign, and possessing any of the four dignities: exaltation, trip, term, or rulership.
4. Born on a waxing Moon: examine the dispositors of the ascendant. If any of its dispositors also aspects the ascendant, the hyleg is the ascendant; otherwise check Fortuna for an aspecting dispositor.

5. Born on a waning Moon: examine the dispositors of Fortuna. If any of its dispositors also aspects Fortuna, then use Fortuna as hyleg; if not, check the ascendant for an aspecting dispositor.
6. If all else fails, see what planet has dignity in the degree of the new or full Moon before birth.
7. If none of these work, then the chart is a third differentia and the child will die before age 12.

While this might look like a very rigorous system, there is actually one point of ambiguity. In Bonatti's original definition, it was not stated that the Sun or Moon, in order to be hyleg, also had to aspect one of its dispositors. The necessity for an aspect between *any* potential hyleg and one of its dispositors was made in Omar of Tiberius's commentary, but it was initially unclear whether this was simply a variation introduced by Omar, or whether it reflected Bonatti's actual usage. With the availability of more classical sources, it is likely that Bonatti simply gave a slightly abbreviated version of his actual working definition.

While this might seem like a relatively minor point, its significance is that one study of the efficacy of the various classical definitions of the hyleg was done, using the data from the March 13, 1996, classroom shootings in Dunblane, Scotland, in which about half the students were killed, and half were not. In an article she wrote for the January 1998 issue of the *Horary Practitioner*, Penny Shelton compared methods from Ptolemy, Dorotheus, Bonatti, William Lilly, John Gadbury, and Henry Coley, and found the Bonatti system to be the most satisfactory in predicting which of the children lived and which died. However, Shelton did not incorporate the necessity for the Sun or the Moon to aspect a dispositor to be counted as hyleg. So perhaps this particular restriction needs reexamination.

The later methods of Lilly, Gadbury, and Coley that Shelton included represent various simplifications of the older system. Later, the simplifications became even more extreme. For one thing, all the earlier definitions were dependent on the five essential dignities, and this became impractical once these dignities were forgotten.

In the Arabic period, the calculation of the hyleg and its derivatives became the principal system for evaluating the length of life. In the Hellenistic period, noted Neugerbauer and Van Hoesen, this function was instead derived from the position of the ascendant.

The calculation of the length of life proceeds as follows. First, Alcocoden is examined, which is the almuten of the hyleg in the case of the Sun or Moon, or the planet which is the aspecting dispositor for the Ascendant and Part of Fortune (also the Sun and the Moon). The alcocoden is also called the "giver of years" in English.

The condition of the alcocoden is then examined with respect to the Table of Years given below. If including only the major dignities (i.e., rulership, exaltation, and triplicity), the alcocoden is essentially dignified, the native's life span is enumerated from the "old years" column. As the transition occurs to lesser dignity to no dignity, and succedent to cadent, then the starting point shifts to one of the other columns.

The final stage, as given by Omar of Tiberius, is to examine whether the alcocoden is aspected by either the benefics or malefics. In either case, an aspect results in either adding or subtracting the lesser number of years.

**Table of Years**

| Planets | Old Years | Mean Years | Least Years |
|---|---|---|---|
| Saturn | 57 | 43 | 30 |
| Jupiter | 79 | 45 | 12 |
| Mars | 66 | 40 | 15 |
| Sun | 120 | 69 | 19 |
| Venus | 82 | 45 | 8 |
| Mercury | 76 | 48 | 20 |
| Moon | 108 | 66 | 25 |

To better exemplify the success of this table, the Table on the Longevity Expectations for Czars of Russia follows. One of the reasons this particular set was selected is that, with the exception of Nicholas II, none were really subject to the modern understanding of hygiene and allopathic trauma care, which arguably could have thrown off the longevity compared to traditional expectations.

**Longevity Expectations for Czars of Russia**

| Czar | Hyleg | Alchocoden | Alchocoden Years | +/-Aspects | Expected Years | Actual Years |
|---|---|---|---|---|---|---|
| Peter I | Asc | Mars | 40 | +12 | 52 | 51 |
| Paul I* | Sun | Saturn | 57 | -15+8+12 | 62 | 46 |
| Alexander I | Fortuna | Jupiter | 45 | n/a | 45 | 47 |
| Alexander II* | Sun | Venus | 82 | -15-30+12 | 49 | 62 |
| Alexander III | Asc | Mercury | 48 | -15+8 | 43 | 49 |
| Nicholas II* | Sun | Venus | 45 | +12 | 57 | 50* |

**Assassinated.*

When freed from being a system of precise longevity calculation, the system does provide some very useful information. Clearly, a person who shows a short to medium longevity is more likely to have serious health consequences earlier in life than a person with greater longevity. This can translate into the necessity of paying more attention to bodily symptoms so that serious conditions are not the only necessary outcome.

—J. Lee Lehman, Ph.D.

**Sources:**

Ferrier, Oger. *Des Jugements astronomiques sur les Nativitez*. Lyon, France: Jen de Tournes, 1550.

Neugerbauer, Otto, and Henry Bartlett Van Hoesen. *Greek Horoscopes*. Philadelphia: American Philosophical Society, 1959.

Omar of Tiberius, *Three Books of Nativities*. Translated by Robert Hand. Project Hindsight, 1997.

Ptolemy, Claudius. *Tetrabiblos*. Translated by F. E. Robbins. Cambridge: Harvard University Press, 1971.

Shelton, Penny. "Awareness of Fate." *The Horary Practitioner* January 1998.
Zoller, Robert. *Tools and Techniques of the Medieval Astrologers*. Privately printed, 1981.

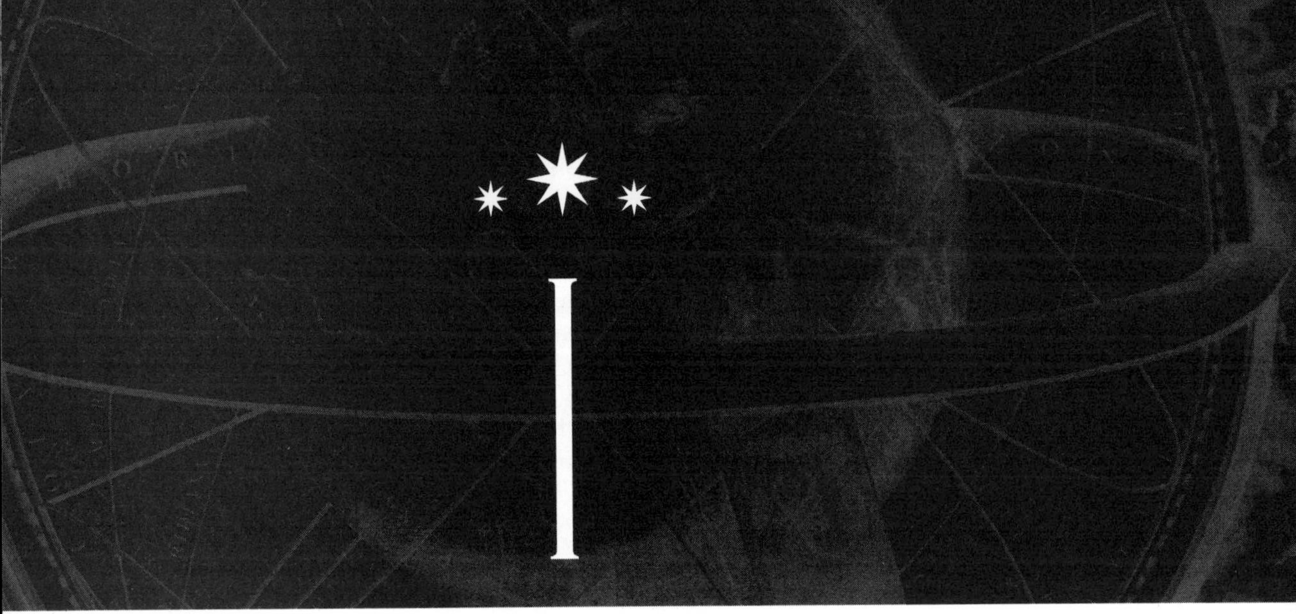


## Iatromathematics

Iatromathematics is a traditional term for medical astrology.

## Ibn Ezra, Avraham

Rabbi Avraham Ben Meir Ibn Ezra was a renowned Jewish scholar born in eleventh-century Spain. He was accomplished in many disciplines and his prolific writing encompassed biblical exegeses; Hebrew grammar; personal, national, and liturgical poetry; philosophy; mathematics; geometry; astronomy; and astrology. In mainstream Judaism, he was known and loved mainly for his Bible commentary as well as his poetry, whereas to the Christian European world he became known through his astrological and mathematical writings. This was the golden era for the Jews in Spain, who flourished economically, scientifically, and culturally, and who were also instrumental in transmitting the Arabic sciences and philosophy to Christian Europe. These were also the times of the Crusades and the wars between the Moslems and the Christians in Spain, and the Jewish communities were caught in the middle, suffering persecutions both in North Africa and Spain. All these circumstances left their mark in Ibn Ezra's life and work.

### His Life

Ibn Ezra was born in in 1089 in Tudela, Spain, but spent most of his life wandering from one country to another, always restless, always seeking knowledge, writing his books, teaching students, and always in great poverty, depending on people's patronage. In one of his personal poems he ironically says that at his nativity the stars changed their natural course to bring him misfortune, so much so that if he decided to sell candles the Sun would never set, and if he decided to sell burial shrouds, no one would ever die. There are many anecdotes and legends about his lack of practicality in worldly matters on the one hand, and his great wit and wisdom in intellectual matters on the other.

At a young age he was married and a son, Itz'hak, was born. Tradition maintains that his wife was the daughter of the renowned Jewish poet and philosopher Rabbi Yehuda HaLevi. Years later, Itz'hak accompanied Yehuda HaLevi on his journey to the Holy Land, but parted ways with him and stayed behind in Baghdad, never to see his father again. In Baghdad, following his host, Itz'hak converted to Islam, and a few years later he died there of an illness. When Ibn Ezra received the news, he poured out his broken heart in a poem, mourning his son's death and lamenting his own fate that deprived him of having a son to comfort him at his old age.

Wandering and material poverty was a way of life for Ibn Ezra. He began his travels going south to the Muslim regions and then proceeded to the Jewish communities in North Africa, which he visited more than once, each time returning to Spain. He was also said to have visited Egypt, the Land of Israel (Palestine), and possibly further east, but there is no real evidence of that.

In 1140, he left Spain for good and began his travels among the Jewish communities in the Christian world—Italy, France, and England. During those years he wrote his greatest works, including astrology. The Jews in those communities had no access to the Islamic sciences, nor did they have sufficient knowledge of the Hebrew grammar, so they welcomed Ibn Ezra's stay among them with great enthusiasm.

Ibn Ezra first went to Rome, where the Jews enjoyed relative prosperity and security under the decrees of the popes. By that time he had become well known, and wherever he went, he found a place to stay, students to teach, and rabbis with whom to discourse. He left Rome heading north to other towns in Italy, never staying long, never settling down, and practicing astrology to make some living.

In 1146, in Lucca, near Rome, he began most of his astrological treatises and completed them a couple of years later. Some sources say that they were written in Beziers (Bedersh) in the south of France, where he arrived in 1147 or 1148.

In 1152, Ibn Ezra went from Provençe towards the north of France, arriving at a town he calls Rodos (Rodez?), where he became very ill at the age of 64. Through the help of a benevolent patron, Moshe Bar Meir, Ibn Ezra recovered and made a vow, which he kept soon after, to write his commentary for the Bible all over again in a long version.

Still restless, at age 70, Ibn Ezra decided to go further north, to London, England, and again he was received very well by the Jewish community. Here, too, he composed important books, dedicated to his benefactors. In 1160, he translated from Arabic into Hebrew the *Explanation of the Tables by Muhammad Al-Matani*.

## His Death

Ibn Ezra died at the age of 75 in the year 1164. In one version, his death took place in Rome. In another, it was in Calahora, Spain. Yet, according to another source, found in a book written 50 years after his death, he never left England and died there. Apparently, he predicted his own death. Israel Levin reports that one of the copyists of Ibn Ezra's commentary on the Torah wrote at the end of the book:

> On Monday, on the First of Addar I, in the year 4924 [which corresponds to Monday, January 27, 1164, on the Julian calendar], Ibn Ezra died, at the age of seventy five, and he wrote for himself in the year of his death in his own hand "Avraham was seventy five years old when he came out from under the wrath of God."

## His Astrological Work

Ibn Ezra wrote nine astrological treatises, as well as a translation from Arabic into Hebrew of two others, covering all branches of astrology—natal, medical, horary, electional, and mundane. He was well versed in the different theories and sources. He knew his predecessors and compared their ideas, frequently coming up with his own conclusions. With proper acknowledgment, he referred to Hindu, Persian, and Arab astrologers, yet mostly following Ptolemy's *Tetrabiblos*.

The contents of Ibn Ezra's work is traditional Hellenistic-Persian-Arabic astrology, rarely mentioning religion or mysticism. Yet, at times, his "Jewishness" shines through in small biblical phrases and in what can be called a Talmudic style, which is apparent in most of the texts.

His writing is concise, scholarly, analytical, critical, and didactic, frequently pointing out how the inner logic of astrology is derived from its elementary components. He is also conversational and personal, often speaking in the first person, addressing the reader directly.

Some of the books were written twice—a short version and a long version—as is the case with *The Book of Reasons* (both are edited and published).

## Ibn Ezra's Works

*The Beginning of Wisdom* (Re'shit Ho'khmah) is Ibn Ezra's best known astrological text. It was edited from Hebrew manuscripts with cross references from an Old French translation (Hagin le Juif, *Le Commencement de Sapience*, 1273) and translated into English for the first time by Raphael Levy and Francisco Cantera in 1939. The ten-chapter book contains basic astrology that encompasses the fundamentals of the horoscope. It describes the tropical and sidereal signs; the fixed stars; the decanates and the images contained in them as well as those that are co-rising; the division of the wheel and the houses; the attributes of the planets and the luminaries; the aspects; the relative strength of the planets; the various ways planets conjoin bodily and by aspect; and an extensive list of the Arabic Parts.

The short version of *The Book of Reasons* (Se'fer Ha'Te'amim) was edited from manuscript by Naphtali Ben Menahem in 1941. The long version was edited by Rabbi Yehuda Fleishman in 1951. It was translated from Hebrew (short version supplemented from the long version) by Meira B. Epstein in 1994. The book contains commentary and additional material for all the topics in *The Beginning of Wisdom*, providing more in-depth discussion meant for those who already know the basics.

Ibn Ezra's *Book of Nativities* (Se'fer Ha'Moladot) was edited from a 1436 manuscript. A translation from Hebrew by Meira B. Epstein was published in 2002. The book contains discussions about the houses in the chart; the specific signification of each house in the chart; the issue of the fate of the individual within that of the collective; astrology's answer to the controversial question of nature vs. nurture, or the relative influence of the environment; chart rectification, including an evaluation of Ptolemy's method (Nimodar), as well as the method base on the moment of conception (the Epoch); some aspects of electional astrology; the timing by the Triplicity Rulers, the Firdar method, Ptolemy's ages of life, the profection method, the solar return chart and its calculation; and an integration of the method of profection with the solar return for annual, monthly, and daily observations.

Ibn Ezra's *Book of Lights* (Se'fer Ha'Me'orot) was edited by Yehuda Leib Fleischer in 1932. It contains discussions on medical astrology; the Decumbiture chart; general motions of the Sun and the Moon and their function in the horoscope; judgments for the condition and recovery from illness from the Moon and eclipses in the decumbiture chart; and evaluations of the effects of benefic and malefic planets, their motions, their strength, and their aspects in the decumbiture chart.

*The Book of Elections* (Se'fer Ha'Miv'harim) was edited from manuscript by Yehuda Leib Fleischer, in 1939. Its contents focus on electional astrology: whether one can affect a desirable outcome by electing a good time to begin an endeavor; the need to also consider the nativity and what to do when it is not known; identifying the appropriate house in the election chart that signifies the purpose of the election; and the various considerations for each house and planet in the election chart.

*The Book of Questions* (Se'fer Ha'She'elot) focuses on horary astrology.

*The Book of the World* (Se'fer Ha'Olam) was edited by Yehuda Leib Fleischer, in 1937. Its contents focus on mundane astrology. The book covers a mathematical formula for calculating the maximum possible number of planetary conjunctions; the Jupiter-Saturn conjunctions; a discussion on the accuracy of the calculations of the rising sign at the time of the Jupiter-Saturn conjunction and the solar annual revolution; using the time of the new or full moon before the Aries ingress; the Firdar periods (from Persian astrologers); the Kabbalistic text (*Sefer Yetsira*); the sign ruler of a country and the Mars-Saturn conjunction (from Mashallah); eclipse interpretation (from Ptolemy); a list of specific signs and degrees associated with countries and cities; predictions of monthly rain amounts; the phases of the Moon; and the lunar mansions.

*Predictions Made in the Year 1154* (He'zionot Rabbi Avraham Ibn Ezra She'haza Al Sh'nat 4914 La'Ye'tsira) was published by Meir Ben Itzhak Bakkal in 1971. Its contents focus on mundane astrology and include a short treatise containing a mundane forecast based on the great conjunction of Jupiter-Saturn in Capricorn, which was coming up in 1166.

*Horoscope Analysis for a Newborn* (Mishpatei Ha'Nolad) was published by Meir Ben Itzhak Bakkal in 1971. Its focus is on the method of chart analysis.

Included is a short treatise on how to read a horoscope, based on birth data that seems to fit October 14, 1160, roughly around 10 P.M., at Narbonne, France. Other topics cover the determination of the hyleg; the rule of not reading the horoscope before the native has reached age four; directing the hyleg to crisis times; and general success and mental quality and observations about both parents.

*The Treatise of the Astrolabe* (Kli Ha'Ne'hoshet) was first edited and published by H. Edelmann in 1845. It was later republished by Meir Ben Itzhak in 1971. The book contains an astronomy treatise, essential for astrological chart calculation. It holds 36 chapters, describing the use of the astrolabe in computing the length of day and night; the diurnal and nocturnal uneven hours; the ecliptical longitude and latitude position of the Sun and the planets; the culminating degree; the rising and setting according to the clime; finding the geographical latitude of a city; whether the planet is direct or retrograde; the disappearance and appearance of the Moon; the Lunar Mansions; computation of the 12 houses of the horoscope; how to determine the astrological aspects; fixed stars of the first and the second magnitudes, including their names and description and computing their precession rate in the tropical zodiac; computing the height of any tall or short or deep object; and what to do when there is no table for the exact geographical latitude or when the astrolabe is not sufficiently accurate.

*Muhammad bin Almatani's Explanations for the Astronomical Tables of Muhammad al-Khwarizmi* (Ta'amei Lu'hot al-Khwarizmi) is a translation from Arabic into Hebrew and includes an introduction by Ibn Ezra. This version was edited and translated into English by Baruch Rephael Goldstein in 1967. The book contains an account of the introduction of Hindu astronomical calculations into Islam; a comparison of the calculations to Ptolemy's *Almagest;* and a discussion of the precession error found in older texts in determining the position of the fixed stars and the constellations. The text is interspersed with Ibn Ezra's additional explanations.

In *A Book by Mashallah on the Eclipses of the Sun and the Moon* (1902), Ibn Ezra provides an Arabic-to-Hebrew translation. It contains a discussion of how the effect of the planets are relative to the clime; a sign classification by elements and by gender, etc. and their effect on the weather; a judgment of the weather and world affairs from the Aries ingress and from total or partial eclipses and from eclipses of the Sun and the Moon; and coverage of the great conjunction of Jupiter-Saturn, the medium conjunction of Mars-Saturn, and the small conjunction of Mars-Jupiter, and their effect in the world.

## Unpublished Books

Naftali Ben Menahem reports on Rabbi Moshe Taku who wrote a book, *Ktav Tamim*, about Ibn Ezra 50 years after his death, in which he mentions a book by Ibn Ezra called *The Book of Life* (Sefer ha-Haim). This book might be the same as *Kohot Shnot ha-Adam*, an autobiography whose possible existence was reported by David Kahanah.

## Translations and Publications

Ibn Ezra's astrological writings were very popular, as evidenced by the numerous translations, manuscript copies, and printings that were made over the centuries.

At least 33 series containing his astrological treatises exist; not all of them are complete but most include *The Beginning of Wisdom*. There are 43 single treatises, eight of which are manuscripts owned by the Library of the Jewish Theological Seminary in New York. Eight more are in the Bibliotheque Nationale in Paris, and others are scattered throughout Europe in private and public collection. The Hebrew University in Jerusalem and the Vatican Library also possess some of the manuscripts.

Ibn Ezra's best-known book, *The Beginning of Wisdom*, was translated from Hebrew into French in 1273 by Hagin le Juif (Hagin the Jew), under the auspices of Henry Bate. This translation served as a basis for three translations into Latin, still extant: one by Henry Bate in 1281 and 1292, another by Peter de Abano in 1293 and a third by Arnoul de Quinquempoix sometime before 1326. A translation was made independently from the Hebrew original into Catalan, by Martin of Osca (or Huesca), Aragon. From this Catalan version, *The Book of Nativities* was translated into Latin by Louis de Angulo in 1448.

Raphael Levy provides a word of caution with regard to the 1507 printing of the Peter de Abano translation:

> It is a Latin translation made from the French translation of the Hebrew, and anyone who has access to it must control it carefully, since the style is considered impure and inaccurate.
>
> The circumstances pertaining to the French translation by Hagin are explained in a colophon, which is reproduced at the end. Many years ago Paulin Paris (1847) remarked: "One can readily see that Hagin was obliged to dictate his translation to a copyist, because he himself did not know how to write them in French; for, if it had been a question merely of having them transcribed clearly and elegantly, he would have probably called upon a better calligrapher than Obert de Montdidier." This procedure of a Jew dictating a French translation to an amanuensis explains the curious fact that it was written in Roman characters, whereas all other contemporary texts, extant in Judaeo-French, were written in Hebrew characters. Consequently it may serve as a guide in deciphering the French texts written in Hebrew characters. Nothing else is known about Hagin le Juif nor about the scribe, but the name of Montdidier is significant because it gives a clue to the Picard dialect of the scribe. Henry Bate, under whose aegis the translation was executed, has already been referred to as one of the three translators from French into Latin.
>
> Naturally, the system of translating the Hebrew of Ibn Ezra into the French of Hagin transcribed by Obert has resulted in an awkward style. Hagin has interpreted the original in a servile manner and often given a literal equivalent word for word. In addition to the large proportion of solecisms and anacolutha, Hagin has interspersed his text with Hebraisms, while Obert suffered from an inevitable confusion in homonyms.

## Ezra's Work as Subject of Scholarly Research

Throughout the centuries, especially in the modern era, a vast number of scholars of various disciplines, studied his works extensively. An especially prominent one was George Sarton (1884–1956), the founder of History of Science. Of Ibn Ezra, he wrote:

> One of the greatest Biblical commentators of the Middle Ages, one of the forerunners of modern criticism, and much admired by Spinoza on that account. He was one of the first to translate writings of Muslims into Hebrew.
>
> He wrote various books on mathematics and astrology, on the calendar, and on the astrolabe; eight treatises on astrology were completed at Lucca in 1148.
>
> One of his main titles to fame is that through his wanderings in Provence, France and England, he helped to propagate among the Jews of Christian Europe (who, unlike their Spanish brethren, did not know Arabic) the rationalistic and scientific points of view which had been developed in Spain by Muslims and Jews on the basis of Greco-Muslim knowledge.
>
> He translated from Arabic into Hebrew three treatises on grammar by Judah Hayyuj (second half of the tenth century), Rome 1140; two treatises on astrology by Mashallah, before 1148; al-Biruni's commentary on al-Khwarizmi's tables, Narbonne 1160. The last mentioned is known only through Ibn Ezra's version.
>
> Ibn Ezra's mind was a strange mixture of rationalism and mysticism. His writings show his deep interest in magic squares and the mystical properties of numbers. He explained a decimal system of numeration using the first nine letters of the Hebrew alphabet, plus a circle for the zero, with place value.
>
> Though they do not directly concern us, Ibn Ezra's commentaries on the Old Testament were so influential, even outside of their own sphere, that something must be said of them. He explained his methods in the introduction to his commentary on the Pentateuch (Perush ha-Torah); he distinguished between the *peshat*, simple or literal meaning; the *derash*, common sense explanation; and the *midrash*, more philosophic explanation; trying hard to steer a middle course between excessive literalism and loose interpretations. As an instance of his boldness, I may mention his conclusion that the Book of Isaiah contains the sayings of two prophets, a view confirmed by modern criticism. The popularity of his commentaries is attested by the large number of super-commentaries.

## Philology and Lexicography

The Old French translation of Hagin le Juif has served Raphael Levy for comparative study with modern French; Frédéric Godefroy in *Dictionnaire de l'ancienne langue française;* Erhard Lommatzsch in Adolf Tobler's *Altfranzösisches Wörterbuch;* A.

Thomas in *Romania;* David Simon Blondheim in *Les Parlers judéo-romans et la Vetus latina;* and Lazar Sâineanu in *Autour des sources indigènes.*

## Citations of the Astrological Treatises of Ibn Ezra

In the introduction to *Beginning of Wisdom*, Raphael Levy writes:

> The number of citations of the astrological treatises of Abraham ibn Ezra is legion. The Hebraists who cited them from the twelfth to the seventeenth century include: Samuel Abu Nasr ibn Abbas, Eleazer ben Juda ben Kalonymos, Jedaiah ben Abraham Bedersi, Levi ben Abraham ben hayyim, Estori Farhi, Mordecai Comtino, Moses ibn Habib, Leon Mosconi, Joseph ben Eliezer of Saragossa, Samuel ibn Seneh Zarza, Samuel ben Saadia ibn Motot, Shem-Tob ben jehudah ibn Mayor, Immanuel ben Jacob Bonfils, Hayyim of Briviesca, Joseph Albo, Moses ben Elijah of Greece, Abraham ben Solomon of Torrutiel, Hayyim Vital, Eliezer of Germany, Joseph Solomon Delmedigo.
>
> In Latin literature, a list of references to these astrological treatises made in the fourteenth, fifteenth, sixteenth and seventeenth centuries is also quite imposing: John of Saxony, Firminus de Bellavalle, Nicolas de Cues, William Raymond Moncada, John of Glogau, Pico della Mirandola, Symon de Phares, Christopher Columbus, Abraham Zacuto, Augustinus Ricius, Johann Stoeffler, Luca Gaurico, Francesco Giuntini, Joseph Scaliger, Johann Bayer, Robert Fludd, Manasseh ben Israel, Athanasius Kircher, Aegidius Strauch.
>
> In modern scientific literature, one finds these treatises mentioned by the leading historians of astronomy and kindred science: R. H. Allen, F. Boll, P. Duhem, C. de la Ronciere, C. A. Nallino, Dr. George Sarton, D. E. Smith, L. Thorndike, E. Tiede.

## Astrology and Religion

Ibn Ezra's Hebrew editors are usually apologetic when it comes to his involvement with astrology and the publication of these works, explaining it by the need to properly understand his Biblical commentaries, in which he extensively resorts to astrological concepts and imagery.

Ibn Ezra was a profoundly religious man, but astrology did not seem to cause any conflict with his faith. Throughout his work it is evident that he fully embraced astrology, in a hard-nosed and intelligent way, with no doubts, no hesitations and no religious dilemmas. Yet, there is hardly any cross-over of religious thought into his astrological writings. Some reconciliation, however, is found in his theological writings and also in the opening of *The Beginning of Wisdom:*

> The beginning of wisdom is the fear of God, for it is the instruction. For when a man does not follow his eyes and heart to fulfill his [worldly] desire, then wisdom will rest in him. Moreover, the fear of God will protect him from the laws and decrees of the heavens all the days of his

life, and when his soul separates from his body it [the fear of God] will endow him with eternity and he shall live forever.

—Meira B. Epstein

**Sources:**

Ben Menahem, Naphtali. *The Book of Reasons*. 1941.

Fleischer, Yehuda Leib. *The Book of The World*. Timishuara, Romania, 1937.

Levin, Israel. *Abraham Ibn Ezra: Reader*. Tel Aviv: Israel Matz Publications, 1985.

Levy, Raphael. *The Astrological Works of Abraham ibn Ezra: A Literary and Linguistic Study with Special Reference to the Old French Translation of Hagin*. Baltimore: Johns Hopkins Press, 1927.

Levy, Raphael, and Francisco Cantera, eds. *The Beginning of Wisdom*. Baltimore: Johns Hopkins Press, 1939.

Sarton, George. *Introduction to the History of Science*. Baltimore: Carnegie Institution of Washington, 1927–48.

## Icarus

Icarus, asteroid 1566 (the 1566th asteroid to be discovered, on June 22, 1949), was named after the character from Greek mythology who died because he flew so close to the Sun that his wings (which were made of feathers and wax) melted. At the time, Icarus and his father were flying away from imprisonment on the island of Crete. The name is appropriate, in that Icarus's eccentric orbit (which takes a little more than a terrestrial year) carries it closer to the Sun than to Mercury. The asteroid is less than 1½ kilometers in diameter and is one of the more recent asteroids to be investigated by astrologers. Preliminary material on Icarus can be found in Demetra George and Douglas Bloch's *Astrology for Yourself*, and an ephemeris (table of celestial locations) for Icarus can be found in the second edition of George and Bloch's *Asteroid Goddesses*. Unlike the planets, which are associated with a wide range of phenomena, the smaller asteroids are said to represent a single principle. George and Bloch give Icarus's principle as "liberation"; their tentative key phrase for Icarus is "My capacity for liberation and risk-taking." Zipporah Dobyns regards the occurrence of Icarus in a prominent house, sign, or aspect related to the element fire as indicating the danger of overreaching oneself or acting prematurely. J. Lee Lehman relates Icarus to the power one gains from reconstituting oneself after the experience of "death" (in one form or another). In a more exoteric vein, Lehman also associates Icarus with flight and accidents. Jacob Schwartz gives this asteroid's astrological significance as "a need to escape quickly from restrictions, speed, risk taking, shamanic power, awareness of evolving through experience."

**Sources:**

Dobyns, Zipporah. *Expanding Astrology's Universe*. San Diego: Astro Computing Services, 1983.

George, Demetra, with Douglas Bloch. *Asteroid Goddesses: The Mythology, Psychology and Astrology of the Reemerging Feminine*. 2d ed. San Diego: Astro Computing Services, 1990.

———. *Astrology for Yourself: A Workbook for Personal Transformation*. Berkeley, CA: Wingbow Press, 1987.

Lehman, J. Lee. *The Ultimate Asteroid Book*. West Chester, PA: Whitford Press, 1988.

Schwartz, Jacob. *Asteroid Name Encyclopedia*. St. Paul, MN: Llewellyn Publications, 1995.

## Immersion

Immersion is a term used to describe the Sun or the Moon as it enters an eclipse. Sometimes the term is applied to occultations.

## Impeded

A celestial body was traditionally said to be impeded or impedited when poorly aspected.

## Imum Coeli

*Imum coeli* (IC) is the point directly opposite the midheaven (which is the most elevated degree of the zodiac). In many systems of house division, it is also the cusp (beginning) of the fourth house. The term *imum coeli* means "bottom of the sky" in Latin. *Imum coeli* is often used interchangeably with nadir, although this usage is technically incorrect: The nadir is the point directly opposite the zenith, not the point opposite the midheaven. The IC is occasionally referred to as the antimidheaven.

## Inception

Inceptional astrology is the branch of astrology dealing with the beginnings of things, and an inception chart is a horoscope calculated for the beginning of a given enterprise. The term was originally coined by Charles E. O. Carter to encompass electional astrology (consciously choosing the most astrologically propitious times to begin projects) as well as the retrospective study of starting points (e.g., casting a horoscope for the launch date of the *Titanic* to determine if its sinking could have been predicted).

## Inclination

An inclination is the angle at which two planes cross. In astrology, it is used to refer to the movement of a celestial body to a position other than the one occupied at birth.

## Inferior Conjunctions

Inferior conjunctions are conjunctions between the Sun and the inferior planets in which Mercury or Venus lies between the Sun and Earth. The antonymous expression superior conjunction refers to conjunctions in which Mercury or Venus is located behind the Sun. None of the other planets is capable of inferior conjunctions, because their orbits never carry them between the Sun and Earth.

## Inferior Planets

The original meaning of inferior was below. In the concept of the universe that was prevalent prior to the Copernican revolution, when Earth was thought to be the stable center around which every other celestial body revolved, the orbits of Mercury and Venus were considered to be closer to the Earth and thus "below" the orbit of the Sun. These two planets were thus referred to as the inferior planets. The current negative connotations of the term "inferior" have caused this expression to be dropped in favor of the term "inner planets."

## Influence

Astrologers often speak of the correlation between planetary positions and earthly events in terms of influence, as if the planets actually exert forces—analogous to gravity or magnetism—that cause a particular incident. If pressed for an explanation, however, the majority of professional astrologers would probably offer a different type of explanation, such as the Jungian notion of synchronicity.

## Infortunes

Traditionally, the planets most likely to lead to difficulties in life—namely, Mars and Saturn—were referred to as the infortunes ("unfortunates"). Mars was further designated as the infortune minor, and Saturn as the infortune major.

## Ingress

Ingress refers to the entry of a planet, one of the luminaries (the Sun or the Moon), or some other celestial body such as an asteroid into a sign of the zodiac. Modern ephemerides (tables of planetary positions) often include information on the exact time one of the planets or one of the luminaries enters a new sign. The term has also been used to refer to the entry of a transiting planet or luminary into a new house.

## Intercepted

With the exception of the equal house system, most systems of house division utilize houses of varied sizes. One result of this variability is that sometimes a wide house will begin in the latter part of one sign, encompass the next sign, and end in a third sign. The middle sign is said to be intercepted. Because houses that are directly opposite each other are the same size, the sign opposite the intercepted sign will also be intercepted. For example, in a given natal chart, the second house begins at 25° Gemini and ends at 3° Leo. The intervening sign, which is Cancer, is thus intercepted in the second house. Correspondingly, the opposite house, which is the eighth house, will begin at 25° Sagittarius and end at 3° Aquarius. Cancer's opposite sign, Capricorn, will be intercepted in the eighth house. Astrologers are divided as to the influence of interception, some asserting that there is a weakening effect on planets placed in an intercepted sign, others asserting just the opposite. At the very least, it is safe to say that the affairs of an intercepted house are usually more complex than those of other houses. When giving a general, introductory interpretation of a natal chart, the majority of astrologers ignore interceptions.

In charts where signs are intercepted, there are other, narrower houses that begin and end in the same sign. This results in two successive houses with the same sign on their cusps (the same sign at the beginning of both houses), which are thus both ruled by the same planet. Some contemporary astrologers interpret this situation as indicating that the affairs of these two houses are linked. Thus, for example, in a natal chart in which the second and third houses are so linked, the native might earn her or his living (second house) through communication, publishing, or travel (third house).

**Sources:**

Filbey, John, and Peter Filbey. *The Astrologer's Companion*. Wellingborough, Northamptonshire, UK: Aquarian Press, 1986.

McEvers, Joan. "Insight on Interceptions." In *Astrology: Old Theme, New Thoughts*. Edited by Marion D. March and Joan McEvers. San Diego: ACS Publications, 1984.

## International Society for Astrological Research

The International Society for Astrological Research (ISAR) was incorporated in Sacramento, California, on December 5, 1979, at 10:30 AM. ISAR is a professional organization that serves the world astrological community with an elected board of directors and a network of vice presidents from many countries.

Since 1980, ISAR has produced annual conferences focusing on professionalism, research, technology, and international outreach, offering scholarships for conference attendance. ISAR was a pioneer among international astrology organizations in initiating professional standards of paying conference speakers, and paying authors for accepted articles published in its quarterly journals.

ISAR's support and backing provided the important gestation phase for Lois Rodden's AstroDataBank, providing accurate birth data to the astrology community. It has given financial grants for research that has helped astrologers earn advanced academic degrees. ISAR keeps a vast library of seminar tapes, including many classic astrologers presenting their specialties. Its *Weekly Online Newsletter*, initiated in 2000, keeps members involved in current events and the latest in research information.

ISAR was the cofounder of the prestigious United Astrology Conference in 1984 and was a cosponsor in 1986, 1989, 1992, 1995, 1998, and 2002. The organization has a code of ethics and is developing a voluntary program that astrological organizations and astrology schools can join in order to share a common standard for the professional practice of astrology. Graduates of these programs can receive a C.A.P. (Certified Astrological Professional) certification from ISAR.

The following ISAR publications have helped support the astrology research community: *Tables for Aspect Research* 1986; *Astrological Research Methods* (volume I, 1995); *ISAR's Financial and Mundane Book* (1996); its quarterly journal, *Kosmos* (1978–99); and *International Astrologer* (1999 to present).

Memberships and selected publications are available from: ISAR, P.O. Box 38613, Los Angeles, CA 90038-0613; phone: 805-525-0461; fax: 805-933-0301; web site: http://www.isarastrology.com.

## Irving, Kenneth

Kenneth Irving's primary interest has been the recognition and understanding of the part of astrology that can be treated as a natural science. He has been instrumental in explaining the work of the late Michel Gauquelin to the astrological public. At the same time, he has been an active participant in defending Gauquelin's work (primarily the Mars effect for sports champions) in the scientific world, and to that end has written or co-written papers in scientific journals as well as making a substantial contribution to the groundbreaking book *The Tenacious Mars Effect* (co-written with Suitbert Ertel), which shows a convergence of opinion (if not agreement) about the Mars Effect from three separate worlds: science, astrology, and skepticism.

Aside from this work, in his lectures and writing he has explored how Gauquelin's findings might be applied in astrological practice. Perhaps the most widely known example of his efforts in this direction is the "angry Venus," a name applied to a pattern of traits that appear to define Venus when it appears in one of the Gauquelin "power zones" in a birth chart. Irving contends that the sweet, flirtatious, harmonious interpretation of Venus seen in astrology is at best one-dimensional, and that though the dominant themes of the Venus personality can include a pleasant and harmonious exterior, the core of the Venus type centers on personal value systems, loyalty, antiauthoritarianism, and freethinking. The "anger" referred to in the name is directed at those who violate the Venusian's closely held values or principles, often without knowing it.

As an editor and column writer (1974 to the present) for *American Astrology*, a general-interest magazine, Irving has been the author of several columns, including "Eye on the Nation" (mundane astrology) and "The New Astrology." He served as the board president of the United Astrology Conference from 1999 to 2001, and as a member of the AFAN Steering Committee from 1992 to 1994. He has been on the AFAN advisory board since that organization's inception, and currently serves on the Correlation Editorial Board. Irving has lectured for numerous local and regional astrology groups, and has been on the faculty of conferences sponsored by the National Astrological Society, the International Society for Astrological Research (ISAR), the National Council for Geocosmic Research (NCGR), the Astrological Association of Great Britain (AAGB), and the United Astrology Conference. He is also coauthor of *The Psychology of Astro*Carto*Graphy* with Jim Lewis.

## Isis

Isis, asteroid 42 (the 42nd asteroid to be discovered, on May 23, 1856), is approximately 94 kilometers in diameter and has an orbital period of 3.8 years. It was named after a major Egyptian goddess. Initially a divinity of fertility, in later mystery religions Isis became a goddess of wisdom. Her chief myth concerns the dismemberment of her husband Osiris, whom she reconstructed. According to Martha Lang-Wescott, Isis may represent sibling relationships, efforts to get or put things or people "together," fragmentation or scattered locations. This asteroid's key word is "collate." According to J. Lee Lehman, Isis, as well as the asteroid Osiris, indicates "something about the

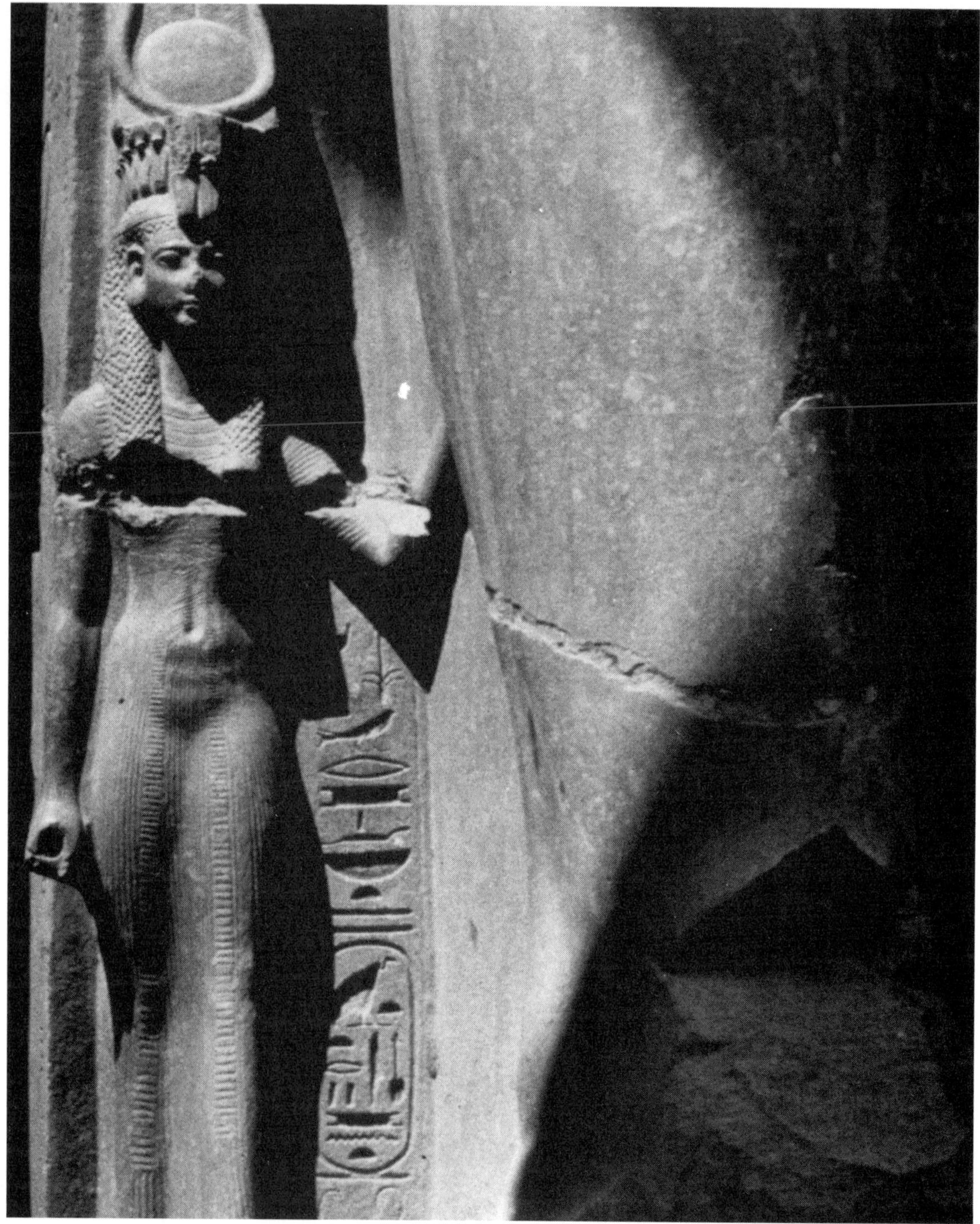

A detail of Isis on a giant statue of Ramses II in the temple at Luxor, Egypt. *Reproduced by permission of Fortean Picture Library.*

masculine-feminine or left-brain–right-brain balance of a person." For people in whose charts either of these asteroids is prominent, androgyny will be an issue. Jacob Schwartz gives Isis's influence as "fragmentation vs. wholeness; sibling issues."

**Sources:**


Lang-Wescott, Martha. *Asteroids-Mechanics: Ephemerides II*. Conway, MA: Treehouse Mountain, 1990.

———. *Mechanics of the Future: Asteroids*. Rev. ed. Conway, MA: Treehouse Mountain, 1991.

Lehman, J. Lee. *The Ultimate Asteroid Book*. West Chester, PA: Whitford Press, 1988.

Schwartz, Jacob. *Asteroid Name Encyclopedia*. St. Paul, MN: Llewellyn Publications, 1995.

## JAWER, JEFF

Jeff Jawer, born May 16, 1946, in New York City, is one of the pioneers of experiential astrology and a leader in astrological organizations. He began his astrological studies in 1973 at the University of Massachusetts, where he earned a B.A. degree in the history and science of astrology. He established OMetrics Astrology Services there with Barry Lynes, his first teacher. Jawer also presented for two years a daily astrological radio program called "High Tides," which continued two more years in Atlanta, Georgia.

In Atlanta, Jawer became corporate astrologer for International Horizons, Inc., and co-invented Astro, the first handheld astrological calculator. He passed the professional-level examination of the American Federation of Astrologers and the professional examination of the City of Atlanta's Board of Astrology Examiners. He later became chairman of the examining board and served two terms as the president of the Metro Atlanta Astrological Society. He also completed Zipporah Dobyns's 16-day intensive course, is a certified Astro*Carto*Graphy (A*C*G) interpreter, and taught at the first A*C*G seminar, which he organized with Jim Lewis.

Jawer coined the now widely used term "astrodrama" in an article for *Astrology Now* magazine and has had numerous articles published on a variety of subjects in journals and in four books. He has led workshops on experiential and other aspects of astrology at over 50 conventions. Jawer has taught astrology throughout the United States and in Canada, Brazil, France, England, Holland, Belgium, Spain, Switzerland and Australia. He lived and worked in France for two years with Alexander Ruperti's Network for Humanistic Astrology.

In 1982, Jawer was one of the founders of the Association for Astrological Networking (AFAN) and served on its steering committee for four years. In 1986, he helped organize the first United Astrology Congress. He has received the Mars Award from the Fraternity for Canadian Astrologers and has been a nominee for the Regulus Award.

Jawer was the director of public relations for Matrix Software in Big Rapids, Michigan from 1995 to 1997, and then in 1998 served as vice president of Astro Communications Services in San Diego. In 1999 Jawer founded StarIQ.com in Redmond, Washington, with Rick Levine. At present he lives with his wife and two daughters in Redmond.

**Sources:**

McEvers, Joan, ed. *Intimate Relationships, The Astrology of Attraction*. St. Paul, MN: Llewellyn Publications, 1991.

———. *Spiritual, Metaphysical & New Trends in Modern Astrology*. St. Paul, MN: Llewellyn Publications, 1988.

Tyl, Noel, ed. *Communicating the Horoscope*,. St. Paul, MN: Llewellyn Publications, 1995.

———. *How to Personalize the Outer Planets: The Astrology of Uranus, Neptune, and Pluto*. St. Paul, MN: Llewellyn Publications, 1992.

## Jayne, Charles A., Jr.

Charles A. Jayne, Jr., born October 9, 1911, in Jenkintown, Pennsylvania, was an eminent astrologer, writer, teacher, and lecturer, who stressed the importance of mathematics and astronomy. He began studying astrology in the mid-1930s. After serving in the U.S. Army during World War II, he became deeply involved in astrological work. During the 1946 fall semester, he served on the astrological faculty of the American Foundation for Metaphysical Arts and Sciences in New York City. He contributed technical material, such as data on eclipses, to Nicholas DeVore's *Encyclopedia of Astrology* and wrote frequently for such astrological periodicals as *Horoscope* magazine.

Jayne joined many astrological organizations and formed several of his own, most notably the Astrological Research Associates in 1958, which published the periodical *In Search*. He was one of the founders of the National Council for Geocosmic Research (NCGR), an officer in DeVore's Astrologic Research Society, and president of the Astrologers Guild (1958–1960). He joined the American Federation of Astrologers in May 1956 and was chairman of the Resolutions Committee at the 1972 convention. He died on December 31, 1985, in Goshen, New York.

**Sources:**

Holden, James H., and Robert A. Hughes. *Astrological Pioneers of America*. Tempe, AZ: American Federation of Astrologers, 1988.

Jayne, Charles A., Jr. *Horoscope Interpretation Outlined*. New York: Astrological Bureau, 1970.

———. *A New Dimension in Astrology*. New York: Astrological Bureau, 1975.

———. *The Technique of Rectification*. 2d ed. New York: Astrological Bureau, 1972.

———. *The Unknown Planets*. New York: Astrological Bureau, 1974.

## Johndro, L. Edward

Lorne Edward Johndro was born in Quebec on January 30, 1882, the same day that Franklin D. Roosevelt was born. While still a young man, he moved south to the United States, settling in Lockport, New York. He became friends with Ernest Wykes, a superintendent of a children's home in Lockport who frequently discussed astrology with him.

Johndro worked as an electrical engineer from 1914 to 1917. He then studied radio and graduated from the National Radio Institute in the 1920s. He perceived parallels between radio/electromagnetism and astrology, and this was reflected in his books and articles, which contain frequent references to radio and electromagnetism. Johndro's writing style is difficult, and his references to electricity only compound these difficulties.

He published two books on the fixed stars in 1919. Their purpose was to assist astrologers in locating terrestrial locations where certain celestial configurations might be anticipated to manifest. Because of their mathematical complexity, these techniques have been infrequently used.

Johndro also introduced the vertex as an important point in the astrological chart, described a technique for constructing a "locality chart" from terrestrial latitude and longitude, and theorized a complex schema of planetary rulership. He continued to write and experiment for the rest of his life. Johndro has a well-deserved reputation as a highly technical astrological writer. He died in the late afternoon of November 11, 1951, in San Diego, California.

**Sources:**

Holden, James H., and Robert A. Hughes. *Astrological Pioneers of America*. Tempe, AZ: American Federation of Astrologers, 1988.

Johndro, L. Edward. *Astrological Dictionary and Self-Reading Horoscope*. 2d ed. Washington, DC: American Federation of Astrologers, n.d.

———. *The Earth in the Heavens*. San Bernardino, CA: Doherty, 1929. Reprint, New York: Weiser, 1970.

———. *A New Conception of Sign Rulership*. Washington, DC: American Federation of Astrologers, n.d.

———. *The Stars: How and Where They Influence*. San Bernardino, CA: Doherty, 1929. Reprint, New York: Weiser, 1970.

## Johnson, Stephanie

Stephanie Johnson holds a Federation of Australian Astrologers' practitioner's certificate and diploma and is a member of the Federation of Australian Astrologers (FAA). She is a student of medieval astrology and the ancient wisdom teachings. She holds a masters of science degree in esotericism from the University of the Seven Rays in Jersey City Heights, New Jersey, as well as the Robert Zoller Certificate of Medieval Astrology. She has lectured at national conferences, and her astrology articles have appeared in Australian publications, including the *FAA Journal* and the *Astrological Monthly Review*. She is also editor of the *Australian Data Collection*. Before beginning her professional astrology career Stephanie was a journalist for 15 years in Australia, England, and the United States.

## Jones, Marc Edmund

Marc Edmund Jones, born October 1, 1888, in St. Louis, Missouri, was a well-known occultist and astrologer. He was educated at the Theological Seminary of the United

Presbyterian Church and Columbia University, where he received a Ph.D. in education in 1948. A long-lived individual, he pursued such diverse careers as astrologer, editorial consultant, Protestant minister, and motion-picture scenarist.

Jones became interest in astrology in 1913 and founded the Sabian Assembly in 1923. He served as president of the American Foundation for Metaphysical Arts and Sciences in New York City some 20 years later. He was an early member of the American Federation of Astrology (AFA) and a member of the Astrologers' Guild of America, serving as the latter's vice president (1941–1942). Late in life he was one of the best-known astrologers in America. He died March 5, 1980, in Stanwood, Washington.

Jones's approach to delineation utilizing horoscope patterns, in *Guide to Horoscope Interpretation*, has proved to be highly popular with astrologers, as has his approach to degree interpretations in *The Sabian Symbols*. These methods were especially popularized by Dane Rudhyar, who built upon Jones's work.

**Sources:**

Holden, James H., and Robert A. Hughes. *Astrological Pioneers of America*. Tempe, AZ: American Federation of Astrologers, 1988.

Jones, Marc Edmund. *Astrology, How and Why It Works*. Philadelphia: David McKay Co., 1945.

———. *Guide to Horoscope Interpretation*. Philadelphia: David McKay Co., 1941.

———. *How to Learn Astrology*. Philadelphia: David McKay Co., 1941.

———. *How to Live with the Stars*. Wheaton, IL: Theosophical Publishing House, 1975.

———. *The Sabian Symbols*. New York: Sabian Publishing Society, 1953.

## Jones Patterns

The Jones patterns are the planetary arrangements first described by the astrologer Marc Edmund Jones, such as the locomotive pattern and the bucket pattern.

## Jubilatrix

Jubilatrix, asteroid 652 (the 652nd asteroid to be discovered, on November 4, 1907), is approximately 15 kilometers in diameter and has an orbital period of 4.1 years. Its Latin name means "woman who rejoices." It was named for the 60th Jubilee Year reign of Austrian emperor Franz Joseph. In a natal chart, Jubilatrix's location by sign and house indicates where and how one is most likely to "rejoice." When afflicted by inharmonious aspects, Jubilatrix may indicate either the opposite of rejoicing or rejoicing for the wrong reasons. If prominent in a natal chart (e.g., conjunct the Sun or the ascendant), it may show an exceptionally joyful person.

**Sources:**

Kowal, Charles T. *Asteroids: Their Nature and Utilization*. Chichester, West Sussex, UK: Ellis Horwood Limited, 1988.

Room, Adrian. *Dictionary of Astronomical Names*. London: Routledge, 1988.

Schwartz, Jacob. *Asteroid Name Encyclopedia*. St. Paul, MN: Llewellyn Publications, 1995.

## Judicial Astrology

Judicial astrology is an older name for mundane astrology, which is the study of celestial influences on nations, cultural movements, world affairs, etc.

## Julian Day

For simplifying certain kinds of calculations, it was found to be helpful to delete references to months and years, and simply number all days consecutively. Each such numbered day is referred to as a Julian Day (JD).

## Jung, Carl

Carl Jung was a turn-of-the-twentieth-century psychoanalyst whose formulation of psychology had a major impact on modern astrology. Jung was born in Basel, Switzerland, on July 26, 1875. After completing medical school, he went on to study psychoanalysis with Sigmund Freud, but later struck off to formulate his own distinctive brand of psychology. Jung utilized astrology in his counseling work, and it was his work with myths and symbols that most influenced modern astrology.

Among other achievements, Jung took the ancient approach to symbolic interpretation and recast it in a form acceptable to the modern world. While astrology has utilized symbolic methods since ancient times, the appeal of the Jungian system has been such that many contemporary astrologers have adopted the language as well as some of the methodology of this school of psychology. The study and integration of Jung's approach by such influential figures of modern astrology as Dane Rudhyar has also had the effect of "psychologizing" contemporary astrology, meaning that the planets and signs are now viewed as representing primarily aspects of one's psychological makeup, as well as psychological types. By way of contrast, traditional astrology was more focused on the prediction of events and on helping clients choose the most auspicious moments to carry out certain actions.

Although many astrologers have attempted to reformulate astrology in terms of Jung (making Jungian psychology the primary component of the mixture), more astrologers have adopted Jungian language to explain what astrologers have always done—interpreted symbols. Three Jungian terms—collective unconscious, archetype, and synchronicity—are almost universally familiar to contemporary astrologers. Practitioners with deeper interests in Jungian psychology have gone so far as to correlate Jung's system of classifying people into psychological types (feeling, thinking, sensate, and intuitive), with the four classical elements.

**Sources:**

Bach, Eleanor. *Astrology from A to Z: An Illustrated Source Book*. New York: Philosophical Library, 1990.

Brau, Jean-Louis, Helen Weaver, and Allan Edmands. *Larousse Encyclopedia of Astrology*. New York: New American Library, 1980.

*The Journal of Geocosmic Research* (Autumn 1975): vol. 1, no. 3.

**The father of psychoanalysis and the introvert/extrovert personality types, famed Swiss physician Carl Gustav Jung.** ***Reproduced by permission of Fortean Picture Library.***

## JUNO

The asteroids are small planet-like bodies that orbit the Sun in a belt that lies mostly between Mars and Jupiter. They first dawned on human consciousness in the early

1800s. The first four asteroids to be sighted were given the names of four of the great goddesses of classical antiquity: Ceres (discovered in 1801), Pallas Athene (discovered in 1802), Juno (discovered in 1804), and Vesta (discovered in 1807).

Many more asteroids were soon discovered, so that by the end of the nineteenth century, over a thousand were known. The first asteroid ephemeris (a table listing planetary positions) was made available to astrologers in 1973 by Eleanor Bach, and it covered only the original four. Today astrologers have computer software developed by Mark Pottenger that tracks the placements of over nine thousand.

Among the thousands of asteroids known, Ceres, Pallas, Juno, and Vesta have a special place. While these are not necessarily the largest asteroids, they were the first to be discovered, and as such they have imprinted themselves on human consciousness in a significant way. They also complete the female pantheon of goddesses, rounding out the system of symbols begun in the usual 10 planets. Of the six great goddesses of Olympus, only Aphrodite (Venus) and Artemis (the Moon) are represented in the conventional astrological symbol system. The other four great goddesses of Graeco-Roman mythology—Demeter (Ceres), Athene (Pallas), Hera (Juno), and Hestia (Vesta)—were missing from astrology until they were reinvoked by their discovery in the early 1800s.

Juno, the third asteroid to be discovered, represents a third stage of life. After the Pallas stage of going out into the world, possibly to have a career, one is ready to encounter one's equal and embark upon the journey of partnership that usually takes the form of marriage.

The glyph for Juno suggests a scepter, befitting the queen of the gods, and a flower, befitting her femininity. In general form, the glyph for Juno resembles that for Venus; but instead of the circle denoting Venus's mirror, there are outward-pointing rays, indicating that the seductive femininity of Venus is about to turn outward, bearing fruit in marriage and children.

In classical mythology, Juno, known to the Greeks as Hera, was wedded to Jupiter (Greek Zeus), supreme king of heaven and earth. As such, she became his queen and the goddess of marriage. In the myths of an earlier time, however, long before her meeting with Jupiter, Juno was one of the primary great goddesses in her own right. As the only one who was his equal, Juno was chosen by Jupiter to initiate with him the rites of legal, monogamous, patriarchally defined marriage. As his queen, she became but a figurehead and was repeatedly deceived, betrayed, and humiliated by her husband's many infidelities. In the myths Juno was portrayed as a jealous, manipulative, vindictive, revengeful, and malcontent wife who, after tempestuous fights, would periodically leave her husband. However, she always returned to try to work things out one more time.

In the human psyche, Juno represents that aspect of each person's nature that feels the urge to unite with another person to build a future together in a committed relationship. This partnership is sustained over time through a formal and binding commitment, whether it be a worldly or a spiritual bond. Juno speaks to one's desire to connect with a mate who is one's true equal on all levels—psychologically, emotionally, mentally, and spiritually.

**A sixteenth-century woodcut of Jupiter, Juno, Neptune, and Mercury from Greek mythology. *Reproduced by permission of Fortean Picture Library.***

When we do not receive intimacy, depth, equality, honesty, respect, and fulfillment in our unions, Juno speaks to our emotions of disappointment, despair, anger, and rage, which can overwhelm us. This is especially true when we have given up a great deal, such as a career, family, home, or religion, to enter the relationship. The Juno in us makes us confront the issues of submission and domination, fidelity and infidelity, trust and deception, and forgiveness and revenge. In her realm, we find ourselves in power struggles for equality as we attempt to balance and integrate ourselves with another person and learn to transform selfish desires into cooperative union.

Within a context of separation and return, Juno encourages us to take the vow of "for better or worse, in sickness and health, till death us do part." She brings the wisdom that conscious relationship is a path to spiritual enlightenment, and the knowledge that relationships allow us to perfect and complete ourselves.

In today's world, Juno is also a symbol for the plight of battered and powerless wives and minorities; for the psychological complexes of love-addiction and codependency; for the rise in divorce rates as people are driven to release unmeaningful relationships; and for the redefinition of traditional relationships in the face of feminism and of gay and lesbian coupling.

To sum up, Juno is the archetype of the wife and partner who maintains her marital commitment to her husband in the face of conflict and struggle. In the birth chart, she, along with other chart factors such as the seventh house, represents your capacity for meaningful committed relationships, your attitude toward such relationships, and the type of relationship experiences that you need in order to feel fulfilled. She represents both what you need and what you attract, and she also signifies the ways in which you act out your disappointment over broken unions. These relationships are usually romantic in nature, but may sometimes assume other forms such as business, professional or creative partnerships.

The Asteroid Goddess Natal Report Writer generates a 40-page personalized interpretation of these four major asteroids in the birth chart. It is available from Astrolabe.

—Demetra George

**Sources:**

Dobyns, Zipporah. *Expanding Astrology's Universe*. San Diego: Astro Computing Services, 1983.

Donath, Emma Belle. *Asteroids in the Birth Chart*. Tempe, AZ: American Federation of Astrologers, 1979.

George, Demetra, with Douglas Bloch. *Asteroid Goddesses: The Mythology, Psychology and Astrology of the Reemerging Feminine*. 2nd ed. rev. San Diego: Astro Computing Services, 1990.

———. *Astrology for Yourself: A Workbook for Personal Transformation*. Berkeley, CA: Wingbow Press, 1987.

Lehman, J. Lee. *The Ultimate Asteroid Book*. West Chester, PA: Whitford Press, 1988.

## JUPITER

Jupiter, the fifth planet from the Sun, is the largest body in the solar system, containing two-thirds the mass of the entire solar system outside the Sun. It is like a miniature planetary system all by itself. Since 2000, Jupiter is now known to have 28 moons of varying sizes. The four largest of them are easily visible with even a small telescope. Galileo discovered these larger moons in 1610. They are called Galilean satellites. Copernicus's model of the heliocentric solar system was supported by the fact that these bodies were noticed to be orbiting another planet.

Jupiter begins a grouping of planets that have a different composition from the four terrestrial planets. These are referred to as the Jovian planets because of their giant sizes. (Jove was the chief Roman deity.) Jupiter's gassy composition is a combination of 90 percent hydrogen and 10 percent helium. It has no solid surface at all. Jupiter rotates once every 10 hours. It orbits the Sun every 11.86 years. Its most distinguishing feature is the giant red spot. Observations from the 1979 *Voyager* mission identified the red spot as the vortex of a violent, long-lasting anticyclonic storm, similar to big storms on earth. Superbolts of giant-sized lightning and giant polar aurorae were also Voyager discoveries about Jupiter.

Early Greek mythology called Jupiter Zeus, and the Romans called him Jove. Jupiter was the son of Saturn (Kronos.) Just as the Oracle of Delphi predicted to Saturn, Zeus was the son to dethrone him, as he had overpowered his own father, Ouranos.

**An engraving from the seventeenth century of Jupiter with his thunderbolt and eagle.** ***Reproduced by permission of Fortean Picture Library.***

Zeus and his brothers drew lots for their share of the universe. Zeus, Lord of the Sky, became chief of the Gods. His power was greater than all the others combined. He was righteous and demanded right action from men, not sacrifices. Jupiter is associated with the idea of justice. His low side made him out of control with his anger and his incalculable use of lightning bolts. He was never a faithful husband. He often acted like a storm cloud, building things up to turbulence. His high side can make things glorious. He gives hope and honors and bestows great gifts. Zeus was known for his great highs and lows.

In Mesopotamian astrology, Jupiter was linked to Marduk, ruler of the gods. Marduk was associated with wisdom, justice, water, and vegetation. Jupiter, known as the Greater Benefic, is the planet of hope, possibilities, expansion, and plenty. It is the most diurnal planet, next to the Sun. Jupiter has beneficial qualities in a nocturnal chart, as well. Jupiter rules the fire triplicity at night. It rules the masculine fire sign, Sagittarius. It is adventurous and robust in a diurnal chart. Jupiter is also the traditional ruler of the feminine water sign, Pisces. It is exalted in Cancer. Jupiter's affinity with water signs makes it more compassionate and generous. In a nocturnal chart, Jupiter is more subdued and moderate. Jupiter is in its fall in Capricorn and its detriment in Virgo, both earth signs. This shows how unhappy Jupiter is when forced to conform and fit into rigid forms.

Jupiter is a social planet. Its influence is open, expansive, and temperate. When in sect, it confirms and radifies what the Sun selects. When contrary to sect, it creates obstacles to stabilization because too much is included. In the hellenistic system, the star Jupiter is assigned the special essence of reputation and crowns of office and expectations.

When Jupiter is dignified its influence is magnanimous, mild tempered, just, wise, and religious. When not dignified its influence can be scattered, over done, shallow, indifferent, and easily led astray. Its real character is good-natured, freedom loving, confident, and conscious of right and wrong, wanting to do what is best. Its optimistic outlook often brings good fortune and opportunity. There is ease to life that allows for luck and happiness.

Jupiter is traditionally associated with begetting children, desire, knowledge, friendships with great men, abundance, great gifts, freedom, trust, possessions, justice, reputation, preferments of priests, government, inheritances, benefaction, confirmation of good things, and deliverance from bad things. It represents officials, administrators, advisors, counselors, aristocrats, aristocracy, and foreign ministry. It rules law, courts, judges, lawyers, and the judicial system, as well as clergy, priests, ministers, and religious leaders. In business, Jupiter rules bankers, brokers, bondsmen, cashiers, clerks, magistrates, managers, merchants, stockbrokers, stocks, treasuries, trusts, and taxes. It is associated with celebrations, coronations, commemorations, grandeur, graduations, inaugurations, monuments, pageants, parades, regalia, rituals, salutes, and winning.

Jupiter gives affluence, amplification, applause, betterment, benevolence, bonuses, charity, chivalry, compensation, credentials, dignity, distinction, elite position, eminence, endowments, enhancement, extravagance, good fortune, gain, generosity, increases, endorsement, inheritance, integrity, joviality, luck, magnanimity, magnificence, opulence, philanthropy, prestige, pride, proclamation, promotion, protocol, protection, purity, recommendation, redemption, reputation, remuneration, restitution, reverence, self-esteem, sincerity, spirituality, splendor, success, superiority, temperance, title, tributes, verification, vindication, wealth, wisdom, worthiness, and worship.

Classical diseases and health problems associated with Jupiter are abscesses, accumulations, arteries, assimilation of food, blood in general and blood pressure, boils, the formation of red blood cells, diabetes, diseases from excess, enlargements, fatty degeneration, glands, growths, hepatic system, liver, upper legs and thighs, obesity, pleurisy, and tumors.

Modern astrology links Jupiter with the level of intelligence that perceives the world around us and puts things into a context that creates our beliefs and our worldviews. It develops the rational thinking processes that lead to conclusion and understanding, bringing opinion and wisdom. Jupiter is the storyteller and is responsible for the dissemination of information on a broad scale. It is influential and inspirational in its delivery of ideas. In modern times it is associated with advertising, sales, and propaganda. Jupiter relates to higher levels of thought: education, philosophy, psychology and religion.

In *Relating: An Astrological Guide to Living with Others on a Small Planet,* Liz Greene identifies Jupiter as the planet symbolizing the myth-making principle:

> Jupiter is thus connected with the urge within the psyche to create symbols, and this takes us into profound depths when we consider the creative power that has shaped the great myths, legends, and religions of the world. It is no less a creative power that shapes the symbolism of our dreams, so that each dream is a masterpiece of meaning and could not be altered in any way for improvement. In this way Jupiter is truly a god of the gateway, for he forms a link between conscious and unconscious through the creation and intuitive understanding of symbols. As we have seen, symbols are the primordial language of life; and Jupiter symbolizes the function which both creates them within man and intuits their meaning.

In Jyotish astrology, Jupiter is associated with the elephant-headed god Ganesh, and the king of the gods, Indra. The myths call Jupiter either Guru, which means "teacher," or Brhaspati, which means "lord of sacred speech." Jupiter is the guru to the gods.

In *The Myths and Gods of India,* Alain Danielou notes that Indra represents the power of the thunderbolt, the all-pervading electric energy, which is the nature of cosmic as well as animal life. He is the deity of the sphere of space, and the ruler of the storm. Indra embodies the qualities of all the gods, hence becoming the greatest. Ever young, Indra embodies all the virtues of youth: heroism, generosity, and exuberance. He stands for action and service but also for the need of force, which leads to power, to victory, and booty. He leads warriors and protects them with his thunderbolt and his bow, the rainbow. Indra loves intoxicants and pleasure. As the embodiment of virility, Indra is represented in the bull, the perfect male. He has numerous love affairs, including the wives of sages. He is given many names. Today, Indra is not the object of direct veneration, but he receives incidental worship and there is a festival in his honor called the "Raising of the Standard of Indra."

—Norma Jean Ream

**Sources:**

Bills, Rex. *The Rulership Book, A Directory of Astrological Correspondences*. Richmond, VA: Macoy Publishing & Masonic Supply Co., 1971.

Crane, Joseph. *A Practical Guide to Traditional Astrology*. Orleans, MA: Archive for the Retrieval of Historical Astrological Texts, 1997.

Danielou, Alain. *The Myths and Gods of India*. Rochester, VT: Inner Traditions International, 1991.

Greene, Liz. *Relating: An Astrological Guide to Living with Others on a Small Planet*. 2d ed. York Beach, ME: Samuel Weiser, 1978.

Hamilton, Edith. *Mythology*. Boston: Little, Brown, 1942.

Pasachoff, Jay M. *Contemporary Astronomy*. 4th ed. Philadelphia: Saunders College Publishing, 1989.

Schmidt, Robert, translator. *Vettius Valens, Book I, Chapter I*. Original Source Texts and Auxiliary Materials for the Study of Hellenistic Astrology and Project Hindsight, Phaser Foundation, 2002.

Wilson, James. *A Complete Dictionary of Astrology*. London: W. Hughes, 1819.

## JUSTITIA

Justitia, asteroid 269 (the 269th asteroid to be discovered, on September 21, 1887), is approximately 35 kilometers in diameter and has an orbital period of 4.2 years. Justitia is a "concept" asteriod. Its name is a personified form of justice. In a natal chart, Justitia's location by sign and house position indicates where one gives or receives justice. When afflicted by inharmonious aspects, Justitia can show injustice or rigid, legalistic justice. If prominent in a natal chart (e.g., conjunct the Sun or the ascendant), it may show an exceptionally fair person or someone for whom justice is a dominant life theme.

**Sources:**

Kowal, Charles T. *Asteroids: Their Nature and Utilization*. Chichester, West Sussex, UK: Ellis Horwood Limited, 1988.

Room, Adrian. *Dictionary of Astronomical Names*. London: Routledge, 1988.

Schwartz, Jacob. *Asteroid Name Encyclopedia*. St. Paul, MN: Llewellyn Publications, 1995.

## JYESHTA

Jyeshta (The Eldest) is one of the Nakshatras (lunar mansions) of Vedic astrology. A hanging earring is the symbol for this Nakshatra found from Scorpio 16°40' to 30°. Considered a good time to act more "mature," people will find it easier to build a better support network of their friends, but may run into family tensions and/or be more scheming. Indra, chief of the gods, presides, and the planet Mercury rules over Jyeshta.

—Pramela Thiagesan

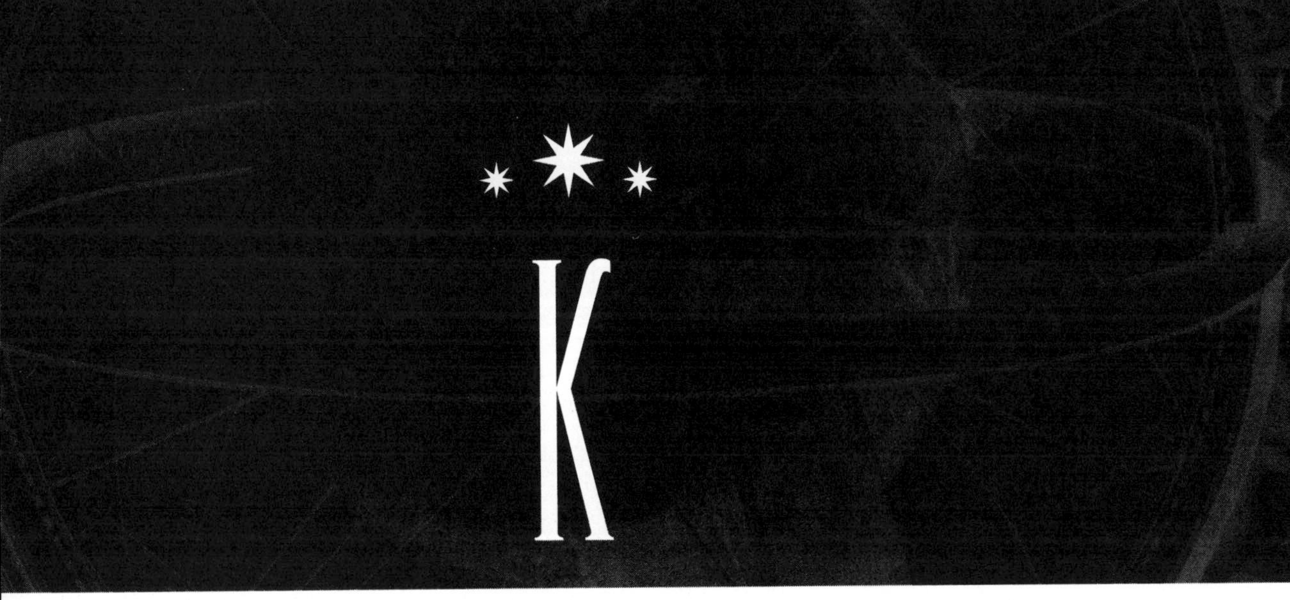


## Kabbalah and Astrology

Astrology is often called "the mother of science" because of its ancient roots and all-embracing qualities. The symbolism used in astrology contains all basic spiritual and esoteric principles. In the Kabbalah, which contains ancient esoteric Jewish teachings, astrological symbolism is used to explain how the structures of universe and men are established.

A very important model used in Kabbalistic teaching is the Tree of Life, which was already used during the era of, or maybe even before, ancient Egypt. The Kabbalistic teaching had worked out this energetic model that shows how the universe came into existence. The different "branches" of the Tree show the stages of this development and provides a view and a key to understanding how the universe is composed. "As above, as below" is a well-known ancient saying, meaning that what happens in macrocosmos reflects in the microcosmos. Therefore, the Tree of Life also shows the structure of a human being from his most divine to his most earthly aspects. It is possible to overlay the personal astrological chart on the Tree to gain insight into these personal levels and how they impact daily life. Combining personal astrology with Kabbalah deepens and enlarges the insights in the soul.

—Lea Manders

## Kassandra

Kassandra (or Cassandra), asteroid 114 (the 114th asteroid to be discovered, on July 23, 1871), is approximately 132 kilometers in diameter and has an orbital period of 4.4 years. Kassandra was the most beautiful of the 12 daughters of Priam and Hecuba of Troy. She was granted the gift of prophecy by Apollo, but, because she refused to honor her promise to make love to the sun god, Apollo pronounced a curse that her prophecies would never be believed. According to Martha Lang-Wescott, Kassandra represents the giving (or receiving) of advice. This asteroid also represents the broadcasting of ideas, but there is usually an issue of whether or not one is believed. Kassandra's key word is "hearing." J. Lee Lehman's interpretation of Kassandra is essentially the same as Lang-Wescott's. Jacob Schwartz gives this asteroid's astrological significance as "wasted speech, talking and having others not follow advice, difficulty accepting advice."

**Sources:**

Lang-Wescott, Martha. *Asteroids-Mechanics: Ephemerides II*. Conway, MA: Treehouse Mountain, 1990.

———. *Mechanics of the Future: Asteroids*. Conway, MA: Treehouse Mountain, 1991.

Lehman, J. Lee. *The Ultimate Asteroid Book*. West Chester, PA: Whitford Press, 1988.

Schwartz, Jacob. *Asteroid Name Encyclopedia*. St. Paul, MN: Llewellyn Publications, 1995.

## Katababazon

Katababazon (also spelled Catahibazon or Katahibazon) is an antiquated but once widely used Arabic term for the south lunar node.

## Katharsis

Katharsis, a now-defunct spiritual community, was begun in 1971 by a group of people attempting to establish a community that would focus on spiritual growth and harmony. The group obtained land near Nevada City, California, in 1974. Katharsis emphasized spiritual growth and self-realization through the study of yoga and related sciences; the development of a natural lifestyle based on diet; cooperative living; and promotion of the practice of astrology as an aid to a fuller life. Katharsis published a solar-lunar calendar every year and sold a line of astrology products.

## Kepler College of Astrological Arts and Sciences

Kepler College of Astrological Arts and Sciences, located in the Seattle suburb of Lynnwood, Washington, is the first college in the Western world in nearly 400 years authorized to grant bachelor's and master's degrees in astrological studies. The dream of returning astrology to the halls of academia began September 3, 1991, when a group of like-minded individuals in the Pacific Northwest met to discuss the possibility of creating a degree-granting college with its complete curriculum designed around astrological studies. On March 10, 2000, Kepler College was granted authorization by the Higher Education Coordinating Board of Washington to open its doors.

The college's mission is twofold: 1) to provide a quality learning environment that promotes academic excellence while furthering education and research in the field of astrological studies; and 2) to promote the reintegration of astrological knowledge and history with modern academia. The college's existence is likely to lead to greater understanding of what astrology can offer society in the twenty-first century.

The first class started July 20, 2000. The distance learning with symposia program enables students from every state and nation to attend Kepler College. The college's interdisciplinary curriculum is comprised of history, philosophy, cultural anthropology, mythology, comparative religion, psychology, astronomy, mathematics, logic, statistics, ethics, and systems theory, with all subjects taught through the lens of astrology. Kepler students not only explore various astrological theories and techniques used throughout history to the present, but critical thinking and open debate are important aspects of the program as well. Kepler's curriculum challenges its students to explore, reason, experience, research, create, write, publish, and become contributing members of society.

The bachelor's program includes three terms of the history of astrology: ancient, medieval, and the modern world. Another three terms comprise a year of studies called "The Art and Science of Astrology," and include an exploration of various traditions, schools of interpretation, and mathematical systems used in astrology. A third year offers each student an opportunity to choose a specialization track among the following five options: 1) astrology and psychology; 2) Eastern and Western astrological traditions; 3) astrology and health sciences; 4) astrology and the social sciences; and 5) the theory and history of astrology. The fourth year of the bachelor's program includes the option of taking numerous electives, studying astrological literature and research, and developing a final project to demonstrate the student's knowledge. Two master's programs are offered: Astrology and Counseling Psychology and Astrology and the Social Sciences.

At least two faculty team-teach each course. The teaching team cocreates the syllabus, and works in partnership the entire term, both with the distance-learning portion of the curriculum, as well as at the on-site six-day symposium. All faculty have higher degrees from accredited institutions, with most holding doctoral degrees. While the curriculum is designed primarily as a full-time curriculum, part-time as well as auditing options are available.

The college uses the services of Blackboard.com for the distance learning aspect of the program. The web site includes an interactive online "classroom" where faculty present questions and challenges that the students are expected to discuss online. The symposium takes place at a residential site in the Seattle area, and includes lectures, seminars, student presentations, debates, and other activities throughout the day and evening.

Kepler College graduates may become practitioners, business consultants, writers, or researchers. In addition to acquiring an excellent astrological education and obtaining a degree, Kepler students also make lifelong colleagues.

**Source:**

*Kepler College of Astrological Arts and Sciences*. www.kepler.edu

## Kepler, Johannes

Johannes Kepler, the last Western astronomer of note to believe in astrology, was born on January 6, 1571, in Weil, Württemberg, Germany. He studied the elliptical orbits of the planets and discovered the three laws of planetary motion that were to lead to Newton's law of universal gravitation. In 1600, Kepler became assistant to Tycho Brahe, succeeding him as court astronomer to Rudolf II. Kepler was deeply mystical, and many of his astronomical discoveries were motivated by a desire to demonstrate that a neoplatonic/Pythagorean mathematical order governed the heavens.

The son of peasants, Kepler erected horoscopes and published almanacs to supplement his income as court astronomer. On the title page of *De fundamentis*, Kepler inscribed, "Discover the force of Heavens O Men: once recognized it can be put to use." He asserted that astrological influence "is so convincing that it can be denied only by those who had not examined it." He also said, "We cannot deny the influence of the stars, without disbelieving in the wisdom of God."

In much the same way as Saint Thomas Aquinas, Kepler felt that human beings could rise above planetary influences. As do contemporary astrologers, he thus cast his predictions in terms of tendencies and probabilities rather than in terms of absolute fate. Kepler's contribution to astrology was his general theory of aspects, and he also invented the quintile, the biquintile, and the sesquiquadrate. Kepler died November 15, 1630.

Kepler is well known to modern science as the discoverer of the three laws of planetary motion named after him. His achievements were momentous, coming on the heels of the Copernican revolution and creating an astronomy of the solar system that was vastly superior to that existing before.

As an astrologer, Kepler's achievements were equally, if not more, substantial. Like his contemporary, Shakespeare, he was "myriad minded." His thinking ranged from the most traditionally Judeo-Christian and Pythagorean in his mysticism, to the most astonishingly modern in his more scientific thinking modes. Full of apparent contradictions, he was in reality the most complex of thinkers in astronomy and astrology, and yet, in some ways, was fundamentally quite consistent. Furthermore, he was a superb writer—lucid and simple, and capable of describing great intricacies clearly, as well as clothing some of his thoughts in magnificent poetic metaphors.

The supposed separation of astronomy and astrology is actually an illusion as far as Kepler was concerned. The contemporary scientific community in particular has all too often been the victim of this illusion, and has oversimplified Kepler's alleged "attacks" on astrology, which are actually heated objections to "bad" astrology and nothing more. The following in particular is a case in point, from his *Tertius Interveniens*:

> This curiosity [about astrology] flourishes, and stimulates one to learn astronomy. And astronomy is not rejected, but highly praised, as is appropriate. Now this Astrology is a foolish daughter.... But dear Lord, what would happen to her mother, the highly reasonable Astronomy, if she did not have this foolish daughter. The world, after all, is much more foolish, indeed is so foolish, that this old sensible mother, Astronomy, is talked into things and put to the lie as a result of her daughter's foolish pranks.... The mathematician's pay would be so low, that the mother would starve, if the daughter did not earn anything.

As devastating as this may seem to astrologers, the passage is not really a condemnation of all astrology. His thoughts must be understood to mean the popular forms of astrology, which he condemned unequivocally.

As for the accusation that astronomers would starve if they did not do horoscopes for pay—this may have some truth in it, but it does not mean that Kepler had to cheapen his science of astronomy by using the popular astrology of "the daughter." And he did cast and interpret horoscopes for pay, but his astrology is on a very high level indeed, as is shown by the two extant delineations of Generalisimus Wallenstein's birth chart (1608 and 1625), and others.

And such astrology was, for Kepler, to be included under astronomy. *This* astrology/astronomy was Kepler's true vocation up to the point in 1619 when he transcended it, but still made it part of a greater scheme of the universe that he called *Harmonice Mundi* (World Harmony), the title of his last major book (1619). Even after then, he still spoke of astrology in these terms, as noted in *Die Astrologie des Johannes Kepler*: "Philosophy, and therefore genuine astrology, is a testimony of God's works and is therefore holy. It is by no means a frivolous thing. And I, for my part, do not wish to dishonor it." That this "genuine astrology" was effective is well proven by the fact that Kepler predicted the manner and time of Wallenstein's death well in advance.

Many astrologers will at first feel offended by Kepler. He was as outspoken against some astrologers as he was against those who condemned astrology. This is seen mainly in his 1610 book *Tertius Interveniens* (Third Party Intervening), in which he takes a "third party" position between those who flatly condemn astrology and those who accept as true everything said in its name. He draws sharp lines between his perceptions of genuine and false practices of the art.

Like Friedrich Nietzsche, his fellow countryman of three centuries later, Kepler was a thinker who skillfully required readers to ponder issues thoroughly while being challenged, irritated, even infuriated. This process is so valuable in helping to gain ever deeper insights. It is advisable at times, when he is attacking with fury, to keep in mind that, like his earlier fellow countryman, Martin Luther, he was a reformer. He definitely did not propose that astrology be abolished, any more than Luther intended to destroy Christianity.

The foundation of his astrology was geometry and, more widely, a universal harmony present in geometry, as demonstrated in *Tertius Interveniens*: "Within this lower world a spiritual nature is concealed that can operate through geometry, which is vitalized through the geometrical and harmonic connections...."; "The geometry or harmony of aspects is not between the stars in the sky, but is located rather down here on earth in the point that collects all their rays." This principle led him to his specific contributions to astrology, among which are: his analysis of planetary interrelationships through Platonic solids; his discovery of additional aspects (the quintile and semisquare); and his cataloging and comments on the fixed stars. Beyond these accomplishments, his theory and philosophy of are indeed major contributions.

—Ken Negus

**Sources:**

Brau, Jean-Louis, Helen Weaver, and Allan Edmands. *Larousse Encyclopedia of Astrology*. New York: Plume, 1980.

Kepler, Johannes. *Harmonices Mundi*.

———. *Tertius Interveniens*.

Kitson, Annabella, ed. *History and Astrology: Clio and Urania Confer*. London: Mandala, 1989.

## KITE

A kite is a configuration in which one of the planets in a grand trine opposes a fourth planet that simultaneously forms sextile aspects (60° angles) with the remaining two planets. This is considered a fortunate configuration in a natal chart: Depending on the indications of the balance of the chart, a grand trine can be *too* fortunate, bringing the native good luck but not challenging the person to develop character. The inclusion of an opposed fourth planet adds an element of challenge and tension that stimulates the native to release the energies of the grand trine in a dynamic manner. The house position of the fourth planet usually indicates the area of life in which this release will occur.

## KOCH HOUSE SYSTEM

When the casual observer looks at an astrological chart for the first time, it is easy to make the incorrect assumption that the 12 "pie pieces" are the 12 signs of the zodiac. The lines indicate the house divisions (sign divisions are usually not represented), which can begin or end at different places in different signs. Astrologers disagree about how to draw the houses, although most agree that the first house should begin on the eastern horizon and the seventh house (180° away) should begin on the western horizon. Also, the great majority of systems begin the tenth house at the degree of the zodiac that is highest in the heavens and the fourth house at exactly 180° away from the cusp of the tenth house.

The Koch house system, also called the birthplace house system, is a very recent one (though not significantly different from the ancient system of Alcabitus) that was put forward in 1971 by Walter Koch. Although a relative newcomer, it has quickly become popular. Like the also popular Placidean house system, the Koch system finds the house cusps intervening between the ascendant and the medium coeli by trisecting the time, in this case the time it takes to rise from the horizon to the ecliptic. In actual practice, Koch house cusps do not vary significantly from Placidean cusps.

## KOCH, WALTER A.

The German schoolteacher and astrologer Walter Koch was born in Esslingen, Germany, on September 18, 1895. His father was a manufacturer. During World War I, Koch was severely wounded in his right leg. He studied classics and history at the Universities of Strasbourg and Tübingen and entered a career of civil service after graduation.

In 1924, Koch began publishing in astrology periodicals. During the Nazi era, he (and most other astrologers) was arrested and spent several years in jail before being transferred to the Dachau concentration camp, where he was held until the end of World War II. After the war, he was an instructor in the Hohenstaufen Classical High School in Göppingen and spent his spare time on astrological research and writing.

Koch was critical of charlatanism and new systems of astrology (as someone trained in classical studies, he was inclined to be a traditionalist). He was especially antagonistic toward fatalism in astrology. He was very interested in colors and in systems of house division, and it is his work in the latter field that made him known in North America. The Koch system is based on the older Regiomontanus system and is discussed in his book *Regiomontanus and the Birthplace House System* (1960). Koch died on February 25, 1970.

**Sources:**

Holden, James H., and Robert A. Hughes. *Astrological Pioneers of America*. Tempe, AZ: American Federation of Astrologers, 1988.

Koch, Walter A. *Psychologische Farbenlehre*. Halle, Germany: Carl Marhold Verlagshuchhandlung, 1931.

———. *Regiomontanus und das Häusersystem des Geburtsortes*. Göppingen, Germany: Sirivsverlag, 1960.

Koch, Walter A., and O. von Bressendorf. *Astrologische Farbenlehre*. Munich, Germany: O. W. Barth Verlag, 1930.

## KOCHUNAS, BRADLEY WAYNE

Bradley Wayne Kochunas was born July 29, 1950, in Hartford, Connecticut. He is a graduate of Baldwin Wallace College in Berea, Ohio (B.A., religion, 1975), Miami University in Oxford, Ohio (M.A., religion, 1985) and the University of Cincinnati (C.A.G.S., counselor education, 1995). He first became interested in astrology in college after reading Grant Lewi's introduction to astrology, *Heaven Knows What,* then immersed himself in the voluminous writings of Dane Rudhyar, which initially shaped his thinking about astrology.

Kochunas majored in religion in graduate school with the express purpose of researching astrology to help it gain academic legitimacy as a field of study. His thesis (available online at cura.free.fr/cura-en) focused upon the religious and therapeutic dimensions within contemporary astrology, applying the hermeneutic methods of religion historian Mircea Eliade (one of the modern founders of religious studies as an academic discipline) to the field of astrology to establish that it could be regarded as a cosmological discipline evidencing structures of sacred space and sacred time as elaborated by Eliade's work in the phenomenology of religions.

Since 1985, his view has been greatly influenced by James Hillman, Thomas Moore, and the other archetypal theorists. Kochunas describes astrology as providing a framework for imagining a profound intimacy between ourselves and our world. He views his contribution to astrology as promoting it as a discipline of the imaginal rather than the literal: In personal communication in 2002, Kochunas said, "It is a poetics of the Imagination, like art and religion, better suited for soulmaking than ego building. It has value in its own right without need for validation from the dominant cultural paradigm. The whole enterprise to concretize astrology, to insist that it is a science, and to pour time and money into research to prove this is simply misdirected." His award-winning writing on counseling and astrology has appeared in both public and professional media in the United States, Ireland, Britain, France, Belgium, and the Czech Republic.

In addition to being licensed as a clinical counselor with board certification in clinical mental health and addictions, working in a correctional setting, Kochunas is also an adjunct instructor in the Department of Religion and Philosophy for Wilmington College and certified as a professional astrologer by the International Society for Astrological Research. He is a member of the Association for Astrological Networking, the Ohio Counseling Association, and the Ohio Association for Spiritual, Ethical and Religious Values in Counseling.

## KOINER, LYNN

Lynn Koiner has been a full-time professional astrologer since June 1969 and a professional member of the American Federation of Astrologers (AFA). She had the opportunity to study directly with Ernest Grant, cofounder of the AFA, and he was her sponsor into this organization in 1969.

Since 1984, she has published an astrological quarterly, the *Amethyst*, dedicated to current astrological trends, planetary cycles, and how they affect the individual personally. From 1994 through 1999, she served as vice president and president of the National Council for Geocosmic Research in Baltimore, Maryland, and she currently serves as newsletter editor for both the Baltimore and Annapolis chapters. With a research specialty since 1972 on Transpluto, she was a contributing author on this topic in Noel Tyl's *Astrology's Special Measurements*.

Koiner's primary areas of research include: medical topics; the Solar Max and its impact upon human behavior; the Nelson Model and solar activity; the phenomena of UFO abductees; esoteric astrology (A. A. Bailey) and the fixed stars discussed by Bailey; Transpluto; and Venus transits (an astronomical term for a rare phenomena when Venus crosses the face of the Sun).

Since the 1970s, Koiner has been examining the psychological patterns shown in the horoscope as connected with specific diseases. The philosophy is that correcting a problematic personality characteristic can impact recovery or prevent onset. The first disease research was blood sugar disorders and some of this research was published in Tyl's book. Subsequent areas of research have been auto-immune system, Alzheimer's disease, respiratory system, skin, addiction (obesity), and Irritable Bowel Syndrome. In July 2000, Koiner received the Sims Pounds Jr. Award from the American Federation of Astrologers for her research lectures on medical astrology.

Since 1999, Koiner has been working and consulting with members of the scientific community (physicists and astronomers). There has been much research conducted in the realm of traditional science that can be incorporated into astrological studies. In this area, she has been examining the data on earthquakes. The Society for Scientific Exploration has been one of the bridging scientific organizations.

## KOLISKO EFFECT (KOLISKO EXPERIMENTS)

The Kolisko effect refers to modifications in the behavior of metallic solutions during certain aspects—particularly during conjunctions—involving the planet traditionally said to rule the metal involved. Rudolf Steiner, the founder of anthroposophy (an offshoot of Theosophy), taught astrology in many of his lectures, including the astrological principle that the Sun, Moon, and planets rule certain metals. Traditionally, the Sun has been thought to rule gold; the Moon, silver; Mercury, mercury; Venus, copper; Mars, iron; Jupiter, tin; and Saturn, lead. Steiner claimed, among other things, that as long as substances were in a solid state, they were subject to the forces of the Earth, but if they were in a liquid state, the planetary forces came into play.

In the early twentieth century one of Steiner's students, Lilly Kolisko, began a series of experiments designed to demonstrate this link empirically. While her experiments were diverse, Kolisko's basic technique was to prepare solutions in which particular metallic salts had been dissolved and then record the pattern that these solutions made when they crystallized onto filter paper. Her hypothesis was that major aspects involving the traditional seven planets (which included the Sun and Moon) would affect the corresponding metal and thus modify the resulting patterns. Kolisko reported marked success. Particularly memorable are experiments during which Saturn was occulted (eclipsed) by the Sun or the Moon. During these occultations, the crystallization of lead salts was either delayed or completely obstructed. These experiments and others are recorded in Kolisko's *Workings of the Stars in Earthly Substance*, *Das Silber und der Mond*, and *Saturn und Blei*.

While some researchers have reported negative or mixed results in attempts to replicate Kolisko's experiments, others have reported success. Theodore Schwenck, in a laboratory of the Swiss Weleda Company, found that the crystallization pattern of a relevant solution was markedly influenced by the Mars-Saturn conjunction of 1949, an experiment that was replicated by Karl Voss in 1964. In 1967, another anthroposophist, Agnes Fyfe, published a paper in which she reported that the precipitation of carefully prepared iron-silver solutions was delayed during the half hour following exact conjunctions between Mars (ruler of iron) and the Moon (ruler of silver). Beginning in 1972, Nicholas Kollerstrom began a series of experiments involving conjunctions and other aspects between Mars and Saturn, the Moon and Saturn, and the Moon and Mars. He succeeded in experiments where the metals used corresponded to the planets involved in the conjunction. He also found that Mars-Saturn conjunctions (which are less fleeting than aspects involving the transiting Moon) produced especially marked effects that typically lasted several days. He also found that the peak influence of conjunctions involving planets other than the Moon always occurred *after* the conjunctions were exact, as if the effect of the disturbance in the Mars-Saturn "energies" was delayed in reaching Earth.

These studies do not exhaust the list of researchers who have successfully replicated Kolisko's experiments. Needless to say, the Kolisko effect stands out as an interesting phenomenon that merits close examination by anyone attempting to either support or debunk astrology from an empirical perspective.

**Sources:**

Davidson, Alison. *Metal Power: The Soul Life of the Planets*. Garberville, CA: Borderland Sciences Research Foundation, 1991.

Fyfe, Agnes. "Uber die Variabilitat von Silver-Eisen-Steigbildern." *Elemente der Naturwissenschaft* 6 (1967): 35–43.

Gettings, Fred. *Dictionary of Astrology*. London: Routledge & Kegan Paul, 1985.

Kollerstrom, Nicholas. "Planetary Influences on Metal Ion Activity." *Correlation* 3, no. 1 (1983): 38–50.

Kolisko, Lilly. *Das Silber und der Mond*.

———. *Saturn und Blei*.

———. *Working of the Stars in Earthly Substance*.

## Krafft, Karl Ernst

Karl Ernst Krafft, a Swiss astrologer, was born in Basel on May 10, 1900. He studied at the Universities of Basel and Geneva. He began to investigate astrology with statistical methods, constructing birth charts from data available from public records. He replicated Choisnard's studies and conducted others of his own.

From 1924 to 1937, Krafft pursued various employments and practiced astrology and astrological research in his spare time. He moved to Germany not long after his marriage in 1937, where he devoted his time to writing and lecturing on his favorite subject. His major work, *Le premier traité d'astrobiologie*, was published in 1939.

Despite work that he performed for the Propaganda Ministry of the German government, Krafft was in and out of jail, eventually dying on January 8, 1945, during a transfer between German detention centers. His importance for astrologers lies in his large-scale statistical work, which began with Choisnard and led to the work of Michel and Françoise Gauquelin.

**Sources:**

Holden, James H., and Robert A. Hughes. *Astrological Pioneers of America*. Tempe, AZ: American Federation of Astrologers, 1988.

Krafft, Karl Ernst *Le premier traité d'astrobiologie*. Paris: Wyckmans, 1939.

## Krittika

Krittika (or the Cutter) is one of the Nakshatras (lunar mansions) of Vedic astrology. Agni, the god of fire, presides over this Nakshatra represented by an axe and located from Aries 26°10' to Taurus 10°, ruled by the sun. This sign gives off the energy of being militaristic, and is a good time to be straightforward and aggressive; individuals may find themselves more motivated and dignified when the moon is in this area, while also being hard-headed or overly excitable.

—Pramela Thiagesan

# KRONOS

Kronos is one of the eight hypothetical planets (sometimes referred to as the trans-Neptunian points or planets, or TNPs for short) utilized in Uranian astrology. The Uranian system, sometimes referred to as the Hamburg School of Astrology, was established by Friedrich Sieggrün (1877–1951) and Alfred Witte (1878–1943). It relies heavily on hard aspects and midpoints. In decline for many decades, it has experienced a revival in recent years.

Kronos indicates elevated matters, both literally and figuratively. Thus, Kronos may represent, on one hand, mountains and airships and, on the other, leaders, executives, and government authorities. It may symbolize authority and expert status as well as the questioning of authority and expertise.

Based on the speculative orbits of the Uranian planets, the Kepler, Solar Fire and Win*Star software program will all locate this hypothetical planet in an astrological chart.

**Sources:**

Lang-Wescott, Martha. *Mechanics of the Future: Asteroids*. Rev. ed. Conway, MA: Treehouse Mountain, 1991.

Simms, Maria Kay. *Dial Detective: Investigation with the 90 Degree Dial*. San Diego: Astro Computing Services, 1989.

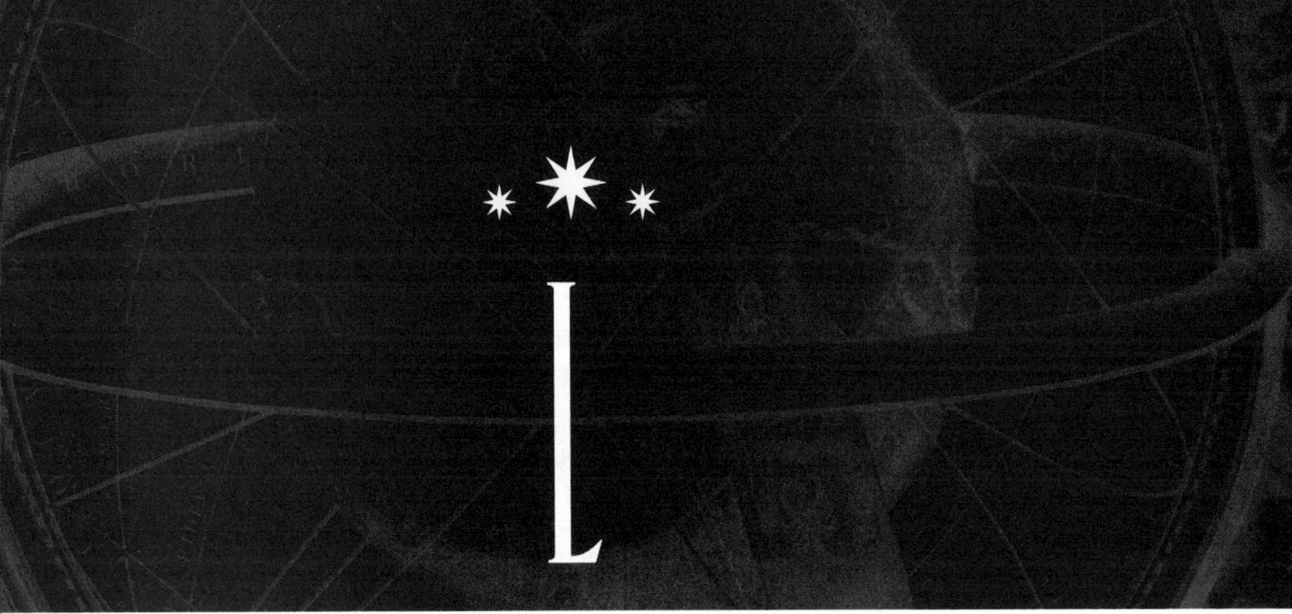

## Lacrimosa

Lacrimosa, asteroid 208 (the 208th asteroid to be discovered, on October 21, 1879), is approximately 48 kilometers in diameter and has an orbital period of 4.9 years. Lacrimosa is Latin for "weeping." The lacrimal glands are tear-secreting glands at the top of the eye. The location of this tiny planetoid by sign and house indicates a source of tears. Crying is not necessarily a negative experience; one can also have "tears of joy." Lacrimosa generally shows where a person's emotions are so deeply invested that the individual experiences extremes of happiness or sadness.


**Sources:**

Kowal, Charles T. *Asteroids: Their Nature and Utilization*. Chichester, West Sussex, UK: Ellis Horwood Limited, 1988.

Room, Adrian. *Dictionary of Astronomical Names*. London: Routledge, 1988.

Schwartz, Jacob. *Asteroid Name Encyclopedia*. St. Paul, MN: Llewellyn Publications, 1995.


## Laetitia

Laetitia, asteroid 39 (the 39th asteroid to be discovered, on February 8, 1856), is approximately 156 kilometers in diameter and has an orbital period of 4.6 years. It was named after the Latin word for gladness and gaiety. When prominent in a natal chart, Laetitia indicates a person with a generally positive attitude. Its location by sign and house indicates potential sources of happiness. When involved in many inharmonious aspects, Laetitia may show a person who is glad about the wrong things or unwisely optimistic.


**Sources:**

Kowal, Charles T. *Asteroids: Their Nature and Utilization*. Chichester, West Sussex, UK: Ellis Horwood Limited, 1988.

Room, Adrian. *Dictionary of Astronomical Names*. London: Routledge, 1988.

Schwartz, Jacob. *Asteroid Name Encyclopedia*. St. Paul, MN: Llewellyn Publications, 1995.

## Lamb

The Lamb was an older, alternate name for the sign Aries. The animal that came to replace the Lamb in contemporary astrology is the Ram.

## Lancelot

Lancelot, asteroid 2,041 (the 2,041st asteroid to be discovered, on September 24, 1960), is approximately 19 kilometers in diameter and has an orbital period of 5.6 years. Lancelot was named after the knight of the Round Table. According to J. Lee Lehman, this asteroid "represents glory thrust on the individual, not due to any personal qualities or actions, but simply from being in the right place at the right time." Schwartz gives Lancelot's associations as "heroic actions resulting from good fortune rather than effort."

**Sources:**

Kowal, Charles T. *Asteroids: Their Nature and Utilization*. Chichester, West Sussex, UK: Ellis Horwood Limited, 1988.
Lehman, J. Lee. *The Ultimate Asteroid Book*. West Chester, PA: Whitford Press, 1988.
Schwartz, Jacob. *Asteroid Name Encyclopedia*. St. Paul, MN: Llewellyn Publications, 1995.

## Latitude

Latitude (properly called terrestrial latitude) refers to a location's distance from the equator. Celestial latitude refers to the angular distance (distance measured in degrees and minutes of an arc) that a planet or other celestial body is located above or below the ecliptic. One can also talk about galactic latitude, which is the distance above or below a plane drawn through the center of the Milky Way, as well as heliographic latitude, which is the distance north or south of the Sun's equator. Clearly, the notion of latitude can be extended to any celestial body.

**Sources:**

DeVore, Nicholas. *Encyclopedia of Astrology*. New York: Philosophical Library, 1947.
Filbey, John, and Peter Filbey. *The Astrologer's Companion*. Wellingborough, Northamptonshire, UK: Aquarian Press, 1986.

## The Law and Astrology

Laws from the near and distant past still restrict professionals who forecast the future, but astrologers are successfully challenging the laws across America, in Europe, and in South America that inhibit their profession. Major court cases have been won in the United States, and dozens of cities have changed their laws on "fortune-telling" or the "occult arts." The Association for Astrological Networking (AFAN) is committed to overturning every law that overly restricts the practice of astrology.

Labeled "fortune-telling," and lumped in with all manner of unrelated and archaic "occult arts" and metaphysical practices—as well as the complete pantheon of New Age philosophies and disciplines—astrological practice is still restricted, or banned, by numerous cities in many states of the union.

AFAN has legal briefs prepared that with little modification can be filed to challenge antiastrology laws in all their various forms. Many cities are unaware of court rulings and legal victories in other jurisdictions, or they ignore them in the face of local civic or religious pressure, or until they get some pressure from AFAN.

The laws astrologers object to include: bonding requirements of up to $10,000 in areas where cities know bonding companies do not issue bonds for astrologers; business license fees that range to $300 per year, when other consulting businesses pay $30; and permits that go for as much as $100 per day, which is not terrible for a one-day event, but is $36,500 for a year in business. Some cities require fingerprints and mug-shot photos, and a license fee in the range of fines, effectively arresting the astrologer before she or he goes into business. All these fees and license requirements are in excess of what other businesses or consultants are charged. Total prohibitions on the practice of astrology for a fee also exist.

The most celebrated case defending an astrologer against charges of fortune-telling is the trial of Evangeline Adams in New York City in 1914. Adams was the best known and most respected astrologer of her era, renowned for her insight and accuracy in forecasting. She was a prolific author and a media celebrity. She was a member of the Boston Adams family, a direct descendant of Presidents John Adams and John Quincy Adams. Her offices were in Carnegie Hall, and her client list included actors, opera stars, politicians, statesmen, kings, tycoons, and high-class brothel madams. Readings were $5.

She was arrested under New York's anti-fortune-telling statute, which made it a crime "to pretend to tell fortunes." Those found to be in violation of the ordinance "shall be adjudged disorderly persons and punished as prescribed therein." Adams, with the support of her clients, specifically J. P. Morgan, decided to defend astrology, rather than pay a minor fine.

Adams contended that she used scientific methods, the measurements of astronomy, logarithms, the rigors of mathematics, and the empirical findings of centuries of astrologers in her practice. She never predicted specific future events, nor did she forecast with certainty, or promote undue reliance on her predictions. Rather, she spoke of planets in particular positions or alignments, indicating a likelihood of a happening or of an opportunity. She did not claim for herself special gifts or mysterious powers, but stated that any knowledgeable astrologer could find the same positions and indications from the proper astrological reference books. Scant mention is found in the transcript that Adams used real planet positions, called transits, which she learned from Dr. Heber Smith, while her contemporaries used the older symbolic system of progressions, or projected positions of the birth planets.

Importantly, this case actually examines the means and methods of astrology. Walter Coleman asserts that it is the *only* case "where the substantive merits of astrology were completely analyzed by a duly constituted judicial authority." Text from *The*

*Encyclopedia Britannica* referred to as "this leading authority of the world," was entered into the court record: "The belief in a connection between the heavenly bodies and the life of man has played an important part in human history.... Men of intellectual eminence ... have convinced themselves that ...astrology has a foundation in truth. [One scientist] insisted indeed that it was a mistake to confuse astrology with fortune-telling, and maintained that it was a physical science just as much as geology depending on ascertained facts, and grossly misrepresented by being connected with magic."

The telling component of the trial came when the judge asked Evangeline Adams to demonstrate her art by interpreting a mystery chart from birth data he supplied. Adams is said to have done a remarkable job on the interpretation. Coleman calls it "perfect" and the judge later said the accurate reading gave him valuable and useful insight into his son's character and behavior. Judge John H. Freschi said, in ruling from the bench, "The defendant raises astrology to the dignity of an exact science." Astrologers have taken great pride in that statement. Adams was found not guilty.

The New York ordinance, and its many similar "siblings" in other jurisdictions, is designed to prevent fraud. Antiastrology laws are also predicated on the false assumption that, without exception, "the business of fortune telling is inherently fraudulent" so that "its regulation or prohibition is required in order to protect the gullible, superstitious and unwary" (from *In re Bartha* [1976]).

These laws may prevent or punish fraud, but they have the unacceptable and unconstitutional result of restricting the honest and helpful speech of astrologers. This is akin to prohibiting drinking to forestall drunkenness and spousal abuse; to banning driving to prevent speeding; or raising a sales or use tax to the level of a fine in an attempt to prevent consumption. The rights of the many cannot be sacrificed to protect or punish the few. Although it is seldom argued, antiastrology ordinances also restrict the public's right to access astrological information and counsel. The public (except for fundamentalists in religion and their counterparts, the skeptics in science) is not clamoring for less astrology, but more.

The most important recent legal victory is known as the Azusa Decision. The California Supreme Court overturned, as an unconstitutional infringement of free speech, an Azusa, California, ordinance that completely banned fortune-telling. The court held that astrologers and fortune-tellers or palmists, have the same constitutionally protected right to express and charge for their opinions as other mainstream forecasters. That the speech may be false is irrelevant, the court held. Banning, or unduly restricting, astrologers' speech is a "content-based" restriction, one of the most egregious violations of the First Amendment.

Astrology's acceptance and popularity actually rose from 22 percent in the early 1970s to 47 percent in the mid-1990s, according to Gallup and *Life* magazine surveys. However, many of the laws on the books in their latest revisions date from the 1950s, an era of fear of the different or unknown. Before that, many laws were revised in the 1920s and 1930s, or in the 1900s, times of economic and social uncertainty. At various points, magnetism, hypnotism, and psychology, which are not noted as predictive sciences, were added to the lists of many practices prohibited in the laws covering occult arts or fortune-telling. They are never called "astrology" ordinances. That is, except for the few that reasonably license astrologers by the same standards applied to "mundane" businesses.

Anti-fortune-telling laws originated in the 1600s with the British Vagrancy Act, designed to curtail "gypsies" and other wandering, poor, vagrants. Colonial America was governed by British law and the new states continued and adopted most city ordinances. While these laws were partly ethnist or racist and partly medical belief (about diseased travelers, going back to the plagues of the 1400s), they were also definitely antifraud, anti-pickpocket, etc., in intent. There may be some historical, and even contemporary, substance to the gypsy stereotype, but it is nonetheless a stereotype—and guilt by association—and a violation of the due process and equal justice guaranteed in the U.S. Constitution.

The Azusa decision was won by a family group of "gypsies," members of the "Rom" or Romany community, who founded a Spiritual Church, and who were doing palm readings, for donations, as a part of their religious practice. The city's ordinance, a total ban on all metaphysical practices, was challenged by one of the ministers when they were ordered to shut down.

The city won in Superior Court, based on the *Bartha* precedent, but lost at the next two levels, where the justices could overturn incorrectly established precedent and rule anew, strictly on constitutional issues. The Appellate Court overturned the Azusa City ordinance and discredited the *Bartha* assumptions based on Article I, section 2 of the California Constitution, which states: "Every person may freely speak, write or publish his or her sentiments on all subjects, being responsible for the abuse of this right. A law may not restrain or abridge liberty of speech or press."

The appellate judges added, consequently, "One need not have a scientific basis for a belief in order to have a constitutional right to utter speech based on that belief." Not only does the broader California Constitution protect astrology but, in addition, the judges found, "the telling of fortunes and prophesying about the future to be a category of speech protected by the United States Constitution."

The City of Azusa then appealed the case to the California Supreme Court, asking for either a review (hoping to overturn the appellate ruling), or a retrial on the facts (including the merits of fortune-telling), and lost again. The California Supreme Court ruled that astrology is not "inherently fraudulent" nor "mere commercial speech" but rather, "protected speech," as fully protected by the Constitution as any other idea. Interestingly, the appellate case was argued primarily on grounds of the Rom's freedom of religion. The Supreme Court asked for a freedom of speech argument.

The Supreme Court majority held that "some persons believe they possess the power to predict what has not yet come to pass. When such persons impart their belief to others, they are not acting fraudulently; they are expressing opinions which, however dubious, are unquestionably protected by the Constitution.... It must also be noted that there are many persons other than professional fortunetellers who purport to predict the future; e.g., astrology columnists in daily newspapers, economists who prognosticate interest rates and other business conditions, investment counselors who forecast stock market trends, sportswriters and odds makers who predict winners of athletic contests, horse race handicappers, pollsters who forecast election returns, and clergymen who describe the concept of a hereafter."

"Under the First Amendment there is no such thing as a false idea," the California Supreme Court said. "However pernicious an opinion may seem, we depend for its correction not on the conscience of judges and juries but on the competition of other ideas." The court did not rule on the validity or the value of astrology, nor separate it from other metaphysical philosophies or occult arts. It leaves those tasks to the marketplace of ideas, and the test of time and events.

In so ruling, the court, throughout its decision, cited federal precedent: cases which were decided based on the protections guaranteed by the First Amendment to the U.S. Constitution. However, they added a footnote at the beginning of their decision stating that their frequent use of the term First Amendment was "merely illustrative" and that the ruling was based on the California Constitution.

This strategic move prevented an appeal to the U.S. Supreme Court, making the California court's opinion the final one. Since the cites in the decision are from federal cases, they, and the ruling, would be very "persuasive" in courts in other states. Their arguments would be influential, but the ruling is not "enforceable" outside California. By law, the Azusa decision is "controlling" in California, which means cities and counties *must* abide by its ruling. However, many cities in this state have ignored the decision until AFAN has reminded them of it and its force of law.

AFAN even had to sue the City of Albany (in the San Francisco Bay Area) to overturn and invalidate that city's ordinance. It was the "arrest first" variety, demanding fingerprints, mug shots, a bond, and high fees. Most cities, in and out of California, are more responsive to AFAN's presentations. City attorneys, council members, and even district attorneys—but seldom police chiefs—recognize the unconstitutionality of prior restraint on the content of a common and popular subject of speech. Quotes and citations from, and commentary on, the Azusa decision, combined with a history of astrology's role and influence in western civilization, taken from trial preparation in the Sundebruch case, and AFAN's *amicus curiae* in the Azusa case, have been collected in a pamphlet titled *The Law & Astrology*, which is AFAN's major tool and reference for overturning laws from the past that restrict those professional astrologers who forecast the future.

—Jayj Jacobs

**Sources:**

*AFAN Newsletter*. Association for Astrology Networking.

Association for Astrology Networking. *AFAN*. www.afan.org.

Brau, Jean-Louis, Helen Weaver, and Allan Edmands. *Larousse Encyclopedia of Astrology*. New York: New American Library, 1980.

*Law & Astrology*. Association for Astrology Networking.

## Leo

Leo, the fifth sign of the zodiac, is a fixed fire sign. It is a positive, masculine sign, and is ruled by the Sun. Its symbol is the lion, and its glyph is said to be a modified version of the initial letter of its Greek name (although this is not universally accepted). It takes its name from the Latin word for lion. Leo is associated with the back and, especially, the heart, and individuals with a Leo sun sign are prone to heart and back problems. The association of Leo with the heart is the astrological background for the common term "lionhearted." The key phrase for Leo is "I will."

Eo ſpectãs ad occaſum ſupra corpus hydrę a capi/
te qua cancer inſtat:uſq; ad mediã partẽ eius con/
ſtitutꝰmedius ęſtiuo circulo diuiditur:ut ſub ipſo
orbe priores pedes habeat collocatos. Occidens
a capite &exoriẽs.Hic habet in capite ſtellas tres
In ceruicibꝰduas.In pectore unam. Interſcapilio tres.In media
cauda unã. In extrema alterã magnã. Sub pectore duas.In pe/
de priore unã clarã.In uentre clarã unam. Et infra alteram ma/
gnam unam.In lumbis unam.In poſteriore genu unam. In pe/
de poſteriore claram unam.Et ita eſt omnino numerus ſtellarũ
decem & nouem.

**The constellation Leo from *Poeticon Astronomicon*, c. 1497. *Reproduced by permission of Fortean Picture Library.***

Like many of the other signs of the zodiac, Leo lacks a developed mythology. It is said to be the Nemean lion slain by Hercules and placed as a constellation in the heavens by Zeus to commemorate the event. Turning to lion symbolism more broadly, the lion is often regarded as the king of beasts, known more for its kindness and mercy than its ferocity. Aesop's fables include a number of lion tales, such as *The Lion and the Mouse*, in which the merciful King of Beasts releases the mouse, who later nibbles through the lion's bonds to rescue him; *The Lion in Love*, in which the lion allows himself to be declawed and detoothed in order to be allowed to marry a woodsman's daughter, only to be driven away after he has rendered himself powerless; and *The Lion's Share*, in which the King of Beasts invites other beasts to hunt with him, but then keeps all of the spoils (moral: Many may share in the labors but not in the spoils).

Like the lions and kings of mythology (the sign is associated with royalty), Leos can embody some of the best as well as some of the worst of human traits. On the positive side, they can be brave and noble to a fault. Associated with the heart, they can give everything for love. On the other hand, they can be ferocious and brutal. Leos have big egos, but these egos are peculiarly sensitive: Whereas ego signs like Scorpio neither need nor seek compliments, Leos require constant acknowledgment. In a group, they often seek to be the center of attention. The need for acknowledgment by others is so great that, like the lion of *The Lion's Share*, they can take credit for the labors of others. Like all fire signs, they are fond of physical and social activity.

The sign that the Sun was in at birth is usually the single most important influence on a native's personality. Thus, when people say they are a certain sign, they are almost always referring to their sun sign. There is a wealth of information available on the characteristics of the zodiacal signs—so much that one book would not be able to contain it all. Sun-sign astrology, which is the kind of astrology found in newspaper columns and popular magazines, has the advantage of simplicity. But this simplicity is purchased at the price of ignoring other astrological influences, such as one's Moon sign, rising sign, etc. These other influences can substantially modify a person's basic sun-sign traits. As a consequence, it is the rare individual who is completely typical of her or his sign. The reader should bear this caveat in mind when perusing the following series of sun-sign interpretations.

One traditional way in which astrologers condense information is by summarizing sign and planet traits in lists of words and short phrases called keywords or key phrases. The following Leo keywords are drawn from Manly P. Hall's *Astrological Keywords:*

> *Emotional keywords:* "Faithful, rich in emotional life, affectionate, idealistic, proud, sympathetic, merciful, chivalrous, domestic, excitable, foreseeing, vain, subject to illusions."
>
> *Mental keywords:* "Commanding, generous, ambitious, self-sacrificing, optimistic, fixed in opinion yet magnanimous, opposed to secrecy, oblivious to enmity, challenging, bold, domineering, autocratic."

At present, there are various astrology report programs that contain interpretations of each of the 12 sun signs. A selection of these for Sun in Leo has been excerpted below:

> More than a bit of a showoff, you love to be the center of attention. But others do not usually mind because they tend to enjoy your genuine warmth and affection. Very spirited and willful, proud and self-important at times, you demand your own way. You are quite honest, however, and the respect of others is very important to you. You never compromise yourself and you pursue your goals with persistence and dedication. Your regal presence and demeanor draw you to positions of leadership and authority. But beware of being overly hardheaded, domineering, ostentatious or patronizing or you will lose the goodwill and admiration that you enjoy. Very theatrical, you live life on a grand scale wherever and whenever possible. Your strength and energy vitalizes those who come in contact with you. (From "Professional Natal Report." Courtesy of Astrolabe [http://www.alabe.com].)
>
> Proud and intensely individual, you really want to stand out, to be the very best you can be, and to be recognized and appreciated for your unique contributions. Doing something well and being respected for it is extremely important to you, and you cannot tolerate being in the background, taking orders from others, or being "just one of the team." You must put your personal stamp on whatever you do, and direct your own course in life. You need to have a place where you can shine, express yourself creatively, and be the one in charge.
>
> You have big dreams and the determination, spirit, vitality, and enthusiasm to bring them into being. You also have a noble, romantic heart, and a love of the dramatic, colorful, and extravagant.
>
> For you it is true that "all the world's a stage" and you secretly (or perhaps not so secretly) desire to be the Star or Hero in the play. You want

to be great, and to receive the love and applause of an adoring audience, even if the "audience" is just one other special person. You need someone to believe in you and your dreams. Though you appear radiantly self-confident and independent, you are actually very much dependent on the affirmation, love, and recognition of others. You cannot bear being unnoticed or unappreciated.

You also love wholeheartedly and generously and really know how to make the person you love feel special. You love the magic of "being in love" and know how to keep the romance alive in your relationships. You are also immensely loyal and will defend your loved ones and stand by them to the end—as long as they never offend your pride or betray your trust. However, you like to be the strong one in a relationship and you really do not share the leading role very easily. Ideally you need to find a person who is as strong-willed as yourself, but who will not try to dominate or compete with you.

Your strengths are your zest and love for life, your creative power, and your warm and generous heart. Your primary fault is your tendency to be very egocentric, so concerned with the impression you are making and with your own creative self-expression that you forget there is another, larger world that does not revolve around you. (From "Merlin," by Gina Ronco and Agnes Nightingale. Courtesy of Cosmic Patterns [http://cosmic.patterns.com].)

When we hear "Lion," we think "fierce." But that's misleading. Go to the zoo and have a look at the "King of the Beasts." He's lying there, one eye open, looking regal. He knows he's the king. He doesn't need to make a fuss about it. The lion, like Leo at its best, radiates quiet confidence. A happy, creative, comfortable participation in the human family—that's what Leo the Lion is all about.

The evolutionary method is deceptively simple: creative self-expression. As we offer evidence of our internal processes to the world, we feel more at home, more accepted, more spontaneous—provided the world claps its hands for us! That's the catch. Leo needs an appreciative audience. That audience can be a thousand people cheering or one person saying "I love you." Either way, it's applause, and for the Lion, that's evolutionary rocket fuel.

Toughing it out, not letting oneself be affected by a lack of support or understanding, may well be an important spiritual lesson—but not for Leo. Here the evolutionary problem comes down to lack of real, ultimate trust in other people. The cure isn't toughness; it's building a pattern of joyful give-and-take. So perform! And if no one claps, go somewhere else and perform again.

With your Sun in Leo, you are naturally creative. Your task is to express that side of your character vigorously and confidently—and to make sure that what you offer is appreciated. What is the best truth you

> know? What's holy and pure in your life, worth living for? That's your gift. Dramatize it. Package it somehow. And perform! You may be drawn to the arts. But just as possibly, you might express your creativity in a business, or in some public service.
>
> Beneath the colorful surface of your character, there is an insecurity. Hardly anyone sees it. It's the fundamental spiritual problem you've come into this life to work out. Your "yoga" lies in tricking the world into clapping its hands for you. Be wary, though: even if you win the Nobel prize, it won't mean a thing unless you win it for expressing your SELF. Otherwise, your deep-seated doubts and insecurities about your SELF go untouched and unhealed. One more thing—if you're doing your best and nobody's clapping, remember this: your act is fine; it's the audience that needs to be replaced. (From "The Sky Within," by Steven Forrest. Courtesy of Matrix Software [http://thenewage.com] and Steven Forrest [http://www.stevenforrest.com].)

Among its several natal programs, Matrix Astrological Software created a unique report based on the published works of the early-twentieth-century astrologer Grant Lewi (1901–1952). Lewi's highly original delineations were recognized as creative and insightful by his contemporaries. One measure of the appeal of his work is that his books *Astrology for the Millions* and *Heaven Knows What* are still in print. The following is excerpted from the report program "Heaven Knows What":

> "We are Earth's best, that learnt her lesson here. / Life is our cry. We have kept the faith!" we said; / "We shall go down with unreluctant tread, / Rose-crowned into the darkness!" ... Proud we were, / And laughed, that had such brave true things to say. / And then you suddenly cried, and turned away." (*Rupert Brooke, born in Leo, August 3, 1887.*)
>
> The mainspring of Leo's great energy, vitality and charm is his instinctive desire for both public acclaim and self-approval. Of all the signs, Leo is perhaps the most aware of himself; in a sense he is always before the looking glass, seeing what effect he is making. In shallow types this makes for mere vanity, pompousness, pride. Add profundity, and all this is changed. Your best Leo type is earnest, sincere, eager to please himself and the world around him and willing, in order to do so, to take on infinite work and go to infinite trouble. He is not genuinely introspective; he has little capacity to discover his inner faults; but he is very sensitive to the effect he makes on others, and studies therefore what to do to make a better effect. There is a difference here from self-analysis to improve character from the inside, but the difference is in method rather than in result.
>
> For Leo, in the process of appearing something desirable, actually becomes something desirable. He knows instinctively the wisdom of the advice Hamlet gave his mother: "Assume a virtue if you have it not." By assuming the appearance of a virtue for the sake of winning approval, he actually acquires the virtue itself, for he is the soul of truth

> and cannot behave as he doesn't feel. He thus removes the curse from his play acting, for his sense of the dramatic is strong, and the roles he assumes are noble. This would be unbearable if in the process Leo did not actually become noble—but he does; some of the greatest spirits who have ever walked the earth are these very Leos who chose for themselves a high role in which to merit the world's approval, lived up to the role, and actually became what they wanted to be admired for. "Such a price do the gods exact for a song, to become what we sing." Whether he is found in business, on the stage (and he often is), or in a love affair (where also he often is), Leo is acutely aware of himself, always standing off and appraising the effect he is making. He will usually be found, if not conventional, at least discreet. Self-approval replaces conscience; he'll do anything if he thinks it is right, and will brave public opinion if his self-approval is sufficiently important to outweigh the loss of public approval. However he behaves, you can rest assured that he is always acutely aware of what people are thinking of him and that he is striving to make them think as well as possible. (Courtesy of Matrix Software [http://thenewage.com].)

The following excerpt comes not from a natal report program, but from David Cochrane's recent book, *Astrology for the 21st Century*. Based on lessons for astrology students, it approaches the signs of the zodiac from a somewhat different perspective than the other short delineations cited here:

> Heightened self-consciousness is the underlying process of Leo. I have not been able to formulate all zodiac sign influences in the energy process perspective, but Leo is one that I view more with an energy process perspective than a list of correlations or symbolic archetypal images. I have repeatedly and consistently found that the person with a great deal of Leo in the birth chart has an acute sense of his own existence and individuality. Symptoms of this acute self-awareness range from shyness to fear of being in front of groups, to feelings of insecurity about one's own competency, to exaggerated feelings of one's own competency and a desire to be in the limelight. Leo is regarded by many, probably the majority, of astrologers as being sunny, outgoing, brash, and egotistical, but I have found the opposite traits of shyness and lack of self-esteem to be just as common. (Courtesy of Cosmic Patterns [http://cosmic.patterns.com] and David Cochrane [kepler@astrosoftware.com].)

A number of specialized report programs have been developed that offer useful supplements to the generic delineations of general reports. The following sun-sign interpretation has been drawn from a program written by Gloria Star (originally part of her book, *Astrology: Woman to Woman*) that generates a specialized report for women:

> With your Sun in Leo you're likely to radiate a sense of regality and power, even if you're just sitting at home in your old jeans. Although you may not demand to be the center of attention, you can certainly

> carry it off when the spotlight is on you. You're driven by a need to create and express yourself, and enjoy playful people and situations. When challenged your pride can get in your way unless you develop some objectivity about yourself, which can be a tough job if you're too self-absorbed. It's okay to think of yourself as royalty some of the time, but just remember that others may not see you that way!
>
> Since you're no stranger to the spotlight, you've probably had ample opportunities to express your assertiveness and personal strength. Your Leo Sun is a magnet for attention, and your actions and attitudes determine whether or not that attention is helpful or detrimental. You have the potential to radiate a powerful energy and may be an inspiration to those who need a stable source of confirmation that life is, indeed, okay. You can be intimidating to men who are unsure of themselves and may even take advantage of this; just try to remember your own insecurity when you first faced raw power! Taking on the challenge of leadership can be one of your most fulfilling experiences, although you can be quite domineering in some situations. If you've been giving away your power to the men in your life, you have probably attracted strong-willed individuals. But to become truly complete, you must learn to embrace and express your own individuality in a manner which opens your creativity and fills your heart.
>
> Well, admit it, sometimes it's just fun to show off with your Sun in Leo. You may even be quite low-key, and gracious about giving others the spotlight. But you know that when you're shining in all your glory, that the light can be blinding for a moment, and then, well, you're just gorgeous! To feel a true sense of success, you may need that few moments of fame and glory. And if you're doing it right, the Universe may even grant you more! (From "Woman to Woman," by Gloria Star. Courtesy of Matrix Software [http://thenewage.com] and Gloria Star [glostar@aol.com].)

Responding to the revival of interest in pre-twentieth-century astrology, J. Lee Lehman developed a report program embodying the interpretive approach of traditional astrology. The following is excerpted from her book *Classical Astrology for Modern Living* and her computer program "Classical Report":

> You are capable of being highly honored, and of gaining wealth and dignity. You are courageous, proud, sober, grave, generous, resolute, strong, valiant, crafty, cruel, discrete, and fierce. You are affable enough, but you must be careful to really mean it, because you are not good at the polite white lie ("But you must have lost weight, Darling, you look absolutely ravishing!"), whatever you might think. You are grave of manner, high-minded, and honest. It is a point of honor to keep your promises. As a bestial sign, you can be quite lascivious. This also means that you can be vicious or violent if angered.

> You are a Fire Sign, which means that you are "hot" and "dry." The "dry" component means, among other things, that you see distinctions easily, and that you are more swayed by intellectual argument than by passion. Being "hot," you react to things quickly: by expressing your anger strongly and immediately, you don't tend to harbor a grudge. You may be perceived by others as angry, but that's only if they are not "hot" as well. You will be perceived as high energy, you are aware of a curious stillness amidst the seeming activity. You may need more sleep than colder types in order to recharge your batteries.
>
> You are fixed, which means you are strong-willed and stubborn. You will want to hang onto people and things long after they have ceased to be useful to you. Being a four-footed sign, you have a strong sex drive. This also means that you can be vicious or violent if angered. (Courtesy of J. Lee Lehman, Ph.D., copyright 1998, [http://www.leelehman.com].)

Readers interested in examining interpretations for their Chinese astrological sign should refer to the relevant entry. A guide for determining one's sign in the Chinese system is provided in the entry on the Chinese zodiac.

**Sources:**

Cochrane, David. *Astrology for the 21st Century*. Gainesville, FL: Cosmic Patterns, 2002.

Forrest, Steven. *The Inner Sky: How to Make Wiser Choices for a More Fulfilling Life*. 4th ed. San Diego: ACS Publications, 1989.

Green, Landis Knight. *The Astrologer's Manual: Modern Insights into an Ancient Art*. Sebastopol, CA: CRCS Publications, 1975.

Hall, Manly P. *Astrological Keywords*. New York: Philosophical Library, 1958. Reprint, Savage, MD: Littlefield Adams Quality Paperbacks, 1975.

Lehman, J. Lee. *Classical Astrology for Modern Living: From Ptolemy to Psychology & Back Again*. Atglen, PA: Whitford Press, 1996.

Lewi, Grant. *Astrology for the Millions*. 5th rev. ed. St. Paul, MN: Llewellyn Publications, 1978.

———. *Heaven Knows What*. St. Paul, MN: Llewellyn Publications, 1969.

Star, Gloria. *Astrology & Your Child: A Handbook for Parents*. St. Paul, MN: Llewellyn Publications, 2001.

———. *Astrology: Woman to Woman*. St. Paul, MN: Llewellyn Publications, 1999.

## LEO, ALAN

Alan Leo, an important turn-of-the-twentieth-century English astrologer, was born in Westminster, London, England, on August 7, 1860. He was brought up by his mother in difficult circumstances and had no formal education beyond grade school. His given name was William Frederick Alan. He pursued various jobs but found nothing satisfactory until he became a traveling salesman for a vending machine company. He stayed in that work until 1898.

Leo taught himself astrology and in 1888 became acquainted with another astrologer, F. W. Lacey. Through Lacey he met W. Gorn Old, who belonged to the inner circle of the Theosophical Society. Leo joined the society in 1890 and formed a partnership with Lacey to publish *Astrologer's Magazine*. For years, the magazine advertised a free chart-reading for new subscribers. (Leo met his wife through such an advertisement.) Although the offer and consequently the magazine proved popular, Lacey withdrew in 1894 to pursue other interests, which left Leo as sole proprietor. He renamed the magazine *Modern Astrology* in 1895.

By 1898, the prosperity of his magazine was such that Leo was able to abandon his sales job and give his full energies to astrology. His Modern Astrology Publishing Company grew steadily and built up a big business in astrological materials. In the early 1900s, he wrote seven substantial books as well as a number of short works on astrology. His books were so popular that they were repeatedly reprinted, and after almost a century they are still in print.

Leo founded the Astrological Lodge of the Theosophical Society in 1915. The lodge thrived and became a permanent part of the society. His success in creating popular interest in astrology was such that he was prosecuted for "fortune-telling" twice. In the first case, in May 1914, he was acquitted on a technicality. In the second case, in July 1917, he was fined 25 pounds (equivalent to thousands of dollars in today's money). These cases were not much different from religious persecution. Some of Leo's friends thought these prosecutions contributed to his death (from cerebral hemorrhage) in 1917.

**Sources:**

Holden, James H., and Robert A. Hughes. *Astrological Pioneers of America*. Tempe, AZ: American Federation of Astrologers, 1988.

Leo, Alan. *The Art of Synthesis*. 9th ed. London: L.N. Fowler, 1968.

———. *Astrology for All*. London: L. N. Fowler, 1969.

———. *Casting the Horoscope*. 11th ed. London: L.N. Fowler, 1969.

———. *Esoteric Astrology*. London: L. N. Fowler, 1967.

———. *How to Judge a Nativity*. London, 1903. Reprint, London: L.N. Fowler, 1969.

———. *The Key to Your Own Nativity*. 10th ed. London: L. N. Fowler, 1969.

———. *The Progressed Horoscope*. 1905. Reprint, London: L. N. Fowler, 1969.

## Levine, Joyce

Joyce Levine's career as an astrological consultant spans more than 25 years. She received professional certification from the American Federation of Astrologers in 1979 and is certified by the National Council for Geocosmic Research (NCGR). She serves on the boards of NCGR and the United Astrology Conference. Frequently interviewed by the media, her picture has appeared in both the *Boston Globe*.

Levine also works with businesses. Businesses also have "birth charts" based upon the date of their incorporation or the beginning of the business. These charts, combined with the charts of key personnel, show the direction the business will take during a particular period of time, what opportunities are available, and what problems are likely to occur.

Levine's second business is Vizualizations publishing. Vizualizations produces self-help and astrology meditation tapes. Through these tapes, people learn how to improve the areas of their lives where they feel trapped or out of control, get in touch with their true selves, learn how planetary cycles affect their energy, unlock their hidden creative sides, release hurtful past experiences, and visualize images of beauty and spirituality.

## Lewi, Grant

Grant Lewi was born June 8, 1902, in Albany, New York. He was educated at Hamilton College and Columbia University. After graduating from Columbia, Lewi taught English at Dartmouth, at the University of North Dakota, and at the University of Delaware. He married Carolyn Wallace, daughter of astrologer Athene Gayle Wallace, in 1926 and began to study astrology with his mother-in-law.

His first career choice was writing, but the economic pressures of the times were difficult, and in 1934 he began working as a professional astrologer. Under the pseudonym Oscar, he provided a short outline of his life in *Astrology for the Millions*. In the late 1930s and 1940s, Lewi edited *Horoscope Magazine*. In 1950, he resigned in order to begin his own magazine, the *Astrologer*. He moved to Arizona in the same period and died July 14, 1951.

Lewi devised a unique approach to astrological interpretation based upon equating house and sign indications. He also utilized certain psychological considerations at a time when astrology was more event-oriented. He used transits exclusively for predictive purposes. This approach was developed in his *Astrology for the Millions* and some of his magazine articles. Lewi's two major works, *Astrology for the Millions* and *Heaven Knows What*, remain popular and have introduced countless numbers of people to astrology. Lewi's interpretations were so highly regarded that Matrix Astrological Software devised a "Heaven Knows What" astrological report program based on Lewi's publications.

**Sources:**

Holden, James H., and Robert A. Hughes. *Astrological Pioneers of America*. Tempe, AZ: American Federation of Astrologers, 1988.

Lewi, William Grant II. *Astrology for the Millions*. New York: Doubleday, 1940.

———. *Heaven Knows What*. New York: Doubleday, 1935.

## Libra

Libra, the seventh sign of the zodiac, is a cardinal air sign. It is a positive, masculine sign, ruled by the planet Venus (some contemporary astrologers want to transfer rulership to several of the asteroids; others assert that an as-yet-undiscovered planet beyond Pluto will rule Libra). Its symbol is the scales, which its glyph is said to represent. It takes its name from the Latin word for "pound weight," or "scales." Libra is associated with the lower back, buttocks, and kidneys, and individuals with a Libra sun sign are susceptible to lower back and kidney problems. The key phrase for Libra is "I balance."

Although many classical accounts say that the goddess Astraea was transformed into the constellation Virgo, Astraea is more properly associated with Libra, which is the next constellation in the zodiac. Older images of Libra represented the

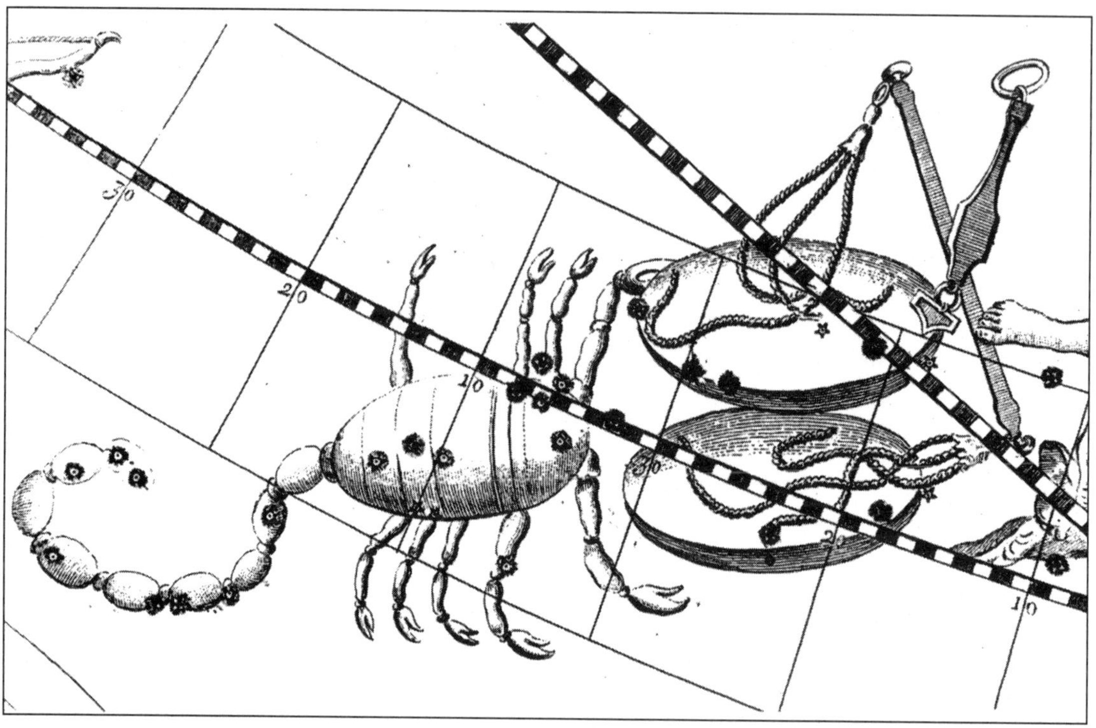

**An engraving of the constellations Scorpio and Libra by Montignot, 1786. *Reproduced by permission of Fortean Picture Library.***

sign as a set of scales being held by a young woman, but the actual constellation is constituted by a handful of stars that form only the scales. To make the figure complete, the tendency was to imagine Virgo holding the scales—thus, the mistaken association of Virgo with Astraea. Although her image was widespread, the classical mythology about Astraea is scanty. The daughter of Zeus and Themis, she spread justice and virtue among humankind during the Golden Age and was the last divinity to leave Earth after humanity had become wicked. The association of scales with justice is very old (e.g., in ancient Egyptian mythology, souls were judged by weighing their hearts on scales), and the modern image of the scales of justice is derived from Astraea's image.

Like their patron goddess, Librans enjoy human company; they find themselves through their relationships with others. While people born under Libra are said to be stubborn, they are more often just sticklers for fairness. They can easily become upset with social injustices. The image of the scales resting at balance conveys a false sense of Libran nature: Even though Librans constantly strive for harmony, the scales can easily become a see-saw, especially when Librans are forced to decide between two alternatives: In many cases, they would rather not choose, but let the circumstances dictate choices for them. Librans are also known for their charm, as well as their attraction to visual beauty. They are natural diplomats.

The sign that the Sun was in at birth is usually the single most important influence on a native's personality. Thus, when people say they are a certain sign, they are almost always referring to their sun sign. There is a wealth of information available on the characteristics of the zodiacal signs—so much that one book would not be able to contain it all. Sun-sign astrology, which is the kind of astrology found in newspaper columns and popular magazines, has the advantage of simplicity. But this simplicity is purchased at the price of ignoring other astrological influences, such as one's Moon sign, rising sign, etc. These other influences can substantially modify a person's basic sun sign traits. As a consequence, it is the rare individual who is completely typical of her or his sign. The reader should bear this caveat in mind when perusing the following series of sun-sign interpretations.

One traditional way in which astrologers condense information is by summarizing sign and planet traits in lists of words and short phrases called keywords or key phrases. The following Libra keywords are drawn from Manly P. Hall's *Astrological Keywords:*

> *Emotional keywords:* "Suave, aesthetic, romantic, enthusiastic, changeable, artistic, easily thrown off emotional balance, secretive in matters of the heart, amorous but fickle."
>
> *Mental keywords:* "Persuasive, imitative, judicial, tactful, undecided, inclined to be a dilettante, fond of show and approbation, intriguing, materialistic, liable to pout, and enjoy feeling abused."

At present, there are various astrology report programs that contain interpretations of each of the 12 sun signs. A selection of these for Sun in Libra has been excerpted below:

> Very sociable, you enjoy being with others and definitely prefer not to be alone. Warm and affectionate, you go out of your way to make others like you. You despise ugliness, so that for you being surrounded by beauty and harmony is a necessity of life. You prefer fine clothing, an attractive home and pleasant surroundings wherever you are. Your refined tastes may apply to music and art as well. Because you have the ability to see both sides of any question, you can at times be indecisive, wavering and faltering when forced to make a choice. The positive part of this is that you are remarkably fair-minded and can be trusted to settle disputes. Your greatest challenge is to make the most of the one-on-one relationships in your life. (From "Professional Natal Report." Courtesy of Astrolabe [http://www.alabe.com].)
>
> Harmony and balance are your keynotes. You instinctively understand the need to accommodate other people's interests and desires, and you are always fair and willing to meet the other person half way. Tactful, diplomatic, and with considerable social awareness, you do all you can to avoid conflict and discord. You express a spirit of cooperation and compromise and often achieve through charm and discretion what would have been impossible to achieve by a direct, forceful approach.

Getting along with others and pleasing them may be TOO important to you, for you can be too dependent on others' approval and opinions to make your own decisions. You will rarely act without getting the counsel and feedback of other people. You prefer sharing and doing things together rather than on your own. Being alone feels very unnatural to you, and you have a strong need for a partner and intimate one-to-one relationships.

You invest a great deal of your energy in personal love and you are very idealistic and romantic about marriage. You seek a partner who is your equal intellectually, and who is capable of a mental relationship as well as a physical and emotional one. You make a thoughtful, considerate friend or lover, and you enjoy the traditional symbols of love—courtship, flowers, etc. Relationships are like an art to you, one that requires time, attention, and creative effort. You appreciate a partner who is subtle and polished, never coarse or dull or blunt.

Fairness and equality, both in your personal life and in the world, are extremely important to you. If you fight about anything, it is often about something you feel is unfair and unbalanced. Balance is very important to you and you believe in moderation in all things, avoiding fanaticism and extremism of any sort.

You also have a strong need for beautiful, harmonious surroundings and a natural sense of artistic style and grace, which is reflected in the way you dress, furnish and arrange your home and workspace, etc. Everything must be aesthetically pleasing and appropriate. Either working with people as a counselor, advisor, consultant, or negotiator—or in an artistic field such as design or photography, would be fulfilling to you. (From "Merlin," by Gina Ronco and Agnes Nightingale. Courtesy of Cosmic Patterns [http://cosmic.patterns.com].)

Perfect equilibrium. That's the spirit of the Scales. When Libra realizes its evolutionary aim, the nervous system is as still as a dark pool on a windless summer evening. Outwardly, Libran energy often looks as though it's already there: it seems graceful and balanced, even unflappable. Inwardly, it's another story: the Libran part of you is tuned as tight as the high string on a violin. Spirit gave you some advice back before you were born: don't pluck it. And don't let anyone else pluck it either.

Inevitably, with your terrific sensitivity, you'll get rattled from time to time. What can you do about it? Watch a ballet, or any other beautiful thing. The outer harmony will internalize; you'll sigh, releasing tension. That's the Libran evolutionary strategy in a nutshell: flood your senses with perceptions of beauty. It will soothe you, lifting you closer to the unbreakable serenity which is the true goal of this sign of the zodiac.

With your Sun in Libra, on the deepest level of your character you are an artist. If you look like one outwardly, painting or playing an instrument, so much the better. Even if you don't, your essence is still

> charged with aesthetic sensitivity. Cultivate it, and you'll feel as though you've come into yourself.
>
> You were born with an instinctive tolerance for paradox. Everything has two sides, and you'll almost always consider both. This gives great clarity of mind, but also presents a problem. Be careful you don't get caught between two equally attractive or (unattractive!) possibilities and just freeze there. Life will crystallize around you again and again in that form: you'll be faced with a parade of morally or practically ambiguous situations. You'll understand them far better than your more dogmatic friends. The question is whether you'll be able to make a choice and get on with your life, burning bridges behind you. (From "The Sky Within," by Steven Forrest. Courtesy of Matrix Software [http://thenewage.com] and Steven Forrest [http://www.stevenforrest.com].)

Among its several natal programs, Matrix Astrological Software created a unique report based on the published works of the early-twentieth-century astrologer Grant Lewi (1901–1952). Lewi's highly original delineations were recognized as creative and insightful by his contemporaries. One measure of the appeal of his work is that his books *Astrology for the Millions* and *Heaven Knows What* are still in print. The following is excerpted from the report program "Heaven Knows What":

> He prayeth best who loveth best / All things both great and small. (*Samuel Taylor Coleridge, born in Libra, October 21, 1772.)*
>
> Libra's aim is to identify himself with as much of the rest of the world as suits the demands of his very eclectic and elegant taste. Despite a gentle and firm sort of independence, he does not put much stock in "being himself," for he values other people a great deal and, if no principle is involved, will please others before thinking of what he wants. In a deep sense, what he wants is what makes others happy. In some this makes weakness. The girl who "made love only to her friends and didn't have an enemy in the world" was very likely a Libran. But so also is the girl whose charm is so great and whose interest so eager that she holds a man's attention without yielding to his carnal passions. And many who have tried to force the apparently yielding Libran along a path counter to his principles have felt the iron hand in the velvet glove.
>
> Libra's willingness to lose his identity in others—in society, in marriage—makes Librans ideal companions, or mates, for those who understand the curious need they have for independence that accompanies their selflessness. They merge with others, but they retain their identity, and will withdraw completely if their identity is attacked or endangered. They are democratic in spirit, but since they identify themselves with elegance, will not allow themselves to be forced into contact with things or people that offend their very strong sense of good taste. Thus they are often thought aristocrats or snobs, when in reality they have the deepest kind of inspect, sympathy and understanding for all sorts and conditions of men.

> They also have a great deal of respect, sympathy and understanding for themselves, and see no reason why they should ever give this up. They are the living embodiment of the cooperative spirit; they will work with you till they drop, but rarely for you. By the same token, if they are executives (and they often are) they treat their subordinates as partners, not as servants. Much is expected of the man who works for a Libra boss, who in return pays him well and treats him as an equal. The aide who does housework for a Libra mistress must keep the place spotless, but is treated with respect, as a fellow mortal whose human dignity must never be violated or imposed on. Libra finds deepest satisfaction in harmonious union with those around him, and with the whole world, which is not too much to be taken in by his warm and tolerant spirit. (Courtesy of Matrix Software [http://thenewage.com].)

The following excerpt comes not from a natal report program, but from David Cochrane's recent book, *Astrology for the 21st Century*. Based on lessons for astrology students, it approaches the signs of the zodiac from a somewhat different perspective than the other short delineations cited here.

> Libra values friendship above all else. Friends are equals. Cancer likes a hierarchy where one person takes care of another person, but Libra prefers that people be equal and take care of one another. People can be different; Libra has no problem with that, but Libra insists that all people be respected and treated as equals, whether the person is an artist, scientist, farmer, or teacher. Regardless of gender or ethnic background all are equal.
>
> Librans frequently avoid direct confrontation in order to maintain harmony and friendship. Avoiding confrontation can lead to outstanding diplomatic skills, but it can also lead to little white lies. Little white lies over time can grow into big ugly dark ones. This tendency to subtle deceit and lies is especially difficult to avoid if the person uses drugs or is under the influence of alcohol.
>
> Libra's acute social awareness can give a special kindness and sweetness to the person. Libra is sensitive to your situation and your needs, and their sincere interest in your well-being inclines them to have many good friends and many people who appreciate them. (Courtesy of Cosmic Patterns [http://cosmic.patterns.com] and David Cochrane [kepler@astrosoftware.com].)

A number of specialized report programs have been developed that offer useful supplements to the generic delineations of general reports. The following sun-sign interpretation has been drawn from a program written by Gloria Star (originally part of her book, *Astrology: Woman to Woman*) that generates a specialized report for women:

> With your Sun in Libra your ego is driven by a need to relate. Now, that doesn't mean that you must be married or in a love relationship. It is through connecting to others that you gain the feedback which allows you to maintain a balance in your life. This can be accomplished through

friendships, work relationships and social situations. You may also crave the best of everything (it's your good taste that can be your downfall if you're on a budget!), and you definitely love the most refined elements of life. At heart, you're artistic, but you can be tough to satisfy.

Claiming your sense of individual autonomy may not be an easy task with the influence of your Libra Sun. Since you tend to think in terms of relativity, it's difficult to extract your own assertive self in a confident manner, especially during your early years. You may have learned to place great importance on your physical appearance or upon proper social behavior, learning to behave like a young lady, assuming that if you were pretty and charming enough then all the other things would just fall into place. Stepping out into the world and discovering that you needed to be known for more than your looks may have been your first reality check. Your sense of relativity can be one of your best assets, however. By making harmonious choices of partners—whether they are friends who share your interests, lovers or husbands—you can gain the type of feedback you need to see yourself more clearly. Then, your autonomy and individuality are strengthened through greater objectivity. But if you seek a partner or husband who will take on the tasks you just don't feel prepared to handle, like dealing with the demands of the world, then you will be continually frustrated and will frustrate your partner, too. Additionally, developing social relationships which support and reflect your true values will help you feel more confident about your identity, instead of just seeking situations which increase your social standing or status.

You may think you don't care much about success as long as it looks good on you. But you know that your Libra Sun is really driving you to reach a stage of getting things right and having life fit your set of specifications. Finding success through your associations with others may seem to be the easy way out, and you may keep trying to change them to fit your desires until you realize that you really are working on changing yourself. So, look in the mirror and start over. What do you want to see reflected back at you? See that confident smile? That's the look of success. The rest should be easy. (From "Woman to Woman," by Gloria Star. Courtesy of Matrix Software [http://thenewage.com] and Gloria Star [glostar@aol.com].)

Responding to the revival of interest in pre-twentieth-century astrology, J. Lee Lehman developed a report program embodying the interpretive approach of traditional astrology. The following is excerpted from her book *Classical Astrology for Modern Living* and her computer program "Classical Report":

You are sincere and just, an interpreter of dreams who can find out secret and hidden things. There is a danger that in the process you will offend others. You are changeable, just, upright, courteous, crafty, cheerful, and conceited.

> While you may be attracted to things warlike or martial, you would do better to avoid them as you could be in danger of dishonor. You are Cardinal, which means that you are better at starting new things than at finishing them.
>
> You are an Air Sign, which means that you are "hot" and "wet." The "wet" component means, among other things, that you blur distinctions, and that you are more swayed by passion than by intellectual argument. At your worst, you see too many connections, becoming lost in conspiracies. At your best, you spot the connection that everyone else missed. Being "hot," you react to things quickly: by expressing your anger strongly and immediately, you don't tend to harbor a grudge. This is the temperament type that is considered the most ideal, because you are the most comfortable within a social situation. You appear warm and friendly to others, and don't seem too eager to hold them to an impossible standard. [Courtesy of J. Lee Lehman, Ph.D., copyright 1998 [http://www.leelehman.com].)

Readers interested in examining interpretations for their Chinese astrological sign should refer to the relevant entry. A guide for determining one's sign in the Chinese system is provided in the entry on the Chinese zodiac.

**Sources:**

Cochrane, David. *Astrology for the 21st Century*. Gainesville, FL: Cosmic Patterns, 2002.

Forrest, Steven. *The Inner Sky: How to Make Wiser Choices for a More Fulfilling Life*. 4th ed. San Diego: ACS Publications, 1989.

Green, Landis Knight. *The Astrologer's Manual: Modern Insights into an Ancient Art*. Sebastopol, CA: CRCS Publications, 1975.

Lehman, J. Lee. *Classical Astrology for Modern Living: From Ptolemy to Psychology & Back Again*. Atglen, PA: Whitford Press, 1996.

Lewi, Grant. *Astrology for the Millions*. 5th rev. ed. St. Paul, MN: Llewellyn Publications, 1978.

———. *Heaven Knows What*. St. Paul, MN: Llewellyn Publications, 1969.

Star, Gloria. *Astrology & Your Child: A Handbook for Parents*. St. Paul, MN: Llewellyn Publications, 2001.

———. *Astrology: Woman to Woman*. St. Paul, MN: Llewellyn Publications, 1999.

Hall, Manly P. *Astrological Keywords*. New York: Philosophical Library, 1958. Reprint, Savage, MD: Littlefield Adams Quality Paperbacks, 1975.

## LILITH

In astrology, Lilith refers to either an asteroid or a cloud of small dust particles that orbit Earth like a second moon. Lilith, asteroid 1,181 (the 1,181st asteroid to be discovered, on February 11, 1927), was named after the legendary first wife of Adam, who was expelled from Eden for not acknowledging Adam's superiority. It has an orbital period of 4⅓ years and is 18 kilometers in diameter.

Lilith is one of the more recent asteroids to be investigated by astrologers. Preliminary material on Lilith can be found in Demetra George and Douglas Bloch's *Astrology for Yourself* and an ephemeris (table of celestial locations) for Lilith can be found in George and Bloch's *Asteroid Goddesses*. Unlike the planets, which are associated with a wide range of phenomena, the smaller asteroids are said to represent a single principle. George and Bloch give Lilith's principle as personal power and conflict resolution; their tentative key phrase for Lilith is "My capacity to constructively release my anger and resolve conflict." Zipporah Dobyns views Lilith as related to many Pluto concerns, namely, a strong will, interest in the occult and the unconscious, and power and control issues. J. Lee Lehman relates Lilith to the "wild women" in each of us (in men, the anima of female shadow self). This aspect of ourselves is often repressed, leading to misogyny in men and self-hatred in women.

Lilith the dust cloud, Earth's "dark moon," received much attention from a handful of important earty twentieth century astrologers, such as Ivy Goldstein-Jacobson and W. Gorn Old (Sepharial). While the very existence of Lilith has been questioned, some astrologers have taken the claimed observations of a dust cloud obscuring—or being illumined by—the Sun and constructed ephemerides for this body. Early investigators regarded the influence of Lilith as malefic, believing the dust cloud to be involved in such unpleasant matters as betrayal and stillbirth. However, the feminist movement—which has strongly influenced the astrological community, if for no other reason than that the majority of practitioners are women—has caused reevaluation of mythological figures like Lilith: Perhaps the rejection of Adam's authority should be seen as commendable, as the first time in history (even though it is a mythological history) that a woman refused to be ordered around by a man. Thus, more recent interpreters have tended to give Lilith a richer range of meanings, including many positive ones.

The majority of contemporary astrologers reject the notion of astrological influence from an obscure dust cloud, and fewer actually use "the dark moon Lilith" in their work. (One measure of its rejection is its absence from such standard twentieth-century reference works as the *Larousse Encyclopedia of Astrology*.) Attributing influence to Lilith persists, nevertheless, particularly among astrologers in the lineage of Goldstein-Jacobson and Sepharial. An important modern treatment of Lilith by Delphine Jay (*Interpreting Lilith*) and her very usable *Lilith Ephemeris* were published in the early 1980s. In 1988 and 1991, respectively, these two books went through their third printing. Thus, like her namesake, Earth's dark moon continues to refuse to submit to the astrological mainstream, which would prefer to deal with more manageable celestial bodies.

**Sources:**

Dobyns, Zipporah. *Expanding Astrology's Universe*. San Diego: Astro Computing Services, 1983.

George, Demetra, with Douglas Bloch. *Asteroid Goddesses: The Mythology, Psychology and Astrology of the Reemerging Feminine*. 2d ed. rev. San Diego: ACS, 1990.

———. *Astrology for Yourself: A Workbook for Personal Transformation*. Berkeley, CA: Wingbow Press, 1987.

Jay, Delphine. *Interpreting Lilith*. Tempe, AZ: American Federation of Astrologers, 1981.

———. *The Lilith Ephemeris, 1900–2000 A.D.* Tempe, AZ: American Federation of Astrologers, 1983.

Lehman, J. Lee. *The Ultimate Asteroid Book*. West Chester, PA: Whitford Press, 1988.

Schwartz, Jacob. *Asteroid Name Encyclopedia*. St. Paul, MN: Llewellyn Publications, 1995.

## LILLY, WILLIAM

William Lilly (1602–1681) was the most important astrologer in England at a time when astrology itself had attained a richness and a degree of influence unmatched before or, probably, since. This stature manifested itself in two ways: his role as an astrologer in the wider social and political world, and his place in and impact on the astrological tradition.

Lilly rose to national prominence in the context of the English Revolution, including the Civil War (1642–49) and so-called Interregnum, lasting until the Restoration in 1662, which saw the return of a king, House of Lords, and bishops. In this time of unprecedented upheaval, astrology—liberated from strict censorship—was among the many ideas that, for a time, took national center stage. And Lilly was, during his lifetime, universally recognized as astrology's preeminent practitioner. Even his disputacious peers made him the leading figure of the London Society of Astrologers, who met annually for a sermon and feast in 1647–58. Lilly consistently issued dire warnings as to the likely fate of Charles I, backed up by inspired and precise astrological exegesis. (Typically, though, he also supplied the beleagured king with private advice, through a royal emissary, as to how to escape it.) His value as chief prophet of the Parliamentarian cause was estimated as equivalent to several regiments, and his annual almanac, *Merlinus Anglicus*, from its start in 1644, rose to sales of nearly 30,000 copies a year throughout the 1650s. There were bitter complaints (particularly by his enemies the Presbyterians) that people put more trust in his almanacs than in the Bible, and that on the occasion of an eclipse in 1652, many in London were too frightened by his dire prognostication to venture outdoors.

After the Great Fire of 1666, Lilly was examined by a parliamentary committee because he was widely believed to have predicted it in a pamphlet of 1651. (A woodcut therein showed twins—Gemini, long held to be ruling sign of London—hanging suspended above a fire that men are struggling to put out.) But on this and other occasions, Lilly was protected by powerful political allies. One was the alchemist and astrologer Elias Ashmole, a firm Royalist and Controller of the Excise after 1662; despite their very different political convictions, the two men became lifelong friends.

In 1652, Lilly left for Hersham, in Surrey, where he became churchwarden of St. Mary's Church in Walton-on-Thames, and married for the third and final time. Here he continued the astrological practice that had begun in his house "by Strand Bridge" in London. From the 1640s through the 1660s, Lilly averaged nearly 2000 consultations a year, and his clients ranged from serving girls to politicans and aristocrats, with a scale of fees paid accordingly. By 1662, he was reported to be earning about 500 pounds a year, a very comfortable sum. He also, however, dispensed free advice and treatment to the parish poor. In 1670, he obtained formal permission from the archbishop of Canterbury to practice medicine as well. Lilly died on June 9, 1681, and was buried in St Mary's, where his marble tombstone, bearing an inscription paid for by Ashmole, can still be seen.

In addition to this remarkable life as an astrologer, Lilly's claim to fame rests on his authorship of the first astrological textbook in English, *Christian Astrology* (1657, with a second edition in 1659 and a facsimile reprint in 1985 that is still in use). While drawing on virtually the entire European corpus then available—more than 200 titles are cited—the book is stamped with Lilly's own unmistakable style, the sample judgments combining the skill of an artist with an authority at once pragmatic and spiritual. Many are horary, reflecting both its importance in a period when many people had no idea of their birth time, but also Lilly's kind of divinatory astrology. It embraced, without any sense of necessary contradiction, a disciplined and systematic approach to knowledge that has since become identified as "scientific"; the magical sense of not only discerning but negotiating with destiny, and thus potentially changing it; and the possibility of religiously inspired, and piously revered prophecy. Within Lilly's lifetime, these three strands started to become seriously estranged. Even within the astrological tradition, there were subsequently only either scientific *or* magical (and sometimes spiritual) astrologers, and these two camps were in perpetual opposition.

Lilly was a genius at something— judicial astrology—that modern mainstream opinion has since decided is impossible to do at all, let alone do well or badly. Only in the final decades of the twentieth century, with a renewal of interest and respect among both astrologers and historians, did he begin to receive proper recognition.

**Sources:**

Cornelius, Geoffrey. *The Moment of Astrology: Origins in Divination*. London: Penguin/Arkana, 1994.

Curry, Patrick. *Prophecy and Power: Astrology in Early Modern England*. Princeton, NJ: Princeton University Press, 1989.

Geneva, Ann. *Astrology and the Seventeenth Century Mind: William Lilly and the Language of the Stars*. Manchester, Eng.: Manchester University Press, 1995.

Lilly, William. *Christian Astrology*. London: Regulus, 1647.

Thomas, Keith. *Religion and the Decline of Magic*. Harmondsworth, Eng.: Penguin, 1973.

—Patrick Curry

## Lion

The Lion is a popular name for the sign Leo.

## Local Mean Time

Before the advent of rapid travel and modern means of long distance communication, particular localities kept time according to the noontime position of the Sun. Because this varied east or west of any given location, the local time also varied as one traveled east or west. The imposition of standard time zones, in which one must set her or his watch forward or backward as an imaginary line is crossed, is a comparatively recent innovation. Time zones serve many purposes, but, to properly cast a horoscope, astrologers must find the true local time during which a native was born. In other words, they must convert a birth time expressed in standard time back into local "Sun time." The more common designation for Sun time is local mean time.

Traditionally, astrologers made this conversion by making certain calculations based on the longitude where a native was born. In more recent years, tables of time conversion (astrologers' atlases, such as *Longitudes and Latitudes in the U. S.*) have been published by people who have made the necessary calculations for most large and medium-size cities, thus saving the astrologer a step in the calculations necessary to set up a chart. The personal computer revolution has largely eliminated the need for such tables, as such calculations have been incorporated into chart-casting programs.

**Sources:**

Dernay, Eugene. *Longitudes and Latitudes in the U.S.* Washington, DC: American Federation of Astrologers, 1945.

DeVore, Nicholas. *Encyclopedia of Astrology*. New York: Philosophical Library, 1947.

Filbey, John, and Peter Filbey. *The Astrologer's Companion*. Wellingborough, Northamptonshire, UK: Aquarian Press, 1986.

## Logarithms

Logarithms, which most schoolchildren are taught but promptly forget, were invented in 1614 to assist in astrological calculations. They constitute the most tedious part of traditional astrological mathematics and have been superseded by the computer.

## Longitude

Longitude (properly called terrestrial longitude) refers to the distance of a given location east or west of 0° longitude (which runs through Greenwich, England, where the system of latitudes and longitudes was worked out in its present form). The expression "celestial longitude" refers to the angular distance (distance measured in degrees and minutes of an arc) that a planet or other celestial body is located east of 0° Aries. The numbers beside planets in a horoscope, which express their position in terms of a certain number of degrees and minutes of a particular sign, are celestial longitudes.

## Lord

Lord is an older term for ruler, as in "Mars is the lord (ruler) of Aries." In the case of the Moon and Venus, traditionally regarded as feminine, the proper term was "lady." Many astrologers want to retain this term but reserve its use for the ruler of a house. Thus, for example, in a horoscope in which Aries is on the cusp (beginning) of the third house, Mars would be the ruler of Aries and the lord of the third house. Most contemporary astrologers have dropped the term lord and use the term ruler for both relationships. One finds the same distinction between sign and house rulership/lordship in Vedic astrology, where this notion is central to the correct interpretation of a chart.

## Lucifer

Lucifer, asteroid 1,930 (the 1,930th asteroid to be discovered, on October 29, 1964), is approximately 21 kilometers in diameter and has an orbital period of 4.9 years. Lucifer was named after the fallen angel of light who became the devil in Western religions. J.

**A sixteenth-century illustration of Dante's vision of purgatory and hell. Lucifer is shown at the center of the Earth, encased in a lake of ice, chewing on the soul of Judas Iscariot. *Reproduced by permission of Fortean Picture Library.***

Lee Lehman associates this aspect with "torch bearers." Jacob Schwartz gives Lucifer's astrological meaning as "a sometimes disruptive bearer of divine light."

Lucifer also means light-bearer and is sometimes applied to Venus.

**Sources:**

Kowal, Charles T. *Asteroids: Their Nature and Utilization*. Chichester, West Sussex, UK: Ellis Horwood Limited, 1988.

Lehman, J. Lee. *The Ultimate Asteroid Book*. West Chester, PA: Whitford Press, 1988.
Schwartz, Jacob. *Asteroid Name Encyclopedia*. St. Paul, MN: Llewellyn Publications, 1995.

**An image of the planetary goddess Luna, the moon, from a fifteenth-century German calendar. *Reproduced by permission of Fortean Picture Library.***

## Lucina

Lucina, asteroid 146 (the 146th asteroid to be discovered, on June 8, 1875), is approximately 140 kilometers in diameter and has an orbital period of 4.4 years. It was named after the Roman goddess of childbirth and the travails of women, who was the daughter of Jupiter and Juno. In addition to indicating something about one's children, Lucina's position by sign and house shows where one "gives birth" to various activities or ideas.

**Sources:**

Kowal, Charles T. *Asteroids: Their Nature and Utilization*. Chichester, West Sussex, UK: Ellis Horwood Limited, 1988.
Room, Adrian. *Dictionary of Astronomical Names*. London: Routledge, 1988.
Schwartz, Jacob. *Asteroid Name Encyclopedia*. St. Paul, MN: Llewellyn Publications, 1995.

## Luminaries

Traditionally, the Sun and the Moon were referred to as the luminaries because, in contrast to the planets, they "lit up" the Earth. The majority of contemporary astrologers have ceased to use the term, in spite of its pleasant connotations.

## Luna

Luna is the Roman name for the Moon, and the root of the adjective lunar. Due to the increasingly eccentric behavior that insane people exhibit during the full moon, the Moon became linked with insanity—hence the terms lunatic and lunacy.

## Lunar Mansions

The lunar mansions are a kind of lunar zodiac, constituted by dividing the Moon's orbital path into 27 or 28 segments. Twenty-seven or twenty-eight roughly corresponds to the number of days the Moon takes to complete its orbit (28 is a day short of a synodic period and a day longer than a sidereal month). The Arabs, the Hindus, and the Chinese all devised systems of lunar mansions, termed, respectively, the *manzils* (from lunar *mansion* is probably derived), *nakshatras*, and *sieu*. Traditionally, these included interpretations of the mansions that approached them in approximately the same way Western astrologers use the signs of the zodiac. The mansions in each system are given in the table that follows.

### Lunar Mansions

| Manzil (Arab) | Nakshatra (Hindu) | Sieu (Chinese) |
|---|---|---|
| Al Thurayya | Krittika | Mao |
| Al Dabaran | Rohini | Pi |
| Al Hak'ah | Mrigasiras | Tsee |
| Al Han'ah | Ardra | Shen |
| Al Dhira | Punarvarsu | Tsing |
| Al Nathrah | Pushya | Kwei |
| Al Tarf | Aslesha | Lieu |
| Al Jabhah | Magha | Sing |
| Al Zubrah | Purva Phalguni | Chang |
| Al Sarfah | Uttara Phalguni | Yen |
| Al Awwa | Hasta | Tchin |
| Al Simak | Citra | Kio |
| Al Ghafr | Svati | Kang |
| Al Jubana | Visakha | Ti |
| Iklil al Jabhah | Anuradha | Fang |
| Al Kalb | Jyestha | Sin |
| Al Shaulah | Mula | Wei |
| Al Na'am | Purva Ashadha | Ki |
| Al Baldah | Uttara Ashadha | Tow |
| Al Sa'd al Dhabih | Abhijit | Nieu |
| Al Sa'd al Bula | Sravana | Mo |
| Al Sa'd al Su'ud | Sravishta | Heu |
| Al Sa'd al Ahbiyah | Catabhishaj | Shih |
| Al Fargh al Mukdim | Purva Bhadra-Pada | Shih |
| Al Fargh al Thani | Uttara Bhadra-Pada | Peih |
| Al Batn al Hut | Revati | Goei |
| Al Sharatain | Asvini | Leu |
| Al Butain | Bharani | Oei |

Traditional cultures attributed great significance to the phases of the Moon, particularly to the waxing and waning cycle. The familiar seven-day week is derived from the ancient custom of further dividing up the lunar month according to new moon, first quarter, full moon, and last quarter. The lunar mansions represent a refinement of this tendency, subdividing the Moon's phases according to its day-to-day increase or decrease in apparent size.

**Sources:**

Brau, Jean-Louis, Helen Weaver, and Allan Edmands. *Larousse Encyclopedia of Astrology*. New York: New American Library, 1980.

Gettings, Fred. *Dictionary of Astrology*. London: Routledge & Kegan Paul, 1985.

## Lunar Year

A lunar year is a year of 12 lunar months (12 synodic periods), or 354.367 days. There are 34 such lunar years for every 33 solar years. The traditional Muslim year is a lunar year. Many civilizations have utilized soli-lunar years, which retain the Moon's synodic period for months but also insert an intercalary month to keep the years aligned with the period of Earth's revolution around the Sun.

## Lunation

A lunation is a complete cycle between two new moons, also referred to as a synodic month. Lunations average 29 days, 12 hours, 44 minutes, and 2.7 seconds. The term "lunation" can also be used interchangeably with "new moon."

## Lysistrata

Lysistrata, asteroid 897 (the 897th asteroid to be discovered, on August 3, 1918), is approximately 46 kilometers in diameter and has an orbital period of 4.1 years. It was named after the heroine of the Greek comedy *Lysistrata*. Lysistrata led a revolt of women across Greece, who as a group withheld sexual favors until the men agreed to stop war. Lysistrata represents the healing as well as the manipulative power of sex. The sign and house position of this planetoid in a natal chart indicates how and where this power manifests for each individual.

**Sources:**

Kowal, Charles T. *Asteroids: Their Nature and Utilization*. Chichester, West Sussex, UK: Ellis Horwood Limited, 1988.

Room, Adrian. *Dictionary of Astronomical Names*. London: Routledge, 1988.

Schwartz, Jacob. *Asteroid Name Encyclopedia*. St. Paul, MN: Llewellyn Publications, 1995.

## Magha

Magha (the Mighty One) is one of the Nakshatras (lunar mansions) of Vedic astrology. Often depicted as either a house or throne room, this Nakshatra is located at Leo 0° to 13°20'. This is considered an ideal time to do activities that necessitate someone being larger than normal, and people will tend to be more positive and big-hearted, yet arrogant and overly demanding at the same time in this period. Pitris, god of ancestors, presides, and Ketu rules over Magha.

—Pramela Thiagesan

## Magic and Astrology

Magic is the art of controlling events by occult (hidden) means. Astrology is not, in the proper sense of the term, magical, but such techniques as electional astrology—determining the best times to perform certain actions—border on magic. Traditional Western magic views astrology as providing insight into the occult forces that are playing on Earth at any given time, and a specialized form of electional astrology is utilized by magicians to determine the best times for performing particular rituals.

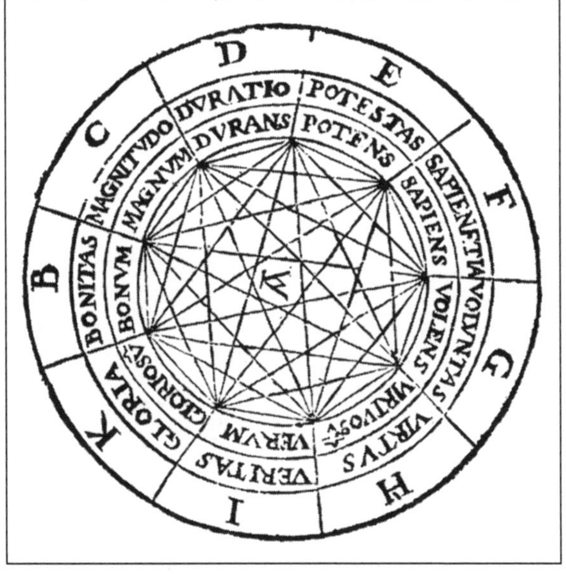


**The alphabetic system of Roman Lull's magical figure. The central "A" represents the Trinity, the nine divisions of the outer circle, the Absoluta (first) and the Releta (second).** ***Reproduced by permission of Fortean Picture Library.***

Much of the astrological lore associated with magic is focused on the days of the week, the planetary hours, and the gems and metals connected with the planets. Each of the traditional seven planets—the Sun, the Moon, Mars, Mercury, Jupiter, Venus, and Saturn—rules, in sequence, the seven days of the week. A similar relationship exists between the planets and the hours of the day. Magicians utilize these relationships and other traditional associations with the planets by, for example, performing rituals to gain love on Friday ("Venusday") during an hour ruled by Venus (the planet of love), performing rituals to gain money on Thursday ("Jupiterday") during an hour ruled by Jupiter (the planet of wealth), and so forth.

Amulets, which are fabricated objects used as charms, are also constructed during days and hours associated with the task the amulet is intended to perform. Additionally, such objects are constructed from materials ruled by the relevant planet. In the above examples, for instance, an amulet designed to attract love might be constructed from copper (the metal traditionally associated with Venus), and an amulet intended to attract prosperity might be made from tin (associated with Jupiter).

Magicians who are competent astrologers also pay attention to the sign in which the relevant planet is placed, as well as the aspects the planet is making at the time of the ceremony. Thus, to once again take Venus as an example, a magician would wait until Venus was in a favorable sign (which, for Venus, would be Libra, Taurus, or Pisces) and favorably aspected (making harmonious aspects with other planets) before performing a love ritual or constructing a love amulet.

**Sources:**

Cavendish, Richard. *The Black Arts*. New York: Capricorn Books, 1967.

Denning, Melita, and Osborne Phillips. *Planetary Magick: The Heart of Western Magick*. St. Paul, MN: Llewellyn Publications, 1989.

## Malefic (Malefic Aspects; Malefic Planets)

Malefic is a traditional term found in older astrological works. It refers to aspects and planets regarded as having an unfortunate, inharmonious influence. Malefic aspects are angles like squares and oppositions (called hard aspects by modern astrologers) and planets like Mars (the Lesser Malefic) and Saturn (the Greater Malefic). The antonym of malefic is benefic. Contemporary astrologers have largely abandoned these older terms, if for no other reason than to avoid frightening clients. There are, however, other good reasons for dropping such language, the primary one being that the "benefics" do not always indicate unmitigated benefits, nor do "malefics" always indicate unmitigated difficulties.

The situation is different in horary astrology, where the traditional malefics can have a distinctly negative bearing on the question being asked. It should also be noted that Vedic astrology, which is very similar to classical Western astrology in this regard, still uses terms like malefic and benefic.

## MANDERS, LEA

Lea Manders was born in Arnhem, the Netherlands, on August 7, 1956, at 1:42 P.M. She started studying astrology at the age of 17. At that time, there were not many books available in the Netherlands, so her self-study began with traditional authors like Maurice Privat. This stimulated Manders to listen very carefully to her clients, because she wanted to test the theories she discovered. Many theories did not work in practice. This has made her an astrologer who has developed her own ideas and methods.

After a few years of study, when Manders was in her late twenties, modern psychological astrology arrived and she was able to buy books from Stephen Arroyo, Liz Greene, and others in the Netherlands. These authors gave her great inspiration, especially during a time when she was developing her therapeutic qualities by following other courses. This led to more depth in her astrological analyses. In the mid-eighties she followed a course in medical astrology. By 1985 she had succeeded in building up a full-time professional practice. She started her own school, offering a four-year course to train astrologers, which is still very successful.

Manders has a special talent for explaining difficult subjects in an simple manner. This is one of the reasons that she is a well-known astrologer in the Netherlands. She is regularly seen or heard on national television and local radio. In the astrological world she is also well known as a teacher and a lecturer. She has written two books and two readers in Dutch and one booklet in English. The subjects range from the more popular to the esoteric. She writes articles for astrologers and for non-astrological magazines. She is currently president of the Astrologische Associatie (ASAS), an association for astrologers which she set up, which aims to make astrology more professional.

With experience in practical and psychological astrological subjects, Manders is now also intensively engaged with the more spiritual side of astrology. She uses the Kaballahistic Tree of Life to create a new vision of astrology and its role in the development of the higher levels in man. She lectured about this theme at the international United Astrology Conference in summer 2002. Manders is also active in politics. Since 1998 she has been a city-counsellor in Arnhem where she lives. Manders is married and has three sons. She speaks Dutch and also lectures in English and German.

—Lea Manders

## MANN, A. T.

A. T. "Tad" Mann was born August 18, 1943, in Auburn, New York. He graduated from Cornell University in 1966 with an architecture degree and worked as a professional architect for a time. He is a member of the Association for Astrological Networkers (AFAN) and the Author's Guild. He lives and works in Hudson, New York, and has a daughter, the woven textile artist Ptolemy Mann.

Mann applied the concept of biological time and the philosophical system of George Gurdjieff, Pyotr Ouspensky, and Rodney Collin to astrology. The resultant logarithmic time scale grades the periphery of the horoscope from the ninth house cusp (conception point) to the ascendant (birth) to the ninth cusp (symbolic death point). During the three periods of gestation, childhood, and maturity, the physical, emotional, and mental bodies are created. There is a fourth period, the transcendent octave, which represents the higher level of gestation influences. *The Round Art of Astrology* (1979 and 2003) first described these ideas with its unique graphic language, *Life Time Astrology* (1984) presented it as a fully functional system for astrologers and therapists, and *A New Vision of Astrology* (2002) includes its revolutionary perceptions.

Mann's life time astrology system is used by astrologers, psychologists, and healers in Europe, the United States, Australia, and the Far East. It is unique as a synthesis of biology, physics, psychology, and astrology. This combination has led to the development of a unique method of treatment at a distance through the horoscope, called Astro*Radionics, as described in *Astrology and the Art of Healing* (1987). Mann applied the principle of logarithmic time scales to the historical process and mechanism of reincarnation in *The Divine Plot: Astrology and Reincarnation* (1986) and *The Elements of Reincarnation* (1995). Astrology is used as an organizing device for understanding the universe, from the subatomic level to the astronomical. *The Divine Life: Astrology and Reincarnation* (2002) combines Life Time Astrology and The Divine Plot.

The application of astrology to tarot led to the development and painting of *The Mandala Astrological Tarot* in 1987. Each card is related to a planet, sign, element, or decanate and is composed of a circular mandala with Eastern, medieval, and symbolic images.

Mann's *Sacred Architecture* (1992) describes the importance of astronomical/astrological, elemental, mythic, and symbolic organizational structures and images in architecture, from megalithic times to the Renaissance, and includes a critique of modern architecture. *Sacred Sexuality* (1995), written with Jane Lyle, shows sacred sexuality as a spiritual dynamic and path for integrating heaven and earth in relationships. A new book, *Reflections on the Sacred Garden* will apply these ideas to the garden as a symbol of the psyche in nature.

Mann has taught design at the International Centre for Creativity, Innovation, and Sustainability (ICIS) in Copenhagen and other universities such as Manchester Metropolitan University in the U.K. and the Denmark Design School in Copenhagen. He has lectured extensively at info-eco design events like the "Doors of Perception" in Amsterdam and "Making Sacred Places" at the University of Cincinnati. He is a graphic designer, web site designer, painter, and Feng Shui consultant.

**Sources:**

Mann, A. T. *Astrology and the Art of Healing*. London: Unwin Paperbacks, 1989.

———. *The Elements of Reincarnation*. Shaftesbury, Dorset, UK: Element, 1995.

———. *Life Time Astrology*. New York: Perennial Library, 1984.

———. *The Mandala Astrological Tarot*. San Francisco: Harper & Row, 1987.

———. *Millennium Prophecies*. Shaftesbury, Dorset, UK: Element, 1992.

———. *The Round Art of Astrology: The Astrology of Time and Space*. Limpsfield, UK: Paper Tiger, 1979.

———. *Sacred Architecture*. Shaftesbury, Dorset, UK: Element, 1993.

Mann, A. T., and Jane Lyle. *Sacred Sexuality*. Shaftesbury, Dorset, UK: Element, 1995.

## Manto

Manto, asteroid 870 (the 870th asteroid to be discovered, on May 12, 1917), is approximately 16 kilometers in diameter and has an orbital period of 3.5 years. It is named after a Greek prophetess. If prominent in a natal chart (e.g., conjunct the Sun or the ascendant), Manto may show a person able to intuit the future or someone who is always seeking information about the future. Manto's location by sign and house may indicate how and where one best intuits the future.

**Sources:**

Kowal, Charles T. *Asteroids: Their Nature and Utilization*. Chichester, West Sussex, UK: Ellis Horwood Limited, 1988.

Room, Adrian. *Dictionary of Astronomical Names*. London: Routledge, 1988.

Schwartz, Jacob. *Asteroid Name Encyclopedia*. St. Paul, MN: Llewellyn Publications, 1995.

## Mantras

Mantra refers to freeing oneself from the mind. The Sanskrit roots of the word *mantra* are *manas*, meaning "mind" and *trai*, meaning "to protect or free from." Therefore the purpose of mantra is to take the mind out of the relative and into spirit. Mantras are used in a variety of ways. Many forms of meditation use mantras as the vehicle to lead the mind from the conscious thinking level and arrive at the source of consciousness itself. Other mantras are used verbally to create an impulse or influence that subtly shifts energy in the physical world.

## Mars

Mars, named after the Roman god of war, is one of Earth's closest neighbors, the next planet from the Sun after the Earth. Because Mars is farther from the Sun than the Earth, it can appear anywhere on the ecliptic, rather than staying close to the Sun, as Mercury and Venus appear to stay when viewed from the Earth. When Mars is at its closest point to the Earth, it is a mere 35 million miles from away and appears as bright as Sirius—the brightest star in the sky. At its farthest point from Earth, the eccentric orbit of Mars may place it approximately 250 million miles away. Mars's orbital period is 686.98 days which is somewhat less than 2 terrestrial years.

In 1726, Jonathan Swift wrote in *Gulliver's Travels* of the discovery of two Martian moons. This occurred 150 years before Asaph Hall actually discovered the two moons that were named Deimos (terror) and Phobos (fear) after Mars's sons. This seems appropriate since Mars is often associated with impulsive or precipitous actions. In traditional astrology, Mars rules over the signs of Aries and Scorpio and is exalted (a place of special import) in the sign of Capricorn. In Hellenistic astrology, it is considered to be of a nocturnal sect, that is, it operates at its best in charts of night births.

In the Mesopotamian astral religion, Mars was associated with Nergal, the god of the underworld. Nergal was also the god of the noonday Sun and said to spread plagues, pestilence, forest fires, fevers, and wars. Robert Powell thinks the Babylonians connected the planet's eccentric movements along the ecliptic—often said to reach

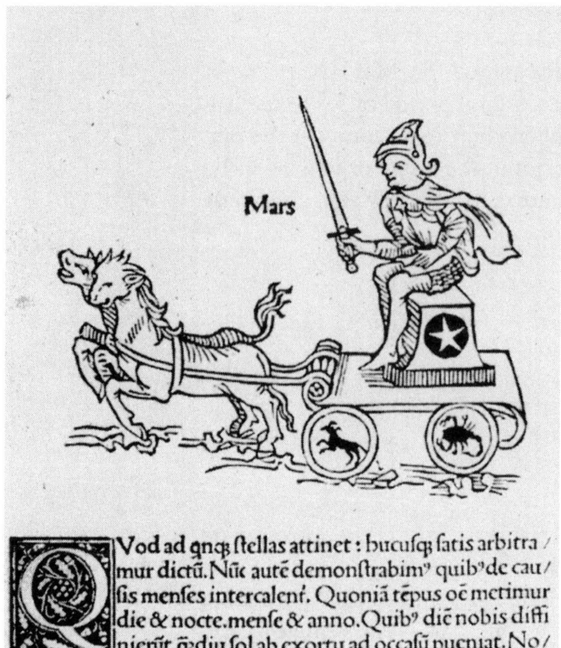


**An illustration of the Roman god Mars in his chariot from the 1494 edition of *Astrolabum Planum*. *Reproduced by permission of Fortean Picture Library.***

6° of south latitude—with the gods' negative associations. Mars was thus known as "he who is constantly wandering about," "the angry fire god," or "the god of war." According to Nick Campion, Mars's malefic qualities were thought to be heightened when it was bright (and therefore closest to the earth), diminished when it was faint, and when at its reddest could signify prosperity but also epidemics. The Babylonian legend of Irra speaks of the gods' attempt to overthrow Marduk, the patron god of the Babylonians. In it, Irra lures the god of good (Marduk) into the underworld and seizes the reigns of power on Earth. As the new ruler of humans, the god perverts their minds and gets them to war against each other so that he may attain his goal to destroy and annihilate Earth. When Marduk returns from the underworld, he finds his worshippers slain and his cities in ruins. In his book *History of the Planets*, Powell said:

> The poem ends with an exhortation to mankind to appease the evil god by allotting a place in their cult to his service, so that he may spare them from another catastrophe like the one described. The subject matter of the legend as well as its treatment implies that, in his quality as a planet, the patron god was unable to protect the community of his worshippers during his periods of absences from the nocturnal sky.

Thus, the Babylonians recognized the need to tame the dangerous, warlike qualities of life by including the god into the sphere of human affairs. This may be looked at as a psychological metaphor for the pacification of man's wrathful and destructive side through its integration into the psyche.

In another story, Nergal stormed into the land of the dead, deposed Ereshkigal, the queen of the underworld, and set himself up as ruler. A variation of the story has him having a passionate affair with her and ruling the underworld alongside her. This second version mirrors the story of Hades and Persephone, king and queen of the netherworld in Greek mythology. Both of these stories therefore connect the planet Mars with rulership over the underworld, a role that was given to Pluto (Hades) by modern astrologers since the planet bore the name of the Roman god of the underworld. Until modern times, when astrologers assigned the rulership of the sign Scorpio to the planet Pluto, Mars had ruled both Aries and Scorpio. Aries, the first sign of the Zodiac and marker of the spring equinox (the month of March is named after Mars), connects the planet to initiations, births, pioneering situations, initiative, impulsiveness, precipitous behaviors, uniqueness, aggression, and survival instincts. This rulership appears to connect better with the solar qualities of Mars and appropriately, the Sun is said to be exalted in Aries. Scorpio, appears to connect to the underworld qualities of Mars and its association with death, sexuality, diseases, adulteries, prostitution, losses, banishments, murders, and bloodshed.

The sexual impulse often connected to Mars also has its roots in his Greek heritage. In the classical Olympian Pantheon, Mars was known as Ares, the god of war. He was the son of Zeus and Hera who allegedly lived in Thracia, a region known for its fierce people. As a warrior god, Mars is often contrasted with his sister Athene, goddess of war and wisdom, who fought and vanquished him in a battle between the gods. Unlike Athene, Ares embodied the more unrefined, evil, and brutish aspects of warfare—prompting Zeus to call him "the most hateful of the gods." Only Aphrodite, the goddess of beauty, could tame the wild Ares through her ability to incite his passions. After one of their illicit affairs—as Aphrodite was married to his brother Hephaestus—Ares was forced by Zeus to endure public humiliation for his adultery. Through Ares's union with the goddess of love, a child named Harmonia (harmony) was produced. Ares also gave birth to two sons, Deimos and Phobos, who gave their names to Mars's two moons and were said to pull his war chariot.

In Hindu mythology Ares is called Mangala, a personification of the planet Mars. He is often depicted with a chariot being pulled by eight fire-red horses. According to some authors, Mangala is a form of the cruel side of Shiva. In one Hindu myth, the gods were being terrorized by a demon who could only be slain by a "seven-day-old son of Shiva." The gods thus created the illusion of a beautifully enticing woman who so moved Shiva sexually, that the great ascetic god ejaculated at the sight of her. His sperm fell into the ocean, which, nourished by the Pleiades (the seven sisters), gave birth to Karttikeya—the god of war who, born out of the necessity, killed the demon.

Although the original Roman Mars may have originated as a vegetation god, he became closely modeled on the Greek god of war. However, among the Romans who valued military prowess, Mars quickly rose to the ranks of most popular deity and patron for all soldiers. He is depicted by the Romans wearing a suit of armor, a plumed helmet, and carrying a shield and spear. In the Roman myths, aside from Mars's affairs with Venus, he is also linked with a vestal virgin Rhea Silvia, who is buried alive for violating the laws of her sisterhood. From this union are born Mars's twin sons, Romulus and Remus, who become the founders of Rome. It became the custom in Rome that generals, before heading out to combat (typically in March when campaigns were started), would invoke the god in his sanctuary.

The myths thus explain the planetary gods' associations with many of the significations listed in *The Anthology of Vettius Valens*:

> The star of Ares signifies violence, wars, rapine, screams, insolence, adulteries, taking away of belongings, losses, banishment, estrangement

> of parents, captivities, ruination of women, abortion, sexual intercourse, weddings, taking away of good things, lies, situations void of hope, violent thefts, piracy, plunderings, breaches of friends, anger, combat, reproaches, enemies, lawsuits. It introduces violent murders and cuts and bloodshed, attacks of fever, ulcerations, pustules, inflammations, imprisonment, tortures, manliness, perjury, wandering, excelling at villainy, those who gain their ends through fire or iron, handicraftsman, workers in hard materials. It makes leaders and military campaigns and generals, warriors, supremacy, the hunt, the chase, falls from heights or from quadrupeds, weak vision, apoplexy. Of the parts of the body, it is lord of the head, rump, genitals; of the inner parts, it is lord of the blood, spermatic ducts, bile, excretion of feces, the hind-parts, walking backward, falling on one's back; it also has that which is hard and severe. It is lord of the essence iron and order, clothes because of Aries, and wine and pulse. It is of the nocturnal sect, red with respect to color, pungent with respect to taste.

Robert Schmidt has extracted from all of the planetary significations a primary principle representing the basic nature of each of the planets. He says Mars represents the principle of separation and severance in a birth chart. Thus Mars's association with impulsiveness or pioneering tendencies are derived from the planet's desire to separate from others; the same may be said of competitive behaviors as one might find in sports, for example. The severing principle is also fundamental in Mars's use of sharp cutting objects and why he is perhaps associated with weaponry and armor, which cuts one off from one's enemy.

Modern astrology, with its emphasis on inner psychological dynamics, focuses more on Mars's correlation with the impulse to act and react. Psychological astrologers point to the planet's representation of one's need to assert, to initiate, to vitalize, to act, to do, to endeavor, to survive. Behaviors characterized as aggressive, self-assertive, enterprising, independent, combative, ambitious, etc., are derived from these basic inner drives. When other factors in the chart point in this direction, these behaviors often make use of Mars-ruled situations or objects such as: new births, enterprises or projects, competitions, accidents, permanent departures and exiles, divorce, mechanical work, fights, operations, sexual acts, etc.

Some of the most conclusive (although not without its detractors) statistical work involving the confirmation of astronomical correlations with human affairs have centered on the planet Mars. In the 1950s French statistician and psychologist Michel Gauquelin began his studies that attempted to demonstrate—under the rules laid down by science—that the planets could be significantly (statistically) correlated with certain professions. While the results showed a statistical correlation between eleven professions and five planets, the statistical effect shown by Mars in the charts of sports champions was by far the greatest. This has been coined the Gauquelin Mars effect in the astrological literature and has yet to be refuted—although many have tried. Gauquelin's work also showed that the positions of the planets just past culminating and just past rising had the greatest strength in producing the professional patterns demonstrated.

**Sources:**

Campion, Nick. *Cosmos: A Cultural History of Astrology*. London: London Books, 2001.

DeFouw, Hart, and Robert Svoboda. *Light on Life*. New York: Arkana Penguin Books, 1996.

Gauquelin, Michel. *Cosmic Influences on Human Behavior*. Santa Fe, NM: Aurora Press, 1994.

Guttman, Ariel, and Kenneth Johnson. *Mythic Astrology*. St. Paul, MN: Llewellyn Publications, 1998.

Holden, James Herschel. *A History of Horoscopic Astrology*. Tempe, AZ: American Federation of Astrologers, 1996.

Perry, Glenn. *Mapping the Landscape of the Soul*. San Rafael, CA: Association of Astrological Psychology, 2001.

Powell, Robert. *History of the Planets*. San Diego: ACS Publications, 1985.

Schmidt, Robert. *Original Source Texts and Auxiliary Materials for the Study of Hellenistic Astrology*. Cumberland, MD: Phaser Foundation, 2002.

Wilson, James. *A Complete Dictionary of Astrology*. London: W. Hughes, 1819. Reprint, New York, S. Weiser, 1969.

—Maria J. Mateus

## Mars Effect

Of the various attempts to demonstrate astrological influence by statistical means, the most successful have been the large-scale studies by Michel Gauquelin and Françoise Gauquelin. The Gauquelins uncovered correlations between vocation and the position of certain specific planets. The most significant of these was the so-called Mars effect, a correlation between athletic achievement and the position of the planet Mars—a planet traditionally associated with physical energy and therefore with athletic achievement—in certain influential sectors of the sky (e.g., close to the eastern horizon and near the zenith) at the time of birth.

**Sources:**

Curry, Patrick. "Research on the Mars Effect." *Zetetic Scholar* 9 (March 1982): 34–53.

Gauquelin, Michel, and Françoise Gauquelin. *Psychological Mongraphs. Series C: The Mars Temperament and Sports*. Vol. II. Paris: Laboratoire d'Etudes des Relations entre Rythmes Cosmiques et Psycholphysiologiques, 1973.

Melton, J. Gordon, Jerome Clark, and Aidan A. Kelly. *New Age Encyclopedia*. Detroit: Gale, 1990.

## Masculine Signs (Positive Signs)

The 12 signs of the zodiac are classified in several different ways, including a division into positive, masculine signs and negative, feminine signs (using negative and positive in the neutral sense of opposite poles rather than as value judgments). The masculine signs are all of the fire signs (Aries, Leo, and Sagittarius) and all of the air signs (Gemini, Libra, and Aquarius). The gender of the signs was originally determined by the Pythagorean notion that odd numbers were male and even numbers female. This caused the signs that came first (Aries), third (Gemini), fifth (Leo), etc., in the zodiac to be classified as masculine. By comparison with the feminine signs, the masculine signs tend to be more active and extroverted.

**Sources:**
Leo, Alan. *The Complete Dictionary of Astrology*. Rochester, VT: Destiny Books, 1989.
Tester, Jim. *A History of Western Astrology*. New York: Ballantine, 1987.

## Masha'allah

Masha'allah (c. 740–815), known to the Latin writers of the Middle Ages under a number of corruptions of that name, among which Messahalla is most common, was an Egyptian Jew who lived and worked in Basra. He practiced the astrological art in the context of Islamic society during the golden age of Arabic astrology. Because of their superior astronomical and astrological skills, he and the Persian Al-Naubakht were selected to elect the time for the founding of the new city of Baghdad in 762, which the caliph Al-Mansur intended as a kind of Muslim Rome—the centerpiece of Islamic high culture.

Masha'allah wrote the first treatise on the astrolabe in Arabic. It was later translated into Latin as *De Astrolabii Compositione et Utilitate* and formed the basis for Geoffrey Chaucer's *Treatise on the Astrolabe*. Masha'allah's astrological writings include *On Conjunctions*, *Religions and Peoples*, which deals with mundane astrology (i.e.,the astrology of world events). This treatise does not survive intact, but it has been preserved in works of the Christian astrologer Ibn Hibinta (c. 900–950). The influence of the Hellenistic/Phoenician astrologer Dorotheus (first century C.E.) on Masha'allah was significant.

Masha'allah also wrote *Liber Messahallae de revoltione liber annorum mundi*, a work on revolutions (the modern term is "Ingresses of the Sun into the cardinal signs"), and *De rebus eclipsium et de conjunctionibus planetarum in revolutionibus annorm mundi*, a work on eclipses. His work on nativities, with the Arabic title *Kitab al-Mawalid*, has been partially translated into English from a Latin translation of the Arabic by James H. Holden in his *Abu 'Ali al-Khayyat—The Judgment of Nativities*. His other works include *Book of Astrological Questions* and *On Conjunctions*, which treats the Jupiter-Saturn conjunctions and their role in mundane (political, religious, military, and meteorological) matters.

Apart from relying on Dorotheus, Masha'allah repeatedly quotes Hermes. His astrology is wholly traditional and not scientific in the modern sense. For instance, his work bears little similarity to that of the Persian Al-Biruni, whose organization of material is orderly, rational, and pleasing to a modern mind. Moreover, Al-Biruni's pedagogical approach is systematic. He gives a thorough outline of the mathematics necessary for practicing astronomy and astrology. Masha'allah, like most medieval astrological authors, regardless of their origin, does nothing more than discuss the practical facts of astrological procedure. Nor does he provide the reader with any theory of astrology as Ptolemy does in *Tetrabiblos*. It is likely that Masha'allah, like Al-Kindi (who died c. 870) and Abū Ma'shar (787–886), had direct contact with the Hermetic cult at Harran (later known as the Sabaeans). According to A. J. Festugière:

> That Mashalla had at his disposal a great number of Hermetic or pseudo-Hermetic works is ascertained by a short Greek extract con-

> tained in the Vatican.... Mashalla says, "I have determined that the ancient sages present ambiguities as to certain fundamental doctrines of astronomy and that these wisemen wrote a considerable number of books. From this it follows that the mind of him who reads them is quite confused. Therefore I have published this book in which I have brought forward the uncontested points and the best doctrines of these treatises, with the help of the books of Ptolemy and Hermes, those great sages of an infinite science, and was also assisted by books which my predecessors left as a heritage to their sons."
>
> Those who published these books are the following: Hermes published 24 books: of these 16 are about genethliology; five on consultations; two on the degrees; and one on the art of calculation. Then follows Plato, Dorotheus, Democritus, Aristotle, Antiochus (of Athens), (Vettius) Valens, Eratosthenes....
>
> Mashalla concludes, "Such are the books which find themselves in our hands today, and on the subject of which, as I have said, I have brought forward (certain ones), in order that you may know that I have taken great care in publishing this book, which you see here as I have made it in four treatises, the synthesis of the aforementioned books."

Masha'allah's importance to astrologers consists in his having edited, and therefore purged, and standardized the Hermetic astrological literature of his day. He also established practical techniques that influenced subsequent astrologers. The Al-Mudsakaret (or Memorabilia) of Abu Sa'id Schadsan, a student of Abū Ma'shar's who recorded his teachers answers and astrological deeds, told of Abū Ma'shar's confession to using a number of Masha'allah's methods.

Masha'allah's practices and theory of astrology greatly influenced Avraham Ibn Ezra (1092–1167), the famous Jewish biblical exegete and astrologer whose astrological works influenced Peter of Abano (1250–1316) and others. Ibn Ezra translated two of Masha'allah's astrological works, *Book of Astrological Questions* and *Eclipses*, from Arabic into Hebrew.

—Robert Zoller

**Sources:**

Al-Biruni. *The Book of Instruction in the Elements of the Art of Astrology*. Trans. by R. Ramsay Wright. London: Luzac & Co., 1934.

Chaucer, Geoffrey. "Geoffrey Chaucer's Treatise on the Astrolabe." In *The Works of Geoffrey Chaucer*. 2d ed. Boston: Houghton Mifflin, 1933.

Dorotheus of Sidon. *Dorothei Sidonii Carmen astrologicum: interpretationem Arabicam in linguam Anglicam versam una cum Dorothei fragmentis et Graecis et Latinis*. Edited by David Pingree. Leipzig: BSB Teubner, 1976.

Festugière, A. J. *L'Astrologie et La Science Occulte*. 3d ed. Paris: Librairie LeCoffre, 1950.

Ibn Ezra, Avraham. *Abrahe Avenaris judei astrologi peritissimi in re iudiciali opera: ab excellentisimo philosopho Petro de Abano post accuratem castigationem in latinem traducta*. Venice: 1507.

Kennedy, E. S., and David Pingree. *The Astrological History of Masha'allah*. Cambridge, MA: Harvard University Press, 1971.
Khayyāt, Yahyá ibn Ghālib. *The Judgments of Nativities*. Translated from the Latin version of John of Seville by James H. Holden. Tempe, AZ: American Federation of Astrologers, 1988.
Ptolemy. *Ptolemy: Tetrabiblos*. Translated by F. E. Robbins. Cambridge, MA: Harvard University Press, 1964.
———. *Ptolemy's Tetrabiblos*. Translated by J. M. Ashmand. London: Foulsham & Co., 1917.
Tester, S. J. *A History of Western Astrology* Woodbridge, Suffolk: Boydell Press, 1987.
Thorndike, Lynn. "Albumasar in Sadan." *Isis* (1954).

## Mathematicians (Mathematicals)

Prior to the advent of modern astrology tables and, especially, the computer revolution, extensive mathematical calculations characterized the practice of astrology. For this reason, the ancients often referred to astrologers as mathematicians or mathematicals.

## Mathesis

Mathesis, asteroid 454 (the 454th asteroid to be discovered, on March 28, 1900), is approximately 88 kilometers in diameter and has an orbital period of 4.3 years. Its name represents the desire for learning and the power of knowledge. In a natal chart, Mathesis's location by sign and house indicates where and how the desire for learning is most likely to manifest. When afflicted by inharmonious aspects, Mathesis may show aversion to learning or attraction to unhelpful subjects of learning. If prominent in a chart (e.g., conjunct the Sun or the ascendant), it may indicate an exceptionally studious person, or an individual for whom learning is a major life theme.

**Sources:**

Kowal, Charles T. *Asteroids: Their Nature and Utilization*. Chichester, West Sussex, UK: Ellis Horwood Limited, 1988.
Room, Adrian. *Dictionary of Astronomical Names*. London: Routledge, 1988.
Schwartz, Jacob. *Asteroid Name Encyclopedia*. St. Paul, MN: Llewellyn Publications, 1995.

## Matrix Astrological Software

Computers were made for astrology, although it took some astrologers a little time to recognize this. Matrix Software, the first company to create computer programs and make them available to the general public, was founded by astrologer Michael Erlewine in 1977 in Ann Arbor, Michigan.

Prior to Matrix, astrologers did their charts using complex log tables, interpolation techniques, and a pencil and paper or, at best, a four-function calculator. Some astrologers even tried to make the argument that the age-old ritual look-up tables had some special meaning in themselves and that computers had no soul. This retro attitude did not last long and astrologers quickly came to love their computers.

Erlewine began programming on handheld-programmable calculators in the early 1970s, in an attempt to research techniques for which there were no tables, such as Local Space and heliocentrics. Erlewine published his own heliocentric ephemeris in 1975 and some of his early programs were published by Hewlett-Packard.

After a centuries-old tradition of creating charts from a series of tables, not all astrologers welcomed the computer. When Erlewine published an astrological calendar in the late 1970s with a cover showing a computer with an astrological program on its screen, he received a letter from a nationally known astrologer berating him for associating computers with astrology. Astrologers were at that time quite computerphobic, even though the computer was to liberate them in such a significant way.

Matrix received the same sort of reaction when it pioneered Astro*Talk, its series of interpretive-report-writing software. These programs printed out complete astrological interpretation reports that astrologers could then make available to their clients. Erlewine recalls a hot debate on these new interpretive reports at an American Federation of Astrologers (AFA) convention forum discussion, where one astrologer burst into tears at the shame of allowing these computer-generated reports to enter the field.

In the beginning, well-known astrologers would buy report-writing software quietly, not wanting other astrologers to know they had and used them. But soon these reports generated enormous revenue for professional astrologers, enabling them to offer a $10–$25 report to clients who could not afford a full sit-down session. One client reported selling more than $300,000 worth of reports from a single $300 program.

Matrix Software relocated to Big Rapids, Michigan, in 1980, where Erlewine was joined by his astrologer/programming brother Stephen Erlewine.

Over the years, Matrix has held dozens of in-depth conferences and meetings, featuring some of the most distinguished astrologers of the time, including Dane Rudhyar, Michel Gauquelin, Charles Harvey, Charles Jayne, Robert Hand, Theodor Landschiedt, Noel Tyl, Roger Elliot, Geoffrey Dean, John Townley, and Robert Schmidt.

In addition to its initial calculations, hi-resolution chart wheels, and report-writing programs, Matrix Software has pioneered a number of astrological techniques, including the first programs that performed simple astrological database research and audio programs that actually spoke astrology, with interpretations available in both masculine and feminine voices. In addition, Erlewine created special programming that offered full-motion video astro-reports, with unique spoken text, recorded over the video for exact birth data. Matrix helped to produce the award-winning Time-Life Astrology CD-ROM. Michael Erlewine, an early pioneer in online and Internet content, created (at the request of Microsoft) the New-Age Forum on MSN, as well as its own TheNewAge.com site, and helped to launch Astro*Net on America Online.

In the late 1970s, Michael Erlewine and Charles Jayne teamed up to create ACT (Astrological Conferences on Techniques). Originally designated by Jayne as a meeting of the minds, by invitation only, Erlewine soon broadened this into a forum format, where invited experts discuss cutting-edge astrological topics in front of an audience. In these sessions, a moderator was also present and the audience was free to participate. ACT conferences were held a number of times, including stints at confer-

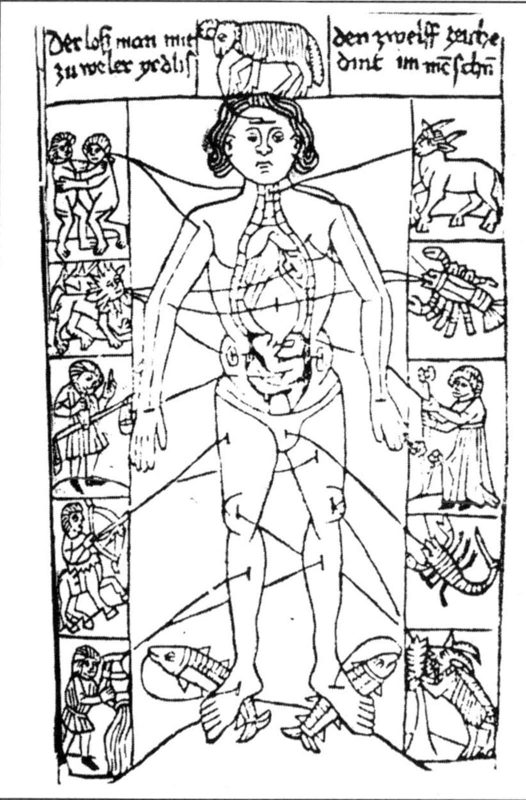

**An image of a zodiacal man representing medical astrology with the rulership of the signs over his body and organs from the late fifteenth century, Germany.** ***Reproduced by permission of Fortean Picture Library.***

ences of both the AFA and the United Astrology Conference (UAC), as well as at Matrix itself. The conferences were always very well attended and participation was very active, reaching incendiary levels at times.

—Michael Erlewine

## Matutine (Matutinal)

Stars that rise in the early morning before the Sun are referred to as matutine. The planets, particularly the Moon, Mercury, and Venus, can be matutinal.

## Mean Motion

Because celestial bodies move in elliptical orbits, their speed varies depending upon their location. Mean motion refers to their average speed.

## Medea

Medea, asteroid 212 (the 212th asteroid to be discovered, on February 6, 1880), is approximately 132 kilometers in diameter and has an orbital period of 5.5 years. Medea was named after the princess who helped Jason obtain the Golden Fleece. J. Lee Lehman associates this asteroid with planning strategy, as well as with bringing together seemingly opposed emotions. Jacob Schwartz gives Medea's astrological influence as "intense emotions and boding with extreme love or hate or both simultaneously."

**Sources:**

Kowal, Charles T. *Asteroids: Their Nature and Utilization*. Chichester, West Sussex, UK: Ellis Horwood Limited, 1988.

Lehman, J. Lee. *The Ultimate Asteroid Book*. West Chester, PA: Whitford Press, 1988.

Room, Adrian. *Dictionary of Astronomical Names*. London: Routledge, 1988.

Schwartz, Jacob. *Asteroid Name Encyclopedia*. St. Paul, MN: Llewellyn Publications, 1995.

## Medical Astrology

There are two completely different components to medical astrology: one that belongs in nativities, and one that is done through interrogations. Both parts have their genesis in Hellenistic astrology.

### Nativities

The early medical applications in nativities involved the following:

1. The general calculation of the length of life through the Apheta, a calculation that later become known as the hyleg.
2. The sign position of the Sun could indicate the nature of infirmities, or even death if sufficiently afflicted.
3. Sickness could also be generally interpreted through the delineation of the 6th house. (This technique did not become typical until the Arabic period. In the Hellenistic era, the 6th and the 12th houses were named after the Bad Spirit, so bad things could happen here, but this would not have been restricted specifically to illness.)
4. Bodily form and temperament could, to a certain extent, indicate particular tendencies toward certain health conditions, as well as ideas for living a more successfully healthy life. Because of the development of astrological methods of computing temperaments, this interfaced to astrology.
5. The calculation of planetary periods of the life, which could have health considerations as well as more general ones, such as riches, marriage, children, etc.

In nativities, the signs were assigned to parts of the body, as shown in the accompanying table.

Thus, for example, the Sun in Sagittarius could mean possible weakness of the hips or the region of the hips.

**Parts of the Body Assigned to the Signs of the Zodiac**

| Zodiac Sign | Body Part |
|---|---|
| Aries | Head, face |
| Taurus | Neck |
| Gemini | Shoulders, arms and hands |
| Cancer | Breasts and stomach |
| Leo | Heart and back |
| Virgo | Intestines |
| Libra | Kidneys, small of the back, genitals |
| Scorpio | Bladder, reproductive organs |
| Sagittarius | Hips, thighs |
| Capricorn | Bones, skin, knees, teeth |
| Aquarius | Shins, ankles |
| Pisces | Feet |

The planets were also assigned parts of the body, as the accompanying table shows. They generally overlapped with their traditional sign rulerships.

### Parts of the Body Assigned to the Traditional Planets

| Planet | Body Part |
|---|---|
| Saturn | Bones, knees, spleen, teeth |
| Jupiter | Arteries, blood, lungs, ribs, sides, veins, reproductive seed |
| Mars | Gall bladder, kidneys, reproductive organs, veins |
| Sun | Left eye (women), right eye (men), heart, sinews |
| Venus | Kidneys, small of the back, reproductive organs and seed, throat |
| Mercury | Brain, hands, tongue |
| Moon | Left eye (men), right eye (women), brain, bladder, stomach, bowels, womb |

These planetary rulerships would be utilized either to delineate the effects through house rulership, or to determine if a planet were particularly compromised in the chart.

In the Arabic and Latin Medieval periods, the sixth house emerged as a focal point for the delineation of illness. The ruler of the sixth house, and particularly its debilities, could show something about the frequency and severity of illness, specifically when that ruler was afflicted by primary direction.

The periods of life were not primarily or exclusively a medical technique. They were used to examine the predominant planetary influence of any given period, much like the Vedic system of *Dhasas* or *Bhuktis*.

As for death, the sign of the eighth house was understood to have something to do with the means or manner of death, although this was usually counted as the eighth from the part of fortune, not the ascendant. In the extant horoscopes from the Hellenistic period, references to death far outnumber references to accidents or disease.

## Interrogations

The other primary system for using medical astrology involves interrogations, which are better known as horary, event, and electional astrology.

The form of delineation is the same for the following two horary questions: What is the cause of my illness? What will be the course of the disease (as for the delineation of any event known as a decumbiture, which is a moment of health crisis)? The following are examples of such moments:

An acute event, such as a heart attack, stroke, breaking a bone, or being in a car accident

The time for checking into a hospital

The time that a diagnostic procedure is performed

The time that the patient is given a diagnosis

Waking up in the morning and finding that you are sick and cannot or should not get out of bed

> Having that feeling that this time, the flu has really got you, even though you don't experience full-blown symptoms, but only something like a tickling in your throat

In all event (decumbiture) charts, the first house is given to the patient. In horary questions about health conditions, the first house is for the person asking the question. When a person asks his or her own question, this is no problem. But when a question is asked about another person (or an animal, for example), the chart *may* need to be turned. The exception is that if a person asks on behalf of someone else, i.e., when the person asking is acting as the agent for the patient, then the patient is considered the first house, and the technical querent (person asking the question) is ignored. If this is not the case, then the chart is turned to give the patient to the house that most closely indicates the patient's relationship to the querent (e.g., to the fifth house if the querent is the parent of the patient).

Before proceeding with the delineation, one of the things the astrologer needs to know is whether the disease is physical, mental, or spiritual. The following table compares some of the astrological indicators of physical vs. mental or spiritual disease.

### Typical Configurations for Physical and Mental Diseases

**Physical/Mental/Spiritual**

Ascendant and Moon afflicted; their rulers not afflicted.
The Ascendant and the Moon not afflicted; but their rulers afflicted.

Mars or Saturn afflicting the Moon, but not the Ascendant.
Mars or Saturn afflicting the Ascendant, but not the Moon.

Jupiter in the first or sixth.
Ruler of the ninth or twelfth in the sixth (witchcraft).

Ruler of the first in the sixth.
Ruler of the sixth is Mercury (witchcraft).

Moon or Ruler of the Ascendant in the twelfth.
Ruler of the Moon or Ascendant in the twelfth.

The debate in classical medical astrology was about whether the Moon and the ascendant, or their rulers, represented the body or the mind. However, the presence of a twelfth house influence was an argument for witchcraft, which, in those days was believed to be a spiritual affliction. In modern parlance, "witchcraft" would be translated as involuntary coercion, a psychological affliction.

Before examining this classification, the astrological houses used in beginning a medical horary analysis need to be defined:

> The first house represents the health and vitality of the patient/querent.
> The fifth house shows the liver, and what virtue(s) are disrupted.
> The sixth house shows the disease.
> The seventh house shows the health care practitioner.
> The eighth house shows the possibility of the death of the patient.

The tenth house shows either the method of cure, or the diagnostic method or technique, depending on the nature of the question.

The normal diagnosis assumes a condition of physical disease. While there are literally thousands of aphorisms that apply to medical astrology, the basic rules are fairly simple. Among the most important rules are:

The Moon represents acute conditions (ones that are less than 90 days in duration); the Sun represents chronic conditions. All the rules that are given as applying to the Moon are subsequently interpreted according to the placement of the Sun after 90 days.

It is better to have as little relationship as possible between the 1st and eighth houses, and the Moon and the eighth house. When there are ties between these, it is an indication of death. Death is defined as meaning that the person would have died in the seventeenth century, prior to the advent of modern medical crisis procedures. In modern times, this would be called a life-threatening illness, although it can still mean death.

A relationship between the first and sixth houses means the patient is the cause of his or her own disease. This usually translates to a lifestyle choice or decision, such as eating the wrong foods or ignoring a serious food allergy, taking a drug that provokes a reaction, or having to cope with too much stress.

A relationship between the sixth and eighth houses means there is a danger of the patient having the disease unto death, meaning the patient is likely to still have the condition at death. This does not mean the patient dies as a result of this condition.

In both decumbiture and medical electional delineation, the basic procedure is to look for an improvement in the patient (first), quite probably as a result of the treatment protocol (tenth), without putting the patient in danger (eighth), and without allowing the disease to become chronic (sixth).

In electional astrology, it is still common to be asked to elect a time for surgery, or other medical procedures. Some basic considerations:

Know the disease or condition. In order to elect a proper time, one needs to understand the context of the condition in question. Appropriate questions include: What is the purpose of the procedure? Is it meant to diagnose, or to cure? What part of the body is being affected (right or left)? What are the odds of survival of the procedure? What days of the week/times of the day does the health care provider operate? How long is the procedure? Is anesthesia given? Is it general or local? How long is the typical recuperation period?

Consider the condition of the Moon. The Moon is unequivocally the paramount concern in all medical charts. In surgery, the cardinal law is never to cut those portions of the body that are ruled by the sign of the Moon.

Consider the qualities (cardinal, fixed, or mutable) of the angles.

Often, the best service the electional astrologer can perform is to scan a period of time, such as several weeks, looking for the best possible time within the range of times specified by the healthcare practitioner. This involves eliminating the worst times, leaving times that, while perhaps not ideal, are at least acceptable.

—J. Lee Lehman

**Sources:**

Burnett, Charles, Keiji Yamamota, and Michio Yano. *Abu Masar: The Abbreviation of the Introduction to Astrology*. Leiden, Netherlands: E. J. Brill, 1994.

Culpepper, Nicolas. *Astrological Judgment of Diseases from the Decumbiture of the Sick*. 1655.

Lehman, J. Lee. *The Martial Art of Horary Astrology*. West Chester, PA: Whitford Press, 2002.

Levy, Rachel. *The Beginning of Wisdom: An Astrological Treatise by Abraham ibn Ezra*. Baltimore: Johns Hopkins, 1939.

Lilly, William. *Christian Astrology*. London: T. Brudenell, 1647. Reprint, Philadelphia: David McKay Co., 1935.

Neugerbauer, Otto, and H. B. Van Hoesen. *Greek Horoscopes*. American Philosophical Society: Philadelphia, 1959.

Saunders, Richard. *The Astrological Judgment and Practice of Physick, Deduced from the Position of the Heavens at the Decumbiture of the Sick Person, &c*. London: Thomas Sawbridge, 1677.

## MEDIUM COELI

Medium coeli is another term for midheaven, which is the most elevated degree of the zodiac in an astrological chart. In many systems of house division, it is also the cusp (beginning) of the tenth House. Medium coeli (frequently abbreviated MC) means "middle of the sky" in Latin. Medium coeli is often used interchangeably with zenith, although this usage is incorrect.

## MEDUSA

Medusa, asteroid 149 (the 149th asteroid to be discovered, on September 21, 1875), is approximately 26 kilometers in diameter and has an orbital period of 3.2 years. Medusa was named after the famous Greek woman whose visage could turn men into stone. J. Lee Lehman associates this asteroid with "volcanic" temperaments, although she adds that in small doses, it may add spice to one's character. Jacob Schwartz gives the astrological significance of Medusa as "the triumph of patriarchal forces over the matriarchal Gorgon Amazons of Lake Triton, or the slaying by Perseus, representing a naval triumph over the Gorgon rulers of the three main Azores islands, thus women of deadly abilities."

**Sources:**

Kowal, Charles T. *Asteroids: Their Nature and Utilization*. Chichester, West Sussex, UK: Ellis Horwood Limited, 1988.

Lehman, J. Lee. *The Ultimate Asteroid Book*. West Chester, PA: Whitford Press, 1988.

Room, Adrian. *Dictionary of Astronomical Names*. London: Routledge, 1988.

Schwartz, Jacob. *Asteroid Name Encyclopedia*. St. Paul, MN: Llewellyn Publications, 1995.

## Melancholic

Melancholic is the traditional name for the personality temperament indicated by an excess of the element earth.

## Melete

Melete, asteroid 56 (the 56th asteroid to be discovered, on September 9, 1857), is approximately 144 kilometers in diameter and has an orbital period of 4.2 years. Its name is derived from the Greek word for care or anxiety. The location of Melete by sign and house indicates a source of anxiety. When prominent in a natal chart, Melete may indicate a native overburdened by cares.

**Sources:**

Kowal, Charles T. *Asteroids: Their Nature and Utilization*. Chichester, West Sussex, UK: Ellis Horwood Limited, 1988.
Room, Adrian. *Dictionary of Astronomical Names*. London: Routledge, 1988.
Schwartz, Jacob. *Asteroid Name Encyclopedia*. St. Paul, MN: Llewellyn Publications, 1995.

## Melothesic Man

The melothesic, or zodiacal, man is the image, often found in medieval astrology works, of a human being with the signs superimposed on the parts of the anatomy they are traditionally said to rule. These anatomical and zodiacal correspondences begin with Aries (associated with the head and face) and follow the order of the zodiac down the body to Pisces (associated with the feet). The sun sign—and, to a lesser extent, the Moon sign and the rising sign (ascendant)—people are born under usually indicates an area of the body with which they are likely to have trouble. Aries natives, for instance, tend to experience a disproportionate number of blows to the head or frequent headaches. Pisces people, on the other hand, tend to have accidents involving the feet (and easily contract such diseases as athlete's foot).

As outlined in Manly P. Hall's *Astrological Keywords*, the anatomical correspondences of the 12 signs of the zodiac are as follows:

Aries: Head and face with their bones and muscles; eyes, cerebrum; upper jaw

Taurus: Neck; cerebellum; upper cervical vertebrae; ears; throat; pharynx; larynx; eustachian tubes; uvula; tonsils; upper part of esophagus; palate; thyroid gland; vocal cords; lower jaw

Gemini: Arms; shoulders; muscles and bones of arms and shoulders; lungs, including trachea and bronchi; thymus gland; upper ribs; capillaries; hands

Cancer: Stomach; armpits; breasts; lacteals; chest cavity; solar plexus; pancreas; epigastric region; diaphragm and upper lobes of liver; thoracic duct; to some extent the womb

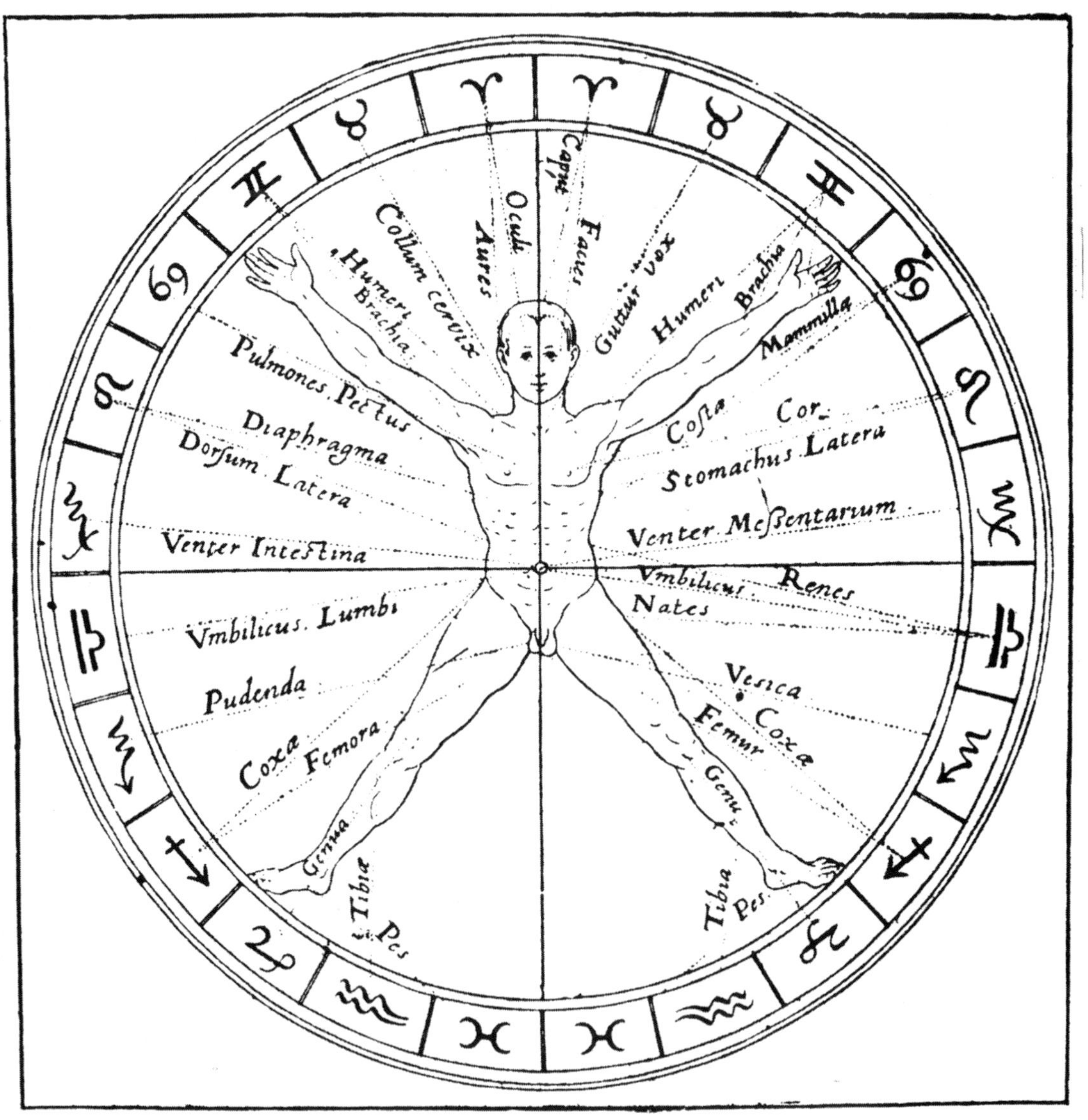


**An illustration depicting the signs in relation to the exterior and interior of the human body. *Reproduced by permission of Fortean Picture Library.***

Leo: Heart; spinal column with its marrow, especially dorsal region; and spinal cord

Virgo: Intestines; alimentary canal; abdominal cavity and its membranes; spleen; lower lobe of liver; duodenum

Libra: Kidneys; ovaries; adrenals; loins; appendix; ureters; lumbar vertebrae and contiguous areas; skin in general

Scorpio: Generative organs; nasal bone; bladder; gall; pubic bone; lower lumbar vertebrae; prostate gland; testicles; colon; rectum

Sagittarius: Hips; thighs; coccygeal vertebrae; sacral region; sciatic nerves
Capricorn: Knees; kneecaps; hair; outer epidermis; various joints of the body; bones in general

Aquarius: Lower leg, including the calves and ankles; teeth; blood circulation in general

Pisces: Feet; toes, especially their bones and muscles; matrix; generative organs; lungs

While there is general agreement on these correspondences, minor variations are often found from one astrologer to the next. The rectum, for example, which Hall associates with Scorpio, is more often associated with Virgo. *See also:* Medical Astrology.

## MERCURY

Mercury is the closest planet to the Sun with an orbit of 88 days. It is a small planet only 3,000 miles in diameter. Because of its proximity to the Sun, Mercury can never be more than 27° away from the Sun in an astrological chart. Therefore Mercury can only be observed shortly before sunrise or shortly after sunset, and even then it is difficult to see.

The name Mercury is from the Latin term *Mercurius*. In the older Greek he is known as Hermes. In Mesopotamia he is known as Nabu, the divine scribe of destiny. In the Vedic culture he is known as "Budha," meaning "intellect," as opposed to *Buddha*, meaning "enlightened one." In ancient Europe Mercury is associated with Odin, the king of the gods.

Of all the planets, Mercury has the most versatile and varied iconography. Mercury is youthful, clever, and often represented as a trickster. He is called both the messenger of the gods and the king of thieves. He is a scribe for the fates, the god of communication, and the god of magic. Because he moves so quickly in the sky and appears to jump to either side of the Sun, he is sometimes a morning star, and sometimes an evening star. This visible trait makes Mercury a chameleon, a planet that is easily influenced by other planets. Mercury is technically neutral in gender although some cultures portray him as a hermaphrodite, half man and half woman.

In Greek mythology Mercury is known for the amazing feats he performed immediately after his birth to Zeus and Maia. One version of the story describes how the newborn discovers a tortoise. He invites the tortoise to join him for a meal followed by music. The tortoise hesitates but soon falls for Mercury's wiles. The child god then kills the tortoise, invents fire to cook the meat, and creates a lyre (harp) out of the animal's carapace. Later the same day he steals fifty of Apollo's cows and sacrifices two of them. When the theft and the thief are discovered, Mercury offers the lyre to Apollo in retribution. It is Apollo's turn to be enchanted by the child, and he gives him the title king of thieves.

From the word Mercury come the words merchant, mercenary, and commerce. It is not only Mercury's charm that won over the offended Apollo, but also his exchange of items: the lyre for two cows. Mercury is an opportunist and loves to wheel and deal. He rules quick transactions and the marketplace. He is the messenger of the gods, delivering Hera, Aphrodite, and Athena to the judgment of Paris, which led to the Trojan War. This demonstrates the mercenary aspect of Mercury. The gods knew that nothing good would come out of the contest, but Mercury performed the deed for the right price.

When Zeus (Jupiter) sojourns on Earth, his favorite companion is Mercury because he is clever, knows how to have a good time, and is skillful. It was Zeus who gave Mercury the winged sandals, and the claduceus that became the symbol of healing and medicine. Mercury is associated with the healing arts, but in Greece he was also associated with death. He could travel between all the worlds, and was responsible for guiding the dead safely and swiftly to the underworld. He was known as the psychopompos who assisted in the transition between different states of reality. In this sense, Hermes functions as a hospice worker.

**A detail of Mercury shown holding two caduceus rods. From an engraving in Maiers' *Atalanta Fugiens*, 1618. *Reproduced by permission of Fortean Picture Library.***

There are similarities in Hinduism with Mercury's association with the god Visnu. In the Rig Veda, Visnu marks out the three worlds with three giant strides spanning the heavens, the earth, and the netherworld. Mercury, as a reincarnation of Visnu, quantifies or defines the different worlds. The Hindu Puranas, like the Greek myths, tell a wonderful story of the birth of Mercury. Jupiter was the guru (teacher) to the gods, and one of his students was the Moon. The beautiful Tara (Star) was married to Jupiter, but fell in love with the Moon. The tryst soon produced a child who was Mercury. Mercury was so delightful and charming that everyone loved him. Both Jupiter and the Moon claimed to be the father of the wonderful child. Mercury has two fathers, and rules the two mutable signs of Gemini and Virgo.

Mercury is also the son of Jupiter in Mesopotamian mythology. Here he is known as Nabû, the scribe of the gods. On the eighth day of the new year, all the gods come together to decide the fate for the coming year. It was Nabu who wrote down the destinies, and thus fixing the fates. Nabu was also a diplomat. One tablet reads, "Nabû who holds the god's Table of Destiny, and can reconcile conflicting things."

By the time of Hellenistic Egypt (300 B.C.E.) Mercury becomes associated with the god Thoth. This god was responsible for all areas of science including medicine, astronomy and astrology, architecture, and magic. Thoth played an important role in Egyptian afterlife. At the time of death a person's soul was magically weighed to determine if he or she had lived a good or bad life. It was Thoth's assignment to document the outcome.

In Alexandria Egypt, around the second century B.C.E., a new form of mysticism was developing from a mixture of Egyptian, Near Eastern, and Greek philosophy. The primary text is known as the "Corpus Hermeticum" and is attributed to Hermes Trismegistus, or the Great-Great-Great Hermes. These Hermetic texts were crucial in the development of astrology and resulted in the development of today's natal astrology. The texts describe the development of the soul through reincarnations that are given qualities based on the planets. Later these writings would evolve into the philosophy of alchemy.

In Europe the god associated with the planet Mercury is the Celtic Lug, known as Odin, or Wotan to the Germanic peoples. He is the master of fine speech, magic, poetry and music, as well as wealth. He is known as the king of the gods, but is also the god of the underworld. His Valkyries transport dead warriors to Valhalla where they celebrate their bravery and conquests. In various myths Odin is shown as an old man wandering the Earth, or exchanging an eye for the wisdom of the world.

Mercury rules all forms of thought and communication. It also represents childhood, education, language, the intellectual mind (as compared to the emotional mind represented by the Moon), movement, business, healing, humor, music and dance, and the derivatives of these key words. For example the key word "language" includes vocabulary, speech, grammar, writing, foreign languages, prose and poetry, oration, understanding, and debate. "Business" includes the concepts of money, exchange or barter, mathematics, marketing, and legal issues pertaining to business.

Mercury rules the zodiac signs of Gemini and Virgo. The mutable nature of these signs is indicative of Mercury's changeable nature. Gemini is an air sign and expresses the mental or intellectual quality of Mercury. Virgo is an earth sign and represents the manual dexterity of Mercury as well as the practical application of knowledge, primarily through service. Mercury is exalted at 15° of Virgo, and in debilitation or fall in the sign of Pisces.

A well-aspected or -placed Mercury will give the native a keen intellect, excellent business skills, and a fine sense of humor. The native can enjoy great diplomatic skills, and excel in logic and debate. They may love to travel and find pleasure in new experiences of all kinds. A weakly placed or aspected Mercury will give a wavering mind that is unable to make decisions. Speech may be affected resulting in harsh or rash language, or excessive gossip.

Mercury in a positive sense is adaptable, but in a negative sense is easily influenced. Close conjunctions and aspects of Mercury with other planets will change the expression of Mercury to a great degree. The one exception is the Sun. Because Mercury spends so much time near the Sun, he can "defend" his self-identity more readily.

Wherever Mercury falls in an astrological chart indicates the area of life where communication is crucial. The house position indicates the field of life where such communication will occur or needs to be developed, while the sign position gives insight into the nature or manner of the communication. Mercury placed in the fifth house indicates communication that is creative, and may involve or be directed at children or lovers. Mercury in the tenth house directs communication to achieve career goals and ambitions, and dealings with people in authority. Mercury placed in the sign of Taurus provides communication that is fixed, focused, and materially practical. Mercury placed in the sign of Gemini is versatile, interested in anything, quick and abstract in communication.

The transits of Mercury are quite fast and thus are not considered very strong. However, the houses and signs of transiting Mercury can indicate areas that are speeded up and activated. These areas or topics of life may experience more communication or thought, and in general require more attention.

There is much discussion about the effects of retrograde planets. The planet Mercury retrogrades on average three times per year, more than any other planet. In the natal chart a retrograde Mercury indicates an introspective mind where there can be more interior dialog than exterior. The individual may experience very deep thoughts, yet have difficulty communicating the depth of their conceptualizations. According to Vedic astrology retrograde planets are considered stronger because they are closer to the Sun.

In mundane astrology retrograde Mercury is often thought of as a negative transit period when there is confusion in communication and decisions will be challenged or undone. Popular culture believes that when Mercury is retrograde, car keys are mislaid, computers crash, and letters are lost. It may be more accurate to say that during these periods people can be distracted due to mental exertion, and this can lead to various mishaps.

**Sources:**

Campion, Nicholas, and Steve Eddy. *The New Astrology: The Art and Science of the Stars*. New Pomfret, VT: Trafalgar Square Publishing, 1999.

Hamillton, Edith. *Mythology: Timeless Tales of Gods and Heroes*. New York: Signet Classics, 1942.

Hinnells, John R., ed. *The Penguin Dictionary of Religions*. London: Penguin Books, 1984.

Hornblower, Simon, and Antony Spawforth, eds. *The Oxford Classical Dictionary*. Oxford, Eng.: Oxford University Press, 1996. Reprint, 1999.

Mani, Vettam. *Puranic Encyclopaedia*. Delhi, India: Motilal Banarsidass Publishers, 1964.

Miller, Susan. *Planets and Possibilities: Explore the Worlds Beyond Your Sun Sign*. New York: Warner Books, 2001.

Wolkstein, Diane, and Samuel Noah Kramer. *Inanna: Queen of Heaven and Earth, Her Stories and Hymns from Sumer*. New York: Harper and Row, 1983.

—Maire Masco

## MERIDIAN

A meridian (from the Latin word for "midday") is formed by taking a line of longitude and projecting it outward from Earth onto the celestial sphere. Another way of imagining a meridian is to picture the circle that would be formed by drawing a line connecting the north pole, the zenith (the point in the sky directly overhead), the south pole, and the nadir (the point directly opposite the zenith).

## Meridian, Bill

Bill Meridian obtained his master's degree in business administration in 1972 and began to study astrology in the same year. He first began applying computers to financial astrology in 1983, and eventually designed the AstroAnalyst. He contributed the efficiency test, first-trade charts, composite cycles, and many other useful tools to AIR Software's Market Trader program.

Meridian has authored *Planetary Stock Trading* and *Planetary Economic Forecasting*. His study of the effect of the lunar cycle on stocks was accepted as part of accreditation for his CMT designation, a finding confirmed by two studies at the University of Michigan. He currently is a fund manager. In the summer of 2002, Meridian's Cycles Research service was ranked number two in the United States for stock market timing in the previous year by *Timer Digest*.

## Merlin

Merlin, asteroid 2,598 (the 2,598th asteroid to be discovered, on September 7, 1980), is approximately 16 kilometers in diameter and has an orbital period of 4.6 years. It is named after Merlin the magician. If prominent in a natal chart, Merlin may signify a person for whom things seem to come together "magically" or, in rare instances, someone who is actually interested in magic. The sign and house position of Merlin in a natal chart indicates how and where this "magic" manifests.

**Sources:**

Kowal, Charles T. *Asteroids: Their Nature and Utilization*. Chichester, West Sussex, UK: Ellis Horwood Limited, 1988.

Room, Adrian. *Dictionary of Astronomical Names*. London: Routledge, 1988.

Schwartz, Jacob. *Asteroid Name Encyclopedia*. St. Paul, MN: Llewellyn Publications, 1995.

## Merriman, Raymond A.

Raymond Merriman is a contemporary astrologer best known for his work in the astrology of the stock market. His formal education and training includes a bachelor's degree in psychology (Michigan State University, 1969); postgraduate studies in clinical psychology (Michigan State and University of Michigan, 1969–71); professional (certified) life member of the American Federation of Astrologers (PLMAFA since 1972); commodities trading advisor (CTA, 1982); and series 3 and 7 exams for commodities, financial futures, securities and investments (1986, 1989).

Currently, Merriman is president of the Merriman Market Analyst, Inc., an investment advisory firm specializing in market timing products and services. He is the editor of the MMA *Cycles Report*, an advisory newsletter issued 17 times a year,

**An illustration of the great wizard Merlin with Vivien.** ***Reproduced by permission of Fortean Picture Library.***

and used by banks, financial institutions, investors, and traders throughout the world since 1982.

Merriman's contributions and awards in astrology are numerous and include: president of the International Society for Astrological Research (ISAR; 1995–2001); recipient of the 1995 UAC Regulus Award for "Enhancing Astrology's Image as a Profession"; recipient of Aquarius Workshops Award for "Service to Astrology" (1994); recipient of Professional Astrologers Inc. (PAI) Award for "Outstanding Activities on Behalf of Furthering Goals of Astrology—Lectures." He has served on the steering committees of UAC in 1989 and 1992, and was a board member of UAC from 1995 to 1998. Merriman is an international lecturer on both financial market cycles and various aspects of astrology as it applies to cycles in human activity. He is the author of several books, including:

*The Solar Return Book of Prediction* (1977)

*The Gold Book: Geocosmic Correlations to Gold Price Cycles* (1982)

*Evolutionary Astrology: The Journey of the Soul through States of Consciousness* (1992)

*The Sun, the Moon, and the Silver Market: Secrets of a Silver Trader* (1992)

*Merriman on Market Cycles: The Basics* (1994)

*Basic Principle of Geocosmic Studies for Financial Market Timing* (1995)

*The Ultimate Book on Stock Market Timing, Vol. 1: Cycles and Patterns in the Indexes* (1997)

*The Ultimate Book on Stock Market Timing, Vol. 2: Geocosmic Correlations to Investment Cycles* (1999)

*The Ultimate Book on Stock Market Timing, Vol. 3: Geocosmic Correlations to Trading Cycles* (2001)

In conjunction with PAS, Inc. Merriman has also developed a financial astrological software system: The FAR (Financial Astrological Research) for the Galactic Trader program, which enable traders to identify potential turning points in various stocks and/or financial futures markets. He is also the text writer for the "Solar Return Report Writer" by Matrix, Inc, and has written the *Annual Forecasts Book* for MMA since 1976.

## Mesoamerican Astrology

As in the ancient Near East, astrology and the birth of civilization were coincident in Mesoamerica, today's Mexico, and northern Central America. During the pre-Classic period, around 600 B.C.E., stone carvings made by Olmec artists are evidence that the key signs utilized in Mesoamerican astrology were already in use. During the Classic period, from about 300 to 900 C.E., the time of the rise and fall of Mayan civilization and the flourishing of Teotihucan in highland Mexico, astrology was a guide to religion, war, and daily life. During this period, ancient Mayan astrologers had considerable power and status, and they devised many sophisticated methods by which to compute planetary and calendric positions. During the post-Classic period, a time during which the Maya were in decline and the Toltecs, and later the Aztecs, dominated the Mexican highlands, the astrological tradition continued to flourish, though it did not develop beyond the high-water mark it had reached in the Classic period. The Spaniards arrived in the early sixteenth century and quickly brought an end to more than 2,000 years of native culture and science.

While the Spanish conquistadors and friars were very thorough burning books and destroying stone inscriptions, the existence of an astrological tradition unique in all the world was not obliterated. From the conquest to the present, an oral tradition among the Guatemalan Maya has kept alive some of the most basic principles of the system. Spanish friars, in their attempts to learn about indigenous practices so as to better eliminate them, described the ancient astrological system in their writings that are today available in college libraries. Archaeologists have translated numerous Mayan inscriptions and also the several surviving Mayan texts, two sources that reveal a deep awareness of planetary cycles and their meanings. Finally, archaeoastronomers have examined ancient ruins with precise instruments and have found numerous astronomical alignments that underscore the importance of celestial phenomena and cosmically inspired ritual to the peoples of ancient Mesoamerica. All of this supports the notion that the astrological tradition in Mesoamerica was a central pillar of native culture, and that it was shared by the several civilizations (Toltec, Maya, Aztec, etc.) that arose in the region. Today, we are able to piece together enough of it to appreciate its high level of sophistication.

Basically, Mesoamerican astrology gives blocks of time the same importance as Western astrology gives blocks of space. The Western zodiac, the aspects, and the houses are all spatial elements in a spatial astrological system. In the Mesoamerican system, blocks of time, with the day being the fundamental unit, serve the same purpose. There are 20 key signs that move in a consistent order, ruling blocks of time that are one day or 13 days in length. An analogy in Western astrology would be the 12 signs of the zodiac and the decans, a set of signs within the signs. In other words, like the zodiac, the 20 key signs of Mesoamerican astrology depict an archetypal evolutionary sequence that is applied to units of time, not to space. Celestial events and births were interpreted according to the symbolism of the block of time in which such events occurred.

The 20 signs of Mesoamerican astrology are grouped in five sets of four. Like the elements in Western astrology, the four directions are important considerations in any evaluation of a Mesoamerican sign. The signs (Aztec names) and their directional compliment are as follows:

### Directions and Signs (Aztec Names)

| East | North | West | South |
|---|---|---|---|
| Crocodile | Wind | House | Lizard |
| Serpent | Death | Deer | Rabbit |
| Water | Dog | Monkey | Grass |
| Reed | Ocelot | Eagle | Vulture |
| Motion | Knife | Rain | Flower |

In the accompanying table, each of the signs, called *tonally* by the Aztecs, rules a single day in the order, from left to right. After 20 days the cycle begins again. Along with these 20 signs run 13 numbers as follows: (1) Crocodile, (2) Wind, (3) House, (4) Lizard, (5) Serpent, etc., to (13) Reed. After that comes (1) Ocelot, (2) Eagle, (3) Vulture, etc. It turns out that there are 20 cycles of the 13 numbers in exactly the same number of days as 13 cycles of the 20 signs. This full cycle is one of 260 days and is called the 260-day astrological calendar; the *tzolkin* of the Maya and the *tonalpouhalli* of the Aztecs. Each sign rules a day and is called a day-sign. The signs that are attached to the number one rule the next 13 days and, since there are 20 of these in the 260-day period, they operate like signs themselves, though in a different order than the days. In other words, any given day in the cycle of 260 days is both a day-sign and a part of a 13-day sign. These are only two of the fundamental building blocks of Mesoamerican astrology, and they are a key to both the classification of individual personality and the analysis of celestial events affecting society at large.

Each of the 20 signs was said to be ruled by a specific deity. Correspondences with the Aztec pantheon are known, but the Mayan correspondences have been lost for the most part. Knowledge of the Aztec gods and goddesses is central to an understanding of the signs, just as an understanding of zodiac signs requires a knowledge of planetary rulers. The few books of symbols and glyphs (called codices) that survived the Spanish conquest reveal even other correspondences and hint at a complex body of symbolic knowledge utilized by priests and astrologers when working with the astrological system. From these books, eclipses and conjunctions could be predicted along with the signs (blocks of time) in which they would occur. In the codices, descriptions of the effects of the various combinations are stated alongside the relevant mathematical detail.

Mesoamerican astrology is a complex subject and was not limited to the astrology of individual personality and destiny. Astrologers practiced a kind of electional astrology, evident from the dates chosen for coronations, wars, and treaties—dates on which important planetary conjunctions or stations occurred. There was also a unique mundane astrology that utilized blocks of time of 7,200 days, a period very close to the length of the Jupiter/Saturn cycle, called a *katun*. The katun was regarded by the Maya as the fundamental unit of time for political and cultural matters. Katuns were grouped in bunches of 13 and 20, and 260 of them made up a creation epoch. Because the Maya were excellent mathematicians and left behind many dates in stone, we are fairly certain that the current epoch began August 11, 3114 B.C.E. and will end December 21, 2112 C.E. The 5,125-year span of 260 katuns (called the Long Count by archaeoastronomers or the Mayan calendar by the new age community) is almost exactly one-fifth of a precession cycle. In Mesoamerican astrology, the passage of the ages is not measured in twelfths of the precession cycle and indicated by signs (as in age of Pisces, Aquarius, etc.); it is divided in fifths that are in turn divided the same way as the 260-day astrological calendar, into 20 units of 13 and 13 units of 20. The Harmonic Convergence of 1987 brought to the world's attention the fact that we are soon to enter the last katun (1/260th) of the entire creation epoch. According to most researchers, this date was April 6, 1993. The Long Count is complete on December 21, 2012, and a new segment of the precession cycle then begins the following day.

Mesoamerican astrologers mathematically worked out the cycles of the visible planets and were able to compute their positions in advance from tables they created. Venus was perhaps the most studied of the planets and its 584-day synodic cycle was apparently both a symbol of the process of cultural evolution and a practical method for determining dangerous periods and cyclic agricultural conditions. The Mayan divided the synodic cycle of Venus into four sections and offered interpretations for each. The first portion of the cycle, the inferior conjunction, which occurs when Venus passes between the Earth and the Sun, was considered extremely dangerous. It was considered to be a time when human errors would lead to disgrace and the high would be struck down. Interestingly, trends like these continue to manifest at the time of the inferior conjunction. The interface between Venus and the Sun (five Venus synodic cycles = eight solar years) was also a component of the larger cycle of 104 years when the cycles of Venus, the Sun, and the 260-day astrological count meshed precisely.

The rehabilitation of Mesoamerican astrology is far from complete. In Mexico and Guatemala today, there is a number of native practitioners who utilize the system in what they believe to be a pure form. In many cases, they reject the work of the academic researchers and devise entirely new rulership schemes. There are also discrepancies over the exact correlation between the ancient pre-Colombian calendar and that of the Christian calendar. However, after much research and painstaking comparisons with colonial documents, oral traditions, and ancient inscriptions, the consensus seems to be that the Goodman-Martinez-Thompson correlation (the GMT), which places the beginning of the present creation epoch (the Long Count) at August 11, 3114 B.C.E., is the correct correlation. The tradition of Mesoamerican astrology is the world's most sophisticated time-based astrological system, and it may eventually be a major contributor to a world-class astrology of the future.

—Bruce C. Scofield

**Sources:**

Aveni, Anthony F. *Skywatchers of Ancient Mexico*. Austin: University of Texas Press, 1980.

*The Book of the Jaguar Priest: A Translation of the Book of Chilam Balam of Tizimin, with Commentary*. New York: Henry Schuman, 1951.

Burland, C. A. *The Gods of Mexico*. New York: G. P. Putnam's Sons, 1967.

Duran, Fray Diego. *The Book of the Gods, the Rites and the Ancient Calendar*. Translated and edited by F. Horcasitas and D. Heyden. Norman: University of Oklahoma Press, 1971.

Jenkins, John. *Maya Cosmogenesis 2012*. Santa Fe: Bear & Co., 1999.

Sahagún, Bernardino de. *Florentine Codex: General History of the Things of New Spain*. Books 4 and 5. Translated by C. E. Dibble and A. J. O. Anderson. Ogden: University of Utah Press, 1957.

Schele, Linda, and David Freidel. *A Forest of Kings: The Untold Story of the Ancient Maya*. New York: William Morrow and Co., 1990.

Schele, Linda, and Joy Parker. *Maya Cosmos: Three Thousand Years on the Shaman's Path*. New York: William Morrow and Co., 1993.

Scofield, Bruce. *Day-Signs: Native American Astrology from Ancient Mexico*. Amherst, MA: One Reed Publications, 1991.

Scofield, Bruce. "Sex and the Plumed Serpent: Venus Cycles in Mesoamerican Astrology." *The Mountain Astrologer*. Issue #94, December 2000/January 2001: pp. 3–10.

Scofield, Bruce. *Signs of Time: An Introduction to Mesoamerican Astrology*. Amherst, MA: One Reed Publications. 1994.

Scofield, Bruce, and Angela Cordova. *The Aztec Circle of Destiny*. 2nd ed. Amherst, MA: One Reed Publications, 2002.

Tedlock, Barbara. *Time and the Highland Maya*. Albuquerque: University of New Mexico Press, 1982.

Thompson, J. Eric S. *Maya Hieroglyphic Writing: An Introduction*. Norman: University of Oklahoma Press, 1960.

## Metals

At least 4,000 years ago, various metals began to be associated with the different planets, including the Sun and the Moon, which in classical astrology were also classified as planets. By the seventh century, the following set of associations had come to be generally agreed upon: the Sun and gold, the Moon and silver, Mercury and mercury, Venus and copper, Mars and iron, Jupiter and tin, and Saturn and lead.

By extension, the signs were also associated with the metals ruled by their ruling planet (e.g., Leo, ruled by the Sun, was associated with gold, the metal ruled by the Sun; Cancer, ruled by the Moon, was associated with silver, the Moon's metal, etc.). The analogical relationship between many metals and their rulers is fairly straightforward. It was natural, for instance, that the most important heavenly body, the "golden" Sun, should be associated with the most precious metal, gold; Saturn, the slowest of the planets known to antiquity, was naturally associated with the heaviest metal, lead; Mars, god of war, had a natural connection with iron, the metal of weapons; and so forth for the other planet—metal associations. Prior to the emergence of the modern world, these planet-metal connections were taken quite seriously as real links, not merely as symbolic analogies. Medieval alchemists, for example, paid attention to the positions of the planets when working with metals, avoiding the use of certain metals when the corresponding planets were involved in hard aspects.

When the "new" planets were discovered, astrologers experienced difficulty expanding the old system of rulerships. Certain associations seemed obvious, such as Uranus's rulership of uranium and Pluto's rulership of plutonium, but no astrologer has really been interested in exploring these new rulerships in any depth, largely because contemporary astrology is focused on individual human beings, with the result that almost all contemporary astrologers are primarily counselors, interested more in the psychological effects of the outer planets. If a significant number of astrologers were also metallurgists, pharmacists, and chemists, the question of the metals ruled by Uranus, Neptune, and Pluto would have been resolved long ago. The testing would be relatively easy: Assuming, as did the ancients, that there is a subtle yet tangible link between metals and planets, then some variation on the Kolisko experiments should determine precisely which metals are ruled by the planets beyond Saturn.

**Sources:**

Bach, Eleanor. *Astrology from A to Z: An Illustrated Source Book*. New York: Philosophical Library, 1990.

Davidson, Alison. *Metal Power: The Soul Life of the Planets*. Garberville, CA: Borderland Sciences Research Foundation, 1991.

Kollerstrom, Nicholas. "Planetary Influences on Metal Ion Activity." *Correlation* 3, no. 1 (1983): 38–50.

## Meteorological Astrology (Astrometeorology)

Correlations between celestial events and the weather have been a longstanding concern in astrology. The very name given to weather study—meteorology—harkens back to a time when the appearance of meteors was associated with changes in the weather. Even contemporary scientific meteorology, which does not generally look kindly on astrological methods, has noted a relationship between long-term weather patterns and sunspot activity.

Ptolemy, whose classic work on astrology exercised a powerful influence on astrologers for centuries, discussed the influence of the planets on weather as far back as the second century B.C.E. Even prior to Ptolemy, the ancient Mesopotamians viewed changes in the weather as being linked to the Moon. According to Hungarian Egyptologist Barna Balogh, the Mesopotamian rule of thumb (which Balogh originally came across in Egyptian sources) is that weather pulsates in two-week cycles. The prevailing weather can only change significantly on the fifth day after a new or full moon, and the weather on the fifth day gives an indication of what the weather will be like for the next two weeks. This rule does not predict the nature of the change, only that there will be a change.

Contemporary astrometeorologists pay attention to the daily positions of the planets, their positions at the times of the new and full moons, and planetary patterns at the beginning of each season. In Nancy Soller's summary of meteorological astrology, *Weather Watching with an Ephemeris*, she notes, for example, that the prominence of particular planets in a seasonal ingress chart (an astrological chart constructed for the exact moment of the Sun's entry into one of the cardinal signs) will indicate seasonal patterns:

> Mercury prominent on an ingress chart signifies strong winds and atypical cooler or colder weather. Venus prominent on an ingress chart indicates a season with more than the average precipitation. Mars prominent indicates weather that will be hotter and drier than normal. Jupiter brings good weather. Jupiter prominent in a Capricorn ingress chart indicates a mild winter. A prominent Saturn indicates cold, wet weather. A prominent Uranus signifies a dry, windy drought, unless Uranus happens to be in a water sign. Neptune prominent signifies precipitation and mild temperatures, and Pluto operates in much the same way as Mars, bringing higher temperatures and little precipitation.

A good ephemeris (table of planetary positions), such as Neil F. Michelsen's *American Ephemeris for the 20th Century*, contains the exact times of ingresses as well as the exact times of the full and new moons.

**Sources:**

Brau, Jean-Louis, Helen Weaver, and Allan Edmans. *Larousse Encyclopedia of Astrology*. New York: New American Library, 1980.

Michelsen, Neil F. *The American Ephemeris for the 20th Century*. San Diego: ACS Publications, 1980.

Ostrander, Sheila, and Lynn Schroeder. *Astrological Birth Control*. Englewood Cliffs, NJ: Prentice-Hall, 1972.

Soller, Nancy. "Weather Watching with an Ephemeris." In *The Astrology of the Macrocosm*. Edited by Joan McEvers. St. Paul, MN: Llewellyn Publications, 1990.

## Metonic Cycle

The ancient Greek Meton discovered that the Moon has a cycle of 19 years, after which a new moon occurs on the same day of the year.

## Michelsen, Neil Franklin

Neil Franklin Michelsen, born May 11, 1931, in Chicago, was the founder and inspiration behind Astro Computing Services (ACS) and ACS Publications. He was a well-known figure in the astrological community for his contributions to contemporary astrology. He was a generous person who gave money, computer time, personal time, technical expertise, and encouragement to many different astrologers, holistic healers, and practitioners of occult arts.

Michelsen graduated magna cum laude from the University of Miami and for 17 years was a systems engineer for IBM. He founded Astro Computing Services in 1973. ACS grew from a one-man business run out of Michelsen's home in Pelham, New York, to the current San Diego corporation staffed by almost two dozen people. A creative individual with solid programming skills, Michelsen became one of the greatest of contemporary astrological technicians. His work in the form of continually refined ephemeredes and books of tables was the standard of accuracy by which other astrological calculations were judged. He has written or contributed to more than 20 reference books, including *The American Ephemeris* (1901–1930, then every decade up to the year 2000); *The American Sidereal Ephemeris, 1976–2000; The American Heliocentric Ephemeris, 1901–2000; Uranian Transneptune Ephemeris, 1850–2050; The American Book of Tables; The Koch Book of Tables; The American Ephemeris for the 20th Century 1900 to 2000, Midnight; The American Ephemeris for the 20th Century 1900 to 2000, Noon; The American Ephemeris for the 21st Century 2001 to 2050, Midnight; The American Midpoint Ephemeris, 1986–1990; The Comet Halley Ephemeris 1901–1996; Tables of Planetary Phenomena* (July 1990); and, with Maria Kay Simms, *Search for the Christmas Star*.

Michelsen was chairman of the National Council for Geocosmic Research (NCGR), and through the NCGR he contributed to projects beneficial to the astrological community. After his death on May 15, 1990, the NCGR set up the Neil F. Michelsen Memorial Fund to continue such projects.

## Midheaven

The midheaven is the most elevated degree of the zodiac in an astrological chart. In most systems of house division, it is also the cusp (beginning) of the tenth house. Midheaven is often used interchangeably with zenith, but this usage is inaccurate.

## MIDPOINT

A midpoint, as the name implies, is a point halfway between two other points. For example, the midpoint between a planet located at 1° Cancer and a planet located at 29° Cancer would be 15° Cancer. Certain schools of contemporary astrology regard midpoints as significant, sensitive points in an astrological chart.

A midpoint between two planets is said to indicate where their combined energies is strongest, and transits to midpoints are particularly important. A third planet located near or in close aspect with a midpoint is particularly significant. In hard aspects such as a square, for instance, a third planet located near the midpoint provides the key to resolving the conflict indicated by the square.

Employed by early schools of astrology, midpoints fell into disuse until revived by Alfred Witte, the founder of Uranian astrology. Witte in turn influenced Reinhold Ebertin, the founder of cosmobiology, who further developed the use of midpoints.

**Sources:**

Brau, Jean-Louis, Helen Weaver, and Allan Edmands. *Larousse Encyclopedia of Astrology*. New York: New American Library, 1980.

Hand, Robert. *Horoscope Symbols*. Rockport, MA: Para Research, 1981.

## MINERVA

Minerva, asteroid 93 (the 93rd asteroid to be discovered, on August 24, 1867), is approximately 168 kilometers in diameter and has an orbital period of 4.6 years. Minerva was the Roman goddess of wisdom, the Roman equivalent of the Greek Athena. Minerva was also the patroness of arts and crafts. According to Martha Lang-Wescott, Minerva represents the principle of analyzing demands in order to alter behavior to please others and get their approval. This asteroid's key word is "calculations." According to J. Lee Lehman, the asteroids Pallas, Athene, and Minerva all represent the application of skill. In contrast with one another, however, "Pallas people are concerned with being right, Athene people are more interested in being competent, and Minerva people with being accomplished." Jacob Schwartz gives this asteroid's astrological significance as "broad perceptual skills and public relations strategies, ideas for pleasing others."

**Sources:**

Lang-Wescott, Martha. *Asteroids-Mechanics: Ephemerides II*. Conway, MA: Treehouse Mountain, 1990.

———. *Mechanics of the Future: Asteroids*. Rev. ed. Conway, MA: Treehouse Mountain, 1991.

Lehman, J. Lee. *The Ultimate Asteroid Book*. West Chester, PA: Whitford, 1988.

Schwartz, Jacob. *Asteroid Name Encyclopedia*. St. Paul, MN: Llewellyn Publications, 1995.

## MITHRAISM AND ASTROLOGY

Mithraism was an enigmatic Hellenistic mystery religion that drew heavily on astrology and astrological symbolism. It was Christianity's last great competitor during the

**A detail of a Mithraic zodiac from an engraving, c. 1870. *Reproduced by permission of Fortean Picture Library.***

period immediately prior to the official conversion of the Roman Empire to the religion of Jesus. As such, Mithraism left its mark on Christianity. For example, the Romans celebrated Mithras's birthday (Mithras was the central deity of Mithraism) on December 25, the time of year when the daylight hours—which had gradually been shortening over the course of the previous six months—begin to lengthen, thus symbolically representing the victory of the forces of light over the forces of darkness. Christ's birthday began to be celebrated on the same date so that Christianity could compete more effectively with Mithraism.

Although Mithraism left a rich heritage of temple art and architecture for archaeologists to uncover, the actual doctrines of Mithraism were not preserved. In the late nineteenth century, the Belgian scholar Franz Cumont put forward a convincing hypothesis about these doctrines that held sway in Mithraic studies for the next 70 years. Beginning with the similarity in name between Mithras and the Persian god Mithra, Cumont developed an explanation that portrayed Mithraism as a form of Zoroastrianism that had branched off and transformed into a mystery religion. If this initial premise is granted, it is then possible to find other Persian myths, often quite obscure, that seem to apply to most of the sculpted forms found in Mithraic sanctuaries (Mithraeum). There were certain problems, however, with Cumont's interpretation—problems that came to a head in 1971 at the First International Conference of Mithraic Studies. At this meeting, devastating critiques were leveled against Cumont's Iranian (Persian) hypothesis. These critiques opened the door for entirely new interpretive approaches.

Freed from the "conventional wisdom" about the meaning of Mithraic statuary, scholars were able to look at Mithras imagery with fresh eyes, and one of the first things they noted was that many of the figures surrounding the tauroctony (the bull-slaying scene that is the central motif in every Mithraeum) seemed to compose a star map of certain constellations. This impression was reinforced by the zodiacal wheels found in many sanctuaries. With these clues as a starting point, contemporary scholars gradually pieced together a picture of a mystery cult that arose out of the religious speculations of a group of astrologically inclined Stoic philosophers in Tarsus (the birthplace of Saint Paul).

David Ulansey, in his *Origins of the Mithraic Mysteries*, has convincingly proposed that this group of philosophers responded to the discovery of the precession of equinoxes by postulating that a previously unknown god was responsible for the gradual movement of Earth's axis (the stars and planets, which were now relegated to positions of lesser importance, had earlier been identified by the Stoics as gods who controlled human fate). This new god, who was clearly more powerful than all the other gods in the heavens because he controlled the very axis of the universe, was linked by these Stoics with the chief local deity, Sandan, who had earlier been identified with the Greek hero Perseus, as well as with the Persian Mithra (hence the name Mithras).

The link between Sandan/Mithras and Perseus is an important key to unlocking the meaning of the tauroctony. In his constellation, Perseus is pictured with an upheld knife and is located immediately above the constellation Taurus. It is thus not difficult to imagine the scene in the star map as leading to the scene in the tauroctony, in which the knife is plunged into the bull. What, however, is the significance of this sacrifice?

Several thousand years ago—during the period when Mithraism emerged—the Sun was positioned at the beginning of the constellation Aries during the spring equinox. Because of the precession of equinoxes, the spring equinox moves slowly backward through the constellations of the zodiac, so that approximately every 2,000 years the equinox begins taking place in an earlier constellation. It has been occurring in Pisces for the past 2,000 years and will begin to occur in the constellation Aquarius in the near future (which is the background for current speculations about the so-called Age of Aquarius). This also means that the spring equinox occurred in the sign Taurus several thousand years prior to the Hellenistic period. Ulansey takes this information and postulates that the tauroctony represented Mithras's destruction of the earlier Age of Taurus.

Ulansey's theory is far more intricate, and his argument far more nuanced, than can be developed here. The theory also leaves some questions unanswered: How did a religion originally devised by a group of intellectuals in Tarsus become one of the most popular religions of the Roman Empire? What did the rituals and other concrete practices of Mithraism actually involve? How did Mithraism change over time? Even though these questions are not addressed, and although many particulars of Ulansey's analysis are open to criticism, the starting place of his discussion—that much of Mithraism's core symbolism is astrological and related to the precession of equinoxes—can be regarded as firmly established.

**Sources:**

Cumont, Franz. *The Mysteries of Mithra*. Chicago: Open Court, 1903. Reprint, New York: Dover, 1956.

Ulansey, David. *The Origins of the Mithraic Mysteries: Cosmology and Salvation in the Ancient World*. New York: Oxford, 1989.

## Mixed Application

Mixed application (applying) is when two planets are moving into an aspect with each other while one is in retrograde motion.

## Mnemosyne

Mnemosyne, asteroid 57 (the 57th asteroid to be discovered, on September 22, 1860), is approximately 116 kilometers in diameter and has an orbital period of 5.5 years. It is named after the Greek goddess of memory, who was the mother of the Muses. The location of Mnemosyne by sign and house indicates something about how one remembers. When involved in inharmonious aspects, this celestial body may indicate a poor memory or unpleasant memories.

**Sources:**

Kowal, Charles T. *Asteroids: Their Nature and Utilization*. Chichester, West Sussex, UK: Ellis Horwood Limited, 1988.
Room, Adrian. *Dictionary of Astronomical Names*. London: Routledge, 1988.
Schwartz, Jacob. *Asteroid Name Encyclopedia*. St. Paul, MN: Llewellyn Publications, 1995.

## Modern Planets

The expression "modern planets" refers to the planets beyond Saturn that were not discovered until the development of modern telescopes, namely Uranus, Neptune, and Pluto. Although technically not "planets," some contemporary astrologers classify asteroids and Chiron as modern planets because they were not discovered until the development of astronomical telescopes.

## Modestia

Modestia, asteroid 370 (the 370th asteroid to be discovered, on July 14, 1893), is approximately 44 kilometers in diameter and has an orbital period of 3.5 years. Its name is a personified form of the Latin word for modesty. In a natal chart, Modestia's location by sign and house indicates where one is most likely to be modest or experience modesty. When afflicted by inharmonious aspects, Modestia may show immodesty or false modesty. If prominent in a chart (e.g., conjunct the Sun or the ascendant), it may show an exceptionally modest person, or someone for whom the seeking of modesty and humility is a dominant life theme.

**Sources:**

Kowal, Charles T. *Asteroids: Their Nature and Utilization*. Chichester, West Sussex, UK: Ellis Horwood Limited, 1988.
Room, Adrian. *Dictionary of Astronomical Names*. London: Routledge, 1988.
Schwartz, Jacob. *Asteroid Name Encyclopedia*. St. Paul, MN: Llewellyn Publications, 1995.

## *Modus Equalis*

*Modus equalis* is the older term for what is now called the equal house system.

## Moira

Moira, asteroid 638 (the 638th asteroid to be discovered, on May 5, 1907), is approximately 41 kilometers in diameter and has an orbital period of 4.5 years. Its name is derived from the Greek word for the Fates. In an astrological chart, Moira's location by sign and house indicates an area of life that is governed by fate or karma. When afflicted by inharmonious aspects, Moira may show negative karma. When prominent in a chart, it shows an individual whose whole life is fated.

**Sources:**

Kowal, Charles T. *Asteroids: Their Nature and Utilization*. Chichester, West Sussex, UK: Ellis Horwood Limited, 1988.

Room, Adrian. *Dictionary of Astronomical Names*. London: Routledge, 1988.

Schwartz, Jacob. *Asteroid Name Encyclopedia*. St. Paul, MN: Llewellyn Publications, 1995.

## Monkey

The monkey is one of the 12 animals of the Chinese zodiac. It refers to one of the 12 earthly branches that are used in Chinese astrology, together with the 10 heavenly stems. Such a branch designates one day every 12 days: the days are named according to a sexagesimal (60) cycle, made of 10 series of 12 branches.

The monkey is often a hilarious live wire even if he is sometimes subject to depression. Energetic (frenetic even), opportunistic, but unpredictable, crafty, inventive and clever, he is not adaptable to routine work. He loves to make an exhibition of himself, and finds losing or being contradicted hard to take.

—Michele Delemme

## The Moon

The Moon is the Earth's only natural satellite. It is technically not a planet; however astrology traditionally groups the Moon, along with the Sun, which is our star, with the planets. The Moon has a diameter of 2,160 miles, and an average distance from the Earth of 328,000 miles. The sidereal month, or the time it takes the Moon to orbit the Earth, is 27 days, 7 hours, and 43 minutes (27.3217 days). The synodic month is the time from New Moon to New Moon and takes 29 days, 12 hours, and 44 minutes (29.5306 days). The synodic month is also known as the lunation cycle.

The Moon is intrinsically linked to the concept of time. The lunation cycle, or month, is one of three natural time cycles observed on Earth. (The other two are the year based on seasons, and the day based on the day/night cycle.) The archeological record shows that humans were documenting the lunation cycle as early as the Paleolithic era (35,000 B.C.E.). There is evidence from around the world that the first calendars were lunar-based. Many contemporary religious calendars are still lunar-based including the Jewish, Islamic, Hindu, and Buddhist calendars. The word "calendar" comes from the Latin *kalendae* and is connected to the Moon. In ancient Rome the *kalendae* was the first day of the month, or day of the New Moon. It was important to the Romans because interest payments were due on the day of the New Moon.

The word "moon" comes from the Greek *mentron*, meaning "to measure." The root is *me*, which means "to mark an appointed time." Expanded, this results in the words "meter," "menses" (the female menstrual cycle), "measure," and "month." The

Latin word for moon is *luna*, from the word *leuk*, meaning "bright" or "shining." The Moon is visible because it reflects light from the Sun. A bright full Moon can cast shadows. Modern words that come from *luna* include lucid, luminous, and lunatic.

The Sun and the Moon are paired in most mythologies throughout the ages. Pairings have included husband and wife, father and mother, and brother and sister. The European culture that developed from Hellenistic Greece believed the Moon was a female deity. However the early European, Oriental, and indigenous American cultures often choose to portray the Moon as male in gender. In all cultures the Moon is linked with fertility and conception. The female menstrual cycle is clearly linked to moon cycles and the period of the month when a woman is able to conceive. Farmers often sow their crops during specific times of the Moon's cycle in order to reap the most beneficial harvest. Just as crops require the Sun to grow, it was the Moon that ensured that the seed would germinate. While the Sun rules the day, the Moon rules the night.

In Sumerian mythology, the Moon is the son of Enlil (Saturn) and Ninlil. Ninlil's mother had warned her daughter not to bathe in the irrigation canal. Ninlil did not obey her mother and washed herself in the water. Enlil, the god of air, saw the beautiful and naked girl, and quickly took advantage of her. His punishment for the rape was exile to the underworld. He left the city, but Ninlil followed. Enlil knew that the girl carried his son, the Moon god Sin. Enlil wanted a bright child (Full Moon) and not a dark child born in the underworld (New Moon). In one version of the myth, he impregnates Ninlil several more times to effect the order and timing of the birth, or appearance, of the Moon. Sin is the bright Moon and his brothers are the dark and waning Moon. In Sumerian mythology, the Moon is best known as the father of Innana, the planet Venus.

In ancient Greece the Moon was associated with three different female deities: Selene, Artemis, and Hecate, known collectively as the Three-faced Goddess. Selene is the goddess in the sky, Artemis is the earthly form, while Hecate is the goddess of the underworld. These manifestations represent the phases of the Moon: Selene is the waxing Moon growing in brightness, Artemis is the full Moon illuminating the Earth, and Hecate is the waning or dark Moon, lessening in light until it is not visible. This is symbolic of the phases of human life: childhood, adulthood, and old age.

Selene is one of the ancient Greek gods, born of the primordial gods called the Titans. She is associated with sleep. Artemis is also ancient, and there is evidence that she was worshipped in Minoan Greece, although she must date from far earlier. She is called a virgin goddess, but this is misleading. She is properly called the unmarried maiden and governed female rites of passage such as reproductive maturation, marriage, childbirth, etc. She is called the Goddess of the Hunt and Mistress of the Animals. Her animal is the deer. If Selene is the expression of the Moon in the heavens, and Artemis is the expression in the physical world, then Hecate is the expression of the Moon in the underworld. She is a chthonic goddess belonging to the graveyard. Hecate is the goddess of the dark Moon and rules witchcraft, potions, crossroads, and death. She is Persephone's attendant during her yearly stay in Hades known as the season of winter. In all her forms, the Greek Moon goddesses are connected with fer-

**Personification of the Moon as ruler of Cancer the crab is shown in this detail from Doge's Palace Venice. *Reproduced by permission of Fortean Picture Library.***

tility, because they protect women and children, and the end of life. A quick, painless death was often attributed to the blessing of the Three-faced Goddess.

In Indian or Vedic mythology the Moon is known as Chandra or Soma. It is interesting that the Vedic sages considered the Moon male in gender, but represented feminine energy. The myth explaining why the Moon waxes and wanes may provide a clue. Chandra was married to Daksa's 27 daughters. Each night he would spend with a different wife, equaling a sidereal month. But Chandra had a favorite wife known as Rohini and he stayed longer with her than with the others. The other wives complained to their father Daksa who cursed Chandra for not treating his daughters more fairly. Chandra immediately fell ill and started to waste away. When the wives saw their husband dying they pleaded with the father to undo the curse. It was not possible to completely reverse the curse, but Daksa was able to lessen the effect. That is why the Moon waxes and wanes.

The Moon rules the zodiac sign of Cancer the Crab. The tides of the oceans are controlled by the Moon, and the tidal zone is the natural environment of crabs and other crustaceans. This is one reason why the Moon represents and governs water in astrology. Water, like the Moon is responsive and adaptable. Just as water assumes the shape of any container that it is put in, the Moon responds to changes in the environment. The Moon is exalted in Taurus, and in debilitation or fall in the sign of Scorpio.

The Moon represents emotions and feelings in the modern natal chart. Daily habits are indicated here, as well as memories of the past. The sign and house placement of the Moon indicate the emotional expression and response of the individual. Planetary aspects to the Moon indicate the areas of life where emotional strengths and weaknesses will develop. Contemporary astrology tends to think of the Moon as representing the unconscious mind as compared to the Sun, which represents the conscious mind.

The Moon is an indicator of early childhood environment, when the first emotional patterns are laid down. In this way, the Moon represents the mother who provides nourishment and guidance. It is the mother who teaches how to respond to external stimuli, and exist in the world. Therefore the Moon is the greatest symbol in the natal chart for how the individual perceives and responds to the external world.

Particular attention is paid to the lunation cycle, which provides insight into the psychological development of the individual. Secondary progressions of the Moon, or advancing the natal chart one day for each year of life, can indicate the long term cycles of an individual's life.

The basic nature of the Moon in Hellenistic astrology is collection and inclusion. The essence of the Moon is *pronoia,* a type of fate suggesting "forethought" and *providentia* meaning "foresight." The Greeks, who loved analytical thought, considered the concept of "foresight" a virtue. There was also an aspect of protection, as *Providentia deorum* was the protectress of the imperial family and the empire. These qualities of forethought, foresight, and protection or continuation of family or empire, are all essences of the Moon in ancient Greek astrology.

In Hellenistic astrology the Moon is the significator for the mother, conception, money, property, travel, and the populace. The Moon rules night births and becomes ruler of the lunar sect, which includes Venus, Mars, and Mercury when an evening star. In Hellenistic astrology the Sun and the Moon are called "the giver's of one's all." The Sun represents the conditions of the soul, while the Moon represents the conditions of the physical body.

In Vedic astrology the Moon, called Chandra, symbolizes the mind (manas), the mother, and the home. In a culture that values stability these are the most important elements. Ambition was not as highly regarded as the ability to lead a happy, contented life. For the ancient Indians, this required a peaceful and calm mind, which was cultivated by a virtuous mother and proper home life. In Vedic astrology the Moon is the key indicator the of the native's ability to enjoy happiness.

Just as the Moon reflects the light from the Sun, the Moon represents the soul expression through consciousness. The Moon represents our personality, or how we relate to others, and our popularity in general. The Moon is considered strongest when waxing towards a full Moon, and weaker when waning. A strong Moon indicates a strong, clear mind allowing productive involvement in family and society. A weak Moon indicates a wavering or confused mind that prevents productive participation in life.

There are 27 lunar Nakshatras, or lunar mansions, that describe the monthly sidereal motion of the Moon. The Moon stays approximately one day in each Nakshatra. The birth Nakshatra of an individual is called his or her star and is the most important planet in the Vedic horoscope. Nakshatras are used extensively in determining personality characteristics, as well as in horary and electional astrology.

Arabic astrologers also used a system of lunar mansions called *manazil*. The 28 manazil were initially used for navigation over the desert, and later took on predictive qualities. The Chinese called their lunar mansions *hsiu*. The three difference systems—Nakshatra, manazil, and hsiu—share a few constellations, but there are significant dissimilarities.

The cycles of the Moon have always been connected with germination and fertility. Specific times during the lunation cycle were considered more supportive of both human and animal conception. Sowing and reaping in farming were optimally timed using the phases of the Moon. The Hellenistic Greeks considered the phases before and after the birth of the child to indicate the general health of the child. A new technique using the lunation cycle was introduced in the twentieth century by Dane Rudhyar (1895–1985), the father of humanistic astrology. He applied the lunation cycle to human psychology. He believed that the lunar cycle one is born under determines the basic psychological outlook of the individual. Over the course of a life, the development of the individual's psychological outlook can be determined through the lunation cycle of the secondary progressed Moon.

Rudhyar defined eight phases of the lunation cycle. The cycle describes the spatial relationship between the Sun, the Moon, and the Earth. Because the cycle is perceived from the Earth, the Moon phases are most easily defined as degrees of separation between the Sun and the Moon as observed from the Earth. The phases according to Rudhyar, the degrees of separation, and a few key words for the eight phases of the lunation cycle are provided below:

*New Moon* (0–45° from Sun to Moon): birth, new beginnings, initiative, creativity, emergence

*Crescent Moon* (45–90°): challenges, effort, change, activity, expansion

*First Quarter Moon (90–135): breakthrough, crisis of action, separation from past, action*

*Gibbous Moon* (135–180°): development, evaluation, perfecting, overcoming

*Full Moon (180–225°):* culmination, illumination, objectivity, vision; fulfillment

*Disseminating Moon* (225–270°): teaching, reaping, maturity, communication, demonstration

*Last Quarter Moon* (270–315°): assimilation, crisis in consciousness, harvest; reorientation

*Balsamic Moon* (315–0°): death, transition, prophetic or future oriented, destiny, release

—Maire M. Masco

**Sources:**

Campion, Nicholas, and Steve Eddy. *The New Astrology: The Art and Science of the Stars*. New Pomfret, VT: Trafalgar Square Publishing, 1999.

Hamillton, Edith. *Mythology: Timeless Tales of Gods and Heroes*. New York: Signet Classics, 1942.

Harness, Dennis M. *The Nakshatras: The Lunar Mansions of Vedic Astrology*. Twin Lakes, WI: Lotus Press, 1999.

Hinnells, John R. ed. *The Penguin Dictionary of Religions*. London: Penguin Books, 1984.

Hornblower, Simon, and Antony Spawforth, eds. *The Oxford Classical Dictionary*. (Oxford, Eng.: Oxford University Press, 1996.

Mani, Vettam. *Puranic Encyclopaedia*. Delhi, India: Motilal Banarsidass Publishers, 1964.

Miller, Susan. *Planets and Possibilities: Explore the Worlds Beyond Your Sun Sign*. New York: Warner Books, 2001.

Rudhyar, Dane. *The Lunation Cycle*. Santa Fe, NM: Aurora Press, 1967.

Wolkstein, Diane, and Samuel Noah Kramer. *Inanna: Queen of Heaven and Earth, Her Stories and Hymns from Sumer*. New York: Harper and Row, 1983.

## MOORE, MARCIA M.

Marcia M. Moore, astrologer and occultist, was born May 22, 1928, in Cambridge, Massachusetts. Her father was Robert L. Moore, the founder of Sheraton Hotels, and her sister was Robin Moore, a novelist who used the pen name Robert L. Moore, Jr. Marcia Moore was a graduate of Radcliffe College, where she wrote a B.A. thesis on the subject of astrology. The thesis was later published in book form by the Lucis Trust. Moore became an active astrologer and a well-known figure in the American astrological community. Moore's second husband, Mark Douglas, collaborated with her on several of her books. Her third husband was Howard Alltounian, Jr. In her final years, Moore was experimenting with mind-altering drugs, which contributed to her death on January 15, 1979, in Bothwell, Washington.

**Sources:**

Holden, James H., and Robert A. Hughes. *Astrological Pioneers of America*. Tempe, AZ: American Federation of Astrologers, 1988.

Moore, Marcia M. *Astrology, The Divine Science*. 2d rev. ed. York Harbor, ME: Arcane Publications, 1978.

———. *Astrology Today—A Socio-Psychological Survey*. New York: Lucas Publishing Co., 1960.

———. *Journeys into the Bright World*. 1978.

——— and Mark Douglas. *Astrology in Action*. York Harbor, ME: Arcane Publications, 1970.

## MORIN, JEAN-BAPTISTE (MORINUS)

Jean-Baptiste Morin (Morinus), the French astrologer and physician, was born in Villefranche, France, in 1583. He received his doctor of medicine degree at Avignon in 1613. Over the next several years, he was a physician to a bishop, an abbot, and the duke of Luxemburg. In 1630, Morin became royal professor of mathematics. He was appointed to draw up the horoscope of the newborn Louis XIV.

Morin developed a method of determining longitudes at sea using the distance of the Moon from a fixed star. He divided the universe into elemental, ethereal, and celestial matter and proposed three layers of earth, which corresponded in reverse order to the three regions of the air. He criticized Ptolemy, rejected Cardan and Kepler, and denied the existence of a vacuum and Toricelli's proof thereof. He advocated the medicine of Paracelsus and opposed the heliocentric astronomy of Copernicus.

As a young child, when both his parents were sick, Morin was asked by his older brother which parent he would prefer to survive. His preference was his father (who eventually recovered), although he loved both parents. When his brother told his mother what he had said, she hated him for the next two days before she died and left him the minimum required by law.

It is not likely that his mother could have given him much even had she wanted to, as his parents had been reduced to poverty by the civil wars, plunder, pillage, lawsuits, and calamities that marked the era of his birth. Because of trying times, his education was interrupted for 10 years.

In *Astrologia Gallica*, Morin wrote: "Each planet in the XII house [he had five if Venus was included, a mere 2° into the XIth] portends a prison cell." Further, "Of this, the course of my youth alone could hardly give more striking confirmation, due to my love of vengeance and pleasures of the flesh." Yet his "prison cells" were metaphorical, he was not imprisoned, but he did suffer servitude. From age of 16 to 46, he worked for 16 masters and had poor relations with them all. Morin characterized his relations with his employers as, "thankless servitude and injurious masters." Even though he saved the life of one of them by performing an operation no other doctor would have attempted, his employer showed him "monstrous ingratitude." He complained that his life was a litany of blasphemy against him by an army of detractors.

Just as his parents seem to have been poor, so was Morin. He wrote that he suffered repeated bouts of chronic illness and faced violent death more than 16 times. In spite of ill health, he lived to 73 years of age. Notwithstanding the enmity he faced, several times in his life he had the love and support of eminent persons, including kings, queens, princes, and cardinals. From 1635 to 1654, he had to fight to offset his detractors' assaults. During this period he developed a method of determining longitudes as sea using the distance of the Moon from a fixed star.

Religiously, Morin was an avid Roman Catholic. He defended Catholicism against the Hussites, Lutherans, and Calvinists. Yet Cardinal Richelieu treated him shamefully, he complained. Morin did not like atheists. He attacked the humanist Pico della Mirandola, who had attacked astrology in his *Disputationes contra astrologiam divinatricem* (1496).

By his own admission, Morinus was fond of "the pleasures of the flesh." His adventures occasionally led to danger, as, for instance, in 1605. In a fight over a woman, he was wounded just below the heart and in the thigh. In true French style, he lost a great deal of blood and only avoided fainting by drinking six cups of wine.

Morin was the author of a number of books. His astrological doctrine is most fully set forth in his monumental 850-page *Astrologia Gallica* which was not published until five years after his death. It is in that book that a great deal of autobiographical information about Morin appears.

*Astrologia Gallica* is divided into 26 books. After an autobiographical preface and another preface advocating astrology, the books cover the following topics:

Book I: the true cognition of God from the light of Nature
Book II: creation
Book III: the division of the world into three regions—elementary, aetherial, and celestial
Book IV: the extension and continuous quantity of created beings
Book V: space, place, and the vacuum
Book VI: motion and time
Book VII: the efficient cause
Book VIII: treats of the alteration of physical bodies
Book IX: mixed bodies
Book X: the experiences, sects, and principles of astrology
Book XI: the simple and primary powers of acting of the celestial
Book XII: the elemental and influential qualities of the celestial bodies
Book XIII: the proper natures and powers of the individual planets and fixed stars
Book XIV: the first physical cause
Book XV: the essential dignities of the planets
Book XVI: the rays and aspects of the stars
Book XVII: the astrological houses
Book XVIII: the fortitudes and debilities of the planets
Book XIX: the elements of astrology
Book XX: the universal action of the celestial bodies with respect to themselves and to sublunary things
Book XXI: the active determination of the celestial bodies and the passive determination of sublunary things
Book XXII: directions
Book XXIII: revolutions of nativities
Book XXIV: progressions and transits
Book XXV: the universal constitutions of heaven
Book XXVI: interrogations and elections

Morin's astrology is based upon Aristotle's philosophy and metaphysics. It is geocentric. His work belongs to a period in Western astrology during which the practitioners of astrology fell over themselves in order to appear rational and scientific. Much space in *Astrologia Gallica* is given to the purging of astrology of what Morin deemed irrational and erroneous procedures. He objected to the Arabic usage of triplicity rulers and replaced it with another of his own devising. He objected to the promiscuous and unregulated use of the universal significations of the planets and introduced his own doctrine of local determination of the Primum Mobile, which he felt enabled the astrologer to make accurate predictions. He stressed the importance of understanding the nature, analogy, and zodiacal state of the planets along with their local determination by the astrological houses in order to get an accurate understanding of their influence on sublunary things. Without such an accurate understanding, correct delineation and prediction is impossible.

For Morin, the natures of the planets were essentially the same as what other astrologers had long believed, but they were not recognized as being as distinct as they were in reality. Aside from their natures, the planets had analogy with specific kinds of manifestation.This analogy was an important factor in delineation.

By zodiacal state, Morin understod the planet's interaction with the sign it is in, its dignity (he recognized rulership, exaltation, and triplicity) or debility (he recognized detriment and fall). He supposed peregrine was a kind of frontier between dignity and debility. His understanding of dignity of triplicity was that a planet in a sign of the same element as the one it rules is in dignity (or honor) of triplicity in that sign (e.g. Mars, who rules the fire sign Aries, in Leo or Sagittarius; Venus, who rules the air sign Libra, in Aquarius or Gemini). Zodiacal state also entailed the planet's relationship with its dispositor (the ruler of the sign it was in), as well as the aspects it received. Zodiacal state modulated the qualitative manifestation of the one planetary nature (Mars, Venus, etc.) giving it a hierarchy of expression from pure to corrupt. The purer a planet's influence, the easier it produced what it promised. Local determination specified the field of action a planet might have, limiting it to the affairs of life corresponding to the house it was in (hence "local") or the one(s) it ruled, or to the affairs of those houses and rulers to whom it was linked by aspect.

Morin regarded astrology as a divine art. Bad astrology was the work of the devil intended to discredit it and to remove it from man's use. He strongly objected to the medieval astrology, which he saw as corrupted by "Arabisms." He questioned the astrological doctrine of combustion, which held that combust planets cease to act on the sublunary world. He favored Regiomontanus houses over equal houses. But he developed his own house system described in *Astrologicarum domorum cabala detecta* (1623). Morin taught that benefic planets could accidentally work evil ("accidental malefics") and malefics could accidentally work good (accidental benefics).

Morin presented the claim that he was reforming astrology. Actually, his reforms were more like rearticulations of the very astrologers he objected to most: Guido Bonatti, Abū Ma'shar, Massa'allah, and Cardanus. Yet upon close study, his assertion that he had improved upon the medieval astrology derived from Arabic and Persian astrologers appeared to amount to his making explicit what was either implicit in the teachings of Bonatti, the thirteenth-century Italian astrologer who resumed the practices of the Arabic astrologers.

For instance, Morin's rule in delineation, "The good or bad signified by a house emanates from the ruler of the house" (Book XXI *Astrologia Gallica*), is found in Bonatti's *Liber astronomiae* and attributed to Abū Ma'shar. So, too, the idea that benefic planets can accidentally work evil and malefics can accidentally work good. In Book XXII, which deals with primary directions, his teaching that the significator indicates the kind of event and the promittor (promissor), the quality is implicit in the earlier medieval and Arabic astrological practice. It can be seen by analyzing the effects of transits. In the final analysis, although Morin's "Rational System of Horoscope Analysis" is of great practical benefit to the practicing astrologer, much of it is not new, nor even Morin's.

It was common to "borrow" the work of one's predecessors in astrology in the seventeenth century and use it without attribution. Indeed, the practice continues in the contemporary astrological scene and related fields. One suspects, reading early modern books on magic, that at least some of the "fathers" of modern science and "inventors" merely published technologies and theories previously handed down secretly within networks of those interested in the occult arts. Certainly a number of astrological doctrines Morin claimed as his own contributions were known to Bonatti and his Arabic sources.

Nevertheless, in most cases Morin made explicit what was implicit or easily missed by Bonatti. For this he deserves the practicing astrologer's respect and gratitude. Also to his credit is his provision of a philosophical and metaphysical context to his astrology, something generally missing in medieval and ancient astrological texts. Morin died in Paris in 1656.

—Robert Zoller

**Sources:**

Morin, Jean-Baptiste (Morinus). *Astrologia Gallica*. The Hague, 1661.

———. *Astrosynthesis*. Translated by Lucy Little. New York: Emerald Books, 1974.

———. *La Vie Devant les Asters*. Translated by Jean Hieroz. Nice, 1943.

———. *My Life Before the Stars, by J.-B. Morin de Villefranche*. Translated by Michael Edwards. In *Astrology, the Astrological Quarterly, the Journal of the Astrological Lodge of London*. Vol. 60, no. 2, Summer 1986, pp. 65–75.

*The Morinus System of Horoscope Interpretation*. Translated by Richard S. Baldwin. Washington, DC: American Federation of Astrologers, 1974.

## Morinus (Morinean) System

The Morinus system of house division, proposed by the seventeenth-century astrologer Morin de Villefranche, is based on equal divisions of the equator, which are then projected onto the ecliptic.

## Morrison, R. J. (Zadkiel)

Richard James Morrison (Zadkiel), an English astrologer, was born in Enfield, London, on June 15, 1795. He enlisted in the navy at age of 11, became a lieutenant in 1815, and retired in 1817, although he later served in the coast guard from 1827 to 1829. In 1828, he rescued four men and a boy from a wrecked vessel and later received a medal for this act of bravery.

Morrison became interested in astrology before he was 30. He was acquainted with the astrologer R. C. Smith, and, inspired by Smith's almanac, the *Prophetic Messenger*, Morrison started his own almanac in 1830. The *Herald of Astrology*, which was renamed *Zadkiel's Almanac* in 1836, was quite successful and was published for the next hundred years. Morrison also had interests in spiritualism, phrenology, and crystal gazing.

In the 1861 issue of his almanac, Morrison predicted an "evil year" for Queen Victoria's husband. As it turned out, Prince Albert died suddenly and unexpectedly of typhoid fever in December 1861. As often happens in the wake of an accurate astrological prediction, some individuals were outraged at the triumph of "medieval superstition." In this case, Edward Belcher, a writer for the London *Daily Telegraph*, attacked Morrison, who responded by suing for libel. The jury found in favor of Morrison, but he was awarded only 20 shillings. He was rewarded, however, by the substantial increase in sales of his almanac that the publicity brought him. Beyond his almanac, Morrison is best known for the abridged edition of Lilly's *Christian Astrology*, which he published. Morrison died on February 8, 1874.

**Sources:**

Holden, James H., and Robert A. Hughes. *Astrological Pioneers of America*. Tempe, AZ: American Federation of Astrologers, 1988.

Morrison, R. J. *An Introduction to Astrology*. London, H. G. Bohn, 1852. Reprint, San Bernardino, CA: Borgo Press, 1980.

## Movable Signs

Movable signs is an alternative expression for the cardinal signs, which are Aries, Cancer, Libra, and Capricorn. Movable signs should not be confused with mutable signs, which refer to four entirely different signs.

## Mrigasira

Mrigasira (or the Deer Head) is one of the Nakshatras (lunar mansions) of Vedic astrology. Represented by a deer's head, this Nakshatra is found from Taurus 23°20' to Gemini 6°40'. Soma, the divine nectar, presides, and the planet Mars rules over this sign associated with the fleetness of a deer. People may be more curious and creative, yet flirtatious and suspicious during this period.

—Pramela Thiagesan

## Muharta

Muhurta serves a purpose similar to that of Western electional astrology in which the astrologer chooses an auspicious time for the commencement of an action. In ancient Vedic times, however, the specific role of muhurta was primarily for the timing of personal and community rites that expressed the spiritual life of the culture.

The central role of such rites is best understood in the context of the philosophy of karma. Although the Western sense of karma is often limited to the results of past action, karma actually means action. In the context of muhurta, karma can be thought of as current actions founded in the will to choose that which can best ameliorate or soften the impact of less evolved past decisions or of simply creating new life trajectories. From this perspective, the wheel of karma is an ongoing cyclical process that encompasses both experiencing the fruits of past action and having the will and responsibility to choose and perform new current actions. In turn, current actions can feed back to patterns created in the past and modify them, carving out new behaviors that are hopefully more beneficial to the individual and to his or her society.

Many Hindus believe that establishing correct patterns of thought and behavior leads to actions (karmas) that will improve life. These patterns (samskaras) are established from birth onward by means of rituals that refine the human being on individual and social levels of life including physical, psychological, intellectual, and spiritual levels. There are usually 16 samskaras, including naming ceremonies, the first feeding of a child, commencement of education, marriage, cremation, and similar rites of passage in human maturation. Because each of these samskaras requires a proper muhurta or commencement time, muhurta is an essential part of the process of evolving towards the state of optimal human maturity known as *moksha* or liberation, whereby the soul completes the wheel of karma. In much of Indian thought, such an enlightened state is the ultimate goal of right action arising from the influence of the samskaras. This function of muhurta is very different from the typical contemporary situation of a client asking the astrologer for a good time to go on a vacation or start a business. Nevertheless, these latter concerns are the subject of most of the muhurtas that the modern jyotishi (practitioner of Vedic astrology) will encounter, whether in the West or in India.

The essential data for establishing a proper muhurta is found in a panchanga, a yearly sidereal almanac used by priests in ancient times as the central guide for arriving at the timing of personal and community rites. To this day, the panchanga is still the primary resource for determining religious festival days in India. Contemporary astrologers use it to arrive at the best available time to start any action within specific parameters. *Panchanga* means "five limbs" and is so named because it sets forth tables for five measurements of time vital for selecting a good muhurta. Panchangas are available worldwide, mostly in Indian communities, and in most Vedic astrology software packages.

The panchanga is organized through the mechanism of soli-lunar cycles. Its five limbs are the seven varanas (day of the week), 27 nakshatras (the Moon's daily position in a lunar constellation), 30 tithis (one of the 30 phases or lunar days in a lunar month), 60 karanas (half of a tithi) and 27 soli-lunar yogas (generated by the relative positions of the Sun and Moon with respect to each other). Although all these contribute to setting a muhurta within the context of a large number of additional ornate rules, primacy is given to the day of the week (varana), lunar day (tithi) and the star group that the Moon is in at the time under consideration (nakshatra). If all the many rules to construct a good muhurta for a particular event are followed, the recommendation might be for a time 200 years in the future due to the infrequent occurrence of all ideal primary astrological patterns. Consequently, secondary considerations are used along with the primary considerations from a panchanga, thereby rendering the process practical.

The varana (day of the week) is the first consideration. Each weekday takes its name from one of the seven main planets including the Sun and Moon. The characteristics of the planet indicate what activities are most appropriate under the influence of its day. In this context, dating might be better on a Friday night (Venus) than on Saturday night (Saturn). Embedded in the varana are the twenty four hours of the day (horas). The first hora or hour of each day is ruled by that day's planetary ruler. In Indian astrology, the day starts at sunrise and therefore, for example, the first hour after sunrise on a Monday would be the hora of the Moon. There follows a set sequence as to the rulers of the subsequent hours for the different days of the week. Since the length of day and night vary as one goes north or south of the equator and at different times of the year, there is the complication that the hora may not be precisely one hour long for a given date and locality. It may be necessary to calculate the horas of the night and day separately to be completely accurate. Use of the horas can be very specific. For example, if someone wants to schedule a job interview, it might be desirable to select the hora of Mercury, provided other considerations are favorable at that time and Mercury is favorable in the birth chart.

A tithi represents one lunar day and is calculated by the position of the Moon relative to the Sun. Each tithi is 12° and there are 15 tithis in the waxing cycle culminating in the full Moon and fifteen in the waning cycle ending with the new Moon. Each tithi is classified as to the purposes for which it is auspicious and inauspicious. Some tithis are completely avoided for almost all important activities. In general, the tithis of the bright half of the lunar month are more favorable than the dark half for activities that have a more outward direction.

Nakshatras are utilized in the context of muhurta to indicate what flourishes and what is counter-indicated under their influence. They have certain archetypes and qualities that lend great richness to astrological interpretation. A modern astrologer can be led by these qualities to choose muhurtas for situations not anticipated in ancient times. For example, the nakshatra of Revati is associated with roads and by association, hospitality, shelter, and protection. If the client wanted to open a bed-and-breakfast inn, an astrologer might choose a time when Revati is prominent in the chart. The relationship between the Moon's nakshatra in the birth chart and at the time of the muhurta is also vital. Certain positions are decidedly inauspicious and should ideally be avoided. A complex matrix of other factors relevant to nakshatras is beyond the scope of this discussion.

Other important considerations give a flavor of the intricacy and detail of muhurta. Points of transition such as the Sun's entry into new sidereal constellations, eclipses, and certain transition times during each day are generally considered unfavorable for initiating most activities. In turn, other such junctures are very auspicious. The position of the Moon is extremely important as well. For example, the Moon in the eighth house from its natal position is said to give inauspicious results. Similarly, it is not desirable for the Moon to be too close to the Sun. Although the consideration of the tithi takes such factors into account to some extent, the underlying principle is that the strength and position of the Moon is always to be optimized. Sometimes, however, there is no choice but to commence something under some of these more obstructive combinations. Fortunately, the system is sufficiently diverse and ornate that these obstructions can be offset by other considerations.

Once a time period has been selected according to these criteria, the most important final step for the purposes of this discussion is to select an ascendant that will empower the client to realize the potential of the chosen time. Although this is technically outside the primary considerations of the panchanga, it is universally recognized that if the ascendant and ascendant lord are not strong, the possibility of a good outcome is greatly reduced. The same reasoning applies to the houses and lords of the houses for the matter under consideration. For example, if the muhurta is for buying a property, the fourth house, fourth, lord and the primary indicators for property in Indian astrology, Mars and Saturn, should be well disposed in the chart of the selected time. The synthesis of all these factors is the great challenge of the art of muhurta.

Selection of the best time possible for a particular endeavor emphatically does not ensure a brilliant outcome if the matter is counter-indicated in the birth chart. If a person has a very difficult pattern with respect to marriage, selecting a beautiful muhurta for marriage will not ensure a smooth or continuous union in and of itself. Muhurta selection, however, is one of the expressions of free will that may modify the outcome of obstructive chart patterns and is therefore an important component of Vedic astrology.

—Penny Farrow

## Muise, Roxana

Roxana Muise, a contemporary second-generation astrologer, was born on October 1, 1935, in Chicago, Illinois. She graduated from St. Catherine's Academy in Lomita, California, and was ordained on February 14, 1974, in the Abundant Life Church of Jesus Christ, a spiritualist, metaphysical church based in San Bernardino, California. She graduated summa cum laude from California State University at Dominguez Hills in 1981 with a degree in health science.

Muise began astrological studies in 1968 with her mother, Patricia Crossley, and graduated from the Scorpio School of Astrology in 1970. Her first teachers were Zipporah Dobyns, Gina Ceaglio, Dane Rudhyar, Virginia Wilson Fabre, Constance G. Mayer, Robert Jansky, Sabrinah Millstein, Al H. Morrison, James Eshelman, Lois Rodden, Edwin Steinbrecher, Buz Meyers, Tony Joseph, Charles Emerson, Robert Hand, Diana Stone, Arlene Kramer, and Manly Palmer Hall.

Muise cofounded the South Western Astrology Conference (SWAC) and served as its director from 1974 to 1985. She is a past president of the International Society for Astrological Research (ISAR) and served on its board for 19 years. She was a founding member of the board of directors of the United Astrology Conference. She keeps the archives for more than 10,000 named asteroids for the Asteroid Special Interest Group (AST-SIG) of the National Council for Geocosmic Research (NCGR) and is the a founding member of the board of directors of Kepler College of Astrological Arts and Sciences in Seattle, Washington.

Muise is the author of *A-Year-at-a-Glance: The 45 Degree Graphic Ephemeris*, which presents her method of creating an overlay of one's natal planets on a yearly graph that shows all hard transiting aspects for an entire year and provides a worksheet that instantly shows dynamic aspects between charts. She is also the author of *The Fourth Sign*, based on research of historical references that give the cat, instead of the crab, as a symbol for the sign Cancer. Muise is author of a learning CD, *The Shadow Ephemeris*, which portrays the entire retrograde subcycle. This begins when a planet first passes the degree at which it will turn direct, and ends when a planet passes the degree where it turned retrograde. The CD includes articles, instruction, examples, and ephemeredes of more than a century of planetary stations and shadow points.

Muise lives with her husband, Ralph, in Lacey, Washington. She is an international lecturer, teaches astrology and metaphysics, and has a private counseling practice. Her *Monthly Astrology Report*, which includes a transit forecast and a symbolism report, is sent by email subscription.

**Sources:**

Muise, Roxana. *A-Year-at-a-Glance: The 45 Degree Graphic Ephemeris*. Torrance, CA: South Western Astrology Conference, 1986.

———. *The Fourth Sign*. Lacey, WA: SWAC Press.

———. *The Shadow Ephemeris*. Lacey, WA: SWAC Press.

## Mula

Mula (the root) is one of the Nakshatras (lunar mansions) of Vedic astrology. The goddess of destruction, Niritti, presides, and the planet Ketu rules over this Nakshatra found from Sagittarius 0° to 13°20'. This is said to be a good time to create something anew, like a garden; an individual may be a better politician and have better fortune during this period, but also may be more unstable or self-destructive.

—Pramela Thiagesan

## Mundane Aspect

A mundane aspect is an aspect (an astrological angle) between two points in space—for example, between two planets—that is measured along the celestial equator. This distinguishes mundane aspects from the aspects relied upon by most astrologers, who usually consider only angles that are measured along the ecliptic (the circle of the zodiac). Mundane aspects are rarely used by contemporary astrologers.

## Mundane Astrology

Mundane astrology is the branch of astrology dealing with history, society, and politics. Traditionally, it had two main functions: First, to understand the past, and, second, to predict the future. Both functions, though, are subsumed within a greater purpose—to manage the present. Indeed, within the context of apocalyptic fears of political disintegration or global catastrophe, mundane astrology's key task has always been to preserve peace, order, and stability. This, at least, was the goal of its cosmology. This is not to deny the existence of more immediate selfish motives, such as the need to gain political advantage over one's rivals. Thus, there may be astrologers who operate according to one agenda, while their political patrons work to another.

As defined by Charles Carter, the most prominent British astrologer of the mid-twentieth century, in his book *An Introduction to Political Astrology*, "The aim then of Political Astrology is the study of all that pertains to the life of politically incorporated body, or nation. It must comprehend the cultural and intellectual life, the religious life, the economic, and so forth." However, bearing in mind the blurring between the personal and professional, it may not always be possible to decide when astrology is mundane and when it is not. For example, if relationships are political (i.e., if, they involve power relationships between men and women, or adults and children), is a composite chart mundane? Also, the birth charts of politicians may be interpreted within the rules of natal astrology, but are clearly of direct importance in mundane work, while horary charts concerning political matters may be also considered mundane. Meanwhile, financial astrology, which is clearly mundane, has tended to evolve into a distinct discipline.

In the Middle Ages, mundane astrology had a narrower remit and was usually known as the study of "revolutions," (i.e., the revolutions of Jupiter and Saturn around the earth), which together were seen as the main timers of history. The term "revolution," used to describe political upheavals, is derived from the word's astrological application. The Sun's ingress into Aries was also known as a "revolution." The three principle technical bases of the study of long periods in relation to Jupiter-Saturn are conjunctions, the casting of horoscopes for the Sun's ingress into Aries, and the use of less frequent events, including predictable ones such as eclipses, and unpredictable ones such as comets or mock suns. New and full moons and planetary transits provided further information between these major events.

The term mundane is derived from the Latin word *mundus*, meaning "world." In the first century the Roman writer Pliny wrote in *De Natura Rerum* that "the Greeks have designated the world by a word that means 'ornament,' and we have given it the name of mundus, because of its perfect finish and grace." Mundus itself is a translation of the Greek word *kosmos*, meaning "world-order" and was probably first used by either the philosopher Parmenides or Pythagoras in the sixth-century B.C.E. The word can also be translated as "adornment," the root of the modern word "cosmetic." The Latin term *mundi* was used to describe the application of astrology to the world from the eleventh century onwards. (The first medieval Latin astrological text was the *Liber Planetis at Mundi Climatibus*, published between 1010 and 1027, and probably written by Gerbert d'Auvergne, who became Pope Sylvester II.) By the seventeenth century, the study of revolutions was also known as "Astrologia Munda." The term "mundane astrology" itself first came into regular use in the nineteenth century and is the title of two "cookbooks" on the subject, one by Raphael and and the other by H. S. Green respectively, both written around the turn of the twentieth century.

While the term itself is modern, it is clear that the earliest known astrology was mundane in nature, being concerned exclusively with affairs of state. Indeed, in ancient Mesopotamia where, according to current records, the technical basis was laid for both western and Indian astrology, the entire cosmos was seen as one political unit in which humanity served the celestial deities, whose deputy on earth was the king. This notion of the "cosmic state is common to most religious societies and persists in the west, shorn of its astrological component, in fundamentalist Christianity. In Mesopotamia, though, the stars and planets were messengers, conveying divine wishes to humanity via the astrologers, whose job it was to scan the skies for signs or omens (i.e., warnings) of divine pleasure or anger.

The earliest Mesopotamian texts, which survive only in fragments, date from around 2200 B.C.E., and the earliest complete text, the *Venus Tablet*, detailing the political and global correlates with Venus' rising and setting, dates from the eighteenth century B.C.E. Most existing written evidence, though, dates from the Assyrian period of the eighth to seventh centuries B.C.E.

Sargon II (reigned 721–705 B.C.E.) was the first of the new line of Assyrian monarchs known to have taken an astrologer on his military campaigns. An inscription from a tablet in the Louvre recording his attack on the city of Musasir, now in northwest Iran, suggests that the timing of his invasion may have been arranged by reference to astronomical factors:

> At the exalted command of Nabû [Mercury] and Marduk [Jupiter], who had moved on a path in a stellar station for starting my campaign, and besides, as a favourable sign for seizing power, Magur ["the boat" = the moon], lord of the tiara [made an eclipse that] lasted one watch, to herald the destruction of Gutium. Upon the precious approval of the warrior Shamash [the sun], who wrote encouraging omens on the text that he would walk at my side ... I mustered my army.

It is fascinating to observe the clear and logical manner in which the military arrangements proceeded. Mercury's movements revealed the mind of Nabû, the Scribe, while Jupiter's position indicated the thoughts of Marduk, the proprietary god of Babylon. Sin, the moon god, confirmed his colleague's intentions, and lastly Shamash, the solar deity, indicated his agreement by giving a positive answer to a question posed via extispicy (i.e., through entrail divination). The gods' intentions would have been clarified against previous events listed in the omen literature, and Sargon would have been informed that a majority of the divine council had approved his action. One can only imagine the crushing effect of the Assyrian army, which was one of the greatest fighting machines of the first millennium. The forces were armed not only with superior numbers and technology, but also with the knowledge that heaven was on its side, which, in turn, must have had an enormous effect on morale. With the sanction of the stars the Assyrian campaign assumed the character of a *jihad*, or holy war, and Sargon's success no doubt convinced him that astrology was an essential tool in his political and military arsenal.

Documented examples of astrology's supposed ability to provide military advantage exist from later European history. As late as the 1640s, a positive forecast from the astrologer William Lilly for either side in the English civil war was considered of more value than the force of a dozen regiments. Further, in spite of the substantial changes in astrological technique and interpretative style since Sargon marched at the head of his conquering army, astrology retains a strict logical procedure, matching each astronomical feature against a corresponding meaning in organized steps in order to arrive at a single conclusion.

The notion of a cosmic state in which the human polity is intimately connected to the celestial world survived into Greek astrology, reinforced by similar conceptions in Egypt, in which the Pharaoh was a representative of the sun god and an incarnation of the star Sopdet (Greek Sothis, modern Sirius), itself identified with the god and mythical king Osiris. Thus, the concept of the sky as an extension of earthly space (the modern signs of the zodiac were known as houses and the modern houses as places) survives from the Greek world, with each part subject to a ruling planet. The Babylonian concept of astrology as the reading of signs continued, but parallel with an alternative cosmology, derived from the fifth- and fourth-century B.C.E. philosophers Plato and Aristotle, in which God's influence descended to Earth via the planetary spheres. Hence, the idea of planetary influences developed only within the context of a divinely ordered cosmos.

The overall framework for most western mundane astrology down to the present day, though, was laid by the second-century Greek astrologer Claudius Ptolemy in his *Tetrabiblos* (in Latin, *Quadripatitium;* in English, "four books"). In particular, Ptolemy revised the Mesopotamian system of equating countries to stars or constellations and identified 72 countries allocated to the 12 signs of the zodiac. He also codified rules for interpreting eclipses and ingresses, and these rules have been repeated down to modern times.

Following astrology's revival in Europe in the nineteenth century, mundane astrology was still broadly laid down by Ptolemy. It was crudely predictive in that there was little concern with history, only with the future. It was crude because, while it relied on classical astrology, it had discarded the complex interpretative structure and multiple logical steps that allowed medieval and Renaissance astrologers to reach precise conclusions. This is not to say that this revived Ptolemaic astrology was more or less accurate, just that its interpretative process was much simpler. However, a series of highly inaccurate predictions did eventually provoke a crisis. These were the high-profile forecasts that there would be no war between Britain and Germany in the late 1930s, made by Charles E. O. Carter, perhaps the most respected astrologer within the profession in Britain, and R. H. Naylor, the most serious of the high-profile British media astrologers. The fact that there were also correct forecasts did not detract from the embarrassment.

The result of the forecasts, after the end of World War II, was a series of innovations designed to increase the efficacy of prediction. First, Carter proposed the creation of sets of data for countries in order to reduce the dependence on the Ptolemaic rulerships, a task he proposed in *An Introduction to Political Astrology,* which was completed in Nicholas Campion's *The Book of World Horoscopes* in 1997. Second, in France, Henri Gouchon and André Barbault pioneered the use of outer planet (Uranus, Neptune, and Pluto) cycles to provide long-term timing measures. Later, in the 1970s, Liz Greene applied Jungian concepts of the collective unconscious, developing an interpretative structure that focused not on more accurate prediction, but on the derivation of meaning from astrological configurations. The result was a set of accurate forecasts of the end of the Cold War and the collapse of the Soviet Union that suggested these postwar innovations might be effective.

In the modern world, outside of the Indian subcontinent, mundane astrology remains a marginal practice among astrologers, whose main concern tends to be with the psychological form of natal astrology. In addition, demand from politicians is low due to astrology's poor standing, in spite of some high-profile patrons, notably former

U.S. president Ronald Reagan and former French presidents Charles de Gaulle and François Mitterand. The popularity of mundane astrology among astrologers tends to ebb and flow with the level of global crisis: in the 1980s, few paid any attention to it, but the collapse of communism and the Gulf War of 1991–92 brought heightened interest, as did the terrorist attacks on the United States on September 11, 2001. Writing during a similar period of crisis—the first years of the Cold War and the height of the Korean conflict—Carter argued in his book *An Introduction to Political Astrology* that mundane astrology "should logically take precedence over all other branches of our science [astrology], especially during the present epoch, when the life of the individual counts for so very little in comparison with that of the community, to which it is increasingly subordinated and by which is ever more coloured."

—Nick Campion

**Sources:**

Baigent, Michael, Nicholas Campion,, and Charles Harvey. *Mundane Astrology: The Astrology of Nations and Organisation*. 2nd rev. ed. London: Aquarian Press, 1991.
Campion, Nicholas, *The Book of World Horoscope*. 2nd rev. ed. Bristol: Cinnabar Books, 1999.
Carter, Charles E. O. *An Introduction to Political Astrology*. London: L. N. Fowler, 1951.
Pliny. *De Natura Rerum*. Book 2, III.

## Mutable Signs

The 12 signs of the zodiac are subdivided according to three qualities: cardinal, mutable, and fixed. The four mutable signs (the mutable quadruplicity or mutable cross) are Gemini, Virgo, Sagittarius, and Pisces. The exit of the Sun from each of these four signs indicates the end of a new season: Gemini, the end of spring; Virgo, the end of summer; Sagittarius, the end of fall; and Pisces, the end of winter. The identifying trait of the mutable signs (sometimes referred to as common signs) is adaptability or flexibility. Mutable signs tend to react to new situations by adapting to them. Negatively, mutable signs can be too malleable or changeable.

The same classification can be found in Vedic astrology—Chara (moveable or cardinal), Dwi-Swabhava (dual or mutable) and Sthira (fixed). The three Vedic qualities, which are associated with the same signs as their Western parallels, have similar connotations.

**Sources:**

Sakoian, Frances, and Louis S. Acker. *The Astrologer's Handbook*. New York: Harper & Row, 1989.
Sutton, Komilla. *The Essentials of Vedic Astrology*. Bournemouth, UK: Wessex Astrologer, 1999.

## Mute Signs

The mute signs are the water signs, Scorpio, Cancer, and Pisces. It is said that when Mercury is afflicted in one of these signs, it results in quietness, difficulty in speaking, or even a speech impediment. The designation mute probably was given because these three creatures are "mute."

## Mutual Application

A mutual application (applying) occurs when two planets are moving toward each other—one in direct motion and the other in retrograde motion—to form an aspect.

## Mutual Reception

Two planets are in mutual reception when they are in each other's signs. If in a given horoscope, for example Mercury is in Aries (which is ruled by Mars) and Mars is in Gemini (which is ruled by Mercury), then Mercury and Mars are in mutual reception. Astrologers interpret mutual reception as being equivalent to a conjunction between the two planets involved.

## Mystic Rectangle

Mystic rectangle is a modern term for a planetary configuration composed of two trines that are connected by two sextiles. To qualify as a mystic rectangle, the pairs of planets on opposite sides of the horoscope from each other must form oppositions. Despite the name, individuals with mystic rectangles in their natal charts need not be mystically inclined. The name seems to have originated with Madame Helena Blavatsky, one of the founders of the Theosophical Society, who had this configuration in her chart.

## Nadir

The nadir is the point in the heavens directly opposite the zenith, which means that it is the point in the heavens on the other side of Earth directly underneath one's feet. It should be carefully distinguished from the imum coeli, which is the point directly opposite the midheaven.

## The Nakshatras: The Lunar Mansions of Vedic Astrology

As in tropical astrology, learning the basics of planets, houses, signs, and aspects is the foundation of learning natal chart analysis. But, to appreciate the depth and uniqueness of Vedic astrology, one must also encounter and explore the *nakshatras*. Nakshatra literally means "that which does not decay." The nakshatras reflect the primordial level of the zodiacal belt, which lies beneath the 12 basic signs. The concept of the lunar mansions extends across many cultures as a natural result of observing the lunation cyle. The Arab, Tibetan, and Chinese cultures also utilized lunar mansion systems in their astrology. The nakshatras can be thought of as the 27 "Moon signs" of the Hindu zodiac. In comparison to the signs or *rasis* as they are called in India, the nakshatras reveal a deeper, more profound effect of the constellations. While the rasis reflect a "mass" or "heap" of the 12 signs, the nakshatras further divide the constellations into 27 segments of equal length. Each nakshatra is 13°20' in length. Multiplying this length by 27 equals the entire zodiacal belt of 360°.

Each nakshatra has a rich mythology and powerful deities that reside within it. It is important to remember that the basis of astrology is mythology. By exploring the myths, symbols, and archetypes of the nakshatras, the constellations are brought to life. One of the best books on this subject is *Myths and Symbols of Vedic Astrology* by

Bepin Behari. As Behari points out, "The Atharva and Yajur Vedas give complete lists of them (nakshatras) and associate them with the oldest Vedic gods." By befriending the particular god or goddess of a given nakshatra, archetypal healing becomes possible. As the great Swiss psychiatrist C. G. Jung once stated, it is important to "feed the gods and goddesses."

The nakshatras represent the fields of activity or environment in which the creative powers of the planets can reveal their multifaceted nature. They are called lunar mansions because the Moon "resides in" each of them for approximately one day. Each lunar mansion of 13°20' length is further subdivided into four quarters of 3°20' called padas. An ancient Vedic myth describes how the Moon god, Soma, was given 27 wives by the lord of creation, Prajapati. Each wife represented one of the lunar mansions which Soma, the Moon god, inhabited during his lunation cycle through the constellations. An ancient Celtic King also had a tower constructed with 27 windows to view the monthly sojourn of the Moon.

Each nakshatra has a particular power or *shakti*. According to Vedic scholar David Frawley, the shakti is "the power of the *devatas* or deities ruling the lunar mansions." Every nakshatra is associated not only with particular deities, but also with a specific planet that rules that asterism. It may fall completely within a particular sign or overlap between two signs. Thus, it is also influenced by the sign or rasi within which it resides and its ruling planet.

Each nakshatra is male or female, as well as *sattwa*, *rajas* or *tamas* in nature. These are the three basic *gunas* in which life reflects, according to the Vedas. *Sattwa* has a quality of spirituality, harmony, balance and purity. Rajas, which is dominant in human experience, is high-energy activity and somewhat "Type A" behavior. Finally, tamas has the basic quality of dullness, inertia, sloth, and darkness. According to Behari, the nakshatras are divided into three groups of nine, called *pariyay*, meaning "cycle." The first nine nakshatras are *rajasic* in nature, the second nine are *tamasic*, and the final nine are described as *sattwic*. A specific animal species, sex, caste, temperament and primary motivation such as *dharma* (life purpose), *artha* (wealth), *kama* (fulfillment of desire), and *moksha* (enlightenment) is reflected through each nakshatra.

Personality characteristics reflecting strengths and weaknesses are also correlated with the basic nature of each lunar mansion. In chapter 16 of his classic text *Brihat Jataka*, Varāhamihira describes the human characteristics of the nakshatras. The chapter focuses primarily on the positions of the natal Moon in the respective lunar mansions. *The Nakshatras: The Lunar Mansions of Vedic Astrology* also provides a good introduction and overview of the personality characteristics of the 27 lunar mansions. It focuses on the meaning of the Moon, Sun, and the Ascendant's natal placement in each of the nakshatras.

In addition, the nakshatras are of primary importance in *muhurtha* or electional astrology. This involves the selection of a particular lunar mansion for the Moon pertaining to the optimal timing to undertake any new venture, i.e., starting a new business, building a new home, or choosing an auspicious wedding date. Finally, a specific archetypal symbol is depicted for each asterism. Because Vedic astrology is a sidereal system, it is based on direct observation of the planets in the constellations. Thus, when observing the Moon at night near the fixed stars of Al Sharatain and Mesarthim, one knows it resides in the first lunar mansion of Ashwini (0° to 13°20' of Aries). In this respect the Vedic or sidereal viewpoint is more in line with an astronomer's picture of the cosmos than the season-based tropical zodiac many people use in the West.

Aspects made from other planets can greatly influence the quality of a planet in a particular nakshatra. The strength of the ruling planet of a nakshatra will also provide furthur insights into the nature of the planet residing there. (It is important to subtract approximately 23° from tropical chart planets and ascendant if a Vedic chart has not yet been calculated.)

### Choosing an Auspicious Lunar Nakshatra

The Moon transits through a specific nakshatra each day (for approximately 25 hours). When the Moon passes through the different 27 lunar mansions, specific activities can bear more productive fruit. The Moon is considered more benefic when it is waxing or moving toward a full moon. The following is a listing of the nakshatras in regard to their qualities and the daily life events that are harmonious under their influence.

The *Laghu* or *Kshipra* (light and swift) nakshatras are Ashwini, Pushya, Hasta, and Abhijit. They are especially good constellations for the Moon to reside in when starting a journey (travel), sports activities, and doing healing work or administering medicines. These lunar mansions are also good for opening a business, sales, trade and obtaining or repaying a loan or debt.

The *Mridu* (soft, mild, or tender) nakshatras are Mrigrashira, Chitra, Anuradha, and Revati. These lunar mansions are excellent for learning music, dance, and drama and performing auspicious ceremonies like marriage. They are also good for buying and wearing new clothes. Lovemaking and romance flow under these stellar influences. These are excellent constellations for making new friends and enjoyment of pleasures that are healing and revitalizing.

The *Sthira* (fixed or permanent) nakshatras are Rohini, Uttara Phalguni, Uttara Ashadha, and Uttara Bhadrapada. These constellations are good for building homes and laying the foundations of communities. The emphasis here is toward permanence, stability, and structure. They are also favorable for ploughing the land, planting trees, and purchasing agricultural property.

The *Chara* (moveable or ephemeral) nakshatras are Purnarvasu, Swati, Shravana, Dhanishtha, and Shatabhisha. These constellations are good for buying automobiles and other vehicles, for going on a procession, and landscaping (gardening). Change of residence or career, travel, and other major life changes can more easily occur under their influence and support.

The *Tikshna* (sharp or dreadful) nakshatras are Ardra, Ashlesha, Jyeshta, and Mula. These lunar mansions are auspicious for creating separation from friends or filing for a divorce. Powerful, bold, and brash activities can occur under their influence.

They are effective for invoking spirits and other incantations. These constellations can be related to black magic, casting spells, exorcism, punishment, and even murder.

The *Krura* or *Ugra* (fierce or severe) nakshatras are Bharani, Magha, Purva Phalguni, Purva Ashadha, and Purva Bhadrapada. They are associated with the assertive and aggressive acts of a spiritual warrior. These constellations can also be related to evil deeds such at setting fires, poisoning, destruction, and other deceitful acts. Imprisonment and other forms of confinement can be experienced here.

The *Misra* (mixed) nakshatras are Krittika and Vishakha. They are generally good for mundane daily activities. Krittika can be good for fire ceremonies due to its deity, Agni.

The following are auspicious lunar nakshatras for specific activities or events:

*Buying a Home:* Mrigrashira, Punarvasu, Ashlesha, Magha, Purva Phalguni, Vishakha, Mula, and Revati.

*Marriage:* Rohini, Mrigrashira, Uttara Phalguni, Hasta, Swati, Anuradha, Uttara Ashadha, Uttara Bhadrapada, and Revati (the first three padas).

*Installing a Deity or Building a Temple:* Rohini, Mrigrashira, Punarvasu, Pushya, Uttara Phalguni, Hasta, Swati, Uttara Ashadha, and Uttara Bhadrapada.

*Laying the Foundation of a Home:* Rohini, Mrigrashira, Uttara Phalguni, Hasta, Chitra, Jyeshta, Uttara Ashadha, and Shravana.

*Learning Astrology or Astronomy:* Ashwini, Punarvasu, Pushya, Hasta, Swati, Mula, and Revati.

*Learning Music or Dance:* Rohini, Pushya, Purva Phalguni, Hasta, Anuradha, Jyeshta, Uttara Ashadha, Dhanishtha, Shatabhisha, Uttara Bhadrapada, and Revati.

*Planting and Sowing:* Ashwini, Rohini, Pushya, Magha, Uttara Phalguni, Hasta, Chitra, Swati, Anuradha, Mula, Uttara Ashadha, and Revati.

*Medical Treatment:* Ashwini, Rohini, Mrigrashira, Punarvasu, Pushya, Hasta, Chitra, Swati, Anuradha, Uttara Ashadha, Shravana, Dhanishtha, Shatabhisha, Uttara Bhadrapada, and Revati.

*Surgical Treatment:* Ardra, Ashlesha, Jyeshta, Mula (Tuesdays and Saturdays). Mars should be strong and the 8th House unoccupied. Waxing moon, but not a full moon.

*Studying Medicine:* Dhanishtha and Shatabhisha.

*Studying the Vedas or the Shastras:* Pushya, Swati and Shravana.

*Travel or Beginning a Journey:* Ashwini, Mrigrashira, Punarvasu, Pushya, Hasta, Anuradha, Mula, Shravana, Dhanishta, and Revati (Tuesday or Mars day should be avoided if possible).

*Making a Will:* Pushya.

In his book *Muhurtha (Electional Astrology)*, B. V. Raman writes that "the constellation of Pushyami or Pushya (the 8th nakshatra) is the most favorable of all the nakshatras. It is said to neutralize almost all doshas or flaws arising out of a number of adverse combinations. Pushya has the power to overcome negative forces and assert its benefic nature. Despite all its positive influence, Pushya is still considered inauspicious for a marriage ceremony." Raman concludes that Pushya is "a constellation par excellence that can be universally employed for all purposes, excepting of course marriage."

—Dennis M. Harness, Ph.D.

**Sources:**

Behari, Bepin. *Myths and Symbols of Vedic Astrology*. Salt Lake City: Passage Press, 1992.

Harness, Dennis. *The Nakshatras: The Lunar Mansions of Vedic Astrology*. Twin Lakes, WI: Lotus Press, 1999.

Raman, B. V. *Muhurtha (Electional Astrology)*. New Delhi: UBS Publishers, 2001.

Sastri, P. S. *Acharya Varahamihiras Brihat Jataka*. New Delhi: Ranjan Publications, 1995.

## Natal Astrology

Natal astrology is the branch of astrology that deals with the astrological forces that influence individuals at the moment of birth. It is the more contemporary term for what traditional astrologers called genethliacal astrology. Natal astrology is to be distinguished from such other branches of astrology as mundane astrology, which interprets the significance of celestial events for cultural trends and national world affairs.

## Natal Chart (Birth Chart; Nativity)

When most people talk about their astrological chart, they are usually referring to their natal (from the Latin word *natus*, meaning "born") chart. A natal or birth chart is a map of the solar system, with respect to Earth (in traditional, geocentric astrology) at the moment an individual was born. Because the planets and signs are usually represented by symbols (referred to by astrologers as glyphs) rather than by words, a natal chart appears confusing to anyone unfamiliar with astrological codes. To the experienced astrologer, however, a natal chart reveals a great deal about the person for whom it was constructed.

The expression natal chart is used exclusively to refer to the birth chart of an individual. It is thus distinguished from such terms as horoscope and radix, which can refer to the chart of an event or to other nonpersonal phenomena. The natal chart is also distinguished from such secondary charts as progressed charts.

## National Council for Geocosmic Research

National Council for Geocosmic Research, Inc. (NCGR), is a nonprofit (501-C) organization incorporated in Massachusetts in 1971 for the purpose of raising the standards of astrological education and research. Its membership of over 3,000 is mostly from the United States, though international membership is growing. Most members affiliate with NCGR's local chapters; as of April 2003, there were 40 established chapters worldwide in 26 countries. Additionally, several special interest groups (SIGs) cross wide geographical areas to foster dialogue among people of similar astrological specialties. A code of ethics, to which members are accountable, provides guidelines for the practice of astrology. NCGR annually publishes two journals—*Geocosmic Mag-*

*azine* and *NCGR Journal*, as well as six newsletters. Many other publications are produced intermittently.

From its 1979 launch in a seminar at Princeton University attended by delegates from chapters, NCGR developed and implemented a four-level education and testing program leading toward certification for astrologers. The first three levels cover basic techniques of astrology and require survey knowledge of its various specialties. The fourth professional level can be tested in four tracks: consulting, research, instructor, or general studies. Each student who achieves Level 4 is entitled to include "CA NCGR" after his or her name, and is identified in a special certified astrologers section on the organization's web site, www.geocosmic.org. Although NCGR does not require that its members be practicing astrologers, more than 1,000 members have participated in the organization's testing program at Level 1 or above, and momentum is building. The education curriculum and testing program are widely respected for their excellence and rigor. Those who have successfully tested at Level 3 or above may use that towards substantial credit for the technical course work required by Kepler College of Astrological Arts and Sciences, the first accredited liberal arts college in the United States to offer bachelor's and master's degrees in astrology.

To briefly summarize the history of NCGR, seven men and women met in Wareham, Massachusetts, on March 6, 1971, at the home of Harry F. Darling, M.D., who became the organization's first chairman. The official signing of the articles of incorporation took place at 9:02 P.M. The founders included astrologers, medical professionals, scientists, and scholars, all interested in exploring astrology as it related to other disciplines. The name they chose, "geocosmic," sought to avoid the popular misunderstanding of astrology and set the tone for their purpose with a serious and scholarly approach to the study of correspondences between life on earth ("geo") and the cycles of the "cosmos"—in particular, that of our solar system.

The first three elected to head NCGR were medical doctors: Darling, followed by Henry Altenberg, M.D., and Donald Wharton, M.D. In 1980, Neil F. Michelsen, a businessman and pioneer of computer technology for astrologers, became chairman, followed by Robert Hand, prominent astrologer, author, and software developer, and the current chair, Maria Kay Simms, astrologer, author, and businesswoman. The late A. Charles Emerson, a teacher, writer, and astrologer in New York City, who was among NCGR's founders, never served as chairman, but is widely considered to be the "father of NCGR" because of his tireless work to build the organization through its first two decades. Through his efforts, along with that of many astrologers' countless hours of volunteer service, NCGR moved beyond an initial "techie" reputation to welcome and assist members of all levels of expertise who share its goals of continuing education and the promotion of the highest professional and ethical standards for astrologers.

## Native

A native is a person born in a particular place. In astrology, this term refers to the person for whom a natal chart was cast. In the latter sense, it is a useful, concise term that, in any extended discussion, is preferable to "person for whom this chart was cast" or some such other unwieldy expression. The term native can also refer to someone born under a particular sign, as when one says that she or he is a native of Cancer.

## Nativity

Nativity is another term for natal chart, which is a horoscope set up for time, date, and place of birth. Other kinds of horoscopes include progressed charts and electional charts.

## Natural Astrology

Natural astrology is the branch of astrology dealing with the motions of the heavenly bodies and the effects of the planets on such natural phenomena as the weather. The former is now called astronomy, the latter meterological astrology or astrometeorology.

## Natural House (Natural Chart; Natural Ruler)

The signs of the zodiac refer to a person's nature, and astrological houses refer to a person's environment, and there is a natural association between each of the 12 signs and each of the 12 houses (e.g., Aries is associated with the first house, Taurus with the second house, Gemini, with the third house, and so forth). Thus, for example, the fourth sign of the zodiac, Cancer, is associated with the home, while the fourth astrological house is also identified with the home and with property. To take another example, the third sign, Gemini, is a sign of communication, and the third house is associated with, among other things, communication. Such correspondences hold between all the signs and houses.

This correspondence is what is referred to, for example, when it is said that a person with Aries on the ascendant (with the first sign on the beginning or cusp of the first house), and with each succeeding sign on the cusp of each succeeding house, has a natural chart: The signs and houses with "natural" links are found together in the chart. Similarly, when a planet is located in the house associated with the sign it rules, it is said to be in its natural house—a placement in which the planet is said to be in accidental dignity. For example, when Jupiter is found in the ninth house, it is in its natural house (and is accidentally dignified), because Jupiter rules the ninth sign, Sagittarius. To complete this series of related terms, the planets are sometimes said to be the natural rulers of the houses associated with the signs they rule.

**Sources:**

Brau, Jean-Louis, Helen Weaver, and Allan Edmands. *Larousse Encyclopedia of Astrology*. New York: New American Library, 1980.

Fleming-Mitchell, Leslie. *Running Press Glossary of Astrology Terms*. Philadelphia: Running Press, 1977.

## Negus, Ken

Ken Negus was born on December 23, 1927, in Council Bluffs, Iowa. He attended the local public schools there, then attended Princeton University, from which he received his

B.A., M.A., and Ph. D. degrees. He served in the U.S. Army (interrupting his undergraduate years) from 1946 to 1950, mostly in the Signal Corps and in the Army of Occupation in Germany and Austria. In 1954 he received a Fulbright grant for one year of study in Germany, where he attended Tuebingen University and did research for his Ph. D. dissertation. He then served in the German departments of Northwestern, Harvard, Princeton, and Rutgers. From time to time at Rutgers, he served temporarily as department chairman and graduate director of German, but he was mainly a teacher and researcher in German literature of the seventeenth through the nineteenth centuries. His main publications are *E. T. A. Hoffmann's Other World* (1965) and *Grimmelshausen* (1972); as well as numerous articles and book reviews on German literature. He retired from Rutgers in 1986 as full professor. Since the beginning of his career as a teacher of literature, he has been translating German poetry into English, and writing his own in both languages. He has self-published several small volumes of poetry, much of which is astrological.

During the sixties, Negus became interested in astrology, as a result of his research on Grimmelshausen, a seventeenth-century German novelist who was also an astrologer and incorporated much astrological symbolism into his writings. Eventually this sideline of astrology became a major interest in itself. In 1972 he helped to found the Astrological Society of Princeton, NJ, Inc., which at times has grown to a membership of over 100. It is one of the most active astrological organizations in the area, with regular meetings, a faculty that teaches on all levels, a referral service for consulting astrologers, a lending library for members, and a journal. Meanwhile Negus has been practicing astrology extensively, writing about it, delivering lectures on it, and filling various offices in several other astrological organizations. Since his retirement from his university career, astrology has become his main activity.

His publications include writings on astrology and literature, harmonics, Chiron, astrology at the university, the validation of astrology, Johannes Kepler, the Cyclic Index, five volumes of his own astrological and esoteric poetry, and numerous translations of poetry and astrological texts. He maintains a regular practice as an astrologer, specializing in rectification; and as a teacher in the faculty of the Astrological Society of Princeton, NJ. He and his wife, Joan, were married in 1952, and remained so until her death in 1997. They have three children and seven grandchildren.

## Nelson, John

John Nelson was an American radio engineer who specialized in the analysis of shortwave radio propagation. In the 1950s and 1960s, he was an employee of RCA Communications and worked on the problem of how to predict fluctuations in the Earth's magnetic field that disrupted radio communication. It was well known that these fluctuations were affected by, among other things, sunspot activity. Using this clue as a starting point, Nelson began investigating correlations between the heliocentric configurations of the planets and radio wave disturbances. His findings were so remarkable that he was eventually able to predict such disturbances with a better than 93 percent accuracy.

His discoveries verified certain elements of traditional astrology to a remarkable extent. For instance, he found that when two or more planets either lined up with the

Sun (thus forming an opposition aspect of 180°) or formed a 90° angle (a square aspect) with the Sun, there would be a disturbance. He also found, again consistent with the principles of traditional astrology, that if yet another planet formed an exact trine (120° angle) to either of these configurations, the disturbance rapidly abated. Because Nelson could further predict the areas of the world where disturbances would be most severely felt, RCA could reroute transmissions without loss of service.

The astronomical and academic communities greeted his discoveries with a thundering silence. But Richard Head of NASA's Electronics Research Center investigated Nelson's studies and found them to be accurate. NASA was interested in the implications of his research for predicting sunspot activity, so that it would be able to avoid the risk of exposing astronauts to excessive solar radiation. NASA thus came to adopt Nelson's methods, under the name gravitational vectoring.

**Sources:**

Brau, Jean-Louis, Helen Weaver, and Allan Edmands. *Larousse Encyclopedia of Astrology*. New York: New American Library, 1980.

Ostrander, Sheila, and Lynn Schroeder. *Astrological Birth Control*. Englewood Cliffs, NJ: Prentice-Hall, 1972.

## Nemesis

Nemesis, asteroid 128 (the 128th asteroid to be discovered, on November 25, 1872), is approximately 116 kilometers in diameter and has an orbital period of 4.6 years. Nemesis was the ancient goddess of vengeance. According to Martha Lang-Wescott, the position of Nemesis indicates one's own Achilles' heel. She also views this asteroid as indicating one's tendency to attribute fault or blame. Nemesis's key phrase is "source of blame."

**Sources:**

Lang-Wescott, Martha. *Asteroids-Mechanics: Ephemerides II*. Conway, MA: Treehouse Mountain, 1990.

———. *Mechanics of the Future: Asteroids*. Rev. ed. Conway, MA: Treehouse Mountain, 1991.

Schwartz, Jacob. *Asteroid Name Encyclopedia*. St. Paul, MN: Llewellyn Publications, 1995.

## Neopagan Spirituality and Astrology

Astrology can be found in the roots of most religions, if not all, and indeed, astrology may be the oldest of them all, just as astrology's evolution to astrology is among the most ancient of sciences. Stone-age artifacts, including the carving of notches on bones coinciding with lunar phases point to very ancient uses of skywatching to keep track of time, presumably to make it possible to anticipate cyclical change. These, along with other carvings and cave paintings, suggest that ancient humans saw both spiritual and practical use of such observations. They saw spirits—gods—within all of nature, within the lights in the sky, and within animal and plant life of Earth. This idea, that deity is immanent within nature, is central to Paganism.

**An engraving of the goddess Nemesis from *Spiegel Der Sibyllen*, 1685. *Reproduced by permission of Fortean Picture Library.***

Over thousands of years, a dualistic philosophy developed that saw deity as transcendent and inherently superior to nature, which was seen as inferior or evil and in need of redemption. This concept of dualism influenced all of the religions of Abraham: Judaism, Christianity, and Islam. A little over halfway through the 20th century, in part spurred by the women's movement, a revival of the Pagan philosophy of immanence began. Though amorphous, with no central organizational structure and many forms of practice, the movement, generally called Neopagan, is growing rapidly and steadily. Contemporary Neopagan practice takes on many forms: Wicca, Native American, feminist spirituality, eco-spirituality, and "new age," are a few of the names by which it may be identified. Both because it is autonomous and as individual as the solitary people or groups that practice it, many of whom are private or even secretive in their practice, the movement is probably much larger than any official count has ever yielded. Some studies, according to the *Encyclopedia of Modern Witchcraft and Neo-Paganism*, suggest that the count of 750,000 people in the United States is likely a conservative estimate of those involved in Neopagan practice.

Virtually all Neopagans use at least some astrology in their practice because their ceremonies and rituals follow the cycles of correspondence between earth and sky: lunar phases, primarily New Moon and Full Moon, and the seasonal holy days based on the equinoxes, solstices, and their cross-quarters (Sun at 15° of each of the fixed signs: Taurus, Leo, Scorpio, and Aquarius). Conversely, it would not be at all true to say that all astrologers are Neopagans. Astrologers come from a variety of religious or spiritual paths. Just as in the general population, though, growing numbers are interested in Neopagan spiritualities and practice.

Modern astrological thought is influenced by similar concepts as those that have emerged within Neopaganism. This can best be defined by additional explanation of the difference between the dualistic split of spirit and matter at the core of established religion and the immanence within nature of Neopagan thought. When deity is seen not as set apart from Mother Nature and self, but instead is seen within nature, within all living things, and within oneself, there is a sense of oneness, of being part of a great Whole. Stemming from that is a greater sense of personal responsibility.

It may have been be the importance of sky movements for timing that first gave root to the idea that deity is "above," and somehow that which is above is inherently superior to that which is below (Earth and its people). That pattern of dualistic thinking developed within patriarchal religion and it also developed within astrology. The residue remains within astrology in language and thought that assigns the power to the planets, in believing that their movements cause both birth characteristics and current events. On the other hand, modern psychological and spiritual astrology, like Neopagan spirituality, emphasizes the power of choice and self-determination. The power is not "out there" with the planets; it is within.

In seeing the power, or deity within, one must realize that the whole of deity means *all* aspects of being, not just the "good" ones. In this, Neopagan thinking is more akin to Jungian psychology in that one must own one's shadow in order to become whole and gain the full power of free will. One is always free to govern one's own response, even when external events occur beyond personal control.

Astrological philosophy is in a state of transition in this time of paradigm shift throughout many aspects of our culture. During the centuries of development of the worldview that characterized God-above as beyond not only Earth but beyond the lights in the sky, as well, astrology, seen as the worship of those lights became condemned as idolatry. Developments of scientific astronomy, although born to serve the interests of astrology, rejected (in the so-called Age of Enlightenment of the 18th century) astrology's correspondence of the cosmos with life on Earth. The detachment of both religion and science from ancient Pagan acceptance of the energy and divine spirit within all of nature and within self has left many in our contemporary culture hungering for a spiritual center. As contemporary students and practitioners of astrology come to realize that astrology is truly a divine science, retaining a place for mystery and deity within its most careful and scientific explorations and observations, a sense of spirituality grows. Of all spiritual paths, those of Neopagan philosophy are by far the most comfortable with astrological roots.

Within the form of Neopagan practice known as Wicca, a very basic form of astrology is taken for granted. Rituals of worship are timed according to the cycles of the cosmos in correspondence with the monthly and seasonal cycles of life on Earth, and symbolism derived from those correspondences permeates virtually all facets of supporting practice. One may or may not learn an advanced level of astrology, but all learn the basic astrological correspondences for the tools used on altars, the herbs and the oils in various preparations, the times to plant and reap, the days and hours of the planets, the planet and sign correlations with the elements, and so on. Modern Wiccans may characterize lights in the sky as gods—the Moon is commonly seen as Goddess (as is also Mother Earth)—but this is with the realization that they are using an archetypal language to describe aspects of an all-encompassing energy. God/dess, the life force, the energy of the Universe, is within self and within everything. In that, the Neopagan view is supported by modern physics.

Beyond merely knowing of the energy, Wiccan/Neopagan practice includes magick, belief in one's ability to learn to focus the mind, to tap into that energy, build it within, and direct it according to will. (For Wiccans, this means primarily to effect creative change within self. The ethic of harm to none bars intent that manipulates the free will of others.) Most have heard the adage "thoughts are things," and so they can become. The use of the "k" among practitioners differentiates the power to direct energy from stage magic, sleight of hand, or sparkly, magical feelings of romance and wonder. It is in choosing appropriate timing that astrological practice comes closest to an act of magick, and a Neopagan practitioner knowledgeable in astrology may use it to select appropriate times for acts of magick and ritual. Other disciplines stemming from "new age" thought, train the mind in various forms of creative visualization, tapping quite similar abilities as the practitioner of magick, but minus the color and flavor of Wiccan/Neopagan spiritual paths, and often without that taken-for-granted use of astrology.

Wiccan/Neopagan ritual work can be practiced as a form of astrology that has been termed "experiential," the dramatizing or role-playing of astrological themes in order to raise personal awareness of them and effect healing. Experiential astrology emerged as a tool of psychological astrology. In recent years experiential astrology has, for many, taken on a more spiritual tone, as astrologers, who others who have become dissatisfied with establishment religion but yearn for a spiritual center, have found within their own study of correspondences a path to Spirit. In perhaps varying levels of consciousness, they recognize that the experience of ritual can give a whole new spiritual dimension to their work, enriching their understanding of astrology and of themselves.

In Wiccan terminology, the effect of ritual on learning can be explained by the need of "young self" (the subconscious or child within) for an experiential form of learning. Young self is bored by objective reasoning or forms of communication, and learns best through the senses: sight, touch, smell, sound, taste, and through the intangible intuition, of the right brain rather than the rational left. Astro-drama (experiential astrology) recognized this, and for some, it worked, whether it had any spiritual meaning or was just for the fun of acting out—role-playing the planets—and in so doing, learning a little more about their meanings. For others, conservative or shy, overt role-playing is not quite comfortable. Group spiritual ritual based on astrological themes, on the other hand, can be comfortable for most anyone, providing one is not singled out for a "solo" part before he or she is ready, or is not deeply conflicted from background within an establishment religion. Ritually invoking the planetary gods within, as personifications of the various aspects of Spirit that are within the Universe and within each individual can enrich one's understanding of astrology, as well of one's purpose in life.

—Maria Kay Simms

**Sources:**

Rabinovitch, Shelly, and James Lewis. *The Encyclopedia of Modern Witchcraft and Neo-Paganism*. New York: Citadel, 2002.

## Neptune

Neptune is a cold planet located between Uranus and Pluto. Visible only with the aid of a telescope, it is a large, gaseous planet with a turbulent atmosphere consisting of hydrogen, helium, and methane. This violent environment is caused by a storm the size of Earth, called the Great Dark Spot, which circles Neptune every 18.3 hours.

The unusual events surrounding the discovery of Neptune, an astrological symbol for illusion, are quite fitting for this elusive planet. Neptune was first sighted by Galileo in December 1612. Instead of identifying Neptune as a planet, Galileo believed it was a moon of Jupiter and did not research it further. It was not until 1845, more than two centuries later, that a British astronomer and mathematician, John Couch Adams, theorized that the growing discrepancy between the predicted and observed positions of Uranus's orbit was the result of an unknown planetary body. He immediately began to analyze Uranus's deviations using Newton's Mechanics. In September of the same year, Adams presented his calculations for the positions of the hypothetical planet to James Challis, director of Cambridge Observatory. However, Challis refused to examine Adams's work, probably considering the likelihood of a young graduate student solving such a complex matter to be ludicrous. As such, Adams's theory was given neither consideration nor observation time by an observatory until after a similar hypothesis with nearly identical placements for the new planet was published by French astronomer and mathematician Urbain Leverrier.

**An image from the sixteenth century of Neptune, Roman god of the sea, riding a whale. *Reproduced by permission of Fortean Picture Library.***

Leverrier independently began researching the same theory—the possibility of another planet influencing Uranus's orbit—approximately one year after Adams's calculations were complete and turned away by Challis. After submitting his third letter to the Académie des Sciences regarding this breakthrough, Leverrier became frustrated at the disinterest of astronomers to actually observe the heavens for this new planet. In September 1846 Leverrier sent his predictions to a German astronomer and acquaintance, Johann Galle, at the Berlin Observatory. Within a few hours on or about September 24, Galle found Neptune with the aid of detailed star maps not far from Leverrier's predicted position. Despite the initial dispute between authorities in England and France about who would receive credit due for the discovery of Neptune, Adams and Leverrier became friends.

After its discovery in 1846, it was suggested that Neptune be named after the Roman god of the sea. In the early 20th century, this name was confirmed after astronomers learned of Neptune's watery interior. Poseidon, the Greek counterpart of Neptune, who is pictured as a bearded and majestic male holding a trident, was the brother of Zeus (Jupiter) and Hades (Pluto). After defeating their father Cronos (Saturn) in the Trojan War, the brothers divided the world into three parts. Zeus took command of the sky, Hades the underworld, and Poseidon rulership of the sea. Poseidon built a grand palace under the sea, yet spent as much time on land in Olympus as in his palace. This accounts for his importance on dry land as well as the sea. He came to rule not only the oceans and seas that lap at the shore, but also the rivers that moisten the land. Mythology reveals Poseidon as having a violent temper as well as a savage and unpredictable nature. When angered, his rage often displayed itself through storms and earthquakes on land and at sea, making them much feared especially by seafarers. Floods and droughts were also common results of his wrath. Yet, he also brought tranquility and stillness to the waters as he skimmed over the waves on his chariot.

Neptune's correlation with the sea is quite symbolic when working with this planet in the natal chart. His association with the sign of Pisces was made by the poet Manilius in the first century C.E., who believed Neptune, as god of the ocean, most likely had a bond with the sign of the Fish. This connection was adopted by many modern astrologers, who consider Neptune the ruler of Pisces. As a seafaring god, Neptune's role in mythology connects him with all maritime matters and liquids. As such, boats, sailing, fish, sea creatures, bodies of water, fog, and floods all fall under his domain. Psychologically speaking, the sea symbolizes the collective and personal unconscious as well as all that is part of the subtle, intangible side of human existence. Thus, Neptune speaks to the intuitive mind, inspiration and imagination, dreams and psychic receptivity. Yet, the depth of water often distorts vision causing illusion or disillusionment, and bringing states of confusion, escapism, and suffering.

In the birth chart, Neptune indicates the ability to see beyond the finite self and world in order to experience unity with a greater whole. It seeks to dissolve the limitations and boundaries of the physical world by beautifying life or raising it to a higher level through displays of compassion, service, and creative force. This inner desire is often sought through artistic or spiritual experience. These activities allow one to escape the bonds of the mundane reality for a time. Through suffering, the wisdom of Neptune helps to flow through difficulties, leading towards levels of consciousness beyond the ego and providing the capacity to see the unity in all. Hence, Neptune teaches empathy and the highest form of love. Neptune is the higher expression or octave of the planet Venus. Venus symbolizes personal love and harmonization with others, while Neptune represents universal love and unity with the cosmos. Neptune refines and sensitizes everything it touches such that one steps beyond the crudeness and coarseness within and embraces the capacity for unselfish devotion and giving.

Individuals with this planet prominent in their horoscope often feel a need to merge or submerge themselves in a group, even to the point of sacrificing their own interests for a collective belief (such as a religious or political movement). It is also possible such individuals are susceptible to victimization or an attitude of being the victim. Neptunian people are extremely sensitive to others in their environment as well as to other realms. They can be clear channels for information from other planes of consciousness. However, this sensitivity also makes them susceptible to becoming a psychic sponge, absorbing and identifying with everyone else's feelings and suffering.

Boundaries, then, become paramount in working with the energy of Neptune. A true Neptunian feels connected with everything. They are naturally kind and caring towards others and display a great love of animals and all helpless creatures. Often individuals with a strong Neptune care for the problems of others as if they were their own and can get so tangled with others' vibrations that they require some degree of solitude in order to revitalize themselves and separate their thoughts and feelings from those of others. Otherwise, it is quite easy for these individuals to become lost in the clouds, unable to separate reality from illusion. This sensitivity supports Neptune's connection with addiction, alcohol, intoxicants, and hallucinogenic drugs as a means of escaping the difficulties of the world and the fear of connecting or merging with a higher source.

Neptune is also the embodiment of imagination and artistic sensitivity. Its gifts include artistic and musical talents, imagination, inspiration, and visionary abilities. Its artistic capacities include film, photography, dance, and painting. This planet is also associated with mysticism and spiritual enlightenment. Thus, matters of religion connect Neptune with saints, nuns, monks, priests, churches, alters, and other dimensions.

Neptune moves very slowly in the sky, completing an orbit of the Sun every 164.79 years, meaning it stays almost 14 years in each sign of the zodiac. Because of its slow movement, its significance in a zodiacal sign is often considered more generational than individual, describing shifts of ideology within society. However, its house placement in the birth chart shows in what area of life it is easiest to delude one's self or where one has and can make use of intuitive sensitivity and creativity in order to fulfill one's highest ideals. There is often a deep sense of mission and a willingness to sacrifice personal interest, rising above the demands of the ego, for the larger good in the attainment of this ideal. Its placement is also where one is most attuned with the higher realms. Negative manifestations of Neptune can include escapism (including addictions), deception (including self-deception), confusion, depression, guilt, and vagueness. Planets in aspect with Neptune are inclined towards fantasy, dreaminess, and a vulnerable nature, making its expression susceptible to disillusionment.

Neptune's glyph, or symbol, resembles the trident that the god Poseidon or Neptune is often shown holding. The crescent is pointing upwards, indicating spiritual receptivity, and is descending to the cross of mater which it rests upon.

—Tishelle Betterman

**Sources:**

Bloch, Douglas, and Demetra George. *Astrology for Yourself: A Workbook for Personal Transformation*. Oakland, CA: Wingbow Press, 1987.

Burk, Kevin. *Astrology: Understanding the Birth Chart*. St. Paul, MN: Llewellyn Publications, 2001.

Campion, Nicholas. *The Practical Astrologer*. New York: Harry N. Abrams, 1987.

Campion, Nicholas, and Steve Eddy. *The New Astrology: The Art and Science of the Stars*. North Pomfret, VT: Trafalgar Square Publishing, 1999.

George, Llewellyn. *The New A to Z Horoscope Maker and Delineator*. 13th ed. Edited by Marylee Bytheriver. St. Paul, MN: Llewellyn Publications, 1986.

Hamilton, Edith. *Mythology*. New York: Little, Brown, 1942.

McEvers, Joan. *Planets: The Astrological Tools*. Saint Paul, MN: Llewellyn Publications, 1989.

Valentine, Christine. *Images of the Psyche: Exploring the Planets through Psychology and Myth*. Shaftesbury, Dorset, UK: Element Books, 1991.

## NERTHUS

Nerthus, asteroid 601 (the 601st asteroid to be discovered, on June 2, 1906), is approximately 43 kilometers in diameter and has an orbital period of 5.5 years. It is named after a Scandinavian goddess of fertility. When prominent in a natal chart, Nerthus may show an exceptionally productive, "fertile" individual. By sign and house, it may show an area of great potential that need only be "cultivated" a little to produce results.

**Sources:**

Kowal, Charles T. *Asteroids: Their Nature and Utilization*. Chichester, West Sussex, UK: Ellis Horwood Limited, 1988.

Room, Adrian. *Dictionary of Astronomical Names*. London: Routledge, 1988.

Schwartz, Jacob. *Asteroid Name Encyclopedia*. St. Paul, MN: Llewellyn Publications, 1995.

## NEW PLANETS

New planets are Uranus, Neptune, and Pluto, which were not part of traditional astrology.

## NEWSPAPER ASTROLOGY

The simplified astrology found in newspapers, magazines, and other popular publications emphasizes sun signs as well as a rudimentary form of solar astrology. While there are many different influences in every individual's natal chart, the single most important astrological influence on personality is usually the sign of the zodiac the Sun was in at birth. Sun-sign astrology has the advantage of simplicity—a person's birthday is all that must be known to figure out her or his sign—but this simplicity is purchased at the price of ignoring all other astrological influences, and hence is rarely 100 percent accurate.

Solar astrology is a system that is often used when an individual's birth time cannot be determined. Rather than beginning the chart's houses from the ascendant (which cannot be calculated when the birth time is unavailable), a solar chart uses the position of the Sun on the day of birth as the place to begin the first house, and then calculates succeeding houses in equal arcs of 30°. Newspaper astrology further simplifies this system by using the 30° arc of the sun sign as the first house, the next sign in order of the zodiac as the second house, and so forth. In other words, for a Scorpio (i.e., a Scorpio sun sign), all 30° of the sign are regarded as the first house, all 30° of Sagittarius (the next sign of the zodiac after Scorpio) as the second house, all 30° of Capricorn as the third house, and so on.

These highly simplified houses are used to determine the influences of the transiting planets that are generic to each sun sign. As a concrete example, the planet Jupiter embodies a principle that expresses itself variously as multiplicity, expansion, joviality, and good luck. When transiting Jupiter is in Capricorn, it is in the solar third house of all Scorpios. The third house represents travel, relatives, communication, and related matters, so the presence of transiting Jupiter in this area indicates a period of time during which one experiences more trips, as well as more communications,

**A nineteenth-century engraving of Sir Isaac Newton, the great scientist and astronomer. *Reproduced by permission of Fortean Picture Library.***

than usual. Relations with relatives also tend to improve. Capricorn is the solar second house for all Sagittarians. The second house has to do with money and possessions, and the presence of transiting Jupiter here usually corresponds with a period of comparative financial abundance. Capricorn is the solar first house for all Capricorns. The first house is the basic self and the physical body, and transiting Jupiter here tends to make one happier and also corresponds with a period during which Capricorns put on weight. These basic principles can be extended to every sign of the zodiac, which is precisely what newspaper astrologers do.

The exact origin of newspaper astrology is difficult to determine, though it probably originated in popular almanacs. Astrology columns have been abundant in the English-speaking world since at least the early twentieth century. Because newspaper astrology ignores all other astrological influences and is thus a hit-or-miss system that works only occasionally, professional astrologers tend to dislike it inasmuch as its inaccuracy can lead nonastrologers to reject astrology as untrue.

**Sources:**

Bach, Eleanor. *Astrology from A to Z: An Illustrated Source Book*. New York: Philosophical Library, 1990.

Gettings, Fred. *Dictionary of Astrology*. London: Routledge & Kegan Paul, 1985.

## NEWTON, SIR ISAAC

Sir Isaac Newton, the scientist famous for formulating the law of universal gravitation, was born January 5, 1642, in Woolsthorpe, Lincolnshire, England, and died on March 31, 1727, in Kensington, England. He was highly regarded in his time, much as Albert Einstein later was. Newton's study of Johannes Kepler's third law of motion led him to theorize that the gravitational attraction between Earth and the Moon—and, by extension, the gravitational attraction between all bodies—is inversely proportional to the square of the distance between them. This law of universal gravitation was put forth in his *Principia Mathematica* (1687). Newton is credited with many other achievements, such as the invention of calculus.

As a young man studying mathematics, Newton also studied astrology. An often-repeated, though probably apocryphal tale, is that the astronomer Edmond Halley kidded Newton about his interest in astrology. Newton, it is said, defended himself by asserting, "I have studied the subject, Mr. Halley, and you have not." In any event, Newton never recanted his belief in astrology, nor did he ever imply that the new science he and his contemporaries were creating invalidated astrology in any way.

## Night Horoscope

A night horoscope is a horoscope in which the Sun is below the horizon.

## Nike

Nike, asteroid 307 (the 307th asteroid to be discovered, on March 5, 1891), is approximately 58 kilometers in diameter and has an orbital period of 5 years. It is named after the Greek goddess of victory. Nike indicates a fortunate outcome to activities undertaken in matters associated with its sign and house position.

**Sources:**

Kowal, Charles T. *Asteroids: Their Nature and Utilization*. Chichester, West Sussex, UK: Ellis Horwood Limited, 1988.

Room, Adrian. *Dictionary of Astronomical Names*. London: Routledge, 1988.

Schwartz, Jacob. *Asteroid Name Encyclopedia*. St. Paul, MN: Llewellyn Publications, 1995.

## Niobe

Niobe, asteroid 71 (the 71st asteroid to be discovered, on August 13, 1861), is approximately 106 kilometers in diameter and has an orbital period of 4.6 years. There were two mythological Niobes. One was the first mortal woman loved by Zeus. The other was a woman who was inordinately proud of her many children and ridiculed the goddess Leto about her children. In revenge, Leto had all of Niobe's children slain, upon which witnessing, Niobe turned to stone. According to Martha Lang-Wescott, the asteroid Niobe indicates inordinate pride in children, creativity, fertility, or virility, which leads to humbling experiences or sorrow. Niobe's key words are "humility" and "fertility." Jacob Schwartz gives this asteroid's astrological significance as "humbling lessons from a source of pride or creativity."

**Sources:**

Lang-Wescott, Martha. *Asteroids-Mechanics: Ephemerides II*. Conway, MA: Treehouse Mountain, 1990.

———. *Mechanics of the Future: Asteroids*. Rev. ed. Conway, MA: Treehouse Mountain, 1991.

Schwartz, Jacob. *Asteroid Name Encyclopedia*. St. Paul, MN: Llewellyn Publications, 1995.

## Nocturnal

Nocturnal means of or belonging to the night. In classical astrology, particular planets were classified as nocturnal or diurnal, no matter where they were in a horoscope. In contemporary astrology, planets are nocturnal if they are located below the horizon (in houses one through six). Many astrologers believe that planets above the horizon line show their influence more in the public sphere whereas planets below the horizon are more private, but this distinction clearly breaks down when considering planets in such locations as the twelfth house (a largely private house situated above the horizon). The expression nocturnal arc refers to the distance, expressed in degrees and minutes of a circle, that a planet traverses between its setting in the west and its rising in the east. Classical astrology also classified signs as diurnal (the masculine signs) and nocturnal (the feminine signs). Contemporary astrologers no longer use the expression nocturnal sign.

**Sources:**

Bach, Eleanor. *Astrology from A to Z: An Illustrated Source Book*. New York: Philosophical Library, 1990.

Brau, Jean-Louis, Helen Weaver, and Allan Edmands. *Larousse Encyclopedia of Astrology*. New York: New American Library, 1980.

## Nodes of the Planets

Take the orbit of Earth around the Sun, imagine it as a flat plane, and project it outward against the backdrop of the stars. This projection is the ecliptic. Although all the principal planets in the solar system orbit the Sun in *approximately* the same plane, none of their orbital paths lies in *exactly* the same plane. The geocentric (earth-centered) nodes are the points at which the planets cross the ecliptic. The point at which a planet moves northward—with respect to our terrestrial perspective—as it crosses the ecliptic is its north node; correspondingly, the point at which it moves southward is the south node. Traditionally, the only nodes regarded as important were the lunar nodes because these were the points where eclipses occurred.

In heliocentric (Sun-centered) astrology, the nodes are located where the orbits of any two planets cross. While only the lunar nodes are significant in traditional, geocentric astrology, the planetary nodes are major points of reference in heliocentric systems. Some astrologers have also tried to develop interpretations of the geocentric planetary nodes, but these have not caught on, partly because the basic astrological tool required to place these points in a chart—an adequate ephemeris (table of positions)—has not generally been available. However, some of the new computer programs include ephemerides for the nodes. The Solar Fire program produced by Esoteric Technologies, for example, will locate the nodes and even place them in a second ring outside of the primary chart.

**Sources:**

Fitzwalter, Bernard, and Raymond Henry. *Dark Stars: Invisible Focal Points in Astrology*. Wellingborough, Northamptonshire, UK: Aquarian Press, 1988.

Gettings, Fred. *Dictionary of Astrology*. London: Routledge & Kegan Paul, 1985.

## Nonplanets

Nonplanets are everything placed in a horoscope that is not the Sun, Moon, or one of the eight planets (e.g., the part of Fortune, the lunar nodes, etc.).

## NORTHERN SIGNS

The northern signs are the zodiacal signs from Aries to Virgo.

## NOSTRADAMUS

Nostradamus (Latin name of Michel de Nostredame), the famous doctor and astrologer, was born on December 14, 1503, in St. Remy, France. He prophesied the manner of death of Henry II, was a favorite of Catherine de Médicis, and served as physician to Charles IX. Nostradamus's fame derives from the *Centuries*, a book of prophecies set to rhyme that was published in 1555. This book has often been reprinted, and is still being reprinted today. The fame of Nostradamus is such that many people have at least heard of "the prophecies of Nostradamus." He died on July 12, 1566, in Salon, France.

**Early seventeenth-century portrait of Nostradamus, likely more famous today for his prognostications than during his lifetime. *Reproduced by permission of Fortean Picture Library.***

## NOVILE

A novile (also called a nonagon or a nonagen) is a minor aspect of 40°, created by subdividing a circle (360°) into nine equal parts. According to Emma Belle Donath, noviles refer to the activity of "brooding," both physical and mental. Noviles are given an orb of influence of 1–2°.

**Sources:**

Donath, Emma Belle. *Minor Aspects Between Natal Planets*. Tempe, AZ: American Federation of Astrologers, 1981.

## NUMEROLOGY AND ASTROLOGY

Like astrology, numerology interprets character and predicts future conditions. Following the Kabbalah (also spelled Kaballahala, Kabalah, Kabbala, Qabbalah, and other variations), which is a system of Jewish mysticism popular in occult circles, the letters of the alphabet are assigned numerical values. When the letters of a person's name are added together, the resulting number indicates her or his basic character—the numerological equivalent of an astrological sun sign. The numbers making up one's birth date are also added together, providing a second number, which is interpreted in a like manner.

Although modern numerology has been mediated to the contemporary world through the Kabbalahalistic tradition, it is rooted in the number mysticism of Pythagoras (c. 580–500 B.C.E.), the ancient Greek philosopher and mathematician. The gender of the signs originated with the Pythagorean notion that odd numbers were male and even numbers female. This caused the first (Aries), third (Gemini), fifth (Leo), seventh (Libra), ninth (Sagittarius), and eleventh (Aquarius) signs in the zodiac to be classified as masculine, and the signs that came second (Taurus), fourth (Cancer), sixth (Virgo), eighth (Scorpio), tenth (Capricorn), and twelfth (Pisces) as feminine.

In numerology, the planets, including the luminaries (the Sun and the Moon) are used to represent the principles of the different numbers. Different systems of numerology utilize different correlations. In the Kabbalahalistic system, the associations were traditionally as follows: the Sun, 1 or 4; the Moon, 2 or 7; Jupiter, 3; Mercury, 5; Venus, 6; Saturn, 8; and Mars, 9. When the "new" planets were discovered, Count Louis Cheiro Hamon popularized a modified version of this system that assigned the extra numbers associated with the luminaries to Uranus, (4) and Neptune (7).

—Evelyn Dorothy Oliver

**Sources:**

Cheiro Hamon, Count Louis. "Astrology and Numbers." In *The Best of the Illustrated National Astrological Journal*. Richard Wagner, 1978.

Gettings, Fred. *Dictionary of Astrology*. London: Routledge & Kegan Paul, 1985.

Westcott, W. Wynn. *The Occult Power of Numbers*. North Hollywood, CA: Newcastle, 1984. (Originally published 1890.)

## Nymphe

Nymphe, asteroid 875 (the 875th asteroid to be discovered, on May 19, 1917), is approximately 13 kilometers in diameter and has an orbital period of 4.1 years. It is named after the mythological spirits of nature, the nymphs. Nymphe represents an exuberance for the natural world. If prominent in a natal chart (e.g., conjunct the Sun or the ascendant), it may show a person somehow deeply involved with nature.

**Sources:**

Kowal, Charles T. *Asteroids: Their Nature and Utilization*. Chichester, West Sussex, UK: Ellis Horwood Limited, 1988.

Room, Adrian. *Dictionary of Astronomical Names*. London: Routledge, 1988.

Schwartz, Jacob. *Asteroid Name Encyclopedia*. St. Paul, MN: Llewellyn Publications, 1995.

## OCCULTATION

An occultation (from the Latin *occultus*, meaning "to hide") is an eclipse of a star or planet by another heavenly body, particularly by the Moon. Despite its seemingly "exotic" connotation, it is a commonly used term in astronomy as well as in astrology. The astrological importance, if any, of occultations has been hotly debated. Part of what is at issue in this debate is competing theories of celestial influence. If, as one school of thought asserts, astrology works via the mechanism of acausal synchronicity, then occultations should have no influence beyond what one would expect from a simple conjunction. If, however, the celestial bodies influence events on Earth through forces analogous to gravity or electromagnetism, then an occultation should have a measurable effect on the star or planet that has been "occulted," especially when it is being eclipsed by a large body like the Sun. Certain experiments, such as those in which the Kolisko effect has been observed, seem to corroborate the latter view.

**Sources:**

Jansky, Robert Carl. *Interpreting the Eclipses*. San Diego: Astro Computing Services, 1979.

Robinson, J. Hedley, and James Muirden. *Astronomy Data Book*. 2d ed. New York: John Wiley & Sons, 1979.

## OCCULTISM AND ASTROLOGY

In the same way the media seized upon the expression New Age in the late 1980s and transformed it into a term of derision, an earlier wave of media interest in the early 1970s seized upon the word "occult" and succeeded in connecting it with such negative phenomena as black magic. Ever since the media sensationalized the "occult explosion" of the 1970s, occult has come to be associated with images of robed figures conducting arcane rituals for less than socially desirable purposes.

*Occult* comes from a root word meaning "hidden," and it was originally interpreted as denoting a body of esoteric beliefs and practices that were in some sense "hidden" from the average person (e.g., practices and knowledge that remain inaccessible until after an initiation). Alternately, it was sometimes said that practices were occult if they dealt with forces that operated by means that were hidden from ordinary perception (e.g., magic, tarot cards, and astrology). Modern astrology is not occult in the sense of secret initiations, but it is occult in the sense that it deals with "hidden" forces.

In earlier times, when there was a widespread knowledge of the science of the stars beyond sun signs, astrology was a universal symbolic code that contained widely recognized archetypes of general principles, types of humanity, and aspects of the personality. Given the completeness of this code, it was natural that astrological language and symbols would be adopted by the other occult sciences, such as tarot and palmistry. In palmistry, for example, the fingers were named after the planets—Mercury finger, Saturn finger, Jupiter finger, etc.

**Sources:**

Cavendish, Richard. *The Black Arts*. New York: Capricorn Books, 1967.

Lewis, James R., and J. Gordon Melton. "The New Age." *Syzygy: Journal of Alternative Religion and Culture*. Vol. 1, no. 3 (1992): 247–58.

## Occursions

Celestial events, from conjunctions to ingresses, are referred to as occursions.

## Odysseus

Odysseus, asteroid 1,143 (the 1,143d asteroid to be discovered, on January 28, 1930), is approximately 174 kilometers in diameter and has an orbital period of 12 years. Odysseus was named after the hero of Homer's *Odyssey*. J. Lee Lehman associates this asteroid with the ability to view a situation from a fresh perspective, without projecting past experiences onto each new moment. Jacob Schwartz gives Odysseus's astrological significance as "cleverness in solving problems."

**Sources:**

Kowal, Charles T. *Asteroids: Their Nature and Utilization*. Chichester, West Sussex, UK: Ellis Horwood Limited, 1988.

Lehman, J. Lee. *The Ultimate Asteroid Book*. West Chester, PA: Whitford Press, 1988.

Schwartz, Jacob. *Asteroid Name Encyclopedia*. St. Paul, MN: Llewellyn Publications, 1995.

## Old, Walter Gorn (Sepharial)

Walter Gorn Old, a well-known astrologer under his pseudonym Sepharial, was born March 20, 1864, in Handsworth, Warwick, England. He attended King Edward's School at Birmingham. He studied astrology and the Kabbalah (which contains ancient esoteric Jewish teachings) from an early age, and for some years studied medicine and psychology along with occultism. He later studied Oriental languages, including Coptic, Assyrian, Sanskrit, and Chinese.

Sepharial moved to London in 1889. Soon thereafter he was admitted into Madame Helen Blavatsky's "inner group." Sepharial introduced Alan Leo to Theosophy, and Leo remained within the Theosophical fold for the balance of his life. Sepharial, on the other hand, left formal Theosophy at some point between Blavatsky's passing in 1891 and Annie Besant's ascension to presidency of the society in 1907. In contrast with Leo, Sepharial was interested in astrology as a practical science rather than as some esoteric art produced by marrying it to theosophy.

Sepharial retained a strong interest in Kabbalah and numerology along with his astrological interests. He was a significant, widely influential astrologer. His reflections on prenatal astrology inspired E. H. Bailey's theorizing on the prenatal epoch. He died on December 23, 1919, in Hove, East Sussex.

**Sources:**

Holden, James H., and Robert A. Hughes. *Astrological Pioneers of America*. Tempe, Ariz.: American Federation of Astrologers, 1988.
Sepharial. *Eclipses*. London: L. N. Fowler, 1915.
———. *The New Manual of Astrology*. London, 1898.
———. *Prognostic Astronomy*. London: L. N. Fowler, 1901.

## Opposition

An opposition is an aspect of 180° between two points—e.g., between two planets—in an astrological chart. An opposition is a major aspect, regarded as challenging and inharmonious. It is sometimes referred to as the aspect of separation. It is difficult, but not as difficult as a square, partially because a 180° angle carries overtones of a polar relationship. By way of contrast to a square, which tends more to signify inner conflicts, an opposition indicates conflicts between internal and external factors. People with a Mars-Saturn opposition, for example, might regularly attract people into their lives whose impulsive, aggressive behavior (Mars) disrupts their sense of security (Saturn).

**Sources:**

Gettings, Fred. *Dictionary of Astrology*. London: Routledge & Kegan Paul, 1985.
Hand, Robert. *Horoscope Symbols*. Rockport, MA: Para Research, 1981.

## Orb of Influence

Few aspects are ever exact (exact aspects are referred to as partile aspects). For this reason, astrologers speak of the orb—or the orb of influence—within which specific aspects are effective. For a sextile, or 60° angle, for example, many astrologers use a 6° orb in a natal chart, which means that if any two planets are making an angle (with respect to earth as the vertex) anywhere in the 54°–66° range, then they are regarded as making a sextile aspect with each other. The closer an aspect is to being exact, the stronger it is. Major aspects (e.g., conjunctions and squares) are given larger orbs than minor aspects (e.g., quintiles and semisextiles), and the more important heavenly bodies, such as the Sun and the Moon, are thought to have larger orbs of influence than the smaller and more distant celestial bodies. Beyond these general principles, there is much disagreement among astrologers as to specifically how large orbs should be. Some allow, for instance, as much as a 12° orb for major aspects, while others allow only a 6° orb for the same aspects.

**Sources:**

DeVore, Nicholas. *Encyclopedia of Astrology*. New York: Philosophical Library, 1947.

Hand, Robert. *Horoscope Symbols*. Rockport, MA: Para Research, 1981.

## Orbit

An orbit is the path in space that one heavenly body makes in its movement around another heavenly body. The Moon, for example, makes an orbit around Earth, while Earth and the other planets make orbits around the Sun. The technical name for the orbiting body is satellite. The orbited body is called a primary. Because primaries are also in motion, the orbits described by satellites are elliptical rather than circular.

Satellites form stable orbits by counterbalancing two forces—their movement away from the primary and the force of gravity drawing them back toward the primary. In other words, in the absence of gravity a satellite would move in a straight line, which would soon take it away from its primary; in the absence of satellite motion, gravity would draw a satellite and its primary together until they collided.

**Sources:**

Robinson, J. Hedley, and James Muirden. *Astronomy Data Book*. 2d ed. New York: John Wiley & Sons, 1979.

Smoluchowski, Roman. *The Solar System: The Sun, Planets, and Life*. New York: Scientific American Books, 1983.

## Orpheus

Orpheus, asteroid 3,361 (the 3,361st asteroid to be discovered, on April 24, 1982), is approximately 12.2 kilometers in diameter and has an orbital period of 5.3 years. Orpheus was named after a masterful player of the lyre who is best remembered for his attempt to rescue his wife Eurydice from the underworld. According to Martha Lang-Wescott, Orpheus represents haunting, lyrical music, mourning or grief, or a sense of loss or longing for what is past. This asteroid's key words are "loss," "grief," and "sad songs." Jacob Schwartz gives Orpheus's astrological significance as "mourning or loss, grieving for a missed opportunity or missing person."

**Sources:**

Lang-Wescott, Martha. *Asteroids-Mechanics: Ephemerides II*. Conway, MA: Treehouse Mountain, 1990.

———. *Mechanics of the Future: Asteroids*. Rev. ed. Conway, MA: Treehouse Mountain, 1991.

Schwartz, Jacob. *Asteroid Name Encyclopedia*. St. Paul, MN: Llewellyn Publications, 1995.

**An Osirian mummy prepared and laid upon a funeral couch by the jackal Anubis. From *The Dawn of Civilization: Egypt & Chaldea* by G. Maspero, 1894. *Reproduced by permission of Fortean Picture Library.***

## Osiris

Osiris, asteroid 1,923 (the 1,923th asteroid to be discovered, on September 24, 1960), is approximately 7.6 kilometers in diameter and has an orbital period of 3.8 years. Osiris was named after the Egyptian god of death and resurrection. J. Lee Lehman associates this asteroid with androgyny. Jacob Schwartz adds that Osiris is associated with death and resurrection.

**Sources:**

Kowal, Charles T. *Asteroids: Their Nature and Utilization*. Chichester, West Sussex, UK: Ellis Horwood Limited, 1988.

Lehman, J. Lee. *The Ultimate Asteroid Book*. West Chester, PA: Whitford Press, 1988.

Schwartz, Jacob. *Asteroid Name Encyclopedia*. St. Paul, MN: Llewellyn Publications, 1995.

## Ox (Buffalo)

The Ox, or Buffalo, is one of the 12 animals of the Chinese zodiac. It refers to one of the 12 earthly branches, which are used in Chinese astrology, together with the 10 heavenly stems. Such a branch designates one day every 12 days: the days are named according to a sexagesimal (60) cycle, made of 10 series of 12 branches.

Reasonable, conservative, austere, taciturn, and materialistic, the Ox hates superficiality and polite conversation. A formidable worker with a will bordering on stubbornness and unlimited patience, his reasoning powers are amazingly effective, even if he may appear a little slow. His memory is surprising. He can be a leader; he is farsighted, independent, and determined, and he wants power. He is an excellent administrator. He also makes a very good, reliable, and responsible friend. Close to nature, he has a robust health, hearty appetites, and minimal romantic capacities.

—Michele Delemme

## Pales

Pales, asteroid 49 (the 49th asteroid to be discovered, on September 19, 1857), is approximately 176 kilometers in diameter and has an orbital period of 5.4 years. It is named after the Roman god of flocks, pastures, and shepherds. When prominent in a natal chart, Pales may indicate a native with an interest in these matters. More often, it indicates more of a metaphorical shepherding; someone with a strong Pales may be involved in some kind of guarding activity, shepherding a congregation, and so on.

**Sources:**

Kowal, Charles T. *Asteroids: Their Nature and Utilization*. Chichester, West Sussex, UK: Ellis Horwood Limited, 1988.

Room, Adrian. *Dictionary of Astronomical Names*. London: Routledge, 1988.

Schwartz, Jacob. *Asteroid Name Encyclopedia*. St. Paul, MN: Llewellyn Publications, 1995.

## Pallas Athene

The asteroids are small planet-like bodies that orbit the Sun in a belt that lies mostly between Mars and Jupiter. They first dawned on human consciousness in the early 1800s. The first four asteroids to be sighted were given the names of four of the great goddesses of classical antiquity: Ceres (discovered in 1801), Pallas Athene (discovered in 1802), Juno (discovered in 1804), and Vesta (discovered in 1807).

Many more asteroids were soon discovered, so that by the end of the nineteenth century, over 1,000 were known. The first asteroid ephemeris (a table listing planetary positions) was made available to astrologers in 1973 by Eleanor Bach, and it covered only the original four. Today astrologers have computer software developed by Mark Pottenger that tracks the placements of over 9,000 asteroids.

Among the thousands of asteroids known, Ceres, Pallas Athene, Juno, and Vesta have a special place. While these are not necessarily the largest asteroids, they were the first to be discovered, and as such they have imprinted themselves on human consciousness in a significant way. They also complete the female pantheon of goddesses, rounding out the system of symbols begun in the usual 10 planets. Of the six great goddesses of Olympus, only Aphrodite (Venus) and Artemis (the Moon) are represented in the conventional astrological symbol system. The other four great goddesses of Greco-Roman mythology—Demeter (Ceres), Athene (Pallas), Hera (Juno), and Hestia (Vesta)—were missing from astrology until they were reinvoked by their discovery in the early 1800s.

Pallas Athene, the second asteroid to be discovered, was named for the goddess who, instead of being born from the womb, sprang from the head of her father and in her later actions exemplified strengths that are often thought of as masculine. Befittingly, this second asteroid to be discovered represents a second developmental stage in people's lives, when they look to their fathers to provide them with the firmness and independence to leave the home and go forth into the world. This is the time of life when one acquires skills and a sense of competence, and starts to formulate oneself as an independent person. In societies where female children were expected to marry at the earliest possible age, this stage was largely neglected in a woman's development, but it is a stage as important for women as it is for men. For either sex, only when this stage is successfully mastered is one truly ready to embark on the next stage, wherein one becomes a partner in a relationship of equals.

The astrological glyph for Pallas Athene pictures the spear that is carried by the goddess in many depictions. The spear points upward and outward toward the world at large. Like the suit of swords in the Tarot, the spear suggests the intellect, which probes and severs, seeking knowledge, and separating one idea from another to achieve clarity. The glyph also suggests a head upon a body; signifying the goddess's origin, her associations with the intellect, and the movement from the womb center to the head, or from the bottom, or IC, of the horoscope wheel to the top, or midheaven.

Pallas Athene was better known to the Greeks as Athene, the goddess of wisdom. She is said to have sprung full-grown, clad in a suit of gleaming war armor, from the crown of the head of her father, Zeus (Jupiter), and to have immediately taken her place at his right-hand side.

As patroness of Athens, she presided over military strategies during wartime and over justice in peacetime. She also fostered useful arts, including spinning and weaving, pottery, healing, and other areas in which human skill and ingenuity improve the quality of life for all. Another art she fostered was horse taming (an interesting association in light of the interest in horses that many girls have in early adolescence).

Among all the goddesses, the classical Greeks held Pallas Athene in a unique position of power and respect. She walked easily and freely through the world of gods, heroes, and men as their colleague, advisor, equal, and friend.

She was idealized as Athene Parthenia, the virgin warrior queen, and she took neither lovers nor consorts. In the myths, she denied her matriarchal origins, claiming that no mother gave her life, as she arranged for the death of her sister Medusa. In all things except marriage, she upheld male supremacy. The price that was extracted from her was the denial of her femininity. She severed her connection from her mother (Metis), her sisters, the community of women, and her sexuality, and she lost touch with her feminine qualities of sensitivity, softness, and vulnerability.

Pallas Athene is mythologically related to an ancient lineage of goddesses from the Near East, North Africa, and Crete who were associated with the serpent as a symbol of wisdom and healing. She affirmed this connection by placing the head of her dark sister, Medusa, the serpent-haired queen of wisdom, in the center of her breastplate. In the yogic tradition, *kundalini* energy is depicted as a serpent that is coiled at the base of the spine ready to rise through the spinal canal and emerge from the top of the head as cosmic illumination. This has similarities to the wisdom of Pallas Athene, who emerged from the head of Jupiter.

Pallas Athene's association with both the serpent and the taming of horses suggests that her basic theme has to do with civilizing the forces of nature for the benefit of humankind. As a woman, she represents the force of nature that brings new life into being, the raw energy that underlies aliveness. As her father's daughter, she executes his will, using that force for the good of society. Administering justice, she is able to discern the truth amid tumultuous emotions. Healing illness, she diverts the life force back into the proper channels. As a weaver and potter, she uses cleverness and dexterity to turn raw materials into useful objects.

Through the ages, women have been major contributors to these arts of civilization. However, in some eras—such as the one from which we are emerging—many of the civilized arts, including the law, medicine, and manufacturing, were largely taken over by men, while the role of most women was limited to handmaiden and reproducer of the race.

In the current culture, women who are smart, powerful, strong, and accomplished are like Pallas in that they may not be considered "real women." They are often pressured to make a choice between career and creative self-expression on the one hand, and relationship and family on the other. In contemporary society, Pallas Athene can be seen in the high school girl who is applauded for her victory on the debate team, but who is not asked to the prom.

The danger of the Pallas Athene archetype is one of severing the feminine side and encasing the wounds in armor. This may lead one to further her ambitions with a kind of cold, ruthless, calculating, expedient strategy.

In order to be healed, it must be remembered that even though the Greek myths had Athene denying her female origins, they still made her not a god but a goddess, one whose unique strength has its roots in the feminine powers of nature. Her story enlarges the possibilities for women, telling women everywhere that they, too, are free, if they wish, to channel their womanly life-creating Venus energy not only through their procreative powers but also through their intellects. This is the Pallas Athene way of enriching and enhancing life. Pallas Athene, that productive and powerful goddess, shows that women do not have to be men to be effective in the world. As women, they are able to impart a special kind of life-promoting energy to intellectual and professional pursuits.

As Zeus's favorite daughter, the archetypal "daddy's girl," Pallas Athene points to another issue: one's relationships to one's own fathers. In birth charts, Pallas Athene reveals the ways in which one emulates the father, seeks his approval, wants to interact in his world, and gives him power over one's lives. A strong, well-placed Pallas Athene in a woman's chart usually shows a girl who was cultivated by her father and who has learned valuable life skills from him.

As a woman dressed in the garb of a warrior, Pallas Athene speaks to calling up and expressing the masculine within women, and the feminine within men. This movement toward androgyny balances and integrates polarities within the self and brings wholeness through the reclaiming of a contrasexual identity.

Pallas Athene's serpent symbolism also connects her to the healing arts. In one of her guises she was called Hygeia, goddess of miraculous cures. Her armor and shield can be likened to the immune system warding off attacks. She especially represents the power of the mind in curing disease.

In summary, Pallas Athene represents the part of a person who wants to channel creative energy to give birth to mental and artistic progeny, or children of the mind. She represents the capacity for creative wisdom and clear thinking, and speaks to the desire to strive for excellence and accomplishment in a chosen field of expression. The model of the strong, courageous, ingenious, artistically creative, and intelligent woman, Pallas Athene shows how to use one's intelligence to seek truth; how to achieve in practical, mental, or artistic fields; and how to work to attain worldly power.

Insofar as Pallas Athene is the military strategist and the administrator of justice, her placement in the horoscope shows how to apply one's intelligence to warding off attack and preserving balance and integrity in one's body, mind, and social interactions. This is not only a matter of self-defense, it is also a fundamental principle of healing. The placement of Pallas Athene in a chart shows the healing modalities that are likely to work best.

In addition, the placement of Pallas Athene may suggest how to relate to ones' father and to what fathers stand for, and how to incorporate the qualities of the opposite sex into ones' own makeup. It may also suggest what life was like before a career was chosen.

—Demetra George

**Sources:**

Dobyns, Zipporah. *Expanding Astrology's Universe*. San Diego: Astro Computing Services, 1983.

Donath, Emma Belle. *Asteroids in the Birth Chart*. Tempe, AZ: American Federation of Astrologers, 1979.

George, Demetra, with Douglas Bloch. *Asteroid Goddesses: The Mythology, Psychology and Astrology of the Reemerging Feminine*. 2nd ed. San Diego: Astro Computing Services, 1990.

———. *Astrology for Yourself: A Workbook for Personal Transformation*. Berkeley, CA: Wingbow Press, 1987.

Lehman, J. Lee. *The Ultimate Asteroid Book*. West Chester, PA: Whitford Press, 1988.

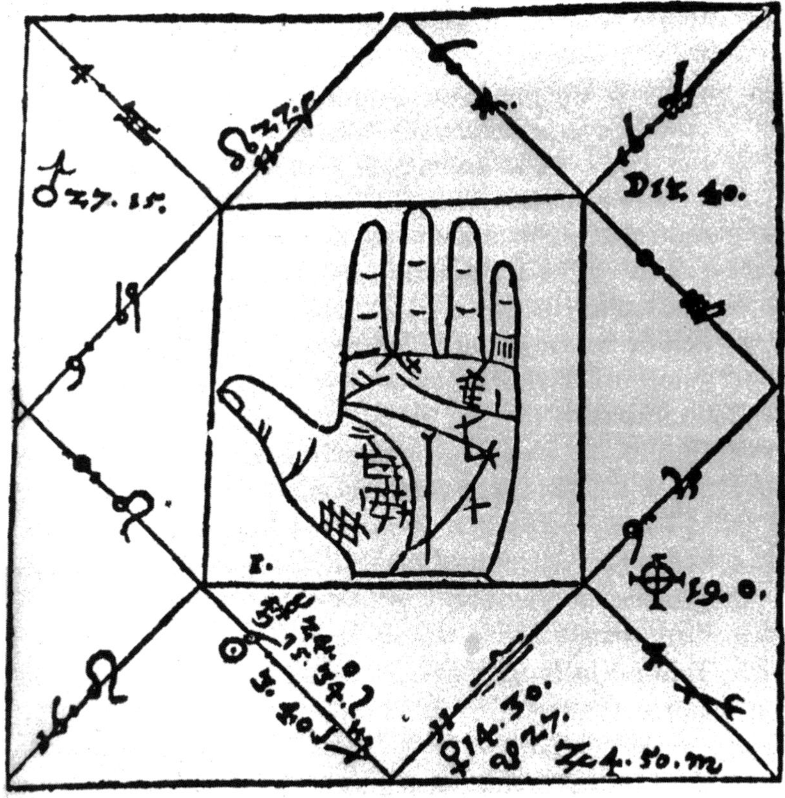

**A diagram depicting the ancient art of palm-reading or handprint analysis.** ***Reproduced by permission of Fortean Picture Library.***

## Palmistry and Astrology (Astropalmistry)

In earlier times when the general populace's knowledge of astrology extended beyond newspaper predictions and sun signs, astrology was more than just the science of the stars. Properly understood, astrology was a universal language or symbolic code that contained widely recognized archetypes of general principles, types of humanity, and aspects of personality. Given the usefulness of this symbolic code, it was natural that astrological language and symbols would be adopted by other occult arts, such as the tarot and palmistry.

In palmistry, the planets, including the luminaries (the Sun and the Moon), were used to name as well as to represent the principles of certain parts of the hand: Mercury, the little finger; the Sun, the ring finger; Saturn, the middle finger; Jupiter, the index finger; Mars, the center of the palm; Venus, the root of the thumb; and the Moon, the lower mound of the hand. Various other lines and areas also bore the names of planets. The classical elements were utilized in certain systems of hand classification, so some palmistry books refer to water hand, earth hand, fire hand, and air hand. As a student of astrology might anticipate, a water hand indicates a sensitive disposition, an air hand indicates an intellectual nature, and so forth. Despite palmistry's wholesale borrowing of astrological terminology, modern astrologers have shown little or no interest in studying correlations between patterns in palms and patterns in astrological charts.

**Sources:**

Gettings, Fred. *The Book of Palmistry*. London: Triune Books, 1974.

Hamon, Louis. *The Cheiro Book of Fate and Fortune: Palmistry, Numerology and Astrology*. New York: Arco Publishing Co., 1971.

## Pandora

Pandora is the name of two distinct celestial bodies: A moon of Saturn and an asteroid. Pandora, the recently discovered (1980) moon in the Saturnian system, is about 55 miles in diameter and orbits Saturn in less than two-thirds of a terrestrial day at an average distance of 88,200 miles. Pandora, asteroid 55 (the 55th asteroid to be discovered, on September 10, 1858), has an orbital period a bit longer than 4½ years, and it is almost 113 kilometers in diameter. Both celestial bodies were named after the mythological Greek woman who released the ills of humanity by opening a box that the gods had sent her but had forbidden her from unsealing. Only the asteroid has been investigated by astrologers.

Pandora is one of the more recent asteroids to be investigated by astrologers. Preliminary material on Pandora can be found in Demetra George and Douglas Bloch's *Astrology for Yourself*, and an ephemeris (table of celestial locations) for Pandora can be found in the second edition of George and Bloch's *Asteroid Goddesses*. Unlike the planets, which are associated with a wide range of phenomena, the smaller asteroids are said to represent a single principle. George and Bloch give Pandora's principle as "curiosity that initiates change." Zipporah Dobyns also associates Pandora with curiosity and has found it prominent in the charts of many astrologers. J. Lee Lehman sees the effect of Pandora as twofold: "to stir a person into doing something, and to produce unintended options of the person." Jacob Schwartz gives this asteroid's significance as "encountering unanticipated ramifications and options of a larger process, caught off-guard, curiosity initiating change."

**Sources:**

Dobyns, Zipporah. *Expanding Astrology's Universe*. San Diego: Astro Computing Services, 1983.

———. *Asteroid Goddesses: The Mythology, Psychology and Astrology of the Reemerging Feminine*. 2d. ed. San Diego: Astro Computing Services, 1990.

George, Demetra, with Douglas Bloch. *Astrology for Yourself: A Workbook for Personal Transformation*. Berkeley, CA: Wingbow Press, 1987.

Lehman, J. Lee. *The Ultimate Asteroid Book*. West Chester, PA: Whitford Press, 1988.

Schwartz, Jacob. *Asteroid Name Encyclopedia*. St. Paul, MN: Llewellyn Publications, 1995.

## Paradise

Paradise, asteroid 2,791 (the 2,791st asteroid to be discovered, on February 13, 1977), is approximately 20 kilometers in diameter and has an orbital period of 3.7 years. Par-

An illustration of Pandora and her box by Arthur Rackman. From A *Wonder Book* by Nathaniel Hawthorne. *Reproduced by permission of Fortean Picture Library.*

adise is a concept asteroid, named after the Garden of Eden. J. Lee Lehman asserts that if this asteroid is well-aspected in a natal chart, the native believes paradise can be found in this existence. If, however, "the asteroid is poorly aspect, then the person is less than optimistic that Paradise exists outside of the movies." Jacob Schwartz gives Paradise's astrological significance as "beliefs in perfection."

**Sources:**

Kowal, Charles T. *Asteroids: Their Nature and Utilization*. Chichester, West Sussex, UK: Ellis Horwood Limited, 1988.

Lehman, J. Lee. *The Ultimate Asteroid Book*. West Chester, PA: Whitford Press, 1988.

Schwartz, Jacob. *Asteroid Name Encyclopedia*. St. Paul, MN: Llewellyn Publications, 1995.

## PARALLEL

The orbits of most of the planets in the solar system lie in approximately the same geometric plane, which is why an astrological chart using only a two-dimensional representation rather than one with three dimensions is drawn. There is, nevertheless, a variation in the tilt or angle of these orbits, so at any given time most of the planets are either north or south of the celestial equator (the plane described by projecting Earth's equator against the background of the stars). This variation is measured in degrees of declination. Two planets are parallel when they are on the same side of the celestial equator and have the same degree of declination. Planets with the same declination are said to have a relationship similar to a conjunction.

## PARAN (PARANATELLON)

A paran (from the same family of words as parallel) is said to occur when two planets cross an angle (whether the same or different angles) at the same time. The notion of parantellon goes back to Ptolemy; it was revived by Robert Hand, who abbreviated its designation to paran. The concept is infrequently employed in modern astrology, although contemporary chart-casting programs can usually calculate it.

## PARSIFAL

Parsifal, asteroid 2,095 (the 2,095th asteroid to be discovered, on September 24, 1960), is approximately 10 kilometers in diameter and has an orbital period of 4.3 years. Parsifal was named after the hero of Chrétien de Troyes's novel *Perceval*. J. Lee Lehman associates this asteroid with the quest for knighthood, as well as with compassion. Jacob Schwartz gives Parsifal's significance as "compassion learned through suffering; those avoiding the learning inflict suffering on others."

**Sources:**

Kowal, Charles T. *Asteroids: Their Nature and Utilization*. Chichester, West Sussex, UK: Ellis Horwood Limited, 1988.

Lehman, J. Lee. *The Ultimate Asteroid Book*. West Chester, PA: Whitford Press, 1988.

Schwartz, Jacob. *Asteroid Name Encyclopedia*. St. Paul, MN: Llewellyn Publications, 1995.

## Part of Fortune

The part of fortune, an imaginary point in an astrological chart, can be determined in two different ways. The first way is to measure the angular distance between the Sun and the Moon, and then find the point in the chart where the Moon would fall if—keeping the angular distance constant—the Sun were to be moved to the ascendant (the sign and degree of the zodiac on the eastern horizon at the moment of birth). The point where the Moon would then fall is the part of fortune. To clarify this with a concrete example, if in a given natal chart the Sun is at 10° Aries and the Moon at 20° Taurus (Aries and Taurus are successive signs), then the Sun-Moon angle (i.e., the angular distance between the Sun and Moon) is 40°. In this same chart the ascendant is located at 5° Libra. If the chart is then imaginarily rotated until the Sun is at 5° Libra, the Moon would be at 15° Scorpio (40° away from 5° Libra). Thus, the part of fortune would be located at 15° Scorpio. This method of locating the part of fortune is actually a simplification of the older method for finding this part.

In the more traditional approach, the above example is correct for daytime births (i.e., for when the Sun is above the horizon). For nighttime births, however, one imaginarily rotates the chart until the Moon rather than the Sun is on the ascendant. Where the Sun then falls is then where one locates the part of fortune. For example, re-envision the above example with the ascendant at 15° Libra. Whereas in the first example the Sun was just above the horizon, in this new example the Sun is just below the horizon. The angular distance between the Sun and the Moon is still 40°, but the part of fortune is now 40° above rather than 40° below the ascendant. Thus in the second chart, the part is located at 5° Virgo.

The house and sign placement of the part of fortune indicate, as the name intimates, good fortune. The placements also indicate areas and activities in which the native finds enjoyment. The part of fortune is but one member of a system of points referred to as the Arabian parts, but which in fact antedates the flowering of Arabic astrology (the part of fortune as well as the other parts were utilized in the pre-Islamic Mediterranean world). Western astrologers, impressed by the compendium of parts written by the great Muslim scholar Al-Biruni, called them the Arabic parts, and the name stuck. The many other parts discussed by Al-Biruni—death, children, commerce, and so forth, which are calculated by measuring the angular distance between various planets and placing one planet or the other on the ascendant or on another house cusp—are rarely used by contemporary astrologers. The part of fortune, however, is utilized by most modern astrologers. Many chart-casting programs can calculate the other parts in an instant, making experimentation with them relatively easy. Thus, a revival of the whole system in the not-too-distant future is possible.

**Sources:**
DeVore, Nicholas. *Encyclopedia of Astrology*. New York: Philosophical Library, 1947.
Granite, Robert Hurzt. *The Fortunes of Astrology*. San Diego: Astro Computing Services, 1980.

## Partile

The astrological aspects—the angles between the planets, such as squares and trines—do not have to be exact (e.g., exactly 90° [square] or exactly 120° [trine]) to be counted as having an influence. (On the basis of the particular aspect and planets involved, astrologers allow aspects a larger or smaller orb of influence, within which they are regarded as having an effect.) Exact aspects are referred to as partile aspects and are considered to have a stronger influence than platic (nonexact) aspects.

## Partridge, John

John Partridge, born January 18, 1643, in East Sheen, London, England, was an influential astrologer and producer of almanacs. Apprenticed to a shoemaker, he acquired enough books to teach himself Greek, Latin, and Hebrew. He may have studied with the astrologer John Gadbury and seems to have given up making shoes when his first publication was issued about 1678. Partridge's first major work, *Mikropanastron*, was published the next year. In 1680, he started issuing an almanac entitled *Merlinus Liberatus*. He left England for political reasons in 1685 and studied medicine in Leyden, Holland, for the next four years. Partridge returned to his native country after receiving his medical degree and married a well-to-do widow. He also resumed his astrological publishing activities.

Partridge came to prefer the Placidian house system, a choice evident in his final major works, including the *Opus Reformatum* (1693) and the *Defectio Geniturarum* (1697), both highly technical analyses of primary directions in sample horoscopes. By 1700, he was the most prominent astrologer in Britain. His almanac was so popular that other people began to publish almanacs in his name.

Partridge is best remembered for his role in promoting the Placidian system and for an incident involving the famous author and social critic Jonathan Swift (1667–1745). Under the pseudonym Isaac Bickerstaff, Swift published a bogus almanac containing a prediction of Partridge's death on March 29, 1708. Swift issued another small tract on March 30, 1708, in which he, as Bickerstaff, claimed that his prediction was correct and gave the particulars of Partridge's supposed death. The trick was believed, and Partridge had difficulty convincing others that he was still alive. He curtailed his almanac for the next four years. When it was reissued, he included some pointed reflections on Swift's character. Partridge died on June 24, 1715, in Mortlake, London.

**Sources:**

Holden, James H., and Robert A. Hughes. Astrological Pioneers of America. Tempe, AZ: American Federation of Astrologers, 1988.

Partridge, John. *Defectio genitvrarvm*. London: B. Tooke, 1697.

———. *Mikropanastron, or an Astrological Vade Mecum*.... London, 1679.

———. *Nebulo Anglicanus, or the First Part of the Black Life of John Gadbury*.... London, 1693.

———. *Opus Reformatum, or a Treatise of Astrology in which the Common Errors of That Art are Modestly Exposed and Rejected*.... London, 1693.

## Patientia

Patientia, asteroid 451 (the 451st asteroid to be discovered, on December 4, 1899), is approximately 280 kilometers in diameter and has an orbital period of 5.4 years. Its name is a personified form of the word patience. In a natal chart, Patientia's location by sign and house indicates where and how one is most likely to be patient. When afflicted by inharmonious aspects, Patientia may show impatience or a pattern of being forced to wait for results. If prominent in a chart (e.g., conjunct the Sun or the ascendant), it may signify an exceptionally patient person or an individual for whom the cultivation of patience is a life goal.

**Sources:**

Kowal, Charles T. *Asteroids: Their Nature and Utilization*. Chichester, West Sussex, UK: Ellis Horwood Limited, 1988.

Room, Adrian. *Dictionary of Astronomical Names*. London: Routledge, 1988.

Schwartz, Jacob. *Asteroid Name Encyclopedia*. St. Paul, MN: Llewellyn Publications, 1995.

## Pax

Pax, asteroid 679 (the 679th asteroid to be discovered, on January 28, 1909), is approximately 72 kilometers in diameter and has an orbital period of 4 years. Its name means peace, and Jacob Schwartz gives this asteroid's astrological significance as "peace." In a natal chart, Pax's location by sign and house indicates where and how one is most likely to experience or seek peace, especially in the sense of outward tranquility. When afflicted by inharmonious aspects, Pax may show conflict or the seeking of peace in situations where a tranquil response is inappropriate. If prominent in a chart (e.g., conjunct the Sun or the ascendant), it may indicate an exceptionally tranquil person or an individual who seeks to create peaceful circumstances.

**Sources:**

Kowal, Charles T. *Asteroids: Their Nature and Utilization*. Chichester, West Sussex, UK: Ellis Horwood Limited, 1988.

Room, Adrian. *Dictionary of Astronomical Names*. London: Routledge, 1988.

Schwartz, Jacob. *Asteroid Name Encyclopedia*. St. Paul, MN: Llewellyn Publications, 1995.

## Pecker

Pecker, asteroid 1,629 (the 1,629th asteroid to be discovered, on February 28, 1952), is approximately 7.6 kilometers in diameter and has on orbital period of 3.3 years. J. Lee Lehman associates Pecker with sex-murder victims and perpetrators.

**Sources:**

Kowal, Charles T. *Asteroids: Their Nature and Utilization*. Chichester, West Sussex, UK: Ellis Horwood Limited, 1988.

Lehman, J. Lee. *The Ultimate Asteroid Book*. West Chester, PA: Whitford Press, 1988.

Schwartz, Jacob. *Asteroid Name Encyclopedia*. St. Paul, MN: Llewellyn Publications, 1995.

## Peregrine

A peregrine (foreign) planet is one so situated as to be neither dignified nor exalted, and simultaneously not in aspect with any other planet. A planet so situated in a natal chart indicates a part of the psyche that seems to operate independently from the rest of the native's personality, and that the native must therefore make a special effort to integrate. The term is seldom used today, except in horary astrology.

## PERIGEE

Every orbit is elliptical. When a satellite is closest to Earth, it is at its perigee (from the Greek *peri*, meaning "near," and *gaia*, meaning "earth").

## PERIHELION

Although they approximate circles, every orbit is elliptical. The point in a satellite's orbit when it is nearest the Sun is called its perihelion (from the Greek *peri*, meaning "near" and *helios*, meaning "sun").

## PERIODICAL LUNATION

Periodical lunation refers to the chart cast for the moment the Moon returns to the exact degree it occupied at birth. It is used for monthly forecasts.

## PERRY, GLENN

Glenn Perry is a contemporary astrologer who started working professionally in 1974. After a brief stint giving traditional "readings," he felt that he was not sufficiently trained as a counselor to provide the kind of help that many of his clients needed. So in 1975 he began graduate work in psychology at Lone Mountain College in San Francisco. During the next five years, he studied under Richard Idemon, who was well known for his integration of astrology and Jungian psychology.

Perry graduated from Lone Mountain College with a master's degree in marriage and family therapy in 1978. His thesis was titled *Inside Astrology: A Psychological Perspective*, a substantial portion of which was devoted to correlating Jungian/humanistic ideas and astrology. After some years as a teacher and therapist, he went back to school in 1981 at Saybrook Institute in San Francisco and graduated with a Ph.D. in psychology in 1991.

In addition to private practice, Perry lectures and conducts workshops throughout the world on the application of astrology to the fields of counseling and psychotherapy. He was featured on the A&E television program *The Unexplained* as a spokesperson for the application of astrology in the mental health professions. Perry has written four books, including *Essays in Psychological Astrology*, and has been an adjunct professor at the California Institute of Integral Studies in San Francisco where he taught astrology to graduate students in psychology. Additionally, he has been employed as a clinical evaluator at Antioch College, Union College, and Goddard College for students integrating astrology into their course work.

In 1987, Perry founded the Association for Astrological Psychology (AAP), a professional organization for astrologers, psychologists, and counselors who are interested in using astrology as a diagnostic tool in therapeutic work with clients. In addition to serving as president of AAP and editing its official publication, *The Journal of AstroPsychology*, Perry served as vice president of the International Society of Astrological Research (ISAR) and has been a board member of the United Astrology Conference (UAC).

## Persephone

Persephone is one of the names given to the hypothetical planet orbiting the Sun beyond Pluto. Peresephone, asteroid 399 (the 399th asteroid to be discovered, on February 23, 1895), is approximately 55 kilometers in diameter and has an orbital period of 5.3 years. Persephone was named after the daughter of Demeter, who was kidnapped by Hades and taken to the underworld to become his queen. According to Martha Lang-Wescott, Persephone represents "separation anxiety; attitudes toward making transitions (that take one away from familiar people and circumstances); experience of feeling separate from family/others." This asteroid's key word is "separation." J. Lee Lehman notes that the location of Persephone may indicate an area where skills are undeveloped. The less pleasant side of this asteroid is that it may indicate where one is an innocent yet willing victim.

**Sources:**

Lang-Wescott, Martha. *Asteroids-Mechanics: Ephemerides II*. Conway, MA: Treehouse Mountain, 1990.

———. *Mechanics of the Future: Asteroids*. Rev. ed. Conway, MA: Treehouse Mountain, 1991.

Lehman, J. Lee. *The Ultimate Asteroid Book*. West Chester, PA: Whitford Press, 1988.

Schwartz, Jacob. *Asteroid Name Encyclopedia*. St. Paul, MN: Llewellyn Publications, 1995.

## Perseverantia

Perseverantia, asteroid 975 (the 975th asteroid to be discovered, on March 27, 1922), is approximately 24 kilometers in diameter and has an orbital period of 4.8 years. Its name is a personification of perseverance. In a natal chart, Perseverantia's location by sign and house indicates where and how one is most likely to be persevering. When afflicted by inharmonious aspects, Perseverantia can show lack of perseverance or a pattern of persevering in situations one should abandon. If prominent in a chart (e.g., conjunct the Sun or the ascendant), it may suggest an exceptionally persevering person or an individual for whom cultivating perseverance is a life goal.

**Sources:**

Kowal, Charles T. *Asteroids: Their Nature and Utilization*. Chichester, West Sussex, UK: Ellis Horwood Limited, 1988.

Room, Adrian. *Dictionary of Astronomical Names*. London: Routledge, 1988.

Schwartz, Jacob. *Asteroid Name Encyclopedia*. St. Paul, MN: Llewellyn Publications, 1995.

## PERSONAL NAME ASTEROIDS

An asteroid is one of thousands of small planets, 95 percent of whose orbits lie between the orbits of Mars and Jupiter. Initially these were given mythological names, but as telescopes increased in strength and more asteroids were discovered, astronomers began naming them after places and people. The various astrologers who have studied the influence of asteroids have reached a consensus, which is, as noted in J. Lee Lehman's *The Ultimate Asteroid Book*, that "asteroids have astrological effects which may be studied," and the "name of an asteroid has astrological significance."

The essential clue with which one begins this type of research is the name of the asteroid, which gives preliminary insight into the asteroid's astrological "temperament." The early asteroids studied by astrologers were named after mythological figures, and an exploration of the relevant myths provided a preliminary clue to the nature of these tiny planets' influence. When researchers began shifting from explicitly mythological asteroids and started examining asteroids with common names like Barry and Patricia, they continued to follow their previous line of exploration by finding initial clues in certain specialized reference works that provided etymologies for common names. Patricia, for example, is derived from the Latin *patricius*, meaning "noble one," which provides "nobility" as an initial clue to the influence of the asteroid.

Astrologers also found that individuals have a special relationship with the asteroid bearing their name. Thus, the natal location of the appropriate personal name asteroid will show something about the character of the individual, and the transits of the same asteroid will give indications about current influences.

**Sources:**

Lehman, J. Lee. *The Ultimate Asteroid Book*. West Chester, PA: Whitford Press, 1988.

Press, Nona Gwynn. *Personal Name Asteroids*. San Diego: Astro Computing Services, 1987.

Schwartz, Jacob. *Asteroid Name Encyclopedia*. St. Paul, MN: Llewellyn Publications, 1995.

## PHILAGORIA

Philagoria, asteroid 274 (the 274th asteroid to be discovered, on April 3, 1888), is approximately 36 kilometers in diameter and has an orbital period of 5.3 years. Its name means fond of assembly in Greek. When prominent in an astrological chart, it may indicate, as the name suggests, an individual who is fond of gatherings of all sorts. The sign and house position offer greater specificity as to where and how the native enjoys assemblies.

**Sources:**

Kowal, Charles T. *Asteroids: Their Nature and Utilization*. Chichester, West Sussex, UK: Ellis Horwood Limited, 1988.

Room, Adrian. *Dictionary of Astronomical Names*. London: Routledge, 1988.

Schwartz, Jacob. *Asteroid Name Encyclopedia*. St. Paul, MN: Llewellyn Publications, 1995.

## Philia

Philia, asteroid 280 (the 280th asteroid to be discovered, on October 29, 1888), is approximately 26 kilometers in diameter and has an orbital period of 5.0 years. Its name is a personification of a Greek word for love. The Greeks distinguished Philia love from Eros love, identifying Philia more with friendship than romance. When prominent in an natal chart, this asteroid indicates a friendly personality. The sign and house position indicates both how one interacts with friends as well as what the friends are like.

**Sources:**

Kowal, Charles T. *Asteroids: Their Nature and Utilization*. Chichester, West Sussex, UK: Ellis Horwood Limited, 1988.
Room, Adrian. *Dictionary of Astronomical Names*. London: Routledge, 1988.
Schwartz, Jacob. *Asteroid Name Encyclopedia*. St. Paul, MN: Llewellyn Publications, 1995.

## Philosophia

Philosophia, asteroid 227 (the 227th asteroid to be discovered, on August 12, 1882), is approximately 60 kilometers in diameter and has an orbital period of 5.6 years. Philosophia is named after *philosophy* (literally, the "love of wisdom"). If other elements of a natal chart concur, this asteroid indicates wisdom or a "philosophical attitude" with respect to the matters indicated by Philosophia's sign and house position.

**Sources:**

Kowal, Charles T. *Asteroids: Their Nature and Utilization*. Chichester, West Sussex, UK: Ellis Horwood Limited, 1988.
Room, Adrian. *Dictionary of Astronomical Names*. London: Routledge, 1988.
Schwartz, Jacob. *Asteroid Name Encyclopedia*. St. Paul, MN: Llewellyn Publications, 1995.

## Phlegmatic

Phlegmatic is the traditional name for the personality temperament indicated by an excess of the element water.

## Phobos and Deimos (Moons of Mars)

The planet Mars is circled by two small, irregularly shaped moons, Phobos and Deimos. Phobos, with dimensions of 17 x 14 x 13 miles, orbits Mars every 7.7 hours in a circular path that never carries it more than 3,720 miles away from its primary (the celestial body around which a satellite orbits). Deimos, which is 10 x 7 x 6 miles, orbits Mars every 30.3 hours, traveling approximately 12,470 miles above the surface. These distances represent the inner and outer extremes for bodies orbiting a planet the size of Mars (i.e., if Phobos were a little closer, it would crash into its primary; if Deimos were a little more distant, it would escape the Martian field of gravity altogether). As in most planetary moon systems, the orbital paths of the Martian moons align with their parent body's equator.

Astronomers speculate that Phobos and Deimos may once have been asteroids (perhaps one asteroid that later split apart into two) that wandered close to Mars and were captured by the planet's gravitational field. Whether or not these satellites are former asteroids, the asteroid connection provides the link between current astrological research and planetary moon studies: Given the growing astrological acceptance of asteroids, many of which are smaller and farther away than the Martian moons, it is only natural that astrologers begin considering the influence of Phobos and Deimos (not to mention the influence of the moons of the other planets).

The moons of Mars constitute a useful starting place for planetary moon studies for three reasons:

1. Mars is the closest planet with moons.
2. The principle indicated by *phobos* (fear; the source of the term "phobia") and *deimos* (panic or terror) is comparatively straightforward and clearly represents the polar opposite principle of Martian assertiveness or courage (other planet-moon relationships are more complex).
3. The moons of Mars have attracted the imagination of human beings more than the moons of the other planets (with the exception, of course, of Earth's moon), indicating that their astrological significance should be more easily retrieved from the collective unconscious.

With respect to the last reason, it is interesting to note that, a century and a half prior to Asaph Hall's discovery of Phobos and Deimos in 1877, Jonathan Swift's fictional hero Lemuel Gulliver found that the Laputans had discovered two Martian moons. Also, later in the eighteenth century, Voltaire wrote about a visitor from Sirius who mentioned the two as-yet-undiscovered moons of Mars. Both Swift and Voltaire based their speculations on the work of Johannes Kepler, who as early as 1610 hypothesized that Mars was circled by two moons. Mars itself has also figured prominently in imaginative literature, having often served as the backdrop for stories of "martial" bravery (e.g., Edgar Rice Burroughs's series of Martian novels featuring the brave and noble John Carter), as well as the home world of fearful and terrifying monsters who invaded Earth (the most well known of which are the Martians in H. G. Wells's *The War of the Worlds*). Although both these subgenres draw on the Mars archetype (war), the latter also draws on what might be referred to as the Phobos-Deimos archetype (fear-panic).

Hall named the Martian moons after the sons of Ares (Aries), who was the Greek equivalent of Mars, the Roman god of war. Phobos and Deimos have no mythological tales of their own. Rather, they are simply mentioned in the context of other myths, where they serve as their father's chariot drivers. Developed myths are not necessary, however, to decipher the meaning of these "brother" moons; unlike the names of many other celestial bodies, Fear and Panic are self-explanatory. Similarly, it takes little reflection to see why they should be associated with Mars: As a psychological principle, Mars represents outgoing energy, assertiveness, courage, and aggression. This planet's placement in a natal chart indicates how, and in what area of life, this principle is expressed most readily. What is not usually mentioned, however, is that where one most tends to express one's self in acts of courage and aggression is also where fear occurs the most. Courage, especially, makes no sense by itself; courage is always courage that overcomes fears, and acts in spite of them.

The significance of Phobos and Deimos for astrology is that astrologers have traditionally associated fears with Saturn (sometimes with Neptune) and cast that planet in a role that belongs to Mars's sons. Psychologically, Saturn represents the principle of security-seeking, and its polar opposite principle, which manifests in the sign and house occupied by Saturn, is insecurity—not fear. Although these two emotions (insecurity and fear) are clearly related, it should also be evident that they are not identical. With this distinction in mind, psychologically inclined astrologers (and astrologically inclined psychologists) can more precisely analyze their clients' anxieties.

This utilization of the Martian moons—delineating fears in terms of the sign and house position of Mars (the position where Phobos and Deimos will also be found)—is fairly straightforward. However, Phobos and Deimos are in constant motion around their parent body, and the constantly changing dynamic of their orbits introduces variations that merit further research. For example, with respect to the geocentric (Earth-centered) perspective, it appears that Phobos and Deimos move forward with Mars half the time and in the opposite (retrograde) direction as the other half. Recent astronomical ephemerides include information from which this alternation can be calculated. It should thus be possible to research the variation that retrograde motion introduces into the astrological influence of the Martian moons.

Also, following the lead of practitioners of heliocentric astrology (the branch of astrology that casts Sun-centered charts, even for individuals born on Earth), investigators should be able to cast areocentric (Mars-centered) charts for the positions of Phobos and Deimos and obtain a more complex delineation of our fears. Perhaps these areocentric positions can even be placed in a geocentric natal chart, as the geo-helio approach does with heliocentric planets. These are just a few lines of potential research.

**Sources:**

Lewis, James R. *Martian Astrology*. Goleta, CA: Jupiter's Ink, 1992.

McEvers, Joan, ed. *Planets: The Astrological Tools*. Saint Paul, MN: Llewellyn Publications, 1989.

Room, Adrian. *Dictionary of Astronomical Names*. London: Routledge, 1988.

Wilford, John Nobel. *Mars Beckons: The Mysteries, the Challenges, the Expectations of Our Next Great Adventure in Space*. New York: Vintage, 1991.

## Photographica

Photographica, asteroid 443 (the 443d asteroid to be discovered, on February 17, 1899), is approximately 32 kilometers in diameter and has an orbital period of 3.3 years. The name derives from a new approach to discovering asteroids with a camera. When prominent in a natal chart, Photographica may indicate interest or skill in photographic representation as well as in other media of visual representation.

**Sources:**

Kowal, Charles T. *Asteroids: Their Nature and Utilization*. Chichester, West Sussex, UK: Ellis Horwood Limited, 1988.

Room, Adrian. *Dictionary of Astronomical Names*. London: Routledge, 1988.
Schwartz, Jacob. *Asteroid Name Encyclopedia*. St. Paul, MN: Llewellyn Publications, 1995.

## Pig (Boar)

The Pig is one of the 12 animals of the Chinese zodiac. It refers to one of the 12 earthly branches that are used in Chinese astrology, together with the 10 heavenly stems. Such a branch designates one day every 12 days: the days are named according to a sexagesimal (60) cycle, made of 10 series of 12 branches.

Kind, affectionate, scrupulous, courteous, and without problems, the Pig is a nice person—too nice, perhaps, for he may get on people's nerves. On the other hand, this generous and peaceful person may prove to be too innocent. Fortunately, he has a lot of luck. He often is a cultured intellectual and he enjoys food. He likes nature and solitude.

—Michele Delemme

## Pisces

Pisces, the twelfth and last sign of the zodiac, is a mutable water sign. It is a negative (in the value-neutral sense of being negatively charged) feminine sign, ruled by the planet Neptune (in traditional astrology it was ruled by Jupiter). Its symbol is the fish (two fish moving in opposite directions, tied together by a rope or, in other versions, by their tails); its glyph is said to be a stylized representation of this symbol. It takes its name from the plural of the Latin word for fish. Pisces is associated with the feet, and individuals with a Pisces sun sign are susceptible to athlete's foot and other foot problems. The key phrase for Pisces is "I believe."

The mythology of Pisces is complex. The image is usually said to represent Aphrodite, the goddess of love, and her son Eros, the god of erotic attraction, who held hands and turned themselves into fish as they jumped into the water to escape a conflict. Both these divinities are the subjects of lengthy mythologies. The fish symbol is similarly complex, with rich associations in Hindu, Buddhist, Christian, Norse, and Sumerian mythologies; it is often a goddess symbol. In classical mythology, fish were sacred to Venus (Aphrodite) and Neptune (Poseidon).

The symbols for the other two water signs are associated with water, but are in a certain sense only "part" watery: Cancer is a crab, sticking close to the shoreline, while one of Scorpio's symbols is the snake, a creature having earth as well as water associations. A fish, however, is a purely marine creature, indicating that Pisceans are more at home in the subtle dimension beyond this realm than they are in everyday life. Unless other factors in a natal chart indicate otherwise, Pisceans have a difficult time coping. They attempt to transcend life through an ethereal art form like music (Aphrodite was patron divinity of the arts), or through some form of mysticism. Negatively, this same tendency can manifest as escapism through daydreaming, drugs, alcohol, or the like. Pisces natives can also be highly intuitive or psychic. Like the divinities of love who became fish, Pisceans can be loving, compassionate people; alternatively, they can be so trapped in the swamp of their emotional insecurities that they become obsessed with themselves.

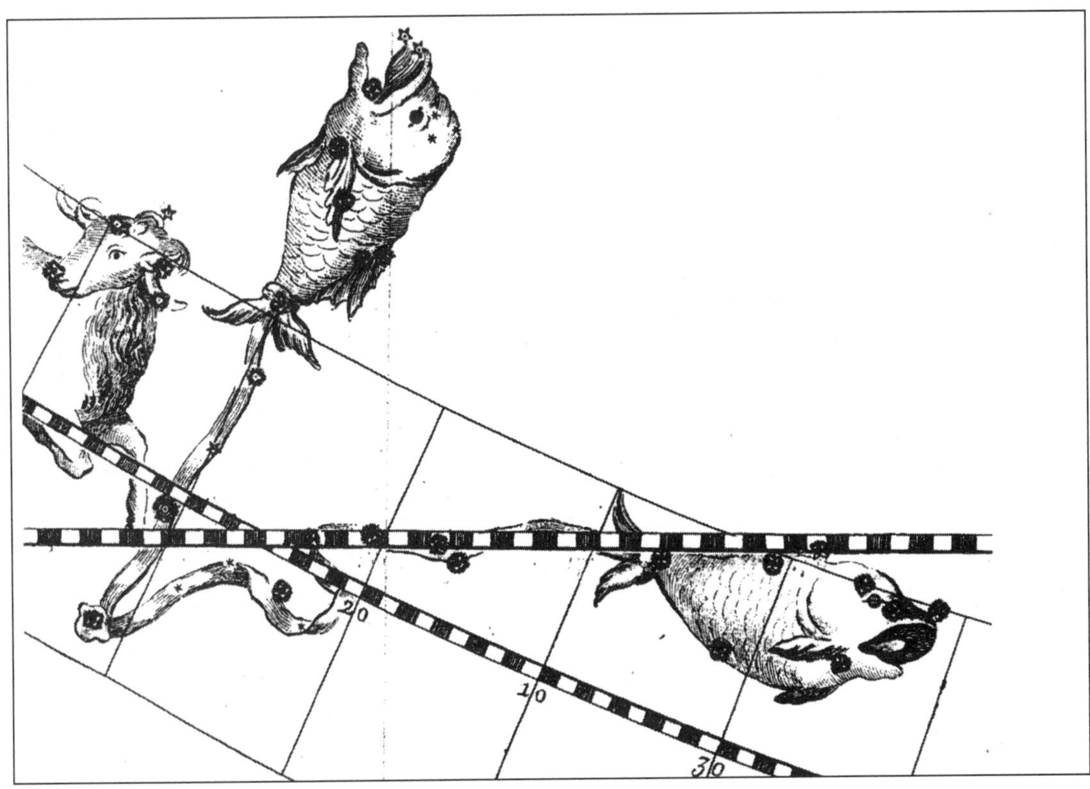


**An engraving of the constellation Pisces by Montignot, 1786. *Reproduced by permission of Fortean Picture Library.***

The sign that the Sun was in at birth is usually the single most important influence on a native's personality. Thus, when people say they are a certain sign, they are almost always referring to their sun sign. There is a wealth of information available on the characteristics of the zodiacal signs—so much that one book would not be able to contain it all. Sun-sign astrology, which is the kind of astrology found in newspaper columns and popular magazines, has the advantage of simplicity. But this simplicity is purchased at the price of ignoring other astrological influences, such as one's Moon sign, rising sign, etc. These other influences can substantially modify a person's basic sun sign traits. As a consequence, it is the rare individual who is completely typical of her or his sign. The reader should bear this caveat in mind when perusing the following series of sun-sign interpretations.

One traditional way in which astrologers condense information is by summarizing sign and planet traits in lists of words and short phrases called keywords or key phrases. The following Pisces keywords are drawn from Manly P. Hall's *Astrological Keywords:*

> *Emotional keywords:* "The emotions are inhibited, native is sensitive and impressionable, psychic, devoted, melancholy, lacks ability to resist environment, secretive, misunderstood."

> *Mental keywords:* "Abstract, intuitive, compassionate, introspective, quick in understanding, executive, philosophical, religious, clairvoyant, versatile, synthetical, loquacious, impractical, procrastinating, lack confidence."

At present, there are various astrology report programs that contain interpretations of each of the 12 sun signs. A selection of these for Sun in Pisces has been excerpted below:

> Extremely sensitive, you absorb the emotions of others (whether positive or negative) like a sponge. Emotionally vulnerable, you are easily touched by the feelings and plights of others. You are at your best when you can structure your environment in such a way that you are surrounded by positive, upbeat people. You are very helpful and understanding of the needs of others. Indeed, at times this can be a disadvantage, because you can be a sucker for anyone who needs help. Rather shy, dreamy, romantic in nature, you delight in retreating into your private fantasy world. Just be careful that you do not get lost in it. Trust your intuitions—you may be quite psychic. (From "Professional Natal Report." Courtesy of Astrolabe [http://www.alabe.com].)

> At heart you are very gentle, impressionable, and receptive—a dreamer. The world of your imagination, feelings, and intuition is as real to you as anything in the outer world, though you may have trouble verbalizing or interpreting your inner experiences in a way others can understand. Mystical, artistic, musical, emotional and imaginative, you have a rich inner life, though you may seem rather unobtrusive and quiet outwardly. You usually keep to yourself.

> You have great sensitivity and empathy with others, and you often sense things psychically or intuitively which prove to be correct. You are tolerant, forgiving, and nonjudgmental, accepting people unconditionally regardless of their flaws, mistakes, or outward appearance. You have deep compassion for the suffering of any fellow creature and often feel others' pain as if it were your own. You sympathize with the needy, the disadvantaged, the misfits of society. You are capable of giving selflessly, living a life of devoted and compassionate service to others, as a healer, physician, social worker, or minister. However, you tend to give indiscriminately, to let others take advantage of your kindness, and to encourage the weak to remain so by becoming dependent upon you. You have little sense of boundaries, of limits, of knowing when to say "no." Moderation and self-discipline are not your strong points.

> You are a lover and a peacemaker rather than a fighter, and you try to avoid open conflict. You will patiently ignore or "tune out" problems and hope they will go away by themselves, rather than directly confronting them, and you tend to lack the positive fighting spirit that is sometimes necessary to overcome challenges. You are fluid, open, nonresistant, and somewhat passive. You do things in a subtle, often covert, manner.

> Your gifts may also lie in the realm of the creative, artistic, or musical, for you have a great sensitivity, inspiration, and limitless imagination. You respond very strongly to beauty and to love.
>
> Your faults include a tendency to be lazy and negligent, and to wallow in self-pity rather than taking strong, definite action to change your life for the better. You also tend to become so detached from your immediate environment that you live in a disorderly, chaotic sort of hodgepodge, though this probably bothers those around you more than it bothers you. (From "Merlin," by Gina Ronco and Agnes Nightingale. Courtesy of Cosmic Patterns [http://cosmic.patterns.com].)
>
> Transcendence. Mysticism. Spirituality. That's Pisces at its best. In this part of your life, you've been given an instinctive sense of mystery and vastness. Something there seems automatically to think in terms of centuries, of high purposes, of divine interventions. Reflexively, when faced with life's vicissitudes, it asks, "What will this matter in five hundred years?"
>
> That's the soul of spirituality. It's also dangerous. Transcendence can run amuck, leaving Pisces in an uncaring, drifting mode, "transcending" while its life descends into entropy. Along that road there are some sad waystations: forgetfulness, spaciness, then escapism—perhaps into alcohol or drugs, perhaps into food, maybe into the television set. Avoid those sorry journeys by feeding your Piscean circuitry exactly what it needs: meditative time, silence, a few minutes each day to sit in the infinite cathedral.
>
> With your Sun in Pisces, you face an astrological paradox: the symbol of identity (the Sun) is shaped by the sign that refers to transcending the identity. There's something inside you that keeps eroding your ego, filling you with a sense of the cosmic joke—we're all spiritual monkeys dressed in perfect human attire, really believing we're insurance salespeople, housewives, and VIPs. And people wonder why you always seem to laugh at "inappropriate" times!
>
> Take care of that spirit-spark inside you. Make certain you have a little bit of time every day to stop being yourself, to float into that vast, luminous space between your ears. Otherwise, you'll start "transcending" at awkward moments: losing the car keys, missing highway exits, losing the thread of conversations. (From "The Sky Within," by Steven Forrest. Courtesy of Matrix Software [http://thenewage.com] and Steven Forrest [http://www.stevenforrest.com].)

Among its several natal programs, Matrix Software created a unique report based on the published works of the early-twentieth-century astrologer Grant Lewi (1901–1952). Lewi's highly original delineations were recognized as creative and insightful by his contemporaries. One measure of the appeal of his work is that his books *Astrology for the Millions* and *Heaven Knows What* are still in print. The following is excerpted from the report program "Heaven Knows What":

Labor to keep alive in your breast that little spark of celestial fire, conscience. (*George Washington, born in Pisces, February 22, 1732.*)

The humblest citizen of all the land, when clad in the armor of a righteous cause, is stronger than all the hosts of error. (*William Jennings Bryan, born in Pisces, March 19, 1860.*)

Pisces seeks salvation within himself, striving always for self-sufficiency, self-knowledge and effacement of self. His aim is deep and worthy, and if he does not succeed, it is because of the difficulty of the goal rather than because he does not try. His early aim appears material, because he knows instinctively that the search for self goes on most successfully if physical wants are not a source of worry. But he is not always equipped by nature for the give-and-take of commerce, and often feels himself a failure when he should not. His "failure" is more often than not that of a square peg in a round hole. When he finds his noncommercial place of service, love, understanding, he goes far toward the deep kind of satisfaction that is his personal, and therefore his true, success.

Because his aim is different, he tries ill-advisedly to accommodate himself to what he thinks he ought to be instead of following what his heart and instinct tell him. And because he wishes deeply to do the right thing, he becomes confused about his true aims and gets bewildered and lost in the business of living. It all comes about because he has forgotten the stir, small voice—because he has allowed himself to be distracted from his true desires—and because in following an uncongenial and unfamiliar path his feet stumble. He thinks he is misunderstood—but this is true only because he misunderstood himself, tried to palm himself off for something that he wasn't, and found he didn't have the heart to go through with it. When he is being his truest, deepest self he is crystal clear—unselfish, sweet, lovable, devoted, demanding little, giving much, eager always to sacrifice himself for others.

It is only in the presence of the material world, when Pisces tries to submerge the sweetness which he may come to be ashamed of, that he is unhappy. It is then that he becomes demanding, jealous, unreliable, self-deceived and perhaps even deceptive—because he is trying to force his meditative spirit into a harness where it must try to be something it isn't. Let Pisces follow his heart, his conscience, his inner desire for service, self-realization and self-knowledge, and the world be damned, and he is the happiest, most useful of mortals, living comfortably with deep spiritual truths that give him an almost mystic grip on other people and on the reins of his own life. (Courtesy of Matrix Software [http://thenewage.com].)

The following excerpt comes not from a natal report program, but from David Cochrane's book, *Astrology for the 21st Century*. Based on lessons for astrology students, it approaches the signs of the zodiac from a somewhat different perspective than the other short delineations cited here:

> Many astrologers associate Pisces with intuition, art, poetry, mysticism, music, and a passive, receptive quality that inclines it to sometimes be dominated by more forceful and aggressive personalities. In my observations, I have not found Pisces to be as "spacey" as is often attributed to it, nor have I found Pisces to be extremely passive, although there is something sensitive and non-aggressive about the Piscean nature.
>
> It appears to me that Pisces seems to approach any subject with a sensitive holistic approach rather than with a singular, well-defined point of view. Pisces sees art in biology and chemistry, and sees science in art. Pisces seems to see past categories and stereotypes and experiences life more honestly and directly, without filtering information through the powerful mental constructs that we unconsciously routinely use in our everyday lives. Pisces does not thrive in our modern day school systems that focus on performance, memorization and getting the "right" answer. (Courtesy of Cosmic Patterns [http://cosmic.patterns.com] and David Cochrane [kepler@astrosoftware.com].)

Many specialized report programs have been developed that offer useful supplements to the generic delineations of general reports. The following sun-sign interpretation has been drawn from a program written by Gloria Star (originally part of her book, *Astrology: Woman to Woman*) that generates a specialized report for women:

> With your Sun in Pisces, your ego dances most freely in the realm of imagination. Your compassion and sensitivity can stimulate your desire to give of yourself for the betterment of life. You may be quite responsive to the energy of your surroundings, and can be tempted, chameleon-like, to adapt to the needs and demands around you instead of determining what you really want, and the manner in which you want to project who you really are.
>
> Your own sense of identity and strength may allude you, especially if you feel confused about your place in the world. The influence of your Pisces Sun may stimulate marvelous dreams about what life could be, but you may not fully realize those dreams unless you can find a way to create positive personal boundaries. This is first accomplished by becoming acquainted with who you are, especially on an inner level. You may feel a special fascination with men, and may believe that they have more influence and power than you. It's tempting for you to project the qualities of power and control onto the men in your life rather than taking the risk of standing up for yourself and your needs. It's also possible that you will unconsciously seek out men who are wounded and need your compassionate support. In truth you have an exceptional strength through your resilience and adaptability. You can flex and bend with the changes happening around you and within you, and emerge quite nicely, thank you! However, in order to fully own and express your will, you may have to struggle with the feelings and sensibilities which make you vulnerable to being victimized by those who

> would take advantage of your gentle spirit. It's also tempting to allow men to see in you whatever they wish instead of establishing an identity which is more readily definable on your own terms. It is this challenge which tests your ability to embrace and fulfill your own needs.
>
> You really don't have to save the world in order to be a success. But with your Sun in Pisces, you may at least try to save a part of it in some way. Your deeper goals may have a more spiritual basis, like achieving a sense of oneness with life. You may never feel satisfied with the everyday successes until you feel connected on the inner level. There is always plenty to do in the world, and sometimes you'll feel wonderful when you've created something that makes a difference. But the real success occurs when your perspective changes and you see yourself and others through the eyes of true forgiveness and compassion. (From "Woman to Woman," by Gloria Star. Courtesy of Matrix Software [http://thenewage.com] and Gloria Star [glostar@aol.com].)

Responding to the revival of interest in pre-twentieth-century astrology, J. Lee Lehman developed a report program embodying the interpretive approach of traditional astrology. The following is excerpted from her book *Classical Astrology for Modern Living* and her computer program "Classical Report":

> You are morally idiosyncratic, trusting yourself over others. You find it easy to withhold information or things because "it's best for them," perhaps forgetting that primarily, it's best for you. You can be quite vicious when angered, and you may stammer when you are stressed. You are libidinous, and addicted to gaming and feasting. Yet you are harmless to others, injuring mainly yourself through your excess generosity and enthusiasm.
>
> Astrologically speaking the sign of Pisces is considered to be ruled by the planet Jupiter. One of the dangers of the Sun in the signs of Jupiter is Jupiter's mythological interest in love affairs (especially when the solar person is perceived as being in a position of power or authority.) In other words, you may treat power (real or imagined) as an invitation to act godlike, with all the trappings and advantages. Yet curiously, this doesn't mean that you go out of your way to seek power. But have a care when it is thrust upon you.
>
> You are mutable, which means that you adapt easily to change. However, you adapt so easily compared to others that they may wonder if you are capable of maintaining a permanent stance about anything.
>
> You are a Water Sign, which means that you are "cold" and "wet." The "wet" component means, among other things, that you blur distinctions, and that you are more swayed by passion than by intellectual argument. At your worst, you see too many connections, becoming lost in conspiracies. At your best, you spot the connection that everyone else missed. You are perceived as being "cold," which in your case simply means you may not be quickly reacting on a surface level. In the

> modern parlance, it fits better with "cold and dry" than with simply "cold." However, a "cold" type is basically lethargic, or slow to react. Here we have an interesting apparent contradiction: your emotions run deep, but that doesn't mean you're talking about them all the time! The quiet quality of "cold" may mislead others about what you're feeling. The "problem" with "cold" is that it makes it hard for you to forget slights. Because you don't tend to lash out immediately, it's hard for you not to allow your anger to build up. (Courtesy of J. Lee Lehman, Ph.D., copyright 1998 [http://www.leelehman.com].)

Readers interested in examining interpretations for their Chinese astrological sign should refer to the relevant entry. A guide for determining one's sign in the Chinese system is provided in the entry on the Chinese zodiac.

**Sources:**

Cochrane, David. *Astrology for the 21st Century*. Gainesville, FL: Cosmic Patterns, 2002.

Forrest, Steven. *The Inner Sky: How to Make Wiser Choices for a More Fulfilling Life*. 4th ed. San Diego: ACS Publications, 1989.

Green, Landis Knight. *The Astrologer's Manual: Modern Insights into an Ancient Art*. Sebastopol, CA: CRCS Publications, 1975.

Hall, Manly P. *Astrological Keywords*. New York: Philosophical Library, 1958. Reprint, Savage, MD: Littlefield Adams Quality Paperbacks, 1975.

Lehman, J. Lee. *Classical Astrology for Modern Living: From Ptolemy to Psychology & Back Again*. Atglen, PA: Whitford Press, 1996.

Lewi, Grant. *Astrology for the Millions*. 5th ed. St. Paul, MN: Llewellyn, 1978.

———. *Heaven Knows What*. St. Paul, MN: Llewellyn, 1969.

Star, Gloria. *Astrology & Your Child: A Handbook for Parents*. St. Paul, MN: Llewellyn, 2001.

———. *Astrology: Woman to Woman*. St. Paul, MN: Llewellyn, 1999.

## PITTSBURGHIA

Pittsburghia, asteroid 484 (the 484th asteroid to be discovered, on April 29, 1902), is approximately 32 kilometers in diameter and has an orbital period of 4.4 years. Pittsburghia is named after the city of Pittsburgh, Pennsylvania. The asteroid's unusual name led to its inclusion in *The Asteroid Ephemeris: Dudu, Dembowska, Pittsburgh, Frigga*, Batya Stark and Mark Pottenger's tour de force of astrological humor.

**Sources:**

Kowal, Charles T. *Asteroids: Their Nature and Utilization*. Chichester, West Sussex, UK: Ellis Horwood Limited, 1988.

Room, Adrian. *Dictionary of Astronomical Names*. London: Routledge, 1988.

Stark, Batya and Mark Pottenger. *The Asteroid Ephemeris: Dudu, Dembowska, Pittsburgh, Frigga*. San Diego: Astro Computing Services, 1982.

Schwartz, Jacob. *Asteroid Name Encyclopedia*. St. Paul, MN: Llewellyn Publications, 1995.

## PLACIDIAN HOUSE SYSTEM

It is easy for a person looking at an astrological chart for the first time to make the incorrect assumption that the 12 "pie pieces" are the 12 signs of the zodiac. These lines indicate the house divisions (sign divisions are usually not represented), which can begin or end at different places in different signs. Astrologers disagree about how to draw the houses, although most agree that the first house should begin on the eastern horizon and the seventh house (180° away) should begin on the western horizon. Also, the great majority of systems begin the tenth house at the degree of the zodiac that is highest in the heavens and the fourth house at exactly 180° from the cusp of the tenth house.

The Placidian house system was developed by a 17th-century Italian monk and professor of mathematics named Placidus de Tito. In this system, the house cusps between the ascendant and the midheaven are obtained by trisecting the time it takes a degree of the zodiac to rise from the eastern horizon to the midheaven. Owing to the widespread availability of Placidian tables of houses, this was the most popular house system in the early 20th century, and it still enjoys widespread use.

## PLACIDUS

Placidus de Titis (1603–1668) was an Italian mathematician and astrologer best known for the house system that bears his name. He joined the Olivetan Order when he was 21. He was a reader of mathematics and physics at the University of Padua for some years, and he was appointed professor of mathematics at the Milanese University in Pavia in 1657, a position he held for the rest of his life. He was also an astrologer to some prominent religious and political figures of the time.

Placidus attributed the initial inspiration for his system of division to a remark made by Ptolemy in *Tetrabiblos*. Ptolemy equated different semidiurnal arcs because they are equivalent to the same number of temporary hours. Analogically, Placidus reasoned, the twelfth-house cusp should begin at one-third of the semidiurnal arc above the horizon, the eleventh-house cusp at two-thirds of the semidiurnal arc above the horizon, and so forth.

Although mistaken, Placidus was convinced he had discovered Ptolemy's lost method of determining houses, and he began to write books in which he described the new system. This system was adopted by John Partridge but rejected by most other English astrologers. At the beginning of the revival of astrology in England in the late 18th century, Manoah Sibly published English translations of Placidus's *Primum Mobile*. The system of Placidus became the dominant system in England, and later the Placidian system was passed to France and Germany. Beyond his house system, Placidus was the inventor of secondary and tertiary directions. He also promoted the use of transits to both the natal and the progressed positions of the planets.

**Sources:**

Holden, James H., and Robert A. Hughes. *Astrological Pioneers of America*. Tempe, AZ: American Federation of Astrologers, 1988.

Placidus. *Physiomathematica sive Coelestis Philosophia Naturalibus hucusque desideratis ostensa principiis....* [Physico-mathematical (questions) or Celestial Philosophy set forth by means of natural principles hitherto lacking....] 2d ed. [Revised by his pupils Brunaccio and Onorati from the 1650 edition.] Milan: Fran. Vigoni, 1675.

———. *Tabulae Primi Mobilis cum … Triginta clariss. natalium Thematibus*. [Tables of the Primum Mobile with thirty horoscopes of famous births.] 2d ed. Milano: Fran. Vigoni, 1675. (Originally published 1657.)

## Planet X

In anticipation of discovering a planet beyond the orbit of Neptune, astronomers referred to the celestial body as Planet X. This planet, now called Pluto, was finally discovered in 1930. A common astrological practice is to assign a newly discovered body a tentative meaning that can be derived from associations with its name. (In the present case, the mythology of Pluto, the ancient Roman god of the underworld, was explored for initial clues about the planet's astrological influence.) Astrologers then study the influence of the body in charts in which it is prominent (i.e., charts in which it is in very close conjunction with another planet or with an angle). After further study of these charts, the preliminary meanings are revised so that they align with the empirical effects of the new body. This astrological principle is based on the well-established observation that the names astronomers give to newly discovered celestial bodies are not coincidental—that by virtue of some kind of unapparent, synchronicity, nonastrologically inclined astronomers give astrologically significant names to things.

Astrologers have not generally considered, however, how alternative names—or, especially, older, abandoned ones—might shed light on the meaning of a celestial body. Pluto, for example, is associated with X rays, sex (which, in contemporary society, is "X-rated"), and the unearthing of what is hidden (as in the "X marks the spot" of treasure maps). These are all meanings of Pluto that could easily have been derived from reflection on the significance of the "X" in the designation Planet X. "X" is also the symbol for multiplication (the Pluto principle of sex "multiplies"). In Roman numerals, "X" is the number 10. If the asteroid belt is considered to be the remains of a planet, Pluto is the tenth-outermost planet in the solar system. It was also the tenth celestial body to be included in the delineation of astrological charts (after the Sun, the Moon, Mercury, Venus, Mars, Jupiter, Saturn, Uranus, and Neptune). Additionally, "X" is a common designation for Christ (as in Xmas), which links Pluto with the redemptive drama central to Christianity: Christ's death on the cross (another "X"), followed by his resurrection (death and rebirth are both ruled by Pluto).

These are all commonly understood associations with the planet Pluto. There are, however, other, less explored associations with "X" that can also be connected with Pluto. "X" is, for example, the biological designation for the female chromosome that everyone carries—females carry two (XX), males carry one (X plus the male chromosome Y). Pluto is thus linked with the primordial female nature. "X" is also used to cross out errors (as in the expression, "to X out an error"), indicating a correcting principle not commonly noted in delineations of Pluto. More associations are possible when entries for cross, crossroads, etc., are explored in a good symbolism dictionary, as well as when such X-words as expose and exorcise are examined in a standard dictionary.

**Sources:**

Littmann, Mark. *Planets Beyond: Discovering the Outer Solar System*. 2d ed. New York: John Wiley & Sons, 1990.

Room, Adrian. *Dictionary of Astronomical Names*. London: Routledge,1988.

## PLANETARY MOONS

The planetary moons are the focus of a branch of astrology devoted to the satellites of Mars, Jupiter, Saturn, Uranus, Neptune, and Pluto. In the past, the principal objection to planetary moon astrology was that, even if these satellites had distinct astrological meanings, such meanings were so blended with their primaries (an astronomical term for the planets around which moons orbit) that their separate influences could not be distinguished. The implication was that the meanings of the moons had already been integrated into existing interpretations of the planets. This objection made logical sense and prevented the emergence of planetary moon studies until relatively recently; however, recent studies have demostrated that this traditional objection is empirically untrue.

Planetary moon studies was significantly influenced by asteroid studies: For several decades, astrologers have been exploring the astrological meaning of the asteroids, and at this stage the idea that asteroids have astrological significance is accepted by the majority of mainstream astrologers. The notion advanced by astronomers that some of the planetary moons may be "captured asteroids" prompted astrologers with asteroid interests to begin investigating the possible independent influence of the planetary satellites. Such research was further prompted by consideration of the mass of some of the moons. Four of the 16 satellites of Jupiter, for example, are larger than the planet Pluto (which is 1,457 miles in diameter, at latest estimate). The Big Four Jovian moons are Ganymede (3,270 miles in diameter), Callisto (2,980 miles), Io (2,260 miles), and Europa (1,950 miles). Europa, the smallest of these four, has a diameter more than three times the diameter of Ceres, the largest asteroid. Thus, four significant celestial bodies larger than Pluto are in conjunction with Jupiter. Jupiter, in other words, constitutes a sort of de facto stellium (multiple conjunction) wherever it is placed in a horoscope.

The importance of the planetary moons has already been convincingly demonstrated. At this stage in the development of the field, planetary moon studies has shown how consideration of the satellites provides insight into the complementary principles of the planet involved (e.g., Mars, the planet of courage, is orbited by Phobos and Deimos, moons whose names mean, respectively, fear and panic). Other lines of research could be explored, such as the constantly alternating direction of the moons (which are retrograde with respect to Earth half the time), as well as use of planet-centered positions of the moons in a geocentric chart.

**Sources:**

Davis, T. Patrick. *Revolutionizing Astrology with Heliocentric*. Windermere, FL: David Research Reports, 1980.

Lewis, James R. *Martian Astrology*. Goleta, CA: Jupiter's Ink, 1992.

## PLANET-CENTERED ASTROLOGY

While traditional astrologers, both eastern and western, use a geocentric chart, research has been undertaken to consider charts centered on other objects within our solar system, notably the Sun and planets. The premise for such a relocation of the center is that the logos of each planet at a specific point in time can be described by looking at such a chart.

From the perspective of Mercury and Venus, the Sun is a vast presence. These two planets have no moons of their own. Both planets can be found in any relationship to the Sun and each other in the chart, unlike the geocentric model in which Mercury and Venus must always be near the Sun.

The planets outside the orbit of the Earth all have moons. For charts centered on these planets, the moons become the dominant factors in the chart. Many of them orbit at high speeds, and their changing positions provide very accurate timers. For example Phobos, one of the moons of Mars, orbits in under eight hours. As the distance from the Sun increases, the significance of the moons increases, as they command the full 360° range of possibility, while the inner planets cluster closer and closer to the Sun.

Stephanie Jean Clement, in her book *Planets and Planet-Centered Astrology*, introduced the subject of planet-centered astrology by examining some of the astronomy of each planet and the more significant moons. This work is based on the premise that the planet-centered perspective is relevant to individuals, even though being on each of the planets is not possible. The planet-centered chart affords the opportunity to consider life from the point of view of the planet, not the individual human being. This transpersonal perspective considers archetypal energies, the mythology surrounding the planet and its moons, and traditional astrological understanding of the planets, against the backdrop of the zodiac.

### Planets, Moons, and Transpersonal (Alchemical) Meanings

| Chart | Planet | Moons | Expression |
|---|---|---|---|
| Hermicentric | Mercury | - | Mediation |
| Venericentric | Venus | - | Concrete Knowledge |
| Geocentric | Earth | - | Intelligent Activity |
| - | - | Moon | Subconscious activity |
| Aricentric | Mars | - | Energy |
| - | - | Phobos; Deimos | Action; Desire |
| Jovicentric | Jupiter | - | Wisdom; Love |
| - | - | Alamthea; Io; Europa; Ganymede; Callisto | Space; Fire; Air; Water; Earth |
| Cronocentric | Saturn | - | Intelligent Activity |
| - | - | Mimas and Enceladus; Tethys; Dione; Rhea; Titan; Iapetus | Transcendant energy; Space; Fire; Air; Water; Earth |
| Uranicentric | Uranus | - | Ritual; Equilibrium |
| - | - | Miranda; Ariel; Umbriel; Titania; Oberon | Space; Fire; Air; Water; Earth |
| Neptunicentric | Neptune | - | Devotion |
| - | - | Triton; Nereid | Prophecy; Compassion |
| Plutocentric | Pluto | - | Will; Power |
| - | - | Charon | Direction of power |

By examining planet-centered charts, an individual can obtain a much clearer view of personal processes and attitudes. Clarity is obtained by considering each chart as coming from the perspective of that planet, and not from one's personal perspective. The Cronocentric (Saturn-centered) chart provides a transpersonal view of Saturn's role in one's life. The major moons of Saturn then offer five specific alchemical possibilities for consideration, providing a freer position of creative choice.

—Stephanie Jean Clement, Ph.D.

**Sources:**

Bailey, Alice. *Esoteric Astrology*. New York: Lucis Publishing, 1951.

Clement, Stephanie Jean. *Planets and Planet-Centered Astrology*. Tempe, AZ: American Federation of Astrologers, 1992.

## Planets

Planets (from the Greek *planasthai*, meaning "to wander") are the familiar celestial bodies orbiting the Sun. They were regarded as stars by the ancients, who referred to them as wanderers because, unlike the so-called fixed stars, the planets were always changing their positions with respect to the background of the celestial sphere. The Sun and the Moon (the luminaries) are also wanderers, and in traditional astrology were referred to as planets. Although they are no longer classified as such by astronomers, many contemporary astrologers still call the two luminaries planets.

Astrological influences manifest themselves primarily through the planets. These basic influences are modified by (1) the signs of the zodiac (i.e., the familiar 12 astrological signs of Aries, Taurus, Gemini, etc.) in which the planets are placed, (2) the aspects (geometric angles) between the planets, and (3) the houses in which the planets are placed. An oversimplified but nonetheless useful rule of thumb is that planetary sign positions indicate personality tendencies, aspects between planets reflect how various components of one's personality interact, and house positions show how the personality manifests in the world.

As an example, consider an individual with natal Mercury (i.e., Mercury's position at birth) in Libra in the second house, with Mercury also trine (at a 120° angle) to Mars. In regard to personality, Mercury represents the mind, particularly the aspect of the thinking mind that deals with day-to-day affairs; this is considered the basic nature of Mercury.

> *Sign:* Individuals born when Mercury was in Libra usually communicate in a refined way and have the ability to be highly diplomatic. It is also easy for them to see both sides of an issue, which can make them indecisive, swaying back and forth between the two alternatives.
>
> *Aspect:* Mars represents the outgoing, assertive, aggressive energies. It also rules mechanical and other kinds of physical skills. Trine aspects often indicate where two influences blend together harmoniously. In this case, Mercury trine Mars shows, among other things, an individual who can tap her or his assertive energies in a positive manner and

**The seven planets and their corresponding days of the week. The zodiac signs over which they rule appear in black circles. From an English shepherd's calendar, c. 1510. *Reproduced by permission of Fortean Picture Library.***

express them through powerful communications. This person also has a mind that can easily understand mechanical skills, or any other subject associated with Mars.

*House:* The second house is the house of earned income and personal possessions. Mercury here shows someone who can earn money with her or his communication skills. She or he also acquires possessions related to Mercury, such as books and other forms of communication media.

The planets have a special relationship with the signs of the zodiac whereby each planet is said to "rule" a certain sign (or signs). The relationship between the planets and the signs is one of kinship in their basic traits and associations. Prior to the discovery of Uranus, a general consensus about these relationships had endured since the time of Ptolemy. The traditional system held that the Sun ruled Leo, the Moon ruled Cancer, Mercury ruled Virgo and Gemini, Venus ruled Taurus and Libra, Mars ruled Aries and Scorpio, Jupiter ruled Sagittarius and Pisces, and Saturn ruled Capricorn and Aquarius. This is still the primary rulership system used in Hindu astrology. After the more recently discovered planets were studied, astrologers gradually came to assign Uranus to Aquarius, Neptune to Pisces, and Pluto to Scorpio, leaving Saturn, Jupiter, and Mars as the rulers of Capricorn, Sagittarius, and Aries. Only Mercury and Venus are still viewed as ruling two signs each.

The planets are classified in various ways, such as according to whether they are inferior (circle the Sun within Earth's orbit) or superior (circle outside the terrestrial orbit), exert benefic ("good") or malefic ("bad") astrological influences, and so forth. (*See* the individual entries on the planets for more information.)

**Sources:**

Campion, Nicholas. *The Practical Astrologer*. New York: Harry N. Abrams, 1987.
DeVore, Nicholas. *Encyclopedia of Astrology*. New York: Philosophical Library, 1949.
McEvers, Joan. *Planets: The Astrological Tools*. Saint Paul, MN: Llewellyn Publications, 1989.

## Platic

Astrologers allow individual aspects a particular orb of influence within which they are regarded as having an effect. Nonexact aspects are referred to as platic aspects and are considered to have a weaker influence than partile (exact) aspects.

## Plato

Plato, the most famous of all Greek philosophers, lived in Athens from approximately 427 B.C.E. to 347 B.C.E. Although some sources have claimed that Plato lived for a period in Egypt and studied astrology, this is not reflected in his writings. Plato's significance for astrology is that directly through his own surviving works and indirectly through the Neoplatonic tradition, he was the most influential advocate of the idea that the human being is a miniature version (microcosm) of the larger universe (macrocosm). The microcosm and the macrocosm are linked by—and affect each other through—certain correlations. This notion is basic to ancient astrology.

## Plotinus

Plotinus, the greatest Roman neoplatonist, lived from approximately 205 to 270 C.E. He studied in Alexandria, Egypt, one of the centers of learning that preserved classical astrology, magic, and medicine (Alexandrian neoplatonists were responsible for the survival of astrological science in the West). Plotinus accepted astrology but was opposed to a deterministic view of planetary influence. Like Plato (from whom the term neoplatonism is derived), Plotinus is not important for any direct contribution to astrology but for the elaboration and propagation of the Pythagorean view that the individual human being is linked to the greater cosmos through a system of correlations—a view that is a foundation stone of ancient astrological theory.

## Pluto

Pluto is the farthest known planet from the Sun and by far the smallest with a diameter of 1,444 miles and a mass only 2 percent that of the Earth. Pluto completes an orbit of the Sun every 247.69 years, meaning that it spends more than 20 years in each sign of the zodiac. Thus, an entire generation is born while Pluto is transiting each sign.

The existence of a ninth planet was suspected when astronomers detected a gravitational affect on the orbit of Neptune. Percival Lowell, an American astronomer, built a private observatory in Flagstaff, Arizona, called Lowell Observatory in order to locate the hypothetical planet, which he termed Planet X. He began his search for this planet in the early 1900s without success. In December 1929, a young amateur astronomer, Clyde Tombaugh, was hired to continue the search. His research eventually led to the first sighting on February 18, 1930 after conducting a very careful sky survey and examining hundreds of plate pairs. The official discovery was announced March 13 on Lowell's 75th birthday.

**Pluto, ruler of the underworld, with the three-headed dog, Cerberus, at his feet. From Jack Bryant's *New System*, 1774. *Reproduced by permission of Fortean Picture Library.***

Scientists at the Lowell Observatory requested suggestions from the public for the naming of Planet X. Many names were proposed, including Atlas, Minerva, Apollo, Zeus, Perseus, and Vulcan. However, its name came as a result of a letter from Venetia Burney, an 11-year-old schoolgirl in Oxford, England, who recommended it be named after the Disney character, Pluto. It is possible that this idea was accepted based on the fact that the planet is in perpetual darkness (from the myth of Pluto, the Roman god of the underworld) and because the first letters, "PL," are the initials of Percival Lowell.

Pluto, also known as Hades, the brother of Zeus and Posiedon in the Greek culture, was a grim deity, yet not a totally evil one. He rarely ventured from the underworld, which he inherited following the defeat of the Titans. When he did travel the overworld, he hid himself with a helmet of invisibility. He was also called the God of Wealth from not only the precious metals hidden in the earth, but also the fact that the number of his subjects—the dead—could only increase. Over time, a gradual idea of judgment entered the myths of Hades, associating him with the idea of punishment and reward. Most souls were said to spend life after death in the dreary Meadows of Asphodel. Evil sinners were doomed to torture for eternity in Tartarus, while heros resided in Elysium enjoying feasts and games.

The myth surrounding Pluto's wife, Persephone, is symbolic of the origins of the seasons. Persephone was the only daughter of the goddess Demeter. While Persephone was out picking flowers, a chasm opened up revealing Pluto. He quickly pulled her into the underworld and made her his wife and Queen of the Lower World. Demeter scoured the land looking for her daughter and once she discovered what had occurred, she was grief-stricken. She wandered the land alone, bringing famine to the earth in her grief. The people called out to Zeus for assistance and he answered by ordering Hades to release Persephone. However, she had already eaten a pomegranate seed. Having fed upon and drank from the goods of the underworld, she was obligated to spend a third of the year with Pluto. Thus, the winter when the Earth is cold and barren is the time Persephone resides in the underworld and Demeter travels the Earth alone and yearning for her only daughter. At Persephone's release in the spring, the Earth begins to grow and flower again.

In ancient Mesopotamia, the ruler of the dead and the underworld was the goddess Ereshkigal, the Queen of the Great Below. Unlike her Roman and Greek counterparts, Ereshkigal was an unhappy figure who resented her exclusion from the divinities of the upper world and agonized over the fate of those souls unlucky enough to die in early childhood. Ereshkigal had a sister Ianna who was goddess of the sky and heavens. After Ereshkigal's husband died, Ianna attended the funeral in the underworld. However, Ianna was not welcomed by her sister. Instead, Ereshkigal forced Ianna to meet the same tests that all souls encounter when they enter the underworld.

When traveling to the underworld, there are seven doors. At each door, each soul must give up a garment or jewel to pass through it. Ianna did the same thing and thus as she passes through the seventh door, she is completely naked. Upon her entrance into the underworld, she is forced to bow to Ereshkigal, who then kills Ianna and places her on a meat hook to rot. However, Ianna was prepared in case of any problems. Before leaving, she requested the help from two small men called mourners. Hearing that Ianna is in trouble, they go to the underworld to seek out Ereshkigal. When they arrive, they find the Queen of the Great Below in great pain not only from losing her husband, but also from the process of giving birth. The two men provide her with their company and the needed space to cry, moan, scream, and complain. Ereshkigal, grateful for the comfort the men offered, offered them the choice of a gift. They chose the freedom of Ianna, who was then brought back to life and permitted to return to her kingdom.

The myths of Ereshkigal and Persephone cover many aspects of Pluto—stripping away things one identifies with, forcing vulnerability, and understanding one's shadow or dark side. It allows a transition beyond areas of habit where one becomes stuck in life. It helps to understand that the attitudes, people, or things once so strongly attached to are not part of one's our true self. Pluto is ultimately about life-changing transformation from something old into something beautiful and new like the caterpillar transitioning into the butterfly, never to be the same again. One must die to the old to be transformed into the new.

Death and rebirth are Pluto's primary associations. This powerful planet represents the ultimate threat to the ego because it obliterates the ego's facade by penetrating deeply into the true self and exposing the shadows and pain that must be dealt with. Pluto characterizes the will, or a person's inclinations or disposition in the sense of what drives them in life. Pluto's sign in the natal chart describes how the person expresses these drives. Its house placement indicates where there is a tendency to control and dominate.

The reason for this association is it is human nature to fear life-altering changes, so there is an attempt to hold on tighter, to control the process and outcome. However, when undergoing a Plutoian experience, it becomes impossible to maintain this control because it is only by letting go that the transformation process can take place. Ultimately, Pluto's placement in the natal chart exposes the areas of life where the individual is learning to surrender control and let go of old patterning. If a person works with this force throughout his or her life, the Plutoian experience can be renewing; by fighting it, the experience can be much more difficult and painful.

Like the mythological figure, Pluto is not evil. He governs the regenerative process which eventually leads to physical and psychological healing. In order to heal, an individual must first recognize and eliminate the toxins, whether physical, emotional, or mental. When Pluto is prominent in a chart, the individual often possesses intuitive knowledge of the healing process which can be used to help themselves and others.

Modern astrologers place Pluto as the ruler of the sign of Scorpio. Like Scorpio, Pluto represents hidden matters, power, metamorphosis, oppressiveness and extremes. Before Pluto's discovery, Mars was considered the ruler of Scorpio. Interestingly, Pluto is considered the higher expression of the planet Mars. Mars rules sexual desire while Pluto is associated with orgasm and the conception, which brings about new life. Mars is also tied to aggression and courage; Pluto with intensity and the courage to let go.

—Tishelle Betterman

**Sources:**

Arroyo, Stephen. *Astrology, Karma, & Transformation*. 2d ed. Sebastopol, CA: CRCS Publications, 1992.

Bloch, Douglas, and Demetra George. *Astrology for Yourself: A Workbook for Personal Transformation*. Oakland, CA: Wingbow Press, 1987.

Burk, Kevin. *Astrology: Understanding the Birth Chart*. St. Paul, MN: Llewellyn Publications, 2001.

Campion, Nicholas. *The Practical Astrologer*. New York: Harry N. Abrams, 1987.

Campion, Nicholas, and Steve Eddy. *The New Astrology: The Art and Science of the Stars*. North Pomfret, VT: Trafalgar Square Publishing, 1999.

George, Llewellyn. *The New A to Z Horoscope Maker and Delineator*. 13th ed. Edited by Marylee Bytheriver. St. Paul, MN: Llewellyn Publications, 1986.

Hamilton, Edith. *Mythology*. New York: Little, Brown and Co., 1942.

McEvers, Joan. *Planets: The Astrological Tools*. Saint Paul, MN: Llewellyn Publications, 1989.

Valentine, Christine. *Images of the Psyche: Exploring the Planets through Psychology and Myth*. Shaftesbury, Dorset, UK: Element Books, 1991.

## Poesia

Poesia, asteroid 946 (the 946th asteroid to be discovered, on February 11, 1921), is approximately 40 kilometers in diameter and has an orbital period of 5.5 years. Its name is a personification of the word poetry. In a natal chart, Poesia's location by sign and house indicates one's poetic sensitivity, or where and how one is most likely to experience poetry. If prominent in a chart (e.g., conjunct the Sun or the ascendant), it may show a poetically talented individual.

**Sources:**

Kowal, Charles T. *Asteroids: Their Nature and Utilization*. Chichester, West Sussex, UK: Ellis Horwood Limited, 1988.

Room, Adrian. *Dictionary of Astronomical Names*. London: Routledge, 1988.

Schwartz, Jacob. *Asteroid Name Encyclopedia*. St. Paul, MN: Llewellyn Publications, 1995.

## Polyhymnia

Polyhymnia, asteroid 33 (the 33rd asteroid to be discovered, on October 28, 1854), is approximately 62 kilometers in diameter and has an orbital period of 4.8 years. Polyhymnia is named after the Greek muse of singing, mime, rhetoric, and sacred dance, who was a daughter of Zeus and Mnemosyne and whose symbol is the veil. Like its mythological namesake, the asteroid Polyhymnia confers talent in singing, dance, mime, and rhetoric to natives in whose chart it is prominent.

**Sources:**

Kowal, Charles T. *Asteroids: Their Nature and Utilization*. Chichester, West Sussex, UK: Ellis Horwood Limited, 1988.

Room, Adrian. *Dictionary of Astronomical Names*. London: Routledge, 1988.

Schwartz, Jacob. *Asteroid Name Encyclopedia*. St. Paul, MN: Llewellyn Publications, 1995.

## Porphyry System

The Porphyry, or Porphyrian, system is one of the older systems of house division, obtained by evenly trisecting the ecliptic in each of the four quadrants. It was named after the neoplatonic philosopher Porphyry, who is said to have devised it.

## Poseidon

Poseidon is one of the eight hypothetical planets (sometimes referred to as the trans-Neptunian points or planets, or TNPs for short) utilized in Uranian astrology. The Uranian system, sometimes referred to as the Hamburg School of Astrology, was established by Friedrich Sieggrün (1877–1951) and Alfred Witte (1878–1943). It relies heavily on hard aspects and midpoints. In decline for many decades, it has experienced a revival in recent years.

On the one hand, Poseidon is mind, spirit, and ideas; on the other, it is enlightenment, inspiration, spirituality, and "vision." Thus, for example, a Mercury-Poseidon connection may indicate spiritual perception; Venus-Poseidon connection, pure love, or religious faith.

**Sources:**

Lang-Wescott, Martha. *Mechanics of the Future: Asteroids*. Rev. ed. Conway, MA: Treehouse Mountain, 1991.

Simms, Maria Kay. *Dial Detective: Investigation with the 90 Degree Dial*. San Diego: Astro Computing Services Services, 1989.

## Posited

Posited (from the Latin word for "placed") is where a planet is located or placed in an astrological chart.

## Precession of Equinoxes

The phenomenon known as the precession of equinoxes was said to have been discovered by Hipparchus in the second century B.C.E., but there is evidence that some groups of people were aware of the phenomenon much earlier. To recall some basic science, the seasons are the result of the slant of Earth's axis: When the Earth's hemisphere is inclined away from the Sun, this results in winter; when the hemisphere is inclined toward the Sun, this is summer. The spin of Earth makes it behave like a gyroscope (always tending to maintain the same angle), but, because Earth is not perfectly round, it tends to "wobble" a little. One result of this wobble is that each year the Sun appears to have moved ever so slightly backward (against the backdrop of the relatively unmoving stars) from where it was at the same point (e.g. at a solstice or an equinox point) the preceding year (at the rate of 1° every 71.5 years).

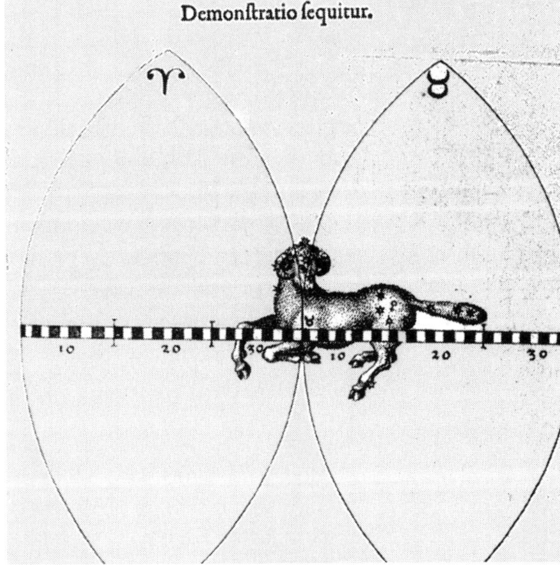

DE SIGNIS ZODIACI. 575

Generaliter hîc notandum eſt, ſtellas fixas corpora animalium cœleſtium conſtituentes propriis ſuis intervallis, & locis ſeu domibus non eſſe contẽtas, ſed partem corporis cujuſque ſigni in ſua ſede propria comprehendi, & reliqua ejus membra in loco alterius ſigni ei proximi contineri. Sic minor Arietis pars reperitur in poſteriore parte longitudinis ei attributa, nempe verſus finem 30. graduum, ejus domum commenſurantium, videlicet ejus tibiæ, cornu dextrum & dimidia cervicis pars cum capitis ejuſdem portione. Reliquæ verò ejus partes in Tauri dominium ſe extendunt, & 21 ferè gradus illius longitudinis occupare videntur.

Demonſtratio ſequitur.

**Robert Fludd's attempt to illustrate the theory of precession. From the 1617 edition of *Technica Macrocosmi Historia*. Reproduced by permission of Fortean Picture Library.**

This precession is the reason that the tropical zodiac, which most Western astrologers use, is a "moving" zodiac: Following the admonitions of Ptolemy, the great astrologer-astronomer of antiquity, the beginning of the Zodiac—0° Aries—is located where the Sun is positioned during the spring (vernal) equinox. Thus, each year the zodiac is moved very slightly. This movement keeps the zodiac aligned with the seasons, but it is always slipping backward with reference to the stars. This is disconcerting to anyone who feels that sign influence emanates from the constellations after which the signs of the zodiac take their names. However, if one switches over to one of the sidereal zodiacs (which align the zodiac with the stars), then the zodiac—which contains much seasonal symbolism—slips out of alignment with the seasons. This means that it is possible to make a good argument for either system.

**Sources:**

Bach, Eleanor. *Astrology from A to Z: An Illustrated Source Book*. New York: Philosophical Library, 1990.

Filbey, John, and Peter Filbey. *The Astrologer's Companion*. Wellingborough, Northamptonshire, UK: Aquarian Press, 1986.

## Prime Vertical

The prime vertical is the great circle that intersects the east point, the west point, the nadir, and the zenith at any given point on Earth. It is perpendicular to both the meridian and the horizon. Some systems of house division utilize this great circle as their primary point of reference, deriving the house cusps by dividing the prime vertical into 12 equal subdivisons.

## PRISON

Prison is an obsolete term for fall (when a planet is in a sign opposite the sign of its exaltation).

## PROBITAS

Probitas, asteroid 902 (the 902d asteroid to be discovered, on September 3, 1918), is approximately 12 kilometers in diameter and has an orbital period of 3.8 years. Its name is a personification of the Latin word for "probity" or "uprightness." In a natal chart, Probitas's location by sign and house indicates where and how one is most likely to be honest and upright. When afflicted by inharmonious aspects, Probitas may show improbity or projecting a false image of integrity. If prominent in a chart (e.g., conjunct the Sun or the ascendant), it can show a person of exceptional integrity, or an individual for whom integrity is a major life theme.

**Sources:**

Kowal, Charles T. *Asteroids: Their Nature and Utilization*. Chichester, West Sussex, UK: Ellis Horwood Limited, 1988.

Room, Adrian. *Dictionary of Astronomical Names*. London: Routledge, 1988.

Schwartz, Jacob. *Asteroid Name Encyclopedia*. St. Paul, MN: Llewellyn Publications, 1995.

## PROGNOSTICATION (PROGNOSIS)

Astrological prognostication refers to astrological prediction, although prognosis is more accurate for what astrologers actually do. If the future were rigidly fated, then, no matter what anyone did, only one future would be possible. Given this assumption, one should be able to predict the future. The term *prognostication*, however, does not imply a rigidly fated future. Instead, the term seems to suggest that human willpower can, within certain limits, change the future. Like a weather reporter, an astrologer can only predict upcoming conditions. Whether or not one chooses to go for a picnic on a day a meteorologist predicts rain—or on a day an astrologer advises staying at home—is a matter of personal will.

## PROGRESSIONS AND DIRECTIONS

Progressions and directions are two related astrological methods for predicting future conditions and developments. Prediction is the oldest element of the astrologer's craft: Whereas contemporary astrologers tend to be more concerned with understanding individuals and their potential, traditional astrology tended to focus on prognostication (predicting the future). The most ancient and still the most important astrological tool for prognostication is transits, current and forthcoming movements of the planets that are transiting the sky. Progressions and directions are other ways of examining a natal chart for prediction purposes.

Secondary progressions (sometimes called secondary directions), the most popular method of prognostication other than transits, use the formula "a day for a year" to predict the future. This method's underlying notion is that there is a relationship between the first day of life and the first year of life, between the second day of life and the second year of life, and so forth. The actual technique involves finding a person's current age and moving the planets and house cusps of the natal chart to the positions they occupied at the same number of days after birth as the individual's current age in years. These positions are then examined and tell the astrologer about the client's life for the current year.

An oversimplified but nevertheless useful generalization of the transit/progression distinction is that transits indicate external conditions, whereas progressions indicate inner development (in the sense of changes in one's personality and personal interests). Thus, transits are used to predict future environments, whereas progressions are used to predict inner changes (although, because there is always a relationship between inner and outer influences, these two cannot be so neatly separated in actual practice). For readings, astrologers often erect a chart consisting of three concentric circles. The inner circle contains the natal chart, the intermediate circle contains the progressed positions (in what is referred to as the progressed chart), and the outer circle records the positions of the transiting planets, usually calculated for the time of the reading. This tripartite chart allows the astrologer to view the interactions between the various levels at a glance.

The method of secondary progressions examines changes in the progressed chart, as well as how planets in a progressed chart interact with the natal chart. For example, John Smith was born when the Sun was at 4° in the sign Sagittarius. The Sun (which in astrological parlance is one of the "planets") represents John's basic self, so the sign Sagittarius colors his entire personality. Unless this sun sign is counterbalanced by other factors in the chart, John is probably a fun-loving guy who does not like to be tied down by obligations to anybody. Around age 26, his progressed Sun will enter the sign Capricorn. This sign tends to be focused on business and duty—very different from John's sun sign. The progressed Sun's change of sign does not indicate that John will suddenly drop his Sagittarian traits and be transformed overnight into a Capricorn. Rather, his personality will acquire an overlay of the latter sign's orientation, becoming somewhat more serious and mature. Business matters may become more important, and the commitments entailed by such relationships as business partnerships and marriage will seem less unappealing.

Another method of progression, termed tertiary progressions, could be referred to as "a day for a month" system. In a manner parallel to secondary progressions, this approach takes each day after birth as representing a month (a lunar month, which is shorter than a calendar month) of life. This method, devised by the twentieth-century astrologer Edward Troinski, is used far less frequently than secondary progressions. Another infrequently used method, converse secondary progressions, entails using each day before birth as equivalent to a year of life.

Primary directions (also termed Placidean arcs, primary arcs, and equitorial arcs) is the name for another method of astrological prognostication—"a degree for a year" system. As one might anticipate, this method involves predicting events according to the movement of a planet through degrees, although primary directions uses degrees of right ascension (measured along the celestial equator) rather than degrees of the zodiac (measured along the ecliptic). Prior to the advent of computer chart-casting programs, primary directions was a comparatively difficult method to use, and thus fell into disuse.

Other degree-for-year systems are solar arc directions, which measure movement in degrees of celestial longitude (along the ecliptic), and solar declination arc directions, which measure movement in terms of degrees of declination. Yet other systems of directions are ascendant arc directions, vertical arc directions, radix directions, and symbolic directions. The very overabundance of these approaches is a primary (if not *the* primary) reason most astrologers stick with transits and secondary progressions. Nonetheless, the best contemporary chart-casting programs allow one to calculate all of them, a provision that vastly simplifies experimentation and research. Many if not all of these methods are thus likely to be the subjects of renewed interest to computer-equipped astrologers.

**Sources:**

Brau, Jean-Louis, Helen Weaver, and Allan Edmands. *Larousse Encyclopedia of Astrology*. New York: New American Library, 1980.

DeVore, Nicholas. *Encyclopedia of Astrology*. New York: Philosophical Library, 1947.

## PROMETHEUS

Prometheus, the rebellious Titan from Greek mythology, has given his name to asteroid 1,809 (discovered on September 24, 1960), as well as to one of the moons of Saturn. In contemporary astrological circles, however, Prometheus is most familiar through the work of Richard Tarnas as the mythological figure best expressing the astrological nature of the planet Uranus. Astrologers have long noted, though few expressed the observation, that the traits attributed to the astrological Uranus appear to have no association whatsoever with the mythological Uranus. Using this discrepancy as his starting point, Tarnas took the further step of observing that the mythological figure best expressing the character traits of the astrological Uranus was Prometheus. In an article in the *Journal of the British Astrological Association*,, Tarnas said, "The more I examined the matter the more I realized that every quality astrologers associate with the planet Uranus was reflected in the myth of Prometheus: the initiation of radical change, the passion for freedom, the defiance of authority, the act of cosmic rebellion against a universal structure to free humanity of limitation, the intellectual brilliance and genius, the element of excitement and risk."

Tarnas's ideas have received widespread acceptance in the astrological community. Astrologers who hesitate accepting an exception to the widely held principle that the name given to a celestial body by an astronomer synchronistically corresponds with its archetypal meaning might note that the mythological Uranus is related to the astrological Uranus as its complementary polarity: The Greek Uranus was a tyrant who opposed change, which represents characteristics that must be in place before Prometheus can express his rebellious, freedom-seeking, change-at-any-cost nature.

Other planets embody such polar characteristics. Thus, the astrological Saturn, for example, expresses both security-seeking and insecurity. And Mars indicates both courage and fear, although traditionally astrologers noted only the courageous, assertive nature of Mars and not the corresponding Martian anxiety. In eccentric Uranus, it is the polar opposite principle that is expressed by the planet's namesake. Thus, to acknowledge both Tarnas and the tradition of synchronistic meanings, one could assert that the area of the natal chart where a native feels rebellious (as indicated by the placement of natal Uranus) is also the area where she or he feels most oppressed.

**Sources:**

Schwartz, Jacob. *Asteroid Name Encyclopedia*. St. Paul, MN: Llewellyn Publications, 1995.

Tarnas, Richard. "Uranus and Prometheus." *Journal of the British Astrological Association* (July–August 1989): 187–96.

———. "The Western Mind at the Threshold." *Astrotherapy Newsletter* 3, no. 4 (November 1990): 2–5.

## Promitter

Promitter (from the Latin *promittere*, meaning "to promise") is an older term that refers to the things "promised" by the sign, house, and aspects of a particular planet. The related term significator refers to another planet or important point that, by transit or progression, activates the first planet's "promise." These terms are rarely used in modern natal astrology, although they are common in horary astrology.

## Proper Motion

Proper motion refers to the motion of a planet or other celestial body in space as opposed to apparent motion caused by such factors as the axial rotation of Earth.

## Proserpina

Proserpina, asteroid 26 (the 26th asteroid to be discovered, on May 5, 1853), is approximately 88 kilometers in diameter and has an orbital period of 4.3 years. Proserpina was the Roman name for the Greek Persephone, who was kidnapped by Hades and taken to the underworld to become his queen. According to Martha Lang-Wescott, Proserpina represents rites of passage—infant awareness of separateness, adolescent crisis, leaving home for school, marriage, job change, or personal growth. This asteroid's key word is "transition."

**Sources:**

Lang-Wescott, Martha. *Asteroids-Mechanics: Ephemerides II*. Conway, MA: Treehouse Mountain, 1990.

———. *Mechanics of the Future: Asteroids*. Rev. ed. Conway, MA: Treehouse Mountain, 1991.

Schwartz, Jacob. *Asteroid Name Encyclopedia*. St. Paul, MN: Llewellyn Publications, 1995.

## Prudentia

Prudentia, asteroid 474 (the 474th asteroid to be discovered, on February 13, 1901), is approximately 26 kilometers in diameter and has an orbital period of 3.8 years. Its name is a personification of the word prudence. In a natal chart, Prudentia's location by sign and house indicates where and how one is most likely to be prudent. When afflicted by inharmonious aspects, Prudentia may show imprudence. If prominent in a chart (e.g., conjunct the Sun or the ascendant), it may signal an exceptionally prudent person.

**Sources:**

Kowal, Charles T. *Asteroids: Their Nature and Utilization*. Chichester, West Sussex, UK: Ellis Horwood Limited, 1988.

Room, Adrian. *Dictionary of Astronomical Names*. London: Routledge, 1988.

Schwartz, Jacob. *Asteroid Name Encyclopedia*. St. Paul, MN: Llewellyn Publications, 1995.

## Psyche

Psyche is the name of an asteroid as well as the soul or mind. Psyche, asteroid 16 (the 16th asteroid to be discovered, on March 17, 1852), was named after a beautiful woman in a Greek myth, said to represent the soul. It has an orbital period of 5 years and is 248 kilometers in diameter (making it the same size as Juno). Psyche is one of the more recent asteroids to be investigated by astrologers. Preliminary material on Psyche can be found in Demetra George and Douglas Bloch's *Astrology for Yourself*, and an ephemeris (table of celestial locations) for Psyche can be found in the second edition of their *Asteroid Goddesses*.

Unlike the planets, which are associated with a wide range of phenomena, the smaller asteroids are said to represent a single principle. George and Bloch (1987) give Psyche's principle as "psychic sensitivity"; their tentative key phrase for Psyche is "my capacity to be psychically sensitive to another person." Zipporah Dobyns views Psyche as either the capacity to understand and care for others or the incapacity to do so if one is self-centered or insecure. J. Lee Lehman regards Psyche as representing the unconscious aspect of the mind, particularly one's unconscious mental habits. Jacob Schwartz gives the significance of this asteroid as "psychic and physical bonding, erotic love, raw psychological wounds and recovery."

**Sources:**

Dobyns, Zipporah. *Expanding Astrology's Universe*. San Diego: Astro Computing Services, 1983.

George, Demetra, with Douglas Bloch. *Asteroid Goddesses: The Mythology, Psychology and Astrology of the Reemerging Feminine*. 2d ed. San Diego: Astro Computing Services Publications, 1990.

———. *Astrology for Yourself: A Workbook for Personal Transformation*. Berkeley, CA: Wingbow Press, 1987.

Lehman, J. Lee. *The Ultimate Asteroid Book*. West Chester, PA: Whitford Press, 1988.

Schwartz, Jacob. *Asteroid Name Encyclopedia*. St. Paul, MN: Llewellyn Publications, 1995.

# Psychological Astrology

Psychological astrology is an attempt to reformulate contemporary astrology in terms of psychological concepts and practices. Although psychological astrology received its initial impetus from Carl Jung's analytical psychology and later from Dane Rudhyar's attempts to integrate astrology with humanistic psychology, contemporary astrologers have gone beyond these early forays. More recent attempts include the assimilation of ideas from psychodynamic theory, existential psychology, object relations theory, general systems theory, gestalt therapy, cognitive behavioral psychology, and various other psychological models and perspectives. In this regard, humanistic and Jungian approaches must be regarded as subsets of psychological astrology as a whole.

Perhaps the defining attribute of a psychological approach to astrology is its focus on integrating the birth chart and, thus, supporting the human potential for growth and change. Outside of this one primary focus there is probably no uniform psychological approach, although there are probably few psychological astrologers who are not transpersonally oriented. Almost by definition, psychological astrology is transpersonal, which is that branch of psychology that incorporates spiritual notions into its framework and as such is a more inclusive school of psychology—"a fourth wave," as Abraham Maslow (1968) called it in his 1968 book, *Toward a Psychology of Being*. (The first three waves were psychoanalysis, behaviorism, and humanistic psychology.)

> I consider Humanistic, Third Force Psychology, to be transitional, a preparation for a still "higher" Fourth Psychology, transpersonal, transhuman, centered in the cosmos rather than in human needs and interest, going beyond humanness, identity, self-actualization, and the like.

Given Maslow's assertion, one should not equate psychological astrology with conventional notions of psychology and thereby strip it of its transpersonal dimension. As a transpersonal theory, astrology adds significant breadth and depth to psychology, transforming it into a more spiritualized model that relates psyche to cosmos, just as Maslow envisioned.

Psychological astrology can be differentiated from therapeutic astrology on the basis of it not being limited to psychotherapy. Whereas therapeutic astrology seeks to establish general guidelines, principles, and professional standards for the application of astrology to the fields of counseling and psychotherapy, psychological astrology, per se, is a broader discipline. Just as psychologists must be trained in a variety of different subject areas—psychotherapeutic techniques, personality theory, psychopathology, human development, and research methodology—so the interests of psychological astrologers extend beyond a focus on counseling. Articles and books by practitioners cover a broad array of topics, including developmental stages, sexual dysfunction, learning disabilities, psychopathology, eating disorders, dream analysis, and research methodologies.

## Astrology as a Personality Theory

Although astrology clearly involves counseling, every approach to counseling is founded upon certain presuppositions about the human psyche it hopes to treat. These presuppositions, in sum, constitute the personality theory that supports the therapy. From a psychological perspective, astrology is implicitly a personality theory. Various attempts have been made to organize astrological concepts and precepts into a formal model.

As noted in Calvin S. Hall and Gardner Lindzey's *Theories of Personality*, any adequate theory of personality must accomplish the following minimal objectives: (1) it must be comprehensive, or integrative, in that it deals with the total, functioning person; (2) it must account for what motivates the human being; (3) it must contain a set of empirical definitions concerning the various parts of the personality, thus permitting observation; (4) it must consist of a cluster of assumptions about behavior that are systematically related in accordance with certain rules; and (5) it must be useful in that it is capable of generating predictions about personality characteristics that are testable and verifiable, thus expanding knowledge.

Astrology meets all the qualifications for a theory of personality. First, astrology is a comprehensive system in that it is concerned with all the parts and processes that make up the totality of the human psyche. Second, the signs of the zodiac provide clear referents for the impulses, motives, and instinctual drives that govern and regulate human conduct. Third, the various signs, planets, and houses, which constitute the parts of personality, are empirically defined. Fourth, the rules of chart interpretation—delineation, synthesis, and aspect analysis—represent specific assumptions about behavior that are systematically related. And fifth, astrology is useful in that it not only explains the facts of behavior, it is also capable of generating predictions or propositions that are verifiable, thus promoting research.

Astrology, then, consists of a set of assumptions concerning human behavior together with rules for relating these assumptions and definitions to permit their interaction with observable events. A simple example should suffice to illustrate this. If a person has Saturn on the ascendant, this theory would predict that the function symbolized by this planet would be a salient feature of personality. This prediction is based on the related assumptions that the ascendant is a conspicuous element of personality, and planets conjunct the ascendant will be prominent in the person's appearance and behavior. Since Saturn has an empirical definition, e.g., Saturn represents the process to organize and is associated with orderly, serious behavior geared toward satisfying the need for structure and control, this allows for the testing of the validity of these assumptions, i.e., how do these concepts match up with actual observation of this person's behavior? If this subject does, in fact, appear to be orderly, serious, structured, and the like, then the assumption is confirmed.

This example shows how astrology represents a theory complete with motivational drives, psychological faculties with empirical definitions, systematically related assumptions, and a capacity for generating predictions that are empirically verifiable. Every planet, sign, and house is implicated in the personality, thereby showing how multidimensional and integrative a theory astrology is. There is no behavioral phenomenon of demonstrated significance that falls outside the theoretical framework of astrology.

Astrology is also the only system in which there are external referents—signs and planets—for pieces of psychic structure. These external referents are visible, predictable, and capable of complexity beyond any theory of human behavior devised by psychology. While astrology is simple in its derivation of archetypes (signs), it is complex in its ability to derive individual process from these archetypes (planets in sign, house, and aspect); each piece of psychic structure has concrete meaning yet is infinitely variable in combination. Because astrology has many shades of meaning, it is easily compatible with almost any psychological model, almost all of which can be subsumed into astrological language. For example, Sigmund Freud's tripartite division of the mind into id, ego, and superego is roughly paralleled in astrology by the relations between Mars (id), the Sun (ego), and Saturn (superego). Of course, the many elements of astrology make it a vastly subtler and potentially sophisticated model for depicting the structure and dynamics of the psyche.

Another way that astrology differs from conventional personality theories is that it has no founder. Astrology was not invented, created, or developed by any single individual or group of individuals, as is the case with other personality theories. Invariably, a personality theory bears the stamp of its creator; that is, a theory is a self-portrait of its founder. This can be clearly seen, for example, in Freud's chart, which perfectly symbolizes the Oedipus complex that Freud universalized for every human being. This same principle holds true for the founders of other personality theories. Each theory, with the exception of astrology, starts off as a projection of one person's individual viewpoint and subsequently attracts adherents who resonate with that viewpoint. In each instance, the peculiarities of the theory can be traced back to the prejudices, tendencies, issues, and cognitive styles that are clearly reflected in the horoscope of the founder. Astrology, on the other hand, is a more objective framework since it does not originate with any one individual (or even one culture), is based on empirical observation, and has stood the test of time. In this sense, it can be thought of as a meta-theory that subsumes other models.

## Traditional Event-Oriented Astrology

It was not until the advent of humanistic psychology in the 1960s that astrologers began to think seriously about the chart in terms of growth and transformation. For those who began studying astrology only recently, it might seem that it was always this way. But it was not. Although, in his book *The Secret of the Golden Flower*, Jung said, "Astrology represents the summation of the psychological knowledge of antiquity," the fact is that there was very little in astrology prior to the 1960s that bore much relationship to what today is considered "psychological."

Ancient peoples initially perceived the planets as gods who ruled over the various processes of nature, much as a king ruled over his subjects. The conceived relationship between celestial and terrestrial events was linear, dualistic, and hierarchical: a superior power had dominion over an inferior one. While later and deeper forms of astrological philosophy recognized that macrocosm and microcosm were actually interpenetrating and thus their relationship was not linear or dualistic, this view declined with the collapse of the Hellenistic culture in the third century. A simpler model prevailed during the medieval period and persisted in one form or another right up to the second half of the twentieth century. Human beings were perceived as fated recipients of cosmic forces that could be propitiated but not denied.

Such a gloomy determinism was reinforced by a value-laden terminology that too often described the birth chart in ominous terms, e.g., malefic, evil aspect, debilitation, affliction, detriment, fall, destroyer of life, hell of the zodiac, and so on. Of course, there were "good" parts to astrology as well, such as benefics and exaltations, but these only served to underscore the determinism of the system. Planets were variously conceived as transmitters of mysterious rays or electromagnetic forces that impacted upon the individual at birth. Understandably, this induced individuals to focus their attention outwards to see what malice or affection the gods might have in store for them. The rigid determinism of traditional astrology did not allow for the possibility of change or growth in consciousness. Instead, people more likely consulted the stars as a means of avoiding a calamitous fate or of exploiting opportunities for manipulating circumstances to personal advantage.

The implication of traditional, event-oriented astrology was that the individual was a potential victim of an indifferent universe over which he had little or no control. Accordingly, astrologers were only too eager to give people what they wanted—predictions, advice, warnings, and simplistic solutions to what is now recognized as complex, psychological problems. At best, traditional astrologers were well meaning individuals interested in the prediction of events and the description of character, and they did no harm. At worst, they were fear-peddling individuals who exploited the insecurities and anxieties of the people who purchased their services, and they did great harm.

The vast majority of mundane predictions about illnesses, accidents, divorces, shipwrecks, earthquakes, scandals, inheritances, marriages, job promotions, and the like, were utterly useless except to create an addiction to the astrologer whose pronouncements appeared to offer some promise of control over the events in question. But no astrologer could predict with certainty exactly what the events would be, under precisely what circumstances they would take place, or how they would affect the person. Especially lacking in such predictions was the meaning and purpose that the event might have beyond its immediate effects. What relationship did it have to the consciousness of the experiencer? What opportunities did it offer for self-insight and growth in awareness?

Likewise, the traditional astrologer's description of character was generally limited to superficial trait descriptions heavily laden with moral judgments and glib advice. At best, the astrologer confirmed what the individual already intuitively knew. At worst, the astrologer confused or upset the individual with interpretations that were shallow, insensitive, judgmental, overly negative, or just plain wrong. There was little if any attempt to address the deeper dimensions of the chart that hinted at unconscious beliefs and fundamental drives that underlay surface behavior. Character was seen as either static and unalterable, or easily modified by following the cosmically informed counsel of one's astrologer. Such assumptions appear naive from the perspective of modern, depth psychology. While changing one's inborn character can be extraordinarily difficult, it can be achieved through courage, persistence, and hard work.

## The Birth of Psychological Astrology

It was the Swiss psychoanalyst Carl Jung who first recognized the vast potential of astrology as a tool for exploring the depths of the human psyche. In various writings throughout his life, Jung made reference to his profound respect for astrology. He asserted that astrology had a great deal to contribute to psychology and admitted to having employed it with some frequency in his analytic work with clients. In cases of difficult psychological diagnosis, Jung would draw up a horoscope in order to have a further point of view from an entirely different angle. In a letter to Professor B. V. Raman, published in the June 1948 issue of *American Astrology*, Jung wrote: "I must say that I very often found that the astrological data elucidated certain points which I otherwise would have been unable to understand"

In C. G. *Jung: Letters* (volume II), Jung regarded the signs and planets of astrology as symbols of archetypal processes that originated in the collective unconscious. The archetypes of the collective unconscious were the universal organizing principles underlying and motivating all psychological life, both individual and collective. Whereas mythology placed its emphasis upon the cultural manifestations of archetypes at various times and places in history, astrology utilized archetypes as a language for understanding the basic psychological drives of human beings. "Astrology, like the collective unconscious with which psychology is concerned, consists of symbolic configurations: the planets are the gods, symbols of the power of the unconscious." The gods of mythology represented the living forces of the universe that patterned all things. Like Plato's Forms, an archetype was both subjective and objective; it was evident both in the innate ideas of human consciousness as well as in the fundamental processes of nature; it informed not only human experience but also planetary motions.

It was precisely this dual nature of the archetype that enabled the chart to bridge inner character with the outer events that reflected that character. "There are many instances of striking analogies between astrological constellations and psychological events or between the horoscope and the characterological disposition," wrote Jung in his *Letters*. Archetypes, he concluded, were psychoid, i.e., they shape matter as well as mind. An astrological configuration defined both the innate disposition of the individual and the particular kinds of outer conditions that the individual was likely to experience. In an interview with André Barbault that appeared in the May 26, 1954, issue of *Astrologie Moderne*, Jung stated, "One can expect with considerable assurance, that a given well-defined psychological situation will be accompanied by an analogous astrological configuration."

Jung recognized that the unique and unparalleled ability of astrology to disclose correlations between planetary motions and human experience also made it an accurate way of timing life crises: "I have observed many cases where a well-defined psychological phase or an analogous event has been accompanied by a transit—particularly the afflictions of Saturn and Uranus."

Jung's observance of correlations between psychological phenomena and astrological data contributed to the formulation of his theory of synchronicity. In *The Interpretation of Nature and Psyche*, Jung defined synchronicity as "the simultaneous occurrence of a certain psychic state with one or more external events which appear as meaningful parallels to the momentary subjective state." Accordingly, Jung did not hesitate to take the synchronistic phenomena that underlay astrology seriously. Astrology, he thought, worked precisely because of synchronicity, i.e., the psychic structure of the person about to be born was "meaningfully paralleled" in the positions of the planets at that time.

When looking for a way to test the hypothesis of synchronicity, Jung set up an astrological experiment that correlated planetary configurations, or cross aspects, between the charts of marital partners. He hypothesized that certain cross aspects would appear with greater frequency between the charts of marital partners than between charts of people who had no relationship. "The meaningful coincidence we are looking for is immediately apparent in astrology," said Jung, "since the astrological data ... correspond to individual traits of character; and from the remotest times the various planets, houses, zodiacal signs, and aspects have all had meanings that serve as a basis for a character study."

Although Jung never developed any systematic theory of astrology, it appears that his own theory of analytical psychology was heavily influenced by it. There are so many parallels that one is almost forced to conclude that at least some of his major concepts were borrowed directly from astrology. In addition to his explicit endorsement of planets as archetypes and his theory of synchronicity as a means for explaining astrological coincidences, Jung's notion of two attitude types—extrovert and introvert—is readily recognizable by astrologers as the bipolar division of the zodiac into two polarities—positive/masculine (extrovert) and negative/feminine (introvert) signs.

Likewise, his four function types—intuition, sensation, thinking, and feeling—are roughly paralleled in astrology by the four elements—fire, earth, air, and water. In addition to these more obvious analogues, there are additional correlations that have been explored by astrologers. These include ego/Sun, persona/ascendant, shadow/Pluto, anima/Venus, animus/Mars, and collective unconscious/Neptune. Difficult astrological configurations, especially those involving hard aspects from the outer planets to Mercury, Venus, Mars, Moon, or Sun, have been observed by astrologers to represent trouble spots in the personality similar to what Jung described as psychic complexes, i.e., unconscious, emotionally charged memories, images, and thoughts clustered around a central core.

In the 1930s, Dane Rudhyar began to reformulate modern astrology in terms of Jung's analytical psychology. He especially focused on Jung's idea that the psyche was a dynamic compound of opposing forces in equilibrium, and that the psyche was intrinsically motivated to evolve in the direction of psychic wholeness, a process Jung called *individuation*. Jung believed that the process of personality transformation was innate, or teleologically motivated. Personality was not merely the product of external forces, but strove purposefully towards a final goal of self-realization. As the individual learned from self-created experience, the archetypal structuring of the psyche became increasingly differentiated, integrated, and whole. In Rudhyar's 1936 book *The Astrology of Personality*, he recognized that these ideas were readily adaptable to astrology. The chart, too, was a dynamic compound of opposing forces (signs) in equilibrium. And the various parts of astrology with their myriad aspects and interrelations were symbolic of archetypal forces struggling to transform themselves into an integrated whole. Rudhyar realized that "the process of individuation was implicit in every horoscope."

By the 1960s, Rudhyar's project of reformulating astrology received new impetus from the humanistic movement in psychology. Humanistic psychology, as embodied in the writings of Abraham Maslow, Carl Rogers, Rollo May, and others, had arisen in response to the bleak pessimism inherent in the Freudian psychoanalytic view and the robot conception of human potential implied in behaviorism. Both psychoanalysis and behaviorism were deterministic in that they conceived of personality as the effect of causes external to the person himself, i.e., genetics, parents, environmental conditions, and so on. Humanistic psychologists countered this trend by developing models that could account for the apparent purposiveness and growth-seeking behavior of human beings.

Rather than portray the individual as caught in an interminable struggle between instinctual drives and the inhibiting influence of society (psychoanalysis), or fragment the person into a multitude of conditioned behaviors as seen from an external vantage point (behaviorism), humanists perceived the individual as a unified organism made up of autonomous drives and functions that could be differentiated from one another and integrated into a functional whole greater than the sum of its parts.

Humanistic psychologists challenged Freudian theory by postulating that instinctual drives were not dangerous forces erupting out of a primitive id, but healthy impulses that should be valued and trusted. The individual was perceived as a creative, self-actualizing, and self-determining organism capable of making responsible decisions and growing progressively toward an ideal state. Unlike behaviorists who ignored the internal world of consciousness, humanists emphasized the primacy of the subjective element. Whereas behaviorists contended that behavior was solely conditioned by external causes, humanists focused on the relevance of intentionality as an internal cause of behavior. While behaviorists were concerned with how behavior could be manipulated and controlled, humanists emphasized the capacity for personal freedom and choice. In sum, it was not the outer environment that was of central importance to the humanistic psychologist, but the person's inner world of perceptions, values, thoughts, beliefs, attitudes, expectations, needs, feelings, and sensations.

Rudhyar was the first to recognize how astrology and humanistic psychology complemented one another. The chart, in effect, could be utilized as a tool for mapping the complex inner world that humanists were starting to explore. Just as humanistic psychology was a response to the determinism inherent in psychoanalysis and behaviorism, humanistic astrology was a response to the determinism inherent in traditional, event-oriented astrology. Borrowing from Carl Roger's 1951 book *Client-Centered Therapy*, Rudhyar (1972) developed *Person Centered Astrology*. Rudhyar was less concerned with whether astrology works than on how it could be utilized to assist the process of self-actualization. The real question was, given that astrology works, What is its proper use?

In 1969, Rudhyar founded the International Committee for Humanistic Astrology and declared that astrology was, or should be, primarily a technique for understanding human nature. He decried the implicit determinism of predictive astrology and focused instead on astrology's potential as a symbolic language. Instead of seeing planets as transmitters of physical influence, Rudhyar saw them as symbolic of human functions. As a psychological language and diagnostic tool, astrology could serve as a guide to the integration and transformation of personality. Rudhyar's approach was "person centered" in the sense that every birth chart was unique; a horoscope represented the individual's total potential in which no planet was "good" or "bad," but rather each element was part of an organic whole. Events were not interpreted as isolated occurrences with fortunate or unfortunate effects, but as purposeful, phase-specific manifestations of developmental cycles. An event derived its meaning from the stage it represented in a given planetary cycle and contributed to an ongoing process of growth that lead inexorably toward self-realization.

In the 1970s, the humanistic banner was taken up by such astrologers as Zipporah Dobyns, Richard Idemon, Stephen Arroyo, Robert Hand, Donna Cunningham, and others. Humanistic astrologers asserted that there is no absolute separation between human and divine; rather people and planets are woven into the same seamless web of being. Every individual is a focus and channel for the numinous energies that permeate the entire cosmos. Consciousness, not matter, is the primary reality of the universe. As the human psyche is both reflective of and embedded within the universal psyche, it partakes of the creative power of this parent consciousness. The psyche is bound and animated by the laws and formative principles of the one being of which all lesser beings are parts. While the universal laws of absolute being cannot be violated, the individual is free and self-determining within the boundaries of these laws.

Rudhyar held that each person was born in response to a need of the universe at a particular time and place. The birth chart, in effect, represents the solution to this need, i.e., it reveals the purpose of the life and the key to one's destiny. Put another way, the horoscope is like a "seed plan" that shows a person's unique path of development. Just as a seed packet depicts a picture of the plant that the enclosed seeds may eventually become, so the horoscope symbolizes the kind of adult that the individual may become. In this view, nothing occurs in a human life except for a purpose, and this purpose is the purpose of the whole acting through the individual. This whole is often referred to as the core self, the indwelling divinity that is rooted in a living, purposive universe. The question then becomes not what is going to happen, but what is its meaning? Astrology, said Rudhyar, can be utilized as a kind of karma yoga in which everything that happens is related to who the person is and what he or she may become. Thus, the humanistic astrologer should not be concerned with events, per se, but only with the response or meaning that the client gives to them. "It is not the predictable events which are important, but the attitude of the individual person towards his own growth and self-fulfillment," Rudhyar wrote in *Person Centered Astrology*.

The advantage of the birth chart is that it depicts the individual as a whole and thus provides a means for understanding how internal conflicts result in personality fragmentation and the exteriorization of conflict. Individuals split off and deny certain parts of themselves when the needs that underlay the expression of these parts meet with pain and frustration. Various functions get repressed and projected, and thus the individual is reduced to only part of what he or she potentially is. Unintegrated functions are typically experienced in the outer world in the guise of people and situations the individual attracts. What the individual experiences as a problematic situation or relationship can be seen in the chart as an aspect of his or her own psyche. In this way, the horoscope indicates what functions have been denied and projected, and through what circumstances (houses) they will likely be encountered.

While the birth chart provides insight into the client's internal conflicts, transits and progressions reveal when these conflicts will be targeted for healing. These planetary movements indicate the nature, meaning, and duration of various developmental periods, each of which presents its own challenges and opportunities. While transits may correlate with outer events that seem to impinge upon the individual, astrology suggests that these events are the synchronous external manifestation of inner changes. In other words, environment and psyche are reflections of one another. The outer events serve as the trigger or stimulus to promote inner psychological growth. Seen in this way, transits reveal those parts of a person's nature that are ready to be consciously integrated, explored or transformed.

To reengage a split-off part usually results in crisis since it means that the old order has to die in order for a new, more inclusive order to emerge. In his 1975 book *From Humanistic to Transpersonal Astrology*, Rudhyar said the humanistic astrologer:

> ...welcomes crises as signs of growth. He attempts to help the client or patient to reorient himself toward the causes of the crisis, to reassess his goals as well as his motives, to accept what is, but in a new and holistic manner ... which eventually should lead to harmony, inner peace, wisdom and compassion.

The value of astrology, then, is not its power to predict what the gods have in store for humans, but its ability to reveal the god-like powers that reside in the depths of every human being. Accordingly, the focus in humanistic astrology is inward, not outward, and interpretations are made in terms of personal growth and fulfillment. Simply put, the goal is to help the client realize the potentials that are symbolized by the horoscope.

For example, Saturn opposing Venus in the natal chart indicates not simply "misfortune in love," but the potential to love deeply, enduringly, and responsibly along with the patience and determination to overcome obstacles. While realization of this potential may require a certain amount of hardship and suffering, to predict only hardship and suffering with no understanding of the potential gains involved is shortsighted at best and damaging at worst. In *The Astrologer's Casebook*, Zipporah Dobyns put it this way:

> Telling people they are fated to experience specific negative events can be highly destructive. The view taken here is that character is destiny, and that by changing our character (our habitual attitudes, beliefs, and actions) we can change our destiny. With self-knowledge, we can integrate conflicts, overcome weaknesses, further develop talents, and move toward balance. As humanistic psychology puts it, we can achieve self-actualization and self-transcendence.

In many ways, humanistic astrology represents a genuine advancement in the theory of humanistic psychology. Both Jungian and humanistic psychologies have been criticized for their lack of precision in describing the inner nature of the human being. References to archetypes, faculties, functions, impulses, and the like tend to be vague and speculative, with no concrete referents for outlining in a systematic manner the structure of the psyche. Humanistic psychology is more a set of attitudes toward the person than a precise and useful theory of personality and human growth. Astrology, on the other hand, provides objective predictable correlates for the structure and dynamics of the psyche while also indicating the directions that growth might occur. The person with Saturn opposed Venus, for example, may shift over time from a negative, fearful attitude toward relationships, e.g., "I will resist being controlled by my domineering partner," to one of responsible and loyal commitment. Such a shift would reflect a more mature, realistic attitude toward relationship, e.g., "a good marriage requires patience, humility, and hard work," while still being consistent with the astrological meaning of Saturn opposed Venus.

This further implies that the static, fixed meanings that traditional astrology ascribed to planetary aspects reflected a limited understanding of how astrology works. A central postulate of psychological astrology is that a given astrological configuration is multivalent, i.e., capable of manifesting in a variety of ways while still being true to the nature of the archetypes involved. As an individual becomes more integrated, the outer manifestation of his or her chart will change to reflect the growth attained. Thus transits and progressions are not interpreted in terms of specific, concrete events, but as qualities of durations of time that provide opportunities for specific kinds of development. How a transit is experienced—its form and quality—is largely dependent upon the level of consciousness of the experiencer and the meaning s/he attributes to the event.

## Fate and Causality

As a theory of causality, psychological astrology is radically opposed to the mechanistic determinism implicit in most psychological models. It does not assume that psychological problems are invariably the by-products of an unhealthy culture, traumatic experiences, or faulty child rearing. Because the precise nature of the person as well as his or her environment is implicit in the symbolism of the chart from the first breath, astrology suggests that character and destiny are fated. But as Liz Greene pointed out in her book *The Astrology of Fate*, fate is indissolubly bound up with justice and law rather than a random predetermining force that dictates a person's every action and experience. Fate was called *Moira* by the Greeks and evolved from a vision of an orderly, interconnected cosmos. As the guardian of justice, Moira was simply natural law raised to the status of a deity. She embodied the principle that because humans are part of nature they cannot violate nature's laws without suffering the consequences; they cannot repudiate an archetype or express an archetype to excess without exacting a penalty designed to correct the transgression.

In this regard, fate is a cause-and-effect principle analogous to the eastern doctrine of karma. Fate is not simply a blessing or punishment conspired by the gods, but a corrective process in the service of a transcendent purpose. And this purpose is that the individual evolves toward a fuller realization of the divine order that humans naturally embody.

Combining the doctrine of karma with the theory of astrology can account for the fated quality of a person's life and character. The chart may be seen as a seed plan or blueprint of destiny, but in the end it is a self-created fate. This perspective suggests that the infinite wisdom of the cosmos decrees that a person is born when the planets are arranged in a structure that reflects the fate that the individual has earned on the basis of past actions in past lives. Subsequent experiences with one's culture and caretakers derive out of a pre-existent psychic structure. The environment, then, beginning with the body, is not so much a primary as a secondary cause of behavior; it is a mirror reflecting the soul's already existing internal structure.

In regard to the etiology of a pathological condition, the environment confirms, but it does not originate, the child's primary anxieties and inner conflicts. Of course, one cannot dispute environmental deficits and their effects. What needs to be emphasized, however, is the individual's accountability. In this view, the experienced environment constitutes karmic feedback to activate, correct, and refine a person's innate character, however long and painful this process may be. As noted in an article by J. Segal and H. Yahres in the November 1978 issue of *Psychology Today*, some studies indicate the child has as much effect on the parent as the parent has on the child, thus the parent-child relationship is reciprocal. Likewise, recent developments in past-lives therapy suggest that a given life may be but a single chapter in a long and ongoing evolutionary process, as noted in such books as *Coming Back: A Psychiatrist Explores Past-Life Journeys* (Moody), *Many Lives, Many Masters*, (Weiss), and *Other Lives, Other Selves* (Woolger).

Psychological astrology emphasizes character over fate and does so for a simple reason: human beings have more control over character than fate, thus character *deserves* the greater emphasis. As far as fate is concerned, early childhood conditions signify the first and thus prototypical event pattern that reflects psychic structure. This, however, does not mean that the environment is merely the effect of how it is perceived (constructivism). The constructivist position that one constructs a reality on the basis of meaning attributions is only relatively valid. It is valid in the sense that how a person interprets events is going to shape his subsequent experience. His interpretations will influence his feelings and behavior (subjective reality), and these, in turn, will tend to influence subsequent responses from others (objective reality). In this sense, each person *does* construct a reality that conforms to his or her subjective world. That subjective world, however, may derive initially from an objective fate that has been earned on the basis of past actions in past lives, and which was internalized at an early age in the form of emotionally significant childhood experiences—the prototype event pattern. These formative experiences become part of psychic structure, i.e., mental habits, beliefs, expectations, and images of self and other, all of which are symbolized by the horoscope.

This formulation is consistent with Jung's theory of synchronicity and his definition of archetypes as having a *psychoid* factor, meaning they shape matter as well as mind. A basic tenet of Jungian psychology (and psychological astrology) is that archetypes/planets are nonlocal; they do not reside solely *within* the psyche as structural elements, but rather are inherent in nature as a whole. Archetypes are imminent and thus infinitely diffused throughout nature. It is precisely this psychoid quality of the archetype that mediates a meaningful connection between inner, psychic factors and outer, objective events.

Heraclitus's statement, "character is destiny," implied that subjective character and objective fate were two sides of the same issue. Unless this issue is framed in a context that includes multiple lives, astrologers are forced into a deterministic model—the assumption that the planets, a capricious creator, or random chance is the final and ultimate determinant of destiny. Humans *are* creatures of fate, yet have the power to choose. This is the classic paradox in which astrology is embedded. So the horoscope can be interpreted on multiple levels—objective world, subjective world, and the dynamic relations between the two.

It may be that evolution is built into the structure of these relations in that there is an opportunity to learn from self-created experiences (fate). Of course, this is an article of faith, not of fact. However, it is unlikely that all elements of fate are absolutely fixed because that would leave no room for growth or change, and if there is one thing that modern psychology has established it is that people can and *do* change. Fate can be massaged in the direction of more satisfying outcomes to the extent that the individual *learns*. The exact degree to which fate can be altered must remain speculative. Still, this is an infinitely more hopeful vision of human beings than the idea that they are determined by forces beyond their control. Perhaps the greatest contribution of psychological astrology is the idea that character *is* fate, and if humans can alter their character, they can mutate their fate.

## Summary

Psychological astrology is the reformulation of astrology in terms of modern psychological concepts and theories. While it initially derived its impetus from Jungian and humanistic approaches, it has recently expanded to include psychodynamic, cognitive behavioral, and object relations theories, among others. Whereas traditional astrology tended to focus more or less exclusively on outer events and relatively superficial descriptions of personality, without seeing how the former derives from the latter, psychological astrologers try to discern the relationship of character to fate at a deeper level.

Psychological astrology is inherently transpersonal. A key component of this model is borrowed from Jung's concept of synchronicity, which postulates that outer, physical events are meaningfully related to the consciousness of the experiencer. Events are conceptualized as derivatives of consciousness; as such, they provide feedback that catalyzes the further maturation of soul. This formulation is consistent with a reincarnationist perspective, which, when woven into astrology, implies that the horoscope is a symbolic map of both character and fate, the two being mirror images of one another.

The addition of a psychological perspective to astrology contributes to an evolving understanding of the field. Astrology's traditional, event-oriented and predictive dimensions are situated within a context that allows for the growth and development of character. Moreover, psychological astrology makes the evolution of psyche the cornerstone of its model.

—Glenn Perry, Ph.D.

**Sources:**

Dobyns, Zipporah. *The Astrologer's Casebook*. Los Angeles: TIA Publications, 1973.

Greene, Liz. *The Astrology of Fate*. York Beach, ME: Samuel Weiser, 1984.

Hall, Calvin S., Gardner Lindzey, and John B. Campbell. *Theories of Personality*. 4th ed. New York: J. Wiley & Sons, 1998.

Jung, Carl. C. G. *Jung: Letters*. Vol. II. Edited by G. Adler and A. Jaffe; translated by R. F. C. Hull. London: Routledge and Kegan Paul, 1976.

———. "Commentary." In *The Secret of the Golden Flower*. Translated and edited by R. Wilhelm. New York: Harcourt, Brace, & World, 1962.

———. Interview with André Barbault. *Astrologie Moderne* (May 26, 1954).

———. Letter to Professor B. V. Raman. *American Astrology* (June 1948).

———. "Synchronicity: An Acausal Connecting Principle." In *The Interpretation of Nature and Psyche*. Edited by C. Jung and W. Pauli. New York: Pantheon, 1955.

Maslow, Abraham H. *Toward a Psychology of Being*. 3rd ed. New York: J. Wiley & Sons, 1999.

Moody, Raymond. *Coming Back: A Psychiatrist Explores Past-Life Journeys*. New York: Bantam, 1990.

Rogers, Carl R. *Client-Centered Therapy, Its Current Practice, Implications, and Theory*. Boston: Houghton Mifflin, 1951.

Rudhyar, Dane. *The Astrology of Personality*. Garden City, NY: Doubleday & Company, 1936.

———. *From Humanistic to Transpersonal Astrology*. Palo Alto, CA: The Seed Center, 1975.

———. *Person Centered Astrology*. Lakemont, GA: CSA Press, 1972.

Segal, J. and H. Yahres. "Bringing Up Mother." *Psychology Today* (November 1978): 93.

Weiss, Brian L. *Many Lives, Many Masters*. New York: Simon & Schuster, 1988.

Woolger, Roger J. *Other Lives, Other Selves: A Jungian Psychotherapist Discovers Past Lives*. New York: Doubleday, 1987.

## Psychology and Astrology

Because so much of astrology—at least as it is currently practiced—is psychological, the relationship between psychology and astrology is complex. Examined here are some of the issues that psychological researchers have addressed when questioning the validity of astrology.

### Femininity

In the September 1973 issue of the *Journal of Psychology*, Robert J. Pellegrini noted significant correlations between people's sun sign and their score on the California Psychological Inventory's femininity scale. In March 1975, the same journal published another article by Pellegrini in which he noted that the highest femininity scores in the 1973 study corresponded with the consecutive signs from Leo through Capricorn, a correlation that does not correspond with the traditional astrological characterization of *every other* sign as feminine. Later studies failed to confirm Pellegrini's original findings.

### Introversion/Extroversion

In a 1978 *Journal of Social Psychology* article, Jeff Mayo and others found correlations between people's sun sign and their score on a measure of introversion and extroversion. This study found that, congruent with what one might anticipate from astrological tradition, even-numbered signs (Aries, Gemini, etc.) were more extroverted than odd-numbered signs (Taurus, Cancer, etc.). Most later studies failed to confirm Mayo's study, with the exception of one by Jan J. Van Rooij and others in the May 1988 issue of the *Journal of Psychology*, which successfully replicated the Mayo article.

### Occupation

The various studies by Françoise and Michel Gauquelin dealt with in the essay on vocational astrology have successfully demonstrated significant correlations between occupation and the positions of certain planets at birth. Most studies of sun signs have failed to find statistically significant correlations between sun signs and professions, although there was a series that appeared in the *Guardian*, a British newspaper, in 1984 that showed correlations from census data. A disingenuous critique published in the *Skeptical Inquirer* the next year attempted to explain away the *Guardian* study as resulting from the imputed tendency of people to pick professions based on a prior knowledge of the professions associated with their sun signs.

### Belief in Astrology

An interesting line of research that several different researchers have pursued is the correlation between belief in astrology and certain other personality traits, although most such studies are undertaken to demonstrate that "believers" in the science of the stars are weak or defective in some way. Thus, for example, in February 1980, the *Journal of Social Psychology* published an article by Ruth H. Sosis and others that found that a belief in fate was correlated with a belief in astrology. They also found that females were more likely to believe in astrology than males. In 1982, the journal *Personality and Individual Difference* published an article by G. A. Tyson that hypothesized a correlation between astrological clients and stressful social roles. And in 1983, the same journal published an article reporting a study by Michael Startup that found no signs of neuroticism in astrology students, although it did find correlations between astrology students and psychology students.

### Miscellaneous Studies

Other interesting studies have appeared both within and outside mainstream academic psychology. For example, in April 1988, the journal *Perceptual and Motor Skills* published a study by Steven Stack and David Lester that found a correlation between suicide ideation and people born under the sign Pisces (a correlation that one would have anticipated from traditional astrology). Another interesting piece was a 1973 study by John Newmeyer and Steven Anderson that found Geminis, Virgos, and Aquarians most likely to be heroin abusers, and Scorpios and Capricorns least likely.

### Vernon Clark Administers Psychological Tests

The studies conducted by the American psychologist Vernon Clark belong in a class by themselves. In 1959, he designed three tests that were given to 50 astrologers. In the first, astrologers were asked to match the natal charts of 10 people with 10 short biographies that highlighted career, marriage, medical history, and hobbies. All subjects were well established in their chosen profession.

In the second, astrologers were asked, in 10 instances, to match one of two charts with a brief case history. They were not informed that one of each pair was an actual horoscope and the other a chart cast for a random place and time. In the third, astrologers were asked to distinguish natal charts for high-IQ people from charts of victims of brain damage. As a control group, the same tests were given to psychologists and social workers with no background in astrology.

In all three tests, the accuracy of the astrologers was statistically significant. In comparison, the accuracy of the control groups was never more than what would be expected from random chance. Clark's first and second tests, with some variations, were also successfully conducted by both Zipporah Dobyns and Joseph Ernest Vidmar in the 1970s.

Clark's work was important for providing a suggestive model from which to design other experiments. This model has been referred to as holistic because of the way in which it is able to bring the entire astrological chart into the test. Other approaches, such as the aforementioned studies, isolate one factor, such as the sun sign, and ignore other influences.

**Sources:**


Brau, Jean-Louis, Helen Weaver, and Allan Edmands. *Larousse Encyclopedia of Astrology*. New York: New American Library, 1980.

Mayo, Jeff, O. White, and Hans Eysenck. "An Empirical Study of the Relation between Astrological Factors and Personality." *Journal of Social Psychology* 105 (1978): 229–36.

Miller, Neil Z. *Astrology* (Newsletter). Santa Fe: UniSearch, 1991.

Newmeyer, John, and Steven Anderson. "Astrology and Addiction: An Empirical Probe." *Drug Forum* (Spring 1973): 271–78.

Pellegrini, Robert J. "The Astrological 'Theory' of Personality: An Unbiased Test by a Biased Observer." *Journal of Psychology* (September 1973): 21–28.

———. "Birthdate Psychology: A New Look at Some Old Data." *Journal of Psychology* (March 1975): 261–65.

Sosis, Ruth H., et al. "Perceived Locus of Control and Beliefs about Astrology." *Journal of Social Psychology* (Feb. 1980): 65–71.

Stack, Steven, and David Lester. "Born under a Bad Sign? Astrological Sign and Suicide Ideation." *Perceptual and Motor Skills* (April 1988): 461–62.

Startup, Michael. "Belief in Astrology: A System of Maladjustment?" *Personality and Individual Difference* 4: no. 3 (1983): 343–45.

Tyson, G. A. "People Who Consult Astrologers: A Profile." *Personality and Individual Difference* v. 3, iss. 2 (1982): 119–26.

Van Rooij, Jan J., et al. "Introversion-Extroversion and Sunsign." *Journal of Psychology* (May 1988): 275–78.


## Ptolemy, Claudius

Claudius Ptolemy (100–178), sometimes called the father of Western astrology, was a Greek astronomer and astrologer who lived in Alexandria, Egypt. Ptolemy was a highly learned individual, with a broad grasp of geography, mathematics, astronomy, and music. His account of the motions of the planets, which placed Earth as the stable

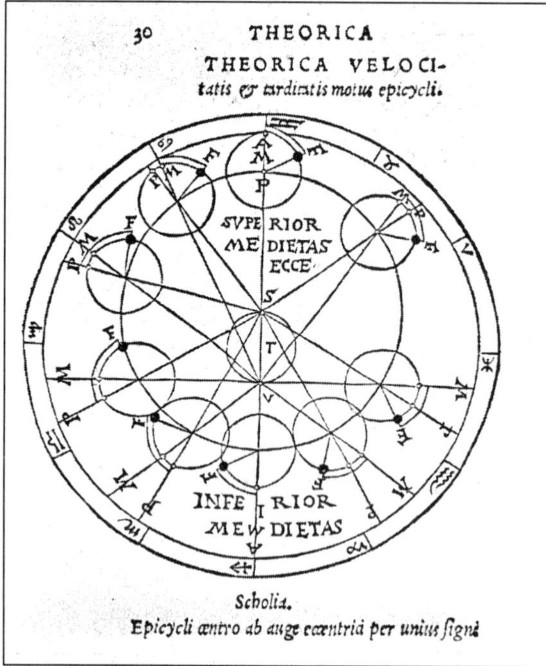


**Late-medieval illustration showing the circular movements of the planets as theorized by Claudius Ptolemy. From George Purbach's *Theoreticae Novae Planetarum*, 1543. *Reproduced by permission of Fortean Picture Library.***

center around which the Sun, stars, and planets revolved, was generally accepted until the time of the Copernican revolution.

In his classic astrological work, the *Tetrabiblos*, Ptolemy attempted to compile the astrological knowledge of his predecessors and systematize it into a unified discipline. He also offered a theory of astrological influence in terms of the science of his day. Despite the shortcomings of his work, Ptolemy's organization of the body of diverse information into a coherent whole made him the most influential single astrologer in Western history.

**Sources:**

Brau, Jean-Louis, Helen Weaver, and Allan Edmands. *Larousse Encyclopedia of Astrology*. New York: New American Library, 1980.

DeVore, Nicholas. *Encyclopedia of Astrology*. New York: Philosophical Library, 1948.

## PUNARVASU

Punarvasu (good again) is one of the Nakshatras (lunar mansions) of Vedic astrology. Depicted as an arrow, this moon sign is thought to be a good time for starting over. It is found from Gemini 20° to Cancer 3°20' and one can expect to be more friendly and generous, but also lack drive or foresight with the moon in Punarvasu. Aditi, mother of the 12 Adityas (forms of the sun), presides, and Jupiter is the ruling planet of this sign.

—Pramela Thiagesan

## PURVA BHADRAPADA

Purva Bhadrapada (former beautiful foot) is one of the Nakshatras (lunar mansions) of Vedic astrology. The Nakshatra is depicted as the front legs of a small bed or couch, and is ruled by the planet Jupiter at Aquarius 20° to Pisces 3°20'. A good time to do something dangerous or risky, one can expect to be better at reading people and more logical, while also being skeptical or worrisome. The deity Aja Ekapad presides over Purva Bhadrapada.

—Pramela Thiagesan

## PURVA PHALGUNI

Purva Phalguni (the former red one or a fig tree) is one of the Nakshatras (lunar mansions) of Vedic astrology. This Nakshatra is symbolized by the front legs of a bed, and is found from Leo 13°20' to 26°40'. This is another good sign for fierce acts, and individuals may find themselves unusually bright and physically active, yet maybe a bit reckless or vindictive. The deity Aryaman presides and the planet Venus rules this sign.

—Pramela Thiagesan

## Purvashada

Purvashada (the former unsubdued) is one of the Nakshatras (lunar mansions) of Vedic astrology. This Nakshatra is usually depicted as a bed or an elephant's tusk, and is located from Sagittarius13°20' to 26°40', where the planet Venus rules it. This is a good time to try to liberate somebody; people may be more wealthy and influential in this period, but also may find themselves settling for less or not open to advice. Apa, god of water, presides or Purvashada.

—Pramela Thiagesan

## Pushya

Pushya (nourishing) is one of the Nakshatras (lunar mansions) of Vedic astrology. One can find this sign, represented by a wheel, in Cancer 3°20' to 16°40'. Brihaspati, the guru of the gods, presides, and the planet Saturn rules over this Nakshatra. Considered one of the best, this moon sign is good for all nourishing activities with the exception of marriage; one may exhibit increased intelligence and spirituality, although zealousness and oversensitivity may also abound in this sign.

—Pramela Thiagesan

## Pythagoras

Pythagoras, a Greek philosopher, mathematician, and astronomer, lived from approximately 580 to 500 B.C.E. Pythagoras was the first to conceive of the heliocentric theory of the universe (the notion that Earth and the planets revolve around the Sun), a notion that did not catch on until Copernicus. Pythagoras and his followers also developed basic mathematical notions, such as the concepts of equation and proportion.

Pythagoras is said to have searched widely for wisdom and is believed to have introduced the idea of reincarnation to the Western world. One of his teachings regards the "music of the spheres," the notion that the intervals between the planets correspond to musical tones and that the movements of the planets produce an ethereal music. Pythagoras's significance for astrology is that he clearly formulated the notion that the human being is a miniature version (microcosm) of the larger universe (macrocosm). The microcosm and the macrocosm are linked by—and affect each other through—certain correlations. This notion is basic to ancient astrology.

An illustration of Pythagoras, considered by some to be the first pure mathematician. From Jacopo Guarama, 1792. *Reproduced by permission of Fortean Picture Library.*

## Quadrant

The quadrants of a horoscope refer to four sets of three houses: Houses one, two, and three (first quadrant), houses four, five, and six (second quadrant), houses seven, eight, and nine (third quadrant), and houses ten, eleven, and twelve (fourth quadrant).

A quadrant is also an instrument used to calculate the position of celestial bodies. In Europe, quadrants superseded the use of astrolabes during the Renaissance.

## Quadrupedal

The quadrupedal signs are the so-called four-footed signs, namely, Aries, Taurus, Leo, Sagittarius, and Capricorn.

## Qualities (Quadruplicities)

The primary categories by which the signs are classified are the four elements—earth, air, fire, and water—and the three qualities—cardinal, mutable, and fixed. Each of the 12 signs of the zodiac is a unique combination of an element and a quality (e.g., Aries is a cardinal fire sign, Taurus is fixed earth, Gemini is mutable air, and so forth). The elemental nature of a sign is said to refer to its basic temperament, whereas its quality refers to its mode of expression.

Cardinal signs are said to be outgoing signs that initiate new activities; fixed signs, by way of contrast, persist with their established activities; mutable signs adapt to changing circumstances. Some modern astrologers use an analogy to certain notions in physics to contrast the nature of the three qualities: cardinal signs are said to represent centrifugal force, fixed signs centripetal force, and mutable signs wave (back and forth) motion.

Although the qualities are on par with the elements as categories for classifying the zodiac, they tend to be treated less fully in most astrological textbooks, partly because the symbols for the elements are more concrete and thus more intuitively obvious, but also because the traits said to characterize each of the qualities do not seem to apply (or, at least, do not seem to apply fully) to certain signs. Thus, for example, individuals born under the cardinal sign Cancer do not typically tend to be outgoing people who initiate new activities (a cardinal trait); rather, Cancers tend to adapt (a mutable trait) or to resist (a fixed trait) changing circumstances. Capricorn, another cardinal sign, is good at initiating new business activities but is also one of the more stubborn signs (a fixed trait).

Although the confusion introduced by these exceptions might lead one to abandon this system of classification altogether, there are certain other sign characteristics that the qualities explain quite well. Fixed signs, for example, are said to manifest the characteristic of stubbornness, and when the fixed quadruplicity is examined, this characterization—with predictable variations introduced by the different elements—works out quite well: Although all the fixed signs are stubborn, Taurus is most stubborn about practical matters (earth), Leo is most stubborn about certain ways of doing things (fire), Scorpio is most stubborn about feelings (water), and Aquarius is most stubborn about ideals (air). Thus, the usefulness of the qualities when they are truly applicable (which is the majority of the time) counterbalances the confusion introduced by a few exceptions.

The same classification can be found in Vedic astrology—Chara (moveable or cardinal), Dwi-Swabhava (dual or mutable), and Sthira (fixed). The three Vedic qualities, which are associated with the same signs as their Western parallels, have similar connotations.

**Sources:**

Hand, Robert. *Horoscope Symbols*. Rockport, MA: Para Research, 1981.

Sakoian, Frances, and Louis S. Acker. *The Astrologer's Handbook*. New York: Harper & Row, 1989.

Sutton, Komilla. *The Essentials of Vedic Astrology*. Bournemouth, UK: Wessex Astrologer, 1999.

## Querent

In horary astrology, the individual asking the question is referred to as the querent.

## Quesited

In horary astrology, the quesited is the person, thing, or event that is the subject of the question.

## Quetzalcoatl

Quetzalcoatl, asteroid 1,915 (the 1,915th asteroid to be discovered, on March 9, 1953), is approximately .4 kilometer in diameter and has an orbital period of 4 years. Quetzalcoatl was named after a god who was simultaneously a creator and a millennialist figure in Aztec mythology and for whom Cortez was mistaken. J. Lee Lehman views this asteroid as a blend of Mars and Sun characteristics, a "Hero-God: more active than the Sun, more creative than Mars."

**Sources:**

Kowal, Charles T. *Asteroids: Their Nature and Utilization*. Chichester, West Sussex, UK: Ellis Horwood Limited, 1988.

Lehman, J. Lee. *The Ultimate Asteroid Book*. West Chester, PA: Whitford Press, 1988.

Schwartz, Jacob. *Asteroid Name Encyclopedia*. St. Paul, MN: Llewellyn Publications, 1995.

## Quincunx

A quincunx (also called an inconjunct) is a minor aspect of 150 degrees. The effect of a a quincunx is comparatively weak. With the exception of double quincunx (yod) configurations, quincunxes received little attention until relatively recently. Their influence was usually regarded as being mildly favorable, like a semisextile, but more recent interpreters regard them as a source of stress, requiring change and adjustment in the areas of the chart that they affect.

## Quindecile

A quindecile is a minor aspect of 24° created when a circle is divided into 15 equal parts. As a third part of a quintile, a quindecile is a very weak but favorable influence that is studied in the branch of astrology referred to as harmonics. It is given a very narrow orb of influence of 1° or less.

## Quintile

A quintile is a minor aspect of 72° created by subdividing a circle into five parts. The great astronomer Johannes Kepler devised quintiles and biquintiles (144°) for his astrological work. Quintiles refer to the aptitudes or talents related to the planets involved in the aspect. It is given an orb of influence of 1° to 3°, depending on the astrologer.

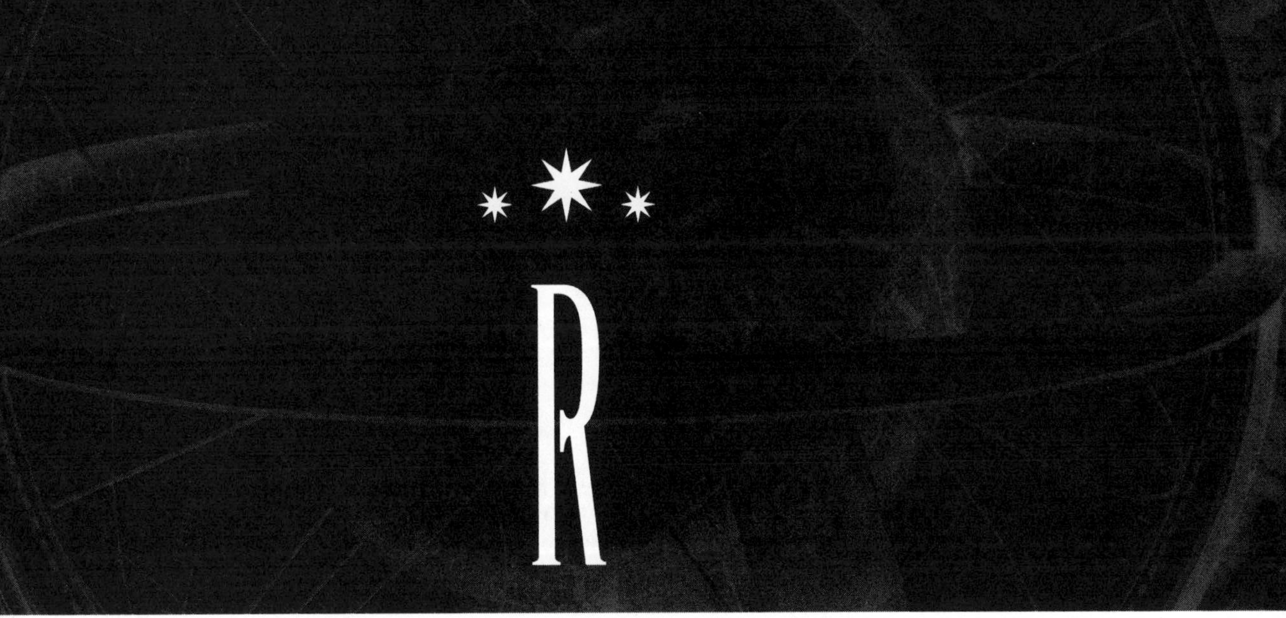

## RADICAL

Radical is an adjective form of the noun radix, as in the "radical" position of the planets, meaning their original position in a horoscope chart.

## RADIX

Radix (Latin for "root") refers to the original horoscope. It is used to distinguish the radix from such secondary charts as progressed horoscopes. In genethliacal astrology it is equivalent to the natal chart. Radix, however, may also refer to the original chart of a horoscope cast for an event (as opposed to a person). It hence has a wider application than natal chart.

## RAM

The Ram is a popular alternate name for the sign Aries.

## RAT

The Rat is one of the 12 animals of the Chinese zodiac. It refers to one of the 12 earthly branches, which are used in Chinese astrology, together with the 10 heavenly stems. Such a branch designates one day every 12 days: the days are named according to a sexagesimal (60) cycle, made of 10 series of 12 branches.

A Rat is jovial (perhaps too much), pleasant, and sociable; with a sense of justice, the Rat tends to want to convince others. On the negative side, he is suspicious, crafty, and may hold grudges if people are disrespectful to him. With a keen interest in everything, he is hardworking, ambitious, and conscientious. He loves money: he knows how to win it, and above all, he knows how to keep it, even if he is generous with those close to him. Easy to get along with, he is persuasive and a successful businessman. Not really faithful, he is nevertheless eager for tenderness.

—Michele Delemme

## The Reagans and Astrology

In May 1988, the late Donald T. Regan, secretary of the treasury (1981–85) and chief of staff (1985–87) for President Ronald Reagan, published *For the Record,* his account of his years in the Reagan White House. Regan's description of the role Joan Quigley, first lady Nancy Reagan's astrologer, played in the Reagan presidency became an occasion for the press to ridicule both astrology and the president. The *New York Post,* for instance, ran the headline "Astrologer Runs the White House." According to Regan, astrology was a daily, sometimes an hourly, factor in Ronald Reagan's schedule. In Regan's book, he made it appear that this control over scheduling amounted to placing the president's life—and consequently the American nation—under the control of Quigley.

Nancy Reagan's memoir, *My Turn,* was published the following year. She devoted an entire chapter to a defense of her reliance on the science of the stars. Reagan defended herself by portraying astrology as a kind of emotional "pacifier." She said, for example, that "each person has his own way of coping with trauma and grief, with the pain of life, and astrology was one of mine." She also downplayed the role astrology had in the Reagan presidency, asserting that Quigley did nothing more than time events.

For her part, Quigley claimed that, in deference to the Reagans, she was reticent to talk about her relationship with the Reagan White House until *My Turn* appeared. Asserting that what Nancy Reagan had "left out about the way she used astrology and my ideas would fill a book," she decided to write her own. *What Does Joan Say?* was published the next year. If *My Turn* underestimated the role the science of the stars played in the Reagan presidency, *What Does Joan Say?* seems to overstate astrology's—or, at least, Quigley's—role. Her book makes it appear not only that her advice was an essential ingredient in most of President Reagan's successes but also that she was responsible for such important advice as persuading the president to stop viewing the Soviet Union as the "evil empire." Quigley, in other words, portrayed herself as the pivotal influence behind the rapprochement between the United States and the Soviet block and, by implication, as responsible for the subsequent collapse of the iron curtain.

For astrologers, *What Does Joan Say?* raises broader issues. In the first place, the relationship between Quigley and the Reagans reminds astrologers that their science was founded by people who studied the stars for the benefit of powerful political figures. Thus, while some contemporary astrologers might condemn Quigley's advice to Ronald Reagan (a president viewed as too right wing by the generally liberal astrology community), she clearly falls into the tradition of court astrologers of former eras—a tradition that nurtured and even gave birth to the type of astrology known today. What are the ethical ramifications of providing astrological information for political leaders? As astrology acquires greater acceptance in the larger society, these issues will become increasingly important to future generations of astrologers.

Another issue raised by the Quigley case concerns the way the practice of astrology is portrayed in *What Does Joan Say?*, which emphasizes electional astrology (determining or "electing" the appropriate times to initiate certain actions) almost to the exclusion of other branches of astrological science. Contemporary astrology has tended to go to the opposite extreme, downplaying the importance of such "elections" and focusing instead on the interpretation of clients' personality and personality potentials. Thus, part of the importance of *What Does Joan Say?* is to remind astrologers of a powerful technique that has been in the background for a long time.

**Sources:**

Quigley, Joan. *What Does Joan Say?* New York: Birch Lane Press, 1990.

Reagan, Nancy. *My Turn: The Memoirs of Nancy Reagan*. New York: Random House, 1989.

Regan, Donald T. *For the Record: From Wall Street to Washington*. San Diego: Harcourt Brace Jovanovich, 1988.

## Reception

Reception is an older term for a relationship between two planets in which one is located in a sign ruled by the other. For example, Mars in Taurus is said to be "received by" Venus (the ruler of Taurus). Contemporary astrologers rarely use this term, except in the expression mutual reception (which occurs when two planets are in each other's sign).

## Rectification

Rectification is the process of adjusting the birth chart to the precise birth time in cases where the birthday is known but the birth moment is inexact or completely unknown. Rectification is accomplished by working backward from the native's personality traits and from important events in the person's life. In other words, an astrologer rectifying a natal chart asks the question, Given certain traits and events, what should this person's birth chart look like?

For example, suppose someone the astrologer knows was born around sunrise. Further assume that before 7:15 A.M. on the day of birth the planet Uranus would have been in the native's eighth house and after 7:15 it would have been in the seventh house. Uranus represents, among other things, sudden, unexpected changes. The eighth house indicates inheritance, other people's money, and the like. The seventh house is partnership and marriage. Thus, if the individual had experienced many sudden beginnings and endings of relationships, the astrologer would infer that the person was born when Uranus was in the seventh house; if, by contrast, the individual had regularly received money from other people in sudden, unexpected ways, the astrologer would infer that the person was born when Uranus was in the eighth house. Through a reasoning process like this, applied to as many different factors as possible, the astrologer could eventually determine precisely when the native was born.

**A sixteenth-century wood engraving of Ptolemy's system called "Regiomontanus."** ***Reproduced by permission of Fortean Picture Library.***

**Sources:**

Foreman, Patricia. *Computers and Astrology: A Universal User's Guide and Reference*. Burlington, VT: Good Earth Publications, 1992.

Gettings, Fred. *Dictionary of Astrology*. London: Routledge & Kegan Paul, 1985.

## REFRANATION

Refranation is a technical term used in horary astrology referring to a situation in which a planet turns retrograde (reverses its apparent motion) before it completes an aspect to which it has been applying. In such a situation, the matter for which the horary chart was cast will not result in a successful conclusion.

## REGIOMONTANUS (JOHANN MÜLLER)

Regiomontanus (born Johann Müller), a German astronomer and astrologer, was born on June 6, 1436, in Königsberg, Germany. He established an observatory at Nuremberg, where he observed Halley's comet. Regiomontanus also published ephemerides (tables of planetary positions) that were used by, among other people, Christopher Columbus. He was brought to Rome by Pope Sixtus IV to help devise the calendar. Regiomontanus was also the translator of Ptolemy's *Almagest*. He died in Rome on July 6, 1476. He is best remembered by astrologers for the system of house division that bears his name.

## REGIOMONTANUS SYSTEM

The Regiomontanus (Regiomontanean) system is a system of house division devised by Johann Müller (Regiomontanus was his pseudonym) in the fifteenth century. At one time it was the most popular sysem in Europe.

## REINCARNATION, KARMA, AND ASTROLOGY

Reincarnation is the theory that each individual soul progressively incarnates in a succession of different bodies. Belief in reincarnation usually carries with it certain other, related notions, such as the idea that one is learning from one lifetime to another and that, in time, every soul will become perfected and consequently no longer need to return to corporeal form. Another idea often associated with reincarnation is the notion of karma, which is the moral law of cause and effect formulated by Hindu and Buddhist thinkers. For example, if one steals money from another person, the thief will eventually have money stolen from her or him, either later in this life or in a future lifetime.

The notions of reincarnation and karma together explain why some people are born into lucky circumstances while other people are born into unfortunate conditions. For astrologers concerned with the issue of why some people come into this life with hardship written large across their natal charts and other people seem to be born under a lucky star, reincarnation and karma provide an important explanatory tool. Reincarnation also provides a framework for explaining why a person should have certain personality traits—they are carryovers from "past lifetimes."

There are different approaches for determining which factors in a chart indicate information about the native's karma and past lifetimes. Planets in intercepted signs and in the twelfth house, for example, are often said to provide insight into one's past lives. The branch of astrology especially concerned with these issues is esoteric astrology.

**Sources:**

Brau, Jean-Louis, Helen Weaver, and Allan Edmands. *Larousse Encyclopedia of Astrology*. New York: New American Library, 1980.

Gettings, Fred. *Dictionary of Astrology*. London: Routledge & Kegan Paul, 1987.

## Reinhart, Melanie

Melanie Reinhart was born in Zimbabwe, whose night skies inspired her vocation of astrology at an early age. She holds a bachelor of arts degree in drama, English, and music, and holds a diploma from the Faculty of Astrological Studies. She has wide experience and training within many different psychological and spiritual disciplines, and also practices spiritual healing. She has been a professional astrologer since 1975, and runs a busy practice of individual consultations in London, Bedfordshire, and Zurich, as well as distance work internationally. She has taught for many astrological schools in the United Kingdom and abroad, including the Centre for Psychological Astrology, the Faculty of Astrological Studies, the Centre for Transpersonal Astrology, and Astro*Synthesis; she has travelled internationally to give lectures, workshops and consultations.

Reinhard is the author of *Chiron and the Healing Journey* (Arkana, 1989), *Saturn, Chiron and the Centaurs* (CPA Press, 1996), and *Incarnation* (CPA Press, 1997), as has contributed to *Modern South African in Search of a Soul* (Sigo Press, 1990) and *Wilderness and the Human Spirit* (Cameron Designs, 1998). She has also contributed articles to many magazines and journals, and writes regularly for *Caduceus* magazine. She has a special interest in meditative, ritual and group work that makes astrology a living experience.

## Revati

Revati (Wealthy) is one of the Nakshatras (lunar mansions) of Vedic astrology. The deity Pushan presides over this Nakshatra that is usually represented by a drum.

Things started at this time will probably flourish, and people are more fortunate and have better hygiene, yet can be more spiteful and overindulgent. Revati rules the planet Ketu at Pisces 16°40' to 30°.

—Pramela Thiagesan

## ROELL, DAVID R.

David R. Roell is a practitioner of contemporary astrology. As a child, he traveled extensively in his native Kansas. The eldest of nine, he was editor of his high school yearbook. He is a graduate of the University of Kansas (bachelor of science degree in journalism) and many years ago spoke fluent French. During a prolonged stay in Europe, he compiled a photographic portfolio of English and French church interiors. He is a former member of the Royal Photographic Society and of Mensa. He was once a factotum to one of the chief financial officers of the United Nations.

Vatican II led Roell on a 30-year study of metaphysics, which eventually included theosophy, Alice Bailey, the seven rays, Gothic architecture, the esoteric church, the Great Ages, alchemy, reincarnation, pyramidology, astral projection, pranic healing, magic, UFOs, Gurdjieff/Ouspensky, the Second Coming, and other subjects. In 1983, he bought his first astrology book. From 1986 to 1990, he worked at the New York Astrology Center. In 1993, on a dare, he and a friend established what eventually became the Astrology Center of America, in Ventura, California. In January 1996, the store moved onto the Internet as AstroAmerica.com. In 1998 he moved to Santa Fe, New Mexico. Since 2000, he has lived in New York City with his wife, Elizabeth, and their daughter, Veracity.

## ROGERS-GALLAGHER, KIM

Kim Rogers-Gallagher has been in the business of astrology for the past 20 years. Her columns have appeared monthly for over 15 years, in *Dell Horoscope*, *Welcome to Planet Earth*, *The Mountain Astrologer*, *American Astrology*, and on the Internet. She was the author of a daily love horoscope called *PassionScopes* for AstroNet (on America Online) for five years. She is also responsible for the "Cosmic Cafe," a creative weekly column published for StarIQ.com and astrocom.com that resembles an astrological soap opera, which was said to demographically attract an 80–90 percent female audience.

Rogers-Gallagher has also published two books. *Astrology for the Light Side of the Brain*, released in 1995, is now in its fifth printing at ACS (Astro-Communications of San Diego), and is the top-selling book in the company's 25-year history. Her second book, *Astrology for the Light Side of the Future*, holds the second-place slot. She has also written chapters in several anthologies for both ACS and Llewellyn Publications. She is the author of the introductory text for Llewellyn's Astrology Calendar, writes the weekly horoscopes for the publisher's *Daily Planetary Guide*, and has been an annual contributor to its Sun-sign and Moon-sign annuals for the past seven years.

Rogers-Gallagher has been a director on the board of the International Society for Astrological Research (ISAR) for eight years. She served as editor for ISAR's quarterly magazine for over four years. She also served as founder and board member for three local groups, in Portsmouth, New Hampshire; Seattle, Washington; and Telluride, Colorado.

—Kim Rogers-Gallagher

## ROHINI

Rohini (or the Red One) is one of the Nakshatras (lunar mansions) of Vedic astrology. Mostly depicted as an ox cart, Prajapati, the god of creation, presides over this Nakshatra located between Taurus 10° and 23°20', ruled by the moon. This sign conveys the brute strength of a bull, and is considered a good time to start new projects; people will tend to be more charismatic and will communicate more clearly during this time, although also perhaps a bit manipulative or indulgent.

—Pramela Thiagesan

## ROOSTER

The Rooster is one of the 12 animals of the Chinese zodiac. It refers to one of the 12 earthly branches, which are used in Chinese astrology, together with the 10 heavenly stems. Such a branch designates one day every 12 days: the days are named according to a sexagesimal (60) cycle, made of 10 series of 12 branches.

A little arrogant and boastful, the Rooster is a nice person. He tries hard to be liked. In fact, he is anxious—he tends to have feelings of self-doubt, and he has to be reassured. Nothing pleases him more than a compliment. He has a quick mind and a quick tongue; and when he is angry, he does not mince his words. Meticulous, efficient, he works at his pace, and shows little ambition. He has many acquaintances but few friends, for he is quite wary.

—Michele Delemme

## ROSICRUCIAN FELLOWSHIP

The Rosicrucian Fellowship was established in 1907 by the well-known astrologer Max Heindel. Heindel moved to the United States from his native Germany and settled in Los Angeles in 1903. He joined Katherine Tigley's branch of the Theosophical Society, lecturing and serving as president of the local lodge in 1904 and 1905. He was also acquainted with Rudolf Steiner, who broke away from the Theosophical Society following the promotion of Jeddu Krishnamurti as the new world teacher.

In 1907, Heindel traveled to Germany where he claimed to have encountered an elder brother of the Rosicrucian order who led him to the Temple of the Rosy Cross, where he "received" his first book, *The Rosicrucian Cosmo-Conception*. After his return to America, he established the first center of his new order in Columbus, Ohio, in 1908. Centers were soon established in Los Angeles; North Yakima and Seattle, Washington; and Portland, Oregon.

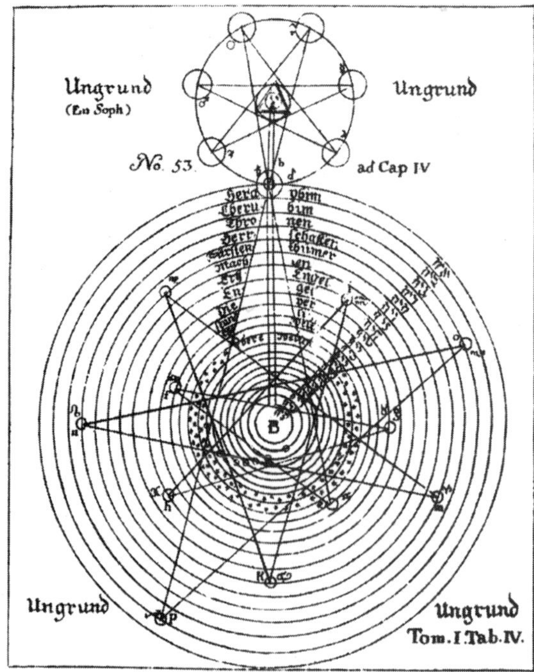


**A Rosicrucian diagram demonstrating Franz von Helmont's theory of reincarnation.** ***Reproduced by permission of Fortean Picture Library.***

*The Rosicrucian Cosmo-Conception* is a variation of theosophy, differing principally in its more extensive reliance upon Christianity and Christian symbols, which reflects the influence of Rudolf Steiner. Heindel also placed a greater emphasis upon astrology. The Rosicrucian Fellowship was a major factor in the expansion of astrology in the early part of century. Until relatively recently, most astrologers, even those not connected with the fellowship, used the ephemerides and table of houses published by the fellowship.

**Sources:**

Heindel, Max. *The Rosicrucian Cosmo-Conception*. Oceanside, CA: Rosicrucian Fellowship, 1937.

———. *Rosicrucian Philosophy in Questions and Answers*. Oceanside, CA: Rosicrucian Fellowship, 1922.

———. *Simplified Scientific Astrology*. Oceanside, CA: Rosicrucian Fellowship, 1928.

Heindel, Mrs. Max [Augusta Foss]. *The Birth of the Rosicrucian Fellowship*. Oceanside, CA: Rosicrucian Fellowship, n.d.

## Royal Stars (Watchers of the Heavens)

The ancients referred to the stars through which the Sun passed during the equinoxes and the solstices as the royal stars. In the third millennium B.C.E., these were Aldebaran (the Watcher of the East, spring), Regulus (the Watcher of the North, summer), Antares (the Watcher of the West, fall), and Formalhaut (the Watcher of the South, winter). Because of the precession of equinoxes, these four stars no longer mark the beginning of the seasons.

## Rudhyar, Dane

Dane Rudhyar was the leading figure in the movement that reoriented twentieth-century astrology from the prediction of events to its present emphasis on the analysis of personality. Born Daniel Chennevierre on March, 23, 1895, in Paris, to a middle-class family of Norman and Celtic stock, he spent his first 20 years in Paris. A serious illness and surgery at age 12 led him to begin developing his mind; he passed his baccalaureate at the Sorbonne at age 16, majoring in philosophy. He began meeting people who introduced him to the artistic and musical world of Paris, then in a great ferment, and to the thought of Friedrich Nietzsche, who freed him from what remained of his past conditioning and introduced him to the concept that all existence is cyclic in character. At this time he wrote *Claude Debussy and the Cycle of Musical Civilization*, in which he saw Western civilization as having reached an autumnal state.

Rudhyar then refocused his attention on music and the piano and was able to meet M. Durand, the music publisher, who read his book on Debussy, commissioned another booklet on him, and published three of Rudhyar's piano pieces. Rudhyar began studying with Émile Pessard at the Paris Conservatoire but broke off his studies when World War I began. He was exempted from military service for health reasons and in 1916 left for New York with two friends to prepare for a performance of their dance-drama *Metachory*, for which he had written some music. His pieces *Poemes Ironique* and *Vision Vegetale* were performed at the Metropolitan Opera under the baton of Pierre Monteux in April 1917 and were the first polytonal music heard in America.

Having met Sasaki Roshi, who later became a Zen teacher, Rudhyar spent much of the summer of 1917 in the New York Public Library, reading about Oriental music and philosophy and Western occultism. In December of that year, he parted ways with his former friends and moved to Toronto, where he stayed with Sigfried Herz, and later to Montreal, where he stayed with Alfred Laliberté, a pupil of Alexander Scriabin. He gave lectures in French and recited some of his recent poetry, published in 1918 under the title *Rhapsodies*. After a summer in Seal Harbor, Maine, where he met Leopold Stokowski, he moved to Philadelphia. There he wrote an orchestral work, *Soul Fire*, which won him a $1,000 prize from the newly formed Los Angeles Philharmonic. He also wrote *Mosaics*, a cycle of piano pieces; *Ravishments*, a series of short preludes; and *Très Poemes Tragique*, for contralto. He also wrote French poems, essays on the Baha'i movement and social organization, and plans for a world city (anticipating those for Auroville, the international community founded by the Indian saint Sri Aurobindo). During the winter of 1918–19, he had free access to the Philadelphia orchestra's rehearsals; at one of them Stokowski introduced him to Christine Wetherill Stevenson, founder of the Philadelphia Art Alliance and initiator of the Little Theatre Movement, who had been producing a play about the life of the Buddha, on the Hollywood grounds of Krotona, then the headquarters of the American branch of the Theosophical Society. She asked Rudhyar to compose scenic music for a play about the life of Christ; it was produced in the summer of 1920 in an amphitheater close to what would become the Hollywood Bowl.

Living among Theosophists and studying astrology, music, and philosophy at Krotona in 1920–21 further deepened Rudhyar's interest in Oriental philosophy, in which he found confirmation of his beliefs about the cyclic nature of civilization and inspiration to dedicate his life to building a new civilization on a non-European basis. Working as an extra in the movies, he met a Dutch woman from Java, Aryel Vreedenburgh Darma, and with her founded a store that imported artifacts from Indonesia. Unfortunately, the store was destroyed by a fire. In other film work, he was cast as Christ in a long-running theatrical prologue at Grauman's Egyptian Theater and also worked with John Barrymore and Alla Nazimova.

After leaving motion picture work in 1927, Rudhyar eked out a living giving lecture-recitals and composing a new type of music, mostly for the piano. He also wrote many articles on music and philosophy, had his *Rebirth of Hindu Music* (1928) published in Madras, India, and published a volume of poems, *Towards Man* (1928). He was a charter member of the International Composers Guild, founded in New York in 1922 by Edgar Varese and Carlos Salzedo, and of the New Music Society of California, begun by Henry Cowell, who featured Rudhyar's orchestral *Surge of Fire* at the society's first concert in the fall of 1925 in Los Angeles and published several of his compositions with financial backing from Charles Ives.

Living in Carmel, California, in 1929, Rudhyar composed music, including a piano piece, *Granites*, a poetic novel, *Rania*, and *Art as Release of Power*. (Except for two works for string quartet written in 1950 and revisions of earlier work, all of Rudhyar's music was written before 1930.) In 1930, he wrote a booklet entitled *Education, Instruction, Initiation*. After moving back and forth between California and New York, on June 9, 1930, Rudhyar married Malya Contento, then secretary to the writer Will Levington Comfort. Through her he met Marc Edmund Jones, then living and teaching in Hollywood, in September 1930; Rudhyar then returned to New York, where Jones sent him his mimeographed courses for the Sabian Assembly, in which he presented astrology in terms of what was then an unprecedented philosophical approach. These courses and a growing acquaintance with the depth psychology of Carl Jung awoke Rudhyar to the possibility of marrying astrology and depth psychology into a new kind of synthesis. In the winter of 1931–32 in Boston, he wrote a series of seven pamphlets under the general title *Harmonic Astrology*; he later renamed his concept "humanistic astrology."

In 1931, Rudhyar started a small magazine, *Hamsa*, but the Depression, ill health, and lack of support led him to drop it in 1934. By then he had met Paul Clancy, who had, in 1932, founded *American Astrology*, the first successful popular magazine in astrology. Clancy was willing to publish anything Rudhyar wanted to write on his new kind of astrology. Month after month, Rudhyar was able to write two to five articles for one, then several, astrological magazines with national circulations of several million readers.

During the summer of 1933, while staying at Mary Tudor Garland's ranch in New Mexico, he was able to read through all of Jung's works that had been translated at that time, and realized he could tie together Jung's concepts and a reformulated type of astrology. Rudhyar used his new approach to write on many topics—politics, philosophy, psychology, esoteric traditions—that no other magazine would have printed, simply by centering the discussion on the birth chart of a person important in one of these fields. Alice Bailey encouraged him to develop these articles into a unified treatise, which he wrote during his summers in New Mexico in 1934 and 1935 and which Bailey proceeded to publish under the title *The Astrology of Personality* (1936). Rudhyar dedicated the book to her in gratitude for her support and for the influence her earlier works had had on him in the 1920s. His next book, *New Mansions for New Man* (1938), was also published under her auspices. Rudhyar was also writing poetry during these years, gathered in a volume entitled *White Thunder* (1938). After 1939, he began developing a style of nonrepresentational painting and composed music during two summers in New Mexico.

In his forties, crises of personal development and marriage difficulties led Rudhyar to question many things he had accepted on faith, and he wrote two more (unpublished) books, *Man, Maker of Universes* (1940) and *The Age of Plenitude* (1942). His circumstances worsened during the war, and his marriage broke down completely. Rudhyar was sustained during this period by his friendship with D. J. Bussell, head of a small, liberal esoteric Christian church.

The crisis over, on June 27, 1945, Rudhyar married Eya Fechin, daughter of a famous Russian painter, Nicolai Fechin, who died in Santa Monica, California, in 1955. They left for Colorado and New Mexico, where Rudhyar did most of his paintings and wrote *The Moon: The Cycles and Fortunes of Life* (1946; reprinted as *The Lunation Cycle*, 1967) and *Modern Man's Conflicts* (1946; rewritten and published as *Fire Out of the Stone*, 1959). He also continued writing his monthly articles for astrology magazines. All of Rudhyar's colored paintings were done between 1938 and 1949, although he continued doing works in black and white during the 1950s.

In 1948, the pianist Bill Masselos discovered and performed Rudhyar's piano piece *Granites*, thus setting off a new period of interest in Rudhyar's music among a small group of musicians. Rudhyar and Fechin moved to New York, where some performances took place. The rendition of a string quartet by the New Music Quartet at the McMillan Theater of Columbia University was particularly memorable.

After several years of apprenticeship to Jacob Moreno, the founder of psychodrama, financial pressure forced Fechin to accept the task of starting a psychodrama department in a mental health institute in Independence, Iowa, where she and her husband lived for two exceedingly difficult years. During this period, Rudhyar turned to science fiction, writing short stories, novellas, and a novel, *Return from No-Return* (1954). When Rudhyar's second marriage collapsed, he returned to California, accepted his 1954 divorce philosophically, and began rebuilding his life at age 60.

After a few months at the Huntington Hartford Art Colony in the Santa Monica hills, where he completed his orchestral work *Thresholds*, Rudhyar began a series of lectures on astrology while still writing his articles, mainly for *Horoscope* and *American Astrology*. With secretarial assistance from a friend, Virginia Seith, he began publishing monthly mimeographed booklets under the series title *Seeds for Greater Living*. These came out regularly for seven years, until 1962. Despite the maturity of his philosophy, he could find no publisher for any of his later works, astrological, musical, or literary.

After years of isolation in a small Hollywood apartment and another painful crisis in 1957–58, Rudhyar accepted an invitation to visit Switzerland from a Madame Honegger, whom he had aided with astrological advice. During this trip, he stopped in Boston, where Marcia Moore arranged lectures for him; in New York, where he lectured under the sponsorship of the astrologer Charles Jayne; and in London, where he was honored at an official dinner arranged by Brigadier Roy C. Firebrace, at which the major British astrologers paid tribute to the effect that his early book, *The Astrology of Personality*, had had on them. In Switzerland, after Madame Honegger became ill, Rudhyar found himself alone in a renovated sixteenth-century tower overlooking the Rhone Valley. There he completed and translated into French *Fire Out of the Stone*.

After a few months of lecturing in Paris, Rudhyar returned to the United States, but after a dismal year in Redlands, California, he returned to Europe for a longer stay.

At a lecture in Holland, he met the Dutch publisher Carolus Verhulst, who offered to reprint *The Pulse of Life*, a Dutch translation of *The Astrology of Personality*, which had been circulated in 1946–47. At last the logjam blocking Rudhyar's career was broken; a gradual stream of his other books was published by Verhulst's Servire Press.

In 1963, Rudhyar, while in Italy on a third journey to Europe, received a letter from a young woman named Gale Tana Whitall, then living in Edmonton, Alberta, Canada, where she had heard about his work from a music teacher. Returning to America on November 22, 1963—the day of President John F. Kennedy's assassination—Rudhyar met Whitall about a month later in Palm Springs, California, during her Christmas vacation. They were married on May 27, 1964, and after a lecture tour to St. Paul, Minnesota, and Boston, they settled in San Jacinto, California, where they lived for the next ten years. Whitall soon became a proficient typist, editor, and organizer of Rudhyar's work and sustained him as he learned to cope with his growing popularity among the young. As often happens to creative innovators who live on into their seventies and eighties, Rudhyar finally received the recognition and respect he had worked so hard for during the last decade and a half of his life.

The far-seeing initiative of Samuel Bercholtz, founder of Shambhala Bookstore and Publications in Berkeley, California, allowed Rudhyar's books to become acceptable to such New York publishers as Penguin, Doubleday, and Harper & Row. Beginning in 1965, life became very full for Rudhyar and his wife, as she diligently typed manuscripts for offset printing in Holland. The volume of correspondence mounted, as did the number of lectures from coast to coast. His books during these years included *The Practice of Astrology* (1966), *Astrological Study of Psychological Complexes and Emotional Problems* (1966), *The Rhythm of Human Fulfillment* (1966), *Of Vibrancy and Peace* (1967; poems) *Astrological Triptych* (1968), and *Astrological Timing: The Transition to the New Age* (1968). In March 1969, feeling the need to promote his approach to astropsychology more vigorously, Rudhyar founded the International Committee for Humanistic Astrology but refused to build an official organization that could lay claim to this new field. About this time, thanks in part to Claudio Naranjo's interest in him, Rudhyar was invited to speak at Esalen, a human potentials institute in Big Sur, California, and to similar groups.

More books followed: *Birth Patterns for a New Humanity* (1969), *A Seed and Directives for New Life* (1970), *Astrological Themes for Meditation* (1971), *The Astrological Houses* (1972), *The Magic of Tone and Relationship* (1972), *Person-Centered Astrology* (1973), *An Astrological Mandala* (1974), and *The Astrology of America's Destiny* (1975). The number of his books in print grew from zero in 1960 to 25 in 1975, and most of them were either entirely new or thorough revisions of older works. Of these, Rudhyar considered *The Planetarization of Consciousness* (1970) to be his most basic work, condensing all his thought into a single integrated statement. It was followed by *We Can Begin Again—Together* (1970), *My Stand on Astrology* (1972), *Occult Preparations for a New Age* (1975), *The Sun Is Also a Star: The Galactic Dimension in Astrology* (1974), *From Humanistic to Transpersonal Psychology* (1975), and *Culture, Crisis, and Creativity* (1977).

Rudhyar's marriage to Whitall ended in 1976, and he married Leyla Rasle in 1977. The last years of his life were especially rich. He wrote *Astrology and the Modern*

*Psyche* (1977), *Astrological Triptych* (1978), *Beyond Individualism* (1979), *Astrological Insights* (1979), *Astrology of Transformation* (1980), and *Rhythm of Wholeness* (1983). Rudhyar died in California on September 13, 1985.

—Aidan A. Kelly

**Sources:**

Brau, Jean-Louis, Helen Weaver, and Allan Edmands. *Larousse Encyclopedia of Astrology*. New York: New American Library, 1980.

Melton, Gordon, Jerome Clark, and Aidan A. Kelly. *New Age Encyclopedia*. Detroit: Gale, 1990.

Rudhyar, Dane. *The Astrological Houses*. Garden City, NY: Doubleday, 1972.

———. *The Astrology of Personality*. New York: Lucis Publishing, 1936.

———. *The Lunation Cycle*. The Hague: Servire, 1967.

———. *The Planetarization of Consciousness*. New York: Harper, 1972.

———. *The Pulse of Life*. Philadelphia: David McKay, 1943.

"Seed Man: Dane Rudhyar," *Human Dimensions* 4, no. 3, 1975.

## Rulership (Ruler)

In astrology, rulership is an association of the planets with the signs of the zodiac whereby each planet is said to "rule" a certain sign (or signs) and, secondarily, certain sets of objects and activities. Since the discovery of Uranus and the other newly detected planets, the question of which planets rule which signs has been a subject of hot debate among astrologers. However, prior to the advent of Uranus, a general consensus about these relationships had endured since the time of Ptolemy. The traditional system held that the Sun and the Moon (the two luminaries) ruled one sign apiece, Leo and Cancer, respectively. The known planets each ruled two signs: Mercury ruled Virgo and Gemini, Venus ruled Taurus and Libra, Mars ruled Aries and Scorpio, Jupiter ruled Sagittarius and Pisces, and Saturn ruled Capricorn and Aquarius. This is still the rulership system held by the great majority practicing Vedic astrology.

The relationship between the planets and the signs is one of kinship in their basic traits and associations. Thus, when the new planets were discovered, astrologers placed them in horoscopes and attempted to determine precisely what the nature of their influence was. From these observations, it was determined that Uranus ruled Aquarius, Neptune ruled Pisces, and Pluto ruled Scorpio, leaving Saturn, Jupiter, and Mars as the rulers of Capricorn, Sagittarius, and Aries. (There often appears in late nineteenth- and early twentieth-century transitional astrological works the term "coruler," an appelation that allowed astrologers to keep the old schema while introducing new rulerships—e.g., Saturn and Uranus were at one time said to be the corulers of Aquarius.) Only Mercury and Venus are still viewed as ruling two signs each.

Because of the attractiveness of a balanced system in which 12 heavenly bodies rule 12 signs, twentieth-century astrologers have often speculated that two new planets would eventually be discovered that would come to be accepted as the rulers of Virgo and Libra. For example, the hypothetical planet Vulcan, which some astronomers said might be found between the Sun and Mercury, was thought to be the ruler of Virgo, while an as-yet-undiscovered planet lying beyond Pluto was thought to rule Libra. Some current astrologers speculate that the planetoid Chiron and/or some of the larger asteroids rule these these signs.

The ruler of the sign on the cusp (i.e., the beginning) of a particular house is said to rule that house, and the ruler of the sign on the ascendant is said to rule the chart. Astrologers who feel that the term "ruler" should be reserved for the planet/sign relationship sometimes prefer to use the traditional term "lord" for the planet-house relationship; hence, the relevance of the expression "lord of a house"; ruler of a sign. "Lord" and related terms are generally not employed by modern astrologers, who tend to use "ruler" to cover all such associations between planets, signs, houses, etc. Finally, the planets are said to rule the matters associated with their signs. Thus, for example, Pluto rules death, the sexual organs, the principle of regeneration, and all of the other matters associated with the sign Scorpio. Neptune rules mysticism, music, the feet, and all Piscean matters.

**Sources:**

DeVore, Nicholas. *Encyclopedia of Astrology*. New York: Philosophical Library, 1947.
Hand, Robert. *Horoscope Symbols*. Rockport, MA: Para Research, 1981.

## Ruth

Ruth, asteroid 798 (the 798th asteroid to be discovered, on November 21, 1914), is approximately 54 kilometers in diameter and has an orbital period of 5.2 years. It was named after the biblical Ruth and represents loyalty. In a natal chart, Ruth's location by sign and house indicates where and how one is most likely to be loyal or to experience loyal devotion from others. When afflicted by inharmonious aspects, Ruth may show disloyalty or overt displays of loyalty that are not felt. If prominent in a chart (e.g., conjunct the Sun or the ascendant), it may signal an exceptionally loyal person or someone for whom loyalty and devotion are important life themes.

**Sources:**

Kowal, Charles T. *Asteroids: Their Nature and Utilization*. Chichester, West Sussex, UK: Ellis Horwood Limited, 1988.
Room, Adrian. *Dictionary of Astronomical Names*. London: Routledge, 1988.
Schwartz, Jacob. *Asteroid Name Encyclopedia*. St. Paul, MN: Llewellyn Publications, 1995.

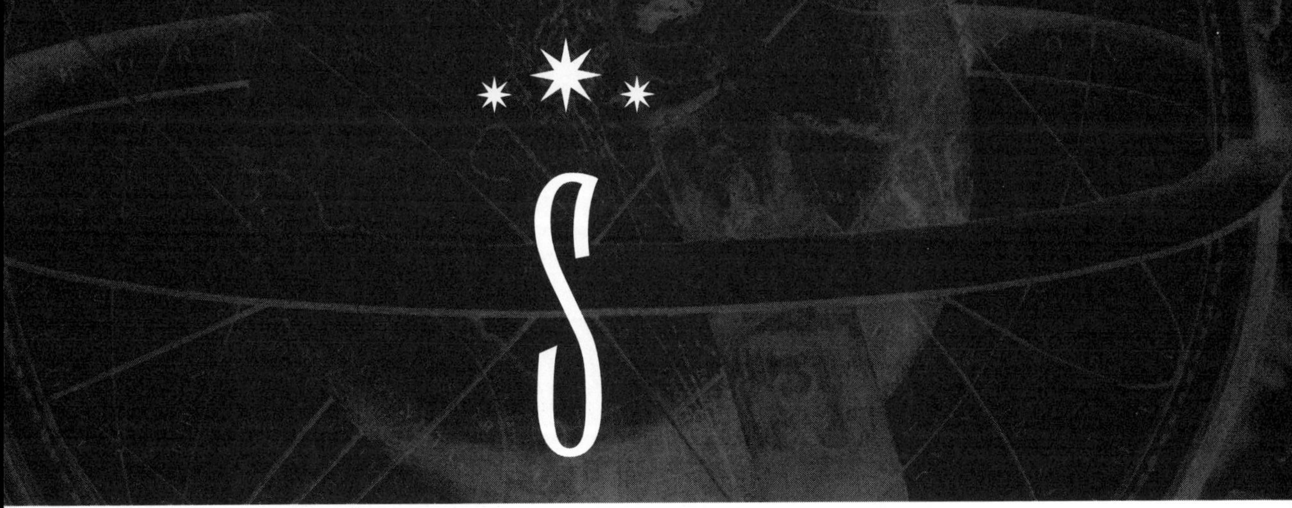

## Sabian Symbols

The Sabian symbols are the unique set of 360 symbolic vignettes or descriptive images for each degree of the zodiac, which were obtained in 1925 by Marc Edmund Jones from an ancient Mesopotamian source.

Several years earlier, Jones had become interested in the psychically obtained astrological symbols of the Welsh seer, John Thomas, better known as "Charubel." He thought about asking permission to recast the descriptions of the symbols, but decided they were too moralized for his purposes. He decided, instead, to try to obtain a more universal set of symbols from one of the "invisible Brothers" who was saturated in the early Egyptian schematism from which the zodiac was originally derived.

With a plan in mind, Jones began looking for someone with psychic abilities but limited life experience (i.e., a person devoid of a sophisticated mindset) to assist him—someone whose consciousness could receive an impression, but form only a simple, modern picture or situation for each of the 360 degrees. For this task, he chose Elsie Wheeler, a Sabian Assembly student who had been wheelchair-bound with arthritis for years. A quiet park lane in Balboa Park, in San Diego, California, behind a row of trees, but close to a busy intersection, was selected as the most opportune place for the project. This setting met the requirement of natural law, that the highest spiritual tasks be performed in everyday situations of high intensity or turmoil.

The project was accomplished in the space of about four hours, in two separate sessions. Jones brought 360 white, unlined, 3" x 5" index cards with him. He had earlier written one of each of the 360 astrological degrees on each card. The role of the invisible brother was to transmit the meaning of each degree to Jones through Wheeler. Her role was to allow her mind to be impressed and describe the pictures she saw. Jones was responsible for supplying the refined cabalistic training needed to critically interpret the pictures.

During the session, Jones constantly shuffled the index cards and randomly placed one of them face down before Wheeler. She would then report on the picture she saw by inward vision. Neither of them knew which degree she was describing. Jones then took back the index card and quickly wrote down the few words that he determined to be the essence of the degree from each picture that Wheeler described.

After the session, Jones put the cards away in a trunk and left them there for several years. He later took them out and typed them in a list that was privately circulated to his astrological students. The response was so encouraging that, in 1931, he worked out the mathematical structure he had discovered in them, expanded the descriptions for each degree, and put the whole thing together in an astrological typescript. Some time afterward, Dane Rudhyar came across the typescript, recognized the value of the symbols, and obtained Jones's permission to modify and include them in his 1936 book, *The Astrology of Personality*. The publication of this book brought the Sabian symbols to first broad public notice.

After some years of reflection, Jones came to the conclusion that he had gone far afield by expanding the descriptions of the symbols on his original index card notes in his 1931 typescript. He also felt he had done precisely what he had tried to avoid in the first place—moralize the symbols. In 1953, he went back to his original notes on the cards, added a new commentary and formula, and published them in his book, *The Sabian Symbols in Astrology*.

Twenty years later, in 1973, Rudhyar reinterpreted his own earlier version of the Sabian symbols and presented them as a contemporary American I Ching in *An Astrological Mandala: The Cycle of Transformations and its 360 Symbolic Phases*.

While the original Sabian symbol descriptions have been modified and reinterpreted more than a few times by various astrologers, the words written on the index cards in Balboa Park in 1925 stand as sole authority as to which version of the symbolic degrees is truly "Sabian." (The original index cards have been reproduced and included in the 1998 book, *The Sabian Symbols: A Screen of Prophecy* by Diana E. Roche.)

The Sabian symbols are most commonly used in astrology to add depth and dimension to the interpretation of the planets, parts, and cusps in a horoscope and for chart rectification. They can also be read for the degrees of new and full moons, moonrise and sunrise, and in horary as well as natal, progressed, and transit charts. The Sabian symbol for the day, which is used for daily guidance by many astrologers, is determined by calculating the degree of the sun at sunrise, at the location of the individual. The symbols can also be used, even by the nonastrologer, in a wide variety of divinatory techniques. The most common one is to open a Sabian symbols book while focusing on a question or problem and, without looking, place a finger on the text and read what is written for that degree.

In order to determine which Sabian symbol to use, it is necessary to consider both the degree and minute of the planet. The Sabian symbol degrees are numbered 1 through 30 for each sign. There is no 0° reading for any sign in the Sabian symbol system. The method used by both Jones and Rudhyar was to read the next higher degree if a planet had reached at least the one minute (1') mark of a degree. Their reasoning was that when consideration is given to moving bodies, as in astrological progressions or directions, the indication is to be seen as in full force from the crossing of any one minute (1') point to the arrival at the threshold of the next one minute (1') point.

Thus, 15° Aries 00' is read as 15° Aries, but 15° Aries 01' is read as 16° Aries, as is 15° Aries 59'. Determining the correct Sabian symbol to use when a planet is found at the very end or beginning of a sign, especially when dealing with seconds, can be particularly confusing. If a planet lies between 29°01' of one sign and 0°01' of the next sign, it is read as 30 degrees. Thus, 29° Pisces 01' is read as 30 Pisces. Following the same line of reasoning, 0° Aries 0'59" is also read as 30 Pisces, but 0°01' Aries is read as 1 Aries.

**Sources:**

Jones, Marc Edmund. *The Sabian Symbols in Astrology*. 3d ed. Stanwood, WA: Sabian Publishing Society, 1969.
Roche, Diana E. *The Sabian Symbols: A Screen of Prophecy*. Victoria: Trafford Publishing, 1998.
Rudhyar, Dane. *An Astrological Mandala: The Cycle of Transformations and Its 360 Symbolic Phases*. New York: Random House, 1973.

—Diana E. Roche, M.Ed., J.D.

## Sabine

Sabine, asteroid 665 (the 665th asteroid to be discovered, on July 22, 1908), is approximately 72 kilometers in diameter and has an orbital period of 5.6 years. It is named after a group of people to the east of Rome whose women were abducted by the Romans. They fought the Romans but finally joined with them to become one people. In a natal chart, Sabine's location by sign and house may indicate where and how one is most able to negotiate conflicts. When afflicted by inharmonious aspects, Sabine may indicate where one is taken advantage of.

**Sources:**

Kowal, Charles T. *Asteroids: Their Nature and Utilization*. Chichester, West Sussex, UK: Ellis Horwood Limited, 1988.
Room, Adrian. *Dictionary of Astronomical Names*. London: Routledge, 1988.
Schwartz, Jacob. *Asteroid Name Encyclopedia*. St. Paul, MN: Llewellyn Publications, 1995.

## Sagittarius

Sagittarius, the ninth sign of the zodiac, is a mutable fire sign. It is a positive, masculine sign, ruled by the planet Jupiter (although some astrologers would say that it is ruled or coruled by the planetoid Chiron). Its symbol is the centaur (sometimes, the archer) and its glyph is an arrow, denoting the arrow in the bow that the centaur is holding. It takes its name from the Latin word for arrow, *sagitta*. Sagittarius is associated with the hips, thighs, and liver, and individuals with a Sagittarius sun sign are susceptible to hepatitis and other liver problems. The key phrase for Sagittarius is "I see."

Unlike many other members of the zodiac, Sagittarius has a complex mythology. Symbolically half human and half animal, the alternative mythical figures for this sign also tend to place Sagittarius between the poles of animal brutality and high refinement. Chiron, the son of Philyra and Chronos, was a highly learned and refined centaur. A wise teacher who tutored Aesculapius, Jason, Achilles, and Hercules, Chiron's vast knowledge encompassed hunting, ethics, music, medicine, and the martial arts. Wounded by a poison arrow, he was unable to heal himself. He gave his immortality to Prometheus so that he could die and put an end to his own misery. Out of pity, Zeus is said to have transformed Chiron into a constellation. The figure of the kindly Chiron, however, is somewhat at odds with the image in the constellation Sagittarius, which points its drawn bow menacingly at Scorpio. Thus, an alternative image for Sagittarius is as an average, nondivine centaur with all the impulsive, savage brutality normally attributed to this mythical species.

Like the worst centaurs, Sagittarians can be crude, wild wanderers, always seeking adventure and freedom from all restraint. They can be reckless, irresponsible, and excessively blunt. Positively, natives of the sign are humorous, entertaining, and optimistic. Like Chiron, they prize wisdom and make inspiring teachers. All Sagittarians strive upward. For the less evolved, this may mean social climbing; for the more evolved, a striving toward higher wisdom and spiritual insight. Like all fire signs, they are fond of physical and social activity.

The sign that the Sun was in at birth is usually the single most important influence on a native's personality. Thus, when people say they are a certain sign, they are almost always referring to their sun sign. There is a wealth of information available on the characteristics of the zodiacal signs—so much that one book would not be able to contain it all. Sun-sign astrology, which is the kind of astrology found in newspaper columns and popular magazines, has the advantage of simplicity. But this simplicity is purchased at the price of ignoring other astrological influences, such as one's Moon sign, rising sign, etc. These other influences can substantially modify a person's basic sun-sign traits. As a consequence, it is the rare individual who is completely typical of her or his sign. The reader should bear this caveat in mind when perusing the following series of sun sign interpretations.

One traditional way in which astrologers condense information is by summarizing sign and planet traits in lists of words and short phrases called key words or key phrases. The following Sagittarius key words are drawn from Manly P. Hall's *Astrological Keywords:*

> *Emotional key words:* "Proud, zealous, energetic, hail-fellow-well-met, buoyant, openhearted, amiable, tender, idealistic, sincere, speculative, daring, impatient, not domestic, self-indulgent."

> *Mental key words:* "Jovial, progressive, philosophic, intellectual, eclectic, frank, just, good-tempered, intrepid, punctilious, oratorical, prophetic, curious, altruistic, extremely ambitious, financially inclined."

At present, there are various astrology report programs that contain interpretations of each of the 12 sun signs. A selection of these for Sun in Sagittarius has been excerpted below:

> You are known for being idealistic, generous, sociable, cheerful and very positive. Full of spirit, you have a huge reservoir of energy within

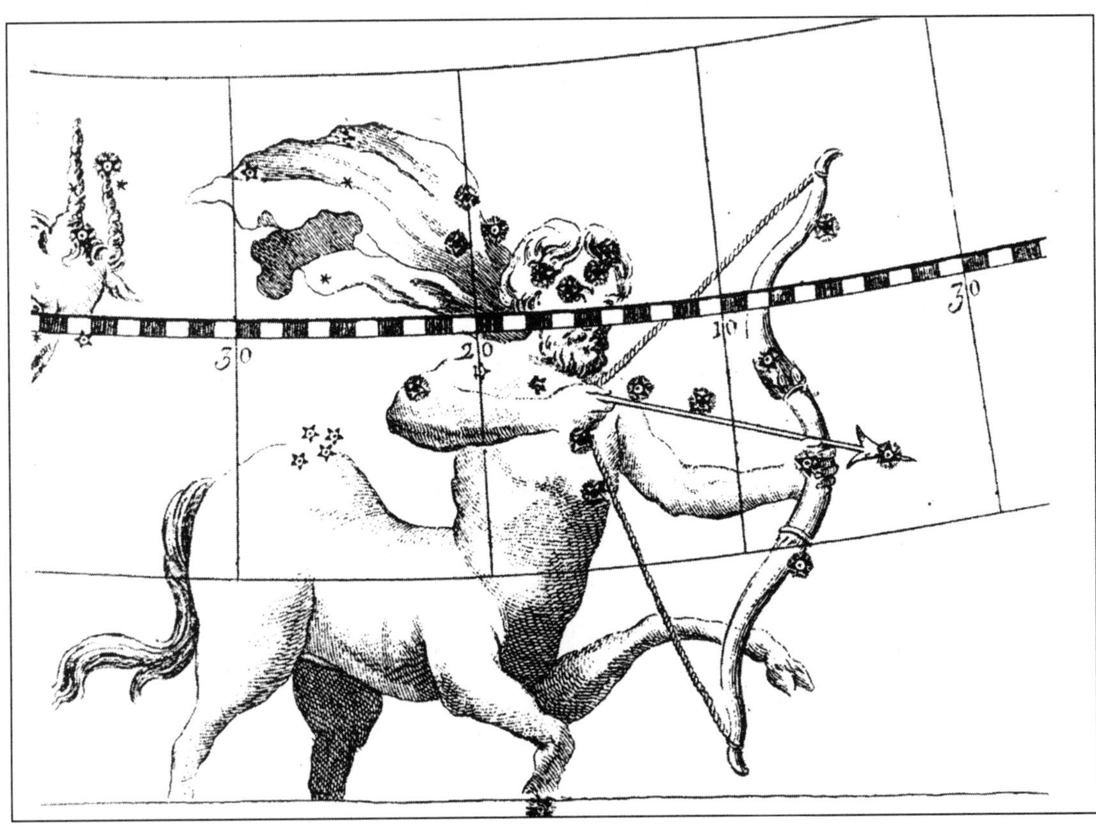

**The constellation Sagittarius in a late 18th-century engraving by Montignot.** ***Reproduced by permission of Fortean Picture Library.***

you that demands to be released. Exercise, either physical or mental, is thus a necessity. Gregarious, you enjoy being with other people, although you tend to avoid emotionally restrictive or overly intimate relationships. You are constantly curious about the broader issues of life, but can be careless and sloppy about details, and may leap to conclusions before all the facts are in. You are probably an avid reader and gatherer of knowledge, and once a subject catches your interest, your enthusiasm for learning all about it is boundless. (From "Professional Natal Report." Courtesy of Astrolabe [http://www.alabe.com].)

You are a gambler and an adventurer at heart, one who loves to take risks, to discover and explore new worlds, and to take the untried path rather than the safe, reliable one. You are an independent soul, freedom-loving, and often very restless. You need a lifestyle that provides opportunities for travel, movement, change, and meeting new people. A steady routine which offers much in the way of security but little in the way of space and freedom is odious to you.

To you, life is a journey, an adventure, endlessly interesting and rich with possibilities, and it may be difficult for you to decide where to focus your attention and efforts. You probably traveled around and experimented with many different paths before you settled on a particular career. Or you may go from one project to the next, for once the challenge and vital interest is gone, you are very quick to move on. Commitment, discipline, focus, and concentration are not your strong points. You can be irresponsible and disinclined to take on the burdens and limitations of adult life.

An incurable optimist, you have big dreams, aspirations, and hopes for the future and are usually pursuing some distant goal. You have a great deal of faith and trust in life and failures don't crush your spirit. You always bounce back from disappointments, often with another bright dream or scheme. You have a sporting, playful attitude toward life and are philosophical about your mistakes. You have the ability to sense future trends, to see the big picture, and you like to theorize and speculate. However, attending to all of the details and practical requirements of implementing your theories is bothersome to you.

You express yourself in a very open, direct, and straightforward manner and are often blunt and tactless as well. Because you do not take yourself too seriously, you may not realize how deeply your candid statements can wound more sensitive souls. In fact, though you may not realize it, your insensitivity and lack of understanding regarding others' feelings is probably one of your worst faults.

You do enjoy friendship and camaraderie, but you need freedom also and do not do well with a possessive, clinging, or emotionally demanding partner. You are quite generous yourself, and heartily dislike pettiness in others. Someone who shares your ideals, your sense of fun, and your zest for life would be the right companion for you. (From "Merlin," by Gina Ronco and Agnes Nightingale. Courtesy of Cosmic Patterns [http://cosmic.patterns.com].)

To the medieval astrologer, there were three kinds of Sagittarian: the gypsy, the scholar, and the philosopher. They're all legitimate, healthy parts of the picture. Sagittarius represents the urge to expand our horizons, to break up the routines that imprison us. One way to do that is to escape the bonds of the culture into which we were born—that's the gypsy. Another is to educate ourselves, to push our intelligence beyond its customary "position papers"—the way of the scholar. Finally, our intuition can stretch outward, trying to come to terms with cosmic law, attempting to grasp the meaning and purpose of life. That's the philosopher's path.

To keep your Sagittarian energies healthy, you need to feed them an endless supply of fresh experience. Travel. Take classes. Learn to scuba dive. Amazement feeds the Archer the same way protein feeds your physical body. Conversely, if there's a cardinal sin for Sagittarius, it is to consciously, willingly allow yourself to be bored.

> With your Sun in Sagittarius, freedom is the most precious arrow in your quiver. You thrive on experience. Your heart beats faster at the sight of a far horizon. Your life is a quest ... for adventure, for experience, ultimately, for meaning. The Gypsy, the Scholar, and the Philosopher all play major roles in your interior existence ... and need to have major input into your existential shopping list! There's a Gypsy-like destiny element in your life that presents you again and again with culture shock, like travel or working with people from different backgrounds. The Scholar manifests as your lifelong desire to learn, to break up your mental routines. And you've been a Philosopher ever since you were born—you popped out of your mother's womb wondering, "Why am I here?" (From "The Sky Within," by Steven Forrest. Courtesy of Matrix Software [http://thenewage.com] and Steven Forrest [http://www.stevenforrest.com].)

Among its several natal programs, Matrix Software created a unique report based on the published works of the early twentieth-century astrologer, Grant Lewi (1901–1952). Lewi's highly original delineations were recognized as creative and insightful by his contemporaries. One measure of the appeal of his work is that his books *Astrology for the Millions* and *Heaven Knows What* are still in print. The following is excerpted from the report program "Heaven Knows What":

> If there were no God, it would be necessary to invent him. *(Voltaire, born in Sagittarius, November 21, 1694.)*
>
> There is no cure for birth and death save to enjoy the interval. *(George Santayana, born in Sagittarius, December 16, 1863.)*
>
> The miracles of the Church seem to me to rest not so much upon faces or voices or healing power, coming suddenly near to us from afar, but upon our perceptions being made finer, so that for a moment our eyes can see and our ears hear what is there about us always. *(Willa Cather, born in Sagittarius, December 7, 1876.)*
>
> The expansion of the ego to the uttermost bounds of human thought, experience and knowledge motivates the Sagittarian, who rushes out eagerly to greet life, equipped with a radiant nature, abundant vitality and a keen, alert mind eager for the fellowship of earth and willing to extend his knowledge to last limits of heaven. The approach to life is straightforward, for the aim is not subtle: it is to experience, to know, to try, to adventure. As a result, the Sagittarian goes far, literally and figuratively. He travels, either geographically or in thought, or both; and however he travels he likes to go fast. If he finishes things at all, it is because he is quick, not patient; life is too short for him to bother with details, and he feels that he will learn more, see more, know more if he goes more. He can thus be superficial, but is rarely shallow, for his sincerity goes right down into his marrow, and a platitude on his lips

can become a great truth because of the wholeheartedness with which he believes it.

> The creative urge is strong; thus does the ego expand and perpetuate itself in its expanded state. Idealism is powerfully marked, as are religious and philosophic tendencies. Sagittarians take naturally to serious thought and, even if uneducated in the formal sense, are at home with abstract ideas, principles, beliefs. They have little use for dogma, and are not conventional in thought, though they are so straightforward that their actions are generally unimpeachable. A low-type Sagittarian is a rara avis. The worst the sign usually gets is mediocre and bromidic. Abundant energy and natural good spirits preserve them from the worst that life throws up. The better types, eagerly questing in the geographical and spiritual world, lead the abundant life up to the hilt. They leave the world better than they found it by the happiness they bring to others, if not indeed by some special contribution to philosophy, religion or science, in which they are especially likely to shine. (Courtesy of Matrix Software [http://thenewage.com].)

The following excerpt comes not from a natal report program, but from David Cochrane's recent book, *Astrology for the 21st Century*. Based on lessons for astrology students, it approaches the signs of the zodiac from a somewhat different perspective than the other short delineations cited here:

> Sagittarius is the archer shooting for a goal. With eyes on the distant horizon, Sagittarius seeks a lofty goal or grand vision. Sagittarians do not get bogged down with details; they understand the overall situation and they travel, negotiate, socialize, and explore on a large scale that provides them the information, contacts, and resources to pursue large scale projects. Because Sagittarians have a broad spectrum of experiences, they tend to avoid getting stuck in a situation; they find another route around the problem and they have enough contacts and alternative resources to find a viable alternative to their current situation. Another trait that helps the Sagittarian is that they rarely take things personally. Their broad view of life allows them to see criticisms or insults from others in proper perspective, and their feelings are rarely hurt. They also often do not realize that others are more sensitive to personal criticism than they are, and consequently can say something without tact and thereby appear to be either insensitive or extremely blunt. (Courtesy of Cosmic Patterns [http://cosmic.patterns.com] and David Cochrane [kepler@astrosoftware.com].)

A number of specialized report programs has been developed that offer useful supplements to the generic delineations of general reports. The following sun sign interpretation has been drawn from a program written by Gloria Star (originally part of her book, *Astrology: Woman to Woman*) that generates a specialized report for women:

> With your Sun in Sagittarius you are a woman who thrives on the grand adventure of life. You may feed this urge through travel or education, but you also fulfill it through your spiritual quests. Your enthusiasm is difficult to miss, and you can inspire others to reach beyond their limitations through the example of your own life. But you can also be difficult to follow, and may head into a new territory before you've even warmed your chair.
>
> Since you've always wondered about everything, a certain level of personal assertiveness has always been part of your personality. Your Sagittarius Sun energy is a powerful driver, stimulating your sense of adventure and endless questioning and giving you an air of excitement. You're the woman who has been comfortable venturing out on your own, particularly if you have a strong interest driving you. As a young girl your experience of your father may have been especially connected to his interest in learning or his philosophical or religious teachings may have been a stronghold in your life. But you may also have a desire to develop these elements of your life in your own way, and in searching for the truth of yourself are likely to discover some differences from your upbringing. Developing your individual identity may be easier said than done because you may always have a tendency toward extreme reverence for your teachers and may take the teachings too literally. Task one: separating the teacher from the teaching will allow you to gain confidence in your individual ability to develop a connection to divine truth. Then, as you explore the vast nature of spirituality, you may discover a path which is uniquely your own. This in turn influences your sense of who you are, not just as a woman, but as a human being on a quest for the ultimate.
>
> You're probably pretty intelligent, like learning, and have an adventurous drive with your Sagittarius Sun. But you may be afraid of success. It's that unknown question about where to aim. If you aim for your high ideals, you could possibly fall short, so you might compromise for something else, just because it's quickly reachable. Then what's that yearning in your heart? Could it be the desire for something more!? There is your drive to success, and it's the adventure itself which gives you the feeling that makes the light in your eyes. After all, when you do reach that pinnacle, you'll just aim for something new! (From "Woman to Woman," by Gloria Star. Courtesy of Matrix Software [http://thenewage.com] and Gloria Star [glostar@aol.com].)

Responding to the revival of interest in pre-twentieth-century astrology, J. Lee Lehman developed a report program embodying the interpretive approach of traditional astrology. The following is excerpted from her book *Classical Astrology for Modern Living* and her computer program "Classical Report":

> You have quick apprehensions, but you are changeable in your opinions. You are fearless, good-natured, high-minded, crafty and inge-

> nious, proud, quick to anger, but soon you are over it. You are stout-hearted, valiant, and witty. You aim at great things, but you can be too severe in the exercise of power. This does not prevent you from achieving success.
>
> You are a Fire Sign, which means that you are "hot" and "dry." The "dry" component means, among other things, that you see distinctions easily, and that you are more swayed by intellectual argument than by passion. Being "hot," you react to things quickly: by expressing your anger strongly and immediately, you don't tend to harbor a grudge. You may be perceived by others as angry, but that's only if they are not "hot" as well. You will be perceived as having high energy levels, and yet you are aware of a curious stillness amidst the seeming activity. You may need more sleep than colder types in order to recharge your batteries.
>
> You are mutable, which means that you adapt easily to change. However, you adapt so easily compared to others that they may wonder if you are capable of maintaining a permanent stance about anything.
>
> Being a four-footed sign, you have a strong sex drive. This also means that you can be vicious or violent if angered. One of the dangers of the Sun in the signs of Jupiter is Jupiter's mythological interest in love affairs, especially when the solar person is perceived as being in a position of power or authority. (Courtesy of J. Lee Lehman, Ph.D., copyright 1998 [http://www.leelehman.com].)

Readers interested in examining interpretations for their Chinese astrological sign should refer to the relevant entry. A guide for determining one's sign in the Chinese system is provided in the entry on the Chinese zodiac.

**Sources:**

Cochrane, David. *Astrology for the 21st Century*. Gainesville, FL: Cosmic Patterns, 2002.

Forrest, Steven. *The Inner Sky: How to Make Wiser Choices for a More Fulfilling Life*. 4th ed. San Diego: ACS Publications, 1989.

Green, Landis Knight. *The Astrologer's Manual: Modern Insights into an Ancient Art*. Sebastopol, CA: CRCS Publications, 1975.

Hall, Manly P. *Astrological Keywords*. New York: Philosophical Library, 1958. Reprint, Savage, MD: Littlefield Adams Quality Paperbacks, 1975.

Lehman, J. Lee. *Classical Astrology for Modern Living: From Ptolemy to Psychology & Back Again*. Atglen, PA: Whitford Press, 1996.

Lewi, Grant. *Astrology for the Millions*. 5th ed. St. Paul, MN: Llewellyn, 1978.

———. *Heaven Knows What*. St. Paul, MN: Llewellyn, 1969.

Star, Gloria. *Astrology & Your Child: A Handbook for Parents*. St. Paul, MN: Llewellyn, 2001.

———. *Astrology: Woman to Woman*. St. Paul, MN: Llewellyn, 1999.

## Sanguine

Sanguine is the traditional name for the personality temperament indicated by an excess of the element air.

## SAPIENTIA

Sapientia, asteroid 275 (the 275th asteroid to be discovered, on April 15, 1888), is approximately 108 kilometers in diameter and has an orbital period of 4.6 years. Its name is a personification of a Latin word for wisdom. If other elements of an natal chart concur, Sapientia shows wisdom with respect to the matters indicated by its sign and house position. When afflicted, it may suggest false wisdom. When prominent in a chart (e.g., conjunct the Sun or the ascendant), it may show a wise person or an individual who seeks wisdom.

**Sources:**

Kowal, Charles T. *Asteroids: Their Nature and Utilization*. Chichester, West Sussex, UK: Ellis Horwood Limited, 1988.

Room, Adrian. *Dictionary of Astronomical Names*. London: Routledge, 1988.

Schwartz, Jacob. *Asteroid Name Encyclopedia*. St. Paul, MN: Llewellyn Publications, 1995.

## SAPPHO

Sappho, asteroid 80 (the 80th asteroid to be discovered, on May 2, 1864), was named after a legendary Greek love poetess of the sixth century B.C.E. who lived on the island of Lesbos (from which the term lesbian derives). Its orbital period is about 3½ years, and it is approximately 84 kilometers in diameter. Sappho is one of the more recent asteroids to be investigated by astrologers. Preliminary material on Sappho can be found in Demetra George and Douglas Bloch's *Astrology for Yourself*, and an ephemeris (table of celestial locations) for Sappho can be found in the second edition of their *Asteroid Goddesses*.

Unlike the planets, which are associated with a wide range of phenomena, the smaller asteroids are said to represent a single principle. George and Bloch give Sappho's principle as "romantic and artistic sensitivity." Zipporah Dobyns has found it prominent in the chart of people involved with poetry and the other arts, as well as in the charts of people involved in nurturing others (the semilegendary Sappho was devoted to nurturing young women). Contrary to the connotations of its name, Sappho does not appear to be associated with homosexuality. J. Lee Lehman associates Sappho with impersonal sexual drive, although the libido represented by this asteroid may be channeled into other endeavors, particularly work. Jacob Schwartz gives the astrological significance of this asteroid as "friendships, artistic expression of sex."

**Sources:**

Dobyns, Zipporah. *Expanding Astrology's Universe*. San Diego: Astro Computing Services, 1983.

George, Demetra, with Douglas Bloch. *Asteroid Goddesses: The Mythology, Psychology and Astrology of the Reemerging Feminine*. 2d ed. San Diego: 1990.

———. *Astrology for Yourself: A Workbook for Personal Transformation*. Berkeley, CA: Wingbow Press, 1987.

Lehman, J. Lee. *The Ultimate Asteroid Book*. West Chester, PA: Whitford Press, 1988.

Schwartz, Jacob. *Asteroid Name Encyclopedia*. St. Paul, MN: Llewellyn Publications, 1995.

## Satabisha

Satabisha (100 Physicians for Healing) is one of the Nakshatras (lunar mansions) of Vedic astrology. Symbolized by a circle or round charm, this Nakshatra is ruled by Varuna, god of the ocean or waves, at Aquarius 6°40' to 20°. One should negotiate or sign contracts at this time, and may be more economically clever and emotionally controlled, though quieter and argumentative.

—Pramela Thiagesan

## Satellite

A satellite is any body that orbits another body. The body being orbited is referred to as the primary. The most familiar examples of satellites are the Moon, a satellite of Earth, and Earth, a satellite of the Sun. This term was originally used to refer to attendants of important people. It was first applied to celestial bodies by Johannes Kepler, who used the term satellite to refer to the moons of Jupiter.

## Saturn

Saturn is the last planet in the solar system that can be seen with the naked eye. Its system of rings makes it stand out as a spectacular sight when seen with a telescope. Saturn has the lowest density of any planet in the solar system and is made up of primarily of hydrogen and helium molecules. Its rings are formed of either matter that was torn apart by Saturn's gravity or material that failed to accrete into a moon when moons were forming. The rings are inclined by 27° to the planet's orbit. According to Jay M. Pasachoff's *Contemporary Astronomy*, there are 9 moons that have long been known and several others have been detected in modern times. Saturn's cycle around the Sun is 29.47 years and mirrors the 29-month lunar cycle. Saturn spends 4½ months a year in its retrograde phase. It annually travels an average of 22° forward and 7° retrograde in zodiacal longitude. Due to its distance from the Sun and Moon the ancients attributed Saturn with the primary qualities of cooling and drying.

In Greek mythology, Saturn was Kronos (Cronos), one of the Titans who were among the first children of Heaven (Ouranos) and Earth (Gaea). Ouranos hated some of the first offspring who were horrible monsters and he hid them in secret places within the earth. Gaia was angered at the treatment of her children and appealed to the Cyclopes and Titans for help. Kronos lay in wait for his father and castrated him with a sickle. From that time on for untold ages, Kronos became lord of the universe, according to Edith Hamilton's *Mythology*. After being overthrown by his son Zeus, Kronos is said to have gone to Italy and ruled over the Great Golden Age. The Romans called him Saturnus, known as the god of agriculture and harvest who founded civilization and the social order. The great feast of Saturnalia is held annually in winter. It was thought that the Golden Age returns during the days the feast lasted. In Christian times, this holiday became Christmas and represents the birth of the Divine Child born at the Winter Solstice. At the turning of the year, old Father Time, who carries a sickle, is replaced by the New Year's Eve baby.

**An illustration of Saturn in his chariot with his zodiacal signs Capricorn and Aquarius as wheels. From a mid-seventeenth-century edition of Johannes Indagines's *Introduciones Apotelesmatica. Reproduced by permission of Fortean Picture Library.***

The passive side of Saturn is solitary, austere, depressive, downcast, miserable, demanding, inactive, sedentary, and immobile. The active side of Saturn is disciplined, determined, driving, sustained, persistent, hard working, and undaunted. In the Hellenistic system, according to Edith Hamilton's *Mythology*, the star of Kronos was assigned the special essence of ignorance and necessity. Saturn traditionally rules the masculine sign Aquarius that opposes the Sun, and the feminine sign Capricorn that opposes the Moon. It is exalted in Libra, in its fall in Aries, and in its debility in Cancer. When Saturn has essential dignity it operates more from the active qualities and can produce positive results. With little dignity its significations manifest in more malefic form. It rules the Air triplicity in a diurnal chart.

Saturn is a diurnal planet by sect. This means that Saturn in a daytime chart is more at his best. Joseph Crane explains Saturn's sect differences in *A Practical Guide to Traditional Astrology*:

> A diurnal Saturn is organized and disciplined, but also responds to novelty and change. He provides the virtues that one needs to flourish in

> the world—self-discipline, self-reliance, consistency, responsibility, and frugality ... a nocturnal Saturn can become more melancholy, more prone to punishing oneself or others. Here gravity can become density and a greater sense of life's futility. Indeed, diurnality balances some of these saturnine extremes!

Saturn is the most important of the planets in relation to terrestrial boundaries. Saturn is associated with agriculture, and the process and handwork of harvest. Things that take time to develop and endure over time are representative of Saturn's nature. Therefore Saturn is linked to time, age, progress, productivity, maturity and wisdom. In the rank of social structure, Saturn is the administrator, taskmaster, tax collector, guardian, and teacher. It procures reputation and notable rank, according to *Vettius Valens, Book I, Chapter I.* Its orientation can be toward perfection that requires diligent and disciplined effort, or efforts that can be blocked and limited by restriction, doubt, and lack of skill. It brings what is deserved or earned. Honors, respect, and authority can be granted after efforts have been made. At its most malefic it judges, punishes, rejects, and brings accusation, tears, captivity, exposure of deceit, and orphanhood.

Classical diseases and health problems associated with Saturn are those proceeding from cold, obstructions, and decay, such as melancholy, agues, all nervous diseases, epilepsy, black jaundice, toothache, cold defluxions, catarrh, atrophy, fistula, leprosy, palsy, apoplexy, and dropsy, according to James Wilson's *Complete Dictionary of Astrology*. Saturn's ailments are chronic and many are associated with aging, such as arthritis, sclerosis, skin diseases, skeletal deformities, hardening of arteries, cancer, congestion, constipation, consumption, deafness, birth defects, falls and bone fractures, gout, growths, halitosis, paralysis, polio, retardation, rheumatism, rickets, starvation, stones in the body, tremors, tooth aches and extractions, weakness, and weight gain, according to Rex E. Bills's *The Rulership Book, A Directory of Astrological Correspondences*.

In modern astrology's psychological view, Saturn's influence in personality lends a restricted bias toward the perception of how life should operate based on parental, social, and cultural standards. It relates to the kind of intelligence that is factual, correlating information into organized, systematically logical knowledge. It is traditional rather than original. Saturn gives strong leanings toward conformity and social acceptance, while resisting change and rejection.

Liz Greene, Jungian psychologist and author of *Saturn: A New Look at an Old Devil,* gives the modern view of Saturn:

> Saturn symbolizes a psychic process as well as a quality or kind of experience. He is not merely a representative of pain, restriction, and discipline; he is also a symbol of the psychic process, natural to all human beings, by which an individual may utilize the experiences of pain, restriction, and discipline as a means for greater consciousness and fulfilment.... The psychic process which Saturn symbolises seems to have something to do with the realisation of this inner experience of psychic completeness within the individual.

Saturn in the natal chart by sign illustrates the lessons necessary for the individual to define himself and his focus in order to integrate into society. Saturn has a 2½-year passage through each sign. The element of the sign highlights the area of greatest restriction that needs to be restructured through the individual's process of development.

Hellenistic astrology gave greater emphasis to planets ruling houses than planets *in* houses. Modern astrology has given more emphasis to planets in houses. The houses in the chart ruled by Saturn are the places where it has greatest influence on the native's life experiences. Saturn rules the natural tenth and eleventh houses and has its joy in the twelfth house. Using traditional rulership of signs, Saturn rules both Capricorn and Aquarius. Modern astrologers have adopted Uranus as the ruler of Aquarius.

In Jyotish (Vedic astrology), Saturn is known as Shani, or Sanaiscara, which means, "moving slowly." Saturn is the farthest visible planet from the Sun. One story tells of how Saturn was born of the Sun. The Sun's wife grew tired of the glare and heat from her husband and decided to visit her family. She left her shadow in her place. The Sun could not tell the difference between his wife and her shadow and had sex with the shadow. Out of this union Saturn was born. When the ruse was discovered the Sun banished Saturn and refused to acknowledge him as his son. This is why Saturn is not a friend to the Sun.

The other important story about Saturn involves Ganesha, the elephant-headed god. After many centuries of practicing meditation and other forms of spiritual practice, Parvoti decided to have a child with her husband Shiva. Shiva stayed up in the mountains meditating while Parvoti went down the mountain and gave birth. The child was exceptional and like any proud mother, Parvoti called all the gods to come and see her beautiful son. All the gods came and cooed and murmured in amazement, except for Saturn who stood away staring at his feet. Parvoti took offense and demanded that Saturn look at the child. Saturn tried to explain that nothing good could come from his glance, but Parvoti insisted. Saturn raised his head and just barely looked at the child, and the child's head was burnt up into ash. Everyone was aghast and very upset, most especially Parvoti. To soothe her Brahma went to find a new head for the child. The first creature he found was a huge bull elephant. He took the elephant's head and fixed it on the body of the child. That is how Ganesha got his head. (There is another version where it is Shiva who cuts off the child's head because he did not know Parvoti had gone off to have a child.)

In the celestial cabinet, Saturn is the servant. He represents the outcasts of society, beggars, and people who do not follow religious practices. His elemental quality is air, and his gender is neutral. He is the indicator for disease, death, and all sorts of bad things. Ironically, a well-placed Saturn indicates good longevity.

**Sources:**

Bills, Rex E. *The Rulership Book, A Directory of Astrological Correspondences*. Richmond, VA: Macoy Publishing & Masonic Supply Co., 1971.

Crane, Joseph. *A Practical Guide to Traditional Astrology*. Orleans, MA: Archive for the Retrieval of Historical Astrological Texts, 1997.

Greene, Liz. *Saturn: A New Look at an Old Devil*. New York: Samuel Weiser, 1976.

Hamilton, Edith. *Mythology*. Boston: Little, Brown, 1942.
Masco, Maire. Jyotish Saturn ideas from correspondence by email.
Pasachoff, Jay M. *Contemporary Astronomy*. 3d ed. Philadelphia: Saunders College Publishing, 1985.
Schmidt, Robert, translator. *Vettius Valens, Book I, Chapter I*. Cumberland, MD: Phaser Foundation, 2002.
Wilson, James. *A Complete Dictionary of Astrology*. Islington Green, London, England: William Hueges, 1819.

—Norma Jean Ream

## Saturnine

There are many common terms and expressions that originate in the science of the stars. Saturn rules, among other matters, sour and depressed dispositions. Hence, someone with a dour, melancholy temperament is sometimes called saturnine.

## Scales

The Scales is a popular alternate term for the sign Libra.

## Schema

Schema (scheme) is an older, medieval term for a horoscope.

## Schermer, Barbara

Barbara Schermer has maintained a vigorous astrological counseling practice in Chicago since 1974 and is known as an advocate and pioneer in the field of experiential astrology. She is the author of *Astrology Alive: A Guide to Experiential Astrology and the Healing Arts*, in which she passionately advocates a holistic, soul-centered (as opposed to prediction-centered) astrology. She has extensive experience as a holistic practitioner integrating archetypal and Jungian psychology, mythology, kriya yoga, flower essences, alchemy, dreams and the arts in her work.

Schermer is an internationally known speaker, having presented at many conferences in the United States, Canada, England, Switzerland, Germany, Norway, Australia, and the Netherlands. She has served as the Media Watch chairman and advisory board member of the Association for Astrological Networking (AFAN), for the board of Kepler College in Seattle, and was twice nominated for the prestigious Regulus award for her contribution to astrology.

She offers a nine-month experiential astrology apprenticeship training in Chicago, mentors astrology students, and for years has been a volunteer teacher for the adult education programs at Francis Parker High School in Chicago and the Chicago Waldorf schools in support of their scholarship funds.

## SCORPIO

Scorpio, the eighth sign of the zodiac, is a fixed water sign. It is a negative (in the value-neutral sense of being negatively *charged*), feminine sign ruled by the planet Pluto (in traditional astrology it was ruled by Mars). The only sign with three symbols—the Scorpion, the Snake, and the Eagle—its symbology is complex. Its glyph is said to represent a serpent (some astrologers say a male member). It takes its name from the Latin word for scorpion. Scorpio is associated with the sexual organs, and individuals with a Scorpio sun sign are susceptible to kidney infections and venereal disease. Male Scorpios are prone to prostate problems; female Scorpios to female problems. The key phrase for Scorpio is "I desire."

Scorpio is associated with the myth of the goddess Artemis calling an enormous scorpion out of the ground to slay Orion. The reasons given for this attack vary in different versions of the tale—some say jealousy, others that she was defending herself from rape, and yet others say that she feared Orion would kill all animals on Earth. In any event, she rewarded the scorpion by transforming it into a constellation. In ancient Mesopotamian mythology, scorpion men guarded the gates of the underworld, which is the original reason Scorpio became associated with death. In European folklore, both scorpions and snakes were associated with evil and treachery, but, outside the Jewish and Christian traditions, snakes were more usually associated with wisdom (they were believed to know the secret of immortality, because when they shed their skins, it appears that they are discarding an old body for a young one). Scorpio's eagle, symbolizing an evolved soul that can soar aloft above earthly concerns, may also represent the Phoenix, a mythological bird that died only to be reborn from its own ashes. On a star map, two alternative symbols can be seen in two constellations above Scorpio: Aesculapius, who is pictured holding a serpent, and Aquila the Eagle, a constellation near the serpent's tail.

All these various mythological associations enter into the sign Scorpio. The sign can be viewed as a form of Artemis herself, and the various versions of Artemis's attack reflect the various ways in which the sign's violent passion can manifest—as intense jealousy, as enraged self-defense, or in defense of others. Scorpios can be debauched, evil, treacherous people who always remember a slight and seek vengeance. They can also be healers and social reformers, manifesting the best traits of humanity. Scorpios are best known for their sexual intensity, although this intense drive can be channeled into other activities. They are also associated with death and, more than any other sign, have within themselves the capacity to "die" to their old selves and be transformed into new beings.

The sign that the Sun was in at birth is usually the single most important influence on a native's personality. Thus, when people say they are a certain sign, they are almost always referring to their sun sign. There is a wealth of information available on the characteristics of the zodiacal signs—so much that one book would not be able to contain it all. Sun-sign astrology, which is the kind of astrology found in newspaper columns and popular magazines, has the advantage of simplicity. But this simplicity is purchased at the price of ignoring other astrological influences, such as one's Moon sign, rising sign, etc. These other influences can substantially modify a person's basic sun-sign traits. As a consequence, it is the rare individual who is completely typical of her or his sign. The reader should bear this caveat in mind when perusing the following series of sun sign interpretations.

One traditional way in which astrologers condense information is by summarizing sign and planet traits in lists of words and short phrases called key words or key phrases. The following Scorpio key words are drawn from Manly P. Hall's *Astrological Keywords:*

> *Emotional key words:* "Extremes of emotions; when highly evolved, the native is impersonal, unselfish, imaginative; when not highly evolved, is revengeful, secretive, quick-tempered, and self-indulgent; not domestic; suspicious"
>
> *Mental key words:* "Scientific, altruistic, executive, penetrating, intellectual, prone to investigate the secret forces of nature, temperamental, sarcastic, vindictive."

At present, there are various astrology report programs that contain interpretations of each of the 12 sun signs. A selection of these for Sun in Scorpio has been excerpted below:

> Intense and complex by nature, you have extremely strong emotional reactions to most situations. Feelings are often difficult for you to verbalize. This gives you a tendency to be very quiet and to brood and think a lot. You seldom get overtly angry, but when you do, you are furious and unforgiving. When you make an emotional commitment, it is total, and so you are not attracted to superficial or casual relationships. If you are challenged, you take it as a personal affront and tend to lash out and fight back in a vengeful manner. You love mysteries and the supernatural. A good detective, you love getting to the root of problems and you enjoy finding out what makes other people tick. You are known to be very willful, powerful and tenacious. (From "Professional Natal Report." Courtesy of Astrolabe [http://www.alabe.com].)
>
> Quiet, deep, emotionally complex and intensely private, you are not a person who is easy to get to know and understand. You are extremely sensitive but disinclined to show it, and you allow only a special few into your inner world. Like a wary animal, you are cautious and mistrustful of those you do not know until you "sniff them out." You are very, very instinctive and intuitive. You usually have a strong, immediate gut reaction to people, even though you may be unable to clearly articulate why you feel as you do. Your feelings and perceptions go deeper than words.
>
> You also have a powerful need for deep emotional involvement and you form very intense love bonds and attachments. You are possessive and often jealous of anyone or anything that you perceive as a threat to your bond with someone you love. When you commit yourself to someone or something, you are wholeheartedly devoted and expect com-

**An image of a dog howling at the moon is the symbol for the third decanate of Scorpio.** ***Reproduced by permission of Fortean Picture Library.***

plete loyalty in return. You merge with or "marry" the person you love at a very deep level and therefore separations are extremely painful for you, and often stormy and nasty. When you have been wounded, you are not inclined to turn the other cheek and will retaliate if at all possible. Certainly you will never forget the injury and often you harbor grievances and resentments for a long, long time. Forgiveness doesn't come easily to you.

Whatever you do, you do with passion and fervor, and you often go to extremes. You are either hot or cold, never lukewarm about anything. You can also be very narrow: either you are 100% involved in something or else it doesn't exist for you at all. Rarely are you emotionally detached and objective. You definitely have a fanatical streak. You are also immensely strong-willed and your tenacity in pursuing your objectives often borders on being obsessive. Fierce pride, courage, and emotional strength are yours in abundance.

You love mysteries and are deeply attracted to the hidden, dark, secret side of life. You never take things at face value and are always probing beneath the surface of people and situations to discover what is REALLY going on. You tend to be more of a cynic than an idealist. (From "Merlin," by Gina Ronco and Agnes Nightingale. Courtesy of Cosmic Patterns [http://cosmic.patterns.com].)

The Scorpion! A spooky image for a spooky sign. There's a scary side to life. People get terrible diseases. Kids get damaged. Old people are forgotten. Everybody dies. Socially we're conditioned to avoid mentioning those things, or to mention them only in ritual contexts—like jokes or political speeches. For Scorpio, the evolutionary aim is to face those shadowy places. To make the unconscious conscious. To break taboos.

The Scorpio part of you is deep and penetrating. It has little patience with phoniness or hypocrisy. Trouble is, a little phoniness or hypocrisy often make life a lot easier for everyone! Be careful of becoming so "deep" that you lose perspective. In the Scorpion part of your life, you could slip into brooding and heaviness. So laugh a little! And find a few friends you can talk to. Do that, and you'll keep you balance well enough to find wisdom.

With the Sun in Scorpio, Spirit's question to you is not "Can you be deep?" You're deep! That's how Spirit made you, and there's not much you can do to alter it. The question is, "Now that you have this depth, can you handle it?" That is, can you avoid being hypnotized by your own depths, slipping into a heavy, tragic feeling in which all the sparkle is drained from life. In avoiding that pitfall, you need to cultivate two allies: a sense of humor and two or three truly intimate friends—people with whom you can discuss anything, however dark or taboo. Make friends with those allies and you'll add the one ingredient that makes it safe to work with this penetrating zodiacal power: a sense of perspective. (From "The Sky Within," by Steven Forrest. Courtesy of Matrix Software [http://thenewage.com] and Steven Forrest [http://www.stevenforrest.com].)

Among its several natal programs, Matrix Software created a unique report based on the published works of the early twentieth century astrologer, Grant Lewi (1901–1952). Lewi's highly original delineations were recognized as creative and insightful by his contemporaries. One measure of the appeal of his work is that his books *Astrology for the Millions* and *Heaven Knows What* are still in print. The following is excerpted from the report program "Heaven Knows What":

> I wish to preach not the doctrine of ignoble case, but the doctrine of the strenuous life.... Far better it is to dare mighty things, to win glorious triumphs, even though checkered by failure, than to take rank with those poor spirits who neither enjoy much nor suffer much, because they live in the gray twilight that knows not victory or defeat. (*Theodore Roosevelt, born in Scorpio, October 27, 1858.*)
>
> The dualism of Scorpio makes it a baffling sign, for the Scorpion combines materialism with spirituality. He is "the world, the flesh and the devil" and also the spirit that renounces them. He is full of the zest of life, which, however, is meaningful only after he has added a unique, almost mystic, significance. The search for inner values, for the key to the riddle of self, of world, of life itself, is Scorpio's basic motivation, and his search, whether it takes him to spiritual heights or into the darkest of subconscious depths, is always intense. To him, "Life is real, life is earnest, and the grave is not its goal." Scorpio takes himself, his work, his ideals, his love seriously and insists that others do the same; yet at the same time he is aware of the fleetingness of it, the futility of it, the smallness of it. Not usually religious in any orthodox sense, he has his own personal religion, which is more mystic than philosophic, and which is part of the depths of his profound nature.
>
> Scorpio is the only sign that never produces a shallow person. The best of the rest dip into nonentities from time to time, but a Scorpion is always consequential. You must reckon with him even if you dislike or despise him. He can sink to the lowest level of them all if the sense of futility turns his great energies inward instead of outward; but to whatever level he may sink, he carries with him an essential dignity, as if to represent the greatness of Lucifer in fall as well as in glory. At its best, Scorpio is a mechanical, spiritual or legal genius, though rarely an executive. Luxurious and extravagant in his tastes, he lacks interest in making money because, when he calls on his maximum powers, they lead him to noncommercial fields. So great is his magnetism that he will generally be found in a position where he can get all he wants without giving his all, which is reserved for private, perhaps secret, pursuits.
>
> Scorpio is careful of appearances, generally a conformist in all that meets the eye, and would not willingly let you into the private details of his life, thoughts and philosophies. Yet these are very clear to him and provide him with an unexpressed viewpoint that gives him great poise. He looks at the world with aware, perhaps accusing, eyes; he does not

> betray the secret he has with himself, which gives him reserve and self-assurance and an uncanny knack of making the other fellow feel that he knows more than he is expressing. Part of the secret of Scorpio (no one can tell you all of the secret except the individual Scorpion himself, and he won't) is the simplicity with which he accepts the merger of the material and the spiritual. He relates all problems of life to a standard of intangibles that is unknown to other men, achieves a practical answer in terms of his secret, perhaps unconscious, doctrine of the worlds, and thus adds to his personality the sort of magic one would have who consulted with an invisible, but ever-present, guardian angel. (Courtesy of Matrix Software [http://thenewage.com].)

The following excerpt comes not from a natal report program, but from David Cochrane's recent book, *Astrology for the 21st Century*. Based on lessons for astrology students, it approaches the signs of the zodiac from a somewhat different perspective than the other short delineations cited here:

> Scorpio is often described as being charismatic, magnetic, sexy, intense, and inclined to intense activities like surgery or the occult. I see Scorpio as an instinctive energy that involves itself directly in life rather than vicariously watching life in a detached fashion. Scorpio immerses itself into the experience. When viewing a good movie we become totally engrossed and lose sense of time and in fact are aware of little else; this is the Scorpio experience. Surgery, which is associated with Scorpio, is another good example of a Scorpio experience; the surgeon is completely engrossed in the process; great concentration is required. Intense experiences such as matters of life and death on the operating table absorb our full attention and the Scorpio nature thrives in this environment. Scorpio bonds intensely, and once bonded will not easily let go. Scorpio marries for life and a divorce is almost excruciatingly painful for Scorpio.
>
> My view of Scorpio given above is similar to the traditional view of Scorpio but with a different slant and emphasis. I see complete immersion into experiences as the essence of Scorpio. Bonding is so strong that the person is, in a way, one with the experience. I remember once when teaching a class many years ago, the class was analyzing the chart of a lady who had several planets in Scorpio, including her Sun. One of the students mentioned that the lady did not seem particularly intense or charismatic, and I also did not detect these traits, although they are common, but not necessary, symptoms of the intense bonding that Scorpio seeks. I shared my views on Scorpio and the lady said that during a difficult period in her marriage her husband wanted a divorce, and she said that she would never let him leave her, and now their marriage was strong again and she felt very happy. To me this revealed that the dynamics of Scorpio were operating in the person, even though the traits that are often attributed to Scorpio were not evident. (Courtesy of Cosmic Patterns [http://cosmic.patterns.com] and David Cochrane [kepler@astrosoftware.com].)

Many specialized report programs have been developed that offer useful supplements to the generic delineations of general reports. The following sun sign interpretation has been drawn from a program by Gloria Scott (originally part of her book, *Astrology: Woman to Woman*) written by Gloria Star that generates a specialized report for women:

> With your Sun in Scorpio your ego is driven by a need to be almost enigmatic. You're more comfortable when at least a little mystery surrounds you, and you can exude a strong level of sensual charm. You're rarely halfway about anything, and your intensity can be daunting to those who are uncomfortable with confrontation. Since your Sun speaks of "who you think you are," you may think that you're more mysterious than you are in actuality! No bother—you're still a mystery to most, so you're safe!
>
> Your deep craving for power which you feel but others may not see accompanies the energy of your Sun in Scorpio. Your father may have seemed somewhat omnipotent when you were young, and he may also have been difficult to understand at times. You have a greater respect for men who can stand up to their own power, and who can respect the unique power of women, too. There is a part of you that will always be fascinated by super heroes and super heroines which stems from your fascination with alterations in energy and transformational change. Throughout your life you may be drawn into situations which need to change and in which you provide the catalyst for these transformations. In many ways you are a natural healer, and you can bring this quality of regeneration into your relationships, your work and your creativity. Embrace the fact that you are a Goddess! Live to create, and own your ability to use the magical ingredients which bring power into your own life, and which effects dynamic shifts in the world around you.
>
> Even though you can be somewhat enigmatic with the Sun in Scorpio, you are also driven to attain the realization of your desires. For anything to be successful in your life, it must be personally meaningful to you, and you must have a strong feeling about it. You simply do not care to waste your energy. But you have to know when to back off because with your intensity, you can set the world on fire. Be gentle. Just remember that after all, as long as you know how to function in a crisis, there's no problem. (From "Woman to Woman," by Gloria Star. Courtesy of Matrix Software [http://thenewage.com].)

Responding to the revival of interest in pre-twentieth-century astrology, J. Lee Lehman developed a report program embodying the interpretive approach of traditional astrology. The following is excerpted from her book *Classical Astrology for Modern Living* and her computer program "Classical Report":

> You are brazen, arrogant, impudent, indecent, ireful, lewd, covetous, cunning, quick and strong in action, and discriminating, deceitful. You can be vicious or violent if angered (anger or sexual arousal?) Your

nature is rugged and ambitious. You are fortunate in matters maritime and surgical.

It is particularly important for you to take care of your health when you are in stressful situations. This is because there is a general sluggishness to your energy which is prone to disease when you are under physical and emotional pressure.

You are a Water Sign, which means that you are "cold" and "wet." The "wet" component means, among other things, that you blur distinctions, and that you are more swayed by passion than by intellectual argument. At your worst, you see too many connections, becoming lost in conspiracies. At your best, you spot the connection that everyone else missed. You are perceived as being "cold," which in your case simply means you may not be quickly reacting on a surface level. In the modern parlance, it fits better with "cold and dry" than with simply "cold." However, a "cold" type is basically lethargic, or slow to react. Here we have an interesting apparent contradiction: your emotions run deep, but that doesn't mean you're talking about them all the time! The quiet quality of "cold" may mislead others about what you're feeling. The "problem" with "cold" is that it makes it hard for you to forget slights. Because you don't tend to lash out immediately, it's hard for you not to allow your anger to build up.

You are fixed, which means you are strong-willed and stubborn. You will want to hang onto people and things long after they have ceased to be useful to you. (Courtesy of J. Lee Lehman, Ph.D., copyright 1998 [http://www.leelehman.com].)

Readers interested in examining interpretations for their Chinese astrological sign should refer to the relevant entry. A guide for determining one's sign in the Chinese system is provided in the entry on the Chinese zodiac.

**Sources:**


Cochrane, David. *Astrology for the 21st Century*. Gainesville, FL: Cosmic Patterns, 2002.

Forrest, Steven. *The Inner Sky: How to Make Wiser Choices for a More Fulfilling Life*. 4th ed. San Diego: ACS Publications, 1989.

Green, Landis Knight. *The Astrologer's Manual: Modern Insights into an Ancient Art*. Sebastopol, CA: CRCS Publications, 1975.

Hall, Manly P. *Astrological Keywords*. New York: Philosophical Library, 1958. Reprint, Savage, MD: Littlefield Adams Quality Paperbacks, 1975.

Lehman, J. Lee. *Classical Astrology for Modern Living: From Ptolemy to Psychology & Back Again*. Atglen, PA: Whitford Press, 1996.

Lewi, Grant. *Astrology for the Millions*. 5th ed. St. Paul, MN: Llewellyn, 1978.

———. *Heaven Knows What*. St. Paul, MN: Llewellyn, 1969.

Star, Gloria. *Astrology & Your Child: A Handbook for Parents*. St. Paul, MN: Llewellyn, 2001.

———. *Astrology: Woman to Woman*. St. Paul, MN: Llewellyn, 1999.

## Second Station

When, from the perspective of Earth, a planet that has been moving retrograde (i.e., appeared to go backward in its orbit) pauses and resumes forward motion, the point at which it pauses is called the second station.

## Sedgwick, Philip

Philip Sedgwick, born November 8, 1950, 2:36 P.M. E.S.T., began his study of astrology in 1969 while serving in the U.S. Navy. Since that time astrology has become a main focus of his life. He has been consulting professionally since 1975, and established his career as a full-time astrologer in 1981.

Sedgwick wrote a weekly column for the Science Fiction Channel online entitled "Space Scopes" from May 1998 to October 2001. He has also contributed regularly to www.StarIq.com as a writer of articles and e-mail transit reports. He now works on a continuing series of articles on the centaurs for *Mountain Astrologer* and comprehensive reports for Cosmic Patterns Software.

A researcher by nature, Sedgwick investigated the astrological signatures of aviation disasters, intensively explored the effects of galactic phenomena on astrology, and is an astrological authority on Comet Halley. Currently, he is working on research relating to planetary cycles affecting commercial aviation and aerospace. He monitors and researches radiation disturbances from not only the Sun, but the newly encountered Soft Gamma Ray repeaters. His latest research passion involves the investigation of the unusual centaur and trans-Neptunian objects found invading our solar system from the depths of space.

He authored three books now in print: *The Astrology of Transcendence*, *The Astrology of Deep Space*, and *The Sun at the Center—A Primer of Heliocentric Astrology*. He was a contributing writer for *Llewellyn's Sun Sign Guide* in 1986, 1988 and 1989, and *Spiritual, Metaphysical & New Trends in Modern Astrology*. His *Galactic Ephemeris* of over 8,700 deep-space objects leads astrologers on discoveries of potent sources profoundly affecting our natal horoscopes. Sedgwick additionally produced a galactic software add-on for the popular Solar Fire program, entitled Galastro. He compiled and published ephemerides for the Centaur objects. He also complied an ephemeris for newly named Kuiper Belt Object, Varuna, the noteworthy KBO 13790 (of great interest as the possible Trans-Pluto), 15874 and 2001KX76. He maintains two taped correspondence courses: one on galactic astrology, the other on the centaurs and Kuiper belt objects.

## Seesaw Pattern

In astrology, a seesaw pattern is a horoscope arrangement in which all of the planets fall into one of two identifiable clusters that face each other across opposite ends of the chart.

## Selene

Selene, asteroid 580 (the 580th asteroid to be discovered, on December 17, 1905), is approximately 41 kilometers in diameter and has an orbital period of 5.8 years. It is named after the goddess of the Moon. She granted a boon to the handsome, vain king Endymion, who chose to sleep forever without aging. Selene was also seduced with a gift of a golden fleece from Pan. The placement of this planetoid in a natal chart shows where and how vanity opens one up to seduction, as well as where and how one is willing to seduce others.

**Sources:**

Kowal, Charles T. *Asteroids: Their Nature and Utilization*. Chichester, West Sussex, UK: Ellis Horwood Limited, 1988.

Room, Adrian. *Dictionary of Astronomical Names*. London: Routledge, 1988.

Schwartz, Jacob. *Asteroid Name Encyclopedia*. St. Paul, MN: Llewellyn Publications, 1995.

## Semioctile

A semioctile (also known as a semisemisquare) is a minor aspect of 22½° that is created by subdividing a circle into 16 equal parts. It exerts a very weak, inharmonious influence and, according to contemporary researchers, is involved in health concerns. It is rarely utilized outside cosmobiology and Uranian astrology.

## Semisextile

A semisextile (also called a dodecile) is a minor aspect of 30° created by subdividing a circle into 12 equal parts. Semisextiles exert a weak though helpful influence. Unlike sextiles, which indicate opportunities, semisextiles often refer to inherited characteristics. The orb of influence is very small, no more than 1° or 2°.

## Semisquare

A semisquare is a minor aspect of 45° created by dividing a circle into eight equal segments. A semisquare, as the name implies, is half a square, and a semisquare acts as a weak square. Though weak, it is perhaps the strongest of the minor aspects, and astrologers give it an orb of influence of 2° to 3°.

## Separating Aspect

When a transiting planet has completed making an aspect with another planet or a house cusp and is beginning to pull away, it is said to be separating. Before the aspect became exact—as the transiting planet was approaching—the aspect was applying. To illustrate, suppose Neptune is located at 25° in the sign Leo. As transiting Venus passes Neptune (e.g., moves past 25° and reaches 26°, 27°, and 28° Leo), Venus is said to be separating from a conjunction with Neptune. Prior to reaching 25° (prior to becoming exact), the aspect was applying.

A doubly separating aspect occurs when both planets are moving away from an aspect. In other words, if in the preceding example Neptune was moving retrograde (backward through the zodiac) as Venus was moving direct (forward through the zodiac) after Venus had passed 25° Leo, the aspect would be doubly separating. For the purpose of interpretation, applying aspects are regarded as being stronger than separating aspects.

**Sources:**

Gettings, Fred. *Dictionary of Astrology*. London: Routledge & Kegan Paul, 1985.
Lee, Dal. *Dictionary of Astrology*. New York: Paperback Library, 1969.

## Septile

A septile is an unusual minor aspect of 51$\frac{3}{7}$° created by dividing a circle into seven equal parts. Because of the numerological association of the number seven with Neptune, it has been regarded as having a mystical or a "beclouding" influence. Such eminent astrologers as John Addey have researched this aspect, and material on septiles can be found in astrology books dealing with harmonics.

## Sesquisquare

A sesquisquare (also called a sesquiquadrate or a sesquare) is a minor aspect of 135°. Like the semisquare, a sesquisquare's influence is like that of a weak square. Though weak, it is, like the semisquare, relatively strong for a minor aspect, and astrologers give it an orb of influence of 2° to 3°.

## Sextile

A sextile is an aspect of 60° between two points—e.g., between two planets—in an astrological chart. This aspect is traditionally regarded as beneficial, although, unlike the trine aspect, the potential contained in a sextile has to be developed. For this reason, it is sometimes referred to as the aspect of opportunity.

## Shravana

Shravana (ear or hearing) is one of the Nakshatras (lunar mansions) of Vedic astrology. Symbolized by a trident, and presided over by Vishnu, this Nakshatra is ruled by the Moon at Capricorn 10° to 23°20'. Favorable actions are usually well supported at this time, and individuals tend to lead more ethical, prosperous lives, though also sometimes be overgenerous or liberal.

—Pramela Thiagesan

## Sidereal Day

A sidereal day is the period of time it takes for Earth to complete one rotation on its axis with respect to a fixed point in space. Specifically, a sidereal day begins and ends when the local meridian for any given location on Earth passes through 0° Aries (the vernal point). Because of the motion of Earth around the Sun, sidereal days are slightly shorter than ordinary solar days. A sidereal day is 23 hours 56 minutes and 4.09 seconds in length; a sidereal hour is $\frac{1}{24}$ the length of a sidereal day.

## Sidereal Month

A sidereal month is the period of time it takes the Moon to complete an orbit of Earth with respect to a fixed point in space, specifically, with respect to a fixed star (hence the designation sidereal, from the Greek *sidus*, meaning "star"). Because of the motion of Earth around the Sun, sidereal months are shorter than months measured from one new moon to the next. A sidereal month is 27 days 7 hours 43 minutes and 11.5 seconds in length.

## Sidereal Period

A sidereal period is the time it takes a celestial body such as a planet to complete an orbit, as measured against the background of the fixed stars. Sidereal months (the time it takes the Moon to complete an orbit) and sidereal years (the time it takes Earth to complete an orbit) are examples of sidereal periods.

## Sidereal Time

Sidereal (from the Greek *sidus*, meaning "star") time, like most ordinary measurements of time, is based on the rotational and orbital motion of Earth. However, unlike other ways of measuring the passing of time, sidereal time uses a fixed point in space (usually one of the fixed stars; hence the name sidereal) as a point of reference for the beginning and ending of a day, month, or year. By way of contrast, ordinary days and years, as well as lunar months (from one new moon to the next), use the constantly changing, relative positions of the Sun, the Moon, and Earth. As a result, there are slight differences in length between sidereal days, months, and years and ordinary days, months, and years. Sidereal time, which is also employed by astronomers, is used in tables of planetary positions (ephemerides) as well as tables of houses. The first step in casting a natal chart is to convert birth time to sidereal time.

## Sidereal Year

A sidereal year is the time it takes Earth to complete an orbit of the Sun relative to the fixed stars. The length of a sidereal year is 365 days 6 hours 9 minutes and 9.54 seconds, which is slightly longer than a solar year.

## SIDEREAL ZODIAC (FIXED ZODIAC)

The zodiac is the belt constituted by the 12 signs—Aries, Taurus, Gemini, Cancer, Leo, Virgo, Libra, Scorpio, Sagittarius, Capricorn, Aquarius, and Pisces. The names of the signs correspond with a belt of 12 constellations ringing our solar system that, several thousand years ago, gave their names to the zodiac. The sidereal zodiac, also referred to as the fixed zodiac, is located where these constellations are actually positioned. Practitioners of Hindu astrology are the most notable users of the sidereal system. The other zodiac originated with Ptolemy, the great astrologer-astronomer of antiquity, who was very careful to assert that the zodiac should begin at (i.e., 0° Aries should be positioned at) the point where the Sun is located during the spring equinox. Because of the phenomenon known as the precession of equinoxes, this point very gradually moves backward every year; currently, 0° Aries is located near the beginning of the constellation Pisces. Astrologers who adhere to the Ptolemaic directive—the great majority of modern Western astrologers—use the tropical zodiac (also called the moving zodiac, for obvious reasons). The sidereal zodiac, however, has become increasingly popular in the West over the last decade or so.

The question of which zodiac to use is more involved than might be initially imagined. When the astrological novice first encounters this issue, the initial tendency is to think that the zodiac should correspond with the constellations; why, after all, should one keep shifting the zodiac just because Ptolemy said to? There is more at stake, however, than the authority of Ptolemy. For example, much seasonal symbolism is associated with the signs: Ever-youthful, pioneering Aries is the sign of spring; cold, restrictive Capricorn is the sign of winter; and so forth. In the tropical zodiac the signs are congruent with the seasons; in the sidereal zodiac these associations are lost. A siderealist, on the other hand, could make the observation that in the Southern Hemisphere, where the seasons are reversed, these associations are meaningless anyway (unless the zodiac is shifted 180° in southern latitudes—a highly problematic but nevertheless logically possible response). There is thus no decisive argument favoring one system over the other.

Some attempts to resolve this problem have been made by assigning different significances to the two zodiacs: The tropical zodiac, some have argued, provides a "map" of the personality (the outer self), whereas the sidereal zodiac provides a chart of the soul (the inner self). Other astrologers, most notably James T. Braha in his *Ancient Hindu Astrology for the Modern Western Astrologer*, have argued that Western, tropical astrology has better tools for analyzing the psyche, but Hindu astrology (the principal form of sidereal astrology) works better in the area of predicting future conditions. Neither of these attempts at reconciliation is likely to become widely accepted. Nor does it seem likely that either zodiac will supplant the other, at least not in the foreseeable future.

**Sources:**

Braha, James T. *Ancient Hindu Astrology for the Modern Western Astrologer*. Hollywood, FL: Hermetician Press, 1986.

Brau, Jean-Louis, Helen Weaver, and Allan Edmands. *Larousse Encyclopedia of Astrology*. New York: New American Library, 1980.

## Significator

In general, every planet is a significator (one who signifies) of the matters associated with the house in which it is located, or with the house it rules. Mars, for example, is a significator of marriage and partnerships if it is located in the seventh house (the house of marriage and partnerships), or if Aries, the sign Mars rules, is on the cusp (at the beginning) of the seventh house. This term is infrequently used outside horary astrology.

## Simms, Maria Kay

Maria Kay Simms, contemporary astrologer, was born in Princeton, Illinois, November 18, 1940, to Anne and Frank Simms. Following her B.F.A. in painting from Illinois Wesleyan University, she taught public school for five years, and later was a gallery painter and commercial artist. She began studying astrology in 1973 while living in San Francisco, and later studied with A. Charles Emerson in New York City, becoming a specialist in Cosmobiology and Uranian Astrology.

In 1976, in New Milford, CT, she combined art with astrology in mystic arts, a metaphysical bookshop and arts and crafts gallery, and also started a local chapter of the National Council for Geocosmic Research (NCGR), serving as president for the first three years. In 1982, after election to NCGR's national board, she served as publications director and editor of the *NCGR Journal* for nine years. Active as an astrological consultant from the mid 1970s, Simms strongly believed that her practice of astrology required credentials beyond her art degree, so she passed the American Federation of Astrologers professional certification exams in 1981, and in 1985, achieved NCGR's Level 4 in consulting. She has been an avid supporter of NCGR's Education Program from its inception.

Simms moved to Florida after divorcing in 1985, did art production for a professional dinner theatre, and freelanced as an astrological consultant and a cover artist for ACS Publications. In 1987, she moved to San Diego, became ACS's art director, and married the owner, Neil F. Michelsen. After Michelsen's passing in 1990, she continued his plan to combine ACS and Astro Computing Services under one corporation, Astro Communications Services, Inc. She served as corporate CEO for eight years, until selling ACS in 1998.

Simms authored several books on astrology and Pagan spirituality, plus text for computer reports and numerous articles. Though her initial approach to astrology was skeptical, and then her specialty technical, Simms found the correspondence of astrology with spirituality to be its highest calling, and the Neopagan path a fulfilling expression of her worldview. In 1988 she began formally studying within an eclectic Wiccan tradition of Gardnerian lineage, and after initiation through third degree, was named a high priestess and began her Circle of the Cosmic Muse in 1991. Through ordination in Community Church of Religious Science (CCRS) in 1994, and also in 1995 through affiliation with Covenant of the Goddess, she holds credentials of legal ministry.

In 1998, Simms moved to New Hampshire, remarried, and in 1999 became the first woman chair of NCGR. She is also on the advisory council for Seattle's Kepler

College of Astrological Arts and Sciences. At this writing, she is serving a second elected term as NCGR chair, and is also working on a new book and new paintings. Simms, who has three grown daughters and two granddaughters, greatly enjoys the serenity of a wooded rural property with plenty of room for family visitors. There she has created a large stone circle garden with marker boulders at the cardinal and solstice points dominated by a seven-foot monolith at Spring Equinox sunrise, as a permanent setting for her Circle gatherings.

Her books are *Twelve Wings of the Eagle* (1988); *Dial Detective* 1988; 2d ed., 2001); *Search for the Christmas Star* (1989); *Your Magical Child* (1994); *Future Signs* (1996); *The Witches Circle* (1996); and A *Time for Magick* (2001).

## SINGLETON

In a bucket (or funnel) chart, all of the planets but one are on one side of an astrological chart. The isolated planet is called the handle or singleton.

## SINISTER

Sinister, from a Latin term meaning left (not evil), refers to one of the many ways of classifying the astrological aspects. The antonym is dexter (right). A sinister aspect occurs when a faster-moving planet makes an aspect with a slower-moving one that is located counterclockwise from it (to its left) in the zodiac. Even though astrologers from Claudius Ptolemy onward have regarded sinister and dexter aspects as having somewhat different influences, the differences are comparatively minor. In most general chart readings, this distinction is ignored.

## SISYPHUS

Sisyphus, asteroid 1,866 (the 1,866th asteroid to be discovered, on December 5, 1972), is approximately 7.6 kilometers in diameter and has an orbital period of 2.6 years. Sisyphus was a mythological figure whose punishment in the underworld was to roll a stone up a hill, only to have it roll back to the bottom, and then have to push it up the hill, over and over again for eternity. According to Martha Lang-Wescott, Sisyphus represents "determination; dogged persistence; to start over (again or anew); to repeat effort." Jacob Schwartz gives this asteroid's astrological significance as "determined action on hopeless or repetitive tasks, 'returning to square one.'" This asteroid's key phrase is "start over."

**Sources:**

Lang-Wescott, Martha. *Asteroids-Mechanics: Ephemerides II*. Conway, MA: Treehouse Mountain, 1990.

———. *Mechanics of the Future: Asteroids*. Rev. ed. Conway, MA: Treehouse Mountain, 1991.

Schwartz, Jacob. *Asteroid Name Encyclopedia*. St. Paul, MN: Llewellyn Publications, 1995.

## SIVA

Siva, asteroid 140 (the 140th asteroid to be discovered, on September 29, 1930), is approximately 104 kilometers in diameter and has an orbital period of 4.5 years. Siva was named after one of the principal Hindu divinities, a complex deity who was, among other things, a god of destruction. According to Martha Lang-Wescott, Siva represents "entrenched beliefs and expectations that are 'wiped out' to enable a liberation ...; interest in India or oriental culture, objects and influences." Jacob Schwartz adds to this, "understanding through catharsis." This asteroid's key words are "insight" and "episodic."

**Sources:**

Lang-Wescott, Martha. *Asteroids-Mechanics: Ephemerides II*. Conway, MA: Treehouse Mountain, 1990.

———. *Mechanics of the Future: Asteroids*. Rev. ed. Conway, MA: Treehouse Mountain, 1991.

Schwartz, Jacob. *Asteroid Name Encyclopedia*. St. Paul, MN: Llewellyn Publications, 1995.

## SNAKE

The Snake is one of the 12 animals of the Chinese zodiac. It refers to one of the 12 earthly branches that are used in Chinese astrology, together with the 10 heavenly stems. Such a branch designates one day every 12 days: the days are named according to a sexagesimal (60) cycle, made of 10 series of 12 branches.

Attractive, smart, hateful of vulgarity, and sometimes narcissistic, the Snake has a disconcerting manner. Reserved and passive, he is a solitary person, but he fascinates. Elusive, he prefers to go around obstacles. Remarkably able to keep his composure, he is materialistic, very perceptive (sometimes visionary), and he makes an excellent organizer. He is also a generous, emotional, even fragile person who can prove to be very devoted, in spite of his apparent reserve. He often seems lazy until he finds his real goal in life.

—Michele Delemme

## SOFT ASPECTS

Soft aspects refer to aspects that present a native with opportunities—namely, trines, sextiles, and the like. Soft aspects is the preferred, contemporary term for what were traditionally termed benefic aspects (the word benefic has dropped out of general usage because soft aspects are not always "good" ones).

## SOL

Sol is the Latin word for Sun and the root of such words as solar and solstice.

## SOLAR CHART (SOLAR ASTROLOGY)

Solar astrology is a system often used when an exact birth time cannot be determined. Rather than begin the natal chart's house cusps at the ascendant (which cannot be

**The Sun driving his chariot with a wheel bearing the image of the zodiacal Leo over which he has rule. *Reproduced by permission of Fortean Picture Library.***

calculated when the birth time is unavailable), a solar chart uses the location of the Sun on the day of birth as the position to begin the first house and then calculates succeeding houses in equal arcs of 30°. For example, if someone was born during a day when the Sun was at, say, 12° in the sign Capricorn, the first solar house would begin at 12° Capricorn, the second at 12° Aquarius, the third at 12° Pisces, and so forth through the remaining signs of the zodiac. This solar chart is interpreted exactly the same way as a standard natal chart.

## Solar Return Chart

A solar return chart provides a wealth of information: It describes the overall themes of the year and the potential, options, problems, and issues associated with those themes. Solar return charts are easy to interpret and give valuable clues regarding major cycles of growth and transformation.

A solar return chart is a chart set for the exact time of the Sun's annual return to its natal position. At the moment one's birth, the Sun has a specific zodiacal position defined in degrees, minutes, and seconds of arc. Each year the Sun returns to this position, and the time of the return can be calculated and known. This time is then used to calculate the solar return chart itself. Calculations are difficult, and, for this reason, computer programs are recommended.

The time of the Sun's return is hardly ever the birth time and sometimes does not even occur on the birthday. The Sun may return a day or two before the birthday, the day of, or the day after. The yearly transit of the Sun through the zodiac is different from the 365 daily rotations (days) experienced on Earth during a year. There is approximately a six-hour difference between the two. In other words, a true solar year (Sun's yearly transiting time) is about 365.25 days long. This is the reason a leap day—February 29—occurs every four years. The extra day corrects for this discrepancy. Because of the difference between the true solar year (Sun's transit) and the number of days in a year, the time of the Sun's return advances approximately six hours each year, while dropping back a day every four years.

Although solar return charts are revealing and easy to interpret, they are not always understood and used. The solar return's lack of astrological prominence is linked to misunderstandings and controversies surrounding calculation and interpretation. These controversies consist of four issues:

> *Tropical versus Sidereal:* What is the difference between a tropical solar return chart and a sidereal one? How would one interpret each kind?
>
> *Precession:* What is precession and should one precess a tropical solar return chart?
>
> *Location:* Which location does one use for calculating the chart? Place of birth? Residence? Present location? And what happens if one is traveling?
>
> *Single chart or double chart interpretation techniques:* Does one interpret the solar return chart in reference to the natal chart or can it stand on its own? In using a two-chart technique, which chart goes in the center and which goes on the outside ring?

Once these questions concerning solar returns have been addressed, the reader should have a clearer understanding of the choices available when calculating and interpreting solar returns charts, and the meaning of each option. Clarity breeds insight, and eventually solar returns will assume their rightful place as a valued astrological tool.

### Tropical or Sidereal

When calculating solar returns, everything becomes clearer if one remembers not to mix tropical and sidereal. Astrology has been divided between these two systems for a long time. The points of reference for these two systems are different. Solar returns are subject to confusion since one has the option of calculating either a tropical or a sidereal solar return chart. Regardless of method of calculation chosen, each solar return chart needs to be handled and interpreted in a manner consistent with the originating system and its customary interpretation techniques.

Tropical astrology is based on the relationship between the Sun and the Earth, and the Sun's apparent path projected on the Earth's surface (ecliptic). Twice a year, the Sun's declination becomes zero as it crosses the equator. The northward crossing is called the vernal or spring equinox, and is defined as the beginning of the zodiac or 0° Aries. The southward passage marks the autumnal or fall equinox and defines 0° Libra. The maximum northern declination of the Sun is the summer solstice and 0° Cancer, while the maximum southern declination of the Sun is the winter solstice and 0° Capricorn. Tropical systems are earth-oriented and consistent with the change of seasons. They have little to do with stellar placements and alignments, or with the precession of the Equinox (primarily a sidereal concern).

Sidereal astrology is star-based. Thus, 0° Aries is always associated with the beginning of the Aries constellation formed by stars. Whenever the Sun is in this part of the stellar sky, in this constellation, it is in Aries, regardless of where the Sun falls in relationship to the equator or what time of year or season it is on Earth. Because of the wobbling of the Earth on its axis and the resulting precession of the Equinox (which is 26,000 years long), sidereal timing shifts every year and the gulf between tropical 0° Aries and sidereal 0° Aries grows. Currently, the timing of the tropical Aries point differs from the timing of the sidereal Aries point by about a month.

Because these two systems have different points of reference, it seems logical to assume that tropical solar returns should be handled differently from sidereal ones. The solar return chart is similar to a temporary natal chart and can be treated as such. Therefore, tropical solar returns could be interpreted like any other tropical chart, and all tropical techniques—such as Sabian symbols, fixed stars, asteroids, house placements. and aspects—should apply. On the other hand, sidereal solar returns could be interpreted like any other sidereal chart, and all sidereal techniques would apply to them. The universe is consistent and it makes sense that what works for one chart in a system will probably work for other charts within the same system, calculated in the same manner and intended for a similar purpose.

Unfortunately in the history of solar returns, this is not what has happened. Until recently, there has been little information available on solar return charts, and the few books that have been published were written almost exclusively by siderealists. However, the majority of astrologers in the western world are tropical astrologers. It was easy to make the mistake of applying sidereal techniques to tropical charts. These techniques would work up to a certain point. The emphasis placed on foreground and background planets (proposed in these books) is not totally foreign to tropical astrology, but its use is primarily emphasized in horary astrology, or in regards to planetary strength based on whether a planet was angular, succeedent, or cadent. For the most part, popular tropical astrology has traditionally dealt with the whole chart, including all the planets, houses, signs, and aspects. Therefore, at first glance, it seems logical to look at the whole chart when interpreting a tropical solar return. Within this approach, the background twelfth house planets would be every bit as important as the foreground first house planets. Equal weight and interpretation would be given to each of the planets in each of these houses.

The same is true of sidereal solar returns. They should be interpreted with sidereal techniques which may include, but are not limited to, foreground-background interpretations and demi-solar returns. One should keep in mind that these sidereal techniques may not work well with tropical solar return charts, and tropical techniques may not suit sidereal solar returns.

## Planets in Signs

An important distinction exists regarding the interpretation of tropical solar return charts. One cannot treat them exclusively like a temporal natal chart since the house position of a solar return planet is more important than the sign. This simplifies solar return interpretation, making these charts easier to interpret than natal charts. There are logical reasons why signs are not particularly important. They are:

1. The Sun is always the same and never changes sign or position.
2. Mercury can only be plus or minus one sign from the Sun and therefore has limited movement.
3. Venus routinely has eight different solar return placements. After eight years, the placements begin to repeat themselves as a new cycle begins. A person can tell a lot about his or her love life by ascertaining what these positions are.
4. Jupiter changes sign each year and consistently goes from one sign to the next.
5. Saturn, Uranus, Neptune, and Pluto will probably stay in the same sign for everyone during the year and it is unlikely that the sign will greatly influence the interpretation.
6. The Moon also has a limited number of placements since it is involved in a 19-year eclipse cycle with the Sun. Once the cycle is completed, the 19 positions are repeated.

Mars is the only planet that is erratic and changes signs regularly and freely; therefore this might be the only planet for which sign is important. So when interpreting a solar return chart, it is more important to emphasize the house position than to focus on a planet's sign.

## Precession

From the previous discussion of tropical and sidereal astrology, it is evident that precession is a sidereal concept that has little to do with the tropical system. Some astrologers feel that a solar return chart should be precessed, or advanced, to make allowances for the gradual shift in the precession of the Equinox. This may be true for sidereal solar return charts, but there is no theoretical basis for precessing a tropical solar return. Precession, by its very nature, indicates stellar influences. There are no stellar, sidereal, or precessional influences innately important to the tropical system.

In all things astrological, one must look at the theoretical basis for what is being done and stay within that theoretical system. If the theory does not hold true, then the chart will not either.

## Location for the Solar Return Chart

There has been a great deal of debate over the location one should use for a solar return chart. Some astrologers believe that the solar return should be calculated using the natal location. Others believe that the solar return should be calculated for the residence or for where one will live most of time during the year. Still others believe that the location at the moment of the Sun's return is the one of greatest importance. It seems that all of these charts work, but there is a difference in how they are understood.

The solar return for the natal residence is a solar return with which one is born. Like a secondary progression for the natal location, these charts cannot be changed, and they are set in motion at the moment of birth. This natal location solar return chart is valid and has good information to offer, but it seems to be more internalized, like a secondary progression. When it is impossible to know where an individual was for the Sun's return, use this chart and it will provide some insight into the year.

The resident solar return chart is set up for where one lives. This chart appears more accurate than the natal solar return chart since it reflects some of the changes that have been initiated since one was born. However, it does not reflect any freewill decisions made to handle issues in a manner different from the one shown in the natal or residential solar return chart. One can change the orientation completely by relocating for the Sun's return. These decisions and adjustments only appear in the solar return calculated for one's exact location at the time of the Sun's return.

Many believe the solar return chart set for one's location at the exact time of the Sun's return is the most accurate. The other charts are valid, but this one seems to be the best. The aspects are the same no matter where one goes. Configurations (T squares, grand trines, and grand crosses) remain. The degrees and minutes of the planets' positions will not change because of travel. This is because the Greenwich Mean Time of the Sun's return stays the same no matter where one goes, but the ascendent, midheaven, and the orientation of the planets in the solar return wheel will slowly rotate as one moves east or west. By relocating or traveling for the solar return, adjustments are made in the focus of attention and the house placements for the planets.

For example, say one has a difficult T square in one's residential solar return that falls in the cadent houses. One might be concerned about health if the opposition falls from the twelfth to the sixth house. Perhaps there is already a plan to move across the country during the year. In anticipation of a major career and domestic changes, one might as well place this opposition in the tenth and fourth houses and deal with problems this way. The orientation of the T square is adjusted by traveling to another part of the country for the Sun's return.

To make adjustments, pick the location carefully, making sure the destination has the qualities needed. Through solar return relocation, an individual can make a conscious choice to grow and face issues in a certain way or through a certain venue. Since energy follows thought, this commitment to a new orientation will carry through. One cannot avoid issues by changing the location; a person can only choose how those issues will be handled.

There are certain things traveling for a solar return cannot do. One cannot negate influences seen in transits, progressions, and solar arcs. Problems or challenges seen in all of these charts will need to be faced and handled even if one seeks to negate them from the solar return chart through relocation. Solar return relocation is only a channeling process. An individual can channel or direct his or her attention to handle matters in a certain way by making a conscious choice. One decides how he or she would like to experience the changes in consciousness that need to occur and in which area of the life is most desirable for the experience. One cannot simply decide to completely hide or avoid. Keep in mind that although human beings have free will, they have only so much latitude. Some events or experiences are necessary for soul growth.

Many astrologers have strong opinions about which location is the most important one to use for solar returns. All of them are valid; individuals may use whichever one they please to calculate their solar returns.

### Single and Double Chart Techniques

Astrologers have tried reading solar returns as a single chart and have also tried to read them in relationship to the natal. Many believe that the solar return chart can only be read in reference to the natal and cannot stand alone. In fact, in the study guidelines for the National Council for Geocosmic Research (NCGR) examination for professional astrologers, this is stated clearly: "Solar returns are meaningless unless compared to the natal chart."

Solar return charts can stand alone and be read as single charts. Ninety percent of the necessary information can come from the solar return chart itself. The information gleaned from the relationship between the solar return chart and the natal is generally a reiteration of what is already seen in the solar return chart itself. Although the added information provides further insight, it is generally unnecessary.

If one intends to look at the solar return chart in relationship to the natal chart, one should use a two-chart technique and place the solar return on the inside wheel. This preserves the integrity of the solar return houses and the placement and orientation of the planets. When the solar return chart is placed outside of the natal chart, it becomes very difficult to obtain a gestalt of what the year will be like, and the interpretation will suffer. One cannot treat a solar return like a secondary progressed chart. It is a birth chart for the new cycle of growth and should be respected in its entire presentation.

—Mary Fortier Shea

**Sources:**

Shea, Mary Fortier. *Planets in Solar Returns: Yearly Cycles of Transformation and Growth*. Rev. ed. Glenelg, MD: Twin Stars Unlimited, 1999.

## Solar System

The solar system is formed by the Sun and all of the various heavenly bodies held within its gravitational field, namely, the planets, their moons, and the asteroids. The orbits of the planets and the asteroids all lie within roughly the same geometric plane, and all move in the same direction around the Sun (all clockwise or all counterclockwise, depending on the position from which they are viewed from outside the system). If the various elements of the solar system were not all within the same plane, it would be difficult to represent astrological influences on a two-dimensional chart. With the exception of some of the fixed stars, all of the influences taken into account by contemporary astrology are confined to our solar system.

**Sources:**

Robinson, J. Hedley, and James Muirden. *Astronomy Data Book*. 2d ed. New York: John Wiley & Sons, 1979.

Smoluchowski, Roman. *The Solar System: The Sun, Planets, and Life*. New York: Scientific American Books, 1983.

## SOLSTICE

The solstices (from the Latin *sol*, meaning "sun," plus *sistere*, meaning "to stand still") are the longest and the shortest days of the year. In the Northern Hemisphere, from the summer solstice to the winter solstice the sunrise occurs a little farther north each day. On the day of the winter solstice, the Sun pauses ("stands still") in its gradual northward movement and begins to move south. This continues until the next summer solstice, when the Sun once again pauses and reverses direction. In the tropical zodiac, the solstices correspond with the moment the Sun enters 0° Cancer (summer solstice) and 0° Capricorn (winter solstice).

## SOPHIA

Sophia, asteroid 251 (the 251st asteroid to be discovered, on October 4, 1885), is approximately 35 kilometers in diameter and has an orbital period of 5.4 years. The name Sophia means wisdom or cleverness in Greek. If other elements of a natal chart concur, Sophia shows wisdom or cleverness with respect to the matters indicated by its sign and house position. When afflicted, it may indicate false wisdom or sly cleverness.

**Sources:**

Kowal, Charles T. *Asteroids: Their Nature and Utilization*. Chichester, West Sussex, UK: Ellis Horwood Limited, 1988.

Room, Adrian. *Dictionary of Astronomical Names*. London: Routledge, 1988.

Schwartz, Jacob. *Asteroid Name Encyclopedia*. St. Paul, MN: Llewellyn Publications, 1995.

## SOPHROSYNE

Sophrosyne, asteroid 134 (the 134th asteroid to be discovered, on September 27, 1873), is approximately 116 kilometers in diameter and has an orbital period of 4.1 years. The name Sophrosyne is Greek for prudence, one of the four virtues in Plato's philosophy. When prominent in a natal chart, Sophrosyne indicates a person with a prudent approach to life. Its location by sign and house position indicates how and where one expresses prudence. When involved in many inharmonious aspects, Sophrosyne may show a person who is imprudent or someone who is inappropriately prudent.

**Sources:**

Kowal, Charles T. *Asteroids: Their Nature and Utilization*. Chichester, West Sussex, UK: Ellis Horwood Limited, 1988.

Room, Adrian. *Dictionary of Astronomical Names*. London: Routledge, 1988.

Schwartz, Jacob. *Asteroid Name Encyclopedia*. St. Paul, MN: Llewellyn Publications, 1995.

## Southern Hemisphere

The Southern Hemisphere is the half of Earth located below the equator. Because most tables of houses are developed for the Northern Hemisphere, casting horoscopes for the Southern Hemisphere involves an extra set of calculations. To construct a southern chart with a northern table, an extra 12 hours must be added to the sidereal time for which it is being cast (for the moment of birth in the case of a natal chart), calculate the house cusps, and then the signs on the cusps exchanged for their opposite signs (i.e., for the sign 180° away). Computer chart-casting programs do these extra calculations automatically.

The reversal of seasons that occurs in the Southern Hemisphere has raised certain questions about how the standard tropical zodiac should be applied below the equator. In particular, there is much seasonal symbolism associated with the signs: Ever-youthful, pioneering Aries is the sign of spring; cold, restrictive Capricorn is the sign of winter; and so forth. In southern latitudes, these associations become meaningless. Some astrologers have proposed shifting the zodiac 180° in the Southern Hemisphere. Thus, someone born on November 2 in Buenos Aires, for example, would be a Taurus rather than a Scorpio; someone born on September 2 in Capetown, South Africa, would be a Pisces rather than a Virgo; and so forth. Despite the apparent logic of this argument, few southern astrologers have found a 180° shift in the zodiac useful in the practice of their craft. It thus does not appear that this proposal will be adopted in the foreseeable future.

**Sources:**

Brau, Jean-Louis, Helen Weaver, and Allan Edmands. *Larousse Encyclopedia of Astrology*. New York: New American Library, 1980.

DeVore, Nicholas. *Encyclopedia of Astrology*. New York: Philosophical Library, 1947.

## Southern Signs

The southern signs are the zodiacal signs from Libra to Pisces.

## Spartacus

Spartacus, asteroid 2,579 (the 2,579th asteroid to be discovered, on August 14, 1977), is approximately 8 kilometers in diameter and has an orbital period of 3.3 years. It is named after the leader of a slave revolt in ancient Rome and represents the breaking of bonds and revolt against oppressive authority. The sign and house position of Spartacus in a natal chart indicates how this tendency manifests. If prominent in a chart (e.g., conjunct the Sun or the ascendant), it can show a person for whom this tendency is a major life theme.

**Sources:**
Kowal, Charles T. *Asteroids: Their Nature and Utilization*. Chichester, West Sussex, UK: Ellis Horwood Limited, 1988.
Room, Adrian. *Dictionary of Astronomical Names*. London: Routledge, 1988.
Schwartz, Jacob. *Asteroid Name Encyclopedia*. St. Paul, MN: Llewellyn Publications, 1995.

## Speculum

A speculum is a table constructed in tandem with an astrological chart that records such information as the planets' declination, right ascension, latitude, etc.

## Splash Pattern

A splash pattern is a horoscope arrangement in which the planets do not appear to organize themselves into any identifiable pattern, but rather seem to have just been "splashed" across the chart.

## Splay Pattern

A splay pattern is a horoscope arrangement in which all or most of the planets group themselves into a number of different identifiable clusters.

## Square

A square is an aspect of 90° between two points—such as two planets—in an astrological chart. A square is a major aspect, regarded as challenging and inharmonious. It is the most difficult of all the hard aspects, though much depends on the nature of the planets involved. A square involving planets like Jupiter and Venus, for instance, will usually bring fewer hardships into a native's life than squares involving planets like Saturn and Pluto. In a natal chart, the planets represent, among other things, various aspects of an individual's psyche. For example, Mars represents the forceful, outgoing, aggressive aspect of self, whereas Saturn represents the security-seeking, self-disciplined aspect of self. Although everyone experiences some tension between these two principles, an individual with a Mars-Saturn square in her or his chart experiences this conflict in an exaggerated manner, often over-repressing outgoing, aggressive urges and at other times exploding with impulsive actions or words.

Many modern astrologers, in an effort to overcome the sometimes frightening delineations of traditional astrology, have tended to go to the opposite extreme. In the case at hand, the square is sometimes presented to clients as a source of "creative tension" or given some other such interpretation. Accurate though such delineations may be, clients ultimately are not served well by calling attention to the silver lining while ignoring the cloud. Squares—and almost everybody has a few—are the most challenging, destabilizing aspects in a natal chart. They demand attention and inner work if they are ever to manifest positively.

**Sources:**

Hand, Robert. *Horoscope Symbols*. Rockport, MA: Para Research, 1981.

Sakoian, Frances, and Louis S. Acker. *The Astrologer's Handbook*. New York: Harper & Row, 1989.

## Standard Time

Before the advent of rapid travel and modern means of long-distance communication, particular localities kept time according to the noontime position of the Sun. Because this varied east or west of any given location, the local time also varied as one traveled east or west. The imposition of today's standard time zones, in which one must set her or his watch forward or backward as an imaginary line is crossed, is a comparatively recent innovation. To properly cast a horoscope, astrologers must find the "true" local time at which a native was born. In other words, a birth time expressed in standard time must be converted back into local "Sun time." The more common designation for Sun time is local mean time.

## Star

A star is a self-luminous celestial body. Although not usually thought of in these terms, the Sun is also a star. Self-luminosity distinguishes stars from planets, which shine by virtue of reflected light. The ancients did not make this distinction but instead referred to the planets as wandering (the etymological meaning of the word planet) stars, and to the stars proper as fixed stars.

## Star of Bethlehem

One of the few biblical accounts in which the practice of astrology can be unambiguously perceived is the story of the three wise men. The Magi were clearly astrologers, and the Star of Bethlehem, as scholars have long pointed out, was actually a major planetary conjunction involving Jupiter and Saturn. The ancients referred to these two celestial bodies as chronocrators—literally, the "rulers of time." Before the discovery of Uranus, Jupiter and Saturn were the slowest-moving of the known planets. As a consequence, their interacting cycles—particularly their conjunctions every 20 years—were taken to mark off longer epochs of time. Around the time of Jesus' birth, this 20-year conjunction occurred in the sign Pisces, which was the sign of the "age" Earth was believed to be entering (by reason of the phenomenon known as the precession of equinoxes). The Magi believed, as do many people today, that Earth was on the verge of entering a "new age," and this particular conjunction was taken to indicate the birth of a new world teacher for the age of Pisces.

**Sources:**

Jacobs, Don. *Astrology's Pew in the Church*. San Francisco: The Joshua Foundation, 1979.

Simms, Maria Kay. *Twelve Wings of the Eagle: Our Spiritual Evolution Through the Ages of the Zodiac*. San Diego: Astro Computing Services, 1988.

## Star Pattern

A star pattern is a horoscope arrangement in which the planets are organized into four, five, or six clusters that form symmetrical angles with one another.

## sTARBABY

The "sTARBABY" incident was a scandal in which the Committee for the Scientific Investigation of Claims of the Paranormal (CSICOP) inserted nonrandom, biased astrological data into a statistical test of astrological influence. The effect of the extra data was to transform test results that verified a particular astrological relationship into test results that appeared to negate the relationship. The unusual name sTARBABY, which was the title of the principal article exposing the fraud, alludes to the Uncle Remus children's tale in which Br'er Rabbit tries to force the Tarbaby to release him—only to become more deeply entrapped.

In the mid-1970s, Paul Kurtz, a professor of philosophy at the State University of New York at Buffalo, collected 186 scientists' signatures in support of an antiastrology statement. This document, "Objections to Astrology," was published in the September-October 1975 issue of the *Humanist* magazine, of which Kurtz was the editor. The tone of the statement was harsh: It portrayed astrology as irrational superstition and called astrologers charlatans. "Objections to Astrology" was also released to the press, and it received widespread publicity. This unexpected publicity encouraged Kurtz and others to found CSICOP, an organization dedicated to debunking "pseudoscience."

"Objections to Astrology" was published in the same issue in which Lawrence E. Jerome's "Astrology: Magic or Science?" appeared. This article attacked, among others, the highly respected French scientists Michel and Françoise Gauquelin. The Gauquelins had undertaken sophisticated statistical tests of astrological claims. These tests largely failed to support traditional astrology, but they also uncovered a few statistically significant correlations. These correlations formed the basis for further studies, and eventually the Gauquelins concluded that they had discovered certain astrological relationships. Michel Gauquelin refuted Jerome's article and intimated possible legal action against the *Humanist* for misrepresenting his views. The Gauquelins's response in combination with the publicity generated by "Objections to Astrology" prompted CSICOP to undertake an empirical refutation of astrology—a refutation that focused on the work of the Gauquelins.

Of the various correlations uncovered by the Gauquelins, the strongest was the so-called Mars effect, the correlation between athletic achievement and the position of Mars—a planet traditionally associated with physical energy—in certain influential sectors of the sky (e.g., close to the eastern horizon and near the zenith) at the time of birth. Confident that any genuine test of astrological influence would disconfirm such correlations, the *Humanist* issued a challenge to the Gauquelins to subject their original findings on the Mars effect to an empirical test. The original research had compared the birth data of athletes against statistical probabilities; the *Humanist* challenged the Gauquelins to test their findings against the actual birth data of nonathletes. Contrary to the expectations of skeptical critics, the Zelen Test (after Marvin Zelen, who carried out the test) confirmed the Gauquelins's original findings. Reluctant to admit defeat, Zelen, Kurtz, and their colleagues quickly changed direction and began questioning the validity of the Gauquelins's original sample of athletes. This disagreement eventually led the Gauquelins to agree to a new test of the Mars effect, which was to be conducted by CSICOP with a sample of American athletes.

Dennis Rawlins, one of the founders of CSICOP and a planetary motion specialist, oversaw the calculations. Anxious to have a "sneak peak" at the preliminary findings of the new test, Kurtz called Rawlins, only to be told that the early results seemed to confirm the Mars effect. According to Rawlins, in an article in the October 1981 issue of *Fate*, a popular magazine on the paranormal, Kurtz responded to the news with a groan and spoke "in a pained voice, as someone cursed with a demon that would not go away." Kurtz then supplied Rawlins with additional samples of athletes. The last sample supplied to Rawlins contained athletes with an extremely low Mars effect—so low as to effectively cancel the Mars effect of the original sample. Rawlins became convinced that the last group of athletes was not a random sample (i.e., that the sample had been intentionally designed to negate the Mars effect).

Rawlins initially attempted to correct what he saw as a cover-up by appealing to other people within CSICOP. That group's leadership responded by ejecting him from the organization. Meanwhile, Kurtz published the results of the "test," claiming that the Mars effect had been decisively disproved. Rawlins, however, soon published his "sTARBABY" exposé in *Fate*. Rawlins's accusations were reinforced by Patrick Curry's article "Research on the Mars Effect," which appeared in the *Zetetic Scholar* soon after the publication of "sTARBABY." The ensuing uproar eventually forced Kurtz and the other CSICOP personnel involved with the test to issue a partial confession. This "reappraisal" acknowledged many weaknesses in the test without admitting either that the data had been manipulated or that the Mars effect might possibly be the result of astrological influences.

To most astrologers, the "sTARBABY" incident has come to epitomize the attitude of would-be debunkers. While many skeptics are far more reasonable than CSICOP, the individuals behind the "sTARBABY" cover-up were clearly more interested in defending a rather narrow interpretation of scientific orthodoxy than in empirical truth. Its image tarnished by the incident, CSICOP has since avoided active experimentation.

**Sources:**

Abell, George O., Paul Kurtz, and Marvin Zelen. "The Abell-Kurtz-Zelen 'Mars Effect' Experiments: A Reappraisal." *The Skeptical Inquirer* 7, no. 3 (Spring 1983): 77–82.

Bok, Bart J., Lawrence E. Jerome, and Paul Kurtz. "Objections to Astrology: A Statement by 186 Leading Scientists." *The Humanist* 35, no. 5 (September/October 1975): 4–6.

Curry, Patrick. "Research on the Mars Effect." *Zetetic Scholar* 9 (March 1982): 34–53.

Forrest, Steven. "Exploring the Fear of Astrology Among the Educated." Paper delivered at the Cycles and Symbols conference, San Francisco, California, July 26–29, 1990.

Jerome, Lawrence E. "Astrology: Magic or Science?" *The Humanist* 35, no. 5 (September/October 1975): 10–16.

Melton, J. Gordon, Jerome Clark, and Aidan A. Kelly. *New Age Encyclopedia*. Detroit: Gale Research, 1990.

Pinch, T. J., and H. M. Collins. "Private Science and Public Knowledge: The Committee for the Scientific Investigation of the Claims of the Paranormal and Its Use of the Literature." *Social Studies of Science* 14 (1984): 521–46.

Rawlins, Dennis. "sTARBABY." *Fate* 34, no. 10 (October 1981): 67–98.

## Stationary

Because of the planets' differing speeds and orbits, they all appear at times to reverse their usual direction and go retrograde. On the day a planet reverses direction, as well as on the day it resumes its direct motion, it is said to be stationary because, against the background of the fixed stars, it appears to have paused in space. A planet that has paused before going retrograde is said to be stationary retrograde, while a planet pausing before going direct is said to be stationary direct. When a planet becomes stationary, it is said to take its station. The stationary period for each planet is regarded as being inversely proportional to the speed of its motion. Thus, for example, the period of Mercury's station would be one day; Venus's, two days; Mars's, three days, and so forth (i.e., the slower a planet moves, the longer it tends to remain stationary).

In an astrological chart, stationary planets are usually indicated by a small "S" that appears at the lower right of the planet symbol. (Many astrologers use "SR" and "SD" to distinguish stationary retrograde from stationary direct.) Someone born when a planet was stationary will have that planet's particular characteristics deeply engraved in her or his nature. For example, someone born when Mercury was stationary will mature into a highly mental person. With respect to transiting, the days that a planet is stationary are considered to be fortunate for the matters associated with the particular planet, although the interpretation varies according to whether the planet is going direct or retrograde. Thus, for example, the day Mercury is stationary direct would be good for embarking on a journey, while the day it is stationary retrograde would be good for beginning a meditative retreat. Some contemporary astrologers regard the points in a chart where planets take their stations as highly sensitive areas that should be watched when other planets transit them.

**Sources:**

Bach, Eleanor. *Astrology from A to Z: An Illustrated Source Book*. New York: Philosophical Library, 1990.

Brau, Jean-Louis, Helen Weaver, and Allan Edmands. *Larousse Encyclopedia of Astrology*. New York: New American Library, 1980.

## Stellium (Satellitium)

A stellium (also called a satellitium) is a multiple conjunction involving three or more planets in one house and/or one sign in an astrological chart. As might be anticipated, this configuration indicates an emphasis on the matters associated with the house and/or sign in which the stellium occurs.

## Strong Signs

In traditional astrology, Scorpio and Aquarius were referred to as the strong signs, presumably because of their fixed natures.

## Sublunar

The ancient geocentric concept of the universe arranged the Sun, Moon, and planets in concentric, moving, crystalline spheres around a stable Earth at the center of the solar system. Because the Moon is closest to Earth, it is the last celestial body. Everything that is sublunar (below the Moon) belongs to this terrestrial, earthly realm. In classical astrology, astrological forces were viewed as having an influence in the sublunar realm, but not in the celestial realm.

## Succedent House

The houses of an astrological chart are classified into three groups of four: angular houses (the first, fourth, seventh, and tenth), succedent houses (the second, fifth, eighth, and eleventh), and cadent houses (the third, sixth, ninth, and twelfth). Traditionally, the succedent houses have been referred to as the resource houses, although this ascription applies best to the second house and the eighth house (the houses of personal resources that are obtained through inheritance and partnership). In classical astrology, planets positioned in succedent houses are said to exercise a stabilizing effect.

**Sources:**

Brau, Jean-Louis, Helen Weaver, and Allan Edmands. *Larousse Encyclopedia of Astrology*. New York: New American Library, 1980.

Hand, Robert. *Horoscope Symbols*. Rockport, MA: Para Research, 1981.

## Sun

The Sun is the star around which Earth and the rest of the planets in the solar system orbit. The earth orbits the sun at an average distance of 93 million miles and takes 365.26 days to complete a revolution—known as a sidereal year. The plane upon which the Earth travels around the Sun is called the ecliptic. From the perspective of the Earth, it appears as if the Sun is revolving around the Earth against a particular band of background stars. This band of 12 constellations is known as the Zodiac. The moon and all the planets orbit within the confines of this 18-degree-wide band, with the Sun apparently traveling on the ecliptic, its center. Therefore the latitude of the Sun is always zero. Although the Sun never appears to retrograde in the sky as the other planets do, it does appear to slow down in speed as the Earth distances itself from it in its annual orbit. This occurs during the northern hemisphere's summer months when the Sun's apparent speed falls under its mean 59 minutes and 8 seconds per day. Astrologically, it rules the sign of Leo where it is most comfortable and is exalted in the sign of Aries where the Babylonians considered it to be held in special esteem.

**A seventeenth-century engraving of the Sun. *Reproduced by permission of Fortean Picture Library.***

The Mesopotamian civilizations were some of the earliest to systematically observe the movements of the Sun and planets in the sky. Because of the difficulty in locating the sun against the map of the stars during the day, the Babylonians had two methods by which they inferred its position in the zodiac. In the first method they noted the phase of the Moon and its zodiacal position and from that inferred where the Sun was located in the sky. Therefore, if the Moon were in its waxing quarter phase and located in the sign of Virgo, one could deduce that the Sun was somewhere in the sign of Gemini. In the other method, the Babylonians located the Sun by observing the constellations rising and setting just before and after the Sun, when its light was dim enough to be able to observe the star map. This second method was also popular amongst the Egyptians who used a solar calendar and had mapped the sky into constellations. In contrast, the lunar Babylonian calendar allowed them to discover that 19 solar years were roughly equal in length to 235 lunar months. This is known as the Metonic cycle, whose 19-year solar period is important in the timing of events in Hellenistic astrology.

In Sumerian the Sun was known as Utu and in Akkadian as Shamash, the names of the two solar deities of Mesopotamia. However, according to Nick Campion, the two words could mean either the visible planet or the hidden power within it, i.e. the god. Campion argues that the Sumerians considered the planets and stars to be under the power or authority of specific deities, but that they were not understood as the planet itself. This is one of the reasons why the sun-god is not the most central figure in the Mesopotamian mythologies nor of that of the Greeks who mapped much of their Pantheon onto the sky religion of the Babylonians. Another related explanation, as Robert Powell points out, is that the Babylonians noted that none of the planets were always visible in the sky, therefore no single deity could have supreme authority. Instead they governed through a council made up of all seven gods. During the Babylonian history, Marduk (the deity associated with the planet Jupiter) established himself as the president of the Council, but the Moon god, Sin, had also been known as "lord of the gods" in a time before the rulership of Marduk. Similarly during the Old Babylonian period of the Amorite king Hammurabi (1792–1750 B.C.E.), the sun god Shamash was considered the "king of the gods." In fact "Hammu" was the old Semitic name for the sun-god and thus, according to Powell, points to the worship of the solar deity.

Shamash was the son of Sin (a male lunar deity) and brother of Ishtar (associated with the planet Venus). He was the great benefactor to humanity because he ignited and supported the growth of life through his light and warmth. However, the early civilizations of the arid Mediterranean and Middle East, were all too aware of the Sun's scorching rays and his ability to burn up crops and dry up rivers and lakes. In Hellenistic and Hindu astrology this translated into a negative influence of the Sun when it was positioned too close to one of the other planets. The planet was designated as "combust" (within 8° from the Sun) or "under the Sun's beams" (within 17°) and was either interpreted as being hidden or operating in secrecy (out of sight), according to Hellenistic astrology, or as weak and ineffective in the Jyotish tradition. This concept of light translating into a higher degree of "sight" finds an echo in the Greek sun-god Helios who was also the god of seeing and often invoked to heal blindness. Medieval astrology, which was largely an Arabic evolution of the Hellenistic tradition, regarded combustion as especially detrimental. Guido Bonatti (thirteenth century) says: "A corporal conjunction with the Sun is the greatest misfortune that can befall a planet." To William Lilly, the Sun is associated with eyesight, cataracts, eye diseases and the brain—and an echo of this can be found in Vedic astrology.

One of the more notable characteristics of the Babylonian sun-god was that he was the arbiter of justice, a role associated with Jupiter in modern astrology. Powell explains this perspective in terms of the interpretation of the Sun's regularity as "infallibility," a desirable trait in the arbitration of justice. In Jacobsen, it is Utu's ability to "enlighten" or to have "clarity of vision" which is considered when he says Utu is the "power in light, the foe of darkness. On the social place he therefore becomes a power for justice and equality.... He is therefore the judge of god and men, presiding in the morning in courts such as the one we know from the Bathhouse Ritual, where demons and other evil doers are sued by their human victims. At night he judges disputes among the dead of the netherworld. He is the last appeal of the wronged who can obtain no justice from their fellow men, and their cry of despair to him, 'i-Utu!' was feared as possessing supernatural power" (as noted in Nick Campion's *Cosmos: A Cultural History of Astrology*.

Conversely, Hellenistic astrologers also noticed that the Sun's close rays could hide other planets and keep them from exerting their powers in an obvious way. This dual nature of the Sun is described in Ariel Guttman and Kenneth Johnson's *Mythic Astrology* in terms of the Greek myth involving the other solar deity, Apollo. While Helios personified the physical Sun, driving his chariot across the sky and ordering the days and the seasons, Apollo represented the Soul of the Sun. After Apollo was born of Leto and Zeus on Delos, he searched for a place where he could build his shrine. He came across a site that was guarded by a giant python, on what became known as Delphi. Apollo slew the serpent and set up his shrine, which became the oracle of Delphi where messages received by a prophetess known as the Pythoness were thought to be direct messages from the sun-god himself. Two admonitions written on the temple gates read: "Know thyself" and "Nothing in excess." According to Guttman and Johnson, the myth and the messages depict Apollo and the Sun as the "reconciler of opposites," the power of the masculine directive principle to unite with the more mystical feminine principle lying beneath directed consciousness. These two polarities are born out in the activities governed by Apollo requiring focused consciousness: mathematics, science, archery; and those requiring a deeper mystical consciousness—prophecy, dreams, oracles. As god of music and healing, Apollo depicts this ability to create order out of the numinous. Similarly, Shamash is often depicted as rising between two mountains, which to Guttman and Johnson represent the boundaries of the world—the polarities of human consciousness.

In Robert Schmidt's reconstruction of Hellenistic astrology, he distills the basic nature of the Sun as one involving the principles of selection and preference. In concrete terms these can be translated into significations of kings, leaders, the father, the head, the heart, friendship, honors, important people, gold, statues, judgment, reputation, rank, etc. Modern psychological astrology interprets the position of the Sun in the natal chart as indicative of one's ego, self-confidence, will, and intention. An exaggeration of these functions can lead to exaggerated pride, conceit, arrogance, and egocentrism. In both conceptualizations, the idea of choice and the elevation of a particular thing over another is fundamental. Glenn Perry describes the role of the Sun as the "decider subsystem" of the psyche. "The Sun is responsible for expressing or suppressing the various functions that the planets symbolize.... The Sun has to regulate the expression of *every* planet." Thus, as in the Apollo myth, the Sun is responsible for reconciling the extreme expressions of the human psyche, much in the same way that its central astronomical position regulates and balances the planets within its gravitational sphere. In a more ancient vernacular, Vettius Valens similarly says: "The all-seeing Sun, existent in a fire-like manner and as the light of the mind, the organ of perception of the soul."

While one may see in Vettius Valen's allusions to the Sun as soul, modern concepts inherent in transpersonal psychology, Schmidt states that this particular text "seems to imply that the Sun has this role in the cosmos as a whole, not in the native." The Hellenistic form of astrology which Valens practiced was rooted in a Neoplatonic conceptualization of the universe as a cosmic animal with intelligence and language. In Plato's Republic, the highest God was called "the Good" and the Sun was envisioned as its archetype or "the son of the Good." Therefore the Good was considered a "transmundane sun" who created the world and everything in it through the power of its reason or Logos. In the Gospel of St. John (1:1–2), the Logos is referred to as the divine word: "In the beginning was the Word (Logos) and the Word was with God. According to St. John, the Logos incarnated as Christ who was therefore identified with the spirit of the Sun. It is against this background that early Christians placed the birth of Christ on December 25, which was the date of the pagan festival of Sol Invictus (Invincible Sun) and the date on which the winter solstice was celebrated (when Helios was thought to be reborn as his light increased until the summer solstice).

A case for the physical, as well as the symbolic influence of the Sun on the affairs of human beings has been made by natural astrologers such as Percy Seymour. It is well known by scientists that the Earth's magnetic field is affected by the Sun's magnetic activity (sunspots and solar flares) which rises and falls in 22-year cycles. Seymour argues that not only does the Sun's magnetic field affect events on Earth, as is evidenced from marks in tree rings every 22 years, but the other planets in the solar system also affect the magnetic activity occurring on the Sun. Specifically, "Jupiter, Saturn, Uranus and Neptune cause the little eddy currents that cause the sun's magnetic field to reverse or flip over." Michel Gauquelin's lesser known studies involving planetary heredity have shown evidence that children born on days when solar activity is more disturbed, are more likely to have the same planets as their parents in certain parts of the birth chart. "The number of hereditary similarities between the child and the parent is *two and a half times greater* if the child has entered the world on a magnetically disturbed day than if the child is born on a calm day."

**Sources:**

Aveni, Anthony. *Stairways to the Stars*. New York: John Wiley & Sons, 1997.
Campion, Nick. *Cosmos: A Cultural History of Astrology*. London: London Books, 2001.
DeFouw, Hart, and Robert Svoboda. *Light on Life*. New York: Arkana Penguin Books, 1996.
Gauquelin, Michel. *Cosmic Influences on Human Behavior*. Santa Fe, NM: Aurora Press, 1994.
Guttman, Ariel, and Kenneth Johnson. *Mythic Astrology*. St. Paul, MN: Llewellyn Publications, 1998.
Holden, James Herschel. *A History of Horoscopic Astrology*. Tempe, AZ: American Federation of Astrologers, 1996.
Lehman, J. Lee. *Classical Astrology for Modern Living*. Atglen, PA: Whitford Press, 1996.
Louis, Anthony. *Horary Astrology Plain and Simple*. St. Paul, MN: Llewellyn Publications, 1998.
Perry, Glenn. *Mapping the Landscape of the Soul*. San Rafael, CA: Association of Astrological Psychology, 2001.
Powell, Robert. *History of the Planets*. San Diego: ACS Publications, 1985.
Schmidt, Robert. *Original Source Texts and Auxiliary Materials for the Study of Hellenistic Astrology*. Cumberland, MD: Phaser Foundation, 2002.
Seymour, Percy. Interview in *Mountain Astrologer*. August/September 1998.
Wilson, James. *A Complete Dictionary of Astrology*. London: W. Hughes, 1819.

—Maria J. Mateus

## Sun Sign

The sign of the zodiac the Sun is in, particularly in a natal chart, is the sun sign (sometimes also called the birth sign). From the viewpoint of Western astrology, the Sun, as the most important celestial body for Earth dwellers, is the most important influence in a horoscope. Consequently, the sign that the Sun is in at birth is usually the single most important influence on a native's personality. Thus, when people say that they are a certain sign, they are almost always referring to their sun sign. Interestingly, the ancient Romans regarded the Moon as the most influential astrological body, so when they said they were a certain sign, they were referring to the sign the Moon was in when they were born. Similarly, in Vedic astrology, the Moon represents a more important influence than the Sun.

Sun-sign astrology, which is the kind of astrology found in newspapers and magazines, has the advantage of simplicity—a person's birthday is all that must be known to figure out the person's sign—but this simplicity is purchased at the price of ignoring all other astrological influences. These other influences make sun-sign astrology a hit-or-miss system that works sometimes but fails miserably at others. Professional astrologers tend to dislike sun-sign astrology because it creates a misconception of the science of the stars (i.e., the misconception that astrology is entirely about sun signs) and because its inaccuracy leads nonastrologers to reject all astrology as untrue.

**Sources:**

Bach, Eleanor. *Astrology from A to Z: An Illustrated Source Book*. New York: Philosophical Library, 1990.

Gettings, Fred. *Dictionary of Astrology*. London: Routledge & Kegan Paul, 1985.

## Superior Conjunctions

Superior conjunctions are conjunctions between the Sun and the two inner planets in which Mercury or Venus lies on the other side of the Sun from Earth. The antonym inferior conjunction refers to conjunctions in which Mercury or Venus is located in front of the Sun.

## Superior Planets

The original meaning of the word superior was "above." In the concept of the universe that was prevelant prior to the Copernican revolution, when Earth was thought to be the stable center around which every other celestial body revolved, the orbits of Mars, Jupiter, and Saturn were considered to be "above" the orbit of the Sun. These three planets were thus referred to as the superior planets. The evaluative connotations of the term have caused this expression to be dropped in favor of outer planets.

## Swati

Swati (the Good Goer) is one of the Nakshatras (lunar mansions) of Vedic astrology. Shown by a sword, this Nakshatra is a good time to "cut loose" and is considered one of the best signs; people under this sign may tend towards gentleness and friendliness during this time, as well as over-generosity and unawareness of debt. The planet Rahu rules Swati and the god of wind, Vayu, presides over this sign located from Libra 6°40' to 20°.

—Pramela Thiagesan

## Sweet Signs

Sweet Sign is an archaic term applied to the air signs, which were said to be sweet (in contrast to the bitter signs).

## Swift

A planet is said to be swift when it appears to be moving faster than average. Because of its elliptical orbit, the Moon, especially, can move noticeably more slowly or more rapidly than its average of 13°10' per 24-hour period.

## Synastry (Chart Comparison)

Synastry, or chart comparison, is the practice of superimposing two or more horoscopes and examining their interactions. Synastry is an especially popular technique for evaluating romantic relationships, but it can also be used for illuminating business partnerships, parent-child interactions, and so forth. The basic idea of chart comparison is very old. In Hindu astrology, for example, the practice of comparing charts to determine marital compatibility is quite ancient. In the Western tradition, Ptolemy mentions synastry in his *Tetrabiblos*, the single most influential astrological treatise in European history. Even the famous Swiss psychiatrist Carl Jung used chart comparison in his work with married couples.

Traditional chart comparison focuses on the aspects between key planets. Thus, if the natal Mercury (planet of communication) of one individual is conjunct the Mercury of the other, the relationship will be characterized by easy communication between the two. Mentally, they will see eye to eye on many issues. In romantic relationships, it is especially interesting to note how Venus (the planet of relating) and Mars (the planet of passion) are aspected. A close conjunction between one person's Mars and the other person's Venus, for instance, is traditionally viewed as a powerful romantic-sexual aspect.

Among astrologers who accept the notion of reincarnation, Saturn is viewed as the planetary ruler of karma (one's ledger of debts and dues from previous lifetimes). Where the Saturn of a person with whom one is in a close relationship falls in one's natal chart indicates something about the nature of one's karmic tie. For example, if a close relative's Saturn is located in one's second house (the house of money and possessions) when the charts are superimposed, there is some sort of financial karma from past lifetimes. If neither person's Saturn is strongly aspected in a comparison, there is no significant karmic tie, and the relationship will usually be transitory.

**Sources:**

Brau, Jean-Louis, Helen Weaver, and Allan Edmans. *Larousse Encyclopedia of Astrology*. New York: New American Library, 1980.

Sakoian, Frances, and Louis S. Acker. *The Astrology of Human Relationships*. New York: Harper & Row, 1976.

## Synchronicity

Synchronicity (from the Greek *syn*, meaning "together," plus *chronos*, meaning "time") is a term popularized by the great Swiss psychologist Carl Jung to explain what might be called "meaningful" coincidences. He defined synchronicity as an "acausal (i.e., noncausal) connecting principle." Jung used synchronicity to refer to connections between events that had no discernible connection. Under normal circumstances, a correlation between two events often indicates that some sort of causal link exists between them. For example, at the time of the first cold snap every year certain birds migrate south. If the same pattern recurs year after year, it can be concluded that event A (cold snap) causes event B (bird migration).

There are correlations, however, with no obvious "causes," which are normally referred to as coincidences. For example, a person is humming a particular song that suddenly begins to play on the radio.

Where Jung departed most radically from mainstream psychology was to assert that quite often these coincidences are not coincidences; rather, the universe is structured so that such correlations occur all the time, and, further, that while there is no causal connection, these correlations are meaningful. A useful example for understanding "noncausal connections" is the correlation between the time on two clocks: just because they both show the same time, should it be concluded that one exerts some kind of force on the other, causing it to read the same? Obviously not. Similarly, Jung postulated that the universe, for reasons and by processes not yet understood, is set up like clocks that have been set in motion so as to infinitely reflect the same "time."

Although not always explicitly stated, synchronicity is assumed in certain forms of astrological research. For example, an accepted astrological practice is to assign newly discovered celestial bodies a tentative meaning that can be derived from associations with their name. This initial step is based on the well-established observation that the designations astronomers assign to newly discovered celestial bodies are not coincidental—that by virtue of some sort of non-apparent, synchronistic process, non-astrologically inclined astronomers give astrologically significant names to things.

Some astrologers also adopt synchronicity to explain astrological influence more generally. Rather than limit the scope of synchronicity to the exploration of the meaning of new celestial bodies, they view the relationship between the stars and human life as two clocks that read the same time. This contrasts with the view that astrological influence is a "force" exerted by the planets and other celestial bodies that is radiated to Earth like the forces of gravity or electromagnetism.

**Sources:**

Brau, Jean-Louis, Helen Weaver, and Allan Edmands. *Larousse Encyclopedia of Astrology*. New York: New American Library, 1980.

## Synodic Period

A synodic period (from the Greek, meaning "to meet or travel together") is the period a heavenly body takes to move from one conjunction with the Sun to the next. A synodic month, for example, is the period of time between successive new moons (which is 29 days 12 hours 44 minutes). Because Earth is always moving forward in its orbit, the time it takes the Moon to complete a synodic month differs from the time it takes the Moon to return to its original position relative to the backdrop of the comparatively stationary stars. Synodic cycle refers to the time between the conjunctions of two planets (not to the time between the conjunctions of a planet and the Sun).

## SYNTHESIS

Synthesis refers to the final stage in horoscope interpretation, when the astrologer weaves the many particular influences into a coherent whole. The ability to meaningfully synthesize astrological information rather than to simply list the interpretations of each individual component of a chart is the mark of an experienced astrologer.

## SYZYGY

Syzygy traditionally referred to a conjunction of the Sun and the Moon, such as occurs during a solar eclipse. By extension, it is currently applied to the alignment of any three celestial bodies in a straight line (such as occurs during eclipses and occultations). The etymology of the term is as follows: The *sy[n]*, which is related to the prefix of such words as synchronic, means "together;" *-zygy* derives from the Greek *zugón*, meaning "yoke," so syzygy literally means to yoke together. This makes syzygy appear to be a macrocosmic parallel to certain yoga practices in which the internal, symbolic (microcosmic) Sun and Moon are joined together—as in alternate nostril breathing, a technique said to join the Sun (right nostril) and Moon (left nostril) energies. What makes this parallel all the more striking is that both *zugón* and *yoga* ultimately derive from the same Indo-European root word *yug* (yoke).

**Sources:**

DeVore, Nicholas. *Encyclopedia of Astrology*. New York: Philosophical Library, 1947.
Gettings, Fred. *Dictionary of Astrology*. London: Routledge & Kegan Paul, 1985.

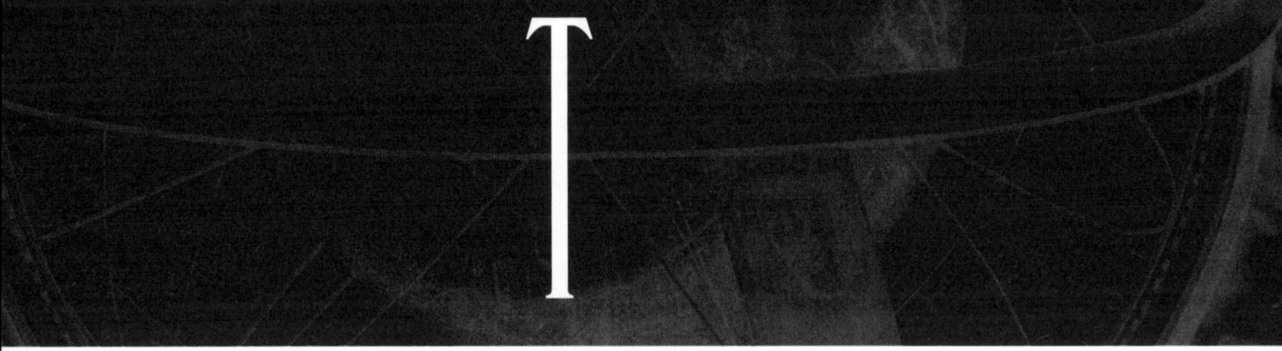

## T SQUARE

Three or more planets that together form a configuration of a "T"—two directly opposite each other and a third at right angles to each of the opposed planets—in a horoscope are referred to as a T square. To qualify as a T square, the planets directly across the chart from each other must be involved in an opposition (180° aspect) and the third planet must make a square (an aspect of 90°) to the first two. Because astrological signs at 90° angles to each other belong to the same quality (cardinal, mutable, or fixed), T squares tend to involve planets in three signs of one quality. Thus, T squares can be classified as cardinal T squares, mutable T squares, or fixed T squares (T squares that involve planets in signs of different qualities are referred to as mixed T squares).

Because all the aspects contained in a T square are hard aspects, an individual with such a configuration in her or his natal chart is presented with more challenges than the average person. At the same time, a T square is a powerfully dynamic configuration (it is considered to be the most dynamic of all configurations, particularly when the constituent planets are in cardinal signs). Once the challenges proffered by a T square have been adequately met, the individual has tremendous personal power.

In certain ways, a T square is like a grand cross (a configuration with four planets in all four corners of a chart) minus one of its "legs." Like a table with only three legs, the T square tends to draw attention to the house where a fourth leg would be required in order to produce a stable table. Imagine, for example, a natal chart in which the three component planets of a T square are in the second, eleventh, and eighth houses. One's attention is thus drawn to the fifth house. This indicates that if natives with this particular T square invested their energy in one or more of the matters associated with this house—children, creations, self-expression, entertainment, and so forth—their lives should become more stable. Simultaneously, this configuration indicates that the lessons learned in houses two, eleven, and eight could be brought to bear on whatever tasks were undertaken in the fifth house.

**Sources:**

Brau, Jean-Louis, Helen Weaver, and Allan Edmands. *Larousse Encyclopedia of Astrology*. New York: New American Library, 1980.

Marks, Tracy. *How to Handle Your T Square*. Arlington, MA: Sagittarius Rising, 1979.

## Table of Houses

A table of houses is, as the name indicates, a table that allows astrologers to locate the position of the houses when casting a horoscope. Tables of houses are usually published in book form, with the house positions arranged according to latitude and sidereal time. This information is incorporated into chart-casting programs, so, with the increasing use of personal computers by astrologers, traditional tables of houses have become obsolete.

## Tarot and Kaballah

The tarot is a set of cards related to contemporary playing cards that are used for divination. Tarot cards are often viewed as being an extension of Kaballah (or Cabbala or Cabala), a form of Jewish occultism. Kaballistic mysticism is built around the Tree of Life, a widespread diagram of the cosmos consisting of 10 circles (spheres) that are connected by 22 paths (lines). Each of the principal 22 tarot cards (the Major Arcana) is associated with one of these lines.

One characteristic practice in traditional occult thought has been to connect the symbol system of a given occult art with other symbol systems. Because of the prestige enjoyed by astrology in past eras, practitioners of other occult systems were especially interested in drawing on astrological symbolism. Palmistry, for example, deploys the symbolism of astrology, particularly in the names given to the fingers and to certain mounds on the palms.

Over the centuries, astrology and astrological symbolism became associated with both the tarot and the Kaballah. However, as systems that grew to maturity independently of the science of the stars, this connection was never quite natural. The difficulty is easy enough to see from a purely mathematical standpoint: How does one appropriately associate 10 spheres or 22 cards with 7 planets (the number of significant heavenly bodies known to the ancients) or 12 signs? Such associations, while useful in some instances, are never really convincing as a complete system.

**Sources:**

Cavendish, Richard. *The Black Arts*. New York: Capricorn Books, 1967.

Gettings, Fred. *Dictionary of Astrology*. London: Routledge & Kegan Paul, 1985.

## Taurus

Taurus, the second sign of the zodiac, is a fixed earth sign. It is a negative (in the value-neutral sense of being negatively *charged*), feminine sign, ruled by the planet

**A German engraving of tarot cards based on the Count de Gebelin pack. *Reproduced by permission of Fortean Picture Library.***

Venus. Its symbol is the bull, and its glyph is said to represent a bull's head and horns. It takes its name from the Greek word for bull. A sign known for its stubbornness, Taurus is the source of such expressions as "bullheaded" and "stubborn as a bull." Taurus is associated with the throat and neck. People with a Taurus sun sign, while they often have beautiful voices, are also prone to sore throats, thyroid irregularities, and other neck problems. The key phrase for Taurus is "I have."

Taurus, like many signs of the zodiac, does not have a developed mythology associated with it. Taurus is most often said to be the bull that kidnapped Europa. As the story goes, the god Zeus saw the princess Europa playing with female attendants on the beach and was filled with love for her great beauty. Zeus then transformed himself into a beautiful white bull, wandered into the group of females, and laid down among them. He presented such a peaceful appearance that they petted him, and Europa climbed onto his back. Zeus then unexpectedly took off swimming, eventually depositing Europa on the beach at Crete, where he made love to her. She bore him three sons and received three gifts from the king of the gods—an unerring spear, an inexorable hound, and a bronze man who drove away strangers.

Like Zeus, Taureans are fond of beauty and sensuality and like to place themselves in beautiful surroundings. They make a special effort to enjoy the good things of life. Similar to the bull of this tale, they are usually handsome and peaceful and are content to lie around and be "petted"; they enjoy receiving massages more than any other sign. They can remain calm when others panic but can explode into rage when pushed too far; though slow to anger, they have the worst temper in the zodiac when aroused. Like the unerring spear and the inexorable hound of the myth, Taureans are "doggedly" stubborn, pursuing a task in the face of all odds. And like the bronze man who chased away strangers, Taureans prefer the familiar over the new.

The sign that the Sun was in at birth is usually the single most important influence on a native's personality. Thus, when people say they are a certain sign, they are almost always referring to their sun sign. There is a wealth of information available on the characteristics of the zodiacal signs—so much that one book would not be able to contain it all. Sun-sign astrology, which is the kind of astrology found in newspaper columns and popular magazines, has the advantage of simplicity. But this simplicity is purchased at the price of ignoring other astrological influences, such as one's Moon sign, rising sign, etc. These other influences can substantially modify a person's basic sun sign traits. As a consequence, it is the rare individual who is completely typical of her or his sign. The reader should bear this caveat in mind when perusing the following series of sun-sign interpretations.

One traditional way in which astrologers condense information is by summarizing sign and planet traits in lists of words and short phrases called key words or key phrases. The following Taurus key words are drawn from Manly P. Hall's *Astrological Keywords:*

> *Emotional keywords:* "Amorous, artistic, gentle, loyal, domestic, proud, quick-tempered, self-indulgent, sensual, moods make definite statements concerning emotions impossible."
>
> *Mental keywords:* "Patient, persistent, thorough, steadfast, conservative, retentive, discriminating, determined, argumentative, stubborn, materialistic"

At present, there are various astrology report programs that contain interpretations of each of the 12 sun signs. A selection of these for Sun in Taurus has been excerpted below:

**A sixteenth-century woodcut of the constellation Taurus the bull.** ***Reproduced by permission of Fortean Picture Library.***

You are known for being patient, slow moving and careful—you love to prolong and savor enjoyable times. You appreciate and need comfort, ease and warm surroundings. Be careful of a tendency to become placid and self-satisfied and to overeat (especially sweets). You require strenuous situations in order to grow and mature properly, even though you try to avoid them. Affectionate, even-tempered and slow to anger—when you do become emotionally upset, you are also slow to forgive and time must pass before your calm returns. You demand real results from any situation—abstractions are very difficult for you to comprehend. Very artistic, your hands love to mold and shape things. You portray an earthy, physical sexiness that others find quite seductive. (From "Professional Natal Report." Courtesy of Astrolabe [http://www.alabe.com].)

You are a steadfast and patient soul, capable of tremendous devotion, dedication, endurance, and constancy. The ability to follow through and stick with things is one of your greatest assets. Once your course is set, you pursue it tenaciously until it is completed, stubbornly resisting any attempts to sway you from your purpose.

You have a very practical nature and want to see concrete, tangible results for your efforts, and you are not one for spinning wild dreams that are unlikely to come into fruition. Most of your "wild dreams" have to do with material achievements, well-being, and security, for you have a great love of the physical world and you want to experience and enjoy it to the full. Though you will work long and persistently, you also have a strong sensual and comfort-loving side, and you want to enjoy what you have worked for. In fact, you can be enormously lazy at times and have a tendency to overindulge in good food and other earthly pleasures. You also love the beauty of the natural world and probably prefer a serene country setting rather than an urban life style.

At heart your needs are simple and you are easy to please. You have a strong desire for security, stability, and peace, and will rarely make changes unless you are forced to do so. You are not very demanding emotionally, though you do crave lots of physical closeness and affection. Because of your faithfulness, emotional steadiness, and gentle strength, others often depend upon you for support. Though you hate upheaval and sudden changes, you usually maintain your poise and equanimity. You also have an innate sense of harmonizing with nature, allowing things to grow and unfold in their own time, and the patience to nurture something into being—be it a garden, a child, or some creative project. You make an excellent mother or father, especially if you follow your instincts more often than "the experts."

You have three major faults: one is your bullheaded obstinacy. The second is your unwillingness to deviate from your safe, predictable routine. And the third is your tendency to always insist upon realism and undervalue the imaginative, speculative, and fanciful—in other words, you lack the ability to play with ideas and possibilities, to open your mind to the new. (From "Merlin," by Gina Ronco and Agnes Nightingale. Courtesy of Cosmic Patterns [http://cosmic.patterns.com].)

Ease, calm, naturalness—those are the spiritual goals of the Bull. Silence too. But not just the kind that comes from keeping your mouth closed. The Bull's silence is deeper: it's a quiet heart. Feel the wind in your hair. Feel the efficiency of your body, the rightness of its rhythms, the easy intelligence of your cells and muscles. That's Taurus. The part of you that's learning the lessons of the Bull is getting more grounded, more present, more receptive to immediate reality. As a result, it has a physical orientation and a practical feeling. It's not so interested in abstract flights of speculation. It avoids the metaphysical Disneylands that seem to fascinate so many people. It specializes in the wordless mysticism of ordinary life.

Feed your Taurean side with hands-on work: gardening, crafting wood or cloth, communing with animals. Soothe it with music. Restore and renew it with time spent close to nature—in the forest, in the mountain valley, by the ocean. Dress it in blue jeans and flannel. And never, ever, ask it to go to a cocktail party!

With your Sun in Taurus, you renew your basic vitality in simple ways. Take a walk in the woods. Paddle a canoe. Build something of oak or maple. Your deepest nature is quiet, stable, solid. You benefit from having a strong tone of continuity in your life—especially in relationships. Keep in touch with old friends. Stay close to people who aren't too quick to get off on "trips," be they guru-scenes, make-a-million schemes, or a new kind of bean sprout that will change your life. At the deepest level, you are learning about calm and naturalness. So keep things simple.

Your practical skills are enormous: you understand the world of raw materials, of money, of daily life. Be careful those skills don't run away with you! A pitfall for you lies in getting so busy keeping all your responsibilities magnificently fulfilled that you starve yourself for quiet time. Then the Sun grows dimmer in you, and every other aspect of your character has less light to reflect. (From "The Sky Within," by Steven Forrest. Courtesy of Matrix Software [http://thenewage.com] and Steven Forrest [http://www.stevenforrest.com].)

Among its several natal programs, Matrix Software created a unique report based on the published works of the early-twentieth-century astrologer Grant Lewi (1901–1952). Lewi's highly original delineations were recognized as creative and insightful by his contemporaries. One measure of the appeal of his work is that his books *Astrology for the Millions* and *Heaven Knows What* are still in print. The following is excerpted from the report program "Heaven Knows What":

"I propose to fight it out on this line if it takes all Summer." (*Ulysses S. Grant, born in Taurus, April 27, 1822.*)

"In all movements, we bring to the front as the leading question in each case, the property question." (*The Communist Manifesto of Karl Marx, born in Taurus, May 5, 1818.*)

"From each according to his abilities, to each according to his needs." (*Karl Marx.*)

The singleness of purpose of the Taurean, his loyalty, his stick-to-it-iveness, spring from one source: his need for security. Self-preservation … is the hub of the Taurean wheel of life; and the Taurean curls and dies within himself when security—emotional or material—is denied him. Not likely to be grasping, sure to be the embodiment of the idealist form of love, Taurus may himself, or herself, be quite unaware of inner motives, for self-analysis is rarely important to this sign. Instincts are powerful and generally right—always right in so far as they serve the perhaps unarticulated motives of the Taurean, who, while not selfish in the ordinary material sense, sees to it that nothing interferes with the gratifying of his instinctual urge, self-preservation and its more abstracted form, self-fulfillment.

The Taurean will not interfere with you if you don't interfere with him in these essentials, but will fight like a bear at bay for his rights to these things. He is the easiest person to live with, if you are willing to live with him and not against him. Anyone who is going to get along with a Taurean must understand that to him or her cooperation doesn't mean doing things together; it means doing things peacefully, in a friendly manner, even if the things are done separately. This kind of cooperation annoys people who are less self-sufficient until they learn that the heart of the Taurean comes home to roost only if you don't try to coerce it, and will break itself against bars of any kind, even if the bars are put up by love itself.

The Taurean is so sure of his need for security that he resents any implication that he needs watching or holding; his instinct is to hold himself to what he needs and wants—and he can't by any force in the world be held to anything else. On the other hand, once he has polarized his instinct on an essential, he will cling to it with hands, teeth and toenails, and no one can tell him that it is unworthy, or wrong, or useless, or low. Once it is his, in that it satisfies his deepest needs, it is his forever, whether it be home, a man, a woman, ambition, love, money or anything. When the Taurean has determined in his deep and sometimes dark subconscious that his emotional or material security lies there, he goes there and stays there forever. (Courtesy of Matrix Software [http://thenewage.com].)

The following excerpt comes not from a natal report program, but from David Cochrane's recent book, *Astrology for the 21st Century*. Based on lessons for astrology students, it approaches the signs of the zodiac from a somewhat different perspective than the other short delineations cited here:

Taurus patiently builds things using an inner instinct. Taurus is attuned to the plant kingdom and a love of nature is usually strong in people who have a lot of Taurus in their charts. Taureans are practical and down-to-earth.

I have not found that love of food and comfort or materialism or acquisitiveness, which are often ascribed to Taurus, are accurate. From my viewpoint Taurus is the builder, plain and simple. Taurus approaches life instinctively, following its own inner sense, and persistently and patiently builds something. Taurus does things in an organic way and does not respond to reason, preferring to follow an unfolding process that works from within. Taurus is attuned to the plant kingdom because Taurus develops organically and slowly, just as plants do. People with strong Taurus in their chart like to build things up step-by-step, unfolding a plan that is within them and as the vision unfolds and materializes, Taurus takes great joy in the process. Others may feel

> bored, as if the Taurean is delighting in watching the grass grow, but patience and tenacity are implicit in the Taurean unfolding process. (Courtesy of Cosmic Patterns [http://cosmic.patterns.com] and David Cochrane [kepler@astrosoftware.com].)

A number of specialized report programs has been developed that offer useful supplements to the generic delineations of general reports. The following sun-sign interpretation has been drawn from a program written by Gloria Star (originally part of her book, *Astrology: Woman to Woman*) that generates a specialized report for women:

> With your Sun in Taurus your steadfast, easygoing energy helps to keep you focused on your priorities. You're interested in a life which provides ample opportunities to grow, and your ego self is driven by a need to experience consistency. The beautiful things in life are most valuable to you, and your capacity for love is immense. Learning the difference between stability and stubbornness can be one of your biggest lessons. Since your Sun shows "who you think you are," you can grow to realize that loving thoughts produce amazing results.
>
> Through your Taurus Sun you experience a sense of continuity and stability, and can express your masculine side through establishing as secure place in the world. Whether you choose a career path or family structure as your focus, you are like an anchor and have the ability to provide strength and consistency. It may be important that you to create a home base, and the energy you put into building your home includes both house and family. Your special sensibility toward the environment can grow as you mature, and you may find that your awareness of the importance of preserving the environment and making the best use of resources is behind your most powerful drives. As a woman, you will take great care to build upon the foundations in your life, and may prefer to assert yourself in a slow, steady pace. Your career path needs to provide opportunities for you to establish yourself and grow steadily. Regardless of your marital status, you function best when you have your own money and resources. Although your father may have been the breadwinner and financial mainstay when you were a child, you may prefer a different situation with a husband or partner. Allowing the man in your life to control your finances will ultimately result in a power struggle, if not externally, then certainly within yourself. You can work cooperatively with a partner toward joint ventures, financially and otherwise, and can feel willing to share and contribute to the financial and other needs of your family. You will feel greater autonomy if you also have a separate fund which you control for yourself.
>
> There's certainly no problem with your desires, since your Taurus Sun qualities may help you create a long wish list. Maintaining your focus is one of the tricks you learned long ago, and when you really want something, there may be no end to your patience. The problem can revolve around determining your priorities and learning the difference between

> what you need and what you want. Sometimes, your stubborn attitudes and refusal to change can interfere with the realization of your needs. In many ways, your success depends upon knowing when to hang on and when to loosen your grasp—at least a little! (From "Woman to Woman," by Gloria Star. Courtesy of Matrix Software [http://thenew age.com].)

Responding to the revival of interest in pre-twentieth-century astrology, J. Lee Lehman developed a report program embodying the interpretive approach of traditional astrology. The following is excerpted from her Classical Report:

> You are a person of few words, with religious or spiritual leanings, and slow to anger. You are sincere and just, confident and bold, an interpreter of dreams who can find out secret and hidden things. There is a danger that in the process you will offend others, and your conceit, or confidence, doesn't help.
>
> You are an Earth Sign, which means that you are "cold" and "dry." The "dry" component means, among other things, that you see distinctions easily, and that you are more swayed by intellectual argument than by passion. You are perceived as being "cold," an outward appearance of unemotional. In the modern parlance, it fits better with "cold and dry" than with simply "cold." However, a "cold" type is basically lethargic, or slow to react. The problem with "cold" is that it makes it hard for you to forget slights. Because you don't tend to lash out immediately, it's hard for you not to allow your anger to build up. Combine this with a tendency, being "dry," to prefer the reasonable approach, and you can end up completely out of touch while your emotions run rampant.
>
> You are fixed, which means you are strong-willed and stubborn. You will want to hang onto people and things long after they have ceased to be useful to you. The Taurus Bull, being a four-footed sign, means that you have a strong sex drive with a tendency to be vicious or violent if angered. (Courtesy of J. Lee Lehman, Ph.D., copyright 1998 [http://www.leelehman.com].)

Readers interested in examining interpretations for their Chinese astrological sign should refer to the relevant entry. A guide for determining one's sign in the Chinese system is provided in the entry on the Chinese zodiac.

**Sources:**

Cochrane, David. *Astrology for the 21st Century*. Gainesville, FL: Cosmic Patterns, 2002.

Forrest, Steven. *The Inner Sky: How to Make Wiser Choices for a More Fulfilling Life*. 4th ed. San Diego: ACS Publications, 1989.

Green, Landis Knight. *The Astrologer's Manual: Modern Insights into an Ancient Art*. Sebastopol, CA: CRCS Publications, 1975.

Hall, Manly P. *Astrological Keywords*. New York: Philosophical Library, 1958. Reprint, Savage, MD: Littlefield Adams Quality Paperbacks, 1975.

Lehman, J. Lee. *Classical Astrology for Modern Living: From Ptolemy to Psychology & Back Again*. Atglen, PA: Whitford Press, 1996.

Lewi, Grant. *Astrology for the Millions*. 5th ed. St. Paul, MN: Llewellyn, 1978.
———. *Heaven Knows What*. St. Paul, MN: Llewellyn, 1969.
Star, Gloria. *Astrology & Your Child: A Handbook for Parents*. St. Paul, MN: Llewellyn, 2001.
———. *Astrology: Woman to Woman*. St. Paul, MN: Llewellyn, 1999.

## Temperaments

The theory of temperaments, or complexions, incorporated four basic qualities: hot, cold, wet, and dry. These four qualities varied by season, gender, age, and person. The ideal of Hippocrates was to lead a balanced life, because if the body is balanced, then disease is less likely to take hold. The method of creating balance combined diet and regimen, and encompassed such lifestyle issues as frequency and type of exercise, time of eating, and sleep patterns.

The entire ancient scheme was based on the four qualities: hot, cold, wet, and dry. Hot and cold were one pair; wet and dry the other. From a behavioral perspective, hot is exactly what one would expect from the common parlance: someone who reacts vigorously to anything even remotely perceived as an attack. "Hot under the collar" is exactly on target. A cold type is basically lethargic, or slow to react, often perceived as being unemotional, but "slow to react" would actually be closer. The expression "cool under pressure" is also a good fit.

Dry represents anything with a discrete shape or structure, while something wet adapts its shape to the container. Dry thinking is characterized by making distinctions, while wet thinking sees connections. A new example of wet thinking is "hyperlinking"; the World Wide Web is a good example. A dry thinker is more easily swayed by intellectual argument than by passion. A wet thinker fits emotion into the picture. Dryness is the position that a moment is unique, that reality can be objectively known. Yet one other way to contrast the two is to say that the epitome of dry thinking is clarity, and the epitome of wet thinking is ambiguity. And yes, the very process of attempting to explain the concept is dry!

Each of the four qualities actually represents a cluster of concepts. For example, the qualities hot and cold do not represent extremes of a temperature continuum, as one might define them. They represent *qualities* of energy, where hot represents high energy or physical heat, and cold represents low energy or physical cold. But these qualities are opposites in a critically different way from the way one normally envisions them. Take temperature: From a purely chemical perspective, molecules in a hotter gas vibrate more rapidly on average than molecules in a colder gas. Mixing hot and cold gases will produce an intermediate result. In other words, the cold portion is completely canceled out by a portion of the hot component. But this is not how it works—at least as far as the qualities, and not chemistry, are concerned. Opposites do *not* cancel each other out.

Thus, people have hot and cold qualities simultaneously. In fact, having "half and half" would be to manifest equal quantities of each, not to have a "zero-sum state" in which hot cancels cold, perhaps producing lukewarm.

Finally, this is where astrology comes into the picture. Hippocrates put forward a workable theory of qualities, but other than general distinctions of age, gender, and physical appearance, he had no way to classify a person as having a particular make-up. But by using the chart, modern astrologers can actually calculate the temperament type. Further, this result can then be used in many ways, including to establish a diet and exercise plan that truly supports well-being. Astrology eventually became the preferred mode for distinguishing the general constitution from its components, or humors.

There are several possibilities for the computation of the temperament type. The general definition includes the following components (the method of computation comes from John Gadbury's *Genethlialogia, or The Doctrine of Nativities Together with the Doctrine of Horarie Questions* and William Lilly's *Christian Astrology*:

1. Sign of ascendant
2. Planet ruling ascendant
3. Planets aspecting ascendant
4. Moon sign and phase
5. Planets aspecting Moon
6. Quarter of year
7. Lord/Lady of Geniture
8. Lord/Lady of Moon

Each component is assigned qualities as follows:

*1. Signs:*
Fire: Hot and Dry
Air: Hot and Wet
Earth: Cold and Dry
Water: Cold and Wet

*2. The Moon is classified by phase.*
New to 1st Quarter: Hot and Wet
1st Quarter to Full: Hot and Dry
Full to Last Quarter: Cold and Dry
Last Quarter to New: Cold and Wet

*3. Seasons are classified as follows:*
Spring: Hot and Wet
Summer: Hot and Dry
Fall: Cold and Dry
Winter: Cold and Wet

*4. Lord/Lady of the Geniture:*
This is a compound Almuten for the hylegical points and angles: the Sun, Moon, Part of Fortune, Ascendant, and Midheaven.

This actually gives nine temperament types, not four. The reason is that often two of the qualities are often in balance, or so close as to have little dominance. These nine types are:

Hot and Wet: sanguine
Hot and Dry: choleric
Cold and Dry: melancholic
Cold and Wet: phlegmatic

Hot: sanguine-choleric
Cold: melancholic-phlegmatic
Wet: sanguine-phlegmatic
Dry: choleric-melancholic
All: balanced

What may appear to be the simpler states, the single-quality ones, are actually more complex. The reason is that the single-quality types are in fact mixtures, because qualities do not cancel out. Having close to an even ratio of hot and cold or wet and dry means that it is easy to become out of balance: stress, the change in season, or even too much to drink.

—J. Lee Lehman, Ph.D.

**Sources:**

Gadbury, John. *Genethlialogia, or The Doctrine of Nativities Together with the Doctrine of Horarie Questions*. London: J. Cottrel, 1658.
Lehman, J. Lee. *Classical Astrology for Modern Living*. West Chester, PA: Whitford Press, 1996.
Lilly, William. *Christian Astrology Modestly Treated of in Three Books*. London: T. Brudenell, 1647.

## Temperaments in Jungian Psychology

The assessment of an individual's underlying type—his or her "complexion or temperament," as noted in William Lilly's *Christian Astrology Modestly Treated of in Three Books*—according to a fourfold division, has long been an important feature of astrological work.

This system of analysis has its roots in the four elements—fire, earth, air, and water—introduced to philosophy by Empedocles in the fifth century B.C.E. and applied to the human organism as an analytical and explanatory tool in the form of the four humors—choleric, melancholic, sanguine, and phlegmatic—by Hippocrates, also in the fifth century B.C.E. Hippocrates's use of the four humors focused on their use for medical diagnosis. Claudius Galen, in the second century B.C.E., developed and preserved Hippocrates's work, and over the centuries a knowledge of the four humors came to be the accepted frame of reference in the West for understanding a human being. This understanding was not only for use in making a medical diagnosis, but also for the description of character in everyday parlance. For example, such writers as Chaucer and Shakespeare used references to the humors as a convenient shorthand for conveying an individual's character or mood.

The relationship between the four elements and the four humors is shown in this table:

| Element | Quality | Humor |
|---|---|---|
| Fiery Triplicity | Hot and dry | Choleric |
| Earthy Triplicity | Cold and dry | Melancholic |
| Airy Triplicity | Hot and moist | Sanguine |
| Watery Triplicity | Cold and moist | Phlegmatic |

The technique for assessing the fundamental temperament from a natal chart is discussed in many standard works of what, as noted in Nicholas Culpeper's *Astrological Judgement of Diseases from the Decumbiture of the Sick*, is now known as traditional astrology. There is general agreement on the importance of four factors: The element of the ascendant sign, the phase of the Moon, the season of the Sun, and the element of the sign of the lord of the geniture (the planet that is strongest by essential dignity while not being accidentally weakened). Additional factors are sometimes added to this list, and different ways of analyzing the information are given. It should also be noted that methods are sometimes given for judging temperament without reference to the natal chart—for instance, as noted by Culpeper, the appearance of an individual or by their behavior or their dreams, according to John Gadbury's *Genethlialogia, or The Doctrine of Nativities Together with the Doctrine of Horarie Questions*.

The advent of modern science saw the humors go out of favor as a tool of medical analysis, and astrologers—with their craft also under attack from the new *zeitgeist*—gradually stopped using them. In Raphael's *Guide to Astrology* from 1877 there is a short section on temperament, in which the four elements are described as giving more or less heat to the nature; this is a clear throwback to the humors, though they are not mentioned by name. By the time Charles E. O. Carter published his *Encyclopaedia of Psychological Astrology* in 1924, the section on humor was concerned only with what makes people laugh. Astrology's connection with the humors was forgotten.

Though by this point the humors were dead and buried so far as astrology was concerned, the psychologist Carl Jung was already working on a study that would lead to their rebirth.

## Jung's Quaternal Heritage

It is fairly well known that Jung had some interest in astrology. Indeed, in a letter to B. V. Raman in September 1947, he wrote:

> I am particularly interested in the particular light the horoscope sheds on certain complications in the character. In cases of difficult psychological diagnosis, I usually get a horoscope.... I have very often found that the astrological data elucidated certain points which I otherwise would have been unable to understand.

Though this probably gives an exaggerated impression of the extent to which Jung used astrology, it is beyond dispute that he read widely among ancient astrological and alchemical literature, and absorbed a good deal of the underlying philosophy that those disciplines shared.

An example of this influence in his work is Jung's emphasis on the quaternity as being archetypal; a mythological motif that was "always collective" and "common to all times and all races," as noted in *The Collected Works of C. G. Jung*. As Jung explicitly states:

> The quaternity is one of the most widespread archetypes and has also proved to be one of the most useful schemata for representing the arrangement of the functions by which the conscious mind takes its bearings.

This opens the way for the consideration of the link between the four elements (as found in astrological and alchemical literature) and the four psychological types that Jung propounded. The following quotation provides the clearest evidence of a direct connection between the two. Jung refers to the last chapter of *De vita longa* (1562) in which:

> Paracelsus makes almost untranslatable allusions to the four Scaiolae, and it is not at all clear what could be meant. Ruland, who had a wide knowledge of the contemporary Paracelsist literature, defines them as "spiritual powers of the mind" (*spirituales mentis vires*), qualities and faculties which are fourfold, to correspond with the four elements.... The Scaiolae, he says, originate in the mind of man, "from whom they depart and to whom they are turned back...." Like the four seasons and the four quarters of heaven, the four elements are a quaternary system of orientation which always expresses a totality. In this case it is obviously the totality of the mind (*animus*), which here would be better translated as "consciousness" (including its contents). The orienting system of consciousness has four aspects, which correspond to four empirical functions: thinking, feeling, sensation (sense-perception), intuition. This quaternity is an archetypal arrangement.

Another passage in Jung's work where the relationship between the "empirical functions of consciousness" and the elements is made explicit comes in his discussion of Plato's *Timaeus*. He analyzes Plato's character, suggesting that although he possessed a preponderance of fiery "spirit" and "airy thought" he was relatively lacking when it came to connection with sensational reality and concrete action ("earth"). As Jung put it, Plato "had to content himself with the harmony of airy thought-structure that lacked weight, and with a paper surface that lacked depth." Jung's equating of the earth element with "concrete reality," of air with "thought" and fire with "spirit" in this analysis allows for the inference of the following relationships between the Jungian functions of consciousness and the astrological elements: thinking-air, intuition-fire, feeling-water, sensation-earth. This is the same alignment of Jungian function to astrological element as was arrived at by the astrologer and Jungian analyst Liz Greene.

## Jung's Psychological Types

Jung's work on *Psychological Types*, first published in 1921, is a work of considerable complexity and the following summary of his typology—the two "attitude-types" and four "function-types" is inevitably cursory.

> The attitude-types ... are distinguished by their attitude to the object. The introvert's attitude is an abstracting one; at bottom, he is always intent on withdrawing libido from the object, as though he had to prevent the object from gaining power over him. The extravert, on the contrary, has a positive relation to the object. He affirms its importance to such an extent that his subjective attitude is constantly related to and oriented by the object.

> The conscious psyche is an apparatus for adaptation and orientation, and consists of a number of different psychic functions. Among these we can distinguish four basic ones: *sensation, thinking, feeling, intuition*. Thus there are many people who restrict themselves to the simple perception of concrete reality, without thinking about it or taking feeling values into account. They bother just as little about the possibilities hidden in a situation. I describe such people as *sensation types*. Others are exclusively oriented by what they think, and simply cannot adapt to a situation which they are unable to understand intellectually. I call such people *thinking types*. Others, again, are guided in everything entirely by feeling. They merely ask themselves whether a thing is pleasant or unpleasant, and orient themselves by their feeling impressions. These are the *feeling types*. Finally, the *intuitives* concern themselves neither with ideas nor with feeling reactions, nor yet with the reality of things, but surrender themselves wholly to the lure of possibilities, and abandon every situation in which no further possibilities can be scented.

Each of these four function-types is mediated by an attitude-type of extraversion or introversion thus giving, in Jung's scheme, a minimum of eight types (although he suggests that this is a relatively crude matrix and that each of the four functions may be subdivided into more refined categories.

## Jung's System in Contemporary Psychological Science—An Introduction to the MBTI

Jung's character typology informs one of the most widely used psychometric tests, namely, the Myers-Briggs Type Indicator (MBTI). According to Isabel B. Myers's *Introduction to Type*, proponents of the MBTI claim it to be the most widely used psychometric test in the world. An estimated 3.5 million MBTI tests are administered each year in the United States alone; it has been translated into two dozen languages and is routinely used in Canada, the U.K., Australia, New Zealand, Japan, Germany, Italy, Singapore, Korea, and many other countries. As noted in Otto Kroeger's *Type Talk at Work*, the popularity of the MBTI owes much to the fact that business communities across the globe have found it of practical value, in part because of empirical evidence correlating "psychological type" (as defined by the MBTI) with occupational role.

The MBTI is commonly deployed to assist decision-making in a variety of management training and personnel areas, including: recruitment and selection; career counseling; team building; organizational change; individual and leadership development. It is also frequently used in post-experience and post-graduate management educational contexts, with students in masters of business administration courses often being exposed to the test at some point in their studies.

The MBTI developed out of the interests of Katherine Cook Briggs (1875–1968) and her daughter Isabel Briggs Myers (1897–1980) in human personality difference. They both read Jung's *Psychological Types* shortly after its initial publication in English in 1923 and were prompted, at the outset of World War II, to try to "operationalize" the typology that he set out. They thought that the construction of a psychometric indicator might, among other things, prove useful in addressing certain pressing military personnel decisions faced at that time in the United States. Early forms of the MBTI testing procedure were thus developed in the period 1942–44, but it was after the war and in the years leading up to 1956 that more systematic research involving medical students, nursing students, and other samples was conducted using the MBTI. Neither Briggs nor Myers had any formal training in psychology or statistics, so Myers's encounter with a young psychology research student named David Saunders in the early 1950s was significant in terms of the statistical enhancement and subsequent development of the instrument.

Although isolated researchers and clinicians showed some interest in the MBTI as it continued to evolve during the 1960s, it was not until Consulting Psychologists Press showed interest in 1975 that the approach became widely available and major commercial success ensued. Work on the development of the MBTI continues to this day, with scales within the test being constantly reevaluated and refined. There are several psychologists associated with the approach: Naomi Quenk, Otto Kroeger, and Linda Kirby are three notable figures, but the most significant contemporary advocate is Mary McCaulley, who, since meeting Isabel Myers and striking up a close working relationship with her in the late sixties, has been a vocal proponent of the MBTI. A membership organization, the Association for Psychological Type, was formed in 1979 and a research publication, the *Journal of Psychological Types*, was established for those working primarily (although not exclusively) with the MBTI.

## Development of Jung's Method in the MBTI

In their interpretation of Jung, Briggs and Myers emphasized the distinction he drew between the rational functions of thinking and feeling—the way in which experience of the world is judged—and the irrational functions of sensation and intuition; that is, the purely perceptive or phenomenological apprehension of the world. Briggs and Myers refer to these two auxiliary functions as judging and perceiving, respectively. In addition to the dominant orientation of consciousness to its environment—the superior function in Jung's scheme—there is a secondary or inferior function.

This means that in the MBTI system there are 16 psychological types resulting from possible combinations of:(1) attitude-type: extraversion (E) or introversion (I); (2) superior function-type: sensing (S), thinking (T), feeling (F), or intuition (I); (3) inferior function-type: S, T, F, or I; and (4)judging (J) or perceiving (P). Hence someone responding to the MBTI questionnaire or engaging in a process of guided self-assessment will arrive at a type for him or herself that can be coded using combinations of four letters: ISTJ, ESTP, ENFP, INTJ, and so on.

## Impact of Jungian and Neo-Jungian Systems on Astrology

In the 20th century, astrology began to reemerge as a subject for serious study, after two centuries of obscurity and neglect. A major issue for astrologers of this period was to try and reclaim the intellectual respectability that the subject had been stripped of by the scientific revolution. The most popular strategy was to link it with the new science of psychology, and in particular with the psychology of Jung. Dane Rudhyar, in his book *The Astrology of Personality*, wrote in 1936: "We are above all stressing values and using a terminology which are found in C. G. Jung's works, because we are deeply convinced of their inherent validity, and also because they dovetail so remarkably with the general set-up of astrological symbolism."

Three other astrologers who have been particularly prominent in promoting the discipline that would become known as psychological astrology have been Stephen Arroyo, Liz Greene, and Howard Sasportas. In addition to her astrological training, Greene holds a doctorate in psychology and is a qualified Jungian analyst. She cofounded, with Sasportas, the Centre for Psychological Astrology in 1983, an organization that defines the main aims and objectives of its professional training course as follows:

> 1) To provide students with a solid and broad base of knowledge, within the realms of both traditional astrological symbolism and psychological theory and technique, so that the astrological chart can be sensitively understood and interpreted in the light of modern psychological thought.
>
> 2) To make available to students psychologically qualified case supervision, along with background seminars in counselling skills and techniques which can raise the standard and effectiveness of astrological consultation. Please note that no formal training as a counsellor or therapist is provided by the course.
>
> 3) To encourage investigation and research into the links between astrology, psychological models, and therapeutic techniques, thereby contributing to and advancing the existing body of astrological and psychological knowledge.

## Typology in Astrology—An Evaluation

As already noted, the way in which Jung's psychology should be applied to astrology has been an object of some controversy among astrologers. It seems safe to conclude that, although it may have been born from astrological ideas, Jung's psychological typology has developed a character of its own, so that it is safer not to try and establish one-for-one correspondences between the elements and the "four functions." This case is argued eloquently by Robert Hand in his book *Horoscope Symbols:*

> Astrology understood as a system of psychology in its own right has a symbolic framework much more powerful than any in orthodox psychology. It would be unrealistic to expect that one man in one lifetime could develop an understanding of symbols as profound as that of astrology, which has been developing for thousands of years.

—Garry Phillipson and Peter Case

**Sources:**

Centre for Psychological Astrology. http://www.cpalondon.com/index.html.

Culpeper, Nicholas. *Astrological Judgement of Diseases from the Decumbiture of the Sick*. London, 1655. Reprint, London: Ascella, 2000.

Ebertin, Reinhold. *Astrological Healing* York Beach, ME: Weiser, 1989.

Frawley, John. *The Real Astrology Applied*. London: Apprentice, 2002.

Gadbury, John. *Genethlialogia, or The Doctrine of Nativities Together with the Doctrine of Horarie Questions*. London: J. Cottrel, 1658.

Greene, Liz. *Relating*. London: Coventure, 1977.

Hand, Robert. *Horoscope Symbols*. Rockport, MA: Para Research, 1981.

Hyde, Maggie. *Jung and Astrology*. London: Aquarian/Harper Collins, 1992.

Jung, C. G. "Letter to Dr. B. V. Raman, 6th September 1947." *Astrological Journal*. Vol. 42, no. 4, July/August 2000.

Jung, Carl Gustav. *The Collected Works of* C. G. *Jung*. 21 vols. Edited by Herbert Read, Michael Fordham, and Gerhard Adler. London: Routledge & Kegan Paul, 1953–83.

Kroeger, Otto. *Type Talk at Work*. New York: Delacorte Press, 1992.

Lehman, J. Lee. *Classical Astrology for Modern Living*. Atglen, PA: Whitford, 1996.

Lilly, William. *Christian Astrology Modestly Treated of in Three Books*. London: T. Brudenell, 1647.

Myers, Isabel B. *Introduction to Type*. 5th ed. Oxford: Oxford Psychologists Press, 1994.

Phillipson, Garry, and Peter Case. "The Hidden Lineage of Modern Management Science: Astrology, Alchemy and the Myers-Briggs Type Indicatork." *Culture and Cosmos (A Journal of the History of Astrology and Cultural Astronomy)*. Vol. 5, no. 2, Autumn/Winter 2001.

Rudhyar, Dane. *The Astrology of Personality*. New York: Lucis Publishing Company, 1936. Reprint, Garden City, NY: Doubleday, 1970.

Tobyn, Graeme. *Culpeper's Medicine*. Shaftesbury, UK: (Element, 1997.

## TERPSICHORE

Terpsichore, asteroid 81 (the 81st asteroid to be discovered, on September 30, 1864), is approximately 122 kilometers in diameter and has an orbital period of 4.8 years. Terpsichore was named after the Greek muse of dance and choral song. According to Martha Lang-Wescott, Terpsichore represents flexibility, agility, dance, body language and gestures, and movement. Jacob Schwartz adds "disciplined physical exercise." This asteroid's key words are "movement" and "body ego."

**Sources:**

Lang-Wescott, Martha. *Asteroids-Mechanics: Ephemerides II*. Conway, MA: Treehouse Mountain, 1990.

———. *Mechanics of the Future: Asteroids*. Rev. ed. Conway, MA: Treehouse Mountain, 1991.

Schwartz, Jacob. *Asteroid Name Encyclopedia*. St. Paul, MN: Llewellyn Publications, 1995.

## *TETRABIBLOS*

The *Tetrabiblos* (literally, "four books") is the oldest existing systematic "textbook" of astrology. Its author, Claudius Ptolemy, is regarded as the father of Western astrology.

## Tetragon

Tetragon is an alternate, though rarely used, term for square, an aspect of 90°.

## Tezcatlipoca

Tezcatlipoca, asteroid 1,980 (the 1,980th asteroid to be discovered, on June 19, 1950), is approximately 6.2 kilometers in diameter and has an orbital period of 2.2 years. Tezcatlipoca was named after the dark god of Aztec mythology. J. Lee Lehman associates it with the dark side of life. Jacob Schwartz gives this asteroid's astrological significance as "the god of darkness, the anti-hero, those who take without giving."

**Sources:**

Kowal, Charles T. *Asteroids: Their Nature and Utilization*. Chichester, West Sussex, UK: Ellis Horwood Limited, 1988.

Lehman, J. Lee. *The Ultimate Asteroid Book*. West Chester, PA: Whitford Press, 1988.

Schwartz, Jacob. *Asteroid Name Encyclopedia*. St. Paul, MN: Llewellyn Publications, 1995.

## Therapeutic Astrology

Therapeutic astrology, or "astrotherapy," can be defined as the application of astrology to psychotherapy. More specifically, it is the attempt to integrate astrological principles with psychological concepts and practices, particularly as these relate to working with clients on an ongoing basis. As clinical psychology is concerned with the examination and treatment of patients, therapeutic astrology would be any form of treatment utilizing astrological precepts for the purpose of treating emotional and behavioral problems, removing or modifying existing symptoms, and promoting positive personality growth and fulfillment.

Just as there are many forms of psychotherapy, there are many forms of astrotherapy as well. Efforts have been made to integrate astrology with humanistic, Jungian, psychoanalytic, gestalt, psychosynthesis, object relations, and transpersonal therapies. There is, in short, no single form of astrotherapy. It is rather a general tool for fostering empathic understanding of the client's internal world.

Like an X ray of consciousness, a birth chart reveals the mental and emotional processes that constitute psychic structure. It assists the therapist in understanding the intrapsychic dynamics that underlay the presenting problem and so enables the therapist to better support the client's efforts at changing emotional, cognitive, and behavioral patterns. Because the language of astrology is symbolic, and thus without restricted meanings for its component variables, it can be translated into almost any psychological model or type of therapy.

### Astrology as a Diagnostic Tool

In its application to psychotherapy, astrology is primarily used as a diagnostic tool rather than as a form of treatment. Because every chart is unique, astrology functions as a diagnostic assessment device of unparalleled richness. Many therapists are beginning to use astrology as a diagnostic tool because of the advantages it presents over traditional psychological tests. Since it is based on an external frame of reference, the chart offers a character portrait that is entirely independent of test responses as occur on traditional psychological questionnaires, thus eliminating any possibility of response bias by subjects who might unconsciously wish to manipulate their scores. Whereas most diagnostic tests provide a flat, static profile based on a quantitative assessment of various personality attributes, astrology presents a qualitative assessment of psychic structure based on psychological processes in interaction (i.e., conscious and unconscious dynamics, areas of repression and conflict, pathways of sublimation, projection, and the like). Thus, the horoscope more closely approximates the psychic geography that therapist and client are exploring.

Because it is based on external referents that are observable and predictable, therapeutic astrology provides an objective reference point to balance the subjectivity of the therapeutic process. Whereas traditional tests are restricted to linear measurements that fragment the personality into a multitude of traits, motives, needs, factors, and scales, a horoscope depicts personality as the overall pattern of behaviors resulting from the unique organization of its underlying variables. Here, again, it is superior to devices that are limited to measuring parts of the personality because such assessments cannot offer an integrative picture of the whole person.

The dysfunctional extremes of zodiacal signs can be precisely correlated to some of the major diagnostic categories of traditional psychology. Generally, however, astrology does not reduce people down to preformed categories with pathological diagnoses. Rather, a chart enlarges one's sense of identity and creates a sense of possibility. Astrology suggests that the individual is not merely a consequence of multiple impinging factors, such as genetics or environmental conditions, but is a mirror of the living universe. The hermetic doctrine of the macrocosm and the microcosm provides the philosophical foundation of astrology and is a counterpart to the modern philosophy of holism. In this view, the psyche is not merely a whole for itself but is also a part of the greater whole that reflects it. Psyche is isomorphic with cosmos. This explains, in part, why human beings are capable of evolving toward communion with the source of individual existence.

Not only does astrology present a comprehensive portrait of the psyche in all its rich complexity, it is also capable of looking backwards into the past or projecting forwards into the future. Astrology is a diagnostic time machine that allows the therapist to gain access to psychological events that span the period from birth to death. For example, by examining the transits and progressions for any year of the life the astrologer is able to discern clues to traumatic events that might have occurred in early childhood, or project into the future and target periods when the individual is liable to face new crises. Such projections do not just predict a generic crisis, but a crisis of a specific type and duration. A chart assists the therapist in both diagnosis and prognosis, for where it symbolizes inborn conflicts, complexes, and areas of repression, it also points to latent potentials and areas (and times) of probable growth. In effect, the chart can be seen as a symbolic map of the process of self-actualization.

An astrological chart has one further advantage over traditional diagnostic schemes. While every assessment device is capable of describing the personality of its subject, traditional tests do nothing to illuminate the specific types of objects that the individual is likely to encounter. In astrology, however, each symbol of the chart is a corollary to both an intrapsychic process and an environmental condition. This means that a chart presents a portrait not simply of the individual, but of the individual in dynamic relation to an environment. Because subject and object define one another, the environment is seen as a reflection of the psyche to which it adheres. The advantage of such a conception is that it shows how interpersonal problems are precisely mirrored in intrapsychic structures. Astrological indications of interpersonal problems are not of a general type, but of highly specialized relations with potential marriage partners, children, authority figures, financial institutions, religious organizations, friends, employers and employees, and just about any other type of relation.

## Basic Needs and Psychopathology

The application of astrology to therapeutic practice can take many and varied forms. Whatever method one employs, however, an immediate advantage of astrology is that it provides a clear framework for understanding a client's needs. Each sign of the zodiac represents a fundamental human need or motivational drive. While all 12 signs are operative in consciousness, constituting the archetypal structure of the psyche, the signs the planets occupy show those needs that are going to be highlighted in the personality. The overall network of planetary aspects symbolizes cognitive structure—that relatively enduring organization of ideas, attitudes, and expectancies by which the individual interprets his world and directs his behavior.

If, for example, a person's Sun squares Neptune, the underlying needs that these planets rule are in conflict (square aspect). The need for validation (Leo) and the capacity for creative self-expression (Sun) are in conflict with the need to surrender ego in selfless service to the whole (Pisces/Neptune). This conflict will emerge into consciousness as a particular way of thinking, perceiving, and behaving. That is, the person may not *believe* that he or she deserves recognition; that others are *perceived* as more important, or disinterested, or invalidating; or that there can be an *expectation* that one will not be acknowledged or appreciated. On a behavioral level, the will is weakened, intentions are unclear, and there is likely to be a tendency toward self-sacrifice, self-sabotage, or self-delusion. The individual may likewise be deceptive with others. Duplicity or fraudulent behavior is a central feature of "the false self" that is characteristic of a Narcissistic personality disorder (i.e., the individual may overcompensate for his perceived deficiencies by developing a behavioral style that seems to say, "I'm special, wonderful, perfect, and superior while you [all other people] are nothing.") The signs that the planets occupy show the particular way this process is likely to unfold.

The point here is that beliefs are cognitive structures that emerge out of the relative integration of underlying needs, while behavior is the observable expression of these internal structures. By examining the client's birth chart, the astrotherapist is able to gain insight into the core ideas that underlie the presenting problem. Psychopathology can be seen as a product of grim, unconscious, pathogenic beliefs that result from a lack of integration of basic needs. These negative or false beliefs predict that the individual will hurt himself and/or others by his attempts to satisfy specific needs. Invariably, false beliefs are rooted in painful childhood relationships that offer the first, and thus prototypical, relational experiences that will later be recreated in adult life. These early formative experiences are the exteriorization of intrapsychic patterns that are symbolized by the birth chart. In other words, the pathogenic beliefs that develop in response to painful childhood experiences are symbolized by certain planetary configurations.

### Summary

Therapeutic astrology, or astrotherapy, is the application of astrological concepts to clinical practice. It presents a complex, multidimensional theory of behavior that depicts the psyche as a hierarchical structure comprised of archetypal needs, cognitive structures, emergent thoughts and behaviors, and corresponding events. It is also a powerful and flexible assessment device that allows the practitioner to discern clues to the formative experiences of childhood, gain insight into the meaning of current events, and target periods of future growth. Unlike traditional, event-oriented astrology, astrotherapy is not concerned with superficial trait descriptions or the prediction of future events. Rather, astrology is used to foster empathy for the client's internal world and thereby enhance the therapist's ability to effectively treat psychological problems, modify or remove existing symptoms, and promote positive personality growth and fulfillment. A birth chart accelerates the assessment phase of therapy by assisting in the formation of hypotheses regarding the patient's psychopathology. As a diagnostic tool, it provides objective information that may confirm, disconfirm, augment, or alter the therapist's subjective perceptions of intrapsychic structure.

—Glenn Perry, Ph.D.

**Sources:**

Perry, Glenn. *Essays in Psychological Astrology: Theory & Practice*. San Rafael, CA: Association for Astrological Psychology Press, 1997.

———. *Introduction to AstroPsychology: A Manual for Students & Teachers*. San Rafael, CA: Association for Astrological Psychology Press, 1998.

## Tibetan Astrology

The Tibetan system of astrology is a combination of Indian and Chinese methods, the greater and most essential (spiritual) part derived from the Chinese, and the technical element coming from the Indian system. The Indian or technical part (ephemerides, lunar tables, etc.) is called Kar-Tsi, and the Chinese, or spiritual part, is called Jung-Tsi.

The Tibetans, who are short on calculation ability, borrowed whatever planetary tables they use from the Indians, and do not depend upon these planetary ephemerides for much of their system. They make great use of the 12-year cycle of the animal signs plus the fivefold element sequence (wood, fire, earth, iron, and water) as used in the various forms of Chinese astrology (Jung-Tsi). The Kar-Tsi came from the Indian system, along with the Kalachakra system. The quintessential portion of the Indian system of value to the Tibetans is the division of the lunar month into 30 equal parts, called tithis in the Indian system.

Tibetan astrology is lunar-based, with the Sun (and all the planets) taking a secondary position to the Moon. One's Tibetan birthday is not the same as one's solar birthday (or yearly return), but is in fact the lunar phase-angle day on which one was born. Thus one's birthday would be celebrated on whatever day of the lunar month the birth took place.

Astrologers in general enjoy manipulating cycles and numbers. The Tibetans make up for their lack of planetary calculations with the manipulation of the various cycles they do use. In Tibetan astrology, numbers are counted forward, backward, and around in many different combinations. It is a complicated procedure that requires an astrologer. The net result of the Tibetan calculation is quite similar in effect or portent to western methods.

The chief exception to this generalization is the use of the lunar cycle in day-to-day life. It is here that the Tibetan system excels and has a great deal to offer Westerners, while in the West the awareness of the lunar cycle has largely been lost.

## Major Elements of Tibetan Astrology

The manipulation of the animal signs, elements, parkhas, mewas, etc., takes considerable skill in calculation and even more expertise in interpretation. What results is a somewhat complex system that claims to explain the status quo, but, like its Western counterpart, allows so much interpretation that firm conclusions can seldom be drawn.

It has been the view of Western observers that the East has a tendency toward fatalism and resignation to what fate has delivered to them. For instance, many Tibetan lamas and teachers are not particularly interested in astrology, outside of using the lunar cycle to plan and time events. To the Buddhist mind, personality makeup is not of great importance. For, no matter what that makeup, good or bad, the remedy remains the same: mind practice of one form or another. In fact, throughout the East, there is little interest in personality psychology as there is in the West. Those in the East have no need to flirt with the deeper areas of the mind, but have long ago been introduced to them, and take them as a matter of course. Keep in mind that reincarnation is the accepted belief system in both India and Tibet and, for that matter, the greater part of the world. A key belief of theirs is continuity of consciousness.

In the West, the awareness of cycles is not self-evident to the majority. Astrologers attempt to bring it to the public's attention, yet society has not come to such a conclusion, much less pushed toward a solution. Buddhist countries, long trained in the analysis of emotions and desires, have little interest in reexamining emotional and personality issues, which have been clarified in ancient times. Instead, the interest in expanding the awareness of the person (happy or sad) beyond such personal issues, and focusing on the root of problems and sufferings is assumed, beginning in childhood.

## Outline of Major Tibetan Techniques

Here are several of the major calculation techniques used by the Tibetan astrologer.

*Cosmic Tortoise Diagram*

*The Wheel of the Twelve Signs:* Century Birth Animal Table; Sign Polarity; Triangles (Thun-Sun); Opposites (Phung-Sun, Dun-Zur); Shi-Sey; Brief Sign Descriptions; Sign Power

*The Five Elements:* Relationship Table; Good, Friends, Filial, Antagonistic

*Major Life Factors:* Life Force; Power; Bodily Health; Luck; Soul

*Tibetan Yearly Calendar:* Months of the Year; Days of the Month; Hour of the Day

*The Eight Parkhas:* Four Good Directions; Four Bad Directions; Month's Direction; Descending Parkhas; Birth Parkha; Gu-Mik (9th Spot); Dur-Mik (Death Spot)

*The Nine Mewas:* The Magic Square; Birth Mewa; Descending Mewa; Daily Mewa; Nine Mewas Described

*Log-Men (not turning back)*

*Deu*

*Day of the Week Cycles*

*Lunar Related Data:* Lunar Day of the Month; Lunar Days for Travel; Losar

*Dar-Ghe*

*Lo-Khak*

*Shi-Shey*

*The Seven Obstacles*

*The Four Mewa Obstacles*

## Turtle's Head

Diagrams like the Turtle's Head are common in writings on Tibetan astrology. Often this diagram is shown drawn on the underside of what is called the Celestial Tortoise. This tortoise represents the universe of both China and Tibet. The upper shell is the dome of heaven, while on the underside is inscribed the essential elements of the astrological mandala. This diagram contains the wheel of animal signs, the elements, and directions/colors.

| Yellow | | | South | South | | | Yellow |
|---|---|---|---|---|---|---|---|
| | Earth | | Fire | Red | | Earth | |
| | | Dragon | Snake | Hare | Sheep | | |
| East | Wood | Hare | | | Monkey | Iron | West |
| East | Green | Tiger | | | Bird | White | West |
| | | Ox | Mouse | Pig | Dog | | |
| | Earth | | Water | Blue | | Earth | |
| Yellow | | | North | North | | | Yellow |

## The Wheel of the 12 Signs

The wheel of the animal zodiac is ancient, arising somewhere in central Asia, and later incorporated by the Chinese. The calendar used by the Chinese is said to have entered Tibet in the year 642 C.E. by way of the Chinese Princess Kong-jo, who married the first Buddhist king of Tibet.

The Tibetan wheel of 12 animals, with its 12-fold division, is similar to its Western counterpart, the zodiac. Unlike the West, where people's signs are determined by the solar calendar, in the East one's sign is determined according to the year of birth. The cycle of 12 animals rotates in strict succession from year to year. The order of the animals is Mouse, Ox, Tiger, Hare, Dragon, Snake, Horse, Sheep, Monkey, Bird, Dog, and Pig. Each animal sign has its own qualities, which are well-known to the general public. Animal sign and their corresponding birth years follow:

*Mouse:* 1900, 1912, 1924, 1936, 1948, 1960, 1972, 1984, 1996, 2008
*Ox:* 1901, 1913, 1925, 1937, 1949, 1961, 1973, 1985, 1997, 2009
*Tiger:* 1902, 1914, 1926, 1938, 1950, 1962, 1974, 1986, 1998, 2010
*Hare:* 1903, 1915, 1927, 1939, 1951, 1963, 1975, 1987, 1999, 2011
*Dragon:* 1904, 1916, 1928, 1940, 1952, 1964, 1976, 1988, 2000, 2012
*Snake:* 1905, 1917, 1929, 1941, 1953, 1965, 1977, 1989, 2001, 2013
*Horse:* 1906, 1918, 1930, 1942, 1954, 1966, 1978, 1990, 2002, 2014
*Sheep:* 1907, 1919, 1931, 1943, 1955, 1967, 1979, 1991, 2003, 2015
*Monkey:* 1908, 1920, 1932, 1944, 1956, 1968, 1980, 1992, 2004, 2016
*Bird:* 1909, 1921, 1933, 1945, 1957, 1969, 1981, 1993, 2005, 2017
*Dog:* 1910, 1922, 1934, 1946, 1958, 1970, 1982, 1994, 2006, 2018
*Pig:* 1911, 1923, 1935, 1947, 1959, 1971, 1983, 1995, 2007, 2019

These years are not measured from either one's birthday or from January 1 of any year. Instead, they are measured from the beginning of the Tibetan New Year, a fluctuating point that marks the new moon that is nearest to the beginning of February. It is important to note that on occasion, the start of the Tibetan and Chinese New Years differ by an entire month. The animal of one's birth year is central to both the Tibetan and Chinese systems of calculation and is the most common form of counting time. The 12-year animal cycle repeats itself from year to year.

The 12 animal signs are divided into male and female signs:

**SIGN POLARITY**

| Male Animal Signs | Female Animal Signs |
|---|---|
| Mouse | Ox |
| Tiger | Hare |
| Dragon | Snake |
| Horse | Sheep |
| Monkey | Bird |
| Dog | Pig |

## Animal Signs

Each of the Tibetan signs, like Western zodiac signs, has its own qualities. The following is a very brief description of the 12 signs as taken from some of the Tibetan manuscripts.

*Mouse:* The mouse is quiet. He is not friendly or outgoing and tends to be stable. He is not rough. Even though he does good to others, others do not seem to respond. On the outside, he is open and relaxed in appearance, but inside he is very strong and critical. Very open-mouthed, he says what he thinks. He is kind, but not generous. He misses the big opportunities, and takes the small ones. He is always searching.

*Ox:* The ox is a difficult person. He is hard to get to work, and is not obedient. He likes to sleep. He often exhibits bad behavior. While it is hard to change him, he is most often an agreeable person. However his slogan is "Don't mess with me!" He is very slow and does not care much if things are satisfactory or not. He postpones everything. He is good tempered. He likes to eat and sleep like a bull.

*Tiger:* The tiger is brave, active, and bright. Always proud and loyal to close relatives, he tends to have rough behavior and speech. He does a lot of thinking. He likes gambling and makes a good businessman.

*Hare:* "I am just for myself." The hare is independent and does not need or ask others for their help. "I can survive. There is much opportunity in the world to be enjoyed. I am satisfied with that." He tends to be indirect, devious, and possibly dishonest, but always skillful. He is stingy, but smiles and is generous on the surface. Possible diseases include those of the stomach and gall bladder.

*Dragon:* The dragon is neither brave nor active, but is good. He never does bad. "I am not very powerful, but nobody harms me." He does not make much effort, but also does not procrastinate or put things off. When the time comes, he does his duty. He has a short temper, but is good-minded. He is talkative. He listens to others talk. He has trouble containing himself. He has less disease than some of the other signs but if he gets sick, it can be serious.

*Snake:* The snake has a bad temper and is always burning his own mind stream. However, he has a good heart and is very optimistic or forward minded. Even if others are jealous of him, no one has the power to put him down. He can, however, destroy himself. He may have a somewhat rough character and can be mean. Once his mind is made up, he will not change it. He tends to diseases of the stomach and liver.

*Horse:* The horse is said to have miraculous power and is capable of great effort. Even though 1,000 enemies chase him, he cannot be defeated. His older life will be better than his youth. He listens to others. He likes horses. He is a fast walker and enjoys play. He has a self-sacrificing character and always helps others. He needs little sleep. His life has a lot of ups and downs.

*Sheep:* The sheep does not talk much and tends to be not too bright. He can be a rough character. He likes to eat. He causes others no harm, but does not sacrifice himself for them either. He is generally good-tempered and good-hearted. Always relaxed, he does not rush. He is not lazy, but cannot get things done on time. He does not show either like or dislike. He is a good provider.

*Monkey:* Monkeys are very smart, not very talkative, and tend to have bad tempers. They have lightweight, weak bodies. They are not always open-minded and are said to have "small" mind power. Not noted for their sense of responsibility, they like to play and enjoy themselves. Their words are not to be trusted and they talk, gossip, and tell lies too much—surface oriented. They look clean but tend to eat dirty things. Very ambitious, they always have great plans. They like to praise themselves.

*Bird:* It is easy for the bird to lose his possessions, legacy, inheritance. They are always advising others, but seldom take their own advice. Possessing a very strong sexual desire, they always need company. They like to be neat and clean, and do not require much sleep. They are prone to blindness. They love style, dressing up, and tend to smile a lot. They enjoy walking and stylish movement. Good with friends.

*Dog:* The dog is proud, mean, and somewhat wrathful. He cannot seem to get kindness from others no matter how hard he tries. He is self-interested, does only for himself, and never for others. His mind is always filled with lots of thoughts. He tries to do things right, but they tend to turn out bad or wrong. He likes meat. He is a fast walker. Very sexual. A traveler. He is high- or good-minded, and elegant people tend to like him.

*Pig:* The pig is not bright. He likes to eat but is not concerned with what type of food. He eats everything. He likes yoga. He has good self-discipline. Can be greedy and often takes advantage of others. He does not benefit himself. He lies. He has a big stomach. He is good with the good people, and bad with the bad people. He seldom smiles and is often mean. He can be a rough character.

## Triangles (Thun-Sun), Opposites (Phung-sun, Dun-Zur), and Shi-Shey

The Chinese call them the three friends, but the Tibetans call them the three destroyers. The triangles or Thun-Sun (three corners) are:

| | | | |
|---|---|---|---|
| 3 Friends = | Pig | Sheep | Hare |
| 3 Friends = | Tiger | Horse | Dog |
| 3 Friends = | Mouse | Dragon | Monkey |
| 3 Friends = | Bird | Ox | Snake |

## Dun-Zur

The worst or opposites (Dun-Zur, which means "seventh corner" or "opposite") are:

| Sign | Dun-Zur (Opposite Sign) |
|---|---|
| Horse | Mouse |
| Ox | Sheep |
| Tiger | Monkey |
| Hare | Bird |
| Dog | Dragon |
| Snake | Pig |

## Shi-Shey

Shi-Shey is the enemy of the fourth one. In addition, the fourth sign over from any given sign (either way) is called Shi-Shey and that is bad, too. The rest of the relationships of the signs are fine (e.g., triangles).

| Sign | Shi-Shey (4th Sign) |
|---|---|
| Snake | Monkey, Tiger |
| Horse | Bird, Hare |
| Sheep | Dog, Dragon |
| Monkey | Pig, Snake |
| Bird | Mouse, Horse |
| Dog | Ox, Sheep |
| Pig | Tiger, Monkey |
| Mouse | Hare, Bird |
| Ox | Dragon, Dog |
| Tiger | Snake, Pig |
| Hare | Horse, Mouse |
| Dragon | Sheep, Ox |

## Power of the Signs

The signs have different power or importance as shown in the following table. By far, the most important are the first four, which are similar to what are called cardinal signs in Western astrology. These signs rule the four major directions as follows: Tiger (east), Pig (north), Monkey (west), and Snake (south).

| Signs | Power |
|---|---|
| Tiger, Monkey, Pig, Snake | Best |
| Mouse, Horse, Bird, Hare | Next-best |
| Ox, Sheep, Dragon, Dog | Lowest |

## The Five Elements

The five elements are taken from the Chinese astrological system. Although somewhat similar to elements as used in Western astrology, the five elements of Eastern astrology are much more defined and depended upon. They are a major factor in

Tibetan astrology. Like the animals signs, the elements also rotate in strict sequence from year to year, but unlike the signs, each element holds for two years before changing. Thus, the elements and signs rotate in combination, the total cycle taking 60 years. The elements are: Wood (air), signifying long life, beauty, good or increasing energy, mental energy, changeable, and not stable; Fire, signifying strong, instant, hot, and warmth; Earth, signifying stable, strength, and ground; Iron, signifying strong, cutting, direct, weapon, changing (it is somewhat similar to earth); and Water, signifying soft, fluid, clear-seeing, flowing, and smooth (often connected to the blood and emotional concerns).

| Element | Color | Body | Function |
|---|---|---|---|
| Wood (Shing) | Green | Veins | Cause to Grow |
| Fire (me) | Red | Warmth, Heat | To Burn |
| Earth (SA) | Yellow | Flesh | Stabilize |
| Iron (Chak) | White | Bones | Hardening |
| Water (Chu) | Blue | Blood | Moistening |

Each year is assigned an element. These elements rotate in a particular order. Each year's element is the son of the previous year's element. In other words, the previous year is considered to be the mother of the following year.

The relationship table shown below is read as follows: Wood is the mother of Fire, Fire is the son of Wood, Water is the enemy of Fire, and Fire is Water's friend.

**Relationship Table**

| Mother | Friend | Son | Enemy |
|---|---|---|---|
| Wood is | Fire is | Fire is | Water is |
| Mother of Fire | Friend of Water | Son of Wood | Enemy of Fire |
| Wood | Fire | Wood | Fire |
| Fire | Water | Fire | Water |
| Earth | Earth | Earth | Earth |
| Iron | Wood | Iron | Wood |
| Water | Iron | Water | Iron |

## Element Relationship Pecking Order

There are preferred relationships between the elements. Mother is the best. Son is the next best. Friend is less important, but acceptable. Enemy is the least desirable. Certain elements go (or do not go) well together. Earth and Water are good, while Wood, Iron, and Fire (in combination) are not as good.

**Relationships**

**Good Relationship**

Water is the Mother of Wood
Iron is the Mother of Water
Earth is the Mother of Iron

Fire is the Mother of Earth
Wood is the Mother of Fire

**Friendly or Beneficial Relationship**

Earth is the Friend of Wood
Wood is the Friend of Iron
Iron is the Friend of Fire
Water is the Friend of Earth
Fire is the Friend of Water

**Neutral or Filial Relationship**

Fire is the Son of Wood
Earth is the Son of Fire
Iron is the Son of Earth
Water is the Son of Iron
Wood is the Son of Water

**Antagonistic Relationship**

Iron is an Enemy of Wood
Fire is an Enemy of Iron
Water is an Enemy of Fire
Earth is an Enemy of Water
Wood is an Enemy of Earth

## Major Life Factors

There are five major factors that are taken into consideration when examining the nature and qualities of a given calendar year. They are listed here in order of their importance:

| Major Life Factors | Tibetan Name |
|---|---|
| Life Force (holder of the life) | Sok |
| Power | Wang |
| Bodily Health | Lü |
| Luck | Lung Ta |
| Soul | La |

Regarding these major elements, the life force is the most important of them, for both sexes. It represents the life strength or *élan vital* (i.e., how one holds one's life). Then comes the power element, how one overcomes obstacles and achieves goals. This is of special interest for women. The function of power is spontaneous, instantaneous. Bodily health, physical health, or sickness is important for all. The luck element, also called "wind horse," is special for men, while soul, which is somewhat similar to the life force but more concerned with the emotional or psychological state, is not used very much. The life force is determined according to the following table. The left-hand column is the animal for the current year, while the right-hand column is the element for that year's life force.

| Current Year Animal | Life Force Element |
|---|---|
| Snake, Horse | Fire |
| Hare, Tiger | Wood |
| Mouse, Pig | Water |
| Monkey, Bid | Iron |
| Dragon, Sheep | Earth |
| Ox, Dog | Earth |

The power element will always be identical to the element determined for the current year. For example, 1991 is the year of the iron sheep. Therefore the power element for 1991 will be iron.

The luck element is determined according to the following table. The left-hand column is the animal for the current year, while the right-hand column is the element for that year's luck. (There is no earth element with luck element.)

| Current Year Animal | Luck Element |
|---|---|
| Tiger, Horse, Dog | Iron |
| Pig, Sheep, Hare | Fire |
| Mouse, Dragon, Monkey | Wood |
| Ox, Snake, Bird | Iron |

With bodily health, calculation is more complicated. First determine the key element:

| Current Year Animal | Health Key Element |
|---|---|
| Mouse, Ox, Horse, Sheep | Wood as Key |
| Tiger, Hare, Bird, Monkey | Water as Key |
| Dog, Pig, Dragon, Snake | Iron as Key |

Next, using this key element, take the power element (as calculated above, this will always be identical to the element determined for the current year) according to the following rules:

| If Power Element Is | Then Bodily Health Element Is |
|---|---|
| Son of Health Key Element | Water |
| Mother of Health Key Element | Wood |
| Enemy of Health Key Element | Earth |
| Friend of Health Key Element | Fire |
| Same Element Health Key Element | Iron |

The Soul Element is always the Mother of the Life Force Element. Use the Relationship Table to determine this.

## The Tibetan Calendar: The 12 Months of the Year

The months always start with the dragon month, which is the first month or Losar (Tibetan New Year), no matter what the year. Each month has an element that is calculated by taking the son of the year's element and making that element go with the first month's sign, Thus, 1988 is the earth dragon year, and the son of earth is iron; therefore the first month is the iron dragon month. Elements are used twice each, so the second month of the year will also be an iron month, and then two water months, and so on in rotation: iron, water, wood, fire, and earth followed again by iron, water, wood, fire, and earth, and so on. The beginning of the next year does not continue the rotation, but starts afresh.

In the earlier Tibetan system, which is still observed for certain calculations, the year started with the new moon *prior to* the Winter Solstice rather than Losar. That moment began the first month, which always took the sign of the tiger, with the other signs following in normal rotation. The elements also start with the calculation of power element for the element of the current year. That power element is then used.

### The Day of the Month's Sign and Element

Each day of the month depends on whether the month is a male (animal sign) or female month. (The male signs are mouse, tiger, dragon, horse, monkey, and dog; the female signs are ox, hare, snake, sheep, bird, and pig.) For all months that are under a male sign, take the tiger for the first day of the month and proceed in strict animal sign rotation to the end of month. For female months, take the monkey and proceed in animal sign rotation. Either way, the rotation ends at the end of the month and the next month's first day takes either the tiger or monkey as a starting point. The first day of the next month depends on the gender of animal sign, etc. The element for each day is derived by taking the son of the month's element (as described earlier). However, in the case of days, elements are used singly and not by twos (as in the case of the months).

### The Hour of the Day's Sign and Element

Start at sunrise and go for 12 hours by two-hour sections. The first two hours after sunrise belong to the hare and each two-hour section follows in strict animal sign rotation. As for the two-hour elements, take the son of the element for the day (described earlier) and use the elements in single rotation (one only, and not two each). Sunrise is determined, when there are no exact calculations, as the moment when the lines on the palm of one's hand can be seen.

### The I Ching Parkhas

Taken from the I Ching or Chinese Book of Changes, each day has a morning and evening *parkha* or trigram. Combined, these parkhas give a complete hexagram for that day that can be used to consult the I Ching.

**The Eight Parkhas (Trigrams from the I Ching)**

| | |
|---|---|
| Li | Fire and South |
| Khon | Earth (Southwest) |
| Dha | Iron and West |
| Khen | Sky and Earth (Northwest) |
| Kham | Water and North (Earth) |

| | |
|---|---|
| Gin | Mountain and Earth (Northeast) |
| Zin | Wood and East (Earth) |
| Zon | Wind and Earth (Southeast) |

## Parkhas: Month's Direction

The triangle of tiger, horse, and dog start on the first day of the month with Li. The triangle of mouse, dragon, and monkey start on the first day of the month with Kham. The triangle of bird, ox, and snake start on the first day of the month with Dha. The triangle of pig, sheep, and hare start on the first day of the month with Zin. The parkhas then follow in strict order, one for each day of the month.

| **Animal Signs for Month** | **Parkha for First Day of Month** |
|---|---|
| Tiger, Horse, Dog | Li, then Khon, Dha, etc. |
| Mouse, Dragon, Monkey | Kham, then Gin, Zin, etc. |
| Bird, Ox, Snake | Dha, then Khen, Kham, etc. |
| Pig, Sheep, Hare | Zin, then Zon, Li, etc. |

## Descending Parkha (Bap-Par)

The descending parkha for the current year is counted differently for male and female persons. For males, start with the parkha Li and count clockwise; females start with the parkha Kham and go counterclockwise. The count, in either case, is to the "agesign," or the number of years from birth to the current year, starting with the birth year as one. Thus, the agesign in 2003 for someone born in 1941 is 63. Once the descending parkha for the current year is determined, refer to the following table to determine the good and bad directions for that year.

### The Eight Parkhas and the Directions

| Cha-Lön | Pal-Key | Dre-Gna | Pal-Key | Cha-Lön | Lü-Chey | Dre-Gna | Lü-Chey | Cha-Lön |
|---|---|---|---|---|---|---|---|---|
| Nam-Men | Zön | Lü-Chey | Sog-Tso | Li | Dre-Gna | Nö-Pa | Khön | Pal-Key |
| Dü-Chö | Sog-Tso | Nö-Pa | Nö-Pa | Nam-Men | Dü-Chö | Sog-Tso | Dü-Chö | Nam-Men |
| Nam-Men | Sog-Tso | Nö-Pa | | South Fire | | Lü-Chey | Dre-Gna | Pal-Key |
| Cha-Lön | Zin | Dü-Chö | East Wood | | West Iron | Dü-Chö | Dha | Cha-Lön |
| Lü-Chey | Pal-Key | Dre-Gna | | Water North | | Nam-Men | Nö-Pa | Sog-Tso |
| Dü-Chö | Nö-Pa | Sog-Tso | Sog-Tso | Nam-Men | Dü-Chö | Nö-Pa | Dü-Chö | Nam-Men |
| Lü-Chey | Gin | Nam-Men | Pal-Key | Kham | Nö-Pa | Dre-Gna | Khen | Sog-Tso |
| Cha-Lön | Dre-Gna | Pal-Key | Dre-Gna | Cha-Lön | Lü-Chey | Pal-Key | Lü-Chey | Cha-Lön |

## Directions

There are four good directions: Nam-Men (sky healer), which is the best one and is particularly good for doctors; Sog-Tso (healthy life), which is the next best and good for sleeping (one should point his or her head in this direction); Pal-Key (generating, glorious), the third best, is the best direction from which to buy or obtain things; and Cha-Lön (bringing auspiciousness, prosperity), which is the fourth best, and is good for traveling.

The four bad directions are: Lü-Chey (body destroying), which is the worst direction and should be avoided; Dü-Chö (devil-cutting), which is second worst; Dre-Gna (five ghosts), which is third worst; and Nö-Pa (evil spirit), which is the least worst.

The four good directions are the good side or Zan-shi, while the bad side or four bad ones are Gnen-shi.

### Birth Parkha

The birth parkha is also important. To find the birth parkha, it is necessary to calculate the descending parkha for the mother of the individual for the year of the individual's birth.

### Gu-Mik (Ninth Spot)

The Gu-Mik, or ninth-eye spot, is calculated as follows: From the birth sign, every ninth sign is Gu-Mik. The parkha Gu-Mik, or ninth spot, with male persons is Li, which is not very good for that year and marks a transition. With females, the same is true for Kham. In addition, Mewa Gu-Mik is when the birth mewa is the same as the current year's mewa.

### Dur-Mik (Death Spot)

Dur-Mik, or death spot, is not as strong as the name suggests. Still, it portends a bad year, and is calculated as follows:

For signs Tiger and Hare, use descending Parkha Khon.
For signs Horse and Snake, use descending Parkha Khen.
For signs Bird and Monkey, use descending Parkha Gin.
For signs Mouse, Pig, Ox, Sheep, Dog and Dragon, use descending Parkha Zon.

If the descending Parkha of the current year is any of the above for the particular signs, then those signs have a year that is Dur-Mik, which is not particularly good.

### The Nine Mewas

*Mewa* means "mole" or "birth mark," and the nine mewas stem from a system of numerology used for centuries by the Chinese. It indicates a karmic relation from life to life. There are nine mewas, and they are often arranged in a so-called magic square that gives totals of 15, whichever way they are totaled up.

### The Magic Square

| Southeast | | South | | Southwest |
|---|---|---|---|---|
| | 4 | 9 | 2 | |
| East | 3 | 5 | 7 | West |
| | 8 | 1 | 6 | |
| Northeast | | North | | Northwest |

| Nine Mewas | Elements |
|---|---|
| 1 White | Iron |
| 2 Black | Water |
| 3 Indigo | Water |
| 4 Green | Wood |
| 5 Yellow | Earth |
| 6 White | Iron |
| 7 Red | Fire |
| 8 White | Iron |
| 9 Maroon | Fire |

These nine mewas are counted backwards starting with the wood-mouse year (1, 9, 8, 7, 6, etc.). An entire circle consists of three 60-year cycles. The current major cycle began in 1864 and will end in 2044 (1924 and 1984 were turning points). The 180-year cycle counts backwards until the year before the wood-mouse year in the third cycle, which is the water-pig year. At that point, the mewa for that year is made to be (2) black, thus making ready for the following year to be (1) white and the start of a new major cycle.

Any number can be put in the center of this diagram and the ascending numbers placed in the corresponding order.

### The Nine Magic Squares

| | | | | | | | | |
|---|---|---|---|---|---|---|---|---|
| 8 | 4 | 6 | 4 | 9 | 2 | 6 | 2 | 4 |
| 7 | 9 | 2 | 3 | 5 | 7 | 5 | 7 | 9 |
| 3 | 5 | 1 | 8 | 1 | 6 | 1 | 3 | 8 |
| | | | | | | | | |
| 7 | 3 | 5 | 9 | 5 | 7 | 2 | 7 | 9 |
| 6 | 8 | 1 | 8 | 1 | 3 | 1 | 3 | 5 |
| 2 | 4 | 9 | 4 | 6 | 2 | 6 | 8 | 4 |
| | | | | | | | | |
| 3 | 8 | 1 | 5 | 1 | 3 | 1 | 6 | 8 |
| 2 | 4 | 6 | 4 | 6 | 8 | 9 | 2 | 4 |
| 7 | 9 | 5 | 9 | 2 | 7 | 5 | 7 | 3 |

## The Nine Mewas (Karmic Relationships)

Here are some very rough translations as to the general meaning of the nine mewas. Traditionally, a birthmark is associated with each mewa, a probable length of life, a specific dharma practice, and mantra for that mewa.

*1 White:* The length of life is 71 years. There will be four difficult times during the life. A birthmark or mole is on the right side. Is left-handed. The practice involves obtaining a Chenresik statue (loving, kindness, and compassion) and practicing this sadhana. The mantra is: "Om mani padme hum." Either an only child, or only one child turns out useful and carries on the generation. He travels a lot. Good in social work, where others are benefited. If a male, then brave. If female, then a strong one.

Could have three children. Likes to move about here and there. Snakes are their protector. Difficult with children, meaning: not so good for the kids—things happen to them. Possessions and jobs are very unstable. He is bad tempered, but has a good mind. A difficult early life, but the longer the life, the better it gets. He is a clean person physically and likes white things like milk, butter, etc.

*2 Black:* The length of life is 61 years. There will be three bad periods. There is a birthmark on the right hand or arm, the heartside, or the neck. The practice is that of Vajrapani, which is strength and the clearing of obstacles. Become like the vajra—indestructible. Get a statue of Vajrapani or a stupa. Mantra: "Om vajra pani hum." If the child is first-born, it will be easy to care for him, an easy child. Is often sick when a child. He has nice speech, but a bad mind. He has a dark appearance, mean and horrible. Always sad. He tries to do good things, but no one likes him. If a monk or a member of the Bon religion, then he is a very strong practitioner. He likes meat and alcohol. He has many friends, whom he loves but seldom has an opportunity to be with them—and thus no result. If sick when an adult, will be hard to cure.

*3 Blue:* The length of life is 50 years. There are three difficult periods. There is a birthmark on the calf of the left leg. The suggested practice is that of Vajrasattva (dorje-sempa) practice. Vajrasattva purifies and removes the limitations, obstacles, and imperfections of the mind. Mantra: "Om vajra sattva hum." He likes to sleep. He has a strong mind, but there is much instability in his life. He is a little bit greedy. At work, he is not able to concentrate, and tends to skip around. If male, he will talk less, and if female will tend to be sad. He is difficult to change. Blame comes even if he does good things for others. He may have many wives (husbands) but no children. He will go to and die in another country. He may have paralysis.

*4 Green:* The length of life is 65 years. There are four difficult periods. On either thigh is a black circle birthmark. The practice is that of Vajrapani, which is strength and the clearing of obstacles. Become like the vajra—indestructible. Get a statue of Vajrapani or a stupa. Mantra: "Om vajra pani hum." He should avoid funerals. Cleanliness is very important; else the nagas (snakes) give a bad disease. He likes to travel. He has a deep mind, but is sometimes bad. Perhaps difficulty having children. If he has property, then farmland. The life is unstable, with a lot of ups and downs. There is sadness sometimes. People gossip about him. He does good things but others get the credit. He does not like to be lower than others, but finds little opportunity to rise. Whatever he has inside, stays with him. The nagas are his protector. He is a vegetarian with four children. No wedding.

*5 Yellow:* The length of life is 50 years. There will be two difficult periods. His birthmark is a certain nervousness. The suggested practice is that of Shakyamuni Buddha, called the diamond vehicle, cutting the vajra. Mantra: "Tadyata om mune mune mahamuni shakyamunaye swaha." This is a dharma person. This is also the astrologer's mewa. A monk's monk. He was a monk in the last life, reborn into a noble family in this life. Here is a very devoted person, with a stable mind. Very intelligent and religious. Obedient to his parents, he follows their customs or carries on their traditions. He does not travel much, or go far from his birthplace. He has a protector coming from his ancestors, whom he has ignored, and who is thus a little bit angry. He has strong dreams because his protector is angry. He is hard to please. Before becoming a monk, he was a saint, also a normal dharma teacher. He talks a lot, but often misses the point. He is very smart, a quick thinker. Should be a religious person in this life. He is restless, moving here and there. He has very high expectations of others. He always helps others, but they become his enemies. They gossip about him. He has five children. He has wealth in the form of property, houses, land. He will live long if he is religious. He is virtuous and educated. His possessions can be somewhat unstable. If female, he gets more gossip from others. If he is angry, it is difficult to please him. He has a good and stable mind. Tends to diseases of the gall bladder, heart attack.

6 *White:* The length of life is 70 years. There will be five difficult periods. There is a birthmark on the calf of the left leg. The practice suggested is that of the long-life (and purification) deity Vijaya Vsnisa (Tsuk Tor Nam Gyal Ma). Mantra: "Om amrita a yur dade swaha." He is intelligent. His mood and appearance are always changing. He travels a lot. If female, then will have nice speech, but the mind is not good. Receives protection from his own local deities. Possibly, he could be very poor. He will not be living near his birthplace, but instead, elsewhere. He will be able to build himself up greater than his parents. He is seldom sick, but if sick, he will be hard to cure. He has many relatives, none of whom offer him much help. There will be many enemies. He does good for others, but is still blamed. He will have three to five children. Children possibly handicapped. There is not much power in the family, but wife is powerful. He is quite bad tempered.

7 *Red:* The length of life is 80 years. There will be four difficult periods. A birthmark is on the backside or chest. The practice is that of tara (green Tara), and thus healing, protection, wealth, and a good birth. Mantra: "Om tare tuttare ture swaha." If female, then she likes to sleep. If married, it will not last long. He likes to fight, has a strong body and a ruddy complexion. Possibly may succumb from a sudden disease. Could die from his love of meat and similar things. His generation always shows suicide and murder. Seven children. The life very unstable.

8 *White:* The length of life is 50 years. There are three difficult periods. A birthmark is on the right cheek. The suggested practice is that of Shakyamuni Buddha called the diamond vehicle, cutting the vajra. Mantra: "Tadyata om mune mune mahamuni shakyamunaye swaha." He should avoid dirty things, stay clean. There is protection by local deities. He could go to another place from where born. Pleasant but proud. Good hands for arts and crafts. Older life will be better than younger life. He is religious and virtuous. Could have four to six children. Elegant people like him. The bad people do not like him. Could have a tendency to gossip, causing bad relations.

9 *Maroon:* The length of life is 73 years. There are five difficult periods. There are birthmarks on the face, neck, or left leg. Suggested practice is that of Manjushri, the development of the mind and intellect. Mantra: "Om ara patsa na dhi." An image of one holding seven glorious flowers in hands. If he keeps flowers well, then will be a very rich man. Could be proud or greedy. His older life will be better than young life. Very brave. He may well live other than where born. Wealth includes cows, animals,

livestock in general. Has to keep his wealth with care or obstacles could destroy it. This is a good mewa for females, but not for monks or Bon.

| Zon | | Li South | | Khon |
|---|---|---|---|---|
| | 4 | 9 | 2 | |
| Zin East | 3 | 5 | 7 | West Dha |
| | 8 | 1 | 6 | |
| Gin | | North Kham | | Khen |

## Birth Mewa

The birth mewa is calculated by counting backward using the current year's mewa in the center up to your agesign. Note that birth year here means the year as measured from the Tibetan New Year, which is approximately the new moon nearest February 1 of the year. The result is the birth mewa.

The current year mewa equals the birth mewa. If the current year's mewa is the same as the birth mewa, that is said to cause the current year to be a little difficult. This is also true for birth mewa and current year's descending mewa—if the same, then that year is not as good.

## Descending Mewa

Another much used calculation is the descending mewa. To calculate one's descending mewa, place the birth mewa in the center of the magic square and count from the center to the east (left) one number. Then, count counter-clockwise if the birth zodiac animal is a male sign and count clockwise if the birth zodiac animal is a female animal zodiac sign. Count to the age sign with the first count (the center) counting as number one. The result is one's descending mewa. When counting, always remember that in the Tibetan system, a person is one year of age at birth. So one is always added to one's Western age.

The meanings of the descending mewa for the current year are:

| | |
|---|---|
| 1, 8 | Iron, Good |
| 2 | Black, Bad (worst one) |
| 3 | Blue (not-so-good) |
| 4, 5 | Medium (5 is the astrologer) |
| 7, 9 | Almost good |

Good (in descending order of goodness): 1, 8, 6, 4, 5 (1 being best). Bad (in descending order of badness): 2, 3, 9, 7 (2 being worst).

## Mewa Daily

One can also calculate a mewa for each day of the lunar month. The following refers to the first day of the zodiac animal month. For example, the first day of the snake month:

The mewa 2, 5, and 8 are ruled by the Tiger, Monkey, Pig, and Snake. Start counting from (1) White.

The mewa 1, 4, and 7 are ruled by the Mouse, Horse, Bird, and Hare. Start counting from (4) Green.

The mewa 3, 6, and 9 are ruled by the Ox, Sheep, Dog, and Dragon. Start counting from (7) red.

These above mewa always occur with these signs. For the above signs, start counting with the indicated mewa, and count each day of the lunar month in a forward (1, 2, 3) direction. For example, the first day of a snake month would start with (1) White, and move forward.

## Log-Men (Not Turning Back)

Log-Men means not turning back or not coming back. This is calculated differently for males and females. For males, always start with the sign of the tiger and, for the element, take the son of the birth power element. Remember, each element is counted twice. The sign and element combination that corresponds to your age sign is the Log-men. Females start with the monkey sign and use the mother of their birth power element and count in reverse direction to the current agesign. That sign and element is their Log-Men.

For males, if Log-Men is the sign Dog then it is called Nam-Go (Door of the Sky), while if the sign is Pig then it is called Sa-Go (Door of the Earth). If Nam-Go, then it is important to avoid climbing, high places, etc., for that year. If Sa-Go, then avoid digging, foundation work, under ground, and the like for that year. For females, the sign of the Dragon marks Nam-Go and the sign of the Snake marks a Sa-Go year.

## Deu

This is a very integral part of the Tibetan astrology system, a means of awarding zeros (good marks) or X's (bad marks) for the current year to one's major elements: Life force, power, bodily health, luck, and soul. This is also part of Keg-Tsi, which is the yearly calculation of the life obstacles.

It is somewhat complex, but well worth working out. To begin, compare the major birth elements and those of the current year elements as follows. For example, using the power element, if the current year's power element is:

| | |
|---|---|
| Mother of my birth power | mark 000 (best rating) |
| Friend of my birth power | mark 00 (2nd best) |
| Son of my birth power | mark 0X (4th best) |
| Enemy of my birth power | mark XX (6th best/least good) |

It is important to calculate these for all of the major elements for each year.

## Days of Week

The day after the new moon is the first day of the month and whatever day of the week it is color the whole month with the tone or quality of the planet of that day (sun for Sunday, etc.). Also, the son of the first day's element is equally powerful for that whole month. The mother of that element is medium powerful, and the friend or enemy is bad for that entire month.

| Planet | Day | Element | Direction |
|---|---|---|---|
| Sun | Sunday | Fire | South |
| Moon | Monday | Water | North |
| Mars | Tuesday | Fire | South |
| Mercury | Wednesday | Water | North |
| Jupiter | Thursday | Wood | East |
| Venus | Friday | Iron | West |
| Saturn | Saturday | Earth | Southeast, Northwest, Southwest, Northeast |
| Rahu | All days | All elements | All directions |

Example: If Sunday is the first day of the month (as above), then every Sunday in that month is very powerful, but if Sunday is friend or enemy (or otherwise not very good), then it dampens the best day of the month.

Further, if the first day of the month falls on a Sunday, then the planet is sun, and the element fire. Therefore, the son of fire is earth, and earth is powerful for the month. The mother of fire is wood, so wood is medium powerful that month. The friend of fire is iron, and the enemy of fire is water. Fire and water are bad for that month.

## Day-of-the-Week Cycles

Depending upon the animal sign for the year of one's birth, three days of the week will have special significance. According to John Reynolds in his *1978 Tibetan Astrological Calendar*, "Days which are best and good are considered to be auspicious for undertaking projects, for doing business and similar activities; while days which are bad are considered inauspicious for any activity at all. In addition, birth on a good or best day indicates long life, while birth on a bad day portends an early death." Using the animal sign for the year of one's birth, enter the following table:

| Sign | Best | Good | Bad |
|---|---|---|---|
| Snake | Tuesday | Friday | Monday |
| Horse | Tuesday | Friday | Wednesday |
| Sheep | Friday | Monday | Thursday |
| Monkey | Friday | Monday | Thursday |
| Bird | Friday | Thursday | Tuesday |
| Dog | Monday | Wednesday | Thursday |
| Pig | Wednesday | Tuesday | Saturday |
| Mouse | Wednesday | Tuesday | Saturday |
| Ox | Saturday | Wednesday | Thursday |
| Tiger | Thursday | Saturday | Friday |
| Hare | Thursday | Saturday | Friday |
| Dragon | Sunday | Wednesday | Thursday |

## Lunar Days of the Month

Certain days of the month are auspicious and inauspicious for a given person. There are three favorable days each month, called foundation days, power days, and success days. There are also three unfavorable days, called obstacle days, disturbance days, and enemy days. In general, it is advised to begin things and take care of important business on the favorable days, and avoid such enterprises on the unfavorable days. The numbers in this table refer to the lunar days of the month for each sign.

| Animal | Foundation | Power | Success | Obstacles | Disturbance | Enemy |
|---|---|---|---|---|---|---|
| Snake | 13 | 12 | 6 | 8 | 9 | 9 |
| Horse | 17 | 12 | 6 | 20 | 5 | 27 |
| Sheep | 8 | 1 | 2 | 20 | 5 | 27 |
| Monkey | 8 | 1 | 2 | 9 | 10 | 17 |
| Bird | 14 | 7 | 25 | 3 | 11 | 24 |
| Dog | 9 | 27 | 5 | 11 | 3 | 12 |
| Pig | 2 | 8 | 11 | 26 | 3 | 12 |
| Mouse | 20 | 6 | 3 | 26 | 10 | 23 |
| Ox | 17 | 14 | 12 | 12 | 18 | 5 |
| Tiger | 5 | 27 | 9 | 14 | 12 | 3 |
| Hare | 7 | 27 | 12 | 26 | 25 | 18 |
| Dragon | 3 | 12 | 17 | 8 | 9 | 11 |

According to Reynolds in his *Calendar,* "When the monthly and weekly cycles oppose each other on the same day, the former is the more powerful due to the planetary energies, but nonetheless, they act together. If, during the monthly cycle, opposing forces manifest on the same lunar day, these two complement each other."

> Lunar days 1, 2, 26: Good for making offerings, requests of high personages, taking vows, religious practices, and, in general, the obtaining of something desired.
>
> Lunar days 3, 11, 20, 23: Excellent days for strong, firm actions; good for beginning construction or obtaining high offices.
>
> Lunar days 4, 13, 16, 25: Days of quickness, clarity, skill, and cleverness; indicative of success in competitions.
>
> Lunar days 5, 8, 17, 18: Very bad reaction days; unethical activities will succeed, moral action will not.
>
> Lunar days 1, 9, 10, 19, 24: Generally good for activities such as marriages, large purchases, collections, teaching, initiation, blessings, building, and ceremonies in general.
>
> Lunar days 2, 15: Barren. Many events will not occur. Neither good or bad for building, meditation practice, and certain ceremonies. Nothing should be undertaken between midnight and 3 A.M.

## Lunar Days for Travel

According to Reynolds's *Calendar*, certain lunar days are good (or not) for travel. Here is a list that he offers:

| | |
|---|---|
| Lunar days 1, 2, 3, 16, 17, 18: | Generally good |
| Lunar days 4, 19: | Unsuccessful |
| Lunar days 5, 20: | Good for business |
| Lunar days 6, 21: | One should not travel |
| Lunar days 7, 22: | Fine for travel |
| Lunar days 8, 23: | Disturbing for emotions |
| Lunar days 9, 24: | Success in covering long distances |
| Lunar days 10, 25: | Fruitful travel |
| Lunar days 11, 26: | Spiritual |
| Lunar days 12, 27: | Wisdom |
| Lunar days 13, 29: | Activity benefits one |
| Lunar days 15, 30: | One should not travel |

## Tibetan New Year: Lo-Sar

Lo-Sar (Tibetan New Year) is the nearest new moon to February first. If there are two new moons, then take the second one. Lo-Sar is the first sunrise after the new moon, the next day.

### Dar-Ghe (going up, increasing)

| | | |
|---|---|---|
| X | Worst (best of) | 1) Ug-len (first breath) |
| X | Worst (best of) | 2) Gnal-ney (conception) |
| 0 | Good (worst of) | 3) Lue-Dzog (Body Complete, full term) |
| 0 | Good (worst of) | 4) Tse-Pa (Birth) |
| 00 | Good (Medium) | 5) True-Jay (Bathing the baby) |
| 00 | Good (Medium) | 6) Goe-Gon (Putting on clothes) |
| 000 | Good (Best of) | 7) Ley-Jey (Working) |
| 000 | Good (best of) | 8) Gar-wa (Prime, full-filled) |
| XX | Bad (Medium) | 9) Gue-Pa (Decaying) |
| XX | Bad (Medium) | 10) Na-wa (Sick) |
| XXX | Worst (worst of) | 11) Shi-wa (Death) |
| XXX | Worst (Worst of) | 12) Dur-shug (Burial) |

In the above table, numbers three through eight are good and nine through twelve and one through two are bad. Numbers three and four are the worst of the good ones, five and six are medium good, and seven and eight are the best of the good. Likewise, numbers one and two are the best of the worst, nine and ten are medium bad, and eleven and twelve are the worst of the worst.

Note that the father's death year sign, if same as the current year, is not very good. If descending Parkha is the same for both husband and wife, this is also not very good. This is true of family members in general.

## Lo-Khak

One might expect that a year that has the same sign as one's birth year would be luck or auspicious. That is not the case in the Tibetan system. If one's birth sign and the current year sign are the same (every 12 years), then this is an example of Lo-Khak, which is very inauspicious. For men, the year before a Lo-Khak (termed Nang-Khah) is a little more difficult than the Lo-Khak itself; for women, it is the year after Lo-Khak (termed Chi-Khak) that is difficult.

During a Lo-Khak year, there are reputedly six months of particular danger when one is most vulnerable:

| | |
|---|---|
| Bird month | Second half very bad |
| Dog month | First half very bad |
| Pig month | Passable |
| Mouse month | Second half very bad |
| Ox month | Firsthalf very bad |
| Tiger month | Passable |
| Hare month | Second half very bad |
| Dragon month | Entire month very bad |
| Snake month | First half very bad |
| Horse month | Passable |
| Sheep month | Second half very bad |
| Monkey month | Entire month very bad |
| Bird month | First half very bad |

If the current year sign is the seventh or opposite of the birth sign, this is called Dun-Zur and is also bad. If the current year is the fifth sign (i.e., Dragon-Monkey), then this is also not good. If the current year is same element as the birth element, then this too is not very good.

## SHI-SHEY

Shi-Shey refers to the signs that are four up and back from the birth year sign. If the current year is either of these signs, then it is called Shi-Shey, which is not very good. Also, for the current year sign, count four up and four back and the months of that year with the same sign are called black months. If these months are Tiger, Monkey, Pig, or Snake, then the whole month is black, but the first ten days are the worst, the second ten days a little better, and the last ten days better still.

If the month signs are the Mouse, Horse, Bird, and Hare, then the days of the month from tenth through the twentieth are the bad ones. If the month signs are Ox, Sheep, Dog, or Dragon, then the last ten days of the month are bad. All days are calculated from the new moon. If the current year is Tiger, Monkey, Pig, or Snake and if the year's mewa is (2) Black, then the whole year is a black year.

## The Seven Obstacles

Quite a bit is made of the so-called seven obstacles. Each of these eventualities affects the entire current year, from Lo-Sar to Lo-Sar. In the following list, "Current year sign" refers to the animal zodiac sign for the current year.

If current year sign = One's birth year sign
If current year sign = Opposite one's birth year sign
If current year sign = Animal sign adjacent (either side) one's birth year animal sign PLUS the same element as one's birth year element. (For example, Snake has Dragon and Horse on either side.)
If current year sign = One of three Destroyers (Friends)
If wife and husband have same descending Parkha for the current year
If current year animal sign = Sign for the year father or grandfather died
If descending Parkha = Birth Parkha

—Michael Erlewine

**Sources:**
Erlewine, Michael. "Lunar Gaps." *Matrix Journal* (1990).
———. "Science and the Lunation Cycle." *Matrix Journal* (1990).

## Tibetan Astrology: Lunar Gaps

The lunar cycle has been observed for ages. The moon, from a Sanskrit term for measure, is the primary means by which the majority of the people in the world measure time and their own lives. Eastern and western astrology use the lunar cycle in the same and different ways. In the West, the lunar cycle is seen as a key to the personality and the birth chart. Although books like Dane Rudhyar's *The Lunation Cycle*, William Yeats's *A Vision*, and many others describe the cycle as a dynamic process that unfolds each month, their focus is more with individual snapshots (the various lunar types) taken from the overall process. The emphasis in the West has been individual birth charts that represent the various lunar phase types.

In contrast, the East seldom mentions the individual birth chart. Their primary interest is in the dynamics of the lunation cycle itself, which they divide and analyze in great detail in order to make use of the opportunities it offers for day-to-day decision-making. In other words, in the East, the lunar cycle is used as a means to determine the kind of activity appropriate for each successive lunar day. This amounts to a form of electional astrology.

In the West, electional astrology is thought of as a means to pick an appropriate time in the future for a particular ceremony or happening. Eastern astrology does the same thing, but it also uses electional astrology as a guide to day-to-day personal living and practice. In India and Tibet, it is the lunation cycle rather than the yearly sun or solar cycle that is the primary indicator used for planning activities and for personal guidance. In other words, in the East they live by and follow the cycle of the Moon.

A very clear illustration of this idea is the fact that, in most eastern countries, birthdays are observed according to the particular day of the moon cycle (lunar phase angle) during which a person was born, rather according to the solar return as in the West. Moreover, due to the fact that lunar months do not fit conveniently within the solar year, a birthday in the East for any given individual can be up to a month away (during some years) from the solar return—one's birthday in the West. This simple fact makes it clear how important the moon and the lunar cycle are in these countries. A study of the existing literature on the meaning and use of the moon in astrology (East and West) shows much similarity but also considerable difference.

There is general agreement (in both East and West) about the nature of the lunation cycle, in that it somehow proceeds from some sort of seed time at the new moon to a fruition at the full, and so on. This is the archetype of a cycle and can be compared to any other cycle such as the circle of the astrological houses or the zodiac itself. If this is done, then the new moon is made equivalent to Capricorn (and the tenth house), while the full moon is similar in cycle phase to Cancer (fourth house).

The Moon receives more attention in Eastern astrology. And it is not just a matter of increased emphasis; there are major qualitative differences in approach. The emphasis is seldom on the type of individual that typifies a given lunar phase. Instead, it is on analyzing the entire lunar cycle in order to take advantage of its ongoing opportunities—using the moon cycle for living. This Eastern approach is very practical.

What interests Eastern astrologers are the opportunities available to them in the monthly lunar cycle. They use the lunar cycle as a way to gauge and measure their life. They have learned how to take advantage of opportunities they have discovered within the lunation cycle. This is an important concept to grasp. These lunar opportunities are sometimes referred to as gaps or openings in the otherwise continuous stream of one's life our lives—windows. They conceive of these gaps as articulation points, much like an elbow is where the arm is articulated. They are natural joints or gaps in time/space upon which time and space turn and through which it is sometimes possible to gain access to information about the larger, dynamic life process that already encapsulates humans.

From a reading of the Eastern literature on this subject, one gets the sense that life is perceived as (on the average) being filled with the noise of one's problems (obscurations), making clear insight often difficult. These obscurations can be many and their accumulation amounts to the sum total of one's ignorance—that which is ignored.

Therefore, in Eastern astrology, these articulation points or windows in time/space are very much valued. In fact, Eastern astrologers analyze the lunar cycle, in minute detail, in order to isolate these moments (gaps in time/space) where insight into one's larger situation can be gained. Much of so-called Eastern religion amounts to a scheduling of precise times for personal practice or activity built around the natural series of gaps that can be found in the continuous lunar cycle. In its own way, it is a very scientific approach. In the East, they have been astute observers for many centuries.

In India and Tibet, the 29.5-day lunar synodic cycle is divided into 30 parts, called tithis. A tithi or lunar day is the time it takes for the aspect between the sun and Moon (elongation, angular separation) to reach a multiple of 12°. Thus each tithi is 12° of solunar angular separation. (Each tithi is further subdivided into two parts, called karanas; this additional subdivision finds wide use in India, Tibet, and other Eastern countries. However, the division of the lunar cycle into 30 parts or lunar days generally suffices.)

The way tithis are measured in Tibet is as follows. The moment of the new moon (0° angular solunar separation) marks the end of the 29th lunar day and the start of the 30th. The 30th lunar day or tithi ends at 12° of solunar separation, and the first lunar day begins. And so it goes, on and around.

In India, the moment of the new moon (0° angular solunar separation) marks the end of the 30th lunar day and the start of the first. The first lunar day or tithi ends at 12° of solunar separation, and the second lunar day begins.

Just as in the West, much is made of the new and full moon days. In fact, in many countries they do not have Saturday and Sunday off. Instead, new and full moon days are considered holy days (holidays), and normal routines are suspended at these times.

It seems that, although East and West agree on the importance of new and full moons, there is less congruence in terms of the quarter moons. In the West, the lunar quarters are next in importance after the new and full moon times. However, in the East, there are other days that are considered of greater importance, such as the 10th and 25th lunar days.

In both traditions, there is agreement that the two or three days preceding the moment of the new moon are difficult ones, which require special observation. In the West, these days have been called the dark of the Moon, or devil's days, days when the darker forces have power. Both traditions affirm a survival of these final days each month. The three days before a new moon can be a hard time. The East is in total agreement on this point, and the days prior to a new moon are set aside for invoking the fierce dharma protectors, those energies that ward off harm and act as protection during the worst of times.

In particular, the 29th day (the day before new moon) is called dharma protector day. It is a time given over to purification and preparation for the moment of the new moon. Ritual fasting, confession of errors, and the like are common practices. In a similar vein, the days just prior to the full moon (the 13th and 14th) are also days of purification, days in which the various guardian and protector deities are again invoked, but in a somewhat more restrained way. For example, the 14th day is often given over to fire puja—a ritual purification. In summary, during days prior to full and new moon, there is some attempt at purification, both physical and mental, in preparation for those auspicious events.

It is clear from the literature that the times of the new and full moon are considered of great importance. These days are set aside for special rituals and worship. Full and new moon (full more than new) are times of collective worship and public confession. In many traditions, the monks and priests assemble for a day of special observance. In the East, the full moon celebration and the entire waxing lunar fortnight are oriented to the masculine element in consciousness, called the father-line deities. The new moon and the waning fortnight are given over to the mother-line deities and the feminine element. The full moon completes the masculine, or active, waxing phase of the cycle, and the new moon completes the feminine, waning phase of the month. This kind of analysis does not exist in the West.

Aside from the new and full moon, the two most auspicious lunar days in the East are the 10th and the 25th. The 10th day (120° to 132°), called Daka Day, is considered auspicious for invoking the father-line deities—the masculine. The 25th day (300° to 312°), called Dakini Day, is given over to the feminine principle and the mother-line deities, in general. These two days, the 10th and the 25th, are formal feast days, days of observation when extra offerings are made and increased attention given to what is happening. There is some sense of celebration at these points in the month. In many respects, these two days even rival the new and full moon days in importance. The fact is that these four days (new, full, 10th, 25th) are the primary auspicious days as practiced in many eastern rituals.

There are many other days of lesser importance, which might also interest western astrologers. Health and healing are important in eastern ritual, and the 8th and 23rd days of the lunar month are auspicious for this purpose. These are the days that straddle the first and last lunar quarters. The 8th day (96° to 108°) is often called Medicine Buddha Day. Again this occurs in the male, or father-line, half of the month. The 23rd day (276° to 288°), occurring in the feminine half of the month, is dedicated to Tara practice. Tara is the female deity connected to health, long life, and healing in general.

The most prominent days given over to purification are the 13th and the 29th. In addition, on a lesser scale, the 9th and the 19th days are also noted as days when the protector deities should be invoked and kept in mind. These, too, are days of purification. And there are more, still finer subdivisions that are made.

How might this Eastern approach to the lunation cycle be of value in the West? A major fact is that the lunar cycle is perceived as having a variety of gaps, joints, or points of articulation that can be used. They can be seen as chinks in the armor of one's particular obscurations. Many Western mystery traditions also observe the times of the full (and sometimes the new) moon. Full-moon meditations are common. The quarter moons are given less attention, and few Western rituals exist for these events.

It is an intuitive fact that moments of clarity and insight (gaps) do come in the course of living. What Eastern astrology seems to suggest is that many of these gaps are not just random, haphazard events that occur in life. They are regular opportunities, joints in the nick of time, when insights are somehow more possible than at other times. Therefore, it is common practice to set aside some portion of these special days for observance, for meditation.

It is unfortunate that the concept of meditation entertained by the public in the West amounts to a type of relaxation therapy or quiet time. This is far from the truth in India, Japan, Tibet, and other Eastern countries. In fact, meditation is a form of observation of what is and of what is happening in one's mind and environment. When the Eastern mind meditates on special lunar days, it sets aside a time to observe with great care the nature of that particular day. Meditation as taught in Tibet and Japan is a technique that increases one's abilities to observe. Unlike in the West, the meditator is not lost in deep inner space; in the East, the meditator is right here, now, observing the mind and life.

Westerners are beginning to learn these techniques of observation. By setting aside a time on these special lunar days for observation, one can be open and aware to the possibilities of insight. This kind of awareness appears to be what is required to pick up on these natural events. If one has an insight at one of these times, one might be more willing to give it credence, knowing that it is happening on a certain a lunar day.

It is clear from Eastern teachings that the moments of full and new moon are times when the various channels in the psychophysical body are somehow aligned. This is not to say the new- or full-moon days are days of peace and quiet. Easterners are taught that, although such a day may tend to be wild or hectic, any patience or forbearance will be much rewarded. In other words, there can be deep insights available at these times. According to these same teachings, an eclipse at the full or new moon is even more auspicious. In the teachings, it is said that, during these very special events, both male and female energies (channels) are in simultaneous alignment—the ultimate opportunity. The lunar cycle and its effects and opportunities have been analyzed in great detail in the Eastern teaching.

—Michael Erlewine

## Tiger

The Tiger is one of the 12 animals of the Chinese zodiac. It refers to one of the 12 earthly branches that are used in Chinese astrology, together with the 10 heavenly stems. Such a branch designates one day every 12 days: the days are named according to a sexagesimal (60) cycle, made of 10 series of 12 branches.

The Tiger radiates gifts, luck, and often beauty. He is a remarkable leader, with a liking for grandeur and a lot of style, but he lacks elementary self-control: he does not like half-hearted people and he proves to be rather explosive. Proud, he fiercely enjoys his independence; he is rebellious and madly reckless. Extremely demanding, he cannot stand treachery. He has a thirst for adventures and exploits. His passionate attitude often borders on self-destruction.

—Michele Delemme

## Toro

Toro, asteroid 1,685 (the 1,685th asteroid to be discovered, on July 17, 1948), was named after the Spanish word for bull. Its orbital period is somewhat more than 1.5 years, and its diameter is 7.5 kilometers. Toro is one of the more recent asteroids to be investigated by astrologers. Preliminary material on Toro can be found in Demetra George and Douglas Bloch's *Astrology for Yourself*, and an ephemeris (table of celestial locations) for Toro can be found in the second edition of George and Bloch's *Asteroid Goddesses*. Unlike the planets, which are associated with a wide range of phenomena, the smaller asteroids are said to represent a single principle. George and Bloch give Toro's principle as "the power of boundless strength"; their tentative key phrase for Toro is "my capacity to use and control power." Zipporah Dobyns hypothesizes that Toro may resonate with the meaning of Taurus, attracted to comfort, beauty, and sensuality, and characterized by a strong will and potential power struggles. Jacob Schwartz gives the astrological significance of this asteroid as "using and controlling power, machismo, using intimidation, competitiveness, and physical work."

**Sources:**

Dobyns, Zipporah. *Expanding Astrology's Universe*. San Diego: Astro Computing Services, 1983.

George, Demetra, with Douglas Bloch. *Asteroid Goddesses: The Mythology, Psychology and Astrology of the Reemerging Feminine*. 2d. ed. San Diego: Astro Computing Services, 1990.

———. *Astrology for Yourself: A Workbook for Personal Transformation*. Berkeley, CA: Wingbow Press, 1987.

Lehman, J. Lee. *The Ultimate Asteroid Book*. West Chester, PA: Whitford Press, 1988.

Schwartz, Jacob. *Asteroid Name Encyclopedia*. St. Paul, MN: Llewellyn Publications, 1995.

## Transit

Transit, from the Latin *trans*, meaning "across," "beyond," or "over" plus *ire*, meaning "go," has two related astrological meanings. The first simply identifies planets that are moving across the sky, in contrast to planets positioned in a birth chart (or in other kinds of horoscopes). For example, a given individual's natal Mercury (Mercury's position at birth) is at 25° Aquarius, whereas transiting Mercury is moving through the early degrees of Sagittarius. One can also talk about a planet's transit (movement) through a given sign or house.

The second meaning of transit refers to a method of predicting conditions on the basis of the interaction between transiting planets and one's natal chart (birth chart). Secondary progressions, the other method of prognostication most in use among contemporary astrologers, entails finding a person's age—say, 40 years—and moving the planets and house cusps of the natal chart to the positions they occupied the same number of days after birth as the individual's age in years, in this case, 40 days. An oversimplified but nevertheless useful generalization is that transits indicate external conditions, whereas progressions indicate inner development (in the sense of changes in one's personality). Thus, transits are used to predict future environments, and progressions are used to predict inner changes. For readings, astrologers often erect a chart that has three concentric circles; the inner circle contains the natal chart, the intermediate circle contains what is referred to as the progressed chart, and the outer circle records the positions of the transiting planets for the time of the reading. This tripartite chart allows the astrologer to view the interactions between the various levels at a glance.

The transiting planets exert generic influences that affect everybody. Thus, the period during which Mercury (which is associated with communication and concrete thinking) is retrograde (appears to move backward in its orbit), for example, is not a good time for anyone to sign contracts. However, when astrologers discuss transits, they usually have in mind the interaction between the planets currently moving through the heavens and the planets in a particular person's natal chart. A natal chart is a bit like a two-way template that shows how a person views the universe as well as how the universe affects the individual. The positions that the planets occupied at the person's birth, in other words, remain sensitive spots that respond to the transiting celestial bodies making aspects to them. Say, for example, that an individual's natal

Mercury (the position Mercury occupied at birth) is 10° in the sign Capricorn. Furthermore, transiting Neptune (a planet that is associated with, among many other things, delusion and foggy thinking) is moving over the person's Mercury, while simultaneously making inharmonious aspects with other planets. For the period this transit is in effect, this individual should refrain from signing contracts. In this situation, unlike the case of retrograde Mercury, the advice is particularized for one person rather than for everybody.

The transiting planets also affect a person according to the house through which they are moving. Thus, for example, a transit of Jupiter (which embodies the principle of expansion and good luck) through the tenth house (career and public standing) would be, unless other transits dictate the contrary, a good period for a businessperson to undertake a business expansion. The length of time a transit has an effect varies according to the relative speed of the planet. Jupiter, for example, usually takes about a year to cross through an average-sized house, giving the hypothetical businessperson in this example a year to take advantage of Jupiter's transit through her or his tenth house. By way of contrast, the Moon transits a house in 2 or 3 days, whereas Pluto takes 15 years.

**Sources:**

Hand, Robert. *Planets in Transit: Life Cycles for Living*. West Chester, PA: Whitford Press, 1976.

Lunstead, Betty. *Transits: The Time of Your Life*. York Beach, ME: Samuel Weiser, 1980.

Sasportas, Howard. *The Gods of Change: Pain, Crisis and the Transits of Uranus, Neptune and Pluto*. London: Arkana, 1989.

## Translation of Light (Borrowed Light)

A translation of light occurs when a transiting planet is separating from an aspect with one planet while simultaneously applying an aspect to another. The transiting planet briefly connects the two planets (which may otherwise not be in aspect with each another), imparting the influence (the "light") from the planet from which it is separating to the planet to which it is applying. For example, say that in an individual's natal chart, Mars is at 12° Aquarius and Venus is at 24° Aquarius. As the transiting Moon reaches 18° Aquarius, it is separating from a conjunction with Mars and applying a conjunction to Venus. While thus in between conjunctions, the Moon is said to be translating (imparting) the light (the energy) of Mars to Venus.

**Sources:**

Bach, Eleanor. *Astrology from A to Z: An Illustrated Source Book*. New York: Philosophical Library, 1990.

Lee, Dal. *Dictionary of Astrology*. New York: Paperback Library, 1969.

## Transpluto

Of the many hypothetical planets postulated by astrologers, the one most likely to have an empirical existence is Transpluto, so called because, if discovered, it would be found beyond the orbit of Pluto. This hypothetical planet has been called by many different names—Persephone, Isis, Minerva, and Bacchus, to name a few—but Transpluto is its most commonly accepted designation. Many astrologers have been attracted by the idea of one or more transplutonian planets, because their discovery would allow astrologers to complete the transferral of sign rulerships that has been in progress since the discovery of Uranus: In the premodern system of sign rulerships, each of the traditional planets ruled two signs apiece, while the luminaries (the Sun and the Moon) each ruled one sign. As the outer planets were discovered, the rulerships of Aquarius, Pisces, and Scorpio were gradually transferred to Uranus, Neptune, and Pluto, leaving Saturn, Jupiter, and Mars as the rulers of Capricorn, Sagittarius, and Aries. Only Mercury and Venus are still viewed as ruling two signs each.

Because of the attractiveness of a balanced system in which 12 heavenly bodies rule 12 signs, twentieth-century astrologers have often speculated that two new planets would eventually be discovered and come to be accepted as the rulers of Virgo and Libra. In particular, it has been speculated that the hypothetical planet Vulcan, which some astronomers said could be found between the Sun and Mercury, is the ruler of Virgo, while Transpluto has been thought to rule Libra. The abandonment of the notion of an intramercurial planet by astronomers has also tended to call into doubt the notion of an extra-Plutonian planet, and some contemporary astrologers have begun to put forward certain asteroids as candidates for the rulerships of Virgo and Libra.

Neptune was discovered by astronomers who used perturbations in the orbit of Uranus to calculate the position of a transuranian planet. Its position was determined mathematically by a Frenchman as well as an Englishman, and German astronomers were actually able to locate the new planet. In a similar manner, some astrologers believe they have enough data to plot the orbit of a transplutonian planet, and more than one ephemeris has been published (Transpluto has even been incorporated into chart-casting programs). The most significant astrological publication in this area is John Robert Hawkins's book *Transpluto, Or Should We Call Him Bacchus, the Ruler of Taurus?* which includes an ephemeris as well as preliminary delineations for Transpluto's house positions, sign positions, and aspects. *Transpluto, Or Should We Call Him Bacchus* has generated enough interest to merit three printings, but the transplutonian planet is still outside the astrological mainstream and will undoubtedly remain so until astronomers definitively establish its existence.

**Sources:**

Corliss, William R. *The Sun and Solar System Debris: A Catalog of Astronomical Anomalies*. Glen Arm, MD: The Sourcebook Project, 1986.

Hawkins, John Robert. *Transpluto, Or Should We Call Him Bacchus, the Ruler of Taurus?* 1976. Reprint, Tempe, AZ: American Federation of Astrologers, 1990.

## TRECILE

A trecile (also called a tresile) is a minor aspect of 108°. Some astrologers place it in the family of aspects created by subdividing a circle into 10 parts (36°, 72°, 108°, 144°, etc.). It could also be regarded as a quintile (72°) and a half and is thus related to that family of aspects. It is given an orb of influence of 1 to 2°.

## Trine

A trine is an aspect of 120° between two points—such as two planets—in an astrological chart. This soft aspect is traditionally regarded as harmonious and beneficial, although too many soft aspects combined with too few hard aspects is regarded as unfortunate because people with this chart pattern do not usually experience enough of life's hard edges to develop strong character. It is sometimes referred to as the aspect of good fortune. Trines indicate an easy flow of energy between two planets. Thus, for example, an individual with a natal trine between Mercury (which represents the mind) and Uranus (which rules, among other sciences, astrology) would have a natural aptitude for understanding astrology.

**Sources:**

Gettings, Fred. *Dictionary of Astrology*. London: Routledge & Kegan Paul, 1985.

Hand, Robert. *Horoscope Symbols*. Rockport, MA: Para Research, 1981.

## Triplicity (Trigon)

Triplicity refers to a group of three, usually three signs of the same element—the fire triplicity, Aries, Leo, and Sagittarius; the earth triplicity, Taurus, Virgo, and Capricorn; the air triplicity, Gemini, Libra, and Aquarius; and the water triplicity, Cancer, Scorpio, and Pisces. Sometimes it is also used to refer to groups of three houses. The traditional term for triplicity is trigon, which comes from the Latin transliteration of the Greek word for triangle (when, on the wheel of the zodiac, lines are drawn so as to connect all the signs of the same element, the resulting figure is a triangle).

## Tripod Pattern

A tripod pattern is a horoscope arrangement in which the planets are organized into three distinct clusters. Ideally, each cluster forms trine aspects with the other two clusters.

## Tropical Signs

The tropical signs are Capricorn and Cancer. The term tropical comes from the Greek *tropos*, meaning "to turn." As the Sun enters these signs during the summer and winter solstices, it appears to reverse its direction (to "turn" around) in its gradual movement north or south of the equator.

## Tropical Year

The tropical year (also called the solar year, the seasonal year, the natural year, the equinoctial year, and the astronomical year) is the time it takes the Sun to go from one spring equinox to the next—365 days 5 hours and 48 minutes. Because of the precession of equinoxes, the equinox point changes slightly (when looked at against the background of the stars), making a tropical year shorter than a sidereal year (a "star" year) by a little more than 20 minutes.

## Tropical Zodiac (Moving Zodiac)

The tropical zodiac, also called the moving zodiac, is the familiar circle of 12 signs that begins at 0° Aries (the point where the Sun is located at the spring equinox). Because of the precession of equinoxes, the equinox point changes slightly so that each year it moves farther and farther back when looked at against the background of the stars. The net effect of this movement is that the signs no longer correspond with the constellation after which they are named, and at this time the tropical sign Aries begins near the beginning of the constellation Pisces. The antonym of tropical zodiac is sidereal zodiac, which refers to the zodiac constituted by the actual constellations. The sidereal zodiac is used in Hindu astrology, and also by a few Western astrologers.

**Sources:**

Bach, Eleanor. *Astrology from A to Z: An Illustrated Source Book*. New York: Philosophical Library, 1990.

Brau, Jean-Louis, Helen Weaver, and Allan Edmands. *Larousse Encyclopedia of Astrology*. New York: New American Library, 1980.

## Turi, Louis

Louis Turi was born and raised in Provence, France. He studied engineering from the FPA college at home while singing and playing in a band. In 1973, he moved to England to pursue his dream to become a pianist. In 1976 he received the highest distinction Musicianship Award Cup and graduated from the Royal School of Music in London. He then worked as a recording artist.

Turi moved to the United States looking for an opportunity to promote his musical career. He started his new life with less than $50 in his pocket. Later he received an ASME section 9 nuclear welding test certification and worked on the U.S. Naval Base in San Diego, California, and Pearl Harbor, Hawaii, while pursuing his passion to fly helicopters.

Turi's life took a sharp turn in 1990 when the U.S. economy, real estate, and construction fields went down. This was his opportunity to turn to his real passion, the stars. He became a full-time astrologer. In 1991 he received a metaphysical doctorate from the Light Institute in Sacramento, California. Disappointed with the conventional jargonized astrology, he spent the last few years, rekindling and practicing the Seer's rare divine astrology method, which he calls astropsychology.

Turi now teaches and counsels people from all walks of life. He has appeared on numerous radios and television shows. In 1999, he launched his own publishing company, Startheme Publications, Ltd. He lectures all over the world.

## Tyche

Tyche, asteroid 258 (the 258th asteroid to be discovered, on May 4, 1886), is approximately 68 kilometers in diameter and has an orbital period of 4.2 years. It is named after the Greek goddesss of fortune and personification of luck and indicates good luck and a fortunate outcome to activities undertaken in matters associated with its sign and house position. A prominent Tyche in a natal chart signals a lucky person.

**Sources:**

Kowal, Charles T. *Asteroids: Their Nature and Utilization*. Chichester, West Sussex, UK: Ellis Horwood Limited, 1988.

Room, Adrian. *Dictionary of Astronomical Names*. London: Routledge, 1988.

Schwartz, Jacob. *Asteroid Name Encyclopedia*. St. Paul, MN: Llewellyn Publications, 1995.

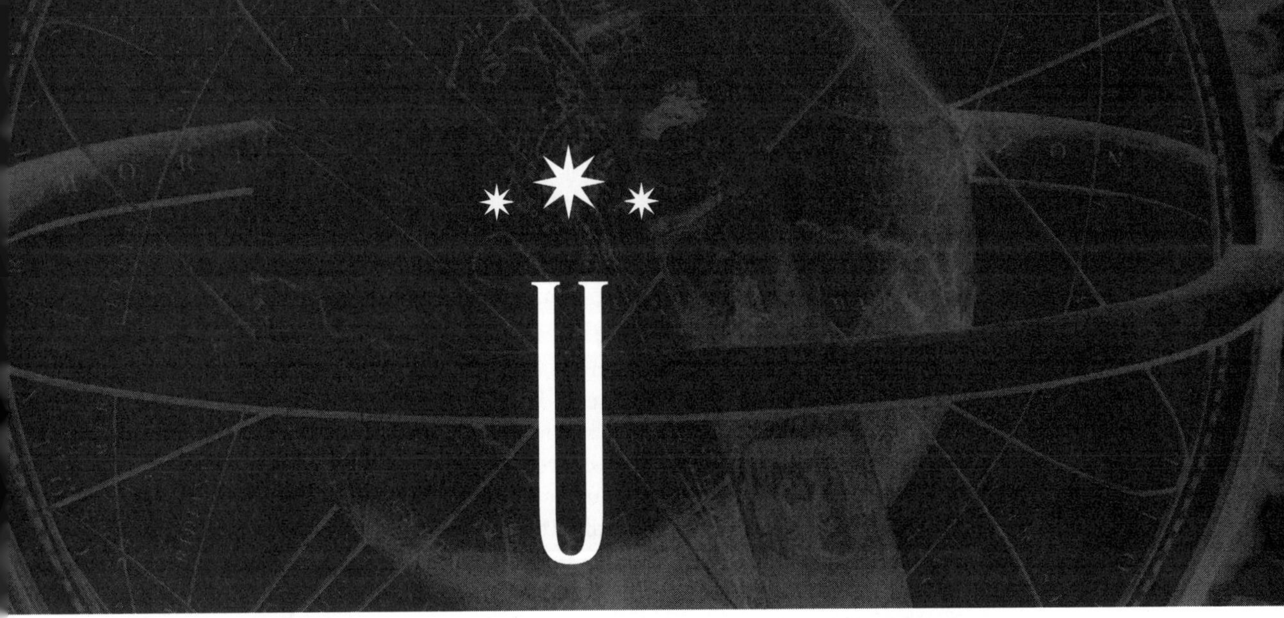


## Ultimate Dispositor

A planet is the dispositor of other planets when they are located in the sign ruled by the first planet. For instance, if both Pluto and Venus are in the sign Leo, then the Sun, the ruler of Leo, is the dispositor of Pluto and Venus. In some charts, a chain of dispositors (e.g., the Sun is the dispositor of Pluto and Venus, while Saturn is the dispositor of the Sun, and so on) can be traced all the way to a single planet that is the final or ultimate dispositor of every other planet in the chart. Such a planet is regarded as having an especially strong influence over the entire horoscope.

## Upaya (Remedial Measures)

Remedial measures are a cornerstone of Vedic astrology. The very first words of the most widely recognized classical work on Indian astrology, *Brihat Parashara Hora Shastra,* are an invocation to Lord Ganesha, the deity for removal of obstacles. This places upaya at the focal point of the Vedic astrology tradition. Scattered through the text, and indeed the texts of most of the classical works of Jyotish, are verses giving methods for relieving the obstructions and suffering caused by various astrological combinations.

The notion that a natal chart is a blueprint for this life that can be improved upon through remedial measures necessitates an understanding of the concept of karma. Jyotisha is not exclusively oriented either to fate or to free will and the resolution of this often hotly debated dichotomy lies in a proper understanding of the different categories of karma and how they integrate into the reality of an indivisible whole.

The Sanskrit word *karma* means "action" or "activity" and by implication refers to the effects that are inherent in any activity or action. Most Westerners have a narrower notion of karma as accrued past actions rather than seeing it as an ongoing process.

The total of karma garnered over many incarnations is known as Sanchita (amassed) karma. This is not knowable or readable in the birth chart of any specific incarnation. The portion of karma that is to be dealt with in a particular lifetime is known as Prarabdha (fructifying) karma. Prarabdha karma is linked to the concept of fate. However, human beings have volition, which is known as Kriyamana (initiated) karma. Humans also have the ability to plan and contemplate actions in the future, known as Agama (impending) karma.

When an astrologer looks at a natal chart only, it is Prarabdha karma that is being assessed. Chart patterns should be understood not only in terms of the areas of life and timing that may be involved but also their intensity. We can understand Prarabdha karma on three levels. If the chart pattern shows a particular area of life to be obstructed in a way that is repeated using multiple techniques of analysis, this is a form of Prarabdha karma known as Dridha (firm) karma. If there are obstructions but also some influences that are helpful, the situation can be described as Dridha-Adridha (firm-unfirm) karma. Chart patterns that do not show any clear pattern or direction for a particular area of life can be described as Adridha (unfirm) karma.

The astrologer should accurately assess the karmic patterns to understand whether the karma is very firm with respect to an issue. In this way proper remediation counseling and recommendations can be set forth commensurate with the intensity of the obstruction indicated.

There is an unending array of upayas, both traditional and contemporary. The most widespread traditional approaches to remediation involve rituals to connect with the Divine, the giving of charity in prescribed ways and service (seva) that is usually specific to the issues in the chart situation.

## Yagyas

Most of the religions of India and indeed almost all human societies involve some kind of ritual. It can be elaborate and performed in a temple or similar setting, or simple and performed privately between a person and the symbol of the Divine for that individual. In the Hindu and Vedic tradition, specific rituals (yagyas or yajnas) are at the heart of the recommendations of the astrologer. Yagyas can be performed on all scales. Some are mind-boggling pageants rivaling analogous spectacles anywhere in the world. These were the rituals of ancient times done for kings who embarked on missions of fame and glory involving power and empires. Even today in India, there are large-scale ritual performances involving hundreds of priests, elephants, horses, etc.

For most individuals seeking remediation, yagyas are on a different order of magnitude. However, there is still a wide range of options available. The power of the yagya increases with the number of repetitions of the sacred sounds prescribed to alleviate the problem in the chart. Therefore, depending on the intensity of the affliction and the financial commitment of the person for whom the rite is being performed, a yagya can last for many days with many priests chanting or take place in a few hours with one priest responsible for the ritual.

In contemporary times, especially in the West, yagyas are performed without the person being present. Westerners often arrange to have them done in India though there are many qualified priests in the West who can perform these ceremonies as well. There are differences of opinion as to the efficacy of a small yagya with the subject present as compared to a larger one in abstentia.

Yagyas are generally comprised of puja and homa. Puja, which is also a ritual in its own right, involves prayers and offerings to a representation of the deity that is being worshipped and/or applied to for relief. Homa is a Vedic fire ceremony in which various symbolic items and mantras are offered into the fire. The fire is the vehicle that carries the offerings to the deities of the planets or whatever aspect of creation is being addressed. Appropriate prayers and chants are part of the performance.

## Mantras

The use of mantras in the yagyas and in an ongoing personal practice is another cornerstone of the recommendations for remediation of an astrological indication. It is well known that sound is a physical vibration. Saying a word couples this physical vibration with a mental intention that gives it energy. In the Vedic tradition, sound is the first manifestation of creation. This is mirrored in the New Testament as well with the phrase "In the beginning was the Word, And the Word was with God and the Word was God."

For the purposes of astrological remediation, Bija (plural) or "seed" mantras are often prescribed. Each planet has an associated Bijam (singular) mantra. These are extremely powerful and proper pronunciation, as with all mantras, is vitally important. The name of the planet can also be used as a mantra when potentized by adding "Om," and "Namaha," words giving respect or reverence. An example for Jupiter would be "Om Gurave Namaha."

Other Vedic mantras specific for each of the planets are more elaborate and very powerful as well. Additionally, there are mantras, verses, and chants for the corresponding deities that are associated with each of the planets that are also prescribed.

Because of the power of mantras, it is important that mantras are prescribed that specifically suit the individual by someone who understands the tradition or the mantras should be suitable for anyone and have no adverse effects even if not pronounced perfectly.

Properly prescribed yagyas and mantras are considered safer forms of remediation than those modalities by which a planetary influence is strengthened, such as wearing gemstones. If the wrong gem prescription is given, one may unwittingly cause an adverse effect by making the "wrong" planet more powerful. This can occur even with an expert gem recommendation if, for example, the birth time is incorrect. There is no corresponding problem with mantra and yagya since these are modalities that propitiate and ask for grace.

## Charity

The classical texts of Hindu astrology prescribe the giving of certain articles, animals, precious metals, etc., for particular planetary combinations. This is considered a propitiation of the planets, causing a problem in the chart.

### Service (Seva)

Performing service is another highly effective way of obtaining relief and grace from a difficult chart pattern. In many ways, this is the safest and perhaps most emotionally satisfying form of remediation. Even if a wrong birth chart is being used, performing a service for uplifting humanity can only have positive outcomes.

In the West, there is a tendency to want to buy one's way out of a difficult situation. In this respect, gems and even yagyas alone can be considered too expeditious to constitute true commitment to changing a negative pattern. However, when one allots some of his or her precious time giving service to another and sustaining that service over time, there is a powerful reorientation that inevitably takes place.

Seva is universally applicable to all cultures, times, and societies. People who are disinclined to perform any ritual or chant mantras can easily find an avenue of service to fulfill the astrological recommendations. The astrologer's interpretation of the talents latent in the chart and the archetypes of the planets involved in the obstructive combinations can give rise to a myriad of possibilities for seva that can be very pertinent and meaningful to the individual.

—Penny Farrow

**Sources:**

Parashara, Maharishi. *Brihat Parashara Hora Shastra*. Vol. I. New Delhi, India: Ranjan Publications, 1989.

## URANIA

Urania, asteroid 30 (the 30th asteroid to be discovered, on July 22, 1854), was named after the Greek muse of astronomy. Its orbital period is 3⅔ years, and its diameter is 94 kilometers. Urania is one of the more recent asteroids to be investigated. Preliminary material on Urania can be found in Demetra George and Douglas Bloch's *Astrology for Yourself*, and an ephemeris (table of celestial positions) for it can be found in the second edition of George and Bloch's *Asteroid Goddesses*. Unlike the planets, which are associated with a wide range of phenomena, the smaller asteroids are said to represent a single principle. George and Bloch give Urania's principle as "inspired knowledge." Zipporah Dobyns speculates that the meanings of Urania are related to those of Uranus, namely, seeking of freedom, the need for variety, intellectual openness, etc. The late John Addey regarded Urania as the ruler of astrology (which Uranus is usually said to rule); he found it prominent in the charts of astrologers. J. Lee Lehman associates it with science (perhaps even "the muse of science"), particularly with the ability to take a range of data and translate them into intelligible form.

**Sources:**

Dobyns, Zipporah. *Expanding Astrology's Universe*. San Diego: Astro Computing Services, 1983.

George, Demetra, with Douglas Bloch. *Asteroid Goddesses: The Mythology, Psychology and Astrology of the Reemerging Feminine*. 2d ed. San Diego: Astro Computing Services, 1990.

———. *Astrology for Yourself: A Workbook for Personal Transformation*. Berkeley, CA: Wingbow Press, 1987.

Lehman, J. Lee. *The Ultimate Asteroid Book*. West Chester, PA: Whitford Press, 1988.
Schwartz, Jacob. *Asteroid Name Encyclopedia*. St. Paul, MN: Llewellyn Publications, 1995.

## URANIAN ASTROLOGY

The Uranian system of astrology, also known as the Hamburg School of Astrology, had its origins in the early part of the twentieth century. Alfred Witte (1878–1943), the founder of the system, was a renowned astrologer in Germany as well as a surveyor. He and his student and colleague, Friedrich Sieggrün (1877–1951), were members of the famed Kepler Circle. During World War I, Witte tried to use the prevailing astrological methods of his day to time battles. He found these methods to be quite lacking, and it was during this time that he developed his revolutionary way of looking at astrology. After the war, he introduced these ideas to his contemporaries in the Kepler Circle. Witte's Uranian astrology is differentiated from other schools of Western astrology by a variety of factors, including the use of dials, the cardinal axis, hard aspects, midpoints, symmetry, and the eight hypothetical planets, as well as its concentration on six personal points and their houses.

Witte postulated that the character and destiny of a person are not solely determined by the aspects between the planets but are seen primarily through the symmetry of the planets. Planets are in symmetry when their arc openings are equal. One of the main tenets of the system states that planets that have equal differences (arc openings) also have equal midpoints and equal sums. These completed symmetrical planetary arrangements are called planetary pictures. A planetary picture may be expressed in the following ways: Planet A + Planet B – Planet C = Planet D; Planet A + Planet B = Planet C + Planet D; Planet A – Planet C = Planet D – Planet B; and, finally, (Planet A + Planet B) / 2 (midpoint of A and B) = (Planet C + Planet D) / 2 (midpoint of C and D).

For example, Planet A, Mars, is at 13° Gemini; Planet B, Jupiter, is at 19° Sagittarius; Planet C, Venus, is at 25° Taurus; and Planet D, Saturn, is at 7° Capricorn. Except for a wide opposition between Mars and Jupiter, these planets would at first seem to be unrelated. However, they actually work in tandem because of their symmetrical relationship. Using whole circle notation we see that:

A + B – C = D
Mars (73) + Jupiter (259) – Venus (55 degrees) = Saturn (277)
A + B = C + D
73 + 259 = 55 + 277
A – C = D – B
73 – 55 = 277 – 259
(A + B) / 2 = (C + D) / 2
(73 + 259) / 2 = (55 + 277) / 2

The system also investigates sensitive points, which are expressed in a similar fashion to Arabic parts, i.e. A + B – C. When these points are completed by a natal, transiting, or solar-arc-directed planet, the completed symmetrical picture is formed. Though many people believe that the system uses thousands of points, in fact, the experience practitioner looks only for these completed symmetrical relationships.

These symmetrical relationships are most easily seen using a rotating dial. Most Uranian astrologers use both the 360° dial and the 90° dial. Some use dials of other harmonics as well, most notably, the 45° and the 22.5° dial. The 360° dial divides the zodiac into 12 30° segments according to sign. The 90° dial divides the circle by four so that all of the cardinal signs are placed in the first 30° of the dial, the fixed signs are posited in the second 30° segment and the mutable signs are found in the last 30° of the dial.

On a 360° dial, there are arrows marking 0° of the cardinal signs and a marking, usually a large dot, indicating 15° of each of the fixed signs. These eight points are collectively referred to as the cardinal axis or the eight-armed cross. In essence, these markings divide the 360° circle by eight. These special markings, therefore, also indicate the hard aspect series, i.e. the opposition, square, semi-square, and sesquiquadrate. There are additional markings on most 360° dials as well as a marking for each segment of 22.5° (sixteenth harmonic aspect). The soft aspects, semi-sextile, sextile, trine, and quincunx are also easily viewed on the dial by using the sign boundaries. Therefore, the dial is not only a tool for examining symmetry, but it is a wonderful aspectarian as well.

Uranian astrologers use the cardinal axis or eight-armed cross to represent the world at large. With the pointer on the cardinal axis, the astrologer looks for planets symmetrically arranged around the axis or in aspect to the axis. When the midpoint of two planets falls around the 0° Cancer / 0° Capricorn axis, they are said to be in antiscia. The use of antiscia is not unique to Uranian astrology, but finding antiscia using the 360° dial is. Contra-antiscia, symmetry around the 0°Aries / 0° Libra axis, is also easily visible using the dial. But Uranians take antiscia even further and examine the symmetry or midpoints of planets around 15° Leo/Aquarius and Taurus/Scorpio. Not only is this technique useful in describing world events on a particular day or place, but the position of the planets at birth relative to this eight-armed cross can also be used to describe the unique connection of the individual with the world at large. After all, the planets are constantly moving in relationship to one another, and they thereby define the course of human history in the broadest sense as well as in everyday ways. How a person fits into this universal, ever-changing rhythm is quite elegantly defined in how the planets were arranged around the cardinal axis at their specific time and place of birth.

In fact, the cardinal axis is the first of the personal points of the Uranian system. It is the outer personal point that represents our connection to the world in general. The second outer personal point is the ascendant. This point describes how a person relates in their immediate surroundings and it rules the place. The third outer personal point is the Moon's node. Through this point, one may examine a person's intimate connections, those that are of a karmic variety.

The next three personal points are considered inner personal points. The first is the Sun, representing the will and ego of the individual. The Sun also rules the day. The Moon is the second inner personal point, representing the emotions of the individual. The Moon also rules the hour. The last of the inner personal points is the MC. The MC represents the person's unique individuality, soul, or spirit of the individual. It rules the moment or minute.

One popular misconception about Uranian astrologers is that they do not use houses. In fact, the seasoned Uranian astrologer uses six house systems for each of the personal points. The Meridian house system is probably the most important of the six since it represents the native's point of view. This house system is divided along the equator rather than the ecliptic and, therefore, the houses are more or less equal in size. The first house of the Meridian system is also known as the equatorial ascendant and describes how the person sees himself. The point known as the ascendant may actually fall in the twelfth house of the Meridian house system.

The Earth horoscope, or houses of the Earth, have 0° Cancer as the tenth house or MC, and 0° Libra on the first house. Therefore, a person with Sun in Sagittarius would have the Sun in the third house of the Earth. The Earth horoscope represents the Earth and the generality; it is how the person operates in the world.

The ascendant is the first house of the ascendant horoscope. Subsequent houses occur at equal 30° intervals. The ascendant horoscope represents the person's connection to their environment and how he or she operates in a specific locale.

The Sun horoscope is found by using the Sun as the fourth house cusp. Subsequent houses occur at equal 30° intervals. The Sun horoscope represents the physical body as well as the relationship to the father.

The Moon horoscope is found by using the Moon as the tenth house cusp. Subsequent houses occur at equal 30° intervals. The Moon horoscope describes the emotional life of the individual as well as the mother.

The node horoscope is found by using the node as the first house cusp. Subsequent houses occur at equal 30° intervals. The node horoscope represents the intimate or karmic connections.

The hypothetical, or "trans-Neptunian" planets, are probably the most controversial aspect of the system. However, after the discovery of Neptune, it was very much in fashion for astronomers to postulate the orbits and existence of new planets. The orbits of the planets were derived by looking back through events and charts and filling in the missing threads. Witte proposed the first four planets, and he and Sieggrün proposed the second four. The planets are: Cupido, Hades, Zeus, Kronos, Apollon, Admetos, Vulcanus, and Poseidon. The fastest of the eight, Cupido, moves slightly more than 1° per year. The slowest, Poseidon, moves about ½° per year. The planets and their meanings are:

*Cupido:* rules marriage, family, groups, society, the arts, cliques, and clannishness.

*Hades:* represents poverty, suffering, garbage, filth, secrets, loneliness, decomposition, antiquity, and service in the highest or lowest sense.

*Zeus:* signifies fire, weapons, the military, machinery, conception, creativity, purposeful action, drive, and obsessions.

*Kronos:* rules authority, government, rulers, nobility, mastery, independence, anything above average, superiority.

*Apollon:* symbolizes great success, expansion, multitudes or the many, open spaces, peace, commerce and trade, science, great intellect, and the "big picture" as opposed to the details.

*Admetos:* symbolizes the beginning and the end (the wheel of life), endurance, depth, focus, specialization, the few, raw materials, real estate, standstill, death, and blockages.

*Vulcanus:* represents great strength, power, mighty forces, fate, destiny, control issues, and violent eruptions.

*Poseidon:* symbolizes enlightenment and wisdom, the life force, spirituality, light, universality, mediumistic, visionary, and the intellectual.

All major astrological software programs contain Uranian astrology tools. Based on the speculative orbits of the Uranian planets, the Solar Fire, Kepler, and Win*Star programs will all locate these hypothetical planets in an astrological chart.

—Madalyn Hillis-Dineen

**Sources:**

Booher, Wayne, Gary Christen, and Arlene Nimark. Various articles. *National Council for Geocosmic Research Journal* (Winter 1991–92).

Simms, Maria Kay. *Dial Detective: Investigation with the 90 Degree Dial.* San Diego: Astro Computing Services, 1989.

## Uranus

Uranus is our solar system's seventh planet, orbiting between Saturn and Neptune at an average distance of about 1.75 billion miles from the Sun. Since it is 20 times further away from the Sun than Earth, it takes Uranus 84 Earth years to travel around the Sun. The blue-green planet also has a day of a little more than 17 hours, 7 hours shorter than an Earth day. The way in which this planet travels is unusual and even eccentric. Rather than rotating on an axis that is perpendicular to the plane of its orbit, Uranus spins on its side with its south pole facing the sun. It also rotates from east to west, the opposite direction of Earth and most other planets.

The third largest planet in our solar system, Uranus is about four times the size of Earth. It is 30,000 miles in diameter, compared to Jupiter's 85,000-mile diameter. As with all gas planets, Uranus has very faint rings around it made up of large chunks of rocky material. Since the rocks are dark in color, the rings cannot be viewed well from Earth. Uranus also has more than 20 moons. The five largest were named for characters in the plays of William Shakespeare and Alexander Pope: Miranda, Ariel, Umbriel, Titania, and Oberon.

Uranus was the first planet to be discovered by an astronomer. Earlier sightings had been made—John Flamsteed first recorded it in 1690—but it had been cataloged as a star. William Herschel spotted Uranus on March 13, 1781, and named the planet Georgium Sidus for George III, the king of England at that time. Many simply called the planet Herschel, after its discoverer. By the mid-1800s the agreed-upon name of Uranus came into common usage, which Bode had proposed as more consistent with the mythological names of the other planets.

The Greek god of the heavens, Uranus was an early supreme god who was the son and mate of Gaia, the creation goddess. An unpredictable, creative, and tyrannical god, he ate his children so they could not usurp his power in the future. He was father of the Titans, of which Cronus (Saturn) was one, and predecessor to the Olympian gods. On Gaia's bequest Cronus castrated Uranus and forced him to release the other children from his stomach, thus usurping his father's power after all.

As the first known planet beyond Saturn, the discovery of Uranus caused something of an upheaval in traditional astronomy and astrology circles. In addition, the timing of Uranus's discovery coincided with the independence revolutions of America and France and the industrial revolution in England. These disruptions of intellectual and political circles gave astrologers reason to believe that Uranus represented rebelliousness, disruptive influences, breaking away from traditional patterns or rules, as well as concern for humanity and brotherhood, progress, and inventiveness. Hence, it was suggested that Uranus ruled or coruled the zodiac sign of Aquarius.

In twentieth-century western astrology Uranus was given rulership of Aquarius, though traditionally and that role belonged to Saturn. Uranus is classified as an outer planet (outside of Saturn's orbit) and stays in each sign of the zodiac for seven years, and is thus considered to have a generational effect. Therefore, assigning rulership of a sign exclusively to an outer planet, including Uranus, is not as simple or appropriate as twentieth-century astrologers had hoped it might be. In light of discoveries from cross-cultural astrological studies and ancient texts, recently translated into English, which make apparent the logic behind Saturn's rulership of Aquarius, it appears more reasonable to continue using the traditional seven planet rulerships of the zodiac signs. However, it can be generally agreed upon that the newly discovered planets can add additional meaning as corulers of signs. Hence, Uranus is the coruler of Aquarius, along with Saturn as its main indicator.

In the Saturn world of the material and the structured, Uranus represents the rejection of rules that no longer serve us and the installation of a new paradigm that sees through the illusion of Saturn's limits. It is the crack in the cosmic view and it is the leap forward into the unknown led by intuition and inspired ideas. Uranus brings the sudden force that tears down unneeded walls so that something newer and better can be built from its foundations. Uranus is associated with humanity, ideals, eccentricity, philanthropy, originality, creative inspiration and genius, but also with chaos, accidents, disasters, antisocial behavior and radical individualism. It is a planet of personal and global transformation, but the way it brings this about is through sudden, swift, unexpected change. Uranus is like lightning—it seemingly comes from nowhere and illuminates with a brilliant flash. It is said to rule astrology, science, electricity, and technology, and is symbolized by inventors, scientists, humanitarians and revolutionaries.

Although the various planets are connected with a wide range of activities and objects, they also, when found in a natal chart, represent different parts of the psyche. Uranus represents the creative, innovative, freedom-seeking part of the self and its placement by sign and house shows much about how and where a person can best express his creative genius and originality, as well as where to anticipate sudden, dramatic change. If the natal chart shows that Uranus was retrograde at birth, and Uranus retrogrades every year for five months, then the urge for freedom may be directed internally, leading to progressive ideas and advanced thinking. A retrograde Uranus afflicted by house placement or hard aspect, however, may indicate a native that is merely erratic or eccentric. In either case, interest in the occult may occur as well. A natal Uranus that is stationary points to a native that is very concerned with humanitarian issues, who may become an instrument of change.

Physically, Uranus is connected to the body's nervous system because of its association with electricity and electrical impulses. Those natives with a prominent Uranus in their chart, particularly if the planet is connected to the first house, can be high strung, oversensitive, and prone to nervous tension and exhaustion. Uranus-type illnesses come on suddenly and disappear just as mysteriously.

—Linda R. Birch

**Sources:**

Arnett, Bill. *The Nine Planets*. www.seds.org/nineplanets/nineplanets/.
*Astronomy for Kids*. www.dustbunny.com/afk.
Bloch, Douglas, and Demetra George. *Astrology for Yourself*. Oakland, CA: Wingbow Press, 1987.
Burk, Kevin. *Astrology: Understanding the Birth Chart*. St. Paul, MN: Llewellyn Publications, 2001.
Campion, Nicholas. *The Practical Astrologer*. New York: Harry N. Abrams, 1987.
Lineman, Rose, and Jan Popelka. *Compendium of Astrology*. Atglen, PA: Whitford Press, 1984.

## Utopia

Utopia, asteroid 1,282 (the 1,282nd asteroid to be discovered, on August 17, 1933), is approximately 35 kilometers in diameter and has an orbital period of 5.5 years. Utopia (literally, "no place") was named after the imaginary republic of Sir Thomas More. J. Lee Lehman associates this asteroid with ideals and, more particularly, with people who act from a blueprint for a better society.

**Sources:**

Kowal, Charles T. *Asteroids: Their Nature and Utilization*. Chichester, West Sussex, UK: Ellis Horwood Limited, 1988.
Lehman, J. Lee. *The Ultimate Asteroid Book*. West Chester, PA: Whitford Press, 1988.
Schwartz, Jacob. *Asteroid Name Encyclopedia*. St. Paul, MN: Llewellyn Publications, 1995.

## Uttara Bhadrapada

Uttara Bhadrapada (latter beautiful foot) is one of the Nakshatras (lunar mansions) of Vedic Astrology. Similar to Purva Bhadrapada, this moon sign is depicted as the back legs of a small bed or couch, and is ruled by the planet Saturn from Pisces 3°20' to 16°40'. People are better problem-solvers and public speakers at this time, though also a bit shy or reluctant, and favorable activities started during this time will have better support. The deity Ahir Budhnya presides over Uttara Bhadrapada.

—Pramela Thiagesan

## Uttara Phalguni

Uttara Phalguni (the latter red one or a fig tree) is one of the Nakshatras (lunar mansions) of Vedic astrology. Represented by the rear legs of a bed, and with the deity Bhaga presiding, this Nakshatra can be found from Leo 26°40' to Virgo 10°. This is considered a good time for new beginnings, such as marriage; with the moon in this position, people tend towards level-headedness and happiness along with vanity and infidelity. The Sun rules Uttara Phalguni.

—Pramela Thiagesan

## Uttarashada

Uttarashada (the latter unsubdued) is one of the Nakshatras (lunar mansions) of Vedic astrology. This Nakshatra, like Purvashada, is represented by a bed or an elephant's tusk, but is ruled by the Sun at Sagittarius 26°40' to Capricorn 10°, and Viswadevas, a combination of all the gods, presides. People may find themselves more fun loving and modest during this time, but also may take on too many others' problems and become very stressed. This is a good time to invest in something for the future.

—Pramela Thiagesan

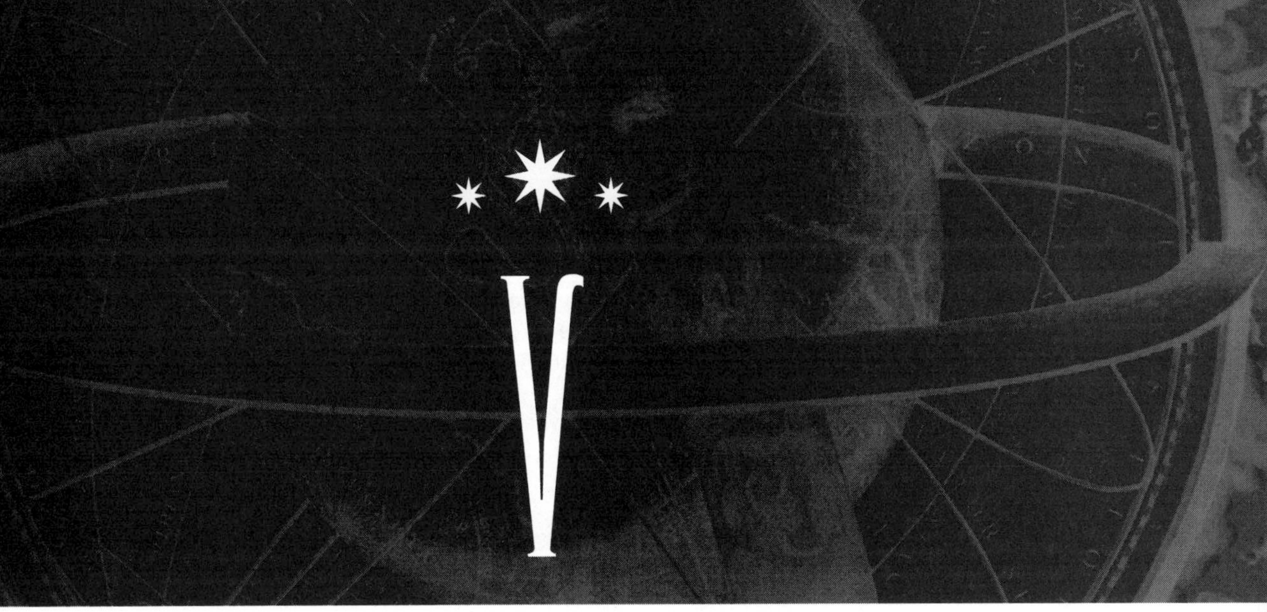

## VEDIC ASTROLOGY (HINDU ASTROLOGY)

Hindu astrology, or Vedic astrology, as it is more commonly referred to by its practitioners, has made tremendous inroads into the Western astrological community in recent years. The origins of Vedic astrology are primarily in India and have flourished for several thousand years. According to modern Vedic scholars, a continuous record of basic astrological knowledge can be traced back to 2500 B.C.E. and the Indus Valley region. As one of the true systems of astrology, Vedic astrology is renowned for its spiritual depth and accuracy in predicting future events. Based on the sidereal zodiac, it reflects an astronomer's perception of the movement of planets through the constellations.

The father of Vedic astrology is Parashara Muni. He was reported to have lived around 1500 B.C.E. and was supposedly one of the first astrologers to actually cast natal charts for individuals. The date of his life is speculative and based on oral tradition. It is recorded that he made a specialized study of medical astrology that reflected health, disease, and longevity issues, and copies of his manuscripts still exist in India. His greatest work was *The Brihat Parashara Hora Shastra*, which was finally compiled around 600 C.E. Parashara also wrote beautiful esoteric hymns in the *Rig Veda* (a Vedic text) that were mantras to the planetary deities. The seer Ranavira was another important astrologer who lived during the same era as Parashara. Ranavira specialized in relationship compatibility, female horoscopy, and other psychological aspects of astrology. In modern astrological practice in India, chart comparisons for marriage compatibility are still commonly utilized.

Vedic astrology is also called *jyotisha*, which means "luminous, brilliant, celestial, shining, belonging to the world of light." It is truly the science of light. Vedic astrology attempts to shine the cosmic light on an individual's true life path. It is a key to understanding the soul's intention or divine plan for this incarnation. Similar to the function of a true guru, the Vedic astrologer attempts to be the "dispeller of darkness." The jyotishi or Vedic astrologer can be viewed as a priest or priestess, life counselor, teacher, and sage.

As in Western astrology, the *rasi* or natal chart is based on the date, place, and exact time of birth. The exact moment of birth is usually considered to be the time of the first breath or cry of the newborn. Many jyotishis also use the time when the umbilical cord is cut. Planetary calculations are based on the sidereal zodiac, which is based on the fixed positions of the stars. Western astrology is based on the tropical zodiac (seasonal). There is an approximate difference of 22° to 24° between the tropical and sidereal zodiacs, depending on in which part of the last century one was born. To calculate the Vedic natal chart by hand, subtract approximately 23° from the tropical positions of the subject's natal planets and ascendant. For example, 3° Virgo sun in Western astrology would be around 10° Leo in the Vedic natal chart.

According to Vedic philosophy, the natal chart represents an individual's past karmic patterns. In Varāhamihara's *Brihat Jataka*, the natal chart reflects "the results of the good and bad deeds done by men in their previous births." Thus, this system is based on the theory of reincarnation and the laws of karma. It is important not to confuse the theory of astrology with fatalism. According to Vedic astrologer Chakrapani Ullal, the Hindu system of astrology emphasizes that "the planets are only the indicative forces and they do not determine the events of life in a fatalistic way. It is for the person concerned, to make use of the indications available, to change the course of one's life by using one's willpower, self-effort and by gaining the grace of God" (personal communication).

## The *Grahas* (Planets)

The basis for understanding astrology is to learn the significations of the planets. The Vedic term for planet is *graha*, which means "demon" or "what possesses a person." The planets represent the *maya*, or illusions that can veil one's divine nature. One must learn to befriend all planets and make them allies. The position of the planets in an individual's birth chart reflects the person's strengths as well as areas that may need to be healed. Each planet signifies certain aspects of life. The following is a list of grahas and their *karakas* or significators (i.e., what they indicate in a person's life):

*Sun/Surya:* Physical appearance, health and general vitality, soul (*atman*) nature, father, nobility, and leadership or status. Heart, circulation, right eye, and head.

*Moon/Chandra:* Emotions and perceptual mind, mother, early childhood, memory and past experience, and influence on the public. Breasts, left eye, stomach, and womb.

*Mercury/Budha:* Rational mind, speech, writing, language systems, intelligence, logic, discrimination, and education. Nervous system, lungs, mouth, tongue, and skin.

*Venus/Shukra:* Wife, beauty, art, music, singing, flowers, gems, cooperation, harmony, happiness, marriage, contentment, and love. Reproductive system, kidneys, and face.

*Mars/Mangala:* Courage, valor, energy, brothers, properties, achievement, dynamism, fires, conflicts, war, enemies, oppression, discord, and accidents. Muscles, sexual passion, and blood.

*Jupiter/Guru:* Religion, higher education, teaching, counseling, consulting, advisor, wealth, children, husband, good fortune, holy places, pilgrimages, travel, and law. Liver, allergies, and fat.

*Saturn/Sani:* Structure, organization, truth, stability, perseverance, discipline, diseases, delay, loss, father (night births), authority figures, separations, and limitations. Bones, teeth, and nerves.

*North Node/Rahu:* Worldly power and desires, fame, foreign lands, travel, the occult and psychology, loss, worry, crime, drugs, and addictions. Mental illness, fears, and phobias.

*South Node/Ketu:* Mystical experiences, liberation, psychic or spiritual insights, ghosts, sleep, dreams, accidents, fires, and injury. Mental confusion, addictions, and death.

The outer planets—Uranus, Neptune, and Pluto—are not usually utilized in traditional Vedic astrology. Vedic astrologers believe that the nodes of the moon reflect the energies of the trans-Saturnian planets adequately. Some modern Vedic astrologers utilize these planets in their natal chart analysis. They believe the planets reflect one's divine birthright and potential soul destiny. All of the grahas operate as cosmic relay stations for the transmission and reception of stellar wisdom.

## The Bhavas (Houses)

The Vedic natal chart is divided into 12 houses called *bhavas*. These houses represent different fields of action or activity. The following are the karakas and significators for the 12 houses that are somewhat similar to those in Western astrology:

*First House/Thanu Bhava:* Bodily appearance, character, early childhood, health and general vitality, personality, ego, strength, fame, and longevity. Dharma house (right action). Head or face. Karaka: Sun.

*Second House/Dhana Bhava:* Money, family life, domestic harmony, food or diet, intellect, powers of speech and writing, jewelry, and dress. Artha house (wealth). Mouth, nose, and right eye. Karakas: Jupiter and Mercury.

*Third House/Sahaja Bhava:* Brothers, younger siblings, fine arts (music, dance, and drama), courage and adventure, skill with hands, short journeys, inquisitive mind, ambition, and will. Karma house (desire). Hands, arms, throat. Karaka: Mars.

*Fourth House/Matru Bhava:* Mother, happiness and contentment, property and real estate, formal education, subconscious mind, and close of life. Moksha house (liberation). Chest, lungs, and heart. Karakas: Moon and Venus.

*Fifth House/Putra Bhava:* Children, love affairs and romance, creative intelligence, *poorvapunya* (past life credit), and wisdom. Dharma house (right action). Stomach (sometimes heart). Karaka: Jupiter.

*Sixth House/Ripu Bhava:* Service, detail work, medicine, catering, pets, enemies, disease, effort and hard work, discrimination, debts. Artha house (wealth). Navel and intestines. Karakas: Saturn and Mars.

*Seventh House/Kalatra Bhava:* Marriage partner, quality of married life, love and passion, social nature, and business partnerships. Kama house (desire). Below navel, kidneys, and veins. Karakas: Venus and Jupiter.

*Eighth House/Ayu Bhava:* Death, longevity, inheritance, mysticism and psychic ability, psychology, delays, fears, and misfortune. Moksha house (liberation). Reproductive systems and chronic illness. Karaka: Saturn.

*Ninth House/Bhagya Bhava:* Wisdom, guru, father, religion, philosophy, long journeys, higher education, law and legal affairs, teachers, and good fortune. Dharma house (right action). Thighs and hips. Karakas: Jupiter and Sun.

*Tenth House/Karma Bhava:* Career or vocation (also first house), status, power, house of action, achievement, and good deeds. Artha house (wealth). Knees. Karakas: Sun, Mercury, Jupiter, and Saturn.

*Eleventh House/Labya Bhava:* Friends, groups, profits and gains, sisters and older siblings, goals, hopes, dreams, and aspirations. Kama house (desire). Legs, calves, and ankles. Karaka: Jupiter.

*Twelfth House/Moksha Bhava:* Enlightenment, bed pleasures, sleep, expenditures, confusion, sorrow, confinement, seclusion, and the next life. Moksha house (liberation). Feet, left eye, and hearing. Karakas: Saturn and Ketu.

To illustrate how the planets and houses are combined, consider pop singer Madonna's natal chart. In viewing her natal Vedic chart, one can see that the houses/signs advance in clockwise fashion. The rasi, or the natal chart, is set up so that each house contains a whole sign. As in Western astrology, there are 12 signs as well as 12 houses. The sign interpretations of Tropical and Vedic astrology are quite similar. The ascendant (rising sign) is of extreme importance in Vedic astrology. In Madonna's Vedic chart, the ascendant, or *lagna*, is at 15° Leo and the entire first house is therefore Leo. Thus, any planets that fall in the sign of Leo (e.g., her retrograde Mercury at 12° Leo) would be considered to be in the first house.

Madonna's second house is the entire sign of Virgo and is empty. Its ruling planet, Mercury, is placed in the first house, creating a *dhana yoga* (wealth producing). The third house is Libra, with Jupiter retrograde at 3° conjoined with Rahu, the fourth house is Scorpio, with Saturn retrograde at 25°, and so on throughout the zodiac. Thus, each house equals 30° or one sign. The bhava chart is also used to fine-tune planetary house positions. It calculates approximately 15° before and after the ascendant as the first house and then uses an equal-house method. Another popular bhava chart calculation is called *sripati*, which takes into account the midheaven point (MC).

In Vedic astrology, the ascendant determines the harmonic pattern of house rulerships as well as how the person acts upon and perceives the world. It is also a reflection of the individual's physical appearance and vitality. As mentioned earlier, in Madonna's Vedic chart the ascendant is Leo or *Simha*. The ruler of the ascendant is the Sun and is located in the twelfth house, indicating career challenges and loss of status. When the ruler of the first house is located in the twelfth, a combination exists that produces tarnished fame and the need for alone time away from the public eye. Fame has its emotional costs. However, Leo ascendants are often driven to be successful on stage. Calculating with the sidereal zodiac, the Leo ascendant is found in the charts of such famous actors and musicians as Tom Hanks, Elton John, Mozart, and Oprah Winfrey, and of such politicians as Franklin D. Roosevelt, Richard Nixon, and the senior George Bush.

Madonna's Sun is located on the cusp, or *sandhi*, of 29° Cancer and is in mutual reception, or *paravartana yoga*, with her Leo Moon, which helps to strengthen the afflicted Sun. The Sun is also located in the sign of its friend, the Moon. The Moon is well placed in the first house in the nakshatra of *Purva Phalguni*, which is ruled by creative Venus. Madonna's ascendant is also placed in this dynamic lunar mansion of success and good fortune.

Madonna also has the planet Mercury residing in her first house conjoined the Moon, which is an excellent placement for speech, writing, intelligence, and communication that will affect the masses. Mercury is in the friendly sign of Leo (Sun and Mercury are considered good friends in Vedic astrology), indicating good communication skills and a large library. Madonna's Jupiter/Rahu conjunction in the third house reflects her good fortune in the fine arts and her strong determination to succeed.

A unique feature of Vedic astrology is planetary periods (*dasa* is the major period; *bhukti* is the subperiod). They can clearly reveal future trends and development cycles in life. They form the basis of a very powerful Vedic technique of dividing life into specific periods of emphasis. Predictions are made based on the strength or affliction of the planetary-period ruler and aspects to it, as well as the houses it rules. It is as if the planet ruling the dasa period becomes the president of one's life during its rulership and the bhukti ruler becomes the vice president during its sway. In examining the charts of famous personalities, one can see periods of introversion during weak planetary periods, followed by speeches before thousands during a strong period.

## Calculating One's Planetary Period

The *dasas* (major periods) are based on a predetermined number of years for each planet or node of the Moon, excluding Uranus, Neptune, and Pluto. The order is based on the rulership of the 27 *nakshatras* or lunar mansions. Each sign of the zodiac contains three nakshatras of varying degrees. From 0° Aries to 13°20' Aries is Aswini, which is ruled by the south node of the Moon (Ketu).

The order of the planetary periods is that of the rulerships of the nakshatras, starting with the first nakshatra of the first sign (Aries), which is ruled by Ketu (south node) and lasts for 7 years. The next nakshatra of Aries is ruled by Venus and lasts 20 years; the next by the Sun, 6 years; the Moon, 10 years; Mars, 7 years; Rahu (north node), 18 years; Jupiter, 16 years; Saturn, 19 years; and Mercury, 17 years. The sequence repeats 3 times through the 12 signs of the zodiac.

The total planetary periods is 120 years, which according to the Vedas (the earliest Hindu sacred writings) would be the potential life cycle for a balanced, healthy person. The beginning planetary period of an individual's life is determined by the nakshatra ruler of the natal Moon. For example, a person born with the Moon at 15° Taurus is in the nakshatra Rohini, which is ruled by the Moon itself (located from 10° Taurus to 23° 20' Taurus).

The task is to calculate how far along the ten-year period is at the time of the person's birth. If the natal moon is exactly 15° Taurus, then it would be 5° into the 13°20' nakshatra of Rohini. Therefore, the planetary period needs to be reduced in proportion. First divide 5° by 13.33°, which equals approximately .375. Then multiply .375 by the total number of years in the planetary period: .375 x 10 + 3.75 years. Finally, subtract .375 from 10 years, which equals 6.25 years, the number of remaining years the person has left in the Moon dasa at the time of birth. This person would have been in the moon dasa for the first 6.25 years of life, followed by 7 years of Mars, 18 years of Rahu (north node) and so forth.

The native's experience of each planetary period is primarily based on the stature of the planet in the natal chart (bhava and navamsa charts should also be utilized). As an example, consider again the chart of Madonna. At the time of the blossoming of Madonna's career, she was under the influence of the planetary period of the Moon dasha. As previously stated, Madonna has both Mercury and the Moon in the sign of her Leo Ascendant. Mercury (representing intellect), placed with the Moon in the first house, gives strong leadership ability, connections in the world of business and commerce, and a high position in society during the Moon planetary period. It was during her Moon dasha and the Mercury bhukti (ruler of the second and eleventh house) that Madonna released her first album and the singles "Lucky Star" and "Borderline." The entire ten-year period of her Moon dasha reflected Madonna's ascent to power, fame, and career success. Also, the Mercury bhukti ruling the second and eleventh houses and placed in the powerful first house brought her increased income and success through friends, social groups, and organizations (eleventh house during this period). The ruler of his tenth house (Venus) is located in the twelfth house (bed pleasures) and indicated the sexual themes of her music and theatrical success.

The seven-year planetary period of Mars began in March 1987 and lasted until March 1994. Mars is Madonna's *yogakaraka*, or planet of power. Placed in the auspicious ninth house in its own sign of Aries conjoined with mystical Ketu, it indicates a spiritual warrior quality with the ability to defeat her competition as well as potential conflict with others. It also aspects her twelfth house Venus reflecting her challenging love affairs and romance. The Mars bhukti started in March 1987, just before the start of her first successful world tour (ninth house) in July. It also revealed the beginning of her bittersweet breakup with her first husband, actor Sean Penn. Their separation occurred during her challenging Mars/Rahu cycle in 1988. Her "Blond Ambition" tour in 1990 reflected the pinnacle of power of her Mars Dasha. Her Mars/Venus period produced the infamous *Sex* book and *Erotica* video.

Madonna is currently running her Rahu dasha (1994–2112) and Mercury Bhukti (March 2002–September 2004). This should reflect an increase in her finances combined with a variety of opportunities in the communications media, such as the television, music, dance, and drama. Her acting career may still be unstable, with her music still her strength. She may become involved in another book project that is autobiographical in nature but less controversial.

### Summary

Vedic or Hindu astrology is an ancient predictive system of esoteric knowledge that is becoming more popular in today's Western culture. As many have embraced the wisdom of the East in other fields of study, such as philosophy and psychology; it is imperative to cultivate this exploration in study of cross-cultural astrology as well.

—Dennis M. Harness, Ph.D.

**Sources:**

Braha, James T. *Ancient Hindu Astrology for the Modern Western Astrologer*. Hollywood, FL: Hermetician Press, 1986.

Cameron, Barbara. *Predictive Planetary Periods: The Hindu Dasas*. Tempe, AZ: American Federation of Astrologers, 1984.

DeLuce, Robert. *Constellational Astrology: According to the Hindu System*. Los Angeles: Deluce Publishing, 1963.

Frawley, David. *The Astrology of the Seers*. Twin Lakes, WI: Lotus Press, 2000.

Harness, Dennis. *The Nakshatras: The Lunar Mansions of Vedic Astrology*. Twin Lakes, WI: Lotus Press, 1999.

Levacy, William. *Beneath a Vedic Sky: A Beginner's Guide to the Astrology of Ancient India*. Carlsbad, CA: Hay House, 1999.

Parashara, Muni. *The Brihat Parashara Hora Shastra*. Translated by R. P. Santhanam. New Delhi, India: Ranjan Publications, 1989.

Varāhamihara. *Brihat Jataka*. Translated by J. R. Satyacharya. New Dehli, India: Ranjan Publications, 1987.

## Vedic Astrology in the West

In the last few years, as part of the greater interest in Hindu and yogic teachings, Hindu, or Vedic, astrology has made tremendous inroads into the Western world. It is now being hailed as one of the most profound and innovative systems of astrology, with tremendous predictive value. Many Western astrologers are now familiar at least with its basic principles. This has been the culmination of several decades of less visible groundwork by a number of people.

Perhaps the point of emergence for Vedic astrology in the West was the First International Symposium on Vedic Astrology, held in October 1992 at Dominican College in San Rafael, California. The keynote speaker was B. V. Raman, who is currently considered by many to be the foremost astrologer of India. He was presented with a lifetime achievement award for his numerous contributions to the field of Vedic astrology.

The symposium was an historic event that symbolized the birth of a new era of Vedic astrology in the West. Since that time, interest in Vedic astrology has continued to flourish. Five annual international symposiums on Vedic astrology have followed, with attendance growing each year. The conferences not only stimulated the interest of individual students of astrology throughout the Western world, but it also led in 1993 to the formation of the American Council of Vedic Astrology (ACVA), a non-profit organization devoted to the promotion of Vedic astrology in the West.

Throughout this century, several individuals have played prominent roles in bringing Indian astrological knowledge into the Western world. The most important has been Raman. In his classic book *Hindu Astrology and the West,* Raman recounted his many visits to America and Europe. He has written more than 30 books and was the chief editor of the *Astrological Magazine*. Some of his famous predictions include the fall of Adolf Hitler and Richard Nixon as well as India's independence. Raman had contact with many of the great political and social leaders of the twentieth century. He even commented that Hitler had once written to him asking for his astrological advice. And in September 1947, Raman received a letter received from Carl G. Jung, in which the prominent Swiss psychiatrist gave his opinon of astrology:

> Since you want to know my opinion of astrology I can tell you that I've been interested in this particular activity of the human mind for more than 30 years. As I am a psychologist, I am chiefly interested in the particular light the horoscope sheds on certain complications in the character. In cases of difficult psychological diagnosis, I usually get a horoscope in order to have a further point of view form an entirely different angle. I must say that I often found that the astrological data elucidated certain points which I otherwise would have been unable to understand. From such experiences I formed the opinion that astrology is of particular interest to the psychologist, since it contains a sort of psychological experience which we call "projected"—this means that we find the psychological facts as it were in the constellations. This originally gave rise to the idea that these factors derive from the stars, whereas they are merely in a relation of synchronicity with them. I admit that this a very curious fact which throws a peculiar light on the structure of the human mind.
>
> What I miss in the astrological literature is chiefly the statistical method by which certain fundamental facts could be scientifically established. Hoping that this answer meets your request.

It is interesting to note that Jung often used astrology as a diagnostic tool in his clinical psychology practice. Psychotherapy and counseling astrology share a common goal of assisting the unconscious aspects of self to become more conscious. As Jung once stated, "That which we do not face in the unconscious, we will live as fate."

World-renowned astrologer Chakrapani Ullal is perhaps the most important astrologer to move to from India to America to spread the word on Vedic astrology. From Kerala, South India, Chakrapani was born into a family of illustrious astrologers and has had continuous contact with many of the leading spiritual teachers of India.

In 1979, he was invited by Swami Muktananda to come to the United States as an astrological consultant and has remained here since. In February 1996, Ullal was awarded a lifetime achievement award for his numerous contributions to the field of astrology by the ACVA. He now resides in the Los Angeles area and travels extensively throughout the world teaching students and providing consultations for his diverse international clientele. He continues to be a popular featured speaker at conferences throughout the United States.

Ullal has always emphasized that an astrological chart is only the indicative of planetary forces and does not determine the events of a life in a fatalistic way. The person can make use of the astrological indications as a karmic road map to change the course of his or her life, by using willpower and self-effort and by gaining the grace of God.

Vedic astrology has followed on the coattails of the interest in yoga and other aspects of Eastern and Hindu spirituality and healing that began in a major way in the United States in the late 1960s. Several yoga, Vedanta, and Hindu movements have promoted it, most notably the Transcendental Meditation (TM) movement founded by Maharishi Yoga that has emphasized Jyotish strongly for more than ten years now. The ISKCON movement (International Society for Krishna Consciousness) is another important group that promotes aspects of Vedic thought, including Jyotish. Sri Yukteswar, the guru, of Paramahansa Yogananda, the founder of SRF (Self-Realization Fellowship), was an astrologer and this had led to much interest in the subject among his disciples. While a decade ago Vedic astrology was almost unknown even in Western yoga groups, now there is interest in it throughout the whole greater sphere of Vedic- and Hindu-based movements.

In particular, Vedic astrology has gained popularity along with Ayurveda, or Vedic medicine, which has recently been growing rapidly as well. Along with the astrology, Vastu or Vedic geomancy (*feng shui*) is gaining its adherents as well. The many Hindu immigrants, including many scientists and computer programmers, to the United States over the last 20 years have also brought with them an interest in the subject.

During the past few decades, numerous books written by Westerners on Vedic astrology have emerged. One of the first books was *Constellation Astrology According to the Hindu System*, written by Robert De Luce in 1963. This groundbreaking book was primarily addressed to Western astrologers to produce a bridge of understanding between followers of the two systems. A Western sidereal astrology (the Fagan-Bradley system) eventually arose, taking aspects of Hindu astrology.

Perhaps the most important single Westerner promoting Vedic astrology has been James Braha. He began with *Ancient Hindu Astrology for the Modern Western Astrologer* in 1986, the first comprehensive book on Vedic astrology published in the West, and has continued with several more important titles. A year later, Tom Hopke (Nalinikanta Das) wrote *How to Read Your Horoscope*, which provided in-depth information on Jyotish from a Vedantic perspective. Then, in 1990, David Frawley wrote *Astrology of the Seers: A Guide to Vedic/Hindu Astrology*. Frawley's extensive background in Jyotish, Ayurveda, and Vedic philosophy provided the reader with much Vedic knowledge.

In recent years, several new books on Vedic astrology have been written. *Light on Life: An Introduction to the Astrology of India*, by Hart Defouw and Robert Svoboda, is already considered a classic in the field. Also, *Beneath a Vedic Sky* by William R. Levacy, *The Astrology of Death* by Richard Houck, and *Vedic Astrology* by Ronnie Gale Dreyer, have been well received.

Many Vedic astrologers from India have come to the West to teach and have brought their books with them. Gayatri Vasudeva and Niranjan Babu, the son and daughter of B. V. Raman, are among these. So are many noted Delhi astrologers, including Bepin Behari, K. S. Charak, Dinesh Sharma, and K. N. Rao. Several of Behari's titles have been published directly in the West. The English literature on Jyotish has burgeoned with many new titles coming every year, producing a veritable renaissance in the subject.

In the computer age Vedic astrology computer programs have come as well. There are now several important programs available devised in the West, including Parashara's "Light," Gorvani's "Jyotish" and "Shri Jyoti," to mention a few. Deepak Chopra uses Vedic astrology to help people find the right mantra for their individual nature.

Many Americans have become professional Vedic astrologers, and several Indians have taken up this occupation here as well. In most major cities, there are professionals who can be consulted for all astrological matters, from birth charts to astrological forecasting. People of all walks of life are drawn to such Vedic astrologers because of the abundance of tools and resources these astrologers have to offer and the support of an entire spiritual tradition that they carry.

This new Western Vedic astrology is taking its own form both by the American-born and Indian practitioners. While in India, clients are concerned about predicting the hard facts of life, such as job and marriage potentials; in the United States, people come to Vedic astrology more for spiritual, psychological, or relationship needs, placing it more in a counseling model. After all, the outer factors of life are not as hard to get or unpredictable as they are in India.

Another interesting difference is that in India few people want to pay astrologers, who are regarded as serving in Brahmical roles that should not charge for services. Informed Americans look upon Vedic astrologers with the same respect as doctors or psychologists and are willing to pay them accordingly. This allows practitioners here to make a livelihood from Vedic astrology, enabling them to spend more time with the system.

There has, of course, been some abuse of Vedic astrology. Partly trained individuals have given wrong predictions. Some charlatans from India have offered magical cures for karmic ills—at the right price. Overly priced gems or *yajnas* (rituals) have left their mark. But instances of such abuse have been rare, probably less than in other occult and psychic pursuits, which always have room for much wishful thinking.

The main potential abuse is that many Westerners do not have the spiritual or ethical background to use Jyotish to its full potential and may be inclined to use it in a more mundane or personal matter, or simply turn it into a business. However, Indians today seem to share the same inclinations. For this reason, the Hindu and Vedic background of the astrology should not be forgotten, particularly if one wants its spiritual benefits.

Some Hindu terms like "karma" and "rebirth" have already entered into Western or New Age Western astrology, but often in a different way. Many New Agers see rebirth not as a cycle of suffering to transcend, but as a way of continued existence, if not enjoyment. The concept of *moksha*, or liberation, is not understood.

Others misunderstand karma and equate it with some sort of fate or destiny. "After all, it is my karma," people will say, meaning that there is nothing they can do about a situation. Karma in the Vedic sense means action, or more specifically, the effect of past actions. According to the Vedic view, people create themselves by their own actions, but as these occur through the course of time, they remain under the influence of what they have done in the past. Vedic astrology helps people to understand their karma and act in such a way in the present that they can alter their karma for the future and gain the liberation of the soul. That is why Vedic astrology emphasizes remedial measures to change the movement of karma and always leads to *sadhana*, or spiritual practice as the real pursuit in life.

—Dennis M. Harness, Ph.D., and David Frawley

**Sources:**

Braha, James T. *Ancient Hindu Astrology for the Modern Western Astrologer*. Miami, FL: Hermetician Press, 1986.

De Luce, Robert. *Constellation Astrology According to the Hindu System*. Los Angeles: De Luce Pub. Co., 1963.

Defouw, Hart, and Robert Svoboda. *Light on Life: An Introduction to the Astrology of India*. New York: Arkana, 1996.

Dreyer, Ronnie Gale. *Vedic Astrology: A Guide to the Fundamentals of Jyotish*. York Beach, ME: S. Weiser, 1997.

Frawley, David. *Astrology of the Seers: A Guide to Vedic/Hindu Astrology*. Twin Lakes, WI: Lotus Press, 2000.

Hopke, Tom (Nalinikanta Das). *How to Read Your Horoscope*. Los Angeles: Vedic Cultural Association, 1987.

Houck, Richard. *The Astrology of Death*. Gaithersburg, MD: Groundswell Press, 1994.

Levacy, William R. *Beneath a Vedic Sky: A Beginner's Guide to the Astrology of Ancient India*. Carlsbad, CA: Hay House, 1999.

## VENUS

Venus is the second planet from the Sun, located between Mercury and Earth. It is the most notable light in the sky, after the Sun and Moon, and has been referred to as Earth's sister planet. Nearly the same size as Earth, Venus orbits around the Sun in a nearly circular path of 225 days. Venus also rotates on its axis in the opposite direction of the Earth and most other planets, turning from east to west, and so slowly that one Venus day is the equivalent of 243 Earth days, longer than its year. In so doing Venus only shows one side of itself to the Earth at its closest orbital proximity.

As a planet nearer to the Sun than Earth, Venus is considered an inferior planet and is never seen to be more than 48° of longitude away from the Sun. As Venus moves along its orbit, it appears from Earth's perspective to periodically slow, stop, and then move backwards. This so-called retrograde motion lasts approximately six weeks, which ends when Venus seems to stop briefly and move forward again. The retrograde motions of Venus happen at regular intervals, taking place five times within the greater eight-year Venus cycle.

It is this eight-year cycle that is recorded on the Venus tablet of Amisaduaq, the tablet of Mesopotamian omens based on the movements of Venus. It dates from approximately 1750 to 1650 B.C.E. and is the earliest known astrological document. In addition, the tablet emphasizes the first and last visibilities of Venus, those times Venus is seen rising just prior to the Sun or setting after it. In the first instance Venus has not been visible for a time, as it has been too close to the sun. Its first visibility is the first morning it can be spotted rising before the Sun, heralding the coming dawn. Similarly, the last visibility is the last time Venus was seen setting on the tail of the Sun. It then disappears for a time behind the Sun's light. These two distinctly different sightings were important as they recognized the dual nature of Venus.

The Sumerian *Inanna* was the goddess of love, fertility, desire, and attraction. She presided over the passions, some of which were destructive ones such as jealousy and anger. Inanna also claimed possession of the Tablets of Destiny, giving her control of the universe. She was the most powerful of deities. Sumerian poetry describes her as Queen of Heaven, Lady of the Evening, as well as Lady of Light, associating Inanna with the planet Venus as both the rising and setting star. Her dual nature ruled over both love and hate, light and dark as seen in her mythology, which includes stories of her descent into the underworld as well as her return to the land of living. The ancients equated the disappearance of Venus with her descent into the underworld. There she had to face herself at her most vulnerable, die, and then rise again as Queen of Heaven and Earth.

When the Akkadians settled in Sumerian territory Inanna's name changed to *Ishtar*. Babylonian poetic descriptions of the descent of Ishtar are nearly identical to the myths of Inanna with the exception of a more forceful warrior like temperament in Ishtar. Thus Ishtar also had the dual characteristics of love and attraction as the evening star as opposed to lust and hostility as the morning star. This was reflected in Babylonian astrological omens where good or evil outcomes were indicated by Ishtar's placements.

While the Mesopotamian lands repeatedly changed hands to be led by the Assyrians and then the conquering Persians, the goddess associated with Venus changed names to the Syrian *Astarte* followed by the Persian *Anahita*. The goddess continued to be seen as the source of all waters and fertility on the earth, the holder of wisdom and benefactress of the human race. Beautiful, bright and adorned with gold, she was the seductive goddess, symbolizing the tradition of temple prostitution. Astrology centered on the reading of omens also continued in Babylon, however by the sixth century B.C.E. the planets began to be seen as either malefic or benefic, rather than dependent on season or rising time, and Venus became overwhelmingly benefic.

The Greeks received knowledge of astrology and the five wandering stars from the Babylonians. In equating the planets to their own pantheon of gods they equated Ishtar with Aphrodite, their goddess of love and beauty. The fertility aspects of Ishtar were seen in Demeter and her mythological descents into the underworld equated with Demeter's daughter Persephone. In addition, Athena was the Greek holder of wisdom as well as the patron goddess of righteous warriors, associations formerly held by Inanna/Ishtar. However, the volatile temperament of Ishtar was fully present in the Greek Aphrodite as indicated by myths displaying her jealousy, anger, and possessiveness.

**A seventeenth-century illustration of the birth of Venus entitled "Imagini Dei Dei."** ***Reproduced by permission of Fortean Picture Library.***

The planet Venus was called the star of Aphrodite in fourth century B.C.E. Greece, recognizing it as the home of the goddess. Sometime during the Hellenic period of Alexandria, the flourishing Greek astrology began referring to the planet as simply Aphrodite. Vettius Valens, who recorded an *Anthology* of Hellenistic astrology in the second century C.E., wrote that the nature of Aphrodite was desire and erotic love, and that it signified the mother and nurse. The star represented priestly rites, parties, weddings, friendships, jewels and ornaments, music, beauty, the arts, as well as a variety of colors. It gave gifts of businesses, involved markets and weights and measures, bestowed favors from female royals or relatives and assured an excellent reputation. It was lord of the neck, face, and lungs, and ruled sexual intercourse. It also indicated the giving of nurturing or pleasure to another. It was the lord of precious stones and the oil of fruits, its color was white, and it belonged to the nocturnal (lunar) sect, along with Ares (Mars) and Hermes (Mercury, as evening star).

Hellenistic astrology included basic functions of the planets, and if one is to assume that Ptolemy's record is representative of astrologers for that period, then a relationship was present between the basic qualities of matter and each of the planets. Aphrodite is listed as temperate (slightly warm) and moist, meaning that it has an active power that attracts as well as a passivity that can include others within its boundaries. Its basic nature was unification and reconciliation. In a solar (daytime) chart Aphrodite is out of, or contrary to, sect so the unions it represents do not come together naturally, but through thought and choice. Whereas in a lunar (night) chart Aphrodite is in sect and relational things come together more easily.

Just as in modern day, Aphrodite ruled the zodiac signs of the Bull (Taurus) and the Balance (Libra), and was exalted in the Fishes (Pisces). It had additional rulerships of Trigons, Bounds, and Faces—divisions that for the most part do not exist in astrology today. Aphrodite as a nocturnal planet was a trigon lord only in a night chart where it ruled all of the feminine signs: the Bull, the Crab (Cancer), the Virgin (Virgo), the Scorpion (Scorpio), the Goat-Horned One (Capricorn), and the Fishes. As for rulerships of bounds and faces (or decans), tables can be consulted to determine these, as they require exact degrees of signs to determine.

Astrology was introduced to the Romans by way of imported slaves. They embraced the Hellenistic practice without alteration, except that they renamed Aphrodite for their goddess of fertility, joy, and beauty—Venus. Through their association with the Alexandrian Greeks, the Romans came to view Venus primarily as the goddess of love and the planet Venus as her abode. Eventually the planet would be thought of as Venus herself, a substitution for the goddess, and the name for the second planet remained Venus on into modern day.

Classical astrology of the Middle Ages had some similarities to the Hellenistic, however the associations for Venus show quite a few variations between them, particularly as to the rulership of body parts, but also in a propensity to expand on the negative, underworld significations of Venus. It represented the force of attraction as well as love and beauty and ruled physical beauty, parts of the face, the throat, the female sex organs, and sense of taste. Like Hellenistic Aphrodite, Venus symbolized women, art, music, and relationships, and was fertile and creative. However, it also signified adulterers, flirts, incest, infertility, kidney and venereal disease, prostitutes, and scandal.

The system of essential dignities had Venus ruling Taurus and Libra and exalted in Pisces, a practice that has not changed throughout history. The classic dignities also included tables of Triplicities, Terms, and Faces that varied according to the practice of the astrologer. William Lilly gave the diurnal, or daytime, triplicities of Taurus, Virgo, and Capricorn to Venus; while the Dorothean, or Ptolemaic, tables added the water signs Cancer, Scorpio, and Pisces to that list. Venus had no nocturnal triplicity rulerships. The terms were signs divided into five parts by degree. The terms of Venus are best consulted in those tables. The faces were essentially decans, or 10° increments of signs. Venus was in her own face in the first 10° of Cancer and Aquarius, the second 10° of Virgo, and the third 10° of Aries and Scorpio.

Vedic astrology, or Jyotish, has some similarities to the Hellenistic methods of astrology. Venus rules Taurus and Libra, and is connected to the wife, marriage, women, beauty, art, and music. Venus is called Sukra (Shukra), but is seen as a male god. The deities associated with Venus are Lakshmi, the goddess of love and pleasure, as well as Indra, the thunderbolt warrior god who also represents desires and yearnings. Sukra rules the face, kidneys, and reproductive system and is associated with harmony, flowers, happiness, and pleasure as well as laziness, vanity, and addictions. He represents love and the ability to relate to another. Sukra's colors are multicolored, his gemstones are diamond and white sapphire, and his day is Friday.

As a benefic, Venus enhances the house in which it is placed as well as providing a good influence on planets associated with it by house or aspect. Sukra (Venus) is a friend to Mercury and Saturn, is an enemy to the Sun and Moon, and neutral with Mars and Jupiter. In the zodiac sign of a friend it is joyful, contented, glad, and rejoicing. In the sign of an enemy it is sleepy, drowsy, and numb. Sukra (Venus), as in western astrology, is exalted in Pisces. Jyotish defines the exact degree of exaltation as 27°

of Pisces (sidereal) and similarly the exact degree of debilitation of Venus is 27° of Virgo (sidereal). As it moves toward the exact degree the intensity of its benefic or debilitated state is increased.

Venus also rules three of the 27 Nakshatras (lunar mansions): Bharani (0 to 13°20' Aries, sidereal), Purva Phalaguni (13°20' to 26°40' Leo, sidereal), and Purva Ashadha (13°20' to 26°40' Sagittarius, sidereal). All three of these Nakshatras share a sense of passion that requires one to learn restraint.

Today's western astrology combines many of the historical attributes of Venus. The planet is associated with the Greco/Roman goddess Venus and rules love and marriage as well as harmony and the ability to attract. The modern Venus is quite feminine in nature, represents grace, elegance, and beauty as well as money and material goods. She is the patron of the arts and music, and reflects one's ability to navigate social situations. Relationships, the capacity for affection, friendships, sensuality, and sexuality all belong under her domain.

The sign that Venus is posited in at birth indicates how one relates to others, what one finds attractive and one's capacity for love and harmony. The house in which Venus resides, as well as the houses the planet rules, describe the areas of life that are most profoundly impacted. For instance, harmony or money issues may be more important in those areas. In addition, the attractive nature of Venus usually brings a love of, or interest in, those things represented by those houses.

The shadow side of Venus recognizes that overindulgence brings out some negative traits, which can be indicated by retrograde motion, or aspects with another planet, as well as placement in a difficult house, such as the twelfth. For example, Jupiter aligned with Venus may seem to be a lucky placement. However, the expansive nature of Jupiter may influence Venus to overspend and to be vain or lazy.

As in the Hellenistic and Jyotish traditions, Venus rules the zodiac signs of Taurus and Libra, is exalted in Pisces, in detriment in Aries and Scorpio, and in its fall in Virgo. Physically, modern Venus rules the female sex organs, the glands, blood in the veins, the throat, and the kidneys. She is associated with the voice, etiquette, sweets, flowers, perfume, copper, Friday, and the number six.

—Linda R. Birch

**Sources:**

Arnett, Bill. *The Nine Planets: A Multimedia Tour of the Solar System*. www.seds.org/nineplanets/nineplanets.

*Astronomy for Kids*. www.dustbunny.com/afk.

Bloch, Douglas, and Demetra George. *Astrology for Yourself: How to Understand and Interpret Your Own Birth Chart*. Berkeley, CA: Wingbow Press, 1987.

Campion, Nicholas. *Mesopotamian Astrology 2,000* B.C.*–O.A.D*. www.nickcampion.com/nc/history/mesopotamia.htm.

Campion, Nicholas, and Steve Eddy. *The New Astrology: The Art and Science of the Stars*. North Pomfret, VT: Trafalgar Square Pub., 1999.

DeFouw, Hart, and Robert Svoboda. *Light on Life*. London: Penguin Group, 1996.

Levacy, William R. *Beneath a Vedic Sky*. Carlsbad, CA: Hay House, 1999.

Lilly, William. *Christian Astrology Modestly Treated of in Three Books*. London: T. Brudenell, 1647. Reprint, Philadelphia: David McKay Co., 1935.
Lineman, Rose, and Jan Popelka. *Compendium of Astrology*. Atglen, PA: Whitford Press, 1984.
Powell, Robert. *History of the Planets*. San Diego: ACS Publications, 1985.

## Vera

Vera, asteroid 245 (the 245th asteroid to be discovered, on February 6, 1885), is approximately 84 kilometers in diameter and has an orbital period of 5.4 years. Its name is Latin for "true." In a natal chart, Vera's house and sign position indicates where one is especially able to perceive or search for the truth. When afflicted, Vera may suggest "false truth."

**Sources:**

Kowal, Charles T. *Asteroids: Their Nature and Utilization*. Chichester, West Sussex, UK: Ellis Horwood Limited, 1988.
Room, Adrian. *Dictionary of Astronomical Names*. London: Routledge, 1988.
Schwartz, Jacob. *Asteroid Name Encyclopedia*. St. Paul, MN: Llewellyn Publications, 1995.

## Veritas

Veritas, asteroid 490 (the 490th asteroid to be discovered, on September 3, 1902), is approximately 128 kilometers in diameter and has an orbital period of 5.6 years. Its name is a personification of the Latin word for truth. In a natal chart, Veritas's house and sign position indicates where one is especially able to perceive or search for the truth. When afflicted, Veritas may suggest "false truth."

**Sources:**

Kowal, Charles T. *Asteroids: Their Nature and Utilization*. Chichester, West Sussex, UK: Ellis Horwood Limited, 1988.
Room, Adrian. *Dictionary of Astronomical Names*. London: Routledge, 1988.
Schwartz, Jacob. *Asteroid Name Encyclopedia*. St. Paul, MN: Llewellyn Publications, 1995.

## Vernal Equinox (Spring Equinox)

Equinox, Latin for "equal night," refers to one of the two days of the year on which daytime and nighttime are equal in duration. The vernal equinox, which occurs on or around March 21, marks the beginning of both the sign Aries and the spring season. The vernal equinox is especially important for Western astrologers, who utilize the Sun's position against the backdrop of the stars at the spring equinox (the vernal point) as the place where the zodiac begins.

## Vernal Point

The vernal (Latin for "of the spring") point is the position of the Sun against the backdrop of the stars at the moment of the vernal equinox (i.e., the spring equinox). The vernal equinox is especially important for astrologers, who use the vernal point as the place to begin the zodiac (i.e., 0° Aries). Because of the phenomenon known as the precession of equinoxes, this point occurs at a slightly different place every year.

## VERTEX

In geometry, a vertex is the pivot point of an angle. In astrology, the vertex is the point in a horoscope where the prime vertical intersects the ecliptic in the west. The antivertex is the corresponding point in the east. The vertex was discovered/invented by L. Edward Johndro and elaborated upon by Charles Jayne. The point where the vertex falls in a chart is said to be the most fated (i.e., least amenable to conscious choices) part of the horoscope. All major astrological chart-casting software programs allow one to calculate the vertex.

## VESPERTINE

Vespertine (from the Latin *vesper*, meaning "evening") refers to the evening, especially the early evening, and in astrology was traditionally applied to a planet or star that dropped below the horizon soon after sunset. Vespertine is the opposite of matutine (which refers to planets and stars that rise above the horizon just before sunrise). Both terms are rarely used in modern astrology.

## VESTA

The asteroids are small planet-like bodies that orbit the Sun in a belt that lies mostly between Mars and Jupiter. They first dawned on human consciousness in the early 1800s. The first four asteroids to be sighted were given the names of four of the great goddesses of classical antiquity: Ceres (discovered in 1801), Pallas Athene (discovered in 1802), Juno (discovered in 1804), and Vesta (discovered in 1807).

Many more asteroids were soon discovered, so that by the end of the nineteenth century, over a thousand were known. The first asteroid ephemeris (a table listing planetary positions) was made available to astrologers in 1973 by Eleanor Bach, and it covered only the original four. Today astrologers have computer software developed by Mark Pottenger that tracks the placements of over 9,000.

Among the thousands of asteroids known, Ceres, Pallas, Juno, and Vesta have a special place. While these are not necessarily the largest asteroids, they were the first to be discovered, and as such they have imprinted themselves on human consciousness in a significant way. They also complete the female pantheon of goddesses, rounding out the system of symbols begun in the usual 10 planets. Of the six great goddesses of Olympus, only Aphrodite (Venus) and Artemis (the Moon) are represented in the conventional astrological symbol system. The other four great goddesses of Greco-Roman mythology—Demeter (Ceres), Athene (Pallas), Hera (Juno), and Hestia (Vesta)—were missing from astrology until they were reinvoked by their discovery in the early 1800s.

After one has been nurtured, gone out into the world, found one's life partner, and reared children, the time comes to turn inward to reconnect with one's spirit. In women, the matron becomes the crone; in the culture of India, the householder sets out on his final spiritual journey as a monk-like wanderer; and in Jungian psychology, the active person of affairs embarks on an inward journey to find the self.

Vesta, the fourth and final of the major Olympian goddesses to give her name to an asteroid, relates to this final stage of life. Although renowned for her shining beauty, she is in fact the eldest of the Olympian gods.

Like Pallas Athene, Vesta was known as a virgin. If Pallas Athene was the pre-reproductive Maiden, Vesta could be thought of as the post-reproductive crone. After their 30-year term of office was up, the Vestal Virgins of Rome were allowed to marry, but they were then often beyond childbearing age. In pre-classical times, the cult of the goddess who later became Vesta included sex as a sacrament. Thus Vesta, insofar as she is sexual, represents a rarefied form of sex that transcends the procreative function and aims to achieve spiritual union rather than physical children.

Vesta was related to Jupiter as his sister. This, too, expresses her non-procreative way of relating, and the fact that she is often thought of as the prototype of the nun, also called "sister."

Besides suggesting the letter V, which points downward and inward, the astrological glyph for Vesta represents a flame burning on either a hearth or an altar. This signifies Vesta's function as keeper of the hearth fire and the temple flame, but it also points to the cultivation of the pure spark of spirit within. Fittingly, Vesta is the brightest object in the asteroid belt.

To the ancient Greeks, Vesta was known as Hestia, a name derived from the word for hearth, and it appears she had to do with the domestication of fire for human use in the home and in sacrificial offerings. As the eldest of the Olympian gods, she was the most venerated, and was always given the first sacrifices and libations. There are few stories about her deeds and the few depictions of her show her in repose, indicating an inward, contemplative nature. She refused the marriage offers of Apollo and Poseidon, and under Zeus's protection vowed to remain a virgin forever.

In Roman mythology, Hestia became Vesta, always veiled, but known as the most beautiful of the deities. In the home she was venerated as the protectress of the hearth and its flame. In public life, she was thought of as the protectress of the state, and her priestesses were the six vestal virgins of Rome. Dedicated to spiritual service, the vestals were responsible for keeping the sacred flame burning, which was thought to ensure the safety of Rome. They enjoyed great prestige, but if they let the flame go out, they were whipped, and if they violated their oath of chastity during their term of office, they were punished by a public whipping and then buried alive.

Vesta became the prototype of the medieval nun. However, several thousand years earlier in the ancient Near East, the predecessors of the vestals tended a temple flame, but also engaged in sacred sexual rites in order to bring healing and fertility to the people and the land.

The original meaning of the word "virgin" meant not "chaste," but simply "unmarried." Whereas Ceres and Juno required relationships to complete themselves,

Vesta's priestesses represent an aspect of the feminine nature that is whole and complete in itself.

When the old goddess religions gave way to those of the solar gods, sexuality became divorced from spirituality, such that a woman desiring to follow a spiritual path had to remain chaste. Earlier, however, a priestess, representing the goddess, could enter into a state of spiritual transcendence through sexual union with an partner in a manner that did not call for marriage or commitment. In the later patriarchal culture, ecstatic illumination was experienced as the descent of the spirit of the god into oneself, and the now-chaste Greek priestesses became the brides of the god Apollo in the sense that the Christian nuns became the brides of Christ.

In the human psyche, Vesta represents the part of each person's nature that feels the urge to experience the sexual energy of Venus in a sacred manner. This may occur in several different ways.

If one is a typical product of one's culture's mores, he or she will most likely internalize this sexual energy. One may devote one's self to following a spiritual, religious, or meditational path, even following in priestly or monastic footsteps. Or, in one's lifelong therapeutic work, one may experience this union with the self as the process of psychological integration. In one way or another, this results in turn inward to attain clarity and energy. The vision that arises when one reaches the whole and self-contained core of one's being then enables one to follow a vocation in which one can be of service in the world.

Vesta the virgin speaks of the importance of the relationship each person has with him or herself. This may lead to a single lifestyle. If a person is married, he or she may not be comfortable with the total surrender asked for in the merging with another.

Vesta protects not only the inner flame of spirituality and sexual energy, but also other precious things that ensure the continuation of human life. As "keeper of the flame," she preserved the state and the institutions of society. She also guarded the home and hearth, including kitchens and the preparation and purity of food. Today she could be seen as a librarian, museum curator, or other sort of worker who preserves the sparks of human culture. She could also express herself in an occupation that deals with housing or food.

Through Vesta, one integrates and regenerates on inner levels in order to focus and dedicate one's self to work in the outer world. In the human psyche, Vesta represents the process of spiritual focus that can lead to personal integration. In a broader sense, she signifies the ability to focus on and dedicate one's self to a particular area of life. When the focus becomes too narrow, it is possible to sometimes feel limited and hemmed in. When the capacity to focus is obstructed, one can feel scattered. This, too, may cause one to experience limitation in the area of life represented by Vesta's sign or house position.

In summary, Vesta is the archetype of the sister and the temple priestess, whose virginity signifies her wholeness and completeness within herself. Her sign, house, and aspect placements in on's birth chart show how one can use the basic sexual energy of Venus to deepen one's relationship to one's self.

—Demetra George

**Sources:**

Dobyns, Zipporah. *Expanding Astrology's Universe*. San Diego: Astro Computing Services, 1983.
Donath, Emma Belle. *Asteroids in the Birth Chart*. Tempe, AZ: American Federation of Astrologers, 1979.
George, Demetra, with Douglas Bloch. *Asteroid Goddesses: The Mythology, Psychology and Astrology of the Reemerging Feminine*. 2d ed. San Diego: Astro Computing Services, 1990.
———. *Astrology for Yourself: A Workbook for Personal Transformation*. Berkeley, CA: Wingbow Press, 1987.
Lehman, J. Lee. *The Ultimate Asteroid Book*. West Chester, PA: Whitford Press, 1988.

## Via Combusta

*Via combusta* is Latin for "burning way," which usually refers to the first half of the sign Scorpio. The first 15° of that sign—and sometimes the last 15° of Libra through the full 30° arc of Scorpio—were taken by the ancients to exert an especially unfortunate influence, particularly for one's natal Moon. Some modern astrologers speculate that this negative ascription may have derived from the many malefic fixed stars that, in older times, were located in the first half of Scorpio (but which, because the Western, tropical zodiac is slowly moving, are no longer located in Scorpio). Although contemporary astrologers no longer use the *via combusta* to interpret natal charts, it is still utilized in horary astrology.

**Sources:**

Bach, Eleanor. *Astrology from A to Z: An Illustrated Source Book*. New York: Philosophical Library, 1990.
DeVore, Nicholas. *Encyclopedia of Astrology*. New York: Philosophical Library, 1947.

## Vibilia

Vibilia, asteroid 144 (the 144th asteroid to be discovered, on June 3, 1875), is approximately 132 kilometers in diameter and has an orbital period of 4.3 years. It is named after the Roman goddess of journeys. When prominent in a natal chart, Vibilia may show someone who is involved in many journeys, either in the sense of travel or in a more figurative way. Vibilia's position by sign and house indicates how and where one journeys.

**Sources:**

Kowal, Charles T. *Asteroids: Their Nature and Utilization*. Chichester, West Sussex, UK: Ellis Horwood Limited, 1988.
Room, Adrian. *Dictionary of Astronomical Names*. London: Routledge, 1988.
Schwartz, Jacob. *Asteroid Name Encyclopedia*. St. Paul, MN: Llewellyn Publications, 1995.

## Vigintile

A vigintile (also called a semidecile) is a minor aspect of 18° formed by dividing a circle into 20 equal subdivisions. The effect of a vigintile is subtle, so it is rarely used. The influence of this minor aspect is mildly favorable; Emma Belle Donath asserts that it represents innate understanding.

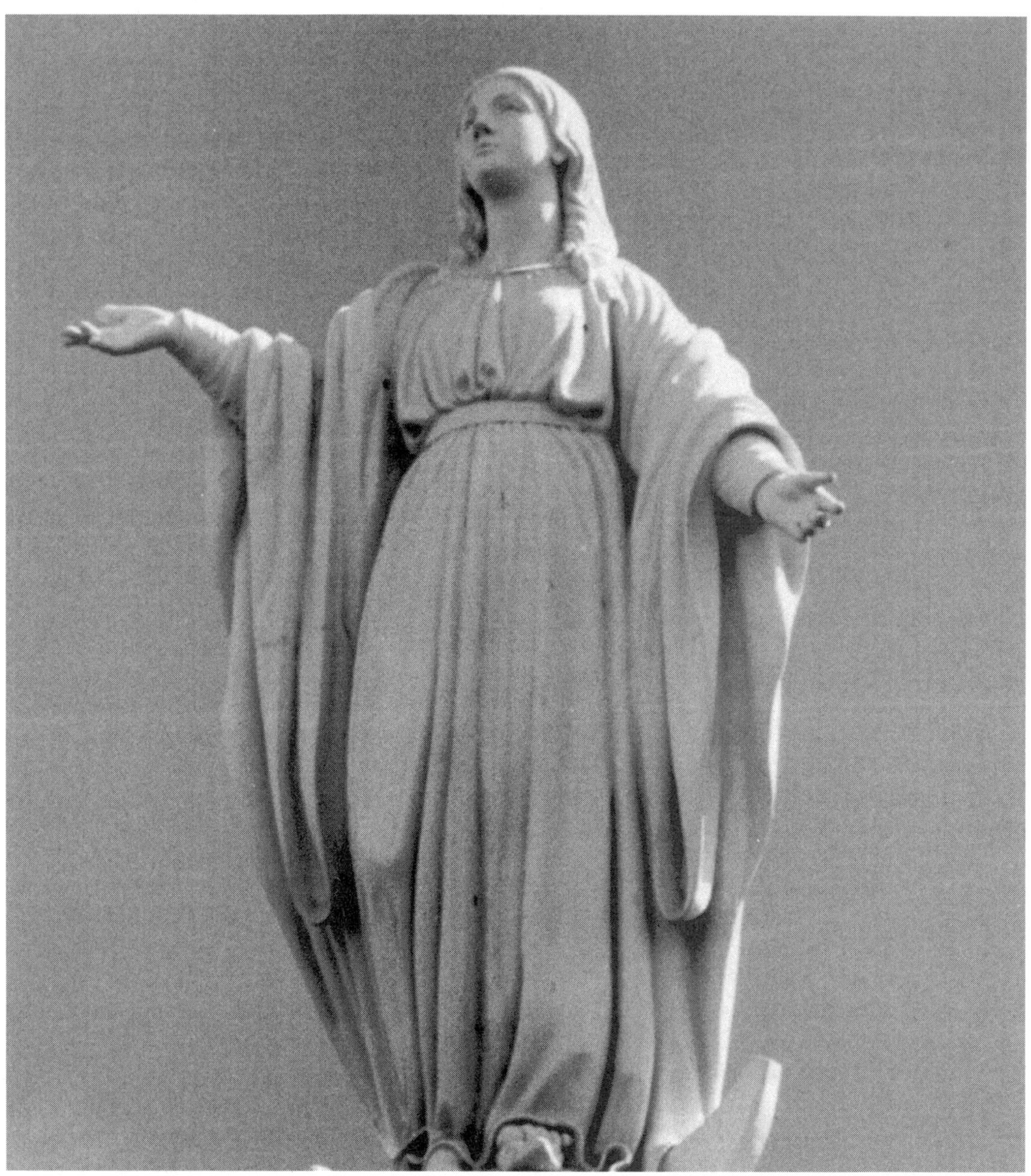

**A gigantic statue in Santiago, Chile, of the Virgin Mary on the lunar crescent.** ***Reproduced by permission of Fortean Picture Library.***

## VIRGIN

The Virgin is a popular (but not particularly appropriate) name for the sign Virgo.

# Virgo

Virgo, the sixth sign of the zodiac, is a mutable earth sign. It is a negative (in the value-neutral sense of being negatively charged), feminine sign, ruled by the planet Mercury—though some modern astrologers dispute this rulership, claiming that it is ruled by several of the major asteroids or by the planetoid Chiron; an older generation of astrologers associated Virgo with the hypothetical planet Vulcan. Its symbol is a young woman, and its glyph is said to represent a serpent that was formerly linked to the serpent-like glyph of Scorpio since it is said that Virgo and Scorpio were once one sign. Virgo takes its name from the Latin word for virgin. Virgo is associated with the nervous system and, especially, with the bowels, and people with a Virgo sun sign are susceptible to bowel problems and ulcers. The key phrase for Virgo is "I analyze."

This sign has either a very simple or a very complex mythology, depending upon which mythological figure is taken to represent Virgo. The constellation Virgo is pictured as a young woman holding an ear of corn, linking the sign to Demeter, the Greek goddess of the harvest (in the Northern Hemisphere, the Sun is in Virgo during harvest time). She taught humanity agriculture, and was the mother of Plutus (wealth). Far from being a virgin, Demeter was a mature earth goddess and the patroness of fertility. Virgo, however, is one of the traditional barren signs. Thus, a better (or, perhaps, an alternative) representative of Virgo is Hygeia, goddess of health and hygiene. Hygeia was the unmarried daughter of Asklepios, the eminent physician, who, attended by his daughter, was often pictured with serpents (commonly associated with doctors; e.g., the serpents twisted around the medical caduceus).

Rather than embodying Demeter's fertility, Virgo represents Demeter's harvest aspect, and people born under this sign are good workers. This, perhaps, is the association with wealth, which is more often built on the foundation of steady labor than on sudden lucky windfalls. Virgos have fewer ego needs than many other signs of the zodiac, and—similar to Demeter who served as a nursemaid, as well as Hygeia who served as her father's assistant—Virgos typically find happiness working under someone else. Like Demeter who taught both agriculture and the Eleusinian Mysteries, Virgos excel at teaching. Like Hygeia, they can also be good doctors and nurses. Virgos are especially concerned with good hygiene, which is derived from the name of the goddess Hygeia.

The sign that the Sun was in at birth is usually the single most important influence on a native's personality. Thus, when people say they are a certain sign, they are almost always referring to their sun sign. There is a wealth of information available on the characteristics of the zodiacal signs—so much that one book would not be able to contain it all. Sun-sign astrology, which is the kind of astrology found in newspaper columns and popular magazines, has the advantage of simplicity. But this simplicity is purchased at the price of ignoring other astrological influences, such as one's Moon sign, rising sign, etc. These other influences can substantially modify a person's basic sun sign traits. As a consequence, it is the rare individual who is completely typical of her or his sign. The reader should bear this caveat in mind when perusing the following series of sun-sign interpretations.

One traditional way in which astrologers condense information is by summarizing sign and planet traits in lists of words and short phrases called key words or key phrases. The following Virgo key words are drawn from Manly P. Hall's *Astrological Keywords:*

> *Emotional keywords:* "Kindly, humane, a high evolved type, lives to serve mankind without thought of self, domestic, melancholy, somewhat petty, fussy, superficial in affairs of the heart."
>
> *Mental key words:* "Ingenious, witty, studious, dextrous, versatile, introspective, scientific, methodical, skeptical, critical, fears disease and poverty, ulterior in motive, self-centered, scheming."

**The constellation Virgo with the caduceus of the planetary ruler, Mercury. From *Abstrolabum Planum,* 1493. *Reproduced by permission of Fortean Picture Library.***

At present, there are various astrology report programs that contain interpretations of each of the 12 sun signs. A selection of these for Sun in Virgo has been excerpted below:

> Careful and cautious by nature, you tend to value neatness and order. You rigorously practice very high standards of living and conduct and you demand the same of everyone with whom you come into contact. At times, you are so supercritical that you are merely nit-picky. You are good at practical skills and handy with tools. You are also greatly concerned with hygiene, cleanliness and personal health problems. Very likely your health is much better than you think it is—don't worry so much. Extremely methodical and analytical, you are a perfectionist, which makes you the perfect person to carry out highly detailed, precise operations. But, at times, you pay so much attention to details that you lose sight of the larger issues. (From "Professional Natal Report." Courtesy of Astrolabe [http://www.alabe.com].)
>
> At heart you are modest and humble, and you rarely strive to be in the limelight or in a position of power. You have a sharp analytical mind, a keen eye for detail, and you prefer to observe, dissect, and study life from a distance. Conscientious and conservative, you can be relied upon to be careful, efficient, and thorough in your work and you take pride in doing a job well. What you may lack in self-confidence you often make up for in skill—developing expertise, technical knowledge, and competency in some specialized area. You are adept at using your hands to create or fix things, and meticulous attention to detail and careful craftsmanship are your forte. Some would say you are a little

TOO meticulous, for you can be extremely critical and petty if everything is not done exactly as you think it should be, and you worry about things that other people consider trivial and unimportant. You like to organize, categorize, and arrange everything into a logical system, and you are often distinctly uncomfortable when something does not fit into a neat category. Disorganization vexes you. You probably wish that you were not such a perfectionist, for besides being a stickler for details, you can be mercilessly self-critical as well. Whether in your environment or in yourself, you tend to focus on the flaws, with a desire to improve, refine, and perfect. You are strictly factual, truthful, and scrupulously honest in your self-estimation, and you often do not give yourself enough praise or credit.

You are also highly discriminating and may be especially particular about your diet, hygiene, and health habits. You have high aesthetic standards and refined sensitivities, and will be bothered by elements in your surroundings (such as disorder, cigarette smoke, etc.) that others overlook. Your tastes are simple, understated, but refined. Coarseness, bluntness, and vulgarity really offend you. You can be difficult to live with sometimes because of your fastidiousness, your sensitivity, and your idiosyncrasies about food and cleanliness.

Though you seem rather cool and self-contained, you have a very helpful nature and you enjoy serving others. You are content to be in a supportive, assisting role rather than in the lead. You are quietly devoted to the ones you care for.

You are careful and cautious in your approach to life, realistic, practical, and disinclined to gamble. You analyze before you act. You are too serious sometimes. Allowing yourself to play and to make mistakes would be HEALTHY for you! (From "Merlin," by Gina Ronco and Agnes Nightingale. Courtesy of Cosmic Patterns [http://cosmic.patterns.com].)

Virginity isn't the point. That's just a kind of inexperience, and in the long run no one learns much from avoiding experience. Virgo means purity. Perfection. Getting everything exactly right. That's a tall order. Perfection is a harsh master. It drives the Virgoan part of you, haunting you with a sense of what could be, a sense of the ideal. It also holds a flawless mirror before you, revealing all the imperfections and shortfalls in your character. The combination is powerful. It fills your spirit with hunger and divine discontent, imbuing you with restlessness, as though you'd taken out an insurance policy against complacency. Be careful, though: Virgo energies can self-destruct, slipping into a crippling hyper-awareness regarding all the flaws and shortfalls inherent in people, oneself, our possessions, our prospects—everything. And nothing kills our climb toward perfection faster than that.

With your Sun in Virgo, sitting around feeling good about yourself doesn't stoke the existential furnace. What drives you, vitalizes you,

> makes you feel alive, is effort. You were born hungry to accomplish things. You're hungry now. You'll die hungry too. That sounds like a baleful prophecy, but it's not as dark as it seems. Another way of describing your innate restlessness is that you're eager to evolve, to learn, to grow, and are never content to rest on your laurels.
>
> Your soul took a risk working with this energy. You sense what you could be, how you'd look if you were wiser, purer, clearer. Just as vividly, you see what you really are, with all your flaws and shortcomings. Ideally, that contrast should inspire you. But if it gets twisted, then you plummet into self-criticism, guilt, and crippling, self-imposed limitations. And that pathology gets expressed outwardly as a critical, nit-picking personality. On the deepest level, you're learning about self-acceptance. But you're doing it in the toughest of all psychological environments: an honest mind. (From "The Sky Within," by Steven Forrest. Courtesy of Matrix Software [http://thenewage.com] and Steven Forrest [http://www.stevenforrest.com].)

Among its several natal programs, Matrix Software created a unique report based on the published works of the early twentieth-century astrologer Grant Lewi (1901–1952). Lewi's highly original delineations were recognized as creative and insightful by his contemporaries. One measure of the appeal of his work is that his books *Astrology for the Millions* and *Heaven Knows What* are still in print. The following is excerpted from the report program "Heaven Knows What":

> "Three things are to be looked to in a building: that it stand on the right spot, that it be securely founded, that it be successfully executed." (*Johann Wolfgang von Goethe, born in Virgo, August 18, 1749.*)
>
> "The happiness of man consists in life. And life is in labor.... The vocation of every man and woman is to serve other people." (*Count Tolstoy, born in Virgo, August 28, 1828.*)
>
> To discover the motivating drive in the life of any Virgoan, it is necessary to look at the work he is doing; for so deep is Virgo's utilitarian sense that he identifies himself with his work and is quite willing to lose himself in it. His personality and character development depend, to a peculiar extent, on the nature of the work he has set himself, for he will be as big or as small as his job or mission. He is capable of becoming single-tracked, absorbed and narrow over whatever he happens to fall into. He is capable of making work his god, and thus going high and far in a chosen direction. He is capable of expanding his spirit by selecting a career somehow related to service. He is capable of the extremes of self-denial if he thinks his work calls him to that. And he is also capable of feeling that his work requires self-immolation, self-limitation and self-sacrifice to an inordinate degree.
>
> However you figure it, the puzzle of his nature will be solved if you find his attitude toward the hub of his universe, his work. So true is this that when you run across an unemployed Virgoan you have the

> most woebegone and incomplete personality in the world. In losing his work, Virgo loses his whole reason for being. In its best forms, this makes for efficiency and brilliance in the performance of duty, and it may take the sense of duty into very humane realms of selflessness. In its worst form, it makes for narrowness of outlook, great inability to talk anything but shop, lack of interest in anything not related to work. So engrossed does Virgo become in his job (talk, mission, message or whatever he calls it) that he sometimes seems intent on destroying all the rest of the personality that doesn't belong to his work. He loses interest in extracurricular activities, so that his life is one long routine of keeping the nose to the grindstone, and he is unhappy when for some reason or other the grindstone stops or his nose gets away from it. To fix the aim high, to select a job that requires diverse talents and wide knowledge, is Virgo's best bet for a well-rounded life. If he has the misfortune to be able to find progress and security in a rut, he is likely to see only the progress and not realize it is a rut. He needs activities, companions, fun, diversions, hobbies to broaden his life, and should seek these along constructive lines lest his overtaxed body and brain force him to seek them in undesirable forms of escapism, brooding and introversion.
>
> Following are the aspects to your Sun. In a general way, the trines and sextiles to your Sun make ease, contentment, happiness, luck; while squares and oppositions give you energy, drive, success, ambition. Conjunctions bring both energy and luck, and are translatable in terms of whether the Sun receives squares or trines, along with the conjunction. Similarly, squares and trines to the Sun together bring success through work and perseverance, and luck develops in proportion to the work done and the effort extended. (Courtesy of Matrix Software [http://thenewage.com].)

The following excerpt comes not from a natal report program, but from David Cochrane's recent book, *Astrology for the 21st Century*. Based on lessons for astrology students, it approaches the signs of the zodiac from a somewhat different perspective than the other short delineations cited here:

> Virgo is notorious for its tendency to categorize, criticize, and try to make everything operate perfectly and immaculately. Of course the world is not perfect and mistakes are made on occasion but Virgo tends to become irritable and disappointed when things do not work perfectly. Striving for perfection is natural for Virgo, but learning how to be patient with error is more difficult.
>
> Virgo is also described as being a helpful sign, and Virgo does love to serve. Virgo loves to fix things, correct errors, and help you fix the problems in your life. However, Virgo, in my opinion, is interested in fixing problems in your life because it seeks perfection and loves to fix your life, but if you want sympathy or a shoulder to cry on, very often it

> is better to seek out someone other than the person with lots of Virgo in their chart. Virgo wants to fix the problem, not indulge it, and Virgo usually has a clear idea of how to fix things and is inclined to become impatient and irritated if there is a lot of discussion and analysis required before the actual improvements can be made. (Courtesy of Cosmic Patterns [http://cosmic.patterns.com] and David Cochrane [kepler@astrosoftware.com].)

A number of specialized report programs has been developed that offer useful supplements to the generic delineations of general reports. The following sun-sign interpretation has been drawn from a program written by Gloria Star (originally part of her book *Astrology: Woman to Woman*) that generates a specialized report for women:

> With your Sun in Virgo your ego is driven by a powerful need to do things well. Although you may not ask for recognition, and may act uncomfortable when it comes your way, you crave the confirmation it brings. Yes, you are a perfectionist and you definitely have opinions. Yet you can be flexible when necessary. Just be sure that flexibility doesn't turn you into a doormat when you run into those people who are the controllers. It's okay to have things your way some of the time, too.
>
> You may be glad you're a woman. In fact, some of the more brutish aspects of manhood may hold absolutely no enticement to you whatsoever. As a Virgo woman, you're not interested in expressing your masculine side as a man might—you would prefer to own your identity and express it just the way you want it! Face it, you can be intimidated by men, and may have given away some of your power because you don't really feel very comfortable tooting your own horn. There is a difference between appreciating yourself and standing up for the recognition and advancement you deserve, and letting someone take advantage of you. Unfortunately, you may not really want to do battle and may prefer to just do your job or attend to your duties and let the blowhards have their fun. You may also get in your own way by being too critical of yourself, or feeling that you are not really "perfect enough," to have all the glory. It's possible that you felt a strong sense of judgment or criticism from your father, and learned to be Little Miss Perfect in order to gain his approval. But that was when you were a little girl. By applying your powerful sense of discrimination and critical judgment to determine if you're getting what you need from your relationship, your job or your family, you can make an honest assessment of your life situation. Then, you can forge a plan of action which will assure that you can achieve a better pathway for your personal fulfillment.
>
> The influence of your Virgo Sun stimulates a need to follow a path which will allow you to utilize your analytical abilities and powers of discernment. Raising a family may be one of your greatest joys, and you can be a supportive and understanding mother. In your choice of career you may be an exceptional educator and will enjoy a career which

> allows you to continue learning. You may also choose designing, health care, writing, editing, or prefer to work in supportive roles in business. If you have your own business, you will enjoy catering to those with discriminating taste, and may promote quality material and workmanship. (From "Woman to Woman," by Gloria Star. Courtesy of Matrix Software [http://thenewage.com] and Gloria Star [glostar@aol.com].)

Responding to the revival of interest in pre-twentieth-century astrology, J. Lee Lehman developed a report program embodying the interpretive approach of traditional astrology. The following is excerpted from her book *Classical Astrology for Modern Living* and her computer program "Classical Report":

> You are given to all manner of learning, and skilled at the sciences, or many areas of knowledge. You are cheerful, discrete and judicious, and a lover of the arts. You are studious, with a wit ingenious but discriminating, and wholly for its own end. You enjoy musical and culinary entertainments.
>
> You are mutable, which means that you adapt easily to change. However, you adapt so easily compared to others that they may wonder if you are capable of maintaining a permanent stance about anything.
>
> You are an Earth Sign, which means that you are "cold" and "dry." The "dry" component means, among other things, that you see distinctions easily, and that you are more swayed by intellectual argument than by passion. You are perceived as being "cold," an outward appearance of being unemotional. In the modern parlance, it fits better with "cold and dry" than with simply "cold." However, a "cold" type is basically lethargic, or slow to react. The "problem" with "cold" is that it makes it hard for you to forget slights. Because you don't tend to lash out immediately, it's easy for you to allow your anger to build up. Combine this with a tendency, being "dry," to prefer the reasonable approach, and you can end up completely out of touch while your emotions run rampant. (Courtesy of J. Lee Lehman, Ph.D., copyright 1998 [http://www.leelehman.com].)

Readers interested in examining interpretations for their Chinese astrological sign should refer to the relevant entry. A guide for determining one's sign in the Chinese system is provided in the entry on the Chinese zodiac.

**Sources:**

Cochrane, David. *Astrology for the 21st Century*. Gainesville, FL: Cosmic Patterns, 2002.

Forrest, Steven. *The Inner Sky: How to Make Wiser Choices for a More Fulfilling Life*. 4th ed. San Diego: ACS Publications, 1989.

Green, Landis Knight. *The Astrologer's Manual: Modern Insights into an Ancient Art*. Sebastopol, CA: CRCS Publications, 1975.

Hall, Manly P. *Astrological Keywords*. New York: Philosophical Library, 1958. Reprint, Savage, MD: Littlefield Adams Quality Paperbacks, 1975.

Lehman, J. Lee. *Classical Astrology for Modern Living: From Ptolemy to Psychology and Back Again*. Atglen, PA: Whitford Press, 1996.

Lewi, Grant. *Astrology for the Millions*.5th ed. St. Paul, MN: Llewellyn, 1978.
———. *Heaven Knows What*. St. Paul, MN: Llewellyn, 1969.
Star, Gloria. *Astrology & Your Child: A Handbook for Parents*. St. Paul, MN: Llewellyn, 2001.
———. *Astrology: Woman to Woman*. St. Paul, MN: Llewellyn, 1999.

## Virtus

Virtus, asteroid 494 (the 494th asteroid to be discovered, on September 7, 1902), is approximately 98 kilometers in diameter and has an orbital period of 5.2 years. Its name is a personification of the Latin word for "virtue." In a natal chart, Virtus's house and sign position indicates where in life one displays virtue in the original sense of power and excellence. When afflicted, Vera may signal false virtue.

**Sources:**

Kowal, Charles T. *Asteroids: Their Nature and Utilization*. Chichester, West Sussex, UK: Ellis Horwood Limited, 1988.
Room, Adrian. *Dictionary of Astronomical Names*. London: Routledge, 1988.
Schwartz, Jacob. *Asteroid Name Encyclopedia*. St. Paul, MN: Llewellyn Publications, 1995.

## Visakha

Visakha (forked or spreading branches) is one of the Nakshatras (lunar mansions) of Vedic astrology. Indragni, both deities Indra and Agni combined, presides and the planet Jupiter rules over this decorated gateway moon sign found from Libra 20° to Scorpio 3°20'. Considered a good sign for construction, land deals, and the like, people in Visakha will be quite clever and enterprising, though overly talkative and greedy at times.

—Pramela Thiagesan

## Vocational Astrology

The two most frequently asked questions in astrology relate to relationships and careers. Of these, career exploration combines the best of traditional astrological methods with the best of modern psychological astrology. In addition, Vedic astrology includes very specific data about the type of career one may pursue.

Exploration of the career includes several factors in the natal chart:

*Individual creative capacity*. Everyone is creative; vocational astrology looks at creativity as it impacts career choices.

*The careers that suit the individual chart*. These reflect the planets, sign, and aspects related to the tenth house and its rulers.

*The actual workplace and the people found in it, reflected by the sixth house and its rulers*. This includes the geographic location, the type of building, and the location within the building where one works.

*The source of one's personal income, reflected by the second house and its rulers*. This house also includes money management, material goods, and self-esteem.

*The personal style of the individual.* This includes myriad factors, with a focus on the Sun, Moon, ascendant, and midheaven signs.

*The place to begin one's career path (indicated by Saturn).*

*The personal activities concerning career (indicated by Mars).*

*Character traits that may affect job performance.* This includes sign and element of the Sun and Moon, speed of the Moon in the birth chart, position of Mercury relative to the Sun, and numerous other factors.

When career considerations are expanded to include the concept of vocation or mission, the astrological delineation of career takes on a philosophical or even spiritual overtone. If one's vocation is a calling, who calls? The ideal career satisfies this calling in a direct way. The astrologer helps the client listen to the inner voice, or *daimon*, to understand the unique personal life path he or she is intended to pursue. The astrologer then uses the above considerations to identify careers that suit the individual mission.

Twenty-first-century vocational astrology has unique demands, considering the rapid changes in the work arena. Significant careers from the past no longer exist, or have metamorphosed into something unrecognizable by a nineteenth-century person. For example, candlemaking was once an essential occupation. The contemporary candlemaker is either working in a highly mechanized atmosphere, or is making candles for the love of the task. Very few people make their living in this career. However, like the butcher and the baker, the candlemaking profession may be seeing a small revival, as people indicate their desire for "the real thing."

The distinctions between work roles have blurred. For example, where a businessperson once had a secretary to prepare all letters, email now is an essential component of an executive's work skill package. Yet skilled letter-writing retains a place in the career mix, and is a creative art to be developed by those who aim to get ahead. The executive has acquired the increased need for written communication skills.

A second example involves libraries. The Internet and computers have resulted in major revisions in the way libraries operate. Once the province of a professional librarian, book cataloging can be done quickly and inexpensively by staff with far less technical training, and a library collection in Pueblo, Colorado, can be viewed by a patron in Italy. In this case, the clerical workload of collection management has been shifted to another staff member, and the professional librarian has moved into the role of collection development and reference services to a large extent.

What do these changes mean for the vocational astrologer? The astrologer has to keep current with career changes. Vocational and professional training information forms an important part of the astrologer's resources. Similar to the career counselor in a school, the astrologer must be able to relate the client's astrological vocational picture to the career market of the day.

The astrologer may act as career coach as well. Help with choosing the career field remains the main focus. In addition, the astrologer may coach the client in how to present his or her skills effectively. A third part of the astrologer's role is to help the client present his deeper character traits effectively. Missing from resumes of the twenty-first century, effective communication of one's character may be the deciding factor in gaining employment in very tough job markets. The astrologer is well positioned to provide essential information in this regard.

Vocational astrology is a growing segment within the broader astrological career field. The use of traditional charting methods and contemporary computer-aided astrology make this a dynamic branch of a profession that dates back at least to the Greeks and their Arabian contemporaries.

—Stephanie Clement

## Voice, Signs of

The signs of voice are those signs of the zodiac said to indicate oratorial capacity—Gemini, Virgo, Libra, Aquarius, and the first half of Sagittarius.

## Void of Course

A planet is void of course after it makes its last major aspect with another planet before transiting out of a given sign. It remains void of course (often abbreviated VOC) until it enters a new sign (almost invariably the next sign) in which it will make another major aspect. This is an old notion, originating in horary astrology, that has begun to enjoy a new wave of popularity. Many contemporary astrologers pay special attention to transiting void-of-course Moons, regarding their influence as being on par with that of retrograde motion—meaning that these are poor periods during which to sign contracts, initiate new projects, or acquire new possessions. It is a good time, however, to reflect and "recharge."

To clarify the mechanics of void of course, imagine that the transiting Moon has just entered Aquarius. Over the course of several days, as the Moon moves from 0° to 26° Aquarius, it will make a half dozen or so major aspects (conjunctions, sextiles, squares, trines, and oppositions) with the Sun and the transiting planets. However, at 26° Aquarius, it will make its last aspect, say, a sextile (60°) aspect with Jupiter. As it sweeps across the next 4° (taking approximately 8 hours to do so), and until it makes its ingress (entry) into the sign Pisces, it is void of course. The length of a void of course varies from a few minutes to more than 24 hours, depending on where the planets are while the Moon transits each sign.

Al H. Morrison, the widely acknowledged expert on void-of-course moons, has observed that "actions taken while the Moon is void of course somehow always fail of their intended or planned results." Morrison studied law enforcement activities and found that whenever investigative actions were initiated during void-of-course moons, individuals violating the law failed to be convicted (although the investigation always managed to upset their criminal operation). Thus, although activities may not turn out as anticipated, the result need not be unfortunate. After 45 years of study, Morrison concluded that the Moon's last aspect has to be a true major aspect with the Sun or one of the planets (not Chiron or one of the asteroids). Minor aspects, such as the semisextile, the quintile, etc., do not save the Moon from being void of course.

Morrison also noted a cyclic mood pattern peculiar to people born during void-of-course moons.

Another astrologer, Janis Huntley, studied 250 charts and found that approximately 1 out of every 12 people was born while the Moon was void of course. She also found a significantly higher percentage—1 out of every 8—among famous people. Thus, this placement does not appear to dampen achievement. Like Morrison, Huntley found that individuals born during void-of-course moons seemed to suffer somewhat from the turmoils of their emotions. They often experience loneliness, feeling "different and misunderstood."

Morrison has published a void-of-course moon ephemeris for many years. Also, some astrological magazines, such as the *Mountain Astrologer,* contain day-by-day accounts of transiting conditions that note when the Moon goes void of course as well as when the Moon enters a new sign. Finally, certain of the major emphemerides, such as the *American Emphemeris*, published by Astro Computing, contain last-aspect and ingress information for the Moon. By all indications, the void-of-course moon has found a permanent niche in the mainstream of modern astrology.

**Sources:**

Huntley, Janis. *Astrological Voids: Exploring the Missing Components in the Birth Chart*. Rockport, MA: Element Books, 1991.

Michelsen, Neil F. *The American Ephemeris for the 20th Century*. San Diego: Astro Computing Services, 1988.

Morrison, Al H. "Notes on the Void-of-Course Moon." *The Mountain Astrologer* 889 (August/September 1989): 11, 29.

## VULCAN

Vulcan (related to the word volcano) is a "hypothetical planet" (sometimes referred to as the trans-Neptunian points or planets, or TNPs for short) that astronomers formerly speculated would be—and that a few astrologers still anticipate will be—found orbiting the Sun inside the orbit of Mercury. The nineteenth-century French astronomer Urbain Le Verrier was the first person to hypothesize its existence and, shortly after he made his theories known, people began to claim that they had observed Vulcan. It was named after the ancient Roman god of fire, who was also blacksmith to the gods. Alice Bailey's system of esoteric astrology makes extensive use of Vulcan, and some esoteric astrologers still utilize it. Many astrologers anticipated that Vulcan, when discovered, would be assigned the rulership of Virgo. As astronomers gradually abandoned the notion of an intermercurial planet, Vulcan slowly faded from astrological discourse. There is, for example, no entry for Vulcan in such standard references as the *Larousse Encyclopedia of Astrology* or Eleanor Bach's *Astrology from A to Z*. Thanks to the *Star Trek* television series, the name is still alive, although Mr. Spock's home planet bears little resemblance to the hypothetical planet of astronomical history.

**Sources:**

Bach, Eleanor. *Astrology from A to Z: An Illustrated Source Book*. New York: Philosophical Library, 1990.

Brau, Jean-Louis, Helen Weaver, and Allan Edmands. *Larousse Encyclopedia of Astrology*. New York: New American Library, 1980.

Corliss, William R. *The Sun and Solar System Debris: A Catalog of Astronomical Anomalies*. Glen Arm, MD: The Sourcebook Project, 1986.

DeVore, Nicholas. *Encyclopedia of Astrology*. New York: Philosophical Library, 1947.

Gettings, Fred. *Dictionary of Astrology*. London: Routledge & Kegan Paul, 1985.

## VULCANUS

Vulcanus is one of the eight hypothetical planets (sometimes referred to as the trans-Neptunian points or planets, or TNPs for short) utilized in Uranian astrology. The Uranian system, sometimes referred to as the Hamburg School of Astrology, was established by Friedrich Sieggrün (1877–1951) and Alfred Witte (1878–1943). It relies heavily on hard aspects and midpoints. In decline for many decades, it has experienced a revival in recent years.

Vulcanus represents powerful and even explosive energy and force, especially the urge that one cannot quite control, or the experience of charismatic coercion. It can also symbolize a person's reservoir of energy and the depletion of that energy.

**The Gallic Vulcan as it appeared on a Celtic monument found under a section of Notre Dame cathedral in Paris in 1711. *Reproduced by permission of Fortean Picture Library.***

**Sources:**

Lang-Wescott, Martha. *Mechanics of the Future: Asteroids*. Rev. ed. Conway, MA: Treehouse Mountain, 1991.

Simms, Maria Kay. *Dial Detective: Investigation with the 90 Degree Dial*. San Diego: Astro Computing Services, 1989.

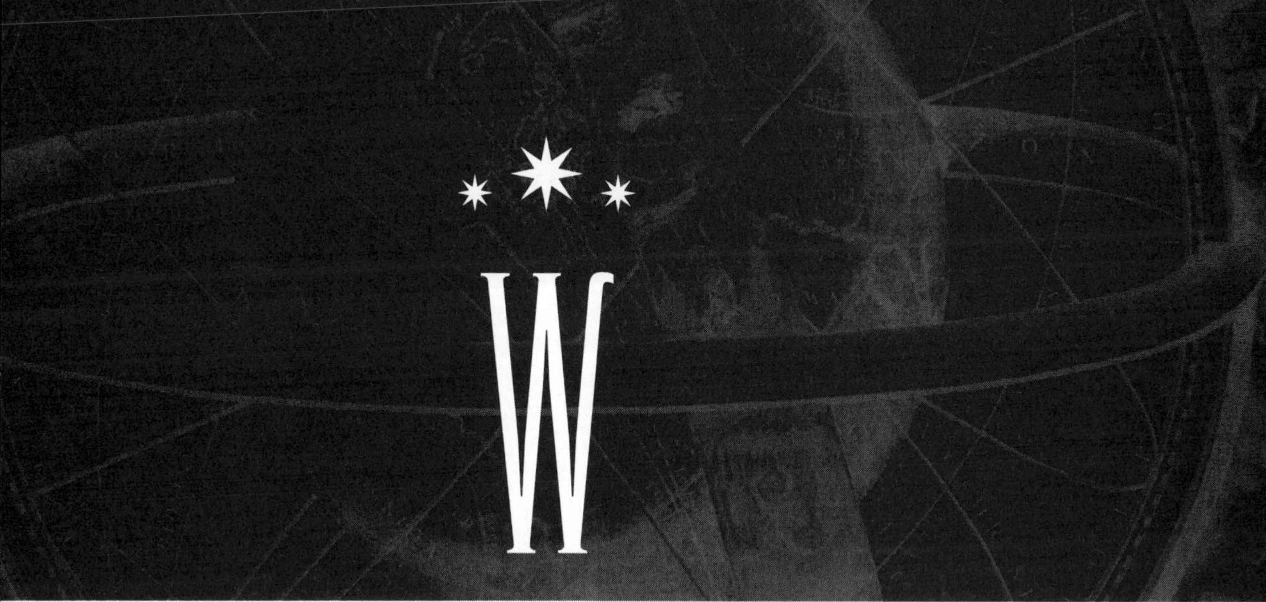

## Walkure

Walkure, asteroid 877 (the 877th asteroid to be discovered, on September 13, 1915), is approximately 27 kilometers in diameter and has an orbital period of 3.9 years. Walkure was named after the maidens in Scandinavian mythology who escorted fallen warriors to Valhalla. J. Lee Lehman asserts that the pattern represented by this asteroid is that of "enjoining the battle, without actually engaging in the fighting."

**Sources:**


Kowal, Charles T. *Asteroids: Their Nature and Utilization*. Chichester, West Sussex, UK: Ellis Horwood Limited, 1988.

Lehman, J. Lee. *The Ultimate Asteroid Book*. West Chester, PA: Whitford Press, 1988.

Room, Adrian. *Dictionary of Astronomical Names*. London: Routledge, 1988.

Schwartz, Jacob. *Asteroid Name Encyclopedia*. St. Paul, MN: Llewellyn Publications, 1995.


## War Time

During World Wars I and II, many countries, including the United States, adopted daylight savings time on a year-round basis to provide a longer workday to meet the increased demands of wartime production. When horoscopes are cast for individuals born during war years, it is thus necessary to subtract one hour to obtain standard time. For natives of the United Kingdom born during WWII, the clocks were two hours ahead of standard time in the summer (this was termed double summer time).

## Water Bearer

The Water Bearer is a popular name for the sign Aquarius.

## WATER SIGNS

The 12 signs of the zodiac are subdivided according to the four classical elements of earth, air, fire, and water. The three water signs (the water triplicity or water trigon) are Cancer, Scorpio, and Pisces. Astrologically, water refers to sensitivity, intuition, emotion, and fluidity. Water-sign sensitivity can manifest as artistic sensitivity, psychic sensitivity, or as sensitivity to others. This element also embodies the traits of compassion, nurture, and protection.

The emotional sensitivity of the water element shows itself somewhat differently in each of the signs of the water triplicity. Cancer's watery nature typically manifests as feelings about home, security, and family. Scorpio's emerges as strong feelings about sex, death, and occult mysteries. Pisces's watery nature appears as mysticism, sensitivity to music, and impressionability.

Negative water people can be moody, depressed, emotionally grasping, and possessive. Unless counterbalanced by other factors, excess water in a chart indicates an individual who is hypersensitive and overemotional. Conversely, lack of water can indicate a person who is insensitive and unemotional.

One finds the same set of four elements and the same classification of signs by element in Vedic astrology. The connotations are basically the same as in Western astrology.

Water is also one of the five elements of Chinese astrology—earth, water, fire, wood, and metal. In this system, the elements are not permanently associated with each of the signs of the zodiac. Rather, each one of the 12 signs of the East Asian zodiac can be a different element. The connotations of water in Chinese astrology do not correspond with the connotations of water in Western astrology.

**Sources:**

Hand, Robert. *Horoscope Symbols*. Rockport, MA: Para Research, 1981.
Sakoian, Frances, and Louis S. Acker. *The Astrologer's Handbook*. New York: Harper & Row, 1989.

## WAXING AND WANING

Waxing refers to indicate the increasing strength of any given astrological influence. More commonly, waxing and waning refers to the Moon's monthly cycle during which the portion of its surface lighted by the Sun increases (waxes) or decreases (wanes) in size. The increase or decrease in the Moon's size is especially important in electional astrology. The basic principle is that activities hoped to quickly expand, such as a new business venture, should be initiated during a waxing (increasing) Moon. Activities hoped to stop or slow down, such as the growth of hair after a haircut, should be undertaken during a waning (decreasing) Moon.

## WEAK SIGNS

Traditionally, the weak signs were Cancer, Capricorn, and Pisces. Although one can perceive the rationale for regarding Cancer and Pisces as "weak," it is difficult to understand why strong, stubborn Capricorn was thus designated.

# Whole Signs (Perfect Signs)

"Whole signs" (also called, in more recent works, perfect signs) is an archaic term referring to certain signs said to indicate strong, healthy bodies. The whole signs are variously listed, but usually include the three air triplicity signs (Gemini, Libra, and Aquarius). This classification has been abandoned by modern astrologers. The antonym is broken signs (imperfect signs).

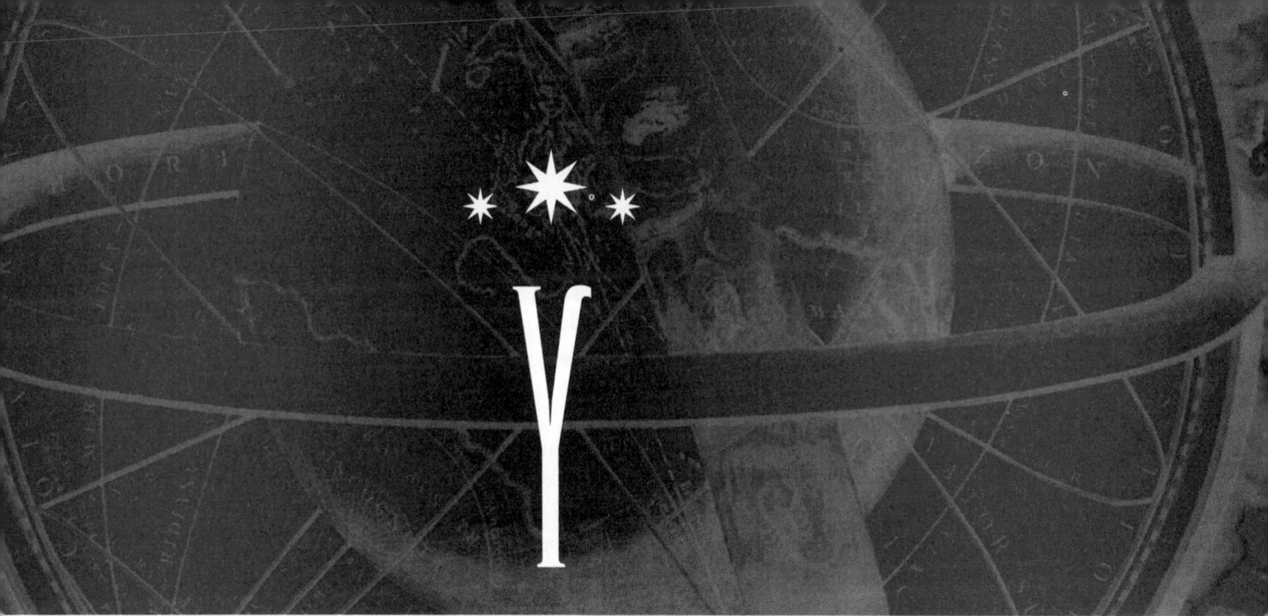

# Yod (Double Quincunx; Finger of Destiny; Hand of God)

A yod is a configuration involving at least three planets in which two of them form a sextile (60°) aspect and both then form a quincunx (150°) aspect with a third planet; hence, double quincunx is one of the several alternative names for this configuration. If lines were drawn to the center of the horoscope from all three planets, the resulting pattern would look like a capital Y—thus the name yod, which is the name of the tenth letter of the Hebrew alphabet and the letter that corresponds with the English "Y" (though, sometimes, with "I" or "J").

The tenth Hebrew letter is an ideogram meaning "hand" or "pointing finger," from which the other names for this configuration derive (finger of destiny, hand of God, etc.). The term "yod," as well as the other, more dramatic names for the pattern, originated with Carl Leipert, a student of history and comparative religion. This configuration has been intensively studied by Thyrza Escobar and Dane Rudyhar.

A yod indicates a strange or unusual destiny. The interpretation often given to a natal yod is that it indicates a life that proceeds along in a certain pattern for a period of time until the established pattern is abruptly interrupted and the native is forced to proceed in a new direction. Often, though not always, the change has been prepared for, as in the case of an unknown understudy who on opening night must fill the shoes of the leading actor (owing to the latter's sudden illness or some other unforeseen event). A yod is not necessarily benefic, in the sense that the interruptions in the life pattern that it indicates are not always pleasant. The disruptive changes foretold by the configuration take place when a transiting or progressed planet makes a major aspect, particularly a conjunction, with the planet at the "fingertip" of the yod. This disruption will be most keenly felt in the affairs related to the house (and, to a lesser extent, the sign) position of this focal planet, though there will also be reactions in the house and sign directly across the chart from the focal planet.

**Sources:**

Brau, Jean-Louis, Helen Weaver, and Allan Edmands. *Larousse Encyclopedia of Astrology*. New York: New American Library, 1980.

Escobar, Thyrza. *Side Lights of Astrology*. 3d ed. Hollywood, CA: Golden Seal Research, 1971.

## YOGAS

The Sanskrit word yoga has multiple meanings including "union" and "join." However, in the context of Vedic astrology, the following two definitions are especially useful. Hart de Fouw defines yoga as "a union of a multitude of astrological factors into a meaningful pattern" and K. S. Charak describes it as "any specific planetary disposition capable of producing some specific result." In a sense, the unique planetary pattern of every chart is a yoga of sorts. However, in practical terms, there are certain well-defined yogas that occur with regularity in charts. These yogas are widely accepted, specifically named and universally applied in the modern practice of Jyotish.

The importance of yogas in Vedic chart interpretation cannot be overemphasized. Experienced practitioners of Vedic astrology scan the chart for yogas as their first priority because the presence of important yogas is one of the most reliable indicators for predicting whether the level of life of a native will be above or below typical human experience. The amplitude in either direction will depend upon the confluence of the yogas, the strength of the component planets to express their indicated themes, and whether the native will experience the dashas (planetary periods) of the planets involved in the yoga combinations at appropriate times of life.

Descriptions of yogas are scattered throughout the ancient texts. Astrologers may never encounter many of these in their practice. By convention, however, yogas can be categorized as follows. Meanings given below represent one possible translation of the Sanskrit word or root:

*Raja Yogas:* Yogas that give rise in life often interpreted along the lines of status and position. Raja means "king."

*Dhana Yogas:* Yogas for wealth and prosperity. Dhana means "wealth."

*Daridra Yogas:* Yogas for penury and poverty. Daridra means "poor."

*Arishta Yogas:* Yogas for misfortune that includes poverty but also illness, loss of loved ones, and other forms of suffering. Arishta means "suffering."

*Pravraja Yogas:* Yogas that incline someone towards spiritual life or renunciation. Vraja means "wandering."

*Ravi or Solar Yogas:* A set of yogas organized around combinations involving the Sun.

*Chandra or Lunar Yogas:* A set of yogas organized around combinations involving the Moon.

*Vividha Yogas:* A huge category of miscellaneous yogas. Vividha means "various."

*Nabhasa Yogas:* Combinations that involve specific clusters or patterns of planets giving a visual impact upon examination of the chart. Nabhasa means "sky."

Yogas can be formed by a single planet meeting certain conditions, but more commonly they are formed by multiple planetary combinations. Sometimes the conditions for forming yogas are a function of the relative positions of specific planets in a chart. An example of such a yoga is a commonly occurring pattern involving an angular relationship between Moon and Jupiter known as a Gajakesari Yoga, which is often given the contemporary interpretation of being good at networking. Many other yogas are formed by planets being the lords of specific houses in certain associations. One of the most easily recognizable forms of the Raja ("rise") Yoga, exemplifies this type of yoga. The condition for its formation is that the lord of an angular or kendra house (houses 1, 4, 7 or 10) must have a mutual relationship with the lord of a trine or trikona house (houses 1, 5, 9). This relationship can be defined by any of the following: mutual association (conjunction), mutual aspect, or an exchange of houses. This latter condition is also known as a Parivartana Yoga.

In order to give some feeling for the breadth and color of this application of Vedic astrology, an example of a yoga in each of the aforementioned categories follows, in a translation of the language of Maharishi Parashara, author of one of the most widely used Vedic scriptures, known as the Brihat Parashara Hora Shastra.

*Raja Yoga:* "Should the lord of the 4th house or of the 10th house join either the 5th lord or the 9th lord, the native will obtain a kingdom."

*Dhana Yoga:* "If the 2nd lord is in the 11th while the lord of the 11th is in the 2nd, wealth will be acquired by the native. Alternatively, these two lords may join in an angle or in a trine."

*Daridra Yoga:* "If the ascendant lord along with a malefic is in the 6th, 8th or 12th houses while the 2nd lord is in an enemy's sign or in debilitation, even a royal scion will become penniless."

*Arishta Yoga:* "The native will be afflicted by illness throughout life if Saturn is with Rahu while the 6th lord and 6th house are conjunct malefics."

*Pravraja Yoga:* "The yoga for ascetism is formed when four or more planets possessed of strength occupy a single house."

*Ravi (Solar) Yoga:* "Barring the Moon, if a planet among Mars etc. be in the 2nd from the Sun, Vesi Yoga is formed. One born in Vesi yoga will be even sighted, truthful, long-bodied, indolent, happy and endowed with negligible wealth. Benefics causing this yoga will produce the above mentioned effects while malefics will produce contrary effects."

*Chandra (Lunar) Yoga:* "If benefics occupy the 8th, 6th and 7th counted from the Moon, Adhi Yoga obtains. According to the strength of the participating planets, the native concerned will be either a king or a minister or an army chief."

*Vividha Yoga:* "If there be exclusively a benefic in the 10th from the ascendant or the Moon, Amala yoga exists. Amala Yoga will confer fame lasting till the moon and stars exist and will make the native honoured by the king, enjoy abundant pleasures, be charitable; fond of relatives, helpful to others, pious and virtuous."

*Nabhasa Yoga:* "If 3 angles are occupied by benefics, Maala yoga is produced while malefics so placed will cause Sarpa yoga. These yogas respectively produce benefic and malefic results."

The study and application of yogas in contemporary astrological practice must include an understanding of the nature of the language of the scriptures. Many of the combinations are worded in language that is hyperbolic. This is a common device pervasively found in the oral tradition of India. It is an effective tool for teaching and memorization but the exaggerated indications are not necessarily meant to be rigidly applied in interpretation and certainly not out of the context of the rest of the chart.

—Penny Farrow

**Sources:**

Charak, K. S. *Yogas in Astrology*. New Delhi: Systems Vision, 1995.

Parahara, Maharishi. *Brihat Parashara Hora Shastra*. New Delhi, India: Ranjan Publications, 1989.

## Zelen Test

Of the various attempts to demonstrate astrological influence by statistical means, the large-scale studies by Michel and Françoise Gauquelin have been the most successful. The Gauquelins uncovered correlations between vocation and the position of specific planets, the most significant of which were those between athletes and the position of Mars. The Zelen Test was part of an extended attempt to disprove this Mars effect by *The Humanist* magazine. The original study had compared the birth data of athletes against statistical probabilities. Confident that an empirical challenge would demolish astrology, *The Humanist* challenged the Gauquelins to test their findings against a control group of nonathletes. Contrary to the expectations of critics, this test, conducted by Marvin Zelen (hence the name), confirmed the Gauquelins's original findings.

**Sources:**

Curry, Patrick. "Research on the Mars Effect." *Zetetic Scholar* 9 (March 1982): 34–53.

Melton, J. Gordon, Jerome Clark, and Aidan A. Kelly. *New Age Encyclopedia*. Detroit: Gale, 1990.

Rawlins, Dennis. "sTARBABY." *Fate* 34, no. 10 (October 1981): 67–98.

## Zenith

The zenith is the point in the heavens directly overhead at any given location on Earth. It should be carefully distinguished from the midheaven (with which it is often confused).

## Zeus

Zeus is both an asteroid and one of the eight hypothetical planets (sometimes referred to as the trans-Neptunian points or planets, or TNPs for short) utilized in Uranian

**A wood engraving of a giant statue of Zeus, the Greek father of the Gods. From *False Gods*, by Frank Dobbins, 1873. *Reproduced by permission of Fortean Picture Library.***

astrology. The Uranian system, sometimes referred to as the Hamburg School of Astrology, was established by Friedrich Sieggrün (1877–1951) and Alfred Witte (1878–1943). It relies heavily on hard aspects and midpoints. In decline for many decades, it has experienced a revival in recent years. As a Uranian planet, Zeus represents the control of strong forces and powers—weapons, anger, willpower, machines, fuel, etc. Although Zeus represents control and restraint, adverse positions of Zeus can also indicate the loss of control.

Based on the speculative orbits of the Uranian planets, the Kepler, Solar Fire and Win*Star software programs will all locate this hypothetical planet in an astrological chart.

**Sources:**

Lang-Wescott, Martha. *Mechanics of the Future: Asteroids*. Rev. ed. Conway, MA: Treehouse Mountain, 1991.

Simms, Maria Kay. *Dial Detective: Investigation with the 90 Degree Dial*. San Diego: Astro Computing Services, 1989.

## Zodiac

The zodiac (literally, "circle of animals," or, in its more primary meaning, the "circle of life" or "circle of living beings") is the "belt" constituted by the 12 signs—Aries, Taurus, Gemini, Cancer, Leo, Virgo, Libra, Scorpio, Sagittarius, Capricorn, Aquarius, and Pisces. This belt is said to extend 8° or 9° on either side of the ecliptic (the imaginary line drawn against the backdrop of the stars by the orbit of Earth). The orbits of the various planets in the solar system all lie within approximately the same geometric plane, so from a position within the system, all the heavenly bodies appear to move across the face of the same set of constellations. Several thousand years ago, the names of these constellations became the basis for the zodiac.

A distinction must be drawn between the sidereal zodiac and the tropical zodiac. The sidereal zodiac is located more or less where the constellations are positioned. The other zodiac originated with Ptolemy, the great astrologer-astronomer of antiquity, who was very careful to assert that the zodiac should begin (i.e., 0° Aries should be placed) at the point where the Sun is positioned during the spring equinox. Because of the phenomenon known as the precession of equinoxes, this point very gradually moves backward every year, and currently 0° Aries is located near the beginning of the constellation Pisces. Astrologers who adhere to the Ptolemaic directive—the great majority of modern, Western astrologers—use the tropical zodiac (also called the moving zodiac, for obvious reasons). If the tropical zodiac is used, it should always be carefully distinguished from the circle of constellations (i.e., from the sidereal zodiac).

The notion of the zodiac is ancient, with roots in the early cultures of Mesopotamia; the first 12-sign zodiacs were named after the gods of these cultures. The Greeks adopted astrology from the Babylonians; the Romans, in turn, adopted astrology from the Greeks. These peoples renamed the signs of the Babylonian zodiac in terms of their own mythologies, which is why the familiar zodiac of the contemporary West bears names out of Mediterranean mythology. The notion of a 12-fold division derives from the lunar cycle (the orbital cycle of the Moon around Earth), which the Moon completes 12 times per year.

From a broad historical perspective, zodiacal symbolism can be found everywhere, and zodiacal expressions are still in use in modern English—e.g., *bullheaded* (an

**The zodiacal calendar, this one adorns the Bracken House in London. *Reproduced by permission of Fortean Picture Library.***

allusion to Taurus), *crabby* (an allusion to Cancer), etc. Throughout the centuries people have drawn parallels between the zodiac and many other 12-fold divisions—such as the Twelve Labors of Hercules, the Twelve Disciples, and the Twelve Tribes of Israel. The popularity of sun-sign astrology (the kind found in the daily newspaper) has kept these ancient symbols alive in modern society, and even such prominent artifacts as automobiles have been named after some of the signs (e.g., the Taurus and the Scorpio).

**Sources:**

Cirlot, Juan Eduardo. *A Dictionary of Symbols*. London: Routledge & Kegan Paul, 1971.
Gettings, Fred. *Dictionary of Astrology*. London: Routledge & Kegan Paul, 1985.
Tester, Jim. *A History of Western Astrology*. New York: Ballantine, 1987.

## APPENDIX A

# READING YOUR OWN ASTROLOGY CHART

The components of your natal chart (birth chart) are not difficult to understand. What follows are the basics needed to interpret your own chart and the charts of friends and family.

Anyone with Internet access who knows the place, date, and time of his or her birth can obtain a free printout of his or her personal natal chart in a matter of minutes. People typically know their place and date, but not their time. This last item of information can almost always be found on one's birth certificate. Although an error of five or ten minutes is not likely to change much, the Rising Sign and the house positions of the planets change approximately every two hours, so an error of an hour or two will make a significant difference.

Armed with this data, go online and find an astrology website that provides online charts. Be careful not to confuse an offer of a free astrology *reading* or a free astrology *report* (which is usually only a Sun-sign reading) with free chart *casting*. I have set up a website as part of this encyclopedia (http://www.astrosoftware.com/astro/06903.htm) to provide readers with this service. If for any reason this site is unavailable when you are seeking to have your chart case online, note that other astrology websites, particularly some of the websites for major astrological software companies, also provide this service.

For any site offering this service, the procedure is to find an appropriate link, which will take you to a data entry page. Data entry is pretty straightforward. After entering your birth data, the final page in the process provides you with a picture of your chart wheel. The first time you look at your chart, it will appear to be an incomprehensible muddle of symbols. Do not despair; these symbols are relatively easy to translate into plain English.

A natal chart is a symbolic picture of the heavens with respect to the Earth at the moment of birth. The center of the chart is the location of the Earth as if one were in outer space looking down at the north pole. The 9:00 position is the eastern horizon, the 3:00 position is the western horizon, the 12:00 position is directly overhead, and the 6:00 position is underneath your feet on the other side of the Earth. Look for a symbol in one of the pie pieces that is a circle with a dot in it. This is the glyph (symbol) of the Sun. If you were born at sunrise, the Sun glyph should be around the 9:00 position; if you were born around noon, the Sun will be at the 12:00 position; around sunset, at 3:00; and at midnight, 6:00.

Astrological influences manifest themselves primarily through the planets (for astrological purposes, the Sun and Moon are both regarded as planets). A glyph for each of the planets is present in the chart. To take some examples, the crescent Moon represents the Moon; the male symbol (circle with an arrow sticking out of it) is the Mars glyph; the female symbol is the Venus glyph, etc. These basic influences are modified according to:

1. The signs of the zodiac (the familiar 12 astrological signs—Aries, Taurus, Gemini , etc.) in which the planets are placed. The glyphs for the signs are present around the perimeter of the chart. Usually the signs are also located close to each planet symbol, between two numbers. These numbers locate the exact position of the planet in terms of degrees and minutes of a circle.
2. The houses in which they are placed. Starting at the 9:00 position (which corresponds with the eastern horizon) and moving counterclockwise, the houses are numbered 1 to 12. Thus, the first house begins at the 9:00 position and ends at the 8:00 position; the second house begins at 8:00 and ends at 7:00, and so forth. In many charts, one will see the numbers of the houses around the center of the chart.
3. The aspects (geometric angles) between them. These can be represented by lines drawn between the planets in the middle of the chart or by a grid. A symbol identifying each angle is drawn along the aspect line or in the grid (this sounds confusing, but it will be clear when you examine your chart). Planets located within seven or eight degrees of one another are conjunct . Conjunctions are typically not represented by aspect lines.

An oversimplified but nonetheless useful rule of thumb is that planetary sign positions indicate personality tendencies, aspects between planets reflect how various components of one's personality interact with one another, and house positions show how the personality manifests in the world.

Visually in an astrological chart, the houses are the 12 pie pieces that together form the basic framework of the horoscope. Sign divisions (where signs begin and end) are *not* represented in a conventional chart. If they were, one would have to draw in another 12 lines, making a total of 24 (which would result in a cluttered appearance). The numbers and symbols that appear around the outside of the wheel indicate where houses begin and end with respect to the signs of the zodiac .

Use a glyph table to locate your planets. Note that the sign at the 9:00 position is your ascendant, also called the rising sign, and that the sign beside the Moon is your Moon sign. Along with your Sun sign, these are your three most important sign influences. It is common for people who know at least a little about astrology to describe themselves in terms of these three signs; e.g., "I'm a Taurus with an Aries Moon and Sagittarius rising" (meaning this individual has a Taurus Sun sign, an Aries Moon sign, and a Sagittarius rising sign). Individuals can all be double signs or even triple signs if the Moon Sign and/or the Rising Sign is/are the same as the Sun Sign.

Aspects can be represented by lines drawn between planets, by an aspect grid, or both. In most chart-casting programs, the aspect symbols are drawn directly on the aspect lines. The major aspects are conjunction, opposition, square, trine, and sextile. Some of the minor aspects are semi-sextile, quincunx, and bi-quintile. (See pages xxxi–xxxi for glyph tables of planets, signs, other points, asteroids, and imaginary planets.)

The balance of this appendix provides concise interpretations for every major component of a natal chart. The reader will find that the interpretations of some positions will say almost exactly the opposite of what other interpretations say. Although these oppositions sometimes indicate conflicting tendencies within the personality, more often than not one tendency will be stronger and win out over the other. The reader should also note that such piecemeal delineations can provide only the building blocks of a chart interpretation. The ability to meaningfully synthesize astrological information rather than simply listing interpretations of individual components of a chart is the mark of an experienced astrologer.

## SIGNIFICANCE OF THE PLANETS AND OTHER POINTS IN A NATAL CHART

*The following was written by Michael Erlewine. For a personal reading, you can contact him at: 315 Marion Avenue, Big Rapids, Michigan, 49307; Michael@erlewine.net.*

At the time of our birth, the planets (through their configurations and relationships) tell us something about how things were when we were born. Each planet points to special qualities within us. Yet, of all the planets, the two most important to astrologers are the "lights," the Sun and the Moon. From where we stand here on Earth, the great shining Sun by day and the reflecting Moon at night are our constant companions. They have much to tell us as to where we have been and where we are headed.

**Sun:** From the Sun comes light—that which draws all of us living on this Earth into life. The Sun in the astrological chart represents the very heart of us, our deepest core essence. It is what we shall become after we work through all of the changes life offers us. In other words, in astrology the Sun represents our identity, or true self.

**Moon:** The Moon provides information about the kind of environment we create around ourselves, our particular life support system—what nourishes us. Endlessly circling the Earth, the Moon is a kind of cosmic mother and has often been called the great provider. And, although the Moon does have to do with the kind of situation we draw around ourselves, it also represents where we have come from, the personal past out of which we have grown including all of the old habits and stages of life that we have discarded.

**Mercury:** Mercury is the light in our eyes, the ever-changing consciousness within us that moves from idea to idea. Thus Mercury has always represented thoughts, ideas, and the mental process in general. It governs not only ideas, but communications, too. Communications—by phone, letter, spoken, or however—are ruled by Mercury. Also, thoughts, connections, phone wires, and everything that connects and conveys—even conversations.

**Venus:** Venus rules our values and sense of appreciation. When we appraise or appreciate something, whether that be another person or a new car, this is Venus—the sense of love and compassion we may feel. By the same token, this planet rules enjoyment of all kinds too. Whether it be self-appreciation or just plain old decadent self-enjoyment—having a good time. This is Venus. When we go shopping or are on a spending spree, it is Venus that allows us to appreciate and value all the good things of life.

**Mars:** Mars is the planet of emotion and inner motivation or drive. When we search for the meaning of something, such as life, it is Mars that urges us on, keeps us searching. Mars also drives us against things, too, and sends us into war and combat. The urgency of Mars—the search for meaning—is identical to the need for union and marriage. Mars is the planet of union or yoga, and marriage is the most common form of yoga. When we have questions about the opposite sex, we are looking at the planet Mars.

**Jupiter:** Jupiter is the planet of success or at least simple survival, the way we have to solve the problems that confront us. Thus Jupiter has to do with the way in which we can be successful, our vocation. The Hindu word for Jupiter is *Guru*. Jupiter is the guru and guide, the way we go through life—our life path or vocation. Jupiter is the method each of us has for dealing with the laws of life, our Saturn, or limitations. Jupiter is our particular light or path. Jupiter provides us with our sense of direction, the path we are on, the way we handle life. It affects how we approach life's problems. It has always been an indicator of how successful we may be, our vocation. The process of finding out who we are (self-discovery) starts when we come to grips with whatever problems life presents to us (our Saturn) and begin to get a handle on them. In other words, if we have not learned to deal with Saturn, or time (that is, if we don't have some control of time), there is little opportunity for other questions. Saturn rules the laws and the particular limitations of this material world we all live in.

**Saturn:** Saturn indicates in each of our astrology charts where we are bound to learn, like it or not. Saturn is said to be the great teacher, the planet that keeps us from getting too carried away in one direction or another. Although it always seeks to limit and determine any thought, word, or action, it also defines and clarifies.

## THE OUTER PLANETS

Up to this point, we have dealt with planets that we can see with our naked eyes. In general, these planets refer to life as we know and live it and are the so-called historical or classic planets. Beyond these are three planets that are not visible in the sky and which have cycles longer than the average human life span. Since they are beyond Saturn or time, astrologers call them the trans-personal or transcendental planets—the planets beyond the physical. One of the ways astrologers learn something about our life beyond time (eternal life) is through these three outer planets: Uranus, Neptune, and Pluto. Here we find information on how we discover ourselves (Uranus), how we understand and accept these discoveries (Neptune), and, in time, how we depend and identify with them (Pluto).

**Uranus:** Our responsibilities can tend to weigh us down, and we each have our particular ways of getting around (or breaking through) the mass of obstructions that tends to congeal around us. The planet that has to do with how we get beyond the difficulties and problems life presents us is Uranus. Here is the way insights come to us, how we discover or come to know and understand ourselves. It has to do with finding new uses for old things, and it rules inventions and sudden insights into our life—everything that is unusual, eccentric, and out of the ordinary. It is the reverse of the status quo and is always unconventional and heretical. Uranus is, in many ways, the opposite, or undoing of Saturn.

**Neptune:** Even the most hard-nosed of us have moments of real understanding, when things are seen as linked together and in one piece. We stop getting the idea in little flashes and just finally get the whole thing. It dawns on us. We each have our own way of letting go, having communion, and (as a poet wrote) letting "the dewdrop slip into the shining sea." These moments and this state of mind are, in fact, the source for all our imagination. There are many ways of seeing through the separateness in the world to the unity behind it. This is the planet Neptune.

**Pluto:** Pluto is the planet of profound change, starting deep within us and moving toward the surface. It often touches upon the most sensitive psychological areas inside us. Once touched, we have no choice but to change and grow. The most sensitive of experiences, the times of greatest vulnerability, are times of complete identification with an experience, a person, or a thing. We know in these instants that we are looking at our self, what we are. The most personal of experiences is one of complete identification with a person, moment, or idea. Perhaps this is only possible for most of us when we look into our child's eyes, and then only infrequently. Love is not the experience here, but total identification. This is very sensitive stuff. To touch upon this material is to go through deep inner change and transformation—inner alchemy. Identification and experiencing that life is our own creation and that, in fact, you are I and I am you. This experience breaks us down and humbles. When we touch upon this experience, we cannot but die to what we have been thinking and doing up to now. It reduces us to our most sensitive because—in a flash—we see or remember that it all is us, our life.

## OTHER IMPORTANT POINTS IN A CHART

The three most important non-planetary points in a chart are the angular position of the Midheaven, (often abbreviated "MC"), the Ascendant ("AC" or "ASC"), and the North

Lunar Node (represented in a chart by [ucL]; sometimes the South Lunar Node is also represented [ucM])

**Midheaven:** The Midheaven is the most elevated degree of the zodiac in an astrological chart. In most systems of house division, it is also the cusp (beginning) of the tenth house. Midheaven is often used interchangeably with zenith , but this usage is inaccurate. The Midheaven tells us something about our vocational and practical abilities. It is here that we can see to do and manipulate. This point is usually associated with our outer standing in the world, our fame, reputation, and fortune. The MC represents fame and honor since it is here that we have our most practical sense and vision. We can see and use; it is our vantage point or perspective. The Midheaven is also the cusp of the tenth house for most astrologers.

**Ascendant:** In Western astrology, the ascendant is usually regarded as influencing the native's appearance and certain outward traits more than the depth of her or his personality. In some systems of esoteric astrology , the ascendant is said to embody positive traits that the native is supposed to be "growing toward." If one was born with Virgo on the ascendant, for example, then the native would need to learn to become more organized or more attentive to details. Whatever one's view of the greater or lesser "depth" of the ascendant, there is general agreement that the ascendant is a peculiarly sensitive point in the horoscope.

**Lunar Nodes:** Imagine the orbit of Earth around the Sun as describing a flat plane, and project it outward against the backdrop of the stars. This projection is the ecliptic. Although all the principal planets in the solar system orbit the Sun in *approximately* the same plane, none of their orbital paths lies in *exactly* the same plane. The point at which the Moon moves northward—with respect to our terrestrial perspective—as it crosses the ecliptic is the north lunar node; correspondingly, the point at which it moves southward is the south lunar node. The lunar nodes are extremely important in Vedic astrology , where they are regarded as being on par with the planets. The north node is seen as representing an area where development is needed, with the south node symbolizing talents already developed. Most astrologers agree that there is an unconscious dynamic at work in the nodes, represented by the nodes' signs, houses, and aspects.

## SUN IN THE SIGNS OF THE ZODIAC

**Sun in Aries:** Go for it! Do it now and ask questions later, for you are a born leader, always first and never afraid to go it alone. Your sense of mission makes for impulsive, sometimes rash (but always brave) actions. Your motto is: Don't think about it, let's get the show on the road.

**Sun in Taurus:** Here is great patience, able to respond to the world and to build upon what is already there and happening. You are willing to listen to others, take cues, and then reflect and build upon that information. Others find you gentle, steady, and, for the most part, kind. You take things in and provide an environment to bring them forth. You make "fertile" your field. A ready ear.

**Sun in Gemini:** You love to investigate, search, and explore. You are also very communicative by any means: talking, writing, broadcasting … even by car. Always going beyond conventions into whatever's new, exciting, and spicy, you are happy when caught up in the variety and complexity of life.

**Sun in Cancer:** You are a very sensitive person who can depend on feelings and intuition to get around in life. Possessing good common sense, you are always very practical and down-to-earth—mothering and protective to all. Security is very important. You also love cooking, growing things, and music.

**Sun in Leo:** You are outgoing, overflowing, and very generous. Always the leader, if not the center of any group, you seldom fail to exhibit strong emotions. You are proud of yourself and of your accomplishments. Dramatic and just plain happy to be here, you are warm of heart, gregarious, outspoken, and independent.

**Sun in Virgo:** You are nothing if not compassionate. Interested in serving others, you worry about their welfare. You like to take care of everything, and are always redeeming, salvaging, and restoring. You believe in conservation in all things. You find yourself through response and service to others, to life.

**Sun in Libra:** Your keyword is responsibility—the ability to respond. You are able to find yourself in others, in relationships, rather than alone—a mirror or clear pool. You can be peaceful, calm, and undisturbed. A genius at bringing out others and getting them to do things, you are a born strategist.

**Sun in Scorpio:** You know how to say "No!" and to go without, if need be. Intense and sometimes driven, you are able to cut through to the heart of things. You are seldom interested in refinement. You can be very magnetic, even wild at times, and have a sense of power and an instinct for survival. Moody.

**Sun in Sagittarius:** You are always out front, frank, and even rough at times—getting to the heart of any subject. On the move, you are a traveler of both the world and the mind—philosophy and religion. Outgoing, friendly, and well-liked, you may enjoy sports and physical activity. Not petty, you like grand themes and big gestures.

**Sun in Capricorn:** You have clear vision and can see what to do. Happy when in control, you enjoy managing anything practical. Not too emotional, you are objective, businesslike, and reliable—disciplined. To you, life is a serious business and you are a great provider, always far-sighted. You are social, or public-oriented. Practical.

**Sun in Aquarius:** You are open-minded and democratic, enthusiastic, and have a definite sense of mission. Above all, you are a progressive and enjoy putting into practice that which is good for all. Your altruism could appear as coolness. At home with different cultures, peoples, and lands, you love to work with (and in) groups.

**Sun in Pisces:** You are long-suffering and able to take a lot for the sake of your beliefs and ideals. In this sense, you are very future-oriented. You are intuitive and at home with the psyche and psychological. A sense of the mystic too. You are able to carry ideas and dreams into reality, to make the spirit matter.

## MOON IN THE SIGNS OF THE ZODIAC

**Moon in Aries:** You can be impulsively direct when relating to others, and may seem fierce or harsh. Independent to the point of loneliness, you don't mind a more Spartan environment than most. You can get by on little. You have a short fuse, and harsh exchanges are not uncommon. Others could feel hurt by this.

**Moon in Taurus:** You have strong, stable emotions and tend to draw around you the perfect environment for your upbringing. The thing you need is always at hand. In addition, you get much support and good fortune from friends and relatives. You value constancy and security in all things and possess a good business sense. You are, by nature, very domestic and enjoy nice surroundings.

**Moon in Gemini:** You are at home where there is lots of communication, investigation, and exploration. Fascinated by social interchange (and gossip too) you tend not to be emotional and are somewhat surface-oriented. You enjoy variety and change. Thinking, writing, researching, and science are good. A teacher.

**Moon in Cancer:** You can sense and understand the mood and feelings of others, and are excellent at counseling and nursing. You are quite emotional, and have a natural sense of that which pleases, knowing the mood of the crowd. You can be overly protective (or protected), but are good at parenting and creating a home. Quite domestic.

**Moon in Leo:** You are gregarious, even to the point of bringing out the performer in others. You somehow always manage to find a creative environment or the creative in any environment. You are great with kids and big on animals, sports, and the outdoors. You are an instant umbrella of warmth, friendship, and self-expression.

**Moon in Virgo:** You are concerned and caring when it comes to the welfare of others. Not dynamic or too emotional, you are attentive, observant, careful, and above all responsible—able to respond. Always competent, you are in fact quite loving, although others could feel scrutinized or inadequate when in your presence.

**Moon in Libra:** You like beautiful surroundings, everything that is calm, tasteful, and harmonious. You are very giving, conciliatory, and even flattering in relationships, able to adjust to any situation. Reflective, tactful, you are able to please others. Above all, you are forever charming and gracious. Also ingratiating and inscrutable.

**Moon in Scorpio:** Yours is a passionate life. Intense feelings and strong attachments make for hot times, and you are fiercely loyal, if not sometimes possessive. Secretive, you are not at all superficial but always get to the heart of things. This is good for business and politics. You have a sense for power, wealth, and passion.

**Moon in Sagittarius:** You are happy even in austere settings, and enjoy getting back to the basics. Religion, truth, and the world of philosophy and ideas are of interest. Your love of simplicity is good for politics too. It brings out the truth and a sense of honesty in a group. You are freedom-loving, independent, and at times, even a trifle remote. You are not bound by relationships and are thus not much of a domestic.

**Moon in Capricorn:** Yours is the most practical of environments. You can manipulate and every idea or situation and put it to good use. Emotions are seldom a priority, and you are always very practical and ambitious. Your career is central to everything you do. Farsighted and traditional, you enjoy success and the successful. You are, for the most part, unmoved by tears and feelings.

**Moon in Aquarius:** You are inspired, for humanity is your family and you are seldom bound by tradition or domestic ties. The big picture is what counts most with you, and large-scale movements and group work are the idea. You seldom find personalities interesting and are democratic in the real sense of the word. You are an altruist and love freedom.

**Moon in Pisces:** The world is a sacred place to you, and you have an absolute commitment to spiritual ideas. Intuition is a fact of life, and you are sensitive, kind, and gentle. A romantic too, with a tender heart. You always work for a real future, doing what has to be done. You love all that is musical and artistic. You have sensitivity to all that is psychic. You have real faith.

## MERCURY IN THE SIGNS OF THE ZODIAC

**Mercury in Aries:** You have a sharp tongue and a quick wit. You speak first, then think about it. Not subtle or complex, you are direct, simple, and to the point. An independent thinker, you would rather speak than listen. Argumentative too. You are quite impulsive when it comes to communicating, and often use strong words.

**Mercury in Taurus:** You enjoy deliberation and have a very methodical mind. Able to develop sound logic and good arguments, you are practical, rather than abstract, and seldom nebulous. You make a good student. A fertile thinker, you are slow and steady but always down to earth. No "pie in the sky" here. You are careful and considerate.

**Mercury in Gemini:** Yours is a lightning wit. You somehow know everything about everybody. Curious, you love finding things out—speculating, investigating. You are clever but not known for your deep thinking, and any and all kinds of communication satisfy. You are always exploring, testing. Debates, games, and puzzles please you. Quick.

**Mercury in Cancer:** You sense things with the mind and understand that feelings are thoughts too. What does this or that thought mean? Where is it pointing? These are questions you ask. You use subjective rather than objective logic—intuition and gut instinct. Poetry, music, and the arts interest you, as do psychology and the psyche.

**Mercury in Leo:** You are dynamic and always expressive in thought and speech—dramatic. You appreciate your own ideas, and tend to be outgoing in speech and manner. Fresh. Warm. You put forth strong views and are hard to influence or change. Emotional and a good entertainer, you are louder than average and tend to exaggerate. You are a lover. There are always plenty of tears and laughter.

**Mercury in Virgo:** You have a fine mind and a great appetite for detail. You appreciate minute differences and distinctions. A craftsman with an innate critical sense, you are always full of suggestions. Your careful, conservative mind wants to salvage every last thing. You possess a love for detail and trivia. Quick-minded.

**Mercury in Libra:** Yours is a reflective mind, a mirror for others. You are equality-minded and easy to talk with—a great mediator or negotiator. You find it easy to accept the ideas and thoughts of others and to hear them out. You are good at relations (politics, diplomacy, sales), not to mention considerate, helpful, and courteous. Calm.

**Mercury in Scorpio:** The original Sherlock Holmes, you are able to ferret out information and all kinds of secrets. You are research-oriented and security minded. A shrewd and penetrating thinker, you have great psychological instincts and are able to get at the causes beneath the surface of life.

**Mercury in Sagittarius:** You are fair-minded and above-board, always direct and honest in thought. You are more interested in eternal thoughts and broad landscapes than in minute details. You always manage to get the picture right away. Farsighted, you have a wandering mind that loves to travel and are at home with the bare bones of truth.

**Mercury in Capricorn:** You have a very clear and analytical mind and are able to grasp ideas and put them to work at once. You have good management and supervisory ability. You use cold reason, are not much moved by emotions, and are always pragmatic. You prefer concrete subjects to "grand ideas" and flights of fancy. Manipulative too.

**Mercury in Aquarius:** You are an impartial thinker, democratic to the point of being impersonal. Fascinated by the latest technology, you have very original ideas, an inventor. Always thinking of the world as a unity, you are idealistic and believe in putting into practice what is preached. You are group-conscious, community-oriented.

**Mercury in Pisces:** You are an intuitive rather than a rational thinker, and psychological thought (the psyche), mysticism and religion are natural. You love poetry and music, tending to feel or sense with your mind the truth of a situation. You are very sympathetic and understanding and have kind thoughts. Compassionate.

## VENUS IN THE SIGNS OF THE ZODIAC

**Venus in Aries:** You exhibit great appreciation, intense love, and always wear your heart on your sleeve—always! Not too sensitive with others, you tend to be rough and ready and can sometimes demand a lot of attention. Shy flowers, stand back! You are independent and single-minded, demonstrative and very loving.

**Venus in Taurus:** Let's get physical! You love to touch and you can be very possessive. You love food and all the creature comforts. Money and what it buys are very important. You are a gentle lover and like a good home life. You are very loyal, loving, and down-to-earth. You may like gardening and gift-giving.

**Venus in Gemini:** You are very friendly indeed, love to communicate and to have deep, searching conversations. You appreciate change, variety, and making local connections. You have many avenues to explore and you love research. You are not too domestic, and loyalty is not a big issue. On the move, you have many different friends and places to go.

**Venus in Cancer:** Homeward bound! With you, the domestic scene is ideal. Marriage, children, animals, gardens—the whole works. You like to feel secure. Sensitive too. You are dependent on others and like to be taken care of, even mothered. You love music, can be very emotional, and tend to be protective.

**Venus in Leo:** Big heart, big love, you are seldom petty. Given to grand gestures and dramatic scenes, you love independence and greatness in all forms and are very regal. You can be generous to a fault. Children and animals are high on your list of priorities. Fervently loyal, you are courageous and demonstrative.

**Venus in Virgo:** Finely wrought or overwrought? You have a fine sense of appreciation and are very attentive. You love to help out and take care of others, expressing a first-rate sense of compassion. You possess an almost infinite ability to respond to the needs and demands of others. Fragile, refined, you are perhaps too prudish.

**Venus in Libra:** A socialite, you love decorum and etiquette, but relationships are the big thing—friends. A peacemaker, sometimes superficial, you avoid all harsh and crude actions, people or things. You appreciate care, concern for life, equality, gentleness, and acceptance.

**Venus in Scorpio:** A passionate one, you are never lukewarm in love. It's hot or not. You are in love with mystery, secrets, and intrigue, anything but that which is open or superficial. You have great personal magnetism and a loyalty verging on possessiveness. You are never dull. You enjoy money and influence too. Politics.

**Venus in Sagittarius:** You love all things plain and true, and possess an innate sense of religion and what's real. Not prudish, even communal, you insist on freedom in all things. You love sports, "great" ideas, and travel. You are anything except too domestic. An idealist, but not dreamy, you are frank and affectionate.

**Venus in Capricorn:** You are in love with what's practical, right down to the last detail. You appreciate tradition and ceremony and are a conservative in all things. You are loyal, seldom emotional, and always proper, even too serious. Cool cucumber. You like to be in control.

**Venus in Aquarius:** Marriage for convention's sake, if at all, is your motto. Let's not get too personal or emotional. A friend's friend. You love to work for a great cause or purpose, and a better world is the place to be. You appreciate what's fair and democratic, and feel most happy in a group or community.

**Venus in Pisces:** You have deep commitments and appreciate sacrifice and duty on the part of others. At home in the world of the dreamer and mystic, you have great intuition. You are always willing to sublimate and take the back seat. Domestic at heart, you love family life. A true romantic. Musical, psychological, poetic, gentle.

## MARS IN THE SIGNS OF THE ZODIAC

**Mars in Aries:** You are powerfully motivated, even driven, have a hot temper, and tend to be impulsive. You are seldom very reflective when it comes to doing something, but act first and ask questions later. Your more fiery emotions are always an insult away. You have blind courage and sheer guts. Aggressive. A self-starter. Energetic.

**Mars in Taurus:** You have great staying power, a drive for security and stability, and can withstand almost anything. You are very dependable, somewhat emotional but stable. You have a natural need to build solid foundations. You are stubborn, but patient and slow to anger. Once angry, watch out!

**Mars in Gemini:** You have an inner need for communication of all kinds and may have too many irons in the fire at times. You can be all over the place, always trying to make one more connection. Speaking and writing are naturals. You have a need for lots of variety, a change of pace. Arguments. Mental energy.

**Mars in Cancer:** You have a real security drive and a need to care and protect others—mother hen. Very sensitive to the slightest emotional change, you have all the artistic traits and talents. If threatened, you can be very defensive, and you hate competition. You love family, children, and animals. You have common sense.

**Mars in Leo:** You are always center-stage and entertaining others. You have an almost fierce sense of pride and are very dramatic and expressive, sometimes forceful. You are a natural at sports, games, anything that "gets it out." Very emotional, you have strong likes and dislikes. You are good with kids, animals—a teacher or coach. You act it out.

**Mars in Virgo:** You have an innate urge to save, salvage, and conserve, and can make a silk purse from a sow's ear. You always want to help and to be of service—to be fully used. You hate waste and are very thorough and precise. For the most part, you are understanding and accepting, but this can turn into criticism and pettiness. You are careful and a perfectionist.

**Mars in Libra:** You have an inner urge to be all things to all people and would rather bend than argue or make an issue. You are a natural diplomat, always courteous and concerned with the comfort and welfare of others. You stay in the background, but are able to manipulate and bring out cooperation in others every time.

**Mars in Scorpio:** You possess a powerful, persistent drive and are a hard, steady worker. Others may find you deep, with a sense of mission and mystery. You are willing to do work others would not go near, quietly bending things to your will, having it your own way. You have strong sexual energy, too, and enjoy getting down to the nitty-gritty.

**Mars in Sagittarius:** With direct drive, you always head straight to the heart of the matter. You are candid, even blunt or brusque in manner. No bells or whistles needed, for you like simple living and could be an outdoors person. You have an urge to be free, to be challenged and tested, and would rather travel far than be stuck in routine.

**Mars in Capricorn:** You are a very hard worker and are driven to accomplish, manage, and be in control. You like to manipulate a situation for its own benefit and would make a natural supervisor. You have an inner urge for order and organization and a great sense of responsibility. You are competent, ambitious, and cool.

**Mars in Aquarius:** You have an inner drive to improve, and reform the world, to share the wealth—true democracy. You have a feel for groups and any large-scale business or community project. Independent with a touch of the impersonal. With you, all persons get the same treatment.

**Mars in Pisces:** You have a sense of true understanding and real sacrifice. Dedication to long-range goals, you are future-oriented. Intuitive, you have an inner drive for all that's psychological, religious, and mystical. Artistic, too. You are sensitive and can get lost in the clouds on occasion. You are not too logical or practical.

## JUPITER IN THE SIGNS OF THE ZODIAC

**Jupiter in Aries:** You could pursue a career as a leader or pioneer. You tend to be the one who takes the initiative and are courageous and often fearless to the point of being foolish. Success for you in most things is second nature. Always "walking point," you tend to be a loner, a warrior. Confident, single-minded, you are sometimes rash but are always direct—straight out.

**Jupiter in Taurus:** You have a green thumb in many areas, able to cultivate and nurture almost any subject. Making money is second nature, and you are able to field ideas and bring forth growth and success. A steady worker, you could also be a backer or money man. Accumulation.

**Jupiter in Gemini:** A career in communications of one kind or another is indicated, for you are a kind of living link or channel. You love investigations, reporting, writing, speaking, broadcasting, advertising—any and all networking. Forever curious, you love searching for answers and following leads.

**Jupiter in Cancer:** A career in big business is possible, for you like broad, secure foundations. It is important for you to feel safe, and you are very domestic—family, home, and kids. Supportive, nurturing, you use your intuition and gut instinct over thought and deliberation. Fiercely loyal, you are a street fighter when protecting your own interests or those you love. Very dependable.

**Jupiter in Leo:** You would love a career that is creative and expressive. Always dramatic, you are a born entertainer and salesman—warm, loud, and gregarious. Proud, you have an inner need to express feelings and emotions to others. You can be self-centered and are driven to leadership positions by a sense of your own inner worth.

**Jupiter in Virgo:** A service career is a perfect choice, for you want very much to be of use, to be used up. You have a fantastic appetite for detail work, and can take it all in and still look for more. Willing and able to respond to almost any emergency, you are responsible and always ready.

**Jupiter in Libra:** You could enjoy a career working with people as a go-between, negotiator, or mediator, for you can be all things to all people—the mirror. You are not interested in what runs deep, but prefer to control what goes on at the surface. That's enough for you. Open and not self-centered, you are a natural diplomat.

**Jupiter in Scorpio:** An in-fighter, with animal-like instincts when it comes to big business, you are always where the action is most intense. Your penetrating mind gets through the B.S. and straight to the bottom line every time. Exciting to be near, you are an entrepreneur, the big wheel. Sometimes restless, driven.

**Jupiter in Sagittarius:** Always on the go, you are a skilled diplomat, negotiator, or representative. Honest, frank, and to the point, you hate routines and love the outdoors, travel, and sports. An eternal optimist, you are open, friendly, and lucky too. Always the philosopher, you are not much taken with emotions. Independent.

**Jupiter in Capricorn:** The perfect manager: conservative and professional in all things. Your career is all-important. A "doer," you are always practical. Never ruled by emotions, you are cool, capable, and competent. You are quick to get the outline or skeleton of a project, to see how things work.

**Jupiter in Aquarius:** A true progressive, especially in community or group work, you are democratic to the point of being radical—an idealist. You are cool and impersonal when it comes to being fair or just, with a great interest in new trends and world affairs. You are future-oriented. Application-minded.

**Jupiter in Pisces:** You are a real humanitarian, with a genuine interest in social work and able to sacrifice yourself to help others. You have a love of what's beyond the surface: religion, psychology, and mysticism. Intuitive, sensitive to emotions, and sympathetic, you are always giving of self and would make an excellent counselor. You are farsighted, future-oriented.

## SATURN IN THE SIGNS OF THE ZODIAC

**Saturn in Aries:** You have a need to be bold, rash, and even a little foolish—to dare. You may have to work on being alone, on being more aggressive, challenging, and willful. You could have difficulty with leadership, self-assertion, and outgoingness, in general. A need to develop impulsiveness, the pioneer spirit, and pride in self.

**Saturn in Taurus:** You have difficulty feeling secure. You avoid routine and can't seem to find the right environment for growth and development. This could include a fear of wealth and possessions. You need to develop the steady domestic virtues: routine work, regular growth, commitments, and so on.

**Saturn in Gemini:** You tend to avoid superficiality, hating small talk and communication in general. You may have difficulty making connections and linking up to others. You need to learn how to investigate, search out answers and explore possibilities. Basic communication skills are required.

**Saturn in Cancer:** You could have difficulty in letting go and feeling life, preferring instead to think about it rather than do it. Afraid of the sense world, you avoid plunging in and fear being caught or tied down. "To be or not to be ..." is your question. There is a need to accept responsibility and limitations, as well as home, family, children, and such.

**Saturn in Leo:** You could be afraid to follow your own heart and to express yourself. Instead, you try to always keep your emotions in control. Children and animals are important in your life. You need to act out and express feelings—let go, learn to be the center of attention, to be loved. Study nature, natural law. Let it flow.

**Saturn in Virgo:** You have a tendency to avoid responsibility or work and to put off taking care of details—delinquency. Application and practice is the remedy. Be specific. Take care of every last detail. Develop and use your critical faculties. Take care of business.

**Saturn in Libra:** You have difficulty with relationships and are very idealistic when it comes to friends. You are inflexible, seldom compromise, and find it hard to give in where other people are involved. You need to developdiplomacy and patience. Learn to give (as in "give in") rather than oppose. Be flexible.

**Saturn in Scorpio:** You have difficulty owning up to any selfishness, sexuality, or mental undercurrents of any kind. You may attempt to deny your passions, but you need to accept instincts, attachments, and all things natural. Allow your desires to function unhindered. Take off the straight-jacket. Feel it.

**Saturn in Sagittarius:** There could be difficulty with long-term goals and philosophies. You don't trust them. Nearsighted, with your nose to the grindstone, you need to travel and explore the length and breadth of the mind and world. Open up. Learn to value freedom, frankness, independence. Look up!

**Saturn in Capricorn:** Organizational problems. You have a tendency to avoid taking charge or responsibility and may need to accept a more disciplined and serious approach to life. Learn to enjoy hard work. Persevere. Learn how to manage. You may feel uncomfortable when in the public eye.

**Saturn in Aquarius:** You have an innate distrust of groups or large organizations and could tend to avoid what is new or future-oriented. You are, perhaps, too conservative and need to develop a sense of community and sharing with others. Learn to be independent. Practice impartiality and altruism. Be innovative.

**Saturn in Pisces:** There could be problems with selfishness. You tend to ignore or avoid opportunities to help out and give of yourself. You fear the deeper, mystical side of life and need to practice putting others before yourself. Also learn to use intuition and feelings. Lend a helping hand.

## URANUS IN THE SIGNS OF THE ZODIAC

**Uranus in Aries:** You are innovative when it comes to leadership, new starts, pioneer-type projects. You have bold and startling insights and tend to break away from tradition. You find freedom in sports, exploration, impulse-buying, and getting out. A standard bearer. You have insights into energy and action.

**Uranus in Taurus:** You have new insight into home, possessions, and the whole domestic scene. Financial independence and novel ways to earn money and make a living interest you. You get away from it all with gardening, building, and family life. You discover freedom in steady, predictable growth—like a plant growing.

**Uranus in Gemini:** You have brilliant insights into communications of all kinds—computers, radio, TV, the press, writing, and speaking. You are inventive and also have deep insights into research and investigations. You like to relax in conversations, telephone, puzzles, and making connections.

**Uranus in Cancer:** You are very innovative in your approach to home, family, and the domestic scene and can really see how to get into traditional values. You have natural insight into sensations, feelings, and just living life. You like to relax by gardening, cooking, and being with family. You get off on the humdrum.

**Uranus in Leo:** You have great insight into matters of personal freedom. You come up with brilliant ways to express, emote, or act things out. New methods of lovemaking, raising kids, and caring for animals are yours. You are outspoken, very dramatic, impressive, and even regal. You relax with children, sports, acting, singing, and such. You really like yourself.

**Uranus in Virgo:** You find new ways to serve others and you have brilliant insights into diet, health, ecology, conservation, and the like. New or alternate lifestyles and ways to make a living interest you. You are economy personified, always able to salvage and redeem anything. You like to tend and care for people and things. You relax by working.

**Uranus in Libra:** You can find new ways to relate and may be innovative in marriage and social conventions. Very tolerant and accepting of differences, you have good insights into all social values. Independent. You like to facilitate, compromise, and otherwise show your breadth of scope—like a coat of many colors.

**Uranus in Scorpio:** You are innovative in sexual matters (anything taboo) and have insights into what makes our darker side tick. All things mystical and occult hold your interest. Drugs, too. You have new thoughts on desires and possessions. You enjoy sex and respect cravings of all kinds.

**Uranus in Sagittarius:** You have new philosophies, ideas for the future, and new approaches to travel and exploration (of all kinds). Long journeys interest you. You may startle others with your direct conversations, always getting right to the nitty-gritty. You enjoy being alone, free, and on the move. The original optimist.

**Uranus in Capricorn:** You are innovative in the political and business arena. You find new ways to manage and control things and people. Ever practical, you come up with new or alternate forms of management—breakthroughs in top-level management and corporate styles. You bring new life to conservative traditions. Your emotions are very staid.

**Uranus in Aquarius:** You have a radical approach to communities and group work. Progressive, with insights into uniting humanity, you understand the true meaning of democracy. You want equal rights for all, and function from an inspired sense of idealism, the urge to make it matter. You would make a great networker and are always working for the benefit of all.

**Uranus in Pisces:** You have new insight into all mystical, occult, and religious matters—a visionary. You find new methods of worship and service. You are very progressive in the areas of philosophy, music, drama, poetry, and the arts. Also innovative in psychology and psychic matters. New dreams, new reality. Movies and films are important.

## NEPTUNE IN THE SIGNS OF THE ZODIAC

**Neptune in Aries:** You believe in action and have the original pioneer-type spirit, forever forging ahead. The ideal you strive for is courage, carrying on—a standard bearer. Not teary-eyed, mystical, or psychological in the least, you welcome the brave new world and are always the hero.

**Neptune in Taurus:** Your ideals are fertile soil and bring real growth. You find a richness in music and the arts. You have a vision of a comfortable dream, a luxurious life, where everything of value flourishes, where every good seed takes root. Romance, wealth, and great art are of interest. A rich field of experience. Sound.

**Neptune in Gemini:** The dream of worldwide communication (networking) where research and science are the key. Fantasy and science-fiction flourish, too. You are a great love of inspired conversation and enhanced communication—all kinds of connections. Great ideas, flights of fancy. Sharing thoughts.

**Neptune in Cancer:** Home and family life are the driving ideal. Your dreams are of a place (perhaps a home) to be or to live in—a body. You tend to lose yourself in life, in just "being there," and feelings and intuitions are much valued. The ride of the body. The chariot.

**Neptune in Leo:** Romance. You are in love with the drama and glamour of the movie star. Forever on stage and always the center of attention. Life is handsome, dramatic. You idolize children, creative artists, and animals. Nature films. Courtship and romance forever.

**Neptune in Virgo:** Practical salvation is the idea, saving the physical. You do this via exercise, diet, vitamins, life-extension aids, and such, and the right livelihood is as important as the right food. Song lyrics. You love to restore and redeem the physical world. A great love of details or trivia.

**Neptune in Libra:** Relationships are the ideal. Nondiscriminating and impersonal in scope, to you all are equal. You are seldom bound by tradition or personal ties and are not domestic. You hold the ideal vision up to the real. You open up in response to others and accept others as yourself.

**Neptune in Scorpio:** Unafraid of the "dark" side of life, you are interested in esoteric religion, everything mystical or occult, and so on. Sexuality and physical desires are encouraged and seen as spiritual. Money, power, and things of this world are OK, too. The physical is ideal. Possessions.

**Neptune in Sagittarius:** Idealism is an innate talent, and you are in love with grand gestures and long thoughts. Religion, politics, and philosophy are natural. The world traveler. You enjoy fair, just, frank, and broad-minded persons. You are gregarious and sports-minded. You dare to dream big. You like new philosophies, long novels.

**Neptune in Capricorn:** The practical is the ideal. Form follows function. You have a dream of being in control—the puppetmaster. You are very interested in tradition and tend to be dignified and conservative. You believe in an orderly society led by benevolent monarchs—those who can see what to do.

**Neptune in Aquarius:** The age of Aquarius marks the ideal. The world community networking with itself. Altruism. Religion is science. Group work is in full swing. Cooperation. Impersonal sharing. Emotions are controlled and managed. The world on the improve. Global co-ops.

**Neptune in Pisces:** The spiritual is seen as the ideal. Intuition, the occult, religion, and all things mystical are desired. Also music, fantasy, and all of the arts. The psyche, psychology, feelings. Also drugs, dreams, and far-out trips. Out-of-the-body. Trance.

## PLUTO IN THE SIGNS OF THE ZODIAC

**Pluto in Aries:** You are very out-front and candid, probably not known for your great sense of diplomacy or tact. Your intensity and passionate approach to life are obvious to all who meet you. You are driven to penetrate the superficial and get at the essential.

**Pluto in Taurus:** You could be a terrific businessperson, as you have an ability to get past the surface of things and separate out that with real worth. In the area of possessions and material goods, you will go through a lot of changes, learn a lot.

**Pluto in Gemini:** A good detective or research person. You can't help but get past all that is superficial. A passion for inquiry, questioning, and searching finds you always in pursuit of some piece of information … communicating, writing, speaking.

**Pluto in Cancer:** You may go through a lot of changes that affect your sense of security. Your home and family situation could be a focus for growth and real learning—an area of great sensitivity or vulnerability.

**Pluto in Leo:** You are very sensitive (even vulnerable) when it comes to expressing yourself, getting it out. Periods of intense creativity enable you to go through changes and inner growth. This creative intensity is good for music, poetry, art, and such.

**Pluto in Virgo:** You tend to be radical when it comes to self-analysis, which means health care, food, physical well-being, and so on. Serving and caring for yourself and others are primary sources of inner growth and changes. You are sensitive to criticism.

**Pluto in Libra:** Change and inner growth tend to come through relationships, both friends and lovers. Marriage or union (yoga) will be very intense and not at all superficial. You get to the heart of a relationship each and every time.

**Pluto in Scorpio:** You tear through appearances in an effort to get beneath, behind, and at the heart or essence. You may find psychology, initiation, mysticism, and the occult of great interest. Intense personal change and inner growth are lifelong habits.

**Pluto in Sagittarius:** You are passionate in your search for truth and essence. Nothing superficial or ephemeral holds your attention. Your intense analytical approach to life cuts through to the heart of things. This directness may not always endear you to others.

**Pluto in Capricorn:** Tremendous practical sense and drive cut through all the red tape and exposes the right decisions every time. You may have an ability to organize and manage all that is vulnerable and sensitive in the human psyche ... the public mind.

**Pluto in Aquarius:** Your burning zeal for the ideal world and your need to be part of a group of like-minded souls are major factors in your makeup. You learn and grow through your efforts to help others, to make into a reality what is seen by your inner vision.

**Pluto in Pisces:** A born psychologist. You can't help but dig beneath the surface of the human psyche and its vulnerabilities. You are passionate about your willingness to give and to sacrifice yourself for what you believe in. You understand and accept others.

## ASCENDANT IN THE SIGNS OF THE ZODIAC (RISING SIGN)

**Aries Rising:** You are bold and impulsive, tending to act first and ask questions later. You come on strong, and others may experience you as somewhat self-centered and possibly arrogant. You appear to be single-minded and daring—a leader.

**Taurus Rising:** You come across as stable, even gentle, and your response to most situations is even-handed and supportive. Sometimes you may seem very stubborn, for you tend to take your time and react to a situation fully.

**Gemini Rising:** You are quick, witty, and much given to talk and communicating with others. You come across as intelligent, verbal, and perhaps a little on the nervous side. You tend to be changeable, being all things to all people.

**Cancer Rising:** You come across as emotional and reactive. You sense things rather than think them through. You tend to mother and include everyone within your protective envelope ... are more comfortable in this role.

**Leo Rising:** You wear your heart on your sleeve and always manage to come across as confident and sure of yourself (possibly egotistical). You are very free with your emotions, which nevertheless tend to stay under your control. You are warm-hearted and effusive.

**Virgo Rising:** You are careful and precise and come across as a caring and responsible person. Your attention to detail and analytical skills (and probably mental, verbal) is obvious to all meeting you. Your appearance is always refined and neat.

**Libra Rising:** You are all things to all people, always responding in a way to please and flatter—a social being. You are so diplomatic and polite that one wonders if you have a viewpoint of your own. You have a natural ability to reflect and mirror others.

**Scorpio Rising:** You appear intense and passionate and probably tend to gravitate to positions of power and control. You come across as somewhat secretive, penetrating, and at all times very sensitive. You can get to the heart of things.

**Sagittarius Rising:** You come across in a frank, candid, and scrupulously honest manner … honest of the point of harshness. You are open-minded and tolerant, and love to travel in the mind (philosophy, religion) and perhaps across the Earth as well.

**Capricorn Rising:** You present yourself in a very practical and conservative manner. Always objective, you come across as very much a sharp business and career person. Others may interpret your clear-mindedness as emotional coolness.

**Aquarius Rising:** Very much a social animal, you communicate yourself best when in a group or when working toward some very worthwhile goal. You come across as impartial, tolerant, and open. Your idealism is apparent to all who come to know you.

**Pisces Rising:** Your manner is very gentle and peace-loving. Your sensitivity and concern for others comes across and is communicated in everything you say and do. You give others the sense that you are long-suffering and capable of much personal sacrifice.

## NORTH LUNAR NODE IN THE SIGNS OF THE ZODIAC

**North Node in Aries:** A vocation and desire to pursue whatever is free, untrammeled, and independent—adventuring, travel, independence, sheer strength.

**North Node in Taurus:** A talent and calling for building and creating environments (mandalas) is indicated. A urge to call forth or fashion a body or structure (to embody ideas). Reaction to new ideas (impulses) resulting in fashioning them forth, embodying them.

**North Node in Gemini:** A calling and vocation for all things connecting and connected—communication in general. Computers, writing, messages, electronics, etc., are indicated.

**North Node in Cancer:** A calling to create something substantial, solid, and secure, be it a home or vehicle of some sort. To experience pure feeling. The thrill and ride of the body.

**North Node in Leo:** A calling to teach, preach, and to express onself. Creativity of all kinds—including children, animals, art.

**North Node in Virgo:** A vocation and talent for healing and caring for all things that otherwise would be lost … to restore and salvage a situation. Restoration.

**North Node in Libra:** A true social calling; a mandate for all that is social and connected to society. An unquenchable thirst for this element.

**North Node in Scorpio:** A calling for all things hidden (occult), taboo, and secret. A drive to penetrate, research, and dig beyond appearances to the core reality. An initiate and initiator.

**North Node in Sagittarius:** A calling to all that is philosophical, true, and real, whether of a traditionally religious or personal-religious nature. A love of the core or kernal truths.

**North Node in Capricorn:** A calling to the practical. Business achievement in management and clear-seeing in general is indicated.

**North Node in Aquarius:** A calling to humanitarian and broad social ideals and issues. An interest and karma for group work and ideals.

**North Node in Pisces:** A calling to all that is inner and psychological. A gift for the psyche and psychic—love of the inner workings of the mind itself.

## SUN IN THE NATAL HOUSES

**Sun in the First House:** You tend to be out front and personable. Your personal appearance is important to you and you put a lot of thought and effort into how you appear or come across. Others notice you, and a position of leadership (prominence) is likely.

**Sun in the Second House:** You are very responsive and probably not a little possessive. You tend to collect things, and material success—money, home, security, possessions—is very important. You tend to be very supportive of others.

**Sun in the Third House:** You are very communicative, not a little curious, and like to talk, speak, write, and so on. Study, research, and investigations of all kinds appeal to you. You are always searching out some answer or another. Siblings are important, too.

**Sun in the Fourth House:** Home, family, and security are important to you. You love to send out roots and build a home base. Sensitive and somewhat private, you tend to be a very feeling (and sometimes vulnerable) person. You sense things and have a good feel for business.

**Sun in the Fifth House:** You are very expressive and outgoing when it comes to your feelings and emotions—you wear your heart on your sleeve. Creativity of all kinds is important to you—music, drama, art, poetry. Also, animals and children play a large role.

**Sun in the Six House:** You are a good worker, always thinking and caring for things. You are naturally service-oriented and enjoy taking care of the needs of others. You are very discriminating and can sort out the good apples from the bad.

**Sun in the Seventh House:** You love a social life—friends and relationships play a major role in your makeup. Close bonds (marriage, yoga) are very important to you.

**Sun in the Eighth House:** "What you see is what you get" is not enough for you. You want more than appearances and are willing to dig down to get at the heart of things. You work through all that is superficial, no matter what kind of personal sacrifice is required.

**Sun in the Ninth House:** You are direct and candid and tend to brush past appearances and settle on the truth within. Ideas—philosophy and religion—are what life is all about. You may travel, counsel, and be a teacher to others.

**Sun in the Tenth House:** You are very career-oriented, and your personal reputation and honor are of the utmost importance. You possess a natural sense of organization and practical insight and may excel at managing or supervising others.

**Sun in the Eleventh House:** Perfect as a group leader, where your innate idealism and love for humanity can blossom. Group or community work—anything that is altruistic or serves the common good—is where you can be found. You strive to make your dreams and ideals real.

**Sun in the Twelfth House:** You naturally are a giving person, sacrificing your own interests for the sake of an inner vision—what you feel is right. A born psychologist, you may find yourself counseling and caring for the mental needs of others.

## MOON IN THE NATAL HOUSES

**Moon in the First House:** You always manage to end up in the limelight, with the support of those around you. You get a lot of mileage out of your appearance and the way you carry yourself and communicate to others. You could make your living from the public.

**Moon in the Second House:** Good things (the support you need) always seem to come to you. Friends, coworkers, and plain old lucky circumstances offer encouragement and backing. You often get what you need, when you need it.

**Moon in the Third House:** You have a knack for putting the feelings of a group into words and may serve as a teacher or spokesperson. Communication is one area where you can always get support and backing from friends and coworkers. Historical ideas may interest you.

**Moon in the Fourth House:** You look to home and family for support and encouragement. History (personal or otherwise) interests you, and you tend toward nostalgia. Security is very important and you need to have real roots in order to be productive.

**Moon in the Fifth House:** You are at your most expressive when urged on by a group or in an environment that you feel is supportive. You may enjoy group sports or working with children or animals. Creativity and its expression are very important in your life.

**Moon in the Sixth House:** You always find support from others when you turn your attention to health, food, nutrition, and areas where service or attention to detail are in high focus. You may enjoy working with a group of others where you can exercise your discrimination.

**Moon in the Seventh House:** Your friends, partners, and relationships mean a lot to you. They are a primary source of strength, and you always look to them for support and encouragement. You are indeed a social being and will no doubt weave this fact into your lifestyle.

**Moon in the Eighth House:** Your keen business sense is never sharper than when you are working with or for others—a group, corporation, and so on. You are great at finding excess and rooting it out, and your actions receive support from those around you. Initiating others.

**Moon in the Ninth House:** Your sense of honesty and truth is something that others sense in you and support. You might find yourself teaching or guiding groups in matters of religion or philosophy. Travel, especially with others, is indicated.

**Moon in the Tenth House:** You have a natural insight and understanding as to what the public wants. Your career gets all kinds of support from other people, and you feel at home making practical and management decisions. You look to your work for strength and encouragement.

**Moon in the Eleventh House:** You need to be part of a group and draw strength and encouragement from your friends and acquaintances. Working with others, especially on community or humanitarian efforts, is perfect for you. You grow through making ideals real.

**Moon in the Twelfth House:** Psychology—in particular group work—is one area that you can always look to for support and encouragement. You may find yourself counseling or ministering to others, helping them to understand and accept their lives.

## MERCURY IN THE NATAL HOUSE

**Mercury in the First House:** You think a lot about appearances—how things come across or might appear to others. You are very personable and aware of personalities.

**Mercury in the Second House:** You have a good mind for business. You tend to think along lines that are practical and conservative, always coming up with sound and productive ideas.

**Mercury in the Third House:** You love to study and question and are always inquiring and searching, using your mind for research. You enjoy communication in all its forms—spoken, written, via computers, and so on. Your mind is active, always testing and searching for limits.

**Mercury in the Fourth House:** Your mind tends to settle on issues of security—home, family, and such. Your thoughts have great substance and feeling. An interest in history, the past, and nostalgia may be lifelong.

**Mercury in the Fifth House:** You can express feelings and put emotions into words. This could give you a flair for the dramatic, public speaking, poetry, and the arts. You are proud of your mind and enjoy using it, solving puzzles—any creative mental outlet.

**Mercury in the Sixth House:** You are skilled at using your mind in an analytical manner, always discriminating. An expert at quality control, you can spot the bad apples every time. You may be skillful when it comes to health-related matters (mental or physical).

**Mercury in the Seventh House:** You love to communicate and discuss ideas with other people. Your ideas are always fair and impartial, especially when it comes to other people, the social scene. You are at your mental best when you are communicating with others.

**Mercury in the Eighth House:** You have a very analytical bent, and your mind excels at making practical decisions. Your ideas run deeper than superficial issues which could mean an interest in depth psychology and even occult and mystical subjects.

**Mercury in the Ninth House:** Your mind and thoughts always gravitate to what is lasting, true, or of the essence. Philosophy and religion are subjects that often occupy you. Your ideas are always to-the-point and candid, never florid or superficial.

**Mercury in the Tenth House:** When it comes to business and career, you have a mind that just can't help but take care of business. Your thoughts and ideas are nothing if not practical, and your clear-sightedness makes some form of management or supervision almost unavoidable.

**Mercury in the Eleventh House:** Your mind runs to humanitarian values and thoughts of what could (and should) be. Ideas connected with group work and goals (making your inner vision real) are natural. You are good at putting your ideas to work in the world, making dreams real.

**Mercury in the Twelfth House:** Your mind is naturally interested in all that is psychological and beneath the surface of things. Ideas of self-sacrifice and compassion—how to serve and help others—are what you tend to think about.

## VENUS IN THE NATAL HOUSES

**Venus in the First House:** You value a good appearance—how people present themselves or come on. You value the personal approach and are very discriminating personally when it comes to matters of taste and art.

**Venus in the Second House:** You have a natural love of possessions and the material world. You value art and all that is beautiful and fine. Your sense of taste and discrimination is excellent.

**Venus in the Third House:** You love to communicate and pursue conversations. The mental world appeals to you, and you are very discriminating (but appreciative) when it comes to concepts, ideas, thoughts, and the like. You value good research and real inquiry.

**Venus in the Fourth House:** You love your roots, whether home and family, ancestors, or history in general. You are probably a collector and very discriminating in this area. You appreciate emotions and like to get a sense or feel for whatever is happening.

**Venus in the Fifth House:** You probably love the theater and all that is creative, expressive, and artsy. You appreciate the dramatic, and emotional scenes are a sign of life to you. You love action, sports, and putting your heart and feelings on the line.

**Venus in the Sixth House:** You like to do things with care and enjoy being discriminating and exact. Your critical faculties are excellent, and you can always pick out what is worth saving and what is not. You appreciate a caring attitude and are service-oriented.

**Venus in the Seventh House:** You love social life and relationships of all kinds—partners, marriages, teachers, and such. You are very responsive yourself and value this in others. You don't play favorites and are quite impersonal when it comes to your responsibilities.

**Venus in the Eighth House:** You don't care much for the superficial. You appreciate getting past the surface and down to the heart—the bare bones of the matter. This could make you a very shrewd and discriminating business person. You value passion in a relationship.

**Venus in the Ninth House:** Your love of truth makes philosophy and religious ideas a lifelong habit. You appreciate things of a global or universal level and could love to travel. Appearances mean little to you, and you value honesty and candidness in friends and partners.

**Venus in the Tenth House:** You love large-scale organization, and career or business will always be close to your heart. Your sense of discrimination when it comes to practical issues is excellent, and you value clearheadedness in others. You like to work.

**Venus in the Eleventh House:** You love community projects and group work of any kind. Your sense of values finds you on the side of altruism and humanism at every turn. You appreciate goals and efforts at the global level.

**Venus in the Twelfth House:** You can appreciate the difficulties of others and be understanding of the problems they may be having. You value a certain amount of self-sacrifice and a giving attitude. You can discriminate between superficiality and the reality beneath it.

## MARS IN THE NATAL HOUSES

**Mars in the First House:** You have a strong drive to be seen and known—to communicate yourself to others. Personal appearance (the way you present yourself) is also a motivating factor.

**Mars in the Second House:** You are motivated when it comes to possessions and material things. An urge to respond, own, and build upon whatever comes your way makes you a natural when it comes to productivity and the business world.

**Mars in the Third House:** A relentless drive to pursue knowledge, to search, research, and follow out leads and pointers. You are very motivated when it comes to communications of all forms—phone, voice, letters, computers, and the like.

**Mars in the Fourth House:** You are driven to send down roots, dig in, and find the limits of whatever you are involved in. This urge to be secure always pushes you to always get to the foundation of things. You are motivated when it comes to home and family.

**Mars in the Fifth House:** You are driven to excel in any form of physical and creative expression—sports, theatrics, arts and crafts, whatever. This urge to express yourself, to speak out and be heard, propels you into many an interesting situation.

**Mars in the Sixth House:** You are very motivated when it comes to matters of care and service—taking care of details. You are up for any task that requires conservation—separating the wheat from the chaff. An urge to salvage everything.

**Mars in the Seventh House:** You are highly motivated when it comes to relationships (social or private) and strive to rise above personalities. An urge to see unity in everything, to marry or join all disparities, may find you going overboard now and again.

**Mars in the Eighth House:** Not content with appearances, you are driven to reduce everything to the bare essentials, the nitty-gritty. This compelling urge for integrity and contempt for the superficial may offend some.

**Mars in the Ninth House:** You may end up traveling the world. An inner urge to find the very heart of truth in all things may propel you endlessly. You are very motivated when it comes to philosophies, religion, and all things essential and lasting. No superficiality.

**Mars in the Tenth House:** You are driven to manage and control things. An urge to organize and be practical amounts to a minor obsession. Your career motivation is constant and relentless.

**Mars in the Eleventh House:** You have real community spirit, a drive to work with others on projects of humanitarian interest. An urge to make your altruistic dreams a reality keeps you moving in the direction of group goals and work.

**Mars in the Twelfth House:** You have a high degree of motivation when it comes to giving and to personal sacrifice. You feel understanding and accepting and are easily moved by the problems of others. Psychology in all of its forms is a driving force in your life.

## JUPITER IN THE NATAL HOUSES

**Jupiter in the First House:** Your career may be built around the way you appear or present yourself—the way you come across to others. Your spontaneous personality and ability to fascinate others are key elements in being successful.

**Jupiter in the Second House:** Your career or lifepath may depend on your talent for responding and making something out of ideas, insights … whatever is new and challenging. The business world may call for your ability to react and build on opportunities.

**Jupiter in the Third House:** A born investigator and researcher, always inquiring, searching, following things to their logical conclusion. Your career will probably be built around these qualities of yours—communication, making connections, thoughts and ideas, and so on.

**Jupiter in the Fourth House:** Your career may be built on your search for roots and security. You find yourself through home and family (all things domestic), and it would be excellent if you could somehow make your living in these areas.

**Jupiter in the Fifth House:** You could be successful working with creativity and self-expression through the arts and theater, in sports, or with the ultimate self-expression, children. You may find yourself a guide and teacher to others when it comes to these matters.

**Jupiter in the Sixth House:** A career in one of the service or health occupations is possible, for you may find yourself automatically taking care of the needs of others. Your occupation involves health, food, and all attempts to restore, salvage, and make the best out of things.

**Jupiter in the Seventh House:** Your life path involves very close relationships with others. This could be through a marriage or another form of yoga (union). Making the two one, joining together what is separate, is the key to your career.

**Jupiter in the Eighth House:** Your life path involves cutting through appearances and superficialities and laying bare the reality of a situation. This could mean that the business world is an open book for you—easy to read. Any career where you get through to what really is there.

**Jupiter in the Ninth House:** Your devotion and search for truth may carry you across the globe and certainly to the far reaches of philosophy and religious thoughts. Your career may hinge on your need to always get at the seed, essence, or heart of every question.

**Jupiter in the Tenth House:** It is natural for you to put your practical and managerial abilities to work. You can make a career out of your keen organizational skills and clear insight into how things work. Supervision and taking charge are your trademarks.

**Jupiter in the Eleventh House:** You could make a career out of group or community work, anything involving attempts to bring large-scale and humanitarian dreams and ideas to reality. Your ideals and inner vision keep what is best for everyone ever on your mind.

**Jupiter in the Twelfth House:** You could excel in a career that involves understanding and self-sacrifice. Psychology, counseling—guiding others to be forgiving and accepting—may be a special skill that you have. Work with mental patients, prison inmates, and the like is possible.

## SATURN IN THE NATAL HOUSES

**Saturn in the First House:** You are very conservative when it comes to your personal appearance and communications with others. You are impartial and don't play favorites or get overly personal. You probably don't waste words.

**Saturn in the Second House:** You could be frugal when it comes to possessions, always limiting your purchases to what is essential and has value. This same theme carries through in your response to people. You don't tend to lavish affection or sentiment. You keep it short and simple.

**Saturn in the Third House:** You don't waste words, and communications tend to be short and to-the-point. You are very determined and deliberate when it comes to mental work and would make an excellent researcher or scientist. You concentrate on what is essential.

**Saturn in the Fourth House:** You have very simple needs regarding home and surroundings. Some might find you frugal. It may be difficult for you to set down roots, build a home-base, and feel secure. Feelings and emotions may be on the sparse side.

**Saturn in the Fifth House:** You find it difficult to let go, emote, and express your feelings, and tend to be cautious and restrained. Feeling creative may be difficult, for you are very hard on yourself in this area. You may have approach/avoidance reactions with children, animals.

**Saturn in the Sixth House:** Your critical faculties are severe, and it may be difficult for you to exercise them. Once you turn your analytical light on, you tend to be relentless in appraisal. This could make working with others difficult. Good for food, health, conservation.

**Saturn in the Seventh House:** Relationships are so important to you that they could be a stumbling block at times. It may be difficult for you to be close, as you are very demanding of others. You are not satisfied with superficialities. You want a lasting marriage (union, yoga).

**Saturn in the Eighth House:** You can be very demanding when it comes to what is essential or central to a situation. You are exacting when it comes to getting down to the nitty-gritty. This is excellent for business or quality control. You like nothing but the best.

**Saturn in the Ninth House:** Religion, philosophy, and truth are essential to your life. You are painstaking and deliberate when it comes to sorting through ideas and values for what is lasting and solid. You may appear to others as too sober or religious.

**Saturn in the Tenth House:** Your career, practical vision, and skills are of central importance to you. You are nothing if not organized and deliberate in this area of life. Your reputation and image are a source of concern, and you do everything you can to make them solid.

**Saturn in the Eleventh House:** You work hard to make your dreams and ideals a reality. You work hard at community or group work. You spare no effort here. Humanitarian goals are central to your life's work.

**Saturn in the Twelfth House:** You are very serious when it comes to self-sacrifice and doing all you can to make things easier for other people. You pursue psychology, the human psyche, and things mystical. You are quite painstaking when it comes to giving and helping others.

## URANUS IN THE NATAL HOUSES

**Uranus in the First House:** A tendency to be eccentric and unconventional in appearance and mannerisms. Perhaps your approach to life—the way you come on—is unusual or different. You may be spontaneous, witty, and unpredictable.

**Uranus in the Second House:** You may have unusual ways of responding to what life offers you, with the result that the way you make your living is somewhat eccentric. Your means of support may be individualistic and different from the group.

**Uranus in the Third House:** You have real insight when it comes to anything connected to research, study, and the world of ideas. Your independent mental approach to problem-solving and communication finds you coming up with connections that are new and different.

**Uranus in the Fourth House:** You are very independent when it comes to your own security and family. This could mean an unconventional-style home or furnishings, or a different approach to sentiment, nostalgia, and history.

**Uranus in the Fifth House:** You are unconventional when it comes to self-expression and enjoyment. You find new and different ways to get it out—possibly sports, the creative arts, and such. Always independent when it comes to emotions, you don't mind feeling a little different.

**Uranus in the Sixth House:** You are innovative when it comes to self-analysis and self-care—food, diet, health, and so on. You can see new ways to make use of the status quo. An unconventional approach to working for/with others may require a special work situation for you.

**Uranus in the Seventh House:** You seem to assert your independence in relationships and the social scene. Unconventional, to say the least, you may well enjoy a different kind of marriage or friendship. You have insight into marriage or yoga—the ties that bind.

**Uranus in the Eighth House:** Lightning fast when it comes to the business deal, you seem to have direct insight into what is worthwhile and worthless in a situation. You have new and unconventional ways to cut through the red tape and get at what is important.

**Uranus in the Ninth House:** Unconventional in matters of philosophy and religion, you always find new ways to get past the fluff and into what is really important. Your insights into truth and the eternal make you independent and somewhat of a loner.

**Uranus in the Tenth House:** You are original and insightful when it comes to practical matters—job, career, and such. Independent, you may have an unconventional approach to work, especially regarding how you organize or manage. You may have a reputation for being different.

**Uranus in the Eleventh House:** You may enjoy eccentric or unconventional friends, and groups with some kind of humanitarian flavor will appeal. You have very original ideas when it comes to community, making our collective dreams into a reality.

**Uranus in the Twelfth House:** You could be unconventional in matters of psychology, the psyche, and all that is mystical or spiritual. Unusual ways to help or care for others—insight into accepting life and self-sacrifice—are yours.

## NEPTUNE IN THE NATAL HOUSES

**Neptune in the First House:** You are a real charmer—able to enchant others and bring them under your spell. You manage to communicate an almost mystical sense to a group. Your ideals and ability to see the whole picture are obvious to all who come to know you.

**Neptune in the Second House:** You are very idealistic when it comes to possessions, finance, and how you choose to make your living. Your response to what life offers you is always very elevated, although not always practical. This could lead to some disappointments.

**Neptune in the Third House:** Your mind tends to be very imaginative and not concerned with facts and figures. Instead, ideas and writing of a mystical or poetic nature appeal. Research into religious or very idealistic subjects is indicated.

**Neptune in the Fourth House:** You don't have to leave home to escape from the rat race. Family, home, and security seem just about ideal to you. You may be very imaginative with your home and domestic setup, or a sense of community and unity pervades your family life.

**Neptune in the Fifth House:** You have great creative imagination, perhaps a strong sense for the dramatic and the ability to express ideas of a mystical or other-worldly flavor. Entertaining children (and adults) with enchanting stories and the like is indicated.

**Neptune in the Sixth House:** You are very imaginative when it comes to your health, the food you eat, and how you take care of yourself. Quick to get the picture, you may find yourself helping others see the benefits that proper care (mental, physical, and such) can bring.

**Neptune in the Seventh House:** You never forsake your ideals when it comes to relationships of any kind. Your imagination is at its best when you are being social or relating to others. You have a real vision of what marriage is all about.

**Neptune in the Eighth House:** You are very trusting and idealistic when it comes to taking care of business, getting down to the nitty-gritty. You see the best in a situation, making it hard to say no or cut yourself the best deal. Initiation and the mystical will appeal.

**Neptune in the Ninth House:** Your dreams and ideals rest in whatever is pure and true. Philosophy and religion are your escape and refuge from the mundane world. An almost mystical imagination provides you with visions into the world as a community—a sense of unity.

**Neptune in the Tenth House:** Your practical skills are linked to your almost mystical inner vision. You manifest your ideals and dreams in an organized and clear-headed manner. You would be great at giving the public a sense of the ideal via films, advertising, spiritual work.

**Neptune in the Eleventh House:** You dream of a world where unity and harmony are a reality. Group or community work with high aims (great altruism) would be ideal for you. Your imagination drives you to make your dreams and inner vision a reality.

**Neptune in the Twelfth House:** You have very high ideals and a vision of unity and togetherness that allows you to be long-suffering and put up with a lot. You tend to be self-sacrificing, understanding, and always interested in whatever is psychological, mystical, and the like.

## PLUTO IN THE NATAL HOUSES

**Pluto in the First House:** You are very out-front and candid, probably not known for your great sense of diplomacy or tact. Your intensity and passionate approach to life are obvious to all who meet you. You are driven to penetrate the superficial and get at the essential.

**Pluto in the Second House:** You could be a terrific business person, as you have an ability to get past the surface of things and separate out that which has real worth. In the area of possessions or material goods you will go through a lot of changes and learn a lot.

**Pluto in the Third House:** A good detective or research person. You can't help but get past all that is superficial. A passion for inquiry, questioning, and searching finds you always in pursuit of some piece of information ... communicating, writing, speaking.

**Pluto in the Fourth House:** You may go through a lot of changes that affect your sense of security. Your home and family situation could be a focus for growth and real learning—an area of great sensitivity and vulnerability.

**Pluto in the Fifth House:** You are very sensitive (even vulnerable) when it comes to expressing yourself, getting it out. Periods of intense creativity enable you to go through changes and inner growth. This creative intensity is good for music, poetry, art, and the like.

**Pluto in the Sixth House:** You tend to be radical when it comes to self-analysis, which includes health care, food, physical well being. Serving and caring for yourself and others is a primary source of inner growth and change. You are sensitive to criticism.

**Pluto in the Seventh House:** Change and inner growth tend to come through your relationships with both friends and lovers. Marriage, union (yoga) will be very intense and not at all superficial. You get to the heart of a relationship each and every time.

**Pluto in the Eighth House:** You tear through appearances in an effort to get beneath, behind, and at the heart or essence. You may find the occult, psychology, initiation, and mysticism of great interest. Intense personal change and inner growth are lifelong habits.

**Pluto in the Ninth House:** You are passionate in your search for truth and essence. Nothing superficial or ephemeral holds your attention. Your intense analytical approach to life cuts through to the heart of things. This directness may not always endear you to others.

**Pluto in the Tenth House:** A tremendous practical sense and drive cuts through all the red tape and exposes the right decisions every time. You may have an ability to organize and manage all that is vulnerable and sensitive in the human psyche ... the public mind.

**Pluto in the Eleventh House:** Your burning zeal for the ideal world and your need to be part of a group of like-minded souls are major factors in your makeup. You learn and grow through your efforts to help others and to make your inner vision into a reality.

**Pluto in the Twelfth House:** A born psychologist. You can't help but dig beneath the surface of the human psyche and its vulnerabilities. You are passionate about your willingness to give and to sacrifice yourself for what you believe in. You understand and accept others.

## NORTH LUNAR NODE IN THE HOUSES

**North Node in the First House:** You are driven to express yourself, to lead, and take charge. This is natural for you and cannot be avoided.

**North Node in the Second House:** You have a strong desire and will to send out roots, to establish yourself, and to draw around you and create an environment that is nourishing and stable. This is a life-long commitment.

**North Node in the Third House:** You have a drive and vocation to explore the world of communication and communications—whatever crosses and re-crosses: wires, sound, light, electric, etc. This also extends to the mind and all of its connections.

**North Node in the Fourth House:** You have an innate desire to build a stable home and environment. You seek strong experiences, real feelings, the thrill and ride of the body.

**North Node in the Fifth House:** You are drawn to all manner of expression and creativity, whether your own or that of a group. Also children and animals. Acting, speaking, and self-expression (teaching!) are unavoidable.

**North Node in the Sixth House:** You are linked to efforts to save, salvage, and restore life—whether in matters of health, mind, or physical matter. You are the savior and redeemer of all things, restoring to purity what would otherwise deteriorate.

**North Node in the Seventh House:** You are linked to public service with no chance of a reprieve. It is your destiny and karma to work with the public and society. Groups, social affairs, and links of all kinds are natural to you.

**North Node in the Eighth House:** A drive to get at the inner core of truth is innate and natural for you. You penetrate to whatever is secret, occult, and hidden—revealing the core. You are, by definition, an initiator.

**North Node in the Ninth House:** Working with truth and all that stands for core truths—religion, philosophy, etc.—is a given for you. You will develop a mastery in these areas. Unavoidable.

**North Node in the Tenth House:** You have a supreme gift for organization and all that is practical. You grasp the practical in every situation and have the ability to manage and be responsible for almost everything that comes your way. This amounts to a vocation.

**North Node in the Eleventh House:** A desire for freedom and the establishment of social ideals will be a lifelong quest for you. You are driven to enact group goals and bring to reality what has been, until now, but a wish or dream.

**North Node in the Twelfth House:** You are steeped in the psychological and the human psyche. This is your karma and the reason you are here. This is your turf and you cannot avoid becoming an expert (and initiated) psychologist.

## PLANETS IN THE ASPECTS

**Sun Conjunct Moon:** A natural go-between or mediator between the generations, you always manage to see it two ways, understanding both sides of any question. Intense and perhaps somewhat private, you have a strong effect on those who come to know you. New ideas.

**Sun Opposite Moon:** You may find yourself torn between two loves or passions, a love of the past versus the future, mother versus father, a younger crowd versus an older crowd. A basic antagonism of home and surroundings against the need to grow, progress, and push on.

**Sun Trine, Sextile, or Semi-Sextile Moon:** A special affinity for old people and for children, plus an innate love of animals, the helpless, and the underdog. An inner vision coupled with the ability to see the "big" picture often finds you working as a go-between with others.

**Sun Square, Semi-Square, or Sesqui-Square Moon:** You are sometimes torn between a desire to progress and be all that you can be versus a tendency to dwell in the past, resting on your laurels. Your inner, more domestic side struggles against authority. You could feel caught in the middle.

**Sun Conjunct Mercury:** You are very bright, and you may be very proud of your mind and all that it can do. You have a high degree of concentration that makes you an excellent student and able to excel in speaking, writing, and all types of communication skills.

**Sun Opposite Mercury:** You have a lot of mental energy and ideas, some of which could be counterproductive or go against your own future interests. Arguments with authorities or more experienced people may find you having to control your tongue and temper your thoughts.

**Sun Trine, Sextile, or Semi-sextile Mercury:** You have a bright, quick mind that is able to get the idea or "big" picture right off. Ever concerned with bringing things down to earth and understanding how things work, you have a natural talent for organization and practical ideas.

**Sun Square, Semi-square, or Sesqui-square Mercury:** You probably say things despite yourself that you regret later. Your ideas and words may get you into trouble now and again, or work against your own best interest. The mental (in all its forms) is something you find more difficult than easy.

**Sun Conjunct Venus:** You have excellent taste and could be expert in all matters of art and discrimination. You can always pick out the valuable and worthwhile. You value and appreciate all that is fine and beautiful. Perhaps an interest in older people or authority.

**Sun Opposite Venus:** You may not always appreciate yourself or your sense of values, and the things you like may be counterproductive or run against your own best interests. You may not care for authority figures or those more experienced than you.

**Sun Trine, Sextile, or Semi-sextile Venus:** An obvious sense of love, understanding, and compassion for others is present. This is coupled with a real feel for the arts (music, poetry, painting, and the like) and also a sensitivity for matters of value and of the heart.

**Sun Square, Semi-square, or Sesqui-square Venus:** Your cravings get you in trouble now and again. You appreciate things that are not always in your own best interest. Your ambition and drive to grow and progress may sometimes be at the expense of your value system, your sense of beauty, and the like.

**Sun Conjunct Mars:** You are very motivated, with a strong drive and urge to do and accomplish. Others could find you a bit pushy. With an eye to progress and the future, you feel compelled to try for what is just out of your reach. You support authority in all forms.

**Sun Opposite Mars:** Your drive and ambition may tend to be counterproductive or work against your own best interest at times. You may feel challenged and competitive with authority figures. Your feelings and emotions can get out of control, go against your will.

**Sun Trine, Sextile, or Semi-sextile Mars:** A natural ability to use emotions in productive ways. Entertaining others is one form this might take. Hard work and all things physical (such as sports and outdoor activities) should be a snap. You are able to manage and see how to work with the energy of others.

**Sun Square, Semi-square, or Sesqui-square Mars:** Your drive to succeed is strong, but you often push yourself in a direction against your own best interests. Your ambitions may find you at odds with authority figures again and again. A tendency towards arguments and emotional drama exists.

**Sun Conjunct Jupiter:** Probably always popular with others and at home in the crowd, you tend to radiate success. Others may value the fact that you can always manage to unravel even the worst problems for them. You could benefit from older people or those in authority.

**Sun Opposite Jupiter:** You could find yourself pursuing options and paths that end up leading away from your own best interests. Your particular solutions to problems may go against, or prove challenging for, those in authority. Your methods may provoke the establishment.

**Sun Trine, Sextile, or Semi-sextile Jupiter:** You have a sense of justice and an innate ability to understand the law, whether natural or manmade. Showing others the way through or beyond the problems in their lives comes easy, for you sense how to manipulate the opportunities of life. Lucky.

**Sun Square, Semi-square, or Sesqui-square Jupiter:** You may tend to take paths at right angles to your real ambitions and self-interest. Trouble with authorities or older people can result. Your struggle to succeed is aided when you show self-control or discipline and find that middle road.

**Sun Conjunct Saturn:** You could be a bit too serious for most, but all would agree that you are organized and able to take care of business. You may seem older than you are, and probably treat authority and the law with great respect. Very disciplined, perhaps too sober.

**Sun Opposite Saturn:** Your sense of order and discipline could, at times, prove to be counterproductive and work against your own better interests. You may feel that others (such as partners or friends) hold you back from organizing your life the way you want.

**Sun Trine, Sextile, or Semi-sextile Saturn:** There is a real love of science and natural laws. You are a hard and tireless worker, with absolute determination and the ability to accomplish great projects with ease. You are fiercely loyal to your friends. Also, very integral ... perhaps too sober.

**Sun Square, Semi-square, or Sesqui-square Saturn:** Your organizational abilities and sense of responsibility can sometimes limit your own true ambitions. Your seriousness may be counterproductive, making it difficult for you to build a foundation. Older men or authorities may prove troublesome.

**Sun Conjunct Uranus:** You are independent and value freedom and the ability to move around and avoid routine. You admire the unconventional and different, and your friends could be eccentric authority figures. Inventions, electronics, computers, and the like would appeal.

**Sun Opposite Uranus:** Your own independence and sense of personal freedom may challenge the establishment or authorities. Others may find you unconventional and eccentric at times. Your solution to problems can be somewhat radical and work against your own interests.

**Sun Trine, Sextile, or Semi-sextile Uranus:** Breakthrough flashes of insight with tremendous originality and independence are typical. A natural sense of invention and a love of all things electrical and of communication in general. A born traveler, not afraid to be alone. You go your own way.

**Sun Square, Semi-square, or Sesqui-square Uranus:** Your need for self-expression and independence may be at the expense of your real growth. You may rebel or find yourself bucking authority figures. It is clear to you that your unconventionality costs you. Part of you wants to conform and go along.

**Sun Conjunct Neptune:** You have a great imagination and probably can entrance an audience in short order with your visions and ideals. You tend to expect the best from others and may find guidance from a spiritual teacher or older person. You are a dreamer, a high floater.

**Sun Opposite Neptune:** Others may not always support your self-image and your personal ideals. At times, your more romantic and idealistic side may even work against your best interests, resulting in disappointments and disillusion with partners, authorities, and such.

**Sun Trine, Sextile, or Semi-sextile Neptune:** A born mother to any and all forms of life. Very compassionate and attentive (aware of) the needs of others. Spiritual ideas and concepts are a way of life here. There is deep appreciation, even love for, movies, big ideas, themes. Visionary director.

**Sun Square, Semi-square, or Sesqui-square Neptune:** You struggle between your sense of ideals and your more practical ambitions. Your self-image and dreams are kept apart from the day-to-day practical concerns. They continue to confront one another. Authorities may not trust you, and vice versa.

**Sun Conjunct Pluto:** Others may find you very intense and too personal. You are very direct and manage to get to the heart of most matters without thinking. Power struggles are not unknown to you, and you may work in politics or with authorities—those older than you.

**Sun Opposite Pluto:** Your personal changes, the need for growth and transformation, can be intense to the point of being counterproductive. Your directness may find you in power struggles with others, especially those in authority. You tend to battle it out.

**Sun Trine, Sextile, or Semi-sextile Pluto:** Innate intensity and seriousness are visible to all. A sense of the eternal aspects of life makes authority and leadership positions natural and unavoidable. A gut sense of how to act in stress situations. Lots of charisma. Power.

**Sun Square, Semi-square, or Sesqui-square Pluto:** You may have a secret life aside from your more public ambitions. Your need for analysis and in-depth probing of every aspect of your life may run counter to your best interests. Power struggles with authorities (and within yourself) can result.

**Moon Conjunct Mercury:** You find it easy to put your feelings into words and are probably interested in psychology, different cultures, and history. You are very clear-headed when it comes to emotional issues, and may excel at writing, speaking, and communicating to groups.

**Moon Opposite Mercury:** You may think and speak in a way that others could find challenging or even antagonistic. Since you don't always listen to your own moods and feelings, some of your ideas may not even feel right to you. You could argue or debate in public.

**Moon Trine, Sextile, or Semi-sextile Mercury:** A great speaker or entertainer. At the very least, the gift of gab. Working with or teaching others and communicating via the mind in general are indicated. A natural storyteller, you are at home in the world of myths and dreams.

**Moon Square, Semi-square, or Sesqui-square Mercury:** You say things you don't mean, and you don't always mean what you manage to say. Your feelings often run counter to what you think or communicate, and you are not at your best when things get emotional. What you say may evoke emotions from others.

**Moon Conjunct Venus:** You have a natural love of history, different cultures, and your own past. You can appreciate the emotional and psychological side of life, and working with groups will be a top priority. Others value you for your sense of appreciation and love.

**Moon Opposite Venus:** Your sense of values and the way you care about things may prove challenging to others. You may not appreciate the emotions and moods you feel, especially when in a group. You may not care much for psychology, history, or the problems of younger people.

**Moon Trine, Sextile, or Semi-sextile Venus:** A born charmer with an innate love and appreciation for other people, especially children. A sense of color, of music, and all of the arts—the beautiful and the comfortable. Always welcome in a group, you are a connoisseur of things bright and kind.

**Moon Square, Semi-square, or Sesqui-square Venus:** Others may not support or feel right about your values. You may be unable to appreciate or show love to someone who supports and provides for you. You may have very little interest in your own past, or history in general. You don't value sentiment.

**Moon Conjunct Mars:** You have an unusual ability to motivate other people, especially in group work. Your enthusiasm and drive is catching, and this makes you ideal as a teacher or group leader, especially with young people. You sometimes push too hard and irritate others.

**Moon Opposite Mars:** Others may find you pushy, for your motivation and drive could run counter to the established values of the group. You tend to go against sentiment and refuse to credit emotions. Culture and history don't fascinate you. You get a lot of reactions.

**Moon Trine, Sextile, or Semi-sextile Mars:** A born coach or teacher, you are at home in the physical and "doing" areas of life. An inspiration and driving force in the lives of others. Quite able to manage a very active and strong emotional life. Strong spirit. Attractive. Direct, perhaps loud.

**Moon Square, Semi-square, or Sesqui-square Mars:** Your own forcefulness and drive can make it difficult for others to offer you nourishment and support. You can be too harsh to allow any real sentiment and feeling to flourish. You tend to ignore personal history and any display of emotions.

**Moon Conjunct Jupiter:** A born teacher or group leader, counselor, or guide. Others find it easy to take direction from you by example alone. You enjoy immersing yourself in a group, solving problems, raising spirits, and so on. People admire your openness and generosity.

**Moon Opposite Jupiter:** You tend to find your own way, which often runs counter to what everyone else is doing. Your solutions to life's problems tend to ignore any moods or feelings you may have. Your career may always seem to be at war with your home and personal life.

**Moon Trine, Sextile, or Semi-sextile Jupiter:** Like a fish in water when in the limelight or in a group, you have an innate social charm. Political and lucky, too! A natural sense of what's right or of the way to get things done brings great popularity, even renown. Law, education. Could be lazy.

**Moon Square, Semi-square, or Sesqui-square Jupiter:** You may have trouble finding support for what you do (your path or career). The way to success for you seems to run counter to emotions and sentiment. You avoid activities having to do with your past environment. Your business is non-domestic.

**Moon Conjunct Saturn:** You are a natural disciplinarian, always extracting the most from others, especially a group. Your no-nonsense approach, which does not always endear you to others, gets to the heart or meaning of any subject. A natural tendency towards solitude.

**Moon Opposite Saturn:** You tend to organize and discipline yourself in a very different manner from the rest of your crowd. Others may complain that your methods may ignore feelings and personal rapport. You could turn your back on the past, ignore sentiment and moods.

**Moon Trine, Sextile, or Semi-sextile Saturn:** A tireless and disciplined worker, you have a tendency to be serious and to prefer being alone over entering the social scene. You can get the most out of others, get them to work under you. A wisdom that comes from simple needs. Conservative. Careful.

**Moon Square, Semi-square, or Sesqui-square Saturn:** Your sense of organization and self-discipline may exist at the expense of your feelings. Others could feel cut off by your no-nonsense approach and may not be as supportive as you might wish. This could result in your being somewhat of a loner.

**Moon Conjunct Uranus:** You may have an unconventional family life and tend to surround yourself with a group of independent and even eccentric friends. You tend to show emotions suddenly or in unusual ways. Your approach to psychology, history, and groups is novel, unusual.

**Moon Opposite Uranus:** Your independence and general unconventionality may sometimes be offensive to others. You like to go against the grain, break free, and relish the unusual and different. You may rebel against tradition, the past, history, and the like.

**Moon Trine, Sextile, or Semi-sextile Uranus:** The life of the party, able to loosen up even the most sober. Great at bringing out the best qualities of others, discovering hidden talents. New and innovative ideas regarding the social scene. Spontaneous, on the move. Independent.

**Moon Square, Semi-square, or Sesqui-square Uranus:** Your flair for the unusual and the unconventional may not receive as much support as you might wish from those around you. Independence at the expense of your feelings is a struggle you know well, and emotional tension a price you may have to pay.

**Moon Conjunct Neptune:** You are a dreamer, with real psychic abilities and prone to visions. You are like a fish in water when it comes to spellbinding a group with images and dreams—entrancing. The psychology of groups and cultures is transparent to you.

**Moon Opposite Neptune:** Your hopes and dreams may be maintained at the expense of your emotions and home life. Others may challenge or find themselves opposed to your ideals or the image you project. Your interest in the occult and spiritual may not always find group support.

**Moon Trine, Sextile, or Semi-sextile Neptune:** A born director and orchestrator of the moods and emotions of a group. A sharp sense of drama and a feeling for spiritual ideas and for art in general. Dreamy. Able to understand the public's mood and what is required to please. Could be deceptive.

**Moon Square, Semi-square, or Sesqui-square Neptune:** The pursuit of your ideals and self-image is often at the expense of your feelings and emotional life. Others may not go along with your sense of mystery and other-worldliness. You struggle to find a balance between dreams and reality as you know it.

**Moon Conjunct Pluto:** You can really psych out a group, always getting to the heart of what is really going on. You could have great political power when it comes to other people and finances. You tend to attract (and enjoy) gut-wrenching, intense, emotional dramas.

**Moon Opposite Pluto:** Your own insistence on analyzing and probing into personal issues may not endear you to the group. Others experience this kind of emotional intensity as unsettling. It goes against how they feel. Power struggles in relationships can be expected.

**Moon Trine, Sextile, or Semi-sextile Pluto:** A born psychologist. Able to understand and handle a crowd and the public in general. Devoted to children and the idea of future changes. Not much given to a misuse of personal power. Always this sense of vision and purpose. Intense. The long haul.

**Moon Square, Semi-square, or Sesqui-square Pluto:** Emotional stress stemming from your insistence on analysis and psychological probing at the expense of feelings—yours and other people's. No one will support it. Your sensitivity and vulnerability often find you at odds with the group or with others.

**Mercury Conjunct Venus:** You love words and ideas and sharing them through writing, speaking, and so on. You love to talk. You appreciate and value the intellect and all mental activities, have great taste and an eye for all that is fine. You are sharp when purchasing, a connoisseur.

**Mercury Opposite Venus:** It could be hard at times for you to put into words what you value and appreciate about someone or something. Sometimes you may not like what you find yourself thinking and saying. Some of your ideas challenge your own set of values.

**Mercury Trine, Sextile, or Semi-sextile Venus:** Lovely words and a flair for description—the artistic in all its many forms. An inner sense of warmth and goodness, and the ability to express this. Kind and easy to be with. Perfect taste in literary and artistic matters. Harmonious.

**Mercury Square, Semi-square, or Sesqui-square Venus:** You don't put much stock in mere words and ideas for their own sake. You have trouble appreciating what you cannot feel and measure. You tend to say and think things that you may not feel are right, that go against your expressed value system.

**Mercury Conjunct Mars:** You think and communicate with great force and in a very direct manner. You are quick with words, quick to anger, and often sorry later for the sharp things you say. You have great mental concentration and perseverance. You can articulate your emotions.

**Mercury Opposite Mars:** You are easily irritated, and conversations have a habit of turning into debates and arguments. You often say things you don't really mean at heart. With all this mental energy and a hair-trigger mind, you often have to exercise self-control.

**Mercury Trine, Sextile, or Semi-sextile Mars:** Language, sound, "the spoken word" are in focus. The ability to give words meaning or to put ideas into words and give others a feeling for what things mean. Communicating with words. Also a sharp and clear mind. Quick, even clever. Entertaining.

**Mercury Square, Semi-square, or Sesqui-square Mars:** You are sharp-tongued. Arguments and debates are probably lifelong companions. You communicate with your emotions and sheer drive as much as by words and thoughts. Your verbal and mental presence (by sheer insistence) is something to behold.

**Mercury Conjunct Jupiter:** You have an eye for legal matters, and are probably great at solving puzzles and finding solutions as well as communicating them to others. A good counselor. Your mind is expert at problems, finding a way through or beyond any roadblock or obstacle.

**Mercury Opposite Jupiter:** Your ideas, thoughts, and words are not always the most practical. You tend to go off in directions that are counterproductive and not in your best interest. Any career moves had best be considered well, until you can separate the wheat from the chaff.

**Mercury Trine, Sextile, or Semi-sextile Jupiter:** Good ability to "get the picture" (the gist of things) and to communicate this to others. In fact, helping others to find their way through life (for example, via vocational counseling) is indicated. Religious ideas and concepts are natural.

**Mercury Square, Semi-square, or Sesqui-square Jupiter:** Your ideas and plans are not always the most practical or expedient. Fond of grand schemes, verbalization, and the like, these ideas don't often boil down to real solutions. Your main path may involve taking many of your ideas with a grain of salt.

**Mercury Conjunct Saturn:** You are a serious thinker and don't often waste words. Concentration is easy for you, and detailed, technical, mental work would suit you just fine. Not free with your words, some may find you a tad on the sober side. A disciplined mind.

**Mercury Opposite Saturn:** You can at times be unorganized and lack discipline in the idea and mental department. You have difficulty limiting and defining what you say or think and may tend to impractical schemes. It could be hard for you to concentrate and to study.

**Mercury Trine, Sextile, or Semi-sextile Saturn:** A real problem-solver, the more tedious the better. Able to reduce any subject matter to the bare bones. Heavy-duty thinker. Could be very serious or philosophical. Enjoy study and thought. Very methodical and practical in approach.

**Mercury Square, Semi-square, or Sesqui-square Saturn:** Your ideas and thoughts often conflict with your sense of responsibility and discipline. You may have trouble concentrating, or may alternate between periods of mental discipline and chaos. Your words and thoughts are not always very practical.

**Mercury Conjunct Uranus:** A genius perhaps—at least others may think so. Your mind always manages to find a new and different way to think and to put your ideas into words. Brilliant, restless, and unusual. Computers, radical methods of thought, and communication are for you.

**Mercury Opposite Uranus:** You have trouble coming up with words and ideas that are truly original, but your mind and thoughts are not as conventional as they may appear. Things that are strange, eccentric, and novel seem to challenge you. Result: An overly conservative response.

**Mercury Trine, Sextile, or Semi-sextile Uranus:** Sharp, nimble mind with ready wit. Quick to get insights and to see new solutions. Approaching genius when it comes to communication skills. Natural physical dexterity. Good hands too. The life of the party when it comes to spontaneity.

**Mercury Square, Semi-square, or Sesqui-square Uranus:** You tend to carry a lot of mental energy and tension, and this can suddenly erupt when you're not kept busy. The way you speak, think, and use your mind can give way to sheer insight and brilliance. At other times you may have very conventional ideas.

**Mercury Conjunct Neptune:** You are a great storyteller, and your mind is at home when working with myths, dreams, and all that is mystical and philosophical. Probably not too technical, you can enchant others with your soaring imagination and words. You could exaggerate a bit.

**Mercury Opposite Neptune:** You can go out of your way to be clear-minded and practical, taking care to remove every vestige of imagination and dreaminess. This is an attempt to ignore your more spiritual and mystical side, which seems to spring up and challenge you at every turn.

**Mercury Trine, Sextile, or Semi-sextile Neptune:** Great psychological talent. Able to sense and feel in the more abstract mental areas and to bring far-out ideas down to earth. Always at the leading edge of social understanding. Great sense of compassion and a real understanding of others.

**Mercury Square, Semi-square, or Sesqui-square Neptune:** Your ideas, thoughts, and mentality may struggle to keep a damper on a tendency towards mysticism and the spirit. Your dreams and ideals may be difficult for you to express or talk about, but are a source of much energy and not a little tension.

**Mercury Conjunct Pluto:** Your intense and probing mind has no trouble getting at the heart of any question. Woe to anyone who tries to argue with you or hide things from you. A natural mind for research, detective work, and any undercover operations. Always curious.

**Mercury Opposite Pluto:** You try hard to be clear-headed and stay away from gossip and a tendency to probe and analyze. However, your inner psychology and that of others (everything secret) challenges and fascinates you. This could be a lifelong friendship/confrontation.

**Mercury Trine, Sextile, or Semi-sextile Pluto:** Penetrating, probing mind that is good for research. Can see far beyond normal concepts in areas of religion and psychology. Always want to get to the bottom of things, get under or beyond the superficial. A sense of the eternal.

**Mercury Square, Semi-square, or Sesqui-square Pluto:** Your personal life and secret thoughts may be something that you have difficulty speaking about or expressing to others. This can produce tension that gives way to bouts of deep searching and analysis, even gossip. The bigger the front, the more it is hiding.

**Venus Conjunct Mars:** You have a natural appreciation for drive and energy, and probably love sports and an active life. Sex is important. You are often moved to appreciate life, and you don't mind emotion and sentiment one bit. You have a strong appetite for almost anything.

**Venus Opposite Mars:** You may have difficulty appreciating force and raw feelings, or at least you may have an approach/avoidance response. Your feelings may run roughshod over your value system. You may not care for those who are ambitious or pushy. You don't love sports.

**Venus Trine, Sextile, or Semi-sextile Mars:** All heart! Feelings are always out front and entirely natural. Love of action, motion (sports, physical, sex, and the like). An expert at matters of the heart. Children, animals, and all creative work get top billing. Always act on instinct, feelings.

**Venus Square, Semi-square, or Sesqui-square Mars:** You may not like displays of emotion and pushy people, or at least find them challenging and thought-provoking. Your basic drive and ambitions may tend to ignore or brush off your more caring and loving qualities. Emotional tension.

**Venus Conjunct Jupiter:** You appreciate a winner and are drawn to the successful and powerful (politics, and such). You may make your living by virtue of your good taste, sense of quality, and discrimination. You love and value guiding others, counseling, and solving problems.

**Venus Opposite Jupiter:** You can't help but overindulge. Your appetites seem to ignore what may be the best choice for you and run to excesses. You have difficulty staying on the straight and narrow. You may have to exercise self-discipline to make career progress.

**Venus Trine, Sextile, or Semi-sextile Jupiter:** Born lucky. A natural when it comes to finding the pot of gold at the end of the rainbow. Very generous with others. Love to spread the good things around. A natural talent for finding your way past the pitfalls of life. A love of travel and puzzles.

**Venus Square, Semi-square, or Sesqui-square Jupiter:** You have a habit of ignoring what is best for you and taking roads that you know will lead nowhere, but might be fun to take. Career decisions may have to be made that don't cater to your particular likes, dislikes, and value system.

**Venus Conjunct Saturn:** You love discipline, organization, and all of your responsibilities. You are uninterested in the frills of life and value only what is essential, the bare bones. Your love of simplicity may appear as austerity and frugality to others.

**Venus Opposite Saturn:** Enjoying yourself at the expense of actual responsibilities may find you in a sorry way from time to time. It can be hard for you to enjoy yourself and appreciate life, so when you do, you tend to do it up right. This is an ongoing condition.

**Venus Trine, Sextile, or Semi-sextile Saturn:** An innate love of truth, essentialness, even adversity. A fierce sense of loyalty for loved ones. Protective and security-minded. You have a love affair with the practical and useful; you love to work and work with love. Form follows function.

**Venus Square, Semi-square, or Sesqui-square Saturn:** You may have trouble enjoying yourself, appreciating the finer things of life. Your no-nonsense, serious approach may tend to limit and cut off feelings of warmth and compassion. The result could be a struggle between binges and responsibility.

**Venus Conjunct Uranus:** You love the unconventional and are drawn to all things new and different. You avoid the mundane and treasure the unusual. You may have very eccentric tastes and ways of showing affection. You value a chance to break away from the pack and be different.

**Venus Opposite Uranus:** You tend not to like things (or people) who are unconventional or different. You appreciate conformity and traditional values, although you may have periods when you break through all this and do the unexpected and let it all hang out.

**Venus Trine, Sextile, or Semi-sextile Uranus:** A love of the new and unusual. Able to grasp and appreciate new trends and concepts at the very forefront of technology. A very free spirit when it comes to friends, lovers, and tastes. In love with what's original. Breaking through.

**Venus Square, Semi-square, or Sesqui-square Uranus:** You may not be able to let yourself appreciate much that is not conventional for fear of going on some kind of a binge. A strong sense of the novel and unusual rears its head every so often and upsets your whole value system.

**Venus Conjunct Neptune:** You love everything mystical and other-worldly. An idealist of the first order, you value dreams, visions, and anything that points beyond mundane reality. Art, poetry, and imagination you appreciate. Needless to say, you are not noted for practicality.

**Venus Opposite Neptune:** Your value system may be less than ideal, even according to your own standards. A tendency to compromise and accept things that don't do much for your self-image is present. There is a basic struggle between dreams or ideals and day-to-day reality.

**Venus Trine, Sextile, or Semi-sextile Neptune:** A mother to every animal, child, or needy person. Generous to the extreme with others. Always sensing the unity in life, as in the phrase "the dewdrop slips into the shining sea." You love movies, myths, and long thoughts. No doubt a dreamer … a lover.

**Venus Square, Semi-square, or Sesqui-square Neptune:** You won't let yourself care for or really go all out for your dreams and ideals. There is something in you that wants to ignore or cut short your mystic and dreamy side. Your dreams tend to intrude and haunt you. There is a real dichotomy.

**Venus Conjunct Pluto:** You love all that is personal, secret, and esoteric. Vulnerability is something you appreciate and value, and you love to sift and analyze what you find within the human psyche. You show affection with passion and intensity.

**Venus Opposite Pluto:** You may find yourself craving the superficial and common. You could have a lot of trouble getting past the surface and appreciating your deeply personal issues and sensitive areas. You may tend to ignore your more passionate desires.

**Venus Trine, Sextile, or Semi-sextile Pluto:** An almost reckless faith in the life process. A natural revolutionary and supporter of change. Fervent feelings for others and deep running emotions mark all relationships. Great personal intensity, even power. Love animals, children, and change.

**Venus Square, Semi-square, or Sesqui-square Pluto:** You may not appreciate displays of emotion or psychological analyzing and probing. This could become kind of a thing with you, trying to avoid sensitive issues that keep coming up all around you. You are fascinated by this stuff, not to mention gossip.

**Mars Conjunct Jupiter:** Your career is most important, and your drive and ambitions in that direction are almost unlimited. You have an uncanny intuitive sense of when and how to make the right moves. Success to you is a succession of successes. You move forward.

**Mars Opposite Jupiter:** Your emotions and drive tend to make things difficult for you, particularly in career decisions. Vocational moves may stifle you and be at the expense of your emotional wellbeing. There is a push/pull sort of thing.

**Mars Trine, Sextile, or Semi-sextile Jupiter:** Tremendous drive to succeed, plus some sheer good luck, brings real accomplishment. Lots of physical energy available too. Very ambitious and motivated. Could serve as group leader or manager. Family person. Career and marriage work well.

**Mars Square, Semi-square, or Sesqui-square Jupiter:** You tend to have trouble coordinating your drive with good career moves. You rush into things, often against your own best interests. You have to be careful selecting a life path, so you don't ignore feelings and emotions.

**Mars Conjunct Saturn:** It is easy for you to push too hard and maybe break something. You may have difficulty learning to use force wisely or efficiently. Learning to contain yourself, foot your energy, and build a good engine will be important to your well-being.

**Mars Opposite Saturn:** You have enthusiasm and drive, but tend to lack the discipline and methods to put your energy to work. Your emotions can cause you to neglect your responsibilities, and you may find yourself going up against authorities or the status quo.

**Mars Trine, Sextile, or Semi-sextile Saturn:** Applied force. Practical competence. Tremendous discipline and a love of routine work. Ability to simplify, code, and reduce a subject to its essential elements. Inner drive to be thorough and responsible in minute details. Self-disciplined.

**Mars Square, Semi-square, or Sesqui-square Saturn:** Your drive and efforts are not always well thought out. They can lack the method and discipline needed to build a firm foundation, a solid footing. You sometimes push against the way things are, the laws of nature ... which is fruitless.

**Mars Conjunct Uranus:** Your temper is a hot one and tends to come bursting forth. A drive for independence and nonconformity takes you beyond the ordinary into the unusual and eccentric. You could pursue electronics, computers, and the like.

**Mars Opposite Uranus:** Your emotional life may tend to get into a rut and lose all spontaneity. Your drive and ambition lead to some rebelliousness in others, especially partners. You may struggle to break through your conventional feelings and do something different.

**Mars Trine, Sextile, or Semi-sextile Uranus:** Powerful urge to be an innovator. Sudden breakthroughs, flashes, or insights. Avoid the common and seek out the unusual, exotic, and unique. Travel to far-off or out-of-the-way places. Energetic/athletic. Inventions with computers and electronics.

**Mars Square, Semi-square, or Sesqui-square Uranus:** Your drive and impetus are sometimes very conventional, and you tend to be very independent or innovative when it comes to feelings and emotions. You may find yourself breaking out of the ordinary with bursts of energy, fits of temper or new ideas.

**Mars Conjunct Neptune:** You are driven to make your dreams and ideals a reality. "What could be and should be, will be and must be" is your slogan. You are committed to ideas like world unity and community. You are living in your own dreams.

**Mars Opposite Neptune:** Your drive and ambitions tend to be unrealistic or go against your ideals and self-image. You are torn between what you have imagined or dreamed as ideal and your more immediate feelings and emotions. You swing back and forth like a pendulum.

**Mars Trine, Sextile, or Semi-sextile Neptune:** Driven towards the communal, to what unifies us all. Always seeing what we hold in common, rather than our differences. Idealism of a high order. Religious themes. Romantic. At home in psychic or psychological realms. The common denominator.

**Mars Square, Semi-square, or Sesqui-square Neptune:** You can be self-defeating, often pushing in directions that go against your own stated ideals and dreams. You have an aversion to foggy-mindedness and lack of clarity, a fear of being misled or duped. Your feelings tend to compromise your own self-image.

**Mars Conjunct Pluto:** Intense and passionate emotions are your trademark, and you have a sense of mission when it comes to pursuing psychological issues and anything that is esoteric, hidden, secret. You search things out and are at home with change and transformation.

**Mars Opposite Pluto:** You sometimes find your ambitions taking you in directions that have no future or limit you from change and growth. Emotionally, you tend to resist change and anything intensely personal and possibly transformative.

**Mars Trine, Sextile, or Semi-sextile Pluto:** Great intensity of emotions and purpose. Could be a spokesperson for a cause or a generation. Fearless in action and not afraid to use power. Will have your way. Know how to get what you want. A very magnetic and perhaps controversial personality.

**Mars Square, Semi-square, or Sesqui-square Pluto:** Your ambition and drive are often at the expense of your inner self and sensitivities. You may find yourself ignoring signals that indicate a need for change, transformation, and vulnerability in general. Bursts of intense anger are possible.

**Jupiter Conjunct Saturn:** Your career moves are always solid, responsible, and based on sound principles. When you make a decision, it is one you can build on and take to the bank. Not frivolous, you don't get involved with superficial projects. You like solid investments.

**Jupiter Opposite Saturn:** You tend to be unorganized and lack planning when it comes to career and life-path decisions. You like to throw caution to the wind, ignore whatever responsibilities you have, and pursue an objective. You fluctuate between conservation and liberality.

**Jupiter Trine, Sextile, or Semi-sextile Saturn:** You possess an architect's vision for what needs to be done and how to do it right to make it last—an expert or true builder. Knowing what tool to use and just how and when to use it. A sense of the right path or dharma. With you, the means and ends are identical.

**Jupiter Square, Semi-square, or Sesqui-square Saturn:** You tend to pursue options and go off in directions without adequate organization and planning. You need discipline but have trouble submitting to learn it, preferring instead to take what appears to be an easier path, ending up short of your goals.

**Jupiter Conjunct Uranus:** Yours is an unconventional path that may take you into unknown and uncharted waters. Inventive and original, you may come up with new and different solutions. Electronics, computers, and the like may be to the fore.

**Jupiter Opposite Uranus:** Any unconventional behavior on your part often ends up affecting your career. Your day-to-day path to success tends to be very staid and lacking in originality, which is what prompts you to leap outside convention and do something unusual.

**Jupiter Trine, Sextile, or Semi-sextile Uranus:** Unusual occupations. Hate the everyday and the rut. Instead, always finding ways to break through or away from what hems you in. Value independence, personal freedom; insist upon and exist on the wildfire at the fringe or very front edge of life.

**Jupiter Square, Semi-square, or Sesqui-square Uranus:** A rebellious streak could affect your career. Your sense of independence may tend to kick over the apple cart and upset everything. Your progress and success may be at the expense of your more unconventional tendencies—a source of struggle.

**Jupiter Conjunct Neptune:** Yours is a path that seeks to make your dreams and ideals a reality. An interest in unity, mysticism, philosophy, and all that is mythical and dreamlike. Your imagination is the key, and esoteric and artistic pursuits of all kinds are indicated.

**Jupiter Opposite Neptune:** You could often be tempted to make career moves that are unethical or at least conflict with your own close-held dreams and ideals. You may feel that your vocation lacks imagination and vision, and this could lead you to various forms of escape.

**Jupiter Trine, Sextile, or Semi-sextile Neptune:** Prefer the forest to the trees, the common to the uncommon or special. At home in ideas of man's essential unity. Religious and psychological ideas are natural. Will act as a minister to others, like it or not. You can sense and see the unity of life.

**Jupiter Square, Semi-square, or Sesqui-square Neptune:** Your goals and ideals are often in contrast to the actual decisions you make, in particular those regarding career. Your tendency to head in directions that are less than ideal, that don't fit your own dreams and self-image, causes tension.

**Jupiter Conjunct Pluto:** Your life-course takes you straight through depth psychology, transformation, regeneration, and all that is vulnerable within us. You may function as a guide or teacher in these realms. You work with areas of the human psyche that are too hot to handle.

**Jupiter Opposite Pluto:** You may make career moves that ignore or trample on your own finer feelings and sensitivities. You could find your vocation to be lacking in opportunities for inner growth and transformation. This conflict could result in tension and confrontation.

**Jupiter Trine, Sextile, or Semi-sextile Pluto:** Organizational genius, especially when it comes to managing other people. You understand what motivates others from the point of view of mass psychology and can get at the heart of things in an instant. You have a great talent for social leadership.

**Jupiter Square, Semi-square, or Sesqui-square Pluto:** You have a tendency to trample on some of your own more sensitive areas and feelings. Your particular path is often at the expense of your inner transformation and growth, a need that keeps building up (again and again) to a crisis and boiling over.

**Saturn Conjunct Uranus:** You are rebellious and innovative, but in a very determined and practical manner. You invent and change things, but always from the very center or heart, never from the periphery. You alter and invent at the deepest symbolical or programming level.

**Saturn Opposite Uranus:** Your natural sense of responsibility struggles against a rebellious streak, a wish to break away and dare to be different. You may find yourself opposing authority now and again or having unusual friends. You overturn the apple cart every once in a while.

**Saturn Trine, Sextile, or Semi-sextile Uranus:** Improvement of existing circumstances. Insights into the status quo, ways to make use of a situation to serve new needs. Making a "silk purse out of a sow's ear" sort of thing. Invention, electronics, computers.

**Saturn Square, Semi-square, or Sesqui-square Uranus:** You are torn between the radical, rebellious, and independent person you feel yourself to be, and a more conservative and traditional bent. Your organized moments may lack originality, and your crazier moments want caution. An ongoing battle.

**Saturn Conjunct Neptune:** You steadfastly go about making your dreams real, putting your ideals into practice. Your imagination excels when it comes to physical reality (physics) and working with time. Your flare for mysticism is never superficial or trivial.

**Saturn Opposite Neptune:** Your more conservative tendencies tend to put a damper on your dreams and deep-seated ideals. You may tend to escape your responsibilities via friends and excursions, mental or otherwise, into the realms of imagination, films, poetry, and the like.

**Saturn Trine, Sextile, or Semi-sextile Neptune:** Making "spirit" matter in day-to-day life, making the ideal real by bringing it down to earth. Incorporation. Perhaps a fear of losing oneself in the beginning, but in the long run, a love of the sea, space, and merging into one. At-one-ment.

**Saturn Square, Semi-square, or Sesqui-square Neptune:** Your sense of responsibility and discipline often are at odds with your dreams and visions, a possible source of depression. You may find yourself escaping routine in flights of fancy and imagination. You soon swing back and grind on.

**Saturn Conjunct Pluto:** You are most practical when it comes to psychology or vulnerable and sensitive issues. You relentlessly insist on stripping away nonessentials and getting at the core of things in an attempt to be secure. Deep inner changes.

**Saturn Opposite Pluto:** Your conservative tendencies may find you somewhat superficial. You avoid looking at or working with inner, emotional, and sensitive areas of your psyche unless forced. You fear and yet are attracted to intense, passionate issues and emotional displays.

**Saturn Trine, Sextile, or Semi-sextile Pluto:** Persistent, intense, and serious. Getting at the heart or root of a situation. Great psychological insight into life problems. Perhaps aiding or counseling, helping others understand difficulties. Fiercely tenacious.

**Saturn Square, Semi-square, or Sesqui-square Pluto:** Power struggles may occur, in particular between your sense of responsibility and an urge to transform yourself utterly. Your more orderly self tends to ignore signs of change until they erupt as major upheavals. An ongoing cycle.

**Uranus Conjunct Neptune:** You could be a visionary, with unusual and direct insight into everything mystical, the dreams and ideals we all have. You are at your most creative when you are using your imagination, pursuing your dreams, creating images.

**Uranus Opposite Neptune:** Your ideals and dreams may be quite conventional, and you tend to avoid that which is strange and unusual. One result of this would be an attraction/revulsion to psychic and mystical ideas.

**Uranus Trine, Sextile, or Semi-sextile Neptune:** A new and waking vision of unity. A powerful sense of music and a faith in making the ideal a reality—for reality to be as we dreamed it and our dreams to become as real. New concepts in group work. "The dewdrop slips into the shining sea."

**Uranus Square, Semi-square or Sesqui-square Neptune:** Your independence and unconventional manner may be at the expense of ideals and dreams. You may alternate between following your more traditional ideals and shattering your self-image via some very erratic and unusual behavior.

**Uranus Conjunct Pluto:** You are insightful, always darting straight to the heart of things and never shy about working with the most sensitive and vulnerable areas of the human psyche. You love new and different ways of self-discovery and transformation.

**Uranus Opposite Pluto:** You go out of your way to avoid intense and meaningful conversations, relationships, and such. You rebel against passionate displays of affection and deep personal probing.

**Uranus Trine, Sextile, or Semi-sextile Pluto:** Spiritual or psychological insight of the first order. Social and/or political revelation. Looking into the inner workings of the mind and psyche. New and fresh viewpoints into the social scene, mass psychology. Intense light.

**Uranus Square, Semi-square, or Sesqui-square Pluto:** Your sense of originality and insight does not go so far as to inquire into areas of psychological sensitivity and vulnerability, which you tend to leave alone. This can produce tension to the degree that you possess a need for inner growth and change.

**Neptune Conjunct Pluto:** Your interests are anything but superficial and always reach beyond the conventional into the realms of mysticism and depth psychology. Imagination and matters of deep personal change are of the greatest importance to you.

**Neptune Opposite Pluto:** Your dreams and ideals tend to be at odds with your instinctive sense of security and survival. You take care of business on the practical level, while imagining better things for yourself.

**Neptune Trine, Sextile, or Semi-sextile Pluto:** A searing vision that cuts through what passes for conventional religion. A vision of the endless process of life ever being born afresh. Great acceptance and faith in the natural process and next generation. Love of children and animals.

**Neptune Square, Semi-square, or Sesqui-square Pluto:** Your self-image and the ideals you strive for tend to ignore an equally important area of yourself, the hidden and vulnerable areas of human psychology. This urge to explore depth-psychology conflicts with a desire to escape and dream.

**Sun Conjunct Midheaven:** You naturally gravitate toward positions of power and authority. Others see in you great practical ability and accept you as a leader or authority figure very easily. Your career may be very important to you, even at the expense of home life.

**Sun Opposite Midheaven:** You tend to be a homebody, and family interests often outweigh career concerns. This could prove difficult if you neglect practical matters or go out of your way to challenge those in authority. Others may find you uninterested in fame and career.

**Sun Trine or Sextile Midheaven:** You seem to shine when it comes to practical matters or those involving work and career. You have an easy way with superiors or those in authority and can always manage to get the most out of any skill or ability you have. You like work and career.

**Sun Square Midheaven:** Your preoccupation with your appearance, how you come across to others, and a social life in general may cut into both your job and your family life. A tendency toward surface and social graces can cost you plenty in career and home goals.

**Moon Conjunct Midheaven:** You are expert at manipulating the public and its many moods. Your practical sense for group psychology may find you in real demand as an organizer and producer of public events. You have real insight into feelings, moods—what makes people work.

**Moon Opposite Midheaven:** You flee from crowds and are most happy when surrounded by home, family, and all that is private. Your home life is most important. It matters not to you that you are not a public person and not at your best when in a crowd.

**Moon Trine or Sextile Midheaven:** Your career always seems to get the support you need, and this is one area of life that runs smoothly. You seem to understand what the public wants, and mass marketing is a natural for you.

**Moon Square Midheaven:** You could find that you are neglecting either your home and family or your career (or both) due to your social and personal life. Relationships, working with other people, and making a good presentation. Home life is secondary.

**Mercury Conjunct Midheaven:** You have a mind for what is practical, organized, and logical. Your employer is probably happy to get you, for you are a natural for management positions. A tendency to be a bit manipulating now and then should be noted. Always planning and scheming.

**Mercury Opposite Midheaven:** Your mind runs to domestic issues; home and family are always on your mind. This trait could work against your career interests, especially if your job requires managerial and organizational skills. Perhaps a home business would be good.

**Mercury Trine or Sextile Midheaven:** Your mind is full of practical ideas, especially related to your job or skills. Always coming up with new ideas to manage things better, make things work—practical thoughts.

**Mercury Square Midheaven:** Your love of talk, ideas, and expressing yourself to others may mean that your family and even your job may suffer. Your mind is often on your appearance, how you come across and relate to the crowd, to those around you.

**Venus Conjunct Midheaven:** You love to take charge, organize, and manage, whether this be in big business or small. You value practical vision and are not above manipulating a situation to the advantage of everyone involved. You love being the boss.

**Venus Opposite Midheaven:** Your love of family and home and lack of interest in external affairs (be they friends or work-related) need to be noted and kept in balance.

**Venus Trine or Sextile Midheaven:** Your love of job and practical skills makes you a fine manager and business person. You bring a great deal of love to your work.

**Venus Square Midheaven:** You love other people, large and small groups, and relationships in general. Your social life could be at the expense of your personal interests and even of your family or job.

**Mars Conjunct Midheaven:** You are very objective and practical when it comes to your feelings and emotions. You seem always to know what things mean and that they are pointing to. You can read feelings the way others read books.

**Mars Opposite Midheaven:** You are moved to secure yourself, always digging in. Home and family are your main focus, even at the expense of career. It would be good if you could work out of your home. Your emotions conflict with the public. You prefer one-on-one.

**Mars Trine or Sextile Midheaven:** You put forth a lot of effort, in particular regarding your career. Your drive and ambitions work well with whatever management skills and practical ability you have, producing a harmonious work environment.

**Mars Square Midheaven:** You are very competitive—even pushy—when it comes to partners and other people. You have a great social drive and love to work in a group or with close friends.

**Jupiter Conjunct Midheaven:** Career is very important, and you have superb management abilities. You are expert at manipulating a situation to the benefit of all concerned.

**Jupiter Opposite Midheaven:** You do best sticking close to home and family, and you enjoy all things domestic and security-based. You would do well working out of you own home, having a home business.

**Jupiter Trine or Sextile Midheaven:** You are gifted and even "lucky" when it comes to career decisions. Things almost always manage to work out for you.

**Jupiter Square Midheaven:** You excel as a social being, and should make a career out of your deep-seated interest in other people, partnerships, relationships, and so on. You find yourself through other people.

**Saturn Conjunct Midheaven:** With a great interest in the business and practical world, your mind works like a steel trap when it comes to making career and management decisions.

**Saturn Opposite Midheaven:** You are very methodical and practical when it comes to matters of home and family, even at the expense of your career.

**Saturn Trine or Sextile Midheaven:** You enjoy working hard and being organized, and you exercise skill and discipline in anything that affects your career and reputation. A perfect combination for an excellent manager.

**Saturn Square Midheaven:** You are very painstaking and deliberate when it comes to partnerships, lovers—relationships of all kinds. You tend toward long-lasting friendships and are very loyal. sometimes too staid.

**Uranus Conjunct Midheaven:** You are most insightful and innovative when it comes to matters of your career and practical matters. You can see how to put ideas (and people) to a better use.

**Uranus Opposite Midheaven:** You are most original when concentrating on areas of home and family where you feel secure. You are a private person and find all the pomp and circumstance of public life repressive and boring.

**Uranus Trine or Sextile Midheaven:** You tend to be creative and original in your work and career, managing to bring new ideas and spontaneity to bear.

**Uranus Square Midheaven:** You have unusual relationships, perhaps a number of them, and not always of long duration. You are creative when it comes to partnerships or lovers; you seem to establish unusual and different relationships.

**Neptune Conjunct Midheaven:** You have an inborn sense of mass psychology, what the public wants and dreams of. You can project images of what is desirable or ideal, using words and ideas that are enchanting and spell-binding. You would make a great film director.

**Neptune Opposite Midheaven:** Your ideal dream is a private one, and heaven is as close as home and family. You find public life and the outer world harsh and unimaginative.

**Neptune Trine or Sextile Midheaven:** You prefer a career that accents your own devotion to the dreams and ideals you stand for. Working with groups in a spirit of cooperation and communion is a natural.

**Neptune Square Midheaven:** You are an idealist when it comes to partners and relationships, always holding out for what your imagination tells you could be. This could result in disappointment when others fail to measure up to your expectations.

**Pluto Conjunct Midheaven:** You have a natural aptitude for describing the most sensitive areas of the human psyche, a practical psychologist of the first order. You can manage and work with touchy issues that others wouldn't touch with a ten-foot pole.

**Pluto Opposite Midheaven:** You have strong family, business, or property ties that affect your public image and goals. There may be tricky finances connected with your business or profession. Obligations involving women, research, or detecting are important in your career.

**Pluto Trine or Sextile Midheaven:** The supportive help of women or a girl can be an important factor that will affect business or reputation and increase your sense of security. You are a fine psychologist, researcher, or detective and are good at dealing with joint or others' finances.

**Pluto Square Midheaven:** Intense and probing partnerships and relationships always find you getting to the heart of things, getting down to the nitty-gritty with others. Some may feel you get too personal.

**Sun Conjunct Ascendant:** You are always out front and manage to spend a lot of time in the spotlight in social situations. A born teacher, others find you easy to watch and learn from. You are very animated, and it is easy for you to convey your ideas or get them across.

**Sun Opposite Ascendant:** Your interest in relationships, romantic and otherwise, is strong and may sometimes work against your personal needs. You could lose yourself in the social world and neglect your ability to present yourself as a separate, unique individual.

**Sun Trine or Sextile Ascendant:** You get along well with older people, especially those in authority. It is easy for you to convey yourself to others, and you always manage to make a good appearance. You have an easy manner and find it easy to communicate with just about anyone.

**Sun Square Ascendant:** Expressing yourself and your relations with others are not always smooth and may tend to get explosive. You could be preoccupied with job and family to the exclusion of a social life. You may have trouble getting your ideas and thoughts across to others.

**Moon Conjunct Ascendant:** You are never more at home than when entertaining and carrying on in front of a group. You wear your heart on your sleeve, and your emotional life is an open book for all to read. Others sense an interest in their welfare when they meet you.

**Moon Opposite Ascendant:** Your love of groups and the social scene may find you less concerned about you as a person and more interested in relationships of all kinds. Others find you very unselfish and open to sharing and cooperation.

**Moon Trine or Sextile Ascendant:** Everything seems to conspire to put you in the limelight. You always come off well in a group and manage to get your ideas across.

**Moon Square Ascendant:** Your close ties with home and family, plus your career interest, may cut into your social life and personal charm. Others may find you somewhat preoccupied and lacking in the social graces. You may feel some regret or tension from this situation.

**Mercury Conjunct Ascendant:** Your bright wit and talkative streak make you always ready for a conversation. You love to get your ideas across to others, and communication in any form is where you are happiest. You always jump right in with your mind, expressing ideas, thoughts, and such.

**Mercury Opposite Ascendant:** You are never funnier, wittier, or more at your mental best than when in a group or lost in a deep conversation with a partner. You may even neglect your personal interests by devoting so much of your time and energy to thinking about other people.

**Mercury Trine or Sextile Ascendant:** Your mind is ever on communication, how you present yourself and come across with others. It is easy for you to express yourself in a crowd, and you are a real smoothie. Everything seems to work out for you when you are talking with others.

**Mercury Square Ascendant:** Your mind is ever on career and family, and this may not make you the most communicative and social animal. You may prefer to avoid crowds and all large gatherings. You may not need relationships other than at home and at work.

**Venus Conjunct Ascendant:** You are a personal charmer, as anyone who ever gets into a one-on-one with you can testify. You seem to appreciate everything and everybody, and this shows. Your sense of love and compassion is an open book for all to read.

**Venus Opposite Ascendant:** You love other people, large and small groups, and relationships in general. Your social life could be at the expense of your personal interests and even of your family or job.

**Venus Trine or Sextile Ascendant:** You love appearances and have a way of pleasing others and coming across as loving and kind.

**Venus Square Ascendant:** Your love of family and home and lack of interest in external affairs (be they friends or work-related) need to be noted and kept in balance.

**Mars Conjunct Ascendant:** Feelings and emotions are an open book with you, and you wear your heart on your sleeve. Others may find your drive and openness threatening and aggressive.

**Mars Opposite Ascendant:** You are very competitive—even pushy—when it comes to partners and other people. You have a great social drive and love to work in a group or with close friends.

**Mars Trine or Sextile Ascendant:** You come on very strong. You have great confidence and a "take charge" sort of manner. You are a great doer, and others accept your commanding nature. You are a good team player.

**Mars Square Ascendant:** You are moved to secure yourself, always digging in. Family and job are your main focus, even at the expense of others. Your emotions tend to conflict with the social and public scene.

**Jupiter Conjunct Ascendant:** You can seem like all things to all people, so able are you to facilitate others. People trust you instantly. You would make a great teacher and counselor.

**Jupiter Opposite Ascendant:** You excel as a social being and should make a career out of your deep-seated interest in other people, partnerships, relationships, and so on. You find yourself through other people.

**Jupiter Trine or Sextile Ascendant:** Your manner is so facilitating and attractive to others that you would make an excellent counselor or teacher. You find it easy to solve the problems that present themselves, and others benefit from this ability of yours.

**Jupiter Square Ascendant:** Your career may well be at the expense of relationships and a social life. Work, home, and family are important to you. Others and the social scene don't concern you.

**Saturn Conjunct Ascendant:** You may have difficulty expressing yourself and getting your ideas across to others, but what you do communicate is very clear and practical. You may use very few words.

**Saturn Opposite Ascendant:** You are very painstaking and deliberate when it comes to partnerships, lovers—relationships of all kinds. You tend toward long-lasting friendships and are very loyal, sometimes too staid.

**Saturn Trine or Sextile Ascendant:** You express yourself deliberately and don't waste your words. You have a natural sense of organization and come across as disciplined and careful, perhaps a little too sober.

**Saturn Square Ascendant:** You are very methodical and practical when it comes to matters of home, family, and career, often at the expense of your social life.

**Uranus Conjunct Ascendant:** Very independent in appearance and communication—the way you come across to others. Your spontaneity and unpredictability make you interesting to any group.

**Uranus Opposite Ascendant:** You have unusual relationships, perhaps a number of them, and not always of long duration. You are creative when it comes to partnerships or lovers and seem to establish unusual and different relationships.

**Uranus Trine or Sextile Ascendant:** You are probably very witty and prefer an unusual method of presenting yourself or communicating to others. Original and quick with words and ideas. Unconventional.

**Uranus Square Ascendant:** You are most original when concentrating on areas of work and family where you feel secure. You are a private person and find all the pomp and circumstance of social life repressive and boring.

**Neptune Conjunct Ascendant:** You have a way of entrancing others and bringing them under the spell that you weave so well with your imagination and sense of communion.

**Neptune Opposite Ascendant:** You are an idealist when it comes to partners and relationships, always holding out for what your imagination tells you what you could be. This may result in disappointment when others fail to measure up to your expectations.

**Neptune Trine or Sextile Ascendant:** You are charming and always manage to enchant others with your words and manner. You bring a sense of the beyond and mystical to any conversation.

**Neptune Square Ascendant:** Your ideal dream is a private one, and heaven is as close as work and family. You find social life and the outer world harsh and unimaginative.

**Pluto Conjunct Ascendant:** You are intense in the way you communicate, to the point of sometimes almost scaring people. Your sense of vulnerability is out there for everyone to see, and you are always passionate, insistent, and direct.

**Pluto Opposite Ascendant:** Intense, probing partnerships and relationships always find you getting to the heart of things, getting down to the nitty-gritty with others. Some may feel you get too personal.

**Pluto Trine or Sextile Ascendant:** You always manage to come across as intense and personal when communicating and presenting yourself to others. Others can be fascinated by the way you come on.

**Pluto Square Ascendant:** You have strong family, business, or property ties that affect your public image and goals. There may be tricky finances connected with your business or profession. Obligations involving women, research, or detecting are important in career.

**North Node in Aspect with the Sun:** Contact with teachers and important authority figures is indicated. Having the extreme good fortune to find a teacher in your life and to learn from them. Love of the Sun.

**North Node in Aspect with the Moon:** A natural affinity with all that is feminine, mysterious, and mystic. The power of the sea. An interest in creating environments (support systems) of all kind. Sustenance always at hand.

**North Node in Aspect with Mercury:** A strong link to the mind and all that is mental—thinking, writing, and communicating.

**North Node in Aspect with Venus:** A natural power of appreciation, and the valuing of objects and things. Fine arts. Criticism. Appraisal.

**North Node in Aspect with Mars:** A link to the emotions and all that drives and pushes the human psyche. Meaning and directionality (of all kinds) is a major focus.

**North Node in Aspect with Jupiter:** A strong link to the ideas of guides, gurus, and all that directs and points the way through life to us. This could take the form of teachers/students. Lawyers, legal.

**North Node in Aspect with Saturn:** A profound interest in and sense of organization and responsibility. Physics. Physical laws. Limitations.

**North Node in Aspect with Uranus:** A very powerful sense of independence, ingenuity, and freedom. The creation of something new from the status quo. The next step. Inventions.

**North Node in Aspect with Neptune:** A natural gift for music, the occult, initiation—whatever serves to unify and dissolve differences into one entity. Mysticism. "The dewdrop slips into the shining sea."

**North Node in Aspect with Pluto:** A gift for all that is not superficial, for all that penetrates the outer and reveals the inner, and vulnerable. The eternal child—to see yourself in the eyes of a child, the same one.

**North Node in Aspect with the Midheaven:** A flare for "big picture" thinking, seeing the forest, not just the trees. A natural affinity for business organization, management in general, and strategic thinking, in particular. Big business.

**North Node in Aspect with the Ascendant:** A lifelong concern with getting across to others, whether it be of ideas or acts. Communication. Would make an excellent teacher, group leader. A communicator.

# APPENDIX B

# ASTROLOGICAL PERIODICALS

This appendix is adapted from the Urania Trust directory of magazines, periodicals, and journals, courtesy of the Urania Trust (http://www.uraniatrust.org/mags.htm).

## ARGENTINA

***Medium Coeli:*** 64-page quarterly written in Spanish with articles on predictive, psychological, mundane, and medical astrology. It includes personal experiences, news, research, data, and reviews. Research astrologers and distributors are welcome. Available by subscription and bookstores. Editor: Jorge Mele, C. C. 3983, 1000 Buenos Aires, Argentina. Tel.: +5411 4641 5724. Email: jmele@formared.com.ar or medium-coeli@excite.com.

## AUSTRALIA

***Australian Astrologer:*** Bimonthly newsletter produced by the Australian Society of Astrologers Inc. President: Renee Badger. Australian Society of Astrologers, P.O. Box 7120, Bass Hill, New South Wales, 2197 Australia. Tel.: +61 7 5445 8017. Fax: +61 2 9754 2999. Email: GJdeMAS@bigpond.com.au. Website: www.angelfire.com/journal/asainc/index.html.

***Federation of Australian Astrologers Journal:*** Journal Editor: Peter Burns. P.O. Box 486, Carnegie, Victoria, 3163 Australia. Email: ambrosia@tpg.com.au.

***Wholistic Astrologer:*** Quarterly journal specializing in quality articles on humanistic and transpersonal astrology, therapeutic approaches, Chiron, healing ethics, philosophy, etc. Editor/Publisher: Candy Hillenbrand. P.O. Box 1796, Macclesfield, SA 5153, Australia. Tel.: 011 61 8 8388 9430. Email: hillen@olis.net.au. Website: www.olis.net.au/~hillen/aplace/ wholisticastrologer.

## BELGIUM

***INFOsophia:*** 25-page newsletter of articles, astrological activities, and data. Editors: Jany Bessier and Michel Mandl. Asbl Star *L, 19, Avenue P.-H, Spaak, B. 1070 Brussels, Belgium.

***Quintile:*** Newsletter. Editor: Astrid Fallon. Federation Astrologique Belge, 300 Chauss, e de La Hulpe, B1170 Bruxelles, Belgium. Tel.: +32 (0) 2 660 7981. Fax: +32 (0) 2 673 7393.

***Vlaams Astrologisch Tijdschrift (VAT):*** Founded in 1973, it provides information about astrology and organizes yearly astrological congress. Editor: Nandy Vermeulen-Geeraert, president of Vlaams Astrologisch Genootschap (VAG). Secretary: Mariette de Marré-Cools. Belgiëlei 149 bus 7, 2018 B-Anwerpen, Belgium. Tel.: + 32 (0) 3 230 75 11. Email: VAG@Pandora.Be. Website: www.geocities.com/VAG_BE/.

## CANADA

***Astrospirale:*** French-Canadian quarterly. Director: Denise Chrzanowska. C. P. 56028/2300, Street Father-Lelievre, Quebec City, Quebec G1P 4P7 Canada. Email: meyer.carl@uqam.ca.

***Shape:*** The astrological journal of the Ottawa Region. P.O. Box 47039, Gloucester, Ontario, Canada, K1B 5P9. Tel.: +1 613 834 9647. Email: sj.rasmith@sympatico.ca.

## CROATIA

***Aster Network:*** This periodical, originally named *Aster E-Zine*, debuted on November 19, 1998, at noon (CET). The idea was to found a Croatian Internet magazine covering astrology, esoterics, alternative medicine, yoga, philosophy, history, nutrition, culture, and other themes related to spirituality. The contents of *Aster Network* can change weekly, even daily if necessary. Subscribers can receive the electronic weekly Aster@News by e-mail. It provides information about the contents of *Aster Network* as well as links to interesting web pages, guides, the latest information and other trends in the world, and free use of a search engine for themes of interest to the magazine's subscribers. Website: www.aster.avalon.hr/aboutus/index.htm.

## CZECH REPUBLIC

***Konstelace:*** A review of the Czech Astrological Society, published four times a year. First published in 1991. Free to members. Editor: Zdenek Bohuslav. Tolsteho 20, CZ-101 00 Praha 10, Czech Republic. Email: bohuslav@comp.cz.

***Rezonance:*** Bulletin of Turnovsky—ISTA (Information Service of Astrology of/in Transformation). First issue November 1996. Contact: Pavel Turnovsky. Svobody 1, CZ-160 00 Praha 6, Czech Republic. Tel.: +420 2 2432 3371. Email: turnov@login.cz and turnovsky@mbox.dkm.cz. Website: www.rezonance.info.

## DENMARK

***Astrologen:*** Bimonthly magazine published by Dansk Astrologforening, the professional organization of astrological practitioners. Chairman: Jesper Bernth. Sdr. Ringgade 24, DK 8000 Aarhus C, Denmark. Tel.: +45 8676 1278. Email: 9heaven@get2net.dk. Website: www.astrologforeningen.dk.

***Horoskopet:*** Published quarterly by Astrologihuset. This huge astrology center has emerged following the highly successful October 1991 Copenhagen Conference and is now the largest center of its kind in the world and includes the world's first astrological museum. Skolegade 12A, Postboks 319, 2500 Valby, Copenhagen, Denmark. Tel.: +45 3645 0545. Fax: +45 3645 0552. Email: horoskop@astrologihuset.dk. Website: www.astrologihuset.dk.

***Stjernerne:*** Monthly magazine published by IC Astrology Institute. Founded in 1956 by Irene Christensen. Director: Christian Borup, Nr Farimagsgade 63, DK-1364 Copenhagen K, Denmark. Tel.: +45 33 123627. Fax: +45 33 141303.

## FINLAND

***Astro Logos:*** Published quarterly by the Astrological Association of Finland. Founded in 1964. Secretary: Pirjo Ahtiainen. P.O. Box 90, FIN-00131 Helsinki, Finland. Tel.: +358 9 495 513. Email: suomi.astro@sunpoint.net or pirah@luukku.com. Website (in English): www.gamma.nic.fi/~astrolog/english/eindex.htm. Website (in Finnish): www.gamma.nic.fi/~astrolog/.

## FRANCE

***Astralis:*** Published by Centre d'Etudes, de Documentation et de Recherche sur l'Astrologie (CEDRA). Runs a very active mailing list. Director: Maurice Charvet. 7 Place des Terreaux, 69001 Lyon, France. Tel.: +33 47823 7276. Fax: +33 42665 6207. Email: mailto:cedra@cedra.net. Website: www.cedra.net.

***Astrologos:*** 64 rue Jean-Jacques Rousseau, 21000 Dijon, France. Website: www.astroariana.free.fr/Web_New/Astrologos/Menu.htm.

***Cahiers Conditionalistes:*** Periodical published by COMAC since 1980. Contact: J. P. Nicola. Sperel, 83170 Tourves, France. Tel/Fax: +33 94 78 88 25. Email: jpnicola@ club-internet.fr. Websites: www.multimania.com/comac, www.conditionalisme.com, and www.comac.free.fr.

***Les Cahiers du Rams:*** Aureas, 15 rue du Cardinal Lemoine, 75005 Paris, France. The journal of the Association de Recherches en Astrologie par des Methodes Scientifiques. Appearing not more than six months apart. First issue published April 1993. Email: rams.rams@online.fr or santoni@aureas.com. Website: ramsfr.org.

***La Lettre du Cadran:*** Monthly reference publication of birth data. Editor: Patrice Petitallot. 10 Lann Fouesnel, 56350 Allaire, France. Tel.: +33 9972 2152. Fax: +33 9972-3703.

## GERMANY

***Astro Woche:*** Published weekly by GmbH ASTROCWeek. Medienstr 5, 94036 Passau, Germany. Tel.: 0851 802 348. Fax: 0851 802 837. Email: service@astrowoche.de. Website: www.astrowoche.de.

***Astrolog:*** Bimonthly magazine focusing on the API/Huber School approach to astrology. Editor: Louise Huber. Obertilistrasse 4, CH-8134 Adliswil., Germany. Tel.: +41 (0) 1 710 3776. Fax: +41 (0) 1 710 3786. Email: huber_api@compuserve.com.

***Astrologie Heute:*** Bimonthly magazine published by Astrodata AG, which offers correspondence, evening, and weekend courses and summer schools both in Switzerland and Germany (in Berlin and

Munich). Runs the biggest astrological calculation service in Europe with a wide range of chart services and computer prepared reports. Albisriederstrasse 232, CH-8047 Zurich, Switzerland. Tel.: +41 01 492 1515. Fax: +41 01 492 1516. Email: info@astrodata.ch. Website: www.astrodata.ch/.

***Cosmo-Trend:*** Covers financial market trends. Contact: Henning P. Schäfer. Kaiserstr 38, 69115 Heidelberg, Germany. Fax: +49 (0) 6221 619 547. Email: cosmo-trend@online.de. Website: www.cosmo-trend.de/.

***FMV:*** Publishing house. Gruenwalder STR 145, D-81547 Munich, Germany. Tel.: +49 (0) 89 648011. Fax: +49 (0) 89 6253069.

***Hamburger Hefte:*** Quarterly dedicated to Hamburg School methods. Founded August 17, 1948. Editor: Michael Feist. Eppendorfer Lds., 158 20251 Hamburg, Germany. Tel.: +49 (0) 40 300 317 68. Fax: +49 (0) 40 300 317 69. Email: Email: mf@Hamburger Hefte.de. Website: www.hamburgerhefte.de.

***Mercury—Trends aus Astrologie und Psychologie:*** Bimonthly publication. Publisher and editor-in-chief: Friedrich Maier. Ferdinand-Miller-Platz 12, D-80335, Munchen, Germany. Tel/Fax: +49 (0) 89 18 54 72. Email: FM.merCur@t-online.de. Website: www. mercur-astrologie.de/.

***Meridian:*** Bimonthly. Editor: Markus Jehle. Moeckernstr. 68, Stairway A, 10965 Berlin, Germany. Tel.: 030 789 90 123. Fax: 030 785 84 59. Email: Markus.Jehle@ online.de. Website: www.meridian-magzin.de/.

***Sternzeit:*** Editor: Beatrix Braukmueller. Astrolog IE Center, Bremen Uhlandstr 2, 28211 Bremen, Germany. Tel.: 0421 700870. Fax: 0421 700888. Email: astrologie-zentrum-hb@freenet.de. Website: www. dav-astrologie.de/sternzeit.htm.

***Uranian Institute Newsletter:*** Published by the Uranian Institute. Intelligent, state-of-the-art astrology for the 21st century, integrating humanistic, transpersonal, geodetic, midpoint, and Uranian techniques. Regular updates on the latest developments in quality Uranian astrology are available via e-mail; contact finblake@mindspring.com. Website: www.finblake.home.mindspring.com/uranbeacon.htm. It is a website for practicing astrologers and serious students of the astrology of the future, unbiased by traditional methods. It includes the material of the Uranian Beacon, a website designed to integrate developments in current astrological techniques and frontier physics with the humanistic developments in Uranian astrology.

## GREECE

***Astrologos:*** Email: astrologos@daphne.gr. Website: www.astrologos.gr/.

## INDIA

***Astrology Magazine:*** The world's foremost and most authentic journal on Jyotisha or Hindu astrology with an international readership. Founded in 1895, it was restarted by Dr. B. V. Raman in 1936. Editor: Mrs. Gayatri Devi Vasudev, "Sri Rajeswari." 28, Nehru Circle, Seshadripuram, Bangalore 560020, India. Tel.: +91 80 3348646 (O), +91 80 3366864 (R). Fax: +91 80 3313260, +91 80 3366864. Email: gdvast@eth.net.

***Express Starteller Magazine:*** India's largest Vedic astrology monthly. 379 George Rd., Point Roberts, WA 98281. Tel.: (206) 295-4791. Website: www.starteller.com.

***Jyotish Darshan:*** First Gujarati Hindu Vedic astrological magazine published outside India (distributed free with advance paid postage). Editor: P. A. Patel (Jyotishi Anand). 8 Cecil Avenue, Wembley, Middx, HA9 7ED, UK. Tel./Fax: 020 8903 6784.

***Vedic Astrology:*** Editor: Dr. K. S. Charak. Systems Vision, A-199 Okhla Ind Area-1, New Delhi 110.020, India. Tel.: +9111 681 1195 or +9111 681 1841. Fax: +911 681 7017. Email: vedicastrology@ poboxes. com. Website: www.parashara.com/news.html.

## IRELAND

***The Dublin Astrologer:*** Quarterly publication of the Dublin Astrological Centre. Articles by Irish and international astrologers on a variety of topics varying from student level to an exploration of the philosophy and theory of astrology. Editor: Andrew Smith. 56 Johnstown Park, Dun Laoghaire, Co Dublin, Ireland. Tel.: +353 1 285 3054. Email: dastroc@iol.ie.

***Réalta:*** Editor: Maurice McCann. Tel.: +44 (0) 20 7272 4208. Email: mcmcann@compuserve.com.

## ITALY

***Datanotizie:*** Italian newsletter published in both Italian and English. Editor: Grazie Bordoni. Centro Raccolta Data Astrologici, Via B Verro 42, 20141 Milano, Italy. Tel.: (00 39 2) 89500925. Fax: (00 39 2) 89501860. Email grabor@tin.it.

***Ricerca '90:*** Quarterly journal; also produces and supplies Astral Software. Director: Ciro Discepolo. Viale Gramsci 16, 80122 Napoli, Italy. Tel.: +39 (0) 81 660420. Fax: +39 (0) 81 680709. Website: www.cirodiscepolo.it. Email: discepol@tin.it.

***Linguaggio Astrale:*** Quarterly 200-page journal published by Centro Italiano di Astrologia (CIDA), the main coordinating body for Italian astrology. First published in 1970. Secretary: Claudio Cannistrà. Via Vizzani 74, 40138 Bologna, Italy. Tel.: +39 (0) 51 342 445. Email: canniclau@libero.it. President: Dr. Dante Valente. Via Monzambano 13, 20159 Milano. Tel.: +39 (0) 269 005 576. Email: linguaggioastrale@libero.it.

***Sestile:*** Monthly journal published since 1992 for the Professional Astrologers Association Board by Centro Italiano di Astrologia (CIDA). Secretary: Claudio Cannistrà. Via Vizzani 74, 40138 Bologna, Italy. Tel.: +39 (0) 51 342 445. Email: canniclau@libero.it. President: Dr. Dante Valente, Via Monzambano 13, 20159 Milano. Tel.: +39 (0) 269 005 576. Email: linguaggioastrale@libero.it.

## NETHERLANDS

***Anima Astrologiae:*** Periodical of traditional classic astrology since 1998. Editor: Oude Arnhemseweg. 29, 3702 BA Zeist, Netherlands. Tel/Fax: +31 30 6911642. Email: mahermes@worldonline.nl.

***ASAScoop:*** Published twice yearly by ASAS since 1997. Editor: Marianne Willems. Jonagold 25, 6662 HV Elst, Netherlands. Tel.: +31 481 376781.

***Astrofocus:*** Published quarterly since 1999 by AVN. Ganzevoortsingel 26, 9711 AM Groningen, Netherlands. Email: redactie@avn-astrologie.nl Website: www.avn-astro logie.nl/.

***Astrologie in Onderzoek:*** Research journal published twice yearly since 1986. Editor: Wout Heukelom. Lederambachtstraat 119, 1069 HM Amsterdam, Netherlands. Tel/Fax: +31 20 6194457.

***AVE-Kroniek:*** Editor: Waling Hieminga. Jongemastate 45, 5655 HN Eindhoven, Netherlands. Tel.: +31 40 2551833. Published monthly since 1981 by AVE.

***BAG-Tijdschrift:*** Published monthly since 1990 by BAG. Clarastraat 120, 5211 LB Den Bosch, Netherlands. Tel.: +31 73 6136938. Email: a.cox@wxs.nl.

**CHTA *Astrokrant:*** Published quarterly by CHTA since 1997. Editor: Joyce Hoen. DFAstrolS, Oudewand 19, 7201 LJ Zutphen, Netherlands. Tel.: 31 575 516479. Email: chta@astrologie.ws. Website: www.astrologie.ws/.

***De Kaarsvlam:*** Published bimonthly since 1946. Editor: Mellie Uyldert. P. J. Lomanlaan 7, 1405 BK Bussum, Netherlands. Tel.: +31 35 6940423.

***Sagittarius:*** Published bimonthly since 1973. Editor: Jan B. Gieles. Karperdaal 147, 2553 PD The Hague, Netherlands. Tel.: +31 70 3912593. Fax: 31 70 3970431. Email: gieles@wanadoo.nl. Website: www.gieles.com/.

***Symbolon:*** Published quarterly since 1990. Editors: Drs. A .J. (Hans) and Dra Karen M. Hamaker-Zondag. Amsterdamseweg 479, 1181 BR Amstelveen, Netherlands. Tel.: +31 20 6436979. Fax: +31 20 6417310. Email: symbolon@wxs.nl. Website: www.symbolon.nl/.

***Urania:*** Published quarterly since 1906 by WVA. Editor: Ingmar de Boer. Oostzeedijk 4b, 3063 BB Rotterdam, Netherlands. Tel.: +31 10 4532708. Fax: +31 10 4531876. Email: ingmardb@zonnet.nl. Website: www.geocities.com/stichtingwva/.

## NEW ZEALAND

***Journal of the Seasons:*** Quarterly journal of the New Zealand Astrological Society. High quality articles across the spectrum of astrology. Contact: Bernard Honey. P.O. Box 5266, Wellesley Street, Auckland C1, New Zealand. Tel./Fax: +64 (0) 9 410 8416. Email: clearavu@ihug.co.nz.

## NORWAY

***Astrologisk Forum:*** Published quarterly since 1983 by the Norwegian Astrological Association. Chairman: Knut A Johnsen. P.O. Box 1432 Vika, 0115 Oslo, Norway. Tel./Fax: +47 23 38 99 86. Email: astrofor@email.com. Website: www.astrofor.freehomepages.com.

## RUSSIA

***Astrologia*** (magazine) and ***Astrolog*** (newspaper): Director: Vladimir Kopylov. Leningradcky prospect 62. Tel.: +7 095 151 8510. Email: astrolog@deol.ru.

***Esotherical Herald:*** Electronic version of the *Herald* published bimonthly by the Moscow Astrology Research Centre (MARC), founded in 1991, and the School of Classical Astrology (SCA), founded in 1994. MARC/SCA is the largest astrological organization of the former Soviet Union. Director: Nikolay

Strachuk. P/Box 373, 103064, Moscow, Russia. Tel.: +7 095 261 1806. Tel./Fax: +7 095 261 3948. Email: astrol.str@relcom.ru. Website: www.astrolog.ru. Online astrocollege: www.astrocollege.ru.

***Kalacakra—The Wheel of Time:*** Published quarterly by the Academy of Global Astrology and Metainformation; contains articles on Western and Eastern astrology and cultural interrelationship. President: Boris Boyko. Box 71, Moscow 115561, Russia. Tel./Fax: +7 095 392 7606. Email: astrology@mtu-net.ru. Website: astrol.ru.

***Urania Magazine:*** *Urania Magazine* has been published in Russia since 1991. *Urania* was the first Russian astrological magazine and its pages have introduced famous Russian and foreign authors. Later, the magazine was supplemented by a book series, *Urania's Anthology*. In 1999, *Urania*'s size doubled and grew into an almanac. Maly Zlatoustinsky 8, Suite 2, Moscow 101000, Russia. Tel./Fax: +7 095 924 7124. Email: Urania.Russia@g23.relcom.ru. Website: www.urania.ru/.

***The Wheel of Time:*** Quarterly information bulletin published by the League of Independent Astrologers: Domodedovskaya St, 6-2, Apt. 59, Moscow 115569, Russia. Tel./Fax: +7 095 392 7606. Email: astrol@astrol.ru. Website: www.astrol.ru.

## SOUTH AFRICA

***Aspects:*** The monthly journal of the Astrological Society of South Africa (ASSA). Contact: Elena van Baalen. P.O. Box 1953, Saxonwold 2132, South Africa. Tel.: (011) 646 3670. Fax: (011) 646 5477. Email: elena@kallback.co.za.

***Mountain Astrologer:*** Distributed by Astrology Services South Africa. Contact: Monica Cromhout. P.O. Box 3777, Somerset West 7129, South Africa. Tel.: (021) 852 4728. Fax: (021) 851 2592. Email: astrolog@iafrica.com. Website: www.AstrologyServices.netfirms.com.

## SWEDEN

***Horoskopet:*** Quarterly magazine published by Skandinavisk Astrologi Skole. Course leader: Karl Aage Jensen. Skolegade 12A, Postboks 319, 2500 Valby, Sweden. Tel.: +45 36 45 0545. Fax: +45 3645 0552. Email: horoskop@astrologihuset.dk. Website: www.astrologihuset.dk.

## SWITZERLAND

***Astrolog:*** Bimonthly magazine produced by Astrologisch-Psychologisches Institut. Contacts: Louise and Michael Huber. Obertilistr. 4, CH-8134 Adliswil/zh, Switzerland. Tel.: +41 (0) 1 710 3776. Fax: +41 (0) 1 710 3786. Email: Huber_API@compuserve.com.

***Astrologie Heute:*** Bimonthly magazine published by Astrodata AG, which offers correspondence, evening, and weekend courses and summer schools both in Switzerland and Germany (in Berlin and Munich). Runs the biggest astrological calculation service in Europe with a wide range of chart services and computer prepared reports. Albisriederstrasse 232, CH-8047 Zurich, Switzerland. Tel.: +41 01 492 1515. Fax: +41 01 492 1516. Email: info@astrodata.ch. Website: www.astrodata.ch/.

***The Sterngucker:*** This unorthodox astro-newspaper appears two to three times annually. Contact: Rosmarie Bernasconi. P.O. Box 263, CH-3000 Berne 13, Switzerland. Tel.: +41 (0) 31 311 01 08. Fax: +41 (0) 31 312 38 87. Email: verlag@astrosmarie.ch. Website: www.sterngucker.ch.

## TURKEY

***The 11th House:*** Turkish newsletter for members of the Astrological Association of Turkey. Address: Ferit Tek Sokak, Sonmezler Apt, B Blok, D2, K1, Moda, Istanbul, Turkey. Tel.: 0212 287 74 37. Email: kirkoglu@superonline.com or gany@turk.net.

## UNITED KINGDOM

***Academy Papers:*** These are papers on different aspects of astrology and significant events, such as the September 11, 2001, U.S. terrorist attacks, that draw astrologers' attention. Email: contact@newlibrary.com.

***Apollon: The Journal of Psychological Astrology:*** Glossy, high-quality journal published three times a year by CPA Press. Editor: Dermod Moore. Tel.: +44 (0) 20 7278 9434. Fax: +44 (0) 20 7209 1648. Distribution: Midheaven Bookshop, 396 Caledonian Road, London, N1 1DN, England. Tel.: +44 (0) 20 7607 4133. Fax: +44 (0) 20 7700 6717. Email: sales@midheavenbooks.com. Website: www.midheaven@compuserve.com

***The Astrologer's Apprentice:*** Contains the finest astrological writing, working within the tradition, yet still provocative and breaking new ground, with a welcome sense of humor. Contact: John Frawley. 85 Steeds Road, London, N10 1JB, England. Tel.: +44 (0) 20 8365 2553. Email: j@apprentice.demon.co.uk. Website: www.apprentice.demon.co.uk

***The Astrological Journal:*** Published bimonthly by the Astrological Association, this is one of the most important journals of its kind and includes material on every aspect of astrology. Free to AA members. Back copies available. Index to the *Astrological Journal* available. Editor: Gerasime Patilas. Unit 168, Lee Valley Technopark, Tottenham Hale, London, N17 9LN, England. Tel.: +44 (0) 020 8880 4848. Fax: +44 (0) 020 8880 4849. Email: astrological.association@zetnet.co.uk Website: www.Astrological Association.com.

***Astrology and Medicine Newsletter:*** Published by the Astrological Association, it acts as a forum and information and resource network for the exchange of views, ideas, and data for all those interested in medical astrology. It promotes the teaching and study of medical astrology and encourages serious research using appropriate methods. Back issues available. Unit 168, Lee Valley Technopark, Tottenham Hale, London, N17 9LN, England. Tel.: +44 (0) 20 8880 4848. Fax: +44 (0) 20 8880 4849. Email: astro logical.association@zetnet.co.uk.

***Astrology Quarterly:*** A very valuable journal with high standards but readily accessible by students at all levels. Editor: Claire Simms. Email: editor@astrolodge.co.uk.

***Company of Astrologers Bulletin:*** Distributed to Friends of the Company fortnightly, on the new and full moons. It contains up-to-the-minute astrology on people and events in the news, as well as quality articles on different aspects of astrology, its tradition, and its relation to psychotherapy and philosophy.

P.O. Box 792, Canterbury, CT2 8WR, England. Tel.: +44 (0)1227 362427. Email: admin@coa.org.uk. Website: www.hubcom.net.

***Conjunction: Journal of Astrological Psychology Institute:*** Focuses on all aspects of astrological psychology and the Huber Method. Acts as a forum for sharing learning and insights into this approach and often includes translations of articles from *Astrolog,* the journal of API Switzerland. Journal included charts, illustrations, diagrams, and photographs. API (UK), P.O. Box 118, Knutsford, Cheshire WA16 8TG, England. Tel./Fax: +44 (0) 1565 651131. Email: huberschool@btinternet.com. Website: www.api-uk.org.

***Correlation:*** The biannual journal of research in astrology by the Astrological Association publishes reports on research and philosophical issues in astrology. Features contributions from top research astrologers from around the world. Editor: Pat Harris. The AA Office, Unit 168, Lee Valley Technopark, Tottenham Hale, London, N17 9LN, England. Tel.: +44 (0) 20 8880 4848. Fax: +44 (0) 20 8880 4849. Email: astrological. association@zetnet.co.uk.

***Culture & Cosmos:*** The first journal to be devoted to the study of the history of astrology and cultural astronomy. If astrology is the use of celestial phenomena to provide meaning for human life, then cultural astronomy is the broader use of astronomical beliefs and theories to regulate and inform society, politics, the arts and every aspect of human life. Published twice a year. Editor: Nicholas Campion; Deputy Editor: Patrick Curry. All articles considered for publication are sent to specialist reviewers for comment. The Astrological Association, Culture and Cosmos Subscriptions, Unit 168, Lee Valley Technopark, Tottenham Hale, London, N17 9LN, England. Tel.: +44 (0) 20 8880 4848. Fax: +44 (0) 20 8880 4849. Email: astrological.association@zetnet.co.uk.

***Gochara:*** The British Association of Vedic Astrology's biannual journal has articles, important festival dates, data, and news on developments in Vedic Astrology in the U.K. and worldwide. *Gochara* is available free to all members. Barn Cottage, Brooklands Farm Close, Kilmington, Devon EX13 7SZ, England. Email: andrew@vedicsoftware.com. Website: www.bava.org.

***Hindu Vedic Astrology:*** Launched in 1994, this is an English bimonthly magazine (free if postage paid in advance) on Vedic Astrology. Editor: P. A. Patel (Jyotishi Anand). 8 Cecil Avenue, Wembley, Middx, HA9 7ED, England. Tel/Fax: +44 (0) 20 8903 6784.

***Horoscope:*** Editor: Mike Kenward. Wimborne Publishing Ltd., 408 Wimborne Road East, Ferndown, Dorset, BH22 9ND, England. Tel.: +44 (0) 1202 873872. Fax: +44 (0) 1202 874562. Email: horoscope@wimborne.co.uk. Website: www.horoscope.co.uk.

***Journal of Spiritual Astrology:*** Editor: Alexander Markin. 8 Rutland Gardens, Hove, E. Sussex, BN3 5PA. Tel.: +44 (0) 1273 726713. Subscribers in the U.S., contact Joseph Polansky, P.O. Box 7368, North Port, FL 34287. Tel/Fax: (941) 426-6915. Email: mzprod@aol.com

***Mercury:*** The official magazine of the British Astrological and Psychic Society (BAPS). Editor: Kim Farnell. 54 Sprules Road, Brockley, London, SE4 2NN, England. Tel.: +44 (0) 20 7252 9252. Email: kimfarnell@duk.co.uk.

**Mountain Astrologer:** P.O. Box 970, Cedar Ridge, CA 95924. Bimonthly. Now distributed in U.K./Europe. Publisher and Editor: Tem Tarriktar. Tel.: (800) 287-4828 (U.S./Canada); (530) 477-8839 (overseas). Fax: (530) 477-9423. Email: subs@mountainastrologer.com. Website: www.mountainastrologer.com. European distributors: *The Wessex Astrologer,* P.O. Box 2751, Bournemouth, BH6 3ZJ, England. Tel./Fax: +44 (0) 1202 424695. Email: wessexastrologer@mcmail.com.

**Prediction:** Magazine contains popular introductory features on astrology. Editor: Jo Logan. Link House, Dingwall Avenue, Croydon, CR9 2TA, England. Tel. +44 (0) 20 8686 2599.

**Predictive Circle Bulletin:** A no-nonsense bimonthly bulletin that incorporates research papers on electional and mundane astrology as well as considerations before judgement and predictions. It also publishes the proceedings of the Predictive Circle. Email: contact@new-library.com

**Realta:** Published twice yearly. Editor: Maurice McCann. Tel.: + 44 (0) 20 7272 4208. Email: mcmcann@compuserve.com. Website: www.ourworld.compuserve.com/homepages/mcmcann.

**Schneider-Gauquelin Research Journal:** *Astro-Psychological Problems (APP):* Françoise Gauquelin's friendly English-language journal also has time-change updates. 8 Rue Amyot, 75005 Paris, France.

**The Traditional Astrologer:** Widely respected magazine covering all aspects of the tradition, history, and development of astrology, with the emphasis on the practical application of all forms of traditional techniques. None published since 1998 but back copies available. Editor: Deborah Houlding. 3 Avondale Bungalows, Sherwood Hall Rd., Mansfield, Notts, NG18 2NJ, England. Tel.: +44 (0) 1623 634012. Fax: +44 (0) 1623 422676. Email: deb@astrology-world.com.

**Tybol Astrological Almanac:** 27 Heversham Avenue, Fulwood, Preston, PR2 9TD, England. Tel.: +44 (0) 1722 465402. Email: Tybolyr@yahoo.co.uk.

## UNITED STATES

**AFA Bulletin:** Monthly publication of the American Federation of Astrologers. P.O. Box 22040, 6535 South Rural Road, Tempe, AZ 85285-1040. Tel.: (480) 838-1751. Fax: (480) 838-8293. Email: afa@msn.com. Website: www.astrologers.com.

**AFAN Newsletter:** Quarterly newsletter of the Association for Astrological Networking includes news, forthcoming events, concepts, and people. Editor: Lorraine Welsh. 42 Grayland Road, Needham, MA 02492. Tel.: (781) 444-4428. Email: lwelsh@ lx.netcom.com.

**American Astrology Magazine:** A quality monthly astrology magazine, founded in 1933, available at most newsstands. It combines both popular features and serious articles on many areas of astrology. Coeditors: Kenneth Irving and Lee Chapman. P.O. Box 140713, Staten Island, NY 10314-0713. Email: am.astrology@genie.gies.com. Subscriptions: Starlog Group Inc, 475 Park Avenue South, New York, NY 10016.

**AstroMind Magazine:** The original free reader-interactive online astrology magazine, *AstroMind* explores astrology beyond sun signs. The publisher and many of the authors are professional astrological counselors. Publisher-Editor: Randall Collins. Email: AstroMind1@aol.com. Tel.: (770) 387-9740. Fax: (603) 719-3655.

***Career Astrologer:*** Produced quarterly by the Organization for Professional Astrology. Editor: Misty Kuceris. P.O. Box 1532, Springfield, VA 22151-0532. Fax: (703) 354-4037. Email: misty@enhanceoneself.com. Website: www.professional-astrology.org/.

***Considerations:*** An independent magazine, unrelated to any astrological group or organization. It has no special ax to grind, no proprietary viewpoint. The subject is astrology in its entirety. Coverage includes the inevitable progress of the seasons, the ordered rhythms of the heavenly bodies, and how these relate to human life. Editor: Ken Gillman. P.O. Box 655, Mount Kisco NY 10549. Tel.: (914) 232-4452. Email: kwgmkg@ aol.com. Website: www.considerations-mag.com.

***Cosmobiology International:*** Contains articles accompanied by charts, dials, and graphs, illustrating the techniques used in chart delineation as developed by Reinhold Ebertin. Cosmobiology Research Foundation, P.O. Box 1844, Englewood, CO 80150-1844. Email: rlg@northlink.com. Website: www.northlink.com/~rlg/crf.

***Crawford Perspectives:*** Leading financial astrology newsletter. Editor: Arch Crawford. 6890 East Sunrise Drive, Suite 120-70, Tucson, AZ 85750-0840. Tel.: (520) 577-1158. Fax: (520) 577-1110.

***Cycles:*** Monthly magazine, not astrological as such but of interest to all researchers. Includes frequent articles on solar, lunar, and cosmic correlations with mundane and business cycles. Editor: Diane Epperson. Foundation for the Study of Cycles, 900 West Valley Road, Suite 502 Wayne, PA 19087-1821. Tel.: (610) 995-2120. Fax: (610) 995-2130. Email: cycles@netaxs.com.

***Data News:*** Birth data, invaluable and entertaining, six issues per year. Editor: Lois M. Rodden. 11736 3rd St., Yucaipa, CA 92399. Tel.: (909) 797-6383. Email: lrodden @aol.com.

***Dell Horoscope:*** Let the stars be your guide with Dell Horoscope, a magazine written for amateur and professional astrologers and for readers who want to be introduced to the ancient art of astrology. Monthly features deal with world and national affairs, personal problems, as well as yearly, monthly, and daily guidance. Dept NS, 6 Prowitt St., Norwalk, CT 06855-1220. Available from www.randomhouse.com.

***Diamond Fire:*** A non-political, non-sectarian, quarterly esoteric review dealing with astrology, meditation, healing, Kabbalah, Vedanta, Buddhism, metaphysics, dowsing, tarot, and all aspects of the inner life. Also includes book reviews, new products, poetry, and esoterically oriented fiction. Editor/publisher: Joe Polansky. P.O. Box 7368, North Port, FL 34287. Email: mzprod@aol.com.

***Geocosmic Magazine:*** A research journal, published by the National Council for Geocosmic Research (NCGR), with articles on the most important topics in astrology today. NCGR is the leading US astrological organization. Issued yearly. Over 100 pages and covers a wide range of provocative editorial content with precis in French, German, and Spanish. Editor: Frances McEvoy. 1359 Sargent Ave., St. Paul, MN 55105. Email: LindaFei@aol.com. Tel.: (651) 698-1691.

***The Horary Practitioner:*** Quarterly magazine devoted entirely to high-quality articles and studies presenting traditional horary material. Editor: Carol A Wiggers. 1420 NW Gilman Blvd., Suite #2154, Issaquah, WA 98027-7001. Tel.: (425) 391-8371. Fax: (425) 392-1919. Email: justus1@msn.com.

***The International Astrologer (TIA):*** Quarterly publication of the International Society for Astrological Research (ISAR). President: David Cochrane. P.O. Box 38613, Los Angeles, CA 90038-8613. Tel.: (805) 525-0461. Fax: (805) 525-0461. Email: maribiehn@hotmail.com or maitreya@csiway.com. Editor: Bette Denlinger. P.O. Box 14 Paris, MI 49338. Tel.: (231) 796-5127. Email: bette@solsticepoint.com. Website: www.isarastrology.com.

***Matrix Journal:*** Bold, daring, yet careful and precise explorations of ideas and theories for understanding astrology. 315 Marion Avenue, Big Rapids, MI 49307. Tel.: (231) 896-2483. Fax: (231) 796-3060.

***Mercury Hour:*** "The Astrologer's Magazine." This quarterly periodical was first published on April 17, 1974 at 11:20 A.M. EDT, in Fairlawn, NJ (074W08 40N56). Contains a wide range of articles and data. In 1989 it was the recipient of the Regulus Award for Community Service. Editor: Edith Custer. 3509 Waterlick Rd. C-7, Lynchburg, VA 24502. Email: mercury-hour@starflash.com.

***MMA Cycles Report:*** One of the most insightful, reliable, and usable market letters in existence today. Used by both small and large traders, individual investors, and financial institutions throughout the world since 1982, it has developed a solid global following for its concrete and timely analysis of the economy, interest rates, stock, precious metals, currencies, and grain markets. Editor: Raymond A. Merriman. P.O. Box 250012, West Bloomfield, MI 48325. Tel.: (248) 626-3034. Fax: (248) 626-5674. Email: mmacycles@msn.com.

***Mountain Astrologer:*** Bimonthly. Now distributed in UK/Europe. Publisher and Editor: Tem Tarriktar. P.O. Box 970, Cedar Ridge, CA 95924. Tel.: (800) 287-4828 (U.S./Canada); (530) 477-8839 (overseas). Fax: (530) 477-9423. Email: subs@mountainastrologer.com. Website: www.mountainastrologer.com. European distributors: *The Wessex Astrologer*, P.O. Box 2751, Bournemouth, BH6 3ZJ, England. Tel./Fax: +44 (0) 1202 424695. Email: wessexastrologer@mcmail.com. Australia/New Zealand: Spica Publications, 617 Stanley St., Woolloongabba, QLD 4102, Australia. Tel.: +1 800 626 402. Email: spica@world.net. South Africa: Options Publishing and Bookseller, P.O. Box 1588, Somerset West 7129, South Africa. Tel.: +27 21 852 4728. Fax: +27 21 851 2582. Email@optpub@iafrica.com.

***NCGR Journal:*** This annual journal of the National Council for Geocosmic Research (NCGR) has been described as the best astrological publication on the planet. NCGR is the leading U.S. astrological organization. Editor: Lorraine Welsh. 1359 Sargent Ave., St. Paul, MN 55105. Email: LindaFei@aol.com. Tel.: (651) 698-1691.

***Welcome to Planet Earth:*** Bimonthly astrological magazine written by internationally recognized astrologers; the articles in *WTPE* offer insights into world events and provide a deeper understanding of contemporary astrology. Editor: Mark Lerner. The Great Bear, P.O. Box 12007, Eugene, OR 97440. Tel.: (503) 683-1760. Fax: (503) 683-8851. Email: markl@efn.org.

## YUGOSLAVIA

***The Astrological Magazine of AFYU:*** Published by the Astrological Federation of Yugoslavia (AFYU). Founders and co-presidents: Marina Talovic and Zeljko Arsenijevic. Karadjordjeva 6/42, 11080 Zemun, Yugoslavia. Email: astro.afyu@net.yu and

# APPENDIX C

# Astrological Organizations, Schools, and Web Resources

This appendix is adapted from the Urania Trust directory of associations, societies, and educational establishments, courtesy of the Urania Trust (http://www.uraniatrust.org/educ.htm).

## ARGENTINA

**Buenos Aires Astrological Centre:** Gral. J. D. Perón 1751 2do. Piso D, 1039 Buenos Aires. Tel./Fax: +541 371 9978. Runs courses to diploma level, workshops, seminars, lectures, and debates. Public library. Contact: Jerry Brignone. Tel: +541 792 1807. Founded April 19, 1961 at 21:25. Email: caba@ciudad.com.ar. Website: www.astrolcaba.com.ar.

**Jorge Mele:** C C 3983, 1000 Buenos Aires, Argentina. Tel: +5411 4641 5724. Email: jmele@formared. com.ar or mediumcoeli@excite.com.

## AUSTRALIA

**Academy of Predictive Astrology:** Offers Internet-based and correspondence courses leading to both certificate and diploma for students in Australia. The work is based on ancient translation and modern research as encapsulated in the works of Robert Zoller and other leading predictive astrologers. Zoller was the teacher of leading Australian astrologers such as Bernadette Brady and others. Unlike many other schools, it pays special attention to the different emphasis that is needed when teaching astrology in the Southern Hemisphere. Students have direct access to the audio lectures, texts with diagrams and tables, an online library, ebooks, and articles. For full details contact The Registrar at contact@new-library.com.

**Astro Logos:** P.O. Box 216, Welland, South Australia 5007. Established in 1990 and is now one of the world's premier astrological centers. Astro Logos is a professional training center for astrologers. Students are educated from beginner through to qualified professional. The first two years of training emphasize solid foundations, chart delineation, and predictive work. Once understood, students move into the more specialized subjects of relationships, research, children's charts, mundane astrology, relocation and mapping, and most importantly, what is required to work as a professional astrologer in the modern world. The qualifications gained are those of the Astrological Guild of Educators, International. Courses are run via Open Learning working with audiotapes, books, and Internet tutorials. Contact: Bernadette Brady. Email: bnbrady@chariot.net.au. Website: www.bernadettebrady.com.

**Astrological Guild of Educators International:** P.O. Box 291, Greenock, South Australia 5360, Australia. Contact: Mari Garcia. Tel./Fax: +618 8562 8358. Email: info@theastrologicalguild.com. Website: www.theastrologicalguild. com. Established in 1998, the Guild is an international organization of professional astrological educators. The Guild is an independent, non-profit body whose charge is to acknowledge the profession of teaching astrology and help those professionals to maintain a high standard in the conduct of examinations, setting and maintaining uniformly high astrological standards at a level acknowledged by the international astrological community and to promote understanding and appreciation of all aspects of astrology.

**Astrology Matters:** Mari Garcia, P.O. Box 291, Greenock, South Australia 5360. Tel./Fax: +61 8 8562 8358. Email: margar@bigfoot.com.au. Website: www.mindbodysoul.com.au/site/astrologymatters. Member of the Astrological Guild of Educators International Inc.

**Astro*Synthesis:** The Chiron Centre, 407 Johnston St., Abbotsford Victoria, Australia 3067. Tel: +61 3 9419 4566. Fax: +61 3 9417 1773. Email: AstroSynthesis@bigpond.com. Astro*Synthesis is a four-year part-time educational astrology program. The program is structured in units and has two levels: the first two years are the basic certificate course, which covers the essentials in contemporary astrology and leads to the certificate in applied astrology. The last two years comprise the advanced program, which leads to the diploma in applied astrology. Supplementary workshops are held on Saturdays throughout the year. The program is available for students who wish to pursue astrology for formal qualifications or for their own interest. The main tutors in the program are Brian Clark and Glennys Lawton. Both are accredited astrology teachers (AAT) with the Federation of Australian Astrologers (FAA) and teach classes in all four years.

**Australian Society of Astrologers, Inc.:** P.O. Box 7120, Bass Hill, New South Wales 2197, Australia. Tel./Fax: +61 2 9754 2999. President: Renée Badger. Tel.: +61 7 5445 8017. Email: GJdeMAS@bigpond.com.au. Website: www.angelfire.com/journal/asainc/index. html. Produces bimonthly newsletter called *The Australian Astrologer*. The Australian Society of Astrologers was born out of some very important astrological needs in today's ever-changing economic and social climate. The first and foremost of these needs was to set up more than one astrological society in Australia that could help temper the monopoly problems that naturally stems from just a single organization. The ASA was formed by a group of dedicated astrologers who recognized the importance of such needs by setting up a society that, additionally, through much greater insight, flexibility and understanding, would allow anyone—novice, student, or professional astrologer alike—to study, learn, teach, and practice, but most importantly grow, in whatever astrological capacity they wish to as individuals.

**Balsama:** Joy Usher, P.O. Box 16, Greenock, South Australia 5360. Tel./Fax: +61 8 8562 8188. Email: balsama@dove.net.au. Member of the Astrological Guild of Educators International, Inc.

**Canopus Academy of Astrology:** Full details online at www.panplanet.com/ or from Canopus Enterprises Pty. Ltd., P.O. Box 774 Kingston, Tasmania 7051, Australia. Tel.: +61 (03) 6267 9902. Fax: +61 (03) 6267 9920. Email: canopus@southcom.com.au. Website: www.panplanet.com/. Offers astrological education online, through its unique mentorship program. All students are offered a personal tutor who works with the student directly by email and correspondence. All reading materials are supplied on CD and hard copy. Canopus also has a correspondence course and face-to-face classes in Australia. The program teaches from beginners to practitioners level and has several specialized short courses including "Astronomy for Astrologers."

**Federation of Australian Astrologers:** The FAA has branches in each of the states. Contacts for inquiries: National FAA secretary: Sylvia Wilson, P.O. Box 466, Woodridge Qld, Australia. Tel.: 4114 617 3200 5449. Email: sylviaw@powerup.com.au. International Liaison Officer: Chris Turner, 24 Berryman St., North Ryde, NSW, Australia. Tel.: 2113 612 9878 2079. State contacts: Sherrynne Dalby, 179 Burns Rd., Springwood, NSW, Australia. Tel.: 2777 612 4751 2568. Sylvia Wilson, P.O. Box 466, Woodridge, Qld, Australia. Tel.: 4114 617 3200 5449. Wendy Linnell, 6 McClements St., Howrah, TAS, Australia. Tel.: 7018 613 6244 6880. Alison Campbell, 5 Vaucluse St., Claremont, WA, Australia. Tel.: 6010 618 9286 2220. Duane Eaks, P.O. Box 331, Heidelberg, Vic., Australia. Tel.: 3084 613 9459 6686. Noelle Rattray, 5 Wright St., Ridleyton, SA, Australia.. Tel.: 5008 618 8267 1579.

**Federation of Australian Astrologers Board of Examiners:** The Coordinator, The Board of Examiners, Gaynor Foster, P.O. Box 70, Northbridge, NSW 1560 Australia. Email: gaynor@zip.com.au. Website: www.faainc.org.au/.

**Sydney Astrological Research Society:** The oldest astrology group in Australia established in 1938. Weekly meetings. Contact: Val Dowling, president. Tel: +61 2 9713 4177. Website: www.planet. net.au/~sars/

**Universal Astrology:** Maggie Kerr AAT, P.O. Box 279, Southport QLD, Australia 4215. Tel.: +61 07 5594 5959. Website: www.universalastrology.com.au/. A course blending of esoteric or soul-centered astrology with the psychotherapies.

## AUSTRIA

**Astromatis:** Österreichische Schule für Astrologie, Maria Luise Mathis, A-2500 Baden bie Wien, Habsburgerstrasse 78, Astrologin, Austria. Tel./Fax: +43 (0) 2252 86 266. Founded in

July 1988, this school runs regular one-year courses in psychological esoteric and classical astrology. Website: www.astromatis.at/frame.htm.

**Studio Moderne Astrologie:** Herbert Hemzal Sandwirtgasse 13, A-1060 Vienna, Austria. Tel.: +43 1 597 30 59. Fax: +43 1 597 30 59 33. Email: sma@hemzal.at. Website: www.hemzal.at. Offers regular courses in astrology as well as computer calculations and interpretations. Also offers professional astrology software programmes for PCs. Contact for free CD.

**Wiener Schule fuer Astrologie (Vienna School of Astrology):** Alserstrasse 26, A-1090 Wien, Austria. Tel.: +43 1 409 35 40. Email: astro@ chello.at. Website: www.sarastro.at. Austria's most successful astrology college. Founded by Peter Fraiss in 1986. Offers three-year course on psychological astrology taking beginners to certified consultants. Weekend seminars for advanced and professional levels with top-level astrologers. Weekly lectures on astrological themes. Astrological bookshop. Development of the astrological software Sarastro, which is well known in German-speaking countries. Center of the astrological community in Vienna.

## BELGIUM

**Anne-Marie Huybrechts:** C Schuermanslaan, 104B-3070 Kortenberg. Belgium. Tel.: +32 2 759 95 18. Seminars and workshops in psychological astrology and mythic tarot. Languages: French, Dutch, English, Spanish.

**Dragana van de Moortel-Ilic:** Boerderijstraat 1, B-9000 Gent, Belgium. Tel./Fax: +32 9 2277036. Email: koenvandemoortel@compuserve.com. Website: www.astrovdm.com. Courses at different levels, lectures, workshops, conferences.

**School voor Astrologie:** Muntestraat 12, B-9860 Munte, Belgium. Tel.: + 32 9 362 23 65. Fax: + 32 9 362 24 65. Email: eline@schoolvoorastrologie.be and rini@schoolvoorastrologie.be. Website: www.schoolvoorastrologie.be. Teaching insight into human nature since 1989. School voor Astrologie is situated in a renovated country house amidst cornfields only 10 kilometers from Ghent. It is a meeting place for spirit, ratio, and art of life. Courses and consultations mainly focus on social relationships.

**Vlaams Astrologisch Genootschap:** Founded in 1973, it provides information about astrology, organizes yearly astrological congress, and publishes a magazine. President: Nandy Vermeulen-Geeraert. Secretary: Mariette de Marré-Cools. Address: Belgiëlei 149 bus 7, 2018 B-Anwerpen, Belgium. Tel.: + 32 3 230 75 11. Email: VAG@Pandora.be. Website: www.geocities.com/VAG_BE/.

## CANADA

**Astrology Montreal:** Contact: Pauline Edward, 6 Harwood Ave., Roxboro, Quebec H8Y 2W2, Canada. Pager: (514) 684-7164. Email: p.edward@videotron.ca. Website: www.astrologymontreal.com.

**Astrology Toronto, Inc.:** President: Dagmar Mikkila. 4 Caracas Rd., Toronto, ON M2K 1A9, Canada. Tel.: (416) 930-9287. Vision Statement: To be the Canadian umbrella organization promoting astrological awareness, education, and research. Its members range from beginning students to full-time professionals. Website: www.astrology- toronto-inc.com.

**Canadian Academy of Astrology and Related Disciplines (CAARD):** Tel.: (613) 722-5975. Fax: (613) 567-0797. Email: cyclespeak@home.com. Website: www.members.home.net/cyclespeak/. On Sunday May 1, 1994, a Canadian school of astrology was initiated in the National Capital District. Classes have now been in progress for several years. As part of an ongoing evaluation of achievement, students are encouraged to write the examinations conducted by the Canadian Association for Astrological Education (CAAE).

**Edmonton Astrological Society:** 66-07-92B Ave., Edmonton, Alberta T6B 0V8, Canada. Email: cmcrae@compusmart.ab.ca. Founded in December 1977 by Chris McRae (honorary life president). Monthly meetings/workshops/seminars.

**Frazer Valley Astrological Guild:** Box 833, Fort Langley BC V1M 2S2, Canada. Tel.: (604) 888-9579. Email: astrologyguild@shaw.ca. Website: www.astrologyguild.com. Twenty-nine astrologers founded the Guild on October 17, 1991, at 7:45 P.M. It is a non-profit astrological association registered as a society in British Columbia, Canada. It holds an annual general meeting on the second Thursday in October usually at 6:30 P.M. Membership is open to all astrologers and astrology students.

**New Alexandria:** Founder and director: Priscilla Costello. Tel.: (647) 433-0501. A center for esoteric studies established in Toronto, Ontario, Canada, to sponsor lectures, workshops, and conferences on the Western esoteric tradition from ancient Greek philosophy and Egyptian wisdom through the Renaissance to the present time.

**Vancouver Astrology School:** Astraea Astrology, Suite 412, 2150 W. Broadway, Vancouver V6K 4L9, Canada. Tel.: (604) 536-3880 Fax: (604) 536-3888. Offers a full range of courses part-time, evenings and correspondence.

**Vancouver Society of Astrologers:** Diana Zoller, #8 1786 Esquimalt Ave., West Vancouver BC, V7V IR8, Canada. Tel.: (604) 926-9027. Email: warwickdiana@hotmail.com.

## COSTA RICA

**Astrological Research Centre (Astrovision):** P.O. Box 290-1150, San Jose, Costa Rica. Tel.: +506 253 9616 or +506 253 8380. Fax: +506 234 9340. Email: abel@interwebcr.com or astrovision@starmedia.com. Promotes astrological research into criminology, earthquakes, political events, and personal consulting.

## CROATIA

**Centre for Astrological Education:** B. Magovca 69, 10010 Zagreb, Croatia. Tel.: +385 1 6684 761. Fax: +385 1 6683 630. Email: igoro@zamir.net. Website: www.geocities.com/alfa019.

Director: Igor Ognjenovic. The Centre's courses have always represented a wide cross-section of astrological thought, from its ancient beginnings to the most recent developments, in theory, practice, and research. Since its inception, the Centre has presented its students with a broad spectrum of astrological thought, in a manner allowing students to develop their own ideas and approaches within the framework of coherent, practical astrology.

## CZECH REPUBLIC

**Astro-Kontakt:** Olbrachtova 52, 140 00 Praha 4, Czech Republic. Tel.: +42 2 439 7661. Email: bohuslav@comp.cz. Website: www.pha.comp.cz/bohuslav/. Consortium of professionals cooperating in research based on classical astrology and producing occasional articles.

**Czech Astrological Society:** Contact: Zdenek Bohuslav, Chairman, Tolsteho 20, 101 00 Praha 10, Czech Republic. Email: bohuslav@comp.cz or Jindra Johanisova, Na Stahlavce 1741/1a, 160 00 Praha 6. Tel.: +420 2 3333 3650. Letters/mail may be sent in English, French, German, Russian and Czech. Website: pha.comp/cz/bohuslav/aaspol.htm (English/Czech). Founded on December 19, 1989, at a meeting of 10 astrologers from Prague, between 5 and 7 P.M. of CET at Prague Strahov monastery. Press announcement was released at 6 P.M., official registration was delivered to hands of chairman on April 10, 1990, at 11:31 Summer CET in Prague. This society is for both professionals and students. Activities: Conferences, regular meetings, library, publishing of review called *Konstelace*. International membership available.

**School of Traditional Astrology:** Teachers: Z Bohuslav, Tolsteho 20, 101 00 Prague 10, R Stribny, Nerudova 39, 118 00 Prague 2, Czech Republic. Email: bohuslav@comp.cz or richard@stribny.cz. Two-year courses in Czech, held once a week, based on tradition of J.B. Morin.

**Turnovsky—ISTA (Information Service of Astrology of/in Transformation):** Contact: Pavel Turnovsky, nam. Svobody 1, CZ-160 00 Praha 6, Czech Republic. Tel.: +420 2 2432 3371. Email: turnov@login.cz and turnovsky@ mbox.dkm.cz. Websites: www.rezonance.info and www.stand.cz/ astrologie/ ceska/index.htm. ISTA offers two-year courses in humanistic and transpersonal astrology, followed by seminars in synastry, mundane astrology, rectification, Sabian symbols in astrological and personal practice, and Astro*symbo*logy in practice. Founded in 1992—800 students joined school, half of them finished school and about 60 work as a full-time or part-time astrologers.

## DENMARK

**Astrologihuset:** Skolegade 12A, Postboks 319, 2500 Valby, Copenhagen, Denmark. Tel.: +45 3645 0545. Fax: +45 3645 0552. Email: horoskop@astrologihuset.dk. Website: www.astrologihuset.dk. This huge astrology center has emerged following the highly successful October 1991 Copenhagen Conference and is now the largest center of its kind in the world. It includes Astrologisk Museum, the world's first astrological museum, which contains a large collection of astrological books and artifacts. In September 2001, Astrologihuset began publishing books. Course leader: Karl Aage Jensen. Students begin with two years of basic education, followed by two years of diploma education and then a one-year extended professional education where students learn how to lecture, teach, and receive media training. Publishes the quarterly magazine *Horoskope*.

**Dansk Astrologforening: the Professional Organisation of Astrological Practitioners:** Sdr. Ringgade 24, DK 8000 Aarhus C, Denmark. Tel.: +45 8676 1278. Website: www.astrologforeningen.dk. Chairman: Jesper Bernth. Founded in 1978 and open to both students and professional astrologers. Provides seminars and conferences and has a large library. Publishes bimonthly magazine *Astrologen*.

**Ekliptika:** Overskousvej 8, 2.tv. DK 2500 Valby, Denmark. Tel.: +45 3630 4947. Email: ekliptika@ekliptika.com. Website: www.ekliptika.com. Chairman: Jytte Koch Littau. Founded in 1980 to provide an open forum for everybody interested in astrology. Offering seminars, library, and monthly meetings. Works primarily in the Copenhagen area.

**IC Astrology Institute:** Nr. Farimagsgade 63, DK-1364 Copenhagen K, Denmark. Tel.: +45 3312 3627. Fax: +45 3314 1303. Director: Pia Balk-Moeller. Founded in 1956 by Irene Christensen. Four-year training program on six levels with final diploma exam. Classes, seminars. Publishes monthly magazine *Stjernerne*.

**International Society of Business Astrologers (ISBA):** Email: info@erhvervsastrologi.dk. Website: www.businessastrologers.com. Founded in Copenhagen on March 10, 1997 at 9:09:00 AM.. by Karen Boesen. Professional members must have five years of experience as a practicing business or financial astrologer and must contribute to ISBA newsletters regularly. Associated members must have experience as a practicing business or financial astrologer. The annual fee for an associated membership is USD 40. Supporting members do not have to meet any requirements except an interest in astrology.

**Skolen for Terapeutisk Astrologi:** Mejlgade 28, DK 8000 Aarhus C, Denmark. Tel.: +45 8625 8062. Director: Holger Stavnsbjerg. Curriculum includes teaching students to use esoteric, psychological astrology to work with themselves and others.

## EUROPE

**Federation of Southern European Astrologers (FAES):** Website: www.astrofaes.org. FAES is an organization consisting of astrologers and astrological associations of southern Europe (from France, Italy, Spain, Greece, and Cyprus). Its existence was confirmed in Mykonos on June 11, 2000. FAES was founded to promote the recognition and the development of southern European astrology. The Federation publishes a monthly multilingual electronic journal with articles and reviews.

## FINLAND

**Astrological Association of Finland:** P.O. Box 90, FIN-00131 Helsinki, Finland. Tel.: +358 9 495 513. Email: suomi.astro@sunpoint.net. Chairman: Raimo K. Nikula, Dobelninkatu 3B, 00160 Helsinki, Finland. Email: mikula@welho.com. Website (in English): www.gamma.nic.fi/

~astrolog/english/eindex.htm. Website (in Finnish): www.gamma.nic.fi/~astrolog/. Secretary: Pirjo Ahtiainen. Email: pirah@ luukku.com. Founded in 1964. Publishes quarterly *Astro Logos*. Annual summer weekend gatherings.

## FRANCE

**Academy of Predictive Astrology:** Offers the only dedicated course in medieval and predictive astrology in the French language. The work is based on ancient translation and modern research as encapsulated in the works of Robert Zoller and other leading predictive astrologers. Students also have direct access to the audio lectures, texts with diagrams and tables, an online library, ebooks, and articles. Email: contact @new-library.com.

**Association Jupitair:** 520 rue de St Hilaire (D8), F34000 Montpelier, France. Tel.: +33 46764 0511. Email: jupitair@astroo.com. Website: www.astroo.com/jupitair/.

**Astroariana:** Association for research and information of natural astrology. Website: www. astroariana.free.fr.

**Centre Associatif de Diffusion et de Recherche d'Actes de Naissance (CADRAN):** Petitallot Patrice, 10 Lann Fouesnel, 56350 Allaire, France. Tel.: +33 9972 2152. Fax: +33 9972 3703. Following the death of Michel Gauquelin, CADRAN has become the key French organization specializing in collecting and providing fully documented birth data and biographical details on historical/contemporary notables/events. It issues a monthly newsletter of fresh birth data and updates.

**Centre d'Études, de Documentation et de Recherche sur l'Astrologie (CEDRA):** 7 Place des Terreaux, 69001 Lyon, France. Tel.: +33 47823 7276. Fax: +33 42665 6207. Email: cedra@cedra.net. Website: www.cedra.net. Director: Maurice Charvet. Founded on September 19, 1986. CEDRA brings together astrologers of all levels—amateurs and professionals—from France and other countries. It places at their disposal various means to improve the knowledge of astrology. CEDRA has approximately 800 members. It is one of the most significant French-speaking astrological associations. It runs seminars and conferences and helps members with research. It keeps close links with national and international organizations. Superb up-to-date databank of current information and events and birth data is accessible to members by phone and the Internet. It publishes valuable non-periodical magazine *Astralis* and runs a very active mailing list.

**Centre d'Organisation des Methodes d'Astrologie Conditionaliste (COMAC):** J.P. Nicola, Sperel, 83170 Tourves, France. Tel./Fax: +33 94 78 88 25. Email: jpnicola@club-internet.fr. Websites: www.multimania.com/comac, www.multi mania.com/comac, www.conditionalisme.com, and www.comac.free.fr. Founded by J. P. and Yen Nicola in 1980, COMAC studies an astrology that is at the same time non-fatalist, experimental, critical, and autocritical—an astrology that is responsive to all approaches to reality.

**Centre Universitaire de Recherche en Astrologie (CURA):** Email: mailto:cura@nomade.fr. Website: www.cura.free.fr. University Centre for Astrological Research is a trilingual site, based in France to promote serious research into astrology, "taking care that this multi-millenary knowledge not be ruined by media hype, does not degenerate into the horoscope trade, and does not become obliterated by partisan research." Useful links, bibliographies, and articles in English as well as French and Spanish.

**Groupe de Recherche en Astrologie par des Méthodes Scientifiques (RAMS):** 15 rue du Cardinal Lemoine, 75005 Paris, France. Tel.: +33 (1) 4354 8888. Fax: +33 (1) 4634 6340. Email: fuzeau.braesch@wanadoo.fr. Website: ramsfr. org. Founded by S. Fuzeau-Braesch, F. Gauquelin, Yves Lenoble, and Francis Santoni. Includes papers or summaries in English.

**Institut d'Astrologie Traditionelle:** 3 Ave. de la Libération, 42000 St. Etienne. Tel.: +33 (4) 77 41 40 40. Fax: +33 (4) 77 38 69 57. Email: astrocours@fr.st. Website: www.astrocours.fr.st. Director: Denis Labouré.

**Société Française d'Astrologie:** 5 rue Las Cases, 75007 Paris, France. Secretary: Colette Cholet, 16 rue Pavée, 75004 Paris, France. Tel.: +33 (1) 4271 5409.

## GERMANY

**Academy of Predictive Astrology:** Email: contact@new-library.com. Offers the only dedicated course in medieval and predictive astrology in the German language. The work is based on ancient translation and modern research as encapsulated in the works of Robert Zoller and other leading predictive astrologers. Students also have direct access to the audio lectures, texts with diagrams and tables, an online library, ebooks, and articles.

**ACS Siegfried Kaltenecker:** Postfach 710504-D-81455, Muenchen, Germany. Tel.: +49 (89) 74 99 53 10. Fax: +49 (89) 74 99 53 11. Email info@kaltenecker.de. Website: www.acs-kaltenecker.de. Classes, courses, and sessions.

**Anthroposophisch-Astrologische Arbeitsgruppe:** Rudolf-Steiner-Haus, Stuttgart, Germany. Dir Ulrike Voltmer, Metzer Str. 65, 66117 Saarbrucken. Tel. +33 (0) 387 873752. Email: uvoltmer@aol.com. Organizes two conferences a year in Stuttgart in May and November on relationship between anthroposophy and astrology.

**ARS Astrologica:** Jürgen GH Hoppmann, 10115 Berlin-Mitte, Schoenholzer Str. 1, Germany. Tel./Fax: +49 (0) 30 440 440 45. Email: jgh.hoppmann@gmx.de. Website: www.arsastrologica.com. TV, radio (MDR), medieval markets, publications, screenwriter. Astrosoftware for PCA, Hermes, and Windows.

**Astro-Center-Bonin:** D-86825 Bad Wörishofen, Kemptener Str.14 A, Germany. Tel.: +49 (0) 8247 2233. Fax: 32438. President: Tony Bonin. Email: TonyBonin@t-online.de. Website: www.TonyBonin.de. Specializes in astro-medical research since 1964, mundane astrology, "genius loci," and astro-psychological research of historical persons.

**Astroclub Zurich:** Dieter Koch: Tel.: +41 (0) 1 401 4660. Email: 100703.3637@compuserve.com. Harald Seeberger: Tel.: +41 (0) 76 373 1870. Email: harald.seeberger@ubs.com.

**Astrodata of Zurich Switzerland:** Sophien-Stiftung, Herzogstrasse 5a, 86981 Kinsau, Germany. Tel.: +49 (0) 8869 1703. Website: www.astrodata.ch/default.htm. Runs weekend courses in Berlin and Munich. Courses and workshops with Robert Powell on astrological biography, medical astrology, karma and reincarnation, hermetic astrology, etc. Specializes in sidereal astrology.

**Astrologische Arbeitsgemeinschaft Stuttgart:** Tel.: +49 (0) 711 6150190. Email: Dieter.Gollong@t-online.de. Website: www.chironverlag.com. This club organizes mainly public lecture evenings (20-25 per year) with speakers of different astrological backgrounds and mostly classical astrology. The speakers are mainly from Germany, but some have connections to Spain, Great Britain, and Switzerland. It has a close connection to the DAV (Deutscher Astrologen Verband e.V).

**Astrologiezentrum Freiburg (Freiburg Center for Research and Education in Astrology):** Astrologiezentrum Freiburg, Lorettostrasse 38, 79100 Freiburg, Germany. Tel./Fax: +49 761 4055653/4098288. Email: info@astrologiezentrum.de. Websites: www.astrologiezentrum.de and www.astrologen.info. Peter Niehenke, Ph.D. and past president of the German Astrologers Association, offers an officially licensed correspondence course for astrology in the German language (if wanted, completely Internet-based).

**Astron-Verlag:** Klaus W. Bonert, Peter-Marquard-Str. 4A, 22303 Hamburg. Tel.: +49 (0) 40 270 1908. Fax: +49 (0) 40 279 5155. Email: astron.bonert@t-online.de. Website: www.astrocalc.com. Sells a wide range of highly sophisticated programmed pocket computers, top software, and books. Gives astrological readings, teaches classes, and organizes astrology seminars with internationally renowned speakers. Publisher of the 1850–2050 *Ephemeris for Ceres, Pallas, Juno, Vesta, Chiron and Transpluto*.

**Deutscher Astrologen-Verband (DAV):** Wilhelmstrasse 11, D-69115 Heidelberg, Germany. Tel./Fax: +49 (0) 6221 18201. Email: davev@t-online.de. Website: www.dav-astrologie.de. President: Detlef Hover. Vice-President: Anne C. Schneider. Niddastrasse 2, 65428 Ruesselsheim, Germany. Email: annecschneider@aol.com. The main German astrological association, established in 1946, DAV organizes conferences, classes, courses, examinations, and study and research groups. It has the main astrological library and data collection in Germany. DAV publishes the bimonthly technical journal *Meridian*. Research programs in cooperation with several universities and considerable contributions from teams and members of DAV have underpinned the truth of astrological teachings. Wherever possible, DAV supports diplomas and Ph.D. theses relating to astrological subjects.

**Ebertin-Institut für Ausdrucks-und Charakterkunde:** Haus Waldesruh, Panoramastrasse 15, 75323 Bad Wildbad, Baden-Württemberg, Germany. Tel.: +49 (0) 7081 9393 40. Fax: +49 (0) 7081 9393 33. Principal: Dr. Baldur Ebertin. Email: brebertib@aol.com. Website: www.

ebertin.de. Classes, courses, and summer schools on astrology and cosmobiology and their applications to psychology, medicine, reincarnation therapy, and related topics.

**Foerderverein Fachbibliothek Astrologie (FFA):** Ulrike Voltmer, Metzer Strasse 65, D-66117 Saarbrucken, Germany. Tel.: +49 (0) 681 52160. Fax: +49 (0) 681 55020. Email: ffabiblio@aol.com. Website: www.astrolog.de. The Fachbibliothek Astrologie (Astrology Expert Library) is a unique institution containing one of the biggest collections of astrology- and branch-related books in Germany. After World War II, the DAV (Deutscher Astrologen-Verband; German Astrological Association) reconstituted, and started organizing the library. During the Nazi regime, astrology had been banned and astrologers persecuted. Only a few books could be saved and they found their place in the library. Due to personal estates and donations of authors and publishers, the stock increased gradually. So today, the library contains rare and out of print books of invaluable worth for astrological work and research. To maintain this special library, in 1991, the FFA was founded, on the initiative of Ulrike Voltmer, the former president of the DAV. The following year, the stock doubled: Edith Wangemann, president of the Kosmobiosophische Gesellschaft, donated parts of her own as well as the society's library to the FFA. Thanks to donations of authors, publishers, and friends of the library, it now contains more than 2,500 books, including English, French, Italian, and Russian books, as well as journals, calendars, collections, and tables. Linked to the library are instructional records and records of lectures and radio and TV broadcasts. Part of the duties of the FFA is acquiring and cataloguing new books and organizing the lending. So, members of the FFA, DAV, and Kosmobiosophische Gesellschaft can profit by a modern and well-organized rental library. In addition to this, the FFA organizes periodical lectures on a variety of astrology-related subjects, held by different speakers from different countries.

**Kosmobiologische Akadamie Aalen:** Tel.: +49 (0) 7541 33722. Fax: +49 (0) 711 681435. Continues work of Ebertin et al.

**Kosmobiosophische Gesellschaft eV:** Rosenthaler Str 52, D-41849 Wassenberg, Germany. Tel.: +49 (0) 2432 49644. Chair: Manfred u Renata Gerling. Organizes courses, seminars, conferences in major towns throughout Germany. Annual conference.

## ICELAND

**Astrological Association of Iceland:** Asgardur 32, 108 Reykjavik, Iceland. Tel.: +354 1 689119.

## INDIA

**Visesh Infosystems Ltd.:** 21 National Park, LajpatNagarIV, 110024, India. Contact: Nishant Bajaj. Email: nishantbajaj@flashmail.com. Astrovedic education.

## ISRAEL

**Polaris:** P.O. Box 39675, Tel Aviv 61396, Israel. Email: stark@netvision.net.il. Director: Isaac Starkman. Rectification program Polaris (for Windows) and offers rectification service.

## ITALY

**Abruzzo:** Bia Gatren, via Silvino Croce 11, 66026 Ortona (Chieti), Italy. Tel.: +39 085 9065565 and via dei Cimatori, 14/A, 00186 Roma. Tel.: +39 06 6877803.

**Academy of Predictive Astrology:** Offers the only dedicated course on predictive astrology that is based on the works on Guido Bonatti, one of the most famous and influential Italian astrologers. Also offers ebooks, including works by leading astrologers who dominated astrology when it was at its height in Italy some 600–700 years ago. Students also have direct access to the audio lectures, texts with diagrams and tables, an online library, ebooks, and articles. For full details contact the registrar at contact@new-library.com.

**Albo Professionale Nazionale Degli Astrologi:** President: Stefano Vanni. Via Montecarlo, 10-41012 Carpi (Modena), Italy. Tel.: +39 059 699569. Vice president: Dr. Vittorio Ruata. Via Antonio Silvani 108, 00139 Roma, Italy. Birth-data coordinator: Enrico Ruscalla. Via Diaz, 5-10023 Chieri (Torino), Italy. Executive Committee: Dante Valente, Grazia Mirti, Claudio Cannistrà, Giuliarosa Bigazzi Vincenzi. Founded in 1989. Exams for admission every two years. Organizes seminars in depth astrological training.

**Centro Italiano di Astrologia (CIDA):** Secretary: Claudio Cannistrà, Via Vizzani 74, 40138 Bologna, Italy. Tel.: +39 (0) 51 342 445. Email: canniclau@libero.it. President: Dr. Dante Valente, Via Monzambano 13, 20159 Milano, Italy. Tel.: +39 (0) 269 005 576. Email: linguaggioastrale@libero.it. The main coordinating body for Italian astrology with well organized branches in most regions of Italy. Good astrological library, printed books, and data collection in Italy. Runs courses, seminars, and conferences in various cities. Publishes a 200-page quarterly journal, *Linguaggio Astrale*, founded in 1970; and a monthly journal, *Sestile*, for the Professional Astrologers Association board.

**Centro Raccolta Data Astrologici:** Contact: Grazia Bordoni. Via Ranzini 30, 27018 Vidigulfo PV, Italy. Tel.: +39 0382 614856. Fax: +39 0382 619787. Email:grabor@tin.it. Website: Archivio online: www.graziabordoni.it/. The biggest data bank in the world—80,000 charts on a database.

**Ricerca '90:** Viale Gramsci 16, 80122 Napoli (NA). Tel.: +39 81 660420. Fax: +39 81 680709. Director: Ciro Discepolo. Website: www.cirodiscepolo.it. Email: discepol@tin.it. Produces quarterly journal *Ricerca '90*. Also produces and supplies Astral Software.

## JAPAN

**Academy of Predictive Astrology:** Offers Internet-based and/or correspondence courses leading to both certificate and diploma. The work is based on ancient translation and modern research as encapsulated in the works of Robert Zoller and other leading predictive astrologers. Students also have direct access to the audio lectures, texts with diagrams and tables, an online library, ebooks, and articles. For full details, contact the registrar at contact@new-library.com.

## MEXICO

**Arc Node:** P.O. Box 2-1011, 44280 Guadalajara, Mexico. Tel.: +52 3823 3448/ +52 3585 8237/ +52 3585 8238. Email: invest.astrolog@megared.net.mx. Contacts: Emilio and Laura Perez Limòn.

## NETHERLANDS

**Academie voor Toegepaste Moderne Astrologie (ATMA):** Antoon van Elenstraat 88-C, 6217 JP Maastricht, The Netherlands. Director: Ben Thomassen. Tel.: +31 43 3472948. Courses.

**ACS (Astrology, Communication, Economics, van Straaten):** Vissenberg 19, 4714 AX Sprundel, The Netherlands. Director: Dr. Han van Straaten. Tel.: +31 165 387770. Fax: +31 165 388204. Email: acesastr@westbrabant.net. Website: www.interweb.nl/aces/. Advice and guidance for people and businesses in their process of growth.

**Adviesbureau Eon:** Plantage 15, 3742 DL Baarn, The Netherlands. Director: Onno Nieveen. Tel.: +31 35 5435338. Fax: +31 35 5435339. Email: info@eon-advies.nl. Website: www.eon-advies.nl/. Esoteric counseling service for organizations using (psychological) astrology, tarot and I Ching.

**Akademie voor Astrologie en Innerlijke Groei Charon:** 108 HS, 1057 HG Amsterdam, The Netherlands. Director: Adrie A van der Ven. van Speijkstraat. Tel.: +31 20 6830405. Email: venvries@compuserve. com. Vocational school for psychological, social, progressive, and medical astrology.

**Akademie voor Esoteriese Wetenschappen:** Graaf Adolfstraat 34, 9717 EG Groningen, The Netherlands. Director: Da Rocha Esteves Rolo. Tel.: +31 50 3186021. Vocational astrology school, lectures/workshops since 1979.

**Antares:** Wezenlaan 171, 6531 MN Nijmegen, The Netherlands. Director: Dr. Jose van Doorn. Tel.: +31 24 3556607. Email: antares@hetnet.nl. Vocational astrology school.

**Ascella Zuid:** Verdistraat 5, 5216 XG Aes-Hertogenbosch, The Netherlands. Director: Gerda E. Roos. Tel.: +31 73 6142221. Email: ascella.zuid@freeler.nl. Vocational astrology school.

**Astroconsult:** Dinant Dijkhuisstraat 12, 7558 GA Hengelo, The Netherlands. Director: Anneke Guis. Tel.: +31 74 2919229. Email: annekeguis@hetnet.nl. Astrology school and consultations.

**Astrologica:** Kanaal B zz 70, 7881 NC Emmer-Compascuum, The Netherlands. Director: Hans Leefkens. Tel.: +31 591 357957. Fax: +31 591 357958. Email: h.leefkens @hccnet.nl. Website: www.astrologica.nl/. Astrology school and consultations.

**Astrological Counseling Hermans:** Regentessestraat 9, 2713 EM Zoetermeer, The Netherlands. Director: Ton Hermans. Tel.: +31 79 3166793. Fax +31 79 3165097. Email: thermans@

wanadoo.nl. Website: www.home.wanadoo.nl/thermans/. Consultations, courses, and personal alphatraining.

**Astrological Star Service:** Val Orea II, nr. 49, 83120 Sainte Maxime, France. Director: Hans W. van Rossum. Tel.: +33 4 94961145. Email: Hans-Van.Rossum@wanadoo.fr. Consultations, courses, workshops, and lectures.

**Astrologie Vereniging Tweestromenland:** Kastanjehof 62, 6533 BX Nijmegen, The Netherlands. Tel.: +31 24 3501218. Email: leo.hunting@12move.nl. Lectures and workshops.

**Astrologisch Adviesbureau Gieles:** Karperdaal 147, 2553 PD Den Haag, The Netherlands. Director: Jan B. Gieles. Tel.: +31 70 3912593. Fax: +31 70 3970431. Email: gieles@wanadoo.nl. Website: www.gieles.com/. Consultations, courses, and monthly lectures.

**Astrologisch Adviesburo de Zon:** Tarwedreef 22, 3204 GR Spijkenisse, The Netherlands. Director: Frans P. D. Hollink. Tel.: +31 181 643131. Email: dezon@flakkee.net. Website: www.flakkee. net/dezon/. Consultations and private lessons.

**Astrologisch Centrum:** Mercatorsingel 68, 2803 ER Gouda, The Netherlands. Director: Nico J. Beens. Tel.: +31 182 518218. Fax: +31 182 678455. Courses.

**Astrologisch Genootschap Aquarius:** Grote Doelenlaan 35, 5491 ED Sint-Oedenrode, The Netherlands. Secretary: Jeanne Peters-Derks. Tel.: +31 413 474736. Email: jeanne.pd@planet.nl. Congress, workshops, and lectures.

**Astrologische Associatie (ASAS):** Den Texstr 32II, 1017 ZB Amsterdam, The Netherlands. Director: Lea Manders. Secretary: Faye Cossar. Tel.: +31 20 6206244. Fax: +31 20 6207710. Email: fcossar@bizzo.nl. Website: www.ASASastrologen.nl/. Association of professional astrologers. Founded April 29, 1996 at 23:30 CED.

**Astrologische Vakopleiding Nous:** Priemstraat 28, 6511 WC Nijmegen, The Netherlands. Director: Willem Kunst Tel.: +31 24 3605093. Email: nous@worldonline.nl. Website: www.home-3.worldonline.nl/~nous/. Vocational astrology school, courses, lectures, and consultations.

**Astrologische Vakvereniging Nederland (AVN):** Prof. Dondersstraat 28, 1221 HN Hilversum, The Netherlands. Director: Carol van de Hoorn. Tel.: +31 35 6831412. Email: info@avn-astrologie.nl. Website: www.avn-astrologie.nl/. Association for professional astrologers, monthly lectures.

**Astrologische Vereniging Eindhoven (AVE):** Weegbreestraat 3, 6026 TA Maarheeze, The Netherlands. Tel.: +31 495 592124. Founded May 11, 1981, at 19:39 GMT in Eindhoven. Monthly lectures; publishes *AVE-Kroniek*.

**Astrologische Vereniging Oost Nederland AstrOn Enschede:** Tel.: +31 74 2919229. Email: annekeguis@hetnet.nl. Secretary: Anneke Guis. Astrological lectures since January 14, 2000.

**Athelas Astrologische Dienstverlening:** Marga Klompelaan 57, 5122 BP Rijen, The Netherlands. Director: A. Aukes. Tel.: +31 161 293145. Email: info@athelas.nl. Website: www.athelas.nl/. Astrology courses, astrological aids, and consultations.

**Aurinko Astrologie Beroepsopleiding Enschede-Heerenveen:** Zuiderkruisstraat 17, 7521 DH Enschede, The Netherlands. Director: Hans Planje. Tel.: +31 53 4350084. Margreet Andriol, Schoterlandseweg 22, 8455 JG Katlijk. Tel.: +31 513 541843 (only in Heerenveen) and Karin Kuijper, Welborchlanden 9, 7542 XH Enschede. Tel.: +31 53 4782358 (only in Enschede). Vocational astrology school.

**Bosch Astrologisch Genootschap (BAG):** Clarastraat 120, 5211 LB Den Bosch, The Netherlands. Secretary: Annemiek Cox. Tel.: +31 73 6136938. Email: a.cox@wxs.nl. Lectures/work shops.

**Capricornus:** Socratesstraat 68, 7323 PH Apeldoorn, The Netherlands. Director: Barbara van Oosterzee. Tel.: +31 55 3668737. Email: b.oosterzee@hccnet.nl. Website: www.capricornus.nl/. Courses in Apeldoorn and Hattum.

**Centrum voor Humanistische & Transpersoonlijke Astrologie (CHTA):** DFAstrolS, Oudewand 19, 7201 LJ Zutphen, The Netherlands. Director: Joyce Hoen. Tel.: +31 575 516479. Email: chta@astrologie.ws. Website: www. astrologie.ws/. Workshops, lectures, and courses. Astrology course also via email.

**Chocmah (de Sfeer van de Zodiac):** Houtlaan 9, 6525 ZA Nijmegen, The Netherlands. Director: Leo Hunting. Tel.: +31 24 3551490. Email: leo.hunting@12move.nl. Website: home-1. wolmail. nl/~cmack/leo/. Vocational astrology school.

**Committee for Objective Research into Astrology (CORA):** De Bese 9, 7722 PD Dalfsen, The Netherlands. Contact: Rudolf H.Smit. Tel./Fax: +31 529 427022. Advice and help regarding research into astrology.

**Cursus-en Opleidingscentrum Ishatar:** Onyx 9, 2719 SG Zoetermeer, The Netherlands. Director: Peter Saarloos. Tel.: +31 79 3617345. Email: info@ishtar.nl. Website: www.ishtar.nl/. Astrology school, courses.

**Dirah Academy International:** Brunostraat 64-B, 5042 JA Tilburg, The Netherlands. Director: Roeland M. de Looff. Tel.: +31 13 4635468. Email: roeland@dirah.org. Website: www.dirah. org/. Institute for Western and Vedic astrology and Astro-Energetics.

**Equilibra:** Schuwacht 322, 2931 BB Krimpen aan de Lek, The Netherlands. Director: Dr Fred Opmeer. Tel.: +31 180 520692. Fax: +31 180 520369. Email: opmeer@ knoware.nl. Website: www.equilibra.nl/. Astrological compatibility and relationship counseling agency; counseling service for business and personal problems.

**Federatie van Astrologische Groeperingen in het Nederlands Taalgebied (FAG):** Prof. Dondersstraat 28, 1221 HN Hilversum, The Netherlands. Tel.: +31 35 6831412. Email:

cc.vd.hoorn@hccnet.nl. Founded April 5, 1981 at 13:00 CED in Soesterberg. Twice yearly meetings.

**Instituut Phoenix:** J. Israelsstraat 34, 9718 GL Groningen, The Netherlands. Director: Berni Thomassen. Tel.: +31 50 3130526. Email: zon@home.nl. Astrology school.

**Instituut voor Holistische Astrologie:** Jac Romansstraat 9, 2321 EX Leiden, The Netherlands. Director: Lydia A. Grevelink-v.d. Erve, Tel.: +31 71 5765620. Courses.

**Inzicht Astrologisch Studie Centrum Goes:** Beukenstraat 159, 4462 TS Goes, The Netherlands. Director: Jopie C. M. Martens. Tel./Fax: +31 113 233115. Email: jopie.martens@wxs.nl. Website: www.home.wanadoo.nl/jopiemartens/. Vocational astrology school, workshops, courses (incl by mail), lectures, and consultations.

**Jupiter:** Keizersgracht 248F, 1016 EV Amsterdam, The Netherlands. Director: Agnes Geveke. Tel.: +31 20 6384148. Vocational astrology school.

**De Kosmische Kring:** Fazantenweg 60-II, 1021 HP Amsterdam, The Netherlands. Director: Marja Winters. Tel./Fax: +31 20 6324130.

**Mellie Uyldert Stichting:** P. J. Lomanlaan 7, 1405 BK Bussum, The Netherlands. Tel.: +31 35 6940423. Lectures and workshops.

**Nederlands Astrologen Congres (NAC):** Mercatorsingel 68, 2803 ER Gouda, The Netherlands. Tel.: +31 182 518218 or +31 75 6401230. Fax: +31 182 678455 or +31 75 6401075. Email: astrocent@ cistron.nl or a.vermist@cable.a2000.nl. Website: www.astrologencongres.nl/. Organizes yearly congress in Soesterberg.

**Nederlandse Vereniging tot Wetenschappelijk Onderzoek v d Astrologie (NVWOA; Dutch Society for Scientific Research into Astrology):** Kasaidreef 19, 3564 AS Utrecht, The Netherlands. Director: Floris J. Methorst. Tel./Fax: +31 30 2617723. Email: lexbruin@worldonline.nl. Website: www.home.worldonline.nl/~lexbruin/index.htm. Monthly lectures and astrological research.

**Opleidingscentrum Astra voor Astrologie en Levensloopanalyse:** Lessinglaan 63, 3533 AT Utrecht, The Netherlands. Director: W. J. M. (Minou) van Hemert. Tel.: +31 30 2966030. Vocational astrology school.

**Persephone: Astrologisch Vormingscentrum:** Klaverstraat 5, 9404 GV Assen, The Netherlands. Director: Karin Klopmeyer. Tel.: +31 592 310160. Website: www.welcome.to/persephone/. Vocational astrology school.

**Rafael Centrum voor Natuurlijke Geneeswijzen:** Kruegerplein 21 hs, 1092 KA Amsterdam, The Netherlands. Director: Wim C. Weehuizen-White Eagle Tel.: +31 20 6942800. Lectures and courses in medical astrology.

**School voor Astrologie:** Metzelaarplein 5, 7416 BV Deventer, The Netherlands. Director: Hermine Merlijn-Hermkens. Tel.: +31 570 636503. Vocational astrology school.

**School voor Klassieke Astrologie:** Oude Arnhemseweg 29, 3702 BA Zeist, The Netherlands. Director: Martien Hermes. Tel./Fax: +31 30 6911642. Email: mahermes@worldonline.nl. Vocational astrology school.

**School voor Toegepaste Astrologie:** Clarastraat 148, 5211 LB Den Bosch, The Netherlands. Director: Threes Brouwers. Tel.: +31 73 6142811. Vocational astrology school.

**Semangat Astrology School:** Beethovenlaan 140, 6865 EE Doorwerth, The Netherlands. Director: A. (Lyke) Bagaya. Tel.: +31 26 3338147. Email: semangat@wish.net. Vocational astrology school, courses, workshops, consultations, and psychoanalytical hypnotherapy.

**Spiritueel Centrum Chiron:** Spinner 36, 1625 VC Hoorn, The Netherlands. Director: Luise Vandemeer. Tel./Fax: +31 229 239827. Email: astron@lvandemeer.demon.nl. 4/5 year holistic astrology school and workshops.

**Stichting Achernar:** Amsterdamseweg 479, 1181 BR Amstelveen, The Netherlands. Director: Karen M. Hamaker-Zondag. Tel.: +31 20 6436979. Fax: +31 20 6417310. Email: symbolon @wxs.nl. Website: www.symbolon.nl/. Vocational astrology school.

**Stichting Ascella:** Abel Tasmankade 29, 2014 AD Haarlem, The Netherlands. Director: J. F. C. M. (Hannie) Vermeulen-Vriend. Tel.: +31 23 5242356. Email: stichting.ascella@ worldon line.nl. Vocational astrology school.

**Stichting Astrologisch Studie Centrum (ASC):** Vechtstraat 77-I, 1079 JA Amsterdam, The Netherlands. Director: Roland M. M. Hepp. Tel.: +31 20 6612433. Fax: +31 20 6440913. Email: ASC@cistron. nl. Astrology school.

**Stichting Astrologische Bibliotheek Centrale (A.B.C.):** Vechtstraat 77-I, 1079 JA Amsterdam, The Netherlands. Director: Roland M. M. Hepp. Tel.: +31 20 6612433.Fax: +31 20 6440913. Email: ASC@cistron.nl.

**Stichting Astro-Visie:** v. Ruysdaellaan 32-A, 3117 XS Schiedam, The Netherlands. Director: Henk Verhoef. Tel.: +31 10 4263292. Courses.

**Stichting Capella:** Venlosingel 209, 6845 JS Arnhem, The Netherlands. Director: Rene Jelsma. Tel.: +31 26 8441956. Email: rljelsma@hotmail.com. Courses, lectures, and workshops.

**Stichting Democratisering Wetenschap en Astrologie (DWA):** Koningsweg 45, 3742 ET Baarn, The Netherlands. Director: Tom de Booij. Tel.: +31 35 5412852. Fax: +31 35 5415980. Email: geopol@worldonline.nl. Founded April 12, 2001 in Baarn. Lectures, publications, and projects to build a bridge between the exact and esoteric sciences.

**Stichting Harmonia Universalis:** Waterlooplein 51, 1011 PB Amsterdam, The Netherlands. Director: Robert D. Doolaard. Tel.: +31 20 6230442.

**Stichting Inspiratie:** Zuwe 32, 2411 ZK Bodegraven, The Netherlands. Director: Jan G. de Graaf. Tel./Fax: +31 172 616363. Email: jang@inspiratiesite.nl. Website: www.inspiratiesite.nl/. Astrotherapy, intuitive astrology and process support, vocational astrology school, workshops, and Astro Cards.

**Stichting Olivijn:** Moutlaan 57, 6681 GX Bemmel, The Netherlands. Director: Marlies van Riel. Tel.: +31 481 463788. Workshops.

**Stichting Opleidingen Astrologie (STOA):** Stroomerlaan 1, 1861 TJ, Bergen (NH), The Netherlands. Tel.: +31 72 58944 56. Email: JenB.Moerbeek@inter.nl.net. Correspondence-course astrology WVA-system.

**Stichting School der Universele Wijsheid:** Postbus 38315, 6503 AH Nijmegen, The Netherlands. Director: Harry A. J. Rump. Tel.: +31 24 3440084. Fax: +31 24 3453033. Lectures, workshops, and courses.

**Stichting Osiris:** Minderbroedersingel 39, 6041 KH Roermond, The Netherlands. Director: Kunnie Gras. Tel.: +31 475 337460. Fax: +31 475 337431. Lectures, workshops, and courses.

**Stichting Skepsis-Astrology Workgroup:** Lederambachtstraat 119, 1069 HM Amsterdam, The Netherlands. Director: Wout Heukelom. Tel./Fax: +31 20 6194457. Email: r.nanninga @wxs.nl. Astrology research.

**Stichting Synthese:** Molvense Erven 200, 5672 HR Nuenen, The Netherlands. Director: Ingrid Rosso. Tel.: +31 40 2838139. Vocational astrology school.

**Stichting Vrienden van het Landhuis:** Vechtstraat 77-I, 1079 JA Amsterdam, The Netherlands. Director: Roland M. M. Hepp. Tel.: +31 20 6612433. Fax +31 20 6440913. Email: ASC@cistron.nl. Organizers of annual fall congress in Oldenzaal.

**Stichting Werkgemeenschap van Astrologen (WVA):** Postbus 13131, 3507 LC Utrecht, The Netherlands. Tel.: +31 10 4532708. Fax: +31 10 4531876. Email: stichtingwva@geocities.com. Website: www. geocities.com/stichtingwva/. Monthly lectures and vocational astrology school.

**Vakopleiding Psychologische Astrologie Apeldoorn:** Vosselmanstraat 299, 7311 CL Apeldoorn, The Netherlands. Director: Liesbeth van Ravenhorst. Tel.: +31 26 3635977. Email: E.van.Ravenhorst@hetnet. nl. Vocational astrology school, courses, workshops, consultations, and lectures.

**Vakopleiding voor Praktische en Toegepaste Astrologie de Verbinding:** Postbus 2354, 7301 EB Apeldoorn, The Netherlands. Director: Frank R Schouten. Tel.: +31 55 3558969. Vocational astrology school.

**Vakopleiding voor Psychologische en Toegepaste Astrologie:** Mr P. J. Oudsingel 114, 6836 PT Arnhem, The Netherlands. Director: Lea R Manders. Tel.: +31 26 3231818. Fax: 31 26

3235609. Email: astrologe-lea. manders@planet.nl. Website: www.AstrologeLeaManders.nl/. Vocational astrology school, consultations, courses, and lectures.

**Vereniging van Astrologen Noord Nederland (VVANN):** Oudeweg 4, 9711 AA Groningen, The Netherlands. Director: N. Helder. Tel.: +31 50 3184911. Email: vvann@home.nl. Lectures.

**Vlot & Van Diepen:** Het Gangwerk 34, 1622 HB Hoorn, The Netherlands. Tel.: +31 229 233733. Vocational astrology school.

**Werkgemeenschap Praktische Astrologie:** Cederstraat 156, 2565 JS Den Haag, The Netherlands. Director: Johanna J. A. Winter. Tel.: +31 70 3630184. School for horary astrology.

**Werkgroep voor Kosmobiologisch Onderzoek (WKO):** Dunantstraat 592, 2713 XD Zoetermeer, The Netherlands. Director: A. J. (Dries) Hoorn. Tel.: +31 79 3164400. Email: dhoorn @box.nl. Founded October 7, 1971 at 13:15 (12:15 GMT) in The Hague. Bi-monthly meetings and mini-congress.

## NEW ZEALAND

**Academy of Predictive Astrology:** Offers advanced Internet-based and correspondence courses that lead to both certificate and diploma. Unlike many other schools, it pays special attention to the different emphasis that is needed when teaching astrology in the Southern Hemisphere. The Academy also works closely with the prestigious Astrology House based in Auckland. The course work is based on ancient translations and modern research as encapsulated in the works of Robert Zoller and other leading predictive astrologers. Many of the techniques that have been uncovered by the Academy are added to the advanced New Zealand astrological software Janus. Students have direct access to the audio lectures, texts with diagrams and tables, an online library, ebooks, and articles. For full details, contact the registrar at contact@new-library.com

**Astrology Correspondence School:** P.O. Box 31-210, Milford, Auckland 1309, New Zealand. Contact principal: Carol Squires. Tel.: +64 9 410 0097. Fax: +64 9 410 0090. Email: caros@ astrologyschool.com. Established in 1983. Tuition by correspondence for beginner, intermediate, and advanced levels. Day/evening classes and regular workshops. For up-to-date information on astrology courses, classes, services, manuals, articles, and time changes in Australia and New Zealand visit www.astrologyschool.com.

**Astrology Foundation Incorporated:** 41 New North Rd., Eden Terrace, Auckland 1003, New Zealand. Tel./Fax: +64 9 373 5304. President: Hamish Saunders. Founded November 7, 1983 at 11.47 A.M. NZDT by Owen Redwood Avis. Granted legal incorporation on November 24, 1984. Honorary Secretary/treasurer: Lianne Plant. The AFI is a friendly non-profit society providing a stimulating environment for those with an interest in astrology. Runs courses for beginners and advanced students. Regular Sunday meetings, library, journals, tapes, and computer services.

**Astrology House:** 41 New North Rd., Eden Terrace, Auckland, New Zealand. Tel./Fax: + 64 9 373 5304. Email: janus-nz@ihug.co.nz. Website: www.astrologyhouse.co.nz/. Astrology House was established in Auckland at the end of 1979 and officially opened at 6:30 P.M. on June 25, 1980. Founded by Owen Redwood Avis, Hamish Saunders, and Mark Griffin with the intention to raise the standard of professional astrological practice in New Zealand. In 1994, Angela Thomas joined Astrology House as a full-time consulting astrologer. Avis studied with Reinhold Ebertin in Germany during the 1950s and learned the astrological system of cosmobiology from him. While cosmobiology is the principal astrological system used at Astrology House, traditional methods of astrology are also employed. The main business of Astrology House is to prepare and interpret personal astrological charts for individuals. Since 1980, Astrology House has built up a clientele numbering in excess of 13,000. They also are the developers and manufacturers of the internationally acclaimed astrological software program, Janus. In addition to client work, Astrology House works closely with the Astrology Foundation. Astrology House and the AFI share the same address and contact details.

**Astrological Society of New Zealand (ASNZ):** P.O. Box 5266, Wellesley St., Auckland C1, New Zealand. Tel.: +64 9 480 8019. Contact: Bernard Honey. Email: clearavu@ihug.co.nz. Formed on July 26, 1973, the society was incorporated on May 8, 1974 at 10.50 A.M. in Wellington. Publishes the quarterly *Journal of the Seasons*.

**Kenobi Networks NZ:** 43 Whatipu Rd., Little Huia, Waitakere Eco City, Auckland, New Zealand. Tel./Fax: +53 9 827 6869. Email: kenobi1@slingshot.co.nz. Founder: Stephen Hill. Publisher of *Palden Jenkins' Historical Ephemeris* (1993). The focus of Kenobi Networks is historical time cycle correlation and motivational futurism. Twenty-five years in astrology.

## NORWAY

**Norwegian Astrological Association:** P.O. Box 1432 Vika, 0115 Oslo, Norway. Tel./Fax: +47 23 38 99 86. Email: astrofor@email.com. Website: www.astrofor.freehomepages.com. Chairman: Knut A. Johnsen. Runs conferences, seminars, workshops, and meetings. Courses for beginners and intermediate students. First meeting January 24, 1980 at 6 P.M. LMT in Oslo. Has arranged the Norwegian Astrology Conference since 1981 and has published the quarterly journal *Astrologisk Forum* since 1983.

## POLAND

**Studio Astropsychologii:** Janusz Nawrocki, 15-762 Biatystok ul Antoniuk Fabryczny 55, 15-950 Biatystok 2 Skrytka Pocztowa 42, Poland. Tel./Fax: (0 85) 654 78 35, (0 85) 653 13 03, (0 85) 653 06 51. Email: biuro@studioastro.com.pl. Website: www.studio astro.com.pl/.

## PORTUGAL

**Jose Prudencio:** Apartado 6110, 1601-901 Lisboa, Tel.: +351 966 036 719. Email: joseprudencio @mail.telepac.pt. Director of Olisippos-Instituto de Astrologia de Lisboa. Philosophical and hermetical astrology. Courses for psychologists and psychiatrists.

## RUSSIA

**Academy of Astrology:** Office 307, 26, 7-th Parkovaya st 105264, Moscow, Russia. Tel.: +7 095 164 9734. Email: astro-academia@mtu-net.ru. Rector: Levin Michail. Founded in 1990. Education (evening, correspondence), consultations, and scientific research.

**Academy of Global Astrology and Metainformation:** Box 71, Moscow 115561, Russia. Tel./Fax: +7 095 392 7606. Email: astrology@ mtu-net.ru. Website: astrol.ru. Founded in 1997. President: Boris Boyko. Educational body (has state educational license for teaching astrology). Classes: Western astrology, Hindu astrology, and Tibetan astrology. Special classes on Western Traditional astrology. Correspondence courses on Western and Hindu astrology. Publishing house. Quarterly magazine *Kalacakra—The Wheel of Time* (articles on Western and Eastern astrology and cultural interrelationship). International congresses and schools. Scientific council for receiving degrees in astrology (in cooperation with Russian Academy of Natural Sciences).

**Institute of Practical Astrology (IPA):** Tel.: +7 095 264 73 47. Email: naasipa@online.ru. Website: www.ipa.f2s.com/. Director: Sergey Kurapov. IPA was created in 1995 in Moscow. The Institute does research work, produces astrological computer programs, teaches astrology, and offers personal and organizational consultations.

**League of Independent Astrologers:** Domodedovskaya St., 6-2, apt 59, Moscow 115569, Russia. Tel./Fax: +7 095 392 7606. Email: astrol@astrol.ru. Website: www.astrol.ru. Founded in 1992, the League has over 1,800 members in Russia and former Soviet Union. President: Karine Dilanyan. Head of council: Boris Boyko. Astrological education, international conferences and schools, largest astrological public library in Russia, computer service, publishing house, research, network, and quarterly information bulletin—*Wheel of Time Herald*.

**Moscow Astrology Research Centre (MARC):** P.O. Box 373, 103064, Moscow, Russia. Tel.: +7 095 261 1806. Tel./Fax: +7 095 261 3948. Email: astrol.str@relcom.ru. Website: www.astrolog.ru. Founded in 1991. School of Classical Astrology (SCA) founded in 1994. Director: Nikolay Strachuk. Online astrocollege: www.astrocollege.ru. MARC-SCA is the largest astrological organization of the former Soviet Union. Evening classes, correspondence courses, online courses, workshops of leading Russian and foreign astrologers, publishing house, specialized book shop, online book shop, service "books by post," bimonthly *Esotherical Herald*, electronic version of *Herald*. Annual International Astrological Conference "Uranus in Aquarius."

**Sanct-Peterburg's Astrological Academy:** Sergey Shestopalov, Chudnovsky st 13, Sanct-Peterburg, 193318 Russia. Tel.: +7 812 580 03 59. Email: sergol13@mail.ru. Rector: Sergey Shestopalov. Founded October 5, 1989. Direction of academy is scientific astrology. Academy has several filials in Russia, Latvia, Estonia, Ukraine. Activities: education, production of computer programmes, consulting, and publications.

**Urania Charity Foundation:** Office 2, Maliy Zlatoustinsky per 8, Moscow 101000, Russia. Tel./Fax: +7 095 924 7124. Email: Urania.Russia@g23.relcom.ru.

**Urania Magazine:** Organizes lectures and workshops on esoteric disciplines with domestic and foreign teachers. Has a center for astrological and psychological consultations. Holds Annual International Urania Congress. Email: urania@antonyan.msk.ru.

## SLOVENIA

**Astrološki Inštitut Matjaža Regovca—Ljubljana Institute for Psychological Astrology (AIMR):** Founder and director: Matjaž Regovec. Contact: The Secretary, AIMR, Cesta XXX/13, 1260 Ljubljana Polje, Slovenia. Tel./Fax: +3861 529 14 14. Email: astroloski.institut@siol.net. Founded in 1993, AIMR focuses on qualitative and in-depth education in psychological astrology. Offers an introductory one-year education program that may lead to the three-year professional diploma training in psychological astrology. Institute's diploma (Dipl Astrol IMR) may be issued upon completion of 50 seminars, 150 supervision hours, at least 50 hours of therapy, and completion of diploma thesis.

## SOUTH AFRICA

**Astrological Institute of Research and Studies:** P.O. Box 10235, Rivonia 2128, South Africa. Tel.: (+27 11) 803 1971. Fax: (+27 11) 807 1071. Email: airs@icon.co.za. Three distance-taught astrology courses are offered (foundation, diploma, or higher diploma) as well as other specialized courses.

**Astrological Society of South Africa (ASSA):** P.O. Box 1953, Saxonwold 2132, South Africa. Contact: Elena van Baalen. Tel.: +21 0 11 646 3670. Fax: +21 0 11 646 5477. Email: elena@kallback.co. za. Website: www.naturalhealth.co.za/assoc/ass_216.html. The Society is seeking to establish relationships with astrologers overseas to facilitate the exchange of information. Produces monthly magazine *Aspects*.

**Astrology Services South Africa:** Contact: Monica Cromhout. P.O. Box 3777, Somerset West 7129, South Africa. Tel.: +27 0 21 852 4728. Fax: +21 0 21 851 2592. Email: astrolog@iafrica.com. Website: www.AstrologyServices.netfirms.com. Promoting astrology in South Africa. Astrology training. Astrology bookseller. Organizers of astrology-related events. Distribution of information to the media, and to astrology students and professionals. Lists professional astrologers. Agents for SolarFire astrological software and *Mountain Astrologer* magazine.

## SOUTH AMERICA

**Academy of Predictive Astrology:** Offers Internet-based and/or correspondence courses leading to both certificate and diploma. The work is based on ancient translation and modern research as encapsulated in the works of Robert Zoller and other leading predictive astrologers. Students also have direct access to the audio lectures, texts with diagrams and tables, an online library, ebooks, and articles. For full details, contact the registrar at contact@new-library.com.

## SPAIN

**Escuela de Astrologia Juan Estadella:** Apdo de Correos no 2.900, 08080-Barcelona, Spain. Contact: Juan Estadella. Tel.: +34 3 395 0956/ (93) 456 24 74. Fax: +34 3 395 5300. Email:

sumitros.cem@retemail.es. Astrological school (basic and advanced courses), conferences, and seminars.

**Escuela Española Huber de Astrologia:** Apartado Correos 96.033, 08080 Barcelona (Spain). Contact: Rosa Solé. Tel.: +34 934 152 530. Email: info@escuelahuber.org. Websites: www.ncsa.es/eschuber.sch and www.escuelahuber.org.

**Gaia:** Apartado de Correos 37109 28080 Madrid (España), Spain. Email: grupo_ gaia@lugar.de. Tel.: +34 91 3262069 - +34 91 3205556. Website: www.arrakis. es/~anagon/gaia.htm.

## SWEDEN

**Skandinavisk Astrologi Skole:** Skolegade 12A, Postboks 319, 2500 Valby, Sweden. Tel.: +45 36 45 0545. Course leader: Karl Aage Jensen in Kobenhavn. Tel.: +45 3645 0545. Fax: +45 3645 0552. Email: horoskop@astrologihuset.dk. Website: www.astrologihuset.dk The students begin with two years of basic education, followed by two years of diploma education, and then a one-year extended professional education where students learn how to write, lecture, teach, and receive media training. Publishes quarterly magazine *Horoskopet*.

## SWITZERLAND

**Astroclub Zurich:** Liduina Schmed-Kik, Hofwiesenstr. 240, CH-8057 Zürich, Switzerland. Email: liduina@compuserve.com. Website: www.astro-club.ch

**Astrodata AG:** Albisriederstrasse 232, CH-8047 Zürich, Switzerland. Tel.: +41 1 492 1515. Fax: +41 1 492 1516. Email: info@astrodata.ch. Website: www.astrodata.ch/. Offers correspondence, evening and weekend courses, and summer schools both in Switzerland and Germany (in Berlin and Munich). Runs the largest astrological calculation service in Europe with a wide range of chart services and computer prepared reports. Publishes the bimonthly magazine *Astrologie Heute*.

**Astrodienst AG:** Dammstrasse 23, Postfach Station, CH-8702 Zollikon/ Zürich. Director: Alois Treindl. Tel.: +41 1 392 1818. Fax: +41 1 391 7574. Offers workshops/seminars with Liz Greene. Website: www.astro.com.

**Astrologisch-Psychologisches Institut:** Obertilistr. 4, CH-8134 Adliswil/ZH, Switzerland. Tel.: +41 1 710 3776. Fax: +41 1 710 3786. Email: Huber_API@compuserve.com. International school in astrological psychology since 1968, with branches in England, South Africa, Spain, Hungary, and the United States. Offers a professional training in a wide range of classes, courses and seminars, and in a correspondence school in English, German, and Spanish languages with a three-year counseling training to diploma level. It also produces a bimonthly magazine *Astrolog* and a series of books on astrological psychology, translated into English and 11 different languages.

**API International:** Postfach 614, CH-8134 ADLISWIL, Switzerland. Professional association for the support and protection of astro-psychological counselors and therapists. Membership 600 in 2001.

**Integrative Astrologie:** Mainaustrasse 28, CH-8008 Zurich, Switzerland. Contact: Frank Sperdin. Tel./Fax: +41 1 380 64 00. Email: frank@sperdin.ch. Website: www.sperdin.ch. Teaching, counseling, and vocational guidance.

**Schule für Erwachsene (SFER):** Albisriederstrasse 232, Postfach, CH-8047 Zürich. Contacts: Claude Weis, Verena Bachmann. Tel.: +41 1 400 53 73. Fax: +41 1 400 53 74. Email: info@sfer.ch. Website: www.sfer.ch. Psychological astrology school.

**Schweizer Astrologen-Bund (SAB):** Postfach 331, CH-8042 Zürich. Tel.: +41 1 700 1012. Fax: +41 1 700 1610, and Chilenholzstrasse 8, CH-8907 Wettswil. Email: info@astrologen-bund.ch. Website: www.astrologenbund.ch. President: Claude Weiss. The major national astrological organization.

## THAILAND

**Planetary Gemologists Association:** 99/22 Soi 7 Lang Suan Rd., Lumpini, Bangkok 10330, Kingdom of Thailand, Tel.: +66 2 252 1230. Fax: +66 2 252 1231. Email: info@p-g-a.org. Website: www.p-g-a.org.

## TURKEY

**Academy of Predictive Astrology:** The only Western school of astrology that caters in particular for students in Turkey who wish to learn the ancient traditions of the West. It offers Internet-based and/or correspondence courses leading to both certificate and diploma. The work is based on ancient translation from leading scholars and astrologers of the West and the East. Students also have direct access to the audio lectures, texts with diagrams and tables, an online library, ebooks, and articles. For full details, contact the registrar at contact@new-library.com.

**Astrological Association of Turkey:** Ferit Tek Sokak, Sönmezler Apt, B Blok, D2, K1, Moda, Istanbul, Turkey. Tel.: +90 212 287 74 37. Email: kirkoglu@superonline.com or gany@turk.net. Group Prometheus transformed itself into the Astrological Association of Turkey on June 11, 2000 at 11:23 A.M. in Istanbul. The Association has a center in the Asian part of Istanbul. Monthly seminars, *The 11th House* (Turkish newsletter for members), and an education program has been carried out since June 2000.

## UKRAINE

**Kiev's Astrological Club:** Contact: Maya Syneokaya. Email: mai@noo. kiev.ua. Tel.: +38 044 5728 513. Administrator: Olena P. Yushchenko. Tel.: +38 044 5195 770. Founded in November 1997. Main activities of the Club are: popularization of astrology, consulting services, experience exchange with other groups, and upgrading of the professional level of the club's members.

## UNITED KINGDOM

**Academy of Predictive Astrology:** New Library London, 27 Old Gloucester St., London WC1N 3XX, England. Email: contact@new-library.com. Specializes in predictive techniques.

A horoscope may tell you what is promised (this is delineation) but the other part of the puzzle that requires consummate skill, is the discovery of when it will happen (this is predictive technique). The course also addresses related topics such as the philosophical exploration of fate vs. Free will, magic, and alchemy. The certificate and diploma courses draw on ancient practice to teach students sound delineation and proper predictive technique. The courses are suitable for the absolute beginner, through to the experienced practitioner. Students have direct access to the teaching of the leading exponent in predictive and medieval astrology, Robert Zoller. They also have access to an online library, ebooks, printed publications, articles, and research papers not generally distributed to the public. Students can also take part in lectures and communicate with tutors by Internet. The Academy also publishes the *Predictive Astrology Bulletin* and *Academy Papers*.

**Advisory Panel on Astrological Education (APAE):** 60 Ivydale Rd., London, SE15 3BS. APAE monitors standards and qualifications in the teaching of astrology. Any person concerned about astrological education or the provision of astrological teaching in their area can have copies of this letter to forward on. APAE represents the major astrological organizations and teaching bodies in UK astrology.

**Association of Professional Astrologers:** Box No. AJI, 80 High St., Wargrave, Berks RG10 8DE, England. Tel.: 01189 404424. Fax: 01189 404858. Email: maureen@ravenhall.fsnet.co.uk. Press Officer: Peta High, Tel.: 0181 498 9850.

**Astrologer's Apprentice:** Tel.: +44 (0) 20 8365 2553 or Email: j@apprentice.demon.co.uk. Website: www.apprentice.demon.co.uk. Offers top level vocational training in traditional astrology (horary, natal, and electional) and studying with John Frawley, author of *The Real Astrology* (winner of the Spica Award for International Book of the Year 2001). Correspondence courses by post or email, or private classes.

**Astrological Association (AA):** Unit 168, Lee Valley Technopark, Tottenham Hale, London N17 9LN, England. Tel.: 020-8880-4848. Fax: 020-8880- 4849. Email: astrological.association @zetnet.co.uk Website: http://www.astrologer.com/aanet. Founded June 21, 1958, 19.22 hrs. GMT, London. The outstanding international astrological organization and the main coordinating body in British astrology. It maintains close links with all the major astrological organizations in Britain and around the world. Membership is open to all levels of interest from students to professionals. The AA publishes the bimonthly *Astrological Journal*, the academic level biannual research journal *Correlation*, the newsletter *Transit*, and specialist newsletters on medical astrology and midpoints through its Special Interest Networks.

**Astrological Library Association (ALA):** Current members are the Heart Center, the Star Centre Library, and the Urania Trust. The ALA was formed to encourage cooperation and exchange of holdings and databases between astrological libraries. Network members are planning seminars with ALA members in the near future.

**Astrological Lodge of London (ALL):** 50 Gloucester Place, London W1H 3HJ, England. The Lodge, which is a registered charity, was founded by the modern father of English astrology, Alan Leo, on July 13, 1915, at 19.15 hrs. GMT in North London, and for many years was under the presidency of the great Charles E. O. Carter and Ronald C. Davison. Historically it is the parent body of the Faculty of Astrological Studies, the Astrological Association, and more recently the Company of Astrologers. Its journal, *Astrology Quarterly*, more commonly known as the *Quarterly*, is one of the finest in the field.

**Astrological Psychology Institute (UK):** P.O. Box 118, Knutsford, Cheshire, WA16 8TG, England. Tel./Fax: +44 (0) 1656 651131. Email: huberschool@btinternet.com. Website: www.api-uk.org is the English branch of Bruno and Louise Huber's influential API based in Switzerland. Formerly the English Huber School, it was founded June 8, 1983, at 12:30 P.M. in London by Richard Llewellyn. Principal: Joyce Hopewell. Teaches a psychological and counseling approach to astrology throughout the English-speaking world, via well-structured correspondence courses, local classes, weekend and one-day seminars and workshops, and an annual residential summer school, "Face to Face." Details of Astrological Chart Data Service from API Chart Data Service, P.O. Box 29, Upton, Wirral, CH49 3BG, England. Tel.: +44 (0) 151 606 8551. Email: r.llewellyn@btinternet.com.

**Astrological Society (UK):** Contact: Peter Howarth, 17 Westbury Rd., Crumpsall, Manchester M8 6RX, England. Tel.: 0161-795-2614. Founded to promote the recognition and development of the Sidereal Body of Man. The Society is interested in the practical value of astrology in daily life through using the astrological framework to deepen understanding of the world and practicing astrological meditation. It actively promotes astrological research including applying the fundamental laws of astrology to the galactic rather than the zodiacal plane.

**Birmingham Astrological Centre:** 22 Denham Court, Park Approach, Erdington, Birmingham, B23 7XZ, England. Email: astro_rainbow@hotmail.com. Website: www.livingnet.co.uk/geminitransformations. Four-year professional courses in astrology, incorporating spiritual and psychological approaches to chart interpretation, plus one-year courses on karmic astrology and the asteroid goddesses.

**Brighton College of Technology:** Tutor: Paul Wade. Tel.: +44 (0) 1273 736491 or Paul Wade on +44 (0) 1435 813479 Website: www.astrologywizard.com. Three years of part-time evening study towards nationally recognized Open College Network GCSE and A-level equivalent accreditation. Comprises introductory studies, intermediate level, and advanced level courses, each lasting for one academic year.

**British Association for Vedic Astrology (BAVA):** Chair: Konilla Sutton. 1 Greenwood Close, Romsey, S051 7QT, England. Tel.: +44 (0) 1794 524178. Email: Komilla.Sutton@btinternet.com. For details of courses, contact membership secretary Rowland Elliott, 52 Church St., Epsom, Surrey, KT17 4DN, England. Tel.: 01372 721047. Email: Rowland2@onetel.net.uk. Website: www.bava.org. Founded at 22:12 hrs. on December 16, 1996 at Romsey, Hampshire, by Vedic astrologers Andrew Foss and Komilla Sutton. Monthly meetings at the

Theosophical Society, 50 Gloucester Place, London. Publishes biannual journal *Gochara*. Yearly conference in September.

**British Astrological and Psychic Society (BAPS):** P.O. Box 363, Rochester, ME1 3DJ, England. Tel.: 0906 4700827. Fax: 01634 323006. Email: info@baps.ws. Founded on March 11, 1976, 19:56 hrs. GMT in Acton, to provide a means of bringing together those working in, or interested in learning about, the many different fields of esoteric study, especially astrology, palmistry, numerology, and various psychic disciplines. BAPS is the only organization that operates a consultant-vetting procedure and publishes a register of approved consultants in disciplines other than astrology. It pursues an educational policy through consultant workshops, lectures, educational institutes, and local groups. Quarterly journal *The Mercury* is free to members or available by annual subscription.

**Centre for Psychological Astrology (CPA):** BCM Box 1815, London, WC1N 3XX, England. Tel./Fax: +44 (0) 20 8749 2330. Email: cpalondon@aol.com. Website: www.astrologer.com/cpa. Director: Liz Greene. The CPA was founded June 12, 1983, at 14:45 BST, London. It is the outstanding center in the world for the study of astrology in relationship to depth psychology. It runs regular courses and seminars in London and occasional additional seminars in Zürich. A three-term Introduction to Psychological Astrology course is run by Clare Martin. This course covers planets, signs, elements, houses, aspects, transits, and progressions, and aims to equip the student with the necessary knowledge to attend the CPA diploma seminars. Seminars are usually on Sundays at Regent's College, Regent's Park, London NW1. The CPA also publishes a wide range of transcribed seminars in book form, all available from the CPA Press. Distribution: John Etherington, Midheaven Bookshop. Tel.: +44 (0) 20 7607 4133. Fax: +44 (0) 20 7700 6717. Email: midheaven@compuserve.com. Website: www.midheavenbooks.com.

**Company of Astrologers (COA):** P.O. Box 792, Canterbury, CT2 8WR, England. Tel.: +44 (0) 1227 362427. Email: admin@coa.org.uk. Website: www.coa.hubcom.net. Founded November 14, 1983, 21:29 GMT, in Queen Square, London. The Company is the home of *Divinatory Astrology*, and seeks to establish a modern craft-based discipline of traditional astrology that acknowledges astrology's connections with psychotherapy and contemporary philosophy as well as reexamining horoscopy in the light of divination. It runs a range of courses and seminars, mainly London-based, covering various aspects of natal, horary, and mundane astrology, plus additional study programs in other forms of divination, especially tarot and I Ching. In the theory and practice of astrology, the COA offers a range of certificate and diploma qualifications, as well as Katarche, a horary astrology correspondence course. Its public seminars are held fortnightly in Hampstead. The Company publishes a fortnightly email bulletin on the new and full moons as part of its Friends of the Company scheme. Complimentary copies are available on request.

**Faculty of Astrological Studies (FAS):** The Registrar, FAS, BM 7470, London, WC1N 3XX, England. Tel.: 07000 790143. Website: www.astrology.org.uk. Generally acknowledged to be the most outstanding teaching body in astrology anywhere in the world. Baldur Ebertin, Liz Greene, Julia Parker, and Robert Hand are all patrons. Its diploma (DFAstrolS) is the highest qualification currently available in astrology. Founded on June 7, 1948 at 19:50 BST in London, it has been raising the standards of education in astrology for over 40 years. One-year foundation (certificate) classes now begin in October and January each year. Diploma (advanced) classes are held each term. Its examinations at certificate and diploma levels are held in the autumn each year. Its summer schools, held in Oxford, are an excellent opportunity for students at all levels to understand astrology under expert guidance. Seminars on every aspect of astrology are held in London on a regular basis and small interpretation tutorials are offered in London for differing levels of ability. Faculty Day in Central London is the annual award ceremony for successful students, with a well-known speaker, and doubles as a gathering of astrologers from far and wide.

**Federation of International Vedic Astrologers:** Founded in 1995. Founder and president: P. A. Patel (Jyotishi Anand). 8 Cecil Ave., Wembley, Middlesex, HA9 7ED, England. Tel.: +44 (0) 20 8903 6784.

**Irish Astrological Association:** Contact: Kay Doyle. Tel.: +353 1 496 9440. email: irishastrology@hotmail.com. Website: www.irishastrology.com.

**London School of Astrology:** BCM Planets, London, WC1N 3XX, England. Tel.: +44 (0) 7002 33 44 55. Email: admin@londonschoolofastrology.co.uk. Website: www.londonschoolofastrology.co.uk. Offers foundation courses for beginners as well as first-year diploma and second-year diploma courses. Examinations are held annually in April for apprentice/certificate level and also professional/diploma level. Monthly seminars, summer schools, and a range of other events, open to all, are also scheduled. Member of the Astrological Guild of Educators International Inc.

**Mayo School of Astrology:** Alvana Gardens, Tregavethan, Truro, Cornwall, TR4 9EN, England. Principal: Jackie Hudson. Tel.: +44 (0) 1872 560048. Email: jackie.h@virgin.net. Website: astrology-world.com/mayo.html. Founded by Jeff Mayo, author of the famous introductory book entitled *Teach Yourself Astrology*, the Mayo School offers correspondence courses at both certificate and diploma level and issues a list of its qualified consultants who have gained the school's diploma (DMSAstrol).

**New Age Foundation (Part of BSY Group):** Contact: Ann Williams, The Registrar, BSY Group, Stanhope Square, Holsworthy, Devon EX22 6DF, England. Tel.: +44 (0) 1409 259214. Fax: +44 (0) 1409 259215. Email: info@bsygroup.co.uk. Website: www.bsygroup.co.uk. Offers a general diploma in astrology and a diploma in applied astrology. Both courses are by correspondence and cover all aspects of astrology as a mantic art.

**Pamela Crane College of Horoscopy:** The Mayor's Arms, 63 The St., Ospringe, Faversham, Kent, ME13 8TW, England. Principal: Rev. Pamela A. F. Crane. Tel.: +44 (0) 1795 532037. Email: seven5zero@aol.com. Short courses, group or individual, in interdimensional astrology and asteroid work. Lectures, research, and publications.

**Urania Trust (UT):** 12 Warrington Spur, Old Windsor, Berks, SL4 2NF, England. Tel.: +44 (0) 1753 851107. Email: urania.trust@ntlworld.com. Website: www.urania trust.org. The UT provided the basis for the current listing. It was formed at 00 hrs MET on November 9, 1970, in London, to encourage the study of astrology in the fullest sense with particular awareness of links to other related disciplines, including astronomy, philosophy, and the arts. The UT sponsors projects and makes grants to individuals and groups as funds permit. It assists research through the Michel Gauquelin Memorial Fund, donations to which are always most appreciated. The UT's publications department works to publish key texts that would otherwise not be available to students of astrology.

**White Eagle School of Astrology:** New Lands, Brewells Lane, Liss, Hants, GU33 7HY, England. Tel.: +44 (0) 1730 893300. Fax: +44 (0) 1730 892235. Email: astrology@whiteagle.org. Website: www.whitealge.org. Head tutor: Simon Bentley. Runs courses at certificate, intermediate, and diploma levels. Training places an emphasis on the esoteric and spiritual dimension of astrology. Occasional lectures and short courses are held.

## UNITED STATES

**Academy of Predictive Astrology:** The largest school of predictive astrology in the United States and the only school that specializes in the teaching of predictive techniques based on the masters who dominated the field in centuries past. Students in America can also draw upon leading articles and texts that relate to astrology that is specific to their own history and outlook. The courses are both Internet-based and/or by correspondence. All students have direct access to audio lectures, texts with diagrams and tables, an online library, ebooks, and articles. Both certificates for the beginner or diplomas for the more advanced students are awarded. For full details, contact the registrar at contact@new-library.com.

**American Council of Vedic Astrology (ACVA):** P.O. Box 2149, Sedona, AZ 86339. Tel.: (928) 282-6595 or (800) 900-6596. Email: acva@sedona.net. Website: www.vedicastrology.org. Executive vice president: Dennis Harness. ACVA is a non-profit organization dedicated to promoting the art and science of Vedic astrology or Jyotish. The Council was founded in November 1993 and reached non-profit status on April 5, 1995.

**American Federation of Astrologers:** P.O. Box 22040, Tempe, AZ 85285-2040. Tel.: (480) 838-1751; (888) 301-7630. Fax: (480) 838-8293. Email: afa@msn.com Website: www.astrologers. com/. Executive secretary: Robert W. Cooper. The AFA, founded on May 4, 1938, at 11:38 AM EST, has members in 48 countries and is dedicated to the advancement of education and research. Membership available. The AFA conducts biannual exams (worldwide). Conventions held on even-numbered years and include over 400 workshops. An extensive product listing includes more than 2,000 titles of study and data astrological books, plus a calendar and almanac.

**American Institute of Vedic Studies:** P.O. Box 8357, Santa Fe, NM 87504-8357. Tel.: (505) 983-9385. Fax: (505) 982-5807. Email: Vedicinst@aol.com. Website: www.vedanet.com/. Founder and director: David Frawley (Pandit Vamadeva Shastri). This comprehensive correspondence course explains Vedic astrology in clear and modern terms, providing practical insights into how to use and adapt the system for the contemporary student. For those who have difficulty approaching Vedic astrology, the course provides many keys for unlocking its language and its methodology, both in terms of chart interpretation and in terms of the practical application of remedial measures.

**Association for the Retrieval of Historical Astrological Texts (ARHAT):** P.O. Box 2008, Reston, VA 21095. Website: www.RobHand.com. ARHAT functions to procure, protect, and publish translations of historical astrological works and secondary source material for all serious astrologers and scholars. Beginning as an informal association in 1992, the "Archive," as it is known today, and the Robert Hand Library now house the original texts and translations of over two dozen ancient and medieval astrologers.

**Association for Astrological Networking (AFAN):** 8306 Wilshire Blvd, PMB 537, Beverly Hills, CA 90211. Email: info@ AFAN.org. Website: www.afan.org/. Communications network for legal research resources, worldwide contacts, astrological community, schools and organizations, magazines, journals, and newsletter. AFAN is a non-profit organization incorporated in California and has been bringing astrologers all over the world together, helping to fight important legal battles and working to improve astrology's image in the press for well over a decade. AFAN produces an annual membership directory and a quarterly AFAN newsletter.

**Association for Astrological Psychology (AAP):** Founder/Director: Glenn Perry. Email: aaperry@home.com. Website: www. aaperry.com. Dedicated to the integration of astrology and psychology. Offers classes and workshops, books, audio tapes, and an outstanding correspondence course (mentorship program) in psychological astrology. No fees to join.

**Astro Economics Inc.:** 1415 W. 22nd St. Tower Floor, Oak Brook, IL 60523. Tel.: (815) 464-8200. Fax: (815) 464-8163. Email: astro@astroeconomics.com. Website: www.astro economics.com/. A financial information service. Grace K. Morris.

**Astrologers Fund Inc.:** 370 Lexington Ave., Suite 416, New York, NY 10017-6503. Contact: Henry Weingarten. Tel.: (212) 949-7211. Fax: (212) 949-7274. Email: hw@afund. com. Website: www.afund.com. Financial astrology.

**Astrological Association of East Tennessee:** P.O. Box 10591, Knoxville, TN 37939-0591. Contact: Billie McNamara. Email: billie@tnhillbillie.net. Website: www.kornet.org/aaet/. AAET meetings are held monthly from September through May. Website offers newsletters concerning these and monthly trends based upon astrological data. Also published are articles of interest to students and friends of astrology.

**Astrological Institute:** 7501 E. Oak St., Room 130, Scottsdale, AZ 85257. Tel.: (480) 423-9494 / (877) 423-9494. Email: astroin@primenet.com. The Astrological Institute is the first nationally accredited school of astrology and psychology in the United States. The Institute is accredited by Accrediting Commission of Career Schools and Colleges of Technology. It is licensed by the

State of Arizona's State Board for Private Postsecondary Education and approved for training of veterans.

**Astrology—A Cosmic Pattern:** Joanne Wickenburg. Email: jwickenburg@foxinternet.net. Website: www. web3.foxinternet.net/jwickenburg/index.htm. This complete correspondence course in astrology takes you through an introduction to signs, houses, planets and their important interrelationships, the techniques for interpreting charts, and finally to examine horoscopes in motion through transits and progressions.

**Astrology Company:** P.O. Box 9237, Naples, FL 34101. Tel.: (941) 261-2840. Fax: (941) 435-0967. Email: Bobmulliga@aol.com. The Astrology Company was founded on June 22, 1974 at 2:30 P.M. CDT in Chicago, Illinois. It offers the mastery of astrology correspondence course, a four-year comprehensive program leading to professional practice. Astrologers educating astrologers since 1974.

**Astrology Masters:** 4250 Fourth Ave., Suite 306, San Diego, CA 92103. Tel.: (619) 298-5577.

**Carol A. Wiggers:** c/o Just Us & Associates, 1420 NW Gilman, Suite 2154, Issaquah, WA 98027- 5327. Tel.: (425) 391-8371. Fax: (425) 392-1919. Email: justus@ speakeasy. org. Website: www.horary.com. Correspondence course in horary astrology.

**Chiron and Friends:** 23 E. Ridge St., Apt. 2, Lansford, PA 18232-1411. Tel.: (570) 645-5982. Contact: Zane B. Stein. Email: zstein@ptd.net. Website: www.geocities.com/ adamlink/chiron_a.htm.

**Church of Light:** 111 S. Kraemer Blvd., Suite A, Brea, CA 92821. Tel.: (714) 255-9218; (800) 500-0453. Fax: (714) 255-9121. Email: churchoflight@light.org. Website: www.light.org. President: Paul Brewer. The Church of Light was founded on November 2, 1932, at 9:55 A.M. LMT, in Los Angeles, California, by Elbert Benjamine (aka CC Zain). The core teachings of the Church of Light follow in the tradition of the Hermetic Brotherhood of Light and are contained in the 21 Brotherhood of Light courses (210 lessons) written by Zain. The Church of Light sponsors a correspondence study program and enjoys a worldwide student/membership base. It is known for its excellent and faithful presentation of the powerful Hermetic tradition of astrology, alchemy, and magic.

**Earthwalk School of Astrology:** P.O. Box 832, Ashland, OR 97520. Tel.: (541) 488-7462. Email: ewastro@ rain.com. Website: www.astrocollege.com/admin/courses/elect.html. Owner, author, and professional astrologer Robert P. Blaschke, a faculty member of the Online College of Astrology, frequently travels to local astrological associations throughout the United States and Canada to lecture and teach astrology workshops. Founded in February 1992 as an outgrowth of Blaschke's full-time professional astrology practice, Earthwalk School of Astrology expanded into a publishing company in 1998. Earthwalk also offers a complete catalog of lecture, class, and workshop tapes by Blaschke. The school is additionally a dealer for both Macintosh and Windows astrology software, as well as offering mail-order chart and report services.

**Exploring Astrology:** Contact: Carole Devine. 1444 Independence Blvd., Virginia Beach, VA 23455-4288. Tel.: (757) 460-0411; (877) 520-2099. Email: cdevine22 @cox.net. Website: www.devineadvantage.com. A hands-on, interactive course. It includes 94 edited tapes, a workbook, homework correction, and a monthly student newsletter sharing others' questions. The course goes from the basics through chart interpretation and advanced techniques.

**Forum on Astrology:** Email: inquiry@forumonastrology.com. Website: www.forumonastrology.com/. An Internet school for astrology offering a two-year program based on the methods of seventeenth-century French astrologer Morin de Villefranche as was taught by Zoltan Mason of New York. This approach stresses seeing the chart as a whole integrated unit. The Forum teaches the interpretation skills required to create an image of the person and to detect their motivations and drives.

**Foundation for the Study of Cycles:** 900 West Vally Rd., Suite 502, Wayne, PA 19087. Tel.: (215) 995-2120. Fax: (215) 995-2130. Fosters and promotes, coordinates, conducts, and publishes scientific research; conducts educational activities in rhythmic fluctuations in natural and social phenomena. It has a unique library of data on cycles of every kind including astrological. Publishes the bimonthly *Cycles*.

**Inner Dimensions:** Astrology training by Emilie Kelso. P.O. Box 440054, Aurora, CO 80044. Tel.: (303) 693-7219. Fax: (303) 400-6404. Email: emilie@emiliekelso.com. Website: www.emiliekelso.com. This course is designed for brand new students of astrology, as well as seasoned students seeking a refresher course in selected basic concepts. Level I, The Basics, will help build a solid foundation for understanding the fundamental principles of astrological symbolism. Students will learn the tools and techniques that will open the door to a deeper understanding of one's self, creative powers, potential for growth, and the themes that influence relationships, career, spiritual path, and all other aspects of life.

**International Society for Astrological Research Inc. (ISAR):** P.O. Box 38613, Los Angeles, CA 90038-8613. Tel.: (805) 525-0461. Fax: (805) 525-0461. Email: maribiehn@hotmail.com or maitreya@csiway.com. Website: www.isarastrology.com. President: David Cochrane. One of the major U.S. astrological organizations, it produces the quarterly *International Astrologer*, publishes a weekly email digest for its members, and hosts a major biennial international astrology conference. It also conducts an ethics awareness seminar as part of its requirements towards professional astrological certification.

**Kepler College:** 4630-200th St. SW, Suite P, Lynnwood, WA 98036. Tel.: (425) 673-4292. Fax: (425) 673-4983. Email: info@kepler.edu. Website: www.kepler.edu. The only college in the western hemisphere authorized to issue bachelor's and master's degrees in astrological studies. The entire curriculum is based on astrology. Kepler's first freshman class began in July 2000. New students can apply/register year-round. In the process of learning astrology, Kepler students earn credits in a number of different subjects. For example, as they explore the history of astrology past, students earn credits in history, astronomy, and a variety of other subjects. As they learn the various methods of horoscope interpretation, they earn academic credits in analytical theory, counseling methods, systems theory, and more. Because of Kepler's unique design, its students not only learn about astrology, but they learn how to think on their feet, reason, solve problems, and communicate. All of the benefits of a well-rounded college education are integrated into the Kepler program, and students learn those skills while studying astrology. Kepler offers a Distance Learning with Symposia Program. Each academic term is 12 weeks long, 11 of which of are presented online. Students complete reading, writing, and research assignments under the email guidance of the faculty. One week each term, students are required to gather in Seattle, Washington, for a seven-day on-site symposium, the centerpiece of the academic program.

**Magi Society:** 847a Second Ave., 245 New York, NY 10017. Tel.: (212) 867-2905. Email: magiastro@aol.com. Websites: www.magisociety.com, www.datewiththestars.com, and www.loveoracle.com. Worldwide membership exceeds 2,000 and provides members with unique computer software. Authors of three books: *Astrology Really Works!*, *Magi Society Ephemeris Including Secrets of Magi Astrology*, and *Magi Astrology—The Key to Success in Love and Money*.

**National Council for Geocosmic Research (NCGR):** Contact: Iva Milson. P.O. Box 38866, Los Angeles, CA 90038. Tel.: (818) 761-6433. Fax: (818) 505-1440. Email: montra@earthlink.net. Website: http://www.geocosmic.org. Membership secretary: Linda Fei. 1359 Sargent Ave., St. Paul, MN 55105. Tel: (651) 598-1691. Email: LindaFei@aol.com. NCGR is an astrological organization dedicated to education and research. The word "geocosmic" refers to correspondences and cycles that relate earthly to celestial phenomena. NCGR was founded in 1971 in Massachusetts and is now a global organization with chapters and members all over the world. Current membership consists of more than 40 chapters worldwide and includes over 3,000 members in 26 countries on six continents. Local NCGR chapters host study groups, hold monthly lectures, and publish their own newsletters. Their SIGS (special interest groups) cover asteroids, declinations, earth and cycles, financial astrology, fixed stars, Sabian symbols, and Uranian/cosmobiology (Uranian Society). NCGR also publishes six member letters per year and the *NCGR Journal*, an educational publication issued at the winter and summer solstices. NCGR's educational program is a four-level program.

**New York Astrology Centre:** 370 Lexington Ave., Suite 416, New York, NY 10017-6503. Tel./Fax: (212) 949-7275. Email: books@afund.com. Website: www.afund.com/shop. Contact: Henry Weingarten.

**Noel Tyl Master's Degree Certification Course in Astrology:** Tel.: (480) 816-0000. Email: njt@mindspring.com. website: www.noeltyl.com. Considered one of the finest courses available in astrology today, the Noel Tyl course has enrolled over 250 students internationally. This correspondence course is designed for students with astrology experience requiring at least 15 to 20 chart interpretations, good astrology software capable of multiple tasks, and word processing capability for clear homework assignments. The course consists of 19 in-depth lessons. Each lesson will require 40 to 50 hours to complete. Tyl studies each lesson personally and returns a tape (25 to 45 minutes) to the student with his personal guidance. Each student proceeds at his or her personal pace, but Tyl recommends that a lesson be completed every four to five weeks. The text for the course is Tyl's classic 1,000-page teaching manual, *Synthesis and Counseling in Astrology*. There is an exam at the end of the final lesson and certification for successful completion of the course, which is acknowledged by the international astrology community. Successful completion of this course prepares the student for professional service and hones skills to a new level for currently practicing professionals. This course may be followed by Tyl's Consultation Skills Training program, advanced guidance for established professionals. Tyl will teach students how to present a horoscope analysis to clients, skills in leading consultation development, and how to involve clients in self-management and development, among other topics. This is a seven-lesson printed course requiring 40 to 60 hours of study for each lesson.

**Northeast Institute of Vedic Astrology and Studies:** 854 Brock Ave., New Bedford, MA 02744. Tel.: (508) 990-7898. Also, One Centre St., Malden, MA 02148. Tel.: (781) 322-5858. Email: crystalx@ici.net or gary.gomes@mailcity. Provides courses in Vedic astrology.

**Oregon Astrological Association:** P.O. Box 6771, Portland, OR 97228. Tel.: (503) 246-3714. Fax: (503) 452-0522. Email: moonmaven@inetarena.com. Website: www.Oregonastrology.org. Founded July 29, 1983 at 8:30 PM PDT, in Portland, Oregon.

**Project Hindsight:** 532 Washington St., Cumberland, MD 21502. Tel.: (301) 724-4463. Fax: (301) 724-3003. Email: phaser@mindspring.com. Website: www.projecthindsight.com/. The main focus of Project Hindsight has been the restoration of the astrology of the Hellenistic period (300 B.C.E. to about 600 C.E.) This is the astrology that developed in Egypt and the surrounding Mediterranean area after the Alexandrian conquest and through the Roman period. It is the primary source for all later Western astrology. Project Hindsight believes it is the first to have restored this ancient discipline to its original form.

**Sabian Symbols Interest Group:** Contact: Alice Kashuba. 10240 Dolphin Rd., Miami, FL 33157. Tel./Fax: (305) 251-4223. Email: 102757.336@compuserve.com. Also, Lynda Hill, 20 Harley Rd., Avalon, NSW 2107, Australia. Tel.: (02) 918-9539. Fax: (02) 973-1453. Email: lhill@peg.apc.org. Launched in 1995, the Group publishes a quarterly newsletter exploring all aspects of Marc Edmund Jones's Sabian symbols.

**San Diego Astrological Society:** 5521 Ruffin Rd., San Diego, CA 92123-1314. Tel.: (888) 405-6825. Website: www.sandiegoastrology.com. Founded in 1974 as an unincorporated, nonprofit association. The purpose of SDAS is to promote the art and science of astrology through education and research, to give the public information to better understand the principles and purposes of astrology, and to cultivate a sense of unity with all astrologers. Members range from beginners and students to world-renowned authors and lecturers. You do not need to have a background in astrology to benefit from these lectures and workshops, only an interest in the intricate workings of the greater macrocosm.

**School of Evolutionary Astrology:** Contact: Jeffrey Wolf Green. Email: blue@pipeline.com. Website: www.jeffreywolfgreen.com. The successful completion of the School will lead to a certificate as a qualified evolutionary astrologer who is competent to counsel people from this perspective.

**Tilton Astrology Association:** 537 Plymouth St., Dept. A, Middleboro, MA. 02346. Tel.: (508) 946-5475. Email: TiltonAstrology@aol.com. Website: www.tiltonastrology.homestead.com/home.html. The Tilton Astrology Association was founded in 1990 by Michele Tilton, a renowned expert in her field. She has been teaching the art and science of astrology to hundreds of people since then. Now she brings her expertise and knowledge into the homes of serious students, who are willing to learn this wonderful art.

**Treehouse Mountain:** 655 Reeds Bridge Rd., Conway, MA 01341-9713. Tel.: (413) 369-4680. Fax: (413) 369-4200. Email: treehsemtn@aol.com. Website: www.treehousemountain.com. Provides classical reference texts, tapes, and services.

**United Astrology Conference:** President of Board of Directors: Donna Van Toen. Tel.: (416) 466-2258. Email: cvantoe@attglobal.net. Conference coordinator: Laura Gerking. Tel.: (206) 545-2912. Email: laurag@astrologyetal.com. Website: www.uacastrology. com. Triennial conference sponsored by three organizations with a major trade show (Association for Astrological Networking, International Society for Astrological Research, and National Council for Geocosmic Research). Over one hundred speakers. International in scope.

**Washington State Astrological Association (WSAA):** P.O. Box 45386, Seattle, WA 98145-0386. Tel.: (206) 664-1004, ext. 1120. Website: www.washingtonastrologers.org. President: Mikel Poulsen. Tel.: (206) 320-1249. Email: twister@oz.net. Vice President: Karen Wennerlind. Tel.: (206) 763-3985. Email: kwennerlind@qwest.net. Founded in 1967, the WSAA membership consists of astrologers of many levels from all over the greater Seattle area and well beyond. Everyone is welcome monthly to exchange ideas, hear the best lecturers from the astrological community, and enjoy each other's company.

**Wisdom School:** P.O. Box 5574, Santa Fe, NM 87502. Tel.: (505) 466-2258. Fax: (505) 466-0510. Email: mail@thewisdomschool.org. Website: www.thewisdomschool. org. The Wisdom School is founded upon two disciplines: those esoteric doctrines revealed by the Masters of the Ageless Wisdom through their various writings, and the study of soul-centered astrology.

## VENEZUELA

**Venezuelan Center Astrologico:** Av. Rómulo Galician, Commercial Ctro. Aloa, Ppal. Plants, The premises 14, Marques, Caracas, Miranda 1070, Venezuela. Robert Gutiérrez. Email: astrorob @cantv.net. Website: www.members.es.tripod.de/CAV/index.html.

## YUGOSLAVIA

**Astarta Astrological Society:** Beogradska 19, Yu-21131 Petrovaradin (Novi Sad), Yugoslavia. Tel.: +381 21 33 96 55. Fax: +1 810 816 2480. Email: astarta@eunet.yu. Chair: Vesna Cubrulov.

**Astrological Federation of Yugoslavia (AFYU):** Contact: Zeljko Arsenijevic. Karadjordjeva 6/42, 11080 Zemun, Yugoslavia. Tel.: +381 11 100 056. Also, Marina Talovic. PF 12, 11183 Beograd 82, Yugoslavia. Email: astro.afyu@net.yu and astro@net.yu. Founders and copresidents: Marina Talovic and Zeljko Arsenijevic. Founded in September 1996. Organizes courses, seminars, and conferences. Publishes *The Astrological Magazine of AFYU* and is the main coordinating body for Yugoslavian astrology. Founders are authors of *The Precise Tables of Houses for Geographical Latitudes of Yugoslavia* and several other books.

**Dragana van de Moortel-Ilic:** DFAstrolS, Cetinarska 38, 21101 Sremska Kamenica, Yugoslavia. Tel.: +381 21 462 278. Email: koenvandemoortel@compuserve.com. Website: www.astro vdm.com. Courses at different levels, lectures, workshops, and astrological computer software.

**Society of Astrologers of Yugoslavia:** Yu-21000 Novi Sad, Filipa Visnjica l/a, Yugoslavia. Tel.: +381 21 21529. Email: soc_astrol_yu@yahoo.com. President: Olga Knezevic.

# APPENDIX D

# ASTROLOGICAL SOFTWARE

## A Brief History of Astrological Calculation Software

When Matrix Software released the first astrology programs for personal computers in 1977, a new era in astrology began. Initially loaded from cassette tapes (and later floppy disks), the programs performed accurate calculations more quickly than possible by hand. They were, however, relatively slow, only accurate for the twentieth century, had no built-in atlas or time changes, and produced crude-looking black-and-white square charts and tables.

By 1986, several important astrology programs were available for IBM PC compatibles, including the then state-of-the-art programs Blue*Star from Matrix, CCRS and Nova from Astrolabe, and Graphic Astrology for Macintosh computers from Time Cycles Research. These programs included circular chart wheels with glyphs, an expanded ephemeris range, greater ability to customize the defaults (e.g., house system, aspect set and orbs, etc.), bi- and tri-wheels, and a wider range of predictive techniques and tables. Ironically, with time, the DOS-based PC programs grew so sophisticated that they offered some techniques and capabilities that are no longer available in today's Windows programs (e.g., Blue*Star by Matrix could find true occultations, and also perform a set of jobs for everyone born in May or named Alice or having Mars square Venus).

In 1992, Esoteric Technologies and Halloran Software released the first serious astrology programs for Microsoft Windows, called Solar Fire and AstrolDeluxe for Windows respectively. The advanced graphical capabilities of the Windows environment ushered in an era of beautifully colored chart wheels, graphs, and maps, much greater ease-of-use and ease-of-learning, trouble-free installation, greater stability, built-in help files, multitasking (the ability to keep several programs open at once and to switch between them), and eventually, tools to design your own charts and page layouts.

In 2003, the most advanced astrology programs are so comprehensive that they have more features than most astrologers will ever use. They now have growing collections of famous peoples' charts, graphic displays of predictive events, chart animation, eclipse mapping, research features, and much more. Nevertheless, software development continues, and these tools for astrologers will only get better.

Astrology software can be divided into four basic types: report programs, research programs, calculation programs, and special-purpose programs.

### Report Programs

Report programs generate interpretations of one of the following topics: birth charts (including specialized topics like asteroids, health, etc.), transits, progressions, relocations, or compatibility. There are two tiers of report programs: personal and professional. The personal report programs usually cost $100 or less and their output cannot be sold. The professional-level report programs produce reports that are licensed for resale, and can be customized with a personal logo.

Some professional astrologers look down upon and don't use report programs, because these programs cannot synthesize, they only take into account one factor at a time. They call up paragraphs describing, for example, a planet in a sign or a planet in a house. Additionally, the authors of a majority of these reports seem to ignore the strong suggestibility of many people. The way they delineate natal and relationship factors and make predictive forecasts can be discouraging and frightening, and thereby cause harm to the reader. Nevertheless, some of today's report programs actually do a remarkably fine job of delineation, given the limitations inherent in this method of chart interpretation.

### Research Programs

Research programs, programs specifically designed to find charts containing single factors or combinations of factors by searching a chart collection (or database), are few and far between. That's because most professional-level astrology calculation programs include at least some research features. The two most notable research programs are JigSaw II and AstroDatabank.

*JigSaw II*. This program (by Esoteric Technologies, Inc., and distributed by Astrolabe) can search chart files for charts that have a specified point (planet, asteroid, angle, node, house cusp, midpoint, Arabic Part, almuten, fixed zodiacal point, ruler of a point, prenatal position, user-defined point, etc.) in a specific placement (specific sign, house, aspect, harmonic aspect, dignity, azimuth, decanate, Gauquelin sector, degree, mode, user-defined division, and more). You can combine any number of searches with "and/or/Xor" logic. The program can also graph the distribution of any one or all of these points in any of these placements, showing which results are above or below the average. JigSaw II can even create control groups to compare with any test group.

JigSaw II also offers the ability to analyze the charts of groups (several people) to find similar placements, including the predominate harmonics, signs, houses, vacant points, and midpoint patterns, complete with excellently written interpretations. Finally, the program allows you to manually or automatically rectify a chart by entering important dates in a person's life.

*AstroDatabank*. This program (by AstroDatabank), is a groundbreaking research program in several ways. First, it includes the Rodden database, the most reliable collection of famous charts (more than 20,000) in the world. Secondly, each of the charts includes biographical information and is placed in categories relating to health, career, personality traits, family patterns, etc. An astrologer can search for both astrological and life factors (e.g., alcoholism) simultaneously. Finally, AstroDatabank introduces the ability to create AstroSignatures, i.e., a tool for analyzing charts using several factors, each with its own weighting. For example, one could create his or her own Saturn signature by giving Saturn on an angle 5 points, Sun in Capricorn 3 points, Sun in Aquarius 2 points, Sun aspected by Saturn 4 points, etc.

## Calculation Programs

Calculation programs fall basically into three tiers, based primarily upon price and capabilities. (A few specialized programs don't fall neatly into any of these categories.) Most of the low-priced programs, i.e., those under $90, are too inaccurate in their calculations for use even by amateurs; they have no built-in atlas or time-change data, and are limited in the range of their functions. The inexpensive programs that *are* accurate include Astrology for Windows from Halloran Software, the Electronic Astrologer report programs (which include the ACS mini-atlas), and the freeware Astrolog, AstroWin, Starlite, and Junior Jyotish.

Intermediate level calculation programs cost between $99 and $200, and are geared towards students of astrology and professionals with fewer requirements. Pegasus, Win*Star Express, AstrolDeluxeReport Writer, and TimePassages are Windows programs that fall into this category. The IO Edition is a Macintosh program and Haydn's Jyotish is a Vedic program in this price range.

All of the intermediate level programs (except Haydn's Jyotish) offer natal, progressed, directed, solar and lunar return, and composite charts, interaspects, several house systems, biwheels, and a transit hit listing. The Windows programs also offer some birth chart interpretation and a time change atlas. In fact, TimePassages, AstrolDeluxe Report Writer, Haydn's Jyotish, and IO come bundled with the full ACS PC Atlas (for auto-lookup of coordinates and time zones for over 250,000 places). Among the distinctive features of each of the intermediate programs are:

TimePassages (by Astrograph Software) includes animation: you can see transiting and progressed planets circle a natal chart and form aspect lines. TimePassages is available for both the PC and the Mac. Pegasus (by Cosmic Patterns) offers mini-reports for natal, transits, major life themes, and synastry. Win*Star Express (by Matrix) has the full *DeVore's Encyclopedia of Astrology* and a nice transit/progressed graph, which shows exact hit dates (but not entering or leaving dates).

Two of the intermediate programs, AstrolDeluxe ReportWriter and IO, have the most features in this price range, and provide a complete software solution for many astrologers. AstrolDeluxe ReportWriter (by Halloran Software) has excellent research features, astro-mapping, report-writing capabilities, and a very wide range of calculations. IO (by Time Cycles Research) has an excellent page designer, the best transit/progressed hit listing (it includes stations), bi-, tri-, and quad-wheels, many tables, and a graphic ephemeris.

Haydn's Jyotish (by Haydn Huntley) has all of the basic Vedic features (and some not-so basic) one would expect: rasi, bhava lagna, varshaphal, and varga charts in North and South Indian formats; dasa/bhukti listing; ashtakavarga; shad bala; bhava bala; and vimshopak listings. It also shows sunrise and sunset times, Kujadosha, moon waxing/waning, moon fullness, Tithis, Dagdha Rasis, Yoga Point, Planetary Yogi, Duplicate Yoga, Avayogi, Karakas, and Raja Yogakarakas. It runs on Windows PCs, Macintosh computers, and MS-DOS. In-depth reviews of each program are available at www.soulhealing.com.

Advanced astrology programs are usually priced at $200 to $300, and have a full range of features and functions. Among Western astrology programs, these include the very complete packages Solar Fire, Kepler, Win*Star Plus, and Janus. Shri Jyoti Star, Parashara's Light, Jyotish Studio, and Käla are the advanced Vedic astrology programs.

## Special-Purpose Programs

Some astrological software doesn't fall neatly in any ordinary category. The ACS PC Atlas, for example, is widely used by astrologers to automatically look up longitudes, latitudes, time zones, and time changes for birthplaces within many professional-level programs, and it also can be purchased by itself. There are several programs designed to help astrologers and astronomers use their telescopes to view stars, planets, and constellations. And there are a group of electional astrology programs designed to help astrologers and lay people to choose the best time for initiating an activity, such as Father Time by A.I.R. Software and Shri Muhurta by GeoVision Software, and another group of horary astrology programs designed to give the answer to a question that the astrologer or lay person asks at the moment, such as Nostradamus by A.I.R. software and VegaSviri Horary by the Center for Temporal Research. An unusual "electional" program called Astrodamus by Nostradamus Corporation automatically rectifies the birth chart, based upon life events, and then predicts the themes for each year.

## Advanced Western Astrology Programs

Every Western astrology program in the $200+ price range offers superb accuracy and a large date range for calculations, as well as transits, progressions, directions, returns, composite charts, interaspect tables, many styles of charts and data tables, astro-mapping and eclipse maps, midpoint trees and dials, the ability to import files from the Quick*Charts format, large built-in time-change atlases (with automatic look up of the coordinates and time zones for most cities), a rectification method (e.g., the ability to change the birth time forward or backwards and immediately see the new chart), at least some interpretations (e.g., of natal planet positions), an astro-clock (i.e., a chart that shows the positions at the present moments and automatically updates when the positions change), ephemeris printing, harmonic charts, and some graphical tables. They all offer the ability to set default colors, house system, zodiac, present location, ayanamsha, true or mean node, a customer's logo, and preferred wheel style. They all run under Microsoft Windows.

*Solar Fire 5*. This program (by Esoteric Technologies, Inc., and distributed by Astrolabe) is perhaps the best-designed for ease of use and the most polished astrology program on the market. It is solid (never crashes), includes the most comprehensive manual, an excellent page designer, easiest and most flexible customizing features (e.g., the ability to create any number of aspect sets), and a huge range of functions. No other program allows you to set different orbs for applying and separating aspects (both in natal chart and for transits, progressions, etc.)

Perhaps its foremost strength is its incredible interactivity. While looking at a chart wheel, you can change the aspect set, type of wheel or page, points displayed, birth time, etc., and immediately see the changes. Another incomparable feature is its Time Map transit/progressed graph. The Time Map shows each predictive event on one line for a period from one day to any number of years, with the entering, exact, and leaving orb dates for each event. In addition to including standard predictive techniques, the Time Map (and transit list) can include eclipses, transits/progressions/directions to and from sensitive points such as midpoints, fixed stars, and many, many asteroids, and to house cusps (not just ingresses), Arabic parts, fixed zodiacal positions, and nodes of any planet or major asteroid. You can also merge separate searches into one listing or Time Map.

Solar Fire also offers the best chart animator, which allows you to view one (or more) biwheels with transiting/progressed/directed planets moving around a chart at any rate you specify with aspect lines forming over time, plus the ability to see up to four wheels or biwheels at once, triwheels or quadwheels or any page of charts, dials, tables, and graphs. Solar Fire includes many pages, including ones for cosmobiology, Vedic, horary, fixed stars, and classical (ancient Western) techniques.

You can record any set of jobs using the program's unique Astrologer's Assistant, and then recreate all of the printouts (charts, graphs, maps, etc.) for a new person with the push of a button. The Eclipse search finds eclipses for a range of 5,000 years, with detailed information on each eclipse. Chart files can be exported in many formats including the Quick*Chart format (for importing into most astrology programs) and can be backed up effortlessly. Solar Fire 5 also includes astro-mapping, an Arabian parts editor, fixed star interpretations, an extensive well-written synastry report, a wonderfully useful graphic ephemeris, and an advanced ephemeris generator that can include Arabic parts, asteroids, transiting midpoints, hypothetical planets, and the ascendant and M.C.

Finally, Solar Fire offers additional advanced features like MultiWheel Superimposition, which allows you to see bi-, tri-, and quad-wheels with each of the charts having their own ascendant, or with all of the charts aligned to any point (e.g., align all of the Suns). It also has an Extra Points wheel, where you can place any set of extra points within a birth chart. You can create any number of sets of extra points, and choose any midpoints, lunations, eclipses, nodes, Arabic Parts, fixed stars, asteroids, hypothetical points, angles, and planets to comprise each set.

*Kepler*. One of Kepler's strengths for many years has been its unrivaled collection of optional add-on interpretive astrological reports. With each new version, Kepler (by Cosmic Patterns) has become more and more powerful and introduced many unique astrological tools. The staff at Cosmic Patterns continually researches time changes throughout the world, and as a result Kepler has the most accurate time-change atlas of any program.

In the area of astro-mapping, Kepler has pioneered incredible advances. Not only does Kepler offer major and minor aspect lines and midpoint lines, but also can show the orb of influence for each line. Beyond this, Kepler includes custom Treasure Maps for specific life themes—like love, career, etc.—that show the places on a map where these goals are most likely to be realized. Kepler takes the same unique thematic approach to its Time Line Profile graph, which indicates, for whatever time period selected, the influence of transits on 14 areas of life, including business success, romance and sexuality, accident proneness, etc.

Kepler is the best program for learning astrology. Its built-in Avalon College includes 47 astrology lessons, an extensive glossary, and many additional articles. Kepler also includes the largest collection (18,000+) of charts of famous people, companies, and events of any professional program. In addition to single factor searches—such as who has a planet in a specific sign or house—Kepler can search for stationary planets, planets conjunct fixed stars, aspects between two charts, planets in another chart's houses, and can even list charts indicating the strength of traits such as logic, originality, impatience, and zeal.

Another unique advance in Kepler is its aspect and interaspect listings showing all of the harmonic aspects between each pair of points. Kepler offers the only graphic ephemeris that allows you to put transits, secondary progressions, and solar arc directions on the same graph. Kepler can read many other programs' files directly and/or import them, as well as export to several formats. It also offers a list of the positions of 1,000 asteroids. Kepler offers stunning new Art Wheels, charts with beautifully rendered backgrounds of sunsets, angels, night skies, and more. Kepler also includes chart pages designed for using Huber methodology.

Finally, Kepler has the most Vedic astrology features of any Western program. Besides displaying wheels and a well-formatted dasa/bhukti/antara listing (with optional interpretations), the program offers divisional (varga) charts, a detailed shad bala table, and a very sophisticated Gochara (transits) graph which takes into account Vedhas.

*Win*Star Plus*. This program (by Matrix Software) inherited many of the capabilities of the powerful Blue*Star program, and offers the largest selection of well-designed wheels and chart pages. It includes a utility to preview each page before choosing it, and a Publisher's Assistant to create wheels of any size for publishing, emailing, and printing. The software includes the complete *DeVore's Encyclopedia of Astrology*, as well as a glossary of astrological techniques. Its DataView function shows a variety of tables, and unique graphs (for any chart) of planets by (geo- or heliocentric) longitude and latitude, right ascension and declination, azimuth and altitude, angular separation, and midpoints.

Win*Star Plus' powerful Searches feature allows you to execute up to six different types of searches at once. You can select the type of search method for each of the six (e.g., transit-to-transit, tertiary progressed-to-natal, etc.), both the search planets and the natal planets to use, search for natal midpoints, the aspect set for each method, and whether to show stations, ingresses, parallels, and entering/leaving dates for each method. Finally, you can select the time range for the set, and then name and save as many sets of searches as you want.

After running a search, you can sort the listing in many ways, create a custom layout of which columns to show and where, merge the listing with another listing (even another person's, whose name will be shown to differentiate both sets of transits—outstanding!), hide or only display some of the items in the list temporarily (e.g., inner transits), and view a bi-wheel chart for any event around the natal chart. No program makes complex searches so easy to create.

Win*Star Plus also excels in the exceptional quality and power of its beautiful astro-maps. It offers the ability to zoom in and out on any area of a map smoothly and easily with the click of a button. Additionally, the program can show the current longitude and latitude and ascendant and midheaven wherever the cursor is placed. Astronomical lines, such as the ecliptic or horizon, and constellations, such as the zodiac, can be shown on maps, as can space-based house cusp lines (e.g., Campanus, Regiomontanus, etc.), and even the region of a map where a planet actually is at the moment of birth, and/or where on the map a planet occupies a specific house (by any house system). The maps produced by Win*Star Plus are by far the highest-resolution and best quality.

The Win*Search function not only allows you to quickly and easily search your chart file (or any subset of it) for a planet by sign, house, specific degree position, aspect or angular separation from another point, dignity, date range, or quadrant, or charts with emphasis of a mode or element, or a lunar day or phase or quarter, but it includes an extremely powerful and unique Astro*Query search language that enables astrologers to create complex "and/or" searches of their own. Win*Search can also create distribution graphs for an entire chart collection (or any subset) showing all or specified planets by sign, house, degree, and many other factors.

*Janus*. This program (by Janus Astrology Software) is the newest professional-level and comprehensive Western astrology program. It is very easy to use, and has the best context-sensitive help screens of any program, which not only document all of the features of the screen you're working on, but also are cross-referenced to allied topics, and include excellent reference tables, and a bibliography on the technique.

Janus offers horary astrologers a fine module specifically designed for their needs, that makes it effortless to turn the wheel, evaluate the considerations of the horary chart, and see the significant factors (e.g., lunar aspects, aspects to Arabic parts and fixed stars, planetary hours, receptions, and dignities). The Electional module is similarly well organized, and adds a graph for the day of changing dignities for each of the Ptolemaic planets, easy time shifting of the chart (by seconds, minutes, hours, days, months, or years), and the ability to adjust what strength aspects are displayed.

Janus also has the best Planetarium/Sky Map, which shows the celestial sphere with the constellations, signs, and stars clearly marked. Its functions include day/night shading, animation, zoom, find (a star, planet, sign, or constellation), and the ability to set colors, select what to display, what coordinate system to use (ecliptic, equatorial, or horizon), and what date to show. It also has information on a large number of fixed stars including both astronomical details and astrological meanings. The astro-mapping feature uniquely offers a general report (i.e., not for a specific city or chart) of interpretations both of planetary lines and of parans.

The predictive search can include void-of-course Moon, lunar phases, unusual methods of progression (e.g., by solar or sidereal days by draconic month, anomalistic year, or eclipse year), arc directions by planetary arcs (instead of just solar arcs), and a remarkably large number of ways to sort the listing of predictive events. Similarly, Janus offers a wider variety of return options than many programs, including planetary midpoint, Synodic, Metonic, and Anlunar returns. The graphic ephemeris can also include lunar phases, house ingresses, and eclipses.

### Specialized Western Professional Astrology Programs

Several additional programs offer advanced astrological functions, and have many but not all of the basic and professional-level features that astrologers expect. They will be treated here as specialized software.

*Millennium*. This program (by A.I.R. Software) offers an incredible number of unique and powerful predictive techniques, most notably the Time Tunnel, a circular graphic ephemeris that can use many predictive methods at once (e..g transits, secondary progressed, solar arc directed, etc.) and show where and when they converge, and an excellent dynamic predictive graph that shows the cumulative effects of transits, progressions, etc. There's a transit calendar, a unique tool for searching complete chart files to see who has the same event happening to them, the capacity to work in many different coordinate systems and to utilize a large number of natal points, planetary phases, and many additional predictive tools. Millennium also has many optional and powerful add-ons, including astro-mapping, electional tools, sophisticated time searching and rectification tools, and much more.

*AstroWorld 2000*. This program (by AstroWorld International) introduces the technique of the Personar chart, which shows the sub-personalities indicated by each planet (by constructing a chart for the moment the Sun first reaches the position of each of the natal planets after birth). It has several nice transit representations, including a lovely transit graph, plus a seven-year rhythm predictive method, which divides the sky into 12 seven-year spans starting at the ascendant and going clockwise around the chart. It also gives full well-written interpretations for natal, transits, and synastry.

*Regulus*. This program (by AstroScan) has a powerful astrological "language" for creating the search conditions for individuals, couples, and progressed charts. For example, it can find individuals in a chart file who meet a set of conditions (e.g., who has Jupiter stationary and weak?). Regulus also offers unusual predictive graphs that include waxing and waning intensities for individual transits and progressions and cumulative graphs for each planet and all of them (and smaller sets of them, e.g., personal planets and angles) combined. It also offers an excellent and innovative predictive report that shows the changes that take place during the year to one's love life, career, money, etc., instead of the standard event-based report (e.g., planet A aspects planet B).

### Advanced Vedic Astrology Programs

Every professional-level Vedic program offers North and South Indian charts, several standard ayanamsas and a user-defined ayanamsa, animated transits, rectification tool(s), a time-change atlas, multiple dasha systems, the ability to import files from the Quick*Charts format, Classical Vedic interpretations (e.g., of natal planet positions), an astro-clock (i.e., a chart that shows the positions at the present moments and automatically updates when the positions change), varga (divisional) charts, research tools, tables and graphs including ashtakavarga, kutams, nakshatras, shri pati house cusps, aspects, panchang, upagrahas, and shad bala. They also offer the ability to design your own screens and pages, and to select the default house system, present location, true or mean node setting, and a customer's logo.

*Parashara's Light*. This program (by Geovision Software) combines beautiful graphics with exceptional ease of use. Its unparalleled Page Designer allows you to precisely control the size and placement of charts, tables, and graphs, and to make as many custom designed pages as you want. The software also allows you to create your own sets of pages to be printed at the push of a button.

Parashara's Light has many unique features including the only Vedic transit and dasha listing that can include entry into signs, nakshatras, navamsas, specific degrees, and kakshas, as well as whole sign and degree transits, sade sati, and dasas up to five levels. The program can also prepare a monthly calendar showing these events, and is the only Vedic program to offer a graphic ephemeris, too.

The software has a wonderful and easy-to-use Muhurta (electional) screen, complete with a simple indicator of general auspiciousness of the date and time that anyone can understand, plus a fine time-shifting tool, as well as rasi and navamsa charts, and detailed tables of planetary information (including avastas, kakshas, and ashtakavarga), five levels of three dasa systems, and the results of the present tarabala, chandrabala, tithi, karana, and nakshatra.

The program has a wonderfully formatted Kaksha report, the ability to graph distributions on groups of charts for signs, nakshatras, dignities, shad bala, aspects, and conjunctions for each planet and the ascendant, a point calculator (e.g., Sun-Moon). It searches from 1001 yogas for those that apply to the chart, and then interprets (and shows the formula for) each yoga. Its auspiciousness graph is an excellent display of each planet's strengths by shad bala, vimsopaka, dignity, number of good vargas, shastiamsha, and two systems of avasthas.

*Shri Jyoti Star*. This program (by ShriSource) excels in the great range of calculations and tables that it offers, including many compatibility features (e.g., Kuta and Yoni for all planets, cross-chart tables of relationships, aspects, lords, ashtakavarga, etc., and the ability to show two different people's charts, graphs, and tables on the same page), and a wealth of graphs and tables for individual charts (such as astronomical data, Arabic parts, panchang, avasthas, argala, udayas, rashmis, latitude, house strengths, and many more).

The Time Shift tool is exceptional in its usefulness in rectification. While viewing any screen(s) of charts, graphs, and tables, you can easily shift the birth date forward or backwards in time by any increment, and see all of the charts, graphs, and tables change accordingly. Shri Jyoti Star also offers a unique Circle Chart display, where you can view two charts concentrically, seeing house boundaries and cusps (bhava madhyas) and sign boundaries, and watch planets transit around a chart.

Another priceless feature is its Yogas and Time Search tool. With incredible ease, you can search for when, in the past or the future, any planets were in specific signs, degrees, or degree ranges (e.g., a Moon at 4° to 6° Aries). You can also search a chart file to see which charts have any individual classical yoga or combination of yogas. Finally, you can construct your own combinations of factors, complete with "and/or" logic, and search your chart file to see who has them. For example, you could look for who has the ascendant hemmed in by malefics while in a particular nakshatra and while the lord of the ascendant is in the navamsha of a great enemy (or, of course, any simpler search.) Shri Jyoti Star's searches are lightning fast, simple to do, and completely accurate. After a search is done, you can click on any of the names listed (of people who met the search requirements) and instantly view their charts.

The newest features include a neat "instant prashna" where you can ask a question and get an answer, and a group muhurta, i.e., find the best nakshatra for a person, couple, or group to initiate an activity. It can draw brilliantly executed aspect lines between points in both rasi and varga charts (a first!) and between any two charts with the ability to set orbs. It also has five tables of Arabic parts, the ability to analyze a rasi chart for a person's inner harmony/tension and compatibility with family members, a Levacy-style South Indian chart, and Arudha Padas in all charts. There is even powerful Astro*Carto*Graphy mapping that allows you to instantly relocate one or two people's charts, as well as the unique ability to see two people's planetary lines on one map.

Shri Jyoti Star offers superb accuracy, many Hart and Iyer options, simple drag-and-drop chart positioning on both the screen and printed page forms, a rich panchang report, a simple chart relocation tool, the largest number of dasa methods, and much more.

*Jyotish Studio (a.k.a. Goravani's Jyotish)*. This program (by Dancing Moon Inc.) has an immense reference section that contains a Vedic tutorial with several lessons, an extensive glossary of Jyotish terminology, valuable tables (e.g., exact degree of exaltation, nakshatras, friendships, etc.), and the full text of both the *Bhagavad Gita* and David Frawley's Vedic astrology book, *Astrology of the Seers*. It also has an incredible list of karakas, i.e., the planets, houses, or signs that signify specific objects, people, etc. (e.g., Epistles and the 3rd house, or Esophagus and the Moon).

The predictive features of Jyotish Studio are diverse and powerful. The Panchang function can show either detailed information on a specific day, complete with the results for an individual chart, or a listing of any duration of all of the relevant factors like the tithi, karana, yoga, nakshatra, paksha, etc. The transit hit list function allows you to see when planets form exact tajika aspects; and shows sign, nakshatra, navamsha, and antardasa ingresses; conjunctions to equal, placidus, and shri pati house cusps, and conjunctions to upagraha, the yogi point, and the part of fortune. The excellently designed tarabala calendar shows a monthly calendar with detailed information for each day on the tithi, nakshatra, moon sign, tara bala from the moon and ascendant, chandra bala from the moon and the ascendant, and the bright/dark quality of the Moon. It also shows changes, to four levels, of the dasa, and planetary station dates.

The Jyotish Studio offers a fine array of truly lovely Vedic charts, some with carefully designed beautiful backgrounds making them suitable for wall hanging. It also has the largest collection of famous peoples' charts (for a Vedic program). You can view and print very useful sorted listings (with many choices of sorts) of the charts in the database, a compact listing of everyone's data and planetary placements, and even compare any chart for similarities with all of the other charts in the database.

The program is packed with a huge variety of nice touches. For example, you can easily rotate any chart to show any sign as lagna. One powerful table shows both the exact degrees for planets in each of the vargas, and a well-thought-out table showing the conjunctions of planets in divisional charts with rasi points. You can also create a listing of planetary stationary times, tertiary progressed stations, kakshas, and custom designed listings of exactly the information you want, from a huge list of attributes.

*Käla*. This program (by Jyotish Academy International) is the newest professional-level Vedic program to be released. As such, it is being enhanced at a rapid rate and many new features—including a Muhurta screen—are likely to be added soon. Käla has a 10,800-year ephemeris range, a very simple-to-learn user interface, the ability to open any number of additional charts and tables at once, and classical text delineations for marriage and sexuality, mental illness, transits, illness and accidents, and dasas.

Käla is most immediately noteworthy because of the quality of its modern interpretations. Its core yoga delineations are impressively thorough and very well written, and its in-depth analysis of planets in combustion, debilitation, and the nodes, as well as the ruler of each house, are very good. Käla also offers very comprehensive information on Vedic compatibility factors.

One of the most valuable features of Käla is its carefully designed screens for specific functions. Its Compatibility screen shows a bi-wheel or composite chart, kuta analysis for all of the planets, tajika aspects between the charts, and more. The Transit screen also shows an animated bi-wheel, with aspect lines drawn in (if they're in the same navamsa portion), as well as valuable animated tables.

Käla's Varshaphala screen is also carefully designed for greatest applicability and includes Mudda, Patyayini, and one-year Vimshottari dasa listings, sahams, three types of Varshaphal strengths, and much more. The Prashna screen allows you to select the Prashna and the Arudha, offering several prashna techniques and the pertinent yogas (from 12 classical Vedic texts).

### Software Limitations

For all of the power and accuracy of today's astrological software, there are still sources of errors. Data entry is of course the primary cause of incorrect charts. Older time-change atlases and incorrect birth times are also common sources of error. A more in-depth look at software limitations can be found at http://www.soulhealing.com/optimal.htm. Many astrology programs have incredible versatility and power, and are built by programmers committed to advancing the field every year. Future programs will be able to help astrologers combine predictive techniques even more effectively and weight factors in relationship to each other. Perhaps they will even achieve chart synthesis.

## Contact Information

**A.I.R. Software:** 115 Caya Ave., West Hartford, CT 06110. Tel.: (800) 659-1247. Website: http://www.alphee.com/.

**AstroDatabank:** 25 Raymond St., Manchester, MA 01944. Tel: (978) 526-8864. Website: http://astrodatabank.com/.

**Astrograph:** 251 Dufour St., Santa Cruz, CA 95060. Tel: (831) 425-3686. Website: http://www.astrograph.com/.

**Astrolabe, Inc.:** P.O. Box 1750, Brewster, MA 02631. Tel: (800) 843-6682. Website: http://www.alabe.com/.

**Astroscan:** Lovstrade 8, DK-1152 Copenhagen K, Denmark. Tel: +45 33 33 85 48. Website: http://www.logos.dk/regulus_uk.htm.

**AstroWorld, International:** P.O. Box 1143, 35001 Marburg, Germany. Tel: +49 (0)6421 13827. Website: http://astroworld.net/eng/.

**Center for Temporal Research:** 41 Lesnaya Str., Moscow 101514, Russia. Tel: (7-095) 924-46-86. Website: http://www.ctp.ru/e_index.html.

**Cosmic Patterns:** 6212 NW 43rd St., Suite B, Gainesville, FL 32653. Tel: (800) 779-2559. Website: http://www.patterns.com.

**Dancing Moon Inc.:** 2852 Willamette St., #353, Eugene OR 97405. Tel: (80) 532-6528. Website: http://www.goravani.com/.

**GeoVision Software, Inc.:** P.O. Box 2152, Fairfield, IA 52556. (800) 459-6847. Website: http://www.parashara.com/.

**Halloran Software:** P.O. Box 75713, Los Angeles, CA 90075. Tel.: (800) 732-4628. Website: http://www.halloran.com/.

**Haydn Huntley:** P.O. Box 1161, Fairfield, IA 52556. Tel: (641) 472-7025. Website: http://www.nlogn.com/.

**Janus Astrology Software:** Tel./Fax: +44 20 7900 2676. Website: http://www.astrologyware.com/.

**Jyotish Academy International:** 1474 Jemez Trail, Yucca Valley, CA 92284. Tel.: (760) 420-5648. Website: http://vedic-astrology.net/.

**Matrix Software:** 407 N. State St., Big Rapids, MI 49307. Tel.: (800) 416-3924. Website: http://astrologysoftware.com/.

**Nostradamus Corporation:** Tel.: (818) 345-6655. Website: http://www.nostradamus2000.net/index.htm.

**ShriSource:** 10610 79th Ave., Suite 202, Edmonton AB, T6E 1S1, Canada. Tel.: (877) 484-7474. Website: http://www.vedicsoftware.com/.

# INDEX

Note: **Boldface** type indicates main entries and their page numbers; (ill.) indicates photos and illustrations.

## D

## N

## O

## P

## Q



## R



## S

Kepler 6.0 introduces a new level of ease of use to astrological software. Simply click to bring back previously selected screens, interactively customize your chart wheels, and use advanced features like auto-adjusting for publishing chart wheels.
Kepler was a leader in providing a complete atlas, AstroMaps and Treasure Maps, a large library of images, a MultiMedia chart reading, extensive educational features, exquisitely beautiful chart wheels, and Vedic calculations. Now we have developed a wonderfully elegant user interface, and added dozens of new features. Kepler also includes a Rectification Assist.
Kepler 6
Superb Astrology Software
NEW USER INTERFACE
Revolutionary
Art Wheels
Vedic
FEATURES
✦ 12 House Systems ✦ Arabic Parts, 8,000 Fixed Stars, Parallels of declination, etc. ✦ ArcTransform Charts and Harmonic Charts ✦ Major and Minor Asteroids, Chiron, Vertex, Equatorial Asc, TransNeptunian Planets, etc. ✦ AstroMaps, Local Space, Geodetic, Zodiac Sign Maps and the spectacular Treasure Maps, relocated charts and relocated aspect listings ✦ Ingress, Eclipse, and Lunation charts, and Eclipse maps ✦ AstroClock ✦ Complete atlas with complete daylight savings time tables ✦ Progressions and Directions ✦ Composite Charts (Asc. midpt, MC midpt, derived, time-space) ✦ Secondary, Tertiary, Minor, Solar Arc, and Degree for a Year charts direct and converse ✦ Solar, Lunar, and Planet Returns ✦ Transits and Progressed Listings and Time Lines (can include midpoint structures, harmonics, eclipses, and declinations) ✦ Time Line Profile graphically shows when a person is accident-prone, athletic performance is good, etc. ✦ Natal Profile gives scores on mental, emotional, and personality traits ✦ Draconic, Declination Longitude Equivalent, Mundoscope, Antiscia, and Tobey Secondary ✦ Heliocentric, Horizon, and Right Ascension wheels, transits, etc. ✦ Midpoint trees in longitude or declination and listings, graphic ephemeris of color-coded natal, progressed, and transiting planets in longitude or declination ✦ 90 Degree Dials, Huber wheels, BiWheels, Tri-Wheels, QuadWheels, MultiWheels, Aspects and Midpoints Comparisons, etc. ✦ Extraordinary research capabilities, including assumptionless research and creating sophisticated astrological signatures. 18,000 charts of famous people, business, earthquakes, etc. included ✦ Avalon College and AstroEncyclopedia, incredible learning tools for anyone from beginner to professional ✦ Natal, Compatibility, and Forecast Interpretive Reports, and the Live Mini MultiMedia birth chart interpretation ✦ Dasas & Bhuktis, Shad Bala, Nakshatras, Vargas, & Gochara ✦ Many advanced capabilities for professionals and technical astrologers ✦ Extensive beautiful astrological graphics library, and True Type astrology font ✦ Graphic Ephemeris of natal, transits, and progressed postions ✦ Rectification assist ✦ 1,000 Minor Asteroid Positions, including recently discovered Ixion, Varuna, and Quaoar! Optional 22,000 Asteroids AND MUCH, MUCH MORE!
OVER 30 STUNNING ART WHEELS
FLEXIBILITY
REPORT OPTIONS
that you can add to Kepler and Pegasus
✦ Merlin ✦ Indra ✦ Alpha Imprints ✦ Life Path Report ✦ Child Report ✦ Flower Essence and Gem ✦ Karmic Insight ✦ Medicine Wheel ✦ Revelation ✦ Astro Analysis ✦ Hidden Messages ✦ Naughty Natal ✦ Adult Report ✦ Vocational Guidance ✦ Cayce Past Life ✦ Karmic Past Life ✦ Personal Security Report ✦ Nature Appreciation Report ✦ Fixed Stars Report ✦ Compatibility ✦ Psyche & Eros Relationship Analysis ✦ Compatibility & Conflict Marriage & Romance ✦ Heaven Sent ✦ The Composite Report ✦ Planets in Solar Return ✦ Basic Forecast ✦ Advanced Forecast ✦ Destiny & Decisions ✦ AstroJourney Forecast for Teens and Young Adults ✦ Poppe Forecast ✦ Mini-Minder ✦ Business Forecast ✦ Love and Romance Forecast ✦ Karmic Forecast ✦ Secondary Progressed ✦ Solar Return ✦ Planets in Solar Return ✦ Many Happy Returns ✦ Lunar Return ✦ Thirteen Moons Lunar Return ✦ AstroQuest Horary ✦ Relocation Information ✦ Cities and Towns ✦ AstroMed ✦ Cosmobiology Health Report ✦ MedScan and Medical Forecast ✦ Canine Report ✦ Galactic Report ✦ Starlight Solutions Forecast ✦ Compatibility & Conflict Bus. or Friends ✦ Senior Report
Many Reports available in Spanish, Portuguese, French, German, Norwegian and Russian.
Easy-to-use
A COMPLETE SYSTEM AT AN EXTRAORDINARY PRICE
Kepler's capabilities are so vast that you may use only a fraction of its capability, but that's OK.
The entire program is $300.
Any one of the following features alone is worth hundreds of dollars: AstroMaps, Advanced Research and database, Graphics library, complete atlas, Avalon College, AstroEncyclopedia, not to mention that Kepler's astrological calculation capability is vast, and the program is a joy to use. We also have the industry's best customer support.
Kepler is a program for everyone, from beginner to the most expert professional.
Pegasus
ASTROLOGY PROGRAM
OTHER NEW FEATURES OF KEPLER 6.0
Many new AstroMap features and improvements, Mundoscope, Declination Longitude Equivalent, Antiscia, ContraAntiscia Charts, Huber style wheels, improvements to time line format transits and progressions, easy selection of series of lunations, Eclipse Charts and Ingress Charts, Munkasey Midpoint Weighting Analysis, positions of recently discovered Ixion, Varuna, and Quaoar, Degree Meanings by 11 authors and harmonic degree meanings, numerology analysis, and much more.
Real Astrology at an Affordable Price! Pegasus is similar to the Kepler program, but has fewer features. Call for details!
Spectacularly Powerful
COSMIC PATTERNS
www.AstroSoftware.com
E - mail: kepler@AstroSoftware.com
6212 N.W. 43rd Street, Suite B
Gainesville, FL 32653
phone: 352 - 373 -1504
(fax: 352 374 8826)
Kepler
Superb Astrology Software